THE FACTS ON FILE
COMPANION TO

THE BRITISH
NOVEL

VOLUME II
20th Century

THE FACTS ON FILE
COMPANION TO

THE BRITISH NOVEL

VOLUME II
20th Century

VICTORIA GAYDOSIK

Facts On File, Inc.

The Facts On File Companion to the British Novel, Volume II: 20th Century

Copyright © 2006 by Victoria Gaydosik

Facts On File, Inc.
132 West 31st Street
New York NY 10001

Library of Congress Cataloging-in-Publication Data

Brackett, Virginia and Victoria Gaydosik
   The Facts On File Companion to the British Novel/Virginia Brackett and Victoria Gaydosik
     p. cm
   v.1. Beginnings through the 19th Century/Virginia Brackett—v.2. 20th Century/Victoria Gaydosik
   Includes bibliographical references and indexes.
   ISBN 0-8160-6377-X (set: hardcover: alk. paper)—ISBN 0-8160-5133-X (v.1: alk. paper)—ISBN 0-8160-5254-9 (v.2: alk. paper)
   1. English fiction—History and criticism—Handbooks, manuals, etc. I. Title: Companion to the British novel. II. Brackett, Mary Virginia. III. Gaydosik, Victoria.
   PR821.F2 2005
   823'.509—dc22   2004020914

Text design adapted by James Scotto-Lavino
Cover design by Cathy Rincon

Printed in the United States of America

VB FOF 10 9 8 7 6 5 4 3 2 1

This book is printed on acid-free paper.

CONTENTS

INTRODUCTION

When I was a youngish reader first attempting a work of serious literature—a fourth-grader grappling with Jane Austen's *Pride and Prejudice*—I quickly realized that I had jumped in over my head. I could understand the words and the sentences, but I could not quite figure out what the characters were doing, aside from a lot of talking, or what the story was about. I did not know it at the time, but I needed a companion to facilitate my reading. Although reading is among the most solitary of human pastimes, reading literature effectively requires its own form of socialization if readers are to recognize and appreciate the conventions that writers have drawn upon in creating the works that make reading possible.

Mercifully, a teacher placed a Newbury award winner in my hands—*Strawberry Girl,* by Lois Lenski—and from there I went on to the other books in our library with the distinctive Newbury seal, including the first book I ever read that featured a girl only a few years older than me in a heroic role, *A Wrinkle in Time,* by Madeleine L'Engle. Through the quality works that had received the Newbury Medal, I was launched on my career as a literate reader; when I came back to *Pride and Prejudice* in high school, I was able to master it and enjoy the author's skill in creating such realistic characters.

Now, many years later, I am a professional companion to readers in training, teaching in a college-level literature program. Through the volume at hand, I am attempting to share my love of reading and of fine literature with a wider audience of high school and college readers who would like to improve their reading. *The Facts On File Companion to the British Novel* is designed to assist high school and college readers of literature in the pleasant task of enjoying their reading assignments more by acquiring a better understanding of the conventions of literature in general and of the specific literary techniques used in particular texts.

I anticipate that the bulk of my audience will consist of readers between the ages of 12 and 22—that most momentous of decades in the span of human life—and that they will be reading both as college English majors and as general high school English students (with perhaps a few precocious middle-school readers in the mix as well). I have chosen works that students in this age range are most likely to read either as assignments for English classes or as personal recreational pursuits, and thus I include canonical titles such as James Joyce's *A Portrait of the Artist as a Young Man* as well as popular phenomena such as the *Harry Potter* series. This volume of the companion consists of more than 500 entries drawn from among the works of the greatest and most commonly taught British authors of the 20th century, as well as noncanonical popular novels and lesser-known works and writers deserving of a wider readership: More than 170 authors are profiled in short biographical sketches, and some 300 works produced by those authors are discussed in suitable detail, along with numerous literary terms of particular relevance.

The first, most challenging, and most enduring task in assembling the entries for a literary companion of use to contemporary students of the British novel has been the identification of the current boundaries of British literature. Because the awarding committees of well-known British literary prizes—such as the recently renamed Man Booker Prize and the Whitbread Book of the Year Award—routinely bestow their highest honors on writers all over a world once dominated by the British Empire, the current boundaries of British literature sometimes seem to be everything originally written in English other than American literature. Additionally, college courses frequently draw on contemporary concepts such as postcolonialism or multiculturalism; consequently, students may be asked to study Joyce Cary and Chinua Achebe in a single course on the contemporary British novel, or to examine Joseph Conrad's novels in light of V. S. Naipaul's work, or to place novels by Rudyard Kipling and Ruth Prawer Jhabvala side by side for comparison. Clearly, an understanding of British experience in the 20th century must be informed by an equally strong understanding of Indian, Caribbean, Canadian, Australian, Nigerian, and other nationalities that have been influenced by the British and that have influenced the British in return.

This volume follows the practices established by British literary prizes in defining British literature broadly: The authors profiled are all native to the countries of the British Commonwealth and Ireland, and the works presented were all written in English and published in England, with a very few exceptions, such as the novels that Samuel Beckett initially wrote in French before producing his own translations of them into English. In addition to the canonical writers of the century, I have covered all of the winners of the Man Booker Prize since it was founded in 1968 and of the Whitbread Book of the Year Award since it was developed in 1977. I have also mentioned other significant prizes, where relevant, such as the James Tait Black Memorial Prize, the *Guardian* Fiction Prize, and the Hawthornden Prize, but it was not possible to cover every winning title or to include every notable

prize currently awarded for British novels. Every title entry has a corresponding author entry; additionally, a few other authors are profiled without a detailed title entry. I also reviewed as many college-level syllabuses as I could find to make sure I had included authors being taught who have not won the approval of prize committees. And a few selections, of course, such as *I Capture the Castle,* by Dodie Smith, and *Cold Comfort Farm,* by Stella Gibbons, won their spot because they were personal favorites that I want others to enjoy too.

The title list of this volume includes works published in every year of the 20th century except three, and the exceptions speak for themselves: 1912, not too long before the outbreak of World War I; 1933, at the height of "the Slump," as the Great Depression was called in England when it occurred; and 1942, when German bombers were pounding London during the blitzkrieg. Books were published during these years, of course, but those titles have not found a place in the curricula of contemporary high schools and colleges. Instead of choosing titles of little use to students and teachers in order to provide complete coverage of the entire century, I have included profiles of lesser-known but prolific authors, such as Netta Syrett, who published in those years.

In addition to choosing novels representative of the entire century and of the entire geographical range of British influence, I have sampled as many genres of literature as possible, including the popular genres of mystery and detective fiction, spy novels, science fiction and fantasy, historical fiction, and romance. Covering popular literature is important, as I have learned in my teaching: Students are more likely to read for pleasure than for literary edification, but any kind of reading can become a conduit to a better understanding of the formal devices and structural techniques that writers use in creating novels. I have had to limit the range of titles and authors I selected to represent popular genres. Sometimes I chose my titles and authors on the basis of critical opinion, as in the choice of John le Carré to represent the genre of spy novels, but a few personal preferences prevailed, such as the choice of the Aubrey-Maturin novels of Patrick O'Brian to represent popular historical fiction.

Although thoroughness in covering the vast range of popular fiction was not possible, I made a point of covering a particular aspect of serious fiction as thoroughly as possible: In the case of the roman-fleuve, which I have come to view as a definitive aspect of 20th-century British fiction, I have individually profiled all of the titles in the most critically acclaimed examples of this kind of writing. Thus I include a title entry for all 12 volumes of Anthony Powell's *A Dance to the Music of Time,* for all 11 volumes of C. P. Snow's *Strangers and Brothers,* for the five volumes of Doris Lessing's *Children of Violence,* and for the four volumes of Lawrence Durrell's *Alexandria Quartet* (although Durrell explicitly distanced his work from this categorization); additionally, I include an overview of each of these series to serve as a guide to the individual title entries. This way, whether readers begin the search for information with the series title or with an individual title, they will quickly gain insight into the work as a whole.

For other trilogies and tetralogies that are now available in one-volume editions, I covered all of the component titles in single entries, discussing the series as a whole and detailing the individual volumes in one long entry with cross-references to the separate titles included in the alphabetical listing. Readers looking for information on *Out of the Silent Planet,* by C. S. Lewis, for example, are referred to *The Space Trilogy,* where the title is profiled along with its companion volumes, *Perelandra* and *That Hideous Strength.* Similarly, readers searching for *The Manticore* are referred to Robertson Davies's *The Deptford Trilogy;* those searching for *The Ghost Road* are referred to Pat Barker's *Regeneration Trilogy.* In choosing this arrangement, my intention is to encourage students to read related titles together and thereby to strengthen their abilities to sustain attention across the entire span of an author's vision.

I have written the title entries so as to make clear to teachers and parents whether a particular book is suitable for all readers, mentioning an author's use of explicit language or content, for example, but leaving the task of passing judgment on such examples to those concerned with the reading choices of students. For example, I include an entry for *Trainspotting,* by Irving Welsh, but I indicate that it may be offensive to some readers; I include *Crash,* by J. G. Ballard, noting that the novel includes violence and perversity as well as insight into the fascination that automobiles hold for

their drivers; I include famously controversial novels such as *Lady Chatterley's Lover,* but I also alert readers to the content that provoked its suppression. It is not my intention to discourage anyone from reading or to encourage teachers and parents to censor student reading; however, I do recognize that not all of the titles included in this companion are appropriate for all of the readers who may consult it. Bold readers may feel that I have erred on the side of caution, while those with more fastidious reading preferences may lean in the opposite direction.

The entries are also designed to alert readers to particular difficulties they may encounter, and in a few cases I have recommended the kind of preparatory reading that may be necessary to develop a full appreciation of a challenging but rewarding text. For example, *Flaubert's Parrot,* by Julian Barnes, is vastly more rewarding *after* the reader has become familiar with, at the very least, "A Simple Heart," by Gustave Flaubert. Novels about Ireland, such as *Fools of Fortune,* by William Trevor, and novels about India, such as *Clear Light of Day,* by Anita Desai, frequently become more enjoyable after the reader is familiar with crucial historical developments in those countries. Throughout, I have tried to imagine what the reader-in-training would need to know in order to understand and appreciate the contexts that writers may have assumed their readers would already share. I include thumbnail sketches of the key events of the 20th century relevant to British history, politics, and culture, with reference to particular novels, as appropriate, but readers should look on these entries merely as starting points for understanding the events that form a background to many British novels. I urge students to make use of the references provided with each entry to develop deeper and more thorough knowledge.

I have paid particular attention to matters of narrative structure, because in my teaching experience I have found that students frequently have difficulty in identifying point of view and other formal features, at least at a first reading of a text. In interpreting texts, I have applied the critical approaches that seemed most appropriate to me, providing an overview of those approaches in a separate glossary. I consider a thorough knowledge of the formal aspects of fiction to be the foundation that best allows students to develop sophisticated reading skills. But formal study is merely a powerfully useful starting point and not an end in itself, and so I include discussions of historical, feminist, Marxist, postcolonial, and postmodern influences, among others, where appropriate.

Although most of this volume resulted from my own reading and writing, I drew on the expertise of a few friends and colleagues as well. Dr. Virginia Brackett wrote all of the materials about Virginia Woolf, and she shared her broad knowledge of English literature freely. Dr. Viki Craig wrote the biography of Graham Greene and the analyses of *The Heart of the Matter* and *The Power and the Glory*; our conversations about Greene's novels helped me expand my coverage of this important writer. Eric Rauscher of the Mythopoeic Society provided an essay about Charles Williams's most noted novel, *Descent into Hell*, and his conference presentations deepened my knowledge of this writer and of the Inklings as well. My student Aleta Bowman

developed the essay on *The Enchanted April* and shared her knowledge of romance literature. At the last minute when I wanted to cover one of the years of the century that did not produce a classic text, Dr. Jill Jones instantly provided a biography of Netta Syrett. And my husband, Marcus Russell, provided daily encouragement and read many of the books I was working on and discussed them with me; he also wrote the analysis of *Hotel du Lac*. I am deeply grateful for all of the assistance and encouragement I received from these avid readers.

I hope that this book leads readers—students and teachers both—to a wider sampling of British literature than they might have found on their own, and that it amplifies their understanding, appreciation, and enjoyment of the texts I have included here. Any success in that endeavor owes a tremendous debt to the English teachers who have helped me to understand and appreciate literature; any shortcomings, however, are entirely my own.

A

A. B. C. MURDERS, THE AGATHA
CHRISTIE (1936)   One of CHRISTIE'S most admired
mysteries and a fine example of MYSTERY AND DETECTIVE
FICTION, *The A. B. C. Murders* pits Hercule Poirot against
someone who kills by the alphabet and who also sends
Poirot an ominous letter before each murder. Christie
constructs her puzzle by having the murderer commit
decoy murders; in a further level of distraction, the
murderer also anonymously hires a patsy (Alexander
Bonaparte Cust) and employs him on bogus sales trips
to the towns where the murders are to be committed.

In addition to having the murderer distract Poirot
through misdirection, Christie works the same angle
on the reader by allowing the telling of her story to
switch from one narrator to another. Usually, Captain
Hastings relates the entire story from a first-person
point of view. In *The A. B. C. Murders,* however, the
story is amplified by means of mysterious asides from
a third-person narrator limited to Cust's thoughts and
behaviors. Initially, these passages are extremely short,
but as Cust is more firmly fixed in the reader's mind as
a suspect, they become more detailed. The coincidence
of his work taking him to all the murder locations
eventually persuades even Cust that he must be guilty
of at least some of these crimes.

As the story opens, Poirot no longer takes routine
cases, but the killer's taunting letter summons him to a
duel of wits. The story unfolds according to the usual
detective formula: After each crime, everyone connected to the victim is questioned to discover the
motive and establish the opportunity for murder. But
as the crimes multiply, so does the pool of potential
suspects. There seems to be no connection between the
victims. Even the murders themselves bear little resemblance to one another, and the fourth murder in Don-
caster seems to miss the mark entirely, since the
victim's name doesn't even start with the letter *D*!

Only after this fourth murder does a smidgen of evidence begin to link poor A. B. Cust to the murder
scenes. Already suspecting himself, Cust flees in a
panic. He knows he has an alibi for the second murder—but could he have committed the other ones in a
deranged state? Dejected, he turns himself in at the
police station. Although Cust is tried and convicted,
when Hercule Poirot interviews the man, he establishes to his satisfaction that Cust could not have committed the crimes. He continues his own investigation.

Although Scotland Yard always suspected a homici-
dal maniac, Poirot remains convinced that the murderer was quite rational and highly clever. The
sensational media circus that attached itself to the
investigation suggests to Poirot that the murderer
intended to create a smoke screen out of many murders to hide the one murder that he or she would benefit from. But which murder is the catalyst, and which
are the distracters? In a detailed exposition, Poirot
assembles the suspects and carries them through the
deductive process that has led him to the truth about

the A. B. C. murders. He flushes his quarry and secures a panicked confession in front of the other witnesses. The case is solved in an unexpected way that demonstrates Poirot's powerful insight into the criminal mind.

In *The A. B. C. Murders,* Christie is at her best. She repeatedly places the guilty party in view, but in such a way that the reader does not draw the right conclusions. Her puzzle is tightly and believably constructed, and through the use of a suspenseful second narrator with a carefully controlled point of view, she keeps attention on the decoy rather than the murderer.

BIBLIOGRAPHY

Bargainnier, Earl F. *The Gentle Art of Murder: The Detective Fiction of Agatha Christie.* Bowling Green, Ohio: Bowling Green University Press, 1981.

Maida, Patricia D., and Nicholas B. Spornick. *Murder She Wrote: A Study of Agatha Christie's Detective Fiction.* Bowling Green, Ohio: Bowling Green University, 1982.

Sova, Dawn B. *Agatha Christie A to Z: The Essential Reference to Her Life and Writings.* New York: Facts On File, 1996.

ACCEPTANCE WORLD, THE ANTHONY POWELL (1955)

The third of 12 volumes in POW-ELL'S ROMAN-FLEUVE entitled *A DANCE TO THE MUSIC OF TIME,* this novel uses a first-person point of view to continue the narrative of Nicholas Jenkins, a writer, as he completes his transition to adulthood in the years 1931–33. In the overall structure of the series, *The Acceptance World* is positioned at the close of the first of four "movements," when the characters are settling into relationships (although not necessarily into marriages) and embarking on careers. The novel follows *A BUYER'S MARKET* (1952) and precedes *AT LADY MOLLY'S* (1957).

As the story opens, Jenkins is employed at a publishing house and has also written his first novel. He worries over the introduction to *The Art of Horace Isbister,* to be written by the elderly Victorian novelist St. John Clarke, a friend of the painter. When Isbister dies, the book's publication acquires greater urgency, and events are set in motion that will move Jenkins's life in new directions. Two school friends, the Freudian poet Mark Members and the Marxist ideologue J. G. Quiggin, become entangled in Clarke's affairs. A chance meeting—a recurring device in the series—reunites Jenkins and Quiggen with Peter Templer; with Peter's wife, Mona; and with his sister, Jean. Mona seems very interested in Quiggin, while Jenkins is interested in Jean, who recently separated from her husband, and to whom Jenkins had previously had a romantic attachment. Both men are soon involved in affairs.

A memorial exhibit of Isbister's portraits provides Jenkins with the opportunity to meet several old acquaintances, and the setting naturally allows the conversations to focus on questions relevant to art—a subject of considerable interest to Powell and a frequent topic of conversation among the characters he creates. Mark Members tells how Quiggin supplanted him as Clarke's secretary; ironically, he has also supplanted Peter Templar. A political demonstration passes by, and in the front ranks they see St. John Clarke with Quiggin—and Mona Templer! Jean learns that Mona has left Peter; other young marriages are breaking up as well.

In the closing event of the novel, Jenkins attends the "Old Boy Dinner," an annual reunion for alumni of his school residential house. He sits between Peter Templer, a golden boy who has outlived his glory, and Kenneth Widmerpool, a man who had been an outcast at school but who is now enjoying great success in the "acceptance world" of futures trading. Widmerpool demonstrates both his folly and his efficiency in the course of the evening, giving an unwanted speech and then taking charge of getting the intoxicated Charles Stringham home. Jenkins goes to visit Jean, but this relationship, too, is fated to end soon. For the moment, Jenkins and Jean agree not to talk about the future.

Formally, *The Acceptance World* brings to a close the first phase of the lives of Jenkins and his friends. Their school years and the social whirlwind of the debutante period is behind them. They are now independent adults, for better or worse, coping with the personal choices they have made with regard to relationships and employment and attempting to fulfill their ambitions. Collectively, they constitute the figures in a vast dance, turning through the required steps, joining hands and then handing off partners, playing out their parts in the grand design of life.

BIBLIOGRAPHY

Joyau, Isabelle. *Understanding Powell's A Dance to the Music of Time.* New York: St. Martin's Press, 1994.

Selig, Robert L. *Time and Anthony Powell.* Cranbury, N.J.: Associated University Presses, 1991.

Spurling, Hillary. *Invitation to the Dance: A Guide to Anthony Powell's A Dance to the Music of Time.* Boston: Little, Brown, 1977.

ACHEBE, CHINUA (1930–   )

One of the most distinguished and honored writers in the world, Albert Chinualumogu Achebe was born in Nigeria on November 16, 1930, the son of Nigerian parents of the Ibo people, who had converted to Christianity—his father was an Anglican preacher. He attended missionary schools and government schools in which English was the only language permitted, since at the time Nigeria was still under the rule of British COLONIALISM. He completed his secondary education at Government College from 1944 to 1947 and then was matriculated at University College in Ibadan, where he received a bachelor's degree in 1953. He worked for the Nigerian Broadcasting Corporation for 12 years, until 1966, spending 1956 in London, where he studied with the British Broadcasting Corporation. In 1961, he was married; he and his wife are the parents of four children.

During this period, Achebe began writing poetry and fiction. His first novel, THINGS FALL APART, appeared in 1958 and is now considered to be a classic of world literature. Achebe chose to write in English in order to regain possession, for Africans, of the narration of African experience. In his view, English writers such as Joseph CONRAD and Joyce CARY had developed an Anglo-centric view of the colonial experience in Africa, particularly in novels like HEART OF DARKNESS and *Mister Johnson,* and Achebe set himself the task of telling that same story of colonialism from the perspective of those who had been colonized. His next three novels continue the story of the Ibo experience of colonialism: *No Longer at Ease* (1960) recounts the disillusionment of an idealistic young Nigerian, trained to undertake the governmental work formerly reserved to the British administrators, who sinks to corruption and alienation; *The Arrow of God* (1964) returns to village life during the early days of contact to explore the replace-ment of the native religion by Christianity; and *A Man of the People* (1966) examines the phenomenon of corruption in Nigerian politics.

When violent civil strife broke out in 1966, Achebe curtailed his writing in order to work in support of Biafra (in secession from 1967 to 1970) and the Ibo people. He worked to publicize the war to the wider world and to raise funds for the cause. He published poetry, short fiction, and children's books; after 1970, when Biafra was reunified as part of Nigeria, he embarked on an academic career that included periods at the University of Nigeria, the University of Massachusetts, and the University of Connecticut. In 1987, he returned to the genre of the novel with *The Anthills of the Savannah,* short-listed for the BOOKER PRIZE. This novel is set in an imaginary African country (modeled on Uganda under Idi Amin) and follows the lives of three boys, one of whom nurtures the desire to become president for life.

In 1990, Achebe was severely injured in a car accident while traveling to the airport in Lagos, Nigeria. The accident left him partially paralyzed. Since then, he has accepted several appointments in the United States and Europe as visiting professor in institutions of higher education such as Stanford University and Bard College. His precarious health and the deteriorated political situation in Nigeria have necessitated a virtual exile, but he has remained active as a writer and a speaker. Numerous universities have awarded honorary degrees to him, and his most famous novel, *Things Fall Apart,* has become widely adopted in high school curricula. His influence on the African novelists who have come after him has been enormous, and his success at placing the African view of the colonial collision with Europe before a worldwide audience is unmatched.

BIBLIOGRAPHY

Achebe, Chinua. *Home and Exile.* New York: Oxford University Press, 2000.

Carroll, David. *Chinua Achebe.* New York: Macmillan, 1990.

Ezenwa-Ohaeto. *Chinua Achebe: A Biography.* Bloomington: Indiana University Press, 1997.

Lindfors, Bernth. *Conversations with Chinua Achebe.* Jackson: University Press of Mississippi, 1997.

ACKROYD, PETER (1949–)

Author of the WHITBREAD AWARD–winning novel HAWKSMOOR (1985), which also received the GUARDIAN FICTION PRIZE in the same year, Peter Ackroyd was an established poet, scholar, biographer, and critic before he turned his hand to fiction. The subjects of his biographies include the poets William Blake, Ezra Pound, and T. S. Eliot; the Victorian novelist Charles Dickens; and the martyr Thomas More. His novels frequently reveal his interest in history and biography, since he draws real people from the past, such as Thomas Chatterton or Oscar WILDE, and uses them as characters in complex stories that unfold in a modern world that remains intimately interconnected with the past.

Ackroyd was born October 5, 1949, in London. He completed an M.A. degree at Clare College, Cambridge, in 1971 and received a Mellon fellowship to attend Yale University from 1971 to 1973. While at Yale he was strongly influenced by the explosion of interest in POSTMODERNISM among scholars there in French literary criticism and philosophy. His studies led him to repudiate the value of realism as a literary form: His own novels often make paradoxical connections between the past and the present that sometimes elude the understanding of the very characters enmeshed in those connections.

Peter Ackroyd has spent his professional life as a writer, serving as first literary editor and then managing editor of the *Spectator* (1973–81) and later serving as television critic and then chief book reviewer for the London *Times* newspaper (beginning in 1981). His biographical writings have been particularly admired; he received the Heinemann Award in 1985 for *T. S. Eliot: A Life,* and he was awarded the JAMES TAIT BLACK MEMORIAL PRIZE for Best Biography in 1998 for *The Life of Thomas More.* His second novel, *The Last Testament of Oscar Wilde,* received the Somerset Maugham Award in 1984.

Peter Ackroyd lives in London and continues to publish fiction and nonfiction works. His novels include *The Great Fire of London* (1982), about a disastrous attempt to film Dickens's *Little Dorrit; The Last Testament of Oscar Wilde* (1983), purporting to be Wilde's diary from the last months of his life; *Hawksmoor* (1984), which combines a murder mystery and a horror story; *Chatterton* (1988), about a minor modern poet obsessed by the possibility that the poet Thomas Chatterton faked his famous suicide in the 18th century; *First Light* (1989), focusing on a contemporary excavation of a neolithic archaeological site; *English Music* (1992), a review of English cultural history; *The House of Doctor Dee* (1993), set in both the Elizabethan era and the modern world and uniting them in the house once owned by an alleged sorcerer; *The Trial of Elizabeth Cree: A Novel of the Limehouse Murders,* published as *Dan Leno and the Limehouse Golem* in Britain (1994), about a series of murders in the Victorian era; *Milton in America* (1997), which imagines that the blind author of *Paradise Lost* traveled to the new world to join the Pilgrim separatists in Massachusetts; and *The Plato Papers: A Prophesy* (2000), set in the distant future and casting a jaundiced eye over the past, including the era we still live in.

BIBLIOGRAPHY

Freiburg, Rudolph, and Jan Schnitker. *"Do You Consider Yourself a Postmodern Author?" Interviews with Contemporary English Writers.* Piscataway, N.J.: Transaction Publishers, 1999.

Onega, Susana. "Peter Ackroyd." In *Postmodernism: The Key Figures.* Edited by Hans Bertens and Joseph P. Natoli. Malden, Mass.: Blackwell Publishers, 2002, 1–6.

ADAMS, DOUGLAS (1952–2001)

Born in Cambridge, England in 1952, Douglas Adams received his early education in Essex before matriculating at St. John's College in Cambridge. He earned a bachelor's degree in English literature there in 1974 and later completed a master's degree as well. His earliest professional work was as a producer and writer for radio and television programs. Adams's first three novels, based on his radio series, *The HITCHHIKER'S GUIDE TO THE GALAXY,* won the Golden Pan award, each selling more (much more) than a million copies. He married in 1991; a daughter was born in 1994. Douglas Adams died unexpectedly of a heart attack at age 49 in 2001 while living with his family in California.

With the airing of *The Hitchhiker's Guide to the Galaxy* as a BBC radio play in 1978, Douglas Adams became a 26-year-old phenomenon. The radio program quickly gained a cult following among SCIENCE FICTION fans; subsequently, recordings of the radio presentation were packaged for sale on audiocassettes, extending the reach of the broadcast to new audiences. Additionally, the story was printed as a set of best-selling novels; it was performed as a television series; and it was getting another makeover as a film screenplay at the time of Adams's death. (The film was released in 2005.) In print form, the story of Arthur Dent's adventures after the destruction of Earth by a Vogon constructor fleet sold millions of copies worldwide and was translated into several languages. The complete series consists of *The Hitchhiker's Guide to the Galaxy,* published in 1979; *The Restaurant at the End of the Universe* (1980); *Life, the Universe, and Everything* (1982); *So Long and Thanks for all the Fish* (1984), and *Mostly Harmless* (1992).

The story's transformation into multiple forms of presentation is characteristic of Adams's interests and talents. He was a noted advocate of the Internet, helping to found a site called h2g2 (subsequently relocated to http://www.bbc.co.uk/h2g2/guide/) and producing a documentary about the Internet for BBC radio. He created an award-winning computer game, *Starship Titanic,* which featured sophisticated language-parsing abilities so that players could converse via the keyboard with the game's characters.

Although the many forms of *The Hitchhiker's Guide to the Galaxy* dominated Adam's creative work, he also wrote two mystery/fantasy novels, *Dirk Gently's Holistic Detective Agency* (1987) and *The Long Dark Tea-Time of the Soul* (1988). Additionally, he collaborated with John Lloyd on *The Meaning of Liff* (1984) and *The Deeper Meaning of Liff* (1990), dictionaries of words (derived from proper names) that do not yet exist but that would be useful if they did. In support of his interest in saving endangered animal species and in order to bring the plight of wild animals to a wider public, he traveled the world and cowrote a nonfiction work, *Last Chance to See* (1990), with zoologist Mark Carwardine. A posthumous collection of miscellaneous writings, *The Salmon of Doubt,* edited by Christopher Cerf, was published in 2002; it includes an unfinished third volume in the Dirk Gently series.

BIBLIOGRAPHY

"Douglas Adams's Official Home on the Web." Available online. URL: http://www.douglasadams.com. Accessed June 2004.

Gaiman, Neil and David K. Dickson. *Don't Panic: Douglas Adams and* The Hitchhiker's Guide to the Galaxy. London: Titan, 1993.

Simpson, Mike. *Hitchhiker: A Biography of Douglas Adams.* London: Hodder & Stoughton, 2003.

ADAMS, RICHARD (1920–) The most famous of Richard Adams's books is his first novel, WATERSHIP DOWN, a modern beast fable published to surprising success in 1972. He originally invented the story to amuse his children, and at their insistence he wrote it out and sought a publisher, enduring numerous rejections before he found one. The book went on to sell more than a million copies and won both the *Guardian* Award for Children's Literature and the Carnegie Medal in 1972.

Adams was born in Newbury, England, on May 9, 1920. After serving in the army during World War II, he entered Worcester College, Oxford, earning an M.A. in 1948. He was married in 1949; he and his wife are the parents of two daughters. Adams was employed as a civil servant from 1948 to 1974, eventually holding the post of assistant secretary of the Department of Environment. After 1974, he worked as a full-time writer. He has taught at the University of Florida (1975) and Hollins College (1976) as a writer-in-residence.

In addition to *Watership Down,* Adams's other published novels are *Shardik* (1974), a mythic FANTASY on an epic scale; *The Plague Dogs* (1977), again using anthropomorphic animals to condemn their use in scientific research; *The Girl in a Swing* (1980), a combination of a love story and a ghost story; *Maia* (1985), a fantasy that follows the adventures of its eponymous heroine, who rises from slavery to save her people; and *Traveller* (1988), which tells the story of the Civil War through the eyes of General Robert E. Lee's horse as he reminisces in later life to the tomcat in the stable.

As a writer, Adams has enjoyed greater success with a popular audience than with critics. He turns a perceptive and sympathetic eye on nature and its nonhuman occupants, reserving his harshest judgments for those human beings who destroy the balance of the natural world.

BIBLIOGRAPHY

Adams, Richard. *The Day Gone By: An Autobiography.* London: Hutchinson, 1990.

———. "Some Ingredients of *Watership Down.*" In *The Thorny Paradise: Writers on Writing for Children.* Edited by Edward Blishen. Harmondsworth, U.K.: Penguin Books, 1975.

Lurie, Alison. *Don't Tell the Grown-ups: The Subversive Power of Children's Literature.* Boston: Little, Brown, 1998, chap. 15.

AERODROME: A LOVE STORY, THE REX WARNER (1941)

This political ALLEGORY predates George ORWELL's *NINETEEN-EIGHTY-FOUR* by seven years, but shares with it a critical view of totalitarian efficiency. *The Aerodrome* features two contrasting settings, highlighting the crucial differences and quintessential weaknesses of both: The unnamed village represents traditional English agrarian life, while the nearby Aerodrome represents modernity and progress. The settings are mutually exclusive examples of open and closed societies, respectively. The ancient village is bound to the fertile earth; it is a somewhat derelict place that tolerates drunkenness, inefficiency, and indulgence in human feeling. The Aerodrome looks to the skies; it is a sterile place that rewards cold indifference, machine-like conformity, and rigorous self-discipline.

The novel's first-person narrator, Roy, relates the events of the year that follows his 21st birthday; the Air Vice-Marshal announces that he is appropriating the entire village and putting it into the service of the Aerodrome, appointing the Flight-Lieutenant to serve as the village "padre." Roy decides to enter the Air Force and hears the Air Vice-Marshal explain his philosophy to the recruits. He is opposed to "words without wings" such as ownership, parenthood, locality, and marriage. Parents transmit the stupidity of history to their children, so airmen should shut their parents out of their minds, along with all their parents' ideas. Sex, on the other hand, is perfectly permissible, as long as no children are fathered. Airmen are to reject the old values of the village through their callous and irresponsible behavior

and indulgence in sexual license without emotional, marital, or filial obligations. The goal of the airman must always be the acquisition of power and freedom.

The positions and attitudes of Roy and the Flight-Lieutenant are slowly reversed. Roy begins to find the village and its traditions distasteful, while the Flight-Lieutenant begins to take his duties as padre seriously. Roy is promoted to serve as attaché to the Air Vice-Marshal, while the Flight-Lieutenant finds himself preaching against the depredations of the Aerodrome against the village. When he openly condemns the Aerodrome from the pulpit, the Air Vice-Marshal orders the Flight-Lieutenant back to the Aerodrome. Roy steadily rises in the estimation of the Air Vice-Marshal and learns how vast his leader's ambition is: He plans to appropriate the entire country to serve the needs of the Air Force.

When the Flight-Lieutenant is killed, Roy confronts the Air Vice-Marshal and asks if he had ordered an execution; disillusioned, Roy indicates that he no longer supports the Air Vice-Marshal's political ambitions. But several secrets are soon revealed about the Air Vice-Marshal and his relationship to the villagers and to Roy—secrets that explain why he molded himself into a military disciplinarian and became the enemy of family and community. His tactics lead to his demise just as he expects to achieve the power he longs for.

Warner's allegory is a chronicle of deeply felt and finely shaded emotions: Roy recounts his transformation from villager to Aerodrome officer and back to villager with clarity and sensitivity. Despite this psychological realism in the characters, the social and political environment of *The Aerodrome* is a dystopia (see DYSTOPIAN NOVELS), although one lacking the crushing dreariness that Orwell thought would dominate a totalitarian state. The Aerodrome's similarity to the fascist regimes that England faced in war at the time the novel was written is apparent; however, there is also a faint allusion to the hedonistic entrapment that Aldous HUXLEY recounted in *BRAVE NEW WORLD*. The Air Vice-Marshal purchases the souls of his recruits with sexual promiscuity and a license to abandon the personal obligations that both complicate and enrich human life; the recruits readily accept the payoff without realizing that they have gotten the worst of the bargain.

BIBLIOGRAPHY

Chialant, Maria Theresa. "The Aerodrome: Prols, Pubs, and Power." In *A Garland for Rex Warner: Essays in Honour of His Eightieth Birthday.* Edited by A. L. McLeod. Mysore, India: Literary Half-Yearly Press, 1985.

McLeod, A. L. *Rex Warner, Writer: An Introductory Essay.* Sydney: Wentworth Press, 1964.

Reeve, N. H. *The Novels of Rex Warner: An Introduction.* New York: St. Martin's Press, 1989.

AESTHETICISM

Also referred to as "art for art's sake," the aestheticism movement affected the visual and literary arts in the last two decades of the 19th century, although its inspirations and influences extend further back into the Victorian era and reach across national boundaries. Advocates of aestheticism sought to overturn the ancient traditional definition of art. As far back as Aristotle, art had been defined as a useful as well as an enjoyable activity; in the famous phrase of the Roman poet Horace, art was required to be both *"dulce et utile,"* or pleasant and useful. The function of art, on this definition, is to teach and delight its audience, and thus the aesthetic aspect of art was yoked to a didactic purpose. On this model, artists function as teachers who deliver lessons to audiences through the instrument of their art. The relationship of artists to their audiences takes precedence over the relationship of artists to their art, and art itself serves that relationship as a vehicle or conduit of the message it carries. The pleasing characteristics of art—the beauty of its form, for example—captures the attention of the audience and facilitates the delivery of a lesson.

In contrast to this traditional definition of art, 19th-century artists (understood in the broadest sense of the term, including painters, poets, novelists, and critics) embraced the notion that art does *not* have utility, that it does not serve a moral or instructional purpose. These aestheticists valued their relationship to art itself and sought to liberate art from the task of proving its worth on the merit of the teaching it could communicate. On this model, form takes precedence over content, and the relationship of artists to their art takes precedence over their relationship to their audience. This attention to form opened the door to extraordinary innovation: Artists began to experiment with the traditional formal aspects of art, and as a result new kinds of painting, poetry, music, and fiction appeared. Some artists abandoned even beauty itself as a component of their art; for example, French symbolist poets such as Charles Baudelaire created poems that used images of decay, and impressionist painters such as Claude Monet produced images that suggested their subjects rather than representing them with strict fidelity to the original source. In this new approach to art, the work of artists would not necessarily teach anything or serve any useful purpose, and it might not even delight its audience, either.

Among British artists, supporters of aestheticism included pre-Raphaelite painters and poets such as Dante Gabriel Rossetti, literary critics such as Walter Pater, and writers such as Oscar WILDE, who was a vocal supporter of aestheticism. His essay "The Decay of Lying" is an ironic affirmation of the primacy of art over reality. In that essay, he asserts that life is an imitation of art and not, as is commonly thought, the other way round. If art is not an imitation of life, then clearly it is not necessary for art to restrict itself to representational modes or to realism. An era of unprecedented experimentation in form and subject matter followed from this simple alteration in the definition of art, marking out the 20th century as an age of innovation in every field of artistic endeavor.

BIBLIOGRAPHY

Bell-Villada, Gene H. *Art for Art's Sake and Literary Life: How Politics and Markets Helped Shape the Ideology and Culture of Aestheticism, 1790–1990.* Lincoln: University of Nebraska Press, 1996.

Dowling, Linda. *Aestheticism and Decadence: A Selective Annotated Bibliography.* New York: Garland Publishers, 1977.

Johnson, Robert Vincent. *Aestheticism.* New York: Barnes & Noble, 1969.

AFFAIR, THE C. P. SNOW (1960)

Volume eight in SNOW's 11-volume ROMAN-FLEUVE *STRANGERS AND BROTHERS, The Affair* covers the years 1953 to 1954. It follows *The CONSCIENCE OF THE RICH* and precedes

CORRIDORS OF POWER, but it is most closely related to volume four in the series, The MASTERS. This earlier novel of academic politics, set in a preeminent British university (Cambridge), establishes many of the characters featured in The Affair some 16 years further on in their careers. Snow continues his examination of modern British life through the eyes of the narrator of the series, Lewis Eliot, an attorney who has also served as a lecturer and a fellow at the university.

The story's conflict begins when a brash young research physicist, Donald Howard, resigns after being accused of using a doctored photograph to support a published thesis. Howard is a vociferous supporter of communism; both his personality and his politics are at odds with the university's status quo. Neither of these factors, however, provides the grounds that would be required to dismiss him legitimately. Lewis Eliot becomes aware of the case when a historian and Laura Howard, the wife of Donald Howard, ask him to use his influence with the senior faculty to reinstate Howard. Eliot satisfies himself that justice has been done; however, new revelations and behind-the-scenes maneuvers alter the circumstances. Eliot's brother Martin, also a physicist, becomes involved. Awkward alliances must be established among old enemies, and future ambitions begin to affect present strategies as the case moves forward through the arcane system of the university's review process.

Unfortunately, Howard himself provides the court with little motivation to favor him. His abrasive personality is ill-suited to the rhetorical subtleties of a case that, if it succeeds, will transfer blame from him to another more distinguished individual. Ironically, many of the members of the university community are simultaneously sympathetic to Howard's cause and yet repelled by Howard's behavior and his politics. The possibility that Howard is innocent of research fraud divides the members of the Senior Court. In the end, AMBIGUITY remains: The two sides in the case serve as a study in the ways intelligent men of goodwill fail to secure either truth or justice, settling instead for the least damaging compromise.

BIBLIOGRAPHY

Bradbury, Malcolm. "New Men: Snow, Cooper, and the Novel of the Fifties." In No, Not Bloomsbury. New York: Columbia University Press, 1987, 173–189.

Karl, Frederick. The Politics of Conscience: The Novels of C. P. Snow. Carbondale: Southern Illinois University Press, 1963.

Ramanathan, Suguna. The Novels of C. P. Snow: A Critical Introduction. New York: Scribner, 1978.

AFRICAN QUEEN, THE   C. S. FORESTER (1935)

Although noted for his Horatio HORNBLOWER series, C. S. FORESTER wrote in many other genres. This romantic adventure flings together a mismatched couple in a struggle for survival against both nature and German aggressors in central Africa in the mid-1930s. Rose Sayer is the sister of a missionary who has died; she is alone until a boat arrives from the nearby mining operation. The Cockney boat captain, Charlie Allnut, barely escaped the Germans with his life and his rickety old steam-powered launch, the African Queen. He is intent on finding a safe hideout, but Rose has decided to "do something for England." Since the boat is stocked with explosives, pipes, and other hardware, she is sure that they can convert the boat into a bomb, get up a good head of steam, set course for a suitable target, and blow it up. As they face white water, leeches, and hostile Germans, Rose and Charlie fall in love before they know it; Forester's story is surprisingly sensitive to the transformation that love brings to Rose in particular. In the final few pages, however, the unexpected introduction of two British boats jars Charlie and Rose right out of the story; the narrative becomes a fast-paced account of a small-scale naval engagement, and the success against the Germans acquires a somewhat anticlimactic quality.

The FILM ADAPTATION directed by John Huston in 1951 with a screenplay by James Agee (also entitled The African Queen) gives Charlie and Rose the conclusion they deserve after their long struggle against the river. Although the final sentence of Forester's novel casts doubt on whether Charlie and Rose will live happily ever after once they are married, the movie version confirms they will indeed do so.

BIBLIOGRAPHY
Hepburn, Katharine. *The Making of* The African Queen, *or How I Went to Africa with Bogart, Bacall, and Huston and Almost Lost My Mind.* New York: Knopf/Random House, 1987.
Sternlicht, Sanford V. *C. S. Forester.* Twayne's English Authors, 320. Boston: Twayne Publishers, 1981.

AFTER LEAVING MR. MACKENZIE JEAN RHYS (1935)

The protagonist, Julia Martin, learns a bitter lesson as her attractiveness to men declines and she enters middle life alone and impoverished and likely to stay that way. Julia has just broken off her affair with Mr. Mackenzie, and the possibility that he has "finished her" lurks in her mind. She soothes herself with drink until his last check arrives. It is not enough money to return home and make a life, nor is there much to look forward to in England, where her stroke-paralyzed mother has been dying for years, tended by Julia's increasingly embittered younger sister.

After an ugly public confrontation with Mr. McKenzie, Julia meets Mr. Horsfield and accepts enough money from him to travel to England. While she is there, her mother dies without recognizing or speaking to her. Her wealthy uncle rebuffs her appeal for assistance insultingly, and her sister seizes all their mother's small estate. A former lover—the man who had first "ruined" her—gives her money for the last time, he says. The third-person narrator provides an unflinchingly scrupulous and dispassionate view of a woman whose life is unraveling and who can do nothing to reverse that process.

Back in Paris, Julia decks herself out in secondhand finery. Her black dress is not as flattering as she would wish; a fashionable hat, however, still lures the occasional man to follow her, at least until he sees the marks of age on the face beneath the brim. Dressed for the seduction she cannot now bring to pass, Julia contemplates the Seine and seems on the verge of throwing herself in. She is filled with frustrated rage: She has done nothing wrong, and yet her life has not gone right. She has lived a desperate and marginal existence so far, and peering dimly into the future, she finally recognizes that henceforth it will only be worse.

After Leaving Mr. Mackenzie contains several autobiographical details from the author's life, such as the loss of an infant and dissolution of a marriage. The story features her characteristic heroine—a woman who is attractive, vulnerable, and unconventional. Jean Rhys relates this painful tale with particular attention to the inconsistency of human thoughts and actions. Repeatedly, characters are of two minds, speaking polite invitations while thinking harsh rejections; wallets may open, but hearts close to Julia, and her options become ever narrower and more distasteful to her. Even though Julia Martin is not entirely likable, readers understand why she has declined to this state of affairs. Given the circumstances in which life has placed her and the risky gambles she has taken, pawning her body in hopes of winning a life of love and comfort, no other end is possible.

BIBLIOGRAPHY
Frickey, Pierrette, ed. *Critical Perspectives in Jean Rhys.* Washington, D.C.: Three Continents Press, 1990.
Gornick, Vivian. *The End of the Novel of Love.* Boston: Beacon Press, 1997.

AFTERNOON MEN ANTHONY POWELL (1931)

This SATIRE of modern life was the first novel published in the long and distinguished career of Anthony POWELL. The targets of Powell's satire are artists, intellectuals, and aristocratic poseurs; his own extensive knowledge of the arts underpins the fully rounded characters he creates to serve as vehicles of the human follies he implicitly condemns.

The story opens with the bored conversation between William Atwater, a museum curator, and Raymond Pringle, a young painter. Others in search of a good time soon join these young men, and all of them are invited by Harriet Twining, a beautiful and idle young woman, to crash a party. Atwater and Pringle amuse themselves observing the party, providing Powell with numerous targets for understated satirical comments. A not unattractive art student named Lola strikes up a meaningless but wittily ironic conversation with Atwater. In the midst of this pursuit, however, he sees a vision of loveliness enter his life when Susan Nunnery arrives. His attraction to Susan is not so strong as to force him to throw over a sure thing such as Lola; nonetheless, he has been stricken with a nascent and half-comprehended love for Susan. For his part, Pringle is soon in pursuit of Harriet, and much to his disappointment he gets her.

The plot follows the romantic entanglements of these friends through bohemian dinner parties, hip night clubs, and summer cottages. Atwater maintains his affair with Lola on the side and becomes an onlooker in Susan's life as newcomers to their circle are attracted to her. One such newcomer is a well-to-do gentleman in his 40s, Verelst, who is simultaneously hated for being a Jew and yet envied for his wealth, refined manners, and flawless sense of style. On Atwater's last date with Susan, he takes her to a boxing match, which serves as a metaphor of their relationship. He loses the struggle; she is going away. Later he learns she has gone to America with Verelst.

The romance between Pringle and Harriet is also a struggle: He has difficulty coping with the intense jealousy she provokes in him with her continual flirtations. At a weekend house party, Pringle stumbles on Harriet and another artist, his friend and rival, in a passionate embrace. When Pringle fails to turn up for lunch, his guests find a suicide note attached to the roast beef. Before they can make their befuddled escape, however, the presumed dead man turns up in fisherman's clothes, having been rescued from his planned expiration. Harriet now appreciates what she nearly lost, and Pringle is ready to forgive her. When the fisherman comes to claim his clothes, one of the funniest passages in the book occurs as the guests try to decide how much they should tip the man for rescuing the intended suicide. Back in London after this holiday, the story ends where it began: Several young people in search of a good time are on the verge of crashing yet another party.

Powell tells this story through the point of view of a third-person objective narrator. The reader sees the characters through descriptions of them and hears the witty banter they spend their lives exchanging, but there is little interior exploration of their feelings and personalities. This approach suits Powell's satirical purpose well: A detailed exploration of their minds would create too much sympathy for them. The effects of Powell's satire occur without the sacrifice of character depth. He is able to make Pringle the target of both ridicule and compassion, for example, and he invests the character of Susan Nunnery with a touching pathos. Although psychological realism is frequently associated with serious narratives, Powell's well-developed characters are as believable to readers as are their own friends and acquaintances, but he uses them to achieve highly comic effects without flattening or stereotyping them.

BIBLIOGRAPHY

Brennan, Neil Francis. *Anthony Powell.* Rev. ed. Twayne's English Authors, 158. New York: Twayne Publishers, 1995.

Gorra, Michael. *The English Novel at Mid-Century: From the Leaning Tower.* New York: Macmillan, 1990.

Tucker, James. *The Novels of Anthony Powell.* New York: Macmillan, 1976.

THE ALEXANDRIA QUARTET LAWRENCE DURRELL (1957–1960) Four novels make up this series: JUSTINE (1957), BALTHAZAR (1958), MOUNTOLIVE (1959), and CLEA (1960); each of these titles receives a detailed treatment under its own alphabetical entry. The story is set in the Egyptian city of Alexandria just before WORLD WAR II, a crossroads of the ancient and the new, simultaneously primitive and cosmopolitan. The main characters include the Irish teacher and writer Darley, who narrates the first two and the last volumes of the quartet in the first person; the two women with whom he has sexually obsessive love affairs, Justine, an Egyptian Jew, and Melissa, a dancer suffering from tuberculosis; Justine's husband, Nessim, a wealthy Coptic Christian and a friend of Darley's who fathers a child by Melissa; Pursewarden, a British diplomat and writer who also has an affair with Justine; Balthazar, the Alexandrian psychiatrist whom Darley consults; David Mountolive, a British diplomat and the lover of Nessim's mother, Leila, and later of Pursewarden's sister Liza, whose child is the fruit of her incestuous relationship with her brother; and the artist Clea, who also has affairs with Justine and Darley. Their stories—all concerned with modern love—unfold in a prose narrative that is highly poetic, evocative of the exotic setting in the city of Alexandria, erotically charged, and distinctly subjective. Overall, the series is noted for its innovations in narrative form.

Durrell uses several extra-narrative elements to help him achieve his goal of breaking the traditional linear structure of the novel as an art form. For example, he prefaces each volume of the series with a note to the reader and with epigraphs from the Marquis de Sade's infamous novel *Justine.* His notes vary, from the plain statement in the first book that the characters are all imaginary, to longer explanations of his plan in composing the series. He takes pains to point out that the series is not and could never become a "ROMAN-FLEUVE." Here, Durrell seems to be distancing his work from the multivolume fictions by writers such as John GALSWORTHY, Anthony POWELL, C. P. SNOW, and the French novelist Marcel Proust. The reader is gently instructed to perceive his series as a work inspired by Einstein's theory of relativity: The first three volumes present different aspects of events occurring in a particular space, viewing those events both subjectively and objectively, but not standing in relation to each other as sequels, while the fourth adds the dimension of time to the story and settles the events of the previous volumes into their proper sequence. In the prefatory note to *Clea,* Durrell uses the term *word continuum* to describe his series of novels.

In addition to opening remarks, Durrell also adds an unusual element to the end of all the novels in the series except *Mountolive*—the story as told from an "objective" stance. These passages are called "Consequential Data," "Workpoints," or simply "Notes." They resemble the rough sketches of a writer's brainstorming session, or they add specific information that the reader might not be able to infer from the text, such as the identification of "the old man" mentioned in the early pages of *Justine* as the Greek poet Cavafy. Like the footnotes to T. S. Eliot's poem *The Wasteland,* these additional materials augment the text and modify both the content and the form that the text takes as a work of art. The "Workpoints" in particular undermine the sense of an ending by opening up new possibilities for the characters. The story is not just what is written—it is also everything else that might occur in the imaginary lives of these people but that didn't happen to be recorded in the volumes in hand. The structure of each volume and of the series as a whole moves from the formality and the historical certainty of epigraphs, quoted from real writers who lived and wrote and died, to the informality of sketchy ideas for plot twists that have not yet happened to imaginary people. In form, the series moves from the actual real past to the possible imagined future, although it does not follow a linear path in getting there.

In his characters as well as his plot, Durrell strives to break with the norms of traditional realism in fictional representations of life. In telling the events of the story from different points of view, he attempts what Justine calls, in the volume named for her, "prism-sightedness." Like a cubist portrait that shows the front and the side view of a face simultaneously, or like the stop-motion effect of Marcel Duchamp's famous painting *Nude Descending a Staircase,* the characters in *The Alexandria Quartet* are layered with AMBIGUITY and potentiality. Readers must actively participate in constructing the characters, the events of their lives, and the motivations for their actions from the array of conflicting evidence Durrell assembles.

BIBLIOGRAPHY

Begnal, Michael H., ed. *On Miracle Ground: Essays on the Fiction of Lawrence Durrell.* Cranbury, N.J.: Associated University Presses, 1990.

Friedman, Alan Warren. *Lawrence Durrell and* The Alexandria Quartet: *Art for Love's Sake.* Norman: University of Oklahoma Press, 1970.

Raper, Julius Rowan, Melody L. Enscore, and Paige Matthey Bynum. *Lawrence Durrell: Comprehending the Whole.* Columbia: University of Missouri Press, 1995.

ALIENATION The definitive modern malaise, alienation is the characteristic of being cut off from sources of meaning or excluded from centers of power, and it crops up repeatedly in 20th-century literature. Alienation is a negative consequence of individualism, particularly when individualism is combined with a skeptical attitude toward the existence of universal truth or the purposefulness of human life. Alienated characters are typically disconnected from the larger world and may be powerless to bring about positive changes either for themselves or for others. They generally experience anger, resentment, frustration, and despair; they may be unable to establish successful personal relationships at home and at work, or they may resort to violence against themselves or against others in order to exert their will in the world. Alienation goes hand in hand with political powerlessness and social oppression; not surprisingly, alienated characters may be members of groups that are marginalized by their class, race, ethnicity, gender, religion, age, political affiliation, or sexual orientation. But since alienation is an outgrowth of individualism, any character—even a member of a powerful and privileged group—may suffer from it. One of the classic fictional studies of alienation is A CLOCKWORK ORANGE, by Anthony BURGESS. Alienation is characteristic of the novels of ANGRY YOUNG MEN such as Alan SILLITOE, John BRAINE, Kingsley AMIS, and John WAIN.

BIBLIOGRAPHY

Read, Herbert Edward. *Art and Alienation: The Role of the Artist in Society.* New York: Horizon Press, 1967.

Schmidt, Richard, and Thomas E. Moody. *Alienation and Social Criticism.* Atlantic Highlands, N.J.: Humanities Press, 1994.

ALLEGORY

A narrative in which each character stands for some particular abstract concept is allegorical in its structure; it was particularly popular as a fictional device in medieval literature. An allegory features characters who are ciphers or metaphors for qualities, sins, behaviors, or attitudes. Allegory is a form of metaphor, since it represents an unfamiliar abstraction in terms of concrete familiarity; more specifically, it is a thorough and systematic application of metaphor to an entire story that effectively doubles the story, making it work consistently on two levels at once. Readers who comprehend only the surface level of an allegorical narrative may enjoy the story, but they will miss the author's point: They must perceive the correspondence between the concrete characters, settings, and actions of the story and the abstract ideas the author represents through those characters, settings, and actions. Allegory is frequently used in religious texts such as parables, but it can also extend across an entire novel, such as John Bunyan's allegory of Christian perseverance, *The Pilgrim's Progress* (1678). Beast fables are usually allegories in which animals represent human beings; their behaviors display human follies that the story condemns. Twentieth-century examples of allegory include ANIMAL FARM, by George ORWELL, which is also a beast fable, and The AERODROME by REX WARNER.

BIBLIOGRAPHY

Bloomfield, Morton. *Allegory, Myth, and Symbol.* Cambridge, Mass.: Harvard University Press, 1981.

Fletcher, Angus. *Allegory: The Theory of a Symbolic Mode.* Ithaca, N.Y.: Cornell University Press, 1964.

MacQueen, John. *Allegory.* London: Methuen, 1970.

Quilligan, Maureen. *The Language of Allegory: Defining the Genre.* Ithaca, N.Y.: Cornell University Press, 1979.

AMBASSADORS, THE HENRY JAMES (1903)

The protagonist of the novel that Henry JAMES himself considered to be his best is Mr. Lewis Lambert Strether, an American editor and a widower with close ties to the wealthy and sternly Protestant Mrs. Newsome. This lady's grown son Chad has been touring Europe for some time, delaying his return to the family fold. Mrs. Newsome turns to Mr. Strether for assistance, offering to send him to Europe on a generous allowance in order to bring Chad home; for Mr. Strether's part, he has reason to expect that he may eventually be accepted as a marriage partner to Mrs. Newsome, and so of course he answers her call for help with her son. As the novel opens, Mr. Strether has only recently landed in England, having been dispatched as Mrs. Newsome's "ambassador" to Chad. At the outset, his mission is clear: Find Chad, separate him from his European attachments, and bring him home as soon as possible. On his very first day in Europe, however, Mr. Strether meets the charming Maria Gostrey, an American expatriate and a lady of independent means and ways.

In Paris, Mr. Strether learns that young Chad is deeply attached to Madame de Vionnet. Since she is older than Chad, Mr. Strether persuades himself as long as he can that the relationship is an innocent one, but circumstances finally force him to recognize the truth of their affair. In the meantime, Mr. Strether has himself become transformed by Europe and given up on his promise to retrieve the young man; his delay in bringing Chad home causes Mrs. Newsome to send another set of ambassadors, her no-nonsense sister, Mrs. Pocock, her brother-in-law, Jim Pocock, and Jim's naive sister, Mamie. These sturdy Americans prove to be immune to Europe's attractions, and they cannot comprehend why Chad and Mr. Strether are entranced by their idyll in the old world. In the end, Mr. Strether decides that he will return to his native land, although he regrets that he will lose the company of Maria Gostry. For his part, Chad remains firm in his intention to stay in Europe.

The clash between the behaviors and expectations of Americans and Europeans was a favorite subject for Henry James. Americans not infrequently come out the worse, as in *The American* (1876–77) and *Daisy Miller* (1878). Europe is James's great symbol of refinement and cultivation inextricably conjoined with decadence; it is the place where materialistic American Protestants can finally find a scale of comparison that dwarfs the achievements of the new world, especially in the arts. Mr. Strether's finer sensibilities blossom in this new environment, as Chad's had also done, but the older man feels the call of duty more strongly and is able to surrender his new enjoyments to go home.

BIBLIOGRAPHY

James, Henry. *The Ambassadors: An Authoritative Text, the Author on the Novel, Criticism.* New York: W. W. Norton, 1964.

Mizener, Arthur. *Twelve Great American Novels.* New York: New American Library, 1967.

Stone, Albert E., ed. *Twentieth Century Interpretations of* The Ambassadors: *A Collection of Critical Essays.* Englewood Cliffs, N.J.: Prentice Hall, 1969.

AMBER SPYGLASS, THE PHILIP PULL-MAN (2001)

This final volume of the trilogy entitled HIS DARK MATERIALS concludes the series that began with *The GOLDEN COMPASS* and continued in *The SUBTLE KNIFE*. It is the first example of children's literature to win the WHITBREAD Book of the Year Award. The story's protagonists, Lyra Silvertongue and Will Parry, complete their transition from childhood to young adulthood by traveling into the afterlife and helping to defeat the totalitarian divinities of the universe. Events draw them together and into their first experience of love only to separate them again, irrevocably and forever.

Pullman removes his heroine from the action in the first third of the novel but uses her like a magnet to draw the story's strands together. No one knows where Lyra is, but everyone wants to find her—some to save her, others to kill her. Will and the armored bear Iorek Byrnison lead the smallest search party, made powerful by Will's possession of the subtle knife. Lyra's father, Lord Asriel, dispatches armed units from the citadel he has raised against the Authority in Heaven; the Church's Consistorial Court contracts an assassin—complete with forgiveness in advance for his intended sin of murder—to kill Lyra, but he is spied on by Asriel's Gallivespian allies, tiny humans only a hand's-breadth tall.

In the novel's middle third, Lyra and Will must first repair the subtle knife, which turns out to have a vulnerability closely linked to Will's developing awareness of sexual attraction, and then use it to travel to the suburbs near the land of the dead. But getting to the afterlife itself, for the living, proves difficult, and no dæmon may proceed there; the separation threatened at Bolvangar in a riveting scene from *The Golden Compass* now becomes a reality. They discover that the land of the dead is terrorized by screaming harpies. Lyra decides to release the spirits of the dead from this torment; since ghosts are confined at the will of the Authority, releasing them will strike a devastating blow. To succeed, Lyra must discover how to appease the harpies.

In Lyra's home world, Church doctrine has decreed that Dust, the mysterious substance that set Lyra's adventures in motion, is the residue of original sin. Theologians think they can eliminate Dust by destroying Lyra; they have created a huge bomb that can kill her no matter where she is. Asriel discovers this plot and weakens the bomb but can't destroy it. The force of the explosion blows an abyss below the bottom of all the worlds, and soul-eating Specters come pouring through. Asriel has neither weapon nor lifeform to resist this attack until Lyra and Will free the ghosts of the dead. They, being spirits, are immune to the Specters.

In the novel's final third, Lyra and Will witness the climactic battle of Asriel's war. Creatures from all the worlds they have encountered are involved: Witches attack angels, armored bears dispatch cavalry, liberated ghosts engage Specters, gyptians battle ordinary humans, and Gallivespians dart through it all. Even afterward, however, Dust drains through the abyss, and more Specters enter through it. Finally, angels loyal to Asriel discover the problem's solution and its connection to the subtle knife; worse, Lyra and Will must return to their own worlds because their dæmons can thrive only in their native environments. The angels can keep only one window open: Either Will and Lyra can have a passageway between their worlds, or else the window from the land of the dead can stay open to liberate the souls of the deceased.

The Amber Spyglass is a thrilling conclusion to a compelling fantasy series. Young readers—and adults as well, armed with the right suspension of disbelief— will be delighted by the story's innovative, imaginative aspects and by the crucial roles that creatures of every age and type play in the resolution of the plot. But Pullman is also addressing an additional audience of educated readers who are familiar with the works of John Milton and with philosophical problems of metaphysics, cosmology, and theology. He achieves remarkable effects by weaving these erudite materials into the text in such a way that they do not become an impediment to readers not familiar with them.

BIBLIOGRAPHY

Bird, Anne-Marie. " 'Without Contraries Is No Progression': Dust as an All-Inclusive Metaphor in Philip Pullman's 'His Dark Materials,' " *Children's Literature in Education* 32, no. 2 (2001): 111–123.

Wood, Naomi. "Paradise Lost and Found: Obedience, Disobedience, and Story-telling in C. S. Lewis and Philip Pullman," *Children's Literature in Education* 32, no. 4 (2001): 237–259.

AMBIGUITY The indeterminate characteristic of being in between two or more possible states of res-

olution or understanding generates ambiguity in a literary text. It has become a common feature of 20th-century fiction, although it is by no means universal. Ambiguity now frequently occurs in the endings of novels; in such cases, authors leave the task of achieving closure for the story to their readers, setting up the PLOT and developing it to the climax without detailing its exact resolution. Certain genres, however, are less likely to employ ambiguity: MYSTERY AND DETECTIVE FICTION generally focuses on resolving uncertainty, at the very least with respect to the identity of the perpetrator of some crime, through the investigative process, and romance fiction exists to bring characters together successfully in unambiguous love, betrothal, or even marriage.

When ambiguity occurs in characters, readers are faced with the same problem that they encounter in all interactions with real people: They must figure out intentions and mental states based on the evidence of behavior and speech. When a story is related through a third-person objective point of view, with no glimpses into the minds of the characters, ambiguity is a possible result; it is not necessarily, however, a flaw in the writing, since fidelity to realism in narrating a story may require the same murkiness and obscurity one can find in ordinary life. And just as real people may deceive others to achieve their own ends, so too characters in novels may be designed to deceive their readers. When this kind of character is also telling the story, the result is an unreliable narrator.

Beginning readers of serious literature are sometimes frustrated by ambiguity in the construction of fiction. Writers who employ ambiguity invite readers to share in the construction of textual meaning, but this strategy *does* place greater demands on readers. Fortunately, the power to resolve ambiguity to one's satisfaction increases with greater experience as a reader; wider reading also helps eliminate the kind of ambiguity that is generated by readers' inabilities to recognize allusion or to catch the subtleties of symbolism. Fully developed readers have generally learned to relish ambiguity, savoring the many possibilities that the ambiguous text opens up and immersing themselves in the pleasant task of probing the uncertainties it provides. This process is the very essence of interpretation, the most important task readers undertake.

BIBLIOGRAPHY

Empson, William. *Seven Types of Ambiguity*. New York: New Directions, 1947.

Scheffler, Israel. *Beyond the Letter: A Philosophical Inquiry into Ambiguity, Vagueness, and Metaphor in Language*. London: Routledge & Kegan Paul, 1979.

AMIS, KINGSLEY (1922–1995)

The author of *Lucky Jim* (1954) and winner of the BOOKER PRIZE in 1986 for *The Old Devils*, Kingsley Amis was born in London to a working-class family. He first attended Norbury College and then moved to the City of London School. In 1941, he was awarded a scholarship to Oxford (St. John's College); there, he met the poet Philip Larkin, a lifelong friend. Amis's studies toward a degree in English literature were interrupted when he received a commission in the Royal Signal Corps at the outbreak of WORLD WAR II. During a three-year military career, he served in France, Belgium, and Germany. Upon his demobilization in 1945, he returned to Oxford, completing his degree in 1947. His first academic teaching post was at University College in Swansea, but after 12 years there he left teaching to work as a full-time writer. His two marriages ended in divorce, but he had three children by his first wife, including the novelist Martin AMIS.

Although he is often cited as one of the ANGRY YOUNG MEN, Kingsley Amis himself disavowed the connection. His politics as a young man were radical, but as he aged, his views drifted to the right and he became an outspoken critic of contemporary culture. He was knighted in 1990. By the time he died in 1995, Kingsley Amis had published more than 40 books, including works of fiction, poetry, essay, literary criticism, SCIENCE FICTION, memoirs, and other genres. He was an authority on James BOND, publishing a critical study, *The James Bond Dossier,* in 1965. After Ian FLEMING died, Amis also wrote a novel featuring James Bond as a main character, *Colonel Sun* (1968), publishing it under the nom de plume Robert Markham. He wrote three books on the topic of alcohol and drinking, a pastime of which he was particularly fond. His volumes of poetry, such as *Bright November* (1947) and *A Case of Samples: Poems 1946–1956* (1956), include meditative lyrics and light verse; additionally, he edited several anthologies of poetry. He also wrote a novel centering on a ghost story, *The Green Man* (1969).

Amis is most noted for fictional SATIRE. *Lucky Jim,* his first novel, won the Somerset Maugham Award and was popular with both the general reading public and critics. Other examples of his novels in this genre include *That Uncertain Feeling* (1956), *I Like It Here* (1958), and *Take a Girl Like You* (1960).

BIBLIOGRAPHY

Amis, Martin, *Experience*. New York: Talk Miramax Books/Hyperion, 2000.

Bradford, Richard. *Lucky Him: The Life of Kingsley Amis*. London: Peter Owen, 2001.

Fussell, Paul. *The Anti-Egotist: Kingsley Amis, Man of Letters*. New York: Oxford University Press, 1994.

Laskowski, William E. *Kingsley Amis*. New York: Twayne Publishers, 1998.

Moseley, Merritt. *Understanding Kingsley Amis*. Understanding Contemporary British Literature Series. Columbia: University of South Carolina Press, 1993.

Salwak, Dale. *Kingsley Amis: A Reference Guide*. Boston: G. K. Hall, 1978.

AMIS, MARTIN (1949–   )

Widely regarded as one of the leading British novelists working in the style of POSTMODERNISM, Martin Louis Amis is the son of the writer Kingsley AMIS. Martin Amis was born on August 25, 1949, in Oxford, England, and grew up immersed in the literary scene and affected by the increasing fame of his father. As a teenager, he acted in the film version of *A High Wind in Jamaica,* by Richard HUGHES. He attended Oxford (Exeter College) and graduated in 1971. He has worked in various editorial positions for the *Times Literary Supplement* and the *New Statesman,* but since 1979 he has earned his living as a full-time writer. His first marriage ended in divorce, and he remarried in 1998; he is the father of two sons and two daughters. Perhaps because of his famous father, his personal life, although no more extraordinary or outrageous than that of other contemporary novelists, has been an object of fascination for the British popular press—even his dental appointments receive scrutiny.

Martin Amis published *The Rachel Papers* in 1973 when he was 24 years old, rather a young age for a debut novel. Just as his father had done before him, Amis won the Somerset Maugham Award for his first novel. The next year *Dead Babies* appeared, followed by *Success* in 1978, *Other People: A Mystery Story* in 1981, MONEY: *A SUICIDE NOTE* in 1984, *London Fields* in 1989, *Time's Arrow: or, The Nature of the Offense* in 1991, *The* INFORMATION in 1995, and *Night Train* in 1997. Although his early works are primarily COMIC NOVELS noted for the use of SATIRE, he has taken up increasingly serious subjects in his career. He is particularly interested in issues of identity (including feminine identity) and in the connections between an author's real world and the world of the fiction the author creates; in fact, one of the characters in *Money: A Suicide Note* is a writer named Martin Amis. But whether comic or serious, his writing is noted for the brilliance of its wordplay, the inventiveness of its plots, and the self-referential nature of his narrative technique.

In addition to novels, Amis has produced two collections of short stories, *Einstein's Monsters: Five Stories* (1987) and *Heavy Water and Other Stories* (1999). His collections of literary essays include *The Moronic Inferno and Other Visits to America* (1986), *Visiting Mrs. Nabokov and Other Excursions* (1993), and *The War Against Cliché: Essays and Reviews 1971–2000* (2001). His recollection of growing up as the son of one of England's most famous writers was eagerly anticipated. *Experience: A Memoir* appeared in 2000 and won the JAMES TAIT BLACK MEMORIAL PRIZE for biography. Martin Amis has also written screenplays and magazine journalism. He continues to live and write in London.

BIBLIOGRAPHY

Diedrick, James. *Understanding Martin Amis*. Understanding Contemporary British Literature. Columbia: University of South Carolina Press, 1995.

Haffenden, John. *Novelists in Interview*. London: Methuen, 1985.

Lane, Richard J., Rod Mengham, and Philip Tew. *Contemporary British Fiction*. Cambridge, U.K.: Polity Press; Malden, Mass.: Blackwell Publishers, 2003.

Reynolds, Margaret, and Jonathan Noakes. *Martin Amis*. London: Vintage, 2003.

AMSTERDAM IAN MCEWAN (1998)

Winner of the BOOKER PRIZE in 1998, *Amsterdam* is the story of four men who have loved Molly Lane, a vivacious woman who has died too soon.

The story, related by a third-person omniscient narrator, opens at Molly's memorial service. There, Clive Linley and Vernon Halliday compare notes on Molly's positive influence on them and on her prolonged death. They are alike in detesting Molly's husband, George Lane, for his dullness, for the tabloid empire that generated his wealth, and for limiting their access to Molly. They also detest Julian Garmony, the foreign secretary and Molly's last lover, for his conservative politics and intimacy with their Molly. Her unexpected death by debilitating disease sets the serious theme of the novel; the slowly revealed vanity and self-importance of her former lovers provide the satirical theme.

The narrative structure alternates between the events of Vernon and Clives's remaining months. Each man faces a risky but life-crowning opportunity: For Vernon, it is the promise of a journalistic coup involving incriminating pictures of Garmony found in Molly's apartment. For Clive, it is the completion of the Millennium Symphony he is writing for the biggest New Year's Eve party in history. The two old friends and rivals are in harmony in their grief until Vernon's journalistic ardor creates a disruption in Clive's compositional life. Handling the scandalous photographs reveals the limits of Vernon's judgment; the mistake he makes with them then recurs in connection to Clive. In both cases, disaster follows.

Vernon's great weakness is his failure to imagine what he has not witnessed. Just as his tastefully displayed pictures are about to hit the stands, Garmony's stalwart wife and children address the nation with a preemptive strike: Mrs. Garmony's speech is a model of the appeal to pity, and Vernon's strategy to topple Molly's last lover unravels in a frantic day. In contrast, Clive's great weakness is his inability to witness and remember the ordinary events of quotidian life in his devotion to the inspired moment. When Vernon's pursuit of Clive's civic duty disrupts the composition of the Millennium Symphony at a crucial stage, only revenge will satisfy the thwarted artist.

By the novel's climax, the old friends are new enemies. Independently, each man sets a plot in motion against the other involving shady Dutch doctors in Amsterdam, where Clive is presenting his botched symphony's premiere. Each man comes prepared with a large cash payment and makes the necessary arrangements. In a perfectly parallel double betrayal, drinks are doctored and doctors are agents of death. Vernon and Clive were very similar: They both loved Molly Lane, they both hated Julian Garmony, and they both die quietly of the same cause.

Of Molly's four lovers, the one who receives the least attention is her dull and conservative husband, George Lane, publisher of sensational tabloids; he, however, winds up with the last word. When the task of concluding the affairs of Vernon and Clive falls to him, he is satisfied that Molly is at last completely his, and he plans a suitable commemoration for her—the sort of event that she, Vernon, and Clive would have hated. But she is dead, and the liberal journalist and the sensitive artist have done each other in, leaving the world to sensible capitalists and conservatives like George Lane and Julian Garmony.

Ian McEwan is himself both a writer and a composer, so he bears a special relationship to Vernon and Clive, constructing them as deeply flawed exponents of their particular arts and then essentially executing them. McEwan's black comedy is at once hilarious and disconcerting. The omniscient narrator mercilessly reveals the weaknesses in the hearts and minds of the main characters, who cannot earn the reader's pity because they are never victimized. Instead, they make sacrificial victims of others for all the wrong reasons: Vernon attempts to sacrifice Garmony to the principles of journalistic truth, hoping to topple a conservative politician by exploiting the very sensationalism he says he loathes in George Lane, and Clive allows a crime to proceed unchallenged in order to preserve a moment of artistic inspiration. Neither character shows mercy

when presented with an opportunity to do so, and neither receives it from his author.

BIBLIOGRAPHY

Annan, Gabriele. "Wages of Sin." Review of *Amsterdam,* by Ian McEwan. *New York Review of Books* 46, no. 1 (1999): 7.

Malcolm, David. *Understanding Ian McEwan.* Understanding Contemporary British Literature Series. Columbia: University of South Carolina Press, 2002, 189–195.

ANGRY YOUNG MEN   In the 1950s, a loosely defined literary movement developed that focused the energies of writers who had been children during WORLD WAR II. England's suffering during and after the war is frequently underappreciated by Americans. The blitzkrieg was particularly hard on children in London and southern England, since many of them were relocated for their safety and separated from family and friends. After the war, there were shortages of food and supplies of every sort, so that rationing had to continue even after the hostilities ended, and some bombed buildings had to remain damaged and unusable in the absence of resources to restore them. While American suburbs were sprawling with new tract homes that featured every modern appliance imaginable, and while the Marshall Plan was pouring money into the reconstruction of the European continent, many English homes still bore the scars of the war and continued to have old-fashioned iceboxes and inadequate heating. The children who endured these hardships grew up to become the writers and dramatists called Angry Young Men because they used hostile, alienated, dissatisfied antiheroes as protagonists.

The playwright John Osborne created his character Jimmy Porter to embody this frustrated and enraged figure as the protagonist in his most famous play, *Look Back in Anger,* but the same kind of character is also present in the fiction of the late 1940s and the 1950s. Novelists such as John BRAINE, Kingsley AMIS, Iris MURDOCH, Alan SILLITOE, John WAIN, and Stan Barstow presented a more strident and harsh picture of British life than had the writers of the previous generation. Their dissatisfied protagonists are projections of their own frustrations and disappointments in the closing years of the British EMPIRE, when the role of Britain in the world declines and the range of options available to British citizens contracts in a seemingly ever-shrinking sphere of influence. In these conditions, working-class writers in particular become the frustrated, angry voice of hope deferred or even denied or dead. They focused their rage not on the global events unfolding at the time but on the British sources of their marginalized lives, especially on the socioeconomic effects of a CLASS system that favored pedigree over talent and ability.

BIBLIOGRAPHY

Feldman, Gene, and Max Gartenberg. *The Beat Generation and the Angry Young Men*. New York: Citadel Press, 1958.

Salwak, Dale. *Interviews with Britain's Angry Young Men*. San Bernardino, Calif.: Borgo Press, 1984.

Stevenson, Randall. *The British Novel Since the Thirties: An Introduction*. Athens: The University of Georgia Press, 1986, 123–131.

ANIMAL FARM GEORGE ORWELL (1945)

Cast in the form of an ALLEGORY, this beast fable is a harsh SATIRE that condemns totalitarianism. In particular, ORWELL targets the Soviet Union's brand of communism as nothing more than the ideology of a police state.

The setting of the story is Manor Farm, and the narrator relates events from an omniscient third-person point of view. The catalyst for the action is a dream that Old Major, a prize pig, tells to the other animals. He has had a vision of a world in which animals are no longer ill-treated by humans, and he urges the animals to rise up in revolution. He advises them to distrust anything human, since animals are the only ones to do productive work, and to respect the equality of all animals. In their misery, the animals are receptive to Old Major's ideas. The pigs Snowball, Squealer, and Napoleon develop Old Major's vision into the doctrine of animalism; eventually, the hungry animals storm the shed where their food is stored, and they run the human owners away. They proclaim the farm to be Animal Farm, writing Old Major's teachings on the barn wall. The most important principle is that all animals are equal, but events soon begin to discredit this ideal.

The pigs, since they are the smartest animals, quickly take charge of the farm's operations. They allocate the food that all the animals help to grow in an unequal manner, reserving the milk for their own exclusive use. Harvests are good at first, and even though the animals work like slaves—harder than they did under Mr. Jones—their morale is good. Snowball emerges as leader, assisted by Squealer, a public relations and propaganda specialist. When the humans try to recapture the farm, the animals stand firm at the battle of the cowshed. Afterward, Snowball begins working on a windmill to provide the animals with electricity so they can enjoy a three-day work week, but before he can accomplish anything, Napoleon stages a coup. He exiles Snowball, backed up by his ferocious dogs, and embarks on a totalitarian program. Whenever necessary, he alters or erases inconvenient principles from the barn wall, and the animals can't discuss these changes, because free speech and open debate have been banned.

Napoleon soon begins making deals with the humans who own farms around Animal Farm, becoming more and more like them, drunken, lazy, and greedy. Napoleon even uses his dogs to attack and kill the farm animals that oppose or criticize him, in order to intimidate the survivors and maintain his domination. His manipulation of the animal's principles has left only one: "All animals are equal, but some animals are more equal that others." At this point, he and his followers have become identical to the human masters the animals had overthrown.

On its own, this sequence of events makes a fine story, but it has another layer of meaning beyond the resolution of the plot. Orwell bases his story on the historical events that led to the founding and early years of the Soviet Union. Old Major represents Karl Marx, who formulated the theory of communism and died before any communist state was established. Snowball seems to represent Leon Trotsky, and Napoleon drives him away in a manner reminiscent of Joseph Stalin's rise to power. However, although the story parallels several details from Soviet history, it also serves as a warning against *any* kind of totalitarian regime. The slow erosion of rights and the decline in civil justice illustrated in *Animal Farm* could occur in any place or at any time. Orwell did not foresee the fall of communism, but the fall of that regime does not mean that *Animal Farm* is a relic: It continues to remind readers how easily a society can slip into the grip of a dictator.

BIBLIOGRAPHY

Gardner, Averil. *George Orwell.* Twayne's English Authors, 455. Boston: Twayne, 1987.

Hammond, J. R. *A George Orwell Companion.* New York: St. Martin's Press, 1982.

Menand, Louis. "Honest, Decent, Wrong: The Invention of George Orwell," *The New Yorker,* 27 January 2003, 84–91.

Meyers, Jeffrey. *A Reader's Guide to George Orwell.* Totowa, N.J.: Littlefield, Adams, 1977.

ANNA OF THE FIVE TOWNS ARNOLD BENNETT (1902)

Set in the Staffordshire potteries district, this novel of romance and self-discovery follows Anna Tellwright's journey to an envied marriage and an unexpected discovery. Arnold BENNETT constructs a narrative by intertwining studies of family dynamics, personal psychology, social relationships, and church politics.

Anna's father, Ephraim, is a pillar of the Methodist church and a financially successful but emotionally volatile miser. The family has returned to Bursley, moving there from another drab, polluted, scorched pottery town. The blasted landscape provides a metaphor for the stunted emotional landscape of the Tellwright household. Two other families are contrasted to the Tellwrights: the loving and wealthy Suttons, and the impoverished Prices. Willie Price, like Anna, finds himself dominated by a harsh father, but under reversed financial conditions, while the Suttons represent everything that Anna can expect from successful upper-middle-class Methodist life.

The story opens on the day when Anna first realizes that a suitable young man, Henry Mynors, is romantically interested in her. The next day, her 21st birthday, her father informs her that she possesses a considerable fortune derived from her mother's money, making her one of the wealthiest eligible young women in the district. In addition to the new experience of romance, Anna must also deal with the management of her fortune and the effect its existence has on every other aspect of her life. In contrast to her new financial enrichment, Anna's spiritual life is impoverished. Although actively involved in church affairs, she lacks any deep inner experience of faith: She is no more able to manage her religious life than she is her financial life. Anna's increase in wealth leads to a rising status in her church through the efforts of Mrs. Sutton, who also takes an interest in Anna's religious life and her romance with Mynors.

Bennett relates this story through an omniscient third-person narrator, using a realistic presentation of working-class details and upper-class mannerisms to capture the social and religious tensions of Bursley. Without overt criticism, he portrays the mundane practices of the midland Methodists, no longer the enthusiastic dissidents that one encounters in *Humphrey Clinker* or even *Adam Bede.* The Methodist faith that is practiced in the Five Towns at the end of the 19th century is a respectable institution with buildings to maintain and investments to nurture. Enthusiasm is channeled into the custom of attending revivals, but Anna's failure to experience a deep emotional response during a revival foreshadows her lack of deep love for Henry Mynors. Anna goes through the motions for the sake of propriety and to provide herself with a sense of belonging. She chooses easy, safe, and respectable solutions over personal satisfaction and integrity. Bennett makes the reader understand the painful and inexorable quality of such choices.

BIBLIOGRAPHY

Anderson, Linda R. *Bennett, Wells, and Conrad: Narrative in Transition.* New York: St. Martin's Press, 1986.

Lucas, John. *Arnold Bennett: A Study of His Fiction.* London: Methuen, 1974.

Preston, Peter. " 'A Grim and Original Beauty': Arnold Bennett and the Landscape of the Five Towns." In *Geography and Literature: A Meeting of the Disciplines.* Edited by William E. Mallory and Paul Simpson-Housley. Syracuse, N.Y.: Syracuse University Press, 1987, 31–55.

ANTIC HAY ALDOUS HUXLEY (1923)

A sensation for its frank presentation of a British-style Roaring Twenties culture of excess, frivolity, and indulgence in sex, alcohol, drugs, modern art, and jazz music, this story follows the adventures of Theodore Gumbril, Jr., who has invented "Patent Small-Clothes" for making the hours spent sitting in church more tolerable (i.e., underwear that inflates to cushion the wearer's posterior). He hopes to become a gentleman of leisure, so he resigns his teaching position to devote himself to the tasks of promoting his invention and indulging in the hedonistic lifestyle he longs to follow. He pursues his crush on melancholy Myra Viveash, a wealthy woman busy drowning the memory of a young man with whom she had an affair before he was killed during WORLD WAR I.

Theodore has friends, such as the painter-poet Casimir Lypiatt and other young gentlemen, who are all quite serious about their role as artists; their main function, however, is to serve as targets for Huxley's satirical attacks against pomposity, self-importance, and empty-headedness. Theodore also secretly rents a flat in London that he visits from time to time, imagining that he might engage in surreptitious adventures there, but mostly he just sits by his gas fire savoring the fact that nobody knows he is there. Sometimes Theodore enjoys an outing disguised as "the Rabelaisian Complete Man" in a beautiful false beard. Wearing it, he can escape his mild and retiring disposition and become a paragon of men; in particular, chatting up girls becomes an easier task from behind the beard. He dreams of wealth and virility, but these are not to be his. In the end, Myra Viveash accepts his company only because no one else is available; the two of them meander through London, desperately searching for drinking companions to provide them with the illusion of fulfillment.

Antic Hay was a scandalous novel when it appeared in 1923, but it became a cult favorite when young people caught up in the club scene of an intoxicated era embraced it and celebrated its author. The farcical story makes a serious criticism of a pleasure-addicted society. As a novel, it is somewhat unevenly constructed, but its satirical jabs are accurately aimed and funny. The novel deserves more attention for its role as a thematic precursor to Huxley's most famous work, *BRAVE NEW WORLD*. In that latter novel he returns to the theme of pleasure-addicted emptiness and the enslave-ment it brings, but his concern is already apparent in this much earlier one.

BIBLIOGRAPHY

Baker, Robert S. *The Dark Historic Page: Social Satire and Historicism in the Novels of Aldous Huxley, 1921–1939.* Madison: University of Wisconsin Press, 1982.

Baker, Robert. "The Fire of Prometheus: Romanticism and the Baroque in Huxley's *Antic Hay* and *Those Barren Leaves,*" *Texas Studies in Literature and Language: A Journal of the Humanities* 19 (1977): 60–82.

ANTIHERO

Traditionally, the main character of a story would also be the hero of the story, possessing the virtues required to resolve the conflict driving the story's PLOT. Sometimes, however, main characters are not admirably heroic, or they may in fact be villainous, and in such a case the term *protagonist* is useful. An antihero is neither an opponent to the hero nor a mere failed hero; instead, an antihero is a character who lacks the traditional qualities associated with heroes but who must carry out the hero's task anyway. The antihero may be sullen and resentful, unattractive, fearful, dull-witted, disrespectful, ill-groomed, clumsy, and awkward, or any other combination of characteristics that do not elicit spontaneous admiration. Nonetheless, this character is called upon to resolve the conflict at the heart of the plot. An antihero is not doomed to failure nor guaranteed of success, but moves toward the climax of a story without catering to the stereotypical expectations readers will have of heroic qualities. As a compositional strategy, the use of an antihero is a daring and risky choice, since the characteristics of the antihero may provoke the antipathy of readers. But since plenty of real-world people must resolve real-world problems without the benefit a heroic constitution, writers striving for realism may prefer to use an antihero as a protagonist.

BIBLIOGRAPHY

Brombert, Victor H. *In Praise of Antiheroes: Figures and Themes in Modern European Literature, 1830–1980.* Chicago: University of Chicago Press, 1999.

Walker, William. *Dialectics and Passive Resistance: The Comic Antihero in Modern Fiction.* New York: P. Lang, 1985.

ANTIREALISM/ANTIREALISTIC NOVEL

Literary works that include elements not found in ordinary life, or which refuse to adhere to conventional expectations about form and content, are antirealistic. Borrowing from the philosophical tradition that begins with Plato, realism may also be contrasted with idealism or transcendent perfection. One of the most widespread kinds of antirealistic fiction is found in the genre of FANTASY, which may include imaginary creatures or supernatural events. Even though the characters in fantasy fiction may behave in realistic, predictable, traditional ways, their actions occur in a context that deviates from the normality of the world to which readers have grown accustomed. In such a case, realism may be embedded into an antirealistic story; for example, in The LORD OF THE RINGS, hobbits, wizards, elves, orcs, and other imaginary creatures are engaged in a realistic struggle between good and evil. The characters think and act the way ordinary real people might do in a similar situation.

But antirealism also refers to fiction that is absurd, illogical, or innovative in its use of formal devices such as PLOT. Some writers deliberately avoid realism in order to prevent readers from relying on comfortable stereotypes or to force them to think in new ways, to see an issue from a new perspective, or to consider unorthodox possibilities. Writers who use this strategy include Flann O'BRIEN in AT SWIM-TWO-BIRDS, Malcolm LOWRY in UNDER THE VOLCANO, Jeanette WINTERSON in SEXING THE CHERRY, James JOYCE in ULYSSES and FINNEGANS WAKE, Martin AMIS in Time's Arrow, and Samuel BECKETT in his fiction and his stage plays.

BIBLIOGRAPHY

Becker, George Joseph. Documents of Modern Literary Realism. Princeton, N.J.: Princeton University Press, 1963.

Graff, Gerald. Literature Against Itself: Literary Ideas in Modern Society. Chicago: University of Chicago Press, 1979.

Norris, Christopher. New Idols of the Cave: The Limits of Anti-Realism. Manchester, U.K.: University of Manchester Press, 1997.

ARCHETYPE

Borrowed from the ideas of Carl Jung and developed by Joseph Campbell and Northrup Frye, an archetype is a pattern of character-istics that can be deployed in many different ways without losing its coherence. Both character and PLOT can draw on archetypes, as can the more abstract devices of imagery and symbolism.

Jung, an early student and protégé of Freud, expanded the concept of the unconscious mind and applied it to the entire human species. After all, if an individual can have hidden memories and desires that influence behavior without rising to the level of conscious recognition, then perhaps the species as a whole also possesses a kind of collective unconscious (sometimes referred to as "racial memory," meaning the shared memory of the entire species). Indirect support for this notion came from the work of 19th-century myth scholars such as James G. Frazer, author of The Golden Bough (1890). Frazer noted that patterns of mythic stories recurred worldwide, and he cataloged numerous examples of related stories in the multiple volumes of The Golden Bough. The gods and heroes serving as the characters of the stories might differ, but the adventures they faced would be similar, as would many symbolic images used to describe those adventures and to endow them with special significance.

Joseph Campbell outlines one of these major archetypal character patterns in The Hero with a Thousand Faces, noting the many heroes of myths around the world who share several features: the extraordinary circumstances of the hero's birth; the early sign of the adult role the hero will undertake; the hero's summons to adventure; his acquisition of a guide, mentor, or helper; his journey into the underworld; the winning of some gift or boon for mankind, usually through great sacrifice or privation by the hero; and, the return to the ordinary world with the prize. Campbell's ideas were a strong influence on George Lucas as he developed the story for Star Wars, and the phenomenal success of that film made it a pattern for many others.

Northrup Frye's key contribution to the theory of the archetype occurs in The Anatomy of Criticism. He creates a system for categorizing literary works based on the cycle of the seasons that so strongly dominated human survival through thousands of years. Thus, there are four major genres: comedy (spring), romance/adventure (summer), tragedy (autumn), and satire (winter). The cycle of human life is also encompassed in this system through birth, youth, and education (spring); maturity, adulthood, and parenthood (summer); and old age, loss of power, and death (autumn). Wintry satire is a kind of subversion of the other genres and can occur in all the stages of life. Frye articulates the characteristics of these genres, citing numerous examples. Our ability to recognize these archetypes is partly the result of simply growing up and living our lives. Writers can exploit the characteristic features in a straightforward manner, but variations on the archetypal patterns are enriched by the recognition of the underlying archetype. For example, Shakespeare achieves a powerful effect by taking a comic story of young love in *Romeo and Juliet* and converting it into a deeply moving tragedy of young death by mixing two of the archetypal patterns.

The strongest and most common criticism of the archetypal theory is that it is a reductionist approach, oversimplifying a complex human activity—the creation of literature, or, more broadly, art—in favor of a systematic explanation. Critics of archetypal theory claim that Frye's approach lops off subtleties or smoothes over discrepancies in the vast field of literature to divide it all into the predetermined categories, like Procrustes, who trimmed or stretched his guests to fit the one bed he already had.

BIBLIOGRAPHY
Campbell, Joseph. *The Hero with a Thousand Faces.* Princeton, N.J.: Princeton University Press, 1949.
Frazer, James George. *The Golden Bough: A Study in Magic and Religion.* Oxford World's Classics. Oxford: Oxford University Press, 1998.
Frye, Northrop. *Anatomy of Criticism: Four Essays.* Princeton, N.J.: Princeton University Press, 1957.
Knapp, Bettina Liebowitz. *A Jungian Approach to Literature.* Carbondale: Southern Illinois University Press, 1984.

ARTIST OF THE FLOATING WORLD, AN KAZUO ISHIGURO (1986)

Winner of the WHITBREAD AWARD in 1986, Kazuo ISHIGURO's debut novel follows the first-person narrative of Masuji Ono, a Tokyo painter, after WORLD WAR II. Masuji has retired and spends his time in meditative seclusion, in contrast to the prominence he once enjoyed as an advocate of Japanese nationalism, imperialism, and militarism. He drinks with old friends at Mrs. Kawakami's bar, the last remnant of the district that once housed the Migi-Hidari, a gathering place for nationalists before and during the war—a kind of Japanese version of the Munich beer halls that helped propel Hitler's Nazi party to prominence.

When the story opens in 1948, the rebuilding of Japan is well under way; young people do not want to be reminded of imperialist aggression, and so Masuji does not display his paintings even in his own home. Although he has survived the war, his reputation has not; his life's work has vanished like the Migi-Hidari. Because of his past and the nation's defeat in the war, he is now a liability rather than an asset to anyone too closely associated with him. This situation would not be a problem except that Masuji has one unmarried daughter, Noriko. Since marriage in Japan is as much a liaison between families as between spouses, she is at a peculiar disadvantage: no respectable family wishes to ally itself with those who supported the war. One negotiation has already ended fruitlessly. The inevitable investigation of family background had turned up—who knows what? Polite excuses were made, and the marriage did not go forward. Noriko has become a prospect in another negotiation, but if this one fails, she is unlikely to get a third chance. The Saito family must accept her; their investigation must not turn up accusations against her father.

The subject is a touchy one, since even to broach it is to imply that Masuji has become an impediment to his surviving children's well-being. A faint hint of ritual suicide suggests itself to Masuji. Many of the leaders of the nationalist movement have killed themselves honorably; others, convicted of war crimes, were still being executed. Having never carried a gun or held a political office or published a treatise urging war, Masuji has been spared this kind of retribution. Now he begins to feel that others may think he has gotten off too lightly.

He spends much of his time recalling his training. His master was influenced by Western notions of three-dimensional depth perception and soft outlines, applying these techniques to subjects drawn from "the floating world" of drinking establishments and geisha houses. When Masuji embraced nationalism, he rejected his master's Western notions for older forms of Japanese painting with hard outlines, flat perspective, and slogans superimposed over the painting's images. Then he had thrown himself into the nationalist movement and placed his art at the service of it; now he is not sure how great a responsibility he bears for the suffering his nation endured, nor how great a price his daughter may yet pay. His concern for her slowly pushes him toward some kind of sacrifice to help her.

With Noriko's marriage, the shadow of ritual suicide would finally cease to haunt him as he looks out over the district once occupied by the Migi-Hidari being converted to offices where young people can shape careers that would have been impossible before the war. Even Mrs. Kawakami's little establishment disappears, leaving no trace of the floating world that once existed there. Masuji finally recognizes that second chances are possible, both for the nation and for people like himself who helped lead it astray.

Since Ishiguro presents this novel as the first-person recollections of an old man partially hiding from his past, the plot unfolds in a digressive and associative manner. Events bring Masuji's past to mind, and he allows his thoughts to wander over recent history and the burden of responsibility it places on the present. Little by little he pieces together the story of his own role in shaping Japan's recent past and then takes responsibility for that role in the name of bringing about a better future for his youngest child. Sometimes Masuji colors the truth so strongly that he can be considered an unreliable narrator; however, his unreliability is merely an effect of his desire to retain some shreds of self-respect in the light of personal and historical events.

BIBLIOGRAPHY

Mason, Gregory. "Inspiring Images: The Influence of the Japanese Cinema on the Writings of Kazuo Ishiguro," *East-West Film Journal* 3 (June 1989): 39–52.

Petry, Mike. *Narratives of Memory and Identity: The Novels of Kazuo Ishiguro*. New York: Peter Lang, 1999.

Shaffer, Brian W. *Understanding Kazuo Ishiguro*. Understanding Contemporary British Literature Series. Columbia: University of South Carolina Press, 1998.

AT LADY MOLLY'S ANTHONY POWELL (1957)

The fourth of 12 volumes in POWELL'S ROMAN-FLEUVE entitled *A DANCE TO THE MUSIC OF TIME*, this novel continues the first-person point of view narration of Nicholas Jenkins, a writer, as he begins his adult life in London. In the overall structure of the series, *At Lady Molly's* is positioned at the beginning of the second of four "movements," following *The ACCEPTANCE WORLD* and preceding *CASANOVA'S CHINESE RESTAURANT*. This portion of the series focuses on the theme of love, including affairs, marriages, and divorces.

Nick becomes an increasingly frequent visitor at Lady Molly's. She has come down somewhat in the world, having divorced her aristocratic first husband and married Ted Jeavons. They keep a large house in London that seems to be continually filled with visitors. There one may find the most extraordinary assortment of guests, some temporary and some permanent, in a setting of pleasant, homey disorder. Among the visitors are the many members of the Tolland family, and his acquaintance widens as he meets more and more of them; by the end of the novel, Nick is on the verge of marrying into this aristocratic group.

Sometime later, Nick runs into J. G. Quiggen and is invited to visit him in the country. The ungainly Quiggen had stolen Peter Templer's beautiful wife Mona in *The Acceptance World;* now this unlikely couple is living together, and Quiggen has acquired a mysterious patron who shares his leftist ideology. More important, Mona has taken a notion to become a film star, and since Nick is writing screenplays, he seems the ideal person to assist her in making the right contacts. While Nick is visiting, the mysterious patron drops by and turns out to be Lord Warminster (called Erridge), the head of the Tolland family and master of Thrubworth, a grand old estate somewhat the worse for Erridge's management of it.

In an eccentric family, Erridge wins the prize for strangeness: His title is wasted on him, and he sometimes wanders in the countryside taking manual labor in the manner of a tramp (a characteristic he shares with George ORWELL) in order to better understand the laboring masses. Erridge invites Quiggen, Mona, and Nick to dine with him in the little apartment that is the only part of Thrubworth not mothballed. At the modest dinner, Erridge proves to be a competent host and Mona begins to flirt with him in subtle ways. Unexpectedly, as dinner concludes, two young women arrive who turn out to be more Tollands. They have dropped by to tell Erridge that Susan, the elder of them, has just gotten engaged. Of greater interest to Nick, however, is the younger sister, Isobel: When he sees her, he knows he has found his future wife. By a lucky stroke, they have a car, and they offer to give Nick a lift home.

Everyone in Nick's circle is pairing up, settling down, or splitting up, and by the novel's end he decides it is time for him to marry. The week that his engagement to Isobel is announced, Erridge unexpectedly departs for a tour of China, taking Mona with him. More sensational events absorb all the conversational attention at the party Lady Molly throws for Nick and Isobel to celebrate their engagement. Nick's old school friend Mark Members, a Freudian and a poet, is there and shares some details about Mona's desertion of Quiggen, including the crucial fact that the two of them were never legally married. The Tollands are eager to know whether their bachelor brother is likely to beget an heir to Thrubworth and the family titles; that future might come to pass if Mona can maintain her hold on him.

One phase of Nick's life closes and another begins in this section of *A Dance to the Music of Time*. In the bright whirl of apparently random social encounters, he finds the permanent partner he has lacked up to this point. He is fully mature, ready to move from the fringes of the marriage dance to the very center. In the remaining two books of this movement, love and marriage continue to be the dominant theme as couples in likely and unlikely combinations try their luck at matrimony. Nick's own choice proves to be the right one, and he and Isobel stay together for a long and amicable marriage.

BIBLIOGRAPHY

Joyau, Isabelle. *Understanding Powell's* A Dance to the Music of Time. New York: St. Martin's Press, 1994.

Selig, Robert L. *Time and Anthony Powell*. Cranbury, N.J.: Associated University Presses, 1991.

Spurling, Hillary. *Invitation to the Dance: A Guide to Anthony Powell's* A Dance to the Music of Time. Boston: Little, Brown, 1977.

AT SWIM-TWO-BIRDS FLANN O'BRIEN (1939)

Written as the first-person narration of an Dublin student who relishes multiple approaches to the representation of reality, this ANTIREALISTIC NOVEL presents a narrator living with an insufferably conventional uncle. The young man has reason to resent his uncle's inquisitiveness: He is an indifferent student, spending as much of his time as possible writing a very unusual book or enjoying a pint with friends.

In the narrator's book, the protagonist, Dermot Trellis, is himself writing a book. The narrator shares passages with his best friend, and at these junctions the story switches to the novel-within-a-novel. In this inner novel, Trellis is writing a condemnation of Ireland's moral decay (the *inner* inner novel). Its villain is John Furriskey, but many of the characters are borrowed, or "hired," from preexisting works and genres. (See also INTERTEXTUALITY.) Whenever Trellis falls asleep, his characters break free of his control. Finn McCool, a mythic Irish hero, tells a long story about mad Sweeny, condemned to flit about Ireland praising its various locations, one of which is Swim-Two-Birds. The characters so much enjoy the autonomy they gain when Trellis is sleeping that they plot to eliminate him and set themselves free.

In his waking moments, however, Trellis fathers a son with a character, the virtuous Sheila Lamont. This boy, Orlick, falls under the tutelage of the Pooka Fergus McPhellimey, a demon who wins him in a card game with the Good Fairy. Orlick is also a writer, and the characters soon persuade him to write a story that will imprison, torment, and execute his father. In a grand courtroom scene, characters from each of the plot layers present arguments, but Trellis escapes death when his manuscript burns. The story returns to the unnamed young student who has written the writing of the writing (all of which is written by Flann O'BRIEN); when he passes his university exams, he also decides he can get along with his uncle.

At Swim-Two-Birds is a showcase of literary styles: When mythological Irish figures are speaking, the narration imitates (and perhaps parodies) the sentence patterns, metaphors, and literary devices of myth and folklore, including the highly romantic translations of ancient Celtic literature that had been popular adjuncts to nationalism earlier in the century; and, when figures out of westerns are speaking, they switch to the style of American "dime novels" of the late 19th century—with an Irish lilt. The novel owes much to James JOYCE, who praised it. It is an extremely complex structure that comments on narrative as a form of literary convention, but it never abandons the author's interest in writing a fierce SATIRE on the hollowness of modern Irish life. It is aware of itself as a work of art, taking advantage of AMBIGUITY in the story, characters, and multiple plots. At the center of the novel, however, is mad Sweeney singing the praises of every part of Ireland. For all its satire, *At Swim-Two-Birds* is also a statement of national pride.

BIBLIOGRAPHY

Imhof, Rudiger. *Alive Alive-O!: Flann O'Brien's* At Swim-Two-Birds. Dublin: Wolfhound Press; Totowa, N.J.: Barnes & Noble Books, 1985.

Shea, Thomas F. *Flann O'Brien's Exorbitant Novels.* Lewisburg, Pa.: Bucknell University Press, 1992.

ATWOOD, MARGARET (1939–)

The author of *The HANDMAID'S TALE* (1985) and *The BLIND ASSASSIN,* which won the 2000 BOOKER PRIZE, Margaret Eleanor Atwood was born on November 18, 1939, in Ottawa, Canada. Because her father's work as an entymologist took him (and his family) into the northern forests on research expeditions, she gained extensive experience as an outdoorswoman and developed a keen appreciation for nature—influences that show up in her later fiction and poetry. She was educated at Victoria College of the University of Toronto, where she was strongly influenced by the ARCHETYPE theories of Northrup Frye, and where she earned a B.A. degree in 1961, and later at Radcliffe College (M.A., 1962) and Harvard University in Cambridge, Massachusetts.

Atwood has taught at numerous universities in Canada, the United States, and Australia, and she has published more than 50 books, as author or editor, including works of fiction, poetry, essays, children's literature, and anthologies. She has been an important voice in advocating the recognition of Canadian literature as a distinctive expression of national identity, supporting this cause by writing theoretical interpretations, collecting the works of Canadian writers, and serving as an editor at House of Anansi Press, a company specializing in Canadian literature. Atwood is also a noted pioneer of contemporary FEMINISM, condemning "phallic criticism"—literary reviews and interpretations driven by stereotypical assumptions about women—in her essay "Paradoxes and Dilemmas: On Being a 'Woman Writer.' " She has also written teleplays, a radio play, reviews, a Canadian history, scholarly studies, and other works; her writing has won numerous awards in Canada and abroad. Margaret Atwood is the mother of one daughter and continues to live and write in Canada.

BIBLIOGRAPHY

Bloom, Harold, ed. *Margaret Atwood.* Philadelphia: Chelsea House, 2000.

Cooke, Nathalie. *Margaret Atwood: A Biography.* Toronto: ECW Press, 1998.

Howells, Coral Ann. *Margaret Atwood.* New York: St. Martin's Press, 1996.

McCombs, Judith, and Carole L. Palmer. *Margaret Atwood: A Reference Guide.* Boston: G. K. Hall, 1991.

Stein, Karen F. *Margaret Atwood Revisited.* New York: Twayne, 1999.

AUBREY-MATURIN NOVELS PATRICK O'BRIAN (1969–1999)

At the time of the author's death in 2000, the adventures of Captain Jack Aubrey of the Royal Navy and his friend and chief of surgery, Dr. Stephen Maturin, stretched through 20 volumes (O'Brian left a three-chapter manuscript of a 21st volume unfinished at his death) and sprawled across the entire navigable world. Set during the Age of Sail from about 1800 to 1820 and exploiting the political environment engendered by Napoleon, the series brings the entire British world to life and has been called the greatest example of historical fiction ever written. The books appeal equally well to men and women: Even though the stories are heavily laced with swashbuckling adventures and bloody battles, O'BRIAN is equally skilled in the development of the characters' personal lives, including romances and family relations, and the effects of career ambitions on these aspects of life. The early volumes in the series caught the attention of writers such as Iris MURDOCH and were read primarily by a coterie audience of writers, scholars, and nautical enthusiasts; however, the readership expanded extensively when an editor at W. W. Norton became enthralled by his first reading of an Aubrey-Maturin novel and decided to print the entire series in the United States.

The books in the series have several dependably recurring features. First and foremost, of course, is the nautical element. Sailing ships of many designs and nationalities are featured, and over the course of many voyages readers become familiar with virtually every sail and rope on a typical frigate. The daily routine of activities aboard a sailing ship of the Royal Navy comes vividly to life: the proper use of navigational instruments, how to measure the ship's speed and position, accurately plotting a course, steering and tacking into the wind, dropping and raising the anchor, and managing the ship's stores—all these contribute details to the texture of the story. Food and wine feature prominently, with the preparation, serving, and relishing of meals described under every condition, from near-famine on wormy biscuits to fine French cuisine to the discovery of human ears and fingers in a Polynesian stew on the fictional island of Moahu. Music, too, is a constant presence, since the sailors entertain themselves with hornpipes and jigs on the forecastle, while in the captain's quarters Jack Aubrey plays the violin accompanied by Stephen Maturin on the cello. Then there is the mission they pursue, providing the framework of a sailing route and a plot for each story. Over the 20 volumes, the series visits every ocean and many seas and harbors around the world; the physical locations, topographical features, geographical orientation, and material resources of numerous ports and anchorages—as they might have appeared at the time of the novel's events—come to life on the page.

These missions frequently involve battles and the wounds that result from them, so the medical conditions aboard ship—appalling by contemporary standards—are faithfully chronicled. The many exotic locations provide Stephen Maturin, a natural scientist as well as a surgeon, with the perfect opportunity to collect plant and animal specimens and to conduct research for the Royal Society, and all are described in specific and precise detail. References to the scientific names of plants and animals are common, along with detailed descriptions of the ecosystems that support the life forms observed and cataloged. But the natural world is also a backdrop for the complexity of human life that is the motivation for every voyage: Each journey is undertaken to achieve human goals, whether political, diplomatic, financial, military, or commercial in purpose. Aubrey and Maturin meet people of numerous cultures and nationalities on nearly every continent in the world in the course of completing their missions, and O'Brian depicts these human interactions with as much detail, insight, and subtlety as he does the nautical, gustatory, musical, and scientific aspects of his stories.

The series opens with *Master and Commander* (1970), in which a youthful Jack Aubrey is still striving to win his first command, while also risking his chances of promotion through his reckless affairs with the wives of his superiors at Port Mahon on Minorca. He meets Stephen Maturin there at a concert at about the time he gets his first command, the tiny *Sophie,* and he persuades his new acquaintance to become his ship's surgeon. He gradually becomes vaguely aware that his friend is a spy for the British government as well as a physician and a skilled linguist. Jack's stunning victory in the western Mediterranean Sea over a larger and better-armed Spanish ship, the *Cacafuego* (modeled on a historical sea battle won by Thomas Cochrane), leads to his promotion. Commissioned to command warships, in *Post Captain* (1972), he is assigned to an ungainly experimental boat, the *Polychrest,* in an action along the eastern French coast, and although the experimental design is nearly worthless in battle, Jack still manages to bring off a victory. He is awarded the temporary command of the *Lively* and sent with a small squadron to intercept Spanish treasure ships sailing from South America, another event modeled on a historical battle. He acquires command of his dream ship, a small, fast, well-armed frigate, in *The H.M.S. Surprise* (1973); Stephen Maturin eventually purchases this sturdy vessel for Jack to sail through many of the later stories. For this first mission in the *Surprise,* Jack carries an ambassador to the East Indies and engages a French squadron preying on British merchant ships bound from China. Aubrey and Maturin embark on another political mission in *The Mauritius Command* (1977), sailing the *Boadicea* through the Indian Ocean; their charge is to install a British governor there as soon as they can liberate the island from the French.

In these early novels, Jack and Stephen are also occasionally in England, where they pursue courtships and endure financial woes. These adventures on land are as fully realized as those at sea, with detailed descriptions of inns, taverns, London districts, country houses, debtors' prisons, gentlemen's clubs, Parliament (where Jack eventually wins a post representing a pocket borough), and various seats of naval governance. Jack succeeds in his courtship of Sophie Williams, eventually marrying her and settling her on an estate not too far inland from the English Channel; they have three children in spite of Jack's frequent and prolonged absences from England. Stephen's pursuit of the beautiful and volatile Diana Villiers takes many detours, but he eventually marries her after a tempestuous courtship, and they have a daughter, Brigid. When they are in England, Jack and Stephen frequently meet with Sir Joseph Blaine, Stephen's spymaster, who is also a keen naturalist eager for news of the exotic plant and animal species encountered in the world's lesser-known quarters.

One of the most thrilling adventures in the series occurs in *Desolation Island* (1978), when Jack commands the *Leopard.* En route to Australia, he sinks a Dutch ship, the *Waakzaamheid,* after being hounded by it into the icy waters of the Southern Ocean. In a gripping account of the deadly combat waged amid 50-foot rollers, Jack nearly cripples his own ship in the process of sinking his enemy, and when his damaged ship later strikes an iceberg, the crew must take refuge at the first landfall they can reach in order to rebuild her. In *The Fortune of War* (1979), Jack and Stephen bring the restored *Leopard* to the Malay Peninsula and are bound home as passengers when their ship is captured by the American frigate USS *Constitution* ("Old

Ironsides") in an action modeled on a historical battle from the War of 1812. They spend some time in Boston as prisoners of war before escaping and joining the *Shannon* in time to witness another historical battle, this time with the USS *Chesapeake.* For *The Surgeon's Mate* (1981), the story moves to the Baltic Sea, where Maturin conducts negotiations to undermine allegiances there to Napoleon Bonaparte. On the way home, adverse winds and currents drive them aground in France, and they once again become prisoners of war, this time in Paris, before escaping home to England. Some of the best food writing occurs in this volume when Jack and Stephen compete with their captors in displaying the sophistication of their palates as they sample a variety of French cuisine.

An action in the eastern Mediterranean extends across both *The Ionian Mission* (1981) and *Treason's Harbor* (1983) as Jack and Stephen engage in various actions among the islands off the west side of Greece and along the North African coast, first in the warship *Worcester* and later in the *Surprise.* Although Jack's mission is not a complete success, in *The Far Side of the World* (1984) he is awarded one further exploit with the *Surprise* before it is to be "sold out of the service": He is to stop an American warship, the *Norfolk,* from harassing British trade in the Pacific. With many mishaps, the voyage takes them to the Galápagos Islands before the *Surprise* finally catches up to the *Norfolk* and defeats the Americans. The voyage home continues through the first third of *The Reverse of the Medal* (1986), but the rest of the book relates how Jack is brought up on charges in London and publicly humiliated before evidence can be produced that exonerates him. In spite of this evidence, he loses his commission in the Royal Navy. The *Surprise* is indeed sold upon its return to England—to Stephen Maturin, who commissions Jack to sail her in *The Letter of Marque* (1990). Jack is awarded a kind of license as a privateer (the "letter of marque" of the title), and wins a fortune taking prize ships from British enemies. He uses some of this wealth to bring the *Surprise* up to his standards as a fighting ship, hoping to win reinstatement into the Royal Navy through some daring exploit—a goal he achieves, much to his satisfaction. He begins this task by "cutting out" the French warship

Diane from its mooring in an armed harbor, another especially thrilling episode of adventure and intrigue.

The Thirteen Gun Salute (1991) begins a four-book exploit that takes the *Surprise* on a circumnavigation of the globe. Aubrey and Maturin sail aboard the *Diane* on a crucial diplomatic mission, intending to rendezvous afterward with the *Surprise* in the East Indies. The mission is a success, but Jack runs aground on an uncharted reef. *The Nutmeg of Consolation* (1991) opens with the crew surviving as castaways on an island near the reef. They capture the *proa* (a ship of native design) of a band of Malay pirates who attack them unsuccessfully; afterward, they sail this craft to Batavia, where they meet Governor Raffles, a historical figure, and receive a Dutch commercial ship from him that Jack renames the *Nutmeg of Consolation*. After engaging the French frigate *Cornélie,* Jack and Stephen reboard the *Surprise,* sending the *Nutmeg* to escort some captured prize ships to market. They sail for Australia without allowing Stephen to stop and collect specimens of rare animals along their little-traveled route. Once on that recently settled continent, however, he has the thrill of capturing a male platypus and discovering firsthand how it uses its previously unknown poisonous spur; he barely survives this encounter.

In *The Truelove* (1992; published in England as *Clarissa Oakes*), the *Surprise* sails eastward from Australia, bound for Peru, but first Jack must settle the situation on the island of Moahu (imagined as part of or near the Hawaiian archipelago). He must figure out which of the warring factions is most sympathetic to British interests and then help that side achieve victory. Having succeeded in this exploit and attended an exotic feast with these new allies, the *Surprise* continues on toward the Peruvian coast in *The Wine-dark Sea* (1993), pursuing the American frigate *Franklin* along the way. Maturin spends much of his time on land while Jack pursues his opportunities at sea, but the diplomatic mission fails when Maturin is recognized as an English agent. He rejoins the *Surprise* after a perilous two-month journey over the Altiplano. Jack's plan is to return to England after first capturing some American merchant ships at Cape Horn, but when the rudder of the *Surprise* breaks in heavy seas, he must let

the wind take him where it will until his good fortune brings another British ship to his aid.

After fretting some time onshore, Jack and Stephen set sail on a double mission in *The Commodore* (1995); Jack, commanding a small fleet in the rank of commodore, is to use a raiding mission against the slave trade along the western coast of Africa as a cover for a covert mission to prevent the French from assisting an Irish uprising. The circumstances of the slave trade are vividly described, and Stephen's activities onshore bring the urban environment of an African colonial slave-trading city to life. By this point in the story, Jack is at a perilous point in his naval career, too senior to continue commanding single vessels, and yet in danger of being passed over, or "yellowed," for promotion to the rank of admiral. For the first third of *The Yellow Admiral* (1996), Jack is at home without a commission and facing both political and financial ruin. When he is finally at sea again, he is limited to the dreary blockade of the French coast. Eventually, he agrees to join Stephen for another visit to South America under the guise of a hydrographical survey in the *Surprise,* but before they can depart Jack is summoned to command a fleet in the western Mediterranean to undermine the buildup of naval forces and allies sympathetic to Bonaparte, who has escaped from Elba. This episode continues in *The Hundred Days* (1998); Jack harasses trade and naval resources, while Stephen enlists allies to burn several yards building ships for the supporters of Napoleon. The action even shifts to North Africa, where Stephen collects intelligence about the allegiance of various Muslim factions and their plans to undermine the land campaign that ultimately culminates in the Battle of Waterloo. In the course of this story, several longtime characters die, including Stephen's wife, Diana Villiers, and Barrett Bonden, Jack's most able sailor. With the passing of these key minor players, O'Brian seems to be winding down the support apparatus of the series.

In *Blue at the Mizzen* (1999), Jack and Stephen travel to Chile in the *Surprise* to assist in preserving that country's independence. Jack is to develop the naval abilities of the country; many of the exploits he performs in the novel were accomplished in history by the famed British naval officer Thomas Cochrane. Jack captures a well-supplied seaport controlled by loyalists to Spain and then cuts out the much bigger frigate *Esmerelda* from her home port, leading the hand-to-hand combat to take the vessel and thereby essentially terminating naval opposition from Peru and Spanish loyalists. The mission is a success in terms of preserving Chilean independence, but the sailors are deprived of their prize money by the very faction they protected. In the end, Jack receives word of his promotion to the rank of admiral in the blue squadron and hoists his flag at the mizzenmast at last.

O'Brian constructs this series with careful attention to historical detail, drawing on naval records from the period he is writing about, mixing real people in among his fictional characters, and basing many of the complex battles he describes on actual events. Sometimes Jack Aubrey's ship substitutes for the historical vessel, and sometimes Jack and Stephen are onlookers to some momentous historical event. But history is the supporting player to the fiction O'Brian crafts. His characters grow and develop in response to the situations they face, but their personalities take precedence over historical detail. For example, when Stephen Maturin restocks his depleted medical supplies, his precision, fastidiousness in his work, and scientific erudition provide a pretext for a discussion of early 19th-century medicine; the substances he stocks later reappear as prescriptions for various ailments, wounds, and accidents that befall the sailors in the course of daily life at sea. Every novel is replete with these kinds of specific details (the best rope for rigging, suitable methods of maintaining the captain's silver tea service, dining customs aboard ship, sailors' rights and duties, and many others), and yet none of them seem expendable or merely tangential. Instead, in O'Brian's series, historical fact and imaginative fiction are inseparably united.

BIBLIOGRAPHY
Grossman, Anne Chotzinoff, and Lisa Grossman Thomas. *Lobscouse and Spotted Dog: Which It's a Gastronomic Companion to the Aubrey-Maturin Novels.* New York: W. W. Norton, 1997.
Kemp, Peter, ed. *The Oxford Companion to Ships and the Sea.* Oxford: Oxford University Press, 1993.
King, Dean, with John B. Hattendorf. *Harbors and High Seas: An Atlas and Geographical Guide to the Complete Aubrey-Maturin Novels.* New York: Henry Holt and Company, 1996.
King, Dean, with John B. Hattendorf and J. Worth Estes. *A Sea of Words: A Lexicon and Companion to the Complete Seafaring Tales of Patrick O'Brian.* 3rd ed. New York: Henry Holt and Company, 1997.
Price, Anthony. *The Eyes of the Fleet: A Popular History of Frigates and Frigate Captains 1793–1815.* London: Hutchinson, 1990.

AUSTRALIA   See EMPIRE and COLONIALISM. For significant Australian novelists, see Peter CAREY, Thomas KENEALLY, and Patrick WHITE.

AVANT-GARDE   The cutting edge in any artistic field at a particular time is known as the avant-garde, a French term. As fashions and tastes change, however, and as surprising innovations become familiar through subsequent imitations of them, yesterday's avant-garde becomes today's normal expectation. Those who consume art—readers of fiction, viewers of films or paintings, listeners to music—become desensitized to the surprising or even shocking innovations of avant-garde artists or else reject them entirely. In both cases, the avant-garde becomes either normal or extinct, and new candidates arise to claim the title. Early in the 20th century, for example, stream-of-consciousness narration was an innovation, and writers such as Dorothy RICHARDSON, James JOYCE, and Virginia WOOLF were on the cutting edge to use this new point of view, but eventually it became one choice in the normal range of options any writer might choose in narrating a story.

See also MODERNISM and POSTMODERNISM.

BIBLIOGRAPHY
Guy, Josephine M. *The British Avant-Garde: The Theory and Politics of Tradition.* New York: Harvester Wheatsheaf, 1991.
Levenson, Michael H. *A Genealogy of Modernism: A Study of English Literary Doctrine, 1908–1922.* Cambridge: Cambridge University Press, 1984.
Peppis, Paul. *Literature, Politics, and the English Avant-Garde: Nation and Empire, 1901–1918.* Cambridge: Cambridge University Press, 2000.

B

BAINBRIDGE, BERYL (1933–) The author of more than 15 novels and several short stories, Beryl Margaret Bainbridge was born on November 21, 1934, in Liverpool, England. She studied dance as a young woman and worked as a professional actress in radio and in various repertory theatres for nearly 30 years. In 1954, she married an artist; she and her husband divorced in 1959.

Bainbridge wrote her first novel during her first pregnancy but could not find a publisher for it. Her first two published novels, *A Weekend with Claud* and *Another Part of the Wood,* met with moderate success in 1967 and 1968. Her writing career began to flourish in 1970, when she met Colin and Anna Haycraft. Colin Haycraft was the head of Gerald Duckworth & Company Publishers, and Anna Haycraft publishes fiction under the pen name Alice Thomas ELLIS; *Harriet Said* was soon published by Duckworth. This title was actually the first novel Bainbridge ever wrote, but it had been rejected as too extreme by other editors, leading Bainbridge to change her voice and style. Anna Haycraft encouraged Bainbridge to continue writing in her original style. Bainbridge's next book. *The Dressmaker* (published in the United States as *The Secret Glass*), was nominated for the BOOKER PRIZE in 1973; in 1974, *The BOTTLE FACTORY OUTING* was also nominated for the Booker Prize and won the GUARDIAN FICTION PRIZE. Four additional novels by Beryl Bainbridge received nominations for the Booker Prize: *An Awfully Big Adventure* in 1992, *EVERY MAN FOR HIMSELF* in 1996, *Master Georgie* in 1999, and *According to Queeney* in 2001. Two of her novels have won the WHITBREAD AWARD: *INJURY TIME* in 1977 and *Every Man for Himself* in 1996. *Master Georgie* won both the W. H. Smith Fiction Prize and the JAMES TAIT BLACK MEMORIAL PRIZE for best novel in 1999.

Beryl Bainbridge lives in London and continues to publish her darkly comic and unexpectedly violent fiction. She has hosted BBC travel programs, written television scripts, and adapted some of her novels for film. She also writes a column for the *Evening Standard* newspaper. In 2000, she was named a Dame Commander of the British Empire.

BIBLIOGRAPHY

Baker, John F. "Beryl Bainbridge: Total Immersion in the Past," *Publishers Weekly* 9 (November 1998): 52–53.

Bing, Jonathan. *Writing for Your Life #4.* Wainscott, N.Y.: Pushcart Press, 2000.

BALLARD, J. G. (1930–) Originally gaining a reputation as an innovative writer of science fiction stories and novels, J. G. Ballard has also produced mainstream fictional and semiautobiographical works. James Graham Ballard was born on November 15, 1930, to British parents in Shanghai, China. He was imprisoned in a concentration camp when Shanghai fell to the Japanese—an experience he fictionalized in *EMPIRE OF THE SUN* in 1984, winning the *GUARDIAN*

FICTION PRIZE and being named to the short list for the BOOKER PRIZE. The novel was the basis for a successful film directed by Steven Spielberg in 1985. From 1949 to 1951 he attended King's College, Cambridge, studying medicine, but before he finished his degree he became fascinated by airplanes, traveling to Canada to train as a pilot. From 1954 to 1957, he served in the Royal Air Force. While stationed in Canada, he got his first exposure to the pulp science fiction magazines that redirected his energies yet again. He was married in 1953, but his wife died in an accident in 1964. He lives quietly—even reclusively—in the suburbs of London, writing innovatively surrealistic speculative fiction and mainstream novels that draw heavily on his interest in human psychology, both normal and extraordinary, and imaginatively conceived landscapes.

Ballard's first four novels form an apocalyptic quartet in which the order and normality of life on earth are destroyed by the four elements of air, water, fire, and earth: *The Wind from Nowhere* (1962), *The Drowned World* (1962), *The Drought* (also published under the title *The Burning World;* 1964), and *The Crystal World* (1966). The interest in apocalypse and the fascination with destruction that these novels display is a recurring theme in Ballard's work, and may grow from his childhood experiences in the battleground that Shanghai became. After the tragic and unexpected death of his wife, Ballard's fiction became darker and even more violent; *CRASH* (1971) was rejected by several publishers and elicited some quite hostile reviews when it appeared; however, Ballard had recognized that the modern love affair with the automobile has a dark, even perverse, underbelly, and he exploited the death wish that forms an unspoken consort to our enjoyment of the automobile. With the publication of *Empire of the Sun,* Ballard adopted mainstream topics and characters for his fiction; he continues to publish in this vein.

BIBLIOGRAPHY

Brigg, Peter. *J. G. Ballard.* San Bernardino, Calif.: Borgo Press, 1985.

Goddard, James, and David Pringle, eds. *J. G. Ballard: The First Twenty Years.* Hays, Middlesex: Bran's Head Books, 1976.

BALTHAZAR LAWRENCE DURRELL (1958)

Volume two of *The ALEXANDRIA QUARTET, Balthazar* opens where *JUSTINE* ended: The time is shortly before WORLD WAR II and the narrator, Darley, is secluded on a Greek island mulling over his life in Alexandria. Instead of moving the narrative forward, however, DURRELL introduces a disruption: Darley has sent his manuscript of *Justine* to Balthazar, the leader of a small group studying the cabala that had included Nessim, his wife, Justine, Darley, and others. One night Balthazar appears at Darley's cottage with the manuscript in hand, heavily annotated and emended. He says that Darley has been completely mistaken, and that Justine in fact loved Pursewarden, conducting an affair with Darley to disguise her true passion from Nessim.

Darley is stunned to learn how wrong he has been about the events in which he was a participant. Amusing details, such as old Scobie hiring him to report on Balthazar's group, turn out to have had deadly significance. Characters who seemed merely charming, such as his flat-mate, the French diplomat Pombal, may have had hidden missions, secret agendas, or concealed lives as spies. As Darley reviews his experiences, he increasingly refers to Balthazar's notes, which he calls "the Interlinear." Readers must pay careful attention to Durrell's use of quotation marks and parentheses in order to keep track of the narrative voice as Darley intersperses his own thoughts with passages from the Interlinear. This combination produces a fractured picture that undermines Darley's confidence in his own perception.

Darley sees Pursewarden as a more sympathetic, deeper character, but the man's suicide remains a mystery. The climax of the story shifts to a carnival ball at which a minor character is murdered. Darley removes himself to the fringe position he now sees he occupied in the lives of Justine, Nessim, Balthazar, and other Alexandrians. The story concludes with a further layering of new perspective as Clea writes to Darley and includes in her letter passages from a letter Pursewarden wrote to her. In her closing, she implies that only a further visit to Alexandria will resolve Darley's struggle to understand the events of his own life.

An early example of POSTMODERNISM, *Balthazar* is a novel cobbled together out of fictional pieces of fiction.

Balthazar's Interlinear undermines the possibility of straightforward storytelling, leaving the fictional author, Darley, adrift in his misguided perceptions. Ironically, volume three of the series, MOUNTOLIVE, reveals that many of Balthazar's "revelations" are actually lies.

BIBLIOGRAPHY

Begnal, Michael H., ed. *On Miracle Ground: Essays on the Fiction of Lawrence Durrell.* Cranbury, N.J.: Associated University Presses, 1990.

Godshalk, W. L. "*Balthazar: A Comedy of Surrogation.*" In *Selected Essays on the Humor of Lawrence Durrell.* Edited by Betsy Nichols, Frank Kersnowski, and James Nichols. Victoria, B.C.: University of Victoria, 1993, 81–91.

Raper, Julius Rowan, Melody L. Enscore, and Paige Matthey Bynum. *Lawrence Durrell: Comprehending the Whole.* Columbia: University of Missouri Press, 1995.

BARKER, PAT (1943–)

Noted for her characterization of women marginalized by patriarchy and men mangled by warfare, Pat Barker was born on May 8, 1943, in the industrial city of Thornaby-on-Tees, England. She graduated from the London School of Economics and Political Science in 1965 with a bachelor of science degree, and in 1978 she was married to David Barker, a zoologist.

Barker's first three novels represent the oppressed lives of working-class women in northern England. *Union Street,* published in 1982, relates the stories of seven women living in the shadow of a factory, all of whom are resigned to lives of suffering. *Blow Your House Down,* published in 1984, presents a similar treatment of the lives of prostitutes in an industrial city, complicated by the presence of a vicious killer. *The Century's Daughter* (1986) is a retrospective both of an elderly woman's harsh life and of the 20th century itself. These novels brought Barker acclaim as a feminist writer, but she did not want to be typecast. She changed her protagonist to a fatherless teenage boy for *The Man Who Wasn't There* in 1989. Her greatest literary success, however, has come from a trio of novels set during WORLD WAR I and collectively titled *The REGENERATION TRILOGY: Regeneration* (1991); *The Eye in the Door* (1993), which won the GUARDIAN FICTION PRIZE; and *The Ghost Road* (1995), which won the BOOKER PRIZE.

Pat Barker has received several honorary degrees and was named a Commander of the Order of the British Empire in 2000. She lives in London and continues to publish fiction.

BIBLIOGRAPHY

Jolly, Margareta. "After Feminism: Pat Barker, Penelope Lively, and the Contemporary Novel." In *British Culture of the Postwar: An Introduction to Literature and Society, 1945–1999.* Edited by Alistair Davies. London: Routledge, 2000, 58–82.

Monteith, Sharon. *Pat Barker.* Devon, England: Northcote House-British Council, 2002.

Perry, Donna. *Backtalk: Women Writers Speak Out.* New Brunswick, N.J.: Rutgers University Press, 1993, 43–61.

BARNES, JULIAN (1946–)

Considered to be one of the three leading writers of his generation in Britain today, with Ian McEwan and Martin Amis, Julian Patrick Barnes was born on January 19, 1946, in Leicester, England. He was educated at the City of London School and Oxford (Magdalene College), earning a B.A. degree in modern languages in 1968. He also studied law but did not undertake a career in that field. He has served in several editorial positions for the *Oxford English Dictionary Supplement,* the *New Review,* the *New Statesman,* the *Sunday London Times,* and as London correspondent for *The New Yorker.* He married in 1979.

Barnes's first novel, METROLAND (1980), features an Englishman, Christopher Lloyd, who experiences his sexual initiation in Paris during the 1968 student uprising there. It shows off Barnes's skill as an objective observer of the details of behavior that reflect the underlying values of the characters. His next novel, *Before She Met Me* (1982), also explores a sexual awakening, but this time it is a case of a man divorcing his wife for a younger, more thrilling woman, only to discover a sordid sexual past that drives him to plan a murder-suicide. Barnes's greatest novel may be his third, FLAUBERT'S PARROT, a work of POSTMODERNISM in which he explores the impossibility of knowing the past in any but a subjective manner.

Julian Barnes also writes MYSTERY AND DETECTIVE FICTION under the pseudonym Dan Kavanagh. His recurring gumshoe is a bisexual former police officer named Duffy; the four novels in this series are *Duffy* (1980), *Fiddle City* (1981), *Putting the Boot In* (1985), and *Going to the Dogs* (1987). Barnes parodies the conventions of the mystery and detective genre while simultaneously demonstrating great skill in exploiting them to best effect, and he also retains the trademark wordplay of his mainstream fiction. The Duffy series features seedy locations and sensationalistic elements, and the novels demonstrate the postmodern difficulty of resolving the many pieces of evidence associated with a crime into a single coherent solution.

Although France is a frequent focal point or source of inspiration for Barnes's fiction, he has also produced insightful novels about his native land. In *The History of the World in 10 1/2 Chapters* (1989), he explores 10 life-or-death scenarios that include a worm on Noah's Ark and the desperate castaways adrift in the painting *The Raft of the Medusa,* all of which are placed in the service of understanding contemporary British life. In ENGLAND, ENGLAND (1999), he imagines a business tycoon trying to turn the Isle of Wight into a kind of Disneyesque theme park with the major icons of British history and culture—Stonehenge, Robin Hood, Big Ben, and others—reproduced for the enjoyment of paying visitors. The novel imagines a world in which England is a mere reproduction of its former glory, serving as a toy to entertain a mass audience, and in the process it satirizes certain recent marketing strategies in favor of British tourism.

BIBLIOGRAPHY

Amis, Martin. "Snooker with Julian Barnes." *Visiting Mrs. Nabokov and Other Excursions.* New York: Vintage International/Random House, Inc., 1993, 154–158.

Moseley, Merritt. *Understanding Julian Barnes.* Understanding Contemporary British Literature. Columbia: University of South Carolina Press, 1997.

Rushdie, Salman. "Julian Barnes." In *Imaginary Homelands: Essays and Criticism, 1981–1991.* London: Granta Books; New York: Viking, 1991.

BARRIE, J. M. (1860–1937)   Born in Scotland on May 9, 1860, James Matthew Barrie wrote as a journalist, a novelist, and a playwright, creating the immortal story of Peter Pan both for the stage and as a work of fiction. Barrie's childhood was marked by a tragic event with lifelong consequences: His older brother David, who was also his mother's favorite, died in a skating accident when Barrie was six. Margaret Ogilvie Barrie became an invalid in her grief, and young Barrie spent the rest of his life trying to revitalize his mother's love by attempting to replace the lost David. The other character-forming aspect of Barrie's youth was physical in nature: His body stopped growing when he was barely five feet tall, and he may have never fully matured sexually, remaining stranded between childhood and adulthood.

After completing his schooling at Dumfries Academy in 1878, Barrie entered the University of Edinburgh and took an M.A. degree in 1882. From 1879 to 1890, he wrote for various newspapers, moving to London in 1885. After 1890, he worked primarily as a dramatist, producing more than 40 works for the stage. He was married to the actress Mary Ansell in 1894, but the marriage was unhappy, and the couple divorced in 1909 without producing any children.

A more important relationship for Barrie may have been the one that developed between him and the five sons of Arthur Llewelyn Davies and Sylvia du Maurier Davies (the paternal aunt of the novelist Daphne DU MAURIER). The children played in Kensington Gardens, near Barrie's home; and he entertained them with stories and accompanied them to pantomime performances. When George and Sylvia Davies died, Barrie became the guardian of the five sons, George, Jack, Peter, Michael, and Nicholas Davies.

These boys all served as models for characters in a story that took many forms. It was first published in the novel *The Little White Bird, or Adventures in Kensington Gardens* (1902). Barrie transformed a part of that novel into the play *Peter Pan: Or, the Boy Who Wouldn't Grow Up,* first performed in 1904. In the wake of the phenomenal success of the play in both London and New York, Barrie also produced the story as a children's book, *Peter Pan in Kensington Gardens,* in 1906 and as a longer prose narration with some additional material, "When Wendy Grew Up," under the title *Peter and Wendy* in 1911. Barrie continued revising and extending his play, publishing a definitive five-act version in 1928.

Most of Barrie's nondramatic works were published in the 19th century or were outgrowths of his plays, so he is not a major 20th-century novelist; however, he created a modern myth that transcends genre in the character of Peter Pan. Barrie continued writing plays until the year before his death and was showered with honors: He was created baronet in 1913 and held the post of rector of St. Andrews University from 1919 to 1922; he was awarded the Order of Merit in 1922; he received honorary doctorates from Oxford and Cambridge Universities in 1926 and 1930, respectively; and he was chancellor of Edinburgh University from 1930 to 1937. Barrie died on June 19, 1937, and was buried in his hometown of Kirriemuir, Scotland, next to his mother and brother.

BIBLIOGRAPHY

Aller, Susan Bivin. *J. M. Barrie: The Magic Behind Peter Pan.* Minneapolis: Lerner Publications, 1994.

Birkin, Andrew. *J. M. Barrie and the Lost Boys.* New ed. New Haven, Conn.: Yale University Press, 2003.

Toby, Marlene. *James M. Barrie, Author of Peter Pan.* Chicago: Children's Press, 1995.

BECKETT, SAMUEL (1906–1989)

Winner of the NOBEL PRIZE in literature in 1969, Samuel Barclay Beckett was born in Dublin, Ireland, on April 13, 1906, to an educated, white-collar Protestant family. He matriculated at Trinity College in 1923 intending to study law and accounting, but he was an indifferent student until he began studying modern languages, especially French. When he completed his degree in 1927, he tried his hand at teaching in IRELAND and in Paris, where he became close to James JOYCE for several years. But Beckett did not want to be an academic or an educator. For more than a decade, he remained only partially and marginally employed, mostly impoverished, as he oscillated between unhappy, depressed stays with his family in Ireland and short stints in London, Paris, and other European cities.

Beckett's depression became especially severe in the early 1930s: in 1932, James Joyce's daughter, Lucia, on the verge of a schizophrenic breakdown, contributed to her father's rejection of Beckett when the younger man did not accept her love, and in 1933, some six months after his father died, Beckett entered psychoanalysis at the Tavistock Clinic in London, where he heard an influential series of lectures by Carl Jung. Beckett was already familiar with the works of Sigmund Freud and had begun studying philosophers such as Descartes, Schopenhauer, and the Belgian Arnold Geulincx, investigating the problems of consciousness and being. This combination of philosophy and psychology became an important influence in his writing.

Beckett's first novel, *A Dream of Fair to Middling Women,* written by 1932 (printed posthumously in 1992), did not find a publisher, and so he reworked parts of it into a series of 10 short stories published as *More Pricks than Kicks* in 1934, but the book did not sell in spite of moderate critical praise. Beckett wrote poems and book reviews to earn a marginal existence and began work on his first published novel, *Murphy* (1938). While this work made the rounds of publishing houses (receiving more than 40 rejections), poverty forced Beckett back to the family home, where he began to take an interest in drama that would later lead to his greatest literary achievement, *Waiting for Godot* (1953), and other innovative plays. When WORLD WAR II began, Beckett was back in Paris, and since Ireland was a neutral nation, he was allowed to stay. He became involved in the French Resistance, but by 1942 he had to flee to unoccupied France, where he worked as a farm laborer.

After the war, Beckett received the *Croix de Guerre* and the *Médaille de la Résistance* in recognition of his service to France. After two more years of wandering, he settled permanently in France and even began to write in French, eventually producing the trilogy of novels *Molloy* (1951), *MALONE DIES* (1955), and *The UNNAMABLE* (1958). During this period, he became instantly famous when *Waiting for Godot* was first performed in Paris. Although Beckett established his literary reputation in the theater, he always considered himself to be primarily a writer of fiction, exploring the riddles of human existence—and of human suffering—in the experimental, abbreviated style of MODERNISM. He continued to write prolifically in various genres from 1960 to 1980, overseeing productions of his plays in several countries, living in Paris and in a country house outside the city with his French wife. Samuel Beckett died on December 22, 1989, in Paris.

BIBLIOGRAPHY

Ben-Zvi, Linda. *Samuel Beckett.* Twayne's English Authors, 423. Boston: Twayne Publishers, 1986.

Bloom, Harold. *Samuel Beckett.* New York: Chelsea House, 1985.

Gordon, Lois G. *The World of Samuel Beckett, 1906–1946.* New Haven, Conn.: Yale University Press, 1996.

Knowlson, James. *Damned to Fame: A Life of Samuel Beckett.* New York: Simon & Schuster, 1996.

BEERBOHM, MAX (1872–1956)

BEERBOHM, MAX (1872–1956)   Although primarily remembered as a humorist and cartoonist, Max Beerbohm also wrote one 20th-century novel, *ZULEIKA DOBSON,* and contributed essays and reviews to numerous literary periodicals. A dandy who associated with the young men of the AESTHETICISM movement, Beerbohm memorialized the late Victorian cultural milieu, nostalgically and lovingly portraying it in gentle parodies.

Henry Maximilian Beerbohm was born on August 24, 1872, and educated at Charterhouse School and at Merton College, Oxford. During his undergraduate years (1890–94), he began contributing to publications such as the *Strand* and *The Yellow Book;* he also became acquainted with Aubrey Beardsley and Oscar WILDE and the artistic circles associated with these men. After leaving Oxford without taking a degree, he traveled several months in the United States as the secretary of his half brother, Herbert Beerbohm Tree, the noted actor-manager. He published a collection of prose pieces, *The Works of Max Beerbohm,* in 1895, and then in 1898 he replaced George Bernard Shaw in the post of drama critic for the *Saturday Review,* continuing in this capacity until 1910. After a journalistic assignment of travel writing about Italy for the *Daily Mail* in 1906, Beerbohm developed a strong attachment to his subject and moved there permanently in 1910, when he married Florence Kahn, an American actress. *Zuleika Dobson* appeared in 1911, and he continued publishing collections of short humor pieces and drawings until 1928. During a long visit to England in 1935, while his wife appeared onstage, he launched a new aspect of his career when he presented a series of popular broadcasts for the BBC, *London Revisited.* In 1939, Beerbohm was knighted. Florence died in 1951, and Beerbohm married his secretary, Elizabeth Jungmann, in 1956. He died May 20, 1956, at his home in Rapallo, Italy.

BIBLIOGRAPHY

Behrman, S. N. *Portrait of Max: An Intimate Memoir of Sir Max Beerbohm.* New York: Random House, 1960.

Hall, N. John, *Max Beerbohm's Caricatures.* New Haven, Conn.: Yale University Press, 1997.

McElderry, Bruce Robert. *Max Beerbohm.* Twayne's English Authors, 111. New York: Twayne Publishers, 1972.

BELLES LETTRES

BELLES LETTRES   Broadly, this French term refers to the kinds of works included in the literary genres of poetry, fiction, drama, essay, and literary criticism; originally, the term valorized literature over the pragmatic, expository prose of science and business. These literary works derive from the imaginations of writers, or from the application of interpretive thought to the imaginative works of others, rather than from the practical explanation of the facts of the world. In the case of realism, imaginative works will use factual descriptions, but these exist to serve the fictional illusions created by the writer, not necessarily to extend or reinforce the reader's knowledge of the world.

In 20th-century references, the term *belles lettres* sometimes suggests a mildly disparaging attitude toward the narrower category of works that feature artifice, stylization, exaggerated charm, or other characteristics of light entertainments rather than serious disquisitions. The term *belle lettrist* refers to a writer who produces such entertainments, considered to be trifles—still literature, but of the second rank—by some critics; the term *belle lettristic* generally dismisses the text it refers to without denigrating it completely. Some critics of the middle and late 20th century find these terms useful in referring to the writing of an era earlier than their own.

BIBLIOGRAPHY

Guillory, John. "Literary Study and the Modern System of the Disciplines." In *Disciplinarity at the Fin de Siecle.* Edited by Amanda Anderson and Joseph Valente. Princeton, N.J.: Princeton University Press, 2002, 19–43.

Wojciechowski, Jacek. "Belles-Lettres in the Library," *Public Libraries* 35.2 (1996): 120–123.

BELLOC, HILAIRE (1870–1953)

Born in France on July 27, 1870, Hilaire Belloc became one of the leading English essayists of the first two and a half decades of the 20th century; he also wrote light verse, including *Cautionary Tales for Children,* travel books, novels, political treatises, journalism, criticism, and both personal and polemical essays, although much of it is not widely read today. Belloc is primarily remembered now for his close association with G. K. CHESTERTON.

Belloc's French father fled with his family from France to his wife's native country, England, during the Franco-Prussian War. Prussian troops despoiled the family's estate and left it devastated, an event that marked the beginning of Hilaire Belloc's lifelong hatred of Germans. A passionate and outspoken supporter of Catholicism, monarchy, and a form of near-medieval economic organization, Belloc saw Germany as the seedbed of Protestantism and capitalism, the twin evils, in his estimation, of the modern world.

Belloc was educated at Balliol College, Oxford University, earning a B.A. degree in 1895. He became a freelance writer for several London periodicals and married in 1896. Around the turn of the century, Belloc found a like-minded friend in the writer and illustrator G. K. Chesterton. Both were advocates of a conservative, even reactionary, return to a Catholic Europe. The dramatist and socialist George Bernard Shaw satirized the two as the "Chesterbelloc," an ungainly beast possessed of fossilized ideas.

Chesterton and Belloc opposed the imperial expansion of British influence through colonialism, particularly when this enterprise led to disasters such as the BOER WAR in South Africa. They envisioned an England (and a Europe) of subsistence farmers and artisans presided over spiritually and politically by the Catholic Church. These ideas offered an alternative, which Belloc called "distributism," to both capitalism and socialism: Essays outlining and defending this system were published in the weekly journal the *Eye Witness,* which Belloc edited before WORLD WAR I.

Although Belloc presented his ideas forcefully in accessible and witty essays, he was frequently an adherent of contradictory claims: For example, he passionately supported monarchy as the preeminent form of political organization, but he also admired the French Revolution that brought the Bourbon monarchy to an end. He was noted (and reviled) as an anti-Semitic writer, yet he despised Hitler for his hostile rhetoric against Jews. Belloc's own anti-Semitism remains a sticking point for contemporary critics; his novels and essays have lost the readership they once enjoyed. In addition to his association with G. K. Chesterton, he is primarily remembered now as an outstanding writer of light verse, in the league of Lewis Carroll and Edward Lear.

Hilaire Belloc died on July 16, 1953, in England, living long enough to see the social practices and political systems that he had so strenuously opposed become accepted institutions throughout the Western world.

BIBLIOGRAPHY

Cheyette, Bryan. *Constructions of "the Jew" in English Literature and Society: Racial Representations, 1875–1945.* Cambridge: Cambridge University Press, 1993.

Corrin, Jay P. *G. K. Chesterton & Hilaire Belloc: The Battle Against Modernity.* Athens, Ohio: Ohio University Press, 1981.

Wilson, A. N. *Hilaire Belloc.* New York: Atheneum, 1984.

BEND IN THE RIVER, A V. S. NAIPAUL (1979)

One of the greatest themes of this monumental 20th-century writer is that of alienation, and this novel provides an intense examination of that theme. The first-person narrator of Indian ancestry, Salim, becomes the proprietor of a small store in the interior of Africa in a nation soon to establish its independence: a quintessential example of postcolonialism. Throwing off the weight of COLONIALISM, however, has removed one familiar problem only to introduce other unfamiliar ones. Before Europeans arrived, the people of this area had an ancestral identity, and after decades of colonial rule their descendants acquired new identities in the struggle to accommodate traditional ways and European dominance. But what is the identity of the new independent nation that "the Big Man"—a dictator for life who has seized power—has carved out for himself? The country is unified on paper and in the political sloganeering of the new regime, but in practice it is a pastiche of rootless and dispossessed individuals: Africans, Europeans, Indians, Arabs, and others, each with faint memories of ancient ways, sharp memories of recent ways, and varying intentions toward the future.

The struggle for independence does not occur without violence, and some people, even in Salim's remote location, have blood on their hands; either through guilt or fear of recrimination, they sit uneasily, waiting for the consequences of their deeds to catch up with them or continuing through violence to keep vengeance at bay. The Big Man has his own debts to pay, and soon Salim's store is confiscated and awarded to citizen Theotime. Even in this remote region, in this insignificant bend of the great river, security cannot be guaranteed. Events lose their comforting predictability. For example, Salim is taken prisoner only to be released later by an unexpected helper. The former colonizers are in no better position: The Frenchman who had advised the Big Man has now been cast off and his wife engages in an illicit affair with Salim, and the collection of tribal masks gathered by the Belgian priest is decaying, a symbol of the decaying memory of the precolonial past. In this new nation, Europeans cannot preserve the past nor can they control the present or shape the future.

Salim visits London and realizes he must set his affairs in order and leave Africa behind, but that he cannot leave his displacement behind. Instead, displacement is the modern condition as populations all over the world grow and shift, adapting to rootlessness. His movement away from Africa will simply be another extension of his alienated status. By the time of his return, the situation in the new nation is tense; everyone is on edge. As violence erupts once more,

Salim slips away on a river steamer. His story does not end in closure because closure cannot come to the displaced and the alienated people of the world. Their rootlessness is like a wound that cannot heal, and all the material goods of the modern world will not assuage the loss of identity, heritage, home, and connectedness to the past. The novel leaves Salim in midlife, in transition from one way station to another, thereby emphasizing the suspended quality of alienation: Individuals persevere or perish, but the mass of humanity moves on, aimless and yet purposeful. The darkness in which Salim makes his escape powerfully echoes the darkness in which human beings everywhere are enmeshed. Naipaul refuses to plaster over the wound of our existence with comforting platitudes.

BIBLIOGRAPHY

Kamra, Shashi. *The Novels of V. S. Naipaul: A Study in Theme and Form.* New Delhi: Prestige Books, 1990.

Morris, Robert K. *Paradoxes of Order: Some Perspectives on the Fiction of V. S. Naipaul.* Columbia: University of Missouri Press, 1975.

Weiss, Timothy. *On the Margins: The Art of Exile in V. S. Naipaul.* Amherst: University of Massachusetts Press, 1992.

BENNETT, ARNOLD (1867–1931)

A prolific writer who is remembered now for several novels set in the Staffordshire district of England (modern Stoke-on-Trent), where pottery and fine china have been made for centuries, Enoch Arnold Bennett was born in that region on May 27, 1867, to working-CLASS parents. His father was ambitious to rise above the station to which he was born, and by studying law at night he was eventually able to qualify as a solicitor and move his family into better accommodations. The elder Bennett's ambition extended to a keen interest in the success of his children, and he objected to his son's pursuit of literature and professional writing, trying to mold the young man instead to the legal profession. Despite Arnold Bennett's intelligence, he failed the exams for the law, preferring to develop his expertise in French literature and the works of English novelists such as Thomas Hardy and George Moore. He was able to secure his father's permission to move to London only by finding employment in the city as a law clerk, but once he was there he began writing and publishing stories. He soon left behind the pretense of developing a legal career.

Bennett's first full-time job as a professional writer began in 1894, when he acquired a position as a magazine editor. By 1898, he had published his first novel, *The Man from the North,* written in the style of 19th-century realism but with a modern awareness of the power of CLASS to shape the lives of the English. He expanded his output as a freelance journalist and also began writing popular novels and nonfiction that would appeal to a mass audience. This kind of writing eventually made him wealthy, but he did not abandon serious literature; in fact, his serious novels such as *ANNA OF THE FIVE TOWNS* (1902) and *The Old Wives' Tale* (1907) secured his reputation as an important novelist of the early 20th century. These stories examine the lives of people in the potteries district, which at that time was an environment ravaged by industrial abuses. Bennett also used this setting for an autobiographical set of novels, *The Clayhanger Trilogy* (*Clayhanger* in 1910, *Hilda Lessways* in 1911, and *These Twain* in 1915), experimenting with form to retell the story of a strong-willed father's sway over his family from different points of view.

Bennett was already in his middle years when WORLD WAR I began. He supported the war effort, although in principle not the war itself, by writing political articles; he was appointed director of propaganda in the last year of the war, 1918. These experiences, along with romantic disappointments in his personal life that included a separation from his first wife, Marguerite Bennett, and an unhappy common-law marriage to Dorothy Cheston Bennett, seem to have darkened his fiction. *The Pretty Lady* (1918) features a French prostitute as protagonist; *Riceyman Steps* (1923, winner of the JAMES TAIT BLACK MEMORIAL PRIZE in 1924) departs from his earlier dependence on realism; and *Lord Raingo* (1926) examines political power and the affair between an older man and a young woman.

Although Bennett was a prolific writer who produced effective examples in numerous genres and styles, his reputation suffered toward the end of his life: Virginia WOOLF attacked him in *Mr. Bennett and Mrs. Brown,* an indictment of the Victorian era, and after his death memoirs by Marguerite Bennett and Dorothy Cheston Bennett undermined his literary importance. Bennett's mix of serious literary works and popular fiction, together with his wealthy lifestyle, provided too many easy targets for his critics. Only since the publication of his letters in the late 1960s has Bennett's contribution to English literature begun to be better understood and appreciated; a new generation of writers typified by Margaret DRABBLE, the author of a biography of Bennett, is finding more to admire in Bennett than Virginia Woolf was managed.

BIBLIOGRAPHY

Drabble, Margaret. *Arnold Bennett: A Biography.* London: Weidenfeld & Nicolson, 1974.

Hepburn, James, ed. *Letters of Arnold Bennett.* 3 vols. London: Oxford University Press, 1966–70.

Woolf, Virginia. *Mr Bennett and Mrs Brown.* London: Leonard & Virginia Woolf, 1924.

Wright, Walter F. *Arnold Bennett: Romantic Realist.* Lincoln: University of Nebraska Press, 1971.

BERGER, JOHN (1926–)

BERGER, JOHN (1926–) Although most of his work has been devoted to painting and art criticism, John Berger has also achieved critical success as a novelist, winning the BOOKER PRIZE in 1972 for his experimental novel *G*. This challenging novel also won the *GUARDIAN* FICTION PRIZE for 1972 and the JAMES TAIT BLACK MEMORIAL PRIZE for 1973. Additionally, in the 1970s Berger contributed to a successful television series on art, *Ways of Seeing,* and he collaborated with the French writer Alain Tanner on the screenplay published in English as *Jonah Who Will Be Twenty-five in the Year 2000* (1983). Berger has also written poetry, plays, translations, and books on photography, and he has acted in films.

John Peter Berger was born in London on November 5, 1926, and studied at Central School of Art and the Chelsea School of Art. He served in the infantry from 1944 to 1946, and taught painting from 1948 to 1955. During this phase of his life, he also exhibited his own paintings at several London galleries; as recently as 1994, he mounted an exhibition in New York. He contributed essays and art criticism to *The*

New Statesman and other periodicals from 1951 to 1960. Berger has been married twice and is the father of three children.

Berger's Marxist political orientation is apparent in his criticism and fiction. He condemns modern capitalism for an increasing impoverishment of the human condition, especially the conceptual and imaginative dimension of human life. His strongest political statements can be found in his essays and art criticism such as *Permanent Red: Essays in Seeing* (1960) and the award-winning *The Seventh Man: A Book of Images and Words About the Experience of Migrant Workers in Europe* (1977). In his fiction, the political aspect of Berger's thought is particularly apparent in the trilogy *Into Their Labors* (consisting of *Pig Earth,* 1979; *Once in Europa,* 1987; and *Lilac and Flag: An Old Wives' Tale of a City,* 1990). Tracing French peasant life from prehistory to the modern era, he demonstrates the losses and costs exacted by progress, modernity, and capitalism.

In his less overtly political fiction, Berger is noted for the humane treatment and dignified presentation of characters marginalized by age, disease, or poverty. *Corker's Freedom* (1964), Berger's third novel, relates the events of one day in the life of an old man who leaves the oppressive home of his sister, embarking on a grand adventure that quickly fails. *To the Wedding* (1995) relates the story of a love that survives the discovery of the female protagonist's HIV-positive status. In *King: A Street Story* (1999), Berger examines homelessness and dispossession. Despite the impoverishment of intellect and spirit that, in Berger's view, the modern world has forced on these characters, the author presents them in ways that underscore the persistence of optimistic potential in the face of crushing oppression.

In the 1970s, Berger settled in the French Alps, where he continues to live and write.

BIBLIOGRAPHY

Dyer, Geoff. *Ways of Telling: The Work of John Berger.* London: Pluto, 1986.

Fuller, Peter. *Seeing Berger: A Revaluation of Ways of Seeing.* Rev. ed. London: Claridge Press, 1988.

Klaus, H. Gustav. *The Socialist Novel in Britain: Towards the Recovery of a Tradition.* New York: St. Martin's Press, 1982.

BILDUNGSROMAN This German word has been adopted in English literary criticism to refer to a novel of transition, the plot of which follows a protagonist from childhood or adolescence to adulthood. Novels of this sort frequently follow the outline of the author's autobiography, but they may also depend on imaginative inventions. The earliest example of the genre is generally considered to be Goethe's *Wilhelm Meister's Apprenticeship* (1796). The protagonist of a bildungsroman may serve a literal or symbolic apprenticeship in the course of the novel; as a result of the plot's effects on his or her character, the protagonist matures and discovers a suitable role in life. The structure of a bildungsroman particularly highlights the character-forming episodes that shape a malleable young psyche into a mature personality, for better or worse.

Related, more specialized terms include *Künstlerroman,* the novel that examines the growth and development of an artist, especially with respect to the artist's particular giftedness, and *Erziehungsroman,* the novel devoted to a young person's education. See *A Portrait of the Artist as a Young Man* by James Joyce for an example of the *Künstlerroman,* or *The Gormenghast Trilogy* by Mervyn Peake (or any volume in the *Harry Potter* series by J. K. Rowling) for an example of the *Erziehungsroman* in the subgenre of FANTASY literature. Phrases used synonymously with bildungsroman include *apprenticeship novel, novel of development,* and *novel of formation.*

Classic examples of the 20th-century bildungsroman include *The Way of All Flesh* by Samuel Butler and *Of Human Bondage* by W. Somerset Maugham. When the protagonist of a bildungsroman is a young woman, the story may focus on her growing experience with and understanding of romance. Such a story may be comic or lighthearted, like *I Capture the Castle* by Dodie Smith, or *Cold Comfort Farm* by Stella Gibbons; alternatively, the young woman's bildungsroman may be a serious or even a disastrous story, like the five-volume *Children of Violence* series by Doris Lessing, or *The Death of the Heart,* by Elizabeth Bowen, or the earlier parts of *The Country Girls Trilogy* by Edna O'Brien. A more specialized type of bildungsroman is the novel that relates the awakening of a young man's or woman's awareness of nonheterosexual desire: *The Swimming Pool Library* by Alan Hollinghurst narrates the growth of a young man's recognition of his homosexuality, making an interesting contrast to the story of a young woman's discovery of her lesbian nature in *The Well of Loneliness* by Radclyffe Hall.

BIBLIOGRAPHY

Abel, Elizabeth, Marianne Hirsch, and Elizabeth Langland. *The Voyage In: Fictions of Female Development.* Hanover, N.H.: University Press of New England, 1983.

Buckley, Jerome Hamilton. *Season of Youth: The Bildungsroman from Dickens to Golding.* Cambridge, Mass.: Harvard University Press, 1974.

Fraiman, Susan. *Unbecoming Women: British Woman Writers and the Novel of Development.* New York: Columbia University Press, 1993.

Hardin, James N. *Reflection and Action: Essays on the Bildungsroman.* Columbia: University of South Carolina Press, 1991.

BLACK PRINCE, THE IRIS MURDOCH (1973)

One of the most complexly philosophical of the many novels by this author, *The Black Prince* is narrated in the first person by Bradley Pearson, a writer who produces a manuscript entitled *The Black Prince: A Celebration of Love* before he dies in prison for a crime he did not commit. Although Bradley's initials point to the title of his manuscript, Murdoch complicates this simple correlation through numerous references to Apollo, to Eros, and to the force of evil in the world. Readers should familiarize themselves with the myth of Apollo and Marsyas in particular: According to the legend, Marsyas boasts of his musical ability and accepts a challenge against Apollo, the god of music (and of poetry, reason, medicine, and other arts), but inevitably loses the contest to face a horrible punishment. Marsyas is thus a figure of *hubris*, or overweening pride that offends even the gods, and of blasphemy in comparing his talent to that of Apollo, and of divine retribution in the flaying Apollo decrees as punishment. Like Marsyas, Bradley Pearson foolishly believes in his own power to transcend the limitations of human abilities; Bradley's act of hubris is to believe that

he can produce literary art that limns *truth,* rather than merely reflecting the appearances of the highly imperfect material world.

The novel opens with layers of artifice: A fictional editor, "P. A. Loxias" (*Loxias* was an epithet sometimes used of Apollo), introduces the "autobiographical" manuscript of Bradley Pearson and vaguely relates a few details of their association. Then Bradley Pearson addresses the reader in his own introduction, in which he proclaims his devotion to art and to truth and excuses the scanty productivity of his literary life on the grounds that he was unwilling to settle for anything less than the truth. After this prologue, Pearson's narrative proper begins, but the reader who skips straight to Bradley's story will miss the opening strategy of Murdoch's framing of her fiction within two further layers of fiction. Similarly, after Pearson's manuscript ends, Murdoch adds fictional postscripts by various characters introduced in Bradley's story and then gives P. A. Loxias the last word. These framing devices create the appearance of truthfulness and amplify the realism of Bradley's autobiography: Ironically, Murdoch uses fiction to make an embedded fiction appear factual.

Bradley's story recounts his decline and fall. After a failed marriage and a career as a tax inspector, he retires to a solitary life in order to bring forth his literary masterpiece, the novel that he believes he harbors within himself. His interpersonal skills are limited, and he thinks that his retirement will free him from the pesky distractions of the world and the flesh. Solitude, however, proves to be elusive. His ex-wife, Christian, returns from America as a widow and suggests that they remarry; Christian's brother Francis Marloe, a doctor who has lost his license through shady prescription practices, distances himself from his own homoerotic feelings by projecting them onto his ex–brother-in-law; Bradley's friend and rival, the enormously popular novelist Arnold Baffin, continually draws Bradley into the stormy domestic life of the Baffin household; Mrs. Rachel Baffin uses Bradley as a diversion, even attempting to seduce him (and denying it later); his emotionally fragile sister, Priscilla Saxe, casts herself on his mercy when her husband abandons her; and, when he least expects it, Bradley falls madly and deliriously in love with Julian Baffin, the 20-year-old daughter of

Arnold and Rachel Baffin, sexually alluring but intellectually shallow. Nothing in his life has prepared him to handle the emotional roller coaster he is soon riding, and he is an easy target for the schemes of others. When Arnold Baffin winds up dead from a blow to the head, Bradley is easily made to seem responsible by the conniving of the actual guilty party.

In prison for a crime he did not commit, Bradley meets P. A. Loxias and finds the solitude he had craved. In retrospect, he has the wisdom that he lacked while the events of his pre-prison life unfolded, and this wisdom of hindsight enables him to pour forth the long-awaited story, which turns out to be the story of his life illuminated by belated understanding. But Murdoch further complicates this picture of artistic fulfillment with the postscripts that P. A. Loxias collects from Christian, Francis, Rachel, and Julian. Speaking in their own voices, these characters undermine the truth of Bradley's story, casting aspersions on his telling of the tale and making him seem to be an unreliable narrator rather than an acolyte of truth. Whatever literary art may be, it is not disengaged from the world of readers nor from the interpretations that each reader will bring to any particular work. Even if artists serve truth, who can guarantee that their readers will do the same, rather than serving their own agendas?

Readers of Iris Murdoch's *The Black Prince* will need a broad acquaintance with the works of Shakespeare and Dostoevsky, with the literary and philosophical classics of antiquity, and with the conventions of realism and POSTMODERNISM in order to appreciate the full range of this complex and demanding novel. It is replete with allusions and parallels to other works; however, Bradley's story is also a well-constructed psychological thriller and a quirky romance. Murdoch demonstrates her virtuoso command of character and plot in the inner story and augments that achievement through her supple control of voice in the ancillary framework in which Bradley's story is embedded. Readers will need a similar level of sophistication in order to decode fully the ironies of the text and to appreciate Murdoch's literary mastery in this novel.

BIBLIOGRAPHY

Antonacchio, Maria. *Picturing the Human: The Moral Thought of Iris Murdoch.* New York: Oxford University Press, 2000.

Dipple, Elizabeth. *Iris Murdoch: Work for the Spirit.* Chicago: University of Chicago Press, 1982.

Todd, Richard. *Iris Murdoch: The Shakespearian Interest.* New York: Barnes & Noble, 1979.

BLACK ROBE BRIAN MOORE (1985)

The title of this novel refers to the name that Indians gave to the French Jesuit priests working to convert them during the settlement of Canada in the 17th century. Praised by literary critics when it was published, the novel won the Heinneman Award from the Royal Society of Literature in 1986. The author adapted this deeply mythic story as a film of the same title in 1991.

In the story, Father Laforgue is chosen to relieve a remote Catholic outpost among the Hurons. He begins his journey eager for the martyrdom it may bring and scornful of the "savages" he must rely on to reach the outpost. Traveling with him is a young man, Daniel Davost, who has come along through an attachment to a Huron girl, Annuka; her father, Chomina, is guiding Father Laforgue on his journey. Part of the ethical structure of the story involves Father Laforgue's motivations: He thirsts for glory and yet he does not respect the people he has come to convert. When the travelers are captured by Iroquois warriors, they are tortured and escape only through Annuka's resourcefulness.

Father Laforgue drifts toward a crisis of faith as he comes to understand the values of the native tribes better; this crisis comes to a head when he finally arrives at his destination, where the dying Father Jerome argues that the ends justify the means in the conversion of pagans to Christianity. The tribe members, sick with fever, suspect the priests of being witches who bring curses on them, but an eclipse saves the Black Robes from destruction. Father Laforgue is unwilling to baptize the Indians until they receive proper instruction in the tenets of the faith, but they wish to receive the protection of the ceremony immediately, whether they understand what it means or not. His experiences in the village create in him a true sense of caring that transcends the strictures of church dogma; the hate he once felt turns to sincere love as he recognizes that his good intentions are part of the destruction of this tribe's way of life.

BIBLIOGRAPHY

Carnes, Mark C. *Past Imperfect: History According to the Movies.* New York: Henry Holt, 1995.

Flood, Jeanne A. "*Black Robe:* Brian Moore's Appropriation of History," *Eire-Ireland: A Journal of Irish Studies* 25, no. 4 (1990): 40–55.

BLIND ASSASSIN, THE MARGARET ATWOOD (2000)

Awarded the BOOKER PRIZE for 2000, this novel is an example of both POSTMODERNISM and FEMINISM and includes elements of SCIENCE FICTION in a complex, multilayered plot rooted in the traditions of realism. The first-person narrator, Iris Chase Griffen, writes out the story of her life in the last weeks before her death as a direct address to her estranged granddaughter, Sabrina. Iris's life story is closely intertwined with that of her sister, Laura Chase, killed at the age of 25 in a dramatic crash when the car she was driving— Iris's car—plummeted over a bridge and burst into flames. Laura has since become a literary phenomenon through the posthumous publication of a novel, *The Blind Assassin.* Graduate students and scholars of literature revere her work, and sometimes they importune Iris for information about Laura; quotations ascribed to Laura appear scrawled on the walls of women's bathrooms. Sensing the approach of her death, Iris writes to memorialize Laura and also to set the record straight on the details of their lives.

As each day passes, Iris begins her self-assigned task by writing about her present conditions: She describes the small routines she is able to follow now that she is in her 90s and analyzes the people with whom she interacts. As she writes, she drifts away from the present and into the past, frequently by way of reminders and associations that point her thoughts back to earlier days. Iris's chief support, Myra, is the daughter of Reenie, the housekeeper for the Chase family while Iris and Laura were growing up; the past and the present are interlaced in Iris's life, and day by day she reenters the world of her childhood and young adult life by way of the ordinary events of the present.

The Chase family had been powerful and wealthy in the little town of Port Ticonderoga, Ontario, Canada. Iris's father owned the button factory there, the town's chief source of employment, having inherited it from a line of Chase entrepreneurs. He expected to hand the business on to his own son someday, but his firstborn child was a daughter, Iris, as was his second-born child, Laura, and his wife died of a miscarriage midway through her third pregnancy. The motherless girls grow up virtually wild, shut out of their father's life and tended by Reenie when she can spare time for them. Iris and Laura are children during WORLD WAR I and then teens as the Roaring Twenties turn into the Great Depression of the 1930s. When economic conditions collapse around the world, the button factory also falls on hard times and the family estate, Avilion, begins to deteriorate. In the most important adventure of their teen years, the girls hide a young man in their attic; he had been trying to unionize the workers at the button factory, and he may know something about the fire that devastated the factory. He fills his enforced idle hours writing to exercise his imagination and makes a safe escape as soon as he can. But his connection to the leftist labor movement and suspicions about his connection to the fire make him a wanted man, and he lives a permanent shadow existence even after he leaves.

This man, Alex Thomas, is later to play another important role in the lives of the sisters and in the creation of *The Blind Assassin.* Segments of that novel are interleaved with the chapters of Iris's memories; like Margaret ATWOOD's novel, also entitled *The Blind Assassin,* the inner story has its own inner story. On the surface, it is the story of an illicit and deeply passionate affair between a hack writer of pulp fiction and a married woman of considerable financial means and social status. In addition to their affair, they share the stories he is inventing, such as "Lizard Men of Xenor"; one draft of a story includes the tale of a blind assassin and a sacrificial maiden he rescues. Gradually, readers become aware of the many parallels and echoes from one level of the story—and of the inner story—to another, and truths that have been hidden for many decades begin to appear between the lines. Additional information comes from newspaper clippings; readers can easily imagine that these, too, have been interleaved with Iris's memoirs as if she were creating a scrapbook of her life. The clippings resemble the experimental technique used by the American novelist John Dos Passos in his trilogy *U.S.A.* (1930–36), and in a similar manner they expand the range of the story and increase the novel's realism.

In *The Blind Assassin,* Atwood has produced a tour de force of literary virtuosity, demonstrating her command of multiple voices and of the changes that occur in a single character's voice over the span of nearly a century. The complex structure of doubly layered double narratives is dizzying, but Atwood's lucid style and consistent characterization keep the story lines distinctive.

BIBLIOGRAPHY

Howells, Coral Ann. "Lest We Forget," *Canadian Literature* 173 (2002): 114.

Stein, Karen F. "A Left-Handed Story: *The Blind Assassin.*" In *Margaret Atwood's Textual Assassinations: Recent Poetry and Fiction.* Edited by Sharon Rose Wilson. Columbus: Ohio State University Press, 2003.

BLOOMSBURY GROUP   The London district in the vicinity of the British Museum provided the name for one of the most influential and least formal organizations of creative people in early 20th-century Britain. Beginning in about 1907 and continuing until the early 1930s, a group of friends met regularly at the homes of Vanessa and Clive Bell (a painter and an art critic, respectively) or of Vanessa's sister, the writer Virginia Stephen (Virginia WOOLF after her marriage to Leonard Woolf in 1912), to talk about art and ideas. Participants in the group, at one time or another, included the biographer Lytton Strachey, the art critic Roger Fry, the economist John Maynard Keynes, the novelists E. M. FORSTER and David GARNETT, and the painter Duncan Grant; occasional visitors included the philosopher Bertrand Russell, coauthor with Alfred North Whitehead of the *Principia Mathematica* (1910–13); the poet T. S. Eliot; and the novelist Aldous HUXLEY.

Members of the group were artists—both painters and writers—or philosophers; many men in the group had attended either King's College or Trinity College at Cambridge, and had been members of the "Apostles,"

an elite club for discussing ideas. While still attending the university, these men became acquainted with the daughters of Sir Leslie Stephen through their brother, Thoby; after college, the group reconfigured itself in London and expanded to include women. The general religious outlook of the group was atheistic; members were determined to expose intellectual shams and sacred cows while searching for definitive examples of truth and beauty. Key texts that influenced the group included the *Principia Mathematica,* in which the authors attempted to convert language into rigorous symbols that could be manipulated logically in the manner of geometric proofs, and G. E. Moore's *Principia Ethica* (1903), in which the author asserts that progress should aim at the enjoyment of philosophical discourse and the appreciation of beauty.

The Bloomsbury group did not advocate a particular aesthetic or political ideology, nor did it present itself as a school of thought. Instead, it served as a source of intellectual stimulation for its members and provided them with an outlet for a rather specialized form of social interaction with like-minded artists and thinkers. As careers thrived or failed, as interests diverged, and as lives changed, the group dissolved; the members were still present in the artistic and intellectual life of London and the university cities, but they had ceased functioning as a group by the early 1930s.

BIBLIOGRAPHY

Bell, Quentin. *Bloomsbury Recalled.* New York: Columbia University Press, 1995.

Caws, Mary Ann. *The Women of Bloomsbury: Virginia, Vanessa, and Carrington.* New York: Routledge, 1990.

Edel, Leon. *Bloomsbury: A House of Lions.* Philadelphia: Lippincott, 1979.

Rosenbaum, S. P. *The Bloomsbury Group: A Collection of Memoirs, Commentary, and Criticism.* Toronto: University of Toronto Press, 1975.

BLUE AT THE MIZZEN PATRICK O'BRIAN (1999)   See AUBREY-MATURIN NOVELS.

BOER WAR (1899–1902)   For the British EMPIRE, the 20th century opened on a sour note when war broke out between Great Britain and the South

African Republic (Transvaal), led by Paul Kruger, and the Orange Free State. The war was expensive and unpopular, with policies that became an international scandal. The British prevailed, but the underlying causes of hostility within the colonial society—cultural, ethnic, religious, and racial differences and socioeconomic problems—were not resolved.

British influence in this region dates to the Napoleonic Wars; after 1806, the British ruled the southernmost Cape Colony and valued the protection it afforded to British shipping routes. Cape Town was a thriving urban environment; in contrast, the earlier Dutch immigrants had followed an agrarian settlement pattern. The discovery of gold in the Transvaal created an urban boomtown at Johannesburg composed mainly of British nationals. Controlling their influence became a priority for Kruger, so he limited voting rights to long-term settlers; however, the wealth generated by the vast gold reserves created a powerful British faction, led by Cecil Rhodes, that demanded plentiful cheap labor and greater access to markets.

Britain's economic and strategic dominance on the entire African continent required the defeat of the Boers, and an ultimatum from Kruger on October 11, 1899, provided the pretext. His edict to limit British reinforcement of its garrison in his territory was received as a declaration of war. At first, British forces fared badly, but as they gained numerical superiority, and as harsher rules of war were implemented under Lord Kitchener, the advantage swung to them. Kruger retreated to Europe, and Boers switched to guerrilla tactics. Because rural Boers provided aid to the commandos, Kitchener initiated a scorched-earth policy, burning crops and homes to destroy the commandos' resources; when this strategy also deprived the noncombatant population of support, these bystanders—women, children, and African natives—were rounded up into camps. Such policies repeatedly aroused Boer solidarity, so that rebellions broke out in British-ruled areas; the strife took on the characteristics of both a territorial struggle and a civil war.

Boer forces were reduced to less than 25 percent of their initial numbers by 1902, after nearly a year and a half of guerrilla fighting. The South Africa Republic and the Orange Free State requested surrender terms and accepted the loss of independence in the Peace of Vereeniging. By treaty, the crucial issue of voting rights for the nonwhite majority was delayed until after the restoration of self-government. When the new nation of South Africa was established in 1910, the voting franchise was denied to blacks everywhere except in the Cape Colony, and even there oppressive policies effectively excluded nonwhites.

At the very beginning of the 20th century, the conflict in South Africa presaged the key issues of the following hundred years: declining support for COLONIALISM and imperialism, increasing demands for universal civil rights, massive forced internment of ethnic populations, and the increasing power of worldwide public opinion expressed through the instrument of a free press to shape politics. Writers responding to the war or affected by it include Thomas Hardy, Rudyard KIPLING, Hilaire BELLOC, G. K. CHESTERTON, H. G. WELLS, Arthur Conan DOYLE, John BUCHAN and others.

BIBLIOGRAPHY

Farwell, Byron. *The Great Anglo-Boer War.* New York: Harper & Row, 1976.

Lee, Emanoel C. G. *To the Bitter End: A Photographic History of the Boer War, 1899–1902.* New York: Viking, 1985.

Pakenham, Thomas. *The Boer War.* New York: Random House, 1979.

BOND, JAMES   Invented by the novelist Ian FLEMING, brought to life for the screen by the actors Sean Connery, George Lazenby, Roger Moore, Timothy Dalton, and Pierce Brosnan (and David Niven, if the 1967 Bond spoof *Casino Royale* is included), and reincarnated after Fleming's death by novelists such as Kingsley AMIS and John Gardner, James Bond is probably the single most famous character in the history of the 20th-century British novel, ranking with Sherlock HOLMES as a cultural icon. Employed as spy number 007 in "MI-6" (the real-world department of military intelligence known as "section six"), Britain's equivalent of the CIA, he is competent with every kind of weapon and operates every imaginable type of vehicle on land, in or under the sea, in the air, or in space. No social interaction is beyond his ability to remain unruffled, from the swankiest casinos of Monte Carlo to the sleaziest dives in Third World dens of iniquity. His suits are impeccably tailored and his speech is accented in the upper-class PUBLIC SCHOOL manner. Women—both the good and the bad—find him irresistible and generally seize the earliest opportunity to succumb to his charms. He drinks his vodka martini "shaken, not stirred"—a phrase that has taken on a life of its own in the popular vernacular. Her Majesty's government has issued him a license to kill (with impunity) in the ordinary performance of his routine duties.

Fleming's adventure series chronicling the exploits of James Bond first appeared in 1953 with the publication of *Casino Royale,* making him a successful author by the time he retired from the foreign desk of *The Sunday Times* in 1959, but the books became a publishing phenomenon after President Kennedy identified *From Russia With Love* as one of his favorite books in 1961. The print hero came to life on the screen in 1962, when Sean Connery portrayed him in *Dr. No,* launching a film franchise that is still in operation more than 40 years and more than 20 films later. Fleming's original 15 Bond stories have all been dramatized for the screen. James Bond has survived the death of his own creator and the fickleness of actors and audiences over the years: New authors have reanimated him and new screenwriters (and new leading men) have reinvented him to adapt to changing tastes and preferences as audiences have become more sensitive to gender stereotyping and ethnic bias. FEMINISM may have been set back two years by the arrival of James Bond as a pop culture icon in the 1960s (as some commentators have claimed), but in the long run Bond has been forced to give ground and make accommodations to the expanded roles women and minorities undertake in the contemporary world—today, even his boss is a woman, and his girlfriend *du jour* is likely to be as skilled in martial arts and target shooting as he is (or very nearly so). Comparative viewings of *Thunderball* (1965), based on an original Fleming text, and *Die Another Day* (2002), custom-made for the screen, make clear the transformation James Bond has experienced.

BIBLIOGRAPHY
Amis, Kingsley. *The James Bond Dossier.* New York: New American Library, 1965.
Banner, Deborah. "Why Don't They Just Shoot Him? The Bond Villains and Cold War Heroism." In *The Devil Himself: Villainy in Detective Fiction and Film.* Edited by Stacy Gillis and Philippa Gates. Westport, Conn.: Greenwood Press, 2002. 121–134.
Carpenter, Rebecca. "Male Failure and Male Fantasy: British Masculine Mythologies of the 1950s, or Jimmy, Jim, and Bond, James Bond," *Minnesota Review: A Journal of Committed Writing* (2002): 55–57.
Chapman, James. *Licence to Thrill: A Cultural History of the James Bond Films.* New York: Columbia University Press, 2000.

BONE PEOPLE KERI HULME (1984)   Winner of the BOOKER PRIZE in 1985, and of the Mobil Pegasus Prize and the New Zealand Book Award in 1984, this novel is the first work by a part-Maori New Zealand author to receive international attention and awards. It is an experimental novel, constructed with three main narrative threads that relate the thoughts, feelings, and interactions of the three main characters: Kerewin Holmes, a painter who lives as a hermit in a tower, Joe Gillayley, a Maori factory worker, and Simon Gillayley, Joe's mute white foster son who washed up on the beach shortly before Joe's wife and infant died of influenza. Their story unfolds in four sections, each divided into three chapters, with a prologue that reveals the family the three of them form in the end and an epilogue that celebrates their union with each other and with their community. The prose style is poetic and fragmented, following the stream-of-consciousness thoughts of the three characters in short turns.

Each of these characters is wounded and hiding something from the larger world, and yet unwilling or unable to become healed separately. Kerewin has broken with her family and prefers an isolated, independent, celibate life; Joe is emotionally ravaged by the loss of his family and his own brutalized childhood, and he beats Simon even though he loves the boy; and Simon had already been traumatized before Joe found him and believes that the beatings he receives are the treatment he deserves—and he commits acts that repeatedly elicit more beatings. When Simon shows up in Kerewin's house one day, he begins the process of bringing the three of them together; however, each will have to suffer and recover from his or her wounds before they can form a meaningful attachment. Each of them, in fact, sinks very nearly to death before a spiritual reconnection with "the bone people," a nonviolent pre-Maori tribe, helps them to reach out to each other and establish emotionally healthy bonds.

Keri HULME's novel is, at times, a challenging reading experience requiring patience, frequent reference to the translations of Maori words and phrases in the back of the book, and imaginative sympathy with three difficult characters. But her plot sheds light not just on a little-known culture in a remote corner of the world, but also on the tension between self-absorption and community involvement that anyone anywhere might experience, and on the recursive tragedies of child abuse and alcoholism. As the characters approach their respective dark nights of the soul (and body), their sufferings become painful to read; this depth of suffering, however, helps elevate the joy of their recovery of interconnectedness with each other and with the larger community.

BIBLIOGRAPHY

Buckman, Jacqueline. "Challenging the Conventions of the Kunstlerroman: Keri Hulme's *The Bone People*," *World Literature Written in English* 35, no. 2 (1996): 49–63.

Hulme, Keri. "Reconsidering *The Bone People*," *Australian and New Zealand Studies in Canada* 12 (1994): 135–154.

Wilentz, Gay. "Instruments of Change: Healing Cultural Disease in Keri Hulme's *The Bone People*," *Literature and Medicine* 14, no. 1 (1995): 127–145.

BOOKER PRIZE   Founded in 1968 to raise the media profile of serious literary fiction in Great Britain, the "Booker Prize" (its formal name has experienced several permutations as its underwriters have changed, including the Booker-McConnell Prize, and its current form, the Mann Booker Prize) has become a powerful force in the British publishing industry. Imitated after the French Goncourt Prize and the Italian Strega Prize, but with a much higher monetary value, the first award was made in 1969 in recognition of SOMETHING TO ANSWER FOR, by P. H. NEWBY. The run-up to the annual ceremonial naming of the winner generates considerable excitement as the panel of judges first announces its preliminary selections (the "long list") and then trims those titles down to the six finalists (the "short list") from which the winning title is chosen. In 1969, the prize value was £5,000, and by 1989 that amount had increased to £20,000; the greatest benefit of the competition, however, seems to be that short-listed and winning titles almost invariably boost their sales as a publicity campaign draws the attention of readers to the titles under consideration. The identity of the title selected as best book is jealously guarded until it is announced at the televised awards ceremony.

The prize is administered by the Book Trust, a charity with funding from Britain's Arts Council, under the leadership of Martyn Goff, and for many years the prize itself was funded by Booker plc, a diversified conglomerate with interests in agribusiness and the food processing industry. The Book Trust also administers other literary prizes, and it has competitors such as the WHITBREAD AWARD, but the Booker Prize has remained Britain's most prestigious literary award since it was founded. Each year the Booker Prize Management Committee assembles a panel of five judges (one of whom is appointed as chair); the judges are charged to identify the "best full-length novel" published in Britain that year.

The judging panel has exercised considerable freedom in defining the terms by which its task is identified, and the members are not restricted to "accessible" fiction that will be easy for the general public to understand. Sometimes the judges have considered very short books to be full-length novels (for example, FELICIA'S JOURNEY by William TREVOR is very nearly a novella), and they have frequently chosen authors from the farther corners of the former British EMPIRE. Since the judges are generally British, the list of prize-winning and short-listed titles makes a kind of de facto definition of "Britishness," at least according to educated readers passionate about quality fiction. Clearly, the British novel and the English novel are different species of fiction. The British novel may well be set in India or Africa or Asia, and its author may be English but born abroad (e.g., J. G. BALLARD or Doris LESSING), or originally non-English but born or educated in England (e.g., Salman RUSHDIE or Kazuo ISHIGURO), or someone English-born who subsequently chooses to live elsewhere (e.g., John BERGER), or someone residing in a former territory of the British Empire but with no direct connection to England (e.g., Keri HULME), or someone from a Commonwealth country who has adopted England as home (e.g., Ben OKRI or V. S. NAIPAUL). Prizewinners have also represented Scottish (James KELMAN), Irish (Roddy DOYLE), Canadian (Margaret ATWOOD and Michael ONDAATJE), Australian (Thomas KENEALLY and Peter CAREY), South African (Nadine GORDIMER and J. M. COETZEE), and other literatures. American authors are not eligible to compete for the Booker Prize, and the suggestion that American fiction be included in the competition has been rather controversial.

See Appendix I for a complete list of the authors and titles that have won the Booker Prize. To access the official Booker Prize Web site, log on to http://www.bookerprize.co.uk/intro/home.html.

BIBLIOGRAPHY

Book Trust Guide to Literary Prizes. London: Book Trust, published annually.

Brett, Simon. *The Booker Book.* London: Sidgwick & Jackson, 1989.

Strongman, Luke. *The Booker Prize and the Legacy of Empire.* Cross-Cultures: Readings in the Post-Colonial Literatures in English 54. Amsterdam: Rodopi, 2002.

Todd, Richard. *Consuming Fictions: The Booker Prize and Fiction in Britain Today.* London: Bloomsbury, 1996.

BOOKS DO FURNISH A ROOM ANTHONY POWELL (1971)

The 10th of 12 volumes in POWELL'S ROMAN-FLEUVE entitled *A DANCE TO THE MUSIC OF TIME,* this novel continues the story of Nicholas Jenkins, a writer, as he returns to a peace-time life at the end of WORLD WAR II. The title refers to the nickname of a key character in the story, the journalist Lindsay "Books-do-furnish-a-room" Bagshaw. But the title also refers to the publishing world as a whole in which Nicholas is professionally situated, and to the comforting refuge he seeks in his writing after the violence of the war. Music and painting have served as key thematic devices in earlier volumes of the series; now the emphasis shifts to literature.

When Nicholas returns to civilian life, many old school acquaintances are dead; in the wake of the war he can think of no better book to study than Burton's *The Anatomy of Melancholy.* He plans a study of it entitled *Borage and Hellebore,* but it is not the kind of project that will sell a large number of volumes. To make some money and move himself back into the spirit of the publishing world, he reviews books for a new liberal (but not communist or even socialist) journal that Bagshaw manages, *Fission.* The publisher of this periodical is Nick's old friend J. G. Quiggen, who has moderated his Marxist politics somewhat. The idea for the magazine had begun with Erridge, Lord Warminster, Nick's eccentric brother-in-law, but he had died before getting it started.

Nick befriends X. Trapnel (modeled on Powell's real-life acquaintance, Julian Maclaren-Ross), who has written a brilliant first novel, *Camel Ride to the Tombs;* he learns that this unfortunate man has fallen in love with Mrs. Pamela Widmerpool. Trapnel is trying to work on a new book, *Profiles in String,* but his personal eccentricities, his anxiety that he will not equal his first achievement, and his affair with Pamela are placing a strain on him. His brilliance is not in doubt, but his life is unstable and gets worse when Pamela deserts Widmerpool to live with Trapnel. She is a demanding woman, essentially unhappy in spite of her stunning beauty, but Trapnel is an equally demanding man needing someone to manage his life.

By chance, Nick witnesses a scene when Widmerpool confronts Pamela and Trapnel in the shabby apartment they share. He announces to the lovers that he is certain that she will return to him, and Trapnel chases Widmerpool out. Widmerpool's prediction, however, comes true in a much worse way: Pamela not only leaves, she also flings the manuscript of *Profiles in String*—the only one in existence—into a filthy canal near their apartment. Bagshaw and Nick are walking Trapnel home when they discover the pages floating away. Like Widmerpool, Trapnel pretends to take this desertion well, but he fades away, his talent steadily eroding and his self-destructive habits gaining ascendancy until his genius is spent.

After a two-year run, *Fission* has also spent itself, and the publishing house closes. Nick manages to finish *Borage and Hellebore* and finds himself ready to turn to greater challenges.

BIBLIOGRAPHY

Joyau, Isabelle. *Understanding Powell's* A Dance to the Music of Time. New York: St. Martin's Press, 1994.

Selig, Robert L. *Time and Anthony Powell.* Cranbury, N.J.: Associated University Presses, 1991.

Spurling, Hillary. *Invitation to the Dance: A Guide to Anthony Powell's* A Dance to the Music of Time. Boston: Little, Brown, 1977.

BOTTLE FACTORY OUTING, THE BERYL BAINBRIDGE (1974)

Inspired by the author's employment as a "cellar woman" in a wine-bottling factory, the protagonists in *The Bottle Factory Outing* are Brenda (BAINBRIDGE'S alter ego) and Freda, two single young women sharing a flat, in spite of their mismatched personalities, and working together in a factory dominated by Italian immigrants with limited English. Freda is a large, dramatic woman with theatrical ambitions, a purple cape, and vocally liberal politics; she frequently urges the workers to rise up and demand their rights, failing to understand the paternalistic patronage relationship between the factory owner, Mr. Paganotti, and the workers he has brought from his homeland. Brenda, on the other hand, scrawny and pinched, is passive and submissive, bottling up her resentments, and incapable either of expressing her desires or of declining unwanted attentions. At 32, she is divorced from her husband, Stanley, although her former mother-in-law, increasingly dotty in her old age, still finds ways to torment the easily intimidated young woman.

Through no particular effort on her own part, Brenda has become an obsession for the married factory manager, Mr. Rossi, who continually tries to lure her into obscure corners of the cellar; in contrast, Freda tries vigorously to secure the interest of the owner's nephew, Vittorio. Brenda's desperation to avoid Mr. Rossi, combined with her inability to reject his unwanted attentions, leads her to invent desperate lies from time to time. In contrast, Freda conducts a vigorous campaign to possess Vittorio, and as part of it she has organized a picnic for the workers on the grounds of an estate open to the public. Freda's goal is to get away from the group and capture her man in a secluded tête-à-tête; when Brenda discovers Freda's murdered body, however, she reluctantly joins her coworkers in the task of disposing of it. As the Italians prepare the body, conduct a kind of funeral, and search for a suitably unobtrusive mode of removing it as far away as possible, Brenda gradually puts together the clues inadvertently dropped in the process, learning the truth about Freda's unexpected demise.

The third-person omniscient narrator relates the plot and reveals the characters' inner natures in a droll, understated manner. The story is an excellent example of the English COMIC NOVEL, juxtaposing quirky characters and unexpected twists with serene aplomb while dispassionately relating Freda's grim fate. With its satirical treatment of CLASS consciousness, sexual harassment, seduction, and death, *The Bottle Factory Outing* won the *GUARDIAN* FICTION PRIZE for 1974.

BIBLIOGRAPHY

Jury, Louise, and Genevieve Roberts. "From Author's Muse to a Squalid Death: The Tragic Story of the Factory Girl Who Inspired Dame Beryl," 18 October 2003. *Independent Digital.* http://enjoyment.independent.co.uk/low_res/story.jsp?story=454580&host=5&dir=205

Schwartz, Lynne Sharon. Review of *The Bottle Factory Outing* by Beryl Bainbridge. *The New Republic* 172, no. 21 (1975): 26.

BOWEN, ELIZABETH (1899–1973)

Most noted for her novels of psychological realism such as *The* DEATH OF THE HEART (1938) and *The Heat of the Day* (1949), Elizabeth Dorothea Cole Bowen was born on June 7, 1899, in Dublin, IRELAND, an only child. The Bowens were a well-to-do Anglo-Irish family; ancestors had come to Ireland from Wales in 1653 to take possession of a large estate in County Cork awarded for service in Cromwell's suppression of the Irish. Bowen's Court, the family seat and the subject of one of Elizabeth Bowen's nonfiction books, had been handed down through succeeding generations for 306 years until Elizabeth sold it in 1959, having no heir of her own to pass it to.

Elizabeth Bowen's mother died in 1912, and the years of her transition from adolescence to adulthood, 1914 to 1923, were years of upheaval and instability in international and domestic politics. WORLD WAR I (1914–18), the Easter Rising of 1916, the Anglo-Irish

War of Independence (1919–21), and the Irish Civil War (1921–23) all occurred during these years of maturation, contributing material for eventual novels. Bowen's Court was occupied by Irish forces, but many of the neighboring homes of the Anglo-Irish were destroyed. Elizabeth depended on her aunts and cousins, and when her aunts disapproved of her engagement to a British officer, she broke it off, spending the winter of 1921 in a tourist hotel in Bordighera with relatives—events that also became material for Bowen's fiction, particularly her first novel, *The Hotel* (1927). In 1923, her life moved in two new directions: Her first volume of short stories was published to good reviews, and she married Alan Charles Cameron. This marriage lasted until 1952, when Alan Cameron died at Bowen's Court.

By 1925, Bowen and Cameron were residing in Oxford and socializing with noted scholars and writers. During the 1930s she frequented the BLOOMSBURY circle and became a friend of Virginia WOOLF, and after 1935 she and her husband made London their home. Elizabeth wrote literary reviews and produced some of her most important fiction during this period. In 1948, she was named a Commander of the British Empire, and in 1949 she received an honorary doctorate from Trinity College in Dublin.

Between 1952, when her husband died, and 1959, when she sold her ancestral home, Elizabeth Bowen remained at Bowen's Court, working on her writing and hosting numerous leading figures of the literary world as her guests. In 1957, Oxford University awarded her an honorary doctorate, and she returned there to live in 1959. Her last novel, EVA TROUT, appeared in 1969. Although it was not uniformly well received by critics, it won the JAMES TAIT BLACK MEMORIAL PRIZE in 1970. In declining health during her last years, Elizabeth Bowen died of lung cancer in 1973.

Although Bowen's fiction is not autobiographical, it does draw on the events of her own life for inspiration. Her characters experience events that she experienced, but they are not confessional portraits of the author herself—instead, they universalize her particular experience. Some of her earliest novels, and some of her best later work as well, present stories of clueless young women who must learn to manage their emotional relationships by discovering themselves under adverse or even hostile conditions. Thus in *The Hotel* (1927), *The Last September* (1930), *To the North* (1932), *The House in Paris* (1935), and *The Death of the Heart* (1938), an ingénue struggles to gain knowledge and find her place in life, with differing results in each case. She is usually cut off from adequate sources of emotional support, isolated from or bereft of parental guidance, and consequently forced to figure out the workings of the world from a position of ignorance. Although Bowen is a master of understated comic interactions, these hapless innocents sometimes stumble into undeservedly tragic circumstances.

Bowen also examines the paths traversed by more worldly women: In *Friends and Relations* (1931), *The Heat of the Day* (1949), and *Eva Trout* (1969), the female protagonist has moved beyond the innocence of youth and must confront threats and opportunities that are more sexual than romantic, again with differing results. But with both of these types of characters—the innocent naïf and the woman of worldly knowledge—Bowen draws subtly nuanced portraits of psychological complexity and shows herself to be a master cartographer of the hearts in many different women's emotional landscapes. Compared favorably by critics with Jane Austen, Henry JAMES, Katherine Mansfield, and Virginia Woolf, Elizabeth Bowen's novels remain important benchmarks in 20th-century British literature.

BIBLIOGRAPHY

Bennett, Andrew, and Nicholas Royle. *Elizabeth Bowen and the Dissolution of the Novel: Still Lives.* New York: St. Martin's Press, 1995.

Glendinning, Victoria. *Elizabeth Bowen: Portrait of a Writer.* London: Weidenfeld & Nicolson, 1977.

Hoogland, Renee C. *Elizabeth Bowen: A Reputation in Writing.* New York: New York University Press, 1994.

Jordan, Heather Bryant. *How Will the Heart Endure? Elizabeth Bowen and the Landscape of War.* Ann Arbor: University of Michigan Press, 1992.

Lassner, Phyllis. *Elizabeth Bowen.* Basingstoke, U.K.: Macmillan, 1990.

BRADBURY, MALCOLM (1932–2000)

A master of the satirical comic novel and a lifelong academic, Malcolm Stanley Bradbury was born in Sheffield on September 7, 1932, to a working-class family. A first-generation college student, he attended University College in Leister from 1950 to 1953, earning a B.A. degree in English, and went on to graduate studies first at Queen Mary College of the University of London, where he earned an M.A. degree in English in 1955, and then at the University of Manchester, where he completed a Ph.D. in American Studies in 1962. He also held graduate fellowships at Indiana University during the 1955–56 academic year and at Yale University during the 1958–59 academic year. Bradbury married in 1959 and was the father of two children. He taught college at the University of Hull and the University of Birmingham before settling permanently at East Anglia University, where he rose from lecturer to reader to professor to professor emeritus between 1957 and his death in 2000. Beginning in 1966, Bradbury was invited to serve as visiting professor at numerous universities in the United States, Australia, Switzerland, and England; he was named a Commander of the British Empire in 1991. His literary output included seven novels, a collection of short stories, numerous scripts for the stage, radio, television, and screen, and a wide array of literary criticism and scholarship, nonfiction, and collections of essays.

Bradbury's fiction generally draws on the parameters of the CAMPUS NOVEL. His first novel, entitled *Eating People Is Wrong* (1959), was generally well received by critics; one noted that it seemed to combine the talents of Charles Dickens, Evelyn WAUGH, and Kingsley AMIS. The story chronicles the transformations occurring in England as the university system expanded after WORLD WAR II to include greatly increased numbers of working-class students—like Bradbury himself—in new "redbrick" colleges (contrasted to the hoary gray stones of Oxford and Cambridge). In *Stepping Westward* (1966), Bradbury places a British academic in a midwestern American university, juxtaposing a representative of the Old World with the monstrous New World that sprang from it. His most famous novel, *The History Man* (1975), is a comic examination of traditional liberal values, again using an academic setting, through the lens of postmodern attacks on foundational concepts. Bradbury's serious interest in the challenges that POSTMODERNISM mounted continued in *Rates of Exchange* (1983), in which a college professor travels to Eastern Europe as an exchange scholar, and in *Dr. Criminale* (1992), in which a journalist researches the life of a famous but mysterious scholar (loosely based on Paul de Mann) for a television documentary.

Bradbury's fiction is frequently a showcase for the academic's love of language, ideas, and arguments; it may give pause to readers satisfied to consume familiar characters managing the twists of recognizable plot structures. But Bradbury also displays a keen moral sense in his satirical treatment of fallible human thought and behavior. His novels are responses to, and comments on, their own historical contexts, defending and questioning traditional liberal humanism while also questioning and exploring postmodern challenges to it.

BIBLIOGRAPHY

Doering, Jonathan W. "Malcolm Bradbury: A History Man for Our Times," *Contemporary Review* 278 (Mar. 2001): 159–64.

Rose, Margaret A. *Parody: Ancient, Modern, and Post-Modern.* Cambridge: Cambridge University Press, 1993.

BRADY, JOAN (1939–)

Originally a ballerina, Joan Brady began publishing novels in 1979. She is one of only two American-born authors, with Paul THEROUX, to win the WHITBREAD Book of the Year Award, qualifying for consideration by living in Great Britain for more than three years. She was born Helen Joan Brady on December 4, 1939, and was a Phi Beta Kappa student at Columbia University. She danced for the San Francisco Ballet from 1955 to 1957 and for the New York City Ballet in 1960. In 1963, she married Dexter Wright Masters; they became the parents of one child. She now lives in London.

In 1979, Joan Brady published her first novel, *The Imposter*. In 1982, she published her absorbing and insightful personal memoir—very nearly a BILDUNGSROMAN—of the demanding world of ballet, *The Unmaking of a Dancer*. Then, in 1993, her second novel, *THEORY OF WAR*, won the Whitbread Book of the Year Award. It was translated into nine languages and also won the French Prix du Meilleur Livre Etranger in 1995. She has also published the novels *Prologue* in 1994, *Death Comes for Peter Pan* in 1996, and *The Émigré* in 1999.

BIBLIOGRAPHY

Brady, Joan. *The Unmaking of a Dancer: An Unconventional Life*. New York: Harper & Row, 1982.

BRAINE, JOHN (1922–1986)

One of the early ANGRY YOUNG MEN, John Gerard Braine was born to a comfortable middle-class family in Yorkshire on April 13, 1922, and reared in his mother's Catholic faith. He attended St. Bede's Grammar School on a scholarship but never studied in a university setting. After numerous entry-level jobs, he decided in 1940 to follow a career as a librarian. From then to 1951, he worked at Bingley Public Library (serving one year, 1942–43, in the Royal Navy) and began to publish freelance articles. He moved to London in 1951 to work full-time as a writer, but the experience was a disaster since he had none of the educational or social ties that would give him entry into literate circles. That same year, his mother was killed in a car accident and shortly after he returned for her funeral he was diagnosed with tuberculosis.

During the year and a half he was hospitalized for the disease, he began writing the novel ROOM AT THE TOP, which would partially fulfill his ambitions as a writer. After leaving the hospital, he was married (1955); he and his wife had three children. He returned to work as a librarian at the Northumberland County Library from 1954 to 1956, and then worked at the West Riding County Library from 1956 to 1957. From 1957 until his death on October 28, 1986, he earned his living as a professional writer, producing a total of a dozen novels, several screenplays and television scripts adapted from or expanding on his novels, and some nonfiction.

Although several publishers rejected *Room at the Top*, when it appeared in 1957 it was an instant success. It expressed the longing for acceptance and success of an entire generation of working-class men who wanted to rise above that station but who were outsiders to the traditional power structure of the educated gentry. The book's hero, Joe Lampton, was unrefined, virile, individualistic, angry, coarse, and aggressively ambitious; he served as a fictional role model capable of articulating the desires of a marginalized group not accustomed to speaking out and not expecting to be heard. Above all, however, Joe Lampton is a modern ANTIHERO determined to succeed on his own terms. He does not want to be transformed into an imitation of the polo-playing, fox-hunting traditional gentry, but instead wants to remain the common man he is and also have all the money and women he can acquire.

After the success of *Room at the Top*, Braine's works have not been as well received critically. *The Vodi* (1959) draws on the author's experience with tuberculosis, following a protagonist who is saved from failure by a love affair with a nurse. *Life at the Top* (1962) returns to Joe Lampton's story as he longs to escape from the empty success he has achieved. *The Jealous God* (1964) examines the conflict between the temptations of the world and the expectations of Catholic faith.

During the 1970s, Braine's political allegiances shifted gradually to a more conservative stance as he became an increasingly outspoken critic of modern liberalism. Ironically, this transformation preserved Braine's status as an outsider protesting the status quo, but where as a young man he had attacked from the Left, as he aged he launched his assaults from the Right. Although his later writings have not matched the achievement of *Room at the Top*, which effectively erased the barrier to serious consideration of "regional novels," he remains an important figure for understanding the social, political, and psychological context of English literature in the period following WORLD WAR II.

BIBLIOGRAPHY

Alrayac, Claude. "Inside John Braine's Outsider," *Caliban* 8 (1971): 113–138.

Burgess, Anthony. *The Novel Now*. London: Faber & Faber, 1967, 140–152.

Lee, James Ward. *John Braine* Twayne's English Authors, 62. New York: Twayne Publishers, 1968.

Salwak, Dale. *Interviews with Britain's Angry Young Men*. San Bernardino, Calif.: Borgo Press, 1984.

BRAVE NEW WORLD ALDOUS HUXLEY

(1932)   This example of a DYSTOPIAN NOVEL opens in a pleasure-dominated but totalitarian future world by touring London's main Hatchery. This expository device allows the author to introduce unexpected features of his imagined future, where human reproduction has been removed from the messy lives of individuals: In a totally mechanized system, the exact kinds of human being that society needs are produced in exactly the right quantity. Divided by intellect into five classes (intellectual Alphas for decision making to near-simian Epsilons for manual labor), these scientifically produced humans arrive in adulthood already trained to do their assigned tasks, subscribing to the motto "Community, Identity, Stability." In place of the family, citizens may indulge in casual sex as long as they don't form permanent bonds, or go to "the feelies" as long as they don't exercise any individual creativity, and enjoy a hallucinogenic recreational drug (soma) instead of developing greater maturity and autonomy.

The key characters are Lenina Crowne, a nurse at the Hatchery; Bernard Marx, a psychologist; and Helmholtz Watson, a scientist. Each of these characters illustrates weaknesses in the new reproductive system. Bernard shows signs of dangerous individualism and ALIENATION; Watson wishes to create a book of his own; and Lenina tends to form lasting emotional bonds with others. Lenina and Bernard begin an affair, and they take a vacation to the uncivilized wilds of New Mexico. They are surprised to encounter two apparent Europeans, Linda and her son John, a young man. She had conceived her child in violation of the hygienic genetic procedures required in the "civilized world" and raised him herself, breaking the civilized taboo on motherhood. Bernard knows that the Director of Hatcheries had traveled here with a woman many years ago and had returned alone, so he suspects that John is the illegal son of this important authority. He invites John and Linda to return to the civilized world, but his motives are hardly charitable.

Linda and John struggle to assimilate to life in the brave new world, but they are pawns in Bernard's power struggle with the Director. Linda adapts by retreating into a haze of soma; meanwhile, John becomes the victim of curiosity seekers. He desires sex, but he is repelled by the promiscuity that is a normal aspect of this world. John's characteristic response to stress is violence, and his disruptions bring him before Mustapha Mond, the Controller.

HUXLEY uses their long debate to form the core of this novel of ideas. John condemns the laws that have limited human beings to an inferior state of infantile happiness delivered by sex, drugs, and feelies. Mustapha Mond tells him, in an argument that recalls Plato's expulsion of poets from *The Republic,* that art stirs the passions and leads to dissatisfaction, unhappiness, social unrest, and political instability. The price to society of allowing individual expression is too high, and the benefits achieved by eliminating it are too great to allow it to continue. Individual freedom must be limited so that collective good can rise to a maximum level. Ultimately, John cannot adjust to this new world, and his presence there changes the lives of the main characters in drastic ways.

In 1957, Aldous Huxley wrote a treatise on his own novel, *Brave New World Revisited.* Many of the cultural features he had imagined in 1932 were coming into existence, especially in the increasing dominance of mass media. The picture of enslavement through pleasure presented in *Brave New World* is innovative; such a world is a much more threatening prospect that the brutal oppression of NINETEEN EIGHTY-FOUR; Huxley's great insight was to see that a world of enjoyment would be a stronger threat to human freedom, and his great literary achievement was to create that world in such a way that it is clearly an outgrowth of the one we actually live in today.

BIBLIOGRAPHY

Baker, Robert S. Brave New World: *History, Science, and Utopia.* Twayne's Masterwork Studies, 39. Boston: Twayne Publishers, 1990.

Bloom, Harold. *Aldous Huxley's* Brave New World. New York: Chelsea House Publishers, 1996.

De Koster, Katie. *Readings on* Brave New World. San Diego: Greenhaven Press, 1999.

BRIDESHEAD REVISITED: THE SACRED AND PROFANE MEMORIES OF CAPTAIN CHARLES RYDER EVELYN WAUGH

(1945)   A best seller that securely established its author's commercial reputation, *Brideshead Revisited* evokes mixed responses from critics, some of whom see it as a flawed novel. Its name became associated with the generation of writers who were children during World War I and middle-aged during WORLD WAR II: WAUGH, Anthony POWELL, Graham GREENE, George ORWELL, and others. In 1980, the novel became a popular dramatic series produced by the BBC and successfully broadcast on PBS stations in the United States.

The novel takes the form of a flashback related by the first-person narrator, Charles Ryder. His military unit is billeted in the vicinity of Brideshead, the family seat of the wealthy and aristocratic Flyte family. Charles's proximity to the house carries his thoughts back through his long association with the Flytes, beginning when he was at Oxford with Lord Sebastian Flyte, the feckless second son of Lord Marchmain. Charles had quickly become a frequent visitor at Brideshead, where he meets the dull family heir, Bridey, and the two daughters of the family, Julia and Cordelia. When he married, Lord Marchmain had returned to the Catholicism of his ancestors, and much of the current generation's story is concerned with the struggle for—and against—faith. In spite of the family's long history, fine house, and financial advantages, the Flytes do not constitute an emotionally successful unit, and the stresses of being a Flyte drive Sebastian into self-destructive bouts of drinking.

Charles's recollections are set within the frame of his current posting as the British army prepares for active duty in World War II; Charles despairs of their prospects, as represented by the incompetent junior officer Hooper. In contrast, his memories of his 20-year association with the Flytes—he nearly marries Julia and nearly inherits the family estate—take on a nostalgic glow, despite the chronicle of the family members' imperfections.

As the friendship with Sebastian had grown, Charles had realized that Sebastian's careless inebriation constitutes an escape from his family, and especially from his charming but possessive mother. Charles and Sebastian visit Lord Marchmain in Venice, where the family patriarch takes refuge from his wife with a mistress, Cara. Sebastian's addiction to alcohol becomes so intense that he leaves Oxford under the supervision of Mr. Samgrass, an associate of his mother's, but this effort to maintain his sobriety fails. At one point,

Charles becomes a facilitator of Sebastian's search for oblivion: When the family members are collected together for Christmas, and the liquor cabinets are all locked up and Sebastian is kept penniless, Charles lends Sebastian two pounds that are immediately spent on a drunken spree. This indiscretion leads to a long break in Charles's connection to Brideshead; Sebastian, too, escapes his keepers and eventually drifts to Morocco.

Charles did not fall in love with Julia until after both of them were married to other people. At first they conduct an affair, but they cannot be accepted in society as an unmarried couple. They each arrange to obtain a divorce; meanwhile, Lord Marchmain returns to Brideshead to spend his final days. He intends to leave the property to Julia and Charles, having disliked Bridey's choice of a wife. But when, on his deathbed, Lord Marchmain makes the sign of the cross in response to a priest, Julia also returns to the church and refuses to divorce her husband—she abandons her love for Charles in preference to her duty to church and spouse. Sebastian, they learn, has attempted to enter an order in Carthage and been refused, so he has taken the position of underporter to the monastery. Faith is restored throughout the surviving members of the family; however, happiness has not come with it.

BIBLIOGRAPHY

Beaty, Frederick L. *The Ironic World of Evelyn Waugh: A Study of Eight Novels*. DeKalb: Northern Illinois University Press, 1992.

Davis, Robert M. "Imagined Space in Brideshead Revisited." In *Evelyn Waugh: New Directions*. Edited by Alain Blayac. New York: St. Martin's Press, 1992.

Lygon, Lady Dorothy. "Madresfield and Brideshead." In *Evelyn Waugh and His World*. Edited by David Pryce-Jones. Boston: Little, Brown, 1973.

Wilson, Edmund. "Splendors and Miseries of Evelyn Waugh." In *Critical Essays on Evelyn Waugh*. Edited by James F. Carens. Boston: G. K. Hall, 1987.

BROOKNER, ANITA (1928–) The first

woman appointed to serve as Slade Professor of Art at Cambridge University (1967–68), Anita Brookner has built dual careers as an academic and novelist. She was born on July 16, 1928, in London and was educated there at King's College, completing her undergraduate studies in 1949. She pursued graduate work in art history at the Courtauld Institute of Art, completing a Ph.D. there in 1953. Her earliest publications were translations from French of contemporary art history and criticism; in 1971, she published her own study of French painting, *The Genius of the Future: Studies in French Art Criticism.* During the following three decades, she produced scholarly studies on the French painters Watteau, Jean-Baptiste Greuze (subject of her doctoral dissertation), and Jacques-Louis David; a collection of essays on art and literature; and an examination of romanticism. She has also written numerous articles on French art for scholarly and mainstream periodicals and has contributed to BBC television programs on art.

Ten years after Brookner published her first original scholarly book, when she was in her early 50s, she published her first novel, *A Start in Life* (1981), brought out in the United States under the apt title *The Debut.* Since then, she has published a new novel nearly every year. Her fourth novel, HOTEL DU LAC (1984), won the BOOKER PRIZE in the year of its publication. Her novels frequently feature educated women coping with loneliness in middle life, although she sometimes explores the emptiness in men's lives as well. Frequently, her protagonists long to find fulfillment in love without sacrificing the tranquility of their lives; however, although they are educated, their ideas of romance are tied to stereotypes of love and marriage. They struggle with their own aging process, or with the burden of caring for elderly parents; sometimes they are scarred by the past, or they have made poor choices in love, or they have been abandoned after love has withered in married life. Her narratives unfold with intelligent humor and praise the ordinary, underappreciated virtues of people who have accommodated themselves to the practice of good habits. Critics see the eye of the artist and of the art scholar in her carefully detailed characterizations, praising the realism she brings to her fictional people. As a novelist, she is often compared to Jane Austen or Henry JAMES.

Anita Brookner has worked full-time as a writer since 1988. She was elected a Fellow of the Royal Society of Literature in 1983, and she was named a Com-

mander, Order of the British Empire, in 1990. She continues to live and write in London.

BIBLIOGRAPHY
Haffenden, John. *Novelists in Interview.* London: Methuen, 1985, 57–75.
Malcolm, Cheryl Alexander. *Understanding Anita Brookner.* Understanding Contemporary British Literature. Columbia: University of South Carolina Press, 2002.
Sadler, Lynn Veach. *Anita Brookner* Twayne's English Authors, 473. Boston: Twayne, 1990.

BUCHAN, JOHN (1875–1940)

A prolific writer who worked successfully in numerous genres, John Buchan (pronounced BUCK-an) also pursued careers in law, publishing, journalism, public administration, and politics. He is most remembered now as the creator of Richard Hannay, the hero of *The THIRTY-NINE STEPS* (1915), *Greenmantle* (1916), and other adventure novels. The film director Alfred Hitchcock perhaps extended the longevity of Buchan's literary reputation when in 1935 he adapted *The Thirty-Nine Steps* into the suspense film of the same title now regarded as a cinematic classic and an important milestone in the development of Hitchcock's signature style.

John Buchan was born in Perth, Scotland, on August 25, 1875. An accidental head injury kept him in bed for a year while he was young; ironically, he died of an accidental head injury after a fall on February 11, 1940. He began his college studies at Glasgow University, but upon winning a scholarship he transferred to Brasenose College at Oxford. While there, he demonstrated the prolific output he was capable of achieving, writing several books and winning the Stanhope Historical Essay Prize in 1897 and the Newdigate Prize for poetry in 1898. By the time he began his legal studies at the Middle Temple in London in 1900, he had published some 10 works of nonfiction, novels, and poetry. He was soon serving as a public administrator in South Africa; after two years of service he returned to England. In 1907, he married and began his career as a publisher with the firm of Thomas A. Nelson and Sons. He later worked for Reuters Press Agency, and during WORLD WAR I he worked as a journalist for the London *Times.* After the war he was again in government service, and he also edited a multivolume history of the war and wrote another of his own. From 1927 until he was appointed governor-general of Canada in 1935, Buchan served in Parliament as the Conservative representative of the Scottish universities.

When Buchan was selected as governor-general, he was also named the first Baron Tweedsmuir. As Canada's chief ceremonial political officer, he hosted important visits from Franklin D. Roosevelt and from King George VI and Elizabeth (parents of Queen Elizabeth II) in 1939. During these many phases of his professional life, he continued writing in his spare time; the bulk of his publications were nonfiction works of history, politics, biography, autobiography, and commentaries on contemporary issues. Critics reviewed his histories favorably in particular. He wrote in several subgenres of fiction, including the historical romance and most notably the espionage adventure story (which he referred to as "shockers"); in the course of his life he produced some two dozen novels and a half-dozen collections of short fiction.

Buchan's fast-paced, plot-thick adventure stories were popular with readers and continue to be his best-remembered works, ensuring him an important place in the historical development of the spy novel. Although he relied on familiar melodramatic situations and plot devices, he avoided sensationalism and brutality, emphasizing the potential for heroism even in modest men of quiet virtue. He used effective landscape descriptions to evoke theme and character, and his prose style was clear, direct, and vigorous. Buchan's historical fiction has been compared favorably with the works of his countrymen Robert Louis Stevenson and Sir Walter Scott; for example, his novel *Montrose: A History* won the JAMES TAIT BLACK MEMORIAL PRIZE in 1928, but Buchan's works currently receive less critical attention.

BIBLIOGRAPHY

Green, Martin. *A Biography of John Buchan and His Sister Anna: The Personal Background of Their Literary Work.* Lewiston, N.Y.: The Edwin Mellen Press, 1990.

Jones, J. D. F. *The Buchan Papers.* New York: St. Martin's Press, 1997.

Lownie, Andrew. *John Buchan: The Presbyterian Cavalier.* London: Constable, 1995.

Smith, Janet Adam. *John Buchan and His World.* London: Thames & Hudson, 1979.

BUDDHA OF SUBURBIA, THE HANIF KUREISHI (1990)

A celebration of London's new multiethnic youth culture, this COMIC NOVEL relates the adventures of the first-person narrator, Karim Amir, the 17-year-old son of a Muslim Indian businessman, Haroon, and an Englishwoman, Margaret. The family resides in the middle-class suburbs south of London, where Karim's father has recently begun to practice yoga and to preach it as well at upscale parties organized by Eva Kay, the mother of the shallow and self-destructive young man Charlie, upon whom Karim has a crush. After the first of Eva's New Age events, Karim sees his father and Eva engaged in illicit intimacies, but when he and Charlie are on the verge of a homoerotic version of the same intimate connection, Haroon sees them and is horrified. Karim's information about his father's affair allows him to control Haroon's homophobic response, but he is helpless to prevent his father's affair from continuing and ultimately breaking up two formerly contented families.

The novel's second half moves into London proper—West Kensington—where Eva and Haroon take an apartment. Karim stays with them and revels in the freedom and the excitement of life in the city. He takes up improvisational acting and connects with new women friends as outlets for his libidinal urges and emotional needs, but he retains a deep crush on Charlie, even as his friend is dissolving into the violent, drunken, punk scene just beginning in London. As Karim begins to find greater success onstage, Charlie discovers an outlet in music, and eventually both young men are drawn to America, the great voracious devourer of popular culture. In New York, Charlie's quest to reach his limits finally allows Karim to shed his crush and return to the city he loves. There, nothing is the same, and yet life is continuing to move forward in familiar ways as Haroon and Eva announce their plans to marry.

The narrative voice of Karim Amir is the great attraction of *The Buddha of Suburbia:* it is frank and fresh, vigorous and contemplative, cheeky and sensitive. Karim is unabashed by the awakening of his amorous drives and uninhibited in the expression of his attraction to both men and women. He finds his place in the larger world without losing the generosity of spirit that makes him such a sympathetic character, continuing to love life—and London—even when events take unexpected turns.

BIBLIOGRAPHY

Carey, Cynthia. "Hanif Kureishi's *The Buddha of Suburbia* as a Post-Colonial Novel," *Commonwealth Essays and Studies* 4 (1997): 119–125.

Lane, Richard J., Rod Mengham, and Philip Tew. *Contemporary British Fiction.* Cambridge, U.K.: Polity Press; Malden, Mass.: Blackwell Publishers, 2003.

BURGESS, ANTHONY (1917–1993)

Widely recognized as one of the most important postmodern writers of British novels in the 20th century, John Anthony Burgess Wilson was born on February 25, 1917, in Manchester. In the following year, he lost his mother and sister to the worldwide influenza epidemic that effectively ended WORLD WAR I. He was reared in a venerable Catholic family that traced its ancestry to the period that preceded the founding of Protestantism in 1517; since England was a Protestant country with a state-supported church, his religious heritage made him an outsider in his native country. Although he turned away from formal religion during his teenage years, his early exposure to it left an indelible mark on his thought so that theological questions—especially those relating to the presence of evil in the universe—form an important recurring theme in his fiction.

Burgess was educated at the University of Manchester and originally wished to pursue studies in music. His father, a pianist, had performed in nightclubs and had passed to his son both an interest in music and a talent for it. But the university curriculum in music required extensive preparation in physics and mathematics, and so Burgess studied English linguistics and literature instead, continuing to play and compose music on his own. When he began writing fiction in his middle years, music played important symbolic and thematic roles in his narrative structure; he even modeled one entire novel, *Napoleon Symphony* (1974),

on a strict formula correlated with a musical composition—Beethoven's *Eroica* symphony—historically related to the story's protagonist.

In 1940, Burgess entered military service and was billeted to an assignment with a musical group that traveled to entertain soldiers in the remote outposts of WORLD WAR II. He married in 1942, forming a union that lasted, with some difficulties, until his wife's death in 1968. In 1943, Burgess was transferred to Gibraltar with the Army Education Corps; in addition to teaching soldiers, he worked in cryptography and intelligence. His wife remained in London, where she became the victim of a brutal assault by American deserters, causing her to miscarry. This event becomes the basis for a key scene in *A CLOCKWORK ORANGE* (1962) in which a gang of thugs assaults a writer and his wife.

Burgess was discharged from military service in 1946 and began teaching in England and pursuing his interest in music. Teaching salaries were low and working conditions were poor in English schools; without much research or planning, Burgess accepted a position teaching in Malayan public schools. There, in midlife, he began writing novels that capture the experience of COLONIALISM, cultural conflict, and ethnic strife. His first three novels form a loose trilogy: *Time for a Tiger* (1956), *The Enemy in the Blanket* (1958), and *Beds in the East* (1959) were published as *The Malayan Trilogy* in 1964 (also known as *The Long Day Wanes*). These first novels already demonstrate the strengths that became the hallmarks of Burgess's style, featuring adroit humor, satire, absence of sentimentality, experimentation in the techniques of narration, and a marked linguistic skill in the contextualizing of foreign words and phrases to make their meaning clear while also sharpening the reader's awareness of an exotic location, culture, or class.

When Malaya became an independent nation in 1957, British nationals were expelled, and Burgess took a teaching position in Borneo. There, he clashed with resident British colonizers and sympathized with the native population of the island. Before he could make too many enemies, however, he suffered a physical breakdown in 1959, collapsing in his classroom in mid-lecture. He was rushed to England for medical care and diagnosed with a brain tumor; doctors gave him a one-year life expectancy. With this perception of a death sentence hanging over his head, Burgess experienced a prolific burst of writing and produced five novels in that one year, hoping that they would provide his widow with financial security after he died. Despite the rapid pace of the writing and the circumstances under which he worked, the novels are excellent and were well received when they were published over the next four years: *The Doctor Is Sick* (1960), *One Hand Clapping* and *The Worm and the Ring* (both 1961), *The Wanting Seed* (1962), and *Inside Mr. Enderby* (1963). Burgess did not die at the end of the year, but the writing he did at that time enabled him to leave teaching and become a full-time novelist.

With restored health, Burgess traveled and wrote more novels. *Devil of a State* appeared in 1961; it comically examines life in a fictional newly independent African nation, showing the influence of Evelyn WAUGH on Burgess. Other sources of literary influence on Burgess's writing include James JOYCE (especially in *The Doctor Is Sick*), about whose work Burgess wrote important and insightful critical interpretations, Vladimir Nabokov, and F. R. Leavis. Travel also provided inspirational material for novels: From his experiences on a visit to Russia in 1961, for example, Burgess developed the plot of *Honey for the Bears* (1963), a comedy about misunderstood relationships and crass smuggling, and he acquired ideas and linguistic material for *A Clockwork Orange*.

After 1964, Burgess diversified his writing to include more criticism and educational treatises on literature; he also wrote for television, reviewed books for newspapers and magazines, produced music and drama criticism for the periodicals *Queen* and *Spectator,* and composed poetry and short fiction. In 1971, Stanley Kubrick adapted the American version of *A Clockwork Orange* (lacking its concluding chapter, so that it ends on a particularly violent note) as a film that became a phenomenal success and a cult classic. The novel had been Burgess's most successful one upon its publication in 1962, but he regarded some of his other titles as superior to it; the success of the film increased the tendency of *A Clockwork Orange* to dominate the public's perception of Burgess as a writer, much to his displeasure.

About six months after his first wife died in 1968, Burgess was married to an Italian translator; they had already produced a son at the time of their marriage, still a scandalous situation at that time. The Burgess family lived in Malta for two years, and in 1971 they bought houses in Rome and in the Italian countryside. But with political turmoil brewing in Italy, they relocated to Monaco five years later. Burgess traveled extensively as a visiting lecturer at numerous universities, but he did not see himself as an academic: Although he was erudite and fluent in multiple languages, he had never pursued advanced studies at the graduate level, and he disliked many characteristics of career college professors. The assumptions underlying liberal humanism made it disappointing to him, and so he was skeptical of the supporters of this ideology, who are frequently to be found clustered in academic enclaves. His novels often interrogate or even condemn courses of action that are too firmly grounded in an unquestioning belief in the power of human beings to perfect themselves through their own efforts.

At the time of his death in 1993, Burgess had written more than 30 novels; nine had been published between 1960 and 1963, and at least two had not yet been published when he died. With the addition of his book-length nonfiction prose, he produced some 60 titles in a 37-year writing career, plus a vast quantity of essays. His narratives generally grew more powerful as he expanded his output, and critics regard the epic novel EARTHLY POWERS (1980) as his masterpiece; it won the Prix de Meilleur Livre Etranger in France in 1981. The range of topics and styles he used demonstrates his command of the novel: he wrote DYSTOPIAN NOVELS (*The Wanting Seed* and *A Clockwork Orange*), historical fiction set in the Renaissance (*Nothing Like the Sun* in 1964, featuring William Shakespeare as a character, and *A Dead Man in Deptford* in 1993, featuring Christopher Marlowe), a spy thriller in the fashion of Ian FLEMING (*Tremor of Intent* in 1966), several more novels about the hapless poet Mr. F. X. Enderby, a satirical attack on the failures of Western cultural values (*MF* in 1971), a verse novel in ottava rima (*Byrne: A Novel,* published posthumously in 1995), novels narrated by uneducated working-class women (*One Hand Clapping* in 1961 and *The Pianoplayers* in 1986), and many others. He wrote two frank and opinionated volumes of memoirs (*Little Wilson and Big God* in 1987 and *You've Had Your Time* in 1990), and produced biographies, histories, translations, and literary monographs. The titles he identified as the best 99 novels of the 20th century are listed in *Ninety-Nine Novels: The Best in English Since 1939* (published in the literarily significant year of 1984). Burgess modestly allowed that readers might perhaps select one of his own novels as the 100th title, but he did not suggest which one was most deserving.

Late in life, Burgess and his wife moved to Monte Carlo; he enjoyed gambling in the casinos, and he became a friend of Princess Grace. He maintained his writing until the end of his life, even through a terminal illness, dying of cancer in London on November 25, 1993. Although he never won a major literary prize in England, he is widely admired by critics, other writers, and discriminating readers as one of the greatest novelists writing in English in the 20th century, and as one of the most important contemporary innovators in fiction-writing technique.

BIBLIOGRAPHY

Aggeler, Geoffrey. *Anthony Burgess: The Artist as Novelist.* Tuscaloosa: University of Alabama Press, 1979.

———, ed. *Critical Essays on Anthony Burgess.* Boston: G. K. Hall, 1986.

Bloom, Harold, ed. *Anthony Burgess.* New York: Chelsea House, 1987.

Burgess, Anthony. *Little Wilson and Big God, Being the First Part of the Confessions of Anthony Burgess.* New York: Weidenfeld & Nicolson, 1986.

———. *You've Had Your Time: Being the Second Part of the Confessions of Anthony Burgess.* London: Heinemann, 1990.

Coale, Samuel, *Anthony Burgess.* New York: Ungar, 1981.

BUTCHER BOY, THE PATRICK MCCABE (1992)

Based on the author's recollection of a radio play he heard as a child, this dark novel was shortlisted for the BOOKER PRIZE in 1992 and became the basis of a FILM ADAPTATION by Neil Jordan in 1998. The first-person narrator, Francie Brady, relates his story through stream-of-consciousness narration in a slang-laden Irish brogue. Because the novel begins with Francie's acknowledgment that he is being hunted for what he did to his nemesis, Mrs. Nugent, his story acquires a dark subtext. The early reveling in boyish pranks cannot be merely amusing: It is a prelude to some grotesque acts of brutality that will be revealed only when Francie is ready to surrender his secret.

The novel is set in the small Irish town Francie has always lived in, where everyone knows everyone else and the rituals of the Catholic Church set the pace of life. Francie's best friend is Joe Purcell, and the two boys enjoy the usual outlets of childhood, riding bikes and reading comics. Francie does not realize how bad his life is nor does he see how incompetent his parents are, since these conditions are all he has ever known. His father, however, is an abusive drunk and his mother is emotionally unstable; both of them plaster over the ugliness of their lives with a variety of lies, including a false story of a happy courtship and honeymoon long ago.

The routine of village life is mildly disrupted with the Nugents' return to the village after living in England for a time. Their son Philip has enjoyed advantages beyond the reach of the village boys, and he has a marvelous collection of comic books that Francie and Joe envy. When the two appropriate the collection for themselves, Mrs. Nugent comes to her son's defense and denounces the members of the Brady family as pigs right on their own doorstep. From that moment, Mrs. Nugent becomes fixed in Francie's mind as the source of all the suffering he soon endures: when his mother attempts suicide, it is Mrs. Nugent's fault, and Francie takes his first revenge by breaking into the Nugent home. His life enters an endless downward spiral as he spends time in a juvenile home, loses his mother and father, and is betrayed by Joe. Each time, Francie blames Mrs. Nugent in order to provide himself with an explanation for the disasters he experiences, but his mental condition is clearly deteriorating.

Francie's slow transition to insanity coincides with the village's absorption in a young girl's vision that the Virgin Mary will personally visit the village. As the frenzied anticipation of her visit mounts, Francie resolves to take care of Mrs. Nugent for good, and since he has been working for the town butcher, he has acquired a chilling set of skills and tools with which to do the job.

Patrick MCCABE captures the full range of Francie's thought, from the cheerful delight of a boy reading comic books to the cold indifference of a deranged executioner. His skill with stream-of-consciousness narration is apparent in the virtually imperceptible shift in Francie's inner monologue from boisterous childhood hyperactivity to obsessive ravings. In many ways Francie seems to be an Irish version of Alex in *A CLOCKWORK ORANGE* by Anthony BURGESS, delighted with himself and indifferent to the moral codes that should restrain him from harming others. But he also demonstrates the exuberance and frankness of other wild-boy narrators such as Huckleberry Finn. As Francie's madness crowds out his humanity, readers are able to pity him because they have been made to see the skewed logic of his mind so clearly. That pity is a tribute to McCabe's storytelling powers.

BIBLIOGRAPHY

Mahoney, Rosemary. "Part Huck Finn, Part Hannibal Lecter," *The New York Times Book Review* 142 (30 May 1993): 9.

Moynahan, Julian. "Never Call a Boy a Pig," *New York Review of Books* 40.16 (1993): 28.

Wallace, Clare. "Running Amuck: Manic Logic in Patrick McCabe's *The Butcher Boy*," *Irish Studies Review* 6, no. 2 (1998): 157–164.

BUTLER, SAMUEL (1835–1902)

Although Butler is generally considered to be a Victorian writer, his novel *The WAY OF ALL FLESH* (1903) was published posthumously in the 20th century and mounts a vigorous satirical assault on Victorian mores and values. Butler thus blazes a trail that numerous subsequent writers who are definitively associated with the 20th century have followed.

Samuel Butler was born the son of a clergyman on December 4, 1835, in Nottinghamshire. His grandfather, Dr. Samuel Butler, had served as bishop of Lichfield and as headmaster of Shrewsbury School; toward the end of the younger Samuel Butler's life, he published an engaging biographical history, in two volumes, of his grandfather's life and times, quoting extensively from the elder Butler's voluminous unpublished writings and letters. (The 17th-century author of *Hudibras* is also named Samuel Butler only by coincidence, not through any family connection.) The affectionate grandson and namesake of Dr. Butler felt no similar identification with his father, who intended him to follow in the traditional family employment and become a clergyman. Even as a young man, Butler wanted to pursue his interests in painting, music, and writing, but he acquiesced to his father's demands and studied at St. John's College, Cambridge, completing a degree in classics in 1858. He even attempted to enter into the clerical life by working with the poor of London's slums as a lay assistant to a clergyman, but he soon decided that his growing religious doubts militated against a career in the church. He was due to receive a comfortable inheritance from his grandfather eventually; his father advanced money on this prospect not to support further study in the arts but to allow Samuel to immigrate to New Zealand.

During a five-year stay in the remoter parts of New Zealand, Butler managed a large "sheep run" he had bought and doubled his investment. His success enabled him to return to England; he lived in London the rest of his life, remaining a bachelor by choice. His father published the series of entertaining and informative letters he had received from New Zealand during his son's five-year absence under the title *A First Year in Canterbury Settlement* (1863); the volume was a kind of guide to frontier life on a sheep ranch. But Samuel Butler's interests were elsewhere: He had already begun publishing articles on Charles Darwin's recently published theory of evolution by natural selection while still in New Zealand, and he had also been working on articles examining the evidence for certain tenets of Christian doctrine. But with the independence gained from his financial success in the farthest outpost of the British Empire, Butler turned to his long-delayed interest in art and began formal studies in painting. He eventually exhibited some of his works at the Royal Academy, although he never achieved great success or reaped financial support as an artist.

Butler continued writing during his 13 years as a student of art and a painter. He also formed a close friendship with a fellow student, Eliza Mary Ann Savage, who took an interest in his writing and commented on his manuscripts. She encouraged Butler to produce his first novel, *Erewhon* (1872), a utopian satire clearly inspired by *Gulliver's Travels.* The novel illustrates the originality of Butler's insights into human psychology and the contemporary science of his day. In 1873, Butler published *A Fair Haven,* again with his friend's encouragement, using the novel as a framework into which he could incorporate his skeptical examinations of the evidence for certain Christian doctrines. The novel's structure looks forward to 20th-century experimentations with narrative form, and it includes an early example of the technique of stream-of-consciousness narration usually identified with Dorothy RICHARDSON and James JOYCE. Shortly after publishing this work, Butler began writing *The Way of All Flesh,* again under the supportive eye of Eliza Savage. But with her death in 1885, Butler put the novel aside; because it contained unflattering portraits based on his own parents, he did not wish to publish it during his lifetime.

George Bernard Shaw became acquainted with Butler and assisted him in finding a publisher for a new treatment of an old subject: In 1901, *Erewhon Revisited Twenty Years Later* appeared, providing Butler with a fresh canvas for his critique of religious superstition. Then in 1902, Butler died of anemia, and when *The Way of All Flesh* appeared the year after, Shaw was one of the early advocates of this wry undermining of all things Victorian. After its publication, the novel slowly built a following, becoming Butler's most successful book and ensuring his place in English literature. In his lifetime, only *Erewhon* had recouped its publishing costs and made a profit for the author, but after Butler's death the novel he withheld from publication made him posthumously famous. Subsequently, Butler's *Note-Books* were published, his letters appeared, and scholars began to devote critical monographs to his literary achievement. The century that he barely lived in has recognized the value and originality of his thought, and the attack on Victorian narrowness and human folly in *The Way of All Flesh* provides a kind of christening for the new era.

BIBLIOGRAPHY

Holt, Lee E. *Samuel Butler.* Twayne's English Authors, 2. New York: Twayne, 1964.

Raby, Peter. *Samuel Butler: A Biography.* Iowa City: University of Iowa Press, 1991.

BUYER'S MARKET, A ANTHONY POWELL (1953)

The second of 12 volumes in POWELL'S ROMAN-FLEUVE entitled *A DANCE TO THE MUSIC OF TIME,* this novel continues the first-person point of view narration of Nicholas Jenkins, a writer, as he enters the social whirl of debutante parties in London, living on his own and making a start in his career as an editor of art books. In the overall structure of the series, *A Buyer's Market* is positioned in the middle of the first of four "movements," after Nick has completed his schooling and university training, but before he has entered into any permanent relationships. It immediately follows *A QUESTION OF UPBRINGING* and precedes *The ACCEPTANCE WORLD.*

In the first of four chapters, Nick presents his recollections of Mr. Deacon, a bad painter fond of the company of young men. These memories crop up when Nick discovers four of Mr. Deacon's paintings at a rummage sale. The paintings' influences fix them in Time—always capitalized in this kind of context—and also turn back the clock and the narration to the days of Nick's youth. These memories lead his thoughts to a house he liked to visit long ago; one of Mr. Deacon's paintings hung there, but more important, there Nick would be likely to encounter the first young lady ever to turn his head, Barbara Goring, best friend of Eleanor Walpole-Wilson. These girls are presented to the social world as debutantes soon after Nicholas has finished college and moved to London. The social whirl of London in the 1920s forms the core of the novel, during an era when the Great War—WORLD WAR I—has carried off too many eligible young men, leaving a buyer's market for those who remain.

Barbara Goring, a boisterous young lady, is elevated to feminine perfection in Nick's mind by his infatuation with her. The novel recounts the building and unbuilding of this state of a young man's mind as Nick floats into a sentimental obsession for Barbara. He mistakes this state of mind for his first adult love attachment before he is disabused of his crush by the young lady herself. After a particularly disastrous party, Nick learns that Kenneth Widmerpool, the tragicomic villain of the entire series, has been suffering the same emotional crush for Barbara that he himself has been experiencing in circumstances that make the discovery a privately hilarious relief.

From the formalities of the ballroom, the story quickly shifts to a "low party" at Mrs. Milly Andriadis's at the invitation of Charles Stringham, Mrs. Andriadis's temporary paramour. Where the debutante ball had been populated by young people and their graying parents, this bohemian party is filled with adults, including a visiting prince from a Levantine country with desirable raw materials and the business tycoon Sir Magnus Donners. The two events on the same evening suggest the transition that Nick is undergoing as he leaves the preoccupations of youth behind and takes up his adult role. His general unpreparedness is indicated by the way he finds himself slipping off from an awkward moment at the party, but in the next chapter he is once again in the presence of many of the same characters at Stourwater, the home of Sir Magnus Donners. Adult life—life in general—is more complicated than he had previously thought, requiring him to adjust quickly.

Soon afterward, he finds himself at the wedding of Charles Stringham and Peggy Stepney, the first ceremony to signal the official transformation of Nick's generation into full adult status. Mr. Deacon dies that day, completing the design of Powell's dance. By the novel's end, Nick is an independent adult, aware of the rapidly rising stakes in the game of life.

BIBLIOGRAPHY

Joyau, Isabelle. *Understanding Powell's* A Dance to the Music of Time. New York: St. Martin's Press, 1994.

Selig, Robert L. *Time and Anthony Powell.* Cranbury, N.J.: Associated University Presses, 1991.

Spurling, Hillary. *Invitation to the Dance: A Guide to Anthony Powell's* A Dance to the Music of Time. Boston: Little, Brown, 1977.

BYATT, A. S. (1936–)

A scholar, a novelist, and a mother, Antonia Susan Drabble was born on August 24, 1936, in Sheffield, England, the elder sister of Margaret DRABBLE. Byatt was educated in literature and art at Newnham College of Cambridge University, graduating with a B.A. degree in 1957; she pursued graduate studies at Bryn Mawr in the United States during the 1957–58 academic year, and at Somerville College in Oxford in 1958–59. She acquired the last name she publishes under through her first marriage in 1959; the Byatts divorced 10 years later in 1969, and A.S. Byatt remarried that same year. Each marriage produced two children.

Beginning in 1962, Byatt worked at various English universities as a lecturer or tutor, in addition to her family responsibilities; her earliest publication was a scholarly examination of the novelist Iris MURDOCH. While Byatt built her academic career, her sister launched a successful career as a novelist. However, Byatt too had been writing fiction at least since her undergraduate days, and she published her first novel, *The Shadow of the Sun,* in 1964, following it in 1967 with *The Game* (a partly autobiographical story). Critics gave her work moderately positive reviews, but she remained overshadowed by the more substantial achievement of Margaret Drabble. Byatt's strength as a novelist became apparent, however, in 1978 with *The Virgin in the Garden,* the first volume of a tetralogy that explores the lives of two literary sisters in the context of the "second Elizabethan Age" (i.e., 1953 to the present). The second volume of the series, *Still Life* (1985) showed equal strength; the series continued with *Babel Tower* in 1995 and concluded with *Whistling Woman* in 2002.

Before this trilogy was completed, however, Byatt's career got a tremendous boost from her novel POSSESSION in 1990. It won the BOOKER PRIZE that year and found a large readership in spite of the fact that the two modern protagonists in the double love story are literary scholars researching a previously unknown romance between two Victorian poets. The love story between the mismatched modern couple follows many of the conventions of the romance genre but raises them to sophisticated heights through the occupation, education, and interests of the main characters in contrast to the poets they are studying. Byatt includes poems and letters from the dead Victorians to advance her narrative, and uses mimetic doubling to intertwine the two love stories into one coherent novel. Her erudition and her stylistic versatility become paramount in "Morpho Eugenia," a novella included in *Angels and Insects* (1992), and in *The Biographer's Tale* (2000); in both these works, she includes long digressive passages allegedly drawn from the reading of the fictional protagonists, altering her style to create these excerpts.

Byatt, like her sister, has become a fixture on the English and American literary scenes, writing reviews and essays for leading newspapers and magazines. But since her career began later, there is less critical and interpretive material available about her. She continues to live and write in London.

BIBLIOGRAPHY

Byatt, A. S. *Passions of the Mind: Selected Writings.* New York: Turtle Bay Books, 1992.

Kelly, Kathleen Coyne. *A. S. Byatt.* Twayne's English Authors, 529. New York: Twayne Publishers, 1996.

C

CAKES AND ALE: OR, THE SKELETON IN THE CUPBOARD W. SOMERSET MAUGHAM (1930) In this roman à clef, the author contrasts Victorian repression with the freer attitudes, values, and behaviors of the 1920s. The novel's protagonist is Willie Ashenden, a representation of Maugham himself. Ashenden, a writer, is friends with another writer, Alroy Kear, whom Maugham based on the novelist Hugh Walpole (eventually admitting the correspondence), a writer of modest talent and large sales of titles he tailors to the tastes of a mass audience. Kear is about to undertake the task of composing a biography of the great Victorian writer Edward Driffield (based on Thomas Hardy), author of the controversial novel *The Cup of Life* (an amalgam of Hardy's *Tess of the D'Urbervilles* and *Jude the Obscure*).

Since Ashenden had been associated with Driffield and his first wife, Rosie (MAUGHAM'S original creation and the symbol of the new century's liberation), Kear wants information about the great man's earlier life. His motivating force is Driffield's second wife, Amy, who has appointed herself to be the guardian of the great man's memory. The biography she wants Kear to write is to be a reverential and heart-warming picture of noble artistry; Ashenden, however, knows that Driffield's early life and his relationship with his first wife do not fit the mold in which Amy and Kear intend to cast the biography. He knows that the true story is much less typically Victorian, much more complex,

and a much greater affirmation of the human potential to create and share joy. He knows that, in order to tell the truth, Kear will have to forgo easy platitudes and comforting stereotypes in preference to the iconoclastic particularity of unique real lives.

Maugham structures his story in a seris of long flashbacks initiated by Kear's request and by an invitation from Amy Driffield. After his first conversation with Kear, Ashenden recalls how he met Edward and Rosie Driffield: As a boy, Ashenden's uncle and guardian served as the vicar of Blackstable, the coastal town that was also the home of the Driffields. While Ashenden was still a boy in PUBLIC SCHOOL, he met the Driffields during school vacation; as a young Victorian enmeshed in a form of training designed to prepare him for a position of influence in the English social hierarchy, Ashenden had not yet learned to question the establishment. He embraced the snobbery of the English CLASS system as a matter of course—and he found Driffield to be a rather common person of no great distinction, drawing this conclusion on the basis of his uncle's report of Driffield's marriage to a local barmaid.

Upon receiving an invitation from Amy to visit her at Blackstable, Ashenden once again returns to his memories of the great man. In time, he had overcome his initial disinterest; in fact, Edward and Rosie Driffield had taught Ashenden how to ride a bicycle and then had invited the boy along on numerous outings. During their acquaintance, Ashenden had gradually realized that Rosie was unfaithful to her husband—but that awareness mystified him, since the two seemed to have a happy and fulfilling personal relationship. By the time Ashenden is a young man studying medicine in London, he is once again introduced into the Driffields' circle, and this time his curiosity about Rosie—a beautiful, loving, and unselfish woman—is resolved in an expected way. Even after the Driffield marriage dissolves, Ashenden maintains an infrequent acquaintance with Rosie, who eventually relocates to New York and lives to be a wealthy and contented widow.

As Ashenden relates what he knows of Rosie and Edward, Kear and Amy present a contrasting view: They see Rosie in particular as a promiscuous woman who need not be given the respect of serious consideration. The sympathetic and admiring view of her that Ashenden presents upsets the simple stereotype of Edward Driffield they had planned to create. Revealing their own backward-looking acquiescence to Victorian repression, they wish to depict Edward Driffield as a pillar of conventional morality, even though his novels constitute an attack on that very concept and despite the fact that his life had been anything but conventional until old age and disease weakened him. In contrast, Ashenden recognizes that Rosie's spontaneous, unself-conscious sexuality and her generous love provided Driffield with the example of a life lived beyond the bounds of repression and enabled him to create characters who could cast off the repression of the past and create a new model of human relationships—a modern story very much worth the telling.

BIBLIOGRAPHY

Curtis, Anthony. *The Pattern of Maugham: A Critical Portrait.* New York: Taplinger, 1974.

Curtis, Anthony, and John Whitehead, eds. *W. Somerset Maugham: The Critical Heritage.* London: Routledge & Kegan Paul, 1987.

Morgan, Ted. *Maugham.* New York: Simon & Schuster, 1980.

CAMPUS NOVEL   Fictionalizations about college life form the subgenre of the campus novel. Although the novel of higher education often receives a comic treatment, such as that found in the novels *Lucky Jim* by Kingsley AMIS and David LODGE's Rummidge series, *Changing Places, Nice Work,* and *Small World,* the field also includes such serious examples as C. P. SNOW's The *Masters* and The *Affair.* The HARRY POTTER series is also a kind of campus fiction, but instead of college life, it explores the world of a private boarding school that trains students in a curriculum approximately equal to American middle- and high-school classes (but devoted to magic).

Colleges and universities present authors with a genteel microcosm of the larger world: The machinations of faculty and administrators provide a perfect opportunity for both parody and analysis of politics in the "real" (i.e., nonacademic) world, and the complex interactions among students and faculty provide opportunities to explore a wide range of relationships. As larger segments of the general population have become college educated, and as university study has become a routine aspect of life for the many and is no longer the exclusive purview of the upper class, campus novels have acquired a wider appeal. Additionally, the traditional age of college attendance occurs during the last period of transition from youth to adulthood, making the college experience a perfect setting for the BILDUNGSROMAN, or novel of personal development.

BIBLIOGRAPHY

Bevan, David, ed. *University Fiction.* Rodopi Perspectives on Modern Literature 5. Amsterdam and Atlanta: Rodopi, 1990.

Bradbury, Malcolm. "Campus Fictions." In *No, Not Bloomsbury.* New York: Columbia University Press, 1987, 329–335.

Kaplan, Carey and Ellen Cronan Rose. *The Canon and the Common Reader.* Knoxville: University of Tennessee Press, 1990.

Lodge, David. "The Campus Novel," *The New Republic* 186.10 (1982): 34.

CANADA   See EMPIRE and COLONIALISM. For significant Canadian novelists, see Margaret ATWOOD, Robertson DAVIES, Rohinton MISTRY, Alice MUNRO, and Michael ONDAATJE.

CANON   An officially recognized collection, anthology, list, or roll is a canon: The writings selected for inclusion in the Bible constitute a canon, as does the list of saints recognized (canonized) by the Catholic Church. More loosely, the "great works" of literature constitute an unofficial canon. Admission to any canon generally follows some kind of testing procedure or juridical review to verify that something or someone proposed for addition to the canon is indeed worthy of selection. And just as individual writings or people can be selected for inclusion, they can also be deselected. Thus Protestant Bibles generally do not include the Apocrypha, or writings previously excluded from the Bible, and some well-known former saints, such as Saint Christopher, have been decanonized, or removed from the list of saints, after modern research determined them to have been mythical rather than historical persons.

In literature, canon formation has been hotly contested in the latter part of the 20th century as various groups have competed to place writers in the canon of literature. In the United States, especially through university course offerings, women and minorities have demanded that their voices be heard, their histories recorded, and their writings recognized. Since there is no official "congress of literary critics" to make a definitive and authoritative selection, scholars debate the issue in literary periodicals, advance their preferences by editing anthologies, and put their choices into effect in college classrooms by including some authors and excluding others. For example, the first edition of the venerable *Norton Anthology of English Literature* (1962) included the writings of only men in volume one; the seventh edition features more than 20 women. In volume two of the first edition, non-English colonial writers were entirely absent from the first edition, while the seventh edition includes postcolonial and Commonwealth writers such as Chinua ACHEBE, Jean RHYS, Salman RUSHDIE, Derek Walcott, J. M. COETZEE, Nadine GORDIMER, Doris LESSING, Alice MUNRO, V. S. NAIPAUL, and Anita DESAI. Although these writers all originate literary works in the English language, and some have taken up permanent residence in England, their diverse nationalities indicate that the definition of the canon of English literature has undergone a shift—a kind of global broadening—in the latter part of the 20th century. Thus both FEMINISM and the legacy of

COLONIALISM have helped to rewrite the canon of English literature.

Although the canon of English literature is an ephemeral entity lacking the imprimature of official recognition, much is at stake in its selection and implementation. Literature textbooks represent an elite selection of outstanding writers, but they are consumed as artifacts of mass culture; when segments of history, or of the population, are excluded from them, the students who study those books receive information biased in favor of the preferences of those empowered to make the selections. Those students who make the mistake of believing that what they learned in college is the whole truth, and is also all they need to know, may also mistakenly assume that anything not taught in college is not worth knowing and valuing. The canon of literature sets a benchmark for cultural value, and so canon formation has become a contested site where those engaged in the struggle to shape the values of the next generation attempt to influence the thinking of the individuals who will eventually make decisions and choices that affect real lives, moral issues, political processes, and social changes.

BIBLIOGRAPHY

Guillory, John. *Cultural Capital: The Problem of Literary Canon Formation.* Chicago: University of Chicago Press, 1993.

Harris, Wendell V. "Canonicity," *Publications of the Modern Language Association* 106, no. 1 (1991): 110–121.

Kaplan, Carey and Ellen Cronan Rose. *The Canon and the Common Reader.* Knoxville: University of Tennessee Press, 1990.

Kermode, Frank. *The Classic.* London: Faber & Faber, 1975.

CAREY, PETER (1943–   )

The second person (with J. M. COETZEE) to win the BOOKER PRIZE twice—in 1988 for *OSCAR AND LUCINDA* and in 2001 for *The True History of the Kelly Gang*—Peter Carey was born in Victoria, Australia, on May 7, 1943. His parents owned a car dealership and sent their son to an exclusive private school; Carey later attended Monash University in 1961 to study science but left without a degree and worked as an advertising copywriter in England and Australia. He was very successful in this field, eventually opening his own firm with a partner. In 1985, he married theater director Alison Summers; they have two sons.

Carey's literary career began with two collections of short fiction: *The Fat Man in History* (1974) and *War Crimes* (1978). His talent was apparent in these first volumes, and critics compared his work to that of Kurt Vonnegut, Franz Kafka, Evelyn WAUGH, Jorge Luis Borges, and other writers of surreal imagination and distinctive narrative voice. His first novel, *Bliss,* appeared in 1981; its protagonist is an advertising executive who awakens from a heart attack to find that the life he has been living is hell. In 1985, Carey published *Illywhacker* (an Australian term for a con artist), the first-person narration of a 139-year-old adventurer and spinner of tall tales. *Oscar and Lucinda* followed three years later. Other notable titles include *The Unusual Life of Tristam Smith* (1994), an odd FANTASY that condemns the universal spread of mass culture using thinly disguised Disney characters, and *Jack Maggs* (1998), inspired by the character of Magwitch in Charles Dickens's *Great Expectations.*

Carey has produced one work of children's literature, *The Big Bazoohley* (1995), about a witch. He is the subject of the 1985 documentary film *Beautiful Lies: A Film About Peter Carey,* and he has written screenplays and a volume of travel writing about Sydney. In 1990, Carey brought his family to New York and taught creative writing at New York University; he has also held an appointment at Princeton University. His writing has transformed Australian literature, breaking the dominance of realism and introducing elements of POSTMODERNISM and postcolonialism. His record of achievement has established him as one of the most important living novelists of any nationality writing in English.

BIBLIOGRAPHY

Hassall, Anthony J. *Peter Carey.* St. Lucia: University of Queensland Press, 1994.

Huggan, Graham. *Peter Carey.* New York: Oxford University Press, 1996.

Woodcock, Bruce. *Peter Carey.* New York: Manchester University Press, 1996.

CARIBBEAN   See EMPIRE and COLONIALISM. For significant Caribbean novelists, see V. S. NAIPAUL (born in Trinidad), Caryl PHILLIPS (born in St. Kitts, West Indies), and Jean RHYS (born in Dominica).

CARR, J. L. (1912–1994)   The author of several COMIC NOVELS that sometimes include elements of FANTASY, James Joseph Lloyd Carr was born and educated in Yorkshire and spent many years as an innovative school teacher—devising a pedagogy designed to appeal to students rather than to administrators—after serving during World War II as an intelligence officer with the Royal Air Force in Sierra Leone. When the war ended, he was married to a farmer's daughter and they settled in Kettering, where Carr remained for the rest of his life. He retired from teaching in 1965 to write full-time. By then, he had published his first novel, *A Day in the Summer* (1964), and earned enough in royalties to support the family. Tragically, his wife was stricken with lung cancer soon afterward and succumbed to this illness 13 years later.

In 1968, Carr published *A Season in Sinji,* drawing on his experiences in Sierra Leone to produce a SATIRE on war. Beginning in 1969, he launched a publishing enterprise for which he produced a number of tiny pamphlets, dictionaries, poetry editions, and maps, which he wrote and illustrated; it was successful enough to enable him to publish his last two novels himself. In 1972, Carr again drew on his own experience, this time as a teacher, for *The Harpole Report,* constructed as a series of letters that include descriptions of his unique approach to teaching. Carr's greatest novel, considered a small masterpiece, was *A MONTH IN THE COUNTRY,* published in 1980. It was short-listed for the BOOKER PRIZE and became a FILM ADAPTATION by the same name in 1987. In *The Battle of Pollock's Crossing* (1985), Carr draws on a year he spent in South Dakota as an exchange teacher, but he reinvents the story as a fantasy in which a British schoolteacher is transported to America and sets his pupils straight about the Sioux Indians and the Battle of Wounded Knee.

A private man throughout his life, Carr made very little factual personal information available, preferring to tell his story through fiction. He died in 1994 in Kettering.

BIBLIOGRAPHY

Holroyd, Michael. Introduction. *A Month in the Country*. J. L. Carr. 1980. New York: New York Review Books, 2000.

Rogers, Byron. *The Last Englishman: The Life of J. L. Carr.* London: Aurum, 2003.

CARTER, ANGELA (1940–1992)

Noted for modern retellings of fairy tales, Angela Olive Stalker was born on May 7, 1940, in Sussex. In 1960, she married Paul Carter; they divorced in 1972. After working as a newspaper journalist in Croydon for four years, she earned a bachelor's degree in English at the University of Bristol in 1965.

Carter's first novel, *Shadow Dance* (1966; published in the United States as *Honeybuzzard*), demonstrates her bold determination to examine sexual stereotypes, as it resolves the mystery of a mutilated girl's sufferings. The next year her second novel, *The Magic Toyshop,* won the John Llewellyn Rhys Memorial Prize; a BILDUNGSROMAN, or coming-of-age story, it revealed her keen interest in fairy tales and their modern reinterpretations. In 1968, her third novel, *Several Perceptions,* appeared, telling the story of a suicidal protagonist and his struggle to cope with the garish world he lives in. It won the Somerset Maugham Prize, which specifically covers travel expenses for young writers. Carter went to Japan for two years, and the experience introduced an element in her writing drawn from theories of FEMINISM. Already known for the use of FANTASY and surreal horror in her novels, Carter also began to draw on the settings and themes of SCIENCE FICTION. Her most noted feminist novel, *The Passion of New Eve,* featured a male character, Evelyn, who falls under the control of a dominating goddess-figure called Mother. Carter's next-to-last novel, *Nights at the Circus* (1985), won the JAMES TAIT BLACK MEMORIAL PRIZE and features a love story between a winged female trapeze artist and a journalist who joins the circus to be with her.

Angela Carter also wrote short fiction, plays, screenplays, children's literature, a book of poetry, and literary criticism; she translated *The Fairy Tales of Charles Perrault* in 1977; and she edited three volumes of fairy tales for Virago Press. Her career was cut short by cancer. In 1992, at the age of 51, Angela Carter died.

BIBLIOGRAPHY

Lee, Alison. *Angela Carter,* New York: G. K. Hall, 1997.

Peach, Linden. *Angela Carter.* New York: St. Martin's Press, 1998.

Tucker, Lindsey, ed. *Critical Essays on Angela Carter.* New York: G. K. Hall, 1998.

CARTLAND, BARBARA (1901–2000)

The author of more than 550 books—most of them romance novels—that have sold more than 600 million copies worldwide, Barbara Cartland became an institution in her long lifetime. She was born Mary Barbara Cartland on July 9, 1901, and educated at Malvern Girls' College and at Abbey House, Netley Abbey, in Hampshire. She was married to Alexander George McCorquodale in 1927; they produced one child and divorced in 1933. In 1936, she married her ex-husband's cousin Hugh McCorquodale. The marriage produced two children and lasted until Hugh died in 1963.

Barbara Cartland worked as a freelance writer beginning in 1925 and developed a formulaic plot that increasingly dominated her romances. The stories, typically set in the 19th century, always featured a virginal heroine and a dashing nonvirginal hero who fall in love and are legally married before indulging in the sexual passions that heat their blossoming romance. At the peak of her career, Cartland could produce a complete romance in seven days, dictating to a stenographer for about two hours a day. She also wrote books on marriage, etiquette, cooking, health, and beauty; biographies of her mother and brother and a variety of royal European figures; five volumes of autobiography; and numerous other topics that capitalized on her name. In later life, she ventured into enterprises outside the publishing world, designing a line of housewares and marketing romantic tours of England.

An active clubwoman who also performed valuable public service during WORLD WAR II, Barbara Cartland was named a Dame of the Order of the British Empire in 1991. She died on May 21, 2000.

BIBLIOGRAPHY

Cartland, Barbara. *I Search for Rainbows: 1946–1966.* London: Hutchinson, 1967.

———. *I Seek the Miraculous.* London: Sheldon Press, 1978.

———. *The Isthmus Years: Reminiscences of the Years 1919–1939.* London: Hutchinson, 1943.

———. *We Danced All Night: 1919–1929.* London: Hutchinson, 1970.

———. *The Years of Opportunity: 1939–1945.* London: Hutchinson, 1948.

Robyns, Gwen. *Barbara Cartland: An Authorised Biography.* London: Sidgwick & Jackson, 1984.

CARTWRIGHT, JUSTIN (1933–)

Justin Cartwright is a South African novelist whose career as a professional writer has not been dominated by the political and racial conflicts of his homeland, although he does occasionally draw on those materials. He was educated at Trinity College, Oxford, and afterward worked as a documentary filmmaker, eventually taking up permanent residence in London. He has published more than 10 books under his own name and has also produced work under the pseudonyms Suzy Crispin and Penny Sutton.

Cartwright's first novel, *The Revenge* (1978), is a roman à clef about an American president (based on Richard Nixon) who tries to arrange for the assassination of a rival candidate. His 1995 novel, *In Every Face I Meet,* was short-listed for the BOOKER PRIZE, and in 1998 LEADING THE CHEERS won the WHITBREAD Book of the Year Award. Other well-reviewed works include *Masai Dreaming* (1993), about a journalist researching the life of an anthropologist who had been studying the Masai tribe in Africa in the period before WORLD WAR II, but who was later sent to Auschwitz with her family, and *Half in Love* (2001), about a protagonist loosely based on British prime minister Tony Blair.

As a stylist, Cartwright has been compared to the great satirist Evelyn WAUGH and to Graham GREENE, the master of shady characters embroiled in moral dilemmas. Very little biographical or critical information on Cartwright is available in standard references or on the Web; he continues to live and write in London.

BIBLIOGRAPHY

Mundy, Toby. Review of *Leading the Cheers. New Statesman,* 25 September 1998, 89.

CARY, JOYCE (1888–1957)

Born on December 7, 1888, in IRELAND, Joyce Cary struggled to become a professional writer and by the end of his life was recognized as one of the leading British novelists of his day. Cary was born into an Anglo-Irish family that had held estates in NORTHERN IRELAND for three centuries before losing them in William Gladstone's 1882 reforms. He grew up in the aftermath of this upheaval in the family's fortunes, which eventually brought the family back to England. During childhood, Cary was sickly and emotionally stricken over the death of his mother in 1898. His father boarded him in the tradition of the English PUBLIC SCHOOLS, where Cary excelled at writing and drawing. At the age of 16, Cary toured France, sketching as he traveled, and at 18 he lived in Paris in the bohemian arts community. His ambition to be a painter ended after a period of study in Edinburgh, Scotland; although he enjoyed his schooling, the most important thing he learned was that his talent was not great enough to support a professional career. Thus he turned to his other talent and began writing. To satisfy his father, he enrolled at Trinity College, Oxford, where he studied from 1909 to 1912. In Oxford, he met his future wife, to whom he was married in 1916.

Cary served with the Red Cross in the Balkans during parts of 1912 and 1913 and then joined the Nigerian Service as an assistant district manager. His experiences there made him skeptical of the purposes and practices of COLONIALISM; increasingly, the British EMPIRE seemed to him to be an unjust imposition on the populations it purported to serve. Four of Cary's first five novels, published long after he had returned to England, are set in Africa and reflect his sense of the conflict between English and African goals. He ended his career in the service in 1919, when he began to place short stories in the *Saturday Evening Post;* the family moved to Oxford, and Cary devoted himself full time to his writing. More than a decade passed before much of his work came to print, but in 1932 his first novel, *Aissa Saved,* appeared, followed by *An American*

Visitor (1933), *The African Witch* (1936), and *Mister Johnson* (1939). The last of these gained some critical attention for the moral conflict that develops between the title character, an African, and the colonial officer who befriends him and later must stand in judgment of him for a murder he commits. It later served as an early influence on the literary thinking of Chinua ACHEBE.

Cary applied for military service during WORLD WAR II but was not accepted (his eyesight had been poor since childhood), so he worked as Oxford's chief air raid warden—a light duty considering that Hitler intended to make Oxford his headquarters after conquering England and therefore preserved it from bombing. Cary's writing changed somewhat as he began to use England and Ireland for settings, but he continued to explore the smaller-scale cultural discrepancies than can still lead to misunderstanding and violence. In *Charlie Is My Darling* (1940), he tells the story of London children evacuated by the thousands to the English countryside during the Blitzkrieg, and in *A House of Children* (1941), Cary returns to his childhood roots in Ireland for an autobiographical novel about the early development of a writer. The novel won the JAMES TAIT BLACK MEMORIAL PRIZE in 1942.

Cary's best works are the two trilogies he completed of the several he began: *Herself Surprised* (1941), *To Be a Pilgrim* (1942), and *The Horse's Mouth* (1944), Cary's first best-seller, later published in one volume entitled *FIRST TRILOGY,* and the *PRISONER OF GRACE* trilogy that includes the title volume (1952), *Except the Lord* (1953), and *Not Honour More* (1955). The two series are similar in structure and method but vary in character and action, although both plots involve the murder of a wife. Both series feature Cary's characteristic use of voice masterfully captured for the first-person narrator—different in each volume—each of whom provides an egocentric view of the novel's action. The events portray Cary's existential view of life as an inescapable freedom derived from the universal burden of human free will.

Cary traveled, lectured, and wrote during the decade of the 1950s, having lost his beloved wife in 1949, the same year he declined appointment as a Commander of the Order of the British Empire. His posthumously published critical work, *Art and Reality* (1958), emphasizes the role of creativity and imagination in linking individuals to the world of reality. Cary died on March 29, 1957.

BIBLIOGRAPHY
Bawer, Bruce. "Why Should We Read Joyce Cary?" *The New Criterion* 11.9 (May 1993): 9–17.
Bishop, Alan. *Gentleman Rider: A Life of Joyce Cary.* London: Joseph, 1988.
Christian, Edwin Ernest. *Joyce Cary's Creative Imagination.* New York: Peter Lang, 1988.
Hall, Dennis. *Joyce Cary: A Reappraisal.* London: Macmillan, 1983.
Roby, Kinley E. *Joyce Cary.* Twayne's English Authors, 377. Boston: Twayne, 1984.

CASANOVA'S CHINESE RESTAURANT
ANTHONY POWELL (1960)   The fifth of 12 volumes in POWELL'S ROMAN-FLEUVE entitled *A DANCE TO THE MUSIC OF TIME,* this novel continues the first-person point of view narration of Nicholas Jenkins, a writer, as he experiences the arts scene in London during 1936–37, meeting musicians, painters, and writers while the threat of war intensifies. In the overall structure of the series, *Casanova's Chinese Restaurant* is positioned in the middle of the second of four "movements," during a period when Nick is working as a screenwriter and becoming better acquainted with his in-laws, the large, eccentric, and aristocratic Tolland family. It immediately follows AT LADY MOLLY'S and precedes *The KINDLY ONES.*

In the opening sentences, Nick is observing the bombed ruins of the Mortimer, a pub where he had enjoyed many evenings with Hugh Moreland, a rising young composer. Nick seems to be writing from a period after the Blitz of WORLD WAR II, but he is thinking back to 1928 or 1929, and the action of much of the novel occurs in 1933 and 1934. As he looks at the ruins, a voice swells up singing a song that he had heard the night he met Moreland here. The song provides a bridge into the flashback and acts as a catalyst unleashing a flood of memories. After establishing a somewhat nostalgic, even elegiac, tone, the story moves to the period of *At Lady Molly's* and immediately afterward. Nick is married to Isobel Tolland, sister of Lord Warminster (also known as Erridge), and they socialize with Hugh and Matilda Moreland.

In these early days of married life, the Jenkinses and the Morelands frequently dine at Casanova's Chinese Restaurant, sometimes joined by the Maclinticks. Although Nick and Isobel are happy in their marriage, the Maclinticks have a destructive relationship that not infrequently erupts into violent shouting matches. Moreland is still establishing his musical reputation; in a key section of the novel, Matilda has persuaded Amy Foxe, the mother of Charles Stringham, to sponsor a reception after the premiere performance of an important composition of Moreland's. Although Stringham had been one of Nick's closest friends while they were at school, his marriage had ended in divorce and he had sunk into alcoholism. Unexpectedly, he arrives at Moreland's reception and shows how low he has fallen in his family's estimation.

At the party, Moreland's attentions to Priscilla Tolland aroused Nick's suspicion that they are having an affair; the Maclinticks quarrel violently. Soon afterward, Nick and Moreland pay Maclintick a call when they learn that his wife, Audrey, has abandoned him for a musician. He lives in near squalor, indifferent to material comforts in his focus on music and music criticism. With Audrey's departure, even the small graces that had formerly been maintained have disappeared. Maclintick is unwilling to admit his loss, trying to gloss over Audrey's absence, but not long after this visit he commits suicide. The shock of this death jolts Moreland out of his pursuit of Priscilla Tolland, and shortly thereafter her engagement to Nick's fellow screenwriter Chips Lovell is announced. Love and death become strangely intertwined as these relationships develop.

The theme of young marriage and the risks that attend it dominates this novel. Nick does not place his own marriage on display; in fact, readers only learn indirectly that Isobel has a miscarriage and her husband only rarely relates bits of their conversations. But through Nick's observation of his family, friends, and acquaintances, readers can see both the humor and the danger that marriage brings. And since desire is not a faucet turned off or contained by marriage, but a permanent subtext for most of human existence, personal relationships are always at risk of becoming more complicated or of flying apart completely.

BIBLIOGRAPHY

Joyau, Isabelle. *Understanding Powell's* A Dance to the Music of Time. New York: St. Martin's Press, 1994.

Selig, Robert L. *Time and Anthony Powell.* Cranbury, N.J.: Associated University Presses, 1991.

Spurling, Hillary. *Invitation to the Dance: A Guide to Anthony Powell's* A Dance to the Music of Time. Boston: Little, Brown, 1977.

CHANGING PLACES DAVID LODGE (1975)

This first volume of an informal trilogy introduces the recurring settings of Rummidge University and Euphoria State and the characters Philip Swallow, a mild-mannered British professor of English literature, and Morris Zapp, a brash American scholar and literary critic. This story combines the features of the COMIC NOVEL and the CAMPUS NOVEL into a SATIRE that contrasts English and American higher education; it is also a roman à clef that draws on some noted members of the literary establishment for its characters.

Rummidge and Euphoria have long exchanged visiting scholars every spring term. In 1969, Philip Swallow and Morris Zapp wind up changing places, and before the novel is over they have changed much more. The novel's plot is ancillary to the author's design of placing selected features of English and American life side by side to contrast them. Each visiting scholar must first find lodging, and each meets a young woman, but where Philip finds a casual sex partner, Melanie, in his apartment building (later to discover that she is Zapp's grown daughter by a previous marriage), Morris finds a pregnant American girl, Mary Makepeace, fleeing to England for an abortion in the days before *Roe v. Wade*. While Morris, who is anything but a traditional man, urges his new acquaintance toward traditional domesticity, Philip winds up allowing his new acquaintance to live with Charles Boon, a young Englishman and Philip's former student, who has become a talk-radio sensation in Euphoria and a squatter in Philip's apartment.

The parallel situations allow LODGE to comment on English and American academic offices, book collections, teaching schedules, student behaviors, scholarly expectations, and party-going manners. Small and large disasters befall each scholar's living quarters, and the adventures of the two men gradually place each one into more frequent contact with the other's wife, so that each winds up living under the roof of his opposite number. The shared domestic arrangements start off properly enough in each case, but Philip's contented domesticity quickly becomes so indispensable to Désirée Zapp that they become lovers, while Hilary Swallow's growing suspicions about Philip eventually push her into the arms of Morris Zapp.

Lodge's narrative strategies in putting this story together vary across the course of the book. He begins with a third-person omniscient narrator relating all the experiences and thoughts of Morris and Philip, Désirée and Hilary. In chapter three, "Corresponding," however, he switches to an epistolary style and provides the reader with the texts of letters (and one telegram) exchanged between the two pairs of spouses. In chapter four, "Reading," Lodge adopts yet another indirect narrative strategy and presents snippets from the *Euphoric Times,* the *Plotinus Gazette,* the *Rummidge Morning Post,* the *Esseph Chronicle,* and various flyers, handbills, and announcements. The first two chapters enable these snippets to stand on their own and advance the plot in a highly efficient and amusing manner. In chapter five, "Changing," Lodge returns to traditional omniscient narration, but it is now dominated by dialogue between Philip and Désirée in Euphoria and Morris and Hilary in Rummidge, with one conversation between Philip and Hilary broadcast by radio to the universe. Then the final chapter, "Ending," turns into a movie screenplay, abandoning narrative completely. Lodge ends his story in a freeze-frame rather than a conclusion, leaving readers to tie up the AMBIGUITY of loose ends for themselves.

Changing Places is a clear example of a novel in the style of POSTMODERNISM: The text makes reference to itself as an artifact of literature both through explicit observations from the characters and from the shifting narrative structure. Although the setting, characters, events, and puns will appeal most strongly to a specialized coterie audience of college English professors,

the satirical contrasts of English and American cultures, attitudes, and behaviors should amuse any well-prepared reader.

BIBLIOGRAPHY

Friend, Joshua. " 'Every Decoding Is Another Encoding': Morris Zapp's Postructural Implication on Our Postmodern World," *English Language Notes* 33, no. 3 (March 1996): 61–67.

Martin, Barbara Arizti. "Shortcircuiting Death: The Ending of *Changing Places* and the Death of the Novel," *Miscelánea: A Journal of English and American Studies* 17 (1996): 39–50.

CHANT OF JIMMIE BLACKSMITH, THE

THOMAS KENEALLY (1972)   Winner of the Heinemann Award in 1973 and the basis of an effective 1978 FILM ADAPTATION, this novel is a tale of cultural conflict in Australia between descendants of English COLONIALISM and an Aborigine who tries and fails to become integrated into the system of cultural values mouthed by whites. The novel fictionalizes the historical case of Jimmie Governor, hanged for murdering whites at the turn of the century.

KENEALLY uses a third-person omniscient narrator to present the story of Jimmie's rising ambition to fit into the white world and of the effects on him of repeated frustrations and humiliations from both whites and natives. Jimmie Blacksmith is half white, half Aborigine; from birth, he straddles these two worlds, not because his white father has a hand in his rearing, but because a white minister, Mr. Neville, makes the effort to mold him to white values. Although Jimmie undergoes the traditional Aborigine initiation into manhood, entitling him to participate in the ancient system of exogamy by which the men of his tribe acquired mates, he chooses to marry a white woman in a Methodist church service. Under the guidance of Mr. Neville, he has sought marriage and employment with whites, but in spite of his sincere efforts at emulation, he is repeatedly abused and cheated: Employers such as Constable Farrell, who uses Jimmie as a tracker, and farmer Healy, who hires him to build fences, cheat him out of wages his labor has earned fair and square. His wife,

Gilda, it turns out, was pregnant with a white man's child when she married Jimmie.

Worse for Jimmie is the betrayal he experiences from his own people, who are crippled by the white man's alcohol and entrapped in the white man's institutions of patronage. The system of tribal and family obligations that he tries to honor leaves him disadvantaged in the white world where time and money are interdependent. His uncle Tabidgi takes his money for drink, and when Jimmie is pushed beyond endurance by the humiliations he endures from whites, Tabidgi helps him in killing the women of the Newby family. On the run, Jimmie and his half brother Mort take revenge on the Healy family. Soon the hue and cry has raised a small army of white men in pursuit of the two brothers. As these events unfold on the local scale, in the larger world Australia is suing to earn its independence among the nations of the world and sending soldiers to the doomed cause of the BOER WAR in South Africa, where another consequence of colonialism is creating a violent upheaval.

Jimmie's story winds to a tragic ending that does not deprive him of his dignity, although it suggests that there is little hope where two cultures so mismatched, so divided, come into violent conflict. Keneally arouses sympathy for the Aborigines, blaming white practices for the degradation of the Australian natives, but he also demonstrates that Aboriginal values contribute their share to the destruction of Jimmie Blacksmith. With neither side free of blame, the long-term prospects for mutual accommodation are bleak.

BIBLIOGRAPHY

Hamilton, K. G., ed. *Studies in the Recent Australian Novel.* St. Lucia: University of Queensland Press, 1978.

Pierce, Peter. *Australian Melodramas: Thomas Keneally's Fiction.* St. Lucia: University of Queensland Press, 1995.

Ramson, William Stanley. "*The Chant of Jimmie Blacksmith:* Taking Cognizance of Keneally." In *The Australian Experience: Critical Essays on Australian Novels.* Canberra: Australian National University, 1974.

CHATWIN, BRUCE (1940–1989) Originally recognized as an outstanding travel writer, Bruce Chatwin reinvented the travel narrative by mixing imaginative and autobiographical materials into his descriptions of locations. He was born on May 13, 1940, in the city of Sheffield, England, and educated at a PUBLIC SCHOOL. He did not go straight to college; instead, while still a teenager, he worked at Sotheby's auction house, beginning as a porter and quickly moving up to a senior staff position by the time he was 25. While there, he met an American woman—a descendant of a wealthy and well-traveled family—who shared his interest in travel; they were married in 1965. He left his position at Sotheby's and studied archaeology for a time at the University of Edinburgh. At the age of 33, he became a travel writer for the *Sunday Times,* but he resigned this position and headed for Patagonia, one of the most remote locations on the planet. The result of this exploration was the very successful travel book *In Patagonia* (1977), which won the HAWTHORNDEN PRIZE in 1978 and the E. M. Forster Award in 1979.

Chatwin's style blends topographic detail, local legend and history, folklore, philosophy, anthropology, imaginative elements, and autobiographical materials that may be fictional. His books *The Viceroy of Ouidah* (1980), about the slave trade in Dahomey and its long-lasting consequences, *On the Black Hill* (1982), set on the Welsh-English border, and *Utz* (1989; shortlisted for the BOOKER PRIZE), about a porcelain collector in Prague, all are generally classified as fiction; *On the Black Hill* won the WHITBREAD Book of the Year for First Novel award and the JAMES TAIT BLACK MEMORIAL PRIZE in 1982. Chatwin also called *The SONGLINES* (1987) a work of fiction, although some references classify it among his travel writings.

Chatwin was confined to a wheelchair in the last years of his brief life. He claimed that he was suffering from a rare bone marrow disease contracted during his travels, but in fact he had contracted AIDS in the years before this disease was very well understood and while it was still hysterically stigmatized; he hid this information even from his family until the very last days of his life. With his wife's assistance, he compiled a collection of short pieces, *What Am I Doing Here,* which was published in 1989, the year he died. Since his death, Paul THEROUX has published the book he and Chatwin wrote collaboratively, *Nowhere Is a Place: Travels in Patagonia* (1992); additionally, Chatwin's photographs and notebooks have been edited and published under the title *Far Journeys* (1993). Bruce Chatwin died at the age of 49 on January 18, 1989, recognized as one of the most innovative and original voices in 20th-century literature in English.

BIBLIOGRAPHY

Clapp, Susannah. *With Chatwin: Portrait of a Writer.* New York: Alfred A. Knopf, 1997.

Meanor, Patrick. *Bruce Chatwin.* Twayne's English Authors, 542. New York: Twayne Publishers, 1997.

Shakespeare, Nicholas. *Bruce Chatwin.* New York: Nan A. Talese, 1999.

CHESTERTON, G. K. (1874–1936)

One of the greatest prose stylists in the genre of the essay, Gilbert Keith Chesterton also wrote poetry, MYSTERY AND DETECTIVE FICTION, novels, literary criticism (he was especially opposed to the AESTHETICISM movement), journalism, biography, works of social, political, and religious philosophy, autobiography, and other forms of literature. He was born on May 29, 1874, in London. His childhood was a happy one, enlivened by his father's imaginative entertainments through storytelling. He attended PUBLIC SCHOOL as a day student at St. Paul's School and then enrolled at the Slade School of Art, although he did not take a degree. By 1895, he was writing reviews for publishers and soon found employment as a journalist—he thrived on the culture of the deadline, producing enough essays to fill 40 volumes. In the publishing district of Fleet Street, Chesterton was noted for his quick wit and his memorable aphorisms; as a conversationalist, he has been compared to Samuel Johnson, the great 18th-century man of letters. Chesterton was married in 1901, and in 1909 he and his wife moved to the London suburb of Beaconsfield, where they lived for the remainder of their lives.

Through his writing, Chesterton met Hilaire BELLOC, another prolific essayist and social commentator, and the two became lifelong friends. Chesterton was also a good friend of H. G. WELLS and George Bernard Shaw, even though Shaw caricatured Belloc and Chesterton as the "Chesterbelloc," an elephantine beast with outdated ideas. Together with Belloc, Chesterton advocated distributism, a kind of decentralized agrarian form of social and economic organization that was to be achieved by dividing all property into small units and distributing the ownership of it throughout the population. Chesterton was the president of the Distributist League, a competitor to the FABIAN SOCIETY for the attention of reform-minded activists. Belloc was a Catholic, and Chesterton converted to Catholicism in 1922. In their vision for a distributist future, the role of the church in political and economic life would resemble the dominance it had during the medieval period.

As a fiction writer, Chesterton is renowned for his short stories, especially the series of detective stories featuring Father Brown. His work as a mystery writer moved the genre toward a greater emphasis on the psychology and motivation of the criminal. He contributed to the formulation of the detective story as a puzzle in which the clues are presented to the investigator (and thereby to the reader) and the crime is solved upon the discovery of the perpetrator's identity. His novels, such as *The Napoleon of Notting Hill* (1904) and *The MAN WHO WAS THURSDAY* (1908), feature convoluted, unrealistic plots. Chesterton used the novel as a platform to expound his social and political ideas, as if he were writing a newspaper editorial or an analytical treatise. Thus, although Chesterton is one of the greatest writers of the EDWARDIAN ERA, he is not among its greatest novelists.

Chesterton suffered a physical and mental collapse in 1914 but soon returned to his work as vigorously as before. Critics generally see some decline in the quality of his writing after WORLD WAR I, when he concentrated more on analytical treatises than on creative efforts. G. K. Chesterton died on June 4, 1936, maintaining his prolific output to the end of his life.

BIBLIOGRAPHY

Belloc, Hilaire. *The Place of Gilbert Chesterton in English Letters.* London: Sheed & Ward, 1940.

Chesterton, G. K. *The Autobiography of G. K. Chesterton.* London: Sheed & Ward, 1936.

Finch, Michael. *G. K. Chesterton: A Biography.* San Francisco: Harper & Row, 1986.

Peters, Thomas C. *Battling for the Modern Mind: A Beginner's Chesterton,* St. Louis: Concordia Publishing House, 1994.

CHILD IN TIME, THE IAN MCEWAN

(1987) Winner of the WHITBREAD Book of the Year Award in 1987, this novel chronicles a father's tragic loss, his deep grief, and his reconciliation to the world of the living. The protagonist is Stephen Lewis, a successful writer of children's books. His life story is a simple and happy one: After a typical period of aimless wandering following the completion of his university studies, Stephen had had an unusual bit of luck when the manuscript he submitted to a leading publisher ended up on the desk of the children's editor. As a novel for adults, *Lemonade* would have been an undistinguished example of competent fiction, but as a book for young readers it was an extraordinary success. Stephen and his loving wife, Julie, a classical musician, are happily settled in London and have begun a financially comfortable and personally satisfying family life with the birth of a daughter, Kate. But at the age of three, Kate disappeared from the grocery story where her father had brought her along on a routine shopping trip. She had been snatched by an unknown stranger; no ransom note followed and no clue to her whereabouts could be found. Stephen and Julie are paralyzed in a suspended state of futile hopes and fruitless waiting, and in the meantime their marriage is falling apart as each spouse copes with his and her separate griefs.

The narrative opens two years later, when Stephen is still haunted by the search for his daughter that has become as integral to his life as breathing. With every step, he is looking for the five-year-old girl she would have become, even as he tries half-heartedly to return to some kind of normal life. His best friend, the publisher Charles Darke, figures at the center of the novel's subplot. While Stephen sinks into a numb despair, Charles enters into politics with unprecedented success. While Stephen and Julie separate, Charles and his wife, Thelma, a physicist, maintain a powerful bond. They try to draw Stephen out of his paralyzed waiting for Kate to return; Charles appoints Stephen as a member of a government commission on childhood, and for the first time in two years the bereaved father begins to venture away from the telephone at home. He even visits Julie at the woodland cottage to which she has retreated, and for a day their marriage seems to have a ghost of a chance of surviving.

Gradually, life imposes itself on Stephen's awareness. In one of the novel's most powerful scenes, he witnesses an accident on the highway and rescues a driver from the crushed wreckage of his truck. The survival of this stranger is a miraculous event, recounted in images of birth pangs and surrounded by inexplicable joy. Other key moments begin to reconnect Stephen to the progress of time, slowly extricating him from the infinite immobility of his grief. He witnesses a reversal in the life of Charles Darke, whose return to childhood ends in tragic petulance. Little by little, scenes of birth and death jolt Stephen from his catatonic state of waiting for Kate. Through his connection to the work of the commission, he rejoins the onward rush of the business of life. When an urgent call from Julie summons him to her side, he is finally ready to put his grief to rest and to embrace the challenges of getting on with the joys and pains of living. In an emotionally powerful and deeply moving conclusion, Stephen and Julie return to life, to love, and to their marriage.

Ian MCEWAN's quiet story emphasizes character development and symbolic imagery over complex plotting. In a simple story of loss and recovery, McEwan captures a tremendous depth of feeling and a wide range of experience at the personal level and in the larger social and political spheres as well. The third-person narrator focuses intently on Stephen's stunned life and his painful recovery, but doing so allows the remaining action of the story to rise to an unforeseen and yet perfectly natural climax. The novel's resolution restores hope and love to their proper places in life, suggesting that harmony restored at the personal level cannot but help to correct the bigger imbalances in the world as well.

BIBLIOGRAPHY

Malcolm, David. *Understanding Ian McEwan.* Understanding Contemporary British Literature Series. Columbia: University of South Carolina Press, 2002, 88–109.

Slay, Jack Jr. *Ian McEwan.* Twayne's English Authors Series, 518. New York: Twayne Publishers, 1996, 115–133.

CHILDHOOD'S END ARTHUR C. CLARKE

(1953) Set in the not-too-distant future, *Childhood's End* forecasts a future for the human race that will simultaneously be a transcendence and a termination as the last generation of children fulfill the destiny of the species.

Reflecting the tensions of the cold war, the novel opens at a test site for nuclear weapons. But as the crucial moment approaches, suddenly the sky is filled by what can only be an alien spacecraft. Within minutes, news flashes around the world announce that similar craft have appeared over Russian test sites and over every major city on every continent. The technology that put these craft in place is obviously vastly superior to anything the human race has achieved, and the whole world comes to a halt, waiting to see what will happen.

The announcement comes quickly. The visitors have no hostile intention toward the Earth and its inhabitants, but they cannot tolerate the continued testing of weapons that could be so destructive to the human race. The visitors intend to impose peace so that human beings can follow a previously unsuspected path of evolutionary development. Human culture can do whatever it wants to as long as it does not destroy itself. Beyond this, the visitors will not reveal what direction or purpose the human species will develop toward, but they do say that they themselves are in the service of a still more superior life form. These tidbits of knowledge leave more questions than answers, especially since the visitors will not reveal themselves.

Eventually, as human hostilities settle down and as the weapons of mass destruction are made inoperative, all but one ship dissolves from the Earth's skies. They had all been mere illusions projected from the one ship still hovering over the United Nations. Gradually, some limited contact with the visitors—the Overlords—is allowed, and the secretary-general of the UN travels regularly to the ship to converse with his contact there. But he never sees this other presence: The meeting room is set up with a glass between them, brightly lit on the visitor's side and darkened on the host's side to create a mirrored surface. Every word and tone exchanged between the secretary-general and the host Overlord is scrutinized all over the Earth as humans try to reassure themselves that this new force among

them is beneficial. Finally, the Overlords announce that they will reveal themselves and interact with human beings in 50 years. On that day, a craft lands, a door opens, and a voice invites a child to come in; then, with the child in his arms, a creature steps out who is indistinguishable from the ancient tales of demons, from the horns on his head to the long tail trailing behind. Even with 50 years to brace themselves, human beings are hardly ready for this.

The Overlords reveal little more about the fate of the human species, saying only that they have come to prepare the way for the one they serve. Just as they are Overlords on the Earth, this superior life form is a kind of Oversoul to the universe, and somehow it will play a part in the fate of the Earth. After the initial shock over their appearance subsides, the Overlords interact freely with humans as observers, attending social events and studying human culture. They seem to have a keen interest in cataloging alleged instances of paranormal activity as they continue to monitor their charges. Human society has reached new heights of achievement since the devastation and expense of war have been eliminated; nation-states are no longer important, and people experiment with new kinds of communities and new forms of social organization. And it is in just such an experimental artist colony located on an idyllic tropical island that the first signs emerge of where the next phase of human existence is headed. A child there terrifies her mother one day by amusing herself with a rattle that she is not touching. Somehow, the infant is controlling the toy with her mind, having bypassed the usual human dependence on the body. Soon more and more reports of these extraordinary mental abilities flood in, and soon it is apparent that nearly all children under a certain age have these mental powers.

But more important, these children lack something crucially human, since they have no use for or interest in their parents and siblings. Completely absorbed in the discovery and exercise of their mental powers, they are indifferent to family life. In some way, they are distinctly not human, even though they occupy, for the present at least, human bodies. The parents of such children are distraught, but there is nothing that can return these children to their ordinary state. Beyond their kinetic control of matter, is also becomes apparent that these new human consciousnesses are aware of one another even at remote distances and are gradually uniting themselves into stronger units, collaborating on greater control of the material world. This is the transformation the Overlords had been sent to foster and protect, and eventually they draw these children together on the continent of Australia, emptied for their use, where the children grow mentally stronger and more united.

The tragedy for those who are not part of this transformation—the parents and older siblings—soon becomes apparent, since no old-fashioned babies are being born. The generation of teens and adults that brought forth this new life form will be the last generation on Earth. The response to this terminal condition of the species runs from despair to wild abandon; some can find no reason to live, while others fling themselves into ever more dangerous recreations and sports. One daring person even stows away aboard an Overlord ship returning to its home world only to discover that there is no future for humans among these creatures, either. The intelligent universe is composed of the Oversoul; the Overlords, of various species, who serve it but will never be part of it; and the developing species who eventually produce the newest additions to the Oversoul and die out. Like salmon that spawn and die, the human race will have completed its mission and exhausted its purpose once the children are taken into the Oversoul. As a final act that demonstrates their readiness, the children destroy first the continent they are on and the Earth itself as they leave it. The Overlords have seen it all many times before and are condemned to continue seeing this spectacle eternally; the stowaway returns on the ship that will carry away the last Overlord supervisor, just in time to witness the end of the world, and, having no other place to go, he stays to be destroyed with it, the last human being in the universe.

Childhood's End is probably Arthur C. CLARKE's greatest novel. Although it is less well known than *2001: A SPACE ODYSSEY,* having never been made into a movie and a pop-culture phenomenon, it shares with that story Clarke's interest in where the human species may be going in the long run. Like the mentally powerful children of *Childhood's End,* the cosmic infant created when Dave Bowman is incubated in a cooling star is both a transcendence of human existence and the purpose toward which human effort has been moving all along without anyone's awareness of it. These novels constitute two of the most original examples of 20th-century SCIENCE FICTION written by an English-born author.

BIBLIOGRAPHY

Hollow, John. *Against the Night, the Stars: The Science Fiction of Arthur C. Clarke.* Athens, Ohio: Ohio University Press, 1987.

Reid, Robin Anne. *Arthur C. Clarke: A Critical Companion.* Westport, Conn.: Greenwood Press, 1997.

CHILDREN OF VIOLENCE DORIS LESSING (1952–1969)

The five volumes in this series include MARTHA QUEST (1952), A PROPER MARRIAGE (1954), A RIPPLE FROM THE STORM (1958), LANDLOCKED (1965), and The FOUR-GATED CITY (1969). Taking the series as a whole, critics rank this work as among the best of LESSING's fictions, exceeded only by The GOLDEN NOTEBOOK (1962).

The series follows the maturation of the protagonist, Martha Quest, so to a certain extent it is a BILDUNGSROMAN spread over many volumes. But because it covers such a large number of characters and such a large range of time—more than 40 years—it also meets the criteria for a ROMAN-FLEUVE. The series begins in psychological realism, but it also includes elements of social and political SATIRE, and by the end of the story the narrative comes to resemble an apocalyptic work of SCIENCE FICTION such as CHILDHOOD'S END. The series is also an important work for FEMINISM, since it is a powerful fictional exploration of the failure of marriage to provide fulfillment for all women. It is also a chronicle of left-wing concerns connected to CLASS and labor in the mid-20th century, since Martha becomes involved with activists who support the Communist Party. And since the novel opens in Africa, where Martha's parents have a farm established through COLONIALISM by a European power, the story also embraces issues of race conflict and cultural clash.

Lessing's series encapsulates the key struggles of the 20th century, but she also projects a new direction for the human race, hypothesizing that a shared or collective consciousness will be the next advance we must make—the next adaptation we must acquire. Starting from actual historical issues, she uses her fiction to articulate an evolutionary direction that would solve the problems of class, race, and gender by allowing human beings to transcend the limitations of individual perceptions of the material world, achieving a higher awareness through thought-powered psychic unity.

BIBLIOGRAPHY

Fishburn, Katherine. *The Unexpected Universe of Doris Lessing: A Study in Narrative Technique.* Westport, Conn.: Greenwood Press, 1985.

Rose, Ellen Cronan. *The Tree Outside the Window: Doris Lessing's Children of Violence.* Hanover, N.H.: University Press of New England, 1976.

Rubenstein, Roberta. *The Novelistic Vision of Doris Lessing: Breaking the Forms of Consciousness.* Urbana: University of Illinois Press, 1979.

Sprague, Claire, and Virginia Tiger, eds. *Critical Essays on Doris Lessing.* Boston: G. K. Hall, 1986.

CHRISTIE, AGATHA (1890–1976)

Born in England on September 15, 1890, to a well-off American father and an English mother, Agatha Christie was never formally educated until, at 16, she studied piano and voice in Paris. Not participating in a traditional program of schooling resulted in a somewhat isolated childhood, but Christie used her imagination to populate her world and began early to create characters (first in the form of other children) and narratives to go with them. Christie's fertile imagination eventually made her one of the most prolific authors of the 20th century: By the time of her death on January 12, 1976, she had published more than 80 books in the genres of MYSTERY AND DETECTIVE FICTION, romance, short fiction, poetry, memoir, drama, and one example of children's literature.

In 1914, Agatha Mary Clarissa Miller was married to Colonel Archibald Christie; the marriage ended in divorce in 1928 and produced one child, a daughter. When Colonel Christie announced that he had fallen in love with another woman, his wife disappeared for nine days: She checked into a resort hotel under the name of the woman her husband was seeing and entertained the other guests by playing the piano. Reports about her disappearance led to her being recognized, and in an embarrassing media circus, Colonel Christie retrieved his wife. A shy and retiring woman, she had suffered a nervous breakdown, and the publicity surrounding her return was so painful to her that she never mentioned this part of her life again, glossing over it in her autobiography.

During WORLD WAR I, in the early days of her first marriage, Christie worked in a hospital dispensary, and there she began to acquire the extensive knowledge of poisons that would be useful in her mystery-writing career. She also began developing a mystery novel featuring a Belgian detective, Hercule Poirot, and his assistant, Captain Hastings. Christie modeled these two loosely on Sherlock HOLMES and Dr. Watson; their first adventure, *The Mysterious Affair at Styles,* appeared in 1920 after receiving several rejections. The mystery genre was growing in popularity, and through a steady, intelligent, output, Christie became the lead writer in the genre and contributed to the shaping of the quintessential mystery format. She constructed inventive, intricate plots, and she communicated information about the case through dialogue rather than through narrative exposition. She played every imaginable variation on the formula she developed; for example, her most sensational early novel, *The Murder of Roger Ackroyd* (1926), features a murderer who narrates his own mystery and is revealed only in the ending after the reader is drawn into the game of looking everywhere else for the perpetrator. And in *Murder on the Orient Express,* the murderer turns out not to have a unified identity. In THE A. B. C. MURDERS, compelling narrative segments that look like clues actually misdirect the reader's attention from the mystery's solution, preserving suspense until the end.

In 1930, Christie married the archaeologist Max Mallowan and spent many summers with him on archaeological digs in the Middle East; her memoir of these travels, *Come, Tell Me How You Live,* appeared under the name A. C. Mallowan in 1946. The decade of the 1930s was particularly fruitful for Christie: With the establishment of a contented home life, she poured out mystery novels under several series, wrote romances under the pseudonym Mary Westmacott, and produced numerous plays. One of her favorite detectives, Miss Jane Marple, first appeared in 1930 in *Murder at the Vicarage.* Other recurring detectives included Tommy and Tuppence Beresford, Colonel Race, and Superintendent Battle. During WORLD WAR II, Christie again worked in a dispensary and continued her voluminous writing. The overall quality of her work declined somewhat after World War II; her last novel, *The Postern of Fate,* appeared in 1973 as her health was becoming frail. Christie received numerous awards during her life: In 1954, the Mystery Writers of America recognized her with a Grand Master Award; in 1956, she was named a Commander, Order of the British Empire; in 1961, she received an honorary doctorate from the University of Exeter; and in 1971, she was made a Dame Commander. She died quietly at her home in 1976 at the age of 85.

BIBLIOGRAPHY

Barnard, Robert. *A Talent to Deceive: An Appreciation of Agatha Christie.* New York: Dodd, Mead, 1980.

Gill, Gillian. *Agatha Christie: The Woman and Her Mysteries.* New York: Free Press, 1990.

Sanders, Dennis, and Len Lovalio, *The Agatha Christie Companion: The Complete Guide to Agatha Christie's Life and Work,* New York: Delacorte, 1984.

Sova, Dawn B. *Agatha Christie A to Z: The Essential Reference to Her Life and Writings.* New York: Facts On File, 1996.

CHRONICLES OF NARNIA, THE C. S. LEWIS (1950–1956)

The seven volumes of this series include (in the order finally preferred by the author) *The Magician's Nephew* (1955), *The Lion, the Witch, and the Wardrobe* (1950), *The Horse and His Boy* (1954), *Prince Caspian* (1951), *The Voyage of the* Dawn Treader (1952), *The Silver Chair* (1953), and *The Last Battle* (1956). The books are examples of Christian ALLEGORY for young adult readers.

Although *The Magician's Nephew* was not written first, it provides the "backstory" that prepares readers to better enjoy *The Lion, the Witch, and the Wardrobe,* the most famous volume in the series. Instead of the four Pevensie children, readers are introduced to Polly Plummer and Digory Kirke, two children living in adjoining row houses in London. One day, they enter an old door and find themselves in a nicely furnished study with Digory's uncle, Andrew Ketterley. He is delighted to have visitors; Uncle Andrew, it turns out, is a magician. He inherited a box of magic from his dying godmother, and with it he has constructed yellow rings to take their bearers to another world and green rings to bring them back.

Digory and Polly travel through the Wood Between the Worlds, a kind of pleasant switching yard filled with trees and a pool for each of the innumerable worlds beyond the wood. From there, they begin exploring these other worlds, and in the very first one, through their curiosity, they awaken a spellbound witch-queen, Jadis. She wants a living world to rule, and so she follows them back to Uncle Andrew's study. Digory realizes he has the power to get her away from this world by touching her as he puts on his yellow ring. Polly joins him, but when they leave through the power of the rings, they bring with them not only the witch but also the horse Strawberry she is riding, Uncle Andrew, and the cabby who owns the horse. In the wood again, they leap into another pool, planning to strand the witch in her old world.

They arrive instead in an empty world. The cabby sings a hymn to keep their spirits up, but soon it is eclipsed by a greater song, and the empty world is slowly transformed into Narnia. They are initially terrified to see that the singer who has brought about this transformation is a huge lion; as he keeps singing, however, more and more of the world comes to life, including a lamppost that grows from a piece of one the witch had brought along as a weapon. She runs away in terror, and the children see the lion select pairs of beasts, dwarves, satyrs, and other creatures as his followers. When all is ready he breathes over Narnia, endowing these beasts with the gift of speech.

Digory seeks out Aslan, as the lion is called, hoping that this lion can somehow save Digory's mother, who is dying. Aslan charges Digory with the task of bringing a fruit from a distant garden so that the seed may be planted in Narnia to fend off the witch's power. Digory succeeds in finding the garden and plucking the apple, but the witch is there as well, and she tempts him to eat the apple himself. The boy survives this temptation and takes the fruit to Aslan, who plants it. The tree grows up immediately, and Aslan gives Digory an apple from it for his mother. Digory obeys Aslan's instructions to dispose of the apple core and bury the magic rings. His mother recovers, and the seeds in the core grow into a fine tree that, many years later, provides the wood to build a wardrobe with the power to bring children to Narnia—the very wardrobe that first brings the Pevensie children to Narnia after Jadis has cast her frozen spell over the enchanted world of the Talking Beasts.

The pattern of the other books in the series is apparent in this volume: Innocent curiosity or pressing need brings unwitting children into contact with some magical connection to Narnia, and there the children have wonderful heroic adventures. Along the way, Aslan, an allegorical symbol of Christ, enacts or brings about some element of Christian doctrine: the creation, Garden of Eden, and temptation of man in *The Magician's Nephew;* the crucifixion and resurrection in *The Lion, the Witch, and the Wardrobe;* punishment of sin in *The Horse and His Boy;* renewal of faith (or perhaps the second coming) and conquest of evil in *Prince Caspian;* baptism in *The Voyage of the* Dawn Treader; rebirth in Christ in *The Silver Chair;* and the end of the world and final judgment in *The Last Battle.*

The main characters change slightly from story to story. In *The Lion, the Witch, and the Wardrobe,* Peter, Susan, Edmund, and Lucy Pevensie enter Narnia and stay for a lengthy adventure, ruling jointly as kings and queens, although no time has passed on Earth when they return. Then the action of *The Horse and His Boy* occurs entirely in Narnia, so no magic device is required to transport human children there; instead, the action restores Prince Cor to the royal family of Archenland with the help of Queen Susan, King Edmund, and Queen Lucy. In *Prince Caspian,* the story opens one Earth year after the children discovered the wardrobe's magic power, but this time they are at a train station when they are summoned back to Caer Paravel, their castle in Narnia, where so many years have passed that their kingdom has fallen into ruin and the true heir has been exiled.

A new protagonist is introduced in *The Voyage of the Dawn Treader:* Eustace Clarence Scrubb, a cousin of the Pevensies. This time, while Edmund and Lucy are visiting Eustace (Peter and Susan having grown a bit too old to go to Narnia), a picture of a ship in the playroom draws the three children back to Narnia. While they are there helping Caspian search to the east for Aslan's home, Eustace's greed turns him into a dragon, and only Aslan can restore him. Then in *The Silver Chair,* another new protagonist enters the story when Eustace, on his own, draws his schoolmate Jill Pole into Narnia as they pass through an ordinary door in the wall around their campus. They rescue Prince Rilian from his imprisonment in the chair of the title. Finally, in *The Last Battle,* Eustace and Jill are summoned to Narnia by Prince Tirian, the seventh descendant of King Rilian, and at a climactic moment Digory, Polly, Peter, Edmund, and Lucy join them (but not Susan, who is "no longer a friend to Narnia"). In the very end, they learn that their lives on Earth have ended in a terrible railway accident and that now they will stay with Aslan forever.

In each story, the narrator relates the events from a third-person omniscient point of view, although the narrator occasionally uses a self-referential pronoun such as "I." The tone of the narration is consistently friendly, seasoned with direct addresses to readers—using "you"—about how they would feel in a similar situation, for example. The allegorical treatment of Christian concepts is accomplished without real-world references to churches or particular religions; the children are always at play, at school, or on the way to school when they enter Narnia, and they are always engaged in the exercise of their imaginations when they cross into this other world. Aslan is never described as a divinity, but clearly he possesses divine and redemptive powers, as well as near-infinite mercy, for those who have faith in him.

Taken as a whole, LEWIS's allegory expands somewhat on the biblical story of creation, since he is explaining how not just the world or the universe came into being but also how multiple universes coexist in space and time, all under the care of a divine creator. Interestingly, artistic creativity plays a key role in Aslan's powers: He sings Narnia into existence, shaping matter through his musical art, in a manner similar to the way J. R. R. TOLKIEN describes Eru composing the music that creates the realm of space and time in *The Silmarillion*. Lewis and Tolkien were both INKLINGS, and Tolkien was instrumental in reconverting Lewis to Christianity—a connection that may be apparent in their use of a similar literary metaphor.

BIBLIOGRAPHY

Holbrook, David. *The Skeleton in the Wardrobe: C. S. Lewis's Fantasies: A Phenomenological Study.* Lewisburg: Bucknell University Press, 1991.

Manlove, Colin. The Chronicles of Narnia. *The Patterning of a Fantastic World.* New York: Twayne: 1993.

Myers, Doris T. "Growing in Grace: The Anglican Spiritual Style in *The Chronicles of Narnia.*" In *The Pilgrim's Guide: C. S. Lewis and the Art of Witness.* Edited by David Mills. Grand Rapids, Mich.: Eerdmanns, 1998, 185–202.

Schakel, Peter J. "The 'Correct' Order for Reading *The Chronicles of Narnia,*" *Mythlore: A Journal of J. R. R. Tolkien, C. S. Lewis, Charles Williams, and Mythopoeic Literature* 23 (Spring 2001): 53–64.

CHYMICAL WEDDING, THE LINDSAY CLARKE (1989)

Winner of the WHITBREAD Book of the Year Award in 1989, this novel combines aspects of romance fiction, HISTORICAL FICTION, and FANTASY to freshen the telling of a double set of complex relationships. Reminiscent of *The FRENCH LIEUTENANT'S WOMAN,* by John FOWLES, the novel moves between sets of characters in the present and the past but uses extensive metaphors drawn from magic and alchemy to describe those characters and suggest the relationships that develop among them.

The story begins in contemporary England with the blocked poet Michael Darken, the first-person narrator of the contemporary part of the plot, and the couple he meets, the former poet Edward Nesbit and his assistant Laura. An additional, historical layer of narrative arises from the research of Edward and Laura into the life of Louisa Agnew, the mid-19th-century ancestor of the current owner of Easterness Hall, Ralph Agnew. Edward and Ralph had had a homosexual affair when they were younger, and Edward had acquired fame from his poetry then, but now, like Michael, he finds himself blocked. Michael's marriage has fallen apart as his poetic inspiration has evaporated, and now he is seeking a respite in the summer cottage of his publisher, in the village dominated by the Gothic presence of Easterness. Gradually Michael becomes involved with the research Edward and Laura are conducting there, and also with the two of them as people to whom he is simultaneously attracted and repelled.

The historical layer of the story begins as a separate narrative thread recounting the work of Louisa Agnew on a treatise called *An Open Invitation to the Chymical Wedding.* Her father Henry is writing a poetic explanation of the practice of alchemy—a practice in which the Agnew family has long been involved. Their quiet world expands when a new vicar comes to the village, Edwin Frere. Marital discord soon dissolves the frail bonds of his marriage, and his wife leaves him for her family's home in Oxford, the seat of reason. By the time Edwin seeks out the companionship and then the passionate love of Louisa, the historical and contemporary narratives have become fused. Their pairing leads to a parallel union of Michael and Laura, with the hint of possession or psychic transfer from past to present. The resulting tensions between Michael and Edward nearly lead to violence, just as the inner tensions of Edwin Frere, due to sexual guilt and self-recriminations, lead to a violent act in his world.

In both worlds, however, there is an unblocking of creative potential: Writers tap new wellsprings of inspiration and words flow forth again. In Louisa's repressive world, her frank portrayals of the sexual imagery of alchemy leads to the destruction of her work, while in the modern world, Laura finds herself set free to shape her own destiny. Enriching both of these stories is the imaginative use of the language of alchemy to elucidate characters and motivate plot actions. Lindsay CLARKE mixes several strong reagents in this absorbing and passionate story, precipitating a double climax and resolution to satisfy both levels of his narrative structure.

BIBLIOGRAPHY

Lund, Mark F. "Lindsay Clarke and A. S. Byatt: The Novel on the Threshold of Romance," *Deus Loci: The Lawrence Durrell Journal* 2 (1993): 151–159.

Sikorska, Liliana. "Mapping the Green Man's Territory in Lindsay Clarke's *The Chymical Wedding*," *Year's Work in Medievalism* 17 (2002): 97–106.

CLARKE, ARTHUR C. (1917–   )

Successful as a scientist, as an underwater explorer, and as a science fiction writer, Arthur C. Clarke is the only 20th-century author to have a celestial zone named after him: The "Clarke Belt," 22,300 miles above Earth, is the location of satellites in geostationary orbits (i.e., they remain above the same location on Earth as they also orbit it, and they have direct sight of each other), and Arthur C. Clarke essentially invented it in 1945 in a scientific article entitled "Extra-Terrestrial Relays." At the time, his highest educational degree was the equivalent of an American high-school diploma.

Born on December 16, 1917, in Minehead, England, Arthur Charles Clarke began work as an auditor at the age of 19 because he could not afford a university education, continuing in that job until 1941. He was already an amateur scientist, having constructed his own telescope and used it to study the moon. He joined the British Interplanetary Society, a group of scientists and enthusiasts who advocated space exploration and worked on problems associated with space travel, serving as president in 1946–47 and 1950–53. When WORLD WAR II began, Clarke joined the Royal Air Force and worked on the new electromagnetic technology of radar (an acronym for "radio detecting and ranging").

Like many demobilized soldiers, after the war Clarke pursued undergraduate studies. He matriculated at King's College in London and earned a degree in physics and mathematics in 1948. But he had already published science fiction stories before 1945, and instead of following a career in science, he began writing seriously and prolifically when he finished school. His first efforts did not succeed financially, and so he worked as an assistant editor of *Physics Abstracts*. But when his 1952 nonfiction book *The Exploration of Space* became the first work of popular science featured as a Book-of-the-Month Club option, and when *CHILDHOOD'S END* sold well in 1953, Clarke became a full-time writer. He also married in 1953; the marriage ended in divorce in 1964.

During the 1950s, Clarke expanded his interests from the unexplored realm of outer space to the nearly equally unexplored realm beneath the sea, developing an interest in scuba diving. He published a series of nonfiction and fiction books about oceans, coral reefs, and underwater exploration, and he moved to Sri Lanka, where he has continued to live. But when he was paralyzed in a 1962 accident, he was forced to give up diving, although he retained his interest in the world's oceans.

Clarke recovered his mobility and began working with the film director Stanley Kubrick on a science fiction film. Kubrick approached Clarke for ideas, and Clarke suggested that they expand his 1951 story "The Sentinel" into a film-length narrative. The project became the film and novel that are both entitled *2001: A SPACE ODYSSEY* (1968), generally regarded as the most important science fiction film ever made. Clarke lived at the bohemian Chelsea Hotel in New York City while he was working on the novel; his neighbors there included American literary artists such as Allen Ginsberg and Arthur Miller. The collaboration between Clarke and Kubrick was unusual, since both had well-established reputations in their own artistic spheres. It did not proceed without clashes of personality and vision, but in the end it produced two distinctive works of art on the screen and in print, each bearing the hallmark style of its main creator.

The success of the movie and the book led to a multibook publishing contract for Clarke, and in the 1970s he worked on the Rama series. He was the sole author of *Rendezvous with Rama* (1973), which won all the major prizes offered for science fiction writing that year: the Hugo, the Nebula, the John W. Campbell Memorial Award, and the British Science Fiction Award. The book sold well and pleased critics, too, with its imaginative descriptions of a vast uninhabited alien spaceship and the technologies that sustain it. Several sequels followed, cowritten with Gentry Lee and others; variations on a Noah's-ark theme, they continued to explore imaginative new ideas speculating on the other intelligent creatures that might inhabit the universe, but they did not equal the success of the first book in the series.

During the 1980s, Clarke became something of a television personality, hosting programs featuring investigative science and sheer speculation, *Arthur C. Clarke's Mysterious World* (1980) and *Arthur C. Clarke's World of Strange Powers* (1984), and he lectured extensively in the United States and Britain. He also began writing sequels to *2001: A Space Odyssey,* producing *2010: Odyssey Two* (1982), *2061: Odyssey Three* (1988), and *3001: The Final Odyssey* (1997). In these continuations of the story, Clarke updates the technological aspects, explains HAL's unexpected breakdown, demonstrates the function of the mysterious monoliths, and even resuscitates Frank Poole when his frozen body is discovered still following its initial trajectory in the outer solar system.

In the 1990s, Clarke continued producing a steady stream of novels, writing both individually and in collaboration with other science fiction authors. He has diversified his subject matter to include the subgenre of disaster fiction in *The Hammer of God* (1993) and *Richter 10* (1996). He continues to live in Sri Lanka, serving as chancellor of the University of Moratuwa since 1979. Now that the technology exists that long ago he speculated would one day expand human capabilities—the personal computer and satellite communication—he stays in touch with the wider world while enjoying his remote home. He has received numerous prizes, awards, honorary doctorates, and fellowships. In 1989, he was named a Commander of the Order of the British Empire, and in 1998 he was knighted. His work to benefit human life has been recognized by the United Nations, and he was nominated for the Nobel Peace Prize in 1994. In 2000, as the millennium turned, a European communication satellite named for Clarke was launched into orbit. Clarke remains optimistic about the future of humankind, and he has provided readers with several provocative visions of the excellence and even the transcendence that we might yet attain.

BIBLIOGRAPHY

Clarke, Arthur. *Astounding Days: A Science Fictional Autobiography.* New York: Bantam Books, 1989.

McAleer, Neil. *Arthur C. Clarke: The Authorized Biography.* Chicago: Contemporary Books, 1992.

Olander, Joseph D., and Martin Harry Greenburg, eds. *Arthur C. Clarke.* New York: Taplinger, 1977.

Rabkin, Eric S. *Arthur C. Clarke.* West Linn, Oreg.: Starmont House, 1979.

CLARKE, LINDSAY (1939–   )

The author of *The* CHYMICAL WEDDING, winner of the WHITBREAD Book of the Year Award in 1989, was born Victor Lindsay Clarke on August 14, 1939, in Halifax, Yorkshire, England. He attended King's College, Cambridge, and graduated in 1961 with a B.A. degree (with honors) in English. Also in 1961, he was married to Sara Pattinson; the couple divorced in 1972. From 1962 to 1965, Clarke served as a teacher in Ghana, and upon his return to England he taught at colleges in Great Yarmouth and Norwich. He has worked full-time as a writer since 1978. In 1980, Clarke married Phoebe Clare Harris.

In 1987, Clarke published *Sunday Whiteman,* his first novel. In addition to *The Chymical Wedding,* a kind of psychic example of romance fiction, he has published *Alice's Masque* (1994) and *Parzival and the Stone From Heaven* (2001). His fiction frequently combines elements of FANTASY FICTION and romance, bringing new readers to both genres.

BIBLIOGRAPHY

"Lindsay Clarke." Available online. URL: http://www.fixstudio.com/lindsayclarke/. Accessed on June 14, 2004.

Moseley, Merritt. *British Novelists Since 1960.* Fourth Series. Detroit: Gale Group, 2001.

CLASS

An aspect of human socioeconomic organization that has been intimately connected with the theories of Marxism in the 19th and 20th centuries, *class* refers to the categories human beings use in order to separate themselves into various degrees of privileged and marginalized sectors as determined by wealth. The related term *status group* refers more specifically to categories based on achievement or birth. The British class system combines aspects of both class and status categories. It is hierarchical, ranging from the nation's monarch and aristocrats with inherited titles who form (along with any extremely wealthy, untitled individuals) the upper class, to the categories of commoners such as the gentry, the yeomanry in rural areas and the middle class in urban areas, and the working class. But it has traditionally been a system tolerant of some degree of social mobility: Commoners can acquire titles by marriage, merit, or purchase, and aristocrats can become commoners as well, generally by choice or by poverty.

The most privileged sector of English society is generally identified by the inheritance of aristocratic titles that are usually associated with the ownership of vast estates and the performance of certain civic duties. This organizational mode has its roots in medieval feudalism, a political and economic system in which dominant lords accepted the fealty of vassal peasants and tradesmen, the lord providing protection while the vassals provided goods and services, primarily of an agricultural nature. Aristocrats gradually became organized into ranks under the authority of a monarch. The inherited ranks of the English aristocracy include the titles (in increasing prestige) of baronet (abbreviated "bt." or "bart." in older works), addressed as "Sir," and viscount, earl, marquess, and duke, all addressed as "Lord." The wife of anyone holding one of these titles is addressed as "Lady." Baronets are not peers of the realm and do not sit in the House of Lords, even though their title is inherited. The title of knight, addressed like baronets as "Sir," is bestowed for the lifetime of the honoree or until the monarch revokes it.

Awareness of class elements is essential in appreciating British literature, so thoroughly does it permeate every aspect of social life. The order in which people are seated at a dining table, which person may go first through a door, what authority an individual may expect to wield over others, and which signs of respect are due to which ranks are all routine considerations in daily life as represented in fiction. In the 20th century, the resistance to this system also appears as authors from working class backgrounds make their voices heard, especially after the end of World War II. In the case of writers from former colonial areas, the awareness of British class customs may be intermixed with colonial history and local social customs, yielding even more complex attitudes toward issues of class.

BIBLIOGRAPHY

Giddens, Anthony, and David Held, eds. *Classes, Power, and Conflict: Classical and Contemporary Debates*. Berkeley: University of California Press, 1982.

Marx, Karl. *Selected Writings in Sociology and Social Philosophy*. New York: McGraw-Hill, 1964.

Vanneman, Reeve, and Lynn Weber Cannon. *The American Perception of Class*. Philadelphia: Temple University Press, 1987.

CLEA **LAWRENCE DURRELL (1960)** Volume four in the series known collectively as *The Alexandria Quartet,* this novel is once again related from the first-person point of view of Darley, the English writer who narrated the first and second volumes, *Justine* and *Balthazar,* respectively. The third volume, *Mountolive,* features a third-person narrator; its events clarify for readers some of the mysteries developed in the first two. Darley, however, has been hiding away on a Greek island after betraying Melissa, his lover, and Nessim, his best friend, through an obsessive affair with Nessim's wife, Justine. But he has been paid back in his own coin, since Nessim and Melissa conceived a daughter born shortly before Melissa dies, and since Nessim, Justine, and other friends of Darley, if Balthazar is to be believed, played Darley for a fool and used him as a patsy. Darley has taken Melissa's child with him to shelter her until Nessim should summon them both back to Alexandria, and in the opening pages of *Clea,* that summons comes.

World War II has begun in the meantime, and Darley returns to an Alexandria under bombardment and must slip into the harbor in a risky venture. Life in the town goes on as usual in spite of the war, but Justine remains a shadow over his mind until he sees her again and discovers that he is free of his obsession for her. Darley and Clea are slowly drawn together into a love affair that surpasses Darley's emotional experiences with either Melissa or Justine. He begins to be healed of the pain that drove him away from Alexandria. They visit the rooms where their old friend Scobie lived— yet another ambiguous individual who may have used Darley for his own clandestine ends. Through the mysterious workings of Alexandrian religion, a shrine has grown up around the bathtub in which Scobie had once brewed a vast quantity of booze—enough to get his entire neighborhood drunk. Darley and Clea witness a procession to the shrine, enthralled by the strange contrast between the man's life and the misshapen memory of it that has developed because of the shrine. This discrepancy echoes a key theme for Darley, whose memory of events during his earlier stay is always at odds with the reports of others.

In a riveting climax, Darley, Clea, and Balthazar take a boat of Nessim's to go skin-diving in the pleasant, secluded cove where a derelict boat lies on the bottom. An accident leads to a life-or-death situation that will irrevocably change the course of a life even in the event of survival. The possessive allure of Alexandria—the spell it casts over its residents and its visitors—continues to hold sway over Darley and Clea as they explore the depths of love and art and puzzle out the mysteries of the reality that lies intangibly beneath the bedazzling appearances of the world.

BIBLIOGRAPHY

Begnal, Michael H., ed. *On Miracle Ground: Essays on the Fiction of Lawrence Durrell.* Cranbury, N.J.: Associated University Presses, 1990.

Friedman, Alan Warren. *Lawrence Durrell and* The Alexandria Quartet: *Art for Love's Sake.* Norman: University of Oklahoma Press, 1970.

CLEAR LIGHT OF DAY ANITA DESAI (1980)

Using a third-person omniscient point of view, this four-part novel follows the four siblings of the Das family of Old Delhi. The eldest son is Raja; now living in Hyderabad and married to a Muslim woman, Benazir, he has become the heir to her wealthy father, the former neighbor (and landlord) of the Das's, Hyder Ali Sahib. The eldest daughter is Bim (also called Bimla and Bim-*masi* by her nieces), a college professor of history who has never married, but who once was courted by Dr. Biswas, a Bengali who attended Raja (for tuberculosis) and Mira-*masi* (for alcoholism-induced delirium tremens) during the summer of independence and the partition of Pakistan, 1947. The third child is Tara, who escaped into marriage to Bakul, a diplomat, that same summer, and who is now the mother of two daughters of traditional marriageable age. The baby of the family is Baba, born late in his mother's life when she suffered from severe diabetes, and who is probably autistic or mildly mentally handicapped, and who is now Bim's dependent in the house where they all were born. The father of these siblings was the part owner of an insurance company; their mother loved playing bridge at the Roshanara Club. Both parents, however, were distant and cold with their children, employing instead an impoverished cousin (Mira) to watch over them. Other neighbors include the Misras, a middle-class family of loutish brothers and two spinster sisters, Jaya and Sarla, who support the family with dancing lessons for girls.

In the opening chapter, Tara and Bakul arrive to visit before going on to the wedding of Raja's daughter. The main characters are introduced through conversations the sisters carry on after many years apart; these conversations establish the underlying tensions between and among the siblings that came to a climax in the fateful summer of 1947. Chapter two returns the narrative to that summer; it was a traumatic year for India and a disastrous one as well for the Das family. The parents die (the mother first); Raja contracts tuberculosis; Mira-*masi* dissolves into alcoholism as the burdens on her increase; and Tara retreats to the neighbors' house and meets Bakul, then marries him and they immediately depart to diplomatic postings abroad. Dr. Biswas's courtship of Bim is a disaster because of his nervous subjugation to a domineering mother (he is her only child and she is a widow). Bim is too strong for these kinds of relationships. In fact, she is the only stable family member that terrible summer, and she winds up making choices that sacrifice her chances of establishing a family of her own. Chapter three takes readers still further back to the period when Baba was born too late in his mother's life to be fully formed and functioning when he is born. Baba's history is depressing, as his limitations become more and more apparent. The girls are being suffocated by the dullness of school—Bim's intelligence exceeds the demands of the curriculum provided to girls, and Tara is indifferent to education.

The most difficult and damaging transformation is the estrangement between Bim and Raja that develops as he matures into a self-absorbed young man, writing poetry and seeing himself as a future hero. In college, he refuses to support the Hindu extremists advocating violence toward Muslim Indians such as Hyder Ali Sahib, and he makes the mistake of openly expressing his support for the partition of India and Pakistan. His attachment to the Hyder Ali family steadily increases, especially as his mother fades into death, followed quickly by his father. He sees his wealthy poetry-loving Muslim landlord as a role model in the absence of a strong father figure. Eventually, everyone escapes but Bim and Baba: Mira-*masi* into death; Raja to Hyderabad and eventually, through marriage, into the Hyder Ali family; Tara into marriage and international travel with Bakul. Bim enrolls in graduate studies and excels in her work, eventually receiving an appointment as a faculty member at a nearby college. But she is trapped in the family home among the memories and disappointments that fill the old house, and Baba will never be able to survive without her. She both envies and resents Raja and Tara even as she tries to believe her life to be satisfactory.

Chapter four returns to the present of the story. Bim must learn to forgive Raja and Tara and accept some responsibility for the choices she made. Tara's presence has stirred up the past, and the sisters have read over Raja's old poems and the letter that finally estranged Bim from him. Bim has reached the end of her patience for the burdens placed on her; after expressing some rage against Baba, suggesting that she may have to send him to live with Raja, she is able to check her frustration and anger, realizing that she must contribute something to heal the rift in the family. Her simple brother is not able to hold a grudge for her outburst, and she determines to forgive Raja. She refuses to attend the wedding, but she asks Tara to invite Raja and his family to visit her and Baba at the old home they grew up in.

On one level, the story of the Das family works as a metaphor for India itself in the early days of independence. The rift in the family parallels the rift between India and Pakistan. But the story is also a carefully rendered example of psychological realism, with a special care to represent the limited options that Indian women have to choose from. The characters' disrupted lives mirror the political disruptions of the nation, but they are also fully rounded individuals with feelings grounded in past experiences that the writer brings to life.

BIBLIOGRAPHY

Chatterji, Partha. "The Nationalist Resolution of the Woman Question." *In Recasting Women: Essays in Indian Colonial History.* Edited by Kumari Sangari and Sudesh Vaid. New Brunswick, N.J.: Rutgers University Press, 1989.

Hashmi, Alamgir. "A Reading of Anita Desai's *Clear Light of Day,*" *International Fiction Review* 10 (1983): 56–58.

Jain, Jasbir. "Airing the Family Ghosts: Anita Desai's *Clear Light of Day,*" *World Literature Written in English* 24 (1984): 416–422.

CLOCKWORK ORANGE, A ANTHONY BURGESS (1962)

An innovative and violent three-part novel that formed the basis for an equally provocative 1971 FILM ADAPTATION of the same name, *A Clockwork Orange* portrays a DYSTOPIAN near-future world. Alex, a teenager who leads a small gang on violent forays against those weaker than themselves, lives with his parents in a faceless block of public housing. Alex and his followers speak a peculiar slang that Anglicizes Russian terms, suggesting a possible result of the cold war that was at its height when Burgess composed this story. They beat up old men and brawl with opposing gangs, and for a special thrill they break into the home of a mild-mannered writer, rape his wife, and beat him so badly he is crippled. On his own, Alex entices two teenage girls to his room for an orgy to the accompaniment of Beethoven's Ninth Symphony. When his gang members challenge his leadership, he forces them to back down but carries through with the robbery they planned without him. The elderly woman whose home they invade manages to call the police and attempts to defend herself; Alex accidentally kills her just before his gang betrays him to the police.

In the middle part of the story, Alex is in prison. In order to minimize his stay, he willingly becomes a well-behaved prisoner, spending time with the chaplain. When he learns of the Ludovico Technique, a method of behavioral conditioning designed to eradicate violent impulses in convicted criminals, he volunteers to become a test subject. The transformation works, but it deprives Alex of his free will, as the chaplain had warned him it would. Additionally, it conditions him to become ill at the sound of Beethoven's symphonies, thereby depriving him of one of his greatest pleasures. He is released back into the world two years after he committed his crimes, a completely new person.

In the novel's last section, Alex experiences the violence that he had dealt out to others in the first part, and he is helpless to defend himself from it. His parents reject him, having acquired a paying lodger, and he encounters his former victims as he roams his old haunts in isolated misery. As for his old friends and enemies, some of them are now policemen, and upon rescuing him from a beating, they carry him out to the country and beat him up themselves. Lost and brutalized, Alex stumbles upon the cottage of the writer he had crippled, whose wife had died after being raped by Alex's gang. Alex's face is recognizable from news coverage about the Lodovico Technique, and his voice, with its distinctive nadsat slang, seals the writer's recognition of his tormentor. He has Alex locked in a room and tortured with classical music. Eventually, Alex's conditioning is reversed through further agonizing procedures.

The novel exists in two editions: The American edition ends with Alex's violent fantasies restored along with his ability to enjoy Beethoven's symphonies, while the editions published in the rest of the world include a further chapter. In this ending, Alex encounters one of his gang members who is married, holding down a job, and speaking standard English; he recognizes that his teenage ways are outdated, supplanted by a younger generation, and imagines himself settled into domestic conventionality. The American version (and the film version) present a bleak, nihilistic view of Alex's future role in the world, while the other suggests the possibility of self-willed reform and redemption in an acceptable way of life.

Anthony BURGESS discussed his intentions for this novel at some length, emphasizing the importance of free will in the story's construction. Alex first chooses to be evil, and then in prison he chooses to be good, but after the behavioral conditioning he is no longer making his own choices. He has been dehumanized and made into an organic automaton—the clockwork orange of the title. Burgess asserts that the freely chosen life, even the *evil* freely chosen life, is superior to the passive existence of the automaton. Alex is no longer a moral agent after his treatment, and therefore his "good behavior" is only an illusory good for society.

BIBLIOGRAPHY

Mathews, Richard. *The Clockwork Universe of Anthony Burgess.* San Bernardino, Calif.: Borgo Press, 1978.

Petix, Esther. "Linguistics, Mechanics, and Metaphysics: *A Clockwork Orange.*" In *Anthony Burgess.* Edited by Harold Bloom. New York: Chelsea House, 1987.

Ray, Philip E. "Alex Before and After: A New Approach to Burgess' *A Clockwork Orange.*" In *Critical Essays on Anthony Burgess.* Edited by Geoffrey Aggeler. Boston: G. K. Hall, 1986.

COETZEE, J. M. (1940–)

An internationally respected writer from South Africa, J. M. Coetzee has won numerous awards for his fiction; he is one of two authors (with the Australian writer Peter Carey) to have won the BOOKER PRIZE twice, in 1983 for *The LIFE AND TIMES OF MICHAEL K,* and in 1999 for *DISGRACE.* In 2003, J. M. Coetzee's literary achievement was honored with the NOBEL PRIZE in literature.

Born in Cape Town on February 9, 1940, into an educated English-speaking family descended from Dutch Afrikaaners, John Michael Coetzee attended the University of Cape Town, earning a bachelor's degree in 1960 and a master's degree in 1963. He began his working life as a computer programmer, employed first by IBM in London, but he also continued his academic studies, earning a doctorate at the University of Texas at Austin in 1969. In 1968, he was appointed to an assistant professorship at the State University of New York at Buffalo, where he remained until 1971. He has also held appointments at the University of Cape Town, Johns Hopkins University, and Harvard University. Coetzee was married in 1963 and divorced in 1980; the couple have two children.

Coetzee published his first fiction, *Dusklands,* a collection of two novellas, in 1974. The two stories in *Dusklands, The Vietnam Project* and *The Narrative of Jacobus Coetzee,* both illustrate the author's concern for the violence that frequently results from the volatile combination of cultural disparity and imperialist aggression, but they are widely separated in setting and plot. In 1977, his novel *In the Heart of the Country* (also known as *From the Heart of the Country*) received the CNA Literary Award; the story examines the simultaneous attraction and repulsion associated with racial inequity, but does so from the perspective of a woman descending into derangement. In 1980, *Waiting for the Barbarians* also received the CNA Award along with the JAMES TAIT BLACK MEMORIAL PRIZE and the Geoffrey Faber Award. The novel revisits the theme of imperialism and racism, relating the story of a magistrate in a remote province who is brutalized by the army "defending" the EMPIRE; the barbarism of the title, it turns out, is not limited to peoples of less developed cultures. Two years later, in 1982, *The Life and Times of Michael K* was equally successful.

Coetzee has also written *Foe* (1987), a retelling of Daniel Defoe's tale of *Robinson Crusoe* (and an example of INTERTEXTUALITY); *The Age of Iron* (1990), about an elderly white South African woman who comes to recognize the horrors of apartheid as she is dying of cancer, and *The Master of Petersburg* (1994), a fiction featuring the Russian author Dostoevsky as its protagonist. Additionally, he has translated works in German, French, Dutch, and Afrikaans, and produced several volumes of nonfiction, including collections of essays and an autobiography. Coetzee continues to live and write in South Africa.

BIBLIOGRAPHY

Attwell, David. *J. M. Coetzee: South Africa and the Politics of Writing.* Berkeley: University of California Press, 1993.

Head, Dominic. *J. M. Coetzee.* Cambridge: Cambridge University Press, 1998.

Huggan, Graham, and Stephen Watson, eds. *Critical Perspectives on J. M. Coetzee.* New York: St. Martin's Press, 1996.

Kossew, Sue, ed, *Critical Essays on J. M. Coetzee.* New York: G. K. Hall, 1998.

COLD COMFORT FARM STELLA GIBBONS (1932)

This delightfully droll COMIC NOVEL follows the adventures of Flora Poste, a proper young lady of modern notions, who finds herself alone in the world at the death of her parents. Since she is not yet ready for marriage and not willing to sacrifice her time for mere money, she writes to all her family members seeking a suitable refuge. The mysterious Starkadders of Cold Comfort Farm are willing and able to take her in; Judith Starkadder's letter of reply alludes darkly to Flora's "rights" and to some wrong done to her late father long ago. The prospect is hardly inviting, but the free room and board is well within her means and will allow her to spend her tiny inheritance on visits to London rather than sustenance. This arrangement allows the author to make both country and city customs the object of her gentle Horatian SATIRE, and with each new character added to Flora's experience, new targets arise. Even literature and literary writers come under scrutiny: The novel is appended to a fictional introductory letter that promises to mark especially fine examples of writing with asterisks—the passages so noted are all examples of purple prose.

Flora is an acolyte of the Higher Common Sense, and upon her arrival at Cold Comfort Farm she sees that she has come to a place direly in need of her ministrations. Cousin Judith is morose and clearly enamored of her second son, Seth, a ravishingly handsome young man whose only love is the movies. His older brother Reuben, however, is a competent, born farmer, devoted to Cold Comfort and hostile to Flora at first, imagining that she has come to take the farm from him, although eventually he falls so far under her sway as to propose marriage as a way of keeping her on. The father of Seth and Reuben is Amos Starkadder, an itinerant fire-and-brimstone preacher of the Quivering Brethren—the sermon Flora attends is a send-up of "low church" excess. The only young woman on the place is Elfine, who is in love with a local scion of the fox-hunting class, Dick Hawk-Monitor of Hautcouture Hall, but her poetry-writing ways and bohemian dress make her completely unacceptable in that proper world. And ruling invisibly over the Starkadder clan is the ancient recluse Aunt Ada Doom—she who saw something nasty in the woodshed as a young girl and who has been banking on the emotional currency of that experience ever since. Flora determines to tidy up all these problems at Cold Comfort Farm, bringing fulfillment to each of these characters, sometimes in unexpected but imaginative ways.

Related by a third-person omniscient narrator, this story achieves its comic effect by the combination of likeable rustic yokels, mildly dysfunctional personalities, and urbane young people. The descriptions are vividly detailed, right down to the intoxicating sukebind flowers that drive young women to surrender to their passions. The primary function of the plot and even the dialogue is to present new topics for the narrator's satiric review; each is dispatched cleverly. The amusing dialogue is archly witty, and since the narrator comments on the disharmony between characters' spoken words and their actual thoughts, readers can stay attuned to the deeper attitudes lurking beneath surface pleasantries.

BIBLIOGRAPHY

Ariail, Jacqueline-Ann. "Cold Comfort from Stella Gibbons," *Ariel: A Review of International English Literature* 9, no. 3 (1978): 63–73.

Hammill, Faye. "*Cold Comfort Farm,* D. H. Lawrence, and English Literary Culture Between the Wars," *Modern Fiction Studies* 47, no.4 (2001): 831–854.

COLLECTOR, THE JOHN FOWLES (1963)

When Ferdinand Clegg, a butterfly collector, turns his attention to human beings, the results are disastrous for Miranda Grey, the young woman he stalks and "collects" to assuage his obsession for her.

Clegg has led a less than satisfactory life; he has been reared by his aunt and uncle, together with their unmarriageable daughter, Mabel. His father was killed in a car accident when he was two, and his mother had then abandoned him to her late husband's older sister. His uncle treats him kindly, taking him on frequent fishing trips and supporting his nephew's growing obsession with collecting butterflies. But he died of a stroke when Clegg was 15, leaving him with the two women. He had served a while in the army and then found a job, but his life-changing event had occurred the day he won a sizable sum in the lottery. He quit his job and sent his aunt and cousin off on a cruise to Australia, where some of the family had settled. Then he devoted his attention entirely to Miranda.

As an experienced collector, Clegg knows how to watch and wait and plan. He assembles everything he needs, purchasing an isolated house with an extensive multiroomed cellar. He buys a van and invests in camera equipment. He decorates the cellar, turning the most remote part of it into a cozy prison, then learns every detail of Miranda's schedule. His attachment to her had begun while she was still in the English equivalent of a high school in his hometown. She had even done business with him at his old job. But Clegg is not an ordinary man with ordinary drives and desires: He does not court Miranda and take the chance of the rejection he is certain he will receive. He prefers to collect her. She is too fine to accept him willingly, but he is still confident of his ability to possess her. Eventually, he captures her and drags her home to his cellar, keeping her there several months until she dies, possibly of pneumonia.

Although Clegg prepares his prison and plans his capture in flawless detail, he does not have a clear story as to what will happen once he has collected Miranda. He has bad thoughts that he tries to keep pushed down, and he looks at pornography with a notion to take pictures of Miranda. At first he thinks he can be satisfied with ordinary pictures. And sometimes he imagines that Miranda will inevitably come to feel for him the way he feels for her, and they will find true, voluntary love. But he has virtually no experience with living, breathing, talking women, and his own responses to his captive are more extreme that he had expected them to be.

At first, Clegg tries to appease Miranda with every material object that might make her happy. She had been an art student in her real life, and so he brings her everything for drawing she might need. And Miranda perceives that she has enough power over him to demand and receive any material comforts she can imagine. He buys the finest materials she asks for, and the books, and the music; he learns to cook and provides the healthy foods she requests prepared the way she likes them. But once she is in the cellar, he will not allow her to have any contact with the outside world. She cannot read newspapers or watch television, and she cannot send a message to her family even to tell them that she is alive and well. Clegg sees their appeals in the papers or on TV, but their suffering doesn't move him. Oddly, her suffering doesn't move him, either. He is obsessed with her, but the fact that he has destroyed her life to possess her makes no difference to him.

Miranda tries everything and finally wins a concession in being allowed outside, under his supervision, at night in the backyard. She waits for her opportunity and lashes out, hoping to escape and run for her freedom. But she only manages to wound him, and after that the conditions of her imprisonment become more severe. Eventually, she wins him back and is allowed into the house for a change of scene, but she cannot stop trying to escape. And finally she tries to earn her freedom by satisfying his desire to photograph her in degrading ways, but none of these stratagems works. When she becomes ill, he is afraid to seek medical treatment for her. If he tries to take her to a hospital, she will be out of his control and will find assistance and gain her freedom, and of course no doctor can be brought to the cellar to treat her. Little by little, her condition worsens, and then one day she dies, after only three months of imprisonment.

After the first week, Miranda had demanded writing paper from Clegg for a diary; knowing she could not get a message past him, he did not care how much time she spent writing. After her death, he finds the diary, but in reading it, all the relationship he imagined they had had evaporates. His plan to atone for Miranda's death by committing suicide seems ludicrous in light of the true feelings she reveals in her diary—all she ever wanted was to get away from him. Before he can even figure out what to do with Miranda's remains, however, he is startled to see what he at first thinks is her ghost in the nearby town. Another beautiful young woman, though not as beautiful as Miranda, crosses the street in front of his van. And even when Clegg tells himself that there could never be another woman for him, he disposes of Miranda's body in a grave in the backyard and cleans out her room as good as new.

John FOWLES tells this chilling story using a first-person point of view, but by employing the device of Miranda's diary, he doubles the story's effect. First Clegg talks, almost confessionally, relating the entire story of his life, his obsession, and his unwilling, doomed "guest." The first half of the novel is a nonstop

explanation of Clegg's capture of Miranda and his experiences with her. He is, of course, rationalizing much of the time, but Fowles communicates much in the hurried, cold, self-justifying sentences. The poor punctuation suggests a lower-class background even as Clegg condemns the educated classes and the rich who, he feels, look down on him. He brings the story to the point at which Miranda is so sick it seems she cannot live much longer without medical attention, and then the focus shifts to Miranda's journal.

As Miranda records her thoughts in a section almost as long as Clegg's opening explanation, the reader already knows where each event is going, and so a certain dread accompanies her accounts of her dealings with her captor. But since she was not quite dead when Clegg's narrative stopped, there is still a faint hope that somehow everything will turn out well for her. Instead, viewing the suffering from her point of view makes it even more harrowing. Early in her journal, Miranda provides the detailed background information about herself that converts her from the object of Clegg's obsession—a flat character—to a fully rounded human being who is suffering through no fault of her own. She recounts her life with a loving family, her artistic ambitions, her attachment to an older man, and her helpless rage toward Clegg. She also relates her version of her escape attempts, and these become more poignant given the knowledge that they will not succeed. Eventually, her journal begins to become incoherent, and then she is too weak to write any more.

Clegg returns as narrator for two additional short sections. First, he explains his pain at losing Miranda and his short-lived plan to kill himself. He falls in love with her all over again and relives the days before he collected her when she occupied his every waking thought. He forgives her, now that she's dead, for her escape attempts and for the lewd behavior he forced her to perform that he simultaneously longs for and loathes. But before these melodramatic and sentimental thoughts can lead to his self-destruction, he finds the diary; afterward, everything is different. The very short closing section shows, in Clegg's own words, how he has grown in his compulsive need to dominate women who have no recourse but to endure him. He speaks of having learned his lesson, but the new object of his attention—the woman who reminds him of Miranda—undermines the reader's ability to believe him. He is repeating a compulsive pattern of anti-social, misogynistic behavior. His experience with Miranda has not made him a better man; it has made him a better collector.

BIBLIOGRAPHY

Laughlin, Rosemary M. "Faces of Power in the Novels of John Fowles," *Critique: Studies in Modern Fiction* 13, no. 3 (1972): 71–88.

Rackham, Jeff. "John Fowles: The Existential Labyrinth," *Critique: Studies in Modern Fiction* 13, no. 3 (1972): 89–103.

Woodcock, Bruce. *Male Mythologies: John Fowles and Masculinity.* Brighton, U.K.: The Harvester Press, 1984.

COLONIALISM

European expansion into other parts of the world dates to 1492 and the discovery of unknown lands west of the Atlantic Ocean, establishment of a sea route around the tip of Africa to the Far East. In Europe, nation-states were emerging and developing as secular kings acquired political power at the expense of papal supremacy, and as the feudal economic organization of the medieval era gave way to capitalism's emphasis on trade and profits. Portugal, Spain, and France—Catholic countries—and England and Holland (the Dutch Republic)—Protestant countries—were soon competing for resources, markets, and labor in North and South America, Africa, India, Southeast Asia, the Pacific islands, Australia, and New Zealand. Belgium and Germany also made colonial forays into Africa on a smaller scale.

From the beginning, colonialism made its presence felt in literature. Travelers' stories became a popular genre of books, and images of the New World became powerful symbols in plays, poetry, political rhetoric, and novels. Europeans set out to explore, but exploration turned to conquests of native peoples and exploitation of natural resources. Slavery also flourished: European enterprises in new lands demanded vast quantities of labor and could be made highly profitable if that labor was obtained at the lowest cost possible. Colonies of Europeans moved into new lands, bringing with them their languages, religions, cultural practices, and artistic styles, but once settled they developed new literatures of pioneering and cultural clashes. The presence of European colonials introduced changes that marked the languages and literatures of conquered populations permanently, affecting colonized peoples even after independence.

The British were particularly effective at spreading the English language to every part of the world, leading to literature written in English by peoples native to the Caribbean, India, Hong Kong, Africa, the Pacific, and most of North America. The British distributed colonists to most of these areas, but natives of colonized regions were also frequently attracted to England by educational and business opportunities. Thus a writer such as Salman RUSHDIE, descended from Indian Muslims but educated in English public schools and universities and a resident of England most of his life, must be considered alongside a writer such as Patrick WHITE, reared and educated in England but renowned as the first Australian to win the NOBEL PRIZE for Literature.

WORLD WAR II struck the death knell for colonial empires; after 1945, colonized countries increasingly demanded independence, frequently with violence, both in warfare against the colonizing Europeans and in civil strife between hostile factions seeking to control power upon liberation. Colonialism had been so widespread throughout the world that the postcolonial phenomenon is a global characteristic of literature rather than a localized effect. In the postcolonial period, writers have pondered the impact of colonialism on their cultures and examined the options open to the nation released from colonial control. In exploring the difficult terrain of the post colonial landscape, writers participate in the process by which the new nation decides how—and whether—to purge itself of its colonial heritage, and they also help explore the paths by which the new nation may move toward a self-directed future.

BIBLIOGRAPHY

Ashcroft, Bill, Gareth Griffiths, and Helen Tiffin. *The Empire Writes Back: Theory and Practice in Post-Colonial Literature.* London: Routledge, 1989.

Boehmer, Elleke. *Colonial and Postcolonial Literature*. Oxford: Oxford University Press, 1995.

Kiernan, V. G. *From Conquest to Collapse: European Empires from 1814–1960*. 2nd ed. New York: Pantheon Books, 1982.

Phillips, Caryl. *Extravagant Strangers: A Literature of Belonging*. New York: Vintage International, 1997.

Thornton, A. P. *Imperialism in the Twentieth Century*. Minneapolis: University of Minnesota Press, 1977.

COMFORT OF STRANGERS, THE IAN MCEWAN (1981)

A dark novella of love and cruelty, *The Comfort of Strangers* is set in the romantic city of Venice, Italy. There, an attractive young English couple, Colin and Mary, spends an idyllic vacation. They have had a relationship for some time, and both feel that they need to decide whether they should get serious and make a long-term commitment to each or perhaps end the relationship so that each can search elsewhere for such a commitment. They do not realize that their decision is about to be stolen from them in an act of predatory cruelty that will lead to one person's death. These modern urban liberals cannot comprehend the danger they are in because they cannot conceive of a world where selfishness trumps generosity so completely as to eradicate it; consequently, they are easy targets for the experienced hunters who are already on their trail.

Colin and Mary meet Robert and Caroline, a middle-aged couple with a luxurious villa in one of Venice's best locations. Although the meeting seems to be the result of coincidence, the young couple has been chosen and stalked: Robert has been following them and photographing them. The appearance of friendship is merely part of the snare that has been painstakingly set to entrap and destroy something genuinely beautiful. Robert and Caroline enjoy the suffering of others, and in several small ways they arrange to make Colin and Mary suffer without being able to connect the situation to Robert and Caroline. Colin and Mary are open to the world and to the people in it, making no effort to protect themselves or to suspect their acquaintances of being anything other than the somewhat pushy and rather presumptuous new friends they seem to be. As Colin and Mary learn more about Robert and Caroline, they are lulled into a degree of pity for the older couple in spite of some odd warning signs that might have alerted a more wary pair; their own relationship is reignited as they come to appreciate the youth, love, and beauty they possess that Robert and Caroline have lost in spite of their privileged status. But even this renewed attachment is part of the punishment that has been planned for them. In a shocking and unexpected twist, the innocent fall prey to unimaginable cruelty.

In 1990, this novella became the basis of a FILM ADAPTATION directed by Paul Schrader, with a screenplay by the noted British dramatist Harold Pinter, and starring Natasha Richardson, Rupert Everett, Christopher Walken, and Helen Mirren. The film has generated as much critical discussion as has the novel upon which it is based, drawing the attention of international scholars to MCEWAN'S work early in his career.

BIBLIOGRAPHY

Hall, Ann C. "Daddy Dearest: Harold Pinter's *The Comfort of Strangers*." In *The Films of Harold Pinter*. Edited by Steven H. Galen. Albany, N.Y.: State University of New York Press, 2001, 87–98.

Richter, Virginia. "Tourists Lost in Venice: Daphne Du Maurier's *Don't Look Now* and Ian McEwan's *The Comfort of Strangers*." In *Venetian Views, Venetian Blinds: English Fantasies of Venice*. Edited by Manfred Pfister and Barbara Schaff. Amsterdam: Rodopi, 1999, 181–194.

Seaboyer, Judith. "Sadism Demands a Story: Ian McEwan's *The Comfort of Strangers*," *Modern Fiction Studies* 45, no. 4 (Winter 1999): 957–986.

COMIC NOVELS

In terms of literary history, the novel differs from the earlier form of the romance (the root of the French term *roman*, or "novel") in depending on realistic characters engaged in real-world actions contextualized in a believable contemporary setting. Within the constraints of realism, however, a wide range still remains of attitudes toward and treatments of character, plot, and theme, and the comic approach is among the most popular and enduring of novelistic forms.

Any of the elements of fiction—plot, character, setting, dialogue, theme, symbolism, imagery, tone, voice, or narration—may bear one of the many stamps of comedy, from low farce to corrosive satire. As a narrative strategy, a comic approach is effective both for entertaining readers and for instructing them, and it is flexible enough to encompass affectionate fun and caustic abuse. A comic novel is, at heart, an optimistic enterprise, since even a tirade of hilarious invective expresses the hope that the recipient may be improved by the experience of receiving it. Where hope has been displaced by despair, comedy does not thrive.

BIBLIOGRAPHY

Finney, Gail, ed. *Look Who's Laughing: Gender and Comedy.* Langhorne, Pa.: Gordon and Breach, 1994.

Harper, Graeme, ed. *Comedy, Fantasy, and Colonialism.* London: Continuum, 2002.

Lodge, David and Malcolm Bradbury. " 'Laughing Matter': The Comic Novel in English," *Moderna Sprak* 86, no. 1 (1993): 1–10.

Wood, James. *The Irresponsible Self: On Laughter and the Novel.* New York: Farrar, Straus & Giroux, 2004.

COMMODORE, THE PATRICK O'BRIAN (1994)   See AUBREY-MATURIN NOVELS.

COMMONWEALTH LITERATURE   Descended from the British Empire, the Commonwealth (called the British Commonwealth of Nations from 1931 to 1946) formally began with the Statute of Westminster in 1931. This legislation recognized the special status of those British possessions occupied primarily by descendants of European immigrants, such as Canada, Australia, New Zealand, and parts of what is now South Africa. In 1947, INDIA AND PAKISTAN became separate sovereign nations and joined the Commonwealth as the first members populated primarily by non-Europeans. Gradually, the former colonies, dependencies, and possessions of the British Empire were transformed into self-governing independent states that could choose membership in the Commonwealth as desired. Eventually, the Commonwealth was organized into four large geographical regions, including Africa, the Caribbean and Canada, Eurasia, and Southeast Asia and the South Pacific. The member nations of the Commonwealth, including the United Kingdom, stand as equals to one another, recognizing the symbolic leadership of the British Crown and maintaining ties of trade, friendship, and historical tradition. The nations of the Commonwealth range from tiny island states to the continent-sized countries of India and Australia.

English is the shared language of the Commonwealth, and writers from nations around the world use it to produce original works of literature. Authors native to places as far removed from one another as Nigeria and Singapore or India and Canada are often united linguistically by the shared language of their former colonial rulers. The range of "British" literature is thus very nearly global. Outstanding achievement by Commonwealth writers has been recognized annually since 1987 by the awarding of the Commonwealth Writers Prize, administered under the direction of the Commonwealth Foundation. Winners of this prize are listed in Appendix I.

See also EMPIRE.

BIBLIOGRAPHY

Ferres, John H., and Martin Tucker, eds. *Modern Commonwealth Literature.* New York: Ungar, 1977.

King, Bruce Alvin. *The New English Literatures: Cultural Nationalisms in a Changing World.* New York: St. Martin's Press, 1980.

Walsh, William. *Commonwealth Literature.* London: Oxford University Press, 1973.

COMPTON-BURNETT, IVY (1884–1969)   Noted for her intensely conversational novels, Ivy Compton-Burnett was born in Pinner, Middlesex, one of 12 siblings, and educated at Royal Holloway College, receiving a degree in classics in 1906. Her life was marked by a series of tragic losses and emotional unrest, including the deaths of two brothers (one due to sickness and the other to war) and the suicides of her two youngest sisters. She had a lifelong friendship with Margaret Jourdain; beginning in the period after WORLD WAR I, the two lived together until Jourdain's death in 1951. Her novel *Mother and Son* won the JAMES TAIT BLACK MEMORIAL PRIZE in 1956, and she was honored with the degree of D.Litt. by the University of Leeds in 1960. She was named a Commander of the Order of the British Empire in 1951 and Dame Commander in 1967. She wrote until the end of her life,

leaving a novel for posthumous publication—*The Last and the First* (1971)—and died in London on August 27, 1969, of bronchitis.

Compton-Burnett typically sets her novels in the last years of the 19th century as the Victorian era was drawing to a close. Her first novel, *Dolores,* was published in 1911; her second did not appear until 14 years later, when she published the novel that establishes her quintessential mature style, *Pastors and Masters* (1925). She presents the nuances of everyday life primarily through conversation, communicating her plot and character development—the swirl of powerful emotion beneath the decorous-seeming surface appearance of the English world—by means of the words the characters exchange, amplified by only a minimum of narrative exposition. Of her 20 novels, 19 in the conversational style, other noted titles include *More Women Than Men* (1935), *A Family and a Fortune* (1939), *Manservant and Maidservant* (1947; published in the United States as *Bullivant and the Lambs*), and *A Heritage and Its History* (1960). This last novel and *A Family and a Fortune* were adapted for television by Julian Mitchell.

BIBLIOGRAPHY

Baldanza, Frank. *Ivy Compton-Burnett.* Twayne's English Authors, 11. Detroit: Twayne, 1964.

Spurling, Hilary. *Ivy When Young: The Early Life of I. Compton-Burnett, 1884–1919.* London: Gollancz, 1974.

———. *Secrets of a Woman's Heart: The Later Life of Compton-Burnett.* London: Hodder & Stoughton, 1984.

CONFLICT

The driving force behind the complications of every plot, conflict arises when two or more things stand in opposition to each other and the circumstances of the story can provide satisfaction for only one (or a fraction) of the opponents. Generally, characters fill the role of "things in opposition"; however, conflict can arise between human beings and nature, between nations, or between institutions. Conflict can also arise inside a single character who must chose between two mutually exclusive alternatives, such as marrying versus remaining single or believing in God's existence versus atheism; conflict also results when a character refuses to accept his or her assigned role in life and attempts to defy destiny. Conflict can be either comic or tragic, depending on the direction the plot takes and the tone the author uses in presenting it. In a COMIC NOVEL, conflict finds resolution in some kind of accommodation, understanding, or even reconciliation of the opposing sides, but tragic conflict typically leads to a victory for one opponent at the expense of the other.

BIBLIOGRAPHY

Forster, E. M. *Aspects of the Novel.* New York: Harcourt, Brace & Company, 1927.

Paris, Bernard J. *Imagined Human Beings: A Psychological Approach to Character and Conflict in Literature.* Literature and Psychoanalysis 9. New York: New York University Press, 1997.

CONRAD, JOSEPH (1857–1924)

A Polish-born seaman who learned his trade in the French and British fleets and chose the identity of English novelist in midlife, Joseph Conrad possesses one of the most unusual biographies in the annals of literature. He was born on December 3, 1857, in the town of Berdyczew, Poland; his birth name was Teodor Josef Konrad Nalecz Korzeniowski. At that time, Russia claimed sovereignty over the eastern part of Poland. Conrad's parents were romantic nationalists who actively supported the reestablishment of their homeland's independence from Russian and German control; his father, a writer and translator, used his skills to support the cause of Polish freedom. In 1862, the family was exiled to Russia, and Conrad's mother died three years later when her son was only eight. Conrad's maternal uncle, the attorney Thaddeus Bobrowski, became the boy's guardian in 1866 and remained an important source of financial and emotional support until Conrad was middle-aged. Conrad's father died in 1869.

In 1874, when Conrad was still a teenager, he traveled to Marseilles, France, and began mastering seamanship in the French commercial marine service. The historical evidence of the four years he sailed on French vessels is sketchy, but he seems to have become involved in a Spanish political cause, the Carlist movement, possibly through an affair with a woman already involved in it. He fought a duel as a result of this affair and may have attempted suicide during this period. In

1878, Conrad relocated to England and began serving on English ships. He rose through the ranks to master, becoming a citizen of Great Britain in 1886, and assuming his first command in 1888. His work carried him to every corner of the globe, including the river trade in the Belgian Congo; these exotic locations, together with the isolation, danger, and emotional stress on humans separated from their homelands, provided Conrad with abundant resources for his subsequent career as a novelist.

An important turning point for Conrad occurred in 1893, when he met the novelist John GALSWORTHY, who had taken passage on Conrad's ship. Conrad was already writing *Almayer's Folly,* and when the novel succeeded upon its publication in 1895, he left the sea, married, and settled in Kent, where he died on August 3, 1924. In the last 29 years of his life, Conrad produced some 16 novels, seven collections of short fiction, and several novellas. Additionally, he produced collections of essays, some plays, and an autobiography. He befriended numerous writers, including Arnold BENNETT, Henry JAMES, Rudyard KIPLING, H. G. WELLS, Ford Madox FORD (with whom he coauthored three novels before breaking off the friendship), and others.

Critics recognize three phases in Conrad's prolific output: the early novels that draw on his experience at sea and in the Congo, including The HEART OF DARKNESS and LORD JIM; the middle period of political novels such as NOSTROMO, The SECRET AGENT, and *Under Western Eyes;* and the late period, including *Chance* and *Victory,* composed of novels that (in the opinions of several commentators) show a decline in Conrad's powers. Throughout his career, Conrad focused on isolated protagonists who must face conflict and overcome challenges without the supports of civilization. His protagonists are frequently isolated because of their employment in the European project of COLONIALISM, but Conrad provides an unflinchingly honest view of the greed that drove colonial enterprises and the inhumanity that resulted from them, questioning the values of the civilized world that inflicted so much suffering in the process of pillaging so many peoples. He is fascinated by the deterioration of moral principles when representatives of the civilized world come face-to-face with tribal cultures. His depiction of

nature is largely unsympathetic and antiromantic; instead, the natural world is the locus of brooding threats to human survival. In terms of narrative technique, Conrad was an innovator who experimented with storytelling modes that would provide inspiration to later writers such as Virginia WOOLF and James JOYCE; his work stands as a bridge between the Victorian moralism of the 19th century and the literary modernism of the 20th century, but it also bridges the lucrative world of mass-market entertainments and the Olympian heights of serious art.

BIBLIOGRAPHY
Bradbrook, M. C. *Joseph Conrad: Poland's English Genius.* Cambridge: Cambridge University Press, 1941.

Gillon, Ada. *Joseph Conrad.* Twayne's English Authors, 333. New York: Twayne Publishers, 1982.

Gordon, John Dozier. *Joseph Conrad: The Making of a Novelist.* Cambridge, Mass.: Harvard University Press, 1940.

Leavis, F. R. *The Great Tradition: George Eliot, Henry James, Joseph Conrad.* London: Chatto & Windus, 1948.

Meyers, Jeffrey. *Joseph Conrad: A Biography.* New York: Scribner, 1991.

CONSCIENCE OF THE RICH, THE C. P. SNOW (1958)

Published as volume seven in SNOW's 11-volume series STRANGERS AND BROTHERS, the events of this story actually place it immediately after the action of the introductory novel of the series. The year is 1927 as the story opens, with the recurring character of Lewis Eliot serving as the first-person narrator. Eliot is in London to take the bar examination that will enable him to enter the profession of law as an apprentice practitioner. At the exam, he encounters Charles March, an acquaintance he wishes to know better, and the two of them have tea afterward. Eliot is virtually impoverished, having spent his entire inheritance in the pursuit of his education to this point, and now his future hinges on achieving the excellent marks that will win him a scholarship for the next year. In contrast, Charles March is from a wealthy family, but Eliot knows little more about him, and Charles is not inclined toward self-revelation. As they enter their legal apprenticeship, they become best friends, and eventually Eliot is invited to visit the March home.

As the story unfolds, Eliot is primarily an observer of this wealthy way of life in which he was not reared but to which he aspires. His outsider status is reinforced by the fact that the March family is Jewish. Eliot is a welcome guest, but he is not an eligible candidate for the courtship of Charles's sister Katherine, a charming young woman who has reached marriageable age. Eliot witnesses the stresses that develop in the March family as the children begin to establish themselves as independent adults, making choices that break with family tradition and that especially displease the family patriarch, Leonard March. Charles becomes involved with Ann Simon, a radical young Jewish woman actively supporting the Communist Party, eventually marrying her. Leonard March is displeased; when Charles decides to leave the legal profession to become a doctor, Leonard retaliates financially, restricting Charles to a small allowance. At stake is Charles's "independence," not from the family but from the obligation of working for a living. Leonard's dissatisfaction with his children multiplies when Katherine marries outside the faith, choosing a young scientist, Francis Getliffe, the brother of Herbert Getliffe, the lawyer who supervises Eliot's apprenticeship.

The focus of the story widens from these family disputes to political and financial intrigues fanned by Ronald Porson, a former admirer of Ann Simon. Porson wishes to get revenge on both the March and the Getliffe families. As the plot thickens, loyalties are strained, and some individuals must choose whether to cleave to their blood relatives or their marital choices, while others must choose whether to advance the interests of their ideological connections or protect the advantages of their loved ones. Relatives issue ultimatums to one another, and emotions are at odds with ideas. Tradition digs in its heels as innovation strains to bring about new ways of being human, conducting business, and controlling government. Eliot relates the unfolding events with sympathy both for the defenders of tradition, such as Leonard March, and for the exponents of change, such as Ann Simon.

As with many modern novels, irony sits at the heart of this one. Family members who should be contributing to one another's success instead wind up in isolated hostility. Acts intended to punish, such as Leonard's eventual disinheriting of Charles, instead have an emotionally liberating effect. Determination to improve the lot of the many, such as Ann's support of the Communists, can only come about at a cost to the beloved few. Good intentions not infrequently lead to bad results, and bad intentions lead to worse results still. Snow's sensitive and sympathetic narrative illustrates how difficult it is for anyone to know how to act in the world, and yet how impossible it is to avoid taking action.

BIBLIOGRAPHY

De la Mothe, John. *C. P. Snow and the Struggle of Modernity.* Austin: University of Texas Press, 1992.

Karl, Frederick F. *C. P. Snow: The Politics of Conscience.* Carbondale: Southern Illinois University Press, 1963.

CONSERVATIONIST, THE NADINE GORDIMER (1974)

A story of racial divisions in South Africa, *The Conservationist* shared the BOOKER PRIZE in 1975 with *HEAT AND DUST,* by Ruth Prower JHABVALA. The story, told by a third-person objective narrator, opens with the arrival of Mehring, a successful South African businessman, at the large farm he owns where he spends his weekends. A divorced man whose one son has been sent to a boarding school, Mehring is the conservationist of the title, but the world that he is conserving is the one of privilege and inequity that apartheid created in South Africa. On this weekend, the body of an anonymous murdered Bantu has been found dumped on the farm, but when Mehring summons the police he learns that no officer can attend to this matter until the next day. The neglected murdered man becomes an ominous symbol of the festering social strife in South Africa: It will cover the land with the stench of death, but whites in power are too busy to pay attention to it in a timely manner.

As the narrator gradually fills in the details of Mehring's character, it becomes apparent that, without being overtly evil, his self-serving and self-centered choices and attitudes nonetheless give rise to human misery. Just as his relationship to his farm is a part-time affair chosen for the financial benefits and emotional satisfactions it will bring to him, so too his relationships with women are selfish exploitations that serve his needs only. Having failed to establish a lasting connection in the human world, Mehring buys 400 acres of the physical world and keeps himself mostly separate from it. His black employees, led by Jacobus, the real steward of the land, keep the empty house in perfect order, tend the cows and the crops, and survive the vagaries of fire and flood while Mehring extracts more wealth from the pig iron business, traveling all over the world in pursuit of it.

The novel features very little plot, allowing the cycle of life's routines in a rural region to stand in for conflict and the complications that are usually associated with plot development. Instead, GORDIMER delivers a richly detailed analysis of a character corrupted by the historical context that has produced him and that supports his life of excess by means of unending deficits in the lives of thousands of oppressed Africans enclosed in the "location"—the shantytown ringed with barbed wire fences 10 feet high—that Mehring must cross to reach his land. Through a careful arrangement of characters who represent the racial tensions of South Africa—white defenders of a legacy of COLONIALISM, descendants of Indian immigrants, and native Africans forced into near-slavery—Gordimer implicitly condemns the myopia of apartheid and the selfish apathy of the white minority who benefit from it.

BIBLIOGRAPHY

Clingman, Stephen. *The Novels of Nadine Gordimer: History from the Inside.* 2nd ed. Amherst: University of Massachusetts Press, 1992.

Cooke, John. *The Novels of Nadine Gordimer: Private Lives/Public Landscapes.* Baton Rouge: Louisiana State University Press, 1985.

King, Bruce, ed. *The Later Fiction of Nadine Gordimer.* New York: St. Martin's Press, 1993.

CORRIDORS OF POWER C. P. SNOW (1964)

Volume nine in SNOW'S 11-volume series *STRANGERS AND BROTHERS*, *Corridors of Power* follows *THE AFFAIR* and precedes the elegiac closing volumes of *THE SLEEP OF REASON* and *LAST THINGS*. The first-person narrator of the series, Lewis Eliot, has achieved a position of enough importance to place him as a witness to the workings of political power in Parliament; the scope of the action has grown from the intrigues of academic politics in *The Affair* to matters of global importance in

the new nuclear era. Snow draws on his real-life experiences to produce verisimilitude in the novel's representation of the machinations of power. In this novel, Eliot is again an observer of the narrative's main events rather than serving as a key participant or the subject of the story.

In the novel's opening event, the Eliots have dinner with a young Conservative member of Parliament, Roger Quaife, and his aristocratic wife, a leading socialite. With his connections and his achievements to date, the story of Quaife's future success could already be written were he prepared to toe the party line rather than to follow the dictates of his conscience. On the matter of the nuclear arms race, however, he feels compelled to oppose the continued participation of Great Britain in spite of the Conservative Party's support for it. Through Eliot, who is experienced in these issues (first dealt with in *The NEW MEN*), Quaife builds a circle of supporters to assist him in exposing the issue to critical examination.

If his project could proceed in a political vacuum, Quaife might have a better chance of success; however, he is immersed in a continually changing scenario among shifting loyalties. When the SUEZ CRISIS of 1956 occurs, Quaife's Conservative connections separate him from his supporters on ending the arms race. As important as the nuclear issue is, it cannot be extricated from the give-and-take negotiations of politics. Additionally, his personal life complicates the political work he is attempting to complete: He has been entangled for some time in an affair with the wife of another member of Parliament, and gossip about this indiscretion surfaces just when it can do the greatest damage to Quaife's credibility with his supporters and to his standing with the public.

Quaife must face a dilemma that will destroy some part of his integrity. He can back down from his opposition to nuclear arms to salvage his political career, or he can stick to his position and suffer the consequences in his professional and personal life. The ramifications of his decision extend beyond his own life and career, however, since Eliot and others are now committed to his project and will suffer no matter which decision Quaife makes. As a consequence of this political battle, Eliot reaches a turning point in his own life. Snow's narrative emphasizes that idealism makes a poor political instrument and is likely to become a sacrificial lamb as compromises chip into it. He echoes the existential message of Jean Paul Sartre's *Dirty Hands* in demonstrating how agents cannot act in the world and simultaneously avoid becoming besmirched by the choices they make to achieve their goals.

BIBLIOGRAPHY

De la Mothe, John. *C. P. Snow and the Struggle of Modernity.* Austin: University of Texas Press, 1992.

Ramanathan, Suguna. *The Novels of C. P. Snow: A Critical Introduction.* New York: Scribner, 1978.

Shusterman, David. *C. P. Snow.* Rev. ed. Twaynes English Authors, 179. Boston: Twayne, 1991.

COUNTRY GIRLS, THE EDNA O'BRIEN (1960–1986)

This trilogy was published in a single volume with added material (*Epilogue*) in 1986; it originally appeared as the separate volumes *The Country Girls* (1960), which was the author's first published novel; *The Lonely Girl* (1962); and *Girls in Their Married Bliss* (1964). In calling attention to the repression of women by the Catholic Church and by the Irish government, and in calling on Irish women to take possession of their own sexuality, the book created an adverse reaction in Ireland, the author's native country: It was banned there, and copies were even burned in O'BRIEN'S hometown.

The narrative of the trilogy's first volume features a double protagonist in Caithleen and Baba, two girls reared in the strict convent tradition of devout Catholics in IRELAND, who are both longing to move into the modern world of Dublin. Caithleen is the first-person narrator, a shy young woman who longs to find a fulfilling love; Baba is her hot-tempered and demanding best friend. When Caithleen's mother drowns, the girls are boarded at a convent until Baba's outrageous behavior gets them expelled. Like drowning, the convent is also a metaphor for the submersion of female existence and the termination of an individual woman's identity. O'Brien returns to this image of submerged death many years after completing the trilogy, bringing one of the protagonists to a similar end.

After the oppressive convent life, the girls are thrilled to go to Dublin, where Baba enters a business school and Cait works in a grocery store. But they have traded small-town frustration for modern urban loneliness. For Cait in particular, love seems impossible because the majority of the men she meets are too badly flawed or damaged to provide a meaningful relationship. The novel leaves Cait with dampened hopes but still with some optimism that she will find love, and in *The Lonely Girl*, set two years later in Dublin, she enters into a relationship with Eugene Gaillard (perhaps an unsympathetic portrait of O'Brien's own husband). The relationship leaves Cait herself feeling damaged, and the two friends leave Ireland for London at the novel's end.

Five years later, when Baba and Kate (Caithleen's Anglicized name) are about 25 years old, their story resumes in *The Girls in Their Married Bliss,* but now Baba becomes the novel's narrator, with additional passages of observation narrated in the third person. The two friends live in London and are married, but both of them are disillusioned with men and disheartened by their marriages. Baba has chosen material comfort over personal fulfillment, and Kate's bitter experience in her failing marriage leads her to elect voluntary sterilization. When O'Brien returned to this story more than 20 years later, when the three books were published in a single volume, she continued her negative perspective on the prospects for women trying to fill the roles laid out for them in a patriarchal society. The country girls mature, but they do so at the cost of their dreams and hopes, turning to despair, indifference, and even self-destruction.

BIBLIOGRAPHY

Eckley, Grace. *Edna O'Brien.* Lewisburg, Pa.: Bucknell University Press, 1974.

Irwin, Archibald E. "Give Us Baba," *Irish Literary Supplement* (Spring 1987): 19.

COVER HER FACE P. D. JAMES (1962)

In this example of MYSTERY AND DETECTIVE FICTION, the author introduces her recurring investigator, Inspector Adam Dalgleish of Scotland Yard, who returns for many more subsequent adventures. In his first appearance, he is faced with a crime that at first seems completely unmotivated: A young servant has been murdered in her attic room at the country house of the Maxie family, Martingale. Further, she was inside a locked room (one of the classic scenarios of the genre) when the murder occurred.

The victim is the beautiful serving-girl, Sally Jupp, who had been a resident at the nearby home for unwed mothers, St. Mary's Refuge for Girls, where she had given birth to her son, Jimmie. She has retained the child and keeps him with her at Martingale; most of the Maxies, and the village as well, are sure that a fallen woman like Sally Jupp should be grateful to have a position as a servant at such a fine estate. But although Sally works efficiently, she does not have a humble spirit, and she quickly alienates the long-tenured housekeeper, Martha, who spends most of her time caring for the senile and bedridden master of Martingale. She has similarly affronted Miss Liddell, warden of St. Mary's, and others. When, during an annual garden party at the estate, she is found in the servants' quarters—to which the entire community has been summoned by Jimmie's howls—it soon becomes apparent that the number of people harboring a score to settle with Sally Jupp is quite large.

The task of sorting out the evidence falls to Inspector Adam Dalgleish of Scotland Yard. The omniscient third-person narrator follows the police proceedings with care, but the narrator controls the flow of information so as to keep the identity of the murderer obscured from the readers. Everyone turns out to have secrets, not the least of which is Sally Jupp's secret. Inspector Dalgleish must sort through the ambiguous testimonies of witnesses, evaluate the conflicting motives, and expose the hidden agendas before he can establish the identity of the murderer and provide the evidence that will prove his accusation. The investigation comes to a climax in the group scene familiar to readers of Agatha CHRISTIE as the detective gathers the suspects together and reviews the evidence before them, eliminating the innocent and zeroing in on the single guilty party.

The novel was a success upon its publication; fans of mysteries recognized the skill with which the story was plotted and the realism with which the characters were delineated. Adam Dalgleish returned in a long and successful series of novels, and his creator, together with Ruth RENDELL, inherited the mantle of Agatha Christie as the leading writers of the mystery and detective fiction genre.

BIBLIOGRAPHY

Gidez, Richard B. *P. D. James*. Twayne's English Authors, 430. New York: Twayne Publishers, 1986.

Hubley, Erlene. "Adam Dalgliesh: Byronic Hero," *Clues: A Journal of Detection* 3 (Fall/Winter 1982): 40–46.

Kotker, Joan G. "P. D. James's Adam Dalgliesh Series." In *In the Beginning: First Novels in Mystery Series*. Edited by Mary Jean DeMarr. Bowling Green, Ohio: Popular, 1995.

CRACE, JIM (1946–   )

Author of QUARANTINE, winner of the 1997 WHITBREAD Book of the Year Award, Jim Crace was born March 1, 1946, in Lemsford, Hertfordshire. He received an education at Birmingham College of Commerce and the University of London, earning a bachelor's degree with honors in English in 1968. He then entered Voluntary Service Overseas (a kind of British Peace Corps), spending a year in Sudan. From 1970 to 1986, he worked as a freelance journalist. He was married in 1975; he and his wife have two children. After 1986, he devoted himself to writing fiction full-time.

Crace published his first novel, *Continent,* in 1986, winning widespread acclaim for his originality, insight, and prose style. The novel is actually a set of seven interconnected stories that examines the effect of change—the price of progress—on an imaginary continent bearing a striking resemblance to Third World nations socially, politically, and economically. His next novel, *The Gift of Stones* (1988), is set in the prehistoric world just as the Stone Age gives way to the Bronze Age. *Arcadia* (1992) uses a modern urban environment to explore the vanity of a rich man who wishes to eradicate the evidence of his impoverished origins. Cultural clash is a frequent object of investigation in Crace's novels. In *Signals of Distress* (1995), he draws on an actual historical event—the grounding of an American ship on the English coast in 1836—to imagine a particular contrast of these two cultures, separated for only 60-some years, in an era when the practice of slavery still flourished in only one of them. *Quarantine* (1997) retells the story of Christ's 40 days in the wilderness, and *Being Dead* (1999) recalls the lives of a murdered couple while also detailing the decay of their mortal remains.

Crace has set forth his principles of fiction writing in interviews, asserting that he is averse to the intense examination of characters' psychology, preferring the larger scale of community interactions. He has won numerous awards for his fiction in addition to the Whitbread Award, including the David Higham Award, the GUARDIAN FICTION PRIZE, and the National Book Critics Circle Award. He continues to live and write in Birmingham, producing novels, radio plays, and shorter works for newspapers and magazines.

BIBLIOGRAPHY

Cooke, Judy. *Jim Crace*. London: Book Trust and the British Council, 1992.

Gussow, Mel. "A Novelist So Revealing His Life Is a Closed Book," *New York Times,* 3 December 2003. Available online. URL: www.nytimes.com. Accessed June 2004.

Lane, Richard J., Rod Mengham, and Philip Tew. *Contemporary British Fiction*. Cambridge, U.K.: Polity Press; Malden, Mass.: Blackwell Publishers, 2003.

CRASH J. G. BALLARD (1973)

This controversial novel, excoriated by some critics for the violent behavior and perverse desires of some of the characters, was the basis of the 1996 film of the same name, also quite controversial, directed by David Cronenberg. The novel features a first-person narrator named James Ballard, a film director, who meets a crash-obsessed man named Vaughn. In surreal and explicit descriptions of car crashes and of the erotic impulses they induce, the narrator tells in the first chapter of Vaughn's last self-inflicted car crash: It was a failed attempt to unite in death with a film star named Elizabeth Taylor, which terminates Vaughn's life in a satisfactorily violent manner in spite of missing the intended target. The narrator goes on in chapter two to recount in vivid detail his own horrific experience in a head-on collision (a life experience the narrator shares with the author) during which a passenger dies in the car he hits. In the aftermath of this crash, the narrator feels drawn to the driver of the other car, a survivor like himself and the wife of the dead passenger. The crash and the attraction to the woman illuminate the erotic role that cars have assumed in contemporary life, especially when combined with the brutal violence of a fatal crash. The narrator is soon obsessed with the event that brought him so close to death without tipping him over into it, and that obsession had brought him to the attention of Vaughn, the master of crash obsessives. Through the crash, he enters into a new perspective on life, on erotic arousal, and on technology.

The novel germinated, for the author, in the experience of surviving a violent crash. Afterward, he mounted an exhibit of crashed cars at an experimental art gallery; the responses of visitors to the exhibit fascinated him and gave rise to ideas for the novel. The story is a departure from the SCIENCE-FICTION settings of BALLARD'S first four novels, but it introduces an array of themes that recur in his next two novels, *Concrete Island* and *High Rise*. He repeatedly depicts a contemporary world of desolation, mechanization, and numbed indifference in which human beings must find a way to survive and thrive however they can. The result is a grim perspective on the wasteland of concrete, metal, plastic, and glass in which modern life is embedded.

BIBLIOGRAPHY

Luckhurst, Roger. *"The Angle Between Two Walls": The Fiction of J. G. Ballard*. New York: St. Martin's Press, 1997.

Stephenson, Gregory. *Out of the Night and into the Dream: A Thematic Study of the Fiction of J. G. Ballard*. Westport, Conn.: Greenwood Press, 1991.

CROME YELLOW ALDOUS HUXLEY (1921)

Using the unifying device of a weekend party at Crome, the country house of Mr. And Mrs. Henry Wimbush, HUXLEY creates a sharp SATIRE on the futile isolation of the human ego. Huxley's protagonist, the poet Denis Stone, observes the many other guests and interacts with them without ever making any meaningful connection. The proprietors and visitors at Crome constitute a catalog of contemporary human solipsism. Henry Wimbush is trapped in his admiration for the past, having devoted three decades to his history of Crome and its inhabitants. His greatest connection to the assembled guests is to read passages from his history to them. His wife (another caricature, with Hermione Roddice in *WOMEN IN LOVE,* of Lady Ottoline Morrell) consults spiritualists and gambles on racehorses. His niece Anne Wimbush has caught the affections of Denis Stone, but she cannot take seriously the emotional attachment of a man four years her junior. Other guests represent cold science, Freudian repression, and failures of communication, in a kind of modernized medieval allegory. Denis eventually picks up the sketchbook of a deaf woman who has anatomized his ineffectual existence with objective honesty. Disheartened, he sends himself an urgent telegram so he can make a polite escape from Crome, and just as he is leaving, he realizes that Anne has begun to be interested in him.

Crome Yellow was Aldous Huxley's first novel, written when he has still in his 20s. Contemporary readers will see its faults, but the author's dry satire and hopeless pessimism for human happiness captured the spirit of his age, or at least of his generation. The survivors of WORLD WAR I were either jaded or devastated by the destruction and death it had wrought, and in the excesses of the 1920s, they settled for a search for pleasure instead of meaning. Huxley's novel captured that outlook and made his reputation among his peers.

BIBLIOGRAPHY

Baker, Robert S. *The Dark Historic Page: Social Satire and Historicism in the Novels of Aldous Huxley, 1921–1939.* Madison: University of Wisconsin Press, 1982.

Bowering, Peter. *Aldous Huxley: A Study of the Major Novels.* New York: Oxford University Press, 1969.

Firchow, Peter. *Aldous Huxley: Satirist and Novelist.* Minneapolis: University of Minnesota Press, 1972.

CROSSING THE RIVER CARYL PHILLIPS

(1993)   This experimental novel includes aspects of both realism and antirealism, and it mixes several narrative strands using different strategies and varying the point of view from one section of the novel to another.

The novel opens with a kind of short prologue spoken by a first-person narrator. This narrator seems to speak as the voice of Africa, recollecting the struggles of the many Africans who have been spread throughout the colonial world—frequently against their will—in a vast diaspora. This narrator also returns at the end in a poetic coda. In the introduction, a desperate African man tells of selling his three children into slavery. His crops had failed and he could not feed them, but he is distraught when they are gone: He calls the sale a desperate foolishness and blames himself for the fates that befall them. The three children are Nash, Martha, and Travis. The bulk of the novel falls into the four parts, set at different times and in different places, that chronicle the lives of these dispersed Africans as they are assimilated into new cultures, along with selections from a slave-trader's journal.

Nash's story is the focus of the first part, "The Pagan Coast," and covers the period from 1834 to 1842. Nash has been a slave, and he calls his former master, Edward Williams, "father." The term suggests a sacred and philosophical connection as well as a family tie. Nash is freed through the deeply religious motivations of his American owner, a man who has also educated his slaves. This man intends to found charitable Christian missions in Africa; Nash has traveled to Liberia to do missionary work—his father's bidding—and to teach the less fortunate natives. Through his letters, readers learn that although the master had inherited his estate, he did not believe in slavery. As he is able to, he educates and frees his slaves and sends some favored few back "home" to Africa.

Nash and Madison, another slave, compete for Edward Williams's favor; they want to please their "father" and be selected to return to Africa and do his work. But Africa (specifically, Liberia) is a harsh land and people in Nash's settlement are dying; he loses the wife and child he brought from America. As the situation becomes more desperate, Nash writes letters to his former master pleading for financial support for the mission and the school. He doesn't hear back, however: Edward Williams's jealous wife is intervening, withholding the letters from him so he will not spend his fortune on this missionary scheme. Nash's letters to Mr. Williams have a prayer-life quality, and his relation to his former master is that of a supplicant to a god; as time goes on, he retreats into greater primitivism. Nash takes on three wives and has many children, and he keeps relocating his settlement farther and farther back up the river. He finally writes to

Edward Williams *not* to come, but he never sends the letter. Edward Williams comes to Liberia, as he had always planned to do, with Madison. His goal is to check on the miracles he expects Nash to have worked there; instead, he discovers that Nash has died in the last outpost farthest up the river. When Madison sees the impoverished and primitive conditions Nash had lived in, he loses respect for Edward Williams for allowing this situation to develop and abandons him in the wilderness.

The second part, called "West," is about Martha; in it, the American West serves as a metaphor for opportunity and fulfillment. The story is revealed from Martha's later life through flashbacks to her youth caused by catalysts that make her think of her lost daughter, Eliza Mae. Both her husband and daughter had been sold away from her, and she too is sold to a Christian family that relocates to Kansas to homestead. There, they cannot make a success of their farm, and so they plan to sell Martha back into slavery; to save herself, she walks away from her owners, and the Emancipation Proclamation frees her before she can be found. She travels to Dodge, farther west, eventually becoming a laundress with her friend Lucy; she has a long-term relationship with a man, Chester, during this period. After Chester is killed in a gambling dispute, Martha and Lucy go to Fort Leavenworth to wash and clean for the "colored troops" stationed there. When Lucy finds a husband who takes her away to San Francisco, Martha, now much older and in ill health, decides she must go still farther west. She attaches herself to a black man who is going west, offering to earn her passage by washing and cooking. Early in the journey, however, she is too sick to go on and she is left in Denver, a frontier town, where a woman finds her and gives her shelter, nursing her through a terminal illness until she dies alone, lost in her memories of her daughter. The woman who has saved her does not even know Martha's name and has to choose one to put on the old woman's headstone.

The third part is called "Crossing the River" and contains the journal of the young captain of a slave ship, along with some letters to his wife. The journal entries are factual rather than ruminative, reporting the weather, purchases of slaves, and events on board. In contrast, his letters to his wife reveal the personality of a loving husband and a sensitive man who finds himself immersed in a hellish world that he is helping to create even as he suffers its effects. The slave trade is merely a business, although a particularly odious one—the captain gets his living and supports his family by this means, but he is no monster. In spite of his misgivings, he facilitates the continuance of this monstrosity.

In the fourth part, called "Somewhere in England," the narrative breaks into two parts that are separated by 20 years. Joyce, a white Englishwoman, tells the story in a first-person narrative that covers the period 1935–45. Her mother is a straitlaced Christian who drives her daughter away from the church; Joyce meets Len, who suffers from black lung, and who therefore cannot fight in the war. Len has little exposure to religion and is a somewhat disreputable figure; nonetheless, he and Joyce marry. Joyce's lot is bitter: Len drinks and beats her and eventually goes to jail for black-market dealings with ration cards. Joyce acquires a bit of freedom with Len's incarceration; eventually, she meets Travis when a unit of black American soldiers is billeted in her village in 1942. Eventually, she and Travis marry, over many objections, and on the conditions that this mixed-race marriage is not brought to the United States. Joyce bears a son, Greer, but Travis is killed in battle. When Len, her divorced husband, turns her out of the business that has sustained her, in desperation Joyce gives her new son up for adoption if anyone will have him. In 1963, the lost son knocks on Joyce's door. She has remarried and has other children now, and she is simultaneously drawn to him and hurt by his presence. She had destroyed every picture and memento of her love for Travis and the existence of this son. She is not prepared to make a place in her heart for him again.

Through the introductory narrator of this novel, Caryl PHILLIPS seems to suggest that Africa as a whole must shoulder some of the burden of responsibility for the sufferings that Africans have endured in the Western strongholds of COLONIALISM. But the existence of slavery among supposedly Christian people is on the conscience of those who maintained this heinous system, as is the racism that continued to mar the lives of Africa's descendents long after slavery was abolished.

BIBLIOGRAPHY

Coetzee, J. M. *Stranger Shores: Literary Essays, 1986–1999.*
New York: Viking, 2001.

Julien, Claude. "Surviving Through A Pattern of Timeless
Moments: A Reading of Caryl Phillips' *Crossing the River.*"
In *Black Imagination and the Middle Passage.* Edited by
Maria Diedrich, Henry Louis Gates, and Carl Pederson.
New York: Oxford University Press, 1999, 86–95.

Law, Gail. " 'A Chorus of Common Memory': Slavery and
Redemption in Caryl Phillips' *Cambridge* and *Crossing the
River,*" *Research in African Literatures* 29, no. 4 (Winter
1998): 122–141.

CRY, THE BELOVED COUNTRY ALAN PATON (1948)

A protest by a white South African writer against the repressive policy of apartheid in his native country, *Cry, the Beloved Country* is a classic of the literature of racial injustice. A third-person omniscient narrator relates the story of the Rev. Stephen Kumalo as he travels from an agrarian village environment into the urban jungle of Johannesburg in search of his son, Absalom, and his sister, Gertrude; he hopes his brother John, a successful merchant, can assist him. Paton uses the land itself as a key thematic symbol in his poetic descriptions of South Africa: in remote places untouched by COLONIALISM, the land remains verdant and fertile; however, where European settlement has affected traditional African ways, the land is desiccated and fails to support its inhabitants. Green hills give way to raw, red valleys, which in turn lead to the sterile pavements of white cities. Stephen Kumalo is summoned to traverse this pathway from the living world of his home village to the deadly world of the city. His mission is to redeem the missing members of his family, and the obstacles to his success are numerous and powerful.

In making his protagonist a Zulu Christian minister, Paton incorporates two conflicting results of colonialism at the heart of his story: European religion—Christianity—has provided a highly idealistic model for the organization of African spiritual and ethical life, but European economics—capitalism—has worked in the opposite direction, devastating the land and destroying the lives of many Africans. The growth of cities and the spread of wage employment in mines and factories have worked together to draw young men and women away from their villages and from the support system of extended families into fragile dependencies on jobs and their own individual resources. When jobs end, or when personal strength fails, these transplanted Africans frequently become even more victimized, with their own weaknesses amplifying the oppressions of apartheid. Thus Gertrude has sunk to prostitution and black-market dealing in liquor, and Absalom has turned to drunkenness and crime. When Stephen Kumalo finds Absalom, the young man is in prison awaiting trial for the murder of Arthur Jarvis.

Ironically, Arthur Jarvis had been a white idealist working to improve the lot of Africans. Two other boys, including the son of Stephen's brother, John, were also accused. Tragically, John uses his influence to help his own son at the expense of Absalom, who alone is sentenced to death for the crime. Stephen Kumalo cannot help his son survive, but he does meet the young woman carrying Absalom's child. He arranges for the couple to be married; Absalom cannot save himself from the hangman, but he does the right thing in giving his own child a family name and a place of refuge with his father. Stephen returns to his village not with Gertrude and Absalom but with the children of these two. PATON suggests that a generation has been lost, but that hope may still flourish in the villages. Stephen's village, starving after the crops have failed, receives help from an unexpected source when Arthur Jarvis's father decides to carry on his son's benevolent work. In the greatest irony of the book, two fathers of different races, both bereft of their sons, work together to make the world a better place in memory of the sons they have lost.

Paton creates a story that is sympathetic to the suffering of the native population oppressed by apartheid, but he also expands the plot to encompass white suffering as well—white suffering that has as its root the policy of apartheid and its effects on the native peoples of the land. Implicitly, South Africa can flourish again only when all of its occupants are working together for their mutual benefit.

BIBLIOGRAPHY

Brutus, Dennis. "Protest Against Apartheid." In *Protest and Conflict in African Literature.* Edited by Cosmo Pieterse and Donald Munro. New York: Africana, 1969.

Callan, Edward. Cry, the Beloved Country: *A Novel of South Africa.* Twayne's Masterwork Studies, 69. Boston: Twayne, 1991.

Paton, Jonathan. "Comfort in Desolation." In *International Literature in English: Essays on the Major Writers.* Edited by Robert L. Ross. New York: Garland, 1991.

D

DANCE TO THE MUSIC OF TIME, A
ANTHONY POWELL (1951–1975)   This 12-volume series of novels—a ROMAN-FLEUVE—follows the life of Nicholas Jenkins, a writer, in a narrative presented through a first-person point of view. The volumes of the series are divided into four movements, in the manner of a classical symphony or the cycle of the seasons: The volumes of the first movement ("spring") include *A QUESTION OF UPBRINGING* (1951), *A BUYER'S MARKET* (1952), and *The ACCEPTANCE WORLD* (1955); those of the second ("summer") include *AT LADY MOLLY'S* (1957), *CASANOVA'S CHINESE RESTAURANT* (1960), and *The KINDLY ONES* (1962); those of the third ("autumn") include *The VALLEY OF BONES* (1964), *The SOLDIER'S ART* (1966), and *The MILITARY PHILOSOPHERS* (1968); and those of the fourth ("winter") include *BOOKS DO FURNISH A ROOM* (1971), *TEMPORARY KINGS* (1973), and *HEARING SECRET HARMONIES* (1975).

The story opens in about 1921–22 and continues through 1971, recounting in fiction the key historical events of the middle two quarters of the 20th century with recollections of childhood experiences during WORLD WAR I. When POWELL published the first volume in this project, he was 46 years old and focusing on events that had occurred 30 years previously; when he published the last, he was focusing as a 70-year-old on events set only four years earlier. The series is simultaneously the story of Nicholas Jenkins's life, which bears some resemblance to the life of the author,

and of the 20th century itself. A low-key narrator who seldom places himself at center stage, Nicholas is a keen observer of the changes occurring in cultural values and social mores, and he has a wide acquaintanceship on which to practice. Although the events of the plot unfold as illustrations of 20th-century history, the series is primarily a story of characters growing, changing, and declining against the historical backdrop.

Nicholas belongs to a privileged CLASS: His father is an army officer, and Nick eventually marries into an aristocratic family. He boards at Eton, a private school (called a PUBLIC SCHOOL in England) and pursues a university degree at Oxford before moving to London to work. His young adult life falls during the first of the two decades between World War I and WORLD WAR II, an era of wealth, social innovation, and excess; he marries and begins his family during the second, after "the slump" that brought about the Depression. For most of his life, he is, like Powell himself, a writer. His first employment is in the publishing industry as an editor of art books, but he also publishes his first novel during this period. He then works as a screenwriter for the British film industry; at the time, regulations required that a British film be shown for every imported (i.e., American) film screened, and so studios in the London vicinity are busily cranking out footage. After his service in the war, he readjusts himself to civilian life by embarking on a scholarly study, entitled *Borage and Hellebore,* of Richard Burton, the 17th-century author of *The Anatomy of Melancholy.* He also works as a magazine journalist, writing reviews for *Fission,* a new liberal periodical, for the two years of its existence. Finally, he returns to writing novels as well.

Art is a constant theme throughout the entire series in the forms of painting, music, and literature. The overarching title of the series derives from a painting by Nicolas Poussin, the French neoclassical artist. The painting is an ALLEGORY of nature in which four women representing the four seasons join hands in a dance as an elderly man personifying Time provides music for them on a lyre. Overhead, gods and goddesses disport themselves in the clouds. The dance—any dance—is a complex pattern of repeated steps, pauses, and turns that carry the dancers together and apart again, and so it provides an excellent metaphor for life itself immersed in the flow of time. The visual image that inspires the title is itself a representation of three art forms: music, dance, and painting. The structure of Powell's novel sequence is also dancelike, since characters perform their steps, pause in their places, make their turns, draw apart, and come together again (or leave the dance entirely). The tone of the interactions among the characters is sometimes sweet and harmonious, sometime martial and discordant, and sometimes elegiac and mournful; additionally, music provides subject matter for the characters, from its centrality for the composer Hugh Moreland to its supporting role as the background music at dances. Instead of capturing the steps and the harmony visually as Poussin did, however, Powell presents his dance in the form of words that make up a complex and richly textured story.

Summaries of the series, because of its many characters and events compressed into short descriptions, can easily resemble soap opera plots rather than outlines of great literature. The actual novels, however, never sink to bathos nor indulge in sentimentality or sensationalism. The insight and erudition of the narrator, casting an interested but dispassionate eye over culture, society, and the historical background against which the action unfolds; the sympathetic presentation of life's comic joys; and the sensitive portrayal of human weaknesses all cooperate to make this series one of the great literary achievements of the 20th century.

BIBLIOGRAPHY

Birns, Margaret Boe. "Anthony Powell's Secret Harmonies: Music in a Jungian Key," *The Literary Review* 27 (Fall 1981): 80–92.

Harrington, Henry R. "Anthony Powell, Nicolas Poussin, and the Structure of Time," *Contemporary Literature* 24, no. 4 (1983): 431–448.

Joyau, Isabelle. *Understanding Powell's* A Dance to the Music of Time. New York: St. Martin's Press, 1994.

Selig, Robert L. *Time and Anthony Powell.* Madison, N.J.: Fairleigh Dickinson University Press, 1991.

Spurling, Hillary. *Invitation to the Dance: A Guide to Anthony Powell's* A Dance to the Music of Time. Boston: Little, Brown, 1977.

DARK-ADAPTED EYE, A RUTH RENDELL writing as BARBARA VINE (1986)

This novel of mystery and detective fiction features a first-person narrator, Faith Severn, who is the niece of the hanged murderess, Vera Hillyard, twin to Faith's father, John Longley. The story is set after WORLD WAR II but looks back to events that happened then and includes further recollections of the 1920s; the action unfolds in a village near London. The catalyst for the telling of the tale is a biographer, Daniel Stewart, who is delving into Vera Hillyard's murder of her younger sister, Eden (Edith Mary), who had been like a daughter to her.

The story is filled with familial attachments and rivalries. The nuclear family expands as its members marry, but new spouses are not always congenial to their in-laws. Thus when John marries an older half-Swiss woman, she does not meet with his family's approval for her age, class, or nationality; for her part, she does not like John's sisters, and this leads to friction between her and John that affects their children, including Faith. John's view of his sisters is highly idealized—he sees them through blinders, incapable of recognizing their faults. In contrast to this theme of attachment, the story also features a strand about the failure to bond: Vera becomes a mother to the orphaned Eden and virtually abandons her own son, Francis, to private schools. He becomes expert at manipulating his mother's emotions for the worse, on his way to a miserable adolescence and adulthood.

Several tragic events happen during Vera's residence at Laurel Cottage, where she grew up and where Eden was born, and these cast a shadow on Vera's life, mental health, and morale. Then, in her middle 30s, Vera delivers a baby boy, Jamie, 10 1/2 months after her husband's last visit home, making her the focus of village gossip. She is deeply attached to this child, who fills her life when Eden marries Tony Pearmain, a wealthy gentleman. But the sisters are soon engaged in a mysterious custody battle for Jamie that divides the tight-knit family; each sister claims that Jamie is actually her child, and each can offer evidence to support her claim. Their quarrel pushes Vera past her limits and she finally resorts to violence. Vera's guilt in the murder is established to the satisfaction of a jury, but the question of Jamie's maternity seems insoluble.

Silence, concealment, repression, and shame stretch the Longley family bonds until they snap, but the novel also shows how the absence of bonding is cruelly corrosive. Since the story is told by an onlooker who must recall events in which she was only a peripheral character, the novel is also about the fragmentation of storytelling and the defect of memory across the generations. Memory can rely on letters, minutes of meetings, and court proceedings to prop it up, as Faith must do at various points in her story, but even the presence of bald facts cannot erase a family's stains nor eradicate their effects on other family members.

Although *A Dark-Adapted Eye* followed the publication of more than 20 mystery novels by Ruth RENDELL, it was the first novel she published under the pseudonym of Barbara Vine. It won an Edgar Allan Poe Award from the Mystery Writers of America in 1986.

BIBLIOGRAPHY

Dubose, Martha Hailey, and Margaret C. Thomas. *Women of Mystery: The Lives and Works of Notable Women Crime Novelists.* New York: St. Martin's Minotaur, 2000.

Klein, Kathleen Gregory. *Great Women Mystery Writers: Classic to Contemporary.* Westport, Conn.: Greenwood Press, 1994.

DARK FLOWER, THE JOHN GALSWORTHY (1913)

A three-part novel about the three great romances in the life of its protagonist, the sculptor Mark Lennan, this novel was one of its author's particular favorites. The third-person omniscient narrator delivers an intimate view of the emotion of passion as it overwhelms Mark and the three women he has loved in his life, and the structure of the story neatly reverses the first and third parts. Unlike the traditional novel, which covers the entire life of a protagonist or even of an entire family or town, *The Dark Flower* concentrates on short periods of intense emotion; it almost forms three novellas about the same character. The three sections bear the titles "Spring," "Summer," and "Autumn," corresponding to Mark's life as a 17-year-old college student, as a 20-something single artist in London, and as a mature married man of about 50.

Mark's first experience of passion occurs when the wife of his college tutor develops a crush on him; when his tutor invites Mark along on their summer vacation, the young man and the middle-aged woman are thrown together in the beautiful scenery of the Alps. The dark red flower his beloved wears, a clove carnation, becomes Mark's favorite, but before this intense swirl of emotion can turn itself into an indiscretion, the party breaks up. Mark must attend the wedding of his sister, and back at the family's estate, the maid of honor, 16-year-old Sylvia, proves to be an enjoyable companion. Mark attends art school in Rome instead of returning to his college, and so he leaves his first love behind and pursues his muse.

As an aspiring artist with some successful commissions behind him in the novel's second part, Mark meets an unhappily married woman, and the two of them fall passionately in love. After meeting secretly to elude her wealthy husband, they are confronted by him with his complete refusal to be parted from his wife. In spite of her coldness, he loves her as passionately as Mark does, and he has the advantage of legal rights. When the lovers try to flee, a disaster puts a tragic close to the affair. Mark once again finds himself in the comforting company of Sylvia, and soon afterward they are married.

With more than 20 years of satisfactory marriage behind him, middle-aged Mark meets the teenage daughter of one of his old school friends. The girl had been born out of wedlock and reared by her father; she is a modern young woman with a forthright manner, and she initiates the passionate connection and repeatedly tries to draw Mark into infidelity. For his part, he too is passionately in love, but he is also tormented by the memory of previous disaster and by the weight of conscience: An affair with this willing young woman would be a betrayal of his wife and his friend. Mark has now taken the position of the woman he first loved, obsessed with an inappropriate love object and on the verge of hurting those who have been faithful to him. In a neat twist that sheds light on the events of the novel's first part, Mark copes with the emotion that has taken possession of him.

Galsworthy's novel has a surprisingly frank erotic element for a mainstream work written under the long shadow of the Victorian era. His sensuous prose points toward the work, much more explicit, of D. H. LAWRENCE, and his detailed exploration of the thoughts and feelings of his characters, male and female, demonstrates the depth of his insight into the workings of the human heart. Everyone who has been passionately in love will recognize the psychological anxieties that Mark and his three love objects suffer and the social games they play in desperate attempts to sustain and perpetuate their inappropriate and yet inescapable passions.

BIBLIOGRAPHY

Gindin, James. *John Galsworthy's Life and Art.* Ann Arbor: University of Michigan Press, 1987.

Rønning, Anne Holden. *Hidden and Visible Suffrage: Emancipation and the Edwardian Woman in Galsworthy, Wells, and Forster.* New York: Peter Lang, 1995.

DARKNESS AT NOON ARTHUR KOESTLER (1940)

When this novel was published, it provided an explanation that the rest of the world could understand of the infamous Moscow purge trials. In the Soviet Union, which had not yet entirely withdrawn from the international stage to the secrecy behind the "Iron Curtain," Joseph Stalin was relentlessly eliminating his opponents in the struggle for power after the death of V. I. Lenin; incomprehensibly, his colleagues were pleading guilty to outrageous charges of plotting to poison masses of workers, collaborating with capitalists to destroy the new government, and other charges for which there was little evidence and less reason. KOESTLER was well positioned to provide the explanation of the mysterious guilty pleas of men who had devoted their lives to the Communist Party, since he had himself been an active member during much of the 1930s, nearly losing his life to the cause during the SPANISH CIVIL WAR. Put simply, Koestler says that the guilty pleas are a last form of service to the party; his novel explicates the mind of a devotee who would make such a choice.

The protagonist of the story is Nicholas Rubashov, a Soviet official and a longtime member of the party who has toed the party line and who has expelled comrades for not toeing that line, even when doing so had led to others' deaths. He has been imprisoned and charged with crimes against the state, including plotting against the life of "Number 1" (Stalin), of which he is not guilty. During his imprisonment, he is interrogated twice. Ivanov, his interrogator, does not care about the particulars of the indictment as long as Rubashov confesses to ideologically defective thinking. He allows Rubashov a two-week interval to think over his options; Rubashov uses the time to write out his statement about his experience with and loyalty to the cause, but he does not confess to plotting to kill Number 1. During this time, he remembers his own acts to enforce party discipline, and he sees prisoners—personal friends of his—dragged off to execution.

Just before Rubashov's deadline has expired, he is hauled under the glare of blinding lights in the office of Gletkin and informed that Ivanov has been executed for the crime of mismanaging Rubashov's case. Gletkin will accept nothing less that a full confession to all the particulars of the indictment. After a grueling, interminable process, Rubashov signs the trumped-up confession. In the days following, he sees a man who had testified against him dragged to execution before the death squad calls for Rubashov himself. A brief moment in the dungeons of the prison closes another minor incident in the party's history.

Much of the interest of *Darkness at Noon* comes from the psychological realism of Rubashov's thoughts through his imprisonment. He recognizes that he, too, has sacrificed others as a means to an end, and that he now is undergoing what he previously had imposed.

But his loyalty to the party survives his ordeal: Having been guilty of actions that led to others' deaths for the good of the party, he can now avoid the full burden of the moral responsibility of those actions only by continuing to serve the party—the agency that bears the responsibility in his stead—and falsely admitting to the crimes he is accused of.

Koestler's portrait of the totalitarian state is an insightful and compelling one, placing his story in the ranks of DYSTOPIAN NOVELS such as NINETEEN EIGHTY-FOUR by George ORWELL. It was not well received in all quarters: Many artists and intellectuals nurtured hopes that the Soviet Union would lead Europe and the world to a better, more just, and more equitable system of governance and economics, and voices that undermined this optimistic view met stiff opposition. Koestler's book had a particularly strong effect in France against the protests of intellectuals such as Jean-Paul Sartre and Maurice Merleau-Ponty. It may have influenced the course of France's political choices by undermining the image of communism in a way accessible to ordinary readers. Not until Aleksandr Solzhenitsyn exposed the abuses of the Communist Party and Soviet Union—especially against artists and intellectuals—in *The Gulag Archipelago* was the Left's lingering idealization of the hoped-for Communist worker paradise finally laid to rest.

BIBLIOGRAPHY

Pearson, Sidney A. *Arthur Koestler.* Twayne's English Authors, 228. Boston: Twayne Publishers, 1978.

Sperber, Murray A., ed. *Arthur Koestler: A Collection of Critical Essays.* Englewood Cliffs, N.J.: Prentice Hall, 1977.

Sterne, Richard Clark. *Dark Mirror: The Sense of Injustice in Modern European and American Literature.* New York: Fordham University Press, 1994.

DAVIES, ROBERTSON (1913–1995)

A Canadian internationally recognized for his fiction, William Robertson Davies was born on August 28, 1913, in Thamesville, Ontario. His literate family published newspapers, and his own skill with language was encouraged from an early age. After learning to read at six, he quickly advanced to the classics of world literature; such a bookish nature in a boy, however, is not always admired by other less academically inclined boys. Davies eventually drew on some of the childhood bullying he endured for episodes in his fiction, turning his suffering to art and immortalizing his tormentors for what they were. Wishing to pursue the best possible education, he traveled to England to study at Queen's University and Balliol College, Oxford, receiving the B. Litt. degree in 1938. Keenly interested in drama, he trained at London's Old Vic Theatre, performing in several plays in 1938 and 1939. In 1940, he married, but with the onset of WORLD WAR II, he and his wife returned home to the safety of Canada.

Back home again, Davies turned to the family tradition of journalism, and beginning in 1942 he edited the newspaper *The Peterborough Examiner.* He created a persona, Samuel Marchbanks, through which to write a column that became so popular it was syndicated throughout Canada for 11 years. Marchbanks was witty and outspoken in his examination of Canadian life as it changed under contemporary pressures; selections of these essays are collected in *The Papers of Samuel Marchbanks* (1985). He also wrote plays and was a founder of the Shakespeare Festival at Stratford, with Tyrone Guthrie. His first novels, known collectively as *The Salterton Trilogy* (1951–58), drew on the adventures backstage of fictional theatrical performers. But Davies became somewhat disillusioned when he had a play produced on Broadway in 1960, *Leaven of Malice,* only to see it fail. As an art form, the novel was completely his own creation since it does not require directors, costumers, and performers, and he began to concentrate on his fiction.

Even though he did not pursue graduate studies, Davies was vastly erudite from his own wide reading and retentive memory. In 1962, he left journalism to become an academic as a faculty member at Trinity College of the University of Toronto, and in 1967 he was appointed the first master of Massey College, a graduate unit at the same institution. Within the microcosm of the university, he was able to continue his interest in theater while also expanding his fiction writing. He began work on the novels that made him internationally famous, *The DEPTFORD TRILOGY: Fifth Business* (1970), *The Manticore* (1972), and *World of Wonders* (1975). These novels explore the lives of three small-town Canadians who, as boys and men, are affected by a tragic accident that two of them cause.

In the 1980s, Davies published another successful set of novels, *The Cornish Trilogy*, consisting of *The Rebel Angels* (1982), *What's Bred in the Bone* (1985), and *The Lyre of Orpheus* (1988). This series explores the life of a mysterious and wealthy painter of fake masterpieces, Francis Cornish. Davies's final novels seemed intended as the first two volumes of another trilogy (sometimes referred to as the "Toronto trilogy"). In *Murther and Walking Spirits* (1991), the narrator is executed in the first sentence of the novel, recounting the remainder of the story post-mortem, and in *The Cunning Man* (1995), an aging physician tells the story of his life—and of Toronto—to an interviewer. Before completing this trilogy, Davies died on December 2, 1995.

BIBLIOGRAPHY

Davis, J. Madison, ed. *Conversations with Robertson Davies.* Jackson: University Press of Mississippi, 1989.

Grant, Judith Skelton. *Robertson Davies: Man of Myth.* Toronto: Penguin, 1994.

Morley, Patricia. *Robertson Davies.* Agincourt, Ontario: Gage Educational Publishing, 1977.

Peterman, Michael. *Robertson Davies.* Boston: Twayne, 1986.

DAY OF THE SCORPION, THE PAUL SCOTT (1968)

The second volume in *The Raj Quartet,* this novel resumes the story of Britain's last days of colonial control over the territory that became INDIA AND PAKISTAN. Where the first volume, *The Jewel in the Crown,* had opened with a rape, in the second volume of the quartet the dominant image is that of ritual suicide by self-immolation; repeatedly, fire plays a role in the events of the story, echoing the scene of an Englishwoman's suicide by suttee, or ritual immolation, in the first volume. The British Raj is essentially trapped in a similarly suicidal ring of fire.

The focus of the story shifts to the Layton family, composed mostly of women who are the dependents of Colonel Layton, a prisoner of war in Germany. Mrs. Mabel Layton manages to endure her situation with infusions of strong drink, and her younger daughter, Susan, married early in the novel to the doomed Teddie Bingham, is emotionally unstable beneath an exterior veneer of cheerfulness. To the elder daughter, Sarah,

falls the duty of managing the family. Ronald Merrick, a police superintendent in the first volume who is now a military intelligence officer, enters the family's life when he serves as Teddie's best man. The Laytons are puzzled that Merrick is hated by the Indians, not knowing of his unjust treatment of Hari Kumar. Merrick likes Sarah and works to impress her. But Sarah is another version of the Englishwoman who is sympathetic to the Indian cause of independence; she lacks Merrick's scorn or Teddie's condescension to the Indians they govern.

The fire image recurs when Merrick tries unsuccessfully to rescue Teddie. Indian soldiers who have joined the Japanese resist Teddie's efforts to return them to the British side, and in the flaming struggle Teddie dies and Merrick is badly wounded. In this action, Merrick shows himself capable of heroism, but his cruelty to Hari outweighs this characteristic. He loses an arm and, at Susan's bidding, Sarah visits him in the hospital in Calcutta. There, he talks about a painting of Queen Victoria receiving tokens of allegiance from her Indian subjects. The painting is another connection to the first volume: It is entitled "The Jewel in Her Crown," and it belonged to Miss Crane, the suttee suicide, in *The Jewel in the Crown.* The paternalistic attitudes of the British toward the Indians are apparent in the painting, but if the Raj is a family composed of British parents and Indian children, it is a dysfunctional family at best. Sarah is the character who best understands that the Raj is in its last days, even though many in charge do not comprehend this simple fact. The Laytons' story continues in the third volume of the series, *The Towers of Silence.*

BIBLIOGRAPHY

Childs, Peter. *Paul Scott's* Raj Quartet: *History and Division.* Victoria, B.C.: University of Victoria, 1998.

Rao, K. Bhaskara. *Paul Scott.* Twayne's English Author, 285. Boston: Twayne Publishers, 1980.

Weinbaum, Francine S. *Paul Scott: A Critical Study.* Austin, Texas: University of Texas Press, 1992.

DEATH OF THE HEART, THE ELIZABETH BOWEN (1938)

Constructed with a third-person omniscient narrator, but interleaved with first-person diary entries and letters, this novel scrutinizes the emotionally empty lives of the prestigious and wealthy Quayne household through the eyes of Portia, the 16-

year-old half-sister of Thomas Quayne. Portia has been orphaned by the death of her mother, with whom she had lived a transient life in European hotels. They had been close, but their life had been rootless. When Portia comes to London to live with Thomas and his wife, Anna, she finds the opposite situation: a couple rooted in respectability and stability but lacking children or even love. In their fine house, material objects are almost fetishized, taking the place of human tenderness and absorbing the reverence usually reserved for religious devotions.

With a teenager's insouciance, Portia is indifferent to the material world of tastefully chosen furniture; from Anna's perspective, Portia is an engine of disorder. When she finds and reads Portia's diary, her distaste for her sister-in-law becomes amplified tenfold: Her pride is wounded as she interprets the diary to mean that Portia is laughing at her. Portia observes and records the interactions and conversations in the Quayne household with an unsparing honesty that disturbs Anna because of the coldness of the accurate picture it creates. Anna is devoted to beauty and refinement, but she is also dependent on hypocrisy and upper-class snobbery to insulate herself from anything too coarse, common, or vulgar.

Portia's social circle remains very narrow in her brother's house, so that her growing awareness of her awakening desires finds few outlets. Lonely old Major Brutt is friendly to her, but she eventually falls in love with Eddie, a 23-year-old employee of her brother. Her feelings toward him are sincere and painfully intense, while he merely toys with her, sending her provocative letters that she hides and rereads in secret. Anna, too, has a stash of secret letters from her former fiancé, and she too relishes them in secret. The woman and the girl are well suited to form a deep and meaningful bond if only they can make the connection.

When Thomas and Anna take a vacation, Portia stays with Anna's former governess, Mrs. Heccomb, and her two stepchildren. The visit to "Waikiki," as Mrs. Heccomb calls her seaside home, is a comic interlude that allows Portia to meet a variety of people her own age who would never be deemed good enough for admittance to the Quayne household. Eddie comes for a visit, and Portia sees him drinking and flirting with other girls, but she decides she can accept these flaws.

For his part, Eddie's inability to take seriously a romantic attachment to a young woman is part of his particular challenge in life: Bowen subtly suggests his suppressed homosexuality, a taboo topic in literature at the time she was writing.

When Portia returns home to welcome the travelers, she learns that Anna has been reading her diary. Angry and resentful, she experiences the same wounded pride that Anna had felt and runs away, sure that Anna is laughing at her. She goes to the sad hotel where Major Brutt rents a room, determined to break with her family permanently. She is luckier than many of the ingénues in literature; Bowen concludes the novel with AMBIGUITY, but also with the suggestion that Portia and Anna and Thomas have a chance to resolve their differences.

BOWEN'S work in general and this novel in particular have benefited from the interpretive insights of FEMINISM. The motherless child and the childless mother of this novel both provoke critical inquiry about the parental role that has been the traditional domain of women. But the novel is also a young woman's BILDUNGSROMAN that refuses to accept the usual formula of courtship and marriage as the rose-strewn path to personal fulfillment. The problems that the young must overcome remain the same—the three sections of the novel are entitled "The World," "The Flesh," and "The Devil"—but the same old solutions may not be enough to make life a more satisfying experience. Bowen illustrates her point in a novel that is both poignant and comic, capturing the insightful freshness of youth without pressing it into a stereotypical conclusion.

BIBLIOGRAPHY

Heath, William W. *Elizabeth Bowen: An Introduction to Her Novels*. Madison: University of Wisconsin Press, 1961.

Lassner, Phyllis. *Elizabeth Bowen*. Basingstoke, U.K.: Macmillan, 1990.

Lee, Hermione. *Elizabeth Bowen: An Estimation*. London: Vision Press, 1981.

DECLINE AND FALL EVELYN WAUGH (1928)

This novel of SATIRE was the first published by Evelyn WAUGH, one of the great English satirists of the 20th century, and many scholars consider it to be his best. The narrative unfolds through a third-person omniscient point of view and relates the misadventures of Paul Pennyfeather, a young divinity student at Oxford. Paul has the misfortune of strolling on the quad one night as the Bollinger Society concludes a drunken revel; the intoxicated aristocrats who make up the society seize Paul and divest him of his trousers. When Paul complains to the university, he himself is expelled for indecent behavior on the quad. Paul's guardian cuts off the legacy that has supported the young man's studies, since a clause in the will of Paul's father allows this action in the event that Paul's performance is "unsatisfactory."

Paul secures a position as a teacher in a private school at Llanabba Castle, where Dr. Augustus Fagan disguises the poor quality of his institution with pious lectures on service. His two daughters are the husband-hunting Flossie and the miserly Diana. Flossie is engaged to Captain Grimes, one of the masters at the school, but Paul learns that this engagement is actually a form of insurance for Grimes, who perpetually manages to land himself in trouble (or, as he says, "in the soup"). Paul's other colleague is Dr. Prendergast, a former clergyman now afflicted by religious doubts. The school's butler is Solomon Philbrick, a con artist with a different story for each of the school's masters: Grimes thinks Philbrick is a novelist conducting research, while Prendergast believes him to be an eccentric aristocrat and shipping magnate. Paul takes up his duties teaching the fifth form (approximately equivalent to an American 11th-grade class); he discovers that his unruly students are susceptible to bribes when he sees how diligent they become after he promises a monetary reward for the longest essay. His best student, he thinks, is Peter Beste-Chetwynde.

At the school's annual sports meet, Paul meets Peter's mother, Margot Beste-Chetwynde, a beautiful widow, and is smitten by her. One of the students at the school, young Lord Tangent, is shot in the heel with a starting pistol; as the term drags on, he dies of infection. Philbrick flees the school as detectives close in, investigating him for false pretense, and Grimes flees his marriage to Flossie, leaving his clothes and a suicide note on a nearby beach.

At the close of the term, Paul is hired to tutor Peter during the summer holiday. He arrives at the Beste-Chetwynde home, King's Thursday, a starkly modernized Tudor site where Margot entertains an unending string of weekend guests. She is being courted by the minister of transport, Sir Humphrey Maltravers, but Paul manages to propose to her, and Peter declares him to be the better of the two options as a stepfather. Shortly before the wedding, Margot sends Paul to Marseilles on a business errand connected with her late father's South American "entertainment" enterprise, which also employs Grimes in some mysterious capacity. Paul does not realize that his errand involves bribes to various political officials—he thinks he is arranging passage for cabaret entertainers headed for Rio de Janeiro. On his wedding day, Paul is arrested for trafficking in the white slave trade and Margot flees to Corfu.

Paul stands trial for Margot's criminal activities and is sentenced to seven years in prison. At Blackstone Gaol, he is reunited with Philbrick, who serves as a trustee, and with Prendergast, who serves as the prison chaplain until he is killed by an inmate. Paul is moved to Egdon Heath Penal Settlement; Grimes is a fellow prisoner there until he manages to disappear into the fog one day. Margot visits Paul to tell him that she is marrying Maltravers, who has been named Lord Metroland and has risen to the post of home secretary. Soon, Paul is removed from Egdon Heath on orders from the home secretary for an appendicitis operation. He finds himself first at a nursing home owned by Dr. Fagan, where he is declared dead and spirited aboard a yacht bound for Margot's Corfu home. Paul rests there and grows a mustache so that he can return to his studies at Oxford. One year after his adventures began, Paul Pennyfeather is back in college, passing himself off as his own cousin. Peter Best-Chetwynde visits him after a drunken evening with the Bollinger Society and warns Paul against involvement with people like himself and his mother; upon Peter's departure, Paul turns his attention back to his textbook on religious heresy.

Evelyn Waugh finds numerous targets for his satire: aristocrats, academics, clerics, the rich, the British government, the Church of England, modern architecture, and human folly of every stripe, among many others. Waugh uses effective name symbolism to give his characters a slightly allegorical dimension, making each of them representative of a class of folly. The tone of the narration is cheerful, with tragic elements revealed indirectly in an understated manner. Paul Pennyfeather (an impoverished lightweight) is the protagonist rather than the hero of the novel: His passive acceptance of life's reversals undermines his character and tarnishes what might otherwise be virtuous fortitude. Since he ends exactly where he began, the deterioration implied by the novel's title has a broader application: Society at large is in decline, the author implies, and those enmeshed in it must cope as best they can in a world that will not reward the good and punish the bad.

BIBLIOGRAPHY

Beaty, Frederick L. *The Ironic World of Evelyn Waugh: A Study of Eight Novels.* DeKalb: Northern Illinois University Press, 1992.

Cowley, Malcolm. "Decline and Fall." In *Critical Essays on Evelyn Waugh.* Edited by James F. Carens. Boston: G. K. Hall, 1987.

DECONSTRUCTION   See POSTMODERNISM.

DEPTFORD TRILOGY, THE ROBERTSON DAVIES (1970–1975)

The three volumes of this series include *Fifth Business* (1970), mainly devoted to Dunstan Ramsay; *The Manticore* (1972), mainly devoted to Boy Staunton; and *World of Wonders* (1975), mainly devoted to Paul Dempsey in his professional guise as Magnus Eisengrim. The setting of the story is originally in the town of Deptford, Ontario, during the middle 20th century, although it moves on to other locations in different volumes as the main characters of each narrative grow and pursue adult lives. This trilogy, and especially the first volume of it, is generally regarded as the best and most characteristic of DAVIES's large creative output. The three protagonist characters live lives that are intertwined at various levels from childhood onward.

Fifth Business follows the life of Dunstan Ramsay, a kind of alter ego for Robertson Davies; Ramsay is recounting his autobiography from the perspective of old age. This first volume opens with an ordinary childhood act—the throwing of a snowball—that has tragic and long-reaching consequences. Ramsay, the intended target, ducks the fateful blow and thereby finds his character altered by the suffering inflicted on Mary Dempster and on the child, Paul Dempster, born prematurely after she is struck by the snowball. The snowball thrower,

Boy Staunton, becomes an important political figure in Canada as an adult; his childhood snowball is so destructive because he has packed it with a stone. As an adult, Ramsay becomes a specialist in hagiology, the study of the lives of saints, perhaps as a compensation for the absence of genuine saintliness in his own life.

The Manticore provides an exploration of Jungian psychology, reviewing the numerous ARCHETYPES Carl Jung defined and applying them in the construction of the story. Boy Staunton's son David is undergoing psychological therapy in Switzerland after an emotional breakdown; his progress into his problems, their sources, and his relationship with his father constitute the bulk of the novel. That paternal relationship is problematic in part because of Boy Staunton's character in relation to his son, and in part because of his mysterious death: His body is recovered from Lake Ontario with the peculiarity of a stone in its mouth—another unexpected death associated with a stone.

World of Wonders is a fictional autobiography of Magnus Eisengrim, undertaken by Dunstan Ramsay. It features a strong emphasis on magic—Magnus Eisengrim is a gifted magician—but the story draws on the concepts of appearance and reality rather than on the recent conventions of magic realism. Davies emphasizes the ways human beings are isolated from the knowledge of the risks they face by acting in the world—in the endless and endlessly interconnected chain of causes and effects—while they are simultaneously condemned to continue acting (with a play of words on "acting," since all the world's a stage and Davies began his career as a professional actor). The snowball incident is seen from yet another perspective, since it was that event that brought about the special giftedness of Paul Dempster.

The three novels display the author's erudition: He was a scholar and a man of letters as well as a novelist, dramatist, essayist, and journalist. Davies demonstrates the psychological depth of his thinking in his use of oppositions such as appearance and reality; his linguistic skill is apparent in his clever wordplay. Characters developed in this series later appear in other works by Davies, and the well-prepared reader encounters them as old friends. Although Robertson Davies writes at a level of literary sophistication that is most fully appreciated by deeply educated and experienced readers, his absorbing plots and fully rendered characters also appeal to readers mainly interested in a good story.

BIBLIOGRAPHY

Lawrence, Robert G., and Samuel L. Macey, eds. *Studies in Robertson Davies' Deptford Trilogy.* English Literary Studies. Victoria, British Columbia: University of Victoria, 1980.

Monk, Patricia. *Mud and Magic Shows: Robertson Davies' Fifth Business.* Canadian Fiction Studies 13. Toronto: ECW, 1992.

———. *The Smaller Infinity: The Jungian Self in the Novels of Robertson Davies.* Toronto: University of Toronto Press, 1982.

Moss, John. *Sex and Violence in the Canadian Novel: The Ancestral Present.* Toronto: McClelland & Stewart, 1977.

DESAI, ANITA (1937–)

DESAI, ANITA (1937–) The daughter of a German mother and a Bengali father, Anita Desai was born on June 24, 1937, in Mussoorie, India. She was reared and educated in Delhi, studying at Queen Mary's School and at Miranda House of Delhi University. At the age of 26, she published her first novel, *Cry, the Peacock* (1963), to critical success, establishing her reputation as an important new author. Desai chooses to write in English, one of the official languages of India, although not one of its native languages; in some circles, her preference for English has drawn unfavorable commentary on her literary choices. She defends her use of English as a legitimate option for writers in India, given the history of COLONIALISM and the consequent pervasiveness of English in India's public life.

Throughout her first six novels, Desai explores a range of Indian women's lives, many of them unhappy. The oppressed protagonist of *Cry, the Peacock* loses her sanity; similarly, the wife in *Where Shall We Go This Summer?* (1975) runs away in an attempt to escape her own fertility and find her true identity. Desai also examines the effects of colonialism in *Bye-Bye, Blackbird* (1971), both on colonizers and natives, and she explores the human crucible of urban life in *Voices in the City* (1965). The ravages and isolation of women in old age provide the subject of *Fire on the Mountain* (1977). But Desai's greatest feminist creation occurs in *CLEAR LIGHT OF DAY* (1980), short-listed for the BOOKER PRIZE in the year of its publication. Bim, a single mid-

dle-aged woman, shapes a fulfilling life teaching college history courses and caring for her mentally handicapped brother, as the stresses tearing apart her family mirror the political rifts that follow India's independence in 1947. Desai expanded her fictional characterizations to include men as protagonists beginning in 1984 with the publication of *In Custody;* this novel charts the decline of Urdu as a significant language in India and was nominated for the Booker Prize. In 1988, Desai narrated a story about a wandering Jew in *Baumgartner's Bombay,* winning the Hadassah Prize. She has also published *Journey to Ithaca* (1995), *Feasting, Fasting* (1999), and *Diamond Dust* (2000).

Anita Desai continues to live and write in India, producing serious fiction and children's literature; she is widely regarded as one of India's most important living novelists.

BIBLIOGRAPHY

Bande, Usha. *The Novels of Anita Desai: A Study in Character and Conflict.* New Delhi: Prestige Books, 1988.

Dhawan, R. K., ed. *The Fiction of Anita Desai.* New Delhi: Bahri Publications, 1989.

Jena, Seema. *Voice and Vision of Anita Desai.* New Delhi: Ashish Publishing House, 1989.

Sharma, R. S. *Anita Desai.* New Delhi: Arnold-Heinemann, 1981.

DESCENT INTO HELL CHARLES WILLIAMS (1937)

DESCENT INTO HELL **CHARLES WILLIAMS (1937)** The plot of this novel occurs one summer during the late 1930s in Battle Hill, a suburb of London. The story's events take place during the preparation and production of a play; as the narrative unfolds, Battle Hill serves as a nexus for activities in differing eras that connect characters to one another across time. Five main characters are involved: Peter Stanhope, the noted poet and playwright; Pauline Ansthuther, a sensitive young woman; Pauline's saintly grandmother Margaret; Adela Hunt, a vain aspiring actress; and Laurence Wentworth, a military historian obsessed with an empty passion for Adela. Some of these characters will find redemption, and some will descend into a living hell.

Peter Stanhope has agreed to allow the town's amateur theatre group to produce his latest play. Adela Hunt and her self-centered fiancé portray the leading roles onstage while Pauline leads the play's chorus and acts as the novel's protagonist. Pauline has been haunted by a doppelganger all her life. It terrifies her, and yet it is a double of her. The lines by Shelley, "The Magus Zoroaster, my dead child, met his own image walking in the garden," serve as a touchstone for her. Peter Stanhope recognizes her poetic nature, and in a conversation with him she reveals her fear. Peter offers to "carry her burden" as an act of spiritual love so that Pauline can find the courage to manage her fear and face the image of her double. To her amazement, it works.

Pauline learns from Margaret that a relative of theirs was burned to death as a heretic on this very hill in the past, during England's bloody conflicts between Protestants and Catholics. Margaret confirms Peter's explanation of sharing others' burdens, and on the night she dies she sends Pauline out into the darkness to help a character in greater suffering than her own—a suicide whose spirit is stranded in Battle Hill. A wretch of a man, he hanged himself while working as a carpenter, part of the group that built the houses on Battle Hill. Pauline helps the spirits of both this man and her ancestor, allowing herself to experience their pain. Margaret passes away in peace shortly after Pauline returns.

The house the suicide killed himself in is inhabited by Laurence Wentworth, an eminent historian who has a recurring dream. In it he finds himself descending a white rope with nothing but darkness around him. At one point, both the suicide and Laurence stand side by side at the same window, looking out into the night as they ponder their lives. Wentworth's obsession for Adela—a sick love rather than a generous one—allows a succubus to insinuate herself into his fantasies; he accepts this false image, knowing it to be false but finding it to be satisfying nonetheless. He further allows a lie to pass for the truth when he approves the designs for the guards' uniforms in the play even though he knows they contain a flaw. Even when he has a chance to reach out to the real Adela, he prefers the imitation of her. Toward the end of the book, Wentworth wanders Battle Hill, lost in his own delusions just like the suicide, both unseeing and unseen. The final chapter relates his trip to London to attend a banquet for historical scholars. It is chillingly told from his self-absorbed and unbalanced perspective.

This mixing of death and life—choices of will and their consequences for either good or evil—forms the matrix upon which the various threads of the characters' lives are woven. Complex and dense, this book has hints of and outright ALLUSIONS to both Shakespeare and Dante. Sodom and Gomorrah also are used as types of existence that can be chosen: not so much as *places* but more as states of mind. For those acquainted with WILLIAMS, Peter Stanhope's role as his doppelganger is apparent. One of the characters in the book comments about Peter, "He's got a number of curiously modern streaks under his romanticism." Additionally, Peter gives Pauline the name "Periel," just as Williams was in the habit of giving people secondary names.

Williams's novels can be dense and daunting, but the rewards for perseverance (and often, rereading) can be great. C. S. LEWIS, a fellow INKLING and Christian, described Williams's novels as "supernatural thrillers"; more recently, this type of fiction has been referred to as modern urban fantasy. Of Williams's eight novels, *Descent into Hell* is considered by many to be his best. Its themes are crafted in a very tight and complex manner, producing layers of meanings that can be a joy to discover.

—Eric Rauscher

BIBLIOGRAPHY

Cavaliero, Glen. *Charles Williams: Poet of Theology.* New York: Macmillan, 1983.

Howard, Thomas. *The Novels of Charles Williams.* New York: Oxford University Press, 1983.

Hillegas, Mark R. ed. *Shadows of Imagination: The Fantasies of C. S. Lewis, J. R. R. Tolkien, and Charles Williams.* Carbondale: Southern Illinois University Press, 1979.

DESOLATION ISLAND PATRICK O'BRIAN (1978)   See AUBREY-MATURIN NOVELS.

DIMINISHING AGE (1945–1960)   In the aftermath of WORLD WAR II, the role of Great Britain in world affairs declined and the nation's economy faltered, making a slow and painful recovery from the war. The nation was bankrupted by the war, sustained by the American Lend-Lease program only as long as the hostilities lasted. Saddled with monumental debt and possessing few exports to trade even for food, the British government borrowed some $4 billion from the United States and Canada. Shortages persisted, requiring the extension of rationing schemes for a few years after the war ended, and the standard of living did not rebound as quickly in the United Kingdom as it did in the United States. The Marshall Plan poured financial resources into the reconstruction of conquered regions, but it provided no relief for the victorious allies, including the British, in spite of the ravages of the blitzkrieg, the disarray of the nation's manufacturing facilities, and the deterioration of such crucial aspects of infrastructure as railroads.

In addition to postwar hardships, the British Empire shrank rapidly during these years. British India gained independence and immediately split into the nations of INDIA AND PAKISTAN in 1947, and gradually other colonial areas became independent nations such as Australia, New Zealand, and South Africa. The cost of administering the EMPIRE in its waning days placed a financial strain on the shrinking resources of the British, but the loss of territory, prestige, and clout in world affairs also had a deleterious psychological effect. In literature, the ANGRY YOUNG MEN attacked the status quo, and increasing numbers of working-CLASS writers challenged the traditional valorization of the upper classes in fiction. These new attitudes and new subjects invigorated British literature at a time when the nation's finances and politics were stagnating.

BIBLIOGRAPHY

Bartlett, C. J. *A History of Postwar Britain, 1945–1974.* London: Longman, 1977.

Havighurst, Alfred F. *Britain in Transition: The Twentieth Century.* Chicago: University of Chicago Press, 1985.

DISGRACE J. M. COETZEE (1999) Winner of the BOOKER PRIZE in 1999—an event that made COETZEE the first author to win that award twice—*Disgrace* presents the elegiac story of a professional and personal disaster in the life of a scholar during his transition from middle age to old age. The novel features a third-person narrator limited to the thoughts of the protagonist, David Lurie; however, at times the narrative voice seems to speak directly from Lurie's con-

sciousness, as if he were speaking about himself, and to himself, in the third person.

Lurie is twice divorced, with one adult daughter living on a farm in Grahamstown. At 52, he is satisfied to live alone and make weekly visits to a prostitute for sexual release until the day he sees her in town with her two children. When he calls her at her home rather than her place of employment, she terminates their relationship. At loose ends, David is soon attracted to a beautiful young woman who is enrolled in his literature class, and his better judgment cannot restrain him from pursuing an affair with her. For her part, she is too young and inexperienced to know how to handle the attentions of an older man who is also her professor, and after entering into the affair, she resorts to the passive-aggressive defense of sending her boyfriend to intimidate Lurie. His handling of the situation soon lands him before an inquiry board, accused of sexual harassment. As the scandal intensifies, Lurie resigns his position and loses his pension rather than plead guilty and apologize.

He goes to visit his daughter, Lucy, while sorting out what to do next. He intends to write an opera to be called *Byron in Italy,* and her farm would provide a bucolic retreat after the glare of the inquiry. Her situation is increasingly precarious, since her farm is directly in the sights of Petrus, an ambitious African whom she first employs and later fears as his control of the farm increases. David volunteers at an animal clinic where the main business is putting to sleep the unwanted pets that have been rescued. A violent attack occurs at the farm; Lucy is raped and beaten, and David is splashed with acid. He is descending into a more and more hellish existence, sometimes because of his folly, and sometimes through no fault of his own. All the while, as an educated and literate man, he is aware of the ironies associated with his misfortunes, and he increasingly feels that the world no longer has a place for him that he would care to accept. Touchingly, David's old-fashioned pride does not obscure his intelligence or prevent him from learning new lessons from those he once would have avoided. He is able to accept responsibility for his disgrace, and even to seek forgiveness from the injured parties. When he remains unforgiven, he is even able to accommodate this snub while also marveling at the human ability to endure ever-greater hardships.

Coetzee uses his aging protagonist, with his self-centeredness and his repulsion for the world that has grown up around him, as an illustration of the inexorably tragic direction of human life toward death. He creates an intense poignancy in David's growing awareness of mortality—his own and that of all life—by highlighting the self-reflexive nature of human consciousness. Not only must we die, David learns; we must go into that darkness knowing full well its finality.

BIBLIOGRAPHY

Barnard, Rita. "J. M. Coetzee's *Disgrace* and the South African Pastoral," *Contemporary Literature* 44, no. 2 (Summer 2003): 199–224.

Cornwell, Gareth. "Realism, Rape, and J. M. Coetzee's *Disgrace*," *Critique: Studies in Contemporary Fiction* 43, no. 4 (Summer 2002): 306–22.

Kossew, Sue. "The Politics of Shame and Redemption in J. M. Coetzee's *Disgrace*," *Research in African Literatures* 34, no. 2 (Summer 2003): 155–62.

DIVISION OF THE SPOILS, THE PAUL SCOTT (1975)

In this novel, the closing volume of *The Raj Quartet*, SCOTT returns to the style of the first volume, *The Jewel in the Crown*, with a complex narrative that both surveys the novel's contemporary moment (1945–47) and also looks back to events of the first three volumes of the series. Scott introduces a character into the story as narrator, Sergeant Guy Perron, who is employed in military intelligence with Ronald Merrick, a key figure throughout the entire story. Perron becomes acquainted with the Layton family as Colonel Layton returns from a prisoner of war camp in Germany at the end of the war to find his world utterly transformed.

Merrick and Perron visit Pankot in the course of their investigative duties, and when Merrick asks Susan Layton Bingham to marry him, she accepts. He is horribly scarred from the fire that killed her husband Teddie, but Susan looks past the surface to the man who risked his own life for Teddie. But Merrick has been too harsh to Indians, and his own end is brutally and savagely violent.

In bringing the entire quartet to its close, the case of Hari Kumar must be resolved, and through an investigation by Nigel Rowan, a suitor to Sarah Layton, readers learn that Hari's innocence is vindicated and that he has been released from prison. But his life has been utterly transformed as well, and he lives in poverty in spite of his upper-class English education. Hari had been something of an Anglophile before his harsh and unjust treatment, but he is left only with the memory of the ideal that England once represented for some Indians. The plight of Indian Muslims also features in the novel's closing portion when the Laytons are unable to save a Muslim friend from a bloodthirsty Hindu mob. Centuries-old religious hatred between the followers of the two faiths boils into a rage that finally tears the land into separate nations. The British are helpless to leave India in good order; nonetheless, they must leave.

BIBLIOGRAPHY

Childs, Peter. *Paul Scott's Raj Quartet: History and Division.* Victoria, B.C.: University of Victoria, 1998.

Johnson, Richard M. " 'Sayed's Trial' in Paul Scott's *A Division of the Spoils*: The Interplay of History, Theme and Purpose," *Library Chronicle of the University of Texas* 37 (1986): 76–91.

Rao, K. Bhaskara. *Paul Scott.* Twayne's English Authors, 285. Boston: Twayne Publishers, 1980.

DOUGLAS, NORMAN (1868–1952)

Only one novel by Norman Douglas continues to draw critical interest: *South Wind* (1917), which built a kind of cult following in England and the United States after its publication. Its popularity with discriminating readers helped extend Douglas's reputation perhaps more than his modest output warranted. He wrote only a few novels and some travel books, memoirs, and literary criticism, but he was well connected to English upper-class travelers and admired by his literary contemporaries. Graham GREENE praised *South Wind,* and the novel's comic style influenced early works by Aldous HUXLEY.

Norman Douglas, although descended from an old Scottish family, was born in Thüringen, Austria, on February 9, 1868, and educated at Karlsruhe. He excelled in languages and published articles on zoology while still in school. He embarked on a career with the British Foreign Office, serving briefly in St. Petersburg, but withdrew to devote himself to his writing. He settled in Italy with his wife, and they collaborated on a collection of stories, *Unprofessional Tales,* published to little attention in 1901. His second book, a volume of travel writing entitled *Siren Land* (1911), required the assistance of noted writers such as Joseph CONRAD and Edward Garnett (father of David GARNETT) to reach publication. Then, in 1917, the cheerful escapism of *South Wind,* coming as it did during the depths of WORLD WAR I, made Douglas's reputation.

Critics continue to admire Douglas's travel writing, especially *Fountains in the Sand* (1912), on Tunisia, and *Old Calabria* (1915), about Italy. Douglas died on February 9, 1952, on the island of Capri.

BIBLIOGRAPHY

Holloway, Mark. *Norman Douglas: A Biography.* London: Secker & Warburg, 1976.

Leary, Lewis. *Norman Douglas.* New York: Columbia University Press, 1968.

Lindeman, Ralph D. *Norman Douglas.* Twayne's English Authors, 19. Boston: Twayne, 1965.

DOWN BY THE RIVER EDNA O'BRIEN (1997)

Inspired by the true story of a pregnant 14-year-old Irish rape victim in 1922, this novel examines the tragedies that follow from attempts to constrain, regulate, and legislate women's fertility, particularly in IRELAND, where Catholicism has been inseparable from politics and law for centuries.

The protagonist of the story is Mary McNamara, the daughter of an abusive and incestuous father. She resists his advances, and when he imposes himself on her physically, she resists facing the reality of her situation, escaping into her thoughts by ignoring what is happening to her body. She flees her home repeatedly, only to be dragged back there repeatedly. When Mary announces her pregnancy to her father, he denies any responsibility for it. She attempts suicide by drowning, but she is saved by Betty Rhodes, who also tries to get her to England for an abortion.

Complicating this plot, already tragic enough, O'BRIEN adds the subplot of Irish women inflamed with antiabortion zeal. They are unwitting tools of the very system that essentially enslaves them; nonetheless, they manage to intervene in Mary's life, preventing her abortion, and bringing her to an Irish court. Mary McNamara is the victim throughout these harrowing events; even the activists who wish to make her a poster girl for women's rights place the ideology they serve ahead of Mary's worth as a person. Mary has more betrayal in her life before a turn of events makes a moot point of her situation.

O'Brien spares neither the Left nor the Right in her examination of women's trampled lives in Ireland. At the end of the story, both ends of the political spectrum have failed to deal with the crisis at the heart of the novel, as have the family, the church, the courts, and the government. With darkly bitter humor, O'Brien paints a world in which women are their own worst enemies even when the means to make the world a better place is well within their grasp.

BIBLIOGRAPHY

Morgan, Eileen. "Mapping Out a Landscape of Female Suffering: Edna O'Brien's De-Mythologizing Novels," *Women's Studies: An Interdisciplinary Journal* 29, no. 4 (August 2000): 449–76.

St. Peter, Christine. "Petrifying Time: Incest Narratives from Contemporary Ireland." In *Contemporary Irish Fiction: Themes, Tropes, Theories.* Edited by Liam Harte and Michael Parker. New York: St. Martin's Press, 2000, 125–44.

DOYLE, ARTHUR CONAN (1859–1930)

The creator of Sherlock HOLMES, one of the immortal characters of literature, Arthur Conan Doyle was born on May 22, 1859, in Edinburgh, Scotland, into a family of Catholic artists, and he continued the family's tradition of creative innovation but shifted his sphere of activity to the world of print narratives. Doyle (he preferred the combination "Conan Doyle" later in life and is frequently referred to as such in academic treatments) read widely as a boy, developing a special fondness for the HISTORICAL FICTION of Sir Walter Scott—a genre he later wrote in himself. He studied at Stoneyhurst, a Jesuit PUBLIC SCHOOL, where he excelled in athletics, and then at a similar school in Austria for a year when he was 16.

Doyle undertook training to become a doctor when he was only 17. He enrolled at the University of Edinburgh, and there he came under the instruction of the man upon whom Sherlock Holmes was later modeled, Dr. Joseph Bell. Doyle completed his medical studies and entered into the practice of medicine, then none too lucrative. But he also began writing and publishing short fiction in 1878, at first anonymously. After serving as a ship's doctor on two voyages, Doyle settled in Southsea, where he practiced medicine until 1890 and was married in 1885. In 1891, he moved his family to London. By this time, he was already writing to supplement his income. His first novel, *A Study in Scarlet,* appeared in 1887 and introduced Sherlock Holmes to the world. He followed this work with two historical novels inspired by Sir Walter Scott, and then returned to Holmes in *The Sign of the Four,* published in 1890. These works were all successful, so that Doyle turned from medicine to writing as his full-time occupation.

Doyle's most popular successes were the many short stories he published about the cases solved by Holmes and Watson. He actually tried to kill Holmes off by 1893, since he wanted to work on other projects rather than serve the public's apparently bottomless appetite for more Sherlock Holmes stories. He worked on other novels, but in 1901 he returned to his great detective in *The Hound of the Baskervilles,* set before Holmes's apparently fatal encounter of 1893. In 1903, Holmes was officially resurrected in a short story, and Doyle continued to use Holmes for short fiction until 1927, producing one further novel about him, *The Valley of Fear* (1914). His short stories about Holmes remain classics of the genre and continue to be read and enjoyed to the present day.

In 1900, Doyle served as a field surgeon during the Boer War, and later he wrote a strong defense of British actions in the war. He received a knighthood in 1902. When his wife died of tuberculosis in 1906, Doyle remarried; he and his new wife had grown close since meeting in 1897. Between 1906 and 1915, Doyle supported causes such as divorce reform and the legal status of women (although he opposed giving women the vote), and he attacked Belgian colonial abuses in Africa. With the outbreak of World War I, he became active in the homeland defense of England. In 1915, he

converted to "spiritualism" as a religion, and he wrote extensively on this subject, traveling far and wide to lecture about it, until his death on July 6, 1930.

Arthur Conan Doyle was a prolific writer with a fertile imagination. In addition to Sherlock Holmes, he also created the popular recurring character of Professor Challenger in *The Lost World* (1912), and of Brigadier Gerard in a series of short stories. He wrote more than a dozen plays, books of poetry, several collections of essays and other nonfiction, and more than 15 works about spiritualism. His many historical novels are not read very much, even though he researched them carefully and expended more authorial effort on them than he did on his one immortal character, Sherlock Holmes. Today, modern authors continue to produce new works featuring Holmes, and he has become an instantly recognizable fixture in movies and television series.

BIBLIOGRAPHY

Booth, Martin. *The Doctor and the Detective: A Biography of Sir Arthur Conan Doyle.* New York: St. Martin's Minotaur, 2000.

Cox, Don Richard. *Arthur Conan Doyle.* New York: Ungar, 1985.

Jaffe, Jacqueline A. *Arthur Conan Doyle.* Twayne's English Authors, 451. Boston: Twayne, 1987.

Orel, Harold, ed. *Critical Essays on Sir Arthur Conan Doyle.* New York: G. K. Hall, 1992.

DOYLE, RODDY (1958–)

Winner of the Booker Prize in 1993 for *Paddy Clarke Ha Ha Ha,* his fourth novel, Roddy Doyle was born in Dublin in 1958. He is married and the father of two children, and since 1980 he has taught English and geography at Greendale Community School in Dublin.

Doyle began his career as a fiction writer with the successful series of novels known collectively as *The Barrytown Trilogy,* including *The Commitments* (1987), made into a film of the same name by director Alan Parker in 1991; *The Snapper* (1990), filmed by Stephen Frears in 1993; and *The Van* (1991), filmed by Stephen Frears in 1996. Each of these novels focuses on a member of the Rabbitte family, residents of a housing project in the working-class district of Barrytown, in north Dublin. Doyle achieves his comic effects partly through the hilarity of his basic concept (an Irish rock band devoted to producing black American soul music in *The Commitments,* or two unemployed middle-aged men running a mobile diner in *The Van*), and partly through the spontaneity and freshness of the characters' witty dialogue. The stories develop through Doyle's presentation of conversations rather than through narration and description; Doyle gives unpretentious working-class Irish men, women, teens, and children an effective and entertaining voice without patronizing his characters or sentimentalizing them.

Doyle takes up increasingly serious topics over the course of the trilogy, including illegitimate pregnancy (in *The Snapper*) and unemployment, and the same trend holds true over the range of novels he published afterward. *Paddy Clarke Ha Ha Ha* presents a troubled boy drifting into greater violence and deeper troubles, and *The Woman Who Walked into Doors* (1996) examines the life of a battered Irish housewife, chronicling the process by which she is able to break free from her abused life. Most recently, Doyle has begun a series of historical novels that takes its departure from the Easter Rising of 1916, opening the series with *A Star Called Henry* (1999). He has also written children's fiction, plays, and the screenplays for the films adapted from the volumes in *The Barrytown Trilogy.*

BIBLIOGRAPHY

Donnelly, Brian. "Roddy Doyle: From Barrytown to the GPO," *Irish University Review: A Journal of Irish Studies* 30, no. 1 (Spring-Summer 2000): 17–31.

Drewett, James. "An Interview with Roddy Doyle," *Irish Studies Review* 11, no. 3 (December 2003): 337–49.

White, Caramine. *Reading Roddy Doyle.* Syracuse, N.Y.: Syracuse University Press, 2001.

DRABBLE, MARGARET (1939–)

The editor of the *Oxford Companion to English Literature* and an admired novelist who has won many awards for her writing, Margaret Drabble is also the younger sister of the scholar and novelist A. S. BYATT. Drabble was born in Sheffield on June 5, 1939; her father was an attorney (or barrister) and judge, and her mother taught English, having completed her college education at Cambridge. The eldest two Drabble children under-

went the same education as their mother, each in her turn, studying at the Quaker-influenced Mount School in York and then matriculating at Newnham College in Cambridge. While Margaret was a student there, she studied with the critic F. R. Leavis, who emphasized the "great tradition" in English fiction of Jane Austen, George Eliot, Henry JAMES, and Joseph CONRAD. Both sisters excelled in their studies, but unlike her sibling, Margaret Drabble turned away from an academic career. She married an actor and for a time worked with him in the Royal Shakespeare Company; when her children were born, however, she began writing novels.

Margaret Drabble became one of the first novelists to write under the influence of the "second wave" of FEMINISM, taking for inspiration the nonfiction work of Betty Friedan and Simone de Beauvoir and the novels of Doris LESSING. Her early novels provided a voice for the increasing numbers of college-educated women who found themselves torn by the conflicting demands of motherhood and their professional lives; although deeply committed to their children, they also wanted to put their abilities to wider use. Her first novel, *The Summer Birdcage* (1962), casts a semiautobiographical eye on the relationship between two educated sisters, the elder a successful scholar. She continues this autobiographical theme in *The Garrick Year* (1964), profiling a married acting couple and the stresses that infidelity inflicts on their marriage. In *The MILLSTONE* (1965; U.S. title: *Thank You All Very Much*), Drabble relates the story of a female graduate student who interrupts her study of the Elizabethan sonnet to have a child even though she has no husband, and who finds her own heart healed as her daughter's congenital heart defect is repaired. The novel won the Rhys Memorial Prize in 1966. Her next novel, *Jerusalem the Golden* (1967), won the JAMES TAIT BLACK MEMORIAL PRIZE in 1968; it examines the relationship between a daughter who gets the chance to pursue the urban, single, academic life and the mother she considers a repressive force but who longed for that same life and lost it when she married. In *The Waterfall* (1969), Drabble allows her protagonist, a woman poet, to experience an awakening through an unexpected sexual passion. In all these novels, the roles that educated women play, the limitations and pitfalls they struggle to escape from, and the challenges they face form the central focus. The novels found their audience among the real-world women whose inner lives these stories illuminated so well.

Drabble's first marriage ended in 1975 after 15 years, and in 1982 she married the biographer Michael Holroyd. The focus of her novels broadened to examine the larger world in which women's lives are situated as they enter middle age: She considers the moral and practical significance of wealth (*The Needle's Eye,* 1972), the market for real estate (*The Ice Age,* 1977), and the world of journalism (*The Middle Ground,* 1980), among other topics. Her own life was also broadened; she became increasingly well known as a commentator on the contemporary cultural and political scene on both sides of the Atlantic in essays and on television. Her work on the revisions to *The Oxford Companion to English Literature* occupied the first half of the 1980s. When she returned to novel writing, she introduced something of a suspense-mystery element in a trilogy of novels, *The Radiant Way* (1987), *A Natural Curiosity* (1989), and *The Gates of Ivory* (1991), still using women protagonists but also including the apprehension of a male serial killer in the story. In the trilogy's final volume, she even carries the story out of England to the destroyed land of Kampuchea (Cambodia).

Margaret Drabble has written notable biographies in addition to her fiction: *Wordsworth* was published in 1966, *Arnold Bennett: A Biography* in 1974, and *A. N. Wilson: A Biography* in 1995. In the second two cases, Drabble was intent on restoring her subjects to critical attention after their literary reputations had faded. She has edited volumes by Jane Austen and written critical studies of women's fiction, Thomas Hardy, Victorian England, the role of landscape in literature, and other topics. She has also written short stories, screenplays, a play, and a teleplay. In 1980, she was named a Commander of the Order of the British Empire. She continues to live in England and write.

BIBLIOGRAPHY
Creighton, Joanne V. *Margaret Drabble.* London: Methuen, 1985.

Rose, Ellen Cronan, ed. *Critical Essays on Margaret Drabble.* Boston: G. K. Hall, 1985.

Sadler, Lynn Veach. *Margaret Drabble.* Twayne's English Authors, 417. New York: Twayne, 1986.

Stovel, Nora Foster. *Margaret Drabble: Symbolic Moralist.* San Bernardino, Calif.: Borgo Press, 1989.

DU MAURIER, DAPHNE (1907–1989)

A writer of romance, HISTORICAL FICTION, biographical works of both nonfiction and fiction based on her family history, psychological thrillers, and short stories, Daphne du Maurier was the daughter of the actor-manager Sir Gerald du Maurier and the granddaughter of the Victorian novelist George du Maurier. She was born in London on May 13, 1907, and spent much of her life in Cornwall—a brooding location frequently featured in her writing. She was educated at schools in London, Paris, and Meudon, France.

Her first novel, *The Loving Spirit,* appeared in 1931 and was moderately well received. A year later, she was married to Frederick Arthur Montague Browning, a military officer. Her first strong critical reception occurred in 1936 upon the publication of *Jamaica Inn;* then, in 1938, she published the Gothic romance for which she is most famous, REBECCA. This novel, considered to be perhaps the finest 20th-century example of the Gothic novel, compares favorably with the work of Charlotte Bronte; it won the National Book Award in 1938, and the 1940 film adaptation by Alfred Hitchcock won the Academy Award for best picture. Hitchcock also filmed her novel *Jamaica Inn* and her short story "The Birds."

Daphne du Maurier was named a Dame Commander, Order of the British Empire, in 1969 and received the Mystery Writers of America Grand Master award in 1977. She died on April 19, 1989, in Cornwall.

BIBLIOGRAPHY
Cook, Judith. *Daphne: The Life of Daphne Du Maurier.* London: Bantam, 1991.

Forster, Margaret. *Daphne du Maurier: The Secret Life of the Renowned Storyteller.* New York: Doubleday, 1993.

Shallcross, Martin. *The Private World of Daphne Du Maurier.* New York: St. Martin's Press, 1992.

DUNSANY, EDWARD JOHN MORETON DRAX PLUNKETT (1878–1957)

Born into an aristocratic Anglo-Irish family (his title was Baron Dunsany, and he frequently published under the name Lord Dunsany), this prolific author is considered to be one of the founders of FANTASY literature, with George MacDonald and J. R. R. TOLKIEN. He lived a privileged and colorful life, receiving his education at Eton College, a PUBLIC SCHOOL, and the Royal Military Academy at Sandhurst (Britain's West Point). He served in the Coldstream Guards and fought in the BOER WAR; he fought and was wounded in the Easter Rebellion in 1916; additionally, he served as a captain in WORLD WAR I and even volunteered for the Home Guard in WORLD WAR II when he was in his 60s. He had inherited the family's title and lands (Dunsany Castle in County Meath) in 1899 but spent much of his time on his estate in Kent, where he and his wife raised their son. He was active in the Abbey Theatre when William Butler Yeats and John Millington Synge were there and wrote his first play at Yeats's request, for performances produced by Yeats. He also was once Ireland's chess champion.

Dunsany considered himself to be a poet and published six volumes of verse, but he also wrote some 25 plays, several of which were produced on Broadway in the second decade of the century. He produced more than a dozen collections of short fiction and six volumes of nonfiction, including a paean to IRELAND and personal memoirs. He translated the *Odes* of the Roman poet Horace in 1947. Dunsany's 14 novels, together with his short stories, are important milestones in the formation of the genre of fantasy. Of these, his masterpiece is thought to be *The King of Elfland's Daughter* (1924). Dunsany's fiction valorizes a lost older tradition of simplicity, nature, and magic; he condemned the industrial devastation of nature, particularly in his 1933 novel, *The Curse of the Wise Woman,* in which Mrs. Marlin (a new version of Merlin) causes a flood to wipe out the factory that has blighted the land. Dunsany's later works are not as admired by readers of his fantasy novels, but his plays have been praised for their literary merit. Lord Dunsany died in Dublin on October 25, 1957.

BIBLIOGRAPHY

Joshi, S. T. *Lord Dunsany: Master of the Anglo-Irish Imagination.* Westport, Conn.: Greenwood Press, 1995.

Smith, Hazel Littlefield. *Lord Dunsany, King of Dreams: A Personal Portrait.* New York: Exposition Press, 1959.

DURRELL, LAWRENCE (1912–1990)

A British writer born abroad who spent a good deal of his working life in government service and who remained nearly a lifelong expatriate, Lawrence George Durrell (pronounced DUR el) was born in Julundur, INDIA, on February 27, 1912. His father, an Irish Protestant of English descent, worked as an engineer in the construction of the Darjeeling Railway; he had never been to England. At the age of 11, Lawrence Durrell was sent "home" to attend a private school. He was not happy in school or in England, and he failed the entrance exams for Cambridge (which he described as an intentional act). He worked as a jazz pianist in nightclubs and left England at the age of 23, disgusted by what he perceived to be its tawdriness and soul-crushing sterility. In 1935, he moved to Corfu with his wife, the artist Nancy Myers, and his mother. Durrell's brother Gerald, a zoologist and travel writer, described their life there in *My Family and Other Animals* (1956).

Durrell spent some time in Paris after reading Henry Miller's *Tropic of Cancer* when it was published in 1934. He and Miller became friends and then corresponded for some 45 years; this exchange was published in 1988 as *The Durrell-Miller Letters, 1935–1980.* In the early 20th century, the literary examination of human sexuality was being transformed by books such as *ULYSSES* (1922) by James JOYCE, *LADY CHATTERLEY'S LOVER* (1928) by D. H. LAWRENCE, and Henry Miller's work. Durrell admired the frank honesty of these works and the criticisms they heaped on the constricted quality of modern life. Although Durrell's first two novels were relatively conventional narratives, in 1938 he published *The Black Book,* which experiments with narrative structure, exploring memory rather than progressing through time, and using multiple narratives by embedding the journal of an absent character within the story of the narrator's life. The subject matter deals with degradation and poverty in an artist's life, treating sexuality frankly. Miller's influence is evident, but Durrell had established his own voice and was already thinking ahead to the work that, when it was published between 1957 and 1960, established his fame as a novelist, *THE ALEXANDRIA QUARTET.* He originally conceived of this work, under the title *The Book of the Dead,* as the third in a trilogy beginning with *The Black Book.*

Before that version could come into existence, however, WORLD WAR II intervened. From 1939 until 1957, Durrell held various government jobs in several locations: During the war, he served first as an English teacher in Athens, and then, as the war advanced, he relocated to Cairo to work in the foreign press office (1941–44) and then to Alexandria as a press attaché. After the war, he accepted appointments, primarily as a public relations officer or press attaché, in Rhodes, Argentina, Belgrade, and Cyprus. He wrote several volumes of poetry, plays, travel narratives, and "island books" during this time, maintaining a prolific output. His first marriage ended during the war; in 1947, he remarried and began working on the first volume of the quartet, *JUSTINE*. This book found a large and appreciative readership, with its lyricism, exoticism, and sensuality. It and the second volume in the quartet, *Balthazar* (1958), won the French Prix du Meilleur Livre Etranger in 1959.

By the time the closing volume of the quartet, *CLEA*, was published in 1960, readers were eagerly awaiting its arrival. Durrell had ended his government service in 1957, and his second marriage was over as well. He settled in the south of France to devote himself to writing, and he married for a third time in 1961. His wife, the novelist Claude-Marie Vincendon, died in 1967. He worked on poems, plays, and essays, and then returned to fiction with the publication in 1968 of the first of a two-novel set. *Tunc* (1968) and *Nunquam* (1970) were republished under the collective title *The Revolt of Aphrodite* in 1974. Critics are divided over whether this futuristic nightmare is a success or not. In this story, an inventor who at first resists the multinational corporation that employs him, only to rise to the supervision of it in the end, creates an artificial woman for his boss so perfectly human that she demands her freedom and ultimately uses it as an opportunity to destroy the men attracted to her. Ironically, the inventor's resistance to the firm began when he believed it was turning him into an artificial man—a robot. Although this inventor is the character of the same name who narrates both volumes, the nature of his character—his personality—is altered from one to the other. Durrell flattens him out, removing his will to resist, and thereby makes a comment on the ways that

humans are co-opted by their circumstances. Misfortune is not forced on human beings; it is embraced by them as they succumb to temptations.

In 1973, Durrell married for the fourth and last time; this marriage, too, ended in divorce. He began working on a five-volume set of novels, collectively known as the Avignon Quintet, that begins with *Monsieur: or The Prince of Darkness* (1974) and continues with *Livia, or Buried Alive* (1978); *Constance, or Solitary Practices* (1982); *Sebastian, or, Ruling Passions: A Novel* (1983); and *Quinx, or, The Ripper's Tale* (1985). *Monsieur* won the JAMES TAIT BLACK MEMORIAL PRIZE in 1975. In form, this first volume resembles the modernist work *AT SWIM-TWO-BIRDS,* by Flann O'BRIEN: It is a nested set of narratives, but instead of beginning with the fictional author, as O'Brien had done, and then moving more and more deeply into layers of embedded narratives, Durrell begins in the most deeply embedded narrative and surprises the reader by revealing his fiction to be someone else's fiction, which in turn is the fiction of yet another writer. Like O'Brien's masterpiece, Durrell has fictional characters interact in the world outside their fiction. In addition to these formal experiments, Durrell constructs a plot about the lost treasure of the medieval Knights Templar; the search for treasure is, metaphorically, a search for enlightenment in the midst of the world's inescapable evil.

Lawrence Durrell continued writing through the last year of his life. He died of a stroke after a lengthy struggle against emphysema on November 7, 1990, in Sommieres, France.

BIBLIOGRAPHY

Bowker, Gordon. *Through the Dark Labyrinth: A Biography of Lawrence Durrell.* New York: St. Martin's Press, 1997.

Fraser, G. S. *Lawrence Durrell: A Critical Study.* New York: Dutton, 1968.

MacNiven, Ian S. *Lawrence Durrell: A Biography.* London: Faber & Faber, 1998.

Weigel, John A. *Lawrence Durrell.* Twayne's English Authors, 29. New York: Twayne Publishers, 1965.

DYSTOPIAN NOVELS   This term has been coined to describe stories that are diametrically opposite to utopian novels: Dystopian novels present a dire world, often in the future, in which the organization of society creates and perpetuates human misery rather than facilitating the fulfillment of human potential. Writers of such stories create relevance by inventing a future that is recognizable as a descendant of the present in which the writer's audience resides. A dystopian novel is thus an implicit attack on those features of the writer's contemporary world that could give rise to a worsening of the human condition. The effectiveness of the attack relies on the widespread acceptance of progress as one of the greatest goods for humankind; the dystopian world follows from ours in time, and is the effect that our world causes, but instead of improving the materials, protocols, and institutions of contemporary life, it turns them into engines that crush the human soul. Some of the classics of 20th-century literature are dystopian novels: BRAVE NEW WORLD by Aldous HUXLEY and NINTEEN EIGHTY-FOUR by George ORWELL are the quintessential exemplars of this literary genre.

See also UTOPIAN NOVELS.

BIBLIOGRAPHY

Booker, M. Keith. *Dystopian Literature: A Theory and Research Guide.* Westport, Conn.: Greenwood Press, 1994.

Rabkin, Eric S., Martin Harry Greenberg, and Joseph D. Olander, eds. *No Place Else: Explorations in Utopian and Dystopian Fiction.* Carbondale: Southern Illinois University Press, 1983.

E

EARTHLY POWERS ANTHONY BURGESS **(1980)** A novel of epic scope, *Earthly Powers* follows the careers of two dissimilar but parallel men of ambition: Kenneth Toomey, a pessimistic homosexual writer of popular works, and Carlo Campanati, a priest—and a brother-in-law to Kenneth—who rises to the position of pope and is under consideration for canonization after his death. Burgess based the character of Kenneth on an amalgam of Noël Coward and W. Somerset MAUGHAM and made him the first-person narrator of the novel; Carlo is based on Pope John XXIII. The action of the story covers the first 70 years of the 20th century and sprawls to numerous locations around the world. BURGESS mixes real people into his fictional world and thinly disguises real events in his complex plot, such as the Jonestown mass suicide, or massacre, at the behest of Jim Jones. Although the narrator is a homosexual, the novel is not a study of homosexuality per se; instead it examines a much broader range of human behaviors, and in particular it explores the ways that good actions can come to evil ends.

The novel opens on Kenneth's 81st birthday. He is living in Malta with a young lover—his "catamite"— when the archbishop calls on him to discuss Carlo Campanati, the late Pope Gregory XVII. To begin the canonization process that leads to sainthood, the performance of a miracle must be documented, and Kenneth had been present many years earlier in Chicago when Carlo, then still a priest, had miraculously saved a boy dying of tuberculosis by blessing him. The archbishop's request sets in motion Kenneth's recollection of his own life and of his connection to Carlo. He did witness the event in question, but he also reveals the horrifying consequences that follow from saving that young man's life: The young man later becomes the leader of a religious cult that murders a congressional representative and commits mass suicide by drinking cyanide. Among the victims in the massacre are the great-niece of Carlo and Kenneth, and her husband. The two men had become brothers-in-law when Kenneth's sister was married to Carlo's brother; this couple in turn became the parents of a set of twins, Ann and John. Ann's daughter is among those who drink the poison, and so in a way Carlo's miracle leads to the destruction of part of his family.

But the ironies extend further. John, the nephew of the two men, travels to Africa with his wife to examine tribal customs among a people who have only recently been proselytized by Catholic priests, including Carlo, and in their fervor to consume the body and blood of communion, the tribe members kill and consume their white visitors. Their death results from a kind of perverse sacrament—a fatally flawed conflation of real and metaphorical consumption. But the mass suicide is also a perverse communion because the celebrants embrace death instead of receiving life everlasting. Burgess exploits the misunderstanding of church doctrine and sacred ritual to demonstrate how the best intentions can lead to the most disastrous results. In the case of Kenneth, a man who will never procreate because of his sexual orientation, and of Carlo, a man who will never procreate because of his vow of celibacy, their closest chance of seeing their genetic existence survive materially is through their niece and nephew: In a bitter twist of irony, these are the very people who are killed as an unexpected result of good works done in the name of God.

Burgess doubles this twisting of good into evil ends in a parallel example from the life of Kenneth during a section of the novel that examines the rise to power of Nazi Germany and Fascist Italy. Kenneth, a world traveler and bon vivant, happens to be present at a moment when a dying woman (Carlo's mother, in fact) devoted to saving Germany's Jews points a gun at Heinrich Himmler. Without thinking—without intending any good deed—Kenneth shoves the Nazi butcher aside and the woman is killed by bodyguards. Kenneth's action to save a particular life dooms millions of other more remote lives to the gas chambers. Good and evil are inextricably intertwined in the construction of Burgess's plot. Kenneth's witnessing of Carlo's miracle virtually guarantees the advancement of the canonization, but Carlo's life-giving miracle itself, and Kenneth's unthinking preservation of a life, both lead to horrible consequences neither man could have foreseen or would have wanted.

In Kenneth Toomey, Burgess creates a protagonist who is cut off from his family, his religion, and his country by his sexual orientation. In a long and eventful life that covers many of the most exotic and glamorous locations of the world and that coincides with some of the 20th century's most notorious events and characters, he pursues an elusive goal of personal fulfillment. In the end, he returns to England to live with his sister and is restored to the institutions that had previously shut him out. He achieves reconciliation, and Carlo is likely to achieve canonization, but the novel's unresolved ethical questions loom larger than either of these men's lives.

BIBLIOGRAPHY

Aggeler, Geoffrey. "Faust in the Labyrinth: Burgess' *Earthly Powers*," *Modern Fiction Studies* 27, no. 3 (Autumn 1981): 517–531.

Ashley, Leonard R. N. " 'Unhappy All the Time': Religion in Anthony Burgess's *Earthly Powers*," *Christianity and Literature* 52, no. 1 (Autumn 2002): 35–45.

EDWARDIAN ERA   Named for King Edward VII, this era begins in the late 19th century, when Edward was Prince of Wales and lasts through the first decade of the 20th century, covering the fin de siècle culture of England and the British EMPIRE. For some writers, it was an age of optimism—the belle epoque—that would usher in a better world, while others pessimistically anticipated the end of civilization as they knew it.

Writers such as H. G. WELLS produced works of UTOPIAN optimism, although Wells also attacked the deleterious effects of the CLASS system in *Tono Bungay*. Under the influence of realism, naturalism, and a widening sense of social rights, novelists such as Arnold BENNETT, John GALSWORTHY, and E. M. FORSTER constructed stories that exposed the flaws they perceived in English provincialism, materialism, and repression; their writing remains optimistic, however, since their novels hold up the mirror to these flaws so their countrymen can take note and correct themselves. They produce novels that meet the Horatian dictum that art must be "*dulce et utile*": It must delight and teach those who experience it.

The development of mass culture begins first in low-cost publishing ventures of the 19th century such as serialized novels in periodicals; popular writers reaching a mass audience of readers primarily interested in the delights of literature, rather than in the instruction they may derive from its study, include Arthur Conan DOYLE, G. K. CHESTERTON, John BUCHAN, J. M. BARRIE, and Max BEERBOHM. Specialized forms such as MYSTERY AND DETECTIVE FICTION, pulp westerns, adventure stories, and SCIENCE FICTION find loyal audiences and begin to fragment the edifice of literature into the domains of serious literature and "fringe genres" or popular fiction. The gap between art and entertainment that begins in the transformation of the 19th into the 20th century continues to widen as new technologies make new expressions of creativity possible in radio, film, television, and now the Internet.

In serious literature, a more elegiac tone comes from the late novels of Henry JAMES, who saw the decline of the English class system as a great loss and a harbinger of a broader decline in civilized values and refinement. In *The WINGS OF THE DOVE* and *The GOLDEN BOWL*, especially, he captures the upper-class decline in moral weight. His contemporary Joseph CONRAD notes a parallel decline in the significance of empire and COLONIALISM in novels such as *LORD JIM* and *HEART OF DARKNESS,* but underlying this critique of social and political arrangements is a deeper pessimism about the nature of the human beings who orchestrate such arrangements. Formerly optimistic writers such as Rudyard KIPLING find reasons to temper their enthusiasm for empire in light of the tragedies and scandals of the BOER WAR, and the trial for homosexuality of Oscar WILDE casts a shadow over the vogue of AESTHETICISM.

These authors differ in their general attitudes toward the future and their diagnoses of present ills, but they share an essentially traditional approach to literary art and to the construction of the novel. But the Edwardian era also includes the beginnings of the radical departures of MODERNISM from both the form and content of the novel (and other literary forms as well). Experimentation with language, narrative point of view, and subject matter becomes a hallmark of 20th-century literature. Wyndham LEWIS and D. H. LAWRENCE make early forays into experimental territory in fiction, while T. S. Eliot and Ezra Pound revolutionize poetry, and by the end of the Edwardian era, James JOYCE is already brooding on the events he will transform into the modernist masterpiece *ULYSSES.*

BIBLIOGRAPHY

Batchelor, John. *The Edwardian Novelists.* New York: St. Martin's Press, 1982.

Hunter, Jefferson. *Edwardian Fiction.* Cambridge, Mass.: Harvard University Press, 1982.

Nowell-Smith, Simon, ed. *Edwardian England, 1901–1914.* London: Oxford University Press, 1964.

ELECTED MEMBER, THE BERNICE RUBENS (1969)

A deeply sympathetic and acutely realistic study of mental illness, *The Elected Member* won the BOOKER PRIZE in 1970, the second year the prize was awarded. The story unfolds through the point of view of a third-person omniscient narrator, allowing readers to examine the behavior of the characters and to listen to their conversations while also gaining access to the secrets they hide—and hide from—in their thoughts.

The novel presents the story of Rabbi Zweck's sad family. His son, Norman, is immersed in a delusional state and addicted to amphetamines; daughter Bella, still living at home, is a spinster with an ugly secret staining her life, and daughter Esther has been shunned for marrying outside the faith. Norman was formerly the family's golden boy, but now his addiction and his madness are torturing his family. He spends most of his time in the bed his mother Sarah died in, remembering her possessive grip on him and watching in delusional horror as imaginary silverfish swarm over him. The plot is set in motion when Rabbi Zweck reluctantly commits Norman to a mental hospital. Norman is enraged by this betrayal and must be forcibly removed by uniformed officers. Rabbi Zweck is anxious to believe that things will soon return to normal. But the family is trapped in a mimetic repetition: Norman has been cleaned up from his addiction before, but he has always reverted to his old habits. The future does not look bright.

In contrast, the past is a rosy and comforting place, at least for Rabbi Zweck. He does not know the secrets harbored by Bella, nor the truth behind Esther's marriage and impending divorce, nor Norman's contribution to both these tragedies. He does remember Sarah's hysterics whenever Norman would try to assert his independence from the family: She drained his will and kept him rooted to the family in frustration. Rabbi Zweck prefers to focus on the happy days when five-year-old Norman first demonstrated his extraordinary linguistic gifts and began mastering foreign languages, one after another, always egged on by his delighted parents. Sarah Zweck had tried to freeze her darling boy in his golden moment when he was nine, refusing to advance his age for three years, and even demanding that his bar mitzvah pass unobserved until he was 16. She is now dead, but her maternal folly continues to exact its toll in the consequences of Norman's arrested development.

The narrative alternates between the daily routine of hospital life in a psychiatric ward and the home life of the guilt-ravaged but sane family members. The strain of Norman's illness wears on Rabbi Zweck, already weakened by age, care, grief, and the chest pains he hides from Bella's knowledge. Norman adapts well to hospital life after he locates a supplier of amphetamines among the other patients. But he is haunted by the suicide of his best friend many years earlier and by a guilty awareness of his own contribution to the circumstances of that death; the suicide of his drug dealer disrupts his contented adaptation to hospital life. Doctors control him with sedation, and when he is finally allowed to emerge from his sleep, he is freed of the cravings and the withdrawal pains, but he suffers an acute sense of guilt and humiliation. He finally understands the punishment he has thrust upon his father and sisters, but this insight comes too late. The Zweck family legacy is a damaged son and two unmarried and childless daughters. In a Job-like despair, Norman sits on his bed and tries to pray, calling on God to help him carry the burdens that God has elected him to bear.

Bernice RUBENS provides a humane but unflinching portrait of madness and family dysfunction in her story. Her compassion for Norman and the other members of his ward is deeply felt and effectively communicated. Since readers can see both the outward behavior and the inward motivations of her characters, they are able to achieve sympathy for Norman and for the others whose lives he has destroyed.

BIBLIOGRAPHY

Kossick, Shirley. "The Novels of Bernice Rubens: 1960–1992," *Unisa English Studies: Journal of the Department of English* 31, no. 2 (1993): 34–40.

Parnell, Michel. "The Novels of Bernice Rubens: An Introduction," *The New Welsh Review* (Summer 1990): 43–45.

ELLIS, ALICE THOMAS (1932–)

Anna Margaret Lindholm was the birth name of the Welsh writer and editor Anna Haycraft, who publishes fiction and nonfiction under the pseudonym Alice Thomas Ellis. She was born in Liverpool, England, on September 9, 1932, and reared in Penmaenmawr, Wales. She was educated in local schools and at the Liverpool School of Art, and she served briefly as a postulant at the Convent of Notre Dame de Namur in Liverpool, having converted to Catholicism as a teenager. In 1956, she was married to Colin Haycraft, a publisher; they became the parents of seven children. In her professional life, she has served as a columnist for the *Spectator,* the *Universe,* and *The Catholic Herald,* and she is a director at Duckworth, a noted publishing house. In her position at Duckworth, she was instrumental in developing the careers of writers such as Beryl BAINBRIDGE, Patrice Chaplin, and Caroline Blackwood; together, these writers created a distinctive style of short witty novels about the lives of contemporary women.

Ellis published her first novel, *The Sin Eater,* in 1977; it presents the fictional Ellis family in Wales as the impending death of the patriarch brings separated family members under one roof. In 1980, *The Birds of the Air* provided a study of grief and an attack on the modern commercialized customs of Christmas. Ellis's third novel, THE TWENTY-SEVENTH KINGDOM (1982), was short listed for the BOOKER PRIZE; it is a satire on modern values. *The Other Side of the Fire* (1983) is a comic modernization of Racine's *Phèdre* (1677), as a middle-aged woman falls in love with her stepson. Ellis's "Summer House Trilogy," consisting of *The Clothes in the Wardrobe* (1987), *The Skeleton in the Cupboard* (1988), and *The Fly in the Ointment* (1989), provided the material for a successful FILM ADAPTATION in 1992, also called *The Summer House.* It tells the story of a misconceived engagement and the clever seduction that puts an end to it.

Anna Haycraft has written passionately about Catholicism, condemning certain modern trends in the church; her essays on this subject are collected in *Serpent on the Rock: A Personal View of Christianity* (1994). She lives in Wales and continues to write under the name Alice Thomas Ellis.

BIBLIOGRAPHY

Conradi, Peter. "Alice Thomas Ellis: Kinder, Kirche, und Küche." In *Image and Power: Women in Fiction in the Twentieth Century.* Edited by Sarah Sceats and Gail Cunningham. London: Longman, 1996. 149–60.

Ellis, Alice Thomas. *A Welsh Childhood.* London: M. Joseph, 1990.

EMPIRE (END OF) Throughout the 20th century, the empire that the British had assembled over some 300 years, and that had reached the height of its extent and influence in the second half of the 19th century, was slowly disassembled and converted into the COMMONWEALTH. Between the time of the Crimean War (1853–56) and that of WORLD WAR I (1914–18), the British military found itself mounting campaigns against rebellious native populations *within* the empire rather than against traditional European foes. The desire for self-government was taking root worldwide. In fact, the 20th century opened to an attempted check on British influence in the South African BOER WAR (1899–1902). Although the British ultimately prevailed, the war signaled a turning point in the relationship between England and the territories it had acquired since the 17th century.

World War I underscored this transformation: When it began, Britain's declaration of war unilaterally committed the resources of the entire British Empire to the struggle, but when it ended, several parts of the empire signed peace treaties as sovereign nations and acquired membership in the League of Nations on an equal footing with the United Kingdom. The Statute of Westminster formalized this arrangement in 1931: Nations dominated by populations descended from British colonists, such as Canada and Australia, were recognized as sovereign governments joined in a voluntary relationship through the Commonwealth. Increasingly, Britain's empire became a loose association designed to promote the best interests of nations with the shared historical connection that the British Empire had brought about.

The pace of change quickened as the century progressed. The Indian subcontinent gained its independence in 1947 and immediately divided along religious lines into two nations, INDIA AND PAKISTAN (East Pakistan became the independent nation of Bangladesh in 1971). Writers from all these countries have shared the task of telling the vast story of COLONIALISM and its consequences, including Anita DESAI, E. M. FORSTER, Salman RUSHDIE, J. G. FARRELL, Arundhati ROY, Rudyard KIPLING, and many others. The British abandoned Palestine in 1948 with the founding of Israel, and its influence in the Middle East essentially ended with the SUEZ CRISIS of 1956, when British troops were forced to withdraw from the Canal Zone in Egypt (compellingly chronicled in P. H. NEWBY's SOMETHING TO ANSWER FOR). Over the next two decades, numerous African colonies—many of which had been under British control for less than a century—became independent countries, including Nigeria, Uganda, Kenya, Tanzania, South Africa, and others. The literature of British-influenced Africa includes the work of Chinua ACHEBE, J. M. COETZEE, Nadine GORDIMER, Ben OKRI, Christopher HOPE, and V. S. NAIPAUL, among others.

Not all the British possessions have achieved independent status. In 1982, Great Britain went to war to regain control of the FALKLAND ISLANDS. Although the effect of the success of that war was to deliver a landslide victory to Margaret Thatcher in her next election campaign, literature of the period occasionally features disparaging references to the government. Additionally, not all former possessions have chosen to join or remain in the Commonwealth: The Republic of IRELAND severed its connection in 1948, and both Myanmar (formerly Burma) and Zimbabwe (formerly Southern Rhodesia) elected not to join the Commonwealth after independence. The last major piece of the empire, the colony of Hong Kong, was returned to China on July 1, 1997, in accordance with a 99-year lease negotiated between China and Great Britain in 1898.

The influence of the British Empire on literature has been enormous; the study of British literature of the 20th century is very close to being a study of world literature. The influence of colonialism, both on the English and on the populations colonized, has been far-reaching. One of the most significant effects has been the spread of English as a *lingua franca* in much of the world, providing much larger audiences—unmediated by translation—for the writings of anyone with a message to communicate and the skill to encode that message in English. As a result, lists of award-winning British literature are as likely to include stories set in African villages or Indian cities as they are in include works set in London or Birmingham or Norwich. It is no more surprising to encounter British characters of Pakistani descent, for example in *The BUDDHA OF SUBURBIA*, than it had been to encounter British citizens

administering another culture's legal system in *A Passage to India*. British colonizers may have transformed
numerous cultures around the globe, but representatives of those cultures have also returned the favor in
transforming contemporary British literature into a
global mosaic of perspectives, ideas, and voices.

BIBLIOGRAPHY

Davies, Norman. *The Isles: A History*. Oxford: Oxford Uni-
versity Press, 1999.
James, Lawrence. *The Rise and Fall of the British Empire*. New
York: St. Martin's Press, 1996.
Knaplund, Paul. *Britain: Commonwealth and Empire,
1901–1955*. New York: Harper, 1957.

EMPIRE OF THE SUN J. G. BALLARD
(1984)   Based on Ballard's childhood experiences in
a Japanese concentration camp outside Shanghai, this
autobiographical novel became a successful film adaptation for director Steven Spielberg in 1985.

The story unfolds in three parts, opening in Shanghai on the eve of the Japanese attack on Pearl Harbor.
The protagonist of the story is Jim, an 11-year-old boy
living in a fine house on Amherst Avenue with his English parents. His father is a businessman, and the family enjoys a comfortable life that includes a swimming
pool, servants, and a chauffeur-driven Packard. But
war has already come to Shanghai: The Japanese army
is encamped nearby, and violence is palpably near.
When the Japanese storm the city, Jim is separated
from his parents in the chaos of exploding shells and
the onslaught of tanks and troops.

Throughout this first section of the novel, Jim roams
the city alone, too naïve to realize the dangers that lurk
on every corner, but becoming wiser to them minute
by minute. He attaches himself to two American merchant seamen, Frank and Basie; they are able to feed
him, although Jim is convinced they're trying to sell
him to one of the Chinese merchants in the open-air
markets. When Jim persuades the two men to visit his
family's house on Amherst Avenue, the three of them
surprise a group of Japanese soldiers who have billeted
themselves there. Soon, Jim and the others find themselves in a fever-infested detention camp, and from

there they go to the Lunghua Camp, a few miles from
the city.

The middle section of the novel skips across two
years of confinement at the camp and opens on 14-
year-old Jim, no longer the child who had first arrived
here at 12. He is a tough survivor. Basie is in the camp
as well, and Jim continues to learn the tricks of survival from him: Bowing to the Japanese, stretching
rations as far as possible, and keeping out of trouble.
Jim helps Dr. Ransome in the hospital and spends restless hours roaming the camp in the golf shoes Dr. Ransome gave him. As the tide of the war turns against the
Japanese, Jim watches the airplanes in the sky change
from Zeroes to Mustangs and B-52 Superfortresses. But
the prisoners are isolated from the larger world and
have no way of knowing whether help is on the way or
when it is likely to arrive. The conditions steadily deteriorate, the rations continually shrink, and the guards
become more brutal as defeat becomes more
inevitable. When Jim sees, or thinks he sees, the flash
of the atomic bomb dropped on Nagasaki, 400 miles
away, he knows that soon the Americans will arrive.
Another wave of chaos engulfs the camp as the Japanese try to rid themselves of the prisoners by marching
them to death around the countryside.

In the final section of the novel, Jim is nearly dead
from starvation and sickness, roaming the countryside
around the camp. He survives an excursion with the
near-dead prisoners being rounded up in the former
Olympic Stadium, lying still among the corpses so he
will not have to join the last death march. Although the
war is over, relief is slow to come to Shanghai because
of sectarian fighting between Communists and other
factions for possession of the city and its lucrative trading port. But finally, American planes begin dropping
food instead of bombs, and Jim inches back from the
delirium of standing at death's doorstep. With astonishing speed, he leaves the hell of the camp and walks
into the house on Amherst Avenue: His parents are
there, having survived internment at Woosung camp.
In the closing pages, Shanghai is bustling back to life,
now with American warships tied up in its ports, and
Jim is aboard a ship bound for the home he had never
previously known in England.

Ballard's fictionalized memoir is a fascinating account strewn with unforgettable images of war's horrors. He places his protagonist in a nightmarishly surreal environment, and every sentence rings with historical accuracy: Surely, this boy's experiences record just what anyone might expect to experience in the wasteland of a wartime prison camp. The third-person objective narrator maintains a dispassionate and factual tone in presenting the life-threatening conditions Jim endures; additionally, the narrator captures the odd child's logic with which Jim views events. As Jim prepares to leave Shanghai for England, the reader may suspect that some part of Jim will always remain at Lunghua, or that he takes the camp with him wherever he goes. Clearly, the boy who entered the camps was a lifetime away from the young man who came out of it bearing the same name, but utterly changed by his three years there.

BIBLIOGRAPHY

Luckhurst, Roger. *The Angle Between Two Walls: The Fiction of J. G. Ballard.* New York: St. Martin's Press, 1997.
———. "Petition, Repetition, and 'Autobiography': J. G. Ballard's *Empire of the Sun* and *The Kindness of Women*," *Contemporary Literature* 35, no. 4 (Winter 1994): 688–708.
Stephenson, Gregory. *Out of the Night and into the Dream: A Thematic Study of the Fiction of J. G. Ballard.* Westport, Conn.: Greenwood Press, 1991.

ENCHANTED APRIL, THE ELIZABETH VON ARNIM (1922)

When four women rent a villa in Italy for a month, they find their lives changed for the better as a result—especially their love lives—in this example of romance fiction. Elizabeth VON ARNIM narrates this story through the third-person omniscient point of view, letting readers see into the hearts of all the characters.

Lotty Wilkins, a wife "still somewhat young," sees an ad in the paper for a villa in Italy for the month of April and notices another woman looking at the same ad. Lotty makes an unusual move and introduces herself to Rose Arbuthnot; the two new friends decide that they can afford to rent the villa if they can find two more to share the cost, and so they advertise for roommates. Mousy Lotty has fallen in love with the idea of the villa and is already being transformed by the place's magic. Only two women answer their advertisement: The beautiful Lady Caroline Dester and Mrs. Fisher, a lonely childless widow who had known many famous Victorian writers when she was a girl. Although these four women are virtually strangers to one another, they decide to go in together and rent the villa.

The ladies arrive severally at their destination in the beautiful spring sunshine of Italy. Mr. Briggs, the owner of the villa, is a single man who grew up as an orphan; he is love-struck by Lady Caroline when he sees her. Getting adjusted to the villa is easy, but adjusting to one another takes a little time. The four ladies are enjoying the spacious villa and the relaxing vacation, so Lotty invites her husband to take his vacation early and join her. Rose dutifully writes to invite her husband to join them, but he has already made his own plans to pursue an illicit romance, not realizing he will find his wife sharing the rented villa of the woman he is pursuing. By good luck, Lotty is the first to meet him when he arrives, and she accidentally saves the day by blurting out his presence and his relationship to Rose just as Lady Caroline walks into dinner; this knowledge confirms Lady Caroline's earlier disinclination to encourage Frederick's attentions. And now that Frederick knows that his marital status is known to Lady Caroline, he comes to his senses. The villa works its magic on him as well, and he and Rose are able to renew their love.

With the two married couples renewed in love and Mrs. Fisher happily attached to Lotty and her husband, only the beautiful Lady Caroline remains to be transformed. Lotty has already recognized the attraction Mr. Briggs feels for Lady Caroline, and she wisely brings them together. Sure enough, the two are soon in love. By the end of this idyllic vacation, two married couples have repaired the ravages that mundane day-to-day life can exact on the fragility of love; an elderly lady has found a loving family to take an interest in her welfare; Lady Caroline has discovered that she is more than just a pretty face and that true love can indeed be found even for beautiful women; and Mr. Briggs finds the fulfillment his orphaned soul has been searching for in the relationship he develops with Lady Caroline. The sentimental but charming novel emphasizes the positive effect that setting can have in shaping character for the better, it shows how love can transform every woman into a beauty and a beauty into a happy woman, and it emphasizes the way that love can allow yet more love to grow in the world.—*Aleta Bowman*

BIBLIOGRAPHY

Joannu, Maroula. *Women Writers of the Thirties: Gender, Politics, and History.* Edinburgh: Edinburgh University Press, 1999.

END OF THE AFFAIR, THE GRAHAM GREENE (1951)

A novel that examines love, faith, fidelity, and saintliness, *The End of the Affair* is one of GREENE'S Catholic novels, along with *Brighton Rock* (1938), *The POWER AND THE GLORY* (1940), *The HEART OF THE MATTER* (1948), and *A Burnt-Out Case* (1961). This novel has been the basis for two successful FILM ADAPTATIONS of the same name: The 1955 version was directed by Edward Dmytryk and starred Deborah Kerr and Van Johnson, and the 1999 version was directed by Neil Jordan and starred Ralph Fiennes and Julianne Moore.

The protagonist and first-person narrator, Maurice Bendrix, works as a professional writer—a novelist—in London, and his story seems to unfold directly from Bendrix's mind to the page, revealing his observations of the people in his fictional world and his more general comments about character, PLOT, and narration. This storytelling strategy is an early and partial example of what eventually comes to be known as POSTMODERNISM: Greene, a novelist, is writing a novel about a novelist who analyzes and interprets his world as if it were the stuff of fiction; this strategy, however, is ancillary to the realistic exploration of love and faith. The story opens in 1946, two years after the end of Bendrix's affair with Sarah Miles, the wife of an acquaintance of his, Henry Miles. Bendrix is angry and hurt because Sarah broke off the affair without cause or explanation; he assumes that she has gone on to some other lover in preference to him. He's sure she didn't simply decide to observe her marriage vows, and he is sure Henry never learned of the affair.

In the first of the novel's many ironic twists, Bendrix encounters Henry one rain-soaked evening and finds that he is contemplating whether he should hire a detective to check up on Sarah, who is not always where he expects her to be nor truthful about her activities. Bendrix offers to manage the sordid business for Henry, saying he will present himself to the detective agency as a jilted lover, which is exactly what he thinks he is. Bendrix follows through in spite of Henry's dismissal of the idea, and in the offices of Mr. Savage he presents a few more details of the affair; Savage assigns Mr. Parkis to the case, and much of the story is revealed through Bendrix's conversations with Parkis. Greene develops a mildly comic CLASS-based contrast between the educated sophistication of Bendrix's use of language and the laboriously mannered jargon of Parkis, but he avoids satire by making Parkis one of the key humanizing influences on Bendrix.

The narration divides as it moves along two time lines—one that follows the unfolding of daily events in 1944, and the other that results from the way the ongoing investigation prompts the piecemeal recollection of the affair's progress between 1939 and 1944. Bendrix occasionally reminisces about the affair, but he can't concentrate on it too intently because of the anger these memories arouse—anger that serves as a defense for the deep wound he received when Sarah broke off the affair. He still doesn't understand: They had been in love, and Sarah's marital status had been no impediment since she was sure Henry didn't see her as anything more significant than the furniture in their home. In an odd way, she was loyal to Henry without feeling compelled to be sexually faithful. That lack of compulsion makes a sticking point for Bendrix, convincing him that Sarah's betrayal of Henry forms the pattern of her relations with men, including Bendrix. He loves her passionately, and yet he also fears and resents the power that his love gives her. That possessive love and the abrupt end of the affair leave him perpetually eaten up with jealousy; he secretly tries to meet the men he believes Sarah has preferred to him, including one man—a vocal rationalist—who would be handsome if his face were not disfigured on the left side.

The investigation makes an important leap forward when Parkis acquires Sarah's journal. Bendrix the writer becomes Bendrix the reader, seeing the affair—and himself as well—through the eyes of the other party. He is shocked to learn that Sarah still loves him and that his opponent in her heart is no ordinary man. In Sarah's voice, the narrative thread following the affair doubles back as the journal entries recount scenes that Bendrix had already dredged up and picked over, such as the time during the blitzkrieg when a bomb exploded near their love nest. However, in spite of the fact that there is no mortal competitor stealing Sarah's love from him, Bendrix is made to realize that he will never regain the relationship they once shared. Sarah has other secrets and other gifts of greater significance than the longing of one ordinary man to possess her exclusively.

For Bendrix, knowledge comes at a terrible price. He cannot have Sarah back, and he cannot accept the miraculous events that continually occur in connection with her. How could an adulterous woman become the saint to sick children and disfigured men? Bendrix finds himself at war with God, left with only his hate, his bitterness, and his skepticism. Without any special effort on her part, Sarah had moved from disbelief to belief, and she had healed and soothed those who came in contact with her except for the one person she most loved and desired to help. Bendrix is left in the paradoxical position of telling the God that he does not believe in to leave him alone forever. But his obsession with confronting his competitors for Sarah's love suggests that he may eventually, albeit unwillingly, find faith himself.

BIBLIOGRAPHY

Isaacs, Rita. "Three Levels of Allegory in Graham Greene's *The End of the Affair,*" *Linguistics in Literature* 1, no. 1 (1975): 29–52.

Sharrock, Roger. *Saints, Sinners, and Comedians: The Novels of Graham Greene.* Notre Dame, Ind.: University of Notre Dame Press, 1984.

Walker, Ronald G. "World Without End: An Approach to Narrative Structure in Greene's *The End of the Affair,*" *Texas Studies in Literature and Language* 26, no. 2 (Summer 1984): 218–241.

END OF THE BATTLE, THE EVELYN WAUGH (1961)

Published in England as *Unconditional Surrender.* See SWORD OF HONOUR TRILOGY.

ENGLAND, ENGLAND JULIAN BARNES (1998)

In this comic novel, Julian BARNES satirizes a publicity campaign to increase tourism in England by reinventing the nation as a commercial brand of entertainment. The novel begins and ends in England—that is to say, in "Old England," the island nation located slightly northwest of Europe proper—but the middle portion unfolds in "*England* England," an amusement park constructed on the Isle of Wight that combines the leisure strategies of Disneyland and colonial Williamsburg. The park's creator, Sir Jack Pitman, hijacks the middle part of the novel just as he plunders his homeland of its monuments in order to capitalize on them and to aggrandize himself.

The novel features a third-person narrator telling the story of Martha Cochrane. In childhood, her favorite pastime is a puzzle of the counties of England, although much of her enjoyment comes from the teasing play with her father as he appropriates various pieces of her puzzle only to make them magically appear somewhere else. When her parents divorce, the puzzle is spoiled—one of the counties is lost. Martha grows up to become an independent and forthright young woman capable of handling everything in life except lengthy romantic commitments. When she applies for a position with Pitco, Sir Jack's commercial enterprise, he is looking for the opposite of a "yes-man," and Martha's cool composure gets her the job. Sir Jack is already undertaking the project that is intended to be the crowning achievement of his business career: a theme park that will consolidate all of England's quintessential features in one convenient location and package the resulting hodgepodge for mass consumption. Along the way, he also intends to enthrone and enshrine himself: unqualified by birth to rule England, he extracts England's essence to the Isle of Wight—which he purchases—and leads the island's politicians to secede from the mainland and enter the European Union as a sovereign nation.

Sir Jack's blatant self-aggrandizement receives a blow when Martha acquires knowledge of his highly peculiar sexual predilections, which Barnes describes in a hilariously deadpan tone. In a brilliant coup, Martha seizes control of the company, leaving Sir Jack all the ceremonial trappings of his "ruling" position—

his coach, his self-awarded medals, and his tricorn hat—and returning the park to a sound footing. She is an effective and devoted administrator, competently managing the tendency of the park's actors to become in reality the historical figures they are supposed merely to impersonate (the episode with "Samuel Johnson" is particularly amusing). But she is unprepared for the depths of Sir Jack's duplicity, and after establishing the park as a phenomenal success, she in turn is forced out of power.

The novel's end relates Martha's return to the land that had been England before Sir Jack turned it into world-class amusement. The decline of the British EMPIRE is so complete that even England, after the founding of "England England," disintegrates into the tiny ancient kingdoms of the Anglo-Saxon period. Martha immigrates to "Anglia" and takes up a modest life of retirement in a quaint village. In a long elegiac denouement, Barnes presents an Edenic picture of English preindustrial village life. Following Sir Jack's crystallization and commercialization of the English stereotype on the Isle of Wight, the rest of the nation is free to follow its own course of de-development. Ironically, the kingdoms that had once been England become even more English, while the theme park intended to capture that quintessence remains patently artificial, although none the less popular for its artifice. Julian Barnes explores the interconnections between reality and artificiality, between being and seeming, between authenticity and simulacra. In the end, he produces a droll, ironic, and deeply nostalgic but highly unsentimental love letter to England—not to *England* England.

BIBLIOGRAPHY

Carey, John. "Land of Make-Believe," *The Sunday London Times,* 23 August 1998, 1.

Moseley, Merritt. *Understanding Julian Barnes.* Understanding Contemporary British Literature. Columbia: University of South Carolina Press, 1997.

ENGLISH PASSENGERS MATTHEW KNEALE (2000)

Winner of the WHITBREAD Book of the Year Award in 2000 and a selection on the short list for the BOOKER PRIZE, *English Passengers* uses multiple narrators and textual devices to tell the 19th-century story of a voyage to Tasmania. The novel opens in 1857 with the first-person narrator Illiam Quillian Kewley, a Manx seafarer and captain of the *Sincerity,* an ingeniously double-hulled ship designed to facilitate the customary Manxman's anti-English indulgence in smuggling. When he runs afoul of the authorities, Kewley must turn to the lowly pursuit of taking on paying passengers. Still bearing his hidden contraband cargo of brandy and tobacco, he reluctantly acquires as passengers the Reverend Geoffrey Wilson and his party; Rev. Wilson is traveling to Tasmania to search for the Garden of Eden—which he firmly believes is sequestered there in Van Dieman's land—and to prove his theory of "divine refrigeration," a rebuttal of Darwin's distasteful claims. The narrative shifts to Rev. Wilson through his letters and tracts, and from him to various members of his party, including his sponsor, the dimwitted but wealthy Jonah Childs, an untalented botanist (a kind of anti-Darwin) named Timothy Renshaw, and a surgeon with an evil and racist agenda, Dr. Thomas Potter. These men are virtual strangers to one another, and they quickly discover they have very little shared common ground or mutual sympathy, and enmities soon fester. Various members of the party pass time during the long hours of the voyage making attempts to proselytize Capt. Kewley's crew to accept their own particular theory of how nature works.

The narrative then moves to a Tasmanian voice and rolls back 20 years to chronicle the fate of the native people of Tasmania. This narrator, Peevay, is the child of a Tasmanian mother and a white father (a seal hunter) who kidnapped and raped her. As an observer of the fate of the Tasmanians, Peevay is torn between the longing for his white father to rescue him from his mother's bitterness against the whiteness in him and the revulsion he feels for the cruelty with which whites dispossessed the Tasmanians of their land. Kneale is drawing on historical records of one of the brutal episodes of COLONIALISM, thinly fictionalizing the historical persons who carried out the extermination of the Tasmanian natives under the guise of protecting them. Capt. Kewley delivers Rev. Wilson and his party into the aftermath of this small holocaust; contacts with colonials on the island confirm the story Peevay related. In the name of religion and civilization, and with no particular intention to perpetrate genocide, British settlers wiped the entire native population of Tasmania off the face of the earth.

KNEALE'S novel satirizes the arrogant self-righteousness of the colonial enterprise by allowing many narrators to damn themselves with their own words. The novel is a virtuoso display of skill with tone and voice; Kneale uses some 20 narrators, but he structures their discourse in such a way that his plot stays on course. His command of characterization is impressive: He does not explain and interpret characters by narration, description, and exposition but instead allows characters to reveal themselves through their interests, writings, and conversations. To do so, he displays his command of a wide range of authentic dialects and accents (the book even comes equipped with a glossary to help readers comprehend the obscure, specific, and archaic terms). *English Passengers* is an engaging story filled with lively characters, some of whom are despicable, but all of whom are believable. Its merit deserves a wider recognition than its prize-winning status has garnered for it.

BIBLIOGRAPHY

Conrad, P. *Behind the Mountain: Return to Tasmania.* New York: Poseidon Press, 1989.

Hines, Derek. "Eden and Empire." Review of *English Passengers. Times Literary Supplement,* 24 March 2000: 24.

Robson, Lloyd. *A Short History of Tasmania.* Melbourne: Oxford University Press, 1985.

ENGLISH PATIENT, THE MICHAEL ONDAATJE (1992)

Toward the end of WORLD WAR II, in the Villa San Girolamo in Italy, four shattered survivors cope with the physical and emotional suffering the war has brought about. They come from different parts of Europe and the dissolving British Empire, but they share similar kinds of pain. Hana, a Canadian nurse, has lost her lover to the war; after his death, she had aborted their unborn child, and then she learned that her father was burned to death on another front of the war. She has suffered a triple loss, and she is also worn out from being immersed in death on a day-to-day basis. When an unidentified burn vic-

tim proves too weak to transport as the unit moves out to follow the troops onward, Hana requests permission to stay behind and nurse the so-called English patient, but she is also using him to assuage her sense of loss for her burned father. Her patient is actually the Hungarian explorer Count de Almásy, who had been involved in an international effort to map the Libyan desert during the 1930s.

Stationed in the nearby town is an Indian officer, Kirpal Singh ("Kip"), trained in England as a "sapper," one who locates and destroys unexploded landmines, booby traps, and bombs. He has seen his comrades killed by the bombs they are trying to disarm, but he remains confident of his ability to carry out this dangerous work. He visits the burn victim, thinking him to be an Englishman, a representative of a distinguished and admired culture, and falls in love with Hana, who returns his love and rediscovers hope through this relationship.

The chief complication to the plot arrives in the form of David Caravaggio, who was tortured in North Africa as a spy by German intelligence agents. He had been a friend of Hana's late father; when he learns that she has remained behind at the villa, he comes there to comfort her. In listening to the hallucinatory reveries of the English patient, he begins to suspect that this man is really Count de Almásy. Caravaggio believes that Almásy provided information to the Germans—information that lead to Caravaggio's arrest and torture—in a doomed attempt to save his injured lover, Katherine Clifton. Vengeance now seems at hand; however, as conversation reveals the details of Almásy's tragic love story, Caravaggio's rage softens.

Michael ONDAATJE, a Canadian born in Sri Lanka (then known as Ceylon) and educated in England, builds a complex narrative than reaches across the boundaries of space and time while remaining anchored in the Villa San Girolamo. By using several smaller stories that the characters relate to each other, Ondaatje is able to contrast different kinds of love, from the destructiveness of Almásy's adulterous obsession with Katherine to the nurturing care that Hana pours out for the doomed man after he has lost his reason to live. Since the smaller stories are set during the earlier stages of the war, and the frame-story in the villa occurs at the war's end, the author is able to examine the ways that war, the most destructive form of hate, leads to disastrous and unavoidable choices that expand outward, ripplelike, with unforeseen consequences for unknown individuals. Good intentions sometimes lead to painful results, and ill will is sometimes transformed into pity. Thus in multiple layers of irony, the novel's conclusion sees Caravaggio save the man who probably caused his own torture from an attacker whose only grudge against him is the mistaken assumption that he is English. For individuals, intention and outcome remain frustratingly dependent on the uncontrollable workings of the larger world in which they are inextricably enmeshed, leading to unavoidable tragedies alleviated by mere moments of joy.

BIBLIOGRAPHY

Barbour, Douglas. *Michael Ondaatje.* Twayne's English Authors, 835. New York: Twayne Publishers, 1993.

Ganapathy-Dore, Geetha. "The Novel of the Nowhere Man: Michael Ondaatje's *The English Patient,*" *Commonwealth* 16, no. 2 (Spring 1996): 96–100.

Michael Ondaatje Issue. *Essays on Canadian Writing* 53 (Summer 1994): 1–262.

EPIPHANY

EPIPHANY   A moment of insight, a revelation of previously hidden truths, or an important instance of self-discovery in literature is an epiphany. A character may grow gradually into this new awareness through a process of maturation, or the discovery may be harshly imposed by circumstance. Not uncommonly, a BILDUNGSROMAN may build to an epiphany on the part of the protagonist, as experiences deepen the character and extend his or her understanding of the ways of the world, the workings of the heart, or other insights.

BIBLIOGRAPHY

Tigges, Wim. *Moments of Moment: Aspects of the Literary Epiphany.* Studies in Literature, 25. Amsterdam: Rodopi, 1999.

EVA TROUT: OR, CHANGING SCENES

EVA TROUT: OR, CHANGING SCENES ELIZABETH BOWEN (1968)   As this last novel by Elizabeth BOWEN opens, Eva Trout is deceiving people into believing that she has been engaged and has trag-ically lost her beloved. In fact, Eva is emotionally stunted: her mother had abandoned her infant daughter upon learning of her husband's homosexuality, and she then died in a plane crash; her father commits suicide over the infidelity of his homosexual lover, Constantine Ormeau; and her teacher, Iseult, leaves the profession in which she excels to marry a working-class mechanic, Eric Arble. As a boarding school student, Eva had lived with Iseult and Eric, and she adored her teacher; unfortunately, Iseult sees Eva as a reminder of the life she gave up for an unsatisfactory marriage. Eric's virile masculinity is small compensation for his limited appreciation of the life of the mind.

Eva will inherit her father's fortune on her 25th birthday; until then, she is the ward of the misogynistic Constantine. Unaware of her own beauty and the added attractiveness her impending wealth gives her, she invents a dead fiancée. In her emotionally handicapped state, Eva vaguely longs for acceptance and normal relationships without knowing how to go about creating either.

At the age of 24, Eva flees to a rural part of England with the assistance of 12-year-old Henry Dancey, son of the local vicar. She charges Henry to sell her Jaguar in order to provide the financial support she will need until her birthday and buys a lonely house far too large for her needs. There, in solitude, she begins to find some satisfaction and autonomy. Soon, however, Eric Arble shows up, having learned of her whereabouts from Henry. Having failed to fulfill the ambitions he and Iseult shared to own a successful fruit farm, he has lost interest in Iseult and the marriage has soured. He tries to make advances to Eva, attracted by her beauty; Eva, however, does not have the emotional resources either to respond or to repel him. When Constantine arrives to assuage his sense of obligation to her as guardian, she is spared further emotional distress, but her sense of autonomy is curbed.

Desiring love but fearing marriage, Eva determines to adopt a child in order to provide herself with a family. She deceives Iseult into thinking that she, Eva, is pregnant, and allows Iseult to believe that Eric is the father. The Arbles divorce as a result of Eva's imaginary pregnancy; they blame Eva even though their marriage had already begun to fail, and both of them are alienated from her. She flees to Chicago upon receiving her inheritance, planning to use her fortune to acquire a child through an illegal adoption.

The second part of the novel picks up Eva's story eight years later, when she returns to England with her adopted son, Jeremy Trout. She wants to reconcile herself to Iseult and Eric by telling them the truth about her imaginary pregnancy. When she inquires after them at the vicarage, she encounters Henry again. He is now 20 years old and a university student; Eva is 32. Henry observes that Jeremy is deaf and mute and feels pity for Eva. Despite the differences between them in age and social position, Eva and Henry are drawn together emotionally. Jeremy goes to a special school in France, and with all her attention now on Henry, Eva recognizes that she is in love with him. Henry is attentive to her, even loving, but unsure of himself and troubled by the obstacles of age and fortune. He rejects Eva's proposal of marriage, which is actually partly motivated by her desire to acquire a father for Jeremy.

Eva retrieves Jeremy from his school and asks Henry to allow her to pretend that they have married and departed for their honeymoon. The appearance of marriage, she thinks, will be enough to acquire for herself the normal status she has always desired: if other people think she has achieved marriage, and if she *seems* to be emotionally fulfilled, perhaps she eventually will become so. Henry agrees to the deception, but then realizes, on his way to meet her at Victoria Station for the departure on the imaginary honeymoon, that he genuinely loves her and that he can overcome his resistance to this unusual alliance. He tells Eva his feelings, and for the first time in her life she sheds tears from the joy of finally achieving the reciprocal love she has always wanted. At that moment, however, Jeremy enters with a gun, which he acquired from Eric Arble, and which he thinks is a toy. He shoots and kills Eva at the height of her emotional development.

Although *Eva Trout* was not well liked by reviewers upon its publication, it won the JAMES TAIT BLACK MEMORIAL PRIZE in 1970. With a narrative style that depends on elliptical conversations to create psychological realism, the novel employs techniques similar to those used by Henry JAMES. The third-person objective point of view requires that readers infer character

development and emotional problems from the contexts in which the characters are placed and from the ways they talk about themselves and their situations. Since Eva distrusts her own emotions and functions with a limited ability to understand and explain even herself, readers must compensate for her semisilence with their own sensitivity to her problems.

BIBLIOGRAPHY

Bennet, Andrew, and Nicholas Royle. *Elizabeth Bowen and the Dissolution of the Novel: Still Lives.* New York: St. Martin's Press, 1994.

Blodgett, Harriet. *Patterns of Reality: Elizabeth Bowen's Novels.* The Hague: Mouton, 1975.

Bloom, Harold, ed. *Elizabeth Bowen.* New York: Chelsea House, 1987.

Hoogland, Renée C. *Elizabeth Bowen: A Reputation in Writing.* New York: New York University Press, 1994.

EVERY MAN FOR HIMSELF BERYL BAINBRIDGE (1996)

Set on the doomed *Titanic* as Europe stands at the threshold of war on a scale never before seen in human history, this novel was named the WHITBREAD Book of the Year for 1996, the second time Beryl BAINBRIDGE won a Whitbread Award (her first award was for *INJURY TIME* in 1977). The narrator is a young man of good prospects named Morgan; his uncle owns the shipping line that has built the *Titanic,* and as the novel opens he is on his way to join two friends and board the ship for its maiden voyage. Bainbridge builds her novel within the historical time frame that begins on August 8, 1912, and ends after only five days of sailing.

Morgan is a likable young man with most of the big events of his life still ahead of him, since he has not yet mastered the art of courting girls, even though he can conceive a tremendous passion for one. He is especially drawn to Wallis Ellery, as are many others. With his friends Van Hopper and Melchett, Morgan spends leisurely days meeting a wide variety of English and American social types—encounters that allow the author to widen her narrative as she also deepens Morgan's character. Since readers all know what is going to happen to the ship, and therefore how the novel must end, the attraction of the story is not so much what happens but to whom it happens and how those individuals are revealed as human beings. The comic and fumbling efforts of the young to cross into adulthood—to master the steps in the dance—come to a crashing halt as the impossible event comes to pass and the unsinkable ship goes down to its grave, taking more than 1,500 passengers to their graves as well. The characteristic Bainbridge novel explores ordinary events that end with unexpected but believable violence, and in the case of *Every Man for Himself,* history provides a ready-made stage for this pattern to play itself out with inexorable force.

BIBLIOGRAPHY

Maassen, Irmgard, and Anna Maria Stuby. *(Sub)versions of Realism: Recent Women's Fiction in Britain.* Heidelberg: Universitätsverlag C. Winter, 1997.

Wenno, Elisabeth. *Ironic Formula in the Novels of Beryl Bainbridge.* Goteborg, Sweden: Acta Universitatis Gothoburgensis, 1993.

EXCEPT THE LORD JOYCE CARY (1953)
See PRISONER OF GRACE TRILOGY.

EYE IN THE DOOR, THE PAT BARKER (1993)   See REGENERATION TRILOGY.

EYE OF THE STORM, THE PATRICK WHITE (1973)   An epic novel that was published the same year Patrick WHITE won the NOBEL PRIZE, *The Eye of the Storm* is set in Australia, White's native country, and covers the period of the first 70 years of the 20th century. The main character is an elderly woman, Elizabeth Hunter, who is declining to death after a vigorous and uncompromising life. She is surrounded by numerous attendants: Her two adult children, Dorothy and Basil, are both now middle-aged and are both scheming to remove their mother to a nursing home; her nurses, Sister Mary de Santis, who has a religious EPIPHANY while caring for the dying Elizabeth, and Flora Manhood, deciding between her boyfriend and a lesbian affair; her brilliant cook, Lotte Lippmann; and her lawyer, Arnold Wyburd. The narrative uses a stream-of-consciousness technique to follow Elizabeth's thoughts as the words and actions of those around her spark a series of recollections. As she reviews her life and interacts with her attendants, all the characters are revealed in their strengths and weaknesses.

On the surface, the novel appears to be a comedy, but the deeper meanings bear a similarity to the tragedy of *King Lear.* Elizabeth had survived a life-changing event on Brumby Island, off the coast of Australia: She had been there when a hurricane passed directly over, so that she witnessed both the violence and then the still eye of the storm. This experience becomes the dominant metaphor of her life and emphasizes her status as a survivor and as one under the eye of God. Her thoughts wander over the past and recapitulate her life, telling how she married a wealthy man in Sydney and brought two children into the world, but at the same time remained determined to experience all of life and to allow no constraints to withhold any aspect of it from her. She had engaged in affairs and become estranged from her husband, only to rediscover her love for him as she nurses him during his fatal bout of cancer. Even this suffering, she realizes, is part of the glorious storm of life.

Elizabeth's last challenge comes from her resentful children, who gather from their corners of the globe to await the division of the spoils. Elizabeth's nurses resort to pleading and even seduction, but Elizabeth herself finally must triumph with her last act of will. Patrick White brings this strong woman fully to life in all its phases from vigorous youth to crippled infirmity and uses her to explore the range of possibilities open to the human spirit as well as the phenomenon of spirituality. Elizabeth's hearty feasting at life's banquet prepares her for her departure and gives her the strength and the peace to let go of life at last.

BIBLIOGRAPHY

Beatson, P. R. "The Skiapod and the Eye: Patrick White's *The Eye of the Storm,*" *Southerly* 34 (March 1974): 219–232.

Shepherd, R. and Kirpal Singh, eds. *Patrick White: A Critical Symposium.* Bedford Park, S.A.: Centre for Research in the New Literatures in English, Flinders University of South Australia, 1978.

Wolfe, Peter. *Laden Choirs: The Fiction of Patrick White.* Lexington: University Press of Kentucky, 1983.

F

FABIAN SOCIETY A socialist organization founded in 1884 and supported by literary figures such as George Bernard Shaw, Edith Nesbit, and (for a time) H. G. WELLS, the Fabian Society helped bring the Labour Party into existence in 1906 and continues its association with that political entity to the present day. Founded by the Scottish philosopher Thomas Davidson, the society takes its name from a Roman general who achieved victories through strategy and tactics rather than confrontation. Fabianism is committed to social change through an evolutionary process rather than the revolution advocated by Karl Marx, and many of the society's policies are at odds with Marxism. The society's goal is the establishment of a democratic socialist government to rule Great Britain, and in support of this goal, it sponsors numerous local chapters, educational activities, lectures, and conferences, and it maintains an active publishing program.

BIBLIOGRAPHY

Cole, Margaret. *The Story of Fabian Socialism*. Stanford, Calif.: Stanford University Press, 1961.

Harrington, Michael. *Socialism: Past and Future*. New York: Arcade, 1989.

Shaw, George Bernard, ed. *Fabian Essays in Socialism*. London: G. Allen & Unwin, 1962.

FACES IN THE WATER JANET FRAME (1961) Drawing on her own experience with mental illness and the institutions that manage those afflicted by it, Janet FRAME creates a novel that is itself a part of her psychiatric therapy: writing used as a path to greater wholeness and self-unity. To capture the experience of mental illness—the discontinuity between inner thought and outer reality, between actual and imagined scenes—Frame resorts to experimental techniques of carefully minimized punctuation and highly poetic phrasing. This novel shares autobiographical roots with Frame's first novel, *Owls Do Cry* (1957), and her third novel, *The Edge of the Alphabet* (1962); some critics loosely group these into a trilogy.

Janet Frame voluntarily entered a mental hospital when she became severely depressed after the second death by drowning in her family—two of her sisters drowned 10 years apart. In Seacliff Mental Hospital, she was wrongly diagnosed with schizophrenia, and as a consequence she underwent more than 200 rounds of electroshock therapy that left her disoriented and terrified. Her memory in particular was affected. In her fictionalization of these experiences, she captures the inner world of the individual at the mercy of an institution she does not understand and cannot control. Frame creates the persona of Istina Mavet as the first-person narrator of her life at Seacliff and later Avondale, called Cliffhaven and Treecroft in the novel. Istina undergoes shock treatment, insulin treatment, and, like Frame, is scheduled for a lobotomy before a doctor recognizes her storytelling skills and "paroles" her to the outside world. At the novel's end, Istina presents the story as evidence that she has obeyed the instructions she received on leaving the hospital—to live a normal life.

Frame's novel exists because, in spite of her own therapy, she continued with her writing and published several stories while confined to the hospital, demonstrating that creativity can be highly resilient under phenomenal stresses.

BIBLIOGRAPHY

Delbaere, Jeanne, ed. *The Ring of Fire: Essays on Janet Frame.* Sydney, NSW: Dangaroo Press, 1992.

Evans, Patrick. *Janet Frame.* Twayne's World Authors, 415. Boston: Twayne, 1977.

Panny, Judith Dell. *I Have What I Gave: The Fiction of Janet Frame.* New York: G. Braziller, 1993.

FALKLAND ISLANDS   A tiny, cold, wind-whipped, and treeless archipelago located about 300 miles northeast of South America's southernmost point, the Falkland Islands became the focus of world attention on April 2, 1982, when Argentina's government invaded this British possession located off its coast. The United Kingdom replied with military forces that included the younger brother of the Prince of Wales. This territorial dispute highlights the 20th-century aftermath of earlier European COLONIALISM: The islands (also known as the Malvinas) were first sighted officially by a Dutch navigator (about 1600), first landed on by the English (1690), and first settled by the French (1764). British settlement on a separate island followed one year later. In 1767, the Spanish purchased the French interests in the islands, and in 1770 Spanish forces drove the British off for a year. The British colony was reestablished under threat of war, but it was removed for economic reasons in 1774, and the Spanish colony withered by 1811.

When Argentina declared itself independent from Spain in 1820, it claimed the islands as part of its sovereign territory, but an American warship destroyed the Argentine settlement on the island in 1830 after three commercial seal-hunting vessels had been detained without legal sanction. The British had never renounced their claim to the territory after leaving it, and in 1833 a British military expedition forced the last Argentineans from the islands and reestablished the colony, which grew to some 2,100 residents and 800,000 sheep. This situation remained in force for nearly 150 years, with an English-speaking colony maintaining possession of the territory that Argentina continued to claim.

The Falklands became an issue for the United Nations when it was founded after WORLD WAR II; formal debate on the fate of the islands began in 1964, and negotiations between Argentina and Britain continued until the invasion of 1982. British forces prevailed 10 weeks afterward, capturing more than 11,000 Argentine troops, inflicting some 750 casualties, and suffering 256. In the wake of the Falkland Islands War, the Argentine military government fell from power and the Conservative Party of Prime Minister Margaret Thatcher won a landslide victory in the next elections. Literary references to the Falklands are often unsympathetic, obliquely communicating implicit criticism of the policies of Prime Minister Margaret Thatcher, especially in novels by Ian MCEWAN, Julian BARNES, and Hanif KUREISHI; the war was also fictionalized in television plays by Charles Wood (*Tumbledown,* 1988) and Ian Curteis (*The Falklands Play,* 1987). Writers sometimes find humor in the slow advance of the British fleet toward the confrontation waiting on the islands: for example, the scene in *A Fish Called Wanda* (1988) in which John Cleese drives a ponderously slow steamroller over an immobilized foe to win a prize of questionable merit recalls the Falklands war in a tongue-in-cheek manner.

BIBLIOGRAPHY

Hastings, Max, and Simon Jenkins. *The Battle for the Falklands,* New York: Norton, 1983.

Perl, Raphael, and Everette E. Larson. *The Falkland Islands Dispute in International Law and Politics: A Documentary Sourcebook.* London: Oceana Publications, 1983.

FAMISHED ROAD, THE BEN OKRI (1991) Winner of the BOOKER PRIZE (known then as the Booker-McConnell Prize) in 1991, this novel of MAGIC REALISM is set in the African nation of Nigeria and serves as an ALLEGORY of Nigeria's transformation from a British colony to an independent country. As such, it is an example of postcolonialism and is sometimes compared with works by writers such as Salman RUSHDIE; like Rushdie, OKRI was influenced by the Columbian novelist Gabriel García Márquez's *One Hundred Years of Solitude.*

Okri draws on the mythic traditions of the Yoruba people (not his own tribal group) to create his protagonist and first-person narrator, Azaro, who is a "spirit-child." In Yoruba myth, the spirit child, or abiku, is a figure of reincarnation, being repeatedly reborn into the world. The multiple journeys through many kinds of reality make the abiku both wise and terrifying. In Azaro's case, he chooses to remain in the human world, resisting the tempting appeals of his fellow abiku to return to the spirit world. Okri telescopes time and condenses space so that Azaro's story unfolds in a human world that is both the primitive past and the modern present, both the insular village and the urban ghetto. This device enables him to capture the reinvention of Nigeria as an independent nation in a single character's lifetime.

Other characters in the novel include Azaro's life-affirming parents, including his long-suffering mother and a father who is in turn a laborer, a boxer, and a politician defending the marginalized poor; his fellow abiku Madame Koto, a barkeeper whose changing establishment helps suggest the movement into the modern world, both for good and for ill; and Jeremiah, a photographer who unintentionally garners the enmity of the new political powers. Okri uses Azaro's travels between the spirit world and the human world to illustrate the permanence of change and the cyclical alternation of drought and torrential rain, and he relies on dreams and visions to suggest the mysteriousness of life and our knowledge of the world that contains it. The oral storytelling tradition acquires a written incarnation as Azaro's father tells him myths, folktales, and fables, recorded in Okri's text, to explain the mysteries and threats the world contains, and to help his son to mature with the strength to bear the crushing burdens of existence such as love and death.

Okri also published a sequel to *The Famished Road* in 1993, *Songs of Enchantment.*

BIBLIOGRAPHY

Hawley, John C. "Ben Okri's Spirit Child: Abiku Migration and Postmodernity," *Research in African Literatures* 26 (Spring 1995): 30–39.

FANTASY   One of the branches or subgenres of speculative fiction, fantasy literature is characterized by supernatural elements in the construction of the plot or the configuration of character. A fantasy story may be set in a world with features that defy the laws of physics, such as traveling through time or parallel worlds or using magic, or it may be set in an ordinary realm in an imagined remote past. In spite of these extraordinary narrative components, the story depends for much of its effects of the readers' appreciation of the conventions of realism. In theme, the fantasy novel shows its greatest affinity to conventional fiction: Fantasy does not redefine heroism and romance but instead creates a particularly spectacular and exotic backdrop against which the familiar conflict of good and evil may provide readers with greater comfort and satisfaction than the same general story would in a realistic narration.

Fantasy shares an affiliation with fairy tales and myths, borrowing heavily from the monsters of folklore such as dragons and demons. It generally depends on the ARCHETYPE of the heroic quest as explained in the mythic criticism of J. G. Fraser, Joseph Campbell, and Northrup Frye. In places it may overlap with horror, another major subgenre of speculative fiction, but it differs in deemphasizing fearsome elements and making them subject to the hero's eventual control. Fantasy differs sharply from SCIENCE FICTION, the third major subgenre of speculative fiction, in declining to explain all the phenomena of the story's fictional world in terms of the known facts of the universe.

The most important 20th-century fantasy writer is J. R. R. TOLKIEN, author of *The HOBBIT* and the three volumes of *The LORD OF THE RINGS*. His work set the benchmark for subsequent fantasy authors, especially with respect to the creation of entire fictional realms. Tolkien borrowed extensively from medieval literature, his academic specialty, and from Scandinavian traditions. He created numerous species of humanlike creatures in varying dimensions: hobbits, elves (not the minuscule ones of British folklore, but their antecedents), dwarves, trolls, orcs, men, wizards, and others. For many of these societies, he developed languages, poems and songs, cultural traditions, social customs, and historical backgrounds. The vast amount of detail he embroiders for his imaginary world creates a palpable texture for the reader; this aspect of his writing has become its most imitated feature. But Tolkien also provided a war between good and evil of mythic scope in which the key characters must struggle against the temptations of power and must overcome evil by repudiating power rather than by using it. In creating fictional realms of magic and adventure, Tolkien's many imitators have understood their task, but in the matter of theme, they have been less uniformly successful.

But Tolkien did not create fantasy literature *ex nihilo*. He followed the example already established by the designer and poet William Morris (1834–96) and the novelist George MacDonald (1824–1905) in drawing on the conventions of myths and fairy tales such as antique or other-worldly settings, characters with supernatural powers, and plot elements that depended on ANTIREALISM. Another key writer in the early stages of the 20th-century development of fantasy was Lord DUNSANY, who also ventured into the subgenres of horror and science fiction.

BIBLIOGRAPHY

Anderson, Douglas A. *Tales Before Tolkien: The Roots of Modern Fantasy.* New York: Del Rey/Ballantine Books, 2003.

Mass, Wendy, and Stuart P. Levine. *Fantasy.* San Diego, Calif.: Greenhaven Press, 2002.

FARRELL, J. G. (1935–1979)

Born on January 23, 1935, in Liverpool, J. G. Farrell was reared with strong ties to family in IRELAND, and as an adult he traveled widely to conduct background research for his novels. Early in his undergraduate career at Oxford, Farrell was stricken with polio, which permanently weakened his upper body. Nonetheless, he took a degree at Oxford in 1960 and then worked in France as a teacher of English. His first novel appeared in 1963, *A Man From Elsewhere.* In his second novel, *The Lung,* published in 1965, Farrell drew on his own childhood battle with polio but gave it a darkly comic twist. In 1966, he won a scholarship to support travel in the United States for two years, and in 1967 he published *A Girl in the Head.* Although his first three novels show the development of his craft rather than the strength of his talent, by this point in his career Farrell was an experienced writer, traveler, and scholar, and these three elements combined to facilitate the composition of his most important fictional works.

The period of Farrell's life roughly coincides with the years during which the British EMPIRE shrank from three blows: the Irish Rebellion; the Japanese conquest of Singapore at the beginning of WORLD WAR II; and the independence of INDIA in 1947, capping decades of strife. When he began writing about these events, HISTORICAL FICTION was in disfavor, but Farrell's fictional retellings of the decline of the empire succeeded with critics and the reading public, and they renewed interest in this genre. Emphasizing character development and plot tension over historical accuracy, Farrell presents the story out of chronological order, beginning with the establishment of Ireland as a separate nation; his childhood experiences in Ireland contributed to his novel *Troubles* (1970), the first in a three-part series. *Troubles* was awarded the Geoffrey Faber Memorial Prize, and the money allowed Farrell to visit India for a year. In 1973, *The SIEGE OF KRISHNAPUR,* the product of his research in India, won the BOOKER PRIZE. To capture the roots of the Indian struggle for independence, Farrell's story reaches back to 1857 and allows British colonials in Krishnapur to explain the Sepoy Mutiny, a turning point in Britain's relations with India. Finally, after a visit to Singapore, Farrell published *The Singapore Grip* in 1978, drawing on personal interviews and historical accounts to tell the story of the fall of Singapore. (This event is also captured by J. G. BALLARD in his autobiographical novel *The EMPIRE OF THE SUN,* published in 1984.)

Taken collectively, this series is the work that established Farrell's reputation as an important contemporary novelist. At the age of 44, he was at the height of his powers. But his career was unexpectedly brief: The very year after he completed his masterwork, Farrell drowned near his home on the southern coast of Ireland.

BIBLIOGRAPHY

Binns, Ronald. *J. G. Farrell*. London: Methuen, 1986.

Bristow-Smith, Laurence. " 'Tomorrow's Another Day': The Essential J. G. Farrell," *Critical Quarterly* 25, no. 2 (1983): 45–52.

FAR SIDE OF THE WORLD, THE
PATRICK O'BRIAN (1984)   See AUBREY-MATURIN NOVELS.

FELICIA'S JOURNEY WILLIAM TREVOR
(1994)   A suspenseful thriller that alternates between the story of a potential victim and that of her potential predator, *Felicia's Journey* follows the title character from her bleak young life in Ireland to an unknown future in England. She is pursuing the hope that the young Irishman who seduced her—whose child she is carrying—and who she believes loves her will welcome her and make everything right. She is a simple girl of few needs and fewer expectations, and she is completely unprepared for the larger world she thrusts herself into. Her naïveté is touching, yet the reader cannot help but fear for her as she faces a world she barely understands. In contrast, Mr. Hilditch runs a well-oiled machine at the cafeteria he manages at a factory. He lives in the large house he had shared with his mother, now deceased, although her clothes still hang in the closets where she left them. He has a sharp eye for a lost lamb such as Felicia, and he knows just how to manage his chances so as to manipulate events into the appearance of chance and coincidence. He is a skilled and resourceful storyteller who can make himself the object of a desperate young woman's pity, effectively disarming her instinct for self-protection.

Felicia is in a danger that she herself cannot recognize as she searches everywhere for her lost love: Everywhere, that is, except the right place, since she is unable to believe that a proper Irish boy could lower himself to serve in the British military. The man she is searching for can be found easily enough in the town's pubs frequented by soldiers, but Felicia, believing his lies, looks everywhere else. Meanwhile, Mr. Hilditch contributes to her growing desperation any way he can, until she has no one to turn to but him. As she sinks into more

and more dire straits, she first receives and then loses the charity of a religious cult before running out of options, which is just where Mr. Hilditch wants her to be. Her life and the life of her unborn child are at risk, but Felicia has none of the skills or the knowledge she needs to fend off her impending doom, and her luck cannot completely save her.

Trevor builds the story's suspense by carefully doling out the details of Mr. Hilditch's previous experiences with women, including his late mother. The narrator presents the story from a third-person limited point of view that peers into the minds of Felicia and Mr. Hilditch but that also withholds information to heighten tension and suspense. In the end, Mr. Hilditch discovers his own vulnerability, providing a sense of closure to the story that he cannot bear to recognize as the story of his life. Felicia narrowly escapes the fate that befell Mr. Hilditch's earlier "friends," but though she survives, she is broken by life's hardships, not saved from them. The grimness of the story is relieved by the humanity with which it is told, a style that won the WHITBREAD Book of the Year Award in 1996.

BIBLIOGRAPHY

MacKenna, Dolores. *William Trevor: The Writer and His Work*. Dublin: New Island, 1999.

Schirmer, Gregory A. *William Trevor: A Study of His Fiction*. New York: Routledge, 1990.

FELLOWSHIP OF THE RING, THE
J. R. R. TOLKIEN (1954)   The success of *The HOBBIT* when it was published in 1937 led Tolkien's publisher to suggest that he write more of this kind of story. Using characters and settings already familiar in *The Hobbit,* but drawing on materials he had been developing for years, Tolkien crafted a monumental quest story in which an unlikely hero must undertake a long and perilous journey in order to defeat evil. The story is tinged both by Tolkien's Christianity and by the historical circumstances occurring when it was written, as WORLD WAR II raged across Europe. Tolkien, however, resisted the formulaic correspondences of biographical and historical criticism and explicitly distanced his story from such interpretations.

This novel is the first volume of the trilogy *The LORD OF THE RINGS*. In a manner similar to the narrative structure of *The Hobbit,* events in the larger world thrust a task upon peaceful, comfort-loving hobbits: The incarnation of evil power, a ring forged by the Dark Lord Sauron, must be destroyed in order to destroy his influence and prevent him from conquering Middle Earth. The quest carries a group of hobbits farther and farther from home and into contact with creatures and cultures from every corner of the world; it begins with the magic ring Bilbo found in Gollum's cave, which he passes to his nephew, Frodo, who in turn is required to end the danger it creates for their homeland by removing it from there.

Ultimately, Frodo must carry it to its origin point at Mount Doom and destroy it. In the process, he himself is at risk from the influence of the ring on its bearer and from others trying to acquire the ring for good or evil purposes. The struggle against the power of Sauron, with Frodo and the ring at its center, unites hobbits, elves (reinvented from the tiny creatures of British folklore), dwarves, and other mythical creatures with human beings of diverse cultures who are on the verge of inheriting the world from them or falling under the subjugation of evil. Hope and goodness can be redeemed only by suffering and sacrifice on the long and dangerous quest.

The story pattern sets the challenge, brings together a band of hero-adventurers to achieve it, subjects them to hardships and dangers that test their courage and resourcefulness, and then breaks the group apart through death, temptation, and violent abduction. Frodo moves into greater isolation to save others from the ring's power; by the end of this novel, only his friend Samwise Gamgee remains with him as he enters the most dangerous phase of his journey, and he has seen his mentor, Gandalf, fall into an abyss while protecting him. He perseveres even as his burden begins to crush his will, and even though he cannot know whether he can succeed in his task and survive beyond it.

See also *The LORD OF THE RINGS; The TWO TOWERS; The RETURN OF THE KING;* TOLKIEN, and FANTASY.

BIBLIOGRAPHY

Ball, Martin. "Cultural Values and Cultural Death in *The Lord of the Rings,*" *Australian Humanities Review* 28 (2003). Available online. URL: http://www.lib.latrobe.edu.au/AHR/archive/Issue-Jan-2003/ball.html. Accessed on March 10, 2003.

Chance, Jane. "Power and Knowledge in Tolkien: The Problem of Difference in "The Birthday Party." *Proceedings of the J. R. R. Tolkien Centenary Conference, 1992.* Edited by Patricia Reynolds and Glen GoodKnight. Altadena: The Mythopoeic Press, 1995.

FEMINISM　　At its simplest, feminism is the ideological position that men and women are entitled to equal opportunities: politically, socially, and economically. These opportunities extend to voting rights, property ownership, the availability of educational and employment options, the right to hold political and other offices, and equal pay for equal work.

The story of feminism in the 20th century, however, even if it is restricted only to its literary elements, must reach back to the Enlightenment and the Victorian era if it is to form a coherent narrative. More than a century passed between the publication of Mary Wollstonecraft's *Vindication of the Rights of Women* (1792) and the establishment of voting rights for women in Great Britain in 1918; more than an adult lifetime passed in the United States between the *Declaration of Sentiments* at 1848's Seneca Falls Convention, which asserted the necessity of voting rights for women, and the enfranchisement of American women in 1920. The founding mothers of the women's movement did not live to cast a vote when their successors finally won the day.

Ironically, the concentrated focus of early feminists on the voting franchise led to a decline in activism once universal suffrage became law. Worldwide strife, economic hardship, and the "baby boom" that followed WORLD WAR II eclipsed feminism for some three decades. With the rise of the Civil Rights Movement in the 1960s, however, activist women were reawakened to the issue of equal rights, and a "second wave" women's movement began to take shape. Centered in the United States but extending to women all over the world, the new feminism seeks equality for women in every sphere of endeavor. The success of first-wave feminism led to new sources of conflict: In the workplace, women appeared in increasing numbers and gradually became more vocal in opposing sexual harassment; in health care, women's demands to control their own bodies helped bring about a Supreme Court decision legalizing abortion in defined circumstances; in their personal lives, women began to take control of their fertility, their sexuality, and the circumstances of their marriages, opposing abuse and exploitation; and in business, politics, education, religion, and other aspects of life, women's voices called for changes that would facilitate their contributions to the larger world.

American colleges and universities have been a key site of transformation for feminism. (For an amusing contrast between American and British higher education systems and attitudes toward women and sexuality during the upheavals of the 1960s, see CHANGING PLACES, by David LODGE.) Courses on women's literature, women's history, and women's health began to appear, and then entire curricular programs developed. Undergraduates began earning degrees in women's studies, and soon their further research brought to light forgotten or neglected female authors and historical figures. Theorists asserted that "the personal is the political," and the fact that an author's gender was female became significant, undermining the domination of objective FORMALISM in literary criticism. The discovery of important women novelists led to heated debates about CANON revision—if women writers were to be added to the curriculum while the length of the academic term remained constant, who among the great writers traditionally studied (sometimes disparagingly referred to as DWEMs, or "dead white European males") was to be removed? A comparison of the first volume of the first edition of *The Norton Anthology of English Literature* with the current edition makes clear the changes feminism has brought about in one part of the public realm. Women writers of every sort are now represented: poets, inspirational writers, fiction writers, historians, dramatists, essayists, and others take their place in the chronological parade of England's greatest writing, next to the men to whom they were contemporaries; however, they were entirely absent in the original edition.

Women's rights are now vigorously defended by well-established organizations and bureaucracies. Women work as lawyers, physicians, pilots, executives, soldiers, truck drivers, and in many other fields once closed to them, and they hold increasing numbers of political offices. In the United Kingdom, the highest offices in the nation, both elected and hereditary, have been held by women. At some universities, women students have begun to outnumber men, and in some churches they are ordained as ministers. The success of women writers in Britain in winning the BOOKER PRIZE led to something of a flap when a special prize for women—the Orange Prize—was founded in the late 1990s. Why should women have their own prize, the argument ran, when they are winning the existing prize so well? And why should men be excluded from consideration for the Orange Prize when they had to compete against women on equal terms for the Booker, the WHITBREAD, and other literary awards? These signs of backlash indicate how far feminism has come but also suggest that the journey to equality is not over.

BIBLIOGRAPHY

Beauvoir, Simone de. *The Second Sex*. New York: Knopf, 1953.

Davis, Flora. *Moving the Mountain: The Women's Movement in America Since 1960*. New York: Simon & Shuster, 1991.

Friedan, Betty. *The Feminine Mystique*. New York: W. W. Norton, 1963.

Gilbert, Sandra M., and Susan Gubar. *The Madwoman in the Attic: The Woman Writer and the Nineteenth-Century Literary Imagination*. New Haven, Conn.: Yale University Press, 1979.

———. *No Man's Land: The Place of the Woman Writer in the Twentieth Century*. 3 vols. New Haven, Conn.: Yale University Press, 1988–94.

Moers, Ellen. *Literary Women*. Garden City, N.Y.: Doubleday, 1976.

Showalter, Elaine. *The New Feminist Criticism: Essays on Women, Literature, and Theory*. New York: Pantheon, 1985.

Steinem, Gloria. *Outrageous Acts and Everyday Rebellions*. New York: Holt, Reinhart, and Winston, 1983.

Woolf, Virginia. *A Room of One's Own*. New York: Harcourt, Brace, 1929.

FIFTH BUSINESS ROBERTSON DAVIES (1970) See *The Deptford Trilogy*.

FILM ADAPTATION

Human beings have presumably created narratives for as long as they have been human, using first the body's own avenues of communication—speech and gesture—and then developing technologies to amplify the effectiveness of the storyteller's art. Speaking, singing, chanting, and acting have been made more persistent, more reliable, and more available by writing, which lasts longer in ordinary circumstances and stays the same from moment to moment and from year to year. Writing in turn has refined, expanded, and diversified the narrative arts, sacrificing some features of the spoken word while also preserving its content beyond the lifespan of the creative speaker and extending its reach to audiences far beyond the range of the speaker's voice. The great advance in writing was the invention of the printing press in about 1450, which enabled the mass production of books that had previously been laboriously handcrafted.

The written narrative has dominated the generation and preservation of literature in the five millennia it has been in use; in the 20th century, however, the new technologies of radio, film, television, and computer began to make it possible to imagine a world devoid of writing that nonetheless could retain all the advantages writing had made possible. With a Web camera, a voice-activated computer, and a broadband connection to the Internet, it's possible to imagine conducting all one's business and personal communication without ever having recourse to the written word. The study of rhetoric—the effective delivery of live (and recorded) messages—may be on the verge of displacing the study of literature's written messages.

Before the technologically spoken work antiquates the written word, however, we can expect to enjoy a long transition of more of less peaceful coexistence between written literature and new technologies, especially film and television. People long accustomed to writing are unlikely to stop doing it overnight; additionally, there is a tremendous backlog of written texts not yet committed to (or adapted to) audiovisual media. Transforming the written work into an electronically preserved spoken form is a delicate business. Just as the written word sacrificed some features of the oral tradition it replaced, the digitized word fails to capture some features of the written tradition; presumably, it will also open previously unimagined opportunities for amplifying the effectiveness of the narrative arts.

The most sophisticated displacement of the written by the spoken tradition is the film adaptation of a work of literature. Film and literature, as media for the creative expression of narrative, differ in several ways, but most crucially in the capacity of each to deal with interiority. The novel is ideally suited to the unlimited exploration of mental states. Writers can choose to reveal or conceal as much of their characters' thoughts as they wish: In first-person narration, the narrator's exploration of interior mental states is limited only by his or her sophistication with respect to self-awareness and self-understanding. The third-person narrator can either reveal all thoughts in all characters (the omniscient narrator) or the thoughts of only one or a select group of characters (the limited narrator). In film, mental states must be inferred by viewers in the same way that they infer the mental states of real people: by drawing conclusions based on statements, facial expressions, and behaviors. Film is quintessentially a medium for showing action that can indicate thought, whereas the novel is quintessentially a medium for exploring thought that can describe action.

In the early history of film, adaptations of literary works were usually carried out by screenwriters; however in the middle and latter 20th century novelists have often adapted their own works for the screen and have diversified their employment by becoming screen writers themselves. After World War II, Hollywood supported a colony of British writers working in the film industry; residents there included Aldous Huxley (who satirized his experience in *After Many a Summer Dies the Swan*), Evelyn Waugh (whose portrait of Hollywood is the much darker short comic novel *The Loved One*), Liam O'Flaherty, Graham Greene, C. S. Forester, Christopher Isherwood, James Hilton, and others. Britain's native film and television industry has benefited from the talents of Anthony Powell, John Braine, Douglas Adams, Fay Weldon, and others. Novelists who have developed original stories directly for presentation in film include Ruth Prawer JHABVALA (who has also adapted her own work for film) and Hanif KUREISHI. Novelists who have adapted their own novels to the screen include John FOWLES, Arthur C. CLARKE, Graham GREENE, Roddy DOYLE, William GOLDING, and others.

Particularly successful films adapted from novels by someone other than the original author include *Schindler's List* (from the novel *SCHINDLER'S ARK*), *WOMEN IN LOVE* and other works by D. H. LAWRENCE, *REBECCA*, *The WINGS OF THE DOVE*, *BLACK ROBE*, *The END OF THE AFFAIR* and other works by Graham GREENE, *The PORTRAIT OF A LADY*, *GEORGY GIRL*, *NINETEEN EIGHTY-FOUR*, *TRAINSPOTTING*, *2001: A SPACE ODYSSEY*, *A CLOCKWORK ORANGE*, *The LORD OF THE RINGS*, *POSSESSION*, *COLD COMFORT FARM*, *The HANDMAID'S TALE*, *LAST ORDERS*, *The SPY WHO CAME IN FROM THE COLD*, *The LORD OF THE FLIES*, and many others. Novels that have been more loosely adapted or that have provided inspiration for films include *The AFRICAN QUEEN*, *The THIRTY-NINE STEPS*, *HEART OF DARKNESS*, numerous adventures featuring Sherlock HOLMES, *The WAR OF THE WORLDS*, *The FRENCH LIEUTENANT'S WOMAN*, the AUBREY-MATURIN NOVELS, *CRASH*, the BOND novels of Ian FLEMING, *LOST HORIZON*, numerous works by Agatha CHRISTIE, *The LIFE AND LOVES OF A SHE-DEVIL*, several works by W. Somerset MAUGHAM, *The PRIME OF MISS JEAN BRODIE*, *The SCARLET PIMPERNEL*, and many others.

The successful adaptation of novels to television has been more common in Britain than in the United States; the British Broadcasting Corporation (BBC) has brought many 20th-century British novels to the small screen that have subsequently appeared on the American Public Broadcast System (PBS) and several cable venues; these adaptations include *The RAJ QUARTET*, *The GORMENGHAST NOVELS*, *BRIDESHEAD REVISITED*, works featuring JEEVES and Bertie Wooster, *The FORSYTE SAGA*, mysteries by Ruth RENDELL and P. D. JAMES, and many, many others.

BIBLIOGRAPHY

Brady, Ben. *Principles of Adaptation for Film and Television.* Austin: University of Texas Press, 1994.

McFarlane, Brian. *Novel to Film: An Introduction to the Art of Adaptation.* Oxford: Clarendon Press; New York: Oxford University Press, 1996.

Naremore, James. *Film Adaptation.* New Brunswick, N.J.: Rutgers University Press, 2000.

Ong, Walter J. *Orality and Literacy: The Technologizing of the Word.* London: Methuen, 1982.

Sinyard, Neil. *Filming Literature: The Art of Screen Adaptation.* New York: St. Martin's Press, 1986.

FINE BALANCE, A ROHINTON MISTRY (1996)

Set in INDIA in 1975 and 1976 under an impending political crisis, *A Fine Balance* follows the lives of four characters in a coastal city in India (Mumbai, formerly Bombay) and the many other figures to whom they are connected. These characters, marginalized in various ways, must work hard to preserve a fine balance between intoxicating hope and numbing despair.

At the center of the story is Dina Delal, a seamstress and a widow of a certain age who rents a tiny apartment and maintains a precarious life by taking in boarders; at the time of the story, Dina's boarders are three: the student Maneck Kohlah, the tailor Ishvar Darji, and Ishvar's nephew Omprakash. Dina has been left impoverished after only three years of marriage, and she does not wish to be obliged to marry again in order to provide herself with financial security. Maneck is the son of a friend of Dina's whose family is threatened with poverty if the political and economic situation does not improve; as a student, Maneck also represents India's hope for a better future. The two tailors are villagers attempting to escape from poverty and caste-based prejudice in their hometown; Dina markets the garments they sew through an export company. These people form the triple stands of the interwoven narrative, struggling to maintain their decency and humanity in spite of poverty and the predation of others wishing to take the little they have.

The political crisis is the "state of emergency" instituted by former Indian prime minister Indira Gandhi: It was designed to save her own grip on power by undermining her opponents' ability to organize themselves against her and was declared despite judicial decisions that ordered her to step down from her position. The novel contrasts the tight, secure, shared existence of the artificial family created in Dina's apartment with the violent, ironbound, and indifferent actions occurring in the larger world and impinging on the four flatmates. Each of them is harmed by the political disaster in which the country is mired: Manek chooses to leave India after a fellow student is murdered, implying that India is driving away its best hope for the future. The tailors return to their village to visit and are forcibly detained and involuntarily sterilized. Dina is left alone, not knowing what has become of her family.

Critics have repeatedly compared *A Fine Balance* to the work of Charles Dickens in light of its large scope, its vast cast of characters, its grim honesty in portraying the ugliness of both poverty and human corruption, and its valorization of human decency, integrity, sympathy, and compassion. The novel was short-listed for the BOOKER PRIZE; additionally, it won the *Los Angeles Times* Book Prize for fiction, The COMMONWEALTH Writers Prize, the Winfred Holtby Prize from the Royal Society of Literature, and other awards.

BIBLIOGRAPHY

Mantel, Hilary. "States of Emergency." In *India: A Mosaic.* New York: New York Review Books, 2001, 181–193.

Moss, Laura. "Can Rohinton Mistry's Realism Rescue the Novel?" In *Postcolonizing the Commonwealth: Studies in Literature and Culture.* Edited by Rowland Smith. Waterloo, Ont.: Wilfrid Laurier University Press, 2000, 157–165.

FINNEGANS WAKE JAMES JOYCE (1939)

A legendarily difficult novel, *Finnegans Wake* is the culmination of James JOYCE'S life and work as an artist. It is a playground, a wrecking yard, a battlefield, of literary experimentation and mythic allegory, placing demands on its readers than can intimidate anyone expecting the familiar and comfortable devices OF PLOT, character, theme, narration, and symbolism—although these *are* there as well. It has been described by scholars as the unique instance of a new literary genre.

The novel is staggeringly ambitious, seeking to form a response to the entire intellectual and creative tradition of the myth, art, philosophy, and history of the Western world. It begins quite literally *in medias res:* not merely in the middle of the action, but in the middle of a sentence, the first half of which can be found at the end of the novel's last line. The text thus circles back on itself, forming a cycle of heroic-quest motifs. At its most basic level, the action covers the events of one night in the lives of a family in the Dublin suburb of Chapelizod: the Protestant innkeeper Humphrey Chimpden Earwicker, his wife Anna Livia Plurabelle, his twin sons Shem and Shaun (the former a sensitive artist, the latter a coarse dullard), and his daughter Issy. Humphrey goes to bed guiltily mulling over an incident in Phoenix Park in which some indecency was proffered to two girls. Like Nietzsche's recognition that all "original" texts are inextricably obscured by centuries of copying errors, misrememberings, editorial emendations, and a host of other "corruptions," Humphrey's thoughts on this incident and Dublin's response to it have blurred the exact nature of whatever it was that happened. In his sleep, Humphrey's dream vision further obscures the original incident while also rehearsing much of European literature and history in terms of it.

The actual words of the text and the syntax in which they are arranged—the formal elements of language itself—take precedence over the traditional forms of narration on a first viewing, requiring readers to tease a meaning (not *the* meaning) out of them. Joyce uses his characters as puppets or actors or instantiations through which he presents, represents, and parodies the key events of European—indeed of human—history and culture. He revisits themes such as the fall— the inauguration of humankind into the world it continues to occupy—through many kinds of falls: the serious kind, such as the fall of the Roman Empire, and the silly kind, such as the fall of Humpty Dumpty. He re-examines a key interest of his, the role of the father and the struggle of sons with their fathers; he also contemplates the contradictions in the double role women must play as mothers and mistresses, engaging one generation of men carnally in order to give rise to a further generation that they must nurture and help to— or hinder from attaining—maturity (or both). He examines the role of the innovator and the imitator through the lives of irresponsible-but-imaginative Shem and dull-but-diligent Shaun. Through it all, he questions how a single universe can accommodate sameness and unity while also allowing the existence of difference and flux: the crucial cosmological paradox in philosophy of the One and the Many.

Joyce gives the reader permission to suspend the dictates of familiar cause-and-effect linearity, inviting a playful interaction with the text. Readers will be helped by a thorough familiarity with the four-stage theory of cultural evolution that Giambattista Vico developed in 1744, popularly known in English as *The New Science* (the phases of which are the theocratic, the aristocratic, the democratic, and the anarchic). Or they may acquire interpretive assistance by recourse to one of the many "keys" to *Finnegans Wake;* in doing so, however, they will have already abandoned the task— the journey, the imaginative exercise—that the author has enjoined them to undertake.

BIBLIOGRAPHY

Attridge, Derek. *The Cambridge Companion to James Joyce.* Cambridge: Cambridge University Press, 1990.

Campbell, Joseph, and Henry Morton Robinson. *A Skeleton Key to* Finnegans Wake. New York: Harcourt, Brace and Company, 1944.

Litz, A. Walton. *The Art of James Joyce: Method and Design in* Ulysses *and* Finnegans Wake. New York: Oxford University Press, 1961.

McHugh, Roland. *The Sigla of* Finnegans Wake. Austin: University of Texas Press, 1976.

FIRST TRILOGY JOYCE CARY (1941–1944)

The three novels in this sequence include *Herself Surprised* (1941), *To Be a Pilgrim* (1942), and *The Horse's Mouth* (1944); Cary's heirs collected the three titles into one volume in 1957 and christened it *First Trilogy.*

Joyce CARY had been publishing fiction for several years, drawing on his youth in IRELAND and his experience as a colonial bureaucrat in Africa, but with these novels he enjoyed his first popular success while also developing new narrative strategies that made effective use of his excellent talent with voice. Cary's innovation is to develop one story but to have three narrators relate its events in the first person. Each novel can stand on its own, but collectively they yield more enjoyment than three unrelated novels would. Cary repeats this strategy even more skillfully in his "Second Trilogy," primarily known as the *Prisoner of Grace* trilogy. Since the narrators each have a particular, partial perspective on the action of the story, each of the three versions of the tale is a unique narration that sheds its own peculiar light on the other two. This technique highlights the modern characteristic of INDETERMINACY: Since the narrators do not completely agree with one another, some or all of them must be lying, and consequently it is impossible for the reader to construct a definitive truth from their three renditions of the story.

The narrator of *Herself Surprised* is Sara Monday, a woman who begins and ends her adult life as a cook but enjoys a period of financial luxury in between through one comfortable marriage and an even better second near-marriage. And if she had not fallen in love with the improvident artist Gulley Jimson, she might have remained in the lap of luxury; however, Sarah has surprised herself more than once in a life crammed with unpredictable twists and turns. As she begins her story, she is writing from jail, where she has landed after doing a sort of wrong thing for a more or less right reason: She claims she has sold unwanted old things— those that her intended second husband had told her to throw away—in order to provide Jimson with the materials he needs to continue serving his muse. From the perspective of her intended's offended family, however, she has been selling off heirlooms to keep a lover (attitudes revealed by the narrator of *To Be a Pilgrim*).

Sara purportedly undertakes her narration as a warning to other women. By presenting her own tale of bad judgment, she hopes to save other women from making her mistakes, although eventually she reveals that a newspaper is paying her for her story. Sara is a loving woman who follows her heart and pours out her favors—she poses nude for a series of paintings by Jimson that eventually becomes the sensation of the art world—without regard for consequences. Her ingenuous generosity makes her an easy target for Jimson's bottomless neediness. She resolves, however, to change her ways when she leaves jail.

In *To Be a Pilgrim,* the narrative switches to Sara's intended second husband, the elderly bachelor Tom Wilcher of Tolbrook Manor. Wilcher is the conservative side of the major love triangle in Sara's life, while the unconventional liberal side belongs to Gulley Jimson. Wilcher's narrative is a study of old age and an old man's love of the disappearing past. While Sara had depicted Wilcher as an insatiable leech, he presents himself as an old fussbudget, happily pottering among his beloved old things (the ones Sara had been selling to provide for Jimson). As the story begins, Wilcher has suffered a heart attack and the family has dispatched Ann, a niece, to keep watch over him and to keep him away from that Sara Monday. But Ann is soon busy with Robert, a nephew who wants to try out the new scientific methods of farming at Tolbrook Manor. Ann and Robert are married (Robert keeps some of the fancy new farming equipment in the living room, to Wilcher's distress). When a local farm girl catches Robert's eye, Wilcher takes advantage of the diversion of attention away from his actions; he totters off to London to find Sara; what he actually finds, however, is that no one can recapture the past or even know for sure what it was really like. A second heart attack forces Wilcher back home, where he soon ends his days without naming an heir for the family property.

The story shifts to the opposite set of personality characteristics in *The Horse's Mouth,* narrated by Gulley Jimson. His tale is an oral history delivered to one of his artistic disciples from a hospital bed after his studio—a derelict shack—had been demolished while he was still in it, still painting, on a scaffold. Jimson's life is a chronicle of Dionysian excess and shady trickster ploys, all placed in the service of Art. Given the socioeconomic arrangement by which most of society governs itself, money is a necessity for everything, but money is the one variable Jimson cannot get under control. He badgers others for money or concocts none-too-savory schemes to get it. Meanwhile, his reputation is growing, some of his paintings are in demand, and he has no way to benefit from this trend since he is already into his next masterpiece. Jimson is something of a wastrel and a profligate, and he is not above slipping valuables into his pocket should any come within convenient reach, but he is also a dedicated artist.

Although Jimson has loved several women, Sara Monday was special, and the nude paintings she modeled for are highly desired by connoisseurs of art. Unfortunately for Jimson, who has attracted the interest of a biographer and an investor, he does not have any of the Sara paintings. She had kept them all when they had broken up their household (for reasons explained in *Herself Surprised*), eventually giving most of them to a collector to whom she owed money. At one point, Jimson actually paints a copy of one of these paintings (it hangs in a public gallery where he can get access to it) and sells the copy as a preparatory study for the original. Jimson's ethical priorities are entirely suborned by his wholehearted and unquestioning devotion to art. He thinks nothing of pawning the furniture of a collector on vacation (after obtaining the key to the man's home by devious means) in order to buy paints so he can create a mural that he's sure the collector will be glad to have immortalized on his plaster walls. Jimson possesses a single-minded devotion that allows him to serve art, and therefore he lacks the compunction that might restrain him from placing other people's lives, possessions, and money into the service of art—*his* art—as well. Concomitant to his devotion is his short temper when anything comes between him and his current obsession—a temper that exercises itself on Sara more than once.

In providing three narrators who address their readers but not one another, Cary creates the perfect circumstances for exploiting indeterminacy: Different narrators have different perspectives—different "truths" to tell—and readers have no way to eliminate the dross and arrive at the gold. Was Sara good-hearted or greedy? Was Wilcher lecherous or restrained? Was Jimson brilliant or nutty? Each narrator presents himself or herself in the special glow of unself-conscious self-reflective appraisal, leaving readers to piece together the reality that lies somewhere in the interstices of their stories, tantalizingly close yet elusively slippery.

BIBLIOGRAPHY

Eskine-Hill, Howard. "The Novel Sequences of Joyce Cary." In *The Fiction of the 1940s: Stories of Survival.* Edited by Rod Mengham and N. H. Reeve. Basingstoke, U.K.: Palgrave, 2001.

Gardener, Helen. "The Novels of Joyce Cary," *Essays and Studies* 28 (1975): 76–93.

Levitt, Annette Shandler. "Joyce Cary's Blake: The Intertextuality of *The Horse's Mouth,*" *Mosaic: A Journal of the Interdisciplinary Study of Literature* 25, no. 3 (Summer 1992): 47–63.

McCrea, Brian. "The Murder of Sara Monday: Art and Morality in Joyce Cary's First Trilogy," *Essays in Literature* 7 (1980): 45–54.

FITZGERALD, PENELOPE (1917–2000)

Belonging to a literary family—her father edited the humor and satire magazine *Punch,* and her paternal uncle wrote detective stories—Penelope Mary Knox Fitzgerald was born on December 17, 1916, in Lincoln, England. In 1939, she earned a degree from Somerville College, Oxford; afterward, she worked for the British Broadcasting Corporation, marrying Desmond Fitzgerald in 1941. The Fitzgeralds collaborated in editing a political journal in the early 1950s; after it folded, she worked in a bookstore and taught English.

Penelope Fitzgerald did not begin publishing until 1975, when she was nearly 60 years old; her first works were biographies, including a dual biography of her father and uncle, Edmund and Ronald Knox. Her first fictional work, *The Golden Child* (1977), was a mystery written to entertain her husband during an illness. Her next four novels drew on her own life experiences; of these, OFFSHORE (1979) won the BOOKER PRIZE. She wrote one more biography (of the poet Charlotte Mew) before turning to HISTORICAL FICTION for her last four novels. In 1998, she became the first non-American to win the National Book Critics Circle Award for her novel *The Blue Flower* (1995), a fictionalization of the life of the German romantic poet Novalis. Critics admire Fitzgerald's nine short novels for the well-chosen details that define character and for the neatly compact complexity of the plotting. She sympathetically presents her characters struggling with their lives but views them with a humorous eye as well.

Penelope Fitzgerald died in London on April 28, 2000. One short story collection has been posthumously published under the title *The Means of Escape.*

BIBLIOGRAPHY

Dooley, Maura. *How Novelists Work*. Bridgend, Wales: Seren, 2000.

Lewis, Tess. "Between Head and Start: Penelope Fitzgerald's Novels," *New Criterion* 18, no. 7 (2000): 29–36.

Sudrann, Jean. "Magic or Miracles: The Fallen World of Penelope Fitzgerald's Novels." In *Contemporary British Women Writers: Narrative Strategies*. Edited by Robert E. Hosmer. New York: St. Martin's Press, 1993, 105–127.

FLAUBERT'S PARROT JULIAN BARNES (1984)

A novel that sometimes disguises itself as a scholarly treatise, *Flaubert's Parrot* was short-listed for the BOOKER PRIZE in 1984. The novel's structure showcases the stylized self-awareness that is characteristic of POSTMODERNISM. The author dispenses with much of the traditional structure of a novel and instead uses striking combinations of imaginative and didactic digressions to sketch the character of the protagonist, Dr. Geoffrey Braithwaite, a retired physician obsessed by the quest to understand fully the 19th-century French novelist Gustave Flaubert.

Braithwaite, the novel's first-person narrator, relates his adventures on the trail of Flaubert's deepest secrets, but along the way he also gradually reveals his own secrets. As a narrator, Braithwaite is witty and learned without being pedantic, and his enthusiasm for all things Flaubertian is contagious. The particular object of his quest is the stuffed parrot Flaubert kept at his desk while writing one of his most famous short stories, "A Simple Heart" ("Un coeur simple"). When he finds stuffed parrots in two different museums that each claim to have the genuine item, his zeal is fired. Braithwaite retraces Flaubert's travels in France and reviews the details of the writer's life, even allowing Louise Colet, the actress with whom Flaubert had an affair while writing *Madame Bovary,* to speak for herself in a chapter redolent of feminine French charm. Everywhere he goes, and in everything he learns about Flaubert, he discovers parrots of one sort or another.

As Braithwaite continues his search, what began as a story of a retired doctor and a deceased novelist expands to become the story of three couples: Braithwaite and his deceased, adulterous wife; Flaubert and Louise Colet, caught up in their illicit affair; and the adulterous Madame Bovary and her cuckolded husband, Charles. Gradually, the reader realizes that Braithwaite's obsessive pursuit of Flaubert is also a compulsive evasion of his own memories of his wife. Her death haunts him, as does the weighty knowledge that he loved her more than she loved him, if she loved him at all.

BARNES places his erudition on display throughout the novel, filling it with literary allusions, ironic jokes, parrot lore, and parody; he does so, however, with a light touch. Readers who are just beginning to enjoy serious literature will miss many of the novel's references, but they should be able to enjoy the many ironies Braithwaite uncovers. Even experienced readers may find that the novel ripens upon repeated readings as greater depths and further parallels become apparent.

BIBLIOGRAPHY

Kermode, Frank. "Obsessed with Obsession," *The New York Review of Books,* 25 April 1985, 15.

Scott, James B. "Parrot as Paradigm: Infinite Deferral of Meaning in *Flaubert's Parrot,*" *Ariel* 21, no. 3 (1990): 57–68.

Updike, John. "A Pair of Parrots," *The New Yorker,* 22 July 1985, 86.

FLEMING, IAN (1909–1964)

The creator of James BOND, Ian Fleming lived a life very nearly as interesting as that of his most famous protagonist. Born into a well-to-do Scottish family on May 28, 1908, Ian Lancaster Fleming grew up in a world of privilege. His father was a Tory Member of Parliament who was killed during WORLD WAR I on the Somme. Ian Fleming attended PUBLIC SCHOOLS such as Eton, and then trained at the Royal Military College at Sandhurst. He chose to pursue a diplomatic career rather than to go directly into military service, training for it by studying languages at universities in Geneva and Munich. He did not receive a posting, however, and in 1931 he went to work for Reuters. His first assignment was in Moscow, where he learned Russian and got a close view of the Soviet system. In 1933, he became a stockbroker to earn a satisfactory income, journalism paying too little. When WORLD WAR II broke out in 1939, Fleming was commissioned in the Royal Navy.

During the war, Fleming gained much of the experience that, combined with his work in Russia, prepared him to create James Bond. Working behind the scenes rather than on the front lines of espionage, he served as the personal assistant to Admiral J. H. Godfrey, the director of Naval Intelligence. Eventually, Godfrey also became the man upon whom James Bond's boss, "M," is based. Fleming acquired insider knowledge of intelligence operations, later using it to create believable details for his stories and especially to capture the tone of the spy bureaucracy. After the war, Fleming worked until 1959 as the foreign manager of *The Sunday Times.* In 1953, he published *Casino Royale,* his first James Bond adventure, followed in the next year by *Live and Let Die.* Until 1966, a new Bond adventure appeared every year—the last two posthumously. In 1964, the year that the film version of *Goldfinger* became Bond's third excursion onto the screen, and the year that he published the children's book *Chitty-Chitty Bang-Bang,* Ian Fleming died of a heart attack.

During his writing life, Fleming genially insisted that his adventure novels were escapist reads, discounting both the detractors and the admirers who found deeper meanings in the Bond stories. Despite the author's disavowals, however, a reader reasonably well informed about the course of British history in the 20th century will note that James Bond's adventures in many ways provide a kind of compensatory denial of the end of the British EMPIRE. His courage and resourcefulness, inflated to superhero size, define a British presence that exceeds the nation's actual unaided clout in the real world, and the power Bond wields over the enemies of civilization seems to constitute a kind of wishful thinking on the author's part as Britain's real power wanes. Although Fleming's work is not the stuff literary prizes were designed to honor, through the transformation of his writing into screen images, his chief fictional character has been viewed by half the globe's 6 billion residents. That kind of influence demands serious consideration.

BIBLIOGRAPHY

Bryce, Ivar. *You Only Live Once: Memories of Ian Fleming.* London: Weidenfeld & Nicolson, 1975.

Lycett, Andrew. *Ian Fleming: The Man Behind James Bond.* Atlanta: Turner Publishing, 1995.

McCormick, Donald. *17F: The Life of Ian Fleming.* London: P. Owen, 1993.

FOOLS OF FORTUNE WILLIAM TREVOR
(1983)   Winner of the WHITBREAD Book of the Year Award in the year it was published, this short novel examines Irish-English relations on the intimate scale of family life. Two "great houses," Woodcombe Park in Dorset, England, and Kilneagh in County Cork, IRELAND, have become interconnected through three marriages over 160 years, and although the English house thrives as a historical ornament, Kilneagh lies in ruins. Each property is emblematic of the effect that strife in Ireland has had on the two countries, leaving England largely untouched while parts of Ireland lie razed to the ground.

TREVOR constructs his narrative by means of two first-person narratives embedded in an anonymous third-person frame narration. Most of the story comes from Willie Quinton, great grandson of the first English lady of Woodcombe Park to marry into Kilneagh, and the son of the second English lady to do so. Willie tells the story of his life, which includes many happy days at home or at his father's mill. All of this happiness, however, is wiped away by an act of cruel vengeance against Kilneagh and its inhabitants committed by the soldiers of the "black and tans"—English troops stationed in Ireland to quell the revolt that ultimately led to Irish independence. Willie remembers, as a small boy, meeting the great hero of that war, Michael Collins, in his father's study. Although the Quintons have a strong English connection, they pay a terrible price for their hospitality to Collins and for other events beyond their control; Mrs. Quinton never recovers from the shock, sinking into genteel alcoholism and neglecting everything around her, including her son.

When Willie's maternal aunt comes to check on her sister, bringing along her daughter, Marianne, the two young people form a close bond. Marianne becomes the second narrator, and so some of the events of Willie's narration are revisited from Marianne's perspective. But her own story broadens the context as she relates information about her life in the rectory—her father presides over the Woodcombe Park parish—and her schooling in Switzerland. At the point in the narrative when events should draw Willie and Marianne into the third generation of connections between the two great houses, they are instead torn apart. Marianne finds herself alone in the world and finally accepts a refuge at Kilneagh, but Willie's actions in the meantime have cut him off from his home and his homeland, possibly forever.

These two stories nest together within the framework of an omniscient narrator's comments. This nameless narrator provides the introductions to each portion of first-person narration; more important, the life of Imelda, the child of Willie and Marianne, is made available in these parts of the text. By using this technique of mixing first- and third-person narrators, Trevor makes his novel both more intimate and more objective. Readers see Kilneagh through the eyes of those who love it best, but they remain connected to the contemporary world that must cope with the consequences of the past.

Trevor's novel creates a deeply moving account of the mixed bonds of love and hate that bind together the Irish and the English while also making that connection so painfully corrosive. Every event in the present stands at the end of generations of causes and effects between the English and the Irish; nothing is simple, new, or accidental. *Fools of Fortune* places the hostile events of the later 20th century into context with the historical background that gave rise to them; however, American readers not familiar with the names and circumstances of the Irish struggle for independence will miss key elements of the story. The pleasures of Trevor's novel will amply repay the effort expended on background reading to prepare for it.

BIBLIOGRAPHY
MacKenna, Dolores. *William Trevor: The Writer and His Work.* Dublin: New Island, 1999.
Schirmer, Gregory A. *William Trevor: A Study of His Fiction.* New York: Routledge, 1990.

FORD, FORD MADOX (1873–1939)   The
grandson of the pre-Raphaelite painter Ford Madox Brown and the son of a music critic connected to a wealthy German family, Ford Madox Hermann Hueffer was born on December 17, 1873, in Merton (now part of London), England. His mother's sister was wife to the brother of Dante Gabriel Rossetti; the Hueffer home was a nexus of artistic appreciation, and young Ford was expected to live up to his connections.

During Ford's childhood, his family immersed him in painting, music, and literature, educating him at University College School in London. The pressure to excel in the shadow of well-known and established artists led to a nagging sense of inferiority and to an unstable emotional life in adulthood. Instead of attending one of the universities, at the age of 18 Ford undertook a tour of Europe and began publishing children's literature. When his German relations urged him to convert to Catholicism, he complied. In 1894, he married and settled in Kent, where he wrote prolifically, producing about a book a year in various genres including fiction, travel literature, poetry, and biography. The strain of his work and his precarious emotional health led to a nervous breakdown in 1902.

Ford became acquainted with Joseph CONRAD in 1898, and the two remained friends and occasional collaborators until 1909. They shared an interest in the techniques of writing fiction; together, they wrote two novels, *The Inheritors* (1901) and *Romance* (1903). Ford may have also made some lesser contribution to other titles published by Conrad before 1909. But Ford's private life—he had an affair with his sister-in-law in 1903—was offensive to Conrad's wife, and so Conrad abruptly broke off their friendship in 1909.

In that same year, the journal Ford edited, *The English Review,* folded, but he was unable to end his unhappy marriage when he was denied a divorce. Despite his continuing emotional problems, Ford produced his masterpiece, *The GOOD SOLDIER,* in 1915, using a technique that he called "literary impressionism." Ford's articulation of this technique did not lead to the founding of an identifiable movement, but it was part of an important shift in narrative technique being advanced by writers such as Dorothy RICHARDSON, James JOYCE, and Virginia WOOLF. At the heart of this change is the use of stream-of-consciousness narration. Just as thought meanders in a recursive, nonlinear fashion, cluttered with inconsequential issues and lacking concentrated focus much of the time, so too literary impressionism unfolds an event from within the subjective thought of someone involved in it. The story focuses not on the conflict that drives the PLOT but on the mental and emotional landscape of the character experiencing it. The narrator's impression may be mis-

taken and reshaped by the course of events, but the narrator may also be deliberately unreliable, hiding from, denying, or even lying about events, other people, and even his or her mind.

With the onset of WORLD WAR I, Ford was fighting in France, where he served until 1919. During the war, he suffered shell shock and was exposed to mustard gas. He changed his name because of British antipathy for all things German; after the war he retreated to a bucolic life in the English countryside with an artist, Stella Bowen. In 1921, he returned to France and edited the *Transatlantic Review* during its short existence, publishing work by such modernists as James JOYCE and Ezra Pound. Ford joined the bohemian culture of English artists and other expatriates living in Paris and conducted an affair with Jean RHYS. His memoir of Joseph Conrad, published shortly after Conrad's death in 1924, made him unpopular in his home country. At the same time, however, he was composing the four novels collected after his death under the single title *PARADE'S END*. Using the technique of literary impressionism, this series relates effects of the modern pressures on its protagonist, Christopher Tietjens, as civilization turns into an ever-bleaker wasteland.

In addition to his innovative fiction, Ford wrote three autobiographical volumes that sensationalize his experiences. Part of his emotional frailty was the result of his weak ability to separate fact and fiction; readers interested in Ford's life should rely on scholarly biographies for factual accounts and read Ford's autobiographies for other insights into the mind of this writer.

BIBLIOGRAPHY

Cassell, Richard A. *Critical Essays on Ford Madox Ford.* Boston: G. K. Hall, 1987.

Delbanco, Nicholas. *Group Portrait: Joseph Conrad, Stephen Crane, Ford Madox Ford, Henry James, and H. G. Wells.* New York: Morrow, 1982.

Judd, Alan. *Ford Madox Ford.* Cambridge, Mass.: Harvard University Press, 1991.

Moser, Thomas C. *The Life in the Fiction of Ford Madox Ford.* Princeton, N.J.: Princeton University Press, 1980.

FORESTER, C. S. (1899–1966) Noted for his seafaring adventure novels featuring Horatio HORN-

BLOWER, a literary character who has, like Sherlock HOLMES and James BOND, transcended his paper origins, C. S. Forester was born in Cairo, Egypt, on August 27, 1899; his given name was Cecil Lewis Troughton Smith. Poor health prevented him from fighting in WORLD WAR I with other young men his age, disappointing him to the extent that he later claimed to have served in the war. Rejected for active duty, he entered medical school. Although high academic achievement had been a hallmark of the entire family, Forester struggled in medical school and turned to writing against his family's wishes, adopting the pen name Cecil Scott Forester. When he changed his name, he also broke with his family.

Without formal training in literature, Forester produced novels that no publisher would accept. He wrote biographies for income and gradually mastered the craft of writing; even so, he later disavowed some of his early fictions. His first novel appeared in 1924, *A Pawn Among Kings*. Two years later, his mystery novel *Payment Deferred* was a financial and critical success and was adapted as a film. He was married to his first wife that year; the marriage produced two children and lasted 20 years before ending in divorce. With his increasing output of stories suitable for film, Forester relocated to California in 1932 and worked successfully as a screenwriter; that experience influenced his writing, sharpening his descriptions into vividly rendered scenes. He published *The* AFRICAN QUEEN in 1935; James Agee adapted the novella as a screenplay for John Huston's 1951 film, widely regarded as a film classic. The romance in the story does not typify Forester's work, but the action-adventure sections do.

Horatio Hornblower first appeared in *Beat to Quarters* (1937), an example of both HISTORICAL FICTION and NAUTICAL FICTION. Set during the Age of Sail and the Napoleonic era, the story introduces Hornblower as a young captain; the popularity of the character led Forester to write several sequels, including *A* SHIP OF THE LINE and *Flying Colours* (both 1938), *Commodore Hornblower* (1945), *Lord Hornblower* (1946), *Mr. Midshipman Hornblower* (1950), *Hornblower and the Atropos* (1953), *Admiral Hornblower in the West Indies* (1958), *Hornblower and the Hotspur* (1962). The series covers the entire career of Hornblower, but Forester composed the episodes out of chronological order.

Generally categorized as popular fiction, Forester's work rises above the formulaic action-adventure story in the author's use of historical detail and fully rounded characters, including a hero who does not always win or choose well. Less complex and erudite than the later nautical fiction of Patrick O'BRIAN (the AUBREY-MATURIN NOVELS), Forester's series provides an enjoyable introduction to this subgenre that is both accessible to younger readers and interesting to adults as well.

After a period of declining health that included arteriosclerosis and stroke, C. S. Forester died of a heart attack at his California home on April 2, 1966.

BIBLIOGRAPHY

Forester, C. S. *Long Before Forty.* Boston: Little, Brown, 1968.

Sternlicht, Sanford. *C. S. Forester.* Twayne's English Authors, 320. Boston: Twayne, 1981.

FORMALISM   Also known as rhetorical criticism and New Criticism, formalism constitutes one of the many lenses through which critics view and interpret literature. A formalist critic pays attention to the form of a literary work, including aspects such as PLOT, character, setting, theme, symbolism, IRONY, the narrator's point of view, and the genre of the work. A formalist approach deemphasizes the author's biography, the reader's personal appreciation of a text, the historical background either of the author or of the text's setting in time, and the social, political, and economic contexts of the author's life and the story's setting. Formalism dominated literary criticism in England, Russia, and the United States from the 1920s to the 1970s; during this period, literary criticism became professionalized in the English departments of an expanding university system, especially in the United States. Formalism is particularly well suited to the academic circumstances of the contemporary university system: It is highly teachable in the format of the large lecture hall, and it carves out a niche for literary study that is distinct from the scholarly territories of history, psychology, sociology, and political science.

Early supporters of formalism in England during the 1920s included two American poets, T. S. Eliot and Ezra Pound; following the poet-critic T. E. Hulme, they rejected the romantic emphasis on the primacy of the poet in favor of an objective approach to the poem. This emphasis on objectivity constitutes an attempt to universalize the experience of literary phenomena: Instead of the unpredictably unique or idiosyncratic musings of individual readers, formalists insist that criticism must prefer the shared properties of the text that all readers can learn to recognize and understand. On this view, criticism as an intellectual activity moves closer to the methods of science and further from the inspirations of art. In addition to this application of formalism to poetry, formalist experiments in fiction include the development of the stream-of-consciousness point of view in novels by Dorothy RICHARDSON, Virginia WOOLF, and James JOYCE.

Important American proponents of formalism included John Crowe Ransom, William K. Wimsatt, Monroe Beardsley, and Cleanth Brooks. Ransom's book *The New Criticism* (1941) became a standard text in the field. In "The Intentional Fallacy," by Wimsatt and Beardsley, these scholars argue that an author's intention in constructing a literary text is unknowable and therefore not relevant to the task of the interpretive critic; in "The Affective Fallacy," the same authors argue that the feelings a literary text produces in readers is similarly irrelevant. Important British formalists include I. A. Richardson (who used the term "practical criticism"), William Empson, author of a classic critical text on the formal elements of AMBIGUITY, F. R. Leavis, and Cyril Connolly.

In minimizing the importance of the expressive quality of an author's work, formalists are reacting against romanticism as canonized in Wordsworth's insistence that poets create art through the spontaneous overflow of powerful feeling. But formalism is not invulnerable to attack: FEMINISM helped to reestablish the relevance of an author's biography to the critical enterprise by arguing that gender *matters* (encapsulated in the slogan "The personal is the political"); structuralists, post-structuralists, deconstructionists, and semioticians questioned the foundational concept of objectivity; New Historicists rediscovered the importance of historical context to counterbalance the cultural bias and myopia that can allow anachronism to flourish in literary criticism. Other schools of thought have arisen as well. In fact, in the last quarter of the 20th century, criticism became a growth industry, albeit to a minuscule market of scholars and graduate students, as competitors struggled for dominance in toppling the hegemony of formalism.

BIBLIOGRAPHY

Abrams, M. H. *The Mirror and the Lamp: Romantic Theory and the Critical Tradition.* New York: Oxford University Press, 1953.

Ransom, John Crowe. *The New Criticism.* Norfolk, Conn.: New Directions, 1941.

Wellek, René. *A History of Modern Criticism: 1750–1950.* Vols. 5–6. New Haven, Conn.: Yale University Press, 1955.

Wimsatt, William K., and Cleanth Brooks. *Literary Criticism: A Short History.* New York: Knopf, 1957.

FORSTER, E. M. (1879–1970)

One of the greatest novelists of the first half of the 20th century, Forster wrote only six novels, publishing five of them during his lifetime. Unlike many of his contemporaries, Forster did not experiment with innovative storytelling modes; his novels follow the structural and narrative conventions of late 19th-century writers. In content, however, he addressed issues of CLASS, COLONIALISM (especially in *A PASSAGE TO INDIA*), gender, and homosexuality (especially in *Maurice*).

The son of an architect who died 18 months after his son's birth, Edward Morgan Forster was born on January 1, 1879, and reared by a devoted mother and several aunts. An inheritance from his paternal great-aunt in 1886 gave him enough financial independence to attend preparatory school and college and to devote himself to his writing immediately afterward. Forster's gratitude to his benefactress appears in his novels, which frequently feature a benevolent—even saintly—elderly woman of insight and sympathy.

Forster received his education as a day pupil at Tonbridge School and matriculated at King's College, Cambridge, in 1897. Through his election to the Apostles, he became acquainted with members of the BLOOMSBURY GROUP; he and Virginia WOOLF formed a lasting friendship. Forster graduated with a second-class degree in 1901, and he traveled in Italy and Greece. In

1905, he published his first novel, *Where Angels Fear to Tread,* about the attempt of a snobbish English woman to gain custody of her late daughter's child, who is under the care of the child's Italian father and his extended family. In 1907, he published *The Longest Journey,* about the troubled relationship between two half brothers, and the following year he brought out *A ROOM WITH A VIEW,* about a young woman who finds the courage to choose love over convention and propriety. *HOWARDS END* appeared in 1910, relating the story of the relationship between the Schlegel sisters and the Wilcox family. Forster suppressed the publication of his fifth novel, *Maurice,* because of its frank and sympathetic treatment of homosexuality; although it was written in 1913, it did not appear in print until 1971, a year after Forster died.

Forster undertook a lengthy visit to India in 1910, at the invitation of a Muslim youth he had previously tutored. The visit aroused his interest in the Anglo-Indian situation, but he did not write about it until after his second visit in 1921. In between, he worked in Alexandria, Egypt, for the Red Cross during WORLD WAR I. He befriended the Greek poet Constantin P. Cavafy in Alexandria and became an advocate of his work, still unknown at that time. Forster's return to India led to the writing of his masterpiece, *A Passage to India,* published in 1924. After that book, Forster wrote no more novel-length fiction, although he remained an active and influential member of the English literary scene. In 1927, he presented the Clark Lectures at Cambridge; these formed the basis of his important critical text, *Aspects of the Novel,* published in the same year.

After WORLD WAR II, Forster was offered an appointment at Cambridge. He became actively involved in the cause of civil liberties and continued writing essays and short fiction. Beginning in 1964, he suffered a series of strokes that impaired his ability to work. He died of a stroke on June 7, 1970. By the middle of the century, Forster had gained an international reputation for his five published novels. After his death, several of his novels became highly successful FILM ADAPTATIONS, bringing his work to the appreciation of even larger audiences.

BIBLIOGRAPHY

Beauman, Nicola. *E. M. Forster: A Biography.* New York: Knopf, 1994.

Iago, Mary. *E. M. Forster: A Literary Life.* New York: St. Martin's Press, 1995.

Stape, J. H. ed. *E. M. Forster: Interviews and Recollections.* New York: St. Martin's Press, 1993.

Wilde, Alan, ed. *Critical Essays on E. M. Forster.* Boston: G. K. Hall, 1985.

FORSTER, MARGARET (1938–)

Author of the popular success *GEORGY GIRL,* which provided the basis for both a hit film and a hit song in 1966, Margaret Forster has also written a definitive biography of Daphne DU MAURIER. Forster was born on May 25, 1938, in Carlisle and educated in her hometown until she matriculated at Somerville College, Oxford, from which she graduated in 1960 with a degree in history. Upon completing her studies, she married the writer Hunter Davies; they remain married and are the parents of three children.

Between 1964 and 2003, Margaret Forster published 31 volumes of fiction, biography, literary criticism, history, and memoir. Her first novel, *Dame's Delight,* was published in 1964; *Georgy Girl* appeared the following year and was an immediate success. She cowrote the screenplay for the movie based on the book. Her novels usually follow the conventions of realism and focus on relationships at the family level; sometimes she draws on personal experience, writing autobiographical fiction. In 1999, her memoir *Precious Lives* won the J. R. Ackerley Prize; it is the sequel to *Hidden Lives* (1995), the story of the lives of her grandmother and mother. Forster's biographical writing has also earned attention, particularly for the work *Daphne du Maurier,* which won the Writers' Guild Award for best nonfiction in 1993 and the Fawcett Society Book Prize in 1994. Additionally, Forster has written biographies of Elizabeth Barrett Browning and Bonny Prince Charlie, and she has produced a fictional autobiography of William Makepeace Thackeray. Forster has written extensive literary reviews for newspapers and has worked as a broadcaster for the BBC. She continues to write fiction and nonfiction; she and her husband divide their time between homes in London and the Lake Country.

BIBLIOGRAPHY

"Margaret Forster." *British Council.* Available online. URL: www.contemporarywriters.com. Accessed February 9, 2004.

"Margaret Forster." Available online. URL: www.visitcumbria.com/mforster.htm. Accessed February 9, 2004.

FORSYTE SAGA, THE JOHN GALSWORTHY (1922)

This title is sometimes loosely applied to the entire sequence of novels and short fiction that relate the story of the Forsyte family; however, it properly refers to only the first three novels in the series: *A MAN OF PROPERTY* (1906), *IN CHANCERY* (1920), and *TO LET* (1921). GALSWORTHY collected these three, together with two short "interludes," "Indian Summer of a Forsyte" (1918) and *Awakening* (1920), in 1922 under the title *The Forsyte Saga;* he then expanded the story with *The White Monkey* (1924), *The Silver Spoon* (1926), and *Swan Song* (1928), which he collected under the title *A Modern Comedy* in 1929. The chronicle continues with *Soames and Flag* (1930) and *On Forsyte Change* (1930), and it extends to the Charwells, country cousins of the Forsytes, in *End of the Chapter* (1934), consisting of *Maid in Waiting* (1931), *Flowering Wilderness* (1932), and *Over the River* (1933).

Galsworthy casts an accurate but critical eye on the upper-middle CLASS as the Victorian era gives way to the modern world. The large Forsyte clan is only two generations down from the country life of the family founder; the governing principles that have guided the acquisition and retention of wealth during the family's rise to prominence are the twin values of property ownership and family solidarity. Galsworthy's critique is directed against the materialism and greed of the Forsytes, and thereby against the upper class they represent. But he also makes a FEMINIST critique of the Victorian marriage laws that allowed men to consider their wives to be property. As the 20th century begins, Galsworthy's sprawling, character-filled novel memorializes the class that will soon lose its overwhelming influence in public affairs, and he anatomizes the problems with the legal bonds that have made marriage into another form of enterprise.

BIBLIOGRAPHY

Johnson, Pamela Hansford. "Speaking of Books: *The Forsyte Saga,*" *The New York Times Book Review,* 12 March 1967, 2, 36.

Ru, Yi-ling. *The Family Novel: Toward a Generic Definition.* New York: Peter Lang, 1992.

Sternlicht, Sanford. *John Galsworthy.* Boston: G. K. Hall, 1987.

FORTUNE OF WAR, THE PATRICK O'BRIAN (1979)

See AUBREY-MATURIN NOVELS.

FOUR-GATED CITY, THE DORIS LESSING (1969)

Volume five in the *Children of Violence* series, this novel follows *Landlocked* (1965) and concludes the adventures of Martha Quest in an apocalyptic vision of a future in which human beings overcome the limitations of communication and mutual understanding through telepathy. This feature has led to the book being included in surveys of SCIENCE FICTION, although it is primarily constructed in the manner of realist fiction. The title refers to a vision that Martha had as an adolescent of a city populated by citizens who have moved beyond the narrow confines of prejudice.

Although the earlier novels in the series had been set in an Africa under the newly liberated influence of postcolonialism, in *The Four-Gated City,* Martha travels to London in the years immediately following WORLD WAR II, returning to her family's historical and cultural roots. With two failed marriages behind her, and disillusioned by some of her experiences as a Communist political activist, she is still seeking independence in a world that defines woman's estate as a dependent condition. In England, she begins to discover her freedom. She has brought with her the manuscript of her late lover, Thomas Stern, a Polish Jew and an idealist with whom Martha had made a complete emotional, physical, and spiritual union. She consults the manuscript periodically, finding it filled with wisdom.

Martha becomes the secretary of the writer Mark Coldridge, who becomes a replacement for Thomas in her life. She shares material from her past, including her visions, and from Thomas's manuscript as well, and these details then become part of Mark's writing, entwined in his thought. His dreams of a UTOPIAN world eventually will carry his cause back to Africa in the attempt to found an ideal city. Mark's wife, Lynda, has suffered institutionalization for years for treatment of her mental illness, and Martha gradually becomes her familiar after Lynda is moved out of hospital care and into the Coldridge's basement. Martha even experiences a kind of madness herself, carrying her inner exploration to the limits of human consciousness and beyond. Ultimately, this "quest" leads her to the goal of self-unity that she had been seeking, throughout her life, in the world around her rather than in the world within her. By sharing Lynda's experience of madness and Mark's vision of the possibilities for a better world, Martha completes her quest and finds personal wholeness and satisfaction.

The epilogue to the novel relates, fragmentarily, the apocalyptic destruction of Great Britain and Martha's escape to an island where the successors to the human race develop and move beyond the violence that engenders them. Connected psychically, these new people are not burdened by the biases inherent in the traditional five senses, tied as they are to race, gender, nationality, or other contingent aspects of identity. Doris Lessing seems to suggest how monumental the challenge of overcoming racism and sexism is: Human beings may have to evolve beyond their current status in order to eradicate injustice and maximize the potential every person has locked inside.

BIBLIOGRAPHY

Karl, Frederick R. "The Four-Gaited Beast of the Apocalypse: Doris Lessing's *The Four-Gated City* (1969)." In *Old Lines, New Forces: Essays on the Contemporary British Novel, 1960–1970.* Edited by Robert K. Morris. Rutherford, N.J,: Fairleigh Dickinson University Press, 1976, 181–199.

Sprague, Claire. "Without Contraries Is No Progression: Lessing's *The Four-Gated City,*" *Modern Fiction Studies* 26 (1980): 99–116.

FOWLES, JOHN (1926–   )

A writer devoted to the motif of the mythic quest and its variations, John Fowles was born on March 31, 1926, and spent much of his adolescence in the English countryside while bombs rained on London during the blitzkrieg of WORLD WAR II. He was educated at Bedford School, excelling in languages and sports and winning election as head boy in his last year. He served in the Royal Marines from 1945 to 1947 and then enrolled at New College, Oxford, studying French and German languages and literatures. Fowles was graduated with honors in 1950.

After college, Fowles taught English, first at the University of Poitiers in France for a year and then on the Greek island of Spetsai until 1953, when he returned to London. While living in the idyllic environment of the Aegean Islands, Fowles wrote *The MAGUS,* although it was not the first of his novels to be published. There, he also met the woman he married in 1954. In England, Fowles taught at Ashridge College for a year and then at St. Godric's College until 1963. He continued writing during this time, and when his first published novel, *The COLLECTOR,* became a popular success in 1963, he left teaching to write full-time. In 1966, Fowles and his wife relocated to the coastal town of Lyme Regis, where they have lived ever since.

Following the success of *The Collector,* Fowles published a philosophical work, *The Aristos: A Self-Portrait in Ideas* (1964), followed by *The Magus* (1965; revised edition, 1977). *The FRENCH LIEUTENANT'S WOMAN* appeared in 1969 and was made into a film in 1981. His other novels include *The Ebony Tower* (1974; a novella), *Daniel Martin* (1977), *Mantissa* (1982), and *A Maggot* (1985). Fowles has been identified as a writer of MAGIC REALISM, and he frequently includes perceptive comments on the visual arts in his novels. He constructs stories that are deeply philosophical but that remain accessible to a wide range of readers. Students who take the time to consult references on art, MYTHOLOGY, and philosophy while reading Fowles's novels will gain added depth in their comprehension of the full complexities of his entertaining and imaginative fictions.

BIBLIOGRAPHY

Acheson, James. *John Fowles.* New York: St. Martin's Press, 1998.

Foster, Thomas C. *Understanding John Fowles.* Understanding Contemporary British Literature Series. Columbia: University of South Carolina Press, 1994.

Huffaker, Robert. *John Fowles.* Twayne's English Authors, 292. Boston: Twayne Publishers, 1980.

Pifer, Ellen, ed. *Critical Essays on John Fowles.* Boston: G. K. Hall, 1986.

FRAME, JANET (1924–2004)   New Zealand's most famous novelist was born on August 28, 1924, in Dunedin, New Zealand, the daughter of a railroad engineer and an educated mother who transferred her appreciation for literature and culture to her children. A sister drowned in 1937, and when another drowned in 1947, Frame admitted herself to Seacliff Hospital, a residential facility for the treatment of mental illness. Repeated depression had led to an earlier suicide attempt; her grief for her sisters proved too much. She was incorrectly diagnosed with schizophrenia, subjected to numerous shock treatments, and even scheduled for a lobotomy before a psychiatrist discovered that she had won a notable literary award for her writing—Frame herself did not know of her prize—and released her.

Frame had already decided to be a writer in 1945 and had published a story in 1946. Despite eight years of hospitalization, she continued to write, publishing *The Lagoon,* a collection of short fiction, in 1951. Her stories brought her to the attention of another writer, Frank Sargeson, and in 1954 she stayed as a guest at his home while writing her autobiographical novel *Owls Do Cry* (1957). With the assistance of a public grant, she traveled for several years, settling in London from 1958 to 1963. During her time in London, she wrote FACES IN THE WATER (1961), *The Edge of the Alphabet* (1962), and *Scented Gardens for the Blind* (1963), and produced another collection of short fiction as well. Her novels draw on her experience with mental illness, exploring the phenomenon of consciousness and the power of the unconscious mind.

In 1963, Janet Frame returned to her homeland and continued writing, producing three more novels in the remaining years of the 1960s: *The Adaptable Man* (1965), *A State of Siege* (1966), and *The Rainbirds* (1968; alternate title: *Yellow Flowers in an Antipodean Room*). Her publishing pace slowed somewhat in the 1970s, when she produced three more novels, as her attention was diverted to traveling, teaching fiction writing, and eventually writing a three-volume autobiography, which includes *To the Is-Land* (1982), *An Angel at My Table* (1984), and *The Envoy from Mirror City* (1985). These volumes were collectively published under the title *An Autobiography* in 1989. An award-winning film

directed by Jane Campion, *An Angel at My Table* (1990), was based on Janet Frame's life.

In addition to fiction and autobiography, Janet Frame has published a volume of poetry and a book of children's literature. Because of her frequent use of mental illness in her characters, her stories are often intensely internal examinations of irrational thoughts and feelings. She presents mental illness in as positive a way as possible, making it a passage to understanding, frequently using a journey metaphor. In 1973, Janet Frame legally acquired the last name of *Clutha,* after a river near her childhood home. Frame was named a Commander of the Order of the British Empire, and she was also nominated for the NOBEL PRIZE in literature. She received an honorary doctorate from the University of Otago in her home country, and she was an honorary foreign member of the American Academy and Institute of Arts and Letters, among other awards and honors.

Janet Frame died on January 29, 2004, of leukemia.

BIBLIOGRAPHY
King, Michael. *Wrestling with the Angel: A Life of Janet Frame.* Washington, D.C.: Counterpoint, 2000.

Stead, C. K. *In the Glass Case: Essays on New Zealand Literature.* Auckland: Auckland University Press, 1981.

FRANCHISE AFFAIR, THE JOSEPHINE TEY (1948)   A mystery, a thriller, and a low-keyed romance, this novel takes the form of a puzzle. Life follows its uneventful course at The Franchise, a somewhat decayed estate inherited by a mother and daughter, Mrs. Sharpe and Miss Marion Sharpe, until one day a young woman claims that she had been held prisoner there for weeks, forced to work for the two women of the house and beaten for refusing to work. The Sharpes protest their innocence, but when the police bring the girl, Elisabeth Kane, to the house, they learn that she has correctly identified details of the interior that she could only have known, it seems, if she had been inside the house. The circumstantial evidence is hardly enough to make a court case against the Sharpes until a former serving girl comes forward claiming that she heard screaming from the attic and that she gave notice in order to escape from the unknown suffering in the house.

Marion Sharpe had wisely retained the legal services of Robert Blair of Blair, Hayward, and Bennet, Milford's most long-established legal practice, as soon as she had learned of the accusation and the imminent arrival of the police investigators. Robert becomes the detective of the story as he searches for holes and contradictions in the false claims of the plaintiff. The role is unfamiliar to him, since his practice generally handles only wills and other kinds of documents, but Robert finds himself reinvigorated by the investigation. Elisabeth Kane is soon an overnight media celebrity, and the Sharpes must endure public humiliation as everyone accepts the outrageous story against them. As newcomers to the close-knit small town, and as quiet residents who keep to themselves, they at first have no friends and defenders other than Robert, who sees immediately that Elisabeth Kane has fabricated the story to cover up some indiscretion. The community is united in its opinion that such an astonishing accusation can only be true, and among the lower elements vandalism and even violence soon breaks out against The Franchise. Finding the truth proves to be a difficult task, but Robert's increasing personal attachment to Marion and his acute sense of the suffering she bravely endures provide all the motivation he needs to stay on the case and see that justice is done.

The Franchise Affair, although it is a fine example of intelligent problem solving, makes an unusual romance in that it features a nearly wordless attraction between two middle-aged people who have never before been married. The narrator provides opinionated and old-fashioned commentary on the tabloid media and the changing social scene in England in the aftermath of WORLD WAR II; the CLASS consciousness of the story is skewed in the direction of the gentry. Clearly, the narrator disapproves of newfangled ways, creating a sense of nostalgia for days long past when servants were not a scarce commodity, when automobiles were not a necessity, and when rank had its privileges. A near-wordless courtship somehow displays the right degree of propriety for the story, although the final resolution involves a twist that borders on FEMINISM.

The third-person limited narrator provides insight into Robert Blair's thoughts, and to a lesser extent into Marion's, but does not explore the other characters; instead, the actions and motives of Elisabeth Kane and the Sharpe's serving girl slowly emerge through the investigation and then through the trial that follows. Truth triumphs, and mendacity receives the exposure and excoriation it deserves. In a style that uses unexpected wordplay, Josephine TEY first sets the world askew and then restores its balance in this well-crafted and intriguing tale.

BIBLIOGRAPHY

Charney, Hanna. *The Detective Novel of Manners: Hedonism, Morality, and the Life of Reason.* Rutherford: Fairleigh Dickinson University Press, 1981.

Roy, Sandra. *Josephine Tey.* Twayne's English Authors, 277. Boston: Twayne, 1980.

FRENCH LIEUTENANT'S WOMAN, THE
JOHN FOWLES (1969)   An example of POSTMODERNISM, the action of this novel is related by an intrusive third-person omniscient narrator who is simultaneously an eyewitness to the events of the plot and yet also a man from a later era. The setting of the novel in time is 1867, 100 years prior to the year when FOWLES began writing it, and the setting in place is at first Lyme Regis, Fowles's hometown, and then shifts to other locations. The story plays with the conventions of the Victorian novel and subverts them in various ways: There are three different endings, including one that occurs in the closing pages when the narrator sets his watch back 15 minutes and replays the action.

The chief characters are the mysterious Sarah Woodruff, widely thought to have been seduced and abandoned, and thereby made to be no longer respectable, and the amateur paleontologist Charles Smithson. Charles is engaged, but during a visit with his fiancée to Lyme Regis, he gradually becomes acquainted with Sarah and is increasingly drawn to her. She reveals herself to be the repudiation of Victorian conformity and repression: She tells Charles that she gave herself willingly to the French lieutenant who abandoned her, but circumstances allow Charles to discover that she is still a virgin—she has deliberately placed herself beyond the pale of Victorian morality by inventing the story of her seduction and, like a novelist, passing it off as the truth. She is a woman who provides her own self-definition rather than accepting the dictates society has laid down for women.

As a Victorian man, Charles would be baffled by such a woman, even if he found her attractive; the novel seems to go in this direction, allowing Charles to marry his fiancée and raise a family with her. But the intrusive narrator dismisses that story after telling it, insisting that Charles really did fall in love with Sarah and that he was transformed by the experience even though he lost contact with her for years. The narrator provides an alternative life for Charles as a man liberated from Victorian repression and conventionality. But even this story is unstable, resulting in two endings that coexist in the same place and time as if they were in parallel universes. This AMBIGUITY is characteristic of 20th-century literature; it is a key distinction between the fiction of the modern world and the fiction of the 19th century. Additionally, the contrast between the conventional fiancée and the self-made Sarah suggests the utility of FREUDIAN CRITICISM in interpreting the story: The fiancée is a kind of superego character bound by social expectations, while Sarah is an id figure bent on following her own will. In the last of the novel's endings, Charles does not embrace either of them, but charts a course of his own instead.

BIBLIOGRAPHY

Foster, Thomas C. *Understanding John Fowles.* Understanding Contemporary British Literature. Columbia: University of South Carolina Press, 1994.

Huffaker, Robert. *John Fowles.* Twayne's English Authors, 292. Boston: Twayne, 1980.

Phelan, James. *Reading People, Reading Plots: Character, Progression, and the Interpretation of Narrative.* Chicago: University of Chicago Press, 1989.

FREUDIAN CRITICISM   Sigmund Freud's theories of the personality and the unconscious mind received international attention in his lifetime as psychoanalysis became an accepted method of treating emotional disorders. Freud's ideas rather quickly became the basis of an approach to literary criticism that remains active and influential in the present, to which his name is usually attached. This approach is also known as psychoanalytic criticism; some specialists distinguish a more general approach as psychological criticism.

Freud hypothesized a three-part structure of the personality. At one extreme is the superego, a self-censoring mechanism oriented toward group needs and community protocols that are protected by rules and laws and that are devoted to order, discipline, and regulation; at the other, unconscious extreme is the id, a wellspring of desires and appetites driven by the will to fulfill them. The ego must mediate between these extremes by bringing the experiences of the external world to bear on the internal forces of order versus disorder, conformity versus individualism, and the accommodation of group mandates versus the gratification of personal desire. Imbalances among these three parts lead to neurotic behaviors: Too much domination of the superego produces highly repressed individuals, while too much domination of the id produces selfish wildness. Freud himself recognized that his method of psychoanalysis could be useful in understanding the products of human activity such as art and culture, and in addition to his clinical and therapeutic works, he wrote interpretive studies of *Gradiva,* a novel by Wilhelm Jensen, and "The Sandman," by E. T. A. Hoffmann, as well as studies of civilization, anthropology, and religion.

One of the most famous of Freud's ideas has a direct connection to literature: The myth of the Theban king Oedipus, fated to kill his father and marry his mother, provided the framework for Freud's explanation of infantile sexuality, an unsettling and revolutionary idea in its day. Freud thought that adult neurosis could develop from the repression, in infancy, of feelings of rivalry toward the parent of the same sex as the infant and longing for the opposite-sex parent. The term *Oedipus complex* refers to males who have not outgrown this triangle of hostility, exclusion, and possessiveness; *Electra complex* refers to females. The conflict that develops when, among three individuals, two of them want the same thing exclusively from the third provides all the necessary ingredients for a PLOT and a narrative. Many fictional examinations of family life and adult maladjustment spring from this universal feature of human emotional experience; however, a writer may clothe the story in such a way that only an interpretive application of Freud's insights can reveal the underlying structure.

In literary criticism, a reader using the Freudian approach examines characters and events in accordance with Freud's theories that may even extend to examinations of authors' lives or of readers' reactions to a literary text. Literary characters not infrequently turn out to be id, ego, or superego figures engaged in conflict as they struggle for dominance. Sometimes flashback or reminiscence will reveal the repressed childhood crisis that is the root cause of adolescent or adult emotional distress. A writer's symbolic choices may reveal a pattern of psychological malfunction, either in the writer's fiction or in the writer's life, just as Freud's techniques in his most famous work, *The Interpretation of Dreams*, distinguish the latent or hidden meaning of a dream from the manifest content that the dreamer recollects. Because psychoanalysis and literature are both about human beings, and because literature and human beings both display a public face that may differ from the hidden underpinnings that create it, Freud's work will continue to be of interest to literary critics even if research into the biochemical functioning of the brain makes it irrelevant to the science of psychology.

BIBLIOGRAPHY

Crews, Frederick. *Psychoanalysis and Literary Process.* Cambridge, Mass.: Winthrop Publishers, 1970.

Fromm, Erich. *Greatness and Limitations of Freud's Thought.* New York: Harper & Row, 1980.

Skura, Meredith Anne. *The Literary Use of the Psychoanalytic Process.* New Haven, Conn.: Yale University Press, 1981.

FROM RUSSIA WITH LOVE IAN FLEMING (1957)

The fifth installment in the ongoing saga of adventures featuring the consummate spy James BOND, this novel helped make the series an international phenomenon when, in 1961, President John F. Kennedy named it as one of his favorite books. As a literary image of the historical cold war, the novel serves a useful purpose, although readers who have only encountered James Bond in films will hardly rec-

ognize him in the dull bureaucratic role in which he makes his entrance in this volume.

Narrated in the third person, the novel opens at a considerable distance from Bond and England, focusing on the murderous apparatus and personnel of SMERSH, a Soviet agency charged with creating mayhem in the West. The narrator provides an insider's report on the locations and hierarchical construction of the Soviet spy system—a report that draws on the experience and knowledge FLEMING acquired from his own years as an intelligence officer in the Royal Navy during WORLD WAR II. The reader gains intimate knowledge of the plot under construction to embarrass the British spy system by drawing 007 into a scandal, including close examinations of an expatriated British citizen now serving as a SMERSH executioner, of the beautiful young woman chosen to bait the trap, and of the evil Rosa Kleb, the mastermind of the operation.

When the novel's focus shifts to London, Bond is sitting at a desk doing paperwork and serving on tedious committees. The humdrum quality of the day-to-day operations of a government agency—even one so exotic as an espionage branch—becomes apparent. But then Bond's phone rings with a summons from M, his boss. A breezy exchange with Miss Moneypenny, a visit with Q, and soon Bond is in Istanbul under the care of Darko Kerim, the head of the British secret service in Turkey. Since readers have acquired the information that Bond seeks as to the nature of the Soviet game he is drawn into, the story builds up tension effectively. The reader sees Bond falling into the trap and is left hoping he can find his way out of it.

The story moves to the *Orient Express* for the climactic confrontation; Bond whiles away some of his time reading a spy novel by Eric Ambler, a writer contemporary to Ian Fleming. As Kerim, Bond, and Tatiana Romanov, the Soviet bait, hurtle day and night from Istanbul to Paris, the net begins to close and the fatalities begin to multiply. Bond learns key information that will be of use if he can only survive the train trip. The novel ends with a cliffhanger, so readers who require closure will have to continue on to other volumes in the series.

BIBLIOGRAPHY

Chapman, James. *Licence to Thrill: A Cultural History of the James Bond Films*. New York: Columbia University Press, 2000.

Price, Thomas J. "The Changing Image of the Soviets in the Bond Saga: From Bond-Villains to 'Acceptable Role Partners,' " *Journal of Popular Culture* 26, no. 1 (1992): 17–37.

G

G. JOHN BERGER (1972) Winner of the BOOKER PRIZE in 1972, this novel traces the life of a 20th-century Don Giovanni (more familiarly known as Don Juan) from birth to death through the key years of the rise of MODERNISM (the late 19th century and the early 20th century to the outbreak of WORLD WAR I). G. is a seducer of women who enjoys risk and danger; he is born in about 1887 and dies in 1914. His father, Umberto, is an Italian distributor of candied fruits; his mother, Laura, is the English mistress of Umberto, whose legal wife, Esther, lives in Livorno. Laura demonstrates her status as a liberated woman by having Umberto's child out of wedlock, but she is not interested in rearing the boy and she will not allow Umberto to bring him up either. Instead, she fosters him with her cousins, the brother and sister pair of Jocelyn and Beatrice, on their farm in the English countryside. G. learns about the life-and-death violence of the world on hunting excursions with Jocelyn. When G. is 15, Beatrice seduces him, initiating him into the mysteries of adult sexuality. He then embarks on a long string of seductions as he relocates to the Alps and then to the Italian town of Trieste, an international crossroads in the last days of the Austro-Hungarian Empire.

G. is a man without allegiances—he scorns "Great Causes." Born outside the law and divided between two nationalities in his parentage, he espouses only the pleasure of seduction. He is a homely man who is nonetheless charismatically attractive to women; he is indifferent to the effect his womanizing has on the husbands of the women he seduces. He is not without male acquaintances, such as his two pilot friends: Charles Weymann makes a daring night flight with G. as passenger, and Geo Chavez makes the first successful airplane flight over the Alps, although he crashes fatally upon landing. G. never allows these friendships, however, to stand in the way of his chief occupation, the seduction of women. While Geo lies dying in a hospital after his daring achievement, G. lies injured in the same hospital, having been wounded by a jealous husband, but he makes no attempt to see his dying friend. When the setting shifts to Trieste, G. is carrying on an affair with an Austrian banker's wife while also attempting to seduce a young Slovenian girl, the sister of a member of the revolutionary "Young Bosnians," the group that claimed responsibility for the assassination in Sarajevo of the Archduke Ferdinand. G.'s dealings with the Slovenians eventually lead to his unmerited death: As he tries to deliver a false passport, he is apprehended by a mob, beaten, and drowned in the Adriatic Sea.

This story of a callous seducer is only a portion of the novel, however. John BERGER is creating a work of POSTMODERNISM that is also a commentary on modernism and on the artistic revolution that accompanied the opening of the 20th century, specifically cubism. Berger's narrator repeatedly breaks into the narration of G.'s story to comment on art, politics, or history, and to discuss the perceptions that other characters have of a particular event. In the same way that the illusion of three-dimensional depth in a traditional painting is shattered in a cubist rendition of simultaneous multiple points of view, Berger's narration is broken up by writerly intrusions into and interruptions of the narrative form that require the reader to see events from other vantage points. A striking innovation in 1972, *G.* has been favorably compared to better-known works by postmodern authors such as the American John Barth.

BIBLIOGRAPHY

Dyer, Geoff. *Ways of Telling: The Work of John Berger.* London: Pluto Press, 1986.

Papastergiadis, Nikos. *Modernity as Exile: The Stranger in John Berger's Writing.* Manchester, U.K.: Manchester University Press, 1993.

Weibel, Paul. *Reconstructing the Past: G. and* The White Hotel, *Two Contemporary "Historical" Novels.* Bern: P. Lang, 1989.

GALSWORTHY, JOHN (1867–1933)

Winner of the NOBEL PRIZE in literature in 1932 just two months before his death, John Galsworthy enjoyed all the advantages of upper-middle-class Victorian society as a young man. He was born on August 14, 1867, to a wealthy family of long standing in Surrey. He was boarded at the elite PUBLIC SCHOOL Harrow, and he took a degree at New College, Oxford. He studied law and then began his practice in 1890.

Galsworthy was well on the way to fulfilling the expectations of a traditional upper-class success story when he fell madly in love with the unhappy wife of his cousin. In an era when divorce was shameful and extramarital affairs were scandalous, the two lived together while Ada was still married to another man; since their personal lives made them social outcasts, they traveled abroad, and Ada encouraged Galsworthy to pursue writing. His first two novels—*Jocelyn* (1898) and *Villa Rubein* (1900)—were published under the pseudonym "John Sinjohn," as were his first two collections of short fiction, *From the Four Winds* (1897) and *A Man of Devon* (1901). These examples of realism demonstrate his talent for capturing the manners and mores of his CLASS, including the details of material setting and social context.

With Ada's divorce in 1905, the two married and resumed a normal life, spending part of the year in their London house and part in a country house. In 1906, Galsworthy published *A MAN OF PROPERTY,* the first volume in the sequence that was eventually collected as *The FORSYTE SAGA.* The novel struck a chord with contemporary readers and became a best seller. Also in 1906, Galsworthy wrote a play, *The Silver Box,* which was as successful onstage as his novel was on the page. Over the next 27 years, Galsworthy published some 20 novels, 26 plays, 11 volumes of short fiction, and six volumes of nonfiction; his poems were published posthumously in 1934. One of Galsworthy's favorites among his works was the passionate triple love story *The DARK FLOWER.*

Although Galsworthy gained great fame in his lifetime, his critical reputation has suffered in subsequent decades, and *The Forsyte Saga,* especially its first volume, remains the sole work of his large output that is now widely read. Novels of social manners that seized the attention of those living in the conditions described therein may later seem outmoded or irrelevant. Galsworthy himself feared that he had not lived up to his potential, and that his novels and plays recorded the particularities of the world he lived in without transmitting any larger vision of human possibilities. He died of a condition that was probably a brain tumor on January 31, 1933; the onset of his illness had prevented him from accepting his Nobel Prize in person.

BIBLIOGRAPHY

Batchelor, John. *The Edwardian Novelists.* New York: St. Martin's Press, 1982.

Dupre, Catherine. *John Galsworthy: A Biography.* New York: Coward, McCann and Geoghegan, 1976.

Gindin, James. *John Galsworthy's Life and Art.* Ann Arbor: University of Michigan Press, 1987.

Mottram, Ralph H. *For Some We Loved: An Intimate Portrait of Ada and John Galsworthy.* London: Hutchinson University Library, 1956.

Sternlicht, Sanford. *John Galsworthy.* Twayne's English Authors, 447. Boston: Twayne, 1987.

GARDAM, JANE (1928–   )   A noted writer of children's literature and the winner of the WHITBREAD Book of the Year Award in 1991 for QUEEN OF THE TAMBOURINE, Jane Gardam was born Jane Mary Pearson on July 11, 1928, in Yorkshire. She matriculated at a selective women's school, Bedford College in London, studying there both as an undergraduate, from 1946 to 1949, and as a graduate student from 1949 to 1952, when she married David Gardam. She worked for three years as a magazine journalist; then, beginning in 1955, she devoted her time to rearing her children.

When she began to write, Jane Gardam first turned her hand to children's literature, publishing her first two books, *A Few Fair Days* and *A Long Way From Verona,* in 1971. By 1993, she had published a dozen children's books, including novels for young readers. Critics place her children's literature in the tradition of E. Nesbit: It features precocious middle-class children learning to handle themselves independently of their parents. In 1975, she published her first collection of short fiction for adult readers, *Black Faces, White Faces,* addressing the legacy of COLONIALISM in Jamaica; this book won the David Higham Prize for first novel and the Winifred Holtby Award. The book features a series of interlinked stories, a form that is characteristic of Gardam's best work. In 1977, her first work of long fiction, *God on the Rocks,* was short-listed for the BOOKER PRIZE, and in 1981 she won the Whitbread Award for Best Children's Book for *The Hollow Land,* another collection of interlinked stories. *The Pangs of Love and Other Stories* (1983), short fiction for adult readers, won the Katherine Mansfield Prize in 1984. In 1985, Gardam was named a fellow of the Royal Society of Literature.

When Gardam relocated from London to a coastal home, she drew on her experience for her most famous novel, *Queen of the Tambourine.* She has published four additional novels and a teleplay. Jane Gardam continues to live and write at her home on the Kent coast.

BIBLIOGRAPHY

Gardam, Jane. "Writing for Children: Some Wasps in the Marmalade." In *Essays by Divers Hands: Innovations in Contemporary Literature.* Edited by Vincent Cronin. Woodbridge, Suffolk, U.K.: The Royal Society of Literature-Boydell Press, 1979.

Something About the Author Autobiography Series. Vol. 9. Detroit: Gale Research Co., 1990.

GARNETT, DAVID (1892–1981)   Son of the influential essayist, playwright, and editor Edward Garnett and of the translator of Russian novels Constance Garnett, David Garnett was born on March 9, 1892, in Brighton. His parents were immersed in the literary world of the late 19th and early 20th centuries: Edward Garnett discovered Joseph CONRAD and D. H. LAWRENCE and counted among his friends and acquaintances H. G. WELLS, W. H. HUDSON, George Bernard Shaw, Hilaire BELLOC, Henry JAMES, and Ford Madox FORD. David Garnett captures charming visits with these luminaries in the three volumes of his autobiography. He was also exposed to international politics through his mother's involvement with revolutionary strife in Russia and enjoyed an adventurous visit to that country with her in 1904.

An indifferent student, Garnett studied botany at the Royal College of Science; during his school years he frequently traveled in Europe and was drawn into the circle of the BLOOMSBURY GROUP. WHEN WORLD WAR I began, Garnett declared himself a conscientious objector and worked with Quakers in France and as a farmhand in England. He began writing after the war and published an inconsequential novel under a pseudonym. In 1922, he published the modernist beast fable LADY INTO FOX, winner of the HAWTHORNDEN PRIZE and the JAMES TAIT BLACK MEMORIAL PRIZE. Garnett failed as a bookseller, turning his experience into a memoir, and then had greater success as a book publisher, cofounding Nonesuch Press. He continued to write novels, short fiction, and nonfiction, and he edited the letters of T. E. Lawrence ("Lawrence of Arabia") and the novels of Thomas Love Peacock. During WORLD WAR II, he worked as an intelligence officer, although he was in his late 40s when the war began. During the war, he also married the niece of Virginia WOOLF.

Although Garnett was a minor writer, his best works continue to hold their worth for their imaginative and droll charm. Garnett continued to write into his late years; he died at the age of 88 on February 17, 1981.

BIBLIOGRAPHY

Garnett, David. *The Golden Echo.* 3 vols. London: Chatto & Windus, 1953–62.

Irwin, W. R. "The Metamorphoses of David Garnett," *Publications of the Modern Language Association of America* 73, no. 4 (September 1958): 386–92.

Raphael, Frederic. "Aspects of Garnett," *PN Review* 23, no. 5 (May–June 1997): 39–42.

GEORGE PASSANT C. P. SNOW (1940)

This novel was published under the title *Strangers and Brothers* in 1940, but it was republished in 1972 as *George Passant.* The earlier title became the name of the entire 11-volume ROMAN-FLEUVE that this novel introduces. See *STRANGERS AND BROTHERS* for the overview of the series considered as a whole and for the detailed discussion of this novel in particular.

GEORGIANS

New generations of writers frequently feel the need to distinguish themselves from those who have gone before, and to do so they must have an identifying stamp. With the accession of George V to the throne in 1910, the Victorian era seemed finally to be in the past; publishers and writers—of poetry in particular—seized the moment and the soubriquet to style themselves "Georgians." Since then, the term has acquired negative connotations. The propensity of Georgian writers and editors toward conservative and conventional literature stands in stark contrast to the innovations of MODERNISM that soon became the dominant mode of literary expression. Writers who published poems in popular Georgian anthologies, but who later went on to greater fame as fiction writers, critics, and exponents of modernism, include D. H. LAWRENCE and Robert GRAVES.

BIBLIOGRAPHY

Swinnerton, Frank. *The Georgian Literary Scene, 1910–1935: A Panorama.* New York: Farrar, Straus, 1950.

GEORGY GIRL MARGARET FORSTER (1965)

A story that captures the changing sexual mores of the 1960s, *Georgy Girl* contrasts the choices two roommates make as birth control expands the range of options women have in their personal lives.

Georgina Parkin is the daughter of Ted and Doris Parkin, the valet and housekeeper of wealthy James Leamington; she has only recently moved out of her family's quarters in the Leamington home, where she received the benefits of wealth such as education and clothing that the childless Leamingtons were pleased to bestow on her. She feels liberated, because James Leamington's smarmy attentions had begun to bother her, while her toadying father could see nothing wrong with his adored employer.

When Georgina finds a flat and advertises for a roommate, her life becomes more complicated: Meredith, her new roommate, plays the violin in the symphony and keeps company with a string of boyfriends, most of whom are musicians. While Meredith is beautiful and aware of the power that her beauty gives her over men, Georgy is a gangly ugly duckling, uncomfortable with her body and with the new freedoms single women are pursuing. She longs for love, and yet she fears it as well, enjoying her independence while remaining aware that she wants more in her life. She doesn't want the attentions she attracts—James Leamington soon propositions her—and she can't attract the attentions she wants. When Meredith becomes pregnant by Jos, her current boyfriend, Georgy and Jos are the only ones pleased with the news, and they prevent Meredith from resorting to abortion, as she had done in the past. Meredith's indifference to her newborn is incomprehensible to Georgy, who soon finds herself making choices that seemed impossible when she first moved out on her own.

In Georgy, Margaret FORSTER creates a predecessor to the kind of heroine one finds in a contemporary novel like *Bridget Jones's Diary:* an independent young woman in charge of her own life and ready to enjoy her physical and emotional freedoms, but one who discovers how powerful are the attractions of such traditional roles as wife and mother. Forster's third-person omniscient narrator gradually makes Meredith and the single life of sexual freedom seem monstrous; consequently, when Georgy decides on a surprising course of action, readers can perceive her choice to be a heroic and modern one when in fact it is actually highly traditional. Forster examines modern sexual permissiveness and rejects it, giving her protagonist a nearly classic resolution to her story. Proponents of FEMINISM are likely to be disappointed by the ending of *Georgy Girl,* but the novel provides a down-to-earth view of an era that has been mythologized for its excesses.

BIBLIOGRAPHY
Kael, Pauline. *Kiss Kiss Bang Bang.* Boston: Little, Brown, 1968.
Thompson, Howard. "Cinderella in London." Review of *Georgy Girl* (film). *New York Times,* 22 September 1996, 62.

GHOST ROAD, THE   PAT BARKER (1995)
See REGENERATION TRILOGY.

GIBBONS, STELLA (1902–1989)

Remembered as the author of *COLD COMFORT FARM,* one of the classic examples of the English COMIC NOVEL, Stella Gibbons was born in London on January 5, 1902, the eldest of three children. Her father was a doctor, but he worked in the poorer parts of London and reared his family there as well. Stella Gibbons was tutored at home and began developing her storytelling skills spinning tales for her two younger brothers. She studied at the North London Collegiate School for Girls and matriculated at University College in London in 1921. After studying journalism for two years, she worked as a professional journalist until 1933, when she married an actor, Alan Bourne Webb. She wrote poetry with some success during this period, although her poems are rarely found in contemporary anthologies. In 1932, her best-known novel, *Cold Comfort Farm,* was published; it is an extremely funny SATIRE on novels set in rural England and features passages that parody the style of writers such as D. H. LAWRENCE.

Stella Gibbons published 17 additional novels by 1970, along with three volumes of short fiction and four collections of poetry. She revisited *Cold Comfort Farm* in her 1949 novel, *Conference at Cold Comfort Farm,* and in her 1940 story collection, *Christmas at Cold Comfort Farm.* In spite of her membership, beginning in 1950, in the Royal Society of Literature, very little critical work has been done on her life or work. Gibbons died on December 19, 1989, in London.

BIBLIOGRAPHY
Oliver, Reggie. *Out of the Woodshed: A Portrait of Stella Gibbons.* London: Bloomsbury, 1998.

GIRLS OF SLENDER MEANS, THE
MURIEL SPARK (1963)

The third-person narrator of this novel follows the lives of several young women living in the May of Teck Club in London during WORLD WAR II and of the young men who take an interest in them. The May of Teck Club is a women's hotel run along the lines of a dormitory dissociated from any academic connection, or of a convent devoid of religious affiliation. It was founded to provide respectable housing in London for ladies under 30 "of slender means" who work for a living in the city. Over the years, some longtime residents have prevailed on the governing committee to overlook the clause about the residents being under 30, but most of the women are of marriageable age, interests, and temperament. The house survived the blitzkrieg of the war—barely. On one occasion, a bomb fell into the backyard, but it failed to detonate and was removed by a bomb squad. Most of the story occurs in 1945, in the short period between the surrender of Germany and the surrender of Japan.

The narrator casts an objective and appraising eye on all the girls of any consequence, but there is not a protagonist who dominates most of the scenes. Readers learn more about Jane, perhaps, because she also appears in the occasional passages that clearly date from a period some time after the war, and because she introduces Nicholas Farringdon to the girls at the May of Teck Club. Nicholas enjoys taking meals with the girls immensely, although clearly he enjoys the company of beautiful Selina much more than he does that of chubby Jane. He is keenly interested in gaining access to the flat roof of the club to meet Selina there, and they find a way to do just this.

The early portions of the novel have almost the quality of a pastiche as the narrator captures bits of song coming from various radios, snatches of conversation, and selections of poetry that are declaimed by Joanna, a lovely young minister's daughter who earns extra money by giving elocution lessons to those wishing to acquire the accepted accent of the educated classes. These captured bits frequently serve to echo a theme or to foreshadow an event in the story. As the narrative unfolds, it begins with the carefree comedy of young single life in the aftermath of war: Everything is still rationed, from cold cream to clothes, and so the girls barter intensely and share almost everything, including the beautiful Schiaparelli ball gown one of them acquires from a wealthy aunt. Slowly, however, the tone darkens as the content of those passages belonging to a future time becomes clearer. The May of Teck Club seems as safe as houses with the war freshly ended, and yet there is a hidden danger lurking that will place many of the girls at risk. Muriel SPARK'S handling of the narrative in transforming it from light comedy to dark tragedy is masterly.

In the closing scene of celebration on VJ day, the narrator allows readers to catch a glimpse of the event that helps explain those passages from the not-too-distant future. This strategy places the reader in the ironic position of knowing what Jane seeks to learn in those passages. The reader knows, too, that Jane's search is doomed to fail. Just as the joy of the war's ending is tainted by the discussion of the terrible new weapon that has secured the final victory, so too is Spark's novel of comedy darkened by bittersweet IRONY.

BIBLIOGRAPHY

Hynes, Joseph, ed. *Critical Essays on Muriel Spark.* New York: G. K. Hall, 1992.

Page, Norman. *Muriel Spark.* Modern Novelists Series. New York: St. Martin's Press, 1990.

Sproxton, Judy. *The Women of Muriel Spark.* New York: St. Martin's Press, 1992.

GO-BETWEEN, THE L. P. HARTLEY (1953)

In 1953, this novel—HARTLEY'S seventh—received the Heinemann Foundation Prize; it is widely regarded as Hartley's best novel. In 1971, director Joseph Losey chose it for a FILM ADAPTATION with a screenplay by the noted British dramatist Harold Pinter. The film received the Grand Prize that year at the Cannes Film Festival.

The protagonist and first-person narrator of the story is Leo Colston. Part of the story arises from a diary Leo kept when, at the age of 13, he spent a school vacation at Brandham Hall in Norfolk. Leo presents the rest of the story in his adult voice when he rediscovers the forgotten diary among his late mother's possessions and decides to revisit Brandham Hall. Reading the diary makes him realize how intensely he has repressed the memory of that summer, and he wishes to determine what degree of moral culpability he must bear for the tragic events that brought his visit to a close.

As an adolescent, much of Leo's thinking was directed toward understanding the world of adults. He is too innocent to recognize the attraction he feels toward Marian Maudsley, the sister of the school friend he is visiting. Additionally, he has recently lost his father, and the two men pursuing Marian represent two kinds of masculine functioning in the grown-up world. Viscount Trimingham possesses social status, a title, and an estate, but he is scarred from wounds he received in the BOER WAR. In contrast, the farmer Ted Burgess possesses practical skills and earthy charm; he easily assumes the role of mentor and surrogate father to Leo.

The chief action of the plot revolves around Leo's role in carrying messages among these three adults. And even as he tries to decide who he would prefer for Marian to choose, he also feels inchoate attraction to her himself. The tragedy that strikes is intertwined with Leo's witnessing of a kind of primal scene between Ted and Marian—the scene that Leo has repressed, along with its consequences, all these years. As an adult who has these hidden memories wrenched back into consciousness, Leo revisits the scene in person and discovers that Marian is still alive. He is at last able to see the larger picture and also to render her a valuable service, thereby assuaging his own need to compensate for his youthful ignorance.

In structuring a first-person narration told by the same person at two widely separated phases of life, Hartley displays a virtuoso control of voice and tone. He adds a symbolic dimension to the story through Leo's fascination with magic and the zodiac, and the story's elements lend themselves to interpretation by means of FREUDIAN CRITICISM. Leo's diary constitutes a record of an interrupted BILDUNGSROMAN, and through the chance rediscovery of it, he recovers the opportunity to complete his growth and move beyond emotional paralysis.

BIBLIOGRAPHY

Mulkeen, Anne. *Wild Thyme, Winter Lightning: The Symbolic Novels of L. P. Hartley.* Detroit: Wayne State University Press, 1974.

Pritchard, R. E. "L. P. Hartley's *The Go-Between,*" *Critical Quarterly* 22, no. 1 (1980): 45–55.

Radley, Alan. "Psychological Realism in L. P. Hartley's *The Go-Between,*" *Literature and Psychology* 33, no. 2 (1987): 1–10.

GODDEN, RUMER (1907–1998)

Born on December 10, 1907, in Eastbourne, Sussex, England, Rumer Godden spent her first 12 years in INDIA (except for a year spent with her grandmother in 1913) and returned there frequently throughout her youth and young adulthood. Her parents followed the custom of educating their children in England; Rumer and her older sister were sent together to a variety of schools, some of which were excessively harsh parochial institutions. In addition to the usual academic subjects, she studied ballet. In 1925, she returned to India, opening a successful school of dance in Calcutta in 1928, the year she also married her first husband.

Godden published her first novel, *Chinese Puzzle,* in 1935, followed the next year by *The Lady and the Unicorn,* a condemnation of English racial prejudice against those of mixed ethnic heritage. She sold her dance studio and returned to England for two years. As WORLD WAR II began, she took refuge with her children first in India and then in Kashmir, continuing her writing in addition to managing the household and rearing her children. She remarried in 1949 when her first husband died; the family took up residence in the English countryside for several years and finally retired to Scotland. Rumer Godden died on November 8, 1998.

Although she began her writing career producing novels for adult readers, by the late 1940s she was writing successful children's literature. In her 21 novels, she frequently addressed the clash of cultures she had witnessed growing up in India; she also memorialized—and attacked—the stringent religious teachers of her English boarding school education, especially in *Black Narcissus* (1939), the story of five unloving Anglican sisters who fail in their mission to found a school at a remote outpost. She revisited this embittered character type in *In this House of Brede* (1969), but also pre-sented a positive picture of the devotional life in *Five for Sorrow, Ten for Joy* (1979). Despite her harsh educational experience, Godden retained a deep spirituality, having witnessed the power of the Christian, Hindu, Muslim, and Buddhist faiths in England and India.

In addition to her novels and children's books, Rumer Godden wrote short stories, memoirs, and nonfiction, including a history of the Pekingese breed of dog, and she edited a cookbook and an anthology of poetry. Her semiautobiographical novel *The* GREENGAGE SUMMER (1958) has become a minor classic of young adult literature.

BIBLIOGRAPHY

Chisholm, Anne. *Rumer Godden: A Storyteller's Life.* New York: Greenwillow Books, 1998.

Simpson, Hassel A. *Rumer Godden.* Twayne's English Authors, 151. New York: Twayne Publishers, 1973.

Tindall, William York. "Rumer Godden, Public Symbolist," *College English* 13, no. 6 (March 1952): 297–303.

GOD OF SMALL THINGS, THE ARUNDHATI ROY (1997)

The winner of the BOOKER PRIZE in 1997 (making the author the first Indian citizen to win that prize), this novel is set in the tropical south of INDIA in the sweltering and fecund province of Kerala, in the town of Ayemenem. The focus of the novel centers on the decaying Ipes family, Anglophile followers of Syrian Christianity. ROY develops a recursive structure for her story, sketching in the essence of a tragic event in the first chapter and then revisiting it repeatedly, but with differing emphases and nuances, in subsequent chapters. Her prose style, admired by some and irksome to others, features playful disruptions of sentences and paragraphs, including random capitalization, idiosyncratic spelling tricks, and made-up combinations of old words to yield new effects.

In addition to its recursive narration, the novel features several kinds of doubling. There are twin protagonists, Estha Ipes (a boy) and Rahel Ipes (a girl), and they are examined at two different times in their lives, at the age of seven in 1969 and at the age of 31 in 1994, after they have been separated for 24 years. Their cousin visiting from England in 1969, Sophie Mol, is a key figure in the tragedy that leads to the separation of the twins, but Roy's light handling of other parts of the novel produces an unusual combination of comedy and pathos. Additionally, the twins' mother, Ammu, provides a further level of complication in her breaking of the social barrier erected between higher and lower castes when she chooses to love a man in the "untouchable" or pariah caste. Sexual transgression in turn becomes an important theme in the way it can serve both as a bridge between isolated individuals and as a weapon particularly wounding to the innocent. Recovering from wounds of various kinds, including guilt, becomes the special challenge for Estha and Rahel.

Arundhati Roy negotiated a million-dollar advance for her novel, creating a sensation before it even reached published form. After publication, the sensation continued as it won the Booker Prize and was translated into numerous languages. It is a distinctive and original work that shines a modern light on a part of the world little known to those outside it, revealing the very human struggles of those living there.

BIBLIOGRAPHY

Dodiya, Jaydipsinh, and Joya Chakravarty, eds. *The Critical Studies of Arundhati's* The God of Small Things. New Delhi: Atlantic Publishers and Distributors, 1999.

Durix, Carole and Jean-Pierre Durix. *Reading Arundhati Roy's* The God of Small Things. Dijon, France: Editions Universitaires de Dijon, 2002.

Khot, Mohini. "The Feminist Voice in Arundhati Roy's *The God of Small Things.*" In *Indian Feminisms.* Edited by Jasbir Jain and Avadhesh Kumar Singh. New Delhi: Creative, 2001, 213–22.

GOLDEN BOWL, THE HENRY JAMES (1904)

One of the greatest of Henry JAMES's prolific output of novels, *The Golden Bowl* focuses on the relationship between a widower, Adam Verver, and his daughter, Maggie. The Ververs are wealthy Americans, freed for a life of cultivated leisure by their financial security; they live in London and spend their time collecting art objects Adam Verver intends to place in a museum he plans to donate to his hometown. Their lives are complete, and their father-daughter relationship is completely fulfilling to them, so they maintain only a limited social circle. Maggie's best friend is Mrs.

Assingham, an American married to a British military officer. Through this friend, she meets the impoverished Italian aristocrat Prince Amerigo. Although she is not passionately in love with him, she thinks he would make a suitable husband; her father arranges the match, essentially adding the prince to the Verver's large collection of European valuables.

Unknown to Maggie, the prince is already in love with Charlotte Stant, who had been a schoolmate of Maggie's but who is herself impoverished like the prince. They both realize that a marriage between them is impossible. They spend their last day together, the day before Maggie's wedding, shopping for a suitable gift from Charlotte. She selects the golden bowl of the title—actually a glass bowl painted with gold leaf—but the prince points out that it has a flaw and relates his fear that the cracked bowl will bring bad luck. Charlotte does not buy the bowl. The next day, Prince Amerigo and Maggie are married; however, for the Ververs, very little changes. Father and daughter continue their close association, enjoying their shared pursuit of antiquities, collectibles, and art objects. Eventually, Maggie comes to think that her father needs a marriage of his own, and she recommends poor Charlotte Stant to him. Circumstances repeatedly throw Charlotte and Prince Amerigo together as the representatives of Maggie and Adam, who prefer spending quiet time together to socializing.

Slowly Maggie realizes that this four-adult family is unusual, and she begins to wonder whether there is a connection between her husband and the friend who has become her stepmother. When she purchases a golden bowl—the same one Charlotte had passed over—a conversation with the shopkeeper arouses her suspicions. But she also realizes that she has played a key role in whatever connection might exist between Charlotte and the prince; her own self-centered behavior in continuing her comfortable connection to her devoted father has helped to undermine her marriage. A parting of the ways becomes inevitable, and the double challenge for Maggie is to let go of her attachment to her father and to ascertain whether her husband loves her for herself or merely for her money.

The Golden Bowl is one of Henry James's finest examples of psychological realism. His complex and indirect style, relating the story through an omniscient third-person narrator, draws out the details and nuances of his characters' thoughts, feelings, motivations, and behaviors. The story contrasts the artificial perfection of material beauty—the things the Ververs collect—with the natural imperfection of human relationships. The golden bowl is a material object of beauty, but its hidden flaw makes it into a metaphor for the relationships in which Maggie is involved. She has tried to convert human beings into collectibles, but the ineradicable nature of human flaws dooms this enterprise. She must learn to deal with people as people, not as objects, and she must accept the flaws ingrained in other people's identities.

The Golden Bowl became the basis of a FILM ADAPTATION in 2000, with a screenplay by the noted writer Ruth Prawer JHABVALA.

BIBLIOGRAPHY

Gargano, James W., ed. *Critical Essays on Henry James: The Late Novels.* Boston: G. K. Hall, 1987.

Jones, Granville H. *Henry James's Psychology of Experience: Innocence, Responsibility, and Renunciation in the Fiction of Henry James.* The Hague: Mouton, 1975.

Macnaughton, William R. *Henry James: The Later Novels.* Twayne's United Stated Authors, 521. Boston: Twayne Publishers, 1987.

GOLDEN COMPASS, THE PHILIP PULLMAN (1996)

The first volume of a trilogy collectively entitled *HIS DARK MATERIALS,* this FANTASY novel introduces Lyra Belacqua, a girl on the threshold of adolescence. Lyra lives in Oxford under the careless supervision of scholars associated with Lord Asriel. Readers familiar with John Milton's great work *Paradise Lost* will pause over that name, recognizing it: The association is apt, because Asriel is mounting a war against heaven, and PULLMAN is retelling Milton's story with unexpected twists.

The most arresting feature of Lyra's world is the presence of daemons. These daemons constitute external manifestations of the soul, and they take the form of talking animals. The daemons of children are shape-shifters, becoming whatever best reflects a child's emotional state at any given moment. Lyra's daemon Pantalaimon is in this stage. During adolescence, the

daemon "settles," assuming its permanent form. This image of a talking, intelligent, caring pet of many forms is a compelling and original device. The connection between daemons and humans becomes the driving force of the plot as Lyra and Pan are drawn into their amazing adventures.

Lyra has a gift for lying—her name is no accident—that is a crucial aspect of Pullman's story; it will draw her into trouble, and sometimes save her life, but her challenge is to rise above it and to embrace truth. Before leaving Oxford, she receives a very different gift from the Master. This small object is the golden compass of the title, but it does not indicate direction in space. It is an aleithiometer—a truth meter. In an ironic pairing, the skilled liar also proves herself to be exceptionally sensitive to the manipulation of this instrument. Only gradually does she learn its subtleties, and as the power of truth grows in her, she finally sees the hollow emptiness that lying brings into the world.

But Lyra is also being pursued. The Magisterium is at work, seeking to retain the absolute power it possesses by obstructing Lord Asriel, capturing Lyra, and eliminating Dust (a kind of elemental life force) from the universe. At Bolvanger, Lyra learns a horrifying truth, discovering the experiments conducted on children and their daemons to make them immune to original sin. Her own experiences there are harrowing before she escapes to travel farther north to Asriel, only to discover that he, too, is conducting horrible experiments. He intends to blast open the borders of his world in order to carry his war to the Authority of all worlds, even though the consequences may be devastating to his own world.

Lyra's adventures teach her hard lessons about appearances and reality, deception and truth, betrayal and trust. In *The Golden Compass,* she begins to leave childhood behind without any clear role model for adulthood. With only her own soul, Pantalaimon, to guide her, she embarks on a quest that fits the pattern of the hero ARCHETYPE. She begins to find her own goodness, her own courage, and her own strength as she discovers how severe the tests of these characteristics can be. At the novel's end, a new and unknown world lies before her on the other side of the Bridge to the Stars, just as, in every child's life, the unknown realm of adulthood lies on the other side of adolescence. She has no choice but to cross into the unknown and be tested there.

BIBLIOGRAPHY

Bird, Anne-Marie. "Dust, Daemons, and Soul States: Reading Philip Pullman's *His Dark Materials*," *British Association of Lecturers in Children's Literature Bulletin* 7 (2000): 3–12.

Nikolajeva, Maria. "Children's, Adult, Human . . .?" In *Transcending Boundaries: Writing for a Dual Audience of Children and Adults*. Edited by Sandra L. Beckett and Jack Zipes. New York: Garland, 1999, 63–80.

GOLDEN NOTEBOOK, THE DORIS LESSING (1962)

An innovative and experimental novel that broke new ground in terms of both form and content, *The Golden Notebook* was identified as a manifesto of FEMINISM when it was published, but the author's examination of the protagonist's life has even further implications that condemn the imperialist traditions of European history and that illustrate the constraints placed on the possibilities of thought by language itself. LESSING'S novel is one of the monumental literary achievements of the second half of the 20th century and a landmark document in the history of feminist thought.

Lessing divides the story into four books, each subdivided into five parts, with an extra part for the golden notebook in the fourth book. Each book contains an opening section entitled "Free Women," followed by writings from the protagonist's variously colored notebooks. The fourth book contains these sections plus the additional writing in the golden notebook, followed by one last installment of "Free Women" that stands on its own and that brings the novel back to the topic it began with, though handling it on a higher plane of understanding.

The novel's protagonist is Anna Freeman Wulf, a novelist who has published a successful book called *Frontiers of War*. In the summer of 1957, she is a divorced mother attempting to live on her own, rear her daughter, and write a new book; the sections of Lessing's novel entitled "Free Women" chronicle Anna's life, her friends, and her work on her novel. As Anna works, she sorts out her thoughts in four different-colored notebooks in which she explores ideas along four axes of inquiry. In the black notebook, she examines literature through her own novel about black and white relations in Africa; in the red notebook, she examines politics, especially the opposition between communism and the capitalist Western world; in the yellow notebook, she develops ideas for fiction by examining women and men in sex and love; and in the blue notebook, Anna examines aspects of herself as a woman, mother, friend, writer, activist, lover—as a user of language and victim of its limits. The blue notebook serves as her day-to-day journal of her life—the place where she turns a critical eye on the bits and pieces of her life and muses on the problem of using language to seek understanding. Finally, when Anna succeeds in moving beyond fragmentation, she begins to write exclusively in the golden notebook. She is no longer divided into fragments of a life. To achieve this unity, however, she must pass through a crisis of disintegration—a breakdown—and reassemble herself on the other side of it.

Doris Lessing constructs her story by creating a relatively straightforward and realistic novel in the "Free Women" sections about Anna, her friend Molly Jacobs, Molly's son Tommy and her ex-husband Richard, and Anna's lover Saul Green. In this novel, which serves as a kind of skeleton or point of departure for Anna's experimental notebook portions, Anna and Molly are free because they are not bound by the legal and personal obligations of marriage. They are old friends and they have long enjoyed getting together to talk over their lives and compare notes. Although they are free women, they remain powerfully bound to men and to the topic of their interactions with men in their conversations. But Anna is growing tired of discussions that seem to be permanently tied to men. She is ready to move beyond the war between the sexes.

Molly's life is complicated by motherhood and by her son Tommy's difficulties as he matures, particularly when his attempted suicide leaves him blind—and leaves both Molly and Anna nagged by their sense of responsibility and the sting of failure. Molly; Tommy; Richard; his second wife, Marion; and various other characters are engaged in a kind of soap-opera existence in the search for love and personal satisfaction.

Anna's life is both more simple and more complicated because she is reaching for difficult goals: transcendence of her limitations, liberation from her social, gender, and cultural conditioning, unity out of her fragmentation, and truth instead of piecemeal facts. As Anna writes in the black notebook, she recreates scenes from her earlier life in Rhodesia but remains dissatisfied that they fall so far short of reality; as she writes in the yellow notebook, she begins a novel called *The Shadow of the Third,* narrated by Ella, an alter-ego for Anna. Ella's affair with a married man ends badly, and so she, too, begins writing, noting all the possible scenarios for how a relationship might go. Anna's life then imitates Ella's art as Saul and Anna play out the possibilities already summed up in the yellow notebook.

The blue notebook is Anna's most personal and challenging work: In it she turns her critical eye on her own life as a woman and a writer. The limitations of thinking and writing become apparent as words begin to fail Anna, as recorded in the blue notebook. She enters psychological therapy in the effort to understand herself and her relationships better. Ultimately, Anna has a breakdown, and the signifier of this breakdown is her loss of control over the words—and their links to meaning in the larger world—in the blue notebook. Anna must cross beyond assumptions and conditioning to achieve a unified identity as a complete and independent human being. She moves to the golden notebook of the title, where she can record her restorative dreams.

In this novel, Doris Lessing demonstrates her prescience in seeing the issues that absorb feminist theory and literary theory in general in the following two decades. The significance of the roles of gender assumptions and political ideology in shaping personal identity, and the power of language in conditioning the very thinking of those who use it, all are present and deeply probed in *The Golden Notebook.* Lessing not only breaks new ground for literary achievement by a woman writer, she breaks new ground by any standard of human identity.

BIBLIOGRAPHY

Cederstrom, Lorelei. "The Principal Archetypal Elements of *The Golden Notebook.*" In *Approaches to Teaching Lessing's* The Golden Notebook. Edited by Carey Kaplan and Ellen Cronan Rose. New York: Modern Language Association of America, 1989, 50–57.

Pickering, Jean. *Understanding Doris Lessing.* Understanding Contemporary British Literature Series. Columbia: University of South Carolina Press, 1990.

GOLDING, WILLIAM (1911–1993)

The author of LORD OF THE FLIES (1954) and one of England's most honored writers, William Golding won the NOBEL PRIZE for Literature in 1983. He was born on September 19, 1911, in Cornwall, the son of a schoolmaster and a suffragette. He enrolled in Brasenose College at Oxford; although he was first drawn to the study of science, he settled on literature and completed an undergraduate degree in 1935 and a belated master's degree in 1960. He was married in 1939; he and his wife became the parents of two children. He taught for a year at Bishop Wordsworth's School in Salisbury before the outbreak of WORLD WAR II, when he joined the Royal Navy. He served on active duty in the North Atlantic—where he witnessed the sinking of the *Bismarck*—until 1945, eventually commanding a rocket ship that sailed in the D-Day armada. When the war ended, he returned to teaching at Bishop Wordsworth's School and remained there until 1961. Golding was also active in several capacities in the London theater world before and after the war.

Back in his role as schoolteacher, Golding wrote steadily despite a lack of success, finishing three novels in manuscript without finding publishers interested in them. These early works were never published, but in 1954 *Lord of the Flies* became a tremendous success in terms of its brisk sales. It was compared to *A HIGH WIND IN JAMAICA* (1929), another book about children thrown prematurely into adult responsibilities. Recognition of its merit in the United States was slower, but by 1961 it was in widespread use on college campuses, and its sales allowed Golding to resign from teaching in order to write full-time.

In the meantime, Golding had continued writing. *The Inheritors* appeared in 1955, presenting a hypothetical exploration of the fatal conflict between Neanderthal and Cro-Magnon hominids. In 1956, Golding published *Pincher Martin,* the story of a sailor cast adrift when his ship is torpedoed during World War II. *Free Fall* (1959) retrospectively examines the psychological development of an artist, Sammy Mountjoy. In 1964 in *The Spire,* Golding turns to another artist, the builder of a monumental medieval steeple, to create an ALLEGORY about Faustian ambition. After 10 years of intensive and successful productivity, Golding published only minor or unsuccessful novels for 15 years, but then in 1979 he published *Darkness Visible,* and this story of a modern struggle between good and evil won the JAMES TAIT BLACK MEMORIAL PRIZE for that year. Then in 1980, *RITES OF PASSAGE,* an example of NAUTICAL FICTION, won the BOOKER PRIZE; it introduces a trilogy that continues with *Close Quarters* (1987) and concludes with *Fire Down Below* (1989).

William Golding has also written poems, short fiction, novellas, plays, radio plays, essays, and a work of travel literature. He was named a Commander of the Order of the British Empire in 1965, and he was knighted in 1988. Numerous universities recognized him with honorary doctorates before he died of a heart attack on June 19, 1993.

BIBLIOGRAPHY

Baker, James, ed. *Critical Essays on William Golding.* Boston: G. K. Hall, 1988.

Dick, Bernard F. *William Golding.* Twayne's English Authors, 57. Rev. ed. Boston: Twayne Publishers, 1987.

Friedman, Lawrence S. *William Golding.* New York: Continuum, 1993.

Gindin, James. *William Golding.* New York: St. Martin's Press, 1988.

GOOD BEHAVIOUR MOLLY KEANE (1981)

Set in the Anglo-Irish world of "great houses" during their days of waning influence in the first half of the 20th century, this SATIRE attacks the emotional frigidity of a society that has allowed propriety and decorum to replace sincerity and affection. The first-person narrator of the story is Aroon St. Charles, the eldest child of a landed family of long pedigree. Although their estate is in IRELAND, in the vicinity of Limerick, they are English and their ways are English ways: dressing for dinner, maintaining a small army of servants, and observing a strict hierarchy of inherited status and privilege. Slowly, however, their world is falling apart.

The story opens when Aroon is 57 years old, on the day when her mother passes away at Gull Cottage, where the two of them have lived in reduced circumstances, tended only by one remaining servant, Rose, for many years. The time of the story's present day is approximately 1960, but the date is immaterial: Aroon is transfixed by the past, especially the period from right before WORLD WAR I until the death of her father during the GREAT DEPRESSION. These were the years when she and her late brother Hubert grew from childhood to adulthood—the years when she and her mother settled into an abiding hostility and an unending power struggle. Aroon launches into the exploration of her past as a way of explaining her present miserable life.

Born into a CLASS of beautiful people who took their own prestige for granted, Aroon was a large and ungainly girl who grew into a graceless and unwanted young woman. In contrast, her beloved brother Hubert was handsome all his short life. As Aroon recollects their governess, Mrs. Brock, and their superficially happy life at the St. Charles family estate, Temple Alice, the reader gradually becomes aware of the deeper unhappiness that permeates every event. Aroon's mother is cold and unloving to her daughter, although appearing to be perfectly behaved in all their interactions. Properly reared, Aroon is oblivious to her own naiveté. Her recollections of her handsome father's popularity with women and of her beautiful mother's emotional fastidiousness explain the family's misery even when Aroon herself seems to be at best vaguely aware of the implications of her story.

At the heart of the story are her brother Hubert, his best friend Richard, and a long summer month that they spend at Temple Alice. Aroon, then in her late teens, has been denied a "season" in London—the traditional presentation of a marriageable daughter to the elite ranks of society in a series of lavish debutante parties—because the family can no longer afford such luxuries after her father loses a leg during the Great War. Aroon's innocence prevents her from seeing that she is merely a convenient camouflage for the two young men's attraction for each other. In her imagination, she is as good as engaged to Richard. As tragedy strikes, and the family finances settle into further indebtedness, Aroon's father has a stroke, and she is left with no ally in a world dominated by her heartless mother. Through Aroon's continued recollections, the reader comes to understand perfectly the choices she has made in the opening chapter of the story.

Molly KEANE draws on her personal knowledge of the Anglo-Irish hunting set in this novel, the first she published under her own name. Born into an old English family on a fine Irish estate, she lived the life she creates for Aroon. Literature was so alien to the world she lived in that she published her first novels under the pseudonym M. J. Farrell; in her story, the only punishment of a child occurs when a boy is caught reading a book of poetry on a fine day for riding. Although Keane's story does not focus on the political, social, or religious differences between the English and the Irish, her satire on the code of behavior to which the English gentry subscribed helps to explain the abyss between the two cultures while it also illuminates the depth of the hostility between them.

BIBLIOGRAPHY

Adams, Alice. "Coming Apart at the Seams: *Good Behaviour* as an AntiComedy of Manners," *Journal of Irish Literature* 20 (September 1991): 27–35.

Lynch, Rachel Jane. "Molly Keane's Comedies of Anglo-Irish Manners." In *The Comic Tradition in Irish Women Writers.* Edited by Theresa O'Connor. Tallahassee: Florida University Press, 1996, 73–98.

GOODBYE TO BERLIN CHRISTOPHER ISHERWOOD (1939)

This book, together with *The Last of Mr. Norris* and *Sally Bowles* (collectively referred to as "the Berlin stories"), provided the source of the play *I Am a Camera,* by John van Druten (also made into a film), and of the popular Broadway musical *Cabaret* and the award-winning film based that musical. ISHERWOOD'S literary reputation rests primarily on these works, which constitute some of the most significant examples of 20th-century political fiction.

Goodbye to Berlin is actually a collection of short stories; however, taken as a whole they create a coherent picture of the disastrous last days of the Weimar Republic in the late 1920s and early 1930s. Rampant inflation and the effects of the worldwide GREAT DEPRESSION have destabilized the nation's economy and opened the door to political and social upheaval. Isherwood intended to write an epic novel about Germany but never got beyond this collection of stories. His famous opening sentence to the novel (beginning "I am a camera . . .") suggests both this larger project that remains to be *developed* and also the nonjudgmental perspective of objectivity that a camera lens brings to bear on the scenes it captures. Isherwood creates an alter-ego in the stories, Herr Issyvoo, who comes into contact with various other characters, allowing him to comment on the lives of entire categories of human beings who will soon become superfluous in the eyes of the intolerant new system already rising to power.

Isherwood drew on his personal experience in Germany during the 1930s as Democratic National Socialism became entrenched in political power and as Adolf Hitler's ambitions, and the threat he posed to European and world peace, became apparent. Berlin was a cosmopolitan city with a thriving art community and one of the earliest activist movements in defense of homosexuality. There, in the nightclubs in particular, but also among the German Jews of various classes, a culture at odds with Nazi totalitarian rule was on display. Isherwood uses his story to explore the extremes of license and discipline, freedom and restraint, as a disorderly system gives way to stringent controls.

BIBLIOGRAPHY

Schwerdt, Lisa M. *Isherwood's Fiction: The Self and Technique.* New York: St. Martin's Press, 1989.

Wilde, Alan. *Christopher Isherwood.* Twayne's English Authors, 173. New York: Twayne Publishers, 1971.

GOOD SOLDIER, THE FORD MADOX FORD (1915)

The story of a disillusionment with respect to a misunderstood marriage, this novel of psychological realism is cast in the form of the recollections—with the full force of hindsight—of John Dowell, a wealthy American who has lost his wife, Florence, and his best friend, the wealthy Englishman Edward Ashburnham; John has only recently learned from Leonora Ashburnham that both deaths were suicides. Dowell has purchased the late Edward's estate in England and is caring for Nancy, the emotionally crippled ward Edward has left behind; Edward's widow Leonora has remarried.

Dowell begins his narrative after these events have transpired and he has arrived at the Ashburnham estate. He is has been bereaved long enough to recover equanimity, but he has only just discovered the truth about Florence and Edward: they had been carrying on an affair for nine years, and many of Florence's travels—ostensibly to improve her health—were disguises for assignations between the lovers. Dowell reflects on the origin and development of the association between the two couples, which he had thought to be a perfectly ideal friendship among four like-minded people of shared values.

The Dowells and the Ashburnhams had met at the German spa of Nauheim. Florence and John were "trapped" on the Continent: Florence had a heart condition (a metaphor for her weak capacity to love her husband), and after crossing to Europe on an ocean liner for their honeymoon, doctors had declared her too weak to make the journey back to the United States. The Dowells are wealthy and at leisure: They can live anywhere they want, and so they enter into a routine of traveling to various resort locations. When they meet the Ashburnhams, John feels that four people have never been so near to being of one mind; ironically, he is the only one clueless as to what is on the minds of the other members of the group. Leonora Ashburnham is experienced in the ways of extramarital affairs because of her husband's repeated infidelities, and so she has no delusions about her sham of a marriage. Edward's profligacy has put his fortune in jeopardy, and Leonora has demanded to manage the family finances and that Edward give up his flings. Since her Catholic upbringing has left Leonora with a mild distaste for human sexuality, this arrangement suits them for a time. But they are neither as wealthy nor as devoted as they appear to be.

But the real shock to Dowell is the discovery of the extent of his wife's deceit. Their marriage had never been consummated because of her alleged heart condition; Dowell believed her to be a virgin too fragile to enter into the full expression of adult passion. In fact, she had had a series of affairs before her marriage; her appetite for sex was healthy; but she didn't find her husband sexually interesting. She seduces Edward in spite of Leonora's vigilance, and for her part, Leonora is glad that Edward has found a paramour who is not after his money nor likely to cause a scandal. The affair also gives her considerable power, since Florence fears what would happen should John ever discover her perfidiousness as a wife. Leonora is perfectly positioned to make this information known to John, and so the affair remains under her partial control.

This perfect friendship ends when Florence dies at Nauheim, clutching a bottle of medicine John believes to be her heart pills. The circumstances of her death, however, represent a case of overdetermination: One of her former lovers shows up at the spa, leaving her in greater fear that her husband will discover her secrets, but she also realizes that Edward has fallen in love with his ward, Nancy. Leonora has a hand in bringing Edward's life and Nancy's sanity to a crisis—she surrenders to spitefulness and manipulation—and then remarries a man not unlike Edward in his infidelity to his wife. John Dowell purchases Edward's home and settles in England, where he cares for the unbalanced Nancy—he, too, has reestablished the pattern of his life, serving as a caregiver to a disabled woman. His one consolation is the knowledge that Nancy's illness is not a lie.

Ford Madox FORD creates a memorable narrative voice in the character of the decent but perhaps somewhat repressed John Dowell, allowing his narration to slide into unreliability. Because John does not know the depths of his own mind and the outer reaches of his own personality, he cannot present a completely accurate, thorough, and orderly account of events. Readers will often infer the truth before John is able to figure it out. His decency cannot always disguise the anger at the bottom of his feelings about his former wife and friend. Becoming acquainted with him, readers also gain experience in seeing the larger story behind the surface meanings of a narration. *The Good Soldier* is written in a lucid and accessible style, but it plumbs the murky depths of the human heart.

BIBLIOGRAPHY

Cassell, Richard. A. *Ford Madox Ford: A Study of His Novels.* Baltimore: The Johns Hopkins University Press, 1961.

Lid, R. W. *Ford Madox Ford: The Essence of His Art.* Berkeley: University of California Press, 1964.

Stang, Sondra J. *Ford Madox Ford.* New York: Frederick Ungar, 1977.

GORDIMER, NADINE (1923–)

Winner of the NOBEL PRIZE in literature in 1991, Nadine Gordimer was born on November 20, 1923, in Springs, Transvaal, South Africa. She was reared in middle-class financial security and educated in private schools and tutored at home. She attended the University of Witwatersrand for a year when she was 21. She was married for the first time in 1949, bearing one child before the marriage ended; she remarried in 1954 and had a second child from that marriage.

Nadine Gordimer became a reader and writer while she was still young, winning her first writing prize when she was 14 and publishing her first short story, "Come Again Tomorrow," when she was 15. In her early 20s, she was made aware of the harsh political realities of South Africa's system of institutionalized segregation, apartheid, and her eyes were further opened while she was in college. There, she became acquainted with an Afrikaans poet who had escaped the separationist ideology of his background. Gordimer had already begun writing, and under his influence she turned her considerable talents to the conditions of social injustice that prevailed in her homeland and the effects of apartheid on both blacks and whites.

Having already published two collections of short fiction, in 1953 Gordimer produced her first novel, an autobiographical story, *The Lying Days.* The protagonist, Helen Shaw, must struggle against the oppressive conventionality of her own home and the idealistic passions of her first love, a man who is devoting his life to eradicating the injustices of apartheid. Her fifth novel, *A Guest of Honor* (1970), won the JAMES TAIT BLACK MEMORIAL PRIZE; it tells the story of an imaginary African nation as it throws off British COLONIALISM and establishes an independent government. *The CONSERVATIONIST,* published in 1974, shared the BOOKER PRIZE with Ruth Prawer JHABVALA's *HEAT AND DUST;* it is admired for its subtle portrayal of racist attitudes, assumptions, and motivations on the part of a white South African urbanite as he tends to his hobby farm. *JULY'S PEOPLE,* published in 1981, describes in post-apartheid future. Gordimer had won numerous international literary awards and had published 10 novels by the time she was awarded the Nobel Prize in 1991.

Gordimer's novels have appeared at four- to five-year intervals. She has also published a dozen collections of short fiction, nine books of nonfiction (some coauthored), and several teleplays. She and her husband have traveled widely. She has lectured at several American universities and received honorary doctorates from Harvard and Yale Universities. In spite of her opposition to white minority rule, she made her home in Johannesburg, South Africa, and continues to live in her homeland and bring it to life through her writing.

BIBLIOGRAPHY

Bazin, Nancy Topping, and Marilyn Dallman Seymour, eds. *Conversations with Nadine Gordimer.* Jackson: University Press of Mississippi, 1990.

Head, Dominic. *Nadine Gordimer.* Cambridge: Cambridge University Press, 1994.

Heywood, Christopher. *Nadine Gordimer.* Windsor, U.K.: Profile Books, 1983.

Smith, Roland, ed. *Critical Essays on Nadine Gordimer.* Boston: G. K. Hall, 1990.

Wagner, Kathrin. *Rereading Nadine Gordimer.* Bloomington: University Press, 1994.

GORMENGHAST NOVELS, THE MERVYN PEAKE (1946–1959)

The three novels in this FANTASY series include *Titus Groan* (1946), *Gormenghast* (1950), and *Titus Alone* (1959). They were composed in the wake of WORLD WAR II as a form of escapist literature that appealed to a writer who had grown too familiar with the reality of the war. The novel became a cult hit of the 1960s.

In the opening novel of the series, Titus Groan is born in the vast recesses of Gormenghast Castle, the heir to old Lord Sepulchrave. Dr. Prunesquallor delivers Countess Gertrude of her baby; at the same time, another child, young Steerpike, goes to work as an apprentice in the kitchens of Gormenghast under the iron rule of the cook Swelter. Steerpike's ambition is at first simple: He wants to escape from the control of Swelter. It soon grows, however, as he gains some small victories and develops a taste for power. Although Titus Groan is ostensibly the hero of the series, in the first volume he necessarily plays a minor role—he is only one year old at the end of the novel, when he is proclaimed the 75th Earl of Groan upon his father's death.

Since its protagonist is an infant and cannot contribute much to the plot nor develop much as a character, the author turns his imagination to the context into which Titus has been born. Gormenghast Castle is a realm complete unto itself, cut off from the rest of the world and uninterested in it. The residents of the castle hold their appointed positions in a fossilized and labyrinthine hierarchy, and all the activities of life are dictated by "the Ritual," a code of conduct so arcane that the reigning earl has a courtier with the exclusive duty of telling him what to do and when and how it do it—no need to ask "why" if the activity is ordained in the Ritual. Steerpike devises a plan for escaping from the kitchen that winds up burning down the library, killing the master of the Ritual, and enabling Steerpike to advance himself to a position from which his manipulations of the castle's occupants will bring him even greater advantages and give freer rein to his cruelties.

Much of the second volume, *Gormenghast,* is a satirical treatment of education and romantic entanglements. Six years have passed since the end of volume one, and Titus's life has been a miserable round of meaningless observation of the Ritual under the stern dictates of Barquentine, who had succeeded to the mastership of the Ritual upon his father's death. As Titus enters his formal schooling, he begins to discover his autonomy and his capacity for rebellion. If Steerpike is a creature of fire, Titus is a figure of water, and water will overmaster fire if there is enough of it. By the time that a flood separates the towers and pinnacles of Gormenghast into a series of islands, there is enough water to undo Steerpike, and Titus has a climactic confrontation with his nemesis. At the end of the novel, Titus is a young man ready to leave his

ancestral home behind in order to explore the larger world beyond it.

In the third volume, fantasy segues into SCIENCE FICTION. Titus finds himself in a city where the residents, if they know of Gormenghast, think it is a mythic place and cast doubt on his stories about it, thereby also casting doubt on his sanity. In a series of adventures and misadventures, he once again must confront authority (he had previously known no higher authority than himself—and the Ritual—at Gormenghast); additionally, he discovers love and acquires self-doubt. In the city, he meets mad scientists and Holocaust survivors, and he is followed (as are others) by automatic spying devices. He spends time in jail and falls into the clutches of a more powerful enemy than Steerpike, the devious Cheeta. His mother had scornfully predicted, when he left home, that he would be forced to return; instead, Titus discovers that he does not need the sanctuary of Gormenghast, but only the knowledge that it—and therefore his entire history—really does exist. After his experiences in and under the city and along the road, he arrives in the familiar vicinity of Gormenghast and turns back, reassured, to continue his journey. The series ends without a firm sense of closure, but the author apparently had intended to add additional material to the story until ill health prevented him from doing so.

Although *The Gormenghast Trilogy* is filled with grotesque exaggerations and draws on some Gothic elements, it differs from the classic fantasy fiction of J. R. R. TOLKIEN in its interest in the realistic exploration of psychological states. Titus Groan's medieval context matches that of fantasy, but his challenges are those that anyone must face in learning to cope with life's restrictions and its freedoms. Like a BILDUNGSROMAN, it follows a young man's coming of age, and it draws on certain ARCHETYPES of mythic storytelling. But it makes a more intimate connection to the interior lives of its many eccentric characters—and to the vast structure of the castle itself, which forms virtually a separate character in the first two volumes—than fantasy stories necessarily do, creating uniquely particular portraits of the residents of an original and innovative imaginary world.

BIBLIOGRAPHY

Batchelor, John. *Mervyn Peake: A Biographical and Critical Exploration.* London: Duckworth, 1974.

Le Cam, Pierre-Yves. "*Gormenghast*: A Censored Fairy Tale," *Peake Studies* 5, no. 2 (Spring 1997): 23–41.

Metzger, Arthur. *A Guide to the Gormenghast Trilogy.* Baltimore: T-K Graphics, 1976.

GOUDGE, ELIZABETH (1900–1984)

A writer and an artist, Elizabeth Goudge was born at Wells in Somerset, the only child of a theologian father and a mother from Guernsey in the Channel Islands. When her father became Regius Professor of Divinity at Oxford, the family moved there, spending summers on Guernsey Island. Goudge eventually drew on these locations for the fiction she began publishing in 1934, beginning with *Island Magic.* Her fiction generally includes carefully researched historical materials, beautiful, evocative landscapes, and positive depictions of Christianity, and it sometimes includes elements of FANTASY, romance, or adventure fiction mixed in with the realism of her characters and settings. Her most important novels include *City of Bells* (1936), about a cathedral town patterned on Wells; *Towers in the Mist* (1938), drawn from the Elizabethan period of Oxford's history; *GREEN DOLPHIN STREET,* a complex romantic triangle; and *The Child from the Sea* (1970), about the secret wife of King Charles II. Goudge also wrote charming children's literature, including *Linnets and Valerians* (1964), about the adventures of several siblings adjusting to village life, and *The Little White Horse* (1947), about an orphaned girl's coming-of-age at Moonacre Manor. She published short fiction, devotional literature, and a volume of autobiography as well.

BIBLIOGRAPHY

Goudge, Elizabeth. *The Joy of the Snow.* New York: Coward, McCann & Geoghegan, 1974.

Gower, Sylvia. *The World of Elizabeth Goudge.* West Mersea, Colchester: Periwinkle Press, 2001.

Mickenberg, Julia. "Misplaced: The Fantasies and Fortunes of Elizabeth Goudge." In *Forgotten Authors.* Edited by Lynne Vallone. Baltimore: Johns Hopkins University Press, 1997.

GRAVES, ROBERT (1895–1985)

A poet who wrote one of the 20th century's most absorbing autobiographies in *Goodbye to All That* (1929), and who is best remembered now for his historical novel *I, CLAUDIUS* (1934), Robert Graves produced an astonishing amount and variety of literature during his life: more than 60 volumes of poetry, 15 novels, 35 nonfiction works, and several volumes of children's literature, short fiction, translations from several languages, and edited anthologies. He was born in Wimbledon on July 24, 1895; his father was an amateur poet and educator, and his mother was German. He was a scholarly and sensitive child tormented by athletic boys at school, but when WORLD WAR I began, the 19-year-old Graves enlisted in the Royal Welsh Fusiliers. He fought under the worst conditions of the war and was severely wounded and shell-shocked; *Goodbye to All That* provides one of the best records of the fighting man's experience of trench warfare ever written.

After the war, Graves married a feminist painter and became acquainted with the leading literary and intellectual figures of his day, including Virginia WOOLF, John GALSWORTHY, H. G. WELLS, and especially T. E. Lawrence. After learning of Lawrence's experience among the Arabs, Graves wrote the biographical account *Lawrence and the Arabs* (1927), later made into a FILM ADAPTATION. In 1929, Graves left his wife to live with Laura Riding, an American poet. They settled on the Mediterranean island of Majorca and remained together for 10 years. After Riding left him, Graves married again, remaining on Majorca the rest of his life. In the 1930s, he wrote his historical novels and began to develop his theories about prehistoric worship of the "triple goddess" in the Mediterranean, which he published in 1948 in his critical work *The White Goddess.* His interest in MYTHOLOGY dominated his writing during the rest of his career. Robert Graves died on December 7, 1985, on Majorca.

BIBLIOGRAPHY

Graves, Richard Perceval. *Robert Graves: The Assault Heroic, 1895–1926.* London: Weidenfeld & Nicolson, 1986.

Seymour-Smith, Martin. *Robert Graves: His Life and Work.* New York: Holt, Rinehart & Winston, 1983.

Seymour, Miranda. *Robert Graves: Life on the Edge.* New York: Henry Holt & Co., 1995.

GRAY, ALASDAIR (1934–) Born to a working-class family in Glasgow on December 28, 1934, Alasdair Gray grew up during a period when Scotland's industrial economy was folding and Glasgow increasingly resembled American "rust belt" cities that had once been economic powerhouses. Problems that resulted from this decline, such as urban decay, unemployment, and disaffected youths, appear in Gray's fictional wasteland settings.

Alasdair Gray lived at home through his middle 20s, receiving a working-class education in state-supported grammar schools and secondary schools; he also attended the Glasgow School of Art, working as a teacher and a painter after graduation. He was already writing fiction in his late teens, and in adulthood he supplemented his income by writing teleplays and radio plays. While he was still relatively unknown in the literary and artistic worlds, he became the subject of a BBC documentary and found his notoriety greatly expanded as a result. He turned this experience into the 1968 teleplay *The Fall of Kevin Walker* and later adapted this work into a novel.

Gray authored eight teleplays, three stage plays, and six radio plays before publishing his first novel, *Lanark: A Life in Four Books* (1981). This story featured an apocalyptic setting and gained the admiration of Anthony BURGESS, one of the century's most important British writers and critics. His second novel, *1982 Janine,* appeared in 1984; it is a study in fiction of pornography. These first two works, along with a collection of short fiction published in 1983, *Unlikely Stories, Mostly,* established Gray as a skilled writer of contemporary SATIRE, an imaginative fictionist, and an insightful critic of society and politics. His next three novels, however, received increasingly cooler reviews from critics: *The Fall of Kevin Walker: A Fable of the Sixties* (1985), *McGrotty and Ludmilla; Or, The Harbinger Report: A Romance of the Eighties* (1989), and *Something Leather* (1990). This last novel, with its themes of sadomasochism and fetishism, was roundly condemned.

Gray's critical reputation revived with the publication of *POOR THINGS* in 1992. This novel won the WHITBREAD Book of the Year Award and received praise for its postmodern innovations: The novel features a reinvention of the Frankenstein story and a thorough examination of FEMINISM, enclosing these elements within a story that is itself a parody of a Victorian novel. Gray published a second collection of short fiction, *Ten Tales, Tall and True,* in 1993, and another novel, *A History Maker* in 1994. He has continued to write stage plays, radio plays, and teleplays, and he has published a collection of poetry, an autobiography, two edited collections of prefaces, and a political treatise supporting Scottish self-rule. In 1996, he published *Mavis Belfrage: A Romantic Novel with Five Shorter Tales.*

BIBLIOGRAPHY

Bernstein, Stephen. *Alasdair Gray.* Lewisburg, Pa.: Bucknell University Press, 1999.

O'Brien, John, and Mark Axelrod, eds. *The Review of Contemporary Fiction* 15.2 (Summer 1995). Special Issue on Alasdair Gray and Stanley Elkin.

Toremans, Tom. "An Interview with Alasdair Gray and James Kelman," *Contemporary Literature* 44, no. 4 (2003): 565–86.

GREAT DEPRESSION (THE SLUMP) (1929–1939) The economic downturn that affected all the industrialized nations of the Western world began in the United States and spread from there to other countries that were dependent on the health of the American economy. The conditions of economic depression actually began six months before "Black Tuesday" occurred on October 29, 1929, when 16 million shares of stock were traded and prices plummeted. The American crisis resulted from a combination of factors that included excessive speculative trading of stocks "on margin" (buying essentially on credit with the expectation of paying the initial cost through monies derived from the increased value of the stock) and inflated confidence in the economic boom of the "Roaring Twenties."

In the post–WORLD WAR I financial world, the United States became a dominant power for the first time in its history. Most European countries were in debt to the United States to some degree, and the countries most in debt were Britain and Germany. As the American economy collapsed and early efforts to stimulate it failed, conditions in these two countries worsened, disastrously so in Germany. In England, the economic events of this period are frequently referred to as "the slump." Anthony POWELL's ROMAN-FLEUVE *A DANCE TO THE MUSIC OF TIME* includes characters affected by the slump, especially in *The ACCEPTANCE WORLD, AT LADY MOLLY'S,* and *CASANOVA'S CHINESE RESTAURANT.*

BIBLIOGRAPHY

Garraty, John Arthur. *The Great Depression: An Inquiry into the Causes, Course, and Consequences of the Worldwide Depression of the Nineteen Thirties, As Seen By Contemporaries and in the Light of History.* San Diego: Harcourt Brace Jovanovich, 1986.

Rothermund, Dietmar. *The Global Impact of the Great Depression, 1929–1939.* London: Routledge, 1996.

GREEN, HENRY (1905–1973)

Born Henry Vincent Yorke on October 29, 1905, Henry Green was a member of a wealthy family that owned factories and had extensive business interests in Birmingham, one of England's industrial centers. He was educated at Eton, England's leading PUBLIC SCHOOL, and later wrote about the experience in short works published in literary journals. He matriculated at Oxford, where his teachers included C. S. LEWIS. Green's first novel, *Blindness,* appeared in 1926; it featured an unflinching self-portrait of the author, who was then only beginning his college studies. Green left Oxford after his second year and went to work in the factories of Birmingham, laboring under a sense of the social inequity that had handed him a silver spoon from birth. His experiences as a member of the working CLASS provided him with a wider range of character types and sharpened his ear for distinctive conversational voices; his novels of quietly comic realism were noted for their sympathetic portrayal of ordinary people without condescension or snobbery. Eventually, he began managing his family's interests and supervising the factories, but he also continued writing novels. *LIVING* appeared in 1929, and *PARTY GOING* in 1939. In the intervening decade, Green had married, begun a family, and continued with both business and literary careers. On the strength of his early novels, Green was compared with George ORWELL and admired by such contemporaries as Evelyn WAUGH, his editor Edward Garnett, and the poet W. H. Auden.

With the outbreak of WORLD WAR II, Green entered the Auxiliary Fire Service, later publishing short works about his experiences putting out fires caused by the German bombing campaign, the blitzkrieg. In 1940, he published a work combining autobiography and criticism, *Pack My Bag,* in which he discussed his theory of the novel, emphasizing the importance of dialogue. During the war, he wrote *Caught* (1943); *LOVING* (1945), frequently identified as his best novel; and *Back* (1946). His three remaining novels increasingly depended on conversations among characters: *Concluding* (1948), *Nothing* (1950), and *Doting* (1952). These novels present readers with greater challenges, since both the action and the ethical structure—the larger picture of the characters' lives—must be inferred from the conversations they carry on.

Green focused on criticism and theory for the rest of the 1950s, retiring in 1958. He was plagued by increasing deafness and became somewhat reclusive. His business interests had kept him separated from participating in literary circles during his writing years, and he continued this isolation. He died on December 13, 1973, leaving behind only a few unfinished works. Although he is perhaps best known now by literary specialists and professional writers, his early novels in particular make accessible and enjoyable reading; they capture the nuances of ordinary English life through fully realized settings and character portraits that are both sympathetic and honest.

BIBLIOGRAPHY

Odom, Keith C. *Henry Green.* Twayne's English Authors Series, 235. Boston: Twayne, 1978.

Ryf, Robert. *Henry Green.* New York: Columbia University Press, 1967.

Treglown, Jeremy. *Romancing: The Life and Work of Henry Green.* New York: Random House, 2001.

GREEN DOLPHIN STREET ELIZABETH GOUDGE (1944)

This novel for young adult readers combines elements of romance, adventure, and FANTASY fiction. The third-person narrator relates the events in the lives of two sisters, Marianne and Marguerite le Patourel, and the boy they grow up with,

Will Ozanne, following them from youth to old age through the complex changes in their relationships and in their inner lives.

The initial setting is in the Channel Islands, where the children live a happy life, each developing according to his or her nature: Marianne ambitious and eager for wealth, Will easy-going and affable, and Marguerite spiritually sensitive and passive. As they reach their young adulthood, Marianne persuades Will to enter the navy; his name is ironic, because he lacks the will to resist her bossy plans for him. He has actually grown to love Marguerite, but Marianne sees him as a conduit by which she can fulfill her ambitions; to her, love is a secondary consideration. When Will's easygoing nature gets him entrapped in a foreign port, clapped in irons, and exiled to New Zealand, both sisters are bereft of their hopes. Will's letters to Marguerite never reach her, and when he has made a home ready to receive a bride, he makes a tragic mistake. Not one to make a bad situation worse, he decides to live with his mistake, but the consequences are painful for all three of the characters.

Only the creation of new life can supply what is missing in each character and complete the lives that have always been only parts of a single whole. With the arrival of baby Veronique Ozanne, new strength, new tenderness, and new faith grow up to complete the personalities of Will, Marguerite, and Marianne. The presence of the child works a magic that unites the souls even of those far separated in space until finally they are brought together in person again. When the secret of Will's tragic mistake becomes known, the three old friends must overcome the effects of this knowledge on the accommodations they have made to life.

Green Dolphin Street was an international best seller and was adapted as a film in 1947. It displays the characteristic features of Elizabeth Goudge's fiction, including lush landscapes described with poetic lyricism, psychological realism, a dash of the supernatural, and an affirmation of the value of Christianity to a life well lived.

BIBLIOGRAPHY

Marsden, Modonna. "Gentle Truths for the Gentle Readers: The Fiction of Elizabeth Goudge." In *Images of Women in Fiction: Feminist Perspectives.* Edited by Susan Koppelman Cornillon. Bowling Green, Ohio: Bowling Green University Popular Press, 1972, 68–78.

Mickenberg, Julia. "Misplaced: The Fantasies and Fortunes of Elizabeth Goudge." In *Forgotten Authors.* Edited by Lynne Vallone. Baltimore: Johns Hopkins University Press, 1997.

GREENE, GRAHAM (1904–1991) Greene was born on October 2, 1904, in Berkhamsted, England, and died in Vevey, Switzerland, on April 3, 1991. He was the son of Charles Henry Greene, headmaster of Berkhamsted School. Greene attended his father's school, as well as Balliol College, receiving his B.A. with a second in history. He was a writer and subeditor for the *London Times* (1926–30), served as editor and film reviewer for the short-lived *Night & Day* (1937), was film reviewer for the *Spectator* (1935–40), and was assigned to the Foreign Office in Sierra Leone (1941–43) and in London (1944). He directed two publishing firms, Eyre and Spottiswoode Ltd. (1944–48), and Bodley Head Publishers (1958–68). During the 1950s, he was Indochina correspondent for *Paris-Match,* the *Sunday Times,* and *Le Figaro.* The experiences of his work life were powerfully integrated into his creative process; an example would be his witnessing of the persecution of the church in Mexico and the subsequent novel, *The POWER AND THE GLORY.*

Greene wrote prolifically—short stories, novellas, "entertainments" (thrillers), serious novels with political and religious themes, book reviews, film reviews, poetry, radio plays, stage plays, autobiography, biography, memoir, travel pieces, screenplays, and in the 1950s, even juvenile literature. He was a contributor to the great publications of his era on both sides of the Atlantic: *Esquire, Commonweal, Spectator, New Statesman, London Mercury, New Republic,* and others. Greene also edited the work of other serious writers, including H. H. Munro (Saki) and Ford Madox FORD.

Greene is always reporting on the external world of his place and time together with the internal terrain that might be called the psyche of the 20th century. He operates on and in borderlands and frontiers—geographically and otherwise; critics say he has created a peculiar terrain of his own called "Greeneland." His themes are consistent throughout the novels—intrigue and espionage, betrayal, responsibility, corruption, sin detection, pursuit. Although his first two novels did not attract attention, his third, *The Man Within* (1929), established him as a strong new voice. When he turned his hand to the thriller with *Stamboul Express* (1932; published in the United States as *Orient Express*), he had a winner; the book was chosen by the English Book Society, and Greene was launched. Other notable thrillers include *A Gun for Sale* (1936; published in the United States as *This Gun for Hire*) and *The Confidential Agent* (1939). Greene injects thriller components such as espionage, intrigue, and detection into his religious novels and the serious novels not focused on Catholicism, such as *The QUIET AMERICAN* (1955). In 1938, he published *Brighton Rock,* followed by what many critics call his Catholic trilogy, *The Power and the Glory* (1940; published in the United States as *The Labyrinthine Ways*), *The HEART OF THE MATTER* (1948), and *The END OF THE AFFAIR* (1951); these novels have generated the most critical debate. However, Greene saw himself as far more a political novelist than anything else. Greene is known in his pursuit novels for making the criminal or corrupted character the focus and the detective secondary. He addresses the territory between the extremes of saint and sinner, creates exotic but seedy settings, explores what he calls "the divided mind, the uneasy conscience, and the sense of personal failure," and renders a fiction ideal for cinematic adaptation. Of all the 20th-century British fictionists, he is likely the one with the strongest tie to film, perhaps because of his career as a film critic. Geographically his early novels, especially the entertainments, focus on England, his Catholic novels extend his range to West Africa and Mexico, and then his travels and his creative output focus on the Far East, Cuba, Russia, Congo, Brazil, Argentina, and other locations around the world. Philip Stratford, in his introduction to *The Portable Graham Greene,* writes that Greene's great contribution to 20th-century letters is the development and exploration of internal travel, surveying "the unmapped region that lies between the risk of betrayal and the risk of love."

—*Viki Craig*

BIBLIOGRAPHY

De Vitis, A. A. *Graham Greene.* Twayne's English Authors, 3. Rev. ed. Boston: Twayne Publishers, 1986.

Hazzard, Shirley. *Greene on Capri.* New York: Farrar, Straus & Giroux, 2000.

Miller, R. H. *Understanding Graham Greene.* Understanding Contemporary British Literature Series. Columbia: University of South Carolina Press, 1990.

Shelden, Michael. *Graham Greene: The Man Within.* London: Heinemann, 1994.

Sherry, Norman. *The Life of Graham Greene: Volume 1, 1904–1939.* London: Jonathon Cape, Ltd, 1989.

———. *The Life of Graham Greene: Volume II, 1939–1955.* New York: Viking Penguin, 1995.

GREENGAGE SUMMER, THE RUMER GODDEN (1958)

An autobiographical novel, this BILDUNGSROMAN tells the story of a summer vacation in France that is by turns frightening and delightful. The five children of the Grey family, ranging in age from about 16 to four, have become a handful for their mother while their father, a naturalist, is away on another of his long expeditions. Finally, at her wits' end, Mrs. Grey declares she will take her children to the battlefields of France; there, she expects that the sight of so many graves will give them a proper respect for propriety. But on the way to France, Mrs. Grey becomes gravely ill, and by the time the six travelers reach the Hotel des Oeillets—the inn on the Marne where they have reserved accommodations—she must be hospitalized. Mademoiselle Zizi, the owner of Les Oeillets, and Madame Corbet, the manager, at first refuse to take the five unsupervised children. But Mrs. Grey appeals to Mr. Eliot, the only other English citizen at the inn, and he prevails on Mademoiselle Zizi to accept the children and help their mother. While Mrs. Grey spends several precarious weeks at the hospital, the children become wards of Mr. Eliot.

The five children consist of four girls and a boy: The eldest, Joss, is just beginning to blossom into the beauty of young womanhood, and her transformation arouses the envy of 14-year-old Cecil (Cecilia), who serves as the story's narrator and the author's alter ego. Then comes practical Hester, still mostly a child, and after her "the Littles": Will, called Willmouse, and

Vicky, only recently out of her toddler years and filled with childhood's irresistible charm. During their first week at Les Oeillets, Joss remains in bed, exhausted by the ordeal of getting her mother and siblings over the English Channel and across France. Cecil becomes the family translator, her schoolgirl French quickly expanding to the demands of her situation. The children are fed with the kitchen staff and confined to the plum orchard while the other guests are dining and touring the inn's attractions. They play with joyful abandon and eat juicy plums until they're stuffed; when Joss recovers, however, she is shocked that the Greys are being treated essentially as servants rather than guests. With a maturity beyond her years, she restores the family to its rightful place, and in doing so earns the admiration of Mr. Eliot and the enmity of Mademoiselle Zizi, who is in love with the mysterious Englishman.

As the hot summer days slowly unwind, tensions in the inn mount as Mr. Eliot's attentions to Joss reveal a romantic attraction, arousing Mademoiselle Zizi's intense jealousy. Cecil becomes the sole eyewitness to key episodes in the family connection to Mr. Eliot, and all the children are forced to grow up in unexpected ways and to shed their English naiveté as it comes into contact with French sophistication. The kitchen boy, Paul, becomes their ally and their antagonist, and they learn about the adult rituals of drinking, smoking, and flirting by observing the ever-fascinating Eliot and Zizi. When the police begin to suspect Eliot of being a notorious bank robber, the children become the unwitting helpers of his escape; their dependence on him is so complete and their emotional bond with him is so strong that they are oblivious to their moral duties.

An absorbing reading experience, *The Greengage Summer* captures the short period when children leave childhood behind and begin to understand the secrets of adulthood. The novel presents a happy past without indulging in nostalgic sentimentality, making the reader aware of the cost of growing up and of the inevitability of doing so. Teenage girls will most likely find a character to identify with in the Grey family; women young and old will be reminded of the anxieties and the enjoyments that accompany the acquisition of an adult identity.

BIBLIOGRAPHY
Rosenthal, Lynne Meryl. *Rumer Godden Revisited.* Twayne's English Authors, 519. New York: Twayne Publishers, 1996.

GREEN MANSIONS W. H. HUDSON (1904)

Exiled for an attempt to overthrow the unjust Venezuelan government, Abel chooses to satisfy a childhood dream: to explore the rain forests of South America. He hopes that a book about his adventures will bring him fame and fortune. As he travels, Abel encounters natives wearing elaborate necklaces of pure gold, and he is seized with gold fever. As he presses forward in this materialist quest, he is welcomed at native villages along his way, where people he regards as savages give him food and shelter, even though they could kill him with impunity. Finding no gold, he decides to become a long-term guest in a native village on the savanna. He hunts when the mood strikes him; he sleeps when he desires. When Abel decides to venture from the domain of the tribe, the savanna, and explore the neighboring forest, he sees a beauty there that is almost otherworldly, the green mansions of the title. The tribesmen are deeply vexed by his exploration: Something dangerous exists in the forest—something worse than fierce tigers or near endless lengths of anacondas. Nonetheless, he decides to reenter the forest.

Abel hears singing in the forest and finds the singer to be a woman of supernatural grace. She is Rima, the bird-girl. Having searched for gold, Abel finds beauty instead, and it begins a change in him that will reorder his place in the green mansions. Back at the village, Abel is warned that the bird-girl is the daughter of the devil and that as long as her voice reigns in the forest, the villagers will not venture forth, not even to hunt. On his next visit to the forest, he comes across a poisonous snake, which he resolves to kill, despite his reverence for the creature's beauty. Unexpectedly, Rima appears and pleads for the snake's protection; it takes refuge with her and coils around her leg in safety. But the snake is not evil; there is a conflict here between two different orientations toward the natural world. Rima is a servant of Good and Beauty, whereas Abel is conflicted. He is able to see beauty, but his desire for riches causes him to keep his eyes toward the ground, hoping to catch sight of a nugget that may reveal the mother-load.

The snake ultimately bites Abel, and Rima disappears. Lost in the forest, he undergoes a fall, from which he will be lifted by Rima, who will enable him to give up the search for gold and plant in him the desire to seek goodness. Abel regains consciousness in the hut of an old man, Nuflo, who claims to be Rima's grandfather. At last, Abel meets Rima in her merely mortal form. She is a plain girl, without the beauty he had previously witnessed in the forest. Later, Abel has the opportunity to talk with Nuflo, who explains that, in honor of Rima, no living being is killed for any reason, not even for food. Her mother is dead, though Rima yearns for her every day. Progressively, Rima begins to show affectionate regard for Abel, but she longs to know the truth about her mother and to find other people like her. She demands to be taken to Rio-lama, her birthplace; during the journey, Nuflo tells his true story: He was part of a violent gang under a curse when they encountered a woman of saintly beauty. Nuflo believed, for the sake of his eternal soul, that he should search for the woman and help her. He found her, saved her life, and took her to a Christian mission, where she later gave birth to Rima and died, giving her child to Nuflo to raise.

Rima was hated by the villagers because she would sing warnings to the animals they hunted. Through superstition and outright lies, the villagers came to believe that Nuflo was the devil and that Rima was his evil daughter. Rima and Abel decide to settle as man and wife in the forest's green mansions, and she goes ahead to prepare their home. When Able and Nuflo make it back, they find that the hut has been burned to the ground; Rima is nowhere to be found. In the village, Abel learns the fate of Rima: A band of hunters happened to see her, and they chased her up a tree. Ultimately, the whole village turned out to kill this enemy. They labored in cutting down trees, leaning them against the tree in which Rima had taken refuge. When the fire was lit, Rima had fallen from her perch into the flames below. After hearing the truth of what happened, Abel can no longer endure the villagers. He quietly escapes to a rival tribe and then leads them to attack Rima's killers, exterminating every villager. He has reverted from civilization to savagery.

Abel collects the burnt remains of Rima in an earthen funerary urn. Thus he lives in the forest and begins a slow sojourn from savagery into madness; he is malnourished, subsisting on insects. The more time he spends in the forest, alone—without the life-sustaining love that keeps us as members of humanity—the more he becomes a madman. Abel finally leaves the forest, regains his sanity, and reaches civilization, where his mission is to mingle Rima's ashes with his own and thereby absolve himself before Eternity.

HUDSON shapes Abel's story as a first-person narrative within a frame story told by an acquaintance of Abel's who reports the man's tale to the larger world. This device allows Hudson to have a dead man narrate his own story with the reader aware of the narrator's demise from the beginning. This knowledge contributes to the story's elegiac quality. Abel undergoes a journey from civilization to paradise to savagery and madness and back to civilization, and Hudson relates this transformative journey in poetically beautiful descriptions of a natural world that, like Rima, is being consumed by flames.

—*Marcus Russell*

BIBLIOGRAPHY

Baker, Carlos. "The Source-Book for Hudson's *Green Mansions*," *Publications of the Modern Language Association of America* 61, no. 1 (1946): 252–57.

Reeve, N. H. "Feathered Women: W. H. Hudson's *Green Mansions*." In *Writing the Environment: Ecocriticism and Literature*. Edited by Richard Kerridge and Neil Sammells. London: Zed, 1998, 134–145.

GUARDIAN **FICTION PRIZE**   Presented by the distinguished English newspaper the *Guardian*, this literary prize carries a monetary award of 10,000 pounds. From 1965 until 1999, the prize was restricted to a work of fiction, but since 1999 the name of the award and the scope of the competition have been changed: The winning book now may be in any field as long as it is a first publication for the author, and the prize has been renamed the *Guardian* First Book Award. The competition is judged by a committee of writers and literary critics under the direction of the *Guardian's* literary editor.

BIBLIOGRAPHY

Book Trust Guide to Literary Prizes. London: Book Trust, published annually.

Todd, Richard. *Consuming Fictions: The Booker Prize and Fiction in Britain Today.* London: Bloomsbury, 1996.

H

HALL, RADCLYFFE (1880–1943)

The author of the classic lesbian text *The WELL OF LONELINESS,* Radclyffe Hall was born on August 12, 1880, at Bournemouth, England. The family owned a large country estate; Hall later drew on her childhood experiences as a tomboy in creating the early life of Stephen Gordon, the heroine of *The Well of Loneliness.* Her father died while she was young, and she received her inheritance when she was 17. Her mother had remarried by then; apparently, the relationship between Hall and her mother and stepfather was an abusive one.

Radclyffe Hall began to write at an early age, and after studying at King's College, in London, she traveled to Germany to continue her education. Between 1905 and 1915, Hall published five books of lyric poems, many of which were set to music. Her first novel, a comedy entitled *The Forge,* appeared in 1924. In the same year, she also published a bolder work, *The Unlit Lamp,* that hints of "sexual inversion," a term then in use to refer to homosexuality; the novel explores the emotional tensions between a mother, her daughter, and the daughter's governess. Hall gained serious critical attention with *Adam's Breed* in 1926, a novel that sympathetically examines the life of a man who earns his living serving others. In 1928, *The Well of Loneliness* was published and became an immediate scandal. It was banned in England in spite of the willingness of leading literary figures such as Virginia WOOLF and E. M. FORSTER to defend it. The awakening of the protagonist to her lesbian identity was considered "unnatural," even though she relinquishes her beloved to a socially acceptable heterosexual marriage.

In her personal life, Hall was herself a lesbian involved in a lifelong relationship with Lady Una Troubridge, who published a biography of Radclyffe Hall in 1961. After the furor over *The Well of Loneliness,* the two lived a quiet country life; Hall produced two more novels in the 1930s, both of which exhibited her deep Christian faith. She also published one short story that revisits the theme of lesbianism, "Miss Ogilvie Finds Herself." On October 7, 1943, Radclyffe Hall died in London of cancer. *The Well of Loneliness* was finally republished in England in 1949.

BIBLIOGRAPHY

Baker, Michael. *Our Three Selves: The Life of Radclyffe Hall.* New York: Morrow, 1985.

Dickson, Lovat. *Radclyffe Hall at the Well of Loneliness: A Sapphic Chronicle.* New York: Scribner, 1975.

Doan, Laura. *Fashioning Sapphism: The Origins of a Modern English Lesbian Culture.* New York: Columbia University Press, 2001.

HANDMAID'S TALE, THE MARGARET ATWOOD (1985)

An example of a DYSTOPIAN NOVEL set in a post-apocalyptic wasteland in the not-too-distant future of the United States, *The Handmaid's Tale* is the story of a world in which fertility has declined drastically and patriarchal institutions have

191

placed women's fertility under state regulation. The ideals of rights and equity enshrined in the Constitution have been replaced by a military dictatorship of men. This new government ostensibly preserves the values of marriage, family, and Christianity; however, some women, including some of the respectable wives of the military men, are infertile. When fertile women are located, they are hauled off to concentration camps for indoctrination into their roles as surrogate child bearers for powerful men with infertile wives. In the camp, the fertile women are abused by the agents of patriarchy—both female and male—and deprived of their individuality and their identities. When this training is complete, they receive designations based on the names of the men they are to provide with off-spring—the protagonist thus receives the name "Offred." Sex is limited to procreative purposes, and all sources of joy, such as dancing and laughing, are allegedly outlawed.

The narrative follows the life of one unfortunate fertile woman who is apprehended, indoctrinated, and handed over to an important man. When she does not immediately conceive, she learns that the plague of infertility is not limited to women: She knows her "master" must be, like his wife and the female servants in his home, sterile. And the larger world is other than she had been taught in the camps: Far from being a paradise of obedience, chastity, and productivity, the powerful men who control the state enjoy the pleasures of speakeasy-type nightclubs, complete with prostitutes who engage in sex merely for the pleasure of the men who purchase their services. But not all men are infertile, and the protagonist is able to find a helper, with the unexpected collusion of the Commander's wife, Serena Joy, and later to attempt a daring escape in the hope of reaching a better world beyond the control of this new totalitarian state. ATWOOD alternates the development of her narrative with passages examining the ways that language contributes to the hegemony of one gender over another, making her text both a work of fiction and a work of theoretical FEMINISM.

This novel was adapted into an effective movie directed by Volker Schlöndorf in 1990, with a screen-play by the noted English dramatist Harold Pinter.

BIBLIOGRAPHY

Atwood, Margaret, and Harold Bloom. *Margaret Atwood's The Handmaid's Tale*. Philadelphia: Chelsea House Publishers, 2001.

Rao, Eleanora. *Strategies for Identity: The Fiction of Margaret Atwood*. New York: P. Lang, 1993.

Wilson, Sharon Rose, and Thomas B. Friedman. *Approaches to Teaching Atwood's* The Handmaid's Tale *and Other Works*. New York: Modern Language Association of America, 1996.

HARRY POTTER SERIES J. K. ROWLING (1997–)

Projected to extend eventually over seven volumes, this enormously popular FANTASY series for young readers includes *Harry Potter and the Sorcerer's Stone* (1997; published in the U.K. as *Harry Potter and the Philosopher's Stone*), *Harry Potter and the Chamber of Secrets* (1999), *Harry Potter and the Prisoner of Azkaban* (1999), *Harry Potter and the Goblet of Fire* (2000), *Harry Potter and the Order of the Phoenix* (2003), and *Harry Potter and the Half-Blood Prince* (2005). The events of each volume correspond to the cycle of a British school year, beginning with the equivalent of approximately an American sixth-grade year. In the first volume, Harry receives an invitation to attend a private school (see PUBLIC SCHOOL), Hogwarts. The conceits that unify the series and set it apart from other examples of the CAMPUS NOVEL include the fact that Hogwarts is a school of magic and that Harry is a born wizard merely needing a bit of training to bring out his natural gifts. On this foundation, ROWLING builds the entire world that is characteristic of fantasy literature, drawing on familiar attributes of magic and sorcery such as cauldrons, broomsticks, magic wands, spells, and potions, but putting them to innovative uses. She harvests numerous creatures and monsters from MYTHOLOGY and folklore to provide challenges, lessons, tests, and traps for Harry and his friends. Rowling's creation of a hidden world lurking behind the facade of reality—just as Diagon Alley, the wizard's shopping district, lies behind a nondescript brick wall—is particularly provocative to an active young imagination.

The story follows the ARCHETYPE of the mythic heroic quest as described by Joseph Campbell: The circumstances of Harry's birth are extraordinary, since he defeats Voldemort while still in his infancy, and he receives a summons to adventure when the invitation to attend Hogwarts arrives. He gains several helpers from among his peers and teachers. He repeatedly travels into an unknown underworld to solve a problem, save a friend, or retrieve an artifact. Harry's return from these adventures serves as a symbolic rebirth; as the series continues, perhaps he will even enter the realm of the dead to acquire the boon that will save the world.

The series achieved its popularity through the recommendations of the children who read it and then urged their friends to read it, too. Without a publicity campaign, the books became cult classics of the playground set. Curious parents also began reading them in an odd reversal of the usual direction of readerly influence. With widespread adult attention, however, came a backlash of criticism, especially from conservative Christian readers who were offended that the stories valorized the instruction of children in magic and sorcery, and who noted that the author provides no model of a benevolent source of divine power in the series, although she definitely represents a recurring evil power (Lord Voldemort, or He-who-must-not-be-named) that seems almost indestructible. Attacks that called for censorship of the books and requests that they be removed from school libraries in turn elicited a keen interest among scholars of literature, education, and popular culture. (The ruckus over *Harry Potter*, in fact, is ironic in the face of the overt criticism of religious authority expressed in the volumes of Phillip PULLMAN's *HIS DARK MATERIALS*, published at the same time as the *Harry Potter* novels and even winning major literary prizes without raising a tempest.)

Literary critics are divided over the merit of the series. Some praise its imaginative development of the fantasy world in which the novel unfolds, which is divided not so much by race and class as by magical ability or the lack thereof. Those with the ability are wizards; those without it, Muggles. But there are also the wizards born of Muggle parentage, providing grounds for discrimination by those whose families have long and unbroken pedigrees as wizards. This treatment places the examination of prejudice in a kind of safe zone, allowing children to examine it and perhaps learn a lesson about it without having their own

hackles raised. But those who express disappointment with the series, including the novelist A. S. BYATT, find that it insufficiently develops genuine moral growth in Harry and his fellow students. Evil is made to be too easily defeated, and Harry frequently triumphs not because of his choices but in spite of them. Flat characters are extremely flat, including Harry's Muggle aunt, uncle, and cousin, and even Lord Voldemort himself.

BIBLIOGRAPHY

Abanes, Richard. *Harry Potter and the Bible: The Menace Behind the Magick.* Camp Hill, Pa.: Horizon Books, 2001.

Anatol, Giselle Liza, ed. *Reading Harry Potter: Critical Essays.* Westport, Conn.: Praeger, 2003.

Granger, John. *The Hidden Key to Harry Potter: Understanding the Meaning, Genius, and Popularity of Joanne Rowling's Harry Potter Novels.* Hadlock, Wash.: Zossima Press, 2002.

Heilman, Elizabeth E., ed. *Harry Potter's World: Multidisciplinary Critical Perspectives.* New York: Routledge, 2003.

Whited, Lana A., ed. *The Ivory Tower and Harry Potter: Perspectives on a Literary Phenomenon.* Columbia: University of Missouri Press, 2002.

HARTLEY, L. P. (1895–1972)

Born Leslie Poles Hartley, the son of an upper-middle-class lawyer and businessman, on December 30, 1895, L. P. Hartley was often compared to Henry JAMES and even to Jane Austen. In his own lifetime, he was recognized as a major novelist, although he is less widely read today than are many of his contemporaries.

Hartley was educated in the British PUBLIC SCHOOL of Harrow and then matriculated at Balliol College in Oxford in 1915. He served briefly as an officer in WORLD WAR I, receiving a discharge for health reasons, and returned to school to complete his degree. His first book—a collection of short fiction—appeared in 1924, and his first novel, *Simonetta Perkins*, in 1925. Hartley earned a living as a book reviewer and critic for some two decades. In 1944, he published *The Shrimp and the Anemone*, the first volume of a trilogy, followed in 1946 by the second volume, *The Sixth Heaven*, and in 1947 by the culminating volume, *Eustace and Hilda*, which won the JAMES TAIT BLACK MEMORIAL PRIZE. Hartley's masterpiece, *The Go-BETWEEN*, appeared in 1953 and received the Heinemann Foundation Prize. He also published 13 other novels, five more collections of short fiction, and a work of criticism, *The Novelist's Responsibility: Lectures and Essays.* The title is apt: Hartley's work reflects his keen concern for moral weight and individual culpability, told through characters invested with psychological realism. Hartley died on December 13, 1972, in London.

BIBLIOGRAPHY
Bloomfield, Paul. *L. P. Hartley.* Writers and Their Work
    Series 217. Rev. ed. Harlow, England: Longman, 1970.
Jones, Edward Trostle. *L. P. Hartley.* Twayne's English
    Authors, 232. Boston: Twayne Publishers, 1978.
Wright, Adrian. *Foreign Country: The Life of L. P. Hartley.*
    London: Tauris, 2001.

HAWKSMOOR PETER ACKROYD (1985)

An example of POSTMODERNISM, *Hawksmoor* won the WHITBREAD Book of the Year Award and the *GUARDIAN* FICTION PRIZE in 1985. For his narrative structure, Ackroyd drew on the conventions of two genres of popular literature, MYSTERY AND DETECTIVE FICTION and horror, but he subverted them both; moreover, he draws on real historical figures such as the great 18th-century architect Christopher Wren, but he is more interested in ideas associated with such figures than he is in producing an example of HISTORICAL FICTION. Still, history—and the uses we make of it in the present—remains crucial to Ackroyd's story. He communicates the essence of a past era through his command of detail and by contextualizing it in its own history. In this case, the 18th-century story unfolds against the backdrop of rampant outbreaks of plague and the Great Fire of London. In terms of plot, Ackroyd creates a double story with settings and characters both in the Enlightenment and in the contemporary world: Odd-numbered chapters occur in the 18th century, even-numbered chapters occur in the novel's present, and numerology plays a role in the intricacies of the case. Events in the earlier period give rise to consequences in the modern world, but linking together the cause and the effect proves to be a potentially insurmountable challenge.

The contemporary protagonist is London police detective Nicholas Hawksmoor. A series of brutal murders has occurred in several old churches built in the 18th century; Hawksmoor is on the case. In the time-honored tradition of Sherlock HOLMES, Hawksmoor is, like many detectives in crime fiction, a proponent of rational thinking skilled in assembling evidence and inferring from it the hidden identity of a criminal mastermind. But rational thinking can only be effective in a rational world: The detective bound by the assumptions of rationalism will be blind to the workings of irrational forces.

In the case of the murders Hawksmoor is investigating, an irrational element continues to cloak the solution he seeks. The churches in which the murders occurred were designed by one Nicholas Dyer, identified as Christopher Wren's most capable assistant. While Wren is, like Hawksmoor, an advocate and defender of rationalism, Dyer secretly allies himself with the irrational. He is a survivor of the plague and the Great Fire who has consecrated his creations with human blood in murderous rituals designed to appease Satanic powers. Thus there are actually two sets of murders to solve: those that Dyer executed to "christen" his churches, and those that Hawksmoor is attempting to solve. There are tantalizing links and similarities between the two events, and Ackroyd reinforces these connections through the formal devices of the language with which he chooses to tell the story.

Unlike the characteristic detective story, Ackroyd does not provide the classic resolution of the crime. Instead, he leaves the solution in the reader's hands, suspending the conclusion in AMBIGUITY—requiring the reader to step into the detective's place—rather than drawing it to closure.

BIBLIOGRAPHY
De Lange, Adriaan M. "The Complex Architectonics of Post-
    modernist Fiction: *Hawksmoor*—A Case Study." In *British
    Postmodern Fiction.* Edited by Theo D'haen and Hans
    Bertens. Amsterdam: Rodopi, 1993, 145–65.
Gibson, Jeremy Sumner Wycherley, and Julian Wolfreys.
    Peter Ackroyd: The Ludic and Labyrinthine Text. New York:
    St. Martin's Press, 2000.
Onega Jaén, Susana. *Metafiction and Myth in the Novels of
    Peter Ackroyd.* Columbia, S.C.: Camden House, 1999.

HAWTHORNDEN PRIZE Founded by Alice Warrender in 1919, the Hawthornden Prize is England's oldest literary prize, although it has not been awarded as frequently as the JAMES TAIT BLACK MEMORIAL PRIZE, founded in the following year. The Hawthornden Prize is awarded annually to a work selected by the panel of judges as that year's "best work of imaginative literature"; neither nominations nor submissions are accepted. The range of works considered to be imaginative includes biography, poetry, travel literature, drama, and various forms of history, as well as fiction. The award value is currently 10,000 pounds.

BIBLIOGRAPHY

Book Trust Guide to Literary Prizes. London: Book Trust, published annually.

Todd, Richard. Consuming Fictions: The Booker Prize and Fiction in Britain Today. London: Bloomsbury, 1996.

HEARING SECRET HARMONIES ANTHONY POWELL (1974)   The final volume in the ROMAN-FLEUVE collectively known as A DANCE TO THE MUSIC OF TIME, this novel follows TEMPORARY KINGS (1973) and concludes the story of Nicholas Jenkins, who has provided his first-person point of view narration for the entire series. The closing action occurs during the years from about 1969 to 1971, when young people are creating a counterculture and when cults of every kind spring up. But these are not new phenomena: In the opening pages of The KINDLY ONES, the followers of Dr. Trelawney jog by Nick's childhood home on a healthful run in their togas. What differs in the volume is the anxiety of seeing a relative caught up in such a cult, as Nick and Isobel find out when their niece, Fiona Cutts, joins the cult of Scorpio Murtlock. They allow the cult to camp on their land. But Nick is not the only character to become involved with the new ways of the young. Kenneth Widmerpool, now a widower and a disgraced politician, wins appointment as chancellor of one of the new universities springing up around the country, and through his public embarrassment at the hands of J. G. Quiggen's twin daughters, he is drawn into the youth-culture world.

Sir Magnus Donners, although dead some time, continues to affect the world of the novel through the great wealth he left. The Donners Prize is established, and Nick is a member of the selection panel the year Russell Gwinnett wins it for his biography of X. Trapnel. But Nick also sees the photographs Donners took of his guests, including Nick, portraying the Seven Deadly Sins, 30 years earlier. The device brings the past into the novel's present and also restates the recurring theme of the role of art in life. But with age come tragedies and, for some, follies; Widmerpool is soon a member of Murtlock's cult and at his leader's command undergoes a humiliating penance—events that unfold at Stourwater, once the home of Sir Magnus Donners.

As in Temporary Kings, Nick is frequently a second-hand reporter hearing about events in the larger world rather than witnessing them himself. Thus it is that he hears of the death of Widmerpool, which occurs on a run with Murtlock's cult. Nick is attending a showing of paintings by Mr. Deacon, an artist of the generation before his, whom he had known personally. Although Nick has dismissed Mr. Deacon's paintings, passing over opportunities to buy several at a garage sale in the opening pages of A BUYER'S MARKET, the changes in the dance of time have brought about a revival of interest in these works. At an exhibit of them, he encounters his first love, Jean Templer Duport Flores. He reflects on his old friends and former loves as he enjoys an autumn bonfire. The novel, and the entire series for which it is the finale, ends on a nostalgic, ruminative, affectionate note. The end will come sometime soon for Nick, but he can take comfort in knowing that he has enjoyed the dance of time to the full and discharged his part with competence and grace.

BIBLIOGRAPHY

Joyau, Isabelle. Understanding Powell's A Dance to the Music of Time. New York: St. Martin's Press, 1994.

Selig, Robert L. Time and Anthony Powell. Cranbury, N.J.: Associated University Presses, 1991.

Spurling, Hillary. Invitation to the Dance: A Guide to Anthony Powell's A Dance to the Music of Time. Boston: Little, Brown, 1977.

HEART OF DARKNESS JOSEPH CONRAD (1902)   This short novel examines the destructiveness of COLONIALISM in Africa while also exploring the capacity of the civilized soul to sink to savagery and even lower into inhumanity. CONRAD uses an innovative narrative structure to present a simple but richly textured narrative. The main story is told by a first-person narrator, Marlowe, a seasoned mariner who is relating a past adventure to a group of fellow sailors; it is set within a slight frame story also told by a first-person narrator.

Looking back to a period when he needed work and had developed an intense curiosity about the blankest part of the world map, Marlowe tell of his experiences as a riverboat captain on a "tinpot steamer" trading along an equatorial African river. When he arrives at the remote trading station, he is taken aback by the suffering of the natives under colonial rule and by the practices of the European traders. Before he can travel the river, he has to make the boat assigned to him watertight and otherwise functional. His ultimate mission is to travel to an even more remote outpost—the farthest extent of European penetration—and retrieve Kurtz, the outpost manager. Kurtz has shipped unprecedented quantities of ivory, and reports indicate he is a man of irreproachable character, intent on civilizing the Africans in addition to extracting ivory from their homeland. Marlowe's task is to find Kurtz, if he is still living, and bring him home.

Marlowe finds the situation to be quite different than he had expected: Kurtz had yielded to the basest temptation for a white man by "going native." This paragon of civilized man has established himself as a kind of god-chief among the untamed tribesmen of the interior. The stringency of his rule is apparent in the severed heads displayed on posts; nonetheless, the natives do not relinquish him willingly. Marlowe finds that Kurtz is physically ill with fever, but worse, he is spiritually ravaged and mentally unstable. He has seen how low a so-called civilized man may stoop in the endless quest for power and domination. With difficulty and at some risk, Marlowe loads Kurtz onto the boat for the journey downriver.

The narrative shifts to Kurtz's story of his decline into savagery; Marlowe is fascinated, compelled to listen, but also disgusted. Kurtz talks of his fiancée—his Intended—and of his shame and the horror of primitive life. He dies aboard Marlowe's boat, leaving Marlowe with the task of deciding what to tell the rest of the world about Kurtz's fall from decency and his death.

Although the story's PLOT is simple, Conrad's objective examination of living conditions under colonial rule is an unmistakable condemnation of colonialism. Issues of race pervade the narrative, intertwined with more subtle references to gender. The story is mythic in scope, highlighted by symbolism that relies on contrasting images of light and dark, male and female, civilized and savage, rational and passionate. Appearing at the onset of the 20th century, *Heart of Darkness* explores many of the key issues that would drive social change in the years to come.

BIBLIOGRAPHY

Adelman, Gary. Heart of Darkness: *Search for the Unconscious.* Twayne's Masterwork Studies, 5. Boston: Twayne, 1987.

Bloom, Harold. *Joseph Conrad's* Heart of Darkness. New York: Chelsea House, 1987.

Firchow, Peter Edgerly. *Envisioning Africa: Racism and Imperialism in Conrad's* Heart of Darkness. Lexington: University Press of Kentucky, 2000.

HEART OF THE MATTER, THE GRAHAM GREENE (1948)

A novel in what is often called GREENE's "Catholic trilogy," *The Heart of the Matter* examines the operations of pity versus compassion. In Greene's view, the former is extraordinarily and necessarily destructive. When pity is compounded with pride, as in the case of the protagonist, Major Henry Scobie, the damage done can be fatal. The common Greene themes—betrayal, responsibility, sin, guilt, and corruption— are all present in the novel. Called "Scobie the Just" by his district commissioner, the central character loves the West African coast of the WORLD WAR II period, and as the novel opens, he has been passed over for promotion to commissioner. Scobie is given the chance to transfer, but he refuses. His unpopular wife, Louise, a woman of artistic and intellectual pretensions, desperately wants to go to South Africa, but Scobie initially fails to secure the necessary money. Louise, frustrated by a loveless marriage and loss of face with the other Brits, begins a flirtation with a younger man named Wilson, purportedly a civilian clerk, but actually attached to MI-5 and assigned to investigate, among others, Scobie.

Thereafter, Scobie searches a Portuguese vessel after a tip that there is contraband aboard, but all he finds is a missive written by the vessel's captain to his daughter. Scobie is required to turn it in, but in a moment of sentiment, remembering his own dead daughter, Scobie decides the letter is not a menace to the war effort and burns it. This act begins his downward spiral of choices based on the heart's demands. Scobie collapses from a dose of fever when he goes to investigate the suicide of another, younger bureaucrat. While Scobie is feverbound, Yusef the Syrian, with whom it is dangerous to associate but who has some regard for Scobie, visits his sickbed and offers to loan him the money for Louise's passage. Although it is a violation of his professional ethics as a policeman, Scobie accepts the loan.

As she leaves for South Africa, Louise warns Scobie that Wilson is a "phoney." After her departure, a group of survivors of a 40-day-at-sea ordeal arrive, and Scobie assists them. One of the last stretcher cases is Helen Rolt, a very young widow who invades the peace of his solitude. They become friends, and "protected" by a vast age difference and by his marriage, they do not recognize lust or infatuation until too late. They become lovers. Meanwhile, Wilson continues to investigate Scobie, and Yusef makes quiet demands of his friend Scobie regarding the investigation of Yusef's rival, Tallit. The investigation backfires, and Scobie feels that Yusef has set him up. As time passes, Helen begins to behave more and more as Louise might, and Scobie fears that love has cooled; all that is left in his heart toward both women is pity and responsibility for their happiness. Louise returns to Scobie with barely any warning, and Scobie must juggle both women in his life.

Furthermore, Louise uses Catholicism to bring her husband to heel, insisting that he go to confession and take communion. He does not intend to give up Helen, so he cannot express real contrition, receive absolution, nor receive communion. Yet he elects to damn his own soul and take the sacrament to make both women happy. Scobie's trusted servant Ali comes upon his master confessing love to Helen and also in possession of a suspect diamond from Yusef, perhaps a payoff. Distressed that his fate and future are in Ali's hands,

Scobie goes to Yusef for help; without Scobie's knowledge, Yusef orders the murder of the faithful Ali. Scobie has betrayed and hurt directly or indirectly everyone who has loved or trusted him. Scobie decides to pretend to suffer from angina pectoris, collect sleeping pills from the doctor, pretend to take them nightly, and then use them to commit a suicide that will appear to be a heart attack. The final question of the novel and its ultimate AMBIGUITY is whether or not Scobie is damned for this mortal sin. The MI-5 bloodhound Wilson finds a subtle clue that Scobie has killed himself rather than died a natural death and then reports it to Louise. Louise takes her concerns to the usually ineffectual priest, Father Rank, who asserts, "The Church knows all the rules. But it doesn't know what goes on in a single human heart."

—*Viki Craig*

BIBLIOGRAPHY

Hynes, Samuel, ed. *Graham Greene: A Collection of Critical Essays.* Englewood Cliffs, N.J.: Prentice Hall, 1973.

Miller, R. H. "Graham Greene's 'Saddest Story,' " *Renascence: Essays on Values in Literature* 51, no. 2 (Winter 1999): 133–143.

Waugh, Evelyn. "Felix Culpa?" In *Catholics on Literature.* Edited by J. C. Whitehouse. Dublin, Ireland: Four Courts, 1997, 89–95.

HEAT AND DUST RUTH PRAWER JHAB-VALA (1975)

With double narratives set in Satipur, INDIA, in 1923 under British imperial rule and in 1975 under postcolonial self-rule, this novel explores the contrasts between European and Indian cultures. It won the BOOKER PRIZE in 1975.

The first-person narrator is Anne, an Englishwoman in her late 20s. She is the granddaughter of a former colonial administrator, Douglas Rivers, who lost his first wife to the exotic allure of assimilation to India, its culture, its values, and its people. When one of Rivers's colleagues, Col. Minnie, publishes his memoirs of colonial India, Anne becomes curious to learn more about her grandfather's first wife, Olivia. She visits the heir of Satipur's colonial Nawab, who had seduced Olivia, but the lives of modern Anglophile Indians in London shed little light on the conditions of 1923. Anne travels to Satipur and rents an apartment from

Inder Lal, a minor official in India's independent government. Gradually, Anne unearths Olivia's story; simultaneously, she also re-creates its events in her own life.

Anne had come to Satipur, a lowland city choking in the heat and dust of the plains, to join her husband. She longs to bear a child; her husband, Douglas, is exhausted and overworked by his administrative duties, but he blames the heat for Olivia's failure to conceive. Bored with the provincial narrowness of the British colonials, who live in a separate enclave designed to mimic an English village, Olivia is drawn increasingly to the charming company of the Nawab, a local prince who maintains his position at the pleasure of the colonial rulers. For his part, the Nawab uses Olivia for a bit of private revenge on the English. When their affair leads to a pregnancy, Olivia decides to have an abortion rather than face the condemnation that would follow upon her delivery of a half-Indian infant. The Nawab's mother enlists Indian midwives to induce a miscarriage, but the narrow-minded English physician who treats her recognizes the signs of the cause of her condition. With her secret known, she flees back to the Nawab's palace, and when he is toppled by the British for taking payoffs from robber barons, she flees with him to a Himalayan village, where she lives out the remainder of her life. Douglas Rivers divorces the wife who has abandoned him and marries the sister of one of the "proper" colonial wives.

As Anne learns the details of Olivia's life, she finds herself increasingly drawn to Inder Lal. They enter into an affair, and Anne gets pregnant. Unlike Olivia, she does not feel obligated to terminate her pregnancy. She brings her child to term and follows Anne's footsteps into the cooler, clearer realm of the Himalayas, deciding to raise her child there rather than return to England. The survival of this child, blending English and Indian identities, is the novel's symbol of hope for a better future and optimism for human possibilities.

Much of the beauty of this novel is found in the careful parallels that Jhabvala develops between the two stories through skillfully deployed minor characters. A long-term guest of the Nawab, Harry, corresponds to the latter Chid, an English convert to Hinduism visiting the Lal family. Each of the attractive Indian men, the Nawab and Inder Lal, houses his strong mother under his own roof. The English doctor of the colonial world corresponds to the Indian doctor of the later period. The Nawab himself, a government officer, corresponds to Inder Lal, the bureaucrat. Anne is virtually a reincarnation of Olivia, but in 1975 she has the option of fulfilling the earlier woman's dream of motherhood, and she has the courage to do so in a world where single mothers cannot count on universal acceptance. The key change between 1923 and 1975 is the absence of the oppressive colonial system with its repressive sense of moral superiority and its paternalistic attitude toward India and its people. Jhabvala's story implicitly condemns the colonial enterprise while also recognizing the necessity, in the face of India's colonial history, of bringing forth some accommodation between East and West. Anne's child represents this accommodation: It is not a part of India assimilating itself to England, like the Nawab's heir in London, nor an English convert to Indian ways, like Chid, the failed Hindu. But it is also left undefined at the novel's end as Anne makes her new life in the village that once sheltered Olivia.

Jhabvala used her novel as a FILM ADAPTATION for the Merchant-Ivory production of *Heat and Dust* in 1983; her work won the BAFTA award (the British equivalent of the Academy Award) for best screenplay that year.

BIBLIOGRAPHY

Agarwal, Ramlal G. *Ruth Prawer Jhabvala: A Study of Her Fiction.* New York: Envoy Press, 1990.

Gooneratne, Yasmine. *Silence, Exile, and Cunning: The Fiction of Ruth Prawer Jhabvala.* Hyderabad, India: Orient Longman, 1983.

Sucher, Laurie. *The Fiction of Ruth Prawer Jhabvala: The Politics of Passion.* New York: St. Martin's Press, 1989.

HIGH WIND IN JAMAICA, A **RICHARD HUGHES (1929)** A novel for young adult readers that appeals to mature readers as well. *A High Wind in Jamaica* tells the story of seven children from two neighboring colonial families who are waylaid by pirates when their parents send them back to England for schooling. Ten-year-old Emily is the protagonist and the middle child of the five Bas-Thornton children. The story is set in the 19th century, with locations in Jamaica, at sea, and in London.

Captain Jonsen is the leader of the pirates; he did not intend to take the children captive, but he is left with them when their ship escapes. The children had already been wound to a state of overexcitement before their voyage by an earthquake and a hurricane—natural disasters that foreshadow the emotional storms the children will encounter as the narrative progresses. Under the indifferent supervision of the pirates, they become wild and careless; Emily's brother dies in an accidental fall while they are briefly in a shady Cuban port, but the children brush off this tragedy as they return to sea. In the confines of the ship, however, there is another risk to the girls. Although Emily does not quite understand the threat Captain Jonsen presents when he shows up drunk in the children's cabin, she bites him when he reaches for her. Mysteriously, the older sister, Margaret, moves into the captain's cabin soon after that, and as if she is ashamed, she no longer associates with the younger children.

A crisis occurs that leads to a crime and some AMBIGUITY as to whether the perpetrator was Margaret or Emily, and soon afterward Captain Jonsen passes the children off to another ship. Emily's chatter inadvertently leads to her blurting out the truth about the ship they had come from, and soon Jonsen and his crew are apprehended and the children arrive in London and are reunited with their parents. The story shifts from the wild and dangerous life on the high seas to the sedate environment of the English judicial system—a highly dangerous place for Captain Jonsen and his crew. With her older brother dead and Margaret in shock, the task of testifying about the children's experiences and the pirates' activities falls to Emily. Once again, deadly forces are at work that are beyond her control.

For his story material, HUGHES drew on a historical event that had also been used by Joseph CONRAD in one of his early works. More important, he rejected the long-held Victorian idea of childhood innocence, drawing instead on the ideas of Sigmund Freud regarding both children's latent awareness of human sexuality and the opposition of libidinal appetite and civilized self-restraint. Although the pirates are operating outside the law, the children are operating outside the civilized world—they have not completed the absorption of civilized values that will mark their admission to the ranks of adulthood. Ironically, the pirates wind up at greater risk from the children than the children ever were from the pirates. Hughes's insight into this IRONY marks a turning point in the literary presence of children, and his novel opens the way for later works such as LORD OF THE FLIES, by William GOLDING.

BIBLIOGRAPHY
Dumbleton, Suzanne M. "Animals and Humans in *A High Wind in Jamaica*," *The Anglo-Welsh Review* 68 (1981): 51–61.
Henighan, T. J. "Nature and Convention in *A High Wind in Jamaica*," *Critique* 9, no. 1 (1967): 5–18.

HILTON, JAMES (1900–1954)

The author of popular adventures and sentimental novels such as LOST HORIZON and *Good-bye, Mr. Chips*, James Hilton was born on September 9, 1900, the son of a schoolmaster. He studied at Leys School and matriculated at Christ's College, Cambridge, receiving an undergraduate degree in 1921. Hilton began his writing career as a journalist while he was still a teenager and published his first novel, *Catherine Herself* (1920), when he was only 20. Since the novel did not sell well, he continued writing articles for newspapers. In 1931, however, he produced two successful novels and began to write fiction full-time: *And Now Good-bye* and *Murder at School: A Detective Fantasia*. This second novel was published under the pseudonym "Glen Trevor" and was later republished under the title *Was It Murder?*

Hilton's two most successful books appeared in 1933 and 1934; both received even greater acclaim upon their American publication and then became more successful still as examples of FILM ADAPTATION. *Lost Horizon* (1933) imagined a utopian world hidden in the Tibetan mountains and contributed the phrase "Shangri-La" to the English language; *Good-bye, Mr. Chips* is a fictional biography of a beloved teacher. *Lost Horizon* won the HAWTHORNDEN PRIZE in 1934, and *Good-bye, Mr. Chips* had its American debut in the pages of *The Atlantic Monthly* that same year. Hilton's success in the United States led him to relocate to

California in 1937, where he wrote screenplays, hosted a radio program, and continued to write novels, although with decreasing success. *We Are Not Alone* appeared in 1937, followed in 1941 by *Random Harvest,* in 1945 by *So Well Remembered,* and in 1953 by *Time and Time Again.* In addition to developing scripts for his own novels, Hilton worked on other film projects; his script for *Mrs. Miniver* won the Academy Award for best screenplay in 1942. Hilton died in California on December 20, 1954, after a battle against liver cancer.

BIBLIOGRAPHY

Sibley, Carroll. *Barrie and His Contemporaries: Cameo Portraits of Ten Living Authors.* Webster Grove, Mo.: International Mark Twain Society, 1936.

Weeks, Edward. Foreword to *Good-bye, Mr. Chips.* James Hilton. Boston, Little, Brown, 1962.

HIS DARK MATERIALS TRILOGY PHILIP PULLMAN (1996–2000)

This FANTASY series for young adult readers takes the form of a double BILDUNGSROMAN in following the growth and development of its two protagonists, a girl and boy of about 12 to 14 years old. The story opens with *The GOLDEN COMPASS,* which relates how Lyra Belacqua acquires and masters a device, the aleithiometer, or golden compass of the title, for discovering unknown truths remote from the seeker in space or time. Her adventures carry her into a parallel world at the novel's end; only gradually over the course of the story's details does the reader realize that her world is not our world, in spite of its many similarities. Along the way, she risks her life and her very soul, which in her world takes material form as an external manifestation; she is very nearly severed from it at one of the novel's most harrowing moments. She witnesses her father's near-maniacal destruction of the barrier between the worlds.

In the second volume, *The SUBTLE KNIFE,* the narrative focus shifts to Will Parry, who does live in the ordinary world of planet Earth. Circumstances bring him to the same world that Lyra has traveled to; there, he meets her and acquires an instrument—the knife of the title—that bestows a terrible power on its keeper. Like Lyra, he must master his device and learn to wield its power to benefit others. Also like Lyra, he has parents who have failed in the task of nurturing him, although for different reasons. The two children reluctantly join forces in order to search for Lyra's father, Lord Asriel; along the way, they also encounter Will's missing father. The children gradually become aware that a war of cosmic proportions is looming, and that Lord Asriel is at the center of it, challenging the very Authority of the universe.

The third volume, *The AMBER SPYGLASS,* was the first example of children's literature to win the WHITBREAD AWARD for the best book of the year. Lyra and Will, who have become close comrades through the adversities that they have shared, must journey into the realm of the dead and free the numberless desolate souls there. Their travels have brought them into contact with many different intelligent species, and in the novel's mammoth climax, all of them are drawn into Lord Asriel's war. Even the dead souls contribute to the struggle, and their assistance proves to be uniquely necessary to the success of the campaign. In a tender and bittersweet denouement, Will and Lyra find themselves in an Edenic world and discover that their friendship has turned to love just before the war's aftermath pulls them apart forever.

Although the series was conceived for and marketed to young readers, Phillip Pullman drew extensively on some of the greatest authors in the English literary CANON. Images, names, and ideas from John Milton's *Paradise Lost* and William Blake's poetry recur throughout the trilogy without overpowering the story of two children leaving their childhoods behind in a chaotic and threatening world.

BIBLIOGRAPHY

Bird, Anne-Marie. "Dust, Demons, and Soul States: Reading Philip Pullman's *His Dark Materials,*" *British Association of Lecturers in Children's Literature Bulletin* 7 (June 2000): 3–12.

Wood, Naomi. "Paradise Lost and Found: Obedience, Disobedience, and Storytelling in C. S. Lewis and Philip Pullman," *Children's Literature in Education* 32, no. 4 (2001): 237–259.

HISTORICAL FICTION

HISTORICAL FICTION   A genre traditionally traced to Sir Walter Scott's novels of medieval romance and adventure such as *Ivanhoe,* and to those that celebrated events in Scottish history, such as *The Heart of Midlothian,* historical fiction had declined in the esteem of serious contemporary literary critics until J. G. FARRELL published *The SIEGE OF KRISHNAPUR* in 1973. The success of that novel opened the way for further work in this genre.

The author of historical fiction attempts to re-create an earlier era through the knowledgeable deployment of detail to support and contextualize the events and people of the fictional narrative: styles of dress, appearances of locations and settings, levels of technology, approved modes of behavior, customs of courtship, economic conditions, political events—any aspect of the past might be useful to the present-day novelist attempting to reanimate it to serve as the context for character and plot development. Historical fiction sometimes uses actual persons from history, but these typically play an auxiliary role to the purely fictional characters who interact with them in the writer's imagined scenario. Clearly, a writer using an actual historical person is limited to a reasonable facsimile of the events that occurred in the historical figure's life, while the fictional character's options are virtually unlimited. The historical novelist is not a historian or a biographer *per se;* instead, history is placed in the service of the fiction writer's purpose.

The greatest risk that the historical fiction writer encounters is that of anachronism, or the inclusion of details that do not belong to the historical era portrayed. Anachronism is a misrepresentation of historical circumstances. In a Renaissance story, the presence of a rifle instead of a musket is as out of place as would be a bustle under an Empire gown during the Regency era. Readers of fiction who are well informed in matters of history may identify such discontinuities between the known facts and the imagined world as compositional flaws that dilute the credibility of the author and detract from the enjoyment of the text. On the other hand, anachronism can be deployed for a purpose, especially in an ANTIREALISTIC novel, an experimental narrative, or a work of POSTMODERNISM.

In addition to J. G. Farrell, other noted writers of historical fiction include Patrick O'BRIAN, especially in the AUBREY-MATURIN NOVELS; Bernard Cornwell, in Sharpe's adventures and in other novels; Pat BARKER, who includes the poet Siegfried Sassoon as a character in the REGENERATION Trilogy; Peter CAREY, particularly with respect to Australian history; Baroness ORCZY, in the series that grew from *The SCARLET PIMPERNEL;* and many others. Rose TREMAIN combines aspects of romance and historical fiction in some of her novels; Ellis Peters combines historical fiction with the devices of the genre of MYSTERY AND DETECTIVE FICTION in the Brother Caedfael series. Lindsay CLARKE in *The CHYMICAL WEDDING,* John FOWLES in *The FRENCH LIEUTENANT'S WOMAN,* and A. S. BYATT in *POSSESSION* interleave a present-day story with a historical narrative. Matthew KNEALE in *ENGLISH PASSENGERS* and Barry UNSWORTH in *SACRED HUNGER* use historical fiction to expose abuses of the past such as COLONIALISM or the race hatred endemic to the slave trade, while Chinua ACHEBE's *THINGS FALL APART* is an example of an African historical novel. Robert GRAVES fictionalizes Roman history in *I, CLAUDIUS,* while Peter ACKROYD bends history to postmodern purposes in *HAWKSMOOR* and other novels.

BIBLIOGRAPHY

Rehberger, Dean. "Vulgar Fiction, Impure History: The Neglect of Historical Fiction," *Journal of American Culture* 18, no. 4 (Winter 1995): 59–65.

Rozett, Martha Tuck. "Constructing a World: How Postmodern Historical Fiction Re-imagines the Past," *CLIO: A Journal of Literature, History, and the Philosophy of History* 25, no. 2 (Winter 1996): 145–164.

HISTORY MAN, THE   MALCOLM BRADBURY (1975)

HISTORY MAN, THE MALCOLM BRADBURY (1975)   A CAMPUS NOVEL that is also an example of both SATIRE and POSTMODERNISM, *The History Man* is set at the imaginary "redbrick" British university of Watermouth (i.e., it has only recently been founded, unlike the ancient institutions of Oxford and Cambridge, which are built of stone). The protagonist, a professor of sociology, is Howard Kirk, a man who has embraced the modern ethos of liberation to the extreme. The action of the plot covers one term of the year, from October to December, beginning and ending with a party thrown by Howard and Barbara Kirk. The third-person narrator describes the characters and the events of the story entirely in the present tense, almost as though the Kirks and their world are coming into existence at the moment the words of the story appear on the page.

The story follows the unfolding of the academic term from its inaugural to its valedictory Kirk party—a party that would be a tradition except that nothing the Kirks do is traditional or conventional. Howard Kirk is bent on implementing his sociological theories, especially the one about sexual liberation, in the everyday life of the campus, and to that end he pursues affairs both with faculty members and students. The third-person narrator, however, gives the lie to Howard's pose of liberation, demonstrating that he is bent on the same kinds of self-serving ends that might occupy the most tradition-bound Machiavelli on earth. Howard is not doing anything particularly new, original, or liberal; he is merely cloaking his pursuit of self-gratification and glory in a jargon that camouflages that pursuit.

Although the Kirks are described as thoroughly contemporary people, readers should be able to discern that they are being condemned—indeed, excoriated—for shallowness, intellectual vapidity, hypocrisy, and a host of other failings of which the characters themselves are oblivious. In other words, they are not so very different from other characters or from real people, even though they perceive themselves to be part of a new order of things. That new order is entirely predictable, since it primarily consists of inverting the old order while refusing to admit that "order" has any part to play in their ordering of their affairs. BRADBURY simultaneously depicts the contemporary world of 1972 and implicitly dismisses it. He expands his critique beyond the realm of characters' personal psychologies by cataloging the architectural features of the campus, the contents of offices and homes, and the vast array of consumer goods that facilitate the Kirks' pose that they are living lives of undesigned, unintended, unmanipulated spontaneity. Bradbury demonstrates that those who live lives of quiet desperation need not be traditional, conventional, old-fashioned, or repressed.

BIBLIOGRAPHY

Acheson, James. "Thesis and Antithesis in Malcolm Bradbury's *The History Man*," *Journal of European Studies* 33, no. 1 (March 2003): 41–52.

Morace, Robert A. *The Dialogic Novels of Malcolm Bradbury and David Lodge.* Carbondale: Southern Illinois University Press, 1989.

Todd, Richard. "Malcolm Bradbury's *The History Man*: The Novelist as Reluctant Impresario," *Dutch Quarterly Review of Anglo-American Letters* 11 (1981): 162–82.

HITCHHIKER'S GUIDE TO THE GALAXY, THE DOUGLAS ADAMS (1979)

This title originally referred to the popular BBC radio series that in turn spawned a five-volume novel sequence and adaptations for television and film. The novels in the series include *The Hitchhiker's Guide to the Galaxy* (1979), *The Restaurant at the End of the Universe* (1980), *Life, the Universe, and Everything* (1982), *So Long, and Thanks for All the Fish* (1984), and *Mostly Harmless* (1992).

The protagonist of the story is Arthur Dent, a mild-mannered Englishman. His adventures begin one day when he discovers that bulldozers are about to knock down his house in order to build a freeway through the site where the house stands. But a friend of Arthur's, Ford Prefect, draws him off to a tavern for a beer, insisting they will need it and that the world is about to end. When they return to Arthur's house after a short absence, the bulldozers have indeed knocked it down. This opening episode, however, is merely a metaphor for what is about to happen to the entire Earth. Ford Prefect is nearly frantic by this time, because he knows that a Vogon constructor fleet is bearing down on the planet to demolish it for a hyperspace bypass. Using his electronic thumb, he hitches a ride for himself and Arthur with the kitchen workers of the fleet just in the nick of time: Earth is destroyed just as completely as Arthur's house had been demolished only moments before.

Arthur is disoriented, as Ford had known he would be, so he hands his friend a copy of *The Hitchhiker's Guide to the Galaxy*. This impressive tome carries a reassuring message on its cover: "Don't Panic." Ford, it turns out, is not an earthling but is an alien from a small planet in the vicinity of Betelgeuse, and he is employed in revising the *H2G2*. Before Arthur can quite comprehend this information, however, Vogon security forces apprehend the two hitchhikers, and the captain plans to eject them into space unless they will tell him how wonderful his poetry is. To their agony, he reads some of it and then ejects them into space in spite of their attempts at flattery.

In the airless cold of space, they should die within seconds, but instead they miraculously find themselves in some kind of smaller, sportier craft. It is equipped with cheerful talking automatic doors and a very morose robot named Marvin, who has, as he continually reminds his human companions, a brain the size of a planet. Thinking himself to be the only human being left alive in the universe, Arthur is astonished to find a young Earth woman, Trillian, on board the ship. Arthur had tried to chat her up at a party, but she now seems to have some attachment to her unusual traveling companion, Zaphod Beeblebrox. The creature is unusual on many counts: He is the inventor of the Pan-Galactic Gargle Blaster; he is the disgraced president of the galaxy; and he has two heads. Zaphod has stolen the ship that so miraculously saved Arthur and Ford. The ship is powered by a prototype of the Infinite Improbability Drive, and at the moment that he and Trillian (whom he saved from Earth) had fired it up, the most improbable event in the universe was the survival of Arthur Dent and Ford Prefect. The Infinite Improbability Drive brings the infinitely improbable event into the realm of the actual.

The travelers wind up on Megatherion, a legendary planet that specializes in the manufacture of planets. There, they meet Slartibartfast, designer of planets who is most happy when he is doing coastlines. Hanging in his workshop is a new construction project for a planet bearing a remarkable resemblance to Earth—the one flattened by the Vogons. Slartibartfast has been commissioned to reconstruct it from his original plans. He explains that Earth was actually a giant computer, the most sophisticated in the universe, designed by the second-most sophisticated computer, Deep Thought, to answer the question of Life, the Universe, and Everything. The Vogons had destroyed it just before the final calculation of that answer had been complete.

But since galactic security forces have already arrived in pursuit of Zaphod, the group has to make a quick retreat, and they wind up at the Restaurant at the End of the Universe—a posh dinner club and also the name of the second volume in the series.

Arthur's adventures continue in the subsequent volumes until at last he is returned to Earth (the new one) and meets a nice girl who, like himself, has acquired the ability to fly in her recent adventures. Ford's update to *The Hitchhiker's Guide to the Galaxy*—the entry that explains the inhabitants of the planet—is finally completed: *Mostly Harmless,* he decides.

The five short volumes of this series show off the imagination and wit of the author, and they are hugely entertaining either as recordings of the original radio broadcasts or as printed texts. Although the plots are unpredictable in advance of the unfolding of the events, once the narrator explains the circumstances, many of which are ironic consequences of scientific theories being carried to extremes, readers can see that the story is perfectly logical and coherent but only on its own terms.

BIBLIOGRAPHY

Batchelor, Murray. "At Sixes and Sevens with the Ultimate Question," *New Scientist* 138, no. 1867 (3 April 1993): 48.

Ditlea, Steve. "An Earthly Prequel to a Galactic Guide," *Technology Review* 103.5 (September–October 2000): 122.

Kropf, Carl R. "Douglas Adams's 'Hitchhiker' Novels as Mock Science Fiction." *Science Fiction Studies* 15, no.1 (March 1988): 61–70.

H.M.S. SURPRISE PATRICK O'BRIAN (1973)
See AUBREY-MATURIN NOVELS.

HOBBIT, THE J. R. R. TOLKIEN (1937)
Initially invented to entertain his young children, J. R. R. TOLKIEN's tales of Middle Earth grew into a heroic epic that eventually sprawled over some 3,000 years of imagined history, numerous cultures, dozens of characters, and several invented languages. Through the stories and novels first published with *The Hobbit,* Tolkien virtually invented the genre of modern FANTASY FICTION.

In the Shire, a rustic place that resembles a preindustrial rural English countryside, lives Bilbo Baggins, the hero of *The Hobbit*. He is typical of his kind: fond of good food, snug burrowlike houses, and good cheer. Gandalf the Grey, a wizard, urges him to go on an adventure; before it is over, Bilbo acquires a sword and the courage to use it, a magic ring and the power it bestows, and a fortune so large he becomes the wealthiest hobbit in the Shire. Gandalf has been enlisted by a group of dwarves to help them recover their ancient home under the Lonely Mountain far to the east. This region and all the treasure in it is now the territory of Smaug the dragon, old, cunning, fierce, and fiery. When 13 dwarves show up for tea, Bilbo agrees to go with them so that the company will not constitute an unlucky number.

As the adventures proceed, Bilbo and the dwarves encounter trolls, elves, goblins, spiders, orcs, eagles, a shape-shifting bear-man, and ordinary human beings. They visit Rivendell, the Misty Mountains, the forest of Mirkwood, the wood-elves, and the men of Lake-Town. They face situations that require cleverness, courage, and magnanimity. The dwarves' quest to reclaim a homeland sparks the Battle of Five Armies, and only the arrival of terrible common enemies forces dwarves, elves, and men (and one hobbit) to cooperate for their mutual survival.

Bilbo faces two special encounters along the way. First, deep under the Misty Mountains, fleeing from Goblins, he finds a ring and then encounters Gollum, the ring's former owner. In a riddling contest, Bilbo outwits Gollum and discovers the ring's power to make its wearer invisible. Then, under the Lonely Mountain, Bilbo wears the ring to examine Smaug's lair and finds the Arkenstone, the dwarves' most valued treasure. He uses his new sources of courage and wisdom to force belligerent opponents to compromise for their mutual benefit. The Bilbo of chapter one lacked the experience to pull off this feat, but the adventures he undergoes make him a stronger and wiser hobbit, to the benefit of himself and his friends.

In content, plot, character, and tone, *The Hobbit* resembles other examples of children's literature, much more so than any of Tolkien's other works. It is a suitable starting place for reading Tolkien, but young readers should be aware that subsequent works are more challenging. Nonetheless, these later works build on the very solid foundation of *The Hobbit*: Tolkien had already imagined many of the characters, themes, and locations that show up later in *The LORD OF THE RINGS* and *The Silmarillion*.

BIBLIOGRAPHY

Foster, Robert. *The Complete Guide to Middle-earth: From* The Hobbit *to* The Silmarillion. New York: Ballantine, 1979.

Tolkien, J. R. R. *The Annotated Hobbit*. Annotated by Douglas A. Anderson. Revised and expanded edition. Boston: Houghton Mifflin, 2002.

Tyler, J. E. A. *The Tolkien Companion: The Indispensable Guide to the Wondrous Legends, History, Languages, and Peoples of Middle Earth*. New York: Gramercy Books, 1976.

HOLIDAY STANLEY MIDDLETON (1974)

Winner of the BOOKER PRIZE in 1974, *Holiday* is a novel of psychological realism. The third-person narrator closely examines the thoughts and feelings of the protagonist, Edwin Fisher, a lecturer in educational philosophy at a small university; occasionally, the narrator expands into near omniscience to relate an anecdote relevant to another character. Edwin, about 30 years old, is spending a week at a middle-class resort on the eastern coast of England, having just left his wife, Meg. His family had always vacationed at this resort, and so Edwin's thoughts are repeatedly drawn to his parents, especially his father, Arthur Fisher, a successful but uneducated shopkeeper. As his meditative and solitary vacation begins, Edwin is surprised to encounter his father-in-law, David Vernon, a wealthy solicitor taking a vacation with his wife at the town's most posh hotel.

The PLOT of the story has more to do with changes of heart than with actions. As the week unfolds, Edwin's thoughts flit back over his childhood, highlighting his struggle against the commanding presence of his father, and then to his meeting and courting the beautiful, willful, and emotionally unstable Meg, and finally over the rocky course of their marriage, which had finally been dealt a mortal blow by the death of their two-year-old son a year and a half previously. As his thoughts move back across time, his life continues on its vacation course: The novel provides a clinical view of one of the classic middle-class English holidays, a week's stay at the seashore. Edwin meets the other guests—all families—at his inexpensive hotel, sharing meals, walks on the beach, and after-dinner drinks at a nearby pub. These activities provide him with the opportunity to examine how other couples handle the stresses of marriage; Edwin's sensitivity to CLASS markers is never far from his perceptions of others or his recollections of the past. The most important events of the week unfold as David Vernon takes it upon himself to repair his flawed daughter's moribund marriage, if it can be done. For Edwin, the possibility of reconciliation begins to take hold through long talks, undertaken somewhat warily and unwillingly, that lead to a closing sequence in his own home.

MIDDLETON'S style is a study in understatement, and yet his handling of contemporary characters is frank and insightful. Through believable conversations and evocative memories, he anatomizes the difficulty of bridging the abyss of silence that separates any two people, suggesting that the persistent presence of the absent past maintains a paralyzing power over the ambiguous present.

BIBLIOGRAPHY

Belbin, David and John Lucas, eds. *Stanley Middleton at Eighty.* Nottingham: Five Leaves Publications, 1999.

HOLMES, SHERLOCK

In the tradition of Edgar Allan Poe's detective Dupin, Arthur Conan DOYLE created a dispassionate investigator and a skilled observer as the central character in a series of novels and short stories that form a cornerstone in the genre of MYSTERY AND DETECTIVE FICTION. Residing in rooms at 221B Baker Street, which he shared with the narrator of his adventures, Dr. John Watson, Sherlock Holmes is an example of a fictional character who has transcended the boundaries his creator set for him and passed into the folklore of popular culture. Even people who have never read one of Arthur Conan Doyle's works about Holmes would be able to describe the great detective's characteristic garb or pick him out of a police lineup (unless he were wearing one of his impenetrable disguises).

Holmes is remembered for his keen eye, his violin, his deerstalker cap, his rigorous devotion to deductive logic, his smarter brother Mycroft, and his occasional drug use, but the really innovative aspect of his creation was how he recurred in independent episodes of stories that provided fresh adventures of the sort that readers had previously enjoyed and were happy to enjoy again with new plot materials. Novels had been serialized in magazines for quite a few decades before Holmes appeared for the first time in the December 1887 edition of *Beeton's Christmas Annual,* but the repetition of an appealing character in episodes of short fiction was something new. Holmes's first introduction to the general public occurred in a novel-length work, *A Study in Scarlet,* followed by his appearance in *The Sign of the Four* in *Lippincott's Magazine* in February 1890, but he thrived in the formal devices of short fiction.

In 1891, Holmes appeared in his first short story, "A Scandal in Bohemia," and the circumstances were right for a huge success: The mass literacy created by universal education was finally complemented by suitable reading material at prices masses of readers could afford. The Sherlock Holmes stories were interesting—even challenging—but not abstruse. The popularity of the stories in the *Strand* in England and eventually in *Collier's Weekly* in the United States was phenomenal.

The success of Sherlock Holmes between 1891 and 1893 continued unabated and grew apace. But Arthur Conan Doyle had other projects he thought were of greater importance, and in 1893 he brought his series to an end in the great struggle between Holmes and his nemesis, Professor Moriarty, at the Reichenbach Falls in Switzerland. The public mourned. Doyle wrote numerous other works and served in the BOER WAR, and then in 1902 Sherlock Holmes entered the 20th century, although *The HOUND OF THE BASKERVILLES* was an adventure that predated his confrontation with Moriarty. But magazine editors would not be denied the circulation-boosting power of such a popular character, and in 1903 Doyle began earning a large fee for new stories of Sherlock Holmes. By the real end of Holmes's career in 1927, Arthur Conan Doyle had written 60 stories featuring his popular detective.

Sherlock Holmes came into the world about the time the film industry did, and the new medium soon undertook the FILM ADAPTATION of the beloved and best-selling character; Holmes also made stage appearances beginning in the early 20th century. Between the birth of film and the advent of television, what must surely have been one of the first fan phenomena occurred, and societies devoted to the great detective sprang up in the United States (the Sherlockians) and Great Britain (the Holmsians). Mock scholarly treatments of Holmes eventually turned into the real thing. Television has carried Holmes to even greater audiences. Whether Holmes will establish as marked a presence on the Internet as he did in books, movies, and television serials remains to be seen.

BIBLIOGRAPHY

Baring-Gould, William S. *Sherlock Holmes of Baker Street: A Life of the World's First Consulting Detective.* New York: Bramhall House, 1962.

Hardwick, Michael and Mollie. *The Sherlock Holmes Companion.* Garden City, N.Y.: Doubleday, 1963.

Keating, H. R. F. *Sherlock Holmes: The Man and His World.* New York: Scribner's, 1979.

Redmond, Donald A. *Sherlock Holmes: A Study in Sources.* Downsview, Ontario: McGill-Queen's University Press, 1982.

Shreffler, Philip A. ed. *The Baker Street Reader: Cornerstone Writings about Sherlock Holmes.* Westport, Conn.: Greenwood Press, 1984.

Tracy, Jack. *The Encyclopaedia Sherlockiana.* Garden City, N.Y.: Doubleday, 1977.

HOMECOMINGS C. P. SNOW (1956)

The sixth volume in the 11-volume ROMAN-FLEUVE collectively known as STRANGERS AND BROTHERS, *Homecomings* (published in the United States in the singular as *Homecoming*) follows *THE NEW MEN* in the publication order of the series, but it skips back to 1938 to pick up the story of the private life of the first-person narrator, Lewis Eliot. At the end of *A TIME OF HOPE,* the third volume in the sequence, Eliot has married the emotionally unresponsive Sheila Knight. In the intervening volumes of the story, Eliot has focused his eye on the lives of his colleagues, friends, and competitors; the tragedy revealed in *Homecomings* suggests why he may have wished to turn his attention somewhere other than to his own life.

Although Eliot's pursuit of Sheila Knight results in the desired goal of marriage, Sheila's pursuit of her own ambition in the publishing world fails. Despite her hints of despair, Eliot is unprepared for the way Sheila copes with her failure. He is left in a withdrawn and wounded condition. His ability to relate to women had been damaged, even before he met Sheila, by his mother's possessive and suffocating love; in midlife, the further events of his marriage make him even less open to the risks inherent in forming emotional bonds with others. Two years pass before Eliot meets a woman to whom he can respond: Margaret Davidson is 24 years old, charming, literate, and intelligent. Before their flirtation can ripen into love and marriage, however, Margaret turns to another man, doubting Eliot's capacity to shed the emotional baggage he has accumulated in his life. She marries and has a child, but two years later, when Eliot and Margaret meet again, he has another opportunity to win her.

In the most intimately personal volume of the series, SNOW explores the inner life of his protagonist so as to demonstrate the lingering presence of the past in individual lives and the power that earlier events have to shape later responses in similar situations. Being a fully complete human being requires each person to break free of the bondage of past experiences in order to navigate through the present moment and achieve a desired future goal. By the end of *Homecomings,* in 1947, Eliot is a father and a husband because he frees himself from the bonds of diffidence his own past has placed on him. He has made the loving connection to a woman he had always longed to establish, helped in the process by the unexpected strength of his love for his son.

BIBLIOGRAPHY

Ramanathan, Suguna. *The Novels of C. P. Snow: A Critical Introduction.* London: Macmillan, 1978.

Shusterman, David. *C. P. Snow.* Twayne's English Authors, 179. Rev. ed. Boston: Twayne, 1991.

HOPE, CHRISTOPHER (1944–   )

Born in Johannesburg, South Africa, in 1944, Christopher Hope was educated in his home country before relocating to London in 1975, where he worked as a journalist and began his publishing career. He is noted both as a keen observer of the telling details of modern life and as a satirist bent on undermining the unquestioned acceptance of existing power structures. Although Hope has returned to South Africa periodically, he makes his home in the south of France, continuing to work as a journalist and a novelist.

Hope's writing career began in 1971 with the private publication, in South Africa, of a collection of poems, *Whitewashes.* In 1981, his first novel appeared, *A Separate Development;* a SATIRE on apartheid, it was promptly banned in South Africa while it also won the David Higham Prize for fiction. In 1984, *KRUGER'S ALP* was named the WHITBREAD Book of the Year; in it, 10 years after leaving South Africa, Hope continued to draw on his homeland's tortured politics and history for satirical targets. In *The Hottentot Room* (1986), his setting shifts to a London pub frequented by South African expatriates. In 1989, he imagined a friendship between an exiled African dictator and a teenage girl in *My Chocolate Redeemer.* His 1992 dark satire set in an English retirement home, *Serenity House,* was shortlisted for the BOOKER PRIZE. In 1996, he created the Society for Promoting the Discovery of the Interior of England, an African institution that is a parody of 19th-century British exploration societies, in his novel *Darkest England.* The Society's emissary, David Mungo Booi, records his impressions of the mysterious island's inhabitants for the benefit of his compatriots back home. In 1997, Hope once again took South Africa for his setting in *Me, the Moon, and Elvis Presley,* a satire on village life in the wake of apartheid's abolition.

Christopher Hope has also continued producing journalism for magazines and newspapers, and he has originated plays for radio and television performance. He has written a volume of autobiography, *White Boy Running* (1988), and volumes of travel writing examining post-Communist Russia and the contemporary world of the Languedoc region of France, where he continues to live and write.

BIBLIOGRAPHY
"Christopher Hope." Contemporary Writers. Available online. URL: http://www.contemporarywriters.com/. Accessed on Feb. 9, 2004.

HOPEFUL MONSTERS NICHOLAS MOSLEY (1990)

Winner of the WHITBREAD Book of the Year Award for 1990, *Hopeful Monsters* follows in the *Catastrophe Practice* series after *Catastrophe Practice* (1979), *Imago Bird* (1980), *Serpent* (1981), and *Judith* (1986). It stands on its own as a separate story, sharing some characters with the others along with the interest of the series in "catastrophe theory" or the idea that evolution proceeds in leaps during disasters with long lulls in between. A "hopeful monster" is some new creature that will either be well adapted to the altered requirements of survival or that will be wiped out as unfit. The story of the same name is a novel of ideas that examines the period between 1918 and the 1970s. Its two protagonists are Max Ackerman, an English physicist who is the son of a biologist father studying genetics and a mother loosely associated in her youth with the BLOOMSBURY GROUP, and Eleanor Anders, a German Jew and an anthropologist. These characters are loosely modeled on the anthropologist Margaret Mead and the theorist Gregory Bateson.

In part, the novel is a love story about two people who meet, fall in love, and sustain their attachment through a separation that would destroy most relationships. By providing these characters with a historical context, Mosley is able to explore the intellectual worlds of Cambridge and Berlin during a period of global upheaval, from the disastrous closing of WORLD WAR I through the GREAT DEPRESSION, the rise of Nazism and communism, to WORLD WAR II, the development of atomic weapons of mass destruction, and the consequences for the contemporary world of that scientific achievement. Much of the story is revealed in the letters Max and Eleanor write to each other when war keeps them apart; the collector of these letters places an epilogue at the end of the novel.

By carefully defining his characters and their settings, MOSLEY is able to integrate discussions of Darwinism, relativity, Heisenberg's recognition of INDETERMINACY in physics, Marxism, FREUDIAN ideas, aesthetic trends, philosophical issues, and historical events. His novel is an overview of 20th-century intellectual history, but it is also a narrative about the lives of characters with whom readers can identify as they cope with the challenges of life that all people must deal with eventually while also experiencing the events and examining the ideas particular to their own place and time.

BIBLIOGRAPHY

Rudman, Mark. "Sudden Jumps," *Pequod: A Journal of Contemporary Literature and Literary Criticism* 34 (1992): 37–48.

HORNBLOWER, HORATIO

The hero of a series of novels in the subgenre of NAUTICAL FICTION, Horatio Hornblower possesses the courage and intelligence of the traditional hero, but his creator, C. S. FORESTER, deepens his hero's character through psychological realism. Hornblower plays the protagonist in nine novels that cover his entire career in episodes that skip around the fictional chronology of his life. He first appears in *Beat to Quarters* (1937) as the young captain of a frigate during the late 18th century; Forester immediately produced two sequels, *A SHIP OF THE LINE* and *Flying Colours* (both 1938), and later combined these three titles to form *Captain Horatio Hornblower*. Upon this character's promotion to command an entire squadron rather than just one ship, he appears in *Commodore Hornblower* (1945), and he is elevated to the peerage in *Lord Hornblower* (1946). Forester then goes back to explore his hero's apprenticeship in *Mr. Midshipman Hornblower* (1950), but he moves forward in the fictional biography in *Hornblower and the Atropos* (1953) and employs Hornblower as a captain to arrange the funeral of Lord Nelson, killed while winning the Battle of Trafalgar. *Admiral Hornblower in the West Indies* (1958) recounts the end of a brilliant naval career, sending the hero into a well-deserved retirement. *Hornblower and the Hotspur* (1962) returns to the early period of Hornblower's career, just after his midshipman days, opening with his marriage to his first wife.

Part of Hornblower's enduring appeal as a character results from Forester's skillful use of realism, his care to capture accurate historical details, and his vividly described action sequences. But more important, Hornblower is a character with whom readers can identify: He is heroic but not perfect. He worries about his receding hairline, for example, and sometimes loses a battle, a ship, or even a beloved wife or close friend. Forester provides Hornblower with the full panoply of human emotions, giving him a rich interior landscape. Additionally, Hornblower is a man of the people, springing from humble origins and earning his career advancements through his successes rather than through his connections. Most recently, Hornblower has gone on to a second career in made-for-cable movies that replay and reinvent his original print career.

BIBLIOGRAPHY

Forester, C. S. *The Hornblower Companion*. Boston: Little, Brown, 1964.

Parkinson, C. Northcote. *The Life and Times of Horatio Hornblower*. London: Joseph, 1970.

HORSE AND HIS BOY, THE C. S. LEWIS (1954)

See *THE CHRONICLES OF NARNIA*.

HORSE'S MOUTH, THE JOYCE CARY (1944)

See *FIRST TRILOGY*.

HOTEL DU LAC ANITA BROOKNER (1984)

An Englishwoman and a writer of romance fiction under the pseudonym "Vanessa Wilde," Edith Hope becomes a guest at the Swiss Hotel du Lac at Lake Geneva in order to take leave from polite society and work on her next book. Edith is in love with David Simmonds, a married man, and she is contemplating what course of action to take after leaving a less interesting man, Geoffrey Long, at the altar. Continuing her affair with David is socially unacceptable, but doing without it will be personally distressing.

The story is set during the off season of September, which will make the stay of the fewer guests more intimate than usual. The Hotel du Lac is a fine hotel, extraordinary in every detail, and the guests are members of a wealthy, untitled aristocracy. Their money and influence ensure the toleration of their behavior. Edith makes her way to the salon, where she is riveted by the spectacle of Iris Pusey, a woman who smiles from her confidence that people have taken notice of her lace dress and sparkling diamond earrings. Her daughter,

Jennifer, is not as glamorous, but she is definitely a vain creature in the making. These women came to stay at the hotel because of the shopping opportunity. They enjoy the wealth left behind by the late Mr. Pusey, a sherry importer. This mother and daughter introduce one of the novel's themes as Brookner allows Edith to tell the story through a letter to David about her stay. In describing the Puseys, she turns to her own mother and their troubled relationship. Although she is already in her 30s, and despite the fact that she earns a very good living from her romance novels, Edith has not yet succeeded in the one arena where women must succeed, that of love, marriage, and family.

Edith next meets Mr. Neville, a charming gentleman who can be relied upon to remove an unwanted spider from a young lady's boudoir, as Edith learns when a scream draws her to Jennifer's door. Edith does not immediately realize that the connection between Mr. Neville and Jennifer Pusey goes further than entomology. Mr. Neville made his fortune in electronics; having no financial care, he is able to spend time in places like the Hotel du Lac, perhaps searching for the perfect wife—his own having left him for a younger man. As Edith and Mr. Neville become better acquainted, he shares his secret: The important thing is not to expect happiness, but instead to seek contentment. Mrs. Pusey's greedy materialism is good, he says, a perfect example of happiness. Accordingly, love is a weakness; it is a state of being that causes such negative experiences as humility and self-effacement. He argues that Edith does not need love, but should instead accept marriage and seek social standing. With her own ethical compass failing, Edith at first finds Mr. Neville's argument of pathological selfishness compelling. But to enter into the community of conventional life, she must first give up her love for David.

Edith imagines married life with Geoffrey Long—a marriage of convention and convenience rather than of true love. All her friends reiterated how lucky she was; he was so good to his mother, they said. To the marriage he brought a new house, security, a noble quality of being, and even a cottage in the country. For her part, Edith brought her loss of solitude, of industry, and of her life as a writer. Through the marriage, she would become a homemaker; never had she been so unhappy as on the day of her wedding. Thus, as she made her way to the Registry Office that day, Edith asked the driver to take her to the park instead. Later, when she apologized to Geoffrey, he said he was grateful his mother had not lived to see that day.

Unexpectedly, Mr. Neville asks Edith to marry him, saying that he needs a wife who will not discredit or embarrass him. He offers her social standing, confidence, and sophistication. She will be able to spend time writing; furthermore, he owns an estate with a fine house. All this, he argues, will rescue her from becoming an old maid. They will not marry for love but to form a partnership based on mutual self-interest. Edith fears that if the proposal is not accepted, she will be forever alone, without even the hope of a simulacrum of happiness. In what she hopes will be her last communication to David, she explains her predicament. It is a night of anguish for her, since she is making decisions that will last a lifetime. Luckily for this woman of solitude and quiet habits, she has an opportunity to see beneath the surface of Mr. Neville's claims, and she plots her course of action with a confidence that she acquires in the Hotel du Lac.

Anita BROOKNER shares an interest with Margaret DRABBLE and A. S. BYATT in exploring the lives of protagonists who are intelligent, cultivated, educated, competent, and ambitious women. Life is not easy for women who have many options and little preparation for how to choose among them. The power of conventional expectations (or in more old-fashioned terms, of peer pressure) on the decisions women make becomes clear as these contemporary writers explore the bumpy terrain of a world where marriage and family constitute only one of the meaningful options available to today's women.

BIBLIOGRAPHY

Hosmer, Robert E., Jr., ed. *Contemporary British Women Writers: Narrative Strategies.* New York: St. Martin's Press, 1993.

Kenyon, Olga. *Women Writers Talk: Interviews with Ten Women Writers.* New York: Carroll & Graf, 1990.

Skinner, John. *The Fictions of Anita Brookner: Illusions of Romance.* New York: St. Martin's Press, 1992.

HOUND OF THE BASKERVILLES, THE
ARTHUR CONAN DOYLE (1902)   One of the most well known characters in twentieth-century literature, Sherlock HOLMES had been absent from the popular press for some nine years when this "prequel" novel appeared. His creator, having grown tired of him, had plunged Holmes to his apparent death in 1893 at the Reichenbach Falls in the Swiss Alps in the short story "The Final Problem." When DOYLE was inspired to write a ghost story after hearing a friend recount a yarn, he chose a time setting for the story before Holmes's death and revived his detective hero to provide the rational explanation to the mystery.

Set in the 1880s on the gloomy moors around Baskerville Hall, the novel is structured to keep Holmes' rational voice absent except at the beginning and the end. Several classic devices of the ghost story are in use, including the ancient family document and the ancestor who entered into a pact with the devil. With the mysterious death of Sir Charles Baskerville, the baying of an allegedly spectral hound, and the eyewitness testimony to the presence of gigantic paw prints around the corpse of Sir Charles, the creepy supernatural details are clear in the readers' mind.

Holmes sends Dr. Watson to Baskerville Hall with the new heir, Sir Henry, claiming that he must attend to a blackmail case in London. Since the estate of the late Sir Charles is worth nearly a million pounds, Holmes suspects that greed, not ghostly hounds, will explain the mystery. As Watson and Sir Henry sit in the crosshairs of an unknown assailant, Holmes carries on his investigation unseen. This device allows Doyle to use the creepy elements of the ghost story to best advantage: Holmes would dispel the mystery too quickly, but Watson does not see through the manipulations of the unknown guilty party. When the danger has reached such a peak of intensity that an attempt is made on Sir Henry's life, Holmes makes his reappearance, and the game is afoot.

Doyle drags several red herrings across the reader's trail and interweaves a mysterious subplot and an attractive woman with the main story. The solution, when Holmes presents it, is plausible and satisfying; the reader can see that the information needed to identify the guilty party was available all along to anyone with the piercing insight to see it. Once again reason prevails over superstitious fear, and Holmes, the exponent of reason *par excellence,* saves the day. Doyle performs a neat bit of narrative sleight of hand, combining the elements of a ghost story to produce a well-made tale of mystery and detection.

BIBLIOGRAPHY

Baring-Gould, William S. *Sherlock Holmes of Baker Street: A Life of the World's First Consulting Detective.* New York: Potter, 1962.

Keating, H. R. F. *Sherlock Holmes: The Man and His World.* New York: Scribner, 1979.

Shreffler, Philip A. ed. *The Baker Street Reader: Cornerstone Writings about Sherlock Holmes.* Westport, Conn.: Greenwood Press, 1984.

A HOUSE FOR MR. BISWAS   V. S. NAIPAUL (1961)   Inspired by his father, V. S. NAIPAUL wrote this comic but warm celebration of one man's trials through a short but personally successful life. In the prologue, the reader learns that Mohun Biswas, 46, has died in his own home after spending time in a hospital to recover from a heart attack. The house is modest, overpriced, ill-designed, and mortgaged to the hilt, but it constitutes a portion of the earth belonging to Mr. Biswas where his family can establish an existence separate from the pressures of the rest of the world. It is no palace, but it is the symbol of Mr. Biswas's fulfillment of his life's goals.

The third-person narrator then returns to the beginning of Mr. Biswas's story, when he was born backwards at midnight (an unlucky time in Hindu tradition) with six fingers on his hands. But this is not a novel of INDIA: Mr. Biswas and his family reside in the Caribbean, descendents of earlier immigrants from India, and although hope may have driven them to the New World, poverty has followed and staked its claim. Mohun Biswas is born in a mud hut, and his father dies when he is still very young—drowns in an effort to save his son. The family barely survives on grudging charity from relatives, and Mr. Biswas leaves home while he is still a boy. In a series of vignettes, he tries out various forms of employment to great comic effect but without any real success; the people he encounters, at this time and throughout his life, form a catalog of eccentricity that readers recognize as a valid picture of a cross section of humanity.

When Mr. Biswas is hired as a sign painter and goes to work in the Tulsi home, where he passes a mash note to Shama Tulsi, his life is changed forever. The Tulsis rig up a marriage in a twinkling, and Mr. Biswas finds that he has become an insignificant satellite in the chaotic but conformist orbit of the sprawling Tulsi clan. His new wife places her birth family ahead of her marriage family very nearly until the end of her husband's life. Having nothing of his own, Mr. Biswas is at first a cranky dependent on his noisy in-laws. He resides in an allotted room in a Tulsi house and works at several Tulsi enterprises.

Mr. Biswas decides that he must have a house of his own if he is ever to establish himself as a person worthy of respect. He acquires three houses in the course of the story; the first two are destroyed, but like the houses of the Three Little Pigs each is sturdier than the last. In the meantime, his fortunes wax and wane as he works in various Tulsi business interests, operates a food shop, becomes a journalist, and is appointed to a post as a civil servant. His family also grows—first a daughter, Savi, then a son, Anand, and then two more children. Each time Shama is due to deliver, she retreats to the Tulsi compound and remains as long as she wants to. Mr. Biswas unwillingly sees his children grow distant, but in one touching episode his son Anand chooses to remain with his father rather than retreat with his mother. Mr. Biswas has made a connection against overwhelming odds.

A House for Mr. Biswas is remarkable for the honesty with which the stresses and discomforts of family life are portrayed without losing the reader's sympathy toward Mr. Biswas. He is a little guy whom anyone can identify with and cheer on in his struggle to assert his human dignity. Naipaul does not romanticize or sentimentalize the family as a social unit, but he does remind readers that it is the cornerstone of human society of every stripe; furthermore, the family is the nursery of the individuals who compose it. In the communal groupthink world of the Tulsis, individualism is devalued, and Mr. Biswas cannot fit in there (nor can he be respected there) because he is preeminently an individual. He has no desire to disappear into the anonymity of Tulsi clannishness, but he does desire to secure his own corner of the globe where he can shelter his wife and children, allowing them to discover how to *be* rather than mindlessly to follow the old ways just because they are already there. By the end of the novel, even Shama has begun, grudgingly, to prefer her husband's awkward little house to the warrens of her family. Mr. Biswas dies content that he has fulfilled his dreams at last.

BIBLIOGRAPHY

Tsomondo, Thorell. "Metaphor, Metonymy, and Houses: Figures of Construction in *A House for Mr. Biswas.*" *World Literature Written in English* 29, no. 2 (Autumn 1989): 83–94.

———. "Speech and Writing: A Matter of Presence and Absence in *A House for Mr. Biswas.*" *Kunapipi* 10, no. 3 (1988): 18–29.

V. S. Naipaul, *A House for Mr. Biswas. Commonwealth Essays and Studies* 9, no. 1 (Autumn 1986): 59–90.

HOWARDS END E. M. FORSTER (1910) A novel that examines the role of both property and propriety in upper-class English life, *Howards End* features double protagonists in the Schlegel sisters, Margaret and Helen, daughters of an English mother and a cultivated German father. These young women possess good taste and the financial means to indulge in fine concerts, fine literature, and leisurely discussions of art. On a vacation in Germany they meet the Wilcox family, and back in England Helen is invited to visit the Wilcoxes at Howards End, the country home that Mrs. Wilcox brought to her marriage. Helen falls in love with Paul, the younger son, but after showing some interest he later behaves coldly to her—she has not met with the family's unqualified approval. The situation would be a private insult except that Helen had already written to her own family with the news, and so her rejection becomes a family matter. The Wilcoxes and the Schlegels break off contact over the awkward incident.

Some time later, Mrs. Wilcox renews her friendship with Margaret when her family rents an apartment across the street from the Schlegel home. Mrs. Wilcox is in failing health, and in her last days Margaret's friendship is a comfort to her. Her own family is in excellent health and caught up in the social whirl of young adults finding marriage partners. Mrs. Wilcox wants to repay Margaret for her generosity to a dying woman, and upon her death she leaves a note saying that Margaret should receive Howards End. Margaret, however, does not learn of the bequest; the Wilcoxes selfishly ignore the note, assuaging their consciences with the claim that their mother had not known what she was doing.

In the meantime, the Schlegel sisters become acquainted with Leonard Bast, an impoverished young clerk who wishes to better himself. He reads poetry and attends lectures, but he has been tricked into marriage by a coarse woman with a questionable past. The sisters try to help Leonard, but the advice they pass on from a chance encounter with Mr. Wilcox leads to a disastrous result for Leonard. When Mr. Wilcox unexpectedly proposes marriage to Margaret, events are set in motion that could tear the sisters apart: Helen loyally supports Leonard, while Margaret feels a sense of obligation to her fiancé, and an unexpected connection between Mr. Wilcox and Leonard's unsavory wife is discovered. The rift between the sisters widens and Helen removes herself to Germany while Margaret seems to make a happy adjustment to the very conventional and unliterary Mr. Wilcox.

With the Schlegels' possessions stored at Howards End, Helen must go there to retrieve some books she wants, and Margaret surprises her there and discovers the secret she has been keeping from her family. The arrival of Leonard Bast, and the foolish attempt at chivalry of Charles Wilcox, the elder son of Mr. Wilcox, leads to a disastrous outcome. Margaret does wind up at Howards End, just as Mrs. Wilcox had wished, but under very different circumstances than anyone had imagined.

FORSTER develops several key contrasts in this novel in order to comment on the social conventions of the Edwardian era. The Schlegel sisters somewhat resemble the sisters in Jane Austen's *Sense and Sensibility,* with both elder sisters displaying a neoclassical sense of decorum and both younger sisters displaying a romantic inclination toward the spontaneous overflow of powerful feelings. The Schlegels and the Wilcoxes form a contrast between the aesthetically sensitive educated elite and the sports-devoted cultural philistines of the upper class. Leonard Bast recalls Jude Fawley of Thomas Hardy's *Jude the Obscure* in his longing to better himself intellectually in a world that reserves such benefits for those already belonging to the privileged classes. Leonard also shares aspects of the identities of both the Wilcoxes and the Schlegels: like the former, he is tied to the business world, although in a much less important role, and like the latter he is devoted to the intellectual and cultural world.

The fate of these three groupings is finally worked out on the grounds of Howards End, a cornerstone of the agrarian way of life that is disappearing from England under the pressure of business and industry, the chief occupations of the Wilcoxes. In the end, it is only possible to make a place for the marginalized victims of the class system (Leonard's child) by placing the reasonable hand of culture (Margaret Schlegel) over the management of wealth and industry (Mr. Wilcox) in the context of England's agrarian history (Howards End). The novel's epigraph is the short phrase "only connect," which has become a shorthand reference to Forster's humanism; through Howards End the three alienated elements of English life finally find their connection.

BIBLIOGRAPHY

Duckworth, Alistair M. Howards End: *E. M. Forster's House of Fiction.* Twayne's Masterwork Studies, 93. New York: Twayne, 1992.

McConkey, James. *The Novels of E. M. Forster.* Hamden, Conn.: Archon Books, 1957.

Trilling, Lionel. *E. M. Forster.* New York: New Directions, 1943.

HOW FAR CAN YOU GO? DAVID LODGE

(1980) Winner of the WHITBREAD Book of the Year Award in 1980, *How Far Can You Go?* addresses the problems of locating boundaries and establishing limits. More specifically, the title refers to the dilemmas faced by Catholics prohibited from using contraception or resorting to abortion to limit their procreative powers, but LODGE uses this real-world issue as a springboard into a broader examination of cultural and religious values and the ways that people circumvent, transgress, accommodate, or ignore them.

The novel opens on Valentine's Day in 1952 during a Thursday morning communion in a Catholic church, Our Lady and St. Jude's, adjacent to a minor urban British university. Ten characters are introduced: nine worshippers in their late teens and the priest, Father Austin Brierley, who conducts the service. The worshippers include the beautiful girls, Angela and Polly, the bad girl Violet, and the plain girl Ruth; the wicked Michael, who cannot stop thinking of women's breasts, the love-struck Dennis, obsessed with Angela; Miles, the recent convert from the Anglican Church who is worried that he has not developed a liking for girls; the repressed Adrian; and the pragmatically virtuous Edward, assisting with the service.

Lodge introduces these 10, noting they are all virgins, and proclaims his intention of following them through the courses of life during which they are initiated into all of its mysteries. The opening chapter also serves as a plain-language introduction to Catholic theology and ritual, liberally seasoned with examinations of the exact state of the souls of the 10 characters. In the subsequent chapters, readers learn "How They Lost Their Virginities," how the wider world in which their lives are contextualized changed, "How They Lost Their Fear of Hell," how they found various forms of liberation, "How They Dealt with Love and Death" (the book's longest chapter), and finally how they are living at the present moment of the novel's composition. Lodge's tone is by turns satirical, plaintive, and ribald as he examines the contemporary practice of Catholicism in England.

Although the narrative initially appears to take the form of a traditional novel of comic realism, Lodge inserts self-referential touches of POSTMODERNISM before the first chapter comes to an end. He lines up his cast of characters at the altar rail and drills the reader in the catechism of their names and personalities, admitting that 10 characters are a lot to absorb at one time. He explicates his own devices, suggesting, for example, that Adrian's glasses indicate both physical and spiritual impairment of vision. And his explicit language and frank presentation of the degree of sexual awareness possessed by each character hints at the scenes yet to come as these 10 move from innocence to experience and from ignorance to knowledge.

BIBLIOGRAPHY

Bergonzi, Bernard. "A Conspicuous Absentee: The Decline and Fall of the Catholic Novel." *Encounter* 15 (August 1980): 44–56.

Moseley, Merritt and Dale Salwak. *David Lodge: How Far Can You Go?* San Bernardino, Calif.: Borgo Press, 1991.

HOW LATE IT WAS, HOW LATE JAMES KELMAN (1994)

Winner of the BOOKER PRIZE in 1994, this Scottish novel follows a short period in the life of Sammy Samuels during a precipitous downward spiral of misfortunes and bad judgment. Sammy wakes up lying in a weed patch wearing athletic shoes and his good trousers instead of his leather boots and jeans. He has no memory of how he got there, although he does remember starting on a drinking binge the day before the missing day. He has a pounding hangover amplified by an inexplicable rage, and his short temper, fueled by a bit of paranoia and a sense of vulnerability, soon lands him in a brawl with authorities. Sammy goes from bad to worse and wakes up in jail unable to see.

Others do not seem to understand his predicament, and in any case they cannot imagine the experience of blindness from the point of view, so to speak, of the newly blinded man, who doesn't fully comprehend his problem either. Eventually Sammy is released to the blank streets of Glasgow. He feels his way home in terror of the street crossings only to find that his girlfriend, Helen, seems to have left for good this time. He has no choice but to fling himself on the assistance of the Department of Social Services; in a particularly surreal exchange, a doctor in that vast bureaucracy examines him uncomprehendingly, and an alleged solicitor offers to represent his case. Sammy tries to find Helen at the pub where she works, but some special event has disrupted the usual routine: Helen is not there, and no one who is there knows who she is. Even in his favorite pub, Glancy's, among his old drinking buddies, Sammy cannot fully grasp his circumstances and force them into a framework of normality. Conversations with old friends are nearly as strange as was the doctor's examination of him earlier. The missing day forms a barrier that cuts off any direct connection to his past, and without his sight nothing in his life is familiar to him any longer. He decides he might as well be somewhere else as here and so he prepares to undertake a journey there.

KELMAN lightly uses a nearly invisible third-person narrator limited to Sammy's thoughts and feelings, but the vast majority of the story unfolds through Sammy's stream-of-consciousness narration. Sammy's mind is active in the absence of his eyesight as he alternates between reasoning out what is going on in the world and reassuring himself that everything will soon be okay if he can just get through this next little minute. He learns how to cope with his blindness, and he learns how to deal with the limitations of those who cannot see, or who will not accept, the fact that *he* cannot see. He displays courage and resourcefulness; since his problems have grown out of his own flaws, he has no one to blame but himself, and he shoulders this knowledge dutifully. As the days pass, Sammy gains dignity, finds a measure of tranquility, and makes peace with the world he had previously neglected. In the departure that closes the novel, Kelman conveys a deep pathos devoid of sentimentality as Sammy accepts his fate. *How Late It Was, How Late* has been compared favorably with the works of Samuel BECKETT and Franz Kafka for the author's handling of menacing absurdity and existential comedy.

BIBLIOGRAPHY

Gilbert, Geoff. "Can Fiction Swear? James Kelman and the Booker Prize." In *An Introduction to Contemporary Fiction: International Writing in English Since 1970,* Edited by Rod Mengham. Cambridge: Polity Press, 1999, 219–234.

Kirk, John. "Figuring the Dispossessed: Images of the Urban Working Class in the Writing of James Kelman," *English: The Journal of the English Association* 48, no. 191 (1999): 101–116.

Pitchford, Nicola. "How Late It Was for England: James Kelman's Scottish Booker Prize," *Contemporary Literature* 41, no. 4 (2000): 693–725.

HUDSON, W. H. (1841–1922)

Born on August 4, 1841, in Quilmes, Argentina, William Henry Hudson was the son of American parents who had left their homeland in search of a climate that would help heal the father's tuberculosis. The son spent his childhood roaming the pampas and becoming more and more fascinated with the natural history of that environment. As a young man, he collected bird specimens for the Smithsonian Museum. After his father died, and finding his own health impaired by rheumatic fever, Hudson moved to England, where he remained from 1874 until the end of his life.

In England, Hudson was impoverished and isolated, finding little work for someone of his talents as a naturalist. He eventually was married to a woman 15 years his senior. He turned to writing out of financial motives, publishing his first novel, *The Purple Land That England Lost,* in 1885, followed by two more novels before the end of the 19th century, along with several nonfiction books on natural history and ornithology. His novels did not originally find an audience among readers or critics, but his reputation grew with his nonfiction books. When he published GREEN MANSIONS in 1904, it received praise from critics without finding an audience in England. Only in the United States after 1916, when Theodore Roosevelt wrote a preface to the American edition of *The Purple Land,* did Hudson find a readership large enough to provide him with an income from writing. Hudson died in 1922, and three years later a bird sanctuary in Hyde Park was dedicated as a memorial to his life and writing.

BIBLIOGRAPHY

Miller, D. *W. H. Hudson and the Elusive Paradise.* New York: St. Martin's Press, 1990.

Ronner, Amy D. *W. H. Hudson: The Man, the Novelist, the Naturalist.* New York: AMS Press, 1986.

Tomalin, Ruth. *W. H. Hudson: A Biography.* Oxford: Oxford University Press, 1984.

HUGHES, RICHARD (1900–1976)

Author of *A HIGH WIND IN JAMAICA* (1929), Richard Hughes was born on April 19, 1900, in Weybridge, England; his parents were Welsh, and later in life he returned to Wales. He was educated at Charterhouse and at Oriel College, Oxford.

Hughes began his literary career as a playwright, earning praise from George Bernard Shaw for the one-act play *The Sisters' Tragedy* in 1922. In the same year, he published a volume of poetry, *The Gipsy-Night and Other Poems.* In 1926, Hughes published his first collection of short fiction, *A Moment of Time,* along with another volume of poetry, *Confessio Juvenis.* He then turned to long fiction; *A High Wind in Jamaica* was his first novel (also published under the title *The Innocent Voyage*), and it remains the work for which he is best remembered. It is a work remarkable for the author's insight into the lives of children and for his objective handling of narrative structure. Hughes published four additional novels—*In Hazard* (1938), *Gertrude's Child* (1966), and two volumes collectively known as *The Human Predicament: The Fox in the Attic* (1961) and *The Wooden Shepherdess* (1973)—a second collection of short fiction, *In the Lap of Atlas* (1979), and some works of children's literature. He died on April 28, 1976, in Wales.

BIBLIOGRAPHY

Hughes, Penelope. *Richard Hughes: Author, Father.* Glouces-ter, U.K.: A. Sutton, 1984.

Poole, Richard. *Richard Hughes: Novelist.* Bridgend, Midglam-organ: Poetry Wales Press—dist. in the United States by Dufour Editions, 1986.

Thomas, Peter. *Richard Hughes.* Cardiff: University of Wales Press—the Welsh Arts Council, 1974.

HULME, KERI (1947–)

Born on March 9, 1947, in Christchurch, on the South Island of New Zealand, Keri Hulme is the granddaughter of a Maori man, but she was reared in a predominantly English-descended family until she was 18. In 1965, she moved to a town where she had close contact with the Maori population, learning the language and traditions of the descendants of New Zealand's occupants before COLONIALISM arrived. She worked at various jobs for the next seven years before deciding to write full-time at the age of 25. She published a book of poetry in 1982, *The Silences Between: Moeraki Conversations,* influenced by her exposure to Maori language and culture. Her first novel, also dependent on Maori and part-Maori characters and language, was THE BONE PEOPLE (1983),

published through the efforts of a feminist collective. It achieved an extraordinary success and won the BOOKER PRIZE in 1984. She has published one additional novel, two collections of short fiction, and one additional collection of poetry. All these works are informed by her connection to the Maori, who constitute a third of the population of contemporary New Zealand. A reclusive person who has made few details of her private life and personal history available, Keri Hulme continues to live and write in New Zealand.

BIBLIOGRAPHY

Fee, Margery. "Keri Hulme." In *International Literature in English: Essays on the Major Writers.* Edited by Robert L. Ross. New York: Garland, 1991.

Stead, C. K. "Keri Hulme's *The Bone People,* and the Pegasus Award for Maori Literature." *Ariel: A Review of International English Literature* 16, no. 4 (October 1985): 101–108.

Williams, Mark. *Leaving the Highway: Six Contemporary New Zealand Novelists.* Auckland: Auckland University Press, 1990.

HUNDRED DAYS, THE PATRICK O'BRIAN (1998)   See AUBREY-MATURIN NOVELS.

HUXLEY, ALDOUS (1894–1963)

A member of a distinguished family of scientists and intellectu-als—his grandfather was the great defender of Darwin-ian evolution, Thomas Henry Huxley; his maternal great-uncle was the poet Matthew Arnold; and his brother was the biologist Sir Julian Huxley—Aldous Huxley was born on July 26, 1894, in England and died on December 22, 1963, in California. Huxley began his formal education at Eton, England's most prestigious PUBLIC SCHOOL, but was forced to leave when an eye disease nearly blinded him. He learned to read Braille and eventually was able to read printed texts with a magnifying glass, so he entered Balliol College, Oxford, where he studied literature and philosophy.

Huxley began his writing career as a journalist while also writing short fiction and poetry. He became a friend of leading writers such as D. H. LAWRENCE, and he was married in 1919—a marriage that lasted until his wife died in 1955. His first novel, CROME YELLOW, was a success and allowed him to devote himself fully to writing novels and essays. His success grew steadily with the series of COMIC NOVELS he published in the 1920s: *Antic Hay* (1923), *Those Barren Leaves* (1925), and *Point Counterpoint* (1928). In these popular novels, Huxley frequently caricatured recognizable figures from the literary and social worlds, satirizing a spectrum of human follies and valorizing a hedonistic youth-oriented culture. But in his greatest novel, *Brave New World* (1932), he presents exactly such a hedonistic society in a story that has become a classic among DYSTOPIAN NOVELS; his implied condemnation of that pleasure-addicted future world suggests a change of heart.

Huxley and his wife relocated to California in 1937. He had developed an interest in Eastern spirituality, studying Hindu and Buddhist theologies; Buddhism especially influenced him. He continued writing novels, though his pace slackened, producing three in the 1930s, two in the 1940s, one in the 1950s, and one in the 1960s. His output as an essayist, however, expanded, and by the end of his life he had published some 24 volumes of nonfiction prose. He also wrote seven plays and several volumes each of short fiction and poetry. He had a keen interest in escaping from the limits of the ego, transcending solipsism, and he experimented with drugs to try to induce the transformation he sought; his book on these experiments, *The Doors of Perception* (1954), contributed to the growing interest in recreational drug use among the young in the late 1950s and early 1960s.

Huxley's literary reputation has waxed and waned: Critics have dismissed most of his novels either for stylized exaggeration of characters and thin plots that merely provide a pretext for satirical jabs at selected targets, or for essaylike treatises artificially divided out as a simulacrum of dialogue. His influence on his peers is undeniable: Satirists such as Evelyn WAUGH used Huxley's style of sharp social SATIRE, and even mainstream novelists learned from him how to cast a jaundiced eye over human folly. *Brave New World* remains firmly ensconced in the literary canon, holding a place for the novel of ideas in a century when literature was largely dominated by the examination of individual psychology.

BIBLIOGRAPHY

Bedford, Sybille. *Aldous Huxley: A Biography.* 2 vols. New York: Knopf, 1974.

Deery, June. *Aldous Huxley and the Mysticism of Science.* New York: St. Martin's Press, 1996.

James, Clive. "Out of Sight: The Curious Career of Aldous Huxley," *The New Yorker,* 17 March 2003, 143–148.

Meckier, Jerome, ed. *Critical Essays on Aldous Huxley.* New York: G. K. Hall, 1996.

I

I CAPTURE THE CASTLE DODIE SMITH
(1948)   A BILDUNGSROMAN with a first-person narrator in 17-year-old Cassandra Mortmain, this COMIC
NOVEL relates the events in the lives of the Mortmain
family as Cassandra and her older sister, Rose, become
young adults during the year that two wealthy American brothers take up ownership of and residence on
the estate that includes Godsend Castle, the derelict
property the Mortmains lease.

The novel's title refers to Cassandra's desire to make
an accurate written record of life among the Mortmains
at Godsend. She keeps her journal in a cheap school
notebook, because that is all she can afford. Her father,
a writer, had published a successful experimental novel
many years earlier, *Jacob Wrestling* (Dodie Smith had
James JOYCE's ULYSSES in mind as the model for Mortmain's book), but he has suffered from writer's block for
years. Every day he goes to his study above the draw-
bridge and produces no new writing, and every day his
family slips into more desperate financial circumstances. His second wife, Topaz, stepmother to the girls,
was once a famous artists' model and occasionally earns
some money still, but she prefers to flit about the castle
grounds communing with the elements. Twenty-year-
old Rose is so desperate for some proper clothes that
she threatens to go out on the street and sell her body;
however, deep in the rural English countryside, she is
secure from making good on her threat.

When Simon Cotton inherits Scoatney Hall and
comes there to live with his younger brother Neil and
his mother, Rose and Cassandra are soon enjoying a
better life through visits with their new landlord. Rose
determines to capture the heart of Simon Cotton and
achieve financial security for herself and her family
through this advantageous marriage. Cassandra has a
suitor in rustic young Stephen, a kind of volunteer
butler and handyman to the Mortmains, but when a
London photographer sees his potential, her pictures
of him make him an overnight celebrity in the art
world. Cassandra begins to think she will never
acquire the skill and success that beautiful Rose enjoys,
but several unexpected turns occur to take the story in
new directions. Cassandra does find love, and in the
most unexpected place.

I Capture the Castle became a best-selling novel both
in England and in the United States, and Dodie SMITH
adapted it for the stage in 1954. It is a novel that one
generation of women passes down to the next: Cassandra's ingenuous charm and the coming-of-age struggles
that she and Rose endure continue to ring true to life.
In addition to the believable voice of the narrator, the
novel features a compelling plot and fascinating characters who balance eccentricity and realism. Dodie
Smith avoids the formulaic quality of romance novels
while also producing a highly romantic story with
unexpected thoughtfulness and a great depth of feeling. Her graceful style makes the novel an effortless

reading experience, beginning with its arresting first sentence: "I write this sitting in the kitchen sink."

BIBLIOGRAPHY

Barnes, Julian. "Literary Executions." In *The Writing Life: Writers on How They Think and Work.* Edited by Marie Arana. New York: Public Affairs, 2003, 382–386.

Blais, Jacqueline. "55 Years Later, "Castle" Keeps Capturing Fans," *USA Today*, 4 September 2003, 5d.

I, CLAUDIUS ROBERT GRAVES (1934)

An example of HISTORICAL FICTION, this novel is based on the lives of the first four Caesars of ancient Rome and the struggles for power that follow the death of Augustus Caesar. GRAVES makes the first-person narrator seem to speak directly out of the past by prefacing his story with the fictional claim that Claudius's lost autobiography has recently been found and translated.

The main character of the story is Tiberius Claudius Drusus Nero Germanicus, thought to be half-witted because of his stuttering and scorned for his lameness. Claudius learns to use his impairments to his advantage, surreptitiously observing those who think him incompetent and storing up information in the historical records he keeps. Since he cannot compete against his peers in physical prowess, he compensates in studiousness and scholarship. He seems harmless and weak in his acceptance of the scorn heaped in him, and the strategy makes him a survivor in a bloodthirsty family driven by lust for power.

The chief villain of the story is Livia, the calculating wife of Augustus. She gets her way by poisoning any who stand between her and the achievement of her goals. She wants her son by a previous marriage, Tiberius, to succeed Augustus, and she makes it happen; she may even have poisoned the emperor himself, her own husband, to place her progeny on the imperial throne. Later, her desire to be declared a goddess after her death leads her to take Claudius into her confidence and to share her murderous secrets with him in return for his assistance in her deification. In this way, Claudius gains the power that such information confers without committing the atrocities that generally serve power.

Atrocity becomes a theme of Roman history when Caligula, son of Claudius's brother, comes to power after murdering the ailing Tiberius. He deceives others into supporting him by suppressing his barbarous nature until he holds the throne, but then he unleashes a reign of bloodshed and degradation until he is assassinated. Mild, nonthreatening Claudius seems an excellent choice for emperor after the brutality of Caligula, and this most unlikely candidate ascends the throne.

Graves's novel was a great success when it was published, and it began a second life in 1976, when it was adapted for television by the BBC. The dramatic interpretation took advantage of the soap opera–like melodrama of the story, and the performance featured numerous well-known actors of the Royal Shakespeare Company. Graves preserved the Roman quality of the pagan religious beliefs of the characters, but he had updated the personality of Claudius to give him a more modern set of political values and pragmatic characteristics, and this device made the adaptation appealing to contemporary audiences. The novel continues to entertain readers, decades after its initial publication, reaching a worldwide audience through its many translations. Readers of historical fiction may also wish to read the sequel, *Claudius the God and His Wife Messalina* (1935), or to read the actual sources for both novels in Suetonius.

BIBLIOGRAPHY

Canary, Robert H. *Robert Graves.* Boston: G. K. Hall, 1980.

Seymour-Smith, Martin. "Claudius." In *Robert Graves.* Edited by Harold Bloom. New York: Chelsea House, 1987.

Suetonius. *The Twelve Caesars.* Translated by Robert Graves. London: Penguin, 1957.

IONIAN MISSION, THE PATRICK O'BRIAN (1981)

See AUBREY-MATURIN NOVELS.

IN A FREE STATE V. S. NAIPAUL (1971)

This novel fits into the pessimistic part of the author's career and won the BOOKER PRIZE in 1971. A study of alienation and exile in the modern world, *In a Free State* consists of two pieces of nonfiction travel writing, "The Tramp at Piraeus" at the beginning and "The Circus at Luxor" at the end, serving as prologue and epilogue, and a short novel in the middle made up of three separate stories that examine the experiences of people who are in exile from their places of origin and yet alienated from their places of residence. These fictional pieces—"One Out of Many," "Tell Me Who to Kill," and "In a Free State"—are unified by their dependence on characters who embrace freedom and discover that alienation is the price of this choice.

"One Out of Many" and "Tell Me Who to Kill" both feature a first-person narrator of Indian descent. In the first, Santosh abandons his family in INDIA to relocate to Washington, D.C., rather than return to his village unemployed. In Washington, he abandons his employer and even his own concept of himself, finding that in repeatedly taking the easy way, he has brought himself to a dead end. In the second story, a West Indian family tries to better itself by educating its brightest hope, the youngest son. The narrator is one of the older sons who has dedicated himself to the elevation of his brother, working endless long days and sacrificing his own life in the process. His nameless condition in the story suggests the unvalued status of his life. He follows his young brother to London, but there he loses his life savings in the failure of a curry restaurant. His brother pursues a course of action—marriage to an Englishwoman—that cannot bring the benefits the entire family wished to achieve through this son. The narrator's life has been devoted to an empty hope, and he sends word to the family that he is dead.

"In a Free State" features a third-person narrator and is set in a postcolonial African nation similar to Uganda. Two characters, Bobby and Linda, are traveling by car to their homes in the southern part of the country. Bobby is a homosexual fleeing from English homophobia who has immigrated to this country to work as a bureaucrat; Linda is a married woman returning to the place she and her husband are temporarily calling home. The trip is fraught with danger since civil unrest is simmering between rival ethnic and political factions in the north and the south of the country. The violent events that unfold demonstrate the outsider status of these two Europeans in Africa on several levels.

The pessimism of these fictional stories is perhaps moderately alleviated by the events of the travel narratives in which they are contextualized. In the prologue, the author sees an example of casual inhumanity and does nothing about it, but in the epilogue a similarly petty and callous event stirs him to intervene. Naipaul seems to suggest that the unremitting gloom of the stories as exemplars of the human condition can be lifted, but only at the cost of every person taking action and sharing responsibility for preserving human dignity and value. The high price and the great risk to those willing to pay it must temper our expectations of what human beings can reasonably expect of a world where displacement and unrootedness have replaced connectedness and tradition.

BIBLIOGRAPHY

Morris, Robert K. *Paradoxes of Order: Some Perspectives on the Fiction of V. S. Naipaul.* Columbia: University of Missouri Press, 1975.

Theroux, Paul. *V. S. Naipaul: An Introduction to His Works.* New York: Africana Publishing, 1972.

Weiss, Timothy. *On the Margins: The Art of Exile in V. S. Naipaul.* Amherst: University of Massachusetts Press, 1992.

IN CHANCERY JOHN GALSWORTHY (1920)

The second volume in the trilogy entitled *The* FORSYTE SAGA, this novel resumes the story of Soames and Irene Forsyte several years after the close of *A* MAN OF PROPERTY, the first volume of the series. The 19th century is turning to the 20th; the British are embroiled in the BOER WAR in South Africa, the beginning of a long process of relinquishing the territories of the EMPIRE. And in the Forsyte family, enmity has arisen to divide the formerly unified clan. The title of this volume of the saga refers to the British court system that handles family law, including divorce cases. Nothing less than divorce can resolve the problems that have plagued the marriage of Soames and Irene.

The two of them have been separated for some time; Irene lives a quiet life in a small flat, earning a modest living by giving music lessons. In a short story that falls in between the first two volumes, readers learn that Soames's uncle, old Jolyon Forsyte, had made a bequest to Irene at his death. She is not destitute, although she hardly enjoys the life that she could have had as the obedient wife of a powerful and wealthy man.

Soames has sublimated his frustrations through his drive to make even more money, but he has begun to long for an heir to whom he can leave his name, his wealth, and his position. Irene will not return to him, and so he looks to other women and soon settles on Annette Lamotte, a young Frenchwoman. According to British divorce laws at that time, divorce cases were routine if one partner had been unfaithful to the other and evidence of that infidelity could be brought before a court. Soames resorts to hiring a detective to ferret out grounds for a divorce; he knows that Irene has been seen in public with his cousin, young Jolyon; this cousin, in fact, is the trustee of the legacy his father left to Irene. Soames's suspicions virtually drive Irene and Jolyon together.

Other branches of the Forsyte clan are also enduring personal problems: Soames's sister, Winifred, finds herself abandoned by her husband, and when two Forsyte cousins go to fight in the Boer War, only one returns. Irene flees to Paris to avoid Soames, and when Jolyon joins her there, the evidence required for the divorce becomes available. Soames and Annette are married, as are Irene and Jolyon. The book ends with the birth of a child in each of these new branches of the Forsyte family. The longed-for heir, however, is a little girl, Fleur, while Irene gives birth to a son, Jon. The story continues in the next volume, *To Let*.

BIBLIOGRAPHY

Gindin, James. "Ethical Structures in John Galsworthy, Elizabeth Bowen, and Iris Murdoch." In *Forms of Modern British Fiction*. Edited by Alan Warren Friedman. Austin: University of Texas Press, 1975.

Rønning, Anne Holden. *Hidden and Visible Suffrage: Emancipation and the Edwardian Woman in Galsworthy, Wells, and Forster.* New York: Peter Lang, 1995.

INDETERMINACY

In the interpretation of literature, rarely does any one explanation fully exhaust the possibilities suggested by the work in question. The other explanations that can also serve to articulate the meaning of a literary text produce AMBIGUITY, and in the 20th century this characteristic has generally been treated as a virtue rather than a vice. A richly textured work of literature offers readers many options for understanding it and yet continues to provoke further thought.

Literary indeterminacy is similar to scientific overdetermination, but science and philosophy generally resort to Occam's Razor and select the simplest of the many possible explanations for a given phenomenon as a starting point for further investigation. Literary scholars in the 20th century have gone in the opposite direction, generating numerous approaches to the interpretation of literature—formalist, feminist, Marxist, psychoanalytic, archetypal, deconstructionist, and historicist are only a few of the possible approaches to a literary text—thereby multiplying the interpretive possibilities rather than cutting them down to a preferred common denominator. For readers ready to discuss a literary text, this indeterminacy suggests the usefulness of keeping an open mind and maintaining a willingness to explore new directions as they become apparent.

See also ARCHETYPE, FEMINISM, FORMALISM.

BIBLIOGRAPHY

Beach, Christopher, ed. *Artifice and Indeterminacy: An Anthology of New Poetics.* Tuscaloosa: University of Alabama Press, 1998.

Iser, Wolfgang. "Indeterminacy and the Reader's Response." In *Twentieth-Century Literary Theory: A Reader.* Edited by K. M. Newton. New York: St. Martin's Press, 1997, 195–199.

Walsh, Timothy. *The Dark Matter of Words: Absence, Unknowing, and Emptiness in Literature.* Carbondale: Southern Illinois University Press, 1998.

INDIA AND PAKISTAN

British interest in the Indian subcontinent began in 1600 A.D. with the creation of the East India Company and the granting of trade monopolies. Portuguese and Dutch explorers had already made some contacts, and the geographical territory of India contained a pastiche of small territories, many of them Hindu, under the rule of the Muslim Mughal Empire. The British originally aimed at establishing a presence in Indonesia in order to profit from the spice trade, but the Portuguese destroyed the British post there. The British broke the Portuguese monopoly on the sea routes to Arabia, with its holy city of Mecca, and formed an alliance with the Mughal empire by 1618.

By the mid-1700s, England traded from three centers of power widely separated around the subcontinent: Bombay, Calcutta, and Madras. Trade goods included spices, cottons, silks, indigo, opium, and saltpeter for manufacturing gunpowder, and later tea was cultivated for trade. But this international undertaking was at first a strictly commercial enterprise; only gradually did the East India Company get into the business of governing parts of India; by 1765, the structure of a corporate government was in place in Bengal, and by 1818 Britain's influence extended over most of the territory of India. Gradually, this corporate state became an imperial territory governed by British administrators; an act of Parliament in 1858 officially transferred political power from the East India Company to the British government, and in 1876 Queen Victoria added the phrase "Empress of India" to her titles. The Raj reached its zenith during the period from 1858 to 1885 after quelling a revolt that began in 1857 (fictionalized in the award-winning novel The SIEGE OF KRISHNAPUR (1973) by J. G. FARRELL). The formation of the Indian National Congress in 1885 formally began the struggle for self-rule that ended in 1947.

British rule in India differed from earlier European colonial enterprises: No large-scale immigrant colonies arrived, and no major conquest was required. British administrators organized and modernized India, profiting from the acquisition of raw materials and markets for manufactured goods, but also building roads, bridges, rail lines, irrigation projects, and other public works. Nonetheless, the British were outsiders, and Indian support for self-rule grew steadily after 1885. By 1906, self-rule was an official demand of the Hindu-dominated Congress, and a parallel Muslim League developed to pursue the same goal. At first, the key supporters of self-rule were English-educated middle-class professionals, but several British policies and harsh military actions converted millions of moderate Indians to support nationalism.

Britain's worst error was probably the assault on a peaceful gathering in Amritsar on April 13, 1919. When the British commander ordered troops to open fire on the 10,000 Indians of every age and station in life, he provided a turning point in the struggle for independence. The charismatic leadership of Mohandas K. Gandhi and Jawaharlal Nehru among Hindus and Mohammed Ali Jinnah among Muslims helped shape Indian outrage into a powerful movement, although the two religious groups remained at odds in every other way. Gandhi's program of nonviolent noncooperation in particular provided an effective strategy that seized the moral high ground from the British. The Congress proclaimed self-rule on January 26, 1930. With a delay due to WORLD WAR II, and violent civil infighting between Hindus and Muslims, India's struggle for independence led to the formation of two nations: At midnight on August 14–15, 1947, British India was simultaneously liberated and partitioned into a two-part Muslim state, West and East Pakistan (later to become Bangladesh), and a Hindu state, the Republic of India.

The connection between England and India has left its mark on literature and produced some of the greatest novels written in English—some by English authors, some by Indian authors, and some by others. Rudyard KIPLING's KIM stands as an eyewitness record of life under the British Raj, and the English author E. M. FORSTER captures the vast three-way cultural gap between British, Hindu, and Muslim interests in A PASSAGE TO INDIA. Many years later, the English novelist Paul SCOTT chronicles the effect of British rule in the volumes of The RAJ QUARTET, and of the aftermath of liberation in STAYING ON. The Indian writer Anita DESAI recounts the tensions in 1947 between Muslim and Hindu families sharing an upper-class neighborhood in CLEAR LIGHT OF DAY; the Indian writer Arundhati ROY, in The GOD OF SMALL THINGS, examines contemporary Indian life in the sovereign nation that India has become in the years since liberation. Ruth Prawer JHABVALA, a German-Jewish refugee to England who married an Indian and resided many years in India, examines the English fascination with her adopted country in HEAT AND DUST; the Canadian-Indian novelist Rohinton MISTRY turns his attention to the Parsi community of India in A FINE BALANCE. In contemporary England, Hanif KUREISHI examines the position in England of Pakistani immigrants and their fully assimilated offspring in The BUDDHA OF SUBURBIA, and Salman

RUSHDIE explores India, Pakistan, England, and the world in MIDNIGHT'S CHILDREN and other novels. A great diaspora has spread Indian culture to Africa, the Caribbean, Europe, the Pacific, and North America, and the greatest chronicler of that vast example of exile is the Indian-descended novelist from Trinidad, V. S. NAIPAUL, particularly in works such as A HOUSE FOR MR. BISWAS and A BEND IN THE RIVER, set not in India but in the places Indians have immigrated to. These are only a few examples of the literary outpouring struck forth from the impact of West and East in the ancient lands of the Indian subcontinent.

BIBLIOGRAPHY

Booker, Keith M. Colonial Texts: India in the Modern British Novel. Ann Arbor: University of Michigan Press, 1997.

Naik, M. K. A History of Indian English Literature. New Delhi: Sahitya Akademi, 1982.

INDUSTRIALISM/POSTINDUSTRIALISM

Beginning with the establishment of factories in the 18th century and reaching its zenith during the first half of the 20th century, industrialism increased productivity and thereby created greater wealth through the centralization of manufacturing processes and the subdivision of the tasks required to produce material goods. Under the factory system, skilled workers no longer manufactured complete products one at a time; instead, unskilled (and therefore lower paid) workers stood on assembly lines and performed only one small part of the total task required to manufacture a product. Combined with the speedy distribution made possible by a railroad system, industrialism changed the face of England and the world: Agrarian regions were crisscrossed with rail lines, and factories arose belching soot from the coal fires that powered their turbines. The decentralized population distribution of an economy dependent on agricultural and cottage industries gradually condensed around manufacturing centers such as Birmingham, Manchester, and the "potteries district" of Stoke-on-Trent.

Writers from the time of William Blake's "dark Satanic mills" onward have captured and commented on this historical transformation of English economic life and of the English countryside. The last decade of the 19th century and the early 20th century in partic-

ular produced a wealth of literature about the new working class: Jude the Obscure by Thomas Hardy features characters repeatedly waiting on train platforms as they chase receding opportunities to secure employment for outmoded skills, and ANNA OF THE FIVE TOWNS by Arnold BENNETT captures the lives of people in the expanding middle CLASS. Additional writers known for depicting the effects of industrialism include George Gissing, George ORWELL, Henry GREEN, John BERGER, the ANGRY YOUNG MEN of the 1950s, and to a lesser extent D. H. LAWRENCE.

Industrialism also led to a greater awareness on the part of workers of the power they acquired through banding together to form unions. Karl Marx and Friedrich Engels urged workers to exercise their power to establish a political voice, giving rise to various movements in support of greater and lesser degrees of socialism, including the FABIAN SOCIETY and even the Labour Party. Marx extended his critique of capitalist economic organization to include a condemnation of the cultural underpinnings that contributed to the oppression of the proletariat, or working class. From a Marxist point of view, art is not simply the outpouring of human creativity; instead, it serves the needs of the bourgeois patrons who commission or buy it. In the earlier history of the English novel, it's true that members of the upper classes frequently served as protagonists and were rewarded with wealth, but by the late 19th century the working classes began to have a meaningful presence in fiction as main characters. This trend has continued into the 20th century: Workers have become commonplace protagonists in mainstream serious literature.

The 20th century is also the starting point for the postindustrialist world through the spread of rapid communication, electronic and digital equipment, and the rise of the Information Age. Workers can once again be decentralized, if they wish, once the products of their labor can be created and delivered electronically. Literature is being transformed by these new technologies as books become FILM ADAPTATIONS, audio recordings, downloadable files, and other digital forms; as computer games develop more and more sophisticated narrative structures; as point-and-click hyperlinks facilitate nonlinear storytelling; as nonprint media come to be as easily manipulated as words and sentences have been for millennia; and as new kinds of expression and collaboration develop through the Internet.

BIBLIOGRAPHY

Keating, P. J. *The Working Classes in Victorian Fiction.* London: Routledge & Kegan Paul, 1971.

Turner, Barry A. *Industrialism.* Harlow, U.K.: Longman, 1975.

INFORMATION, THE MARTIN AMIS (1995)

A work of darkly satiric POSTMODERNISM, this novel features as its protagonist a novelist, Richard Tull, who has painstakingly written two obscure novels, in contrast to the heady success of Gwyn Barry, Richard's old university roommate, who achieves international fame with his second novel, *Amelior.* Richard is working on his newest novel, entiled *Untitled,* and editing a minuscule literary magazine to earn a pittance; mostly his family depends for its support on Richard's patient wife, Gina. The inequity between the reception of Richard's work, in comparison to Gwyn's lightweight fiction, begins to gnaw at Richard's conscience, driving him to take desperate measures in order to right this egregious imbalance in the literary world. Richard's intellect, talent, and hard work have failed to bring him the rewards he longs to possess while showering them on Gwyn. In an ironic American publicity tour, the two writers are yoked together as inequitably as possible, with Gwyn's stunning unearned success continually present to Richard's smarting and envious eye.

While continuing to maintain the appearance of friendly relations with Gwyn, Richard strikes up the acquaintance of Scozzy, a miscreant and one of the few individuals who has read Richard's work. While Richard waffles from one outlandish vengeful scheme to another, Scozzy pursues more traditional methods of harassment, such as breaking and entering. Richard longs to seduce Gwyn's wife or to expose Gwyn's insecurities, but his efforts come to nought through his own bad luck and through Gwyn's steady attempts to shore himself up. Richard even fails at his scheme to type out *Amelior* (with minor emendations) in order to create a fake source as evidence of plagiarism. Meanwhile, Scozzy becomes increasingly difficult to control,

like a libidinal id figure determined to work its will in the world, and his self-assertiveness forces the narrator (gradually revealed as Martin AMIS) to enter the story from time to time. This self-reflexive fictionalizing of the real author, who must enter his fiction in order to keep the products of his own imagination under control, creates one of the key postmodern aspects of the novel. Martin Amis presents the contemporary literary world as a site of intense sibling rivalries and atavistic returns to the ethical standards—or lack thereof— common in childhood.

BIBLIOGRAPHY

Diedrick, James. *Understanding Martin Amis.* Columbia: University of South Carolina Press, 1995.

Nash, John. "Fiction May Be a Legal Paternity: Martin Amis's *The Information,*" *English: The Journal of the English Association* 45, no. 183 (Autumn 1996): 213–224.

INFORMER, THE LIAM O'FLAHERTY (1925)

Set in the 1920s in Dublin, this novel of psychological realism follows the pattern of the Judas story: A member of a marginalized group who betrays a comrade for money then finds himself alienated from all other people, throws away his money, and dies. O'FLAHERTY draws on the violent factions of the Irish Republican Army and the Irish communist movement for characters and situations, but his story focuses on the characters rather than on their political beliefs. The protagonist is Gypo Nolan, and the comrade he betrays is Francis McPhillip, an assassin. Gypo is a man of the earth, slow of thought and powerful in body, and as long as he has a partner to guide him, he carries out his orders. Left to his own devices, however, the difficulties of keeping body and soul together overmaster him. Alone and with no place to sleep, he informs the police that Francis has returned to his family's home after a long period in hiding. The 20 pounds Gypo receives is a virtual fortune to him, but the arrival of the police at the McPhillip home causes Francis to kill himself rather than be taken alive.

With money in his pocket, Gypo needs contact with human beings, but he is incapable of sustaining a positive interaction with others. He visits a prostitute friend, Katy, gives her money, and quarrels with her; he visits the bereaved McPhillip family, quarrels with the father, and gives some money to the mother. The organization he and Francis had supported has expelled them both, but now its leader, Dan Gallagher, sends for Gypo, demanding an explanation as to how he acquired money at the same time Francis died. Once again, Gypo's response is to sacrifice someone else, and he accuses another man. In his dim thoughts, he foresees his restoration to the group, anticipating that he will be exonerated in the "trial" that has been ordered.

Gypo cannot see how near he is to the end of his own life, and he spends the day, and his money, trying to connect with other people. But he is doomed, and O'Flaherty makes it clear that he is the representative of the human condition. We all long to connect with others and to belong to a larger group, but we are also all limited and isolated by the very nature of human existence. Gypo's tragedy is the human tragedy of loneliness, isolation, frailty, and mortality.

BIBLIOGRAPHY

Donoghue, Denis. Preface to *The Informer* by Liam O'Flaherty. New York: Harcourt Brace Jovanovich, 1980.

Sheeran, Patrick F. *The Novels of Liam O'Flaherty: A Study in Romantic Realism*. Dublin: Wolfhound Press, 1976.

Zneimer, John. *The Literary Vision of Liam O'Flaherty*. Syracuse, N.Y.: Syracuse University Press, 1970.

INIMITABLE JEEVES, THE P. G. WODEHOUSE (1922)   See THE JEEVES SERIES.

INJURY TIME BERYL BAINBRIDGE (1977)

In this darkly comic misadventure, four dinner guests and an uninvited friend become hostages of a gang of criminals, much to the consternation of the man who is out with his mistress. *Injury Time* was Beryl BAINBRIDGE'S eighth novel; it won the WHITBREAD AWARD in 1977.

The hostess of the dinner party is Binney, a woman attempting to create some semblance of respectability out of her affair with a married man. Her lover, Edward Freeman—an ironically chosen name—is a tax accountant, and on nights when his wife Helen attends her meetings, he and Binney enjoy a few stolen moments together. Binney is an integral part of those circles of Edward's life not frequented by Helen, but she longs to engage in the more wifely duties of cook-

ing and socializing. Edward has agreed to invite Simpson, a client of the firm, and his wife to a dinner party at Binney's house. The omniscient third-person narrator alternates between Edward and Binney's afternoon activities as the hour of the dinner party draws near.

With the arrival of Simpson and his wife, Muriel, the party proceeds with a moderate degree of success that threatens to collapse at any minute. Beginning with the arrival of Binney's friend Alma, however, events go quickly downhill: She is drunk and petulant, and eventually she throws up on Muriel's fur coat. Soon afterward, the gang of bank robbers bursts in and finds themselves in charge of five miserable hostages. Throughout the remainder of the night and the next day, the dinner party guests and the criminals interact in ways that reveal deeper aspects of character than would be found in ordinary social settings. The narrator provides a mercilessly droll view of the follies and misunderstandings that occur and of the frailties that are revealed before the situation reaches its resolution. Bainbridge prevents the reader from developing sympathy for the hostages by presenting their flawed lives in such a way that every petty lie and insecure vanity is exposed.

BIBLIOGRAPHY

"Books in Brief." Review of *Injury Time*. *National Review* 30, no. 23 (9 June 1978): 732.

Wiehe, Janet. Review of *Injury Time*. *Library Journal* 103, no. 6 (15 March 1978): 682.

INKLINGS   Academic life in Oxford includes, both for students and scholars, the occasional indulgence of that quintessential part of English life, a visit to a local pub to imbibe a pint and enjoy a convivial evening with friends. In the 1930s and 1940s, a group of academics began meeting regularly at various Oxford pubs, including The Eagle and Child, The Burning Babe, and others, and they also met frequently in the rooms of C. S. LEWIS, a leading figure in the group. Those in attendance shared an interest in both academic literature and mythology, and they shared a commitment to Christianity. In these meetings, they discussed their writing projects and their ideas, and they read aloud passages from original works still in development.

They called themselves the Inklings, and their numbers included J. R. R. TOLKIEN, C. S. Lewis and sometimes his brother W. H. Lewis, Charles WILLIAMS, Hugo Dyson, Nevil Coghill, Dr. Havard, and others.

At that time, writing books in popular genres such as FANTASY, MYSTERY AND DETECTIVE FICTION, SCIENCE FICTION, or romance was not a respectable activity for serious scholars; indeed, to the present day, "popular" genres remain a contested ground in many academic circles. Tolkien and Lewis published works of traditional scholarship in their areas of specialty, but they also pursued their academically unacceptable creative efforts, providing and receiving mutual support and interest in the informal meetings of the Inklings. This sharing of ideas is apparent in the similarity, for example, of Aslan's creation of Narnia by singing it into existence in the first volume of The CHRONICLES OF NARNIA, and Eru's creation of space and time by means of music in The Silmarillion. The group never became more than a casual association of friends sharing common interests, and eventually life's other demands occupied the key members. Like the BLOOMSBURY GROUP, the Inklings did not found a school of philosophy or develop a unique critical approach, but both served as important ways for their members to explore ideas and gain fresh perspectives on their works in progress.

BIBLIOGRAPHY

Carpenter, Humphrey. The Inklings: C. S. Lewis, J. R. R. Tolkien, Charles Williams, and Their Friends. Boston: Houghton Mifflin, 1979.

Duriez, Colin and David Porter. The Inklings Handbook: A Comprehensive Guide to the Lives, Thought, and Writings of C. S. Lewis, J. R. R. Tolkien, Charles Williams, Owen Barfield, and Their Friends. St. Louis, Mo.: Chalice Press, 2001.

Fredrick, Candace. Women Among the Inklings: Gender, C. S. Lewis, J. R. R. Tolkien, and Charles Williams. Westport, Conn.: Greenwood Press, 2001.

IN PARENTHESIS DAVID JONES (1937)

Classified as both an epic poem and a novel, this work of MODERNISM, praised by T. S. Eliot, won the HAWTHORNDEN PRIZE in 1938, it follows several young men into the carnage of WORLD WAR I; David JONES drew on his own experience in the war to create this work, admired for its power to show the reader what being in the war was really like. The action of the story covers seven months from December 1915, to July 1916; it follows the lives (and deaths in most cases) of seven characters, all men serving in the Royal Welsh Regiment, 55th Battalion, "B" Company, Platoon number seven; and in structure it is divided into seven sections.

The story moves from the soldiers' training in England through their deployment in France. Readers get to know these men as individuals and share with them their emotional experiences as they come closer to battle and sink further into danger. The connection with the characters creates the powerful effect of the closing section, set at the Battle of the Somme, in which 20,000 British soldiers lost their lives in a single day and 40,000 more were wounded. Of the seven main characters, six are killed. In the end, the lowest ranking man survives, wounded in the leg, and watches other soldiers, from his position under a dead oak tree, hurrying by to their deaths.

Jones wrote an introduction and an extended set of notes for his poem; its use of footnotes to translate Welsh phrases and to identify allusions to obscure Welsh mythic characters makes it resemble "The Wasteland" by T. S. Eliot. Jones's tone is objective and dispassionate, but he also achieves a spiritual quality as well. The men are engaged in a sacrificial ritual, and the writer offers his commemoration of their sacrifice as a kind of prayer or gift to God. In spite of the poem's straightforward depiction of war's gruesome and violent sacrifices, it is not an antiwar poem such as Wilfred Owen's "Dulce Et Decorum Est"; instead, it places the fighting men of this war into the larger context of the heroes throughout history who have fought and died. Novel, poem, autobiography, or prayer, Jones's text remains a compelling document of one of the great tragedies of the early 20th century.

BIBLIOGRAPHY

Dilworth, Thomas. The Shape of Meaning in the Poetry of David Jones. Toronto: University of Toronto Press, 1988.

Rees, Samuel. David Jones. Twayne's English Authors, 246. Boston: Twayne, 1978.

Staudt, Kathleen Henderson. *At the Turn of a Civilization: David Jones and Modern Poetics.* Ann Arbor: University of Michigan Press, 1994.

INTERTEXTUALITY

An extended form of symbolism and allusion, intertextuality describes the characteristic of literature that has its origin in or takes its inspiration from other works of literature. Thus in *Wide Sargasso Sea* by Jean Rhys, the main character of Antoinette Mason is borrowed from *Jane Eyre* by Charlotte Brontë. Rhys's reimagining of Brontë's character gives a voice to a marginalized and demonized character; her novel is an interpretation of Brontë's novel, and each of the two sheds light on and deepens a reader's appreciation of the other. In *Tremor of Intent,* Anthony Burgess deliberately imitates the style and content of a spy novel by Ian Fleming, although without borrowing James Bond or any other character of Fleming's. *At Swim-Two-Birds* by Flann O'Brien borrows characters from Irish mythology and imitates the style of Wild West dime novels and the pulp fiction conventions of mystery and detective novels. The Aubrey-Maturin novels of Patrick O'Brian grow out of and improve on the Horatio Hornblower novels of C. S. Forester. And in *The Blind Assassin,* Margaret Atwood creates a kind of false intertextuality by inserting extracts of a novel also named *The Blind Assassin* (which does not have a correlative text in the "real world" outside her novel, as do the other examples mentioned) into the main narrative of the story.

Some of the familiar literary devices that exhibit this characteristic of intertextuality (the term was coined by the French critic Julie Kristeva) include parody, in which an imitation of the source text is exaggerated for comic effect; simple allusion, in which a later writer makes reference to a preexisting work, usually by quoting a line from it or borrowing a metaphor; translation, whereby a work in one language is transformed into a work in another language but is still considered to be the same as the original work; and adaptation, by which a work in one literary genre is changed to make it fit the conventions of another genre. One of the pleasures of literary study is the expanded ability of a student to recognize the many interconnections among texts and writers as the territory of literature becomes more and more familiar. Only the insider—the reader "in the know"—can appreciate the intertextual elements of literature that make the net output of human creativity so much greater than the sum of its parts.

BIBLIOGRAPHY
Allen, Graham. *Intertextuality.* The New Critical Idiom Series. London: Routledge, 2000.
Lodge, David. *The Art of Fiction: Illustrated From Classic and Modern Texts.* New York: Viking, 1993.

IONIAN MISSION, THE PATRICK O'BRIAN (1981)   See Aubrey-Maturin novels.

IRELAND

The history of Anglo-Irish relations is a long and painful one, dating to 1166, when Anglo-Normans, in the century following their conquest of England, raided and conquered parts of eastern Ireland. King Henry II imposed some degree of order without removing the conquerors, and since then the kings and queens of England have continued to struggle with the connection between these two neighboring islands that differ in religion, culture, and (originally) language. With varying degrees of effectiveness, English kings maintained the title "Lord of Ireland" until Henry VIII was recognized as "King of Ireland" in 1541; he had repudiated Roman Catholicism and founded the Anglican Church in 1532, and the religious struggle in England was to have far-reaching consequences in Ireland.

The early Anglo-Norman raiders had not subdued all of Ireland, and in the west and northwest in particular, the Irish continued traditional Gaelic ways and functioned independently of English politics. The perceived threat of a Gaelic alliance with other Catholic countries such as Spain and France led to the attempt to extend the Anglican Church through Ireland as the official church. During the reign of Elizabeth I (1558–1603), three Irish rebellions arose, and in quelling each of them more Irish lands were seized and made available to Protestant settlers. James I (king from 1603 to 1625) continued and expanded these settlement policies, in particular bringing large numbers of Scottish Presbyterians to Northern Ireland at the point where the two countries are closest geographically. In

1641, under Charles I (1625–49), a Catholic uprising among the settlers in Northern Ireland led to the murder of thousands of people and the destruction of property. During the Interregnum (1649–60), Oliver Cromwell confiscated lands and suppressed the practice of the Catholic religion. Northern Ireland continued to be settled by Protestants, and the Irish were being pushed out of settled regions.

Although Charles II (1660–85) favored religious tolerance, the Protestants of Ireland continued repressive policies against Catholics, and by 1703 the "Protestant Ascendancy" established the minority rule of an Episcopalian elite: Less than 10 percent of the population dominated 90 percent of all land ownership. In 1720, the British House of Lords acquired supreme judicial power to resolve Irish legal issues. World politics began to affect Ireland as British interests expanded around the globe: During the American revolution (1775–83), British military forces in Ireland declined as troops were sent to North America, and as a consequence Irish Protestants organized defensive militias. The Orange Order, a Protestant organization, was founded in 1795. British concessions toward Ireland increased during the French Revolution (1789–99) in order to secure Irish Catholic support against Catholic France. Nonetheless, radical advocates of Irish autonomy sought French support, and the French sent unsuccessful expeditions to Ireland between 1796 and 1798. A rebellion in 1798 led to the consolidation of the Irish and British parliaments and the creation of the United Kingdom in 1801, effectively eradicating any trace of a separate Irish nation for more than a hundred years.

The most important event of the 19th century for Ireland was the Great Potato Famine, beginning in the mid-1840s and continuing until 1850. More than a million Irish citizens died of starvation; another million emigrated from the country, most of them relocating to the United States and some going to English industrial cities. Because the exodus continued after the famine ended, the population of Ireland was halved by 1911. During the latter part of the 19th century, the "Fenian" movement, named for a legendary Gaelic military force, began to advocate the use of any means to obstruct English autonomy and secure

Catholic Irish independence. Also by the end of the century, an artistic movement had begun with an interest in preserving the Gaelic language and in renewing distinctively Irish cultural traditions. Meanwhile, Irish politicians elected to seats in Parliament, including Charles Stewart Parnell, advocated Home Rule. Not all Irish supported Home Rule, however: Protestants in the northern counties fought against Home Rule because they feared becoming a disempowered minority in an independent Ireland dominated by a Catholic majority. In Belfast, the Ulster Volunteer Force was organized in 1912; in Dublin, the Irish Volunteers countered. The stage was set for bloody civil strife when WORLD WAR I intervened. As a political ploy, Home Rule was declared for Ireland and immediately suspended until after the war ended.

But radical efforts to liberate Ireland continued, leading to the Easter Rising on April 24, 1916, organized by a Fenian group, the Irish Republican Brotherhood, and led by Patrick Pearse and others. The fighting was limited to Dublin and continued for about a week, ending in the capture of Pearse and 14 other leaders. These men were tried and convicted by a military court and quickly executed; while their rising had not found widespread support throughout the country, their executions secured the response needed to end effective British rule. A state of chaos and civil strife followed; when Irish police officers resigned rather than suppress the rebellion, British Army units, called the Black and Tans from their uniforms, policed the country harshly. The Irish Republican Army (IRA) was founded under the leadership of Michael Collins to advance the cause of the rebellion. In 1920, the British Parliament passed the Government of Ireland Act, dividing the country into the two political units that persisted through the remainder of the century. On December 6, 1921, the Irish Free State was proclaimed under the leadership of Eamon de Valera, a survivor of the Rising and an active political leader until his death in 1975. Of Ireland's 32 counties, 26 were part of this new state, while the six counties of the northeast, referred to as Northern Ireland, remained part of the United Kingdom.

Violence continued within the Irish Free State due to political differences, and between the Free State and

Northern Ireland. The new government resorted to the suppression of violent factions through arrests and even executions. But slowly, the elements of an organized government fell into place, including a constitution, judicial reforms, and elimination of corruption. In 1937, the Irish Free State took the name Eire (Ireland). During WORLD WAR II, the new nation maintained political neutrality; some British nationals, wishing to avoid the war or the blitzkrieg, took up residence in neutral Ireland. In 1949, the Irish government passed the Republic of Ireland Act and formally severed connections to the British Commonwealth; in 1987, the nation supported membership in the European Community (later changed to the European Union).

During and after the struggle for independence, Irish literature in English was strongly marked by the experience. In the 20th century, Ireland has produced more significant figures of literature than any other English-speaking country, many of whom have written about the Irish struggle, including such poets as William Butler Yeats and Seamus Heaney; novelists such as George MOORE, James JOYCE, Elizabeth BOWEN, Liam O'FLAHERTY, Flann O'BRIEN, Brian MOORE, Edna O'BRIEN, William TREVOR, Jennifer JOHNSTON, Patrick MCCABE, and Roddy DOYLE; playwrights such as Oscar WILDE, George Bernard Shaw, John Millington Synge, Sean O'Casey, and Samuel BECKETT; and numerous writers of short fiction. The sheer quantity of literary brilliance has provoked speculation as to why Ireland has produced so many fine writers; whatever the cause, the world's readers are the beneficiaries.

BIBLIOGRAPHY
Donoghue, Denis. *We Irish: Essays on Irish Literature and Society.* New York: Knopf, 1986.

Foster, R. F. *The Oxford Illustrated History of Ireland.* Oxford: Oxford University Press, 1989.

Kiberd, Declan. *Inventing Ireland.* Cambridge, Mass.: Harvard University Press, 1996.

IRONY   One of the hallmarks of 20th-century literature and criticism, and a key element of SATIRE in any era, irony occurs when a discrepancy arises between actual and expected occurrences in literature or in life. Four kinds of irony are generally recognized:

When writers or speakers say one thing and mean another, with the intended meaning apparent to most readers or listeners, they deploy *verbal* (or *rhetorical*) irony; at its most primitive, verbal irony takes the form of sarcasm. *Situational* irony occurs through events rather than through speech; for example, when Tess is captured asleep on the altar at Stonehenge in *Tess of The D'Urbervilles,* her situation is ironic since sacrificial victims may once have lain there, and Tess is about to be sacrificed through the workings of justice. *Dramatic irony* is a particular kind of situational irony that arises when an audience knows something the hero doesn't know but needs to know in order to resolve a problem; this device can contribute to the suspense and tension a story or play elicits from its audience. In contrast, when a protagonist naively but consistently misperceives his or her situation, *structural irony* is in play, with the protagonist's misunderstanding continually giving rise to fresh sources of humor for the audience. At irony's broadest range, a special form of structural irony called *cosmic irony* occurs when a writer pictures a cruel universe that toys with the hapless human beings trapped in it.

Irony frequently finds expression through the traditional figures of speech: *Hyperbole* is the exaggerated or overly emphatic statement of an intended meaning, while understatement, or *litotes,* works in the opposite way, communicating an opinion by saying less than is expected. Irony is one of the subtlest devices that writers use, and therefore its comprehension may require particular training, or even a certain level of linguistic sophistication, in order for readers to detect and decode it.

BIBLIOGRAPHY
Booth, Wayne. *A Rhetoric of Irony.* Chicago: University of Chicago Press, 1974.

Enright, D. J. *The Alluring Problem: An Essay on Irony.* Oxford: Oxford University Press, 1986.

Muecke, D. C. *Irony.* The Critical Idiom, 13. London: Methuen, 1970.

ISHERWOOD, CHRISTOPHER (1904– 1987)   Born in Cheshire into a family of the English upper CLASS on August 26, 1904, Christopher Isherwood's literary reputation has waxed and waned and waxed again during the 20th century. Isherwood was only 10 when he lost his father, who was killed in WORLD WAR I, and the image of the immature man who suffers for lack of a father figure in childhood, and who seeks to find one among his adult male friends, recurs throughout his fiction. Isherwood's experience of homosexuality, a generation after the infamous trial and conviction of Oscar WILDE, shaped his fiction, altered the course of his life, and determined his relationship to religion.

In 1923, Isherwood moved from his PUBLIC SCHOOL to Corpus Christi College, Cambridge, where he made friends with the novelist Edward Upward, but he left two years later without a degree. He found employment as a secretary and a tutor and began writing autobiographical fiction, strongly influenced by E. M. FORSTER. Isherwood published his first such novel, *All the Conspirators,* in 1928. The next year, he traveled to Berlin with the poet W. H. Auden, whom he had met in school. Isherwood remained in Berlin and Germany during much of the 1930s, using his experiences as the basis of three novels: *The Last of Mr. Norris* (1935), *Sally Bowles* (1937), and *GOODBYE TO BERLIN* (1939). These novels remain the foundation of his literary reputation, strengthened by the vivid portrayal of Sally Bowles in the play *I Am a Camera* (1951) by John van Druten and in the film and musical *Cabaret.*

With the outbreak of WORLD WAR II, Isherwood settled in Southern California, where he remained for the rest of his life. He also converted to the form of Hinduism known as Vedantism; this religion does not proscribe homosexuality. He continued writing autobiographical novels, and in the 1940s he became a screenwriter and television writer. Increasingly, his work dealt with American settings, homosexual sentiments, and religious mysticism, all continuing the autobiographical approach of his earlier fiction. Isherwood kept extensive diaries that provide insight into the real-life sources of his fictional characters; he also published biographies of his parents, some nonfiction accounts of Vedantism, travel writing, plays (cowritten with Auden), short fiction, poems, and several volumes of autobiography. Toward the end of his life, Isherwood became an active supporter of the gay rights movement, especially in his autobiographical volume *Christopher and His Kind: 1929–1939* (1976). Isherwood died on January 4, 1986, in Santa Monica, California.

BIBLIOGRAPHY

Berg, James J., and Chris Freeman, eds. *The Isherwood Century: Essays on the Life and Work of Christopher Isherwood.* Madison: University of Wisconsin Press, 2000.

Izzo, David Garrett. *Christopher Isherwood: His Era, His Gang, and the Legacy of the Truly Great Man.* Columbia: University of South Carolina Press, 2001.

Lehmann, John. *Christopher Isherwood: A Personal Memoir.* New York: Henry Holt, 1988.

ISHIGURO, KAZUO (1954–)

Born in Nagasaki, Japan, on November 8, 1954, Kazuo Ishiguro came to England with his parents at the age of six; the family became permanent residents. With a foot in two cultures, speaking Japanese at home and attending traditional English schools, Kazuo Ishiguro became the unusual combination of a Japanese Englishman. He studied English and philosophy at the University of Kent, receiving an undergraduate degree in 1978. Afterward, he supported himself through employment as a social worker and then enrolled in a graduate-level creative writing program at the University of East Anglia (where Malcolm BRADBURY spent many years as a professor); he completed his master's degree in 1980.

Two years later, in 1982, Ishiguro published his first novel, *A View of Pale Hills,* in which a Japanese immigrant to England—a mother—comes to terms with the suicide of her first child. Although the novel was praised and won the Winifred Holtby Award of the Royal Society of Literature, Ishiguro continued as a social worker until 1986, when his second novel, *An ARTIST OF THE FLOATING WORLD,* won the WHITBREAD AWARD as book of the year. This novel is set in Japan in the aftermath of WORLD WAR II and presents a compelling portrait of that ravaged land and the psychological scars left by defeat, even though the author had not visited the country of his birth in more than 25 years. Ishiguro's third novel, *The REMAINS OF THE DAY,* won the BOOKER PRIZE in 1989 and became a FILM ADAPTATION in 1993. Once again, his plot examines the aftermath of World War II and the consequences of poorly chosen allegiances in the past, but in this case his setting and characters are entirely English.

Ishiguro was married in 1986, when he became a full-time writer. He and his wife live in London, and he continues to publish novels, including *The Unconsoled* (1995) and *When We Were Orphans* (2000). Additionally, he writes film and television scripts and magazine pieces.

BIBLIOGRAPHY

Lewis, Barry. *Kazuo Ishiguro.* Contemporary World Writers. Manchester: Manchester University Press; New York: St. Martin's Press, 2000.

Shaffer, Brian W. *Understanding Kazuo Ishiguro.* Understanding Contemporary British Literature. Columbia: University of South Carolina Press, 1998.

Vorda, Allan. *Face to Face: Interviews with Contemporary Novelists.* Houston, Tex.: Rice University Press, 1993.

J

JAMES, HENRY (1843–1916) Originally an American, Henry James became a British citizen in 1915 shortly before he died, having spent most of his adult life in England. He was born on April 15, 1843, in New York City to a wealthy and distinguished family that produced three brilliant offspring—his brother William James was a noted philosopher and his sister, Alice James, was a political radical and diarist. His father, a noted philosopher of his day, was acquainted with Ralph Waldo Emerson, Henry David Thoreau, James Russell Lowell, Nathaniel Hawthorne, and other leading thinkers and writers and chose to educate his children in European cities; Henry James studied in France, England, Italy, Germany, and Switzerland. He made a brief attempt at studying law at Harvard University as the Civil War was beginning. When he suffered an injury while helping to put out a fire, he became incapacitated and spent a long recovery unable to participate in the war effort. During this time, he began writing reviews and short fiction, publishing his first story in 1865.

Beginning in 1865, James spent several years traveling through Europe, making the acquaintance of writers, artists, and socialites. He published a novel, *Watch and Ward,* in 1871, and a collection of stories, *The Passionate Pilgrim,* in 1975. The stories were a success, and he settled in England to concentrate on writing, establishing a prolific pace. During the first 10 years of his publishing career, from 1875 to 1885, his work received popular sales and critical approbation as he explored the collision of American innocence and world-weary European experience. His novel *The American* (1877–78) marked out the territory, contrasting the pragmatic, wealthy, and egalitarian protagonist with the impoverished but aristocratic family of the beautiful Frenchwoman he is courting. Among his most noted works of this period are many that have become standards of the high school literature CANON: *Daisy Miller* (1878) and *Washington Square* (1880). The greatest work of this phase of James's career is *The Portrait of a Lady* (1880–81); in it, a young American woman unexpectedly inherits a fortune and becomes the spouse and victim of a cultured but ruthless European man. The novel displays the skill with which James is able to create complex and authentic female characters with depth and subtlety.

In 1885, James entered a second phase of his career, lasting until 1897. He began to experiment with formal technique and to intensify his exploration of personal psychology in his characters; the most notable works of this period include *The Bostonians* (1885–86) and *The Princess Casamassima* (1885–86). His success began to decline both among readers and critics. James turned to the stage, disappointed in his publishing failures, but he was even less successful as a playwright. In 1895, his play *Guy Domville* was virtually booed off the stage and closed quickly. His experiences are reflected in the short fiction he wrote about this time, focusing on the fate of artists who lose touch with reality, including "The Real Thing" (1893) and *Embarrass-ments* (1896).

The last phase of James's career began when he returned to the novel form in 1897 with *The Spoils of Poynton,* a study of the material avarice that underlies the most refined tastes. He produced the novella *The Turn of the Screw* in 1898, elevating the ghost story in the process. His work as a 20th-century novelist begins with *The Sacred Fount* (1901) and continues with *The Wings of the Dove* (1902), a story about the corrosive power of money on love, and includes his own favorite work, *The Ambassadors* (1903), which returns to his theme of comparing American and European characters. In 1904, *The Golden Bowl* combined his interest in art with his observations of New and Old World values. James undertook an extensive revision of his complete works from 1906 until 1910, producing the uniform volumes of the New York edition. He continued writing to the end of his life. In 1915, dismayed at the American reluctance to enter World War I, he changed his citizenship. James died at his home in Rye, England, on February 28, 1916, after having suffered a stroke two months earlier.

The writers who influenced Henry James were the French novelist Honoré Balzac, the English Victorian novelist Charles Dickens, and the American Nathaniel Hawthorne. His own work—some 20 novels, more than a 100 works of short fiction, a dozen plays, and an extensive body of literary criticism—marks the beginning of literary MODERNISM in English. James's experiments with narration, point of view, and character development were to point the way for writers such as James JOYCE and Virginia WOOLF. In addition to his professional influence through his art, he also had a personal influence through his wide acquaintance with the literary circles of England, America, and Europe. Several of his works have provided the material for FILM ADAPTATION in the latter part of the 20th century, and he has also become a fictional character in the work of postmodern (see POSTMODERNISM) novelists such as David LODGE, Colm Toibin, Alan Hollinghurst, and others. The stature of Henry James in both American and English literature has continued to grow, boosted in recent decades by an impressive body of biographical and interpretive scholarship.

BIBLIOGRAPHY

Bell, Millicent. *Meaning in Henry James.* Cambridge, Mass.: Harvard University Press, 1991.

Edel, Leon. *Henry James : A Life.* Rev. ed. New York: Harper & Row, 1985.

Graham, Kenneth. *Henry James, a Literary Life.* New York: St. Martin's Press, 1996.

Jolly, Roslyn. *Henry James: History, Narrative, Fiction.* Oxford: Clarendon Press, 1993.

Kaplan, Fred. *Henry James: The Imagination of Genius.* New York: Morrow, 1992.

Lewis, R. W. B. *The Jameses: A Family Narrative.* New York: Farrar, Straus & Giroux, 1991.

Novick, Sheldon M. *Henry James: The Young Master.* New York: Random House, 1996.

Yeazell, Ruth Bernard, ed. *Henry James: A Collection of Critical Essays.* Englewood Cliffs, N.J.: Prentice Hall, 1994.

JAMES, P. D. (BARONESS JAMES OF HOLLAND PARK) (1920–)

A noted writer of MYSTERY AND DETECTIVE FICTION, Phyllis Dorothy James was born in Oxford, England, on August 3, 1920. She attended Cambridge High School for Girls until the age of 16, when she followed her father's example and entered civil employment in the English equivalent of the Internal Revenue Service. She continued working until 1979 in various managerial roles, including hospital and police administration, forensic lab work, and employment in the Department of Home Affairs; after retirement, she served as a magistrate in London. She was married to a doctor in 1941; however, when his experience in WORLD WAR II left him emotionally impaired, she became the head and financial support of the household. She published her first novel, *Cover Her Face,* in 1962, featuring her recurring detective, Adam Dalgliesh of Scotland Yard, and continued writing part-time until her retirement, publishing six additional novels during that period. She has published eight novels since retiring, all in the mystery and detective genre except a thriller, *Innocent Blood* (1980), and a work of science fiction, *The Children of Men* (1992). In addition to the Adam Dalgliesh novels, she has produced two books featuring the female private eye Cordelia Gray, *An Unsuitable Job for a Woman* (1972) and *The Skull Beneath the Skin* (1982).

P. D. James is often identified as the successor to Agatha CHRISTIE, the first queen of crime writing. James, however, writes in a distinctively more mainstream style, carefully developing her detective as an intelligent, sensitive, and fully rounded character and exploring the lives of those connected to and affected by the crime in detail. She makes it clear that crime occurs in the real world of ordinary people suffering the same stresses and pressures that afflict her readers, not in some exaggeratedly mysterious realm. She also draws on her extensive personal experience in the English medical, civil, and judicial systems to intensify the realism of her characters' interactions.

James has received numerous awards for her mysteries, beginning with a 1967 prize from the Crime Writers Association, for her novel *Unnatural Causes.* Nine of the novels featuring Adam Dalgliesh have been effectively brought to life on television, and although he is not as distinctively recognizable as Sherlock HOLMES, nonetheless he has developed a devoted following both in print and on the small screen. Cordelia Gray has taken on a life of her own in a television series titled *An Unsuitable Job for a Woman,* but originated by other writers. James has also written short fiction in the mystery genre, one play, a nonfiction work about a historical crime, and a volume of autobiography. In 1991, she was elevated to the rank of baroness.

BIBLIOGRAPHY

Gidez, Richard B. *P. D. James.* Twayne's English Authors, 430. Boston: Twayne Publishers, 1986.

James, P. D. *In Time to Be in Earnest: A Fragment of Autobiography.* New York: Knopf, 2000.

Porter, Dennis. "Detection and Ethics: The Case of P. D. James." *The Sleuth and the Scholar: Origins, Evolution, and Current Trends in Detective Fiction.* Edited by Barbara A. Rader and Howard G. Zettler. New York: Greenwood Press, 1988.

JAMES TAIT BLACK MEMORIAL PRIZES

Awarded annually to a work of fiction and to a work of biography, the James Tait Black Memorial Prizes were founded in 1919 by Mrs. Janet Coats Black in memory of her late husband, who had been a partner in the publishing house of A. & C. Black Ltd. The original bequest has since been supplemented by the Scottish Arts Council; two awards of 3,000 pounds each are presented. Publishers submit novels and biographies that have been published in the 12 months previous to the September 30 deadline. Authors may be of any nationality, but their works must have been published in English in the United Kingdom, and the author must not have previously won the prize in a given category. The selection of the winning titles falls to the professor of English literature at the University of Edinburgh.

BIBLIOGRAPHY

Book Trust Guide to Literary Prizes. London: Book Trust, Published annually.

Todd, Richard. *Consuming Fictions: The Booker Prize and Fiction in Britain Today.* London: Bloomsbury, 1996.

JEEVES SERIES P. G. WODEHOUSE (1919)

The short story collection entitled *My Man Jeeves* (1919) introduces one of the great character combinations of the 20th-century British COMIC NOVEL in the form of its eponymous hero, who serves as the valet to the wealthy and idle (but good-hearted and generous) young man Bertie Wooster. Bertie is the privileged character, educated at Oxford and a member in good standing of the Drones Club, while Jeeves is the ever-resourceful problem solver. These two characters appear in some 20 novels that are generally regarded as the best of Wodehouse's long fiction. After publishing a number of short stories about Wooster and Jeeves, Wodehouse combined several of them to create a novel entitled *The Inimitable Jeeves* (1922; also known as *Jeeves* in a later reissue). He published additional collections of short fiction before writing a complete and new novel, *Thank You, Jeeves,* in 1934.

In pairing these two complementary halves of one complete person, Wodehouse draws on the well-established tradition of the servant who is cleverer than the master, familiar in the Roman comedies of Plautus, Ben Jonson's humor comedies of the English Renaissance, Molière's French comedies of the 17th century, and many other sources from many other nations. Since the characters are stereotypes, and thereby flat rather than fully rounded and well developed, and since the plots are mostly variations on a recurring theme, the interest of the story lies more in the manner of its telling than in the substance it presents to the reader. Wodehouse is noted for his distinctive prose style, with its exaggerated poetic language, numerous allusions drawn from literary classics, and imaginative wordplay. He also develops Jeeves in particular as the series continues, endowing him with astonishing erudition for a servant, and with the deductive perspicacity of a Sherlock HOLMES.

In the typical plot, Bertie or a friend becomes ensnared in an engagement, frequently through some degree of scheming on the part of either the lady engaged or Bertie's formidable Aunt Agatha. These engagements may be undesirable for many reasons, but generally they involve some effort made to transform Bertie into a better man through intellectual application or physical exertion—two aspects of life repugnant to him. Bertie sometimes becomes entangled in these awkward situations because he is too well bred not to go along with the proper thing—and sometimes he just falls head over heels for the nearest girl. In *The Inimitable Jeeves,* the doomed groom-to-be is Bertie's old school friend "Bingo" Little, who has a penchant for proposing marriage to waitresses and an uncle inclined to withhold funds from nephews who go so far as to marry waitresses. Jeeves devises various schemes to resolve Bingo's problem repeatedly, since the poor man hardly escapes from one scrape before he lands himself in another. The multiple complications reflect the creation of this novel by combining preexisting short stories. In the end, a clever twist resolves Bingo's last engagement in such a way that he can marry his waitress and maintain his financial security as well. The series goes on in this manner to many upscale locations and events, with Bertie perpetually attempting to maintain the idyllic freedom of careless youth (he almost seems to suffer from Peter Pan syndrome) and Jeeves enabling him to do so in spite of Bertie's loveable ineptness.

BIBLIOGRAPHY
Jaggard, Geoffrey. *Wooster's World: A Companion to the Wooster-Jeeves Cycle of P. G. Wodehouse.* London: Macdonald, 1967.

Love, William F. "Butler, Dabbler, Spy: Jeeves to Wimsey to Bond." In *Dorothy L. Sayers: The Centenary Celebration.* Edited by Alzina Stone Dale. New York: Walker, 1993, 31–43.

Watson, George. "The Birth of Jeeves," *Virginia Quarterly Review: A National Journal of Literature and Discussion* 73, no. 4 (1997): 641–652.

JEWEL IN THE CROWN, THE PAUL SCOTT (1966)

The first volume in *The RAJ QUARTET,* this novel is set in Mayapore, INDIA, in 1942. The movement for Indian independence, stalled by the onset of WORLD WAR II, has reached a fever pitch of intensity in the "Quit India" campaign as Indians bring their struggle to the individual British citizens serving the Raj or merely attached to those who serve it. The novel opens with two unrelated assaults against British women: An enraged crowd attacks and beats Miss Crane, the supervisor of the Protestant Mission schools and a sympathizer with the independence movement, and a gang of young men rapes Daphne Manners, an English girl who, like Miss Crane, is inclined to sympathy with the independence cause and who is in love with an English-educated Indian, Hari Kumar. The male Indian teacher accompanying Miss Crane is killed, so great and so indiscriminate is the rage of the mob.

The police become involved in these cases, and at that time the police force is still under the control of British supervisors and administrators. The district superintendent is Ronald Merrick, a man incapable of handling the cases objectively, in part because of the solidarity of the British community, in part because Daphne once rejected his offer of marriage, in part because of his racial prejudice against Indians, and in part because of his resentment of the advantages conferred by PUBLIC SCHOOL educations such as that completed by Hari Kumar. In this one character, Scott brings together issues of CLASS, race, and gender, the three monumental social issues of the 20th century. Merrick resents Hari as an Indian and as the product of an upper-class education, and he sinks so low as to plant evidence and extract false statements under torture. In this manner he succeeds in sending an innocent Indian man to prison.

The narrative structure is complex, with various voices and sources of information contributing to the total effect. The PLOT does not provide closure and resolution since justice has been perverted, and since that perversion has not been redressed by the novel's end. The imagery and events of the novel set the stage for the story's continuation in *The DAY OF THE SCORPION*, but the deaths of both Miss Crane and Daphne Manners suggests the dark direction the story will take as Indian determination clashes with British tenacity. In particular, Miss Crane's suicide by ritual immolation or suttee is a foreshadowing of the violently destructive resentment the Raj faces.

BIBLIOGRAPHY

Bachmann, Holger. "Speaking of the Raj: Language in Paul Scott's *The Jewel in the Crown,*" *English: The Journal of the English Association* 46, no. 186 (Autumn 1997): 227–249.

Rao, K. Bhaskara. *Paul Scott.* Twayne's English Authors, 285. Boston: Twayne Publishers, 1980.

Swinden, Patrick. *Paul Scott: Images of India.* New York: St. Martin's Press, 1980.

JHABVALA, RUTH PRAWER (1927–)

An admired and respected writer of international experiences, Ruth Prawer Jhabvala was born in Cologne, Germany, on May 7, 1927, to Jewish parents. The family fled from Nazi persecution to England in 1939; 12-year-old Ruth then attended English schools. She became a British citizen in 1948 and earned a master's degree from London's Queen Mary College in 1951, the same year she was married to a Parsi Indian architect. The couple moved to New Delhi and became parents to three daughters. Ruth Jhabvala began working full-time as a writer, publishing her first novel, *To Whom She Will,* in 1955 (known in the United States as *Amrita*). She published four additional novels and a collection of short fiction by 1963, producing social and romantic comedies that critics compared in style to the novels of Jane Austen; Jhabvala, however, developed the materials of Indian culture and social customs. A generally positive and optimistic view of INDIA prevails in her next few novels: *The Nature of Passion* (1956), *Esmond in India* (1958), *The Householder* (1960), and *Get Ready for Battle* (1962).

Her career took a turn in 1963, when she entered a creative partnership with Ismail Merchant and James Ivory and began writing or cowriting screenplays and developing classic fictional works as FILM ADAPTATIONS. Between 1963 and 2000, she produced 21 screenplays for Merchant-Ivory films, including her adaptation of her masterpiece *HEAT AND DUST,* which won a 1984 BAFTA (British Academy of Film and Television Arts) award for best screenplay. She adapted Henry JAMES's *The Bostonians* and *The GOLDEN BOWL.* Her adaptations of E. M. FORSTER's works include *A ROOM WITH A VIEW* (which won an Academy Award in 1986 for best adapted screenplay), *Maurice,* and *HOWARDS END* (which won another Academy Award in 1992 for best adapted screenplay). She also wrote an adaptation of Kazuo ISHIGURO's *The REMAINS OF THE DAY* (nominated for an Academy Award), an adaptation of *Jefferson in Paris,* and of *Surviving Picasso,* and she created several original narratives as well. Additionally, she has written three television plays, *The Place of Peace* (1975), *Jane Austen in Manhattan* (1980), and *The Wandering Company* (1985).

During this period, Jhabvala also continued to write novels and short fiction, but her tone began to darken, and SATIRE replaced comedy. *A Backward Place* appeared in 1965, examining the tensions produced by East-West cultural clashes, followed in 1972 by *A New Dominion* (U.S. title, *Travelers*), which exposes the exploitation of Westerners seeking spiritual renewal in India. Beginning in 1974, Jhabvala moved to New York City for nine months of the year to facilitate her screenwriting work for Merchant-Ivory films, and her residence in the United States provided new materials for her fiction. Her narrative approach also became more complex, and in 1975, her novel *Heat and Dust,* with its double story of two generations of a family coping with similar experiences in India, won the BOOKER PRIZE. In 1983, she published *In Search of Love and Beauty,* her first novel set in the United States, relating the multigenerational story of a family of Jewish immigrants. *Three Continents* (1987) moves between the United States, England, and India to record the destruction of an American sister and brother duped by an Indian mystic. *Poet and Dancer* (1993) stays in Manhattan, following two cousins who become detached from the outside world. *Shards of Memory* (1995) is another critique of the power an Indian guru wields among his followers, with settings in Manhattan, London, and India.

Jhabvala is neither exclusively European nor British nor Indian nor American; instead, all these aspects of identity find expression, in one way or another, in her writings. She generally presents her narratives from the point of view of a third-person omniscient observer with a journalist's eye for the telling detail. Because her characters are not deeply particularized, readers of all kinds can identify with them and appreciate the ways they cope with the challenges of living in the shrinking modern world.

BIBLIOGRAPHY

Booker, Keith M. *Colonial Texts: India in the Modern British Novel.* Ann Arbor: University of Michigan Press, 1997.

Crane, Ralph J. *Ruth Prawer Jhabvala.* Twayne's English Authors, 494. Boston: Twayne, 1992.

Shahane, V. A. *Ruth Prawer Jhabvala.* New Delhi: Arnold-Heinemann, 1976.

JOHNSTON, JENNIFER (1930–)

The author of such popular HISTORICAL FICTION novels as *The Captains and the Kings* (1972), Jennifer Johnston's 1977 novel *Shadows on our Skin,* a BILDUNGSROMAN with a romance doomed by civil strife in IRELAND, was shortlisted for the BOOKER PRIZE, and she received the WHITBREAD Book of the Year Award in 1979 for *The Old Jest.* She was born on January 12, 1930, in Dublin; her father was a leading playwright in Ireland, and her mother was an actress. Johnston was educated at Trinity College in Dublin. Her first marriage began in 1951 and produced four children; her second marriage began in 1976. She has written plays, both for the stage and for radio, and several short stories for periodical publication in addition to her 11 novels.

Johnston has been associated with novelists of the Anglo-Irish "big house" tradition in Ireland, such as Elizabeth BOWEN, William TREVOR, Molly KEANE, and others; she is also a novelist who makes effective use of warfare and violence in a manner similar to the English writer Pat BARKER, but relying on Irish characters. Johnston has frequently explored the coming-of-age scenario through the painful experience of betrayal; her portraits of girls on the cusp of womanhood are particularly effective, as in her second novel, *The Gates* (1973), and in *The Old Jest.* In *The Illusionist* (1995), she makes use of some autobiographical touches to explore the life of a middle-aged woman who becomes a novelist. The title refers both to the work of her late husband, a magician, and to the writer's task of making illusions through words.

Jennifer Johnston currently resides in Derry, where she continues to write.

BIBLIOGRAPHY

Fauset, Eileen. *Studies in the Fiction of Jennifer Johnston and Mary Lavin.* Fort Lauderdale, Fla.: Nova Southeastern University, 1998.

González, Rosa. "Jennifer Johnston." In *Ireland in Writing: Interviews with Writers and Academics.* Edited by Jacqueline Hurtley, et al. Amsterdam: Rodopi, 1998, 7–19.

Rosslyn, Felicity. "The Importance of Being Irish: Jennifer Johnston," *Cambridge Quarterly* 32.3 (2003): 239–249.

JONES, DAVID (1895–1974)

One of the most prominent Welsh-English writers of the 20th century, David Jones is noted primarily as a poet; however, his book-length poem *IN PARENTHESIS* is also an autobiographical novel that relates the horrors of WORLD WAR I and its effects on the men of Jones's generation. This work won the HAWTHORNDEN PRIZE in 1938.

David Michael Jones was born on November 1, 1895, in Brockley, England; his father was Welsh and his mother English. Jones originally trained and worked as a visual artist, studying at the Camberwell School of Art until the outbreak of WORLD WAR I. He joined the Royal Welsh Fusiliers in 1915 and was wounded at the Battle of the Somme in July 1916. He spent three months recuperating in England before returning to the front for the remainder of the war.

After the war, Jones returned to art. In 1921, he converted to Catholicism and joined an artists' community. He began writing in 1928, working on *In Parenthesis* for nearly 10 years. His style drew its inspiration from T. S. Eliot's *The Wasteland,* with its elliptical density and extensive footnotes. By the time Jones finished his poem, Eliot was working at Faber and Faber, the publisher to which Jones submitted his manuscript. Eliot recognized its merit, and the poem's success confirmed his judgment.

Jones suffered from depression and a debilitating nervous condition; although he continued to work both as a writer and an artist, he was uninterested in bringing his work to the public. His major poem *The Anathemata* appeared in 1952; it is a very dense modernist work. In poor health, Jones lived in retirement homes for the last two decades of his life. He died on October 28, 1974. More of his work, in the form of poems, essays, and letters, was published after his death than during his life. *In Parenthesis* remains his only work classified as a novel, although its complexity and its connection both to the author's life and to historical events cast doubt on that classification.

BIBLIOGRAPHY

Blamires, David. *David Jones: Artist and Writer.* Toronto: University of Toronto Press, 1971.

Rees, Samuel. *David Jones.* Twayne's English Authors, 246. Boston: Twayne, 1978.

JOYCE, JAMES (1882–1941)

Widely considered to be one of the most important novelists of the 20th century, and intensively studied by a vigorous and devoted scholarly community, James Joyce carried the narrative experimentation of MODERNISM to new territory in both the forms he developed for telling his stories and the subject matter he chose to write about. Although his literary output is relatively small in quantity, its impact on world literature has been powerful. Numerous writers worldwide have been influenced by Joyce's innovations in fiction, including the British novelists John FOWLES and Malcolm LOWRY; Samuel BECKETT was a close friend for several years and was also influenced by Joyce's approach to literature.

Joyce was born in Dublin on February 2, 1882; both of his parents were musically gifted, and Joyce himself had an excellent tenor singing voice. He was educated in Jesuit parochial schools before entering University College, also a Jesuit institution, in Dublin, where he studied modern languages and philosophy. Aspects of his youth and young adulthood appear in the semiautobiographical character of Stephen Dedalus in *A PORTRAIT OF THE ARTIST AS A YOUNG MAN* and *ULYSSES*. After completing his undergraduate studies in 1902, Joyce left IRELAND in a self-imposed exile from homeland, church, and family. He made a brief return in 1903 to visit his mother in her final illness, but after her death in 1904, he left again. This time he was accompanied by Nora Barnacle, who became his common-law wife until 1931, when the couple was formally married in order to secure inheritance rights for their two children. Joyce made two additional short visits to Ireland but remained an exile from it for the rest of his life.

Joyce taught English in Trieste, Italy (at that time under the Habsburg Empire), until 1915, when the outbreak of WORLD WAR I forced him to relocate his family to politically neutral Zurich, Switzerland. They remained there for five years and in 1920 moved again, this time to Paris. At that time, life in Paris was highly affordable and expatriated artists from many countries lived there on shoestring budgets. The Joyces lived in poverty, alleviated on occasion by support from the British government arranged by friends such as Ezra Pound. Joyce's eyesight was weak, requiring numerous surgeries; nonetheless, it continued to decline, leaving him nearly blind by the end of his life. The family's life was also strained by the unstable emotional condition of Joyce's daughter, who spent some of her life in institutions.

Joyce published essays and criticism as early as his 18th year, and he produced a volume of poetry, *Chamber Music,* in 1907. His first work of serious fiction was the short story collection *Dubliners* (1914), which included stories that have become classics of the high school and college literature curriculum, such as "Araby," "Eveline," and "The Dead." These stories, all set in Dublin, as is Joyce's entire CANON, feature middle- and lower-CLASS characters, some of whom experience an EPIPHANY that may be couched in AMBIGUITY, requiring the reader to engage the stories more intensively in order to achieve some closure to the narrative. Although some of the stories appeared in periodicals as early as 1904, finding a publisher for the entire collection took several years. During that time, Joyce was already writing his first novel, *A Portrait of the Artist as a Young Man,* originally called *Stephen Hero* (the surviving portion of which was published in 1944). It underwent radical revisions, beginning life as a traditional narrative in the style of 19th-century realism that grew to more than 900 pages before it was half finished. Ironically, it appeared in the same year that Joyce was finally able to publish *Dubliners,* 1914.

After a pause in his attention to fiction writing in order to write a play, *Exiles* (1918), Joyce turned his hand to composing his epic masterpiece, *Ulysses,* which he worked on from 1915 until it was published in 1922. By then, he and his family were settled in Paris, where they remained until the hostilities of WORLD WAR II once again forced them to seek residence in Switzerland. After the publication of *Ulysses,* the book was banned in the United States for obscenity, but a 1933 verdict ruled it was not obscene, and in 1934 the American edition appeared. In the meantime, Joyce had begun writing FINNEGANS WAKE, which he worked on until it was published in the spring of 1939. Its publication was immediately overshadowed by the war. In Zurich again, Joyce underwent an operation for a perforated ulcer. After the operation, he sank into a coma and died on January 13, 1941.

Literally hundreds of scholarly works are available on every aspect of Joyce's life and works, tailored to virtually every level of reader. His experimentation with narrative devices such as stream-of-consciousness point of view, although already used by novelists such as Dorothy RICHARDSON and Virginia WOOLF, has reshaped the writing of fiction in the 20th century. The 1922 publication of *Ulysses* marks the high point of modernism in literature. To the extent that Joyce wished to expand, open, and diversify the interpretive possibilities of literature, the vast extent of the critical tradition that has developed since his death stands as a testament to his staggering success.

BIBLIOGRAPHY

Attridge, Derek, ed. *The Cambridge Companion to James Joyce.* Cambridge: Cambridge University Press, 1990.

Beja, Morris. *James Joyce : A Literary Life.* Columbus: Ohio State University Press, 1992.

Benstock, Bernard, ed. *Critical Essays on James Joyce.* Boston: G. K. Hall, 1985.

Blades, John. *How to Study James Joyce.* Houndmills, England: Macmillan, 1996.

Bowen, Zack R., and James F. Carens, eds. *A Companion to Joyce Studies.* Westport, Conn.: Greenwood Press, 1984.

Costello, Peter. *James Joyce: The Years of Growth, 1882–1915.* New York: Pantheon Books, 1993.

Ellmann, Richard. *James Joyce.* 1959. Rev. ed. New York: Oxford University Press, 1982.

Kenner, Hugh. *Joyce's Voices.* Berkeley: University of California Press, 1978.

Potts, Willard. *Joyce and the Two Irelands.* Austin: University of Texas, 2001.

Reynolds, Mary T., ed. *James Joyce: A Collection of Critical Essays.* Englewood Cliffs, N.J.: Prentice Hall, 1993.

JULY'S PEOPLE NADINE GORDIMER (1981)

A political FANTASY set in a very near future world in which a race war has forcibly removed South Africa's white minority from power, *July's People* vividly demonstrates how racial oppression affects a marginalized population. The educated, liberal, upper-middle-CLASS white protagonists of the story, Bamford and Maureen Smales and their three children, find themselves hiding under the protection of their former houseboy, July (also known as Mwawate), when a native revolt turns into a bloody war. The Smales reluctantly and disbelievingly flee Johannesburg, and they take shelter in the bush in July's village with his already large extended family. Ironically, Bamford Smales, an architect, finds himself living in a hut made of sticks and mud.

As time passes, the Smales try to adapt to the circumstances of their precarious survival; the parents cling to the few possessions they brought with them and to the hope that life will soon return to "normal," while the children make a swift accommodation to village life, laying aside the values of the old white-dominated world, forgetting their schooling, and growing apart from their parents as they find ways to fit in with African children. Gradually, the Smales are separated from their material goods: July takes the keys to the small pickup truck in which the family escaped from the city, and his assistant Daniel eventually steals Bamford's shotgun in order to join the rebels. Bamford and Maureen have no meaningful way to contribute to village life—they cannot even speak the language of the village—and they come to realize that their dwindling possessions have greater value than they themselves do. Even when they try to work to gather food or hunt, their efforts are ineffectual and the existing social structure has no place for them to occupy.

Power—how it is exerted and how it is organized—is key to the story. Eventually, the Smales discover that the protection July has extended to them is only partial, since July in turn must obey a district chieftain who has his own needs and goals. When they are summoned before this chieftain, their absence provides the opportunity for their last possessions, including the shotgun the chief is interested in, to disappear. Gordimer suspends the narrative in AMBIGUITY rather than resolving the ethical, psychological, and political issues that the story raises. Helicopters approach the village and Maureen runs to them, thrilled to think that whites have finally regained power, forgetting the military might that neighboring African nations have extended to the rebels. After bringing the estrangement of the Smales family vividly to life in the many practical crises they must face, Gordimer leaves their fate unresolved, allowing readers to imagine the story's ending.

BIBLIOGRAPHY

Bodenheimer, Rosemarie. "The Interregnum of Ownership in *July's People*." In *The Later Fiction of Nadine Gordimer.* Edited by Bruce King. New York: St. Martin's, 1993, 108–20.

Brink, Andre. "Complications of Birth: Interfaces of Gender, Race, and Class in *July's People*," *English in Africa* 21, no. 1–2 (July 1994): 157–80.

Smith, Rowland. "Masters and Servants: Nadine Gordimer's *July's People* and the Themes of Her Fiction." In *Critical Essays on Nadine Gordimer.* Edited by Rowland Smith. Boston: Hall, 1990, 140–152.

JUSTINE LAWRENCE DURRELL (1957) In this opening volume of THE ALEXANDRIA QUARTET, Lawrence DURRELL develops the cast of characters he revisits from different angles in BALTHAZAR, MOUNTOLIVE, and CLEA. One of his most important characters is the ancient city of Alexandria itself, which forms the backdrop for the impassioned actions of the story's characters. A city long devoted to the lust for knowledge both intellectual and carnal, Alexandria in the years before WORLD WAR II served as a political, historical, cultural, and linguistic crossroads for French, English, Greek, Egyptian, and Arab nationals, as well as for Jews, Muslims, and Christians. It is a place where anything can happen and everything is permitted.

The first-person narrator through whose eyes readers see the tale unfold is Darley, an Englishman ambitious to write novels but earning his living as a schoolteacher. He tells the tangled story of his love for two women, Justine and Melissa, retrospectively: He has fled Alexandria to seek refuge on an obscure island in the Greek Cyclades. For reference, he has various notes of his own, a novel about Justine by her first husband, entitled *Moeurs,* some volumes of Justine's diaries, and some writings by Justine's current husband, Nessim Hosnani. Darley intersperses his own account with selections from these other texts in a way that disrupts the linear chronology of the story; he also quotes from the work of Pursewarden, a successful English novelist. Durrell deliberately breaks up the narrative line in this manner in order to achieve what he has Justine refer to as "prism-sightedness"; he also frequently describes characters mirrored in multiple reflective angles, and sometimes he makes Darley's narration unreliable or even self-contradictory. These characteristics mark this novel as an early example of postmodern (see POSTMODERNISM) experimentation that splits the narrative and the characters into disjointed parts to be examined from many angles more or less simultaneously.

Darley relates that in Alexandria he had shared an apartment with a sensual minor French diplomat, Pombal. Whenever Pombal was away on extended business, he would sublet his part of the apartment to Pursewarden, who eventually commits suicide at the height of his literary success and leaves Darley a bequest of 500 pounds. Darley falls in love with Melissa, a cabaret dancer, and she virtually moves into the apartment, but they have hardly settled into a domestic routine when Darley also falls in love with Justine, the beautiful and alluring wife of a fabulously wealthy Coptic Egyptian businessman. He is soon obsessed with Justine, whose libertine ways excite and frustrate him. Gradually, he learns that her nymphomania results from having been raped when she was young by a mysterious and powerful man whose identity she knows but keeps secret, revealing only that he wears an eye patch. Her first husband had coped with her sexual compulsions by taking her to every psychologist in Europe, including even the great Freud, and then by writing a novel about her; Nessim interprets her infidelities to be signs of her love for him as she attempts to rid herself of the demon memory of rape, but Darley does not understand this at first. Ironically, he becomes Nessim's friend and a regular member of the wealthy circle in which the Hosnanis socialize.

Justine and Nessim also draw Darley into the Cabal, a study group led by Balthazar and dedicated to the Jewish Kabbalah and gnostic texts. Justine was born a Jew, Darley learns; he himself has a scholarly and literary interest in the ancient texts. He sees the group as a collection of harmless amateurs, and he is amused when he is recruited as an informant by Scobie, an elderly Englishman employed in the Egyptian Secret Service. Gradually, Nessim and Melissa become aware of the connection between Darley and Justine, but Nessim denies the possibility of a meaningful love relationship between his wife and his friend until Melissa herself tells him of Justine's infidelity. Darley learns only later, from diaries, that Melissa and Nessim find themselves drawn together in their common misery and engage in a fling that leads to the conception of a child just before Melissa travels to Jerusalem for an extended course of medical treatment.

Justine becomes convinced that Nessim intends to kill Darley at the annual duck hunt on Lake Mareotis, but Darley decides to attend anyway; only en route there does he realize that another of his acquaintances also in attendance, Da Capodistria, is undoubtedly the man who had raped Justine long ago. Darley's narration of the events of the duck hunt creates the novel's suspenseful climax; afterward, in the story's denouement, Justine has disappeared, and Darley takes a two-year teaching appointment in Upper Egypt. Melissa has given birth to Nessim's daughter, and when she lies dying in an Alexandria hospital, Darley is summoned to her side only to arrive too late. He takes her child and uses the small inheritance from Pursewarden to leave the passions of Alexandria behind and make sense of them by writing the novel readers have just finished—*Justine*.

Durrell's style in telling this story is lush in its descriptions and frank in its treatment of human sexuality. He had become acquainted with Henry Miller after reading that novelist's erotic sensation, *Tropic of Cancer,* and the two carried on a lifelong correspondence. Miller's influence is apparent in Durrell's treatment of Darley's two affairs and the private lives, at least in passing, of nearly all the characters. His fictional people do not just have families and jobs and emotional lives—they also routinely have sex lives deserving literary attention. Durrell's prose style in creating the hothouse erotic atmosphere of his story is admired by many critics, but like Hemingway's style, it has also been the subject of parody.

BIBLIOGRAPHY

Begnal, Michael H., ed. *On Miracle Ground: Essays on the Fiction of Lawrence Durrell.* Cranbury, N.J.: Associated University Presses, 1990.

Friedman, Alan Warren. *Lawrence Durrell and* The Alexandria Quartet: *Art for Love's Sake.* Norman: University of Oklahoma Press, 1970.

K

KEANE, MOLLY (1904–1996) Born Mary Nesta Skrine in County Kildare into an old Protestant Anglo-Irish family that lived in a "Big House" and kept horses for fox hunting, Molly Keane wrote under the pseudonym "M. J. Farrell" for most of her life, since writing novels was not a good fit for the social circles she frequented. The source of the pseudonym, she said, was a sign for a pub that she noticed when driving home one night. Mary Skrine married a gentleman farmer, Robert Lumley Keane, and settled with him in County Waterford in 1938; they reared two daughters.

Molly Keane wrote her first novel, *The Knight of the Cheerful Countenance,* when she was 17 years old and published it in 1926 to earn extra money for buying clothes. She published 10 additional novels by 1961, all under her pen name. She also wrote four plays, three with cowriter John Perry, between 1938 and 1961. Her husband's death led to a 20-year break in her writing career; when she next published a novel— *Good Behavior,* in 1981—it appeared under her own name. It was short-listed for the Booker Prize, and interest in Molly Keane's novels was revived. Keane wrote two more novels, *Time After Time* (1983) and *Loving and Giving* (1988). These titles are all examples of the comic novel in which Keane presents the customs, behaviors, and oddities of the Anglo-Irish class to which she was born. Keane also wrote nonfiction, including a cookbook and a travel book about Ireland. She died at the age of 92 in 1996.

BIBLIOGRAPHY

Cahalan, James M. *The Irish Novel: A Critical History.* Boston: Twayne, 1988.

O'Toole, Bridget. "Three Writers of the Big House: Elizabeth Bowen, Molly Keane, and Jennifer Johnston." In *Across the Roaring Hill: The Protestant Imagination in Modern Ireland.* Edited by Gerald Dawe and Edna Longley. Belfast: Blackstaff, 1985, 124–138.

Weekes, Ann Owen. *Irish Women Writers: An Uncharted Tradition.* Lexington.: University Press of Kentucky, 1990.

KELMAN, JAMES (1946–) A Scottish writer of short fiction and novels, James Kelman was born in Glasgow on June 9, 1946. By the time he was 15, he had left secondary school for an apprenticeship as a type compositor. He left this training without completing it when he was 17 in order to join the rest of his family in immigrating to the United States, but he returned to Scotland before long and worked at numerous jobs or went on the dole during periods of unemployment, moving from Glasgow to London and back. Heavy industry in England and Scotland was beginning to collapse under the pressure of Asian competition, and the economy that had depended on it was in decline; unemployment and disillusionment were widespread, and Glasgow was especially hard hit.

Kelman had begun to write fiction in his early 20s without impressing English publishers enough to get his work in print. His first publications were collections

241

of short fiction: In 1970, *An Old Pub Near the Angel and Other Stories* appeared in the United States. He matriculated at Strathclyde University in 1974 at the age of 28—in a era before the "nontraditional student" had become a commonplace at universities—to study English and philosophy, but he left three years later without taking a degree. In 1983, the student press at Edinburgh University published *Not Not While the Giro and Other Stories.* His short fiction was also beginning to appear in anthologies of regional writers. His first novel, *The Busconductor Hines,* was published in 1984 to mixed reviews, and his second, *The Chancer,* published the following year, met a similar fate. Also in 1985, his work appeared in *Lean Tales: James Kelman, Agnes Owens, Alasdair Gray.* He expanded his audience in 1987 with the short stories in *Greyhound for Breakfast,* displaying his capacity for scabrous humor.

In a different vein that demonstrated the extent of his range as a fiction writer, Kelman published *A Disaffection* in 1989. This novel of a schoolteacher's loss of faith in her vocation and in her life received wider recognition and admiration for Kelman's control of voice and tone, winning the JAMES TAIT BLACK MEMORIAL PRIZE for that year. In 1991, he published another collection of short fiction, *The Burn,* and in 1993 he produced a collection of nonfiction pieces, *Some Recent Attacks.* Then in 1994, he published his introspective masterpiece, *HOW LATE IT WAS, HOW LATE,* winning the BOOKER PRIZE for that year. After this triumph with the novel form, Kelman returned to short fiction, publishing the story collections *Busted Scotch: Selected Stories* in 1997 and *The Good Times* in 1999; he also wrote several plays and published politically motivated nonfiction. Kelman returned to the novel in 2001 with *Translated Accounts,* an experimental novel that received mixed reviews. In 2004, Kelman published the novel *You Have to Be Careful in the Land of the Free.*

Kelman writes about the interior landscapes of working-CLASS Glasgow Scots in a realistic manner that captures the logic of their thinking, the hierarchy of their concerns, and the tenor of their feelings, all in the expletive-filled dialect of English peculiar to that socioeconomic and geographic corner of the world. Kelman, married and the father of two children, continues to live and write in Glasgow.

BIBLIOGRAPHY

Baker, Simon. " 'Wee Stories with a Working-Class Theme': The Re-imagining of Urban Realism in the Fiction of James Kelman." In *Studies in Scottish Fiction: 1945 to the Present.* Edited by Susanne Hagemann. Frankfurt: Peter Lang, 1996, 235–50.

Bernstein, Stephen. "James Kelman." *Review of Contemporary Fiction* 20, no. 3 (Fall 2000): 42–79.

McGlynn, Mary. " 'Middle-Class Wankers' and Working-Class Texts: The Critics and James Kelman." *Contemporary Literature* 43, no. 1 (2002): 50–84.

KENEALLY, THOMAS (1935–) One of Australia's leading novelists, Thomas Keneally won the BOOKER PRIZE in 1982 for *SCHINDLER'S ARK* (published in the United States as *Schindler's List,* the title also used for the award-winning 1993 FILM ADAPTATION by Steven Spielberg).

Keneally was born on October 7, 1935, in Wauchope, New South Wales, Australia. His family was descended from Irish immigrants, and he was reared in the Catholic faith. He completed studies for the priesthood but did not take orders; he also studied law. From 1960 to 1964, he taught high school in Sydney, but he was also writing during this time. He published his first novel in 1964, *The Place at Whitton,* and his second, *Fear,* in 1965. These novels both won Australian literary prizes, but Keneally later distanced himself from them as apprentice work.

Keneally's two dozen novels cover a wide range of settings, character types, and narrative techniques. He writes novels both of contemporary characters trapped in moral dilemmas, as in *The CHANT OF JIMMIE BLACKSMITH* (1972), and of historical figures such as Joan of Arc (*Blood Red, Sister Rose,* 1974) and Oskar Schindler. His passionate commitment to social justice on the large scale and ethical conduct at the personal level serves as the unifying characteristic of his diverse body of fiction.

Keneally has also written play, teleplays, several books of nonfiction, a children's book, and a memoir. In his personal life, he has worked as a political activist in support of Australian nationalism and global human rights. He has lectured at the University of New England in New South Wales and at the University of California at Irvine. He has been honored with the order of Australia for Literary Services, and he has been named a fellow of both the American Academy of Arts and Sciences and the Royal Society of Literature. Thomas Keneally continues to live and write in Australia.

BIBLIOGRAPHY

Keneally, Thomas. *Homebush Boy.* London: Hodder & Stoughton, 1995.

Quartermaine, Peter. *Thomas Keneally.* New York: Viking-Penguin, 1991.

Willbanks, Ray. *Australian Voices.* Austin: University of Texas Press, 1992.

KIM RUDYARD KIPLING (1901)

Primarily remembered for his short stories, poems, and nonfiction works, KIPLING also published four novels that are generally less effective in terms of character development and structure—with the exception of *Kim,* his affectionate farewell to INDIA, the place where he spent the happiest years of his life. The protagonist of the title is an Irish orphan boy born in India who eventually becomes a follower of the Red Lama of Tibet (the Venerable Teshoo Lama). This emphasis on Buddhism through one of the two main characters in the novel is important: India has been torn by religious strife between Hindus and Muslims for centuries—strife that led to the partitioning of British India into India and Pakistan in 1947. Buddhism originated in India before spreading to other parts of Asia, where it thrived after withering in its original home, and the Buddhist principle of "the Middle Way" becomes an implicit theme of the novel, suggesting that wholeness can be achieved only by avoiding the sectarian and racist extremes that lead to violence and hatred.

Kim is reared by a native foster mother, but eventually contacts his father's military regiment and becomes a kind of teenage intelligence agent. He is able to provide greater assistance to the Lama through the knowledge he gains, and he foils a hostile plot against British interests along the way. These elements of the SPY NOVEL maintain the story's liveliness, but Kipling keeps the maturation of Kim and the spiritual quest of the Lama as the focus of the story. He incorporates some of his own short stories into episodes in the larger narrative and draws on the traditions of Indian folklore and Buddhist scripture to add exotic, colorful, and authentic details to his narrative. Juxtaposed with these Indian and Asian elements is Kipling's vivid picture of the English presence in India, especially through the British-molded Indian Army. Kipling concludes his novel with enough AMBIGUITY to allow strong debate about whether Kim becomes an exponent and tool of imperialism or someone more individually transformed by his contact with Indian spiritualism.

With its vivid eyewitness accounts of the vast range of human, cultural, political, military, and religious influences in India at the turn of the century, *Kim* stands as one of the greatest novels of English COLONIALISM, and one of the best novels about India by an English writer.

BIBLIOGRAPHY

Bloom, Harold, ed. *Rudyard Kipling's* Kim. New York: Chelsea House, 1987.

Coates, John. *The Day's Work: Kipling and the Idea of Sacrifice.* Madison, N.J.: Fairleigh Dickinson University Press, 1997.

Orel, Harold, ed. *Critical Essays on Rudyard Kipling.* Boston: G. K. Hall, 1990.

KINDLY ONES, THE ANTHONY POWELL (1962)

The sixth of 12 volumes in POWELL'S ROMAN-FLEUVE entitled *A DANCE TO THE MUSIC OF TIME,* this novel opens with a prolonged reminiscence of a WORLD WAR I childhood and then continues the narration through the first-person point of view of Nicholas Jenkins, a writer, as the world once again hovers on the verge of global conflict. In the overall structure of the series, *The Kindly Ones* is positioned at the end of the second of four "movements," following *CASANOVA'S CHINESE RESTAURANT* and preceding *The VALLEY OF BONES.* The title refers to the euphemism employed by the ancient Greeks to refer to the Furies—punitive divinities who pursued wrongdoers to torment them in retribution of those wrongs. They were so feared that they were called *eumenides,* or kindly ones, as a form of appeasement. As the attempts by Britain and its allies to appease Hitler gradually fail and war becomes inevitable, Nick's thoughts take him back to the days when the "great war" was looming. His governess had told him of the myth of the kindly ones; as world tension mounts, those days come alive again.

The most interesting people in Nick's young life had been the servants in the Jenkins household: Albert, the cook; Billson, the high-strung parlor maid who sees ghosts; Miss Orchard, Nick's tutor; Edith, his nurse; Mercy, the housemaid; and the occasional helpers, Bracey, a "soldier-servant" or a sort of valet and handyman, and Mrs. Gullick. The setting for this large household is Stonehurst, a country house in the vicinity of Aldershot. Nick is absorbed in the fascinating private lives of the servants, with whom he spends much of his time. He knows of Albert's alleged dislike of women, especially the one in Bristol who keeps writing him long letters, and he knows of Billson's crush on Albert in spite of her reiterated contempt for men in general. He is puzzled by Bracey's "funny days" when the man broods obsessively on something, but he knows that Bracey loves Billson. Less prominent than the servants—to young Nick, at least—are the friends of his parents, such as General and Mrs. Conyers, and the neighbors, such as the eccentric cult leader Dr. Trelawney.

All the characters and the tensions flowing among them come to a boiling point one Sunday when General and Mrs. Conyers have driven over for lunch in their newfangled motorcar. Albert gives his notice that day; he has married the letter-writing girl from Bristol and will be moving away to join her. No one can guess the effect this news will have on Billson, who had already been jilted once. To make matters worse, Uncle Giles has wired to say he will arrive that evening to visit for a while. Then, when the luncheon guests are enjoying their coffee and chatting after lunch, Billson comes into the parlor to give *her* notice, but she is stark naked, unhinged by Albert's new plans. General Conyers saves the moment, and Uncle Giles arrives at the peak of confusion with the news that some Austrian archduke has been assassinated. The outbreak of the war seems a fitting end to this domestic upheaval.

Later, in the present-day of the narrative (about 1938–39), Nick's friend Hugh Moreland moves to the country for a while, taking a house near Stourwater Castle, the seat of Sir Magnus Donners. Matilda Moreland invites Isobel and Nick to visit them there, and the entire group is invited to dinner at Stourwater, since Sir Magnus has become a kind of patron to Moreland, even though—or perhaps because—Matilda had once been the mistress of Sir Magnus. Nick encounters several old friends and acquaintances at the dinner, and for amusement the guests act out a pageant of the Seven Deadly Sins, which is photographed by Sir Magnus. Years and years later, in a closing volume of the series, Nick finally sees these comic scenes of his youth.

Soon afterward, Nick's Uncle Giles dies of a stroke at a seaside hotel, and the job of settling his affairs falls to Nick. Several coincidences occur, like a conjunction of planets in an astrologer's chart: The hotel is owned by Albert, the old family cook; Nick encounters Bob Duport in the bar and learns of Jean Duport's many affairs and also of Widmerpool's duplicitous business and political dealings. Even more amazing, and more threatening in light of the earlier flashbacks, is the presence in the hotel of Dr. Trelawney; he has become, for Nick, a harbinger of war. He predicts the arrival of war, and Mrs. Erdleigh, a psychic who had made previous appearances in Nick's life, soon arrives; when Uncle Giles's will is read, Mrs. Erdleigh is his sole beneficiary.

War arrives, and everyone's life is changed as stockbrokers, workers, businessmen, and even novelists enter the military. Nick is searching for a commission with no luck. Confusion is mounting as people's lives are convulsed by the preparations for war. On a visit to Lady Molly's, Nick meets Ted Jeavon's brother, a man still on active duty in an administrative role. He is preoccupied with some task, sorting piles of papers, as they converse. When Nick at last realizes that this new acquaintance is assigning applicants to military positions, he mentions his own fruitless search. On the spot, his seemingly impossible problem is solved. As he leaves, Ted Jeavons is fiddling with the blackout curtain, trying to seal up the house's light so that German bombers can't find it.

The story has reached its midpoint at the end of this volume, and Nick is near the midpoint of his life as well. He has weathered the first loss of a family member to death, and his first child has been conceived.

The future has never looked more uncertain as he departs from Lady Molly's home, where he had become a guest at the beginning of this "movement" and where his marriage had been feted; he is uncertain whether he will ever call here again. Powell suspends his characters in uncertainty, reflecting the uncertainty of English life on the brink of WORLD WAR II, masterfully constructing a complex and nostalgic narrative. The past glows cheerfully, in contrast to the dire prospects that the near future offers and that Nick has no choice but to plunge into. At the midpoint of a massive literary undertaking, *The Kindly Ones* is a powerful, superb novel on its own, made even richer by the five volumes that precede it.

BIBLIOGRAPHY
Joyau, Isabelle. *Understanding Powell's* A Dance to the Music of Time. New York: St. Martin's Press, 1994.

Selig, Robert L. *Time and Anthony Powell*. Cranbury, N.J.: Associated University Presses, 1991.

Spurling, Hillary. *Invitation to the Dance: A Guide to Anthony Powell's* A Dance to the Music of Time. Boston: Little, Brown, 1977.

KING OF ELFLAND'S DAUGHTER, THE

LORD DUNSANY (1924)   An early work in the nascent genre of FANTASY literature, this novel draws on the traditions of Irish mythology and folklore for characters and plot devices, but it also makes a philosophical comment on the nature of mundane reality.

The protagonist of the story is a hero who undertakes a quest. In the earthly land of Erl, members of the parliament wish to bring innovation to their world from the magical realm of Elfland; they send the king's son, Alveric, to find and retrieve it for them. Alveric enlists the aid of a witch, Ziroonderel, knowing he will need magic powers, not merely an earthly sword, if he is to succeed in his quest. His goal is to marry Lirazel, the king of Elfland's daughter, and to bring her with him to earth. He ultimately prevails in this quest, overcoming the obstacles and impediments thrown up against him. Back in the land of Erl, Alveric and Lirazel create a son, Orion. But all is not well, because Lirazel is unaccustomed to life in the material and temporal world of matter and decay. Her father sends a letter of magic runes of fetch her back, and although she resists the letter's power for a while, gradually she realizes she must return in order to survive. Her return, however, leaves Alveric and Orion bereft.

The father and son each undertake further quests in the direction of Elfland or on its borders, but since Lirazel has departed from the earth they lack the magic to succeed. Finally, through her intercession with her father, she wins his consent to reunite the family. The unexpected result, however, is the absorption of the entire land of Erl into Elfland, causing it to disappear from the world of men. The longing of the Parliament of Erl to bring magic into their world ultimately results in more success than they had wished for when magic brings them permanently into Elfland.

DUNSANY captures the charm of folktales in his story, but he also preserves the clash of cultures and religions that such stories frequently disguise. Christianity has come to the land of Erl by the time Lirazel marries Alveric; her refusal to convert to Christian ways becomes a key motivation for her return to Elfland. Later, when the land of Erl is subsumed into Elfland, only the sacred ground of a Christian friar's garden remains behind. The land of Erl cannot be both a part of the earth and also possessed of Elfland's magic; that magic, however, is powerless against the new faith on earth. The story offers no reconciliation between the two worlds, although it does allow love and family to find a refuge beyond mortal limits.

BIBLIOGRAPHY
Cantrell, Brent. "British Fairy Tradition in *The King of Elfland's Daughter*," *Romantist* 4–5 (1980–1981): 51–53.

Joshi, S. T. *Lord Dunsany: Master of the Anglo-Irish Imagination*. Westport, Conn.: Greenwood Press, 1995.

KIPLING, RUDYARD (1865–1936)   The

first British writer to win the NOBEL PRIZE for Literature (1907), Rudyard Kipling was born in Bombay, INDIA, on December 30, 1865. His father was a scholar and artist, and his mother was related, through her sisters' marriages, to leading artists and politicians of the day. He grew up tended by Indian servants, learning to speak their language fluently and absorbing their oral folktale tradition. Like most children of English families serving in India, Kipling and his sister were sent to England for their formal education, but the experience was an unhappy one. He attended the United Services College and edited the school newspaper there. At 16, in 1882, he returned to India. Between the ages of 18 and 22, he served as assistant editor of *The Civil and Military Gazette* in Lahore, where his father worked as a curator in the Lahore Museum. He was already writing short fiction and poetry, and in 1886 he relocated to Allahabad to help edit *The Pioneer.* His stories proved to be popular and were soon appearing in newspapers throughout India and eventually gained him notice in the London literary establishment.

Between 1889 and 1892, Kipling traveled extensively, taking the long way round to England. He also suffered an emotional breakdown and an unrequited love for a painter, Violet Flo Garrard, events that feature in the semiautobiographical novel *The Light That Failed* (1891). During this time, Kipling befriended the American writer Wolcott Balestier, the brother of Kipling's future wife, and they collaborated on a novel, *The Naulahka: A Story of East and West* (1892). That same year, Kipling's most famous poetic work, *Barrack Room Ballads and Other Verses,* was published; it became a tremendous success. After a last trip to India, Kipling and Caroline Balestier were married in January of 1892, and they settled for five years in Vermont, where Kipling became friends with Mark Twain and wrote the popular work of children's literature *The Jungle Book.* He also studied the New England cod-fishing industry as background for his novel *Captains Courageous* (1897), the story of a spoiled rich boy's acquisition of self-discipline. Longing for greater privacy than the American press allowed him to have, Kipling and his family relocated to England in 1897, although they roamed to different locations until 1902.

During the BOER WAR (1897–1902), Kipling was in South Africa; there, he wrote his best novel, *KIM,* publishing it in 1901. By then, he was well established in the literary firmament of British letters, a position cemented by his winning the Nobel Prize in 1907. His health declined in his later years, and his only son was a casualty of WORLD WAR I in 1915. Kipling died on January 18, 1936, and his ashes were buried in Westminster Abbey in Poet's Corner. Increasingly, in his later years, Kipling was perceived as an ardent apologist for imperialism, and as the British EMPIRE failed, his reputation declined with it. More recently, scholars have begun to reconsider his work on its own merits. As a short story writer, he is ranked with the Frenchman Guy de Maupassant and the Russian Anton Chekhov, and his voluminous production of poems covers a vast range of styles and subjects, showing greater ambivalence toward the English enterprise in the world than had originally been recognized. With growing interest in the legacy of COLONIALISM and the rise of postcolonialism, Kipling's reputation is in debate, but the fact that scholars take such a keen interest in his work is a positive indication.

BIBLIOGRAPHY

Gilmour, David. *The Long Recessional: The Imperial Life of Rudyard Kipling.* New York: Farrar, Straus & Giroux, 2002.

Laski, Marghanita. *From Palm to Pine: Rudyard Kipling Abroad and at Home.* New York: Facts On File, 1987.

Orel, Harold, ed. *Critical Essays on Rudyard Kipling.* Boston: G. K. Hall, 1990.

Ricketts, Harry. *Rudyard Kipling: A Life.* New York: Carroll and Graf, 2000.

Wilson, Angus. *The Strange Ride of Rudyard Kipling: His Life and Works.* New York: Viking Press, 1978.

KNEALE, MATTHEW (1960–   )

Born on November 24, 1960, Matthew Kneale grew up in a literary family: His father is a playwright and his mother is a writer. He matriculated at Magdalen College of Oxford University, completing an undergraduate degree in English in 1982. He spent the next year teaching English as a second language in Tokyo, and the experience provided the basis for his first novel, *Whore Banquets* (1987), which won him the Somerset Maugham Award in 1988. After leaving Japan, he also taught English as a second language in Rome. Kneale is an avid traveler, having toured extensively in Australia, Latin America, Asia, and having spent longer periods in Italy. His travels have made him a witness of varieties of human existence, ranging from Stone Age tribal cultures in New Guinea to doomed student protests in China.

In 1989, Kneale published his second novel, *Inside Rose's Kingdom.* His third novel, *Sweet Thames* (1993), won the John Llewellyn Rhys Award the year it was published; it is an examination of Victorian life set in 1849 during an epidemic of cholera in England. Kneale traveled extensively during the 1990s, partly to conduct research for his fourth book, ENGLISH PASSENGERS, another example of HISTORICAL FICTION set during the Victorian era. It satirically relates a colonizing voyage to Tasmania undertaken by a biblical literalist hoping to refute Charles Darwin's new idea of evolution and a racist physician seeking proof for his theory on the human species. *English Passengers* was short-listed for the BOOKER Prize and won the WHITBREAD Book of the Year Award in 2000. In that year, Kneale also was married. He continues to live and write at his home in Oxford, England.

BIBLIOGRAPHY

Bruns, Ann. "Matthew Kneale." Interview. Bookreporter.com, March 24, 2000. Available online. URL: http://www.bookreporter.com/authors/au-kneale-matthew.asp. Accessed February 6, 2004.

Yates, Emma. "Five Minutes with Matthew Kneale." Interview. The Guardian Unlimited, January 18, 2001. Available online. URL: http://books.guardian.co.uk/whitbread 2000/story/0,,424148,00.html. Accessed February 6, 2004.

KOESTLER, ARTHUR (1905–1983)

Born on September 5, 1905, in Budapest, Hungary, Arthur Koestler grew up in a multilingual household, the son of a Jewish inventor. His grandfather escaped from Russia during the Crimean War; his mother was from a Jewish family in Prague, Czechoslovakia, and his governesses were frequently English or French. Young Arthur knew German, French, English, and Hungarian while he was still a child. The family relocated to Vienna after financial reversals caused by WORLD WAR I. Koestler attended school for a while, developing his interests in science, but he became inspired by Zionism and left his family for Palestine in 1926. There, he held numerous jobs without finding a career until he began working as a journalist. His fluency with languages helped him secure a position with the Ullstein newspaper chain. He was posted to the Middle East, then to Paris, and by 1930 he was serving as science editor in Berlin, Germany, as the Nazi Party gained a grip on power.

During the 1930s, the only strong opponent to Nazi domination was the Communist Party; Koestler became a member in 1932. In 1932 and 1933, he visited the Soviet Union but was barred from returning to Germany. He spent three years at loose ends performing various work for the party in Vienna, Paris, and London. Then in 1936, he got a job as a reporter covering the SPANISH CIVIL WAR for a London paper, but he went to Spain primarily to help the Republican cause that the Communist Party supported. He was apprehended by the right-wing Nationalist forces of General Franco and would have been executed had the British government not intervened and saved him. He published the story of his experiences in *Spanish Testament* in 1938 and left the Communist Party that same year in disgust over the purges Stalin was conducting in Moscow to secure his power. After Spain, he was in France and was taken prisoner when it fell to the Nazis, but he escaped to England, which became a home base for him. He became a naturalized citizen of Great Britain after WORLD WAR II.

In 1940, Koestler published his masterpiece, *DARKNESS AT NOON,* a study of party loyalty. He had previously published one novel, *The Gladiators* (1939), an examination of the means and ends of acquiring political power through the revolt led by the Roman slave Spartacus. Koestler's third novel was *Arrival and Departure* (1943), another study of revolutionary motivation. During this period he was also working for the British Broadcasting Corporation. His opposition to communism placed him at the center of an intellectual storm: Many leading European (and American) writers, artists, philosophers, and other thinkers were supporters of socialism or communism, hoping it would solve longstanding problems of economic inequity and political abuses. In France in particular, the philosopher Maurice Merleau-Ponty attacked *Darkness at Noon* in his collection of essays entitled *Humanism and Terror* (1947); the quarrel is fictionalized in Simone de Beauvoir's roman à clef *The Mandarins* (1954).

Koestler turned to nonfiction political writing, autobiographical writing, science writing, and finally to explorations of paranormal phenomena such as extrasensory perception (ESP). His personal life remained somewhat unsettled: He was married three times. His health began to decline due to Parkinson's disease; he and his third wife committed suicide on March 3, 1983.

BIBLIOGRAPHY

David Cesarani. *Arthur Koestler: The Homeless Mind.* London: William Heinemann, 1998.

Harris, Harold, ed. *Stranger on the Square: Arthur and Cynthia Koestler.* New York: Random House, 1984.

Levene, Mark. *Arthur Koestler.* New York: Ungar, 1984.

KRUGER'S ALP CHRISTOPHER HOPE (1984)

Set in southern Africa, this novel, which won the WHITBREAD AWARD, is about the struggle to overcome racism and opens with a first-person narrator walking on the grounds of a church school that is slated to be bulldozed to make way for progress. The narrator had been a student in this school, where the kindly priest taught black and white children together and allowed black children their first experience of relaxing in the shade for a story while white children worked in the sun nearby. As he looks on the setting where the scenes of his youth had transpired, the narrator enters into a dream vision about the lives of four childhood friends from this school. HOPE structures the dream vision—a literary form common during the medieval period—as an ALLEGORY of South Africa. One of the friends, Theodore Blanchaille, follows in the footsteps of the boys' mentor and becomes a priest himself. He sets out on a quest to locate the mountain retreat in Switzerland allegedly created by the founder of South Africa, Paul Kruger, who had been forced into exile during the BOER WAR. Legends of Kruger's gold enter into the story, echoing an irony about South Africa, a country incredibly rich in natural resources yet plagued by poverty and lacking in opportunity for all its citizens.

Kruger's Alp is an advanced reading experience since it demands a certain degree of background knowledge about South Africa's history and politics and deploys literary devices that challenge the reader. But with preparation, its humor becomes apparent and its passionate appeal for a more humane, just, and equitable world becomes accessible.

BIBLIOGRAPHY

Maltz, Harold P. "Narrative Mode in Christopher Hope's *Kruger's Alp,*" *English in Africa* 14, no.2 (1987): 45–58.

KUREISHI, HANIF (1954–)

Born and reared in London of Pakistani and English descent, Hanif Kureishi received his education at King's College in London. He began his career in the theater as a playwright, winning a prize in 1981 for his play *Outskirts* (published in 1983) and serving as the resident playwright of the Royal Court Theatre in 1982. He expanded his work to film with his screenplay for *My Beautiful Laundrette* (1985); the story followed the adventures of two young men, one a Pakistani and the other his English lover, who open a coin-operated self-service laundry that doubles as a hip social center. Three years later, his screenplay for *Sammie and Rosie Get Laid* presented the street violence and racism of London, satirizing the social conditions condoned under Prime Minister Margaret Thatcher. Kureishi's first novel, *The BUDDHA OF SUBURBIA,* was published in 1990; it draws on his autobiographical experiences growing up in the middle-class suburbs of London and then working in the London theater world. Primarily a writer of COMIC NOVELS that rely on realism, Kureishi uses a style that is funny, frankly erotic, sexually explicit, and unflinching in its portrayal of the seamier aspects of urban life in the multiethnic world of contemporary England.

BIBLIOGRAPHY

Moore-Gilbert, B. J. *Hanif Kureishi.* Contemporary World Writers Series. Manchester, U.K.: Manchester University Press, 2001.

L

LADY CHATTERLEY'S LOVER D. H. LAWRENCE (1928)

The center of one of the most notorious censorship battles involving 20th-century literature, this novel broke new ground in its benign portrayal of an adulterous affair and its frankly casual use of taboo words pertaining to human sexuality. The book was banned in England and the United States from the time it was privately published until 1959 (in the United States) and 1960 (in England), when high-profile court decisions permitted its unexpurgated publication and distribution. Despite its illicit status, the book was available on the Continent; educated tourists to Europe not uncommonly made a point of acquiring a copy to bring home, giving it the status of an underground cult classic even before it was freely available.

The central character of the novel is Lady Constance Chatterley, wife of Sir Clifford Chatterley, who has been paralyzed from the waist down since being wounded in WORLD WAR I. Connie helps her husband with his short fiction projects, but she is growing restless in her asexual marriage. She wanders the Chatterley estate, Wragby, and briefly inters into an affair with an Irish playwright, Michaelis. Connie is the daughter of an artist and an aesthetically sensitive woman, and she becomes dissatisfied not just with her lover, but with his entire approach to art as a commercial enterprise. When she stumbles across the cottage of her husband's gamekeeper, Mellors, on one of her walks, she meets a man unlike any she has known. Mellors is well educated and artistically sensitive, but he is also a man of the earth and a man of the people. Despite some initial disagreements, he and Connie are soon drawn into a deeply passionate affair. The explicit description of the consummation of their love created the censorship case that kept the novel out of print for so many years.

Connie discovers the extent of her love for Mellors when her sister Hilda visits her: Mellors alienates Hilda with his forthright frankness of opinion, and Connie realizes that she prefers to side with Mellors rather than with Hilda. When the sisters vacation in Europe, visiting Paris and Venice, Connie again realizes that her future lies with Mellors, not with her husband or her family. By this time, she is carrying his child, but she agrees to go along with her father's plan to identify the father of the child as Duncan Forbes, an artist of his acquaintance. Mellors derides Forbes's painting—evidence of Mellors's aesthetic refinement—but he himself has as great an obstacle to a permanent union in his life as Connie has in hers. Mellors has an estranged wife whom he never got around to divorcing and a daughter who lives with his family. Before the lovers can unite their lives, each must be freed of obligations already undertaken.

Connie at first tries to go along with her father's plan—it will spare her husband's pride and be less of an affront to his position in the CLASS hierarchy—but in revealing her pregnancy to Sir Clifford, she winds up telling him the whole truth. For his part, Sir Clifford is enraged and hurt; he refuses to grant his wife a divorce. Connie leaves to stay with her sister Hilda in Scotland, and Mellors takes a job at a farm, waiting for his divorce to become final. The future resolution of their lives remains suspended in AMBIGUITY, but the novel ends with Mellors's tender and loving letter to Connie. It appears that their love will survive despite the obstacles presented by other people in their lives and by society's conventional expectations.

Having been certified of its literary worthiness in the court systems of Great Britain and the United States, *Lady Chatterley's Lover* faces new critics in the contemporary academic world. Proponents of FEMINISM have called into question the positive image of Mellors and Connie, seeing him as a glorified double for LAWRENCE himself and her in particular as a projection of male fantasy and wishful thinking—a woman sexually free and grateful for the fulfillment of her desires. But Mellors is a complex and compelling character even if he is Lawrence's projection of himself into perfected fictional form, and the depiction of Connie's growing self-awareness is an insightful presentation of a woman's life.

BIBLIOGRAPHY

Balbert, Peter. *D. H. Lawrence and the Phallic Imagination.* New York: St. Martin's Press, 1989.

Britton, Derek. *Lady Chatterley: The Making of the Novel.* Winchester, Mass.: Unwin Hyman, 1988.

Holbrook, David. *Where D. H. Lawrence Was Wrong About Woman.* Cranbury, N.J.: Bucknell University Press, 1992.

Squires, Michael, and Dennis Jackson, eds. *D. H. Lawrence's "Lady": A New Look at* Lady Chatterley's Lover. Athens: University of Georgia Press, 1985.

LADY INTO FOX DAVID GARNETT (1922)

Silvia Tebrick (née Fox) is strolling out with her husband one afternoon as a fox hunt rushes by their property; when the uproar has settled, Mr. Tebrick sees that his wife has been metamorphosed into a vixen—a female fox, and a very beautiful one, too. Thus begins a novella that teeters between impish comedy and solemn tragedy. The comic elements all relate to the events of the story (except the last event), and the tragic air derives from the complete seriousness with which the tale is related to the readers by a first-person narrator. Mr. Tebrick's attachment to his wife is not the least lessened by her transformation, but his situation becomes more and more ludicrous as he gently tries to impose his wife's refinement and delicacy on the vixen she has become. The picture of the fox dressed in Mrs. Tebrick's negligee, for example, related in a completely deadpan manner, is one of the delights of the story.

On one level, GARNETT's story simply seems to reinscribe the proverb "Clothes make the man"—or, in this case, the woman. The longer Mrs. Tebrick remains in fox form, the more strongly the natural behavior of foxes comes out in her: She acquires a taste for fresh-killed fowl, and she begins running off to be with other foxes when mating season arrives. At a more abstract level, Garnett is exploring the tension between nature and nurture in the constitution of the human personality, and nature definitely has the stronger sway over Mrs. Tebrick once she assumes her fox form. But she never completely forgets her connection to Mr. Tebrick, so that when she has a litter of fox cubs, she brings him to see them and allows Mr. Tebrick to become a kind of honorary member of her fox family. But this idyllic life cannot last long: People in the neighborhood are talking, and the season for fox hunting approaches once more.

Garnett's tale has drawn a moderate amount of critical commentary, but the record lacks a feminist reading, and the story cries out for one. It is filled with issues of gender identity and gender stereotypes, marital fidelity and infidelity, sexual continence and license, family structure, emotional bonds, personal freedom, self-development, and others. *Lady into Fox* has the potential of becoming a minor classic of FANTASY literature if it can find its readership.

BIBLIOGRAPHY

Ross, Michael. "Ladies and Foxes: D. H. Lawrence, David Garnett, and the Female of the Species," *D. H. Lawrence Review* 18, no. 2/3 (Summer/Fall 1986): 229–238.

LANDLOCKED DORIS LESSING (1965)

This novel follows *A RIPPLE FROM THE STORM* (1958) in the ROMAN-FLEUVE *CHILDREN OF VIOLENCE,* and it precedes the apocalyptic conclusion to the series, *The*

FOUR-GATED CITY (1969). The protagonist, as in the other volumes, is Martha Quest, born in the fictional African country of Zambesi to white English parents during the period of COLONIALISM.

At this point in the series, Martha is still living in Africa and she has been married and divorced twice. She is politically involved with the Communist Party, but she has also become disillusioned with politics, especially after her second marriage—to a Communist allegedly planning to reshape the world—turned out to be utterly conventional. Still in her 20s, she has a job as a secretary; and she continues to pay attention to her visions. In one, she must work to keep the many rooms of a house scrupulously separated; in another, she is stranded on barren land as others sail away, but she is locked in place, unable to reach the water. It is time for her to go on to other challenges—to return to England—but before she can leave, she has more to learn.

Martha meets Thomas Stern, a Polish Jew who survived the concentration camps of the Holocaust but who has a deteriorating grasp on his mental faculties. With him, Martha finally learns about love emotionally, bodily, and psychically. In neither of her marriages did she have the complete union she achieves with Thomas. But larger causes must also be served, and Thomas travels to Palestine to fight for the security of Israel's precarious existence. Martha is left behind, stranded, as in her vision, waiting for Thomas to return. He does come back, but he doesn't seem to be the same person, and he doesn't stay, choosing instead to work in impoverished African villages. There, he dies of fever, leaving Martha in possession of a manuscript he had been working on.

This manuscript is something of a catchall pastiche, blending the everyday and the numinous, the routine and the extraordinary, the ridiculous and the sublime. Martha studies the manuscript—Thomas's gift that begins to reconnect her to the larger world and that dislodges her from the barren land where she is locked. After one last political meeting, where she confirms for herself that she has no role to play in Africa any longer, she packs her few possessions to leave for England, taking with her Thomas's nurturing manuscript.

BIBLIOGRAPHY
Greene, Gayle. "Doris Lessing's *Landlocked:* 'A New Kind of Knowledge,' " *Contemporary Literature* 28, no. 1 (Spring 1987): 82–103.

LAST BATTLE, THE C. S. LEWIS (1956)
See *The* CHRONICLES OF NARNIA.

LAST ORDERS GRAHAM SWIFT (1996)
As the oldest survivors of "the greatest generation"—the victors of the greatest conflict of the 20th century—pass into memory all these years after the end of WORLD WAR II, Graham SWIFT provides a novel that commemorates England's sacrifices, large and small, during that war. *Last Orders* won the BOOKER PRIZE in 1996 at a time when the world was marking the half-century anniversary of the war; the story creates a small-scale tragedy in the death of an old soldier, and the ceremony of remembrance his friends conduct for him traces the large-scale history of the war's effect on England.

The old soldier who has died of cancer at the opening of the novel is—was—Jack Dodds, a master butcher by trade, like his father before him, who owns the little shop in a rapidly changing neighborhood. His friends are Ray, Lenny, Vic, and Vince; his widow is Amy. The action that drives the PLOT along is Jack's last request: He wishes to have his ashes strewn into the sea from the end of Margate Pier. These are the "last orders" of the title, although the phrase also refers to the bartender's signal prior to closing time that the taps are about to be shut off. Jack, Ray, Vic, Lenny, and Vince have been drinking buddies in the local pub through most of their lives, but Jack's passing has altered their routine in several ways.

Graham Swift develops his story by passing the narration from one man to another, and occasionally to Amy or other characters more peripheral to the central action. Each speaks as a first-person narrator, his or her voice and accent captured by Swift's ear and translated to the page. These are working-CLASS people without the benefit of exclusive educations or elaborate pedigrees, and Swift invests them with gritty charm and unassuming decency. Much of the novel's artistry lies in the tapestry of voices, interwoven in short chapters and elliptical conversations, that gradually reveal individual personalities and histories. As is typical among the bereaved, much of the conversation is designed to commemorate Jack's life and to reinscribe it on the memories of his friends; additionally, however, the several characters rehearse their own lives through the connections they had with Jack. The mystery of Amy's absence from the "funeral" the friends create in carrying Jack's ashes to Margate is also slowly resolved, along with the unexpected betrayal bound up in her refusal to attend.

The route the friends take carries them past several locations key to Jack's life, to their own lives, and to the life of the nation as well. In particular, they visit a monument erected to the memory of the war dead, and they pass by the scene of an old hop-farming operation where city dwellers often spent time playing in the country and working at the harvest. The significance of the location Jack has chosen for his final resting place also becomes apparent as various characters reveal their thoughts to the reader and contribute their words to the conversation. Swift modulates the emotional landscape over a wide range of feelings as differing perspectives on Jack's life are contrasted. These many vantage points round out Jack's character and bring him to life for the reader as his friends carry him, in death, to a last farewell.

Last Orders served as the basis of a FILM ADAPTATION—an increasingly common occurrence for winners of the Booker Prize. The film was released in 2001, directed by Fred Schepisi and starring Michael Caine, Bob Hoskins, and Helen Mirren; however, readers should be warned that seeing the movie first completely steals the thunder from the book. The character portraits created by the fine cast and the cinematic approximation of the narrative strategy leave very little for the reader to do upon opening the book.

BIBLIOGRAPHY

Parker, Emma. "No Man's Land: Masculinity and Englishness in Graham Swift's *Last Orders*." In *Posting the Male: Masculinities in Post-War and Contemporary British Literature*. Edited by Daniel Lea and Berthold Schoene. Amsterdam, Netherlands: Rodopi; 2003, 89–104.

Pedot, Richard. "Dead Lines in Graham Swift's *Last Orders*," *Critique: Studies in Contemporary Fiction* 44, no. 1 (Fall 2002): 60–71.

LAST POST FORD MADOX FORD (1928)
See *PARADE'S END*.

LAST THINGS C. P. SNOW (1970)
The closing volume in SNOW's 11-volume ROMAN-FLEUVE, collectively known as *STRANGERS AND BROTHERS*, *Last Things* follows *The* SLEEP OF REASON (1968). As in all the stories, the first-person narrator is Lewis Eliot; in this case, he is the main subject of his own narration rather than an observer of someone else's life.

Lewis had already returned to life in his hometown in *The Sleep of Reason,* and in *Last Things* his semiretired life is even quieter. But he has reached the age at which he begins to see his contemporaries die, and his own health is not entirely robust. In particular, Eliot must undergo an eye operation to fix a detached retina. Afterward, he learns he had suffered a cardiac arrest during the surgery: He has literally died and been resurrected. Even with assurances from his doctor that he is healthy, Eliot finds himself in a meditative mood, contemplating the scope of his life and the finality of death. His closing thoughts are on the future and what it may bring, especially for his son's generation. With some trepidation, even though Eliot himself has been a lifelong liberal, he sees his son becoming engaged in leftist political causes. But he can do nothing about the onslaught of time and age, and his opportunities to change the world—to set the agenda for the future—have come and gone. He closes his long study in moderate optimism for what may come after.

The most famous volumes of Snow's series are the CAMPUS NOVELS *The MASTERS* (1951) and *The AFFAIR* (1960), and the political intrigues in *The NEW MEN* (1954) and *CORRIDORS OF POWER* (1964). *Last Things* is an introspective and valedictory novel, as is appropriate to the end of the long series and to the advanced age Eliot has reached. It is an suitable summing-up to an epic examination of English life through the most momentous events of the 20th century.

BIBLIOGRAPHY

Jones, Richard. "The End of the C. P. Snow Affair," *Atlantic Monthly* 226, no. 3 (September 1970): 112.

Weintraub, Stanley. "Last Things: C. P. Snow Eleven Novels Afterwards," *Mosaic: A Journal for the Interdisciplinary Study of Literature* 4, no. 3 (1971): 135–141.

LAWRENCE, D. H. (1885–1930)

Hailed as the greatest English novelist of the 20th century by some critics and reviled by others, David Herbert Lawrence was born on September 11, 1885, in Nottinghamshire, to a semiliterate, hard-drinking coal miner mismatched with a pious, educated wife. Lawrence's childhood was marred by the strife between his parents and by his mother's emotional dependence on her children. His sickly body and quick intelligence made him the antithesis of his virile father, and his mother concentrated her attention and affections on him, encouraging him to educate himself and escape the grim world of the coal-mining district.

After a bout with pneumonia in 1902, Lawrence took up teaching in his hometown of Eastwood. He experienced his first emotional attachment in a complex relationship with a local girl, Jennie (later portrayed as Miriam in *Sons and Lovers*); his mother's domination of his emotional life made Lawrence's transition to adult love difficult. Jennie encouraged him to write, and by 1905 Lawrence was composing short stories and poems and working on *The White Peacock,* his first published novel; in 1908, she sent poems of his to Ford Madox FORD, who was impressed with Lawrence's writing. On his recommendation, the firm of William Heinemann published *The White Peacock* in 1911.

The years of 1910 and 1911 were emotionally draining for Lawrence: He broke off his first relationship, his mother died, and he undertook an ill-fated engagement. But he also wrote a second novel, *The Trespasser* (1912). Then, during a visit to Eastwood in 1912, Lawrence fell in love with Frieda von Richthofen Weekley, a married woman and the mother of three children, whom she abandoned for him. They eloped to the Continent, where Lawrence completed the manuscript for *Sons and Lovers* (1913). The chief editor of Duckworth publishers, Edward Garnett (father of David GARNETT), was so impressed by Lawrence's nov-

els that he arranged to publish *Sons and Lovers;* first, however, Garnett eliminated some of Lawrence's more explicit discussions of sexual desire and mother-son relationships.

Lawrence and Frieda married in 1914 after she obtained a divorce. When WORLD WAR I broke out, they were living unhappily in England. Their marriage was stormy, and they were impoverished. Upon its publication in 1916, *The RAINBOW* was banned for its political and sexual content, and then publishers were unwilling to bring out the novel now considered to be Lawrence's greatest, *WOMEN IN LOVE*. These two books tell the story of the Brangwen family and were originally conceived as a single novel under the title *The Sisters. Women in Love* finally appeared in 1920 in the United States. Lawrence's literary acquaintances did not adequately defend his work when it was suppressed, and in 1919 Lawrence and his wife left England, embittered and alienated; he never returned, spending the last 10 years of his life wandering the world, searching for a tolerable society and for a warm, dry climate that would help him recover his health. The Lawrences finally settled on a ranch in Taos, New Mexico, making occasional extended trips into Mexico proper.

Lawrence continued writing as he traveled, publishing *The Lost Girl* (1920), *Aaron's Rod* (1922), and *Kangaroo* (1923). In New Mexico, he became interested in Aztec culture, and his studies about it, together with his travels in Mexico, form the basis for his novel *The Plumed Serpent* (1926). These novels are less successful artistically than those that preceded them, since Lawrence uses his fiction as an outlet for preaching his ideas about the importance of reuniting primal urges, such as sexual desire, with the rational thought that has suppressed them for centuries. He also wrote literary criticism, travel narratives, essays, poems, and plays. His health continued to decline, and in 1926 he returned to Europe. There, he produced three versions of *LADY CHATTERLEY'S LOVER,* the novel that is widely associated with his name, even though critics do not include it among his best works. The prohibition of the novel in England and the United States prompted Lawrence to write some outstanding essays attacking the censorship of literature, but when he died in 1930, of tuberculosis, the novel was still banned on the grounds of obscenity. After sensational trials in the United States and England, and after having become an underground cult classic despite its prohibition, Lawrence's last novel was finally legally declared to have literary merit and published in 1959 in the United States and in 1960 in England.

After his death, Lawrence's literary reputation suffered somewhat from the widespread association of his name with vague notions of pornographic content. In fact, Lawrence's novels are deeply concerned with morality, but he boldly addresses those aspects of human existence most densely circumscribed by taboo and thereby suppressed in human personalities without being eliminated from human psychology. He explores the functioning of desire and the expression of sexuality in men and women, breaking new ground through his insights and producing lyrical and symbolic language for the description of the physical consummation of the emotion of love. In the 1950s, critics began revising their assessment of Lawrence under the influence of F. R. Leavis especially, who identified Lawrence as one of the great English novelists, placing him in the company of Jane Austen, George Eliot, Henry JAMES, and Joseph CONRAD in his crucially influential book *The Great Tradition* (1948). Most recently, some feminist critics have taken Lawrence to task for his portrayal of women, but these criticisms have not unseated him from the CANON of the great 20th-century English novelists.

BIBLIOGRAPHY

Ellis, David. *D. H. Lawrence: Dying Game 1922–1930.* Cambridge: Cambridge University Press, 1998.

Heywood, Christopher, ed. *D. H. Lawrence: New Studies.* New York: St. Martin's Press, 1987.

Kinkead-Weekes, Mark. *D. H. Lawrence: Triumph to Exile 1912–1922.* Cambridge: Cambridge University Press, 1996.

Pilditch, Jan. *The Critical Response to D. H. Lawrence.* Westport, Conn.: Greenwood Press, 2001.

Worthen, John. *D. H. Lawrence: The Early Years, 1885–1912.* Cambridge: Cambridge University Press, 1991.

LEADING THE CHEERS JUSTIN CARTWRIGHT (1998)

Winner of the 1998 WHITBREAD Book of the Year Award, this novel by a South African author is set in Michigan and features as its pro-

tagonist Dan Silas, an Englishman and a former advertising executive who had spent his high school years in small-town America, where his father worked as an executive for General Motors. When Dan returns to Hollybush to deliver the keynote address at his 30-year high school reunion, he is shocked to learn from his former girlfriend that, at the end of those long-ago high school days, he had fathered a daughter with her, but that the young woman that baby grew up to be has recently become the victim of a brutal serial killer. These revelations draw him into a series of actions that constitute the story's main PLOT, but as he searches for ways to help his old girlfriend ease her pain and as he tries to find out the truth for himself, new information continually disrupts his view of his own past and of the life he missed out on when his family returned to England.

In the key subplot, Dan's old high school buddy Gary now believes himself to be a 19th-century Native American. Gary experienced a mental breakdown during his undergraduate days at Harvard and has since been in and out of various psychiatric institutions. He is living with his widowed mother, but his mental state has not returned to the normality that ordinary people expect in everyday life. Dan spends his travel time poring over his old yearbook and contemplating the choices he has made in his life and the unexpected directions the lives of his old friends have gone in. Having sold his share of the advertising agency he cofounded, he is at loose ends and is trying to connect to the better and nobler aspects of human existence. In revisiting Hollybush, he discovers unlooked-for opportunities to reconnect with his friends and to help them cope with and survive the burdens life has placed on them.

Justin Cartwright constructs his story through a first-person narrator, and much of the book's compelling quality derives from the narrator's keen observation of the American experience through the eyes of someone who is simultaneously an insider and an outsider. Dan Silas grew up admiring Thomas Jefferson and Thomas Edison, and his own character has been shaped by his Americanized teenage years. His reconnection to his old girlfriend and his old best friend, however, bring him face-to-face with dimensions of irrationality that nothing in life has prepared him to understand. He finds himself carrying out requests he could never have imagined being made of him. But he succeeds in his quest to open himself to new dimensions of possibility and to new appreciations of the human mystery.

BIBLIOGRAPHY

Kurtz, J. Roger. Review of *Leading the Cheers*, *World Literature Today* 74, no. 2 (Spring 2000): 363+.

Sayers, Valerie. "Most Likely to. . . ." Review of *Leading the Cheers*. *New York Times Book Review*, 17 October 1999, 24.

LE CARRÉ, JOHN (1931–)

Born David John Moore Cornwell on October 19, 1931, John le Carré is a writer whose SPY NOVELS are admired by some critics for their mainstream literary qualities, especially in the development and exploration of character. Le Carré learned about secrecy and deceit early in life: He was the son of a father who made his living as a swindler and confidence artist (and who eventually served a prison term for fraud) and of a mother who abandoned her two sons and left her husband for another man. He later turned his childhood experience into fiction in *A Perfect Spy* (1986). Le Carré attended a PUBLIC SCHOOL, Sherborne, which he hated, and entered college at Berne University in Switzerland, where he studied French and German.

In the wake of WORLD WAR II, le Carré worked for a short period of mandatory military service as an intelligence officer in Vienna. Afterward, he entered Lincoln College at Oxford, where he earned a degree in modern languages in 1958. His first marriage began in 1956 and lasted until 1971, when it ended in divorce; he later remarried. He is the father of four sons, three from his first marriage and one from his second. After leaving Oxford, le Carré turned to teaching, securing a position at Eton as an instructor of Latin and French. In 1960, he entered the British Foreign Service; biographers have speculated that he may have worked as a spy in this employment.

Le Carré published his first novel in 1960, *A Call for the Dead,* combining elements of the spy novel and of MYSTERY AND DETECTIVE FICTION in a story of a murder and its solution. George Smiley makes the first of many appearances in this novel, presenting the world with an intelligence man who is the diametric opposite of James BOND. Smiley recurs in le Carré's second novel, *A Murder of Quality* (1962), which is a mystery set in an elite boys' school. These novels attracted the attention of mystery readers, but with his third novel, *The SPY WHO CAME IN FROM THE COLD* (1963), le Carré's career as a novelist of international reputation took off. He resigned his position in the Foreign Service to write full-time. Since 1965, he has written 16 additional novels, almost all of them in the genre of spy fiction, and many featuring George Smiley. Some of his most noted titles include *Tinker, Tailor, Soldier, Spy* (1974), *The Little Drummer Girl* (1983), *The Russia House* (1989), *The Tailor of Panama* (1996), *Single and Single* (1999), *The Constant Gardener* (2000), and *Absolute Friends* (2004). Le Carré has had a hugely successful career as a writer of popular fiction while also winning positive notices for his spy novels as serious literary fiction.

John le Carré continues to live and write at his seaside home in Cornwall.

BIBLIOGRAPHY

Beene, Lynn Diane. *John le Carré.* Twayne's English Authors Series 496. New York: Twayne, 1992.

Cobbs, John L. *Understanding John Le Carré.* Understanding Contemporary British Literature Series. Columbia: University of South Carolina Press, 1998.

Lewis, Peter E. *John le Carré.* New York: Frederick Ungar, 1985.

LEITCH, MAURICE (1933–)

Author of *SILVER'S CITY,* the novel that won the WHITBREAD Book of the Year Award in 1981, Maurice Leitch was born to a working-CLASS family on July 5, 1933, in County Antrim, NORTHERN IRELAND. He was educated in Belfast and taught school for several years before going to work for the BBC as a producer, a career that he eventually followed, in 1970, to London, where he continued working for the BBC until 1988. His first creative efforts, in the early 1960s, were radio dramatizations.

Leitch published his first novel, *Liberty Lad*, in 1965; it is the semiautobiographical story of Frank Glass, born to a small town that is losing its economic base as the linen industry collapses. Through a homosexual friend, he becomes an eyewitness to the customs of Northern Ireland's gay culture, confined at the time to a limited, low profile. Four years later, his second novel, *Poor Lazarus* (1969), won the GUARDIAN FICTION PRIZE; set along the border that divides the island of IRELAND into two realms, it is the story of two men, one a Canadian filmmaker and the other—his intended subject—a Protestant Irishman. These novels were both banned in the Republic of Ireland when they were published. In 1975, Leitch published *Stamping Ground,* followed in 1981 by *Silver's City.* In the 1980s, he published primarily short fiction or novellas, and he also wrote professionally for film and television. In 1989, his novel *Burning Bridges* begins in London before moving the action back to Ireland.

Leitch wrote and published three novels as the 20th century was ending: *Gilchrist* (1994), *The Smoke King* (1998), and *The Eggman's Apprentice* (2001). *Gilchrist* features a reprobate Protestant preacher who falls in with a shady couple after he rips off his church's funds; *The Smoke King* is a double murder mystery involving American soldiers stationed at a camp in Northern Ireland. In *The Eggman's Apprentice,* a naïve young man with a beautiful singing voice becomes involved with Irish gangsters. Leitch's fiction is noted for the unadorned style in which believable characters carry on with realistic plots. He makes frequent reference to cinema as a metaphor for life in the modern world, and he often uses characters who would fit comfortably into American hard-boiled detective fiction. Leitch continues to live and work in London.

BIBLIOGRAPHY

"Maurice Leitch." Interview. In *Banned in Ireland.* Edited by Julia Carlson. London: Routledge 1990, 99–108.

Mills, Richard. "Closed Places of the Spirit: Interview with Maurice Leitch," *Irish Studies Review* 6, no. 1 (April 1998): 63–68.

Paulin, Tom. "A Necessary Provincialism: Brian Moore, Maurice Leitch, Florence Mary McDowell," In *Two Decades of Irish Writing: A Critical Survey.* Edited by Douglas Dunn. Chester Springs, Pa.: Dufour Editions, 1975, 244–256.

LESSING, DORIS (1919–)

One of the most important writers of the 20th century, and a key thinker with respect to FEMINISM in particular, Lessing was born Doris May Taylor in Persia (now Iran) on October 22, 1919. Her parents were both English, but they had immigrated to Iran after WORLD WAR I, and they subsequently moved to a farm in Southern Rhodesia (now Zimbabwe). Her years at home were impoverished and not especially happy in light of her parents' disappointments in life. Lessing attended a boarding school in Salisbury for a time, but after the age of about 14 she educated herself through wide reading.

Doris Taylor relocated to Salisbury in 1938, and the next year she was married to Frank Charles Wisdom. They had two children, and the marriage ended in divorce in 1943. She remarried, to Gottfried Lessing, in 1945, and this marriage produced one child and also ended in divorce, in 1949. That year she moved to London and published her first book, *The Grass Is Singing,* a novel of racism's crippling effects and the limited roles available to women. She had a strongly developed social conscience, and she joined the Communist Party in England for a time in the 1950s but formally ended her association with it in 1956. During this period, she also actively opposed the proliferation of nuclear armaments, while also traveling, writing, attending rallies, and giving speeches. She began a ROMAN-FLEUVE, *CHILDREN OF VIOLENCE,* in 1952 and completed it in 1969; its five volumes include *MARTHA QUEST* (1952), *A PROPER MARRIAGE* (1954), *A RIPPLE FROM THE STORM* (1958), *LANDLOCKED* (1965), and *THE FOUR-GATED CITY* (1969).

During this period, she published other novels as well, including her masterpiece, *The GOLDEN NOTEBOOK* (1962), which is widely considered to be one of the great treasures of world literature created in the 20th century. She turned her attention to SCIENCE FICTION in the 1970s through the early 1990s, publishing novels such as *Briefing for a Descent into Hell* (1971), *The Memoirs of a Survivor* (1974), and five novels in the series *Canopus in Argos: Archives* (collected in 1992). In 1983 and 1984, Lessing published two novels under the pseudonym Jane Somers to make a point and to put her work to the same test unknown writers must face: She submitted *The Diary of a Good Neighbour* and *If the Old Could . . .* under her nom de plume and several publishers rejected it. Most recently, she has returned to realism in her fiction writing.

In addition to some 25 novels, Doris Lessing has written plays for the stage, a volume of poetry, several collections of short fiction, and an extensive body of nonfiction, including her autobiography that began in 1994 with *Under My Skin*. Although Lessing's prolific output has slowed in recent years, she continues to remain active as a socially conscientious citizen and as a writer.

BIBLIOGRAPHY

Fishburn, Katherine. *Doris Lessing: Life, Work, and Criticism.* Fredericton, New Brunswick, Canada: York Press, 1987.

Greene, Gayle. *Doris Lessing: The Poetics of Change.* Ann Arbor: University of Michigan Press, 1997.

Pickering, Jean. *Understanding Doris Lessing.* Understanding Contemporary British Literature Series. Columbia: University of South Carolina Press, 1990.

Sprague, Claire, and Virginia Tiger, eds. *Critical Essays on Doris Lessing.* Boston: G. K. Hall, 1986.

Whittaker, Ruth. *Modern Novelists: Doris Lessing.* New York: St. Martin's Press, 1988.

LESS THAN ANGELS BARBARA PYM (1955)

A novel of human observation and interpretive commentary, *Less Than Angels* uses for its point of departure a gathering of anthropologists—specialists in the art of human observation and interpretive commentary. A pair of these academics has been observed arriving for a party by another specialist in human observation, a romance writer named Catherine Oliphant who happens to live with an anthropologist, Tom Mallow, when he's not "in the field."

The third-person omniscient narrator begins with Catherine and from her passes easily to Professors Fairfax and Vere, then on to Professor Mainwaring and his elite life of retirement in the country, and from him into the new anthropological facility he has persuaded a wealthy American widow to fund, along with some grants for field research. In the new center, Miss Lydgate and Miss Clovis, an anthropologist and a linguist, are preparing the sandwiches and sherry for the party and trying to figure out how to get rid of the six students studying in the library. Lacking the firmness required to evict the students, the two women invite them to join the gathering of distinguished scholars as representatives of the new generation of young anthropologists. Thus Deirdre, Digby, and Mark, all English aspirants to the field, and some French and American ones as well, wind up rubbing shoulders with the eminent men of their intended profession. Through their conversation, references to Alaric Lydgate (Miss Lydgate's brother), neighbor to Deirdre's family, and to the suburban setting of Deirdre's family life complete Pym's introduction. By the end of the first chapter, the ground is prepared for a series of interactions among these people, and the tone of light and droll SATIRE, somewhat influenced by FEMINISM, suggests the primarily comic nature of the exploration.

Although absent from the opening and the closing of the novel, Tom Mallow is very much the center of it. Three women are in love with him in the story: He and Catherine already have a relationship of some maturity, living together as they do whenever he is in London, but this time, while he's home to work on his dissertation, he cannot resist the unquestioning adoration of young Deirdre, and on a reluctant visit to his upperclass family, he cannot avoid a meeting with his first love, a woman still in love with him. These relationships with Tom also acquire an additional dimension from the connections that exist, or that develop, among these women, especially Catherine and Deirdre. Tom ultimately moves out of Catherine's cozy flat, even though he is not seriously interested in Deirdre—only in being adored by her on occasion—and his temporary quarters with Digby and Mark (one of whom has his own interest in Deirdre) complicate matters more.

In addition to the observation of these contrasts among people, Pym also contrasts the differing settings to which each of her characters belongs, allowing her satire to extend, by implication, across a range of the socioeconomic and CLASS arrangements of the English. The students and the young academics, of course, are at the bottom, living modest lives, wearing modest—if not shabby—clothes, and drinking modest sherry. Above these are the suburbanites, such as Deirdre's family and their neighbor Alaric, who begins to look more and more interesting to Catharine on her visits to the well-regulated routines of that environment. Higher still is the class of the gentry: those born to it but in rejection of it, such as Tom Mallow, and those aspiring to recline permanently in its embrace, such as Professor Mainwaring.

Barbara Pym's treatment of these materials never loses its decorum, but it also never relinquishes its satirical edge. In her sympathetic treatment of her female characters, she presents the dilemma of women, which is to be generally competent, especially in the art of making the world a more comfortable place in which to be human, and perpetually dismissed by the men who cannot doubt that they themselves are the pinnacle of life on earth and reason enough for women to keep busy making it comfortable. Pym's treatment of her topic never acquires the bitter edge of sarcasm, even though she sees clearly the inequities of the world she observes so insightfully.

BIBLIOGRAPHY
Liddell, Robert. *A Mind at Ease: Barbara Pym and Her Novels.* London: Peter Owen, 1989.

LETTER OF MARQUE, THE PATRICK O'BRIAN (1988)   See AUBREY-MATURIN NOVELS.

LEWIS, C. S. (1898–1963)   Born Clive Staples Lewis—familiarly called Jack—on November 29, 1898 in Belfast, IRELAND, C. S. Lewis succeeded in three literary spheres: as a scholar, a fantasist, and a Christian essayist. He grew up in a book-loving family, but the death of his mother when he was only 10 was a devastating emotional experience. Reading, studying, and writing provided him with solace, and he won a scholarship to University College, Oxford, just as WORLD WAR I broke out. He had to delay his studies until after the war. Like his colleague and friend J. R. R. TOLKIEN, he served on the front lines in France, where he was wounded.

At Oxford, Lewis devoted himself to the study of literature in the specialty area of the medieval and Renaissance periods. With the spread of modernist experimentation in virtually all forms of art, appreciation of older literature was waning, and Lewis worked to restore the reputations of such great writers as Edmund Spenser, author of *The Faerie Queene,* and John Milton, author of *Paradise Lost.* His scholarly work, *The Allegory of Love* (1936), established his academic reputation. But

Lewis also wrote in the popular genres of SCIENCE FICTION and FANTASY, and he delivered public lectures and radio talks about Christianity, and neither of these activities conformed to the expectations of senior academics. His advancement at Oxford was stymied, and in 1954 he relocated to Cambridge, accepting a chair in his specialty at Magdalene College.

Lewis's first publications were volumes of poetry and scholarship, but in 1938 he published the first volume of his SPACE TRILOGY, also referred to as the *Ransom trilogy. Out of the Silent Planet* was followed in 1943 by *Perelandra* and in 1945 by *That Hideous Strength;* these novels feature the unusual combination, for this genre, of Christian doctrine and science fiction in a story of the cosmic struggle between good and evil. Its protagonist, the philologist Professor Ransom, is modeled on J. R. R. Tolkien. The two men were members of the INKLINGS, a loose association of like-minded writers in Oxford who met in a local pub to discuss literature, ideas, and writing. In 1942, Lewis published *The SCREWTAPE LETTERS,* a comic novel in the form of a series of letters written by a senior demon in hell. In 1950, Lewis produced the first of seven volumes in *The CHRONICLES OF NARNIA,* a children's Christian ALLEGORY and adventure series. His last novel, *Till We Have Faces* (1956), was a retelling of the myth of Cupid and Psyche.

C. S. Lewis died on November 22, 1963—the day President Kennedy was assassinated. Since then, numerous posthumous publications have appeared, primarily essays of Christian "apologetics" or explanations of and explorations into the theological principles of the faith. His unusual but intensely romantic marriage to Joy Davidson Gresham, an American divorcée, has been captured in the play and film *Shadowlands.*

BIBLIOGRAPHY
Carpenter, Humphrey. *The Inklings: C. S. Lewis, J. R. R. Tolkien, Charles Williams, and Their Friends.* Boston: Houghton Mifflin, 1979.
Manlove, C. N. *C. S. Lewis: His Literary Achievement.* New York: St. Martin's Press, 1987.
Sayer, George. *Jack: C. S. Lewis and His Times.* San Francisco: Harper & Row, 1988.
Wilson, A. N. *C. S. Lewis: A Biography.* New York: W. W. Norton, 1990.

LEWIS, WYNDHAM (1882–1957) A writer, painter, and intellectual, Wyndham Lewis poured out creative and critical works prolifically and was strongly praised by contemporaries such as T. S. Eliot. Percy Lewis Wyndham was born on his wealthy American father's yacht off Nova Scotia, so his birthplace is considered to be Canada. His parents divorced when he was about 11 years old, and his English mother boarded him in a series of PUBLIC SCHOOLS. In 1898, he entered the Slade School of Art in London and studied painting until 1901, when he undertook a lengthy tour of Europe, establishing his reputation as a painter. He also began writing seriously during this period, and by 1909 he was publishing short fiction in *The English Review.* Back in London in 1912, Lewis published *Blast,* a magazine (lasting for only two issues) that introduced vorticism, his brainchild, to the world. In both graphics and text, *Blast* was innovative and influential, shaping the direction of British MODERNISM and virulently attacking the aesthetics of the 19th century. The magazine's writing showed the influence of imagist poetry on Lewis; the graphic design was heavily influenced by the industrial compositions of Italian futurism, focusing on machines and experimenting with ways to suggest movement in static pictures. The two issues comprise the founding documents of the vorticist movement in art and literature, building a connection between the massive and pragmatic designs of industry and the traditional arts of painting and poetry. As articulated by Lewis, vorticism opposed romanticism and turned away from nature, preferring abstraction bounded by hard outlines in graphic design. Although vorticism's advocates worked in multiple artistic disciplines, including writing, painting, and sculpture, the movement had only a limited influence. The attraction of radical thinkers such as Lewis and Ezra Pound to the Italian dictator Mussolini, and their admiration for the political systems of fascism, further undermined the appeal of the movement.

With the onset of WORLD WAR I, Lewis's literary career faltered as he entered military service. Like his contemporaries J. R. R. TOLKIEN, Ford Madox FORD, Robert GRAVES, Herbert Read, and David JONES, Lewis witnessed the horrors of trench warfare. After the war, Lewis wrote prolifically, producing more than two dozen books in about half as many years. But he also alienated himself both by attacking (and satirizing) mainstream figures in print and by writing eccentrically structured novels; he also expressed admiration for Adolph Hitler in the early 1930s. Lewis's opinions demonstrate an odd mix of revolutionary aesthetics and reactionary politics that pleased no one and resulted in his own marginalization.

Lewis moderated his style in fiction in the early 1930s and began writing thrillers such as *The REVENGE FOR LOVE* (1937) that, while they still dealt with political and philosophical issues, presented readers with more traditional plots and characters. Lewis also began to question his own earlier extremes of opinion. In the autobiographical *Self Condemned* (1954), an English historian spends a miserable isolated period in Canada during WORLD WAR II, just as Lewis did, and ends up crushed and hollowed by his experiences. After the war, Lewis contributed art criticism to *The Listener* until 1951, when blindness ended this aspect of his career. The tumor that caused his blindness killed him in 1957, but in the last decade of his life, he produced nearly a book a year, including some of his best criticism and commentary.

BIBLIOGRAPHY

Foshay, Toby. *Wyndham Lewis and the Avant-Garde: The Politics of the Intellect.* Montreal: McGill-Queen's University Press, 1992.

Kenner, Hugh. *Wyndham Lewis.* Norfolk, Conn.: New Directions, 1954.

Materer, Timothy. *Vortex: Pound, Eliot, and Lewis.* Ithaca, N.Y.: Cornell University Press, 1979.

Sherry, Vincent B. *Ezra Pound, Wyndham Lewis, and Radical Modernism.* New York: Oxford University Press, 1993.

LIFE AND LOVES OF A SHE-DEVIL, THE FAY WELDON (1984) A dark example of both SATIRE and FEMINISM, this bleakly funny novel traces the revenge taken by Ruth Patchett when her husband, Bobbo, a handsome and successful self-employed accountant, enters into an extramarital affair with the celebrated romance novelist Mary Fisher, who is one of his richest clients. When Ruth announces the affair at a dinner party with Bobbo's parents, he calls her a she-devil and storms off to stay with Mary in the lighthouse she has had converted into a charming and stylish home. The name-calling liberates Ruth, who had up to that point been a dutiful and conscientious wife: She embraces her identity as a she-devil and begins to plot the course of a thoroughgoing program of revenge on both Bobbo and Mary.

Ruth is a large and ungainly woman, with coarse dark hair, six feet two inches tall, raw-boned, unfeminine, and vigorously healthy. Mary Fisher is a petite and lissome blonde possessed of conventional but perfect prettiness. Ruth has two children from her marriage, and because she had devoted herself to the work of a full-time wife and mother, she has no education or employment skills. Mary Fisher has a successful career writing conventional and highly lucrative romance fiction, unencumbered by familial responsibilities. Ruth—her very name is part of the novel's ironic structure—decides that Mary and Bobbo must experience what Ruth has experienced: Mary must walk in the shoes that cruelly pinch the feet of ordinary women, and Bobbo must learn what it is like to live with unrequited love. Ruth sets about the task of transferring the burdens she has borne to their untroubled shoulders. She brings about the colossal assortment of accidents that burn down the suburban home in Eden Grove where Bobbo had established his wife and children, and she leaves the two children on the doorstep of the lovers in the converted lighthouse. She disappears from sight and begins a long process of bringing Bobbo to humiliation, of reducing Mary to the mundane lives of the women who buy her novels and thereby ensure her own luxurious lifestyle.

In order to achieve her revenge, Ruth must acquire vast sums of money and undergo the self-imposed torments of cosmetic and reconstructive surgery. She is able to do so thanks to Bobbo's act of converting her to a she-devil. With no moral restraints to bind her, and without the emotional bondage of feminine subjection to love and family ties, Ruth amasses the wealth she needs, destroys the financial resources of Bobbo and Mary, and reshapes herself into the image of stereotypical beauty that Bobbo could not resist. She becomes fully empowered and takes her revenge at her leisure.

WELDON constructs this story by alternating between Ruth's wounded first-person narration of her experiences and a coolly disinterested third-person narration that confirms Ruth's reports. Sometimes readers look through Ruth's eyes, experiencing her rejection, her wrath, and her cold determination at firsthand, and at other times they look on the larger scene, seeing Ruth and the other characters in context. This strategy moderates the novel's tone while also multiplying the author's opportunities to take satirical jabs at the way society has wasted the resources of half its population. Ruth will stop at nothing to have her revenge, and the result is a novel that is both funny and incisive in its condemnation of the world we take for granted.

BIBLIOGRAPHY

Barreca, Regina, ed. *Fay Weldon's Wicked Fictions.* Hanover, N.H.: University Press of New England, 1994.

Dowling, Finuala. *Fay Weldon's Fiction.* Rutherford, N.J.: Fairleigh Dickinson University Press, 1998.

Smith, Patricia Juliana. "Weldon's *The Life and Loves of a She-Devil,*" *Explicator* 51, no. 4 (Summer 1993): 255–257.

LIFE AND TIMES OF MICHAEL K, THE

J. M. COETZEE (1983)   A simple story that may be read as a political and social ALLEGORY of the disintegration of minority rule in South Africa in the 1980s, *The Life and Times of Michael K* won the BOOKER PRIZE in 1983. The novel's title proclaims its affiliation with the surreal works of Franz Kafka, and its odyssey of a dying woman to her birthplace suggests aspects of William Faulkner's *As I Lay Dying.* COETZEE contextualizes his work in the decay of South Africa's misbegotten government, but he also creates a story that rises above its time and place to condemn injustice and inhumanity in general.

Coetzee effectively combines the vague and the specific to develop his novel's atmosphere of oppression and confusion. As a noted South African writer—his previous novel, *Waiting for the Barbarians* (1980), had won the JAMES TAIT BLACK MEMORIAL PRIZE—he could depend on readers understanding the political context in which he was writing: A tradition of white minority rule through apartheid was collapsing into chaos as the majority black population organized itself into more effective forms of resistance. But Coetzee is vague about matters of race. Michael K is born into poverty and disfigurement (his harelip, like his poverty, could be corrected, but no one bothers to do so) to a mother nearly broken by the hard labor of servitude, but their race is never specified, and neither is that of the other characters, bad and good, whom they encounter in the story. Whether they are black or white, that fact becomes secondary to the conditions of oppression under which they live.

The long first section of the novel, related by a dispassionate third-person narrator, follows Michael's life from birth to the schooling that prepares him for a second-rate existence in his employment as a gardener in the parks of Cape Town. His life, it appears, will follow this inconsequential routine indefinitely, but then his mother, Anna, becomes ill as her limbs swell and weaken with dropsy. Michael K is a dutiful son, so he does all he can to help his mother. When she wishes to return to the farm where she grew up, he sets about the task of making it possible. He purchases train tickets, but the vast and labyrinthine bureaucracy that regulates the issuing of permits to travel proves to be impenetrable. Michael K sets off with Anna in a cart, and along the way she dies in a hospital that is in fact an inhospitable institution.

Michael K continues the journey and spreads his mother's ashes on a farm that might be the one she remembered so fondly. He begins tending the farm— he is a trained gardener, after all—but soon he flees when the purported owner returns. He takes refuge in the wilderness, where he nearly starves, but is captured and confined in a so-called resettlement camp (clearly a kind of concentration camp). He escapes back to the farm and finds it deserted, but he is once again captured, nearly starved from living alone on the land, and sent back to Cape Town for retraining. Even though the oppressive government seems to wish his kind would disappear from the face of the earth, when he arrives at the retraining center, he is hospitalized for malnutrition: In a horrible IRONY, the system that is driving him to the brink of survival also does its utmost, having brought him there, to keep him alive.

Clearly, oppressors need the oppressed more than the oppressed need their oppressors.

The short second part of the novel has as a first-person narrator the doctor who treats Michael K and takes an interest in him. Things are going badly for the oppressors, and the doctor worries about what he may suffer once the oppressors are no longer in charge. The doctor sees that Michael K, in his simplicity and ability to endure suffering, is a representative of the survivors. Michael needs very little and expects very little from life, and he is therefore well prepared to succeed in a world that has little to offer. The very short third section of the novel follows Michael K after he escapes from the retraining facility. He joins a group of other marginalized survivors, and as a community they seek refuge in the neglected, ruined parts of the city until the more demanding components of society can finish fighting over who will be in charge of it. But Michael K does more than just survive: In spite of his deformity, he finds a sexual partner, and in this connection he has a chance of extending his survival into an unknown future. In making this humble survivor his protagonist, and in avoiding the specifics of racial identity, Coetzee broadens his story into an implicit attack on those who wield oppressive power over others and those who lust for the opportunity to do so as well.

BIBLIOGRAPHY

Brink, Andre. "Writing Against Big Brother: Notes on Apocalyptic Fiction in South Africa," *World Literature Today* 58 (Spring 1984): 189–194.

Gallagher, Susan V. *A Story of South Africa: J. M. Coetzee's Fiction in Context.* Cambridge, Mass.: Harvard University Press, 1991.

Moses, Michael Valdez, ed. *The Writings of J. M. Coetzee.* Durham, N.C.: Duke University Press, 1994.

LIGHT AND THE DARK, THE C. P. SNOW (1947)

The second volume to be published in the ROMAN-FLEUVE collectively entitled STRANGERS AND BROTHERS, this novel follows *George Passant* (1940; originally titled *Strangers and Brothers*) and continues the life story of the first-person narrator of the entire series, Lewis Eliot. In order of publication, it immediately precedes *A TIME OF HOPE* (1949); however, in the chronology of Eliot's life, it follows the action related in *The* CONSCIENCE OF THE RICH (1958). In *The Light and the Dark,* Eliot is an observer of another man's behaviors and choices rather than a main character in the PLOT; in this case, the focus of Eliot's narration is his university friend Roy Calvert, a scholar of the Orient—specifically, of the Manichean heresy that posits equally strong forces of good and evil at work in the universe. Roy is brilliant but unstable, exhibiting patterns of behavior that might today be diagnosed as bipolar disorder. His life is a cycle of light and dark as he alternates between manic periods of great activity and depressive periods of self-destructiveness. Roy is prone to uncontrollable abusiveness toward his colleagues and toward women, many of whom nonetheless find him attractive. Unable to live a normal life or to exercise consistently rational judgment of his best course of action, Roy eventually volunteers for service as a bomber pilot when WORLD WAR II breaks out—an expression of his passively suicidal tendencies, since the survival rate for this duty is very low, especially in the early days of the war. In a bittersweet IRONY, Roy does find love and some degree of fulfillment, but he is not fated to enjoy it for very long.

Roy belongs in the same category as Eliot's mentor, George Passant, and his friend Charles March. These three men are the earliest influences on Eliot's character as a young man just beginning to make a start in his own independent life. Each of the three is flawed in a different way, possessing giftedness or financial advantages, but lacking the ability to put these to best use. Eliot examines their flawed lives with compassionate sympathy and psychological insight, demonstrating his own giftedness in doing so.

BIBLIOGRAPHY

Davis, Robert Gorham. "C. P. Snow." In *Six Contemporary British Novelists.* Edited by George Stade. New York: Columbia University Press, 1976, 57–114.

Widdowson, Peter J. "C. P. Snow's *Strangers and Brothers* Sequence: Lewis Eliot and the Failure of Realism," *Renaissance & Modern Studies* 19 (1975): 112–128.

LION, THE WITCH, AND THE WARDROBE, THE C. S. LEWIS (1950) See *The* CHRONICLES OF NARNIA.

LIVELY, PENELOPE (1933–) Born Penelope Margaret Low in Cairo, Egypt, on March 17, 1933, Penelope Lively is a prolific author of children's books, short fiction, television plays, and novels for adult readers. After WORLD WAR II, she attended boarding schools in England, and in 1956 she earned an undergraduate degree in history from St. Anne's College of Oxford University. She was married in 1957 to Jack Lively; they are the parents of two children.

Penelope Lively began her publishing career in 1970, writing books for children; she won a Carnegie Medal from the Library Association in 1974 for *The Ghost of Thomas Kempe,* and a Whitbread Literary Award for *A Snitch in Time* in 1976. She began writing for adult readers in 1977; that year, *The Road to Lichfield* was short-listed for the BOOKER PRIZE. It is the story of a woman who discovers that her conventional father, whom she tends in his lonely old age, had been involved in an extramarital affair. After several more novels that presented realistic depictions of contemporary life, she was again short-listed for the Booker Prize in 1984 for *According to Mark: A Novel,* in which a biographer learns that the life of his research subject had several distinct aspects that do not fit easily into a single identity. Lively's best-received book was MOON TIGER, which won the Booker Prize in 1987. She has also drawn on historical themes for novels such as *Cleopatra's Sister* (1993), set in an imaginary African nation, and she has returned to the theme of old age in *Spiderweb,* about a woman who retires from a career in anthropology to live out her life in a small village setting. Lively lives in England and continues to produce novels and other works for both children and adults.

BIBLIOGRAPHY

Moran, Mary Hurley. *Penelope Lively.* Twayne's English Authors, 503. New York: Twayne, 1993.

LIVES OF GIRLS AND WOMEN ALICE MUNRO (1971) A novel constructed from a series of interlinking short stories, *Lives of Girls and Women* is a special kind of BILDUNGSROMAN known as a "kunstlerroman" or novel of the development of an artist's gifts. The first-person narrator of the eight stories that make up the novel is Del Jordan, daughter of Addie Jordan.

The stories follow Del's life from about the age of 11 until shortly after her graduation from high school. Del is observant enough to recognize her desire to wield power over her own life when it crops up, and she is strong enough to choose a course of action that will make it possible for her to do so.

In the introductory story, Del awakens from childhood on her father's fox farm in Ontario to an awareness of the ordinary beauty of the world. She senses her calling to be an observer of the exquisite details of this world. In the remaining stories, Del encounters a variety of women and girls living lives that illustrate the options open to her: Her friend Naomi accepts the predefined life society offers her and becomes a nurturer in the role of wife and mother, and at the darkest extreme a marginalized girl escapes that fate through suicide, while other characters fall within this range of passive acceptance and violent rejection. Del makes her own exploration of the lives offered to girls, of the tenets of religion, and she eventually has an initiation into adulthood that also presents her with a defining moment when she must accept or reject the standard option.

The most important woman in Del's life turns out to be her mother. Addie has the wisdom to urge her daughter to use her brain and to accept a life of independence and struggle rather than one of utter dependence on a husband. Addie looks to a future—a world that has not arrived for her—in which women will finally take control of the choices in their lives and lay claim to full equality with the rest of the human race. In the novel's epilogue, Del embarks on the task of writing the stories she has lived, accepting her mother's challenge.

Lives of Girls and Women is a quintessential example of the fiction of Alice MUNRO. It is her only novel, and yet it can also be read as independent stories—the form Munro has made her own. The novel is also a semiautobiographical study of Munro's own experience of maturing as a young woman and choosing to become a writer.

BIBLIOGRAPHY

Carrington, Ildikó De Papp. *Controlling the Uncontrollable: The Fiction of Alice Munro.* DeKalb: Northern Illinois University Press, 1989.

MacDonald, Rae McCarthy. "Structure and Detail in *Lives of Girls and Women,*" *Studies in Canadian Literature* 3 (Summer 1978): 199–210.

Rasporich, Beverly J. *Dance of the Sexes: Art and Gender in the Fiction of Alice Munro.* Edmonton, Alberta: University of Alberta Press, 1990.

LIVING HENRY GREEN (1929)   Written in an experimental style and set primarily in the English industrial city of Birmingham, where in real life the author managed and worked in factories owned by his family, this novel of social realism presents an array of characters who depend on the Dupret Foundry. Among the workers, the characters include Mr. Craigan, one of the most skilled workers in the foundry, who heads an extended "family" of boarders drawn from among his coworkers. Mr. Craigan works with the half-hearted assistance of his best friend and housemate, Joe Gates, the father of beautiful and frustrated Lily Gates. Mr. Craigan's other boarder is Jim Dale, a handsome young foundry worker who loves Lily but lacks the words to tell her so. Not realizing what she has in her own household, Lily falls in love with Bert Jones; too inexperienced to see this young man's callow, weak character, she elopes with him to Liverpool, but there she finds herself abandoned. Lily longs to escape from the dreary world of the foundry, but she returns there deprived of both love and hope, expecting that her ambitions will never be fulfilled.

Inside the foundry, the senior owner, Mr. Dupret, clings to the business methods he is familiar with, refusing to modernize. The supervision of the workers is haphazard and frequently unfair: Mr. Bridges, the shop manager, relies on the malicious tattling of Mr. Tupe, a man who compulsively betrays his coworkers, who in turn hate him but can do nothing about his snitching. With the death of Mr. Dupret, his son Richard begins to run the factory under the modernizing plans of a young engineer, Mr. Tarver. Men begin to lose their jobs, some because of poor work habits and some because of age. Coping with retirement or unemployment proves difficult for most of them, and drink becomes a major preoccupation.

GREEN's experimentation consists of violating basic rules of syntax, such as the consistent use of articles and complete sentences. This strategy heightens the importance of conversations among the characters, since those are accurate representations of the accents and speech patterns typical of each character's social status and economic standing. The oddly structured expository passages may also make the reader suspend judgment of the characters based on their manner of speaking: Even the least-educated speaker sounds better in dialogue than the choppy fragments and ungrammatical phrasing of the third-person narrator. Green's experiment is a distinctive example of the desire to do in fiction what artists were doing in painting in the early 20th century, but it did not become the pattern for an artistic movement and remains something of a literary curiosity.

BIBLIOGRAPHY

Holmesland, Oddvar. *A Critical Introduction to Henry Green's Novels: The Living Vision.* New York: St. Martin's Press, 1985.

North, Michael. *Henry Green and the Writing of His Generation.* Charlottesville: University of Virginia Press, 1984.

Russell, John. *Henry Green: Nine Novels and an Unpacked Bag.* New Brunswick, N.J.: Rutgers University Press, 1960.

LODGE, DAVID (1935–)

Noted especially for his CAMPUS NOVELS, David Lodge was born on January 28, 1935, to a working-class Catholic family in London. During childhood, he experienced the wartime ravages of the German bombing campaign against Britain, the blitzkrieg. In 1955, he earned an undergraduate English degree from University College, London; he was already practicing the art of fiction, although he did not publish the novel he wrote in college. For the next two years, he fulfilled his National Service obligation (a policy no longer in force today) with an unhappy tour of duty in the armed forces, where he composed the novel that he first published, *The Picturegoers* (1960), the story of an aspiring novelist lodging with a Catholic family and struggling with his own religious experience.

Lodge returned to University College and earned a master's degree in 1959. Also in that year, he was married; he and his wife are the parents of three children, including a son afflicted with Down syndrome. After a year of employment with the British Council (an organization that makes British culture available to the rest of the world in the form of lecturers and publications), he accepted a teaching appointment at the University of Birmingham. He earned a doctorate from this institution in 1969, rising to the position of full professor in 1976 and retiring to write full-time in 1987.

After 1960, Lodge published steadily, both fiction and scholarly works. His second novel, *Ginger, You're Barmy* (1962), drew on his military experiences. At Birmingham, he became friends with Malcolm BRADBURY, also a faculty member there at that time. Bradbury's influence led Lodge to experiment with comic novels, resulting first in *The British Museum Is Falling Down* (1965), the story of a Catholic graduate student rushing to complete a dissertation as his young family grows. Lodge received a fellowship to study in the United States during the 1965–66 academic year and published a well-received scholarly book, *The Language of Fiction,* in 1966. His fourth novel, *Out of the Shelter* (1970) was a semiautobiographical BILDUNGSROMAN, relating the coming-of-age experiences of a 16-year-old Catholic boy visiting Germany in about 1950. In 1971, he published his critical study *The Novelist at the Crossroads,* in which he develops the innovative self-reflexive ideas that soon appear in his own fiction.

In 1969, Lodge served as a visiting professor at the University of California at Berkeley, experiencing the upheaval and euphoria of the Free Speech Movement on that campus. He converted his observations and experiences into *CHANGING PLACES: A TALE OF TWO CAMPUSES* in 1975; the novel gained him a readership on both sides of the Atlantic, especially among literary academics, and won the HAWTHORNDEN PRIZE. He traveled widely in the late 1970s, attending numerous academic conferences in far-flung locations and collecting experiences for further comic explorations of the academic world. In 1980, he published his SATIRE on the troubled link between Catholicism and birth control entitled *HOW FAR CAN YOU GO?* and won the WHITBREAD AWARD. Lodge reduced his academic duties to spend more time writing. He published *Working with Structuralism* in 1981, followed in 1984 by *SMALL WORLD,* a comedy about academic conferences. In 1988, *NICE WORK* was short-listed for the BOOKER PRIZE; it completes the so-called "Rummidge Trilogy" of comic novels with an academic theme.

In the 1990s, Lodge published *Paradise News* (1991), about a Catholic theologian's family vacation in Hawaii, and *Therapy* (1995), about an unhappy television scriptwriter. He also published the scholarly collections entitled *After Bakhtin: Essays on Fiction and Criticism* (1990) and *The Art of Fiction* (1992). He has also written short fiction, television screenplays, and satirical stage revues in collaboration with Bradbury and Jim Duckett. Lodge's most recent novels are *Home Truths* (200) and *Thinks . . .* (2001). He continues to live and write in Birmingham.

BIBLIOGRAPHY

Haffenden, John. *Novelists in Interview.* London: Methuen, 1985.

Martin, Bruce K. *David Lodge.* Twayne's English Authors, 553. New York: Twayne, 1999.

Moseley, Merritt, and Dale Salwak. *David Lodge: How Far Can You Go?* The Milford Series, Popular Writers of Today 16. San Bernardino, Calif.: Borgo Press, 1991.

LOITERING WITH INTENT MURIEL SPARK (1981)

A comic novel and the 16th work of full-length fiction in SPARK'S long and diverse career, *Loitering with Intent* features a first-person narrator, Fleur Talbot, who is herself a novelist. In post–WORLD WAR II London, having nearly finished her novel *Warrender Chase,* she takes a job as a typist for the Autobiographical Association, a curious organization founded by Sir Quentin Oliver. Its ostensible mission is to bring its members together to encourage the writing of their autobiographies; however, Fleur soon realizes that Sir Quentin's organization exists so he can play god in the lives of those he has ensnared. As she continues working for the Association, she sees repeated correspondences between the characters in her novel and the collection of humdrum eccentrics Sir Quentin has assembled. After she allows Sir Oliver to read *Warrender Chase,* she also realizes he is plagiarizing her manuscript to enliven the dull life stories of the Association's members. Fleur has also been altering the dull manuscripts as she types them, but she invents incidents, whereas Sir Quentin steals them from her.

Fleur admires two great autobiographical texts and knows them so well, she can quote from them: *Apologia Pro Vita Sua* by John Henry Newman and *The Autobiography of Benvenuto Cellini.* While Fleur's tone is light and her story comical, there are serious literary questions under examination: What is the purpose of life? Does art imitate life, or does life imitate art? What constitutes good autobiographical writing? Ironically, the fictional Fleur is writing her own autobiography, entitled *Loitering with Intent,* a story loosely based on the experiences of the real Muriel Spark, the author of *Loitering with Intent,* in her days as a beginning novelist.

As the novel unfolds, it develops a keen element of FEMINISM. Fleur meets the mousy women of the Association, along with Sir Quentin's housekeeper, and the wife of Fleur's soon-to-be ex-lover. These women are characterized as "English roses," passive and submissive to male domination and to the conventional expectations of a society determined to limit women to marriage and childrearing. Fleur, too, is a flower, but in name only. She lives independently, makes her own decisions, and dares to challenge Sir Quentin as his treatment of the Association's members becomes emotionally abusive. In contrast to the English roses, with whom Fleur cannot identify, Sir Quentin's raucous, elderly, incontinent mother, Lady Edwina, soon becomes her friend. Fleur's outcast status is underscored by her identification with a woman thought to be crazy by Sir Quentin, but her genuine sympathy for the old woman's suffering points up her compassionate humanity.

In spite of these serious elements, the novel remains a comedy throughout. The eccentric characters and the complex plot that requires Fleur to wrest her manuscript back from Sir Quentin and a scurrilous publisher counterbalance Fleur's musings about art, life, and autobiography. Several scenes are hilarious, and throughout the book, Fleur's droll, witty, intelligent narration maintains the light tone.

BIBLIOGRAPHY

Bold, Valerie. "Fun and Games with Life-Stories." In *Muriel Spark: An Odd Capacity for Vision.* Edited by Alan Bold. Totowa, N.J.: Barnes & Noble, 1984.

Sproxton, Judy. *The Women of Muriel Spark*. New York: St. Martin's Press, 1992.

Whittaker, Ruth. *The Faith and Fiction of Muriel Spark*. New York: St. Martin's Press, 1982.

THE LONELINESS OF THE LONG DISTANCE RUNNER ALAN SILLITOE (1959)

This book consists of the novella of the title and eight other short stories; together, the collection represents an excellent example of fiction typical of the ANGRY YOUNG MEN in post–WORLD WAR II Britain. The stories are mostly constructed on the model of the BILDUNGSROMAN, or novel of a young person's maturation, and most of them feature a first-person narrator struggling to move from the dependency of childhood to the independence of adulthood. The stories are set among working-CLASS young men facing bleak futures during the "diminishing age" as the British EMPIRE declines and the options available to British citizens shrink.

The title novella features a protagonist drawn from the working class who is disenchanted with the values and norms of English life. The protagonist is also the first-person narrator, Smith; he is a young man reflecting on his experiences in a juvenile detention facility, the Essex Borstal. He had been apprehended in a robbery from a bakery. In the Borstal, the Warden encourages him to take up the sport of running and Smith complies. He enjoys the solitude of running and the privilege of leaving the grounds of the Borstal. As he runs, he thinks; the narrative becomes a stream-of-consciousness record of Smith's reflections on his life, his capture, the jail, the Warden, and the future. He is confident that he understands the minds of those in power such as the Warden, and that the Warden is more interested in seeing a victory for his team than in any rehabilitative effect running might have on his young prisoners.

Smith divides the world into the "in-laws," who live conventional and obedient lives, and the "out-laws," like him, who rebel against the injustices ingrained into the quotidian rounds of class-dominated English life. He is searching for a way to win against the "in-laws," but he fails to comprehend that such a victory may be insignificant in light of the larger problem. He becomes an excellent runner, fast and full of stamina, but when he has victory in his grasp during an actual competition, he throws it away to spite the Warden, running in place as the other contestants, whom he had earlier outdistanced, pass him on their way to the finish line. In doing so, he demonstrates his power to deprive the Warden of a desired achievement, but he also shows that he cannot do so without defeating himself as well. Upon his release from prison, Smith returns to theft as a way of life, pleased to be more successful at evading capture. SILLITOE does not resolve this moral AMBIGUITY in the novel's closing: Smith's consciousness concerning class inequity and social injustice is raised, but he can only respond with spite, not with constructive change in himself or in the larger world against which he continues his ineffectual rebellion.

BIBLIOGRAPHY

Craig, David. "The Roots of Sillitoe's Fiction." *The British Working Class Novel in the Twentieth Century*. Edited by Jeremy Hawthorn. London: Edward Arnold, 1984.

Hutchings, William. "The Work of Play: Anger and the Expropriated Athletes of Alan Sillitoe and David Storey," *MFS: Modern Fiction Studies* 33, no. 1 (Spring 1987): 35–47.

Slack, John S. "A Sporting Chance: Sports, Delinquency, and Rehabilitation in *The Loneliness of the Long Distance Runner*," *Aethlon: The Journal of Sport Literature* 17, no. 2 (Spring 2000): 1–9.

LONELY PASSION OF JUDITH HEARNE, THE BRIAN MOORE (1955)

A tragic novel that displays the effects of alcoholism, *The Lonely Passion of Judith Hearne* is set in Belfast, NORTHERN IRELAND, in the 1950s. The life of Miss Hearne, an impoverished spinster in her 40s, in many ways reflects the dull, impoverished world of lower-CLASS Belfast, and alcohol is the anodyne of choice for both the fictional character and the real world she is imagined to occupy. In terms of literary antecedents, Judith Hearne is a descendant of the quintessential heroine of Jean RHYS in novels such as *AFTER LEAVING MR. MACKENZIE*: a woman who is vulnerable, flawed, and excluded from the sources of life's stereotypical joys such as family.

Judith Hearne had been orphaned young; a crabby old aunt reared her, and in turn Judith sacrificed her youth and its few opportunities so she could repay her debt by nursing the old woman through her last years. She is now alone in the world with a tiny income that barely covers her living expenses even in the degraded material conditions of her life in shabby boarding houses. At the beginning of the novel, she arrives at a new boarding house after remaining sober for six months. But a misunderstanding with Mr. Madden, another boarder, and the insulting treatment of her landlady soon drive her to the numbness of intoxication and the temporary oblivion it brings.

Miss Hearne seeks other forms of solace in the one respectable friend she has left—a married woman with a family—and in the rituals of the Catholic Church. Much of the imagery of the rest of the novel involves Miss Hearne's painful realization that she has lost her faith and recounts her ineffectual efforts to rediscover it. Instead she discovers, when she visits the former friend who first taught her the anesthetic utility of alcohol, what happens to old women who lack homes, family, friends, faith, and sobriety. At the Earnscliffe House, silent despair is her former friend's only companion. Judith sinks further into self-destructiveness after seeing what her friend has sunk to and takes most of her money out of the bank for one last fling before she too enters that final stopping-off place.

Brian MOORE relates this story through a nonjudgmental third-person omniscient narrator without either appealing to pity or resorting to condemnation. Judith Hearne's life takes on a fatalistic quality, as if she is fulfilling a foreordained end even as she loses the ability to believe in any divinity that might have such fateful power. She cannot save herself, and no one else is responsible for saving her—the belated efforts of a priest and her one friend are ineffectual. But the narrator's objectivity does have the effect of leaving open to the reader the option of voluntarily taking pity on Judith Hearne, just as we must all do for our compatriots in real life if mercy is to persist in the world.

BIBLIOGRAPHY

Dahlie, Hallvard. *Brian Moore.* Twayne's World Authors, 632. Boston: Twayne Publishers, 1981.

Maher, Eamon. "Belfast: The Far From Sublime City in Brian Moore's Early Novels," *Studies: An Irish Quarterly Review* 90, no. 360 (Winter 2001): 422–431.

LORD JIM JOSEPH CONRAD (1900) The story of a man's fall from grace and his later fatal redemption of his honor, *Lord Jim* is one of Joseph CONRAD's best works, with *HEART OF DARKNESS* and *NOSTROMO.* Like *Heart of Darkness,* its first-person narrator is Captain Marlow, although there is an introductory section narrated anonymously in the third person. This introduction reveals the circumstances of Jim's fall: On the *Patna,* a ship loaded with hundreds of religious pilgrims, the crew members panic when they believe the ship is sinking, and they abandon the pilgrims to their fate. The *Patna,* however, does not sink. The crew members are found and charged with desertion. Marlow enters the story as Jim is found guilty, effectively ending any kind of respectable career at sea.

Marlow likes Jim's stoic acceptance of the consequences of his action, and he finds jobs for him. Jim achieves occasional happiness, especially when he works as a chandler at a seaport, sailing a small craft out to incoming ships to take orders for the goods needed. He succeeds because he works hard, sails first, and ventures farther than others are willing to go. But always the story of his involvement with the *Patna* catches up with him and terminates his employment. Finally, Marlow secures a remote post for Jim at Patusan; it is so remote that perhaps there he can escape his past.

Jim once again succeeds, but once again his past catches up with him. He has never learned how to handle the dishonor of his choice on the *Patna,* seeking instead only to escape from the memory of it rather than to face the fact of it. In spite of the success and respect he has earned at Patusan, when faced again with his past he again makes a disastrous decision— one that costs another man his life. But Jim's situation is complicated by the fact that he now lives in a native culture with a different set of rules governing each man's honor. COLONIALISM has reached this outpost but has not yet eradicated the old ways of the native population. Jim has the opportunity to redeem his honor—unlike in the civilized world, where he was condemned to a kind of permanent shadow world of dishonor—but only at a terrible price.

Key aspects of Conrad's complicated narration of this story include IRONY and AMBIGUITY, both juxtaposed with a murky moral problem. No injury results from the *Patna* incident, and yet some wrong had been done and had to be redressed. But what form of punishment or retribution can wipe away an individual man's memory of his own cowardice, even if it has harmed no other person? Jim's failure to resolve this problem ultimately leaves him with nothing but tragic choices: He can live in shame, or he can die in honor.

BIBLIOGRAPHY

Henthorne, Tom. "An End to Imperialism: Lord Jim and the Postcolonial Conrad," *Conradiana: A Journal of Joseph Conrad Studies* 32, no. 3 (Fall 2000): 203–227.

Stape, J. H. *The Cambridge Companion to Conrad.* New York: Cambridge University Press, 1996.

LORD OF THE FLIES WILLIAM GOLDING

(1954) A modern classic by a writer awarded the NOBEL PRIZE in 1983, this novel reveals the author's pessimism about the human power to do evil. It shares with *A HIGH WIND IN JAMAICA* (1929) the conviction that children are not innocent and pure, but instead must be restrained from brutality and trained to be civilized.

In the opening of the novel, the destruction of an aircraft evacuating a group of schoolboys, apparently after an atomic war, leaves the unsupervised children stranded on a tropical island. Clearly, this event is a return to an Edenic existence: The island abounds with fruit trees, and the tropical climate is mild. The boys devote themselves to joyous play, but they choose a leader to supervise duties such as keeping a signal fire going to attract the attention of rescuers. Ralph—literally the fair-haired child—becomes the first leader, to the dissatisfaction of his rival, Jack, and Jack's enforcer, Roger. Dissent soon follows, but not because of any failure, incompetence, or unfairness on the part of Ralph. Instead, Golding's plot suggests that dissent arises because human beings are contentious, envious, ego-driven, and thirsty for power.

Jack soon challenges Ralph's authority; the boys who follow Jack hunt the island's wild pigs for meat and for the thrill of the chase and the kill. "Piggy" is also the nickname of an unpopular boy who is intellectually strong but physically weak. And later, when the boys have degenerated to primitive savagery, a pig's head is offered to appease the thing in the jungle that becomes the symbol of the boys' irrational fear. These images of sacrificial offerings, especially in the context of placating the thing in the jungle, suggest that the wild boys are worshipping death rather than nurturing life; they also indicate that Jack's kind of leadership is regressive and degenerative, allowing the boys to slip into uncivilized ways. The outburst of murderous impulses on the island confirms this descent into baseness.

In addition to the boys' loss of moral understanding, as they degenerate they also become more foolish, fearful, and superstitious. In the heat of passion, dominated by their feelings in the absence of the balancing force or reason, the boys make the short step from hunting and sacrificing pigs to hunting and persecuting Ralph. A clever idea to drive him out of safe hiding—setting fire to the vegetation—soon gets out of hand and leads to the destruction of their Eden: The trees are burned, and the smoke of this unintended signal fire attracts the attention of adults who will restore the boys to the fallen world of the human community. When the boys have cast off all vestiges of civilization and are hunting their own kind as a means of resolving a rivalry, their rescuers arrive. The IRONY of the adult surprise at the appearance of the boys is the novel's final dark note: Adults believe the lie of innate human goodness, but the behavior of the boys on the island points in the opposite direction.

BIBLIOGRAPHY

Bloom, Harold, ed. *William Golding's* Lord of the Flies. Philadelphia: Chelsea House, 1999.

Dickson, L. L. *The Modern Allegories of William Golding.* Tampa: University of South Florida Press, 1990.

Nelson, William, ed. *William Golding's* Lord of the Flies: *A Source Book.* New York: Odyssey Press, 1963.

Reilly, Patrick. Lord of the Flies: *Fathers and Sons.* Twayne's Masterwork Studies, 106. New York: Twayne Publishers, 1992.

Whitley, John S. *Golding:* Lord of the Flies. London: Edward Arnold, 1970.

LORD OF THE RINGS, THE J. R. R. TOLKIEN (1954–1955) This three-volume sequence includes *The FELLOWSHIP OF THE RING* (1954), *The TWO TOWERS* (1954), and *The RETURN OF THE KING*

(1955); however, it was conceived by its author as a single epic story. It shares the Middle Earth setting that Tolkien established in *The HOBBIT* (1937) and revives the characters of Gandalf the Gray, a wizard charged with protecting Middle Earth from evil, and Bilbo Baggins, a Hobbit who had found a magic ring in the earlier story but who now must retire from the action and pass the ring to his nephew, Frodo Baggins. The story is narrated from the third-person omniscient point of view and recounts the adventures of the heroes who destroy Bilbo's ring when it is identified as the source of evil power in Middle Earth.

Although published in the 1950s, Tolkien had been working on this story for years. When *The Hobbit* proved to be a success, Tolkien's publisher had urged him to carry the story further. During WORLD WAR II, and the years leading up to it and following it, Tolkien worked on the new book. Although many commentators have observed the parallels between Middle Earth and Europe, with the Shire in the northwest representing England, and Mordor in the southeast representing Germany, Tolkien himself disavowed this reading of the text as merely a political ALLEGORY. He drew inspiration from many sources other than current events, including his vast knowledge of medieval literature, MYTHOLOGY, and languages. Additionally, Tolkien's Christian faith informs the story symbolically at least as much as, if not more than, the events of World War II.

In a century that saw the novel shrink virtually to short Story proportions while it also elongated into the ROMAN-FLEUVE, Tolkien wrote an old-fashioned heroic epic in the tradition of Homer, Virgil, Dante, Milton, and the unnamed bards of the oral tradition. His story is filled with songs and poems of his own composition that hearken to an earlier world and imbue his text with the flavor of an antiquity that never existed in our world; instead, we must imagine that the newest events of Middle Earth, coming at the end of an already lengthy history, predate us and pave the way for our dominion over the world. The traditional quest motif and the simple good-versus-evil ethical structure of the novel have appealed to readers of all ages all over the world, creating one of the largest and best-organized fan followings in popular culture. A scholarly following has developed more slowly, but Tolkien's work seems to be making a rapid transition to canonical (see CANON) status.

BIBLIOGRAPHY

Chance, Jane. The Lord of the Rings: *The Mythology of Power.* New York: Twayne Publishers, 1992.

Clark, George, and Daniel Timmons. *J. R. R. Tolkien and His Literary Resonances: Views of Middle Earth.* Westport, Conn.: Greenwood Press, 2000.

Shippey, T. A. *The Road to Middle Earth.* Boston: Houghton Mifflin, 1983.

Stanton, Michael N. *Hobbits, Elves, and Wizards: Exploring the Wonders and Worlds of J. R. R. Tolkien's* The Lord of the Rings. New York: St. Martin's Press, 2001.

LOST HORIZON JAMES HILTON (1934)

An example of UTOPIAN fiction, *Lost Horizon* imagines a Tibetan monastery, or lamasery, hidden away in the Himalayan Valley of the Blue Moon. This idyllic retreat is named Shangri-La, a term that has since become a synonym for paradise.

The narrative takes the form of a story within a story. Rutherford, a British diplomat, finds his old friend Hugh Conway in a hospital, disoriented and exhausted. Conway should be at the prime of his life; however, having survived the brutal ravages of WORLD WAR I, he had become jaded and disheartened long before his most recent adventure began. He relates the amazing story of his travels during the months he has been missing. It had all begun in the spring of 1931 at a British consulate in Baskul, on the Indian subcontinent; trouble leads to the evacuation of white Europeans, and Conway is among the last to leave. He tells of escaping in a plane with a zealous missionary named Miss Brinklow; Henry Barnard, an American suspected of the crime of embezzlement; and Capt. Charles Mallinson, an upper-class British diplomat devoted to the ideals he absorbed in his education. The passengers become uneasy as they realize that their pilot is carrying them deeper into the Himalayas rather than to their intended destination. They suspect they are being kidnapped for ransom. When their plane makes a hard landing and the pilot dies from his injuries, the passengers doubt they can survive in the frigid air of the high mountains. Soon, however, they are rescued by a small search party and led to the lamasery of Shangri-La.

Eventually, Conway is invited to meet the High Lama, and in a series of conversations, he learns the story of Father Perrault, a Capuchin friar who wandered into this valley in 1734. After converting to Buddhism, Perrault had built the lamasery and discovered the life-lengthening properties of the pure mountain air. Other Europeans and Asians had joined him and built the ideal community of Shangri-La. Eventually, Conway learns that the High Lama is indeed Father Perrault himself. Just before Perrault dies, he predicts the coming war that will destroy Western civilization, and he appoints Conway to replace him in leading the community of Shangri-La so it can be ready to restore civilized culture to the world. In the meantime, Capt. Mallinson has entered into an affair with Lo-Tsen, a Chinese woman who appears young and beautiful but who is already over 60. They have arranged to hire guides and porters to lead them out of Shangri-La and back to "civilization."

Out of a sense of responsibility (a key moment in the narrative, viewed by some as a weak plot point), Conway ultimately goes with them. Before he can finish telling Rutherford his tale, however, he leaves the hospital in search of Shangri-La. Rutherford learns that Conway had been brought to the hospital by an elderly Chinese woman and begins to wonder if the fantastic tale he had heard from his friend might be true. The novel ends with Rutherford's hope that his friend will once again find Shangri-La.

Lost Horizon is an example of escapist FANTASY, but the long conversations between Conway and Father Perrault elevate it above the level of a typical adventure story. These conversations serve as a point of departure for exploring the definition and characteristics of an ideal community. The values of Aristotle's *Nicomachean Ethics,* with its emphasis on the "golden mean," or the middle way between extremes, dominate the decision making in Shangri-La; the exotic Tibetan and Buddhist elements serve as set decoration rather than as a viable alternative to Western philosophical traditions and cultural customs. Appearing in 1934, when another vast war threatened to engulf Europe, the novel provided an outlet for wishful thinking and was a huge success, making its author one of the highest-paid writers in the world.

BIBLIOGRAPHY

Crawford, John W. "The Utopian Dream: Alive and Well," *Cuyahoga Review* (Spring/Summer 1984): 27–33.

Heck, Francis S. "The Domain as a Symbol of a Paradise Lost: *Lost Horizon* and *Brideshead Revisited,*" *The Nassau Review* 4 (1982): 24–29.

Whissen, Thomas R. *Classic Cult Fiction: A Companion to Popular Cult Literature.* Westport, Conn.: Greenwood Press, 1992.

LOVED ONE, THE EVELYN WAUGH (1948)

Set in Hollywood among British expatriates in the wake of WORLD WAR II, this dark example of a COMIC NOVEL satirizes the Californian way of death. The protagonist, Dennis Barlow, gained acclaim for the book of poetry that grew out of his war experience, and Megalopolitan Studios brought him to America first class. As a screenwriter, however, he did not prosper or even suffice, and he soon found his contract not renewed. The generosity of his countrymen keeps him afloat: He is a guest of Sir Francis Hinsley, once a successful screenwriter, but now reduced to public relations. When Dennis takes a job as a mortician at the Happier Hunting Grounds pet cemetery, however, the thoroughly British members of the Cricket Club are appalled—the burial of American pets is hardly a suitable form of employment for a British poet, they feel. But Dennis persists in his chosen line of work, especially after meeting Miss Aimée Thanatogenos in the groves of the legendary Whispering Glades cemetery, which adjoins (and dwarfs) the Happier Hunting Ground. She works there as a cosmetician, restoring the colors of life to embalmed corpses just before they are positioned to receive their mourners in a tastefully appointed Slumber Room.

For her part, Miss Thanatogenos is in a quandary, since she also receives the attentions of Mr. Joyboy, the highly refined embalmer-artist head mortician at Whispering Glades. Although she is flattered by Mr. Joyboy's perfectly proper middle-aged obsequies, touchingly expressed in the smiles of the corpses he sends to her care, she is attracted to the handsome but impoverished young poet, except for his un-American cynicism about patriotism, citizenship, and the attenuated niceties of Whispering Glades. In order to understand her feelings better, she writes repeatedly to "The Guru Brahmin," an advice column in the local newspaper. She finally settles on Dennis and accepts his proposal, only to learn, at the funeral of the ancient parrot of Mr. Joyboy's mother, that the poems Dennis had been sending her were copied from an anthology. She then becomes formally engaged to Mr. Joyboy but despairs of the future when Dennis refuses to release her from her promise to him. The Guru Brahmin provides his last advice to her from the public telephone at Mooney's Saloon; when she follows it, the resolution of the novel is set in place, and Dennis finds a way to return to his native country in the same manner he left it—first class.

WAUGH shapes his comedy as an example of Juvenalian SATIRE but restrains his tone through understated humor and offhand factual comments that, in context, acquire great hilarity.

BIBLIOGRAPHY

Decker, James M. and Kenneth Womack "Searching for Ethics in the Celluloid Graveyard: Waugh, O'Flaherty, and the Hollywood Novel," *Studies in the Humanities* 25, nos. 1–2 (June–December 1998): 53–65.

Wells, Walter. "Between Two Worlds: Aldous Huxley and Evelyn Waugh in Hollywood." In *Los Angeles in Fiction: A Collection of Essays: From James M. Cain to Walter Mosley.* Edited by David Fine. Albuquerque: University of New Mexico Press, 1995, 187–206.

LOVE IN A COLD CLIMATE NANCY MITFORD (1949)

A sequel to the novel *The PURSUIT OF LOVE,* having the same narrator and observing the same aristocratic set, *Love in a Cold Climate* is a kind of comic soap opera of the British upper CLASS written by one of its own members. The events of the plot are recounted by Fanny, the narrator of the earlier story as well; this time, she focuses on the household of Lord and Lady Montdore, whose beautiful daughter Polly surprises everyone when she marries the middle-aged man who has only recently become a widower through the death of Polly's paternal aunt. This situation is particularly

trying to Polly's mother, since that lady had previously been the mistress of her daughter's new husband, "Boy" Dougdale. The marriage has transformed her lover and brother-in-law into her son-in-law. In retaliation, she shuts Polly out of her life and turns her attention to a nephew from Nova Scotia, Cedric Hampton, who is the heir of Lord Montdore's title. Cedric is such a charmer that he eventually draws Lady Montdore to a reconciliation with her daughter.

MITFORD presents her comic story as a mild SATIRE on human folly in the special context of the aristocratic upper class. It is a pleasant and amusing read that may shed some light on the British class system for young American readers unfamiliar with that social milieu as long as they keep in mind that behavioral mannerisms have been made to serve comic ends and that, consequently, stylized exaggeration trumps realistic representation.

BIBLIOGRAPHY

Hepburn, Allan. "The Fate of the Modern Mistress: Nancy Mitford and the Comedy of Marriage," *MFS: Modern Fiction Studies* 45, no. 2 (Summer 1999): 340–368.

LOVING HENRY GREEN (1945)

Set during the privations of WORLD WAR II among the English gentry and servants in a "great house" located in the recently independent (and politically neutral) nation of Eire (IRELAND), *Loving* relates the development of attachment between Charley Raunce and Edith, two servants employed in the house. Without focusing on the historical background of the setting in *place* or the current events of the setting in *time*, GREEN manages to convey fully the hostility between the English landowners and the Irish natives as well as the risks and suffering of life in England during the war. The house is filled with English citizens who are glad to have a refuge from England: they are not being bombed, not being conscripted, and not dealing with scarcities of food and consumer goods. Their greatest fear is that the IRA—the Irish Republican Army—will burn down the house, since so many other of the English estates have been destroyed.

The novel opens with the death of Eldon, the old butler. Raunce is merely a footman, but knowing the scarcity of servants created by the war effort, he seizes the opportunity to better himself. His employer, Mrs. Tennant, has little choice but to promote him. This change of station causes an emotional tempest in the teapot of the servants' hall as a former peer, familiarly addressed by his first name, becomes the supervisor who must be addressed by his surname and a courtesy title. "Mr. Raunce" is almost more than the house-keeper can tolerate after the tragic loss of Mr. Eldon.

Charley is a good observer of life in the great house and quickly learns to turn his new position to best advantage, helped by the secret notebooks Eldon had kept for years. He is also interested in the young women serving in the house, finally settling on Edith. Love is the novel's recurring subject, in the many forms it takes. Charley's loving courtship of Edith, the cook's protective love for her nephew and her addicted love for her tipple, Mrs. Jack Tennant's illicit love for a neighboring squire while her husband is away at war, Mrs. Tennant's negligent love of her estate and her absentminded management of it, the children's rau-cous love of mischief, and the pigeons' mating-season love of each other all contribute elements to the com-edy of life in the great house that shelters rich and poor while England is being pounded to smithereens. Green avoids sentimentality by presenting his characters through the objective narration of their charms and their faults. His portrait of life on the estate is fully developed, showing the good and the bad of both the upper and lower classes, but he allows the reader to pass judgment on them.

BIBLIOGRAPHY

Bassoff, Bruce. *Toward Loving: The Poetics of the Novel and the Practice of Henry Green.* Columbia: University of South Carolina Press, 1975.

Holmesland, Oddvar, *A Critical Introduction to Henry Green's Novels: The Living Vision.* New York: St. Martin's Press, 1985.

Russell, John. *Henry Green: Nine Novels and an Unpacked Bag.* New Brunswick, N.J.: Rutgers University Press, 1960.

LOWRY, MALCOLM (1909–1957)

A writer whose short and self-destructive life produced a mas-terpiece of modern fiction, UNDER THE VOLCANO (1947), Malcolm Lowry was born to a comfortable MIDDLE-CLASS life, the son of a Liverpool cotton merchant, on July 28, 1909. He was educated briefly at a PUBLIC SCHOOL to ready him for university study; he had already fallen under the influence of alcohol in his early teenage years. In 1927, Lowry worked for five months as a deckhand on the freighter S.S. *Pyrrhus,* bound for Yokohama (he was 17 at the time he shipped aboard), and he studied for a time in Bonn, Germany, in 1928, absorbing the ideas of German expressionism. In 1929, he visited for a summer with the American writer Conrad Aiken—the author of the 1927 novel *Blue Voyage,* which had captured Lowry's seagoing imagination.

Lowry enrolled in Cambridge University and earned an undistinguished degree there. At Cambridge, he cultivated the two aspects of his life that would domi-nate his remaining years: his impressive writing and his extensive drinking. A tragedy occurred in his first term at school when his roommate committed suicide, an event that haunted Lowry's life and that he later claimed responsibility for (although biographers cast doubt on some of Lowry's autobiographical state-ments). He was already writing his first novel, *Ultrama-rine* (1933), which drew on his experiences at sea and also addressed issues of CLASS bias in an unusual way by exploring working-class rejection of a worker born to the upper class. Upon completing his studies in 1932, Lowry was not obligated to work for a living; instead he was supported by his father, who wanted to encourage his son's writing without enabling his drinking.

In 1934, Lowry was married to an American Jewish writer, Jan Gabrial, in Paris. The relationship was marred by Lowry's drinking bouts, leading to a separa-tion by 1935. During this time, Lowry produced a manuscript, a thousand pages long, for a novel to be titled "In Ballast to the White Sea." It was never pub-lished, and in 1944 it was destroyed in a fire. He trav-eled to the United States in 1935, to New York, and landed in Bellevue Hospital—the psychiatric ward—to be treated for his alcoholism. He wrote about this excruciating experience in a novella that was finally published posthumously under the title *Lunar Caustic* (1968). After his release, he was reconciled to Jan, and the two of them went to California, where Lowry failed as a screenwriter. Their next stop was Cuernavaca,

Mexico, and there Lowry's compulsive drinking led to the collapse of the marriage in 1937. Lowry was imprisoned in Oaxaca that year and deported to Los Angeles in 1938. During this period, he was already working on *Under the Volcano,* and his suffering in Mexico provided additional material for the novel. In Los Angeles, he met Margerie Bonner, a former child star during the silent era, and when his American visa expired in 1940, they relocated to British Columbia and were married there.

Lowry and his wife spent 14 relatively happy years in a beach hut near Vancouver; he wrote and rewrote but had little success publishing his work, other than *Under the Volcano.* The couple occasionally traveled, returning to Mexico for a disastrous visit in 1945 and later visiting Haiti, New York, France, and Italy. Lowry's creative powers ebbed, and in 1949 he wrote a long screenplay of the novel *Tender Is the Night* by the American novelist F. Scott Fitzgerald. Because he was able to finish the script, this event marked a turning point, and Lowry began to write again but lost his publishing contract in 1954. He and his wife moved to England, where Lowry declined for three years before committing suicide on June 27, 1957. Critics continue to debate the importance of Lowry's contribution to literature, agreeing on the importance of *Under the Volcano* while also recognizing the limited appeal of the rest of his works.

BIBLIOGRAPHY

Binns, Ronald. *Contemporary Writers: Malcolm Lowry.* London: Methuen, 1984.

Bowker, Gordon. *Pursued by Furies: A Life of Malcolm Lowry.* New York: HarperCollins, 1993.

Costa, Richard Hauer. *Malcolm Lowry.* Twayne's World Authors Series, 217. New York: Twayne, 1972.

Grace, Sherrill, ed. *Swinging the Maelstrom: New Perspectives on Malcolm Lowry.* Montreal: McGill-Queen's University Press, 1992.

LUCKY JIM **KINGSLEY AMIS (1954)** One of the funniest novels written in English in the 20th century, *Lucky Jim* follows the misadventures of its eponymous first-person narrator, Jim Dixon, who is a new faculty member in the fusty English department of a minor ("red brick") English university. The book is one of the outstanding examples of the CAMPUS NOVEL and a SATIRE on English CLASS snobbery and on the hopelessly inextricable entanglement of the academic world with England's social and cultural elites. AMIS creates a narrative that suggests that competent individuals will be saved from their own willingness to "sell out" because their worst behavior will not sink as low as the level of the mind-numbed conformity and petty protocols of the establishment to which they are attempting to peddle their talents. In other words, the truly fortunate are those who are doomed to be blessed with failure in their attempts to accommodate themselves to complacency.

In attempting to preserve his undesirable academic appointment, Jim makes the obvious strategic choices: a romantic alliance with a more securely entrenched colleague, dovetailed with unobtrusively obsequious fawning on his department's chief powerbroker, with both of these supplemented by a knee-jerk compulsion to accept every mindless simulacrum of academic achievement for which he can claim credit. He thus betrays himself in his personal life, in his professional life, and in his communal life, developing a quasi-relationship with Margaret Peel, striking sycophantic postures with Professor Welch (or in any case *attempting* to do so), and committing himself to deliver a suitable speech at the college's annual symposium. As the academic year progresses, Jim botches each of these efforts, generally in some way that involves alcohol, but if necessary resorting to fire as well. He is without a doubt the worst weekend guest to whom the Welches ever played host.

Along the way, he is vouchsafed a vision of the better life to which he would like to become accustomed. He meets Christine, the beautiful girlfriend of Professor Welch's son; he meets Julius Gore-Urquhart, a wealthy patron with a position at his disposal. These things seem infinitely beyond his grasp until after he has utterly destroyed the false life he is living, alienating himself from the goodwill of the girlfriend he does not love, from the support of the superior he does not admire, and from the protection of the community he does not respect. Jim's ejection from the place where he doesn't want to be anyway is the unsuspected first step toward the life he had been longing for.

Considering Jim's adventures from a somewhat more cynical perspective, one might also say that Kingsley Amis wants readers to conclude that the connection between effort and reward is entirely random, such that bad work may lead to good results; however, the INDETERMINACY of the narrative structure allows readers to see a positive connection between Jim's destructive behaviors and the improvement in his circumstances that he finally achieves.

BIBLIOGRAPHY

Bell, Robert H., ed. *Critical Essays on Kingsley Amis.* New York: G. K. Hall, 1998.

Kenyon, J. P. "*Lucky Jim* and After: The Business of University Novels." *Encounter* (June 1980): 81–84.

M

MAGICIAN'S NEPHEW, THE C. S. LEWIS (1955) See *The Chronicles of Narnia*.

MAGIC REALISM
After more than a century of focusing on realism, in the second half of the 20th century novelists reinvented FANTASY in a realistic mold. Where traditional fantasy writing featured mythical species such as elves and dragons and depended on a medieval setting, magic realism features ordinary characters who undergo supernatural experiences. A key text in the development of magic realism is *One Hundred Years of Solitude* (1967), by the great Colombian novelist Gabriel García Márquez. Many notable writers of magic realism were concentrated in Latin America, including Jorge Luis Borges, Miguel Ángel Asturias, Laura Esquivel, and Isabel Allende, but rather than remaining a regional literary device, magic realism is a worldwide artistic phenomenon particularly prominent in the visual arts and in fiction. Established writers of renown, such as the American novelist John Updike, have experimented with elements of magic realism, and internationally famous writers such as Italo Calvino (Italy), Günter Grass (Germany), Salman RUSHDIE (England), and John FOWLES (England) are commonly identified as magic realists.

Novelists incorporate magic realism by violating, or appearing to violate, the known limits of the world of possible experience. Dreams, trances, and drug-altered consciousness may serve as rational explanations for the supernatural elements of the PLOT, but the point is not how to explain those elements but how characters respond to them and cope with them; additionally, these elements may serve a symbolic or metaphorical function, standing in for features of the contemporary world without merely reflecting them. Magic realism does not depend on the nostalgic development of a longed-for lost Golden Age as do works of traditional fantasy, and it does not focus on scientific and technical details as does the genre of SCIENCE FICTION. Writers of magic realism frequently draw on mythology and psychology to create situations that carry their characters beyond the quotidian world of work and love, but they do not abandon that world or substitute another for it.

BIBLIOGRAPHY
Zamora, Lois Parkinson, and Wendy B. Faris, eds. *Magical Realism: Theory, History, Community*. Durham, N.C.: Duke University Press, 1995.

MAGUS, THE JOHN FOWLES (1965)
Probably the most important novel of this important 20th-century author, *The Magus* draws on the experiences of the author in the Greek Aegean Islands; it is an engrossing, hypnotic novel featuring layer upon layer of illusion. The story is deeply informed by classical MYTHOLOGY, Jungian psychology, and archetypal (see ARCHETYPE) literary devices. The first-person narrator, Nicholas Urfe ("earth," as FOWLES explains in the preface to the revised edition), takes a job in the early

1950s teaching English at a private Greek school modeled on the English PUBLIC SCHOOL system. He accepts the position more out of desperation than love of teaching English: No better prospects for employment have turned up, and he wishes to end his love affair with Alison Kelly, an intelligent and independent Australian woman. Nicholas imagines that on Phraxos (inspired by the real-life island of Spetsai), he will spend his abundant and isolated leisure time writing poetry. He fancies himself to be a great poet, although he has yet to produce significant examples of verse.

Nicholas arrives on Phraxos primed for an encounter with the owner of a large estate that covers the southern part of the island: Before leaving London he meets the previous English master, who warns him to beware "the waiting room." Once he arrives on the island, Nicholas makes inquiries but cannot assemble a coherent picture of the estate owner, Maurice Conchis ("conscious"). Some people despise the man and claim that he collaborated with the Nazis during the war. Memories of the brutal oppression inflicted on the islanders are still vivid. But some people speak well of Conchis and say that he made a noble sacrifice and survived a firing squad. Nicholas spends his free time rambling through the woods and enjoying the island's beaches; he writes the occasional poem and allows his memories of Alison to fade, knowing, from previous experience with failed affairs, that his longing for her will die. The novel's first section ends with Nicholas at a particularly low point in his life, believing that he has contracted syphilis from a prostitute in Athens.

As the long second section opens, Nicholas meets Conchis and becomes a frequent weekend guest at Bourani. Conchis is a spellbinding storyteller, and the story of his life provides fascinating material for the telling. Conchis claims to be psychic, and in the dead of night strange things do happen at Bourani, always associated in some way with the portion of his life story Conchis had told Nicholas over dinner. At first Nicholas takes Conchis to be an eccentric millionaire creating illusions to entertain and mystify his single guest, but gradually he realizes that some elaborate game is under way, although he cannot discern the purpose of the game or the reason why he has been chosen to participate in it. Other people are somehow present as well, acting out the "masque" the old man presents, including a beautiful young woman who is impersonating Lily, Conchis's tragic first love. The nocturnal performances always include mythic elements, and the appearances of Lily sometimes seem to be as supernatural as Conchis claims her to be. Nicholas reasons that there must be a twin sister present to help create the mysterious encounters he has with Lily.

Sure enough, there are two sisters involved in the performances. When Nicholas succeeds in speaking to Lily, she tells him she is an actress named Julie Holmes, and that her twin sister June is also present, and that both of them are acting under the direction of Conchis. Nicholas is strongly attracted to Julie, so he is astonished when Conchis explains that she is a schizophrenic under his care. He enlists Nicholas to assist him in an innovative program of therapy that includes acting out delusional fantasies. Nicholas joins in the game, obsessed with the desire to possess Julie and suspicious of everything Conchis tells him. He struggles with the two versions of reality that Conchis and Julie have presented to him; everything that happens to him is doubly laden with possibilities, and he yearns to have Julie's version turn out to be the real one. He repeatedly compares Julie to Alison, always deciding that Julie will be the better option for him if she is indeed an ordinary actress and not a psychiatric patient.

When Nicholas's visit to Bourani is suspended one weekend, he agrees to meet Alison in Athens. She has taken a job as an airline flight attendant. By now, Nicholas is in love with his hoped-for version of Julie/Lily; nonetheless, he allows Alison to rekindle her hopes for him. He knows he is misleading her, but his conscience hardly bothers him, so powerful is his desire for Julie. When he returns to Phraxos, he lies about his connection to Alison and resumes his pursuit of the person he hopes Julie really is. The game continues as before, with Conchis relating a new episode of his life story after dinner, but eventually Julie becomes a dinner guest rather than a mere performer. Although Conchis warns him not to believe her and explains that she uses her attractiveness to enlist the assistance of men gullible enough to fall for her, Nicholas is already incapable of heeding the warning. He is soon making plans to help Julie so they can be together, certain that the more enjoyable version of the two realities he has been presented with will turn out to be real. But soon the game becomes too deep and events take a turn that Nicholas could not have anticipated. He finds himself trapped in circumstances beyond his control, and he learns beyond a doubt that nothing is what it seems to be. At the close of the novel's second section, Nicholas has been expelled from Bourani, he has lost his job, and he has experienced a harrowing trial in which—although he himself is nominally the judge—he is judged and found to be unworthy. To his shock he learns that Alison has had an invisible hand in the game, and that Conchis and Julie had always known when he lied to them even though he was never able to discover the truth behind their game.

The novel's third section is approximately the same length as the first section; in this denouement, Nicholas is obsessed by the desire to understand what has happened to him. His compulsion to find out the truth is only part of the story: He also longs to confront "Julie," or whoever she really is, and condemn her for misleading him. He has rediscovered the qualities in Alison that made him fall in love with her in the first place, but now he cannot locate her. He conducts exhaustive research in the effort to find some trace of truth about Conchis and Julie, visiting libraries, consulting records in Greek and English government agencies, writing letters, and following faint leads. Although he never finds Julie or Conchis, he does locate Julie's mother, and in a long and revealing conversation he hears truths that he does not want to acknowledge. When Alison finally consents to see him, he realizes that he has lost her.

Nicholas's experiences follow the archetypal pattern of the mythic hero's adventures: he has a summons to a quest, he acquires "supernatural" helpers, and he enters the underworld to face a challenge. In this case, however, Nicholas fails to perform the hero's tasks. He does not return from his adventure with a boon for his fellow man; he does not mend the faults in his character; he does not win the approval of the women he encounters. Fowles draws on the psychological and mythic theories of Carl Jung (Conchis relates that he had met Jung personally) to construct the game

Nicholas uncomprehendingly plays; he also uses aspects of existentialism, insisting on each person's freedom to choose how to act in life. Nicholas does not embrace his freedom nor does he take responsibility for his choices, and so he cannot complete his quest successfully. In contrast, Conchis has shouldered the burden of freedom, having survived his own harrowing trial during the war. In his case, however, his summons to adventure was no game but a very real ordeal at the hands of Nazi executioners. In a riveting passage, Conchis explains to Nicholas that everyone is always free to choose and therefore always responsible for the choices that are made. This lesson is the one Nicholas cannot comprehend.

Readers are likely to be as charmed by Nicholas as Alison was. Since Nicholas is relating his own experiences in the first person, the reader's perception is limited to Nicholas's telling. But Fowles includes details in the telling of the story that allow the reader's understanding to exceed the narrator's capacity to comprehend the events of his life. The theme of appearance and reality, together with the epistemological problem of distinguishing between them, spills over into the reader's experience of the novel. Nicholas appears to be the hero of his life, but a more sensitive and honest perception reveals the unflattering reality he cannot or will not acknowledge.

BIBLIOGRAPHY

Huffaker, Robert. *John Fowles.* Twayne's English Authors, 292. Boston: Twayne, 1980.

Palmer, William J. *The Fiction of John Fowles: Tradition, Art, and the Loneliness of Selfhood.* Columbia; University of Missouri Press, 1974.

Wolfe, Peter. *John Fowles: Magus and Moralist.* Lewisburg, Pa.: Bucknell University Press, 1976.

MALONE DIES SAMUEL BECKETT (1951)

This second volume in BECKETT'S *Trilogy* was initially published in French under the title *Malone Meurt;* it follows MOLLOY (1951) and precedes The UNNAMABLE (1953). Beckett published his English translation of *Malone Dies* in 1956.

The title character also serves as the first-person narrator of the minutes and days leading up to his death.

Malone thinks he remembers being in a hospital after a blow to the head; in any case, he is confined to a bed that is confined to a room. For diversion and activity, he has only his own solitary thoughts and his thoughts about his thoughts. He occupies himself with writing stories that may be memories or fictions, recording his thoughts, imagining complex lives for characters such as young Saposcat or old Macmann (apparently his alter-egos), and inventorying his minuscule store of possessions, some of which were also possessions of Molloy (his sucking stones and his knife rest). As he lies on his deathbed, Malone becomes less coherent and finds his control of his life, apparently never firm, slipping away into chaos and feebleness. When his stick rolls away from him, for example, he works for two days to regain possession of it. And when the old woman dies who had brought him soup each day and who had emptied his chamber pot, he is helpless to care for himself and so knows that his end is near. Malone's story does not build to closure; like life, it merely unravels to its end.

Beckett is the leading practitioner of literature of the absurd in 20th-century fiction in English. Like his renowned play *Waiting for Godot, Malone Dies* is a work of surprising comedy in the midst of stark circumstances. Although it lacks rigorous narrative structure, it is linked to the two volumes of the *Trilogy* that precede and follow it in sharing a concern for the mundane spaces of everyday life—bedrooms and beds, for example—and for the most insignificant objects with which people concern themselves, such as bicycles or pencils. The characters of the *Trilogy,* although they differ in name, also share a vaguely Irish identity and a faintly Catholic heritage; however, these elements are seasoned by a distinctly French context, and neither Irishness nor Catholicism is valorized. Just as Malone struggles with his faltering mortality encapsulated within his room, continually aware of deeper levels of consciousness encapsulated within his self-awareness, the novels struggle to capture the multilayered mysteries of identity, existence—and nonexistence.

BIBLIOGRAPHY

Fletcher, John. *The Novels of Samuel Beckett.* New York: Barnes & Noble, 1970.

O'Hara, John. *Twentieth Century Interpretations of* Malloy, Malone Dies, The Unnamable: *A Collection of Critical Essays.* Englewood Cliffs, N.J.: Prentice Hall, 1970.
Webb, Eugene. *Samuel Beckett: A Study of His Novels.* Seattle: University of Washington Press, 1970.

MAN COULD STAND UP, A FORD MADOX FORD (1926)   See *PARADE'S END.*

MAN OF PROPERTY, A JOHN GALSWORTHY (1906)   The protagonist of this first volume of *The FORSYTE SAGA* is Soames Forsyte, a lawyer who has married the beautiful Irene Heron. The marriage is failing; Irene does not love Soames and, in fact, has come to loathe him. Soames, however, is determined to hold onto Irene as a key piece of his property. The struggle between these two, Soames actively possessing Irene while she passively resists him, forms the central story of the novel.

Galsworthy opens the novel with an effective device: the gregarious Forsytes are gathered to celebrate the engagement of June, in the youngest generation, to the architect Philip Bosinney. The large clan provides Galsworthy with an expansive canvas upon which to create the numerous types of upper-class Victorian personalities. The party is a grand event, but it is also one of the last times the family will find itself this united and harmonious. As competent as the Forsytes have been in piling up material wealth, they have as much difficulty with their personal lives as any other less advantaged family does, and those difficulties will divide the family and thereby undermine one of the Forsyte principles.

Soames is not a bad man by any means, but he is possessive. He genuinely loves Irene, as he shows her through ostentatious gifts. But Irene, a symbol of abstract beauty, longs for something better than the conspicuous consumption of wealth. As a grand gesture, Soames decides to build a spectacular country house for Irene, and he turns to the soon-to-be-family architect Philip Bosinney to design the house and supervise its construction. The construction runs over budget, and Soames argues over costs and design details; worst of all, Irene and Philip fall in love and embark on an affair. This double betrayal of Forsytes—Philip's fiancée is Soames's cousin—helps to split the family into two factions. Once in place, these divisions and their consequences continue to affect new generations who do not even know the reasons for the split. Soames finally "repossesses" his property—he rapes his wife to assert his rights over her. Philip Bosinney's accidental death leaves Irene with no option but to return to the house of the husband she despises.

Galsworthy ends the novel without resolving the problem of the unhappy marriage between Soames and Irene. He continues the story in the second volume of *The Forsyte Saga,* IN CHANCERY.

BIBLIOGRAPHY

Kettle, Arnold. "John Galsworthy: *A Man of Property.*" In *An Introduction to the English Novel.* Vol. 2. Edited by Arnold Kettle. New York: Hutchinson's University Library, 1967.

MANTICORE, THE ROBERTSON DAVIES (1972)   See *The* DEPTFORD TRILOGY.

MAN WHO WAS THURSDAY: A NIGHT-MARE, THE G. K. CHESTERTON (1908)

This novel presents a response to the worldwide rise in anarchism during the late 19th century and the early 20th century. This political movement had inspired a series of political assassinations, including an Italian king, a Spanish prime minister, an Austrian empress, and two presidents, one in France and one in the United States (William McKinley). But anarchism suffers from an apparent inconsistency in its own principles, since it is a system of thought and behavior that renounces system as a principle of thought and behavior. Anarchists wish to eliminate government, laws, and forms of regulation based on law, claiming that the natural state of human beings liberated from the oppressions of government and law will be one of voluntary goodness, mutual aid, and absence of crime. CHESTERTON develops an anarchic story that moves toward order under the guiding hand of a benevolent central authority, using a dream ALLEGORY to puzzle out the inconsistencies of anarchism as a political philosophy.

The protagonist is Gabriel Syme, a police officer for Scotland Yard; he encounters Lucien Gregory, an anarchist poet, and engages him in a heated discussion. Syme denies the possibility of anarchism as a movement, and in response Gregory invites Syme to attend a meeting of anarchists. There, Gregory intends to run for election to the central council, which is organized according to the days of the week: Sunday rules the council, assisted by the Secretary (Monday), Gogol (Tuesday), the Marquis de St. Eustache (Wednesday), Professor de Worms (Friday), and Dr. Bull (Saturday). The position of Thursday remains unfilled, and when Syme wins the election instead of Gregory, he apparently becomes a mole in the organization. He learns of the plan to conduct assassinations in Russia and France, and is amazed when Sunday announces the presence of a spy in their midst, accusing Gogol, not Syme, as the turncoat. Gogol flees, and Syme becomes linked with Professor de Worms, who eventually admits to being yet another Scotland Yard detective. Their goal is to prevent the planned assassination; to do so, they must intercept Wednesday, but more surprises are in store before Sunday draws the group together for a revealing exposition of hidden truths.

Chesterton's COMIC NOVEL provides a model for many elements of subsequent spy stories, but it also draws formally on the work of James BUCHAN. By its very nature, spying is a dubious enterprise founded on lies, misdirection, betrayal, and misinformation. In this case, each of the seven members of the council turns out to be something other than he appears to be, so the plot becomes a tangled web of unmaskings, and the very concept of character becomes unstable. Additionally, Chesterton adds a theological element to the climactic revelation scene as Sunday "preaches" his doctrine to the reassembled council. Along the way, he deploys several chase scenes using every imaginable vehicle—a clear source for the adventures of more recent spies such as James BOND. Chesterton uses SATIRE to develop a critique not of espionage but of the nihilistic philosophies that proved alluring to many young writers and thinkers during the period of the fin de siècle. He reaffirms the value of order in nature and of reverence for the divine creative force that gave rise to it.

BIBLIOGRAPHY

Boyd, Ian. *The Novels of G. K. Chesterton: A Study in Art and Propaganda.* New York: Barnes & Noble, 1975.

Hunter, Lynette. *G. K. Chesterton: Explorations in Allegory.* London: Macmillan, 1979.

MARTHA QUEST DORIS LESSING (1951)

Volume one in the *CHILDREN OF VIOLENCE* series, this novel introduces the eponymous heroine as a 15-year-old girl in the colonial African territory—based on the author's childhood home in southern Rhodesia—that eventually becomes the independent nation of Zambesia. It leads directly into the second volume of the series, *A PROPER MARRIAGE.* Since this first volume narrates a young woman's coming of age, it is a BILDUNGSROMAN; since it stands as the introduction to a ROMAN-FLEUVE, it establishes the range of themes that will recur as the series unfolds.

Martha Quest is a rebellious girl who, like many adolescents, rejects her parents' values. In her case, she is rejecting the specifically Victorian values that lingered in the British territories still subject to COLONIALISM after those values had been supplanted by MODERNISM in England. Martha engages in an intense period of self-exploration, but she also begins to enter the larger world and to discover the intoxicating thrill of political activism. This alternation between the interior world of the self and the larger community in which selves are contextualized becomes a major narrative strategy in the series. In this novel, Martha explores the dimensions of her own psyche (she has a vision of an ideal city in which inequities based on race have disappeared), of the social and political worlds she must learn to navigate, and of the adult roles typically available to a young woman of her era.

Martha's early influences grow out of her reading, her exposure to the vast natural world of the veldt, and her contacts with other young people such as the Jewish brothers Joss Cohen, a socialist, and Solly Cohen, a Zionist. She breaks with her family and her roots in this journey of self-discovery, leaving her family and the farm they live on for the racially divided confines of the city of Zambesia. There, she finds two worlds: a social world of attractive young white partygoers, empowered in their world by virtue of their whiteness, and an ideologically passionate world of Communist political activists seeking to end the damages of European colonial domination in Africa. Martha is involved in both these somewhat incompatible worlds and finds a way to arouse criticism in both of them simultaneously. Her consciousness is raised by an experience of injustice she witnesses, but before this process can come to full maturity, she meets Douglas Knowell, an alleged radical. Martha lacks the perspicuity to understand the perfunctory nature of Douglas's connection to radical causes, and she marries him before she knows what she is doing. The volume closes with predictions of impending failure in her marriage and upheaval in her personal life.

Martha's quest, in part, is a search for wholeness—for personal unity—in a world that seeks to analyze, simplify, categorize, and divide human identity. Fragmentation continually threatens Martha, but she continually searches for a unity that can bring together the pieces of her life in a single but complete identity. Along the way, she will have many disappointments in love, in politics, in marriage, in motherhood, and even within her own mind. She does not forget her vision of the four-gated city (the subject of her vision becomes the title of the final volume in the series), and she does not lose her determination to search for the means to a better world. Since no one can show her the way to that better world, her own life perforce becomes the territory of experimentation as she continues her quest.

BIBLIOGRAPHY

Daymond, M. J. "*Martha Quest*: The Self and Its Spatial Metaphors." In *Women and Writing in South Africa: A Critical Anthology.* Edited by Cherry Clayton. Marchalltown: Heinemann Southern Africa, 1989, 163–181.

Rosen, Ellen I. "Martha's 'Quest' in Lessing's *Children of Violence,*" *Frontiers: A Journal of Women Studies* 3, no. 2 (1978): 54–59.

Tiger, Virginia. *Critical Essays on Doris Lessing.* Boston: Hall, 1986.

MASTER AND COMMANDER PATRICK O'BRIAN (1970)   See AUBREY-MATURIN NOVELS.

MASTERS, THE C. P. SNOW (1951) The
fourth volume in the 11-volume ROMAN-FLEUVE collectively entitled STRANGERS AND BROTHERS, this novel finds the first-person narrator of the series, Lewis Eliot, restricting his law practice in London in order to lecture at Cambridge. The story is set in 1937 and is colored by the looming threat of the conflict eventually known as WORLD WAR II. On a much smaller scale, internal strife breaks out on the campus when the faculty members must elect a new master. The politics, alliances, negotiations, and rising discord form a microcosm that mirrors the impending strife in the larger world of diplomacy, intimidation, and brinkmanship. The Masters is an outstanding example of the subgenre of the CAMPUS NOVEL; its characters and themes reappear in The AFFAIR, the eighth novel in the Strangers and Brothers series. Both books were critical and popular successes when they were published, and both are among the most admired volumes in the series.

As the story begins, Lewis Eliot holds an appointment as a tutor, a junior faculty member. He learns from Jago, one of the senior members, that the present master of the college, Vernon Royce, is dying of cancer. A new master must be chosen from among the members of the college; Jago is interested in the position, and Eliot offers his support. At first Jago's chances look good, but when the issue is first addressed in a faculty meeting, a second candidate, the physicist Crawford, makes a bid for the position and splits the college into two rival factions. Eliot finds himself in opposition to his old friend Francis Getliffe, who supports Crawford; the increasing acrimony between the two sides threatens to ruin their friendship. At first the advantage remains with Jago, although his support comes from junior members, but when Nightingale switches sides, the two sides are more evenly divided. On Jago's side, efforts are under way to win a large donation to the college from Sir Horace Timberlake. The funds will greatly benefit the college, and success in this financial matter may sway some of Crawford's supporters to vote for Jago.

The interactions between the factions degenerate into name-calling, insults, and ridicule: Nightingale sinks so low as to threaten junior members with the loss of their position, and when he circulates a broadside attacking Jago's wife as a woman of questionable

character, she is deeply hurt by the attack. The death of the old master raises the stakes and adds a new complicating factor when the proceedings fall to the supervision of the senior member of the college, Gay, a man who has become moderately senile in his old age. When Jago's side wins the financial grant, this benefit is offset by the defection of another supporter, Pilbrow, to Crawford's faction. Eliot and another Jago supporter decide to appeal to Gay in an attempt to win his vote for Jago. An extra burden hangs over the proceedings, since the issue will revert to the choice of the local bishop if the faculty cannot come to an agreement. When the votes are cast, Jago appears to have a tiny advantage if Gay supports him; however, another defection at the last minute—Chrystal claims to be dissatisfied with both candidates—swings the election to Crawford.

The Masters is an absorbing portrait of academic politics and of the effect of strife in placing stress on the workings of individual consciences and collective values. Eliot is an insightful and well-informed observer of his colleagues, and his analytical reportage of the events leading to the election demonstrates how stress magnifies the flaws in individuals' characters, which in turn exaggerate the cracks in the ethical conduct of social interactions. The action of the story consists entirely of people trying to influence one another through courageous and courteous personal contact on the part of some partisans and ignoble backstabbing on the part of others. Despite its quiet setting and low-key action, the narrative has a gripping effect as the two sides battle for advantage. The small worth of the issue that has given rise to this conflict actually highlights the reader's awareness of the degree to which human passions can be stirred. SNOW suggests there is reason to maintain hope for the resolution of human conflict: He ends his novel with a magnanimous gesture of reconciliation from the defeated Jago who offers a toast to the new master after the elections are over.

BIBLIOGRAPHY
Meckier, Jerome. "Modern or Contemporary? Mastering an Academic Question with Evidence from Snow, Enright, and the Angry Young Men." In University Fiction. Edited by David Bevan. Amsterdam: Rodopi, 1990, 157–168.

MAUGHAM, W. SOMERSET (1874–1965)

A prolific writer, William Somerset Maugham was born on January 25, 1874, in Paris. His father was a lawyer and his older brothers followed the profession as well, but Somerset Maugham developed a stutter that made arguing cases in court impossible. Maugham was reared by an elderly uncle after 1884, because by then both his parents had died. Isolated in his uncle's small-town vicarage, Maugham read for entertainment. He succeeded academically but was unhappy in school. When he had completed the "sixth form," the approximate equivalent of an American high school degree, he decided to travel and did not attend an undergraduate college. He did earn a medical degree in London in 1897, but in that year his first novel appeared, *Liza of Lambeth,* and it was so successful that Maugham abandoned medicine for a career as a professional writer.

In 1898, Maugham began writing plays, and by 1907 he had a hit with *Lady Frederick.* This play was the first of a long series of popular successes, primarily with comedies of manners and light SATIRES on marriage. Maugham had a good ear for realistic but witty dialogue and was a skillful creator of dramatic characters. He wrote 29 plays by 1933, but he also continued to write short fiction, publishing more than a dozen collections, and some 20 novels. Of his novels, the most important is the BILDUNGSROMAN OF HUMAN BONDAGE (1915), drawing on his own experiences growing up.

Maugham served as an intelligence agent during WORLD WAR I, traveling to Switzerland and Russia; later, he turned his experience with the world of spying into a series of short stories featuring the recurring main character of Ashenden. After the war, he published *The MOON AND SIXPENCE* (1919), drawing on the life of the impressionist painter Paul Gauguin, who abandoned his responsibilities in France to live in Tahiti. In 1926, Maugham relocated to a villa on the French Riviera, where he continued pouring out novels, plays, short stories, and works of nonfiction. In 1930, he wrote CAKES AND ALE, his own favorite among his novels. During WORLD WAR II, he resided in the United States, publishing *The RAZOR'S EDGE,* one of his most serious works of fiction, in 1944. After the war, he returned to his villa and continued to write. His health began to decline in his old age and he died on December 16, 1965, nearly 92 years old.

BIBLIOGRAPHY

Calder, Robert. *Willie: The Life of W. Somerset Maugham.* New York: St. Martin's Press, 1989.

Curtis, Anthony, and John Whitehead, eds. *W. Somerset Maugham: The Critical Heritage.* London: Routledge & Kegan. Paul, 1987.

Loss, Archie K. *W. Somerset Maugham.* New York: Ungar, 1987.

MAURITIUS COMMAND, THE PATRICK O'BRIAN (1977)   See AUBREY-MATURIN NOVELS.

MCCABE, PATRICK (1955–)   Author of *The BUTCHER BOY,* the basis for the 1998 FILM ADAPTATION of the same name, Patrick McCabe was born on March 27, 1955, in the small town of Clones in County Monaghan. He pursued his education at St. Patrick's Training College, Dublin, and for much of his adult life he has worked in England teaching learning-disabled children. He was married in 1981; he and his wife are the parents of two children.

McCabe's first creative efforts were radio plays, including presentations for children. He published his first novel, *Music on Clinton Street,* in 1986, followed in 1989 by *Carn,* the story of an economic boom in an Irish town and the Americanization that prevails until long-simmering hostilities resurface. These novels did not find an audience outside IRELAND. In 1992, however, *The Butcher Boy* was short-listed for the BOOKER PRIZE, and it won Ireland's Aer Lingus Prize for that year. Since establishing an international reputation, McCabe has published *The Dead School* (1995), about two teachers locked in a mutually destructive hatred; and *Breakfast on Pluto* (1998; nominated for the Booker Prize), about an Irish transvestite obsessed with 1960s pop-diva Dusty Springfield. His most recent books include *Mondo Desperado: A Serial Novel* (1999), *The Emerald Germs of Ireland* (2001), and *Call Me the Breeze* (2004).

In contrast to other contemporary Irish writers such as Roddy DOYLE, McCabe presents a darker and more violent picture of a world that is obsessed with popular culture yet ignorant of history while also in thrall to the forces it has put in place. He is particularly admired for his ability to capture the voice of an unusual first-person narrator such as a deranged boy or transvestite prostitute, illuminating the context that produced such a human outcome. Patrick McCabe continues to live and write in England and Ireland.

BIBLIOGRAPHY

Kearney, Richard. *Transitions: Narratives in Modern Irish Culture.* Dublin: Wolfhound Press, 1988.

MCEWAN, IAN (1948–)

Widely considered to be one of the most important living writers in England today, Ian Russell McEwan was born on June 21, 1948, in Aldershot, England. Because of his father's military career, McEwan's childhood included stays in Libya and Singapore. He attended a boarding school before matriculating at the University of Sussex; he graduated in 1970 with an undergraduate degree in English. He then entered the graduate program at the University of East Anglia, completing a master's degree in 1971.

McEwan's first publications were short stories. His collection of stories, *First Love, Last Rites,* drawn from the work he completed for his graduate degree, appeared in 1975, followed in 1978 by another story collection, *In Between the Sheets.* That year, McEwan also published his first novel, *The Cement Garden,* and he has continued to focus primarily on longer fiction since then. McEwan also began to write for stage, film, and television productions; in 1983, he wrote an oratorio on the subject of nuclear holocaust, *Or Shall We Die?* McEwan's interest in and knowledge of music is sometimes apparent in his fiction; one such example is the conductor co-protagonist of *AMSTERDAM* (1998).

McEwan followed *The Cement Garden* with the chilling novella *The COMFORT OF STRANGERS* (1981), the basis for a FILM ADAPTATION in 1990; the novel is set in Venice and follows the fatal intersection of two couples, one a young couple vacationing from England, the other increasingly mysterious and demanding. In 1987, *The CHILD IN TIME* won the WHITBREAD AWARD for Best Book. Then in 1997, *Enduring Love* was a phenomenal best seller in England, and the next year *Amsterdam* won the BOOKER PRIZE. McEwan's next novel, *Atonement*

(2002) was short-listed for the Booker Prize; additionally, he has published *Saturday: A Novel* (2005).

McEwan's novels and stories frequently feature a violent or perverse element, but his chief interest is in the ways societies cope with the fact of such events. Laws prohibit such things, and people are repelled by them, and yet they continue to occur. McEwan frequently anatomizes his characters' weaknesses with a wickedly dark satiric verbal wit, probing the unstable foundations of the moral structures that govern their actions. Frequently grouped with writers such as Julian BARNES, Martin AMIS, Angela CARTER, and J. G. BALLARD, McEwan's fiction forms part of the bridge between the CLASS-conscious works of the 1950s and 1960s associated with the ANGRY YOUNG MEN and the more recent influence and innovation of POSTMODERNISM.

BIBLIOGRAPHY

Malcolm, David. *Understanding Ian McEwan.* Understanding Contemporary British Literature Series. Matthew J. Bruccoli, ed. Columbia: University of South Carolina Press, 2002.

Ricks, Christopher. "Adolescence and After: An Interview with Ian McEwan," *Listener* (April 12, 1979): 527.

Slay, Jack Jr. *Ian McEwan.* Twayne's English Authors, 518. Kinley Roby, ed. New York: Twayne Publishers/ Simon & Schuster Macmillan, 1996.

MEN AT ARMS EVELYN WAUGH (1952)

See SWORD OF HONOUR TRILOGY.

METROLAND JULIAN BARNES (1980)

This BILDUNGSROMAN won the Somerset Maugham Award when it was published. It features an ingenuous first-person narrator, Christopher Lloyd, who examines his life at three different periods. As he begins his narration in 1963, Christopher is 13 years old; he despises the part of London—the Metroland of the title—where he lives, condemning it for its bourgeois materialism. He and his best friend, Toni, are attempting to take possession of the attitudes and behaviors of adulthood while still enamored with childhood's pranks. They are excessively grown-up in their reading tastes, having chosen to model themselves on such decadent French writers as Charles Baudelaire and Gerard de Nerval, and yet they attempt to discomfit shopkeepers and middle-aged men through droll examples of mild impudence. They crave the satisfaction of provoking an irritated response, since that is how they will know that they have successfully exercised some power in the adult world. In fact, they are very much on the periphery of life, too shy to speak to the girls whom they spy on through binoculars.

In the novel's middle section, five years have elapsed, and Christopher is an 18-year-old living in Paris in 1968, a year of violent student protests and civil unrest. He falls passionately in love with the young Frenchwoman Annick, to whom he loses his virginity, while he also pursues studies in comparative literature. He remains a person of introspection rather than a person of action, even as one of the great periods of contemporary social activism unfolds around him. His nonconformist adolescence has impelled him to live the exotic life he dreamed of when he heaped scorn on the bourgeois values of Metroland's suburbs, and he appears to be on the verge of making a decisive split from his past. But his middle-CLASS English origins have stamped him more strongly than he could have guessed: Like his adolescent pranks, his French adventure does not transform him; instead, he marries an English girl and settles in London.

The novel's third segment opens nine years afterward, in 1977; Christopher and his English wife, Marion, own a house in Metroland. They are coping with the financial pressures of a mortgaged life and rearing a child. Christopher supports this bourgeois lifestyle by editing coffee-table books, and occasionally he spends an evening with his old friend Toni, who still talks the radical talk, even going so far as to suggest that Christopher's middle-class conventionality is a sellout. But the comforts of life in Metroland make up for the criticisms the young Christopher and Tony once lodged against it. Christopher has become the thing he once condemned, but he has grown into this role in contrast to his teenage strategy of clothing himself in ideas as if they were garments.

BIBLIOGRAPHY

Jenkins, Mitch. "Novel Escape." The [London] Times Magazine, 13 January 1996, 18.

Moseley, Merritt. Understanding Julian Barnes. Understanding Contemporary British Literature. Columbia: University of South Carolina Press, 1997.

Sesto, Bruce. Language, History, and Metanarrative in the Fiction of Julian Barnes. New York: Peter Lang, 2001.

MIDDLETON, STANLEY (1919–)

Writing about middle-CLASS characters residing in the Midlands of England, Stanley Middleton produced more than 35 novels between 1958 and the end of the 20th century; he won the BOOKER PRIZE in 1974 for HOLIDAY. He was born in the Midlands district of Nottingham on August 1, 1919, and he was educated at High Pavement School and at the University of Nottingham. He served in the military during and after WORLD WAR II (1940–46), in the Royal Artillery and the Army Education Corps. He was married in 1951 and became the father of two daughters. He returned to his hometown and to his home school, serving as an English teacher at High Pavement College from 1947 until 1981. During the 1982–83 academic year, he was the Judith E. Wilson Visiting Fellow at Emmanuel College of Cambridge University.

Middleton's novels have been admired for their realistic portrayal of ordinary people who must cope with such stressful events as divorce, mediocre success in their careers, the suicides of friends or peripheral characters, or the inexorable process of growing older and less capable. He frequently uses music and painting as tropes, although his musical and artistic characters are more likely to be, at best, middling successes in their fields. His novels form a consistent body of work in both form and content; only a few of them have been published in the United States, including *Entry into Jerusalem* (1983), *Valley of Decision* (1985), and *Vacant Places* (1990). Middleton continues to live and work at his home in Sherwood, Nottinghamshire.

BIBLIOGRAPHY

Middleton, Stanley. Ends and Means. London: Hutchinson, 1977.

———. The Other Side. London: Hutchinson, 1980.

MIDNIGHT'S CHILDREN SALMAN RUSHDIE (1981)

A novel enriched by the technique of MAGIC REALISM, *Midnight's Children* won the BOOKER PRIZE in 1981; it was RUSHDIE'S second work of long fiction. Its structure shares characteristics of HIS-

TORICAL FICTION and ALLEGORY as Rushdie retells the story of the independence of INDIA AND PAKISTAN from the EMPIRE of British COLONIALISM and the subsequent division of Pakistan first from India and then into the two nations of Bangladesh and Pakistan. The novel contains autobiographical elements as well: The author is a man born in India just weeks before independence to a Muslim family with strong ties to England and Pakistan, so the events in the life of the novel's protagonist, Saleem Sinai, form a rough parallel to the life of Rushdie himself.

The novel's central device is the notion that children born during the hour of India's independence—midnight on August 15, 1947—were endowed with special powers. On a practical level, this belief (historically voiced by Nehru, India's first prime minister) affirms the crucial role of the first generation born under self-rule to shape India's future; in Rushdie's metaphorical treatment, the children born coincidentally with the birth of the nation of India acquire mythic identities and supernatural powers. Saleem Sinai enters the world stage at the moment India does, arriving at the upper-class home of a Muslim family in Bombay, and in childhood he realizes that his supernatural abilities allow him to contact the other "midnight's children" telepathically. Nightly, he summons them to the Midnight Children's Conference. The children learn of each other's abilities and begin to demonstrate the contributions they may be able to make to India's future. As Saleem grows and learns of his family's history and its role in the events of the 20th century, he also learns of India's colonial history

When Saleem enters school, a series of accidents leads to the discovery that he is not the biological child of the Sinai family: In Rushdie's variation on the worldwide myth of the "changeling" child, a nurse had switched two infants, causing the Sinais' biological son to be reared in poverty and in the Hindu tradition—he is named Shiva, after the Hindu god of chaos and destruction, and he functions like his namesake—and placing a child from the slums, Saleem, in the care of the Sinai family, who rear him as a Muslim. From his telepathic powers, Saleem discovers a further secret about Shiva: This boy, too, is not completely the biological child of the Sinai family, for he had been fathered by an Englishman who abandoned India upon its independence. The Sinai family now resides on the estate once owned by this departed Englishman. Saleem's adoptive parents—the family with whom he has lived since birth—choose not to sort out the nurse's mix-up, continuing to rear him as a son and leaving Shiva to the vagaries of his life on the streets of Bombay's slums. Saleem and Shiva form an interlocked pair or opposites, rich and poor, Muslim and Hindu, their fates repeatedly bound up in each other's lives.

The Sinai family next relocates to Pakistan rather than remain among the hated Muslim minority in India. Saleem ends the Midnight Children's Conference: He wants to avoid Shiva, and in Pakistan his telepathic powers abandon him. Instead, he uses his sensitive nose—so large that it is repeatedly compared to an elephant's trunk or a cucumber—to sniff out corruption and injustice in the new Pakistani nation. Two historical events come to dominate the direction of the story: the 1965 war between Pakistan and India, and the 1973 civil war that leads to the establishment of East Pakistan as the separate nation of Bangladesh. Saleem's family is wiped out in these violent upheavals, except for his sister (in name only, since he is essentially adopted) Jamila. He loves Jamila passionately, and yet their upbringing as blood relatives prevents that love from producing any happiness for him. His life reaches a nadir following the civil strife that divides Pakistan into two nations, and at his hour of greatest desolation one of the other midnight's children, Parvati (bearing the same name as a Hindu mother-goddess), uses her magical powers to bring Saleem back to India. He and Parvati are married, but the marriage remains unconsummated, obstructed by Saleem's love for Jamila. As a consequence, Parvati takes Shiva as a lover and bears him a son, Aadam. Just as Saleem was not the biological son of his father, he now becomes the father in name only to a son he acknowledges as his own, knowing full well that the child does not carry his biological identity.

Shiva's destructive force grows as his stature in the Indian bureaucratic establishment rises: He bulldozes slums that are still occupied by their residents, killing Parvati in the process. Rushdie uses Shiva's program of "urban renewal" to criticize the policies of the government of Indira Gandhi and in particular the management by her son Sanjay of real-world public-works projects and attempts at population control. Saleem and the other midnight children are among the victims of Shiva's "eugenics": They are all sterilized. Metaphorically, Rushdie seems to suggest that the productivity of India's first generation of free citizens has been eliminated by endemic destructive forces. The explicitness of his criticism of particular policies and politicians led to the banning of *Midnight's Children* in India. In the end, the midnight child who once seemed to have the brightest future comes to a sour end: He must support himself by taking a job in a pickle factory; ironically, the factory's owner is the very nurse who had switched Saleem and Shiva in their infancy.

Readers unfamiliar with the mythic traditions of the Indian subcontinent will benefit from perusing a general survey of Indian mythology and legends before turning to *Midnight's Children;* familiarity with the outline of Indian and Pakistani history in the late 19th century and the entire 20th century will also increase the reader's ability to appreciate the many levels on which Rushdie's novel operates. Although the novel offers enjoyable reading on its own imaginative terms, the larger significance of the story becomes apparent only by placing it in the historic circumstances and the narrative traditions that shaped the author's life and thoughts.

BIBLIOGRAPHY

Hogan, Patrick Colm. "*Midnight's Children:* Kashmir and the Politics of Identity," *Twentieth Century Literature: A Scholarly and Critical Journal* 47, no. 4 (Winter 2001): 510–44.

Rao, M. Madhusudhana. *Salman Rushdie's Fiction*. New Delhi: Sterling Publishers, 1992.

Trevedi, Harish. "Post-Colonial Hybridity: *Midnight's Children*." In *Literature and Nation: Britain and India, 1800–1990*. Edited by Richard Allen and Harish Trivedi. London: Routledge, 2000, 154–65.

MILITARY PHILOSOPHERS, THE ANTHONY POWELL (1968)

Volume nine in the 12-book ROMAN-FLEUVE collectively entitled *A DANCE TO THE MUSIC OF TIME*, this novel closes the third of four movements in the series, following *The SOLDIER'S ART* (1966) and preceding *BOOKS DO FURNISH A ROOM*

(1971). It is the last of the novels that chronicle the experiences of the first-person narrator, Nicholas Jenkins, during WORLD WAR II, and as such it sums up the war's toll on Britain. The grimness of events in *The Soldier's Art*—the destructiveness of the blitzkrieg on London's population and property—continues in *The Military Philosophers* as several of Nick's friends meet violent deaths in war, while the opportunistic Kenneth Widmerpool continues his rise to power and influence.

The story opens in 1942, at the height of the war. Nicholas had transferred to a branch of the army working with underground resistance in several European countries at the end of *The Soldier's Art:* His work in England is primarily administrative in nature, but it is deadly enough on the battlefronts. At first he serves as a liaison officer to the Poles, who are headquartered in his uncle's former London home, the Ufford Hotel. Nick's work continually brings him into contact with old friends, such as Sunny Farebrother and Peter Templar, one of his best friends from his days in PUBLIC SCHOOL and university. His best friend, Charles Stringham, has recovered from a long bout of alcoholism and shipped out as an enlisted man for the Far East. On routine business, Nick meets Stringham's niece Pamela Flitton, now a beautiful young woman of easy virtue and voracious sexual appetite; Pamela has news that Stringham has been captured in the fall of Singapore (a historical event chronicled in the autobiographical novel of J. G. BALLARD, *EMPIRE OF THE SUN*).

Nicholas is promoted to the supervision of the Belgians and the Czechs; he continues to encounter familiar faces in unfamiliar roles. Pamela has a short affair with Peter Templar, once a renowned ladies' man, but now oddly dejected and fatalistic about his future. She then turns to Odo Stevens, another old acquaintance of Nick's, and Nick is present when a quarrel breaks up the affair. Nick is promoted again, and for the first time his duties take him to Europe, where he tours Normandy and Belgium. He meets Bob Duport, the man who had been married to Nick's first love, Jean Duport, sister of Peter Templar, and he learns that Templar has been killed in a covert operation in the Balkans. By now it is 1944, and the end of the war—and the victory of the Allies in Europe—is in sight.

Back in London, Nick learns that Pamela Flitton has inexplicably become engaged to Widmerpool, who now influences policymakers in Whitehall at the highest levels. As the war is winding down, Pamela makes a scene and accuses Widmerpool of murder by knowingly sending Templar to his death. With the fall of Berlin and the celebration of Victory in Europe Day, Nick attends a memorial service at St. Paul's Cathedral, where he sees Jean Duport, now the wife of Flores, a colonel in the army of a Latin American country; ironically, Nick does not recognize his former flame.

By this point in the story, POWELL'S series is so rich with characters, places, and incidents that passing references are laden with significance from earlier encounters in the course of Nick's life. The poignancy of the deaths of Templar and Stringham is partly due to the long connections readers have had with them as they developed from boyhood to young manhood and maturity. The mere presence of Widmerpool is cause for alarm, since he has shown himself to be capable of anything other than nobility of character. The tumultuous joy of the war's ending is tempered by its staggering cost in lives, and Powell is able to emphasize this cost through the loss of Nick's dear old friends and the questionable natures of the new acquaintances he makes. Recovering from the war will require a long and peaceful period of healing; Powell provides that interlude in the opening of *Books Do Furnish a Room* as Nick settles down to study Burton's *Anatomy of Melancholy*.

BIBLIOGRAPHY

Frost, Laurie Adams. *Reminiscent Scrutinies: Memory in Anthony Powell's* A Dance to the Music of Time. Troy, N.Y.: Whitson Publishing Co., 1990.

Joyau, Isabelle. *Understanding Powell's* A Dance to the Music of Time. New York: St. Martin's Press, 1994.

Selig, Robert L. *Time and Anthony Powell.* Cranbury, N.J.: Associated University Presses, 1991.

Spurling, Hillary. *Invitation to the Dance: A Guide to Anthony Powell's* A Dance to the Music of Time. Boston: Little, Brown, 1977.

MILLSTONE, THE MARGARET DRABBLE (1966)

Published in the United States as *Thank You All Very Much,* this novel examines the options available to contemporary women through the life of its first-person narrator, Rosamund Stacey, who is happy in the dry academic world and pleased to be an independent and modern young woman. As a graduate student in a literature department, Rosamund is immersed in her study of the Elizabethan sonnet. The poetic form she studies devotes itself to love, but in her life Rosamund is on the verge of empty emotional sterility: She dates men, but she cannot establish a permanent bond with the men she knows, and she is afraid of sex in an era that has been granted unprecedented license by the invention of the birth control pill. Rosamund finally encounters a man as unthreatening as she is and allows herself a one-night fling only to discover she has become pregnant from this, the only sexual experience in her life.

The emotional connection to another person Rosamund had longed for grows not from a romantic attachment to a man but from her maternal attachment to her daughter, Octavia. Rosamund loves her daughter as any married woman would; her experience makes an interesting contrast to the heartless single mother of *GEORGY GIRL,* who has substituted casual sex for maternal bonding. Many women will recognize the way that Drabble's heroine fears the sexual freedom that began to become common in the 1960s, and also the way she becomes a new human being through her experience of motherhood. Octavia is born with a defective heart, mirroring her mother's crippled emotional powers. But in saving her daughter by placing this fragile human life ahead of her own ambitions, concerns, and preoccupations, Rosamund also saves herself and becomes reintegrated into the human community by allowing herself to depend on others. Her satisfaction and fulfillment are completely unexpected and yet also completely natural. Implicitly, Drabble's story points out that the role of women in the world cannot merely be an imitation of the traditional masculine pursuit of success: There is much more at stake, and without a serious examination of family responsibilities, gender inequities cannot be resolved.

BIBLIOGRAPHY

Myer, Valerie Grosvenor. *Margaret Drabble: Puritanism and Permissiveness.* London: Vision Press, 1974.

Roxman, Susanna. *Guilt and Glory: Studies in Margaret Drabble's Novels 1963–1980.* Stockholm: Almquist & Wiksell, 1984.

Sadler, Lynn Veach. *Margaret Drabble.* Twayne's English Authors, 417. Boston: Twayne, 1986.

Stovel, Nora Foster. *Margaret Drabble: Symbolic Moralist.* San Bernardino, Calif.: Borgo Press, 1989.

MISTRY, ROHINTON (1952–)

Born in the Parsi community of Bombay (now Mumbai), India, Rohinton Mistry has lived in Canada since 1975; he immigrated there upon completing his studies for a bachelor of science degree at the University of Bombay. In Canada, Mistry pursued a bachelor of arts degree at the University of Toronto (conferred in 1984) and found employment as a banker in Toronto while he worked on his fiction in his spare time. Since 1985, he has devoted himself to his writing full-time. His first publication was a collection of short stories, *Tales from Firozsha Baag* (1987; published in the United States as *Swimming Lessons, and Other Stories from Firozsha Baag*). His first novel appeared in 1991, *Such a Long Journey;* it received the Canadian Governor General's Award for that year and the Commonwealth Writer's Prize for 1992. The novel also became the basis of a film adaptation and was named to the BOOKER PRIZE short list. It is characteristic of Mistry's work to date, taking an ordinary Indian citizen as protagonist and placing him in the context of contemporary life in independent INDIA—specifically, the struggles with Pakistan in the 1960s and the independence of Bangladesh from Pakistan in 1971. Mistry's second novel, *A FINE BALANCE* (1996), was also named to the Booker Prize short list and continues the approach of creating a world of characters coping with life in modern India. Mistry's third novel, *Family Matters,* was published in 2002 and was nominated for the JAMES TAIT BLACK MEMORIAL PRIZE (won that year by Jonathan Franzen's *The Corrections*).

Mistry is generally regarded to be among the finest writers developing fiction in English about India, writing stories that are as vivid and compelling as is the work of Salman Rushdie, although Mistry's style also shows the more traditional influence of Charles Dickens, preferring the daily drama of ordinary lives to the self-consciousness of POSTMODERNISM. He continues to live and write in Toronto.

BIBLIOGRAPHY
Leckie, Barbara. *Rohinton Mistry.* Toronto: ECW Press, 1995.

MITFORD, NANCY (1904–1973)

Born into the English aristocracy on November 28, 1904, Nancy Mitford was the eldest of the famous Mitford sisters. Daughters of David Bertram Ogilvy, the second Baron Redesdale, the girls grew up intimately connected to the political pressures that preceded WORLD WAR II, because their parents strongly supported the British Union of Fascists under the leadership of Oswald Mosley (the historical figure who provides the approximate model for Lord Darlington in *The REMAINS OF THE DAY* by Kazuo ISHIGURO). Two of the sisters, Diana and Unity, followed their parents' political bent: Diana became the wife of Mosley, and Unity traveled to Germany, where she met Adolf Hitler and other members of his government whose names have since become infamous. Nancy and Jessica Mitford moved to the other end of the political spectrum as socialists; they both also became writers. A selection from Jessica Mitford's nonfiction work *The American Way of Death* is frequently anthologized in undergraduate composition texts.

Nancy Mitford lived the kind of life vividly described in *A BUYER'S MARKET* by Anthony POWELL: She entered adult society as a debutante during the early 1920s as one of the "bright young things" satirized by Evelyn WAUGH and Aldous HUXLEY. In London, she socialized with bohemian artists and writers as well as aristocrats and other members of the upper class. Following the example of her literary friends, she published a novel. *Highland Fling* appeared in 1931, the first of many works that, at their best, have been compared with the gently comic and pragmatically romantic style of Jane Austen. In 1935, Mitford published *Wigs on the Green,* a satirical look at her sisters' involvement with fascism. Her two most enduring works are *The PURSUIT OF LOVE* (1945) and *LOVE IN A COLD CLIMATE* (1949); these wry comedies feature the same narrator and are generally read together. After 1949, Mitford turned increasingly to nonfiction, writing biographies, histories, essays, and sociological examinations of the

English aristocracy. She was a prolific letter writer, and many of her correspondents were professional writers or other notable figures. Two volumes of her letters appeared during the 1990s, one devoted to her correspondence with Evelyn Waugh. Nancy Mitford died on June 30, 1973.

BIBLIOGRAPHY

Carpenter, Humphrey. *The Brideshead Generation.* London: Faber & Faber, 1989.

Hastings, Selina. "The Pursuit of Nancy Mitford." In *Essays by Divers Hands: Being the Transactions of the Royal Society of Literature.* Edited by Richard Faber. Wolfeboro, N.H.: Boydell, 1988, 91–102.

Lovell, Mary S. *The Sisters: The Saga of the Mitford Family.* New York: W. W. Norton, 2001.

MO, TIMOTHY (1950–)

Born on December 30, 1950, in Hong Kong when it was securely in British possession, Timothy Peter Mo was the son of a British mother and a Chinese father. In 1960, the parents relocated to England and sent their son to a college preparatory school. Timothy Mo then matriculated at St. John's College, Oxford, completing his undergraduate degree in 1971. He worked as a journalist, writing book reviews and covering boxing matches; he himself was a bantamweight boxer. His first novel, *The Monkey King,* appeared in 1978 and won the Geoffrey Faber Memorial Prize in the next year. In 1982, his second novel, Sour Sweet, was short-listed for the Booker Prize and the Whitbread Award but won the Hawthornden Prize. Both of these novels focus on the differences between the cultures of the East and the West, using a comic touch to examine how his characters cope with displacement into alien worlds. Mo shifted his strategy for his third novel, *An Insular Possession,* writing a work of Historical fiction but using some of the self-referential techniques of Postmodernism. The story is set during the struggle between British and the Chinese during the First Opium War of 1839–42 but views both sides through the eyes of a young American couple. Mo has continued to write, publishing three additional novels by the end of the century.

BIBLIOGRAPHY

Ho, Elaine Yee Lin. *Timothy Mo.* Manchester, U.K.: Manchester University Press, 2000.

Ramraj, Victor. "The Interstices and Overlaps of Cultures." *International Literature in English: Essays on the Major Writers.* Edited by Robert L. Ross. Garland Reference Library of the Humanities, Vol. 1,159. New York: Garland, 1991, 475–485.

Vlitos, Paul. "Timothy Mo." *World Writers in English Volume 1: Chinua Achebe to V. S. Naipaul.* Edited by Jay Parini. New York: Scribner, 2004, 307–324.

MODERNISM

The tension between traditionalism and originality—between imitation and innovation—has a long and distinguished history in literature. From time to time, some new school of thought arises and sets itself apart from it predecessors, sometimes to the accompaniment of howls of indignation. Jonathan Swift's *The Battle of the Books* (1697) records (and satirizes) one such literary fracas; William Wordsworth's "Preface" to the second edition of *Lyrical Ballads* (1800) proclaims—without satirical commentary—the separation of a new poetic style from the conventions then dominating poetic composition; and, in the early 20th century, Wyndham Lewis proclaimed a new artistic spirit in his two-issue periodical *Blast.* Where the proponents of a new style also maintain that their approach is superior to the old, a dust-up on the printed page is almost inevitable—and who would follow a new style if it weren't superior, or stick with an old style without confidence in its merit as well as its longevity? Human beings compete to be held in the highest esteem by their peers in literature just as in other spheres of endeavor.

Modernism is the result of a discontinuity in artistic conventions that arose in the second half of the 19th century and affected the arts of painting, literature, music, theater, and other genres. It is generally characterized by the importance of experimentation with conventions of form and by expanded definitions of acceptable subjects for content. In literature, modernism is associated with experiments in point of view (particularly stream-of-consciousness narration), alterations of the conventions of syntax and punctuation, and innovations in the use of extraliterary materials in extreme cases (song lyrics, bits of news) to create the effect of a narrative collage. Additionally, as the 20th century began, writers experimented with content, drawing increasingly on sympathetic working-CLASS protagonists and using the entire range of human experience—including sexual experience—as sources of narrative. Concepts drawn from the theories of Sigmund Freud and Carl Jung became particularly influential.

English literary modernism is generally dated from 1914, when WORLD WAR I began, but scholars vary as to when it ended, some placing the terminus as the beginning of the GREAT DEPRESSION and others placing it at the end of the DIMINISHING AGE, 1965. Important modernist figures, some of whom were innovators in form and some in content, include Dorothy RICHARDSON, Virginia WOOLF, James JOYCE, D. H. LAWRENCE, Aldous HUXLEY, Evelyn WAUGH, Somerset MAUGHAM, Graham GREENE, and Joyce CARY. Literary modernism is preceded by the EDWARDIAN ERA and followed by the work of the ANGRY YOUNG MEN.

The modernist narrative becomes more sharply focused on the interior landscape of a protagonist, following from Henry JAMES'S detailed and absorbing examinations of his characters' mental and emotional lives. As an account of interiority, a modernist literary work is less interested in and committed to either the contexts in which characters are placed or the historical processes that brought about those contexts. Critics of modernism focus on the solipsism of characters' interior lives and on the anticommunal and antihistorical aspects of modernist texts. The interior life of modernist literary characters is frequently an alienated one, and the disconnection from context and history can produce AMBIGUITY or INDETERMINACY in the construction and resolution of the PLOT. Advocates of modernism see these effects as strengths, while detractors see instead weaknesses.

BIBLIOGRAPHY

Bradbury, Malcolm. *Modernism: 1890–1930*. Harmondsworth, U.K.: Penguin, 1976.

Kramer, Hilton. "Modernism and Its Institutions," *New Criterion* 22, no. 2 (October 2002): 4+.

Thormählen, Marianne, ed. *Rethinking Modernism*. Basingstoke, U.K.: Palgrave Macmillan, 2003.

MOLLOY SAMUEL BECKETT (1951)

Although Samuel BECKETT'S reputation as a dramatist of absurdity—most notably for *Waiting for Godot*—dwarfs all other aspects of his literary creativity, he wrote several novels that have received serious attention from literary scholars. Like his plays, these novels exploit absurdity, AMBIGUITY, and INDETERMINACY to create works of literature that are simultaneously compelling and yet elusive. His most noted novels form a loose trilogy: *Molloy*, MALONE DIES (1951), and *The* UNNAMABLE (1953).

Molloy bears some similarities to *Waiting for Godot:* It consists of two parts that are strikingly similar and yet distinctly different. In chapter one, readers meet Molloy, a disoriented and marginalized old man who has returned to his mother's room; in chapter two, they meet Jacques Moran, who receives an assignment to search for Molloy. Molloy is writing out his story under compulsion; by the end of his fruitless adventures, Moran writes out his story, too. Molloy has lost his ability to walk, and his crutches and his bicycle are important parts of his story; Moran is nearly crippled by the time he begins writing, and both crutches and a bicycle have figured in his journey. Before Molloy returned to his mother's room, he witnessed two men from a distance as they had a brief encounter; Moran encounters another man as he searches for Molloy. Molloy has a complicated relationship with an old widow, Lousse; Moran has a complicated relationship with his son, also named Jacques Moran. Molloy obsesses over his "sucking stones," devising elaborate schemes for their rotation; Moran obsesses over the wearing of his shirt. Molloy is uncertain who has brought him to his mother's room and ordered him to write his story; at the opposite extreme, Moran is employed by Youdi and receives his commands from Gaber, Youdi's messenger.

Beckett's novel stands up under numerous critical approaches without yielding all its secrets. Readers taking a Freudian approach emphasize Molloy's attachment to his mother and his return to the room/womb; his immobile condition resembles the condition of the infant who has not yet learned to walk. In Moran's part of the story, the protagonist relates to a son rather than a mother, suggesting some Oedipal connection. From a philosophical perspective, both Molloy and Moran seem to be trapped in existential angst, committed to meaningless actions in a manner similar to Sisyphus's endless rolling of his boulder uphill. Some readers see "Youdi" as a version of Yahweh and "Gaber" as a truncation of Gabriel; Moran receives his instructions from God and tries to act on them, even though the process of doing so seems to drain away his life. Beckett's novel accommodates these and other interpretations, but those interpretations do not exhaust its possibilities. As a work of art, *Molloy* appears to be resistant to definitive explication, suggesting that literature and criticism really are different enterprises, and that the relationship between them is a hierarchical one, with the literary text in ascendancy to the criticism of it.

BIBLIOGRAPHY

O'Hara, J. D., ed. *Twentieth Century Views of* Molloy, Malone Dies, *and* The Unnamable. Englewood Cliffs, N.J.: Prentice Hall, 1980.

Pilling, John. *The Cambridge Companion to Beckett.* Cambridge: Cambridge University Press, 1994.

Rabinovitz, Rubin. *Innovation in Samuel Beckett's Fiction.* Urbana: University of Illinois Press, 1992.

MONARCHY A form of government in which power is concentrated in the hands of a single ruler who makes decisions and dispenses laws is a monarchy; the designated ruler may be chosen by some form of election or may acquire the position by the default of inheritance. The British monarchy—an inherited position that has from time to time been realigned by force, by the failure to produce heirs, and by an act of Parliament—is one of the oldest governmental institutions in the Western world, although in its contemporary form it is more culturally and historically symbolic than politically functional. From early times, monarchic government in England coexisted with the rights of various claimants: the Magna Carta ("Great Charter") first limited the king's prerogative in 1215 under the rule of King John I; wealthy landed barons were the beneficiaries of this document, but slowly the protection of rights spread to wider segments of the population, and the power of the monarch was correspondingly circumscribed.

In the 20th century, two dynasties have occupied the British throne: the House of Hanover and the House of Windsor. As the century began, Queen Victoria ruled in the final years of her life as the last representative of the House of Hanover. She was a descendant of George I (1714–27), the founder of the Hanoverian line who succeeded Queen Anne, a descendant of the Stuarts, by an act of Parliament designed to restrict the crown to a Protestant line of inheritance. George I and George II (1727–60) were German by birth and by language, but with George III (1760–1820; the person about whom the American Declaration of Independence complained so bitterly), the House of Hanover became native to England. George IV (1820–30) ruled as regent during parts of his father's life, lending his title to a historical period—the Regency era of the late 18th and early 19th centuries. At the end of the brief reign of William IV (1830–37), a son of George IV, the crown passed to Victoria, the niece of the deceased king. Queen Victoria reigned from 1837 until 1901 and gave her name to the century in which most of her life occurred. During her long reign, the monarchy became the largely symbolic institution that it is today; without her determination, it might have disappeared entirely.

In 1901, Albert Edward Saxe-Coburg-Gotha, the eldest son and second child of Queen Victoria and Prince Albert, ascended the throne as Edward VII and ruled until 1910. Prince Albert had presaged in his youth the new and freer directions that cultural values would take after the death of Queen Victoria. Known popularly as "Bertie," Albert Edward was born on November 9, 1841, and was named Prince of Wales shortly afterward. As a boy he showed little interest in scholarship, but he was the first British monarch to pursue his studies to the college level. He attended both Oxford and Cambridge Universities during the period from 1859 to 1861 without taking a degree, but after a scandal with an actress in 1861, his parents determined that he should marry soon. Princess Alexandra, daughter of the heir to the Danish throne, was selected as a suitable match, but the death of Prince Albert in 1861 delayed the union until 1863. Edward and Alexandra produced five children: two sons, Albert Victor (Duke of Clarence, 1864–92) and George (Duke of York, Prince of Wales, and King George V, 1865–1936), and three daughters, Maud (Queen of Norway), Louise Victoria (Princess Royal and Duchess of Fife), and Princess Victoria.

The long period between Edward's marriage and his coronation in 1901 was marked by numerous scandals that brought the Prince of Wales into courtrooms as a witness. Queen Victoria withheld political power from her son because of these examples of poor judgment, but the prince attained a widespread popularity nonetheless through his personal charm and social skills. He enjoyed the pageantry of diplomatic visits and ceremonial occasions, so he was an effective figurehead for the state. As king he supported reforms in the navy and army, advocated racial and religious tolerance, founded the Order of Merit, adopted the newfangled automobile, and set standards of taste for the era that has been named after him.

The second son of Edward VII succeeded him as George V (1910–36), the eldest son having died in 1892. George had served in the Royal Navy until his older brother's death placed him in the direct line to inherit the throne. The following year, he married his late brother's fiancée, Princess Mary of Teck, and in 1901 he acquired the title Prince of Wales when his father inherited the throne. He then succeeded his father in 1910; coronation ceremonies were held on June 22, 1911.

The reign of George V occurred during some of the most disastrous years of the 20th century, including the carnage of WORLD WAR I and the economic hardship of the GREAT DEPRESSION. As king, George was politically active, involved in and influencing crucial decision making with respect to Parliament, cabinet posts, and the selection of prime ministers. He made extensive visits to the battlefield during the war, thereby earning the respect of his forces and of his countrymen. In response to anti-German sentiment during World War I, in 1917 George V officially abandoned the royal family's German name in favor of "Windsor," the name of one of the chief palaces of the British monarch. In spite of illness during the last eight years of his life, he remained politically active in the nation's government. As a constitutional monarch, his influence depended on his personal skills as a negotiator and statesman rather than on any real authority assigned to the crown.

Upon the death of George V in 1936, the late king's eldest son became Edward VIII, but he held the crown for less than a year, abdicating on December 10, 1936, to his next brother when it became apparent that his intended wife, the American divorcée Wallis Warfield Simpson, was unacceptable as the consort of a British king. This event was a scandal of huge proportions because no previous British king had ever voluntarily repudiated the throne. The former king became the Duke of Windsor and then married the woman for whom he had surrendered a throne in 1937 in Paris, where the couple continued to live (except for 1940–45, when they resided in the Bahamas). Virtual exiles from the royal family until the 1960s, the Duke and Duchess of Windsor traveled widely, becoming noted arbiters of style. Edward died in Paris in 1972 and was buried at Windsor Castle; in 1986, the Duchess of Windsor died and was buried beside him. The scandal over the abdication was a key event for the monarchy; the literature of the period frequently makes reference to it or to Mrs. Simpson with fictional conversations reflecting the passions aroused by the prospect of an American as queen of England.

The second son of George V and the younger brother of Edward VIII, George VI became king on December 10, 1936. He had already served in the Royal Navy and the new Royal Air Force (1913–19) and had attended Trinity College at Cambridge for a year, and in 1923 he had married Lady Elizabeth Bowes-Lyon, later the Queen Mother. Their two daughters, Elizabeth and Margaret, were then young girls. George suffered from a severe stutter—a serious handicap in an age of live radio broadcasting of speeches. But during the bombing of England in WORLD WAR II, George and Elizabeth gained the love and admiration of the British people when they chose to remain in London rather than to seek safe shelter elsewhere. Like many Londoners, they sent their children away to safety, but they stayed through the blitzkrieg and frequently toured bombed sites, comforting those who had lost homes and loved ones and standing firm as symbols of British determination to resist Hitler's onslaught. After the war, George VI became the first monarch of the COMMONWEALTH of Nations that developed from the old British EMPIRE. His health declined after 1948, and he died of lung cancer in 1952. His daughter succeeded him to the throne as Elizabeth II, and his wife, Elizabeth, one of the most beloved and popular members of the royal family, lived past the age of 100, maintaining an active public role as Queen Mother to the end of her life in 2002.

The daughter of George VI, the niece of Edward VIII, the granddaughter of Edward VII, and the great-granddaughter of Queen Victoria, Elizabeth Alexandra Mary Windsor was born on April 21, 1926, while her uncle was king. She was proclaimed the nation's monarch upon her father's death, and her accession to the throne was formalized with a grand coronation ceremony on June 2, 1953—the first to be broadcast on television. She had married Philip Mountbatten in November 1947, and the royal couple produced four children: Prince Charles (b. 1948), Princess Anne (b. 1950), Prince Andrew (b. 1960), and Prince Edward (b. 1964). The royal family continues to use the name Windsor, but those members not holding the title of prince or princess use the name Mountbatten-Windsor. Elizabeth and Philip's eldest son Charles, the Prince of Wales, is the heir apparent to the British throne.

Elizabeth has traveled extensively to all parts of the British Commonwealth and much of the rest of the world during her reign, always appearing composed, dignified, and regal. Her personal touch has increased the popularity of the monarchy: she walks out among crowds of well-wishers to shake hands, her invitations to social and ceremonial events reach across all classes of the population, and her prime ministers generally praise her knowledge of domestic and international affairs. During the reign, the honors of aristocratic titles have been extended to icons of popular culture such as rock stars and actors. She has expanded the participation of the royal family in the ceremonial duties of the monarchy, continuing to use her father's metaphor for the family, "The Firm."

This expansion has not been without its drawbacks: The greater public exposure of her children and grandchildren has generated considerable fascination with their private lives in the tabloid press, especially the marriages of Prince Charles and Lady Diana Spencer and of Prince Andrew and Sarah Ferguson. The monarchy has been besieged by scandal as unhappy royal marriages multiplied, with the queen explicitly urging Charles and Diana to divorce in 1995 (the divorce was finalized in 1996). The death of Diana in 1997 was another crisis for Queen Elizabeth, and in response to a public outcry she addressed the nation on television prior to the funeral to commemorate the life of her former daughter-in-law.

Although the governing power of the British monarch had declined steadily, especially during the 19th and early 20th centuries, the work of the monarch as a national representative increased proportionately. At the beginning of the century, King Edward VII spent about a month's time out of a year engaged in official duties, while at century's end Elizabeth II sponsors more than 700 societies and is perpetually in demand for public appearances. The future of the monarchy remains a question of keen interest in Great Britain, becoming a matter of national debate from time to time.

BIBLIOGRAPHY

Bradford, Sarah. *The Reluctant King: The Life and Reign of George VI, 1895–1952.* New York: St. Martin's Press, 1989.

Donaldson, Frances. *Edward VIII: A Biography of the Duke of Windsor.* Philadelphia: Lippincott, 1975.

Flamini, Roland. *Sovereign: Elizabeth II and the Windsor Dynasty.* New York: Delacorte Press, 1991.

Pearson, John. *The Selling of the Royal Family: The Mystique of the British Monarchy.* New York: Simon & Schuster, 1986.

Rose, Kenneth. *King George V.* New York: Knopf, 1983.

Weintraub, Stanley. *Edward the Caresser: The Playboy Prince Who Became Edward VII.* Detroit: Free Press, 2001.

Wilson, A. N. *The Rise and Fall of the House of Windsor.* New York: W. W. Norton, 1993.

MONEY: A SUICIDE NOTE   MARTIN AMIS (1984)

The first-person narrator of this novel, the Englishman John Self, is a vulgarian who longs for moneyed refinement and yet lacks the will, the ability, and the skills to achieve it. He is a director of raunchy television commercials, but he is trying to elevate himself to the ranks of film directors, and so he searches for the funding to create his presumed masterpiece, entitled *Money*. Self's name symbolizes the source of his problems and frustrations: He epitomizes the voracious, appetite-driven, and pleasure-addicted id. He lacks the education, talent, and discipline that would enable him to fulfill his grand ambitions. His knowledge of literature is so incomplete, in fact, that he does not recognize the many allusions to Shakespeare—and particularly to *Othello*—that litter the novel. Like the duped Roderigo of that play, Self is caught up in other people's games. He actually dares to think of himself as an artist; instead of creating and inventing, however, he devotes himself to alcohol and sex, substituting busy unceasing activity for genuine achievement. Nonetheless, John Self manages to charm readers: Like many of us, he is just trying to have a good time in a world that keeps pleasure—especially in its most intense forms—under tight control. Despite his potbelly, the "bad rug" on his head, and his raging abscessed tooth, Self is recognizably human and clearly the product of a world in which greed, materialism, consumerism, and self-indulgence are out of control.

John Self jets back and forth between London and New York in pursuit of his goals and dreams. These two cities become the twin centers of greed, which have trapped him in frantic orbit. He is tormented by his love for the unfaithful Selina Street, and this love forms a festering, touchy sore spot in his chaotic life. His 26-year-old producer, Fielding Goodney, is an unflappable Californian amalgamated out of Teflon and vast inherited wealth. Goodney—his name is ironic—invisibly dominates Self's progress toward the goal of financing his film and eventually dupes Self in an underhanded financial scam. Famous film stars just past their prime are eager to attach themselves to Self's movie and to monopolize his time in endless self-promoting telephone calls. Through it all, Self immerses himself in drink and sex in an endless effort either to find bliss or to anesthetize his existence without it.

The novel takes a distinctly postmodern (see POSTMODERNISM) turn when Self hires a writer named Martin Amis to revise the screenplay of *Money*. Rather than maintaining control of his art, Self is trying to accommodate the conflicting ego-driven demands of his actors, who in turn are serving their own agendas in demanding alterations to their parts. Martin Amis (the character—but necessarily also the author) engages Self in long conversations about protagonists, realism, and irony; eventually his rewrite of *Money* succeeds in satisfying the demands (and the vanity) of the actors, thereby thwarting some of Goodney's callous and malevolent plans for Self's movie. Fixing the script, however, is a far cry from fixing the conditions that have produced the Fielding Goodneys of the world. Self is so changed by his experiences that the font representing his words changes to italics at the end of the novel.

The greatest attraction of this novel is the distinctive voice of a narrator who lacks the guile to disguise his unappealing characteristics. Like Philip Roth's Portnoy in *Portnoy's Complaint,* the narrator's frankness is compelling even when it is sordid. The narrative gushes forth, mirroring the frantic pace of Self's hectic life and revealing more than its originator intends to show. Martin Amis displays his characteristic lushness and inventiveness in the words he piles on to construct the world of Self—the novel is full of word play, allusions, puns, and convoluted syntax. It is a banquet fit for lovers of language, as intoxicating to them as booze is to John Self.

BIBLIOGRAPHY

Dern, John A. *Martians, Monsters, and Madonna: Fiction and Form in the World of Martin Amis.* New York: Peter Lang, 1999.

Diedrick, James. *Understanding Martin Amis.* Understanding Contemporary British Literature. Columbia: University of South Carolina Press, 1995.

MONTH IN THE COUNTRY, A   J. L. CARR (1980)

A quietly COMIC NOVEL fashioned as a pastoral elegy, this text was short-listed for the BOOKER PRIZE the year it was published. The setting of the story is the English village of Oxgodby in Yorkshire, and the protagonist, who also serves as the first-person narrator, is a former soldier still suffering from shell shock after the war, Tom Birkin. He recalls the events of his youth from many years later, thus giving the novel its unusual mix of the comic and the elegiac.

Birkin has taken a job uncovering a tempera wall painting in an ancient Yorkshire church. While he works, he lives in the belfry of the church. In the nearby pasture, Charles Moon, another veteran whose war experiences had gone a very different route, is doing another kind of uncovering, searching for an ancient tomb. Both projects have been set in motion by the bequest made in the will of an eccentric spinster. As Birkin peels back the grime and plaster of five centuries, and as Moon scrapes at the ground in the pasture, following his own purposes, the two men also relive the events of their lives that have brought them to this rural village. Their respective tasks serve perfectly as metaphors for their psychological quest.

Within days, the curious villagers begin to drop by, and soon Birkin is virtually a member of the Methodist Ellerbeck family. But when he meets Alice, the beautiful young wife of the Reverend Keach, his supervisor, Birkin finds himself unexpectedly in love—hopelessly in love. As the idyllic summer ambles onward, and as his restoration and Moon's excavations move toward completion, Birkin begins to be healed of the many wounds that life has inflicted on him. The two projects turn out to have an unexpected connection that explains a mystery Birkin uncovers, but the novel's real crux is what Birkin learns about himself.

J. L. Carr was a painter as well as a writer, and his knowledge of church architecture and ornamentation deepens the story's realism and rounds Birkin into a fully developed character. The author avoids the obvious choice and the stereotypical outline; even though he is dealing in the familiar materials of ordinary life, he outfits his story with a melancholy charm that never fails to please.

BIBLIOGRAPHY

Allen, Brooke. Review of *A Month in the Country. Atlantic Monthly* 287, no. 3 (March 2001): 92.

Holroyd, Michael. Introduction to *A Month in the Country.* J. L. Carr. 1980. New York: New York Review Books, 2000.

MOON AND SIXPENCE, THE W. SOMERSET MAUGHAM (1919)

Loosely inspired by the life of the French postimpressionist artist Paul Gauguin, this novel follows the progress of Charles Strickland as he transforms himself from a middle-CLASS London stockbroker, husband, and father into an impoverished Parisian art student and finally into a recluse in Tahiti, painting masterpieces to please himself rather than to earn a living. The story is presented from the first-person point of view of an objective narrator who describes people and events in scrupulous detail without passing judgment on them. It forms a bridge between the author's first novel, *OF HUMAN BONDAGE,* a BILDUNGSROMAN in a traditional setting, and his later work in unusual or exotic locations.

The most compelling feature of Charles Strickland as a character is his complete indifference to the effect he has on other people's emotional lives. As he places himself in the service of his vision and his gift, he is uniformly destructive to others: He abandons his wife, children, and career in midlife to study painting in Paris, where he destroys the marriage of one of his first admirers, his fellow artist Dirk Stroeve, and contributes to the suicide of Blanche Stroeve by discarding her after he no longer desires her services as a model. He finds a measure of happiness in Tahiti with a 17-year-old native girl who serves as his wife and caretaker without asking anything of him for herself. The single-mindedness of Strickland's selfishness is offset by his devotion to his calling. He does not use his artistic abilities to turn out products for sale to others; he does not paint to please the critics and is in fact indifferent to the critical rejections of his early work. His service to art is so pure that he instructs his Tahitian wife to burn down their hut when he dies, destroying the masterpieces on its walls, and her service to him is so pure that she complies with this request.

The novel's structure falls into three acts determined by setting and unified by the presence of the narrator and the protagonist in each of them. The first part chronicles the upper-middle-class life of London professionals, providing a sympathetic picture of Mrs.

Strickland as a wife, mother, and hostess. She is not a dazzling woman, but she fills her role in life competently. Her settled existence is disrupted when Charles abandons her and goes to Paris, the second setting of Charles's story and the second phase of the novel: Mrs. Strickland thinks her husband has run off with another woman, and she sends the narrator to reason with him and fetch him back to his family. Through the narrator's conversations with Charles in Paris, the depth of Charles's callousness to other human beings is apparent as he describes his indifferent cruelty to his wife and then destroys the Stroeves. In Tahiti, the narrator picks up Charles's story from conversations with those who knew him there, learning of the leprosy that slowly killed him after a period of brilliant painting. In an epilogue, the narrator brings the last news of Charles—the story of his death—to Mrs. Strickland and sees that she has reproductions of Charles's paintings hanging on her walls. She was his first victim, and if anyone has a reason to reject the art that displaced her in Charles's life, she does; nonetheless the mastery of the paintings wins even her admiration.

BIBLIOGRAPHY

Daniels, Anthony. "W. Somerset Maugham: The Pleasures of a Master," *New Criterion* 18, no. 6 (February 2000): 23–28.

Macey, David J. "Fantasy as Necessity: The Role of the Biographer in *The Moon and Sixpence*," *Studies in the Novel* 29, no. 1 (Spring 1997): 61–73.

MOON TIGER PENELOPE LIVELY (1987)

Winner of the BOOKER PRIZE in 1987, *Moon Tiger* recounts the life of historian Claudia Hampton, the protagonist of the novel. The author mixes passages of third-person objective narration about Claudia, who is an elderly woman on her deathbed in the novel's present, with passages of Claudia's own first-person point of view. In her head, she is writing the history of the world and placing the story of her life within it. Old and frail and near death, she cannot know exactly when it will come, but she has the will to continue the work of the living as long as she is alive. Nurses and doctors go about their routines dealing with her physical needs while in her mind her life and the life of the world flashes before her historian's eyes.

One of the highlights of Claudia's life had been a love affair with a tank commander in the deserts of northern Africa during WORLD WAR II. This man, Tom Southern, had kept a journal of his military days and had written to his family about Claudia without ever identifying her by name. LIVELY generates Claudia's memories of this event and its consequences in complex flashbacks. An article Claudia had written about her personal experiences during the war leads Tom's sister to send his journal to Claudia; her reading of it provides a re-creation of the affair and its wartime context through the other participant's perspective. Virtually the last event of Claudia's life is the re-creation of the last days of Tom's life when he was thinking of her and writing a journal with no knowledge of whether she would ever read it.

Penelope Lively draws on her own years in Egypt to capture the British experience there in Claudia's retrospective review of her life and her century. The alternation of third- and first-person narration enables her to avoid the sentimental elements that might be inevitable in an old woman's deathbed thoughts, as does the choice a trained historian as protagonist. The novel's title refers to a coil of incense burned at night to ward off insects and associated in Claudia's mind with Tom—their nights together were sanctified by the smoldering pungent glow. Claudia's heated recollections circle this key relationship in her life that gives meaning to everything else and that emphasizes the role of individuals within the sweep of historical events.

BIBLIOGRAPHY

Moran, Mary Hurley. "Penelope Lively's *Moon Tiger*: A Feminist 'History of the World,' " *Frontiers: A Journal of Women Studies.* 11, no. 2–3 (1990): 89–95.

Raschke, Debrah. "Penelope Lively's *Moon Tiger*: Re-Envisioning a 'History of the World,' " *ARIEL: A Review of International English Literature* 26, no. 4 (October 1995): 115–132.

MOORE, BRIAN (1921–1995)

Born in Belfast, NORTHERN IRELAND, on August 25, 1921, Brian Moore began his education at Catholic schools, but left St. Malachi's College in 1940, when he entered wartime service. During WORLD WAR II, he traveled widely in Europe and North Africa, and afterward he lived and worked in Poland and Scandinavia. In 1948, he immigrated to Canada and settled in Montreal to work as a journalist. He wrote formulaic dime-store novels to eke out a living, but established his reputation as a serious writer with the publication of *The Lonely Passion of Judith Hearne* in 1955. Retaining his Canadian citizenship, Moore moved to the United States in 1955. A Guggenheim Fellowship in 1959 allowed him to finish *The Luck of Ginger Coffey,* a study of an Irish immigrant in Montreal who fails to fulfill the dreams that drew him away from his homeland. The novel is admired for its vivid portrait of Montreal and draws some of its power from the author's projection into it of his own fear of becoming an Irish failure.

Moore's novel *The Great Victorian Collection* won the James Tait Black Memorial Prize in 1975. It tells the story of Tony Maloney, whose intense dreams bring a collection of Victorian artifacts into existence in a California parking lot and who subsequently becomes the victim of his own dreaming, revealing the shallowness of material culture and the helplessness of imagination to deliver us from it. Three of Moore's novels were short-listed for the Booker Prize: *The Doctor's Wife* (1976), centering on an adulterous affair; *The Color of Blood* (1987), about Catholicism and communism in the declining days of Russian influence over the Soviet Bloc; and *Lies of Silence* (1990), examining Irish terrorism instigated by the Irish Republican Army. The latter two novels demonstrate a marked shift in Moore's writing, since they are thrillers that examine contemporary political issues. Moore also wrote a noted historical adventure novel, *Black Robe* (1985), adapting it as a screenplay in 1991, and he wrote television and movie scripts, including the screenplay for Alfred Hitchcock's political thriller *Torn Curtain* (1966).

Although his later works seem to have been tailored for a mass audience, and although he continued to draw praise from critics, Moore never produced a best seller. His 19 serious novels skillfully revisit themes of Irishness, expatriation, sexual desire, Catholicism, ambition, imagination, and fear of failure, and his sensitive portrayals of women's inner lives demonstrate keen psychological insight. Moore remained an active writer until his death in 1999.

BIBLIOGRAPHY

Dahlie, Hallvard. *Brian Moore.* Twayne's World Authors, 632. Boston: Twayne, 1981.

O'Donoghue, Jo. *Brian Moore: A Critical Study.* Montreal: McGill-Queen's University Press, 1991.

Sampson, Dennis. *Brian Moore: The Chameleon Novelist.* Dublin: Marino Books, 1998.

Sullivan, Robert. *A Matter of Faith: The Fiction of Brian Moore.* Westport, Conn.: Greenwood Press, 1996.

MOOR'S LAST SIGH, THE SALMAN RUSHDIE (1995)

A large novel of epic scope, *The Moor's Last Sigh* is the story of Moraes Zogoiby, fourth child and only son of Aurora da Gama and Abraham Zogoiby. Moraes is familiarly known as "the Moor"; his family blends East and West, with roots in the Muslim, Christian, and Jewish religions. On his mother's side, the da Gamas trace their lineage back to Vasco da Gama, the Portuguese explorer who first opened a sea route to Asia in 1498; the Zogoibys trace their lineage to the last Moorish king of Granada, Boabdil the unfortunate (el Zogoybi), who was expelled from Spain by Ferdinand and Isabella in 1492, a year generally remembered in the West for another project supported by this busy royal couple, Columbus's voyage across the Atlantic Ocean. According to family traditions on both sides of Moraes' lineage, illicit liaisons with these famous persons produced the Indian families that continue to bear their names. The double family narrative unfolds in Cochin, a city on the western coast of India where Europeans first made contact, and in Bombay, the modern dynamo of Indian culture.

Moraes explores 100 years of history on both sides of his family; in the process, he produces a vast canvas illustrating "Mother India," the name of a popular Hindi film that appeared in 1957, the year Moraes was born. The story of his parents' marriage is structurally important to the symbolism of the story: His mother, Aurora, is an artist who has been enormously popular at some periods of her career, while his father Abraham is a master capitalist who keeps his fortunes afloat in difficult times through extreme measures such as exporting heroin or managing prostitutes and who eventually even sinks to dealing armaments as he helps fund the development of nuclear weapons for the Arab world. In the characters of Abraham and Aurora, Rushdie combines aesthetics and commerce, exploiting the tensions endemic to such a contrastive pair. Although they live together as man and wife, they do so without civil or sacred sanction, since both families opposed the union (just as the Montagus and Capulets opposed their children's love) and no official of state or religion would countenance the marriage. In creating this couple, Rushdie unites numerous pairs of opposites, detailing a vivid picture of the hybrid nature of the modern world, especially the modern Indian world.

In terms of the protagonist's plot, the story follows the search of Moraes for true love on several levels: love of family, love of nation, and love of another person—in his case, the beautiful but treacherous Uma Sarasvati, an artistic rival to his mother. The power of art is a constant support to him, and part of his life is devoted to the quest for some Moorish paintings that, his mother says, will tell him much about his own life. In addition to the role of love and art, RUSHDIE draws on the imaginative conventions of MAGIC REALISM for some of his PLOT turns, and he alludes to other great texts of world literature with erudite familiarity. Although this novel is less challenging than is *The SATANIC VERSES,* it still makes substantial demands on its readers; its storytelling exuberance, however, should sustain the interest of diversely prepared readers.

In the end, Rushdie produces a novel that attempts to survey the vastly complex culture and history of India itself, and in the process he creates a lovingly burnished portrait of the land of his birth that is simultaneously idealized and yet also truthful. The last sigh of Moraes is uttered for the India that Rushdie cherishes, and although it is tinged with melancholy, it is also an expression of guarded optimism for the future, if not for the utterer.

BIBLIOGRAPHY

Rose, Charlie. *"The Moor's Last Sigh."* In *Conversations with Salman Rushdie.* Edited by Michael Reder. Jackson: University of Mississippi Press, 2000, 199–215.

Su, Jung. "Inscribing the Palimpsest: Politics of Hybridity in *The Moor's Last Sigh,*" *Concentric: Literary and Cultural Studies* 29, no. 1 (January 2003): 199–226.

Weiss, Timothy. "At the End of East/West: Myth in Rushdie's *The Moor's Last Sigh,*" *Jouvert: A Journal of Postcolonial Studies* 4, no. 2 (Winter 2000): 47 paragraphs (electronic journal).

MOSLEY, NICHOLAS (1923–)

Author of the 1990 WHITBREAD Book of the Year, HOPEFUL MONSTERS, Nicholas Mosley has been publishing novels since 1951. He was born on June 25, 1923, the son of Oswald Mosley. This connection has had a shaping force in Mosley's life: His father was the founder of the British Union of Fascists. Ironically, while his father spent WORLD WAR II in jail without specific charges against him, Nicholas Mosley spent the war fighting fascism in the British army. He has struggled to cope with the heritage of an infamous father, writing a widely admired two-volume memoir-biography, *Rules of the Game: Sir Oswald and Lady Cynthia Mosley, 1896–1933* (1982) and *Beyond the Pale: Sir Oswald Mosley and Family, 1933–1980* (1983).

Mosley's fiction has been admired for its innovative formal qualities. His subject matter has varied widely, mirroring his own personal and spiritual journey. His first three novels, all published in the 1950s, address the impact of World War II on individuals and on nations. By the end of that decade, he was writing for the Anglican Christian magazine *Prism,* and he turned to nonfiction writing about religious experience for several years. He returned to fiction in 1962; his most notable novel of that decade was *Accident* (1965), the story of a fatal car crash and its effects on those responsible for it, which became the basis of a FILM ADAPTATION directed by Joseph Losey with a screenplay by the noted British playwright Harold Pinter.

Ironically, a car accident left Mosley bedridden for a year in the early 1970s, and he published no fiction for nearly a decade. He returned to fiction with the "Catastrophe Practice" series of five novels: *Catastrophe Practice* (1979), an experimental combination of fiction and drama; *Imago Bird* (1980), about a sex scandal in a renowned family; *Serpent* (1981), about a writer developing the story of the mass suicide of Jews at Masada in A.D. 70; *Judith* (1986), a series of letters from the title character to the main characters of the other books in the series; and *Hopeful Monsters* (1991), which actually accounts for the beginning of the series and presents the panorama of 20th century history as well.

Nicholas Mosley was made a peer in 1966 as the third Baron Ravensdale, and he succeeded to his father's baronetcy in 1980. He continues to live and write in London.

BIBLIOGRAPHY

Mosley, Nicholas. *Efforts at Truth: An Autobiography.* Normal, Ill.: Dalkey Archive Press, 1995.

"Nicholas Mosley Issue," *Review of Contemporary Fiction* 2, no. 2 (1982).

MOUNTOLIVE LAWRENCE DURRELL (1958)

Volume three in THE ALEXANDRIA QUARTET, *Mountolive* differs from its three "siblings," as DURRELL terms JUSTINE, BALTHAZAR, and CLEA, in having a traditional omniscient third-person narrator. The story focuses intensely on the characters previously introduced in the first two volumes of the series, and in his analysis of the thoughts, feelings, and motivations of his characters, Durrell reveals himself to be a deeply insightful observer of the human condition.

The central character of the story is David Mountolive, a remote figure in *Justine* and *Balthazar* seemingly uninvolved in the lives of the Hosnanis and the other Alexandrians so central to the life of the novelist, Darley, who narrates those volumes. During the PLOT action that had been the focus of the first two books, Mountolive was the head of the British embassy to Egypt, a remote and presumably powerful figure of impeccable manners and imperturbable aplomb. In this third volume of the series, however, the story reaches further into the past to reveal his very intimate connection to the Hosnani family: He had spent some months with them when he was new to the diplomatic service, improving his Arabic. Nessim Hosnani became his close friend, and Mountolive even entered into an affair with the mother of Nessim, the brilliant and vivacious Leila. From Nessim's slowly dying, wheelchair-bound father, Mountolive learns the ill-starred history of the Coptic Christians under British rule in Egypt: Misunderstood and distrusted by European Christians, the Copts have become increasingly marginalized in their native land after centuries of service as the nation's educated elite.

With his Arabic perfected, Mountolive is posted to virtually every part of the diplomatic world that has no need for mastery in that language. During these long years, Leila maintains a vigorous correspondence that allows her to live vicariously through Mountolive's experiences, while his long stay with the Hosnanis slowly becomes mythologized in his own memory. Through Leila's tutoring of him in art and literature through her letters, Mountolive is led to contact the novelist Pursewarden to request him to sign a book for Leila. They become friends, sharing their experience of serving in the diplomatic corps—Mountolive as a career officer and Pursewarden as a contract employee. Nessim becomes friends with Pursewarden through Mountolive and provides a valuable social contact when the novelist is posted to Alexandria. As the omniscient narrator follows Pursewarden to Egypt's "European city," scenes that have already been related in *Justine* and *Balthazar* are revisited from yet another perspective. Sometimes Durrell repeats exact passages of dialogue, but readers see the exchange through a completely different perspective unfiltered by Darley's perceptions.

The omniscient narrator also provides a close examination of the complexly motivated courtship of Nessim and Justine. They share a political passion that completely escaped Darley's notice and that drives them to support the violent establishment of a Jewish state in Palestine. As political machinations and diplomatic realignments undermine Mountolive's confidence in himself and in his government, he finally settles for the life of a bureaucratic functionary. His unfolding story provides a deeper perspective on Darley's narration of events and on Balthazar's emendation of that story, but even the objective point of view fails to dispel all the mysteries and ambiguities of Alexandria. Such resolution is impossible, because Mountolive's story is a modern tragedy, telling not of the hero's death or disgrace but of his acquiescence to the workings of an imperfect and sometimes corrupt system that he fails to master.

BIBLIOGRAPHY

Begnal, Michael H., ed. *On Miracle Ground: Essays on the Fiction of Lawrence Durrell.* Cranbury, N.J.: Associated University Presses, 1990.

Friedman, Alan Warren. *Lawrence Durrell and* The Alexandria Quartet: *Art for Love's Sake.* Norman: University of Oklahoma Press, 1970.

MRS. DALLOWAY VIRGINIA WOOLF

(1925) Clarissa Dalloway, an upper-CLASS English wife, is throwing a party on the day chronicled in this novel, and Septimus Smith, a troubled survivor of WORLD WAR I, is reaching the end of his modest abilities to cope with the stresses of modern life. Switching between these two stories, the narrative creates an elegiac picture of a tragically beautiful world that is perpetually dying.

Virginia WOOLF wrote this novel with a vision of caves and tunnels in mind, described in entries later published in the second volume of her diaries. Those excavations would serve to link characters who might, on the surface, appear disconnected. She feared that reviewers would miss the connections between her sane protagonist, Clarissa Dalloway, and the shell-shocked Septimus Warren Smith. Incorporating many of her own experiences with madness into those of Smith, she also projects details from her life and those of family and acquaintances onto Mrs. Dalloway, supporting fictional connections with those that occurred in real life.

The novel began as a short story titled "Mrs. Dalloway in Bond Street," while Woolf also imagined another story featuring an insane protagonist named Septimus Smith who plans an assassination of England's prime minister. When she decided to include both characters in the same novel to represent what she labeled in her diary entry of October 1922 "a study of insanity & suicide," she at first titled the project *The Hours.* That title would be coopted later in the century for a novel, made into an award-winning movie, by American writer Michael Cunningham based on *Mrs. Dalloway,* an indication of the long-lasting effect of Woolf's "mining" for "gold," one way she described in her diary the process of writing the novel. As for her own influences, she had been reading T. S. Eliot's epic

poem "The Wasteland," published by her Hogarth Press and had recently reread James JOYCE's revolutionary novel ULYSSES (1922). Critics note Joyce's influence on the form of Woolf's novel, as well as the fact that her Septimus Smith was called Stephen Daedalus in early notes, and that in drafts Woolf occasionally incorrectly called her female character Sally Seton Molly, like Joyce's characters.

Woolf employs a stream-of-consciousness narrative approach to reveal the thoughts of Clarissa Dalloway in a plot completed in a single 24-hour period. Mrs. Dalloway prepares for a party to be held that evening, where she and her husband, an MP named Richard, will greet important persons. She moves from the past into the present and back again, remembering herself at 18 at home at Bourton. Big Ben strikes the time as she leaves her house to purchase flowers on the morning of her party, contributing to the imagery of existence measured in small bits and pieces that extends throughout the novel. She recalls a verse from William Shakespeare's *Cymbeline* that will also recur: "Fear no more the heat o' the sun / Nor the furious winter's rages." Although for Mrs. Dalloway the verse seems to mean she may shed her fears and look forward to a pleasant evening, when the reader later encounters the verse as Septimus Warren Smith observes the light on the wall of his room, it takes on a far more ominous significance, foreshadowing his eventual suicide.

Smith's story runs parallel to that of Mrs. Dalloway. As she plans her party and enjoys memories of her former love, Peter Walsh, whose marriage proposal she refused, Smith battles serious mental illness with symptoms including delusions caused by his participation in the war while stationed in France. Smith's wife, Rezia, walks with him in the park on the way to visit a nerve specialist, despairing over his recent threat of suicide. Some passersby are described, and an airplane flies overhead, uniting Mrs. Dalloway, Smith, and others on the London streets as they gaze at it. Smith's paranoia leads him to believe that the plane is bringing "them," evil beings that pursue him. Another intersection occurs when Rezia notes the sad song of an old woman, also noticed by Peter Walsh, who has been walking in the park and gives the woman some money. Walsh has seen the

Smiths, guessing they are having an argument, as Smith continues to murmur aloud to himself.

Walsh anticipates seeing Clarissa, although he is presently in love with Daisy, a woman he plans to help divorce her present husband. Although Mrs. Dalloway also thinks about Walsh, her specific memory of the day he proposed to her is focused more on an "exquisite" kiss she shared with Sally Seton, which Walsh's proposal interrupted. That scene counters what appears to be Clarissa's cold nature.

Other characters include Clarissa's daughter, Elizabeth, who eventually shakes off the attentions of Miss Kilman, a religious woman whose views Clarissa worries will negatively affect her daughter. The reader also meets Hugh Whitbread, whose wife, Evelyn, is unwell. He plans to join Lady Bruton and Richard Dalloway for lunch, where the two men will assist Lady Bruton in writing a letter on the subject of emigration, which she hopes to submit to the *Times*. Hugh brags of buying a gift for his wife, annoying Richard, who buys a large bunch of roses, the quintessential symbol of female sexuality, for Clarissa. Ironically, Walsh will later note the sound of an ambulance, unbeknownst to him on its way to the tragic scene of Septimus Smith.

Walsh arrives at Clarissa's party and feels strange, not knowing many of the guests, as Clarissa begins to feel her party is not successful. Then Sally Seton, or Lady Rosseter as she is now titled, arrives to revive Clarissa's joviality and complete the reassembling of the group present at Bourton for Clarissa's 18th birthday, decades earlier. Clarissa grows angry, endangering the fragile atmosphere of the celebration, when she learns of Richard's delay due to a man's nearby suicide. When Clarissa leaves the group to sit in a room alone, she feels somehow connected to the young man who is, of course, Septimus Smith. While she seems to identify with Smith, she cannot determine why, and the emotion quickly passes. When Clarissa reemerges, her party is ending, and the novel closes with a scene of Sally and Walsh on a couch together.

Themes of the war and British rule of INDIA, from which Walsh has recently returned, would have proved familiar to contemporary readers. Later feminist critics, including Elaine Showalter, would theorize that Woolf wanted to demonstrate a connection between men shell-shocked from physical combat and women repressed by a patriarchal society, the connection being the "nerve specialist" appointed to treat both groups. Other critics classify Woolf's narrative format, presented mainly in Clarissa's and Septimus's points of view, as symbolizing two different views of the world. Some note the 24-hour period as indicative of all time or even timelessness, seemingly completed, but destined to simply begin again in a new cycle. Others consider the novel as not representing an existing unity, but rather symbolizing each individual's perception of unity, reflecting a basic component of postmodern theory known as contingency, in which each person's world view is contingent upon his or her private construct of the environment.

The book remains an important subject for study and continues to influence feminist critics and novelists.

—*Virginia Brackett*

BIBLIOGRAPHY
Beja, Morris. *Critical Essays on Virginia Woolf*. Boston: G. K. Hall, 1985.
Dowling, David. *Mrs. Dalloway: Mapping Streams of Consciousness*. Twayne Masterwork Studies, 67. Boston: Twayne, 1991.
Hussey, Mark. *Virginia Woolf: A–Z*. New York: Facts On File, 1995.

MUNRO, ALICE (1931–)

Especially noted for short stories that seem to equal novels in their complexity and scope, the Canadian writer Alice Munro has also produced story cycles that function as novels by relating episodes in the life of a single central character. Thus LIVES OF GIRLS AND WOMEN (1971), published as a novel, is sometimes viewed as a story collection.

Born Alice Laidlaw in rural Ontario on July 10, 1931, Munro matriculated at the University of Western Ontario in 1949 and married in 1951. That year, the couple relocated to British Columbia, first to Vancouver and later to Victoria. The marriage produced three daughters, but Munro also continued writing the stories she had been creating since childhood. Her first story collection, *Dance of the Happy Shades*, was published in 1968 and won the Governor General's Literary Award in 1969. In 1972, a year after the publication of *Lives of*

Girls and Women, Munro and her husband separated, and she moved back to Ontario; the marriage ended in divorce in 1976. Soon afterward, Munro remarried and moved to a rural Ontario town. She published *Something I've Been Meaning to Tell You: Thirteen Stories* in 1974, *The Beggar Maid: Stories of Flo and Rose* in 1979 (winning the Governor General's Literary Award), *The Progress of Love* in 1986 (another winner of the Governor General's Literary Award), and other collections. Her stories continue to appear in distinguished periodicals such as *The New Yorker* and *The Atlantic Monthly* and are appreciated by a wide public and lauded by critics.

BIBLIOGRAPHY

Blodgett, E. D. *Alice Munro.* Twayne's World Authors, 800. Boston: Twayne, 1988.

Miller, Judith, ed. *The Art of Alice Munro: Saying the Unsayable: Papers from the Waterloo Conference.* Waterloo, Ont.: University of Waterloo Press, 1984.

Ross, Catherine Sheldrick. *Alice Munro : A Double Life.* Toronto: ECW Press, 1992.

MURDOCH, IRIS (1919–1999)

One of the outstanding English novelists of the 20th century, Jean Iris Murdoch was also noted as a philosopher and an academic. She was born into an Anglo-Irish family—an only child—on July 15, 1919, in Dublin, IRELAND, and she boarded at Badminton School in England before entering Somerville College at Oxford. She was briefly a member of the Communist Party during her student days. Upon completing her undergraduate studies in 1942, she entered the Civil Service in the Treasury, experience that later provided material for her fiction. As WORLD WAR II ended, she served as a relief worker for the United Nations, traveling to Belgium and Austria; in Belgium, she was first exposed to the philosophical ideas of existentialism—a school of thought she later opposed. In 1947, she won a scholarship to Newnham College at Cambridge to study philosophy; in 1948, she was appointed a tutor at St. Anne's College, Oxford, where she remained until 1963, when she retired to pursue full-time writing. In 1956, Iris Murdoch married the Oxford literary scholar John Bayley.

Murdoch maintained a prolific writing schedule, publishing 26 novels during her life, along with eight works of nonfiction and philosophy, several plays, and a collection of poetry. Her first novel, *Under the Net,* appeared in 1954; the title refers to the web of language-based structures by which individuals limit and constrain the phenomena of experience. The novel received high praise from critics, and Murdoch frequently returned to the theme of how human beings can discover reality between the surface distractions of appearances. Murdoch's training as a philosopher informs her novels—especially her interest in moral issues—without overwhelming them.

Among her novels, some of her best-loved titles include *A Severed Head* (1961), which satirizes Freudian psychology in a contemporary sex farce; *The Nice and the Good* (1968), a treatment of human folly in matters of love and power; *A Fairly Honourable Defeat* (1970), about a manipulative attempt to split up a happily united homosexual couple; *A Word Child* (1975), which follows the path of a street urchin to literacy and to two disastrous affairs; and *The Green Knight* (1994), a retelling of the story of Sir Gawain and the Green Knight. Murdoch's most critically acclaimed fiction includes *The BLACK PRINCE* (1973), which won the JAMES TAIT BLACK MEMORIAL PRIZE, and *The SEA, THE SEA,* (1978), which won the BOOKER PRIZE. In *The Black Prince,* a writer falsely convicted of murdering another writer produces his masterpiece, a novel called *The Black Prince,* while in prison. In *The Sea, the Sea,* a retired theater director copes with life after a long and successful career. Murdoch draws extensively on her training in philosophy to construct her stories, but she also frequently uses examples of well-known paintings as literary tropes.

In 1976, Iris Murdoch was named a Commander of the Order of the British Empire, and in 1986 she was named a Dame Commander. She received honorary doctorates from Oxford University in 1987 and from Cambridge University in 1993. By 1995, Murdoch was suffering from Alzheimer's disease, which she at first thought was a serious case of writer's block. Her tragic deterioration was recounted in two poignant memoirs that her husband published after her death, and these were adapted as the film *Iris* in 2001. Iris Murdoch died on February 8, 1999.

BIBLIOGRAPHY

Antonacchio, Maria. *Picturing the Human: The Moral Thought of Iris Murdoch*. New York: Oxford University Press, 2000.

Bayley, John. *Elegy for Iris*. New York: St. Martin's Press, 1999.

———. *Iris and Her Friends: A Memoir of Memory and Desire*. New York: W. W. Norton, 1999.

Conradi, Peter J. *Iris Murdoch*. New York: W. W. Norton, 2001.

Todd, Richard. *Encounters with Iris Murdoch*. Amsterdam: Free University Press, 1988.

MUSIC AND SILENCE ROSE TREMAIN
(1999) An example of HISTORICAL FICTION, *Music and Silence* won the WHITBREAD Book of the Year Award the year it was published. It is set in 1629, in the Danish court of King Christian IV, as the king broods over his disastrous finances and the adulterous affairs of his much younger wife, Queen Kirsten. The protagonist of the story, Peter Claire, is an English lutenist who has only recently arrived for a period of miserable employment at the court. He possesses an angelic beauty, and the beleaguered king soon relies on Peter as a confidant—as his personal "angel." In a parallel plot, Queen Kirsten acquires a new lady-in-waiting, Emilia Tilsen, who is entirely the opposite of the queen's sexually voracious and selfishly cruel personality.

Peter and Emilia have both come to the Danish court in flight from adverse circumstances: Peter had been involved in an affair with the wife of his former employer, an Irish nobleman, while Emilia had been driven out of her family by a new stepmother. The two are soon in love—or in any case, Peter is in love with Emilia; unfortunately for him, so is Queen Kirsten, who jealously advises Emilia to avoid Peter and later intercepts Peter's letters so Emilia will not know of his sincere efforts to reach her. Their love is a genuine one, however, and it transcends Kirsten's manipulative attempts to destroy it. Kirsten's abuse of her husband comes to an end when he unexpectedly rejects her and sends her home to her mother. The two women then set several stratagems to regain favor at court, but these either fail or backfire—the final gambit of sending a seductress to win the king's confidence leads to his decision to divorce Kirsten and marry the seductress, a commoner. The hapless king, who has pursued numerous ludicrous schemes to restore his kingdom's finances, finds unexpected happiness when he frees himself from his bootless obsession for Kirsten.

Rose TREMAIN combines elements of fairy tales, historical events, and passionate romance to develop an engrossing story. Her large cast of characters allows her to contrast good and bad examples of parenting, marriage, and love, while the setting in a royal court introduces themes of power, politics, finance, and intrigue. By making her hero and heroine attractive, sincere, and capable of virtue, but also realistic in her full development of their emotional lives, she takes the historical romance to a higher level of sophistication than it ordinarily achieves.

BIBLIOGRAPHY

Acocella, Joan. Review of *Music and Silence*. *The New Yorker*, 5 June 2000, 92.

Kaiser, Mary. Review of *Music and Silence*. *World Literature Today* 74, no. 4 (Autumn 2000): 815.

MYSTERY AND DETECTIVE FICTION
Edgar Allan Poe is widely regarded as the founder of the literary genre of mystery and detective fiction with his creation and development of Chevalier Dupin in "The Murders in the Rue Morgue" (1841) and other stories. The genre moved to England some dozen years later in Charles Dickens's use of the judicial system as the primary backdrop for *Bleak House* (serialized 1852–53). In 1868, *The Moonstone,* by Wilkie Collins, centered on the resolution of a jewel theft; some critics have identified this title as the first full-length English detective novel, while others reserve that honor for Arthur Conan DOYLE's *A Study in Scarlet* (1888), one of the great adventures of the immortal Sherlock HOLMES.

The readership for mystery and detective fiction expanded greatly during the late 19th and early 20th centuries under the influence of low-cost pulp magazines, many of which featured sensationalized short stories of lurid crimes with the reassurance that wrongdoers would be apprehended and punished in the end. Several related literary forms developed, but in the classic detective story an investigator—a professional police detective, a private investigator, or an amateur sleuth—examines the evidence left at a crime scene (typically a murder) in order to identify the unknown perpetrator of the crime. Noted early British writers of short stories of detection, in addition to Arthur Conan Doyle, included G. K. CHESTERTON (his "Father Brown" series) Ernest Bramah (who created a blind detective), and R. Austin Freeman. By the 1920s, the short story was displaced by the more expansive canvas of the novel as the quintessential form of the genre: an important 20th-century influence was E. C. Bentley's *Trent's Last Case* (1913), although Sherlock Holmes also made a 20th-century appearance in novel form in *The Hound of the Baskervilles* (1902).

In 1928, the mystery writer Ronald Knox (paternal uncle of the novelist Penelope FITZGERALD) published "The Decalogue," a set of guidelines that defined the "best-practice" conventions of the genre. The 1920s and 1930s are widely regarded as the golden age of mystery and detective fiction in both Britain and the United States: Writers organized themselves into professional associations, and stellar examples of novel-length mysteries were pouring from publishers. Noted British writers included Agatha CHRISTIE, A. E. W. Mason, Michael Innes, the poet C. Day Lewis writing under the pseudonym Nicholas Blake, Dorothy SAYERS, H. C. Bailey, Margery Allington, Ngaio Marsh, and numerous others. During this period, Christie created Hercule Poirot and Captain Hastings on the model of Sherlock Holmes and Dr. Watson, introducing them in *The Mysterious Affair at Styles* (1920); these detectives are gifted amateurs with extraordinary insight into the workings of the criminal mind. Noted Poirot mysteries include *The Murder of Roger Ackroyd* (1926), *Murder on the Orient Express* (1934), and THE A. B. C. MURDERS (1936). Christie also created Miss Marple, another amateur sleuth, during this golden age, introducing her in *The Murder at the Vicarage* (1930) and continuing her adventures in numerous additional novels.

Although the American "hard-boiled" novel of violence, brutal crimes, and private investigators (typified most famously in the novels of Dashiell Hammett and Raymond Chandler) did not successfully take root in British mystery and detective fiction, writers since the 1930s have increasingly used a story model that focuses on the realistic representations of police departments at work. Interest in realism has also led to more attention to the development of criminals as characters and more use of social criticism regarding the circumstances that lead to criminal acts. As a result, the amateur sleuth has been replaced by the professional police detective. Writers such as Josephine TEY, P. D. JAMES, H. R. F. Keating, Ellis Peters, and Ruth RENDELL (writing under her own name and under her pseudonym Barbara Vine) have developed the novel of the professional crime investigator.

In the later part of the 20th century, some writers have shown the influence of POSTMODERNISM on the genre of mystery and detective fiction. For example, Peter ACKROYD's award-winning novel HAWKSMOOR doubles a contemporary crime story with its historical precedents, and the noted postmodern novelist Julian BARNES writes mysteries under the pseudonym Dan Kavenaugh. The genre of mystery and detective fiction has also been cross-pollinated with the genres of SCIENCE FICTION and FANTASY in the novels of Jasper Fforde, featuring his literary detective Thursday Next, and in the two detective novels by Douglas ADAMS, *Dirk Gently's Holistic Detective Agency* and *The Long Dark Teatime of the Soul*. Most recently, stories of crime and punishment have proved their popularity yet again through the new media of movies and television; the public appetite for mystery and detective fiction in one form or another shows no signs of abating.

BIBLIOGRAPHY

Barzun, Jacques and Wendell Hertig Taylor. *A Catalogue of Crime.* New York: Harper & Row, 1989.

Binyon, T. J. *Murder will Out: The Detective in Fiction.* Oxford: Oxford University Press, 1989.

Symons, Julian. *Bloody Murder: From the Detective Story to the Crime Novel: A History.* New York: Viking, 1985.

MYTHOLOGY The study of the sacred stories of the world's various religions has a long and distinguished history. Throughout the 18th and 19th centuries, when any university worth the name featured a strong classics department and when philology ruled the study of language, scholars undertook massive projects to collect and analyze the mythologies of the various regions in the British EMPIRE and the rest of the world. Indeed, George Eliot mildly satirized this enterprise in the character of Mr. Casaubon in *Middlemarch*:

He is ostensibly writing a "key to all mythologies" as his great lifework. Despite Eliot's portrayal of Casaubon, this extensive and rigorous scholarship laid a strong foundation for 20th-century interest in mythology, providing a wealth of texts and interpretations for new generations of readers, scholars, and literary critics.

Among the scholarly texts produced in the 20th century, one of the most important was the monumental multivolume comparative study *The Golden Bough* (1922) by Sir James George Frazer. In it, Frazer traces the significance, influences, and interconnections of a single mythic story, that of the "King of the Wood" (*rex nemorensis*), through every source he can find. In so doing, Frazer demonstrated the underlying worldwide unity of mythic stories in the common human experiences of birth, maturation, procreation, senescence, and death. The great surface disparities among the stories of the world's historic and prehistoric religions disappeared as the underlying metaphors demonstrated the common function of mythic systems to explain the cycle of human life while also preserving that explanation for the future. From the recognition of globally shared features of storytelling it is only a small step to Carl Jung's theory of the "collective unconscious," featured in novels as diverse as *The MAGUS, The CHYMICAL WEDDING,* and *WOMEN IN LOVE.* Other influential critics and scholars of mythology's relevance to literature include Joseph Campbell, whose book *The Hero with a Thousand Faces* built on the work of both Frazer and Jung, and Northrup Frye, who established strong connections between the cycle of the seasons and the genres of literature in his masterwork, *The Anatomy of Criticism.*

The influence of the classics—the study of the Latin and Greek languages and the literature created in them—persisted in the British education system long after American schools had discarded Latin in favor of modern English; consequently, American students reading British literature of any era may need some preparatory study in mythology in order to appreciate the numerous mythic allusions they will encounter. An understanding of the pantheon of Greek and Roman gods and goddesses, together with Nordic and Celtic mythology, should be a prerequisite for the study of serious literature and even for the enjoyment of popular literature. And as the authors of literature in English continue to spring from the diverse cultures of the world that have been influenced by the spread of the English language, other mythologies may also become important sources for understanding the images, symbols, and metaphors that such authors deploy to express their literary visions.

BIBLIOGRAPHY

Campbell, Joseph. *The Hero with a Thousand Faces.* 1949. Princeton, N.J.: Princeton University Press, 1968.

Frazer, Sir James George. *The Golden Bough: A Study in Magic and Religion.* 1922. Abridged edition. New York: Collier Books-Macmillan Company, 1950.

Frye, Northrop. *Anatomy of Criticism: Four Essays.* Princeton, N.J.: Princeton University Press, 1957.

Jung, C. G. *Psyche and Symbol: A Selection from the Writings of C. G. Jung.* Translated by Cary Baynes and R. F. C. Hull. Garden City, N.Y.: Doubleday, 1958.

N

NAIPAUL, V. S. (1932–   )   The winner of the NOBEL PRIZE in literature in 2001, Vidiadhar Surajprasad Naipaul was born on August 17, 1932, in Trinidad into a family descended from Indian immigrants. His father, a journalist, published a collection of short stories. Naipaul and his father were close; nonetheless, the younger man was eager to leave Trinidad. He matriculated at University College, Oxford, in 1950, earning a degree in English. His father died, only 47 years old, while Naipaul was an undergraduate.

In 1955, Naipaul married, settled in London, and began to work as a professional writer—the only career he has ever followed. For eight years he wrote fiction reviews for *The New Statesman,* and during this time he also published his first four novels: *The Mystic Masseur* (1957), *The Suffrage of Elvira* (1958), *Miguel Street* (1959), and *A HOUSE FOR MR. BISWAS* (1961).

In 1961, Naipaul embarked on a series of travels intended to stimulate his imagination; these journeys led to the publication of several volumes of travel writing that are as admired and as well respected as his best fiction. At different times, his travels have taken him to Trinidad, India and Kashmir, Uganda, Iran under the Ayatollah Khomeini, Pakistan, Malaysia, and Indonesia. From his travels to Muslim countries, he has produced two controversial volumes of journalistic commentary critical of Islamic nationalism, *Among the*

Believers: An Islamic Journey (1981) and *Beyond Belief: Islamic Excursions Among the Converted Peoples* (1998); the second volume revisits many of the same places presented in the first and examines the effects of Islamic politics. Naipaul's pro-Western stance is at the heart of the controversies these books produced.

While he traveled, Naipaul also continued to write fiction. *Mr. Stone and the Knights Companion* (1963) is set in London and features an English protagonist retired from colonial service, but it was written in the contested border province of Kashmir; it won the HAWTHORNDEN PRIZE the year it was published. Naipaul's next novel, *The Mimic Men* (1967), was written in Uganda; it won the W. H. Smith Prize. It is the semiautobiographical story of Ralph Kirpal Singh, a man who feels that he has a history but no escape from the absurdity of life. Naipaul's seventh novel, *IN A FREE STATE* (1971), won the BOOKER PRIZE. It contains three interlinked stories about the dispossessed rootlessness of modern life—a problem that afflicts the entire modern world. *Guerrillas* (1975) studies the delusional idealism of self-styled revolutionaries in a Caribbean state on the verge of violent collapse. *A BEND IN THE RIVER* (1979) carries Naipaul's themes of rootlessness and cultural displacement to a postcolonial nation in central Africa, where a shopkeeper of Indian descent tries to survive in the face of violent social and political transformations.

V. S. Naipaul was knighted 1989, and he won the David Cohen Literature Prize for Lifetime Achievement in 1993. He remarried in 1996 after his first wife died, settling in the English countryside. He continues to live and write in England.

BIBLIOGRAPHY

Feder, Lillian. *Naipaul's Truth: The Making of a Writer.* Lanham, Md.: Rowman & Littlefield Publishers, 2001.

Gorra, Michael. *After Empire: Scott, Naipaul, Rushdie.* Chicago: University of Chicago Press, 1997.

Mustafa, Fawzia. *V. S. Naipaul.* Cambridge: Cambridge University Press, 1995.

Naipaul, V. S. *Reading and Writing: A Personal Account.* New York: New York Review of Books, 2000.

Theroux, Paul. *Sir Vidia's Shadow: A Friendship Across Five Continents.* Boston: Houghton Mifflin, 1998.

NAUTICAL FICTION   A more specialized

subgenre than MYSTERY AND DETECTIVE FICTION, romance, HISTORICAL FICTION, SCIENCE FICTION, or FANTASY, nautical fiction consists of those novels that are set on ships—usually sailing ships—and that feature the adventures of the ship's crew for story material. When nautical fiction goes ashore, it does so in order to follow the adventures of seamen while they are on solid ground. Nautical fiction springs from the popularity of nonfiction accounts of sailing triumphs during the Age of Sail at the end of the 18th century. As the British EMPIRE pushed out to every corner of the globe and the Royal Navy grew in size, more and more British families sent loved ones to sea, and the nation had a greater stake in the success of its ocean-going enterprises. Newspaper accounts of naval battles and autobiographies of sailors were soon amplified by novel-length fictions that used realism to capture the spirit of the sailing world while also giving free range to the authorial imagination. In addition to the professional seamen who turned to writing novels on land, professional writers also turned to stories of the sea for new material. The American novelist James Fenimore Cooper wrote nautical fiction in the early 19th century, along with Herman Melville, whose nautical fiction *Moby Dick* is recognized as one of the greatest novels of any kind ever written.

Successful writers of nautical fiction include some of the greatest novelists of the 20th century, such as Joseph CONRAD. C. S. FORESTER (creator of Horatio HORNBLOWER) and Patrick O'BRIAN (author of the AUBREY-MATURIN NOVELS) both had tremendous popular successes with their series of seafaring books. Less well-known writers who have produced popular and even award-winning nautical fiction include Matthew KNEALE, who won the WHITBREAD Book of the Year Award for *ENGLISH PASSENGERS* in 2000, and Richard HUGHES, author of *A HIGH WIND IN JAMAICA* (1929).

BIBLIOGRAPHY

Peck, John. *Maritime Fiction: Sailors and the Sea in British and American Novels, 1719–1917.* Basingstoke, U.K.: Palgrave, 2001.

NEWBY, P. H. (1918–1997)   Born on June 25,

1918, Percy Howard Newby won the first BOOKER PRIZE in 1968 (for his 14th novel for adult readers, *SOMETHING TO ANSWER FOR*) from a list of contenders that included works by better-known authors such as Muriel SPARK and Iris MURDOCH. He attended St. Paul's College for two years before entering the Royal Army Medical Corps. Between 1939 and 1942, he fought in WORLD WAR II, serving in France and Egypt. During the second half of the war and until 1946, he taught in Egypt at King Fouad I University. This experience of living in a foreign land was an important influence, stimulating Newby's imagination and providing materials for several of his novels.

Newby was married in 1945. He spent three years as a freelance journalist before joining the BBC in 1949, where he remained until 1978, working as a radio producer and eventually reaching the position of managing director. In his spare time, Newby wrote fiction, publishing his first novel, *A Journey to the Interior,* in 1945; it won the Atlantic Award of the Rockefeller Foundation and the Somerset Maugham Prize. By 1995, when he produced his last novel, *Something About Women,* Newby had published 20 novels for adults and some children's books as well, along with a collection of short fiction and some nonfiction works of history, biography, and criticism. Throughout his career, Newby remained a relatively unknown writer primarily read by professional critics, but generating positive responses from them and receiving consistent notice in overviews of contemporary writers. In 1972, he was named a Commander of the Order of the British Empire. P. H. Newby died on September 6, 1997.

BIBLIOGRAPHY

Bufkin, E. C. *P. H. Newby*. Twayne's English Author Series, 176. Boston: Twayne, 1975.

Fraser, G. S., and Ian Scott-Kilvert. *P. H. Newby*. Writers and Their Work 235. Harlow: Longman, for the British Council, 1974.

NEW MEN, THE C. P. SNOW (1954)

The fifth volume in the ROMAN-FLEUVE entitled STRANGERS AND BROTHERS, this novel follows The MASTERS, a story of political machinations in the microcosm of an academic setting, and it precedes HOMECOMINGS, the personal story of the narrator's adult family life as an unhappy marriage ends and a second one blossoms. In *The New Men,* Lewis Eliot, the first-person narrator of the entire series, has left the academic world and entered the larger political sphere as a public administrator. In particular, Eliot is working in the defense world, and his younger brother, the physicist Martin Eliot, is working on the British project to develop an atomic weapon. Eliot is pained to see his brother ruthlessly pursue power as he struggles to control the bomb project; for Martin's part, he is establishing himself in the world of science and politics, and he is driven by the need to achieve influence through his own efforts and not indirectly through his older brother's connections and skills as a lawyer, academic, and bureaucrat.

SNOW combines the classic elements of a cold war–era suspense thriller: Martin must deal with the risks of the research work itself—his competitor to head the project suffers radiation sickness at a crucial point—and with the political sympathies of other scientists, some of whom are communist fellow travelers or outright supporters. The work is going on at the same time that WORLD WAR II is happening; as German bombs turn into V-2 rockets, the scientists have a vivid motivation to carry on their deadly work. Observing from outside the main action but intimately connected to it through his brother, Eliot has the opportunity to comment on the ethical issues at stake in creating a weapon of such terrible power. As an academic, he can also contemplate the distinction between the two paths that science can take: the pure research that makes new discoveries for their own sakes, and the applied research that makes new discoveries to fulfill predetermined purposes in the world, such as blowing up cities. For Martin Eliot, this last issue becomes the deciding factor in the way he ultimately shapes his life course.

BIBLIOGRAPHY

Boytinck, Paul. *C. P. Snow: A Reference Guide*. Boston: G. K. Hall, 1980.

Widdowson, Peter J. "C. P. Snow's *Strangers and Brothers* Sequence: Lewis Eliot and the Failure of Realism," *Renaissance & Modern Studies* 19 (1975): 112–128.

NEW ZEALAND

See EMPIRE and COLONIALISM. For New Zealand novelists who have significant British careers, see Janet FRAME and Keri HULME.

NICE WORK DAVID LODGE (1989)

Shortlisted for the BOOKER PRIZE in 1988, this closing volume of the "Rummidge trilogy" parallels CHANGING PLACES, the first volume in the trilogy, in the way that the narrative brings together two different realms of experience. But where the earlier book contrasted British and American academic practices in the context of university English departments, *Nice Work* brings together the rarefied thinking of the British academic world and the practical action of the British manufacturing world—two realms of experience that are perhaps even more widely separated than are those of American and British English departments.

The omniscient third-person narrator begins with the quotidian rounds of Vic Wilcox, an engineering manager of a manufacturing firm that is an arm of a vast corporation. The opening chapter is a textbook case of realism in fiction writing. In the second chapter, however, with the introduction of the academic character, Robyn Penrose, LODGE shifts his narrative style to reflect the ideological style of this new character. Robyn—a teaching assistant at Rummidge University—is so thoroughly postmodern (see POSTMODERNISM) that the third-person narrator must break the convention of the anonymous outside observer and use the first-person pronoun "I" in order to discuss the difficulty of properly presenting Robyn Penrose, a character who does not believe in the existence of characters. The first task the plot must then complete is to bring these two diametrically opposed characters together; Lodge achieves this result with an imaginary government program designed to integrate the academic world into the practical world of business and industry by having selected academics follow selected business managers around one day a week for a term. Thus Robyn Penrose becomes Vic Wilcox's shadow, and the juxtaposition of the two characters allows Lodge to explore their ideological differences and to exploit their comic potential.

Since, as every postmodernist knows, it is not possible to observe a phenomenon without also interacting with it and thereby changing it, Robyn's task of observing Vic soon changes both the observer and the observed. As the practical, traditional, and masculine entity collides with the abstract, unconventional, and feminist one, Vic and Robyn come together in unpredictable ways. Lodge's canvas is large enough to allow him to contrast 19th- and 20th-century narrative conventions, since Vic is at the endpoint of the earlier century's historical influence and Robyn is at the beginning of a new way of thinking and writing. Ironically, Lodge bestows the happy ending of 19th-century novels on Robyn, the anticharacter, while leaving old-fashioned Vic in a position of AMBIGUITY.

BIBLIOGRAPHY

McLemee, Scott. "David Lodge Thinks . . . The British Novelist of Ideas Takes on the Literary Implications of 'Consciousness Studies,'" *The Chronicle of Higher Education* 49, no. 2 (1 November 2002): A14–A17.

Womack, Kenneth. *Postwar Academic Fiction: Satire, Ethics, Community*. Basingstoke, U.K.: Palgrave, 2002.

NIGERIA   See EMPIRE and COLONIALISM. For significant Nigerian novelists, see Chinua ACHEBE and Ben OKRI.

NINE TAILORS, THE DOROTHY SAYERS (1934)   This novel of MYSTERY AND DETECTIVE FICTION introduces SAYERS'S recurring sleuth, Lord Peter Wimsey, the younger brother of the Duke of Denver. The title refers to the traditional tolling of nine deep melancholy tones on a church bell to denote the death of a person in an English parish; it has nothing to do with a guild of artisans devoted to the production of quality menswear. In the opening chapter, set in 1930, a minor car accident strands Lord Peter and his manservant, Bunter, in an East Anglia village where flu has struck down one of the local bellringers on New Year's Eve, just as the time approaches for a special nine-hour ringing of the local church's eight famous bells. Lord Peter, it turns out, is an initiate skilled in the mysteries of campanology, or bell ringing, and he fills in for the sick man, allowing the remarkable event to proceed as scheduled. Three months later, when a corpse is discovered very much out of place in the church graveyard, the rector writes to request Lord Peter's assistance, having learned that his bell-ringing guest is the most renowned investigator in England since the passing of the great Sherlock HOLMES.

Sayers constructs her puzzle as a double intrigue: The identity and death of the dead man must be explained, but there is also the matter of an emerald necklace stolen 15 years previously from a guest at the village's manor house. The necklace, worth thousands of pounds, was never recovered, but the lord of the manor drained the family fortune to pay the necklace's owner for her loss in his home. The butler and a London jewel thief had been convicted and sent to jail, but the trial never did extract the truth from their conflicting testimonies. Clues suggest that the corpse in the graveyard is connected to the earlier theft, but it remains for Lord Peter and Bunter to resolve both mysteries.

Sayers emphasizes the novel's puzzle-solving structure by opening with the completely mysterious and virtually incomprehensible—to the uninitiated—jargon of "change-ringing" on church bells, an art grounded in the mathematical relationships between the notes of the scale. The novel captures a distinctly English peculiarity: Visitors to London have remarked on the English love of bell ringing since the Renaissance, and every village throughout the countryside features its community's Anglican church with a bell tower housing varying numbers of bells. Readers not familiar with English church architecture and bell-ringing practices might wish to consult an illustrated guide while reading this novel, since various scenes take place in every corner of the church and the nearby rectory. Other useful knowledge includes the hydrological engineering by which the fens of East Anglia are drained (or flooded).

The precise and accurate use of recondite terminology contributes to the authoritative and knowledgeable tone of the narration, delivered by a third-person omniscient narrator, but the main focus of the story remains on the characters and the interactions among them. An English village comes vividly and memorably to life in Sayers's presentation. The closing scenes of the villagers, with their children, their animals, and their furniture, taking refuge in the church—built on the parish's only hill—as flood waters drown the surrounding terrain is as vivid as other water scenes in the works of renowned canonical writers such as Thomas Hardy and George Eliot. Lord Peter's polite charm, his unpretentious manner with persons of every CLASS, and his zest for resolving an intrigue make him an appealing and memorable character, leaving the reader with a longing to know him better. Textual references make it clear that the author intends to create a worthy successor to Holmes—a modern master of deduction and inference—and the novel is a testament to her success. *The Nine Tailors* is recognized as one of the outstanding examples of its genre.

BIBLIOGRAPHY

Hall, Trevor H. *Dorothy L. Sayers: Nine Literary Studies.* Hamden, Conn.: Archon Books, 1980.

McGregor, Robert Kuhn, and Ethan Lewis. *Conundrums for the Long Week-End: England, Dorothy L. Sayers, and Lord Peter Wimsey.* Kent, Ohio: Kent State, 2000.

NINETEEN EIGHTY-FOUR GEORGE ORWELL (1948)

One of the most important novels of the 20th century, *Nineteen Eighty-Four* presents the paradigm of DYSTOPIAN NOVELS: The setting is a near-future world that is a recognizable descendant of the world the readers live in, but instead of an improvement on the present, it is a regression to totalitarian control. ORWELL makes this future particularly harrowing by imagining the means by which the few dominate the many. His protagonist, the nervous and unhappy Winston Smith, works in the Ministry of Truth changing the records of the past to make them consistent with present events and decrees. The world of the novel consists of three superpowers, Oceania, Eurasia, and Eastasia, constantly at war with one another in ever-shifting alliances. The ruling political system, Ingsoc, venerates the leader (possibly mythical) Big Brother; members of the Inner Party exercise the real power behind the ubiquitous face of Big Brother. Winston, a lowly member of the outer party, has no power to wield, and the state is interested only in his obedience to the will of the Party.

Winston was born before the revolution placed Ingsoc in power, and he is sure the world used to be a better place; ironically, his activities in the Ministry of Truth contribute to the eradication of any evidence that the present is anything but an improvement on the past. In a world where surveillance is universal and betrayal of divergent thought is patriotic, where activities of every sort are mandated and regulated, where the thought police set traps for unwary souls who dare to think independently in their private thoughts, and where the official language, Newspeak, is nothing more than a tissue of lies that serve the ends of power, Winston longs for spontaneity. He begins the subversive activity of keeping a journal, and he embarks on a love affair with Julia, another worker in the Ministry of Truth.

The lovers make the crucial mistake of trusting O'Brien, a member of the Inner Party, believing that he belongs to a counterrevolutionary group. Winston and Julia have a few happy meetings before they are apprehended by the ruthless and inexorable machinery of the thought police. Julia essentially disappears from the story as the third-person narrator focuses on the process by which O'Brien tortures and breaks Winston. In betraying his love for Julia, Winston destroys the only refuge of hope in his mind and comes to embrace "doublethink": the ability to believe two contradictory propositions simultaneously. In a chilling ending, when he is released back into the world to wear out his days under the anodyne of drink, he is happy to realize that he loves Big Brother.

Although Orwell's title suggests a particular future time that is now in the past, his novel remains relevant for contemporary readers as an ominous portent of the direction the world might still go. Lust for power can occur at any time, and when it is yoked to an efficient bureaucracy of anonymous cruelty and faceless inhumanity, the stage is set for cultural depredation and even holocaust. Our task, Orwell suggests, is to prevent that future from happening.

BIBLIOGRAPHY

Bloom, Harold. *George Orwell's* 1984. New York: Chelsea House, 1987.

Hynes, Samuel Lynn, ed. *Twentieth Century Interpretations of* 1984: *A Collection of Critical Essays*. Englewood Cliffs, N.J.: Prentice Hall, 1971.

Reilly, Patrick. Nineteen Eighty-Four: *Past, Present, and Future*. Twayne Masterwork Studies, 30. Boston: Twayne, 1989.

Sandison, Alan. *George Orwell After* Nineteen Eighty-Four. London: Macmillan, 1986.

NOBEL PRIZE   Founded in 1895 by Alfred Nobel, the Swedish inventor of dynamite, and first bestowed in 1901, Nobel Prizes are awarded annually in the fields of physics, chemistry, physiology and medicine, literature, and peace, with a prize for economics added in 1969. These prizes are widely considered to be the most distinguished awards for achievement in the world, although recently other prizes have been established of equivalent merit and financial worth, such as the Templeton Prize in religion. In the field of literature, the Nobel Prize recognizes a body of literary writings rather than a specific genre or work; the literary achievement recognized by the prize must have made a contribution to the betterment of mankind with global significance. Responsibility for awarding the prize in literature rests with the Swedish Academy, a national institution of scholars and writers.

The first British recipient of the Nobel Prize in literature was Rudyard Kipling, in 1907, for works that included poetry, short fiction, and novels. Other recipients who have resided in the British Commonwealth (or in the colonial territories that preceded it) include the Bengali poet and writer Rabindranath Tagore in 1913, the Irish poet William Butler Yeats in 1923, the dramatist George Bernard Shaw in 1925, and the novelist John Galsworthy in 1932. During World War II, no prizes were awarded in literature. After the war, the American poet T. S. Eliot, who eventually became a British citizen after a long residence in England, won the prize for literature in 1948, followed in 1950 by the philosopher and nonfiction writer Bertrand Russell. In 1954, Winston Churchill won the Nobel Prize in literature for his historical writings. The Irish dramatist and novelist Samuel Beckett, long expatriated to France, won the prize in 1969. The first Australian to win the Nobel Prize in literature was Patrick White, a novelist, in 1973. In 1983, the English novelist William Golding became a Nobel laureate. The Nigerian playwright Wole Soyinka received the prize in literature in 1986; the South African novelist Nadine Gordimer won in 1991; and, in 1992, the West Indian poet Derek Walcott was honored. In 1995, the Irish poet Seamus Heaney won the literature prize. In the 21st century, two Commonwealth novelists have won: the Trinidadian V. S. Naipaul (2001) and the South African J. M. Coetzee (2003).

BIBLIOGRAPHY

Feldman, Burton. *The Nobel Prize: A History of Genius, Controversy, and Prestige*. New York: Arcade Pub., 2000.

Kidd, Walter E. *British Winners of the Nobel Literary Prize*. Norman: University of Oklahoma Press, 1973.

NO LAUGHING MATTER ANGUS WILSON (1967)   Referred to by the author as an "anti-Forsyte" saga, *No Laughing Matter* is an experimental novel, differing from John Galsworthy's *The Forsyte Saga* both in form and content. It displays its literary roots in the author's many allusions (one character calls himself a "Micawber," after Charles Dickens's model of misfortune and failure) and in his imitation of several dramatists' characteristic styles in scenes that take the form of plays. Where Galsworthy used a realistic approach to fiction, Wilson uses modernist techniques such as stream-of-consciousness point of view, a disordered plot line, and genre-bending scenes of drama to follow the lives of the members of the Matthews family, consisting of six children and two self-absorbed unloving parents. Where the Forsyte clan was wealthy, the Matthews family teeters on the brink of poverty; where the Forsytes were united in their ambitions to maintain their wealth and to exercise power in the world, the Matthews family—both the parents and the children as adults—strive to outdo each other in failures of various kinds.

The father of the family, Billy Pop, fails as a novelist, even though his failure casts his family onto the mercy of wealthy relatives; the mother, known as The Contessa, fails unashamedly as a wife, conducting affairs as a way of humiliating her husband. Each of the six children fails in some sphere of life, even when they succeed in other endeavors. The eldest, Quentin, fails as a political idealist, drifting from support of radicalism into cynicism. Gladys Matthews fails in love and business when she mixes the two, landing in prison after she acquires illicit funds to help the man she loves. Rupert Matthews acquires a measure of fame as a film actor, but his marriage is a cruel mess and he assuages his unhappiness with alcohol. Sukey hides from life in a colorless marriage; her twin Margaret writes novels that only critics read. The youngest Matthews, Marcus, displays effeminate behavior in childhood, earning his mother's scorn, and becomes a financial success when an elderly male lover sets him up in business as an antiques dealer.

The novel sprawls across the events of the entire 20th century, incorporating some into the plot, as when Quentin serves in the armed forces during WORLD WAR I, and suggesting some of them metaphorically, as when the Matthews parents exterminate their children's kittens despite promises to the contrary—a small-scale betrayal that mirrors the heartlessness of Nazi anti-Semitism. Wilson takes up issues of CLASS, gender, and sexuality through his large cast of characters, but his main point is the way that human life is stamped by the experiences of childhood, a time when the people and the events that are beyond our control imprint behaviors and attitudes that last a lifetime. Before the term *dysfunctional family* became a byword of pop psychology, Wilson created a model example,

using it as a lens through which to view the history-making events of the 20th century.

BIBLIOGRAPHY

Faulkner, Peter. *Angus Wilson: Mimic and Moralist.* New York: Viking Press, 1980.

Halio, Jay L., ed. *Critical Essays on Angus Wilson.* Boston: G. K. Hall, 1985.

NO MORE PARADES FORD MADOX FORD (1925)   See *PARADE'S END*.

NORTHERN IRELAND   A component part of the United Kingdom, Northern Ireland's separate identity from the rest of the island on which it is located began in the 18th century; as a strategy to bind Ireland more tightly to England and to reduce the power of Catholicism in the country, Protestant English settlers, many from Scotland, were awarded lands in the counties closest to the crossing to Scotland. This strategy did not succeed. Instead, it led to a Protestant enclave concentrated in the six counties of the north-easternmost part of the island, although Protestants are also present in other parts of Ireland as well in lesser numbers. When the movement for Home Rule in IRELAND began, the Protestant northern counties resisted this change, fearing to become a permanent minority in a nation ruled by a Catholic majority. When the Irish Free State was declared in 1921, the Protestant counties maintained their membership in the United Kingdom.

BIBLIOGRAPHY

Bartlett, Jonathan. *Northern Ireland.* New York: H. W. Wilson, 1983.

Bell, J. Bowyer. *The Irish Troubles: A Generation of Violence, 1967–1992.* New York: St. Martin's Press, 1993.

Holland, Jack. *Hope Against History: The Course of Conflict in Northern Ireland.* New York: Henry Holt, 1999.

NOSTROMO JOSEPH CONRAD (1904)
Widely considered one of CONRAD's best novels, though not a perfect one, *Nostromo* is set in the imaginary South American nation of Costaguana. The land, situated along the northern coast of the continent, is

divided by a mountain range, and rebels under Montero have seized the eastern part. In the west, the wealth of the nation, the San Tomé silver mine, under the management of the Englishman Charles Gould, serves as a powerful incentive to summon the revolutionaries over the mountain.

Montero's revolution is designed to place the nation's wealth and power at his personal disposal rather than to right wrongs or relieve the oppression of the poor. Gould unites with newspaper editor Martin Decoud and other leading townspeople of varying ranks; they decide to resist the revolution and establish the Occidental Republic. The key to their success is to keep the semi-annual silver shipment, ready at the customs house, from falling into the hands of Montero. They choose Gian' "Nostromo" Battista—his nickname means "Our Man"—as their chief protector of the silver. Nostromo is a popular leader of the working class, a stevedore himself, and he is widely thought to be incorruptible. He is carefully following the plan to save the silver when an unexpected turn of events throws him on his own resources; his alternative plan initially works, but in the ensuing chaos he winds up being the only man who knows where the silver is located. That knowledge transforms him, and the lure of material wealth entraps him. Although his country honors him for his role in creating its independence, he secretly begins converting the stashed silver to his personal benefit.

Nostromo's secret is soon at risk in the ordinary process of growth and expansion in the new republic. He essentially becomes the tool of the hidden silver, compromising his honor and even his love to protect his valuable secret. With his judgment impaired, he acts unwisely and is accidentally shot. Carried to the hospital, he asks to speak to Charles Gould's wife and tries to tell her the location of the silver. But Mrs. Gould has become disheartened by the destruction that the silver has brought; she refuses to receive the information.

Conrad creates an impressive multinational cast of characters to play out this story of greed, materialism, idealism, and corruption. The Englishman Gould is an agent of COLONIALISM: His father owned and managed the silver mine before him, and although Charles was born in Costaguana, he remains an Englishman thanks in part to his Oxford education. The Frenchman Decoud is a modern skeptic who cannot resist the temptation to build an independent republic. The Italian Nostromo possesses the virtues of a hero until the corrupting force of secret knowledge tarnishes his soul. In addition to this international diversity of characters, Conrad creates an extensive range of social and economic niches to which these characters belong. His detailed descriptions of the landscape, the mine, the capital city of Sulaco, and its adjacent harbor and the islands beyond all work to bring the scene vividly before the reader's eyes as a realistic setting in which the large cast can perform the many actions of the PLOT. Despite these many qualities, the novel fails to carry them out consistently, shifting its focus in the later third of the story from the large sweep of politics, economics, and revolution to the small scale of one man's struggle with his own flawed nature. Nonetheless, *Nostromo* remains in the first rank of Conrad's large and diverse body of work.

BIBLIOGRAPHY

Bloom, Harold, ed. *Joseph Conrad's* Nostromo. New York: Chelsea House, 1987.

Carabine, Keith, Owen Knowles, and Wieslaw Krajka, eds. *Contexts for Conrad.* Boulder, Colo.: East European Monographs, 1993.

Watt, Ian. *Joseph Conrad:* Nostromo. Cambridge: Cambridge University Press, 1988.

NOT HONOUR MORE JOYCE CARY (1955)

See *PRISONER OF GRACE* TRILOGY.

NUTMEG OF CONSOLATION, THE PATRICK O'BRIAN (1991) See AUBREY-MATURIN NOVELS.

O

O'BRIAN, PATRICK (1914–2000) Creator of the 20 volumes of NAUTICAL FICTION in the AUBREY-MATURIN NOVELS, Patrick O'Brian is the pseudonym and perhaps the alter ego of Richard Patrick Russ. Born in Chalfont St. Peter, Buckinghamshire, England, in 1914, O'Brian was the son of an English-German union. His mother was English; his father, a German-descended physician specializing in venereology. After starting a writer's life as Richard Patrick Russ, publishing fiction, marrying, fathering two children, and serving as an intelligence officer during WORLD WAR II, O'Brian abandoned his family, adopted his new name, and crafted a fictional identity for himself as an Irishman, a sailor, and a Catholic by birth. He remarried, to Mary Tolstoy, the ex-wife of Count Nicholai Tolstoy, and after a period in Wales, he and his wife relocated to the Rossillon coast of France. There, O'Brian earned a living writing novels and biographies, and translating French works into English, including texts by Simone de Beauvoir. He became acquainted with his neighbor, Pablo Picasso, and drew on that experience for an award-winning biography published in 1976. His biography of the great English naturalist, Joseph Banks, was equally well received in 1993.

O'Brian is best known, however, for his nautical fiction. His two young-adult novels, *The Golden Ocean* (1956) and *The Unknown Shore* (1959), as preparation for *Master and Commander* (1969). With the death of C. S. FORESTER in 1966, and the end of the popular Horatio HORNBLOWER series, the book market had room for more sailing novels for adult readers. As the suggestion of an editor, O'Brian accepted the challenge: He elaborated the basic concept of two contrasting friends at sea and created Captain Jack Aubrey and Dr. Stephen Maturin. For the first 20 years of the novels' existence, they remained relatively unknown, but sold well enough to warrant continuing the series. Iris MURDOCH and other English scholars and writers were fans of the series, and O'Brian continued to write in contented obscurity. In 1990, an editor at W. W. Norton read *The Reverse of the Medal* (1986), the 11th book in the series, and decided to publish the forthcoming volumes while also reissuing the earlier ones. A superlative review by Richard Snow in *The New York Times Book Review* helped the new series reach a wide readership, and the series was soon a publishing phenomenon. O'Brian was 75 years old when Norton began reissuing his books, and he produced seven additional volumes in the series, for a total of 20, before he died in January 2000.

O'Brian's great nautical series combines the carefully detailed research of quality HISTORICAL FICTION, but it also demonstrates a keen understanding of human psychology. His portrayals of the personal lives of Aubrey and Maturin form key elements in the success of the novels, along with his thrilling battle sequences and the fully realized depiction of 18th-century manners, morals, speech patterns, and behaviors. Although his creation of the series may have had a financial motive to supply texts for a preexisting demand, in his style, erudition, and narrative skill, he succeeded in hitting a much more literarily significant target.

BIBLIOGRAPHY

Cunningham, A. E. *Patrick O'Brian: Critical Essays and a Bibliography.* New York: W. W. Norton, 1994.

King, Dean. *Patrick O'Brian: A Life Revealed.* New York: Henry Holt, 2000.

Lapham, Lewis. "Stupor Mundi." *Harper's Magazine* 300, no. 1799 (April 2000): 9–13.

Mamet, David. "The Humble Genre Novel, Sometimes Full of Genius," *The New York Times,* 17 January 2000, E1.

O'BRIEN, EDNA (1930–)

An Irish writer noted for her portrayal of women in their search for love and fulfillment, Josephine Edna O'Brien was born in County Clare, in the western part of IRELAND least affected by English and Scottish settlement, on December 15, 1930. Her father was a farmer and horse breeder who drank to excess while her mother suffered in silence; the life of the village was provincial and insular. These details form the background for much of her fiction, in which women ill prepared for the larger world nonetheless escape into it, chasing a dream that might be impossible to attain. The story is the outline of the plot of O'Brien's own life: She left the village of Scarriff for an independent life, spending some time boarding at a convent in County Galway before moving to Dublin. There, she discovered the works of James JOYCE and studied pharmacy, receiving a license in 1950. In 1952, she was married to the writer Ernest Gebbler; the union lasted 12 years and produced two sons, who were the focus of the bitter divorce proceedings that ended the marriage in 1964.

By then, O'Brien was living in London and publishing long fiction. Her first novel appeared in 1960, the introductory volume in *The COUNTRY GIRLS* series that eventually extended to three volumes and an epilogue: *The Country Girls* begins the story of Cait and Baba, which continues in *The Lonely Girl* (1962), *The Girls in Their Married Bliss* (1964), and the *Epilogue* (1986). O'Brien does not bestow happy endings on her characters, and the relationships in which they become involved are often poorly chosen because the girls lack a realistic understanding of their own hearts and of the psychology of men. O'Brien advocates FEMINISM beginning with her earliest novels by focusing on the validity of women's needs and desires, including sexual ones. She also makes strident criticisms of the Catholic Church; the combination of her frank presentation of desire and her hostile treatment of Catholicism has led to the banning of some of her books in her own home country.

By the end of the 20th century, O'Brien had written 15 novels, seven collections of short stories—the literary genre for which she is most admired—several plays, screenplays, and teleplays, a volume of poetry, five works of children's literature, and six works of nonfiction, including a memoir, *Mother Ireland* (1976), and two studies of James Joyce. Her most receptive and appreciative audience is in the United States; her stories frequently appear in American introductory literature textbooks as exemplars of short fiction, and new works appear in distinguished periodicals such as *The Atlantic Monthly* and *The New Yorker.* Critics remain divided on the place of her novels in the CANON of 20th-century literature in English, while also recognizing her facility with language and her fastidious re-creation of the quotidian details of life in her novels of psychological realism.

BIBLIOGRAPHY

Eckley, Grace. *Edna O'Brien.* Lewisburg, Pa.: Bucknell University Press, 1974.

O'Brien, Edna. Interview by Molly McQuade. *Publishers Weekly* May 18, 1992, 48–9.

O'Brien, Peggy. "The Silly and the Serious: An Assessment of Edna O'Brien," *The Massachusetts Review* 18 (Autumn, 1987): 474–88.

Roth, Philip. "A Conversation with Edna O'Brien," *The New York Times Book Review,* November 18, 1984, 38–40.

O'BRIEN, FLANN (1911–1966)

The Irish writer Brian O'Nolan published his fiction under this pen name; he also wrote a newspaper column for the *Irish Times,* "The Cruiskeen Lawn," under the name Myles na Gopaleen ("Myles of the Little Ponies"), and used additional pseudonyms such as George Knowall, Great Count O'Blather, Brother Barnabus, and others.

Flann O'Brien was born in Strabane into a family that spoke both Irish and English. The family eventually moved to Dublin; O'Brien matriculated at University College, majoring in Celtic Studies. While working on a master's thesis about contemporary Irish poetry, O'Brien also wrote his masterpiece, AT SWIM-TWO-BIRDS (1939). This COMIC NOVEL was praised by critics, but it did not find a popular audience—it is an ANTIREALISTIC NOVEL—until it was republished in 1960. O'Brien obtained employment as a civil servant and earned his living in this manner until he retired in 1953. He continued to write, both as a journalist and a novelist. But when his publisher discouraged him over his second novel, *The Third Policeman* (not published until after O'Brien's death), he focused more and more on his journalism and other incidental writing. His third novel was published in Irish as *An Béal Bocht* in 1941 and translated into English for publication in the United States as *The Poor Mouth* in 1973. Again, the work was not a success, except with "Gaelic revivalists" who advocated the preservation of the native Irish language; ironically, Gaelic revivalists were the targets of the novel's SATIRE.

After a hiatus from novel writing for two decades, O'Brien gained fame upon the republication of *At Swim-Two-Birds* in 1960. Ambitious to find success as a novelist, O'Brien moderated his style more and more toward the forms of realism, which he had masterfully satirized in *At Swim-Two-Birds*. His last two novels, *The Hard Life* (1961) and *The Dalkey Archive* (1964), were not as skillful as his earlier work. In 1966, afflicted by alcoholism and cancer, Flann O'Brien died at the age of 55.

BIBLIOGRAPHY

Asbee, Sue. *Flann O'Brien.* Twayne's English Authors, 485. Boston: Twayne Publishers, 1991.

Cronin, Anthony. *No Laughing Matter: The Life and Times of Flann O'Brien.* 1989. New York: Fromm International, 1998.

Hopper, Keith: *Flann O'Brien: A Portrait of the Artist as a Young Post-Modernist.* Cork, Ireland: Cork University Press, 1995.

Kenner, Hugh. *A Colder Eye: The Modern Irish Writers.* New York: Knopf, 1983.

OFFICERS AND GENTLEMEN EVELYN WAUGH (1955)   See *SWORD OF HONOUR TRILOGY.*

OFFSHORE PENELOPE FITZGERALD (1979)

Winner of the BOOKER PRIZE in 1979, this autobiographical novel is set among the barge-dwellers along the Thames River at Battersea, and draws on the author's own residence in a barge community along the Thames in the 1960s. *Offshore* explores the liminal world that is neither dry land nor open water but a threshold between the two, and this space becomes a metaphor for the lives of the people who reside there, who are in various ways living in-between existences. The novel's protagonist is Nenna, a married woman living aboard the *Grace* apart from her husband; their two daughters, 11-year-old Martha and six-year-old Tilda, run wild on the banks, enjoying the freedom of life in the houseboat community. Tilda lives in the happy oblivion of early childhood, while Martha has become prematurely grown up. Although Nenna loves her husband, she cannot bring herself to join him in their landlocked suburban home at Stoke Newington. She finds herself drawn to Richard, a retired officer of the Royal Navy who owns the retired minesweeper that towers above the neighboring barges. He is orderly and disciplined, and yet also sensitive and reasonable; above all, however, he is competent and reliable, especially in a crisis. He is coping with his own marital stresses as Nenna's story unfolds.

Other members of the barge community are more eccentric: Maurice the male prostitute serves as a community confidant, listening to the troubles of others as his own life spirals out of control. The communal cat, Stripey, is not large enough to chase full-grown rats—they chase her instead. Woody, a painter of marine subjects whose commissions have dried up, lives on a boat that is becoming one with the sea as it slowly sinks—and as its owner tries to sell it while it's still afloat. Fitzgerald concentrates on meticulously nuanced character development and evocative descriptions of setting rather than on strong PLOT lines; the power of the novel's suggestive quality belies its short length. By suggesting possibilities rather than defining realities, and by providing enough motivational details to allow readers to think about why the characters perform as they do, Fitzgerald's story can assume larger dimensions in the imaginations of readers. Like the barge community, the novel resides between certainty and AMBIGUITY, between firmness and vagueness. It is a characteristic example of Fitzgerald's economical style—she is often praised as a "miniaturist"—capturing marginalized lives that suggest the larger world to which they are peripheral.

BIBLIOGRAPHY

Sudrann, Jean. "Magic or Miracles: The Fallen World of Penelope Fitzgerald's Novels." In *Contemporary British Women Writers: Narrative Strategies*. Edited by Robert E. Hosmer. New York: St. Martin's Press, 1993, 105–127.

OF HUMAN BONDAGE W. SOMERSET MAUGHAM (1915)

A partially autobiographical BILDUNGSROMAN, this novel inaugurated its author's distinguished career in fiction and is generally regarded as his masterpiece. The story's protagonist is Philip Carey, who is orphaned at the age of nine and then reared in the unloving environment of his uncle, a narrow and miserly vicar in an isolated church. In addition to the emotional and financial hardship of his childhood, Philip is burdened with a disability: He has a clubfoot, and other children taunt him cruelly. The only delight in his life is his access to his uncle's library, where he gives his imagination full play as often as possible. His bondage to the torments of a disabled orphan's life are broken when he turns 18 and receives a small inheritance that allows him to study abroad. In Germany, he meets new friends who talk freely and skeptically about religion, and Philip discovers that he does not believe in God. His new friends introduce him to a world of books and ideas not represented in his uncle's library, and among the most important of these new works is *The Life of Jesus* by Ernest Renan—an example of a book from the real world having an influence in the realm of fiction. Just as books had given him joy in childhood, as a young adult he finds that they open unsuspected vistas and depths of thought.

Having broken free of the strictures of poverty and religious dogma, Philip wishes to learn the secrets of love. He returns to his hometown and enters into an affair with a much older woman, with the result that he is disappointed by the experience. But again a book changes the direction of his life when his mistress introduces him to *The Bohemians of the Latin Quarter*. Philip decides to plunge himself into the Bohemian life of Paris and study painting, and for two years he attempts to learn whether he has enough of a gift to be an artist. He makes new friends and sees what happens to those who have a thirsty ambition to achieve artistic glory but who lack the gifts to fulfill that ambition. Disillusioned once again, especially when one of his moderately talented ambitious friends commits suicide, he decides to return to London and study medicine. Although he learned that he is not gifted enough to sustain an artistic career, he is satisfied that he understands himself better now and can proceed with his adult life with greater confidence.

It is during his studies in London that Philip experiences one of the defining relationships of his life. He meets and falls obsessively in love with Mildred Rogers, a woman who presents no apparent attractions to create such a passion. She is a waitress, coarse, uneducated, and not particularly attractive. Nonetheless, a love for her has taken possession of Philip's soul, and he is helpless to command his own reasoning until he breaks free—until he recovers from the disease of his love for Mildred. For her part, she is indifferent to him and finds opportunities to humiliate his feelings for her and to exploit his limited financial resources. Repeatedly, Mildred betrays Philip, and repeatedly he takes her back again.

In the meantime, another and more positive influence comes to bear on Philip. He meets Thorpe Athelney in the course of his studies to become a doctor when Thorpe is admitted as a hospital patient. After his discharge, Thorpe frequently invites his new friend to visit; at the Athelney home, loving parents shower affection on their happy children. This is the life Philip lost when he became an orphan, and he rediscovers the simple joys of domesticity by observing the happy interactions among the members of the Athelney household. But Mildred reenters his life when he finds her selling herself as a streetwalker. The example of Thorpe and his well-adjusted family has helped Philip recover from his obsession for Mildred, and although he once again helps her, he no longer loves her or suffers for that love. Their final parting is costly to Philip in terms of material goods, but he is truly free of the binding power she once exerted over him.

Philip exhausts his inheritance and leaves school until his uncle dies and he once again comes into financial security. He finishes his medical studies and takes a vacation with the Athelneys. After the vacation, he intends to become a ship's doctor and travel to exotic locations around the world on an extended working adventure. During the vacation, however, he discovers that one of the Athelney daughters has grown to adulthood and he falls in love. Philip faces one last struggle with the bonds that tie human beings as he chooses the best course for finding his own happiness during his mature life.

MAUGHAM'S record of one person's interior journey of self-exploration is virtually flawless: Philip discovers the many forms of bondage to which human life is inevitable subject by examining his own thoughts, feelings, behaviors, assumptions, and responses. By implication, if this man can reason his way out of misunderstanding and unhappiness, so too can the rest of us, given the leavening of even a small amount of good fortune in one's circle of friends. Philip rises above the limitations he has placed on himself and those that circumstance have imposed on him as well. In the end, he is ready and able to choose the path that will secure to him the greatest personal happiness for the rest of his life.

BIBLIOGRAPHY

Loss, Archie K. Of Human Bondage: *Coming of Age in the Novel.* Twayne's Masterwork Studies, 40. Boston: Twayne Publishers, 1990.

O'FLAHERTY, LIAM (1897–1984) Liam

O'Flaherty was born in IRELAND'S remote and rugged Aran Islands on August 28, 1896. He excelled scholastically, attending Catholic parochial schools and Holy Cross College, a seminary in Dublin. He earned a scholarship to University College, Dublin, and matriculated there to study medicine. The outbreak of WORLD WAR I disrupted his education in 1915, when he left school to join the British Army, where he served with the Irish Guards. He experienced combat in Belgium and France, and he suffered shell shock in 1917

at Langemarck. He was "invalided out" of the army in 1918 and entered a two-year period of wandering, working as a sailor on Atlantic and Mediterranean trading routes and later traveling and working in the United States and Canada. His brother was the writer Robert O'Flaherty, living in Boston; he encouraged Liam to write, drawing on the wide-ranging experience of the past two years for story material.

Liam O'Flaherty tried his hand at fiction but was displeased by the results and destroyed his earliest work. He returned to Ireland in 1920 and became politically active, joining the Communist Party and supporting the struggle for Irish independence from Great Britain; he also formally abandoned the Catholic Church. He led a march that occupied a Dublin landmark in 1922, but his left-wing allegiances ultimately drove him out of Ireland. In London, he began writing seriously, and in 1923 a story he placed in a magazine there, "The Sniper," gained the interest of the influential critic and publisher Edward Garnett. Through this connection, O'Flaherty's first novel—still the work of a writer learning the craft—was published. *Thy Neighbor's Wife* is set in the Aran Isles and brings that remote location to life. His next novel was *The Black Soul* (1924), also set in the Aran Isles, and it showed greater sophistication in handling the interior lives of the characters; then in 1925, his third novel, *The INFORMER,* made his reputation and won several literary prizes, including the JAMES TAIT BLACK MEMORIAL PRIZE. It later became the basis of a FILM ADAPTATION that won two Academy Awards in 1935.

During this period, O'Flaherty was also writing short fiction; he published collections of stories in 1924, 1925, and three in 1926. In that year he was also married, a union that lasted until 1932, when it ended in a separation. Also in 1926, his novel *Mr. Gilhooley* appeared; it is a study of isolation, alienation, and obsessive love. In 1930, he visited the Soviet Union and became disenchanted with communism. As a result of these travels, he published the nonfiction book *I Went to Russia* in 1931. His literary output in the 1920s and 1930s was voluminous, placing him in the first ranks of Irish writers of his day, in the company of James JOYCE and others. In 1932, he was a founding member of the Irish Academy of Letters. That year he also published one of his most critically admired novels, *Skerrett,* the story of a schoolmaster in the Aran Isles. His other most noted novel is *Famine* (1937), which follows the lives of an Irish family during the Great Potato Famine of the 1840s.

Most of O'Flaherty's writing predates WORLD WAR II, when he again traveled extensively and began dividing his residence between Ireland and the United States. He published two volumes of autobiography in his life, *Two Years* in 1930 and *Shame the Devil* in 1934. He also wrote a biography of Tim Healy, a critical study of Joseph CONRAD, and a work of children's literature published the year of his death. Liam O'Flaherty died in Dublin on September 7, 1984.

BIBLIOGRAPHY

Doyle, Paul A. *Liam O'Flaherty.* Twayne's English Authors, 108. New York: Twayne Publishers, 1971.

Kelly, A. A. *Liam O'Flaherty the Storyteller.* New York: Barnes & Noble, 1976.

O'Brien, James H. *Liam O'Flaherty.* Lewisburg, Pa.: Bucknell University Press, 1973.

OKRI, BEN (1959–)

Born into the Urhobo people of Nigeria on March 15, 1959, Ben Okri was the son of an African executive in the British colonial system. Nigeria achieved its independence in 1960, and Okri's youth was marked by the convulsions of postcolonial civil strife as different factions, many based on tribal affiliation, vied for power. He attended Urhobo College in Warri (the equivalent of a secondary education) and the University of Essex in Colchester, England. He later moved to London, where he has remained as a voluntary expatriate ever since. He has edited a journal of African poetry and has worked as a commentator for the British Broadcasting Corporation.

Okri's first novel was *Flowers and Shadows* (1980); it used the device of an unsuspecting son discovering his father's corrupted business dealings to suggest the political situation in Nigeria, a nominal democracy. In *The Landscapes Within* (1981), he uses the fictional experiences of an artist whose paintings draw the wrath of the powerful on his head, a device he also uses with a photographer in *The* FAMISHED ROAD (1991); he seems to suggest that the artist has a role to play in creating an awareness of injustice in the wider world, but that the price for doing so may be very high. Okri has also published two collections of short fiction, *Incidents at the Shrine* (1986) and *Stars of the New Curfew* (1988).

In 1991, *The Famished Road* made Ben Okri the first black African writer to win the BOOKER PRIZE (South Africa's J. M. COETZEE had won it in 1983 for *The* LIFE AND TIMES OF MICHAEL K.). *Songs of Enchantment* (1993) continues the story begun in *The Famished Road,* reemphasizing its positive view of life in the midst of Africa's harsh realities. In 1995, Okri produced a philosophical novel, *Astonishing the Gods,* about understanding the difference between appearance and reality. *A Dangerous Love* (1996) places a love story in the realistic setting of modern Lagos, Nigeria's capital. He has also published three additional novels, *Birds of Heaven* (1996), *Infinite Riches* (1998), and *Mental Flight* (1999). In 1992, he produced a collection of poetry, *An African Elegy,* and in 1997, a collection of essays, *A Way of Being Free.* His novels preserve traditional aspects of African storytelling by incorporating them into internationally recognized narrative devices such as MAGIC REALISM; his poems and essays are sympathetic polemics to his fellow Africans to resolve their differences and make a place for themselves in the modern world.

BIBLIOGRAPHY

Falconer, Delia. "Whispering of the Gods: An Interview with Ben Okri," *Island Magazine* 71 (Winter 1997): 43–51.

Fraser, Robert. *Ben Okri: Towards the Invisible City.* Devon, England: Northcote House-British Council, 2002.

Quayson, Ato. *Strategic Transformations in Nigerian Writing: Orality and History in the Work of Rev. Samuel Johnson, Amos Tutuola, Wole Soyinka, and Ben Okri.* Bloomington: Indiana University Press, 1997.

OLD DEVILS, THE KINGSLEY AMIS (1986)

Winner of the BOOKER PRIZE in 1986, THIS COMIC NOVEL follows the lives of several old friends in the south of Wales who find their settled retirement disrupted by the arrival of a former member of the group—a man whose literary achievement has considerably outstripped that of his old friends. Alun Weaver, a professional Welshman (one of the novel's themes is "Welshness"), and his wife, Rhiannon, return to their hometown after many years in London; Alun has become a television personality, a writer noted for his poetry, and an authority on the Welsh poet Brydan (a thinly disguised Dylan Thomas), but he is also the former lover of Gwen Cellan-Davies, who is the present wife of Malcolm Cellan-Davies, the man Alun is about to displace as the leading local man of letters. Malcolm is an amateur poet (and retired insurance salesman), and he senses he will soon be eclipsed by his old friend's notoriety. Rhiannon, on the other hand, is the former lover of Peter Thomas, who is now a retired chemical engineer unhappily married to Muriel Thomas. She is nobody's former lover, but she is a native of Yorkshire displaced to Wales by her marriage. The other key characters include the Norrises, Sophie and Charlie: Sophie was once the lover of Alun Weaver and she would be happy to renew that affair, while Charlie is a part owner of the Owen Glendower Hotel and a man morbidly afraid of the dark even in his sunset years.

Kingsley AMIS builds much of his humor on the foibles and facts of old age. Malcolm worries continually about the state of his bowels, but he resents efforts from Gwen to show any concern for him in this matter. Peter has grown too fat to clip his own toenails; Muriel's nagging has become honed to a deadening degree. The characters are all in their 60s or beyond, and yet they remain immersed in a kind of soap-opera existence in their own day-to-day lives. The poets in the group are jealous of their status as poets and deeply resent any intimation that their current work may be in any way less significant than was the rest of their oeuvres. Alun Weaver even goes to the extreme of taking revenge on Charlie Norris, who had opined (when urged to give an "honest opinion") that Alun's current poetic efforts were of no value: His revenge takes advantage of Charlie's well-known fear of the dark. But Alun's fame and success are no guarantee of longevity, and when he dies unexpectedly of a heart attack, as any elderly person might be expected to do in his waning years, the lives of his friends are thrown into disarray. A game of musical spouses becomes possible once Alun has departed the scene, and the rearrangements lead to several unexpectedly happy outcomes.

The great strength of this novel is its characterization of the lives of the elderly from an interior perspective. The omniscient third-person narrator is both droll and merciless in depicting the thoughts, hopes,

obsessions, and fears of the characters. Amis presents the elderly as ordinary people with the same concerns that any of us might have, plus the extra concerns forced on them by old age—many of which have to do with the declining capacity to pursue their concerns to satisfactory conclusions. His treatment of the characters makes them fully human, not pitiable husks of people who once were human: They have full lives, sharp appetites, and all the follies of self-importance, vanity, and desire that plague the young and the middle-aged, too. Optimistically, Amis shows that people can find happiness even on death's doorstep, and he reminds readers that humor is the leavening of a life well lived.

BIBLIOGRAPHY

Bell, Robert H., ed. *Critical Essays on Kingsley Amis.* New York: G. K. Hall, 1998.

Farringdon, Jill. "When You Go Home Again to Wales," *The Anglo-Welsh Review* 86 (1987): 87–92.

OLD JEST, THE JENNIFER JOHNSTON (1979)

Set along the eastern Irish coast near Dublin in 1920, the year leading to the establishment of the Irish Free State, this novel covers a few days in the life of Nancy Gulliver, beginning on her 18th birthday. Nancy's family has a long history of service to the British government: Her elderly grandfather is a retired general, and her uncle Gabriel died in uniform. They trace their ancestry back to the 17th century, but the family is in the last days of its decline. Nancy is an orphan; her mother died when she was born, and only her aunt Mary and her grandfather remain, tended by a longtime cook and an old gardener. They live in a beautiful and peaceful corner of IRELAND, but changes are coming to their world. The family finances are drained and the house they have owned by the sea for generations must be sold if they are to have enough to live on.

Nancy is just at the threshold of adulthood, and so these cares have been kept from her. She is very young and very naïve, but she is also determined to grow up and crack the mystery of adulthood. She has long had a crush on Harry, a young man employed as a businessman in Dublin, but he is in love with Maeve Casey and thinks of Nancy as just a kid. She is experiencing desires she doesn't understand, and at the same time the political situation in her country is equally as passionate and as uncertain as her own unsettled state of mind.

JOHNSTON uses two narrative devices so that readers can examine Nancy from the inside and from an outside third-person perspective: The novel opens with the first entry in the journal Nancy buys for herself as a birthday present, and then the third-person narrator takes over the story to fill in the context, the other characters, and the action of the plot. The conflict arises out of two sources: from Nancy's desire to know about her father, who is never mentioned in the family, and who is not present in any of the family photographs, and from the presence of a strange man, who appears to be about the age her father should be, in the little beach hut sequestered from view where Nancy sometimes goes to read, write, and think. This mysterious person has a gun, in an era of daily sniping, assassinations, and manhunts, but he asks nothing of Nancy until one day he needs a message taken up to Dublin. Nancy is unwittingly, though willingly, drawn into the violent world of adulthood.

Johnston's short novel won the WHITBREAD Book of the Year Award in 1979. It is an accessible evocation of a person, a place, and a time, filled with beautiful descriptions of the Irish coast and a touching portrait of a young girl facing the daunting task of crossing into adulthood virtually alone. Johnston captures the uneasy coexistence of settled domesticity and unexpected violence—of old English loyalties and growing Irish nationalism—as one girl arrives at a turning point in her life.

BIBLIOGRAPHY

Lanters, José. "Jennifer Johnston's Divided Ireland." In *The Clash of Ireland: Literary Contrasts and Connections*. Edited by C. C. Barfoot and Theo D'haen. Amsterdam: Rodopi, 1989, 209–222.

Lynch, Rachael Sealy. "Public Spaces, Private Lives: Irish Identity and Female Selfhood in the Novels of Jennifer Johnston." In *Border Crossings: Irish Women Writers and National Identities*. Edited by Kathryn Kirkpatrick. Tuscaloosa: University of Alabama Press, 2000, 250–268.

ONCE AND FUTURE KING, THE T. H. WHITE (1958) A modern retelling of the Arthurian legends, this book was originally published in four parts, with a fifth part remaining unpublished at the author's death. The series has appeared in print as a single volume since 1958, when T. H. WHITE combined and revised *The Sword in the Stone* (1938), *The Witch in the Wood* (1939; renamed *The Queen of Air and Darkness* in the consolidated edition), *The Ill-Made Knight* (1940), and *The Candle in the Wind* (1958), together with selections from *The Book of Merlyn*, then unpublished, to form *The Once and Future King*. This book in turn became the inspiration for the Broadway musical *Camelot* in 1960, which, in turn, became part of the American mythology of John F. Kennedy's presidency. White developed his story by adapting freely from Thomas Malory's *Le Morte D'Arthur*, itself a 16th-century redaction of centuries of storytelling about the knights of the Round Table.

In the first section of 24 chapters, a third-person omniscient narrator relates how Merlyn became the tutor of the Wart, the orphaned foster-brother of Kay, son of Sir Ector. Merlyn uses his magical powers and his influence with the animals of the world to teach Arthur about politics and morality, sometimes changing Arthur into various animals to help drive the lesson home more vividly. Arthur draws Excalibur, the sword of Uther Pendragon, from the stone into which Uther had driven it upon his death and is begrudgingly proclaimed king. Merlyn reveals that Arthur is in fact Uther's son; through his teaching, he has made Arthur ready to assume the responsibilities he was born to undertake.

In the second section of 14 chapters, the setting shifts to the northern Scottish island kingdom of Orkney, where four noble brothers—Gawaine, Agravaine, Gaheris, and Gareth—are growing up under the thumb of a demanding but loveless mother who has failed to instill in them any useful understanding of right and wrong. Their untaught, aimless amorality is the metaphor for the condition in Arthur's lands that he must eradicate before he can unite its squabbling tribes and clans and form them into a nation. The narrator intertwines the stories of Arthur and the sons of King Lot, ending with the decision of Lot's wife, Morgause, who is also Arthur's half sister, to entangle

Arthur with magic so that she can conceive his son, Mordred.

The knight for whom the third section is named is Sir Lancelot, who is described as ugly and sinful and yet mighty in feats of arms and devoted to religious fervor, if not to purity in his behavior. Arthur comes to the height of his power and establishes his court and the Round Table, achieving his goals for a brief period before human frailty can topple order into chaos again. T. H. White was a pacifist in life who fled England to avoid the risk of conscription for military service during WORLD WAR II; his presentation of a medieval world of military might contains his SATIRE on the use of force to win political or other ideological goals. His pessimism about the human race becomes evident in the ways that innocence and hard work fail to instill enduring states of justice among the envious, vain, deceitful, and violent men and women of the world.

In *The Candle in the Wind,* White shows the dissolution of the Round Table when the affair between Lancelot and Guenevere is brought to light. Civil war replaces order, unity, and peace, and Arthur departs for Avilion, leaving his story in the charge of a young boy, knowing that eventually the world will be a fit place for peace again. Readers interested in White's original conception of the closing of the series should also consult *The Book of Merlyn: The Unpublished Conclusion to The Once and Future King,* edited by Sylvia Townsend Warner and published in 1977 by the University of Texas Press.

BIBLIOGRAPHY

Brewer, Elisabeth. *T. H. White's* The Once and Future King. Cambridge: D. S. Brewer, 1993.

Gallix, François. "T. H. White and the Legend of King Arthur: From Animal Fantasy to Political Morality." In *King Arthur: A Casebook.* Edited by Edward Donald Kennedy. New York: Garland, 1996, 281–311.

Worthington, Heather. "From Children's Story to Adult Fiction: T. H. White's *The Once and Future King,*" *Arthuriana* 12, no. 2 (Summer 2002): 97–119.

ONDAATJE, MICHAEL (1943–   )   Born on September 12, 1943, in Colombo, Sri Lanka (called Ceylon at that time), Michael Ondaatje is a leading contemporary novelist and poet. His parents divorced when he was two, and his mother relocated with her children to London in 1954. Michael Ondaatje attended secondary school at Dulwich College. In 1962, at the age of 19, he moved to Canada and matriculated at Bishop's College, Quebec. Two years later, he married an artist some dozen years older than he was who had previously been the wife of one of his professors. The couple became part of a Canadian artists' colony during the summers, when they entertained writers and friends at their farm in the Great Lakes countryside. The marriage produced two children and ended in a separation in 1980.

During the 1960s, Ondaatje was writing award-winning poetry, and his poems were showcased in anthologies of "new wave" Canadian literature. He also continued his academic studies, receiving a bachelor's degree from the University of Toronto in 1968 and a master's degree from Queen's University. He was appointed to a faculty position at the University of Western Ontario, and in a supremely ironic twist he was fired in 1971 for not pursuing a Ph.D. degree only days before winning Canada's highest literary recognition, the Governor-General's Award—the first of three he has received.

By then, Ondaatje was also experimenting with performance art and making short films, and he had published *The Collected Works of Billy the Kid: Left Handed Poems* (1970; the impetus for his first Governor General's Award), an AVANT-GARDE novel. His next two novels received further attention from literary prize committees: *Coming Through Slaughter* (1976) won the *Books in Canada* First Novel Award, and *In the Skin of a Lion* (1987) was nominated for the Ritz Hemingway Literary Prize. His fourth novel, *The ENGLISH PATIENT* (1992), won the BOOKER PRIZE, making Ondaatje the first Canadian to win that award. The novel became the basis of a popular FILM ADAPTATION in 1996, winning the Academy Award for Best Picture and bringing Ondaatje's work to a worldwide audience. In 2000, he published the novel *Anil's Ghost*. Michael Ondaatje continues to live and write at his home in Toronto, Canada.

BIBLIOGRAPHY

Barbour, Douglas. *Michael Ondaatje.* Twayne's World Authors, 835. New York: Twayne, 1993.

Jewinski, Ed. *Michael Ondaatje: Express Yourself Beautifully.* Toronto: ECW Press, 1994.

Mundwiler, Leslie. *Michael Ondaatje: Word, Image, Imagination.* Vancouver: Talonbooks, 1984.

ORCZY, BARONESS (1865–1947)

Born on September 23, 1865, into the privileged world of her aristocratic parents in the town of Tarna-Örs, Hungary, during the height of the doomed Austro-Hungarian Empire, Emmuska Magdalena Rosalia Maria Josepha Barbara Orczy (pronounced ORT-zee) enjoyed an opulent childhood. Her father was a noted conductor and composer who counted among his friends the musicians Wagner and Listz. When she was five, however, as she recounted in her autobiography, peasant unrest imprinted a scene on her mind when a Luddite mob burned her father's barns, stables, and crops to protest his program of agricultural modernization.

By the time Emmuska was 15, the family was settled in London after several years of relocation in Brussels and Paris, where she had been educated in convent schools. Baroness Orczy later described England as her spiritual home; at 15, she learned the English language quickly and adapted to her new nationality. She wanted to be an artist, but since she had none of her father's musical talent, she enrolled in the West London School of Art and at Heatherly's studio. There, she met her future husband, the illustrator Montagu Barstow. They were married in 1894. They collaborated on illustrations for periodicals and books, including a collection of Hungarian folktales. Emmuska also began writing detective stories featuring the recurring "armchair detective" called The Old Man in the Corner—someone who bears a faint similarity to Mycroft Holmes, but who is less reclusive than Sherlock HOLMES'S smarter brother. She conceived of the Scarlet Pimpernel while visiting in Paris in 1901 and began developing a novel for this dashing character. In an era of literary MODERNISM, however, her swashbuckling historical thriller was repeatedly rejected by London publishers.

The Barstows were enthusiastic about the theater, attending performances in London frequently. When they met the actors Fred Terry and Julia Neilson, who were searching for new material for plays, the Barstows offered to adapt the unpublished Pimpernel volume for the stage. They collaborated on this work, as on their illustrating projects, and the play of The SCARLET PIMPERNEL appeared in Nottingham and later moved to London in 1904. Critics did not praise it, but it was a great popular success nonetheless—so great, in fact, that the novel quickly found a publisher, and the story became a success in the print medium as well. Sir Percy Blakeney went on to appear in some 16 additional novels, counting stories of his ancestor Diogenes and his descendent Peter. He also made a successful transition to the screen, appearing in a FILM ADAPTATION in 1935 in which Leslie Howard acted the part of Sir Percy. Others who have played Sir Percy include the renowned actors David Niven and James Mason; Daffy Duck has parodied him as the Scarlet Pumpernickel.

Baroness Orczy also wrote many additional series of detective stories featuring Lady Molly of Scotland Yard and the Irish lawyer Patrick Mulligan. By the end of her life, she had published more than 30 volumes of fiction. Royalties from the many stage performances of *The Scarlet Pimpernel* and from sales of the book in the many languages into which it was translated allowed the Barstows to move to Monte Carlo when WORLD WAR I began, and they remained there until 1943, even through the Nazi occupation. Montagu Barstow died in 1943 and Emmuska Orczy returned to London. She continued writing, working on new material to the end of her life. She died in London on November 12, 1947.

BIBLIOGRAPHY

Orczy, Baroness. *Links in the Chain of Life.* London: Hutchinson, 1947.

Rutland, Arthur. "Baroness Orczy," *The Bookman,* April 1913, 193–201.

ORLANDO VIRGINIA WOOLF (1928)

This unusual FANTASY novel, atypical of the works of Virginia WOOLF, draws its protagonist from a specific model: Woolf's lover Vita Sackville-West served as a major inspiration for the ambiguously gendered Orlando, especially with respect to the legal bias in favor of men that led to the loss of her family home to an uncle under laws requiring that males inherit some family property. Woolf dedicated the novel to Sackville-West and completed the lengthy work in an incredibly short time during the creative rush that moved her from TO THE LIGHTHOUSE (1927) through The WAVES (1931).

Woolf believed that, contrary to popular belief, biographers rarely told the "truth"; she originally planned a parody of that genre in her novel. She toyed with many traditions of biography, including the concept of time and gender. Woolf drew inspiration for the novel's ironic "preface" from the traditional biography form, thanking her creative influences including Sir Walter Scott, Emily Brontë, and Walter Pater. She also "acknowledges" the help of members of her inner circle, including her nephew Quentin Bell, "an old and valued collaborator in fiction," alluding to their cowritten Christmas dramas performed each year for their family. She also inserted posed photos of supposed factual subjects, including "The Russian Princess as a Child," featuring her niece, Angelica Bell.

In the character of Orlando, Woolf made a statement about women's lack of rights, prompted in part by the traditional "law of entail" from which Sackville-West had suffered. The story had grown in Woolf's imagination for some months, indicated by a March 1927 diary entry noting her desire to write a fantasy and her thought that "Vita should be Orlando, a young nobleman." By the end of 1927, she had stopped all critical writing to focus on the novel.

The novel opens with Orlando as a 16th-century 16-year-old youth favored by Queen Elizabeth I. At work on a five-act tragedy, Orlando's sexuality is awakened by various women, including the Russian Princess Sasha, whom he cannot marry. By the second chapter, no longer in favor with the court ruled by James I, Orlando mourns the loss of Sasha, who has returned to Russia. In a morbid mood, he spends large amounts of time in the family crypt but is inspired, writing 47 plays by the age of 25. However, he decides that poetry is the best of all arts, and that the battle to produce exquisite art proves just as difficult and valuable as any of the military exploits of his ancestors. Woolf's antiwar sentiment guided her insertion of that theme. She introduces famous writers of the era, including Shakespeare,

Christopher Marlowe, and Ben Jonson. By age 30, Orlando still lives alone and burns all his writing except for a single poem, "The Oak Tree," which he continues to revise. The chapter concludes with his falling in love with the Archduchess Harriet of Roumania, who believes that Orlando looks just like her sister, and with Orlando's appointment as ambassador to Constantinople. Each subsequent chapter continues to suggest that the attitude of its age toward marriage determines Orlando's fate, as the author continues to reference "historical sources" for her biographical account. Much of the detail throughout the novel Woolf actually based on the history of the Sackville-West family, long involved in English history and literature.

Orlando begins chapter three as an ambassador and then earns a dukedom and the Order of Bath from King Charles. He enters a trance, is discovered to have married the Gypsy Rosina Pepita, a character based on Sackville-West's grandmother Pepita, and is captured by Turks during a revolution. While in the trance, Orlando is ministered to by our Lady of Purity, our Lady of Chastity, and our Lady of Modesty; "he" then awakes as a woman. She lives with Gypsies and is well received until accused of worshipping nature. Orlando's work on her poem deepens her accusers' suspicions and some seek to kill her. She returns to England on the ship Enamoured Lady, and in chapter four begins to learn the meaning of womanhood. Seeing St. Paul's Cathedral reminds Orlando of a servant poet from her earlier life as she arrives in 18th-century London. There she sees notables including John Dryden and Alexander Pope, a result of Woolf's telescoping of time: Dryden died when Pope was about two years old. Woolf emphasizes the antiquated law of entailment still in use in the 20th century as Orlando discovers that not only has she been declared dead, but also that she cannot inherit her own property due to her present gender. Her sons through her previous marriage, while male, to Rosina Pepita have claimed all her property. Orlando again begins work on her poem, "The Oak Tree," at which point the shadow previously cast across the page by Archduchess Harry again appears, but the archduchess is now Archduke Harry, who wants to marry Orlando. Orlando enjoys high-society life, romances both males and females, and meets Samuel Johnson and James Boswell. Critics later noted that Woolf avoided the perils inherent in the theme of "sapphism," the cause of the ban of Radclyffe HALL'S *WELL OF LONELINESS,* printed three months before *Orlando.*

By the fifth chapter, Orlando has been working on her poem for 300 years. She dwells in a society of enormous-sized families with her lawsuits settled. As she attempts to finish her poem, large inkblots mar it, and she seems able to produce only garble. Her Turkish lawsuit settled, she is officially declared a woman and marries Marmaduke Bonthrop Shelmerdine, who had previously rescued her when she sustained a broken ankle. The book concludes in chapter six at midnight on October 11, 1928. During this final age, Orlando seems to find approval in society for her marriage, and her work on her poem progresses. Nick Greene, an influential critic, declares that "The Oak Tree" must be published, and he longs aloud for the spirit of the Renaissance or the 18th century. Orlando sets out to learn all about literature as she corresponds with Shelmerdine in a coded language, representative of Woolf's own correspondence with her husband, Leonard. She retains some memory of her 400-year-long life, with the image of the poet in the servant quarters recurring as she drives through the countryside where she once lived. "The Oak Tree" has won an award, as well as comparison to writing by John Milton, and she decides to bury a copy beneath her favorite real tree. Woolf based Orlando's poem on Sackville-West's Hawthornden Prize–winning poem, "The Land," a work Woolf quotes in chapter six. Orlando places the book on the ground and calls out "Shel," her husband's name. He appears, parachuting to earth from an airplane flying overhead, as the clock strikes midnight.

Some critical reaction proved negative, with Arnold Bennett terming it "a high-brow lark." Woolf had at one point confessed to Leonard that she began the book as a joke, but later adopted an entirely serious attitude toward it. Others, like the American Rebecca West in an article titled "High Fountain of Genius," pronounced *Orlando* "a poetic masterpiece." West praised Woolf's clear contempt for realism, evident in her adoption of the most realistic of presentations, the biography, for a fantasy. Sackville-West's mother detested the book, but

likely based her reaction on her belief that Woolf's affections alienated her from her daughter. Later critics have seen it as an important work of FEMINISM, making clear the social conventions that discourage creativity and intellectual development in women in a patriarchal society, as many continue to investigate its various sources. Despite any negative reactions, the work proved extremely popular, with an immediate sell-out of first printings in England and America. When the book appeared in paperback in the late 1940s, the printing ran to 278,000 copies. Woolf proved that experimental fiction did sell, and by the year's close, *Orlando* had entered its third printing. It remains a popular work and appeared in film version in 1992.

—*Virginia Brackett*

BIBLIOGRAPHY

Brackett, Virginia. *Restless Genius: The Story of Virginia Woolf.* Greensboro, N.C.: Morgan Reynolds, 2004.

Hoffmann, Charles G. "Fact and Fantasy in *Orlando*: Virginia Woolf's Manuscript Revisions," *Texas Studies in Literature and Language* 10 (1968): 435–444.

Hussey, Mark. *Virginia Woolf: A–Z.* New York: Facts On File, 1995.

Lawrence, Karen R. "Orlando's Voyage Out," *Modern Fiction Studies* 38.1 (Spring 1992): 253–277.

Woolf, Virginia. *The Diary of Virginia Woolf.* Vol. 3. New York: Harcourt, Brace, 1982.

ORWELL, GEORGE (1903–1950)

Born Eric Arthur Blair, George Orwell produced two of the most important works of political fiction in English in the 20th century, *ANIMAL FARM* (1945) and *NINETEEN EIGHTY-FOUR* (1949), and is admired as one of the finest English prose stylists of the century. His works have been translated into languages all over the world, and his essays are commonly included in composition textbooks as models of good writing.

Orwell was born on June 25, 1903, in INDIA, where his father was a career administrator under the British Raj during the height of COLONIALISM. In 1905, Orwell's mother returned to England with her children. Eric attended St. Cyprian's preparatory school and then was enrolled at England's premier PUBLIC SCHOOL, Eton, where his classmates included Anthony POWELL. Eric entered the Indian Imperial Police and served in Burma for five years, resigning in 1927 to become a writer. His financial resources were limited, and at that time life in Paris was cheaper than life in London, so Orwell relocated. He wrote articles for newspapers on political, social, and ethical issues, and he wrote novels and short fiction that publishers uniformly rejected. He sank into poverty, unable to develop an adequate income from writing, and eventually returned to London in impoverished circumstances, living for some time as a homeless drifter. His experiences formed the basis for his first published book, a work of nonfiction, *Down and Out in Paris and London* (1933). Orwell was to maintain his identification with the disempowered poor and with the working CLASS throughout his writing career, in spite of his upper-middle-class origins and elite education.

Orwell began publishing fiction in 1934 with *Burmese Days,* drawing on his experiences in the Imperial Police for the background of a tragic romantic triangle that symbolizes the hopeless project of colonialism. His next two novels moved away from autobiographical connections to explore human interactions: *A Clergyman's Daughter* (1935) and *Keep the Aspidistra Flying* (1936), which follows an idealistic young man disgusted by middle-class complacency. Then in 1937, he wrote a nonfiction work about the coal miners in Yorkshire and Lancashire, *The Road to Wigan Pier.* His experience with the working conditions and the poverty the miners endured provided a platform from which Orwell could advocate a position sympathetic to socialism. But he did not embrace Marxist ideology, much less communism, with wholehearted approval; during the Spanish civil war, which he covered as a journalist and fought in as a partisan, he came to distrust the communists. Out of that experience, he wrote *Homage to Catalonia* (1938), generally regarded as his best nonfiction book.

Orwell's health was not robust, and his first serious pulmonary problem occurred in 1938, forcing him to seek treatment for tuberculosis in the warm climate of Morocco. During this period, he wrote *Coming Up for Air* (1939), the story of an insurance salesman who longs for the "good old days" as WORLD WAR II looms, and who journeys in search of the world of his childhood, only to find it wiped out by the sprawl and violence of the modern world. When World War II arrived, Orwell was not healthy enough for military service; instead, he became a broadcaster for the BBC. He also began writing *Animal Farm* but had difficulty finding a publisher until 1945; ironically, upon its publication it was instantly recognized as a modern classic of ALLEGORY and SATIRE, in a league with works by Jonathan Swift, the most brilliant satirist in English. Orwell's health was failing as he worked on *Nineteen Eighty-four,* and his first wife died in 1945 as he was starting to compose; he sequestered himself on a Scottish island to work on the book. By the time he finished it, he was suffering severely from tuberculosis. He remarried in October 1949, and in January 1950 he died in London.

Orwell continues to receive serious attention from scholars, and his two political novels have become standard components of high school and college curricula. He was simultaneously a leftist reformer, advocating democratic socialism, and a critic of abuses by any form of totalitarian regime. By keeping himself at arm's length from communist literary circles he incurred the displeasure of Marxist critics, but his literary legacy is devoid of dogmatic or propagandistic elements. *Animal Farm* and *Nineteen Eighty-Four* rise above specific political squabbles to address the universal issues of human needs and rights within the contexts of shared social communities of conflicting interests.

BIBLIOGRAPHY

Crick, Bernard. *George Orwell: A Life.* Boston: Little, Brown, 1980.

Davison, Peter. *George Orwell: A Literary Life.* New York: St. Martin's Press, 1996.

Gardner, Averil. *George Orwell.* Twayne's English Authors Series, 455. Boston: Twayne, 1987.

Hitchens, Christopher. *Why Orwell Matters.* New York: Basic Books, 2002.

Ingle, Stephen. *George Orwell: A Political Life.* Manchester, U.K.: Manchester University Press, 1993.

Sheldon, Michael. *Orwell: The Authorized Biography.* New York: HarperCollins, 1991.

OSCAR AND LUCINDA PETER CAREY **(1988)** Winner of the BOOKER PRIZE in 1988, this novel of mismatched love and futile ambition is set in late 19th-century Australia. The novel features a double protagonist: Oscar Hopkins is a defrocked (for gambling) Anglican priest with a fanatical personality who comes to sacrifice himself to Australia, and Lucinda LePlastrier is a Victorian feminist and compulsive gambler who hopes to change the world through the establishment of factories—she herself owns a glass factory. These two individuals of extreme personalities and strong passions need the counterbalancing force of moderation, but they find each other instead. The novel's narrator is Oscar's present-day great-grandson; Lucinda, however, is not the narrator's great-grandmother.

Oscar and Lucinda meet on a ship and discover their shared weakness for risk; they embark on a kind of evangelical gambling tour of the Australian frontier. CAREY pays careful attention to historical detail in presenting the rampant settlement of the antipodean continent, allowing an Aboriginal narrator, Kumbaingiri Billy, to present an alternative version of how Oscar brought Jesus to the outback. With the product of her failing factory, Lucinda provides Oscar with a glass church—a veritable cathedral—to serve as his benefice in the outback. First, of course, Oscar must get the church to its intended location, and the long journey is marred by murder and human rapacity. Although Oscar and Lucinda have a sweet and touching love, they are driven apart by scandalized Victorian propriety.

Oscar and Lucinda is characteristic of Peter Carey's style in its careful attention to a wealth of historical detail and in its dependence on idiosyncratic characters who become sympathetically believable through their reactions to the events of the PLOT. The novel served as the basis for a FILM ADAPTATION in 1997 in a movie directed by Gillian Armstrong that starred Ralph Fiennes and Cate Blanchett.

BIBLIOGRAPHY

Hassall, Anthony J. *Dancing on Hot Macadam: Peter's Carey's Fiction*. St. Lucia: University of Queensland Press, 1998.

Krassnitzer, Hermine. *Aspects of Narration in Peter Carey's Novels: Deconstructing Colonialism*. Lewiston, Me.: E. Mellen Press, 1995.

OUT OF THE SILENT PLANET C. S. LEWIS **(1938)** See *SPACE TRILOGY, THE*.

P

PADDY CLARKE HA HA HA RODDY
DOYLE (1993) Winner of the BOOKER PRIZE in
1993, this novel chronicles the life of 10-year-old
Patrick Doyle in 1968, the year that his family disintegrates. The story in set in the north Dublin neighborhood of Barrytown, which also served as the setting for
Doyle's earlier novels, *The Commitments* (1988), *The
Snapper* (1990), and *The Van* (1991). Doyle's narrative
strategy is notable for the way he captures the thoughts
and feelings of a 10-year-old Irish boy in a manner that
is realistically believable while still allowing for the
indirect development of the plot out of the child narrator's scattered and unsophisticated observations.
Paddy sees the world and reports it, but he does not
yet have the reasoning capacity to analyze his observations or to make cause-and-effect connections among
the day-to-day ephemeral events of his life.

Paddy is unaffectedly honest in presenting the casual
cruelty of the world of children. He tells of the adventures of his group of friends, implying the pecking order
that has imposed a hierarchy on the group long before
its members can articulate or even understand concepts
of power, privilege, and dominance. Paddy belongs to
the group because he is Catholic and lives in a house
where a father is the breadwinner and a mother is the
family caretaker. But his position in life is about to
undergo a reduction in status: He notices that life at
home is changing, and that it is getting worse, not better. His parents fight—not just arguments anymore, but

bouts of physical abuse; to solve their problems, Paddy
tries to stay awake all night, or he asks endless questions
to keep their attention on him instead of on their disagreements, and he finally even tries running away so
that they will *have* to stay together. Nothing he does
helps, however. His situation at school deteriorates:
Teachers he once successfully dodged now catch him
sleeping in class, and the boys he plays with sense his
changing home life and "demote" him, making up the
cruelly insulting rhyme that completes the novel's title:
"Paddy Clarke—Paddy Clarke—Has no Da—Ha ha ha."

Although it is a story of a child's life told from the
child's point of view, *Paddy Clarke Ha Ha Ha* is no children's book: Its true audience is the adult reader who
has survived childhood's joys and pains, acquiring the
consciousness that fills out Paddy's partial construction
of his world into its full dimensions of divorce, humiliation in several contexts, and displacement of the natural world. Part of the tragedy of this highly COMIC
NOVEL is the reader's recognition that had some other
boy's family fallen apart, Paddy would have been
among the chanters of a similar rhyme. Roddy Doyle's
great achievement in this novel is to use the materials
of childlike speech and thought to build a complete
narrative of ordinary life in all of its mundane glory.

BIBLIOGRAPHY
Cosgrove, Brian. "Roddy Doyle's Backward Look: Tradition
and Modernity in *Paddy Clarke Ha Ha Ha,*" *Studies: An Irish
Quarterly Review* 85, no. 339 (Autumn 1996): 231–242.

PARADE'S END TETRALOGY FORD MADOX FORD (1924–1928)

Four novels compose this series, also known as the *Tietjens Tetralogy: Some Do Not . . .* (1924), *No More Parades* (1925), *A Man Could Stand Up* (1926), and *Last Post* (1928). The protagonist of the story is Christopher Tietjens, an old-fashioned Englishman who essentially represents all that is swept away by the disastrous events of WORLD WAR I. He is a younger son of the upper CLASS, although he expects that he may eventually inherit the family estate, Groby, since his older brother Mark keeps a French mistress in preference to the conventions of wife and family. If Mark dies without legitimate issue, Christopher will own the estate and its incomes; however, he has little interest in material comforts or social status.

Christopher Tietjens is a man of virtue and honor, but he is married to a woman bent on destroying him *because* he is virtuous and honorable. Sylvia, his wife, flaunts her infidelities as a way of tormenting her husband and satisfying her own desire for power over others; she also lies repeatedly to others about Christopher's treatment of her. For his part, Christopher protects his wife's reputation and accepts responsibility when she conceives a child, even though he cannot be sure whether or not it is the product of one of her liaisons. To tidy up his life, he moves Sylvia to Groby for safety while he is away fighting in "the war to end all wars." Before he leaves, he tries to express his love for Valentine Wannop, a suffragist and the daughter of a family friend. The two come to recognize their mutual attraction without consummating their desires. Given Sylvia's determination to make her husband suffer, there seems little hope that the love between Valentine and Christopher can ever flourish.

Christopher's virtue extends to his military unit and to the trenches—as does Sylvia's venom. She falsely tells Christopher's superior, General Campion, that her husband beats her, hoping to wreck Christopher's military standing. General Campion has reasons of his own to find fault with Christopher, who has difficulty staying neat enough for the general's satisfaction and who extends too warm a hand of friendship to the men in his unit rather than imposing a properly upper-class distance between the ranks. Although Christopher performs heroically during actions at the front and saves the lives of others, he fails to satisfy General Campion's idea of an officer: Christopher sees incompetence thrive as officers fail to prosecute the war with any degree of effectiveness, and he believes the war will destroy everything he ever valued.

Valentine and Christopher are reunited when he returns from the war suffering from stress and shell shock. She goes to nurse him, willing to be his mistress if she cannot be his wife; eventually they reside in a cottage at Groby. There, Sylvia had worked her poison as best she could, renting the estate to vulgar rich Americans and giving them permission to deface the property by cutting down an ancient tree. Both brothers forgave her; in her complete inability to wound either of them, Sylvia finally agrees to grant Christopher a divorce so she can marry General Campion and live a regal life in India.

Mark had increasingly retreated from life after a stroke, and in the last volume of the series, the narration focuses on his interior realm as he waits to die, convinced that the modern world is no place for him or any of his family. Mark and Christopher are relics of an earlier world that has lost its status and power as a result of World War I. For his part, Christopher works as an antiques dealer, happy in his little cottage with Valentine, who is expecting their child. Mark's thoughts range back across events of the earlier volumes, such as his father's death—thought to be a suicide resulting from Sylvia's lies—and the son born to Sylvia, who will inherit Groby since Christopher claimed paternity. Mark thinks himself into a happy resolution to these troubling issues.

Ford Madox FORD uses several narrative strategies in this novel of comic MODERNISM. The time sequence is loosely managed through a series of vividly presented scenes: The narrative voice shifts from third-person point of view to stream-of-consciousness and back, and he focuses on the minds of different characters at different stages of the story. The first three volumes capture Ford's bitterness over the human potential lost in World War I and England's loss of status as a result of the war; the final volume implies that happiness may yet be possible, but it is a muted and qualified version of happiness. The hero for whom this happiness is conjured remains offstage throughout the last novel, pursuing a profession beneath his training and living in circumstances beneath his social standing and economic resources, but thriving in a genuine and mutually shared love for the first time in his life.

Christopher Tietjens finally receives his reward for nobly enduring his marriage to Sylvia and his country's wanton destruction of life and tradition during the war. Ford seems to suggest that Englishmen who wish to find happiness henceforth will need to emulate the modesty and self-sacrificing devotion modeled by the hero of *Parade's End:* Only in such reduced circumstances can happiness thrive.

BIBLIOGRAPHY

Longenbach, James. "Ford Madox Ford: The Novelist as Historian," *Princeton University Library Chronicle* 45, no. 2 (Winter 1984): 150–66.

Meyer, Eric. "Ford's War and (Post)Modern Memory: *Parade's End* and National Allegory," *Criticism: A Quarterly for Literature and the Arts* 32.1 (Winter 1990): 81–99.

Mulvihill, James. "Ford Madox Ford's *Parade's End* Tetralogy and Evelyn Waugh's *A Handful of Dust,*" *Notes on Contemporary Literature* 32, no. 3 (May 2002): 8–9.

PARKS, TIM (1954–   )

A novelist, translator of Italian works, essayist, scholar, and literary critic, Tim Parks was born in 1954 in Manchester, England, and educated at Cambridge and Harvard Universities. With his Italian wife, he moved to Verona, Italy, in 1981 and has remained there since. He lectures at the University of Milan; his specialty is literary translation. His first novel, *Tongues of Flame,* an autobiographical work, appeared in 1985 and won the Somerset Maugham Award; in 1997 his dark comic novel, *Europa,* was shortlisted for the Booker Prize. His prize-winning translations include such noted Italian writers as Roberto Calasso, Alberto Moravia, and Italo Calvino. Parks has written a key text on the art of translating modern English literature into Italian, *Translating Style* (1997), and a collection of literary essays on topics ranging from Dante to Borges, *Hell and Back: Essays* (2001). His short fiction and essays appear in periodicals such as *The New Yorker.* Tim Parks continues to live and write in Verona.

BIBLIOGRAPHY

Fenwick, Gillian. *Understanding Tim Parks.* Understanding Contemporary British Literature Series. Columbia: University of South Carolina Press, 2002.

PARTY GOING HENRY GREEN (1939)

On the surface, this mildly experimental novel provides a humorous view of the "bright young things" examined in the early COMIC NOVELS of Aldous HUXLEY and Evelyn WAUGH. In terms of both PLOT and character, virtually nothing happens in the story: A group of wealthy, privileged young men and women are gathering at a London train station to begin a pleasant journey to the south of France, where they will be the guests of a popular London playboy. Various relatives and servants are also gathering at the train station to see them off. Dense fog, however, has paralyzed the transportation system, leaving the idle rich truly idle. The young people carry on silly flirtations and reveal the shallow triviality of their lives and their minds as they fritter away the hours of their delayed departure.

GREEN deepens this slight material by the careful deployment of death symbols. In the opening scene, a pigeon flying in the fog crashes into an invisible wall and drops dead at the feet of Miss Fellowes, an elderly aunt of one of the partygoers. The pigeon remains in the story: Miss Fellowes picks it up, washes it, and wraps it in brown paper and string, and carries it with her, even though its presence causes her to become faint and dizzy with nauseous dread. The fog imposes a paralyzed ignorance on the world of the partygoers. Like the pigeon, they are going about their lives oblivious to the larger world; such obliviousness, however, does not make them immune to death.

In the early two-thirds of the novel, the omniscient third-person narrator dominates the story, sometimes allowing only fragments of conversation in. But as the characters form into a group, conversation begins to dominate the narrative, and readers must take over the job formerly performed by the narrator. Clearly, Green is developing a SATIRE; however, he leaves it to readers to pass judgment on the materials he places before their eyes and to apply the lesson of the text to their own lives.

BIBLIOGRAPHY

Mengham, Rod. *The Idiom of the Time: The Writings of Henry Green.* Cambridge: Cambridge University Press, 1982.

North, Michael. *Henry Green and the Writing of His Generation.* Charlottesville: University of Virginia Press, 1984.

Treglown, Jeremy. *Romancing: The Life and Work of Henry Green.* New York: Random House, 2001.

PASSAGE TO INDIA, A E. M. FORSTER
(1924) A masterful double examination of COLONIALISM and Victorian sexual repression, *A Passage to India* is a novel of social and psychological realism with a simple PLOT: A young Englishwoman visits her fiancée in INDIA and allows an accusation of rape to be lodged against Dr. Aziz, a Muslim Indian, after a trip to the mysterious Marabar Caves; during the trial, she recants the accusation, alienating herself from both the colonizing British and the colonized Indians. Supporting and extending this simple PLOT, however, is Forster's three-part structure that examines British, Muslim, and Hindu characters in the settings of the mosque, the cave, and the temple (the titles of the novel's three sections) during the three seasons of the tropical Indian year, the pleasant spring, the punishingly hot summer, and the drenched monsoon.

Adela Quested comes to India with Mrs. Moore, the elderly mother of Adela's fiancée, Ronald Heaslop, the city magistrate of Chandrapore and a rising young colonial official. The two women want to experience the "real India"; at a spring garden party hosted by a friend of Ronald, they note that Indian and British guests do not intermingle. The British sense of cultural superiority and the Indian perception of their inferior status in British eyes create such tension and awkwardness that the party is a miserable failure. Adela and Mrs. Moore's search for real experiences brings them into contact with Cyril Fielding, a school principal who treats the Indians as his peers rather than his inferiors. He invites the women to tea, along with a Hindu teacher at his school, Professor Godbole, and Dr. Aziz, whom Mrs. Moore had met by chance. When Ronald calls for the ladies, he is angered that Fielding has left Adela alone with Dr. Aziz in order to show Mrs. Moore the school. The relationship between Ronald and Adela cools, and it becomes apparent that their attachment to each other is motivated more by convention and convenience than by genuine love.

Dr. Aziz had invited the ladies to visit the Marabar Caves near the city, famous for their mysterious echo, so they could see more of the real India. Once again, the outing is an awkward and tense situation that leads this time to a disastrous failure. Cyril and Dr. Godbole miss the train taking the party to the caves. The day is hot and the caves are primitive. Mrs. Moore experiences an existential crisis as she listens to the incoherent echo with a crowd of Indians; Adela enters a cave alone and then runs out frantically, injuring herself in a headlong rush downhill away from the caves. Under medical care in the British compound, she claims that Dr. Aziz assaulted her, and he is arrested. The trial is a sensation that divides the city into opposing camps along dogmatic nationalist lines. When Mrs. Moore expresses support for Dr. Aziz's innocence, Ronald sends her home; she dies at sea while the trial is underway and is buried in the Indian Ocean. Her absence becomes a crucial element during the trial, since it appears that the British have suppressed and manipulated the available testimony—crowds outside the courthouse chant her name and soon confuse it with the name of a Hindu deity. When Adela recants her accusation, the city bursts into a chaotic celebration with the potential to turn ugly.

The scandal of the trial forces Dr. Aziz to leave the tropical lowlands of Chandrapore for the cool Himalayan slopes of an interior province. There, he meets Cyril Fielding one last time. Dr. Aziz is bitter, and even the discovery that Fielding has married the daughter of Mrs. Moore, the only English person other than Fielding ever to treat Aziz with dignity and respect, does not soften his heart. The Hindus are celebrating the renewal of the seasons in a festival dedicated to the god Krishna, a chaotic scene similar to the aftermath of the trial but suffused with joy rather than injured pride. Dr. Aziz and Fielding meet, but they cannot connect after the events that have pushed them apart.

FORSTER'S conclusion to the novel does not offer an optimistic promise that people can overcome the vast differences that separate them: nationality, religion, culture, race, and gender open chasms between individuals and groups. Sadly, bridging those chasms may take more resources than individuals can develop in the short spans of their lives.

BIBLIOGRAPHY
Bradbury, Malcolm, ed. *E. M. Forster,* A Passage to India: *A Casebook.* London: Macmillan, 1970.

Herz, Judith Scherer. A Passage to India: *Nation and Narration.* Twayne's Masterwork Studies, 117. New York: Twayne, 1993.

Shahane, V. A., ed. *Perspectives on E. M. Forster's* A Passage to India: *A Collection of Critical Essays.* New York: Barnes & Noble, 1968.

PATON, ALAN (1903–1988)

On January 11, 1903, when Alan Stewart Paton (PAY-ton) was born in Pietermaritzburg, the province of Natal was still a British colony and the BOER WAR had only recently ended; in 1910, Natal became part of the Republic of South Africa, the nation that Paton loved, served, and worked to shape during his adult life. Paton was educated at the University of Natal, completing his studies in science and education in 1922. He was already writing plays and poems, but his career as a published novelist did not begin until after he had worked as an educator and administrator for some 25 years. He served as assistant master at Ixopo High School from 1925 to 1928, then worked at Pietermaritzburg College from 1928 to 1935, and finally was named principal of the Diepkloof Reformatory near Johannesburg in 1935; he retired in 1948 when his first novel proved to be a financial success. He was an innovative and humane administrator at this facility, which served as a prison for black juvenile delinquents from South Africa's burgeoning slums.

Paton's first and greatest novel, *CRY, THE BELOVED COUNTRY,* appeared in 1948 and became a classic of world literature, although in South Africa it was ignored by many whites and criticized by many blacks for using racial stereotypes. It chronicles the tragedies of two fathers, one a black minister and the other a privileged white, who are drawn together when the minister's son kills a young white man. Beginning in 1948, Paton was deeply involved in organizing opposition to the ruling Nationalist party's policy of apartheid ("separateness"), or institutionalized racial oppression, that kept the white minority in power after the end of COLONIALISM. He helped found the Liberal Party of South Africa—an organization open to whites and blacks and dedicated to nonviolent social change—and traveled extensively to raise awareness of the harshly oppressive conditions in his home country. Under his leadership, the Liberal Party worked against apartheid until the Nationalist government outlawed mixed-race political parties in 1968, when the Liberal Party disbanded rather than comply with the new law. Although Paton was spared the exile, prosecution, and imprisonment that some activists faced, he was deprived of his passport for nearly 10 years in the 1960s.

Paton continued writing fiction and nonfiction throughout his retirement. He published the novel *Too Late the Phalarope* in 1953, featuring an interracial love story; the book was banned in South Africa. He wrote several nonfiction books about South Africa and produced several short stories, collected in *Tales from a Troubled Land* (also known as *Debbie Go Home*) in 1961. His third novel, *Ah, But Your Land Is Beautiful,* appeared in 1981; it relates the story of a young Indian girl's act of protest against apartheid—reading in a library, an act forbidden to nonwhites—and it follows the historical record of social and political activism against apartheid in the 1950s and 1960s.

Paton was already suffering from ill health, and so he turned his attention to his autobiography, publishing it in two volumes, *Towards the Mountain: An Autobiography* (1980) and *Journey Continued: An Autobiography* (1988). In the closing years of his life, world attention was focused on South Africa, including an economic embargo intended to punish the government for its policy of apartheid, and violence was increasingly replacing protest and negotiation. Although Paton had long opposed apartheid, he refused to endorse violence as a means of political change, and he opposed the embargo because it punished poor blacks more than anyone else. He had already earned the enmity of white supporters of apartheid; his moderate positions made him unpopular among many blacks as well. He died on April 12, 1988, of throat cancer, six years before the all-race voting of 1994 effectively ended apartheid as a state policy.

BIBLIOGRAPHY

Alexander, Peter F. *Alan Paton: A Biography.* New York: Oxford University Press, 1994.

Callan, Edward. *Alan Paton.* Twayne's World Authors Series, 40. Rev. ed. Boston: Twayne Publishers, 1982.

PEAKE, MERVYN (1911–1968)

The son of a physician and a nurse serving as missionaries in China, Mervyn Peake was born on July 9, 1911, in central China. Except for the first two years of WORLD WAR I, the family remained in China until Mervyn was about 12 years old in 1923. Upon their permanent return to England, the Peakes enrolled their son in the PUBLIC SCHOOL of Eltham College, where he was an excellent athlete also noted for his artistic skills. Upon completing his studies at Eltham in 1929, Peake attended art school in London and began working on projects that brought him into contact with the London art scene. He taught at Westminster School of Art, where he met his future wife, Maeve Gilmore. Their happy marriage began in 1937, producing three children. During this period, Peake was illustrating books and writing his own poetry.

In 1940, the onset of WORLD WAR II disrupted Peake's life with military service in the British army. Peake had always been a nervous and intense adult of indifferent health, and service in the military pushed his emotional stability beyond its limits; he was discharged after experiencing a breakdown. By then, he had begun writing the series upon which his reputation as a novelist rests: the GORMENGHAST novels, comprising *Titus Groan* (1946), *Gormenghast* (1950), and *Titus Alone* (1959). His health continued to decline, and in 1957 a second breakdown led to a diagnosis of Parkinson's disease or early-onset senility. Peake was eventually placed in a residential care facility, where he died in 1968. His deteriorating health affected his writing adversely: Although he had planned additional volumes about Titus Groan, the final volume of the trilogy is generally thought to be less successful than the first two.

BIBLIOGRAPHY

Gardiner-Scott, Tanya J. *Mervyn Peake: The Evolution of a Dark Romantic.* New York: P. Lang, 1989.

Smith, Gordon. *Mervyn Peake: A Personal Memoir.* London: V. Gollancz, 1984.

Watney, John. *Mervyn Peake.* New York: St. Martin's Press, 1976.

PERELANDRA C. S. LEWIS (1943)   See SPACE TRILOGY, THE.

PHILLIPS, CARYL (1958–)   Born in the Caribbean of African decent, but reared and educated in England, Caryl Phillips is the author of several novels that explore the history of slavery and the international effects of the African diaspora under the sway of European COLONIALISM. He was born in St. Kitts on March 13, 1958, and soon afterward his family relocated to England. He entered Queen's College of Oxford University, where he studied English and was active in theatrical productions. By the time he completed his undergraduate studies, he had decided to be a professional writer.

For several years, Phillips supported himself through employment in theaters and by writing for stage, radio, and television. His first novel, *The Final Passage,* appeared in 1985; it won the Malcolm X Prize for Literature for its story of the racism experienced by Caribbean immigrants to England. Phillips produced a controversial work of nonfiction, *The European Tribe,* in 1987, which condemned European cultural hegemony. It won the Martin Luther King Memorial Prize. Phillips received several visiting professorships in INDIA, Africa, and the United States beginning in 1987, and in 1992 he was awarded a Guggenheim Fellowship. The following year he published *CROSSING THE RIVER,* a study of African experiences in various locations and times using several narrative voices. The novel won the JAMES TAIT BLACK MEMORIAL PRIZE and was on the BOOKER PRIZE short list.

Caryl Phillips continues to teach in various universities, and he contributes to numerous publications. He writes screenplays in addition to novels, including the adaptation of V. S. NAIPAUL's *The Mystic Masseur* for Merchant-Ivory Productions in 2001. He divides his time between London, the Caribbean, and the United States.

BIBLIOGRAPHY

Bell, C. Rosalind. "Worlds Within: An Interview with Caryl Phillips," *Callaloo: A Journal of African-American and African Arts and Letters* 14, no. 3 (1991): 578–606.

Eckstein, Lars. "The Insistence of Voices: An Interview with Caryl Philips," *ARIEL: A Review of International English Literature* 32, no. 2 (April 2001): 33–43.

Sarvan, Charles P. "The Fictional Works of Caryl Phillips: An Introduction." In *Twayne Companion to Contemporary World Literature: From the Editors of World Literature Today.* Edited by Pamela A. Genova. New York: Twayne-Thomson Gale, 2003, 422–439.

PICTURE PALACE PAUL THEROUX (1978)

The narrator of this novel is Maud Coffin Pratt, an elderly woman who has established fame as a portrait photographer, having created pictures of numerous celebrities. From the vantage point of old age—she is in her 70s—Maud reviews a life that had been marked early on by her incestuous love for her brother, Orlando, who is dead at the time Maud narrates her story. He, in turn, had been involved in an incestuous relationship with his and Maud's sister, Phoebe. Maud has the proof of that connection—of the proscribed relationship that she desired but that her sister achieved—in the form of a photograph she took without her siblings' knowledge. Her own love for them enables her to see their embrace as an expression of innocence, and yet she locks the photograph away from sight. Theroux's narrative explores the familiar trope of the artist's vision as a metaphor for forbidden knowledge: Some events that can be seen and captured by artists can be destructive, just as desire can be addressed to proscribed objects—or persons.

THEROUX based the character of Maud, considered as a visual artist, on the real-life photographer Jill Krementz—wife of Kurt Vonnegut—who is noted for her photographic portraits of literary figures. *Picture Palace* was Theroux's 10th work of long fiction. It appeared in the period between the publication of two best-selling travel books that resuscitated the field of travel writing and that made Theroux's literary reputation, *The Great Railway Bazaar: By Train Through Asia* (1975) and *The Old Patagonian Express: By Train Through the Americas* (1979). Although he is most noted as a travel writer, in *Picture Palace* Theroux demonstrates his control of voice in creating a female narrator—an artist—and imagining her view of the world. The novel won the WHITBREAD Book of the Year Award in 1976.

BIBLIOGRAPHY
Bell, Robert F. "Metamorphoses and Missing Halves: Allusions in Paul Theroux's *Picture Palace*," *Critique: Studies in Contemporary Fiction* 22, no. 3 (1981): 17–30.
Coale, Samuel. " 'A Quality of Light': The Fiction of Paul Theroux," *Critique: Studies in Contemporary Fiction* 22, no. 3 (1981): 5–16.

PILGRIMAGE DOROTHY RICHARDSON (1915–1938)

This modernist work, the first to use stream of consciousness narration in English, originally appeared in 12 separately published volumes, but these were collected by the author into a four-volume set of "chapter-novels" in 1938. The four-volume edition, some 2,000 pages in length, includes the following titles (original publication years are in parentheses after each title): in volume one, *Pointed Roofs* (1915), *Backwater* (1916), and *Honeycomb* (1917); in volume two, *The Tunnel* (1919) and *Interim* (1919); in volume three, *Deadlock* (1921), *Revolving Lights* (1923), and *The Trap* (1925); in volume four, *Oberland* (1927), *Dawn's Left Hand* (1931), *Clear Horizon* (1935), and *Dimple Hill* (1938). A further edition, in 1967, adds a new section entitled *March Moonlight* to the end of volume four; this unfinished section of the novel was found among the author's possessions upon her death in 1957 at the age of 84.

Pilgrimage is an autobiographical novel and a BILDUNGSROMAN that begins in the adulthood of the protagonist, Miriam Henderson. The title refers to Miriam's journey—and the author's—toward the fulfillment of her mission in life, which is the writing of fiction. Individual volumes seem to dispense with PLOT, but the series as a whole chronicles Miriam's assertion of her independence and the discovery of her calling. Because the story unfolds from within the thoughts of the woman serving as protagonist, it provides a vivid picture of an emerging awareness of FEMINISM as Miriam discovers that she does not wish to accept the role that the larger world has reserved for women—the domestic role of wife and mother. She comes to realize that her identity combines elements of both the feminine and the masculine, while the standard life reserved for women provides an outlet primarily for the feminine. For Miriam, fulfillment comes not from the formation of a love-bond with another human being of either sex, but from the act of artistic creation through writing.

BIBLIOGRAPHY
Gray, Nancy. *Language Unbound: On Experimental Writing by Women.* Urbana: University of Illinois Press, 1992.
Thomson, George H. *Notes on* Pilgrimage: Dorothy Richardson Annotated. Greensboro, N.C.: ELT Press, 1999.
Winning, Joanne. *The Pilgrimage of Dorothy Richardson.* Madison: University of Wisconsin Press, 2000.

PLOT The sequence of events in a novel, driven by some form of conflict, is the plot. Novels vary considerably as to the construction of the plot. Character-driven novels that focus on the growth (or decay) of a fictional person's emotional or intellectual maturity may require merely low-key incidents that are only loosely interconnected; the novel of psychological realism requires very little plot action to produce transformative conflict in the personality of the protagonist. Plot-driven novels such as MYSTERY AND DETECTIVE FICTION, action-adventure stories, SPY NOVELS, and thrillers feature tightly interconnected sequences of causes and effects, and may require mere stereotypical characters to carry the story forward.

Plots sometimes incorporate details from the real world. Examples of HISTORICAL FICTION and NAUTICAL FICTION derive part of their satisfactions from the readers' knowledge of events and equipment in the real world; the effectiveness of the plot may depend on or correlate to the reader's knowledge of the period or the technology central to the story. At the other extreme, plots in works drawn from the genres of speculative fiction (FANTASY, SCIENCE FICTION, and horror) may require readers to imagine events that are not possible in the real world. In these cases, the exercise of the imagination takes precedence over the accumulation of knowledge.

BIBLIOGRAPHY

Graesser, Arthur C. "Agency, Plot, and a Structural Affect Theory of Literary Story Comprehension." In *The Psychology and Sociology of Literature.* Edited by Dick Schram and Gerard Steen. Amsterdam: Benjamins, 2001, 57–69.

Honeywell, J. Arthur. "Plot in the Modern Novel." In *Essentials of the Theory of Fiction.* Edited by Michael J. Hoffman and Patrick D. Murphy. 2nd ed. Durham, N.C.: Duke University Press, 1996, 147–157.

Richardson, Brian. *Narrative Dynamics: Essays on Time, Plot, Closure, and Frames.* Columbus: Ohio State University Press, 2002.

POINT COUNTER POINT ALDOUS HUXLEY (1928)

This roman à clef presents a satirical view of HUXLEY'S literary, artistic, social, and intellectual contemporaries, as did his three earlier novels, *CROME YELLOW* (1921), *ANTIC HAY* (1923), and *Those Barren Leaves* (1925). In *Point Counter Point,* however, Huxley demonstrates greater sophistication in developing his characters and in complicating his plot. Although *BRAVE NEW WORLD* is Huxley's most famous and enduring novel, some critics consider *Point Counter Point* to be his masterpiece.

Huxley unites his characters by exploring the various branches of the Quarles and Bidlake families and examining their connections to friends and lovers. Philip Quarles (Huxley's avatar) writes novels but remains emotionally distant from the rest of humanity, including his wife, Elinor Bidlake Quarles, and his doomed little son, also named Philip. Sidney Quarles, Philip's father, writes history—or, in any case, he represents himself to be writing a history, although he never seems to make much progress toward a conclusion. Women (other than his wife, Rachel) distract him; he enjoys flirtations, but when things get out of hand he relies on Rachel to resolve his affairs discreetly. She accepts this rather degrading role with Christian humility, finding satisfaction in the traditional role of supportive nurturer.

Philip's in-laws exhibit similar frailties. Elinor's brother Walter, a critic writing for Denis Burlap's *Literary World,* has abandoned his wife to live with Marjorie Carling, who is a married woman; after less than two years, Marjorie is pregnant, and Walter has grown so bored with her that he begins to pursue the promiscuous Lucy Tantamount. She is the daughter of Lord Tantamount, a brilliant scientist with the emotional maturity of a child; Lord Tantamount's laboratory assistant, Illidge, festers with the revolutionary ideas of Everard Webley (based on the British fascist Oswald Mosley) and holds utter contempt for the aristocratic socialites of his employer's class. Elinor's father, John Bidlake, flirts with Lucy's mother, Lady Edward Tantamount; she had formerly been his mistress. John Bidlake used to be a ladies' man like Sidney Quarles, going through three wives in the process, and he once had a successful career as an artist, but his creative and procreative powers have waned, leaving him embittered. Unlike Rachel Quarles, Elinor's cast-off mother, Janet, is helpless in her old age, unable to assist her children with their emotional problems, although she does provide a home for her grandson Philip when his parents travel abroad, and she allows her former husband to return to her house when he learns he is dying of cancer.

Several key events in the lives of Philip and Elinor Quarles drive the later part of the PLOT. When Lucy Tantamount runs off to Paris, Philip persuades his brother-in-law to bring Marjorie Carling to the Quarles's country home; there, Rachel Quarles befriends the unhappy woman. Marjorie is possessed by jealousy over Walter's affair, but the arrival of her child will provide her with the emotional clarity and focus she had previously lacked. For his part, Walter doesn't want to be a heel, but he has become so obsessed with Lucy that he hurts Marjorie in spite of his good intentions. Eventually, Lucy's betrayal and Walter's guilt work in Marjorie's favor to create a reconciliation with Walter. In the meantime, Elinor has begun to doubt her husband's capacity to love her: He possesses a vast understanding of life, but he is unable to develop genuine emotions. Elinor yearns for romantic attentions and is on the verge of pursuing an affair with Everard Webley, who had courted her many years earlier. When little Philip contracts the fatal illness of meningitis, however, she abandons her planned tryst to rush to her son's bedside, where she is joined by her husband. As Everard Webley arrives for his meeting with Elinor, he is murdered by the nihilistic cynic Maurice Spandrell, who in turn enlists the aid of Illidge in disposing the body. Philip and Elinor are devastated by the loss of their child, and to cope with their pain they once again immerse themselves in endless diversions by traveling abroad.

The novel's title refers to the musical technique of combining contrastive melodies to create complex harmonies, suggesting the organizing principle Huxley used in shaping his narrative. He pairs characters with similar personality traits or quirks in order to examine the contrasting behaviors that may arise from such traits. Among the many dysfunctional personalities, one character, the artist Mark Rampion, exhibits the attitudes and behaviors that make possible a well-balanced and positive approach to life and to marriage. Rampion is based on the novelist D. H. LAWRENCE, one of the most controversial authors in the CANON of 20th-century British fiction. Huxley presents Lawrence as a voice of reason who also appreciates the sensual and passionate aspects of human life. In contrast, the literary magazine editor Denis Burlap sometimes finds moments of childlike glee with his mistress, Beatrice Gilray, but he lacks the completeness of Rampion's balanced enjoyment of a full intellectual and physical existence.

Huxley alternates scenes in much the same way that a film director intercuts simultaneous action. Indeed, the events of the first half of the book all occur over the span of only one night and the following day, with a long flashback chapter that relates the courtship of Mark and Mary Rampion. A musical party hosted by Lady Tantamount provides the pretext for bringing together the large cast of characters, either in person or as the topic of others' conversations, allowing Huxley to explore a wide range of social behaviors in detail. Lucy Tantamount and Walter Bidlake then carry the action to a nightclub, where they meet the Rampions, Spandrell, and numerous minor characters who represent the self-absorbed and pleasure-addicted "bright young things" of youth culture in the 1920s. By the time Huxley follows various characters to their separate homes in the wee hours of the morning, the contrastive strands of the narrative are well established.

The plot continues to unfold in a similar manner, following one character to another and occasionally dipping into the past by means of a flashback or relying on the diaries of Philip Quarles to shed light on his friends and relatives; letters from Lucy Tantamount in Paris or conversations with empty-headed paradigms of vanity such as Molly d'Exergillod embroider the main line of the story. Above all, however, *Point Counter Point* is a novel of absorbing character development and exploration, seasoned with a few sensational plot elements. These moments provide situations of extreme pressure through which the characters may be pushed to their limits. In Huxley's treatment, plot becomes yet another means of character development.

BIBLIOGRAPHY

Baker, Robert S. *The Dark Historic Page: Social Satire and Historicism in the Novels of Aldous Huxley, 1921–1939.* Madison: University of Wisconsin Press, 1982.

Firchow, Peter. *Aldous Huxley: Satirist and Novelist.* Minneapolis: University of Minnesota Press, 1972.

Meckier, Jerome, ed. *Critical Essays on Aldous Huxley.* New York: G. K. Hall, 1996.

Watt, Donald, ed. *Aldous Huxley: The Critical Heritage.* London: Routledge & Kegan Paul, 1975.

POOR THINGS: EPISODES FROM THE EARLY LIFE OF ARCHIBALD MCCANDLESS M. D. SCOTTISH PUBLIC HEALTH OFFICER EDITED BY ALASDAIR GRAY

ALASDAIR GRAY (1992) An example of POSTMODERNISM, *Poor Things* received the WHITBREAD Book of the Year Award and the GUARDIAN FICTION PRIZE in

1992. It could be described as a cross between Mary Shelley's *Frankenstein* and Laurence Sterne's *Tristram Shandy* updated with an eye to contemporary SATIRE. Set in Glasgow, Scotland, beginning in the 1880s, the story is presented as a collection of actual documents about a bizarre medical incident: When a pregnant woman in her eighth month—Bella—commits suicide in order to escape an abusive husband by drowning herself, a doctor—Godwin Bysshe Baxter—resurrects her by transplanting the brain of the unborn fetus into the head of the 25-year-old mother's body. The result is a completely unrestrained id empowered by a fully mature—and fully sexual—adult body. Baxter's fellow doctor, the McCandless of the novel's title, falls in love with the beautiful and uninhibitedly libidinous Bella and the two become engaged, but she runs off with the playboy Duncan Wedderburn and drives him to death by sexual exhaustion. After a stay in a Paris brothel, Bella returns to Scotland, and McCandless has his second chance to win the hand of the beautiful and sexually voracious young woman.

McCandless serves as the narrator of this first portion of the novel, aided by letters that Bella sends from her wanderings on the Continent. GRAY'S satire appears in his control of McCandless's voice and his references to the seamy underside of Victorian attitudes and behaviors. But upon concluding the reunion of Archibald and Bella, Gray adds a further level of revisionism in the form of a letter from Victoria "Bella" McCandless that comments upon the text Archibald McCandless created about his connection to Bella. Her version of events provides an entirely different perspective of them, and the voice she brings to the story is that of a sharp intelligence. In his final twist, Gray adds a section of notes and comments purportedly in his own voice as he fills out the alleged sources, persons, locations, and odd references of the McCandless story. Gray (an artist as well as a novelist) even adds his own drawings and hand-lettered (or hand-scrawled) typography where it is needed to complete the illusion of verisimilitude for his novel.

Perhaps the best thing about this very funny novel is the character of Bella. She is a strong woman, but she is also a naïve innocent who gives the lie to the veneer of Victorian high-mindedness and civilized restraint. Read-

ers get to see her through the lustful eyes and the prurient desires of the uxorious McCandless, but then they get to hear her speak in her own calm, strong, and reasonable voice in her commentary on McCandless's text (Gray's introduction ironically refers to Victoria's letter as the ravings of a disturbed mind). In the end, the reader is left with two versions of reality plus the fiction of a researcher's commentary on both versions from an author masquerading as a historian. In full postmodern fashion, Gray makes his readers into his cocreators in determining how to put the parts together.

BIBLIOGRAPHY

Crawford, Robert, and Thom Nairn, eds. *The Arts of Alasdair Gray*. Edinburgh: Edinburgh University Press, 1991.

Kaczvinsky, Donald P. "Making Up for Lost Time: Scotland, Stories and the Self in Alasdair Gray's *Poor Things*," *Contemporary Literature* 42, no. 4 (Winter 2001): 775–99.

Moores, Phil. *Alasdair Gray: Critical Appreciations and a Bibliography*. Boston Spa: British Library, 2002.

PORTRAIT OF THE ARTIST AS A YOUNG MAN, A   JAMES JOYCE (1916)

An autobiographical novel that is also a BILDUNGSROMAN and a *kunstlerroman*—a story that recounts the development of a gifted artist's talent—*A Portrait of the Artist as a Young Man* marks a technical advance in JOYCE'S literary technique over the short fiction in *Dubliners* (1914), while it also paves the way for the much more experimental work in ULYSSES (1922). The novel was first published in serialized form in *The Egoist*, edited by Ezra Pound, who recognized its importance and secured a patron for Joyce on the basis of its merit.

Over the course of the novel's events, related in five chapters that extend from earliest childhood memories to young manhood, the protagonist of the novel, Stephen Dedalus, grows in intellectual stature and, more slowly, emotional sophistication. As he grows, his language evolves, exhibiting greater complexity, subtlety, refinement, and power; his interior growth as a human being, however, is less straightforward. Stephen is caught in a cycle of excess, inherited from his alcoholic father and symptomatic of IRELAND'S ongoing struggle to attain self-rule. He moves from one form of excess to another, occasionally managing to make a virtue of his vice, as when he suffers as excess of spiritual rectitude.

His earliest memories are of the excessively heated arguments between his father, Simon—a supporter of Parnell and an opponent of the priesthood's power in Irish life—and his aunt, Dante Riordan, a supporter of the priesthood and a passionate critic of Parnell's failings. Their reiterated battles over the best course for Ireland establish Irish nationalism and the Irish national character as one of the key themes of the story. Rooted in these extremes of passion and constrained by them as well, Stephen must find a more temperate ground from which to launch his artistic career.

Stephen is educated in the Jesuit tradition at the Clongowes Wood College (as was Joyce) until the family's fortunes fail. At first, his memories of school are dominated by his fear of the other boys, who easily bully the shy and retiring young man. But as Stephen's academic prowess becomes apparent, and especially after he courageously complains about an unjust punishment he received, he wins approval from his peers. When, at the age of 16, he wins several prizes for his work at school, he uses the money to help his family, but he also hires a prostitute in order to discover the mysteries of love. Joyce structures episodes such as these so that each climaxes in an EPIPHANY—an experience that will feature prominently in Stephen's aesthetic manifesto toward the end of the novel. As he grows, his insight and understanding are deepened, but the experience of sex leaves him awash in guilt.

Ridding himself of that guilt leads to a new phase of excess: Stephen is ashamed to unburden himself to his parish priest, choosing instead to seek out an anonymous counselor in Dublin. The consolation he receives restores him to a course of righteousness, and when his schoolmasters praise him as the kind of young man who would make a good Jesuit, Stephen decides to devote himself to the church. He values sinlessness and fears the torments of hell that his imagination vividly re-creates from the words of sermons he hears, but his desire to pursue the priesthood has more to do with selfish reasons than with self-sacrifice.

The last stage of Stephen's development begins, as it has done for so many young people, when he enters the university. In the freer environment of his advanced studies he discovers doubt and skepticism instead of finding confirmation of his life's goal of joining the priesthood. Stephen himself, however, is among the last to understand the change in his thinking: His friends—especially Emma, a young woman he has liked since the two of them first met in childhood—point out that he is more of a heretic than a believer. That outside perspective sparks his ultimate epiphany, allowing him to let go of the script he has prepared for himself as a priest and reimagine a life that will enable him to fulfill—and to live fully—his artistic potential. Stephen decides that he must leave Ireland. Having separated himself ideologically from his family, from the Irish nationalist movement, and from the church, he must separate himself physically from Ireland if he is to pursue his dreams wholeheartedly. In one of the most famous sentences in 20th-century literature, he proclaims his intention to "forge in the smithy of my soul the uncreated consciousness of my race." Stephen's—and Joyce's—art will be the product of that forging.

BIBLIOGRAPHY

Ryf, Robert S. *A New Approach to Joyce:* The Portrait of the Artist *as a Guidebook.* Perspectives in Criticism 8. Berkeley: University of California Press, 1962.

Staley, Thomas F., and Bernard Benstock. *Approaches to Joyce's* Portrait: *Ten Essays.* Pittsburgh: University of Pittsburgh Press, 1976.

Swisher, Claire, ed. *Readings on* A Portrait of the Artist as a Young Man. San Diego, Calif.: Greenhaven, 2000.

POSSESSION: A ROMANCE A. S. BYATT (1990)

Winner of the BOOKER PRIZE the year it was published, *Possession* presents a double love story as it follows the search of two scholars, Roland Michell and Maud Bailey, for the evidence of a love affair between two Victorian poets, Randolph Henry Ash and Christabel LaMotte, who had not previously been known to be acquainted with each other. A. S. BYATT crafts her novel as a story within a story: In the outer, contemporary story, the characters are trying to discover the details of the inner story. Both stories unfold simultaneously as Roland and Maud move from clue to clue; as others catch the scent of something important, the two find themselves racing to be the first to uncover the truth that the Victorian lovers had kept so secret for so long. As the search continues, Byatt displays a virtuoso's control of voice and style, creating the poems and letters of

Ash and LaMotte, the pages of other people's journal entries about them, and the essays of subsequent scholars' critical assessments of their separate poetic CANONS, while simultaneously bringing Roland and Maud into a slow awareness of their own developing love.

Roland and Maud are not just two scholars: Roland is specialist in Ash while Maud is a specialist in LaMotte and a descendant of LaMotte's family. Roland has failed to secure a university teaching post, so he works as a researcher for a British scholar of Ash, James Blackadder; Maud is a feminist who manages the Women's Resource Center in Lincoln. By structuring her characters in this way, Byatt can use her narrative to comment on nationalities as well as on gender discrepancies. The contemporary supporting characters also show this division, including the leading American scholar on Ash, Mortimer Cropper, an acquisitive and aggressive competitor for the ownership of the correspondence that Roland and Maud uncover, and Leonora Stern, the most prominent American specialist on LaMotte, who is interested in defending the accepted belief that Christabel LaMotte was a lesbian. Roland and Maud also have preexisting romantic entanglements: Roland's lover Val has supported him for years and has become unhappy with her lot, while Maud's former lover Fergus Wolff—a young British specialist on Ash who forms a counterpart to Roland—breaks the story of the correspondence to other British scholars of Ash when he learns of it without Maud's knowledge.

Just as the contemporary story has a large supporting cast to complicate the plot, so too does the Victorian story. Ash was married for more than 40 years to Ellen Best Ash, who kept a coded journal that has been studied by the contemporary scholar Beatrice Nest; LaMotte lived for several years with the painter Blanche Glover, who committed suicide shortly before Christabel moved to Lincolnshire to live with her sister and brother-in-law. Blanche's suicide note has been preserved, and from journal entries it becomes apparent that she had tried to break up Ash and LaMotte's relationship by revealing it to Ellen Ash. LaMotte also had cousins in France whom she visited after Blanche's suicide, including Sabine, who kept a journal of her own and included in it her suspicion that Christabel was

pregnant when she came to visit in France. Clues lead Roland and Maud to the locations that Ash and LaMotte visited, including a hotel by the sea where they vacationed together, the French villa to which LaMotte retreated after breaking with Ash, and the home of her sister that she retired to—still in the Bailey family.

The double structure of past and present romances that somehow become intertwined has also been used in the novels *The* FRENCH LIEUTENANT'S WOMAN, by John FOWLES and *The* CHYMICAL WEDDING by Lindsay CLARKE. Byatt adapts this form into a novel that defies easy categorization. *Possession* is part detective story, part HISTORICAL FICTION, part romance, part Gothic thriller, and entirely literary—all without taking itself too seriously. Because Byatt builds such likeable and believable characters and places them in such a compelling situation, her novel achieves a broad appeal; however, college English majors and graduate students will particularly relish its many treasures.

BIBLIOGRAPHY

Hulbert, Ann. "The Great Ventriloquist: A. S. Byatt's *Possession: A Romance.*" *Contemporary British Women Writers: Narrative Strategies.* Edited by Robert E. Hosmer, Jr. New York: St. Martin's Press, 1993.

Lehmann-Haupt, Christopher. "When There Was Such a Thing as Romantic Love," *New York Times,* 25 October 1990, C24.

Parini, Jay. "Unearthing the Secret Lover." *New York Times Book Review,* 21 October 1990, 9+.

POST CAPTAIN PATRICK O'BRIAN (1972)

See AUBREY-MATURIN NOVELS.

POSTMODERNISM

Once MODERNISM had a name and a definition, artists could also conceive of and create works that consciously went beyond that definition; critics and theorists kept pace. While modernist writers of the early 20th century abandoned history and experimented with form and content, they nonetheless continued the long-held view that a work of art is a coherent entity with its own separate existence. By this view, even an experimental novel is something other than and distinct from the rest of the universe, and just like traditional novels it can be discussed, examined, and explained. Theorists gave the term *metalanguage* to those words devoted to the analysis, explication, interpretation, and criticism of other creative works (novels, poems, paintings, architecture, musical compositions, philosophical essays, histories, laws, and other constructions). However, in the case of literature—the art of words—the creative artifact and the analytical theories about that artifact are both made of the same constituents: words. Where modernist writers or critics persist, with their non-modernist predecessors, in drawing a line around a work of art and contemplating its distinctiveness, the postmodernist points out that any such line is no more than a line in the sand: there is sand on the one side, and sand on the other side, and the line itself is nothing more than a particular arrangement of sand. The presumed distinction between language and metalanguage cannot be sustained.

Although the term *postmodern* was in minor use early in the 20th century, the path from modernism to postmodernism in literature and criticism was long, traversing the terrain of linguistics, philosophy, anthropology, and numerous other fields of study. In the first decade of the 20th century, the Swiss linguist Ferdinand de Saussure, teaching at the University of Geneva, presented lectures that were eventually published under the title *Course in General Linguistics.* Saussure emphasized that signs such as words (which he called *la parole*) possessed meaning only within the context of the system (*la langue*) of which they were merely a part. Communication is a process of encoding, transmission and reception, and decoding; it can only occur if those doing the encoding and the decoding possess the knowledge both of the correlation between signs and the things they refer to *plus* the system of rules that govern how such signs may be combined in order to convey a message. By placing the study of signification within the total system of words and rules that make it possible, Saussure shifted attention to the understanding of the structures of language that underpin the human ability to communicate.

Scholars in other fields quickly recognized the utility of structural study to their own disciplines. During WORLD WAR I, Russian scholars such as Victor Shklovsky and Vladimir Propp extended Saussure's ideas from language to literature, developing the school of thought that came to be known as Russian formalism and its related term, narratology. In their view, a body of literature was analogous to the system of rules (*la langue*) by which individual components could be combined, and an individual work (*la parole*) was like a single instantiation of that system. In the 1950s, the French anthropologist Claude Lévi-Strauss successfully applied Saussure's structural approach to myths and kinship systems. The study of literature in this manner demanded much more of the scholar than a knowledge only of the history and formal conventions of a genre: Literary scholars desiring to use a structuralist approach would also need to study psychology, sociology, anthropology, and many other fields in addition to literary history and generic form. Other effects of the structuralist approach include the de-emphasizing of the authorial role in the creation of a work of literature and a preference for the theoretical study of literature as a whole rather than the practical interpretation of particular texts.

The literary application of structuralism expanded through the work of scholars identified with "the Paris school" in the 1950s and 1960s, including Roland Barthes, Tzvetan Todorov, and Michel Foucault. These theorists and other argued that in order to understand a work of literature, readers had to possesss knowledge of the literary code—the system of rules, or *la langue*—in order to comprehend the meaning of a particular text. Barthes's crucial work *S/Z* (1970) explored five codes that readers use to understand works of fiction: the codes of actions (relevant to PLOT), puzzles (the questions raised by the text), cultural values, connotative themes (relevant to characters), and symbols. Structuralist ideas spread to the English-speaking world through the popularizing works of the American scholars Jonathan Culler (especially in *Structuralist Poetics*) and Robert Scholes (*Structuralism in Literature*).

In the mid-20th century, structuralism and semiotics carried the examination of literary texts as forms of language to more technical extremes that discounted the origin and significance of the work itself, favoring the perceptions of readers. Works of postmodern literary art explored and exploited disorder and fragmentation; critics pared the task of examining literature to a minimalist extreme by eliminating the author and the historical context of a work from the interpretive equation while simultaneously expanding the task of reading the signs encoded in texts. Novels were seen as instances of a larger cultural practice derived from and dependent upon human use of language and of literary narrative as communication systems. In this approach, critics seek to explain *how* literature functions—or fails to function—rather than *what* a particular work of literature means.

Poststructuralism carried this analysis still further by emphasizing that criticism is literature by other means: Literature is a phenomenon of language, and criticism is also a phenomenon of language, but one that takes literature as its point of departure while also remaining in the realm of language. Postmodern works are frequently said to be self-reflective, as when a novel includes a character who is writing the novel that contains him or her; postmodern criticism is similarly aware that the task of examining language phenomena is constrained by the fact that language is the only tool available by which the examination may be conducted.

Beginning in the 1970s, academic literary circles in university English departments experienced a particularly intense wave of interest in French criticism. Following terminology developed by the French philosopher Jacques Derrida—the first proponent of these ideas to lecture in the United States—this critical approach came to be known as deconstruction. Derrida argued that the Western tradition of seeking truth through language is an enterprise doomed to self-contradiction because of the failure of language to create or impose *necessary* connections between "signifiers," or words, and "signifieds," or things in the world. This critical approach is skeptical of the possibility that texts can achieve coherence by not contradicting themselves. The application of deconstructive literary interpretation generally proceeds by first searching a text for oppositional pairs of terms—a "binary" opposition—and then examining the logical consequences of this opposition until a contradiction is identified.

Deconstruction had a radical effect in literary interpretation: During most of the 20th century, the goal of any analysis of literature was, whether explicitly stated or not, the demonstration of a literary work's unity or

coherence. But deconstruction began from the premise that unity and coherence were not features of language fabrications and that any carefully conducted examination could turn up the inconsistencies and contradictions in a given text. These inconsistencies and contradictions were not failures on the part of the author; instead, they were inherent failures on the part of language. Meaning necessarily is always in play and cannot be nailed down by explaining metaphors and other traditional elements of literature. Since meaning cannot be resolved to a particular truth, said deconstructionists, the task of interpreting a literary text becomes an open-ended realm of possibilities. From one perspective, this approach might seem to be good news, since literary scholars using this approach will never run out of work to do. Critics of this approach, however, claim that deconstructive analyses can begin to seem redundant since they all lead to the conclusion that nothing can be concluded.

Schools of criticism multiplied quickly in the 1970s as scholars worldwide carried literary theory as far as possible. Examples of such new approaches include poststructuralism (also known as deconstruction), reader-response theory, Lacanian psychoanalysis, post-colonialism, cultural poetics, and aspects of Marxism, historicism, and feminism. Postmodern thought has been applied to the visual arts, including film, to history, to the study of law, and to cultural studies such as anthropology and sociology. The British novelist David LODGE has drawn the definitive fictional portrait of the state of academic literary study in the late 20th century in his COMIC NOVEL *SMALL WORLD,* which follows the adventures of several scholars as they compete for preeminence while traveling to conventions to present papers that argue their different positions.

BIBLIOGRAPHY

Calinescu, Matei and Douwe Fokkema, eds. *Exploring Post-modernism.* Amsterdam: J. Benjamins, 1987.

McGowan, John. *Postmodernism and Its Critics.* Ithaca, N.Y.: Cornell University Press, 1991.

Norris, Christopher. *Deconstruction: Theory and Practice.* London: Methuen, 1982.

Selden, Raman. *A Reader's Guide to Contemporary Literary Criticism.* Lexington: The University Press of Kentucky, 1985.

Tompkins, Jane. "A Short Course in Post-Structuralism." *College English* 50 (1988): 733–747.

POWELL, ANTHONY (1905–2000)   The son of a military officer and well connected to aristo-cratic circles, Anthony Dymoke Powell (pronounced *PO*-el) produced one of the most significant literary achievements to be found in 20th-century literature in English. His 12-volume ROMAN-FLEUVE, *A DANCE TO THE MUSIC OF TIME,* compares favorably with the nationalist masterpieces of Marcel Proust and Leo Tolstoy, sustain-ing a complex but unified narrative among a large number of compelling characters during the history-making upheavals of the century. The events in the life of the narrator, Nicholas Jenkins, also bear a marked similarity to the events in Powell's own life.

Born on December 21, 1905, Powell was educated at the leading English PUBLIC SCHOOL, Eton, beginning in 1918; he entered Balliol College, Oxford, in 1923, taking a degree in 1926. At various times, his class-mates included literary figures such as Cyril Connolly, Graham GREENE, George ORWELL, and Evelyn WAUGH—a group of writers representing what Waugh called "the Brideshead generation." Upon completing his undergraduate degree, Powell worked for the dis-tinguished literary publishing house Duckworth, which had broken new ground with early works by D. H. LAWRENCE. Powell married Lady Violet Paken-ham in 1934; they became the parents of two sons and remained married until death parted them.

Like his fictional alter ego, Nicholas Jenkins, Powell became a screenwriter for the English film industry, but Powell's adventures took him briefly to Hollywood in pursuit of screenwriting work. Powell also published five novels during the years of the Depression, begin-ning in 1931 with *AFTERNOON MEN* and continuing with *Venusberg* (1932), *From a View to a Death* (1933), *Agents and Patients* (1936), and *What's Become of Waring* (1939). These novels established Powell's reputation as an effective and successful writer but did not suggest the full powers displayed in *A Dance to the Music of Time.* Like Jenkins, Powell gave up writing and entered military service with the outbreak of WORLD WAR II, ris-ing to the rank of major by the war's end and serving in several postings, including intelligence work.

Also like Jenkins, after the war Powell had difficulty returning to fiction writing, so he undertook a schol-arly study; whereas Jenkins studied Robert Burton, the 17th-century scholar, Powell himself studied John Aubrey, the 17th-century biographer. He also, again like Jenkins, wrote extensively as a literary critic. When he finally returned to fiction, he began writing his masterwork, publishing the first of its 12 volumes in 1951 and concluding the cycle in 1975, producing a new title about every two years.

For nearly a decade after completing *A Dance to the Music of Time,* Powell published his multivolume mem-oirs, collectively titled *To Keep the Ball Rolling,* produc-ing *Infants of the Spring* in 1976, *Messengers of the Day* in 1978, *Faces in My Time* in 1980, and *The Strangers All Are Gone* in 1982. His last novel, *The Fisher King,* appeared in 1986 to resounding critical praise. In the 1990s, Powell published two collections of his literary reviews and three volumes of his journals. He received numerous honors, beginning long before his master-piece was completed: He was named a Commander of the British Empire in 1956, and he received honorary doctorates from Sussex University in 1971 and from Oxford in 1980. Anthony Powell died on March 28, 2000, at the age of 94, widely honored as one of the finest British novelists of the 20th century.

BIBLIOGRAPHY

Anthony Powell Society. Available online. URL: http://www.anthonypowell.org.uk/indexnf.htm. Accessed February 2004.

Barber, Michael. *Anthony Powell: A Life.* London: Gerald Duckworth & Co. Ltd., 2004.

Brennan, Neil Francis. *Anthony Powell.* Rev. ed. Twayne's En-glish Authors, 158. New York: Twayne Publishers, 1995.

McEwan, Neil. *Anthony Powell.* New York: St. Martin's Press, 1991.

POWER AND THE GLORY, THE GRAHAM GREENE (1940)   Characterized by some critics as a type of medieval morality tale, Graham GREENE'S *The Power and the Glory* is considered to be one of the finest, if not *the* finest, of his novels. It is the second of Greene's religious novels, after *Brighton Rock* (1938), and stands as a part of his great "Catholic trilogy," which also includes *The HEART OF THE MATTER* (1948) and *The END OF THE AFFAIR* (1951). *The Power and the Glory* borrows strongly from the thrillers which pre-ceded it during the 1930s, since it is a fiction of pursuit:

The pursuit of a fugitive priest by the police, but also the pursuit of a tortured soul by his own conscience and by God. The novel was based closely on Greene's peregrinations in Mexico, especially in Chiapas and Tabasco, during the winter of 1938. Many of the images, characters (Tench, Coral Fellows, the mestizo, the police chief, and others), and themes of the novel appeared first in Greene's *The Lawless Roads* (1939), an unusual and evocative travel book.

The novel opens with the first of a number of one-on-one encounters between a fugitive priest, known as the "whiskey priest," who has been on the run for some time, and the other characters—in this case, a dentist named Tench. The political situation is treacherous: The state is in the hands of an atheistic, prohibitionist, anticlerical regime patterned on the historical repressions inflicted by dictator Garrido Canabal. The fugitive priest is trying to escape to Vera Cruz by boat when he meets Tench; they drink and talk together, Tench happy at discovering another English speaker. The priest's escape is aborted when a child arrives looking for a doctor for his dying mother. The priest leaves with the child to administer last rites, but he feels angry with himself for being a slave to his duty and to the faithful even though he himself is profoundly flawed, being an alcoholic and the father of a bastard child.

Meanwhile, the priest's principal antagonist, a fanatical young police lieutenant who is an atheist and who detests the church, suggests a plan to his superior to catch the priest—that is, to take hostages among the villagers and execute them if they do not turn in the priest. The lieutenant genuinely believes the priest to be more dangerous than a murderer-thief from Texas who is also on the loose, and in pursuing the priest he believes he is making the world a better place. Another scene at this point introduces Padre Jose, a former priest who has married and renounced his faith under duress, in counterpoint to the fugitive whiskey priest. Jose ponders the living death of having abandoned his church—his vocation—and of being yoked to his former housekeeper by the marriage sacrament he once administered to others.

The whiskey priest next seeks refuge on a banana plantation from 13-year-old Coral Fellows, daughter of Capt. Fellows, one of the overseers. She hides him and lies to the lieutenant about the priest's whereabouts. Later she and the priest talk, and the uncompromising, formidable young woman suggests he renounce his faith, admitting that she renounced hers at age 10. She urges him to return to hide if he needs to in the future, and she also offers to teach him Morse code as a means of communicating clandestinely. They are two of a kind, Coral being "ready to accept any responsibility," as Greene's third-person narrator states, and the priest remaining duty-bound, as Greene's characters often are. Coral ultimately dies from an illness contracted while working in the place of her father, just as the priest will die at book's end.

The whiskey priest then flees to the village of his former lover, Maria, and their child, Brigida. Next to his original parish town, Concepcion, this is his safest hideout. He learns of the lieutenant's execution of hostages and worse—that the executions started in Concepcion. With the police close on his heels, he still agrees to hear confession and celebrate Mass in the town during the wee hours. When the police arrive and question the townspeople about the priest, Brigida, an already corrupted and malicious child of seven, saves him by acknowledging him as her father. Maria tells him to leave the village and the country; for him to become a martyr is abomination, given his past.

On his way south to Carmen, following the police at a safe distance, the priest meets a mestizo by the river who insists on traveling with him. This mixed-blood man will serve as the priest's Judas, ultimately betraying him for money. But when they arrive in the town, the priest betrays himself, first in searching for and buying illegal drink; the authorities discover his contraband and throw him in jail, where he remains while he works off his fine. Ironically, while he is in jail, his nemesis the lieutenant talks to him, pities him, and gives him five pesos. After leaving the town, the priest comes upon an Indian woman who speaks little Spanish; he understands her enough to know that her child is in trouble, so he goes with her. The child is dead, having been shot by the authorities after the murderer-thief had taken the child as a human shield, in an ironic contrast to the lieutenant's use of human beings as bait for religious treason.

The priest continues his flight into the next state, where a German brother and sister named Lehr give him sanctuary. He plans to go to the city and report to his bishop, but before he can do so, the mestizo arrives, imploring him to come and give last rites to the murderer-thief, who is now dying in the neighboring state. Knowing he will be apprehended and executed, the priest still goes back to help the mortally wounded man. The murderer-thief urges the whiskey priest to take his knife and run, but the police close in on the priest right after the murderer dies, and they take him away for trial and execution in the city.

On the trip and while he is in prison the night before his death, the priest engages his opponent in the most significant dialogue of the book. The lieutenant softens toward him and offers to get Padre Jose to hear a confession. Jose refuses to comply, however, fearing the duplicity of the police and his wife's ire, so the whiskey priest dies unshriven, leaving one final word overheard by the dentist Tench, a witness to the execution: "Excuse." Even though the whiskey priest is supposedly the last priest in the area, following his death another priest comes in the dark of night to hide with a family of the faithful. Greene called his novel the story of two antagonists: "the idealistic police officer who stifled life from the best possible motives, the drunken priest who continued to pass life on."

—*Viki Craig*

BIBLIOGRAPHY

Greene, Graham. *The Power and the Glory.* Edited for text, background, and criticism by R.W. B. Lewis and Peter J. Conn. New York: Penguin, 1977.

Malamet, Elliott. "The Uses of Delay in *The Power and the Glory,*" *Renascence: Essays on Values in Literature* 46, no. 4 (Summer 1994): 211–23.

Pearson, Sheryl S. " 'Is Anybody There?' Graham Greene in Mexico," *Journal of Modern Literature* 9, no. 2 (May 1982): 277–290.

PRIME OF MISS JEAN BRODIE, THE

MURIEL SPARK (1961)   A romantic and political SATIRE on education and educators, this novel follows the life of a Scottish teacher at the Marcia Blaine School, a private secondary school for girls; since much of the action occurs at the school, it is thus also an example of a CAMPUS NOVEL. Although Jean Brodie is a devotee of the finer things in life such as art and music, her refinement in matters of taste does not entail a parallel sense of discrimination in matters of politics; she is also an admirer of Mussolini and other examples of strong, forceful leaders, eventually including even Hitler. In fact, as the novel unfolds, Jean Brodie demonstrates a marked lack of judgment in several aspects of her life, including her romantic connections to the married-but-alluring art teacher, Mr. Lloyd, and to the available-but-dull music teacher, Mr. Lowther. Her failures of judgment even extend to her pupils; her attempts to shape her acolytes—"the crème de la crème"—in accordance with her own muddled principles lead to disaster and betrayal.

When the novel opens, Miss Brodie's students are about 11 years old and turning into adults as quickly as they can, helped and hindered by their teacher's goals for them. A spinster deprived of love and marriage when her intended was killed in WORLD WAR I, Miss Brodie considers herself to be in her prime as the story begins in about 1930. Although Mr. Lloyd has a crush on her, she will not embark on an adulterous affair; instead, she becomes Mr. Lowther's lover, thereby providing a pretext for her supervisor's animosity—Miss McKay advocates the cooperative spirit fostered by sports and the rational exercise of the mind, in opposition to Miss Brodie's self-absorbed and idiosyncratic individualism. Any excuse to dismiss Jean Brodie would be a boon to Miss McKay; ultimately, one of Miss Brodie's own girls provides the evidence needed. This girl, Sandy Stranger, is inversely parallel to Miss Brodie, possessing the rational understanding her mentor lacks, but lacking in empathy and mercy.

In its compressed structure, this novel shares the strategy of multiple time frames also used in SPARK'S novel *The GIRLS OF SLENDER MEANS.* Readers see Miss Brodie's influence on her followers over several years and observe how the teachings that sounded fascinating and iconoclastic in the classroom or in lunchtime conversations can later turn to unexpectedly bad results. Deprived of a full life—and especially of love and family—by circumstances and temperament, Miss Brodie uses her girls as her own fantasy alternates, inspiring them to pursue adventures and romances for which she has left them woefully unprepared. Unwilling to "settle" for Mr. Lowther's marital conventionality, she eventually loses him, and in coping with her attraction to Mr. Lloyd she imagines that one of her girls can substitute for her. In the end, she loses everything—love, employment, admiration—when she fails to understand all the effects her teaching produces.

The novel's intensely developed characters provide apt material for transformation to the performance arts. *The Prime of Miss Jean Brodie* was adapted for the stage in 1966 and the dramatic script was subsequently transformed into a MOVIE screenplay in 1969. In a legendary performance, Maggie Smith brought Jean Brodie to life on the screen, winning the Academy Award for Best Actress.

BIBLIOGRAPHY

Montgomery, Benilde. "Spark and Newman: Jean Brodie Reconsidered," *Twentieth Century Literature* 43 (Spring 1997): 94–106.

Randisi, Jennifer Lynn. *On Her Way Rejoicing: The Fiction of Muriel Spark*. Washington, D.C.: Catholic University of America Press, 1991.

Sproxton, Judy. *The Women of Muriel Spark*. New York: St. Martin's Press, 1992.

PRINCE CASPIAN C. S. LEWIS (1951) See *The* CHRONICLE OF NARNIA.

PRISONER OF GRACE TRILOGY JOYCE CARY (1952–1955)

The three novels in this series include *Prisoner of Grace* (1952), *Except the Lord* (1953), and *Not Honour More* (1955); collectively, these novels are also known as "the Second Trilogy" or as the "political trilogy." In his FIRST TRILOGY, consisting of *Herself Surprised* (1941), *To Be a Pilgrim* (1942), and *The Horse's Mouth* (1944), CARY pioneered the technique of dividing a story among three independent narrators and allowing the AMBIGUITY produced by multiple narrators to remain unresolved; in the second trilogy, he perfected the technique. Although the first-person narrator of each volume produces an internally consistent story, readers of all three volumes in either trilogy will notice inconsistencies that cannot be resolved from the evidence of each character's narration of events. Each narrator has a particular perspective on the events of three shared lives, and the truth lies somewhere in between these particular stories. This effect, according to Cary, captures the indeterminate quality of life as it is actually lived: No one sees the entire picture clearly, and yet everyone must make decisions based on such partial knowledge.

The *Prisoner of Grace* series focuses on the world of politics and on the natures of politicians, but it extends the concept of politics into the domestic sphere of marriage and personal relationships. The narrator of the first volume, *Prisoner of Grace*, is Nina, a woman who is at first married to Chester Nimmo, an important politician, despite her love for her cousin Jim Latter, a soldier for many years, and the father of her three children to whom she is eventually married. These two men are first seen through the eyes of Nina as she examines herself and her world, and later they become central characters in their own self-obsessed stories, in which Nina fades to the periphery while still remaining crucial to the plot. Although she marries Chester out of convenience—she is a 17-year-old girl of the upper middle CLASS pregnant with Jim's child—she also becomes an essential support to Chester's political career. She never loses her love for Jim, but having married Chester, she never abandons her connection to him and his legacy, even after they are divorced. Her cooperation with Chester as he works on his memoirs, and her continued affection for him, drive the possessively jealous Jim to extreme measures.

In the trilogy's second volume, *Except the Lord,* the narrator is Chester Nimmo, an old man who enjoys expounding on the details of his life in politics. Chester is modeled on the historical figure of David Lloyd George, British prime minister from 1916 to 1922. More broadly, his personal narrative follows the rise and collapse of the British Liberal Party in the late 19th and early 20th centuries. Whereas Nina's story is dominated by the men in her life, Chester barely makes mention of his wife and completely omits the existence of his rival for her attention, Jim Latter. Chester focuses on his impoverished working-class origins and the effect on him of his father's failure as an evangelical preacher. He loses his faith in God but replaces it with a devotion to evangelical politics—the British socialism of the FABIAN SOCIETY (called the Proudhon Society in the novel) given form in the Liberal Party. Chester rises to increasing political importance, serving as a minister during WORLD WAR I and then becoming prime minister only to lose his grip on power and his position in the government. His narration is both retrospective and prospective: He looks over his life and his achievements, but he also returns to his roots, rediscovering his faith and determining to rejoin the political fray in a new role.

Chester's plans are thwarted through the intervention of Jim Latter, as related in the third volume, *Not Honour More*. The narrative task shifts to Jim, a reactionary bent on bringing down the political edifice exemplified by Chester Nimmo in *Except the Lord*. Where Chester makes compromises in his principles in order to achieve worthy political goals, Jim holds to his code of honor with unbending and unforgiving rigidity. At heart, however, Jim's opposition to Chester derives from his possessive jealousy over Nina rather than from any deep political commitment. Despite the fact that Jim had declined to leave his regiment in order to marry Nina when he got her pregnant, he blamed Nina for marrying someone else. His code of ethics is both simple and inflexible: Nina should not have avoided the social stigma of her unmarried pregnancy by marrying Chester. Jim's intermittent presence in her life produces two additional children, including a late-life pregnancy that begins when she is 45, after her first child by Jim has grown to maturity and committed suicide. Even when he persuades Nina to divorce Chester—after that event can no longer damage the political career of "the great man"—he is frustrated that he cannot eradicate Chester's 30-year connection to Nina. Jim indirectly contributes to Chester's death and then murders Nina. In his view, the world that the Liberal Party fostered has *no* values since it does not have *his* values. To make an example of Nina and to punish her, he ends her life. His narrative is dictated from jail as he awaits his execution.

Cary's second trilogy is a remarkably successful example of modernist experimentation with point of view. Through the development of three vivid characters and the detailed exploration of the world through the eyes of each of them, he expands the range of first-person narration to make it a vehicle for social, political, and historical observation.

BIBLIOGRAPHY

Adams, Hazard. *Joyce Cary's Trilogies: Pursuit of the Particular Real.* Tallahassee: University Presses of Florida, 1983.

Fisher, Barbara. *Joyce Cary: The Writer and His Theme.* Atlantic Highlands, N.J.: Humanities Press, 1980.

Nyce, Benjamin. "Joyce Cary's Political Trilogy: The Atmosphere of Power," *Modern Language Quarterly* 32 (1971): 89–106.

PROPER MARRIAGE, A DORIS LESSING (1954)

The second volume in the ROMAN-FLEUVE collectively entitled *CHILDREN OF VIOLENCE,* this novel follows *MARTHA QUEST* and precedes *A RIPPLE FROM THE STORM*. The protagonist, Martha Quest, has left behind the first stage of her journey of self-discovery with her marriage to Douglas Knowell, a man she had believed to be a deeply committed political radical. *A Proper Marriage* covers the second stage of her life during the years of her first marriage, first child, and first divorce.

As the violence of WORLD WAR II approaches—Martha herself had been born during the violence of WORLD WAR I—she finds herself pregnant and alone, since her husband is off fighting in the war, leaving her to manage her delivery as best she can. Douglas returns before the end of the war on a medical discharge, suffering from ulcers, and moves his family to a suburban setting. Martha finds herself subordinated to the demands of household domesticity as a member of the highly conventional world of the colonial equivalent of a country club. Several years evaporate in this manner before Martha renews herself first through reading and then through a reconnection with her politically active friends. Douglas, whom she had once admired for what she thought was an enlightened political awareness, now resents Martha's resurgence of political idealism. Their marriage deteriorates into emotionally distraught shouting matches, until finally Martha leaves Douglas and her daughter as well. The cozy suburban world sides with Douglas, seeing Martha as the villain in the breakup of her marriage: a woman who abandons her duties as wife and mother in order to work toward change for the better in the larger world.

In this novel, LESSING is exploring the clay feet of three important idols of womanhood: marriage, motherhood, and community. The pull of these connections fragments her life, but Martha is searching for wholeness. Whatever benefits marriage, motherhood, and community may confer on women, the price for those benefits is high; for Martha at this stage in her life, this *particular* marriage and this *particular* community exact their toll without helping her to reach her personal goals. Saving herself from the marriage and the community imposes the further cost of losing her role in motherhood itself as she goes back to an independent life with nothing more than her wits and her hope for a better world to help her along.

BIBLIOGRAPHY
Stitzel, Judith G. " 'That's Not Funny': Attitudes Towards Humor in Doris Lessing's *A Proper Marriage* and *A Ripple from the Storm*," *The Bulletin of the West Virginia Association of College English Teachers* 5, no. 1–2 (1979): 40–46.

PUBLIC SCHOOLS (I.E., PRIVATE SCHOOLS)
In England, public school education has been a crucially important and influential aspect of life for centuries. More commonly referred to today as "independent schools," English public schools are roughly the equivalent of American private college preparatory schools, but with longer pedigrees and more ancient traditions. The curriculum taught was traditionally dominated by the study of Roman and Greek classical civilization; when the British EMPIRE sprawled across the world, England's public schools provided the administrators who controlled it. Public schools generally board their students in dormitories, although some also take "day students" who go home at night. Although public schools educate only a small percentage of the population, that small group has an inordinate influence on the management of the nation's affairs. Young men who attend public schools have traditionally acquired a common set of values, attitudes, behaviors, and speech: The "public school accent" is a hallmark of this form of education and helps reinforce the widespread awareness of CLASS distinctions between those who have been so educated and those who have not.

Many of the major authors of the 20th century have been educated in public schools, including George ORWELL, Evelyn WAUGH, Anthony POWELL, Salman RUSHDIE, Christopher ISHERWOOD, Bruce CHATWIN, Joyce CARY, John GALSWORTHY, and Ian FLEMING. Other authors, such as William TREVOR, have taught at public schools, while still others, such as P. G. WODEHOUSE, have taken the public school for a recurring setting or an essential feature of a character's identity.

England's oldest public school is Winchester College, founded in 1382; its largest and most prestigious is Eton College, founded in 1440 by King Henry VI. Eton College is the traditional public school of the Prince of Wales, the heir to the British throne. Other important public schools of long standing include Harrow School (founded 1571); Rugby, where the game of the same name was invented, and where the father of the poet Matthew Arnold was headmaster (founded 1567); Westminster School (founded 1560); Merchant Taylor's School (also 1560); Charterhouse School (1611); and many others. These schools came to be called "public" because they accepted paying pupils from anywhere in the realm, not just the children of the local town. Additionally, their traditional purpose was to train men to work in the public sphere of government and business. Public schools for girls began to appear in the latter 19th century, along with religious-sponsored campuses and private schools located in colonial realms. Ambitious families of colonized countries frequently sent their sons to England to acquire a public-school education and thereby advance the families' standing, and in this way the public school educational tradition spread beyond its original sphere of influence.

BIBLIOGRAPHY
Middleton, Peter. "The Recognition of British Public-School Masculinities in Modernist Fiction." *Forum for Modern Language Studies* 34, no. 3 (July 1998): 237–249.

PULLMAN, PHILIP (1946–)
Author of the FANTASY trilogy for young adult readers *HIS DARK MATERIALS,* Philip Pullman was born in Norwich on October 19, 1946. As the child of a father, and later a stepfather, in the Royal Air Force, he traveled widely before entering Exeter College at Oxford, where he studied English. After completing college in 1968, he worked at several jobs before settling down in Oxford to teach middle school for 12 years. Eventually, he also taught part-time at Oxford's Westminster College, offering courses on the Victorian novel, MYTHOLOGY, and other subjects. In 1986, he left teaching to write full-time.

Pullman's first published novel appeared in 1978, entitled *Galatea;* it is his only novel written specifically for adult readers. His books for young adult readers include the Sally Lockhart series set during and after the Opium Wars of the British Empire, *The Ruby in the Smoke, The Shadow in the Plate, The Tiger in the Well,* and

The Tin Princess. These novels have been praised for their finely detailed historical settings, their well-developed characters, and their vigorously paced adventures; they share characteristics with the Victorian novels of Charles Dickens and Wilkie Collins. Pullman's best-reviewed books for children include *Count Karlstein* (1991), *I was a Rat* (2000), and *Puss in Boots* (2001), an updated telling of the familiar fairy story. Pullman's most noted books are the volumes of the trilogy collectively titled *His Dark Materials: The* GOLDEN COMPASS (1996; originally published in England in 1995 as *Northern Lights*), *The* SUBTLE KNIFE (1997), and *The* AMBER SPYGLASS (2001), winner of the WHITBREAD Book of the Year Award. These novels have been compared with *The* LORD OF THE RINGS by J. R. R. TOLKIEN; like that wellspring of fantasy literature, they create a richly detailed alternate reality in which various articulate species must cooperate to overthrow evil; unlike Tolkien's work, Pullman's story locates evil in the oppressiveness of organized religious tyranny.

In 2003, Pullman was named a Commander of the Order of the British Empire. He continues to live and write in Oxford.

BIBLIOGRAPHY

Gallo, Donald R., ed. *Speaking for Ourselves, Too.* Urbana, Ill.: National Council of Teachers of English, 1993.

Wood, Naomi. "Paradise Lost and Found: Obedience, Disobedience, and Storytelling in C. S. Lewis and Philip Pullman," *Children's Literature in Education* 32, no. 4 (2001): 237–259.

PURSUIT OF LOVE, THE NANCY MITFORD (1945)

A novel of upper-CLASS life and love in the first half of the 20th century, this story features a first-person narrator, Fanny Logan, whose parents leave her to the care of an aunt. Fanny spends a great deal of her time visiting her friend and cousin Linda at Alconleigh; there, Linda's father, Uncle Matthew Radlett, sends his bloodhounds out to hunt for his children. This large family's eccentricities create the novel's endearing charm and maintain a comic tone in a story that includes bittersweet elements as well.

The novel is loosely autobiographical, with the character of Linda based on a combination of the author and some of her sisters. Much of the story is devoted to Linda's unsettled love life as she begins in a conventional marriage to a banker—everyone but Linda can see the error of her ways in uniting herself to such a dull man—before falling in love with a Communist supporter and then finding true happiness in an affair with a French aristocrat. The onset of WORLD WAR II severs this relationship, but not before Linda conceives a child with her lover. His death in the war leaves her alone in the world, and her own compromised health makes her an unsuitable candidate for pregnancy. Although Fanny has been an onlooker to Linda's more exciting life, in the end Fanny must step in for her best friend in a way she never anticipated.

Readers enjoy the exuberant comedy of the Radlett household, the affection picture of a bygone age, and the sentimental bond between the two friends. Fanny's narration continues in the sequel to this novel, LOVE IN A COLD CLIMATE.

BIBLIOGRAPHY

Hepburn, Allan. "The Fate of the Modern Mistress: Nancy Mitford and the Comedy of Marriage," *MFS: Modern Fiction Studies* 45, no. 2 (Summer 1999): 340–368.

PYM, BARBARA (1913–1980)

Born in Shropshire, near the English border with Wales, on June 2, 1913, Mary Crampton (Pym's birth name) was the elder daughter of a successful lawyer. Her mother belonged to a well-to-do family of notable Welsh descent, and the two Crampton sisters grew up in a world of material comfort and secure leisure. They were encouraged to express their imaginations, so Barbara Pym's writing life began in childhood with plays that she and her sister and cousins performed for the family. Pym was educated at a Liverpool boarding school during her teenage years and then entered St. Hilda's College at Oxford University in 1931, where she studied English literature, and from which she was graduated with honors in 1934. Beginning that year, she wrote her first novel, *Some Tame Gazelle,* an autobiographical fiction featuring herself, her sister, and other friends as models for the main characters; she did not find a publisher for it, however, until 1950. Three additional novels written during the years of the GREAT DEPRESSION remained unpublished until after Pym's death. During her college years, Pym developed an intense but unrequited love for a fellow student; her disappointments in love—she never married—inform her characteristic fictional picture of talented, capable women and the preening, self-absorbed men they love.

With the outbreak of WORLD WAR II, Pym first worked at a canteen of the YMCA in her hometown and then was relocated to Bristol in 1941 to censor letters as a form of wartime national service. While in Bristol, she fell in love with a married man. In 1943, she entered military service in the Women's Royal Naval Service (WRNS), serving in England and Italy, with time off to care for her dying mother. After the war, she worked as an editor for the International African Institute from 1946 until 1974; there, she became acquainted with the world of professional anthropologists, which enters into much of her fiction. Barbara Pym died of cancer on January 11, 1980.

Pym's writing career began long before her publishing career and was interrupted by a 16-year hiatus (1961–77), during which publishers snubbed her work despite her earlier successes. Beginning in 1950, she published six novels in 11 years: *Some Tame Gazelle* (1950), *Excellent Women* (1952), *Jane and Prudence* (1953), *LESS THAN ANGELS* (1955), *A Glass of Blessings* (1958), and *No Fond Return of Love* (1961). These novels are comedies of manners set in the drawing rooms of middle-CLASS English homes and relating the personal lives of rather old-fashioned individuals of no great importance. Pym's skill in character development and her psychological insight elevate these uneventful lives, endowing them with the significance that even the least important member of society feels for the events of her or his personal life.

Tastes had changed by 1963, when her novel *An Unsuitable Attachment* was rejected by her longtime publisher—and by several others as well. Pym suffered a crisis of confidence in her writing, but she kept on writing for her personal enjoyment and for the enjoyment of her friends. Then, in 1977, her career was revived when she was named as one of the most underrated of living authors in *The Times Literary Supplement;* she submitted *Quartet in Autumn* for publication and was successful: The novel was short-listed for the BOOKER PRIZE, and it achieved a popular success as well. It is a sympathetically comic study of retirement and its effects on four longtime coworkers. Pym's earlier novels immediately went into reprint and found an appreciative readership in Britain and the United States. In 1978, *The Sweet Dove Died* (actually written in 1968) was equally successful, as was *A Few Green Leaves* (1980).

By this time, Pym was suffering from breast cancer, which ended her life at the age of 66. Her friend and coworker Hazel Holt managed Pym's literary estate, bringing out *An Unsuitable Attachment* in 1982, *Crampton Hodnet* (written about 1940) in 1985, and *An Academic Question* (written during her exile from publishing) in 1986, along with collections of essays and short fiction. *Crampton Hodnet* is perhaps the most cheerful of Pym's narratives; it and *An Academic Question* are both examples of CAMPUS NOVELS, exploring the lives of students and professors in university settings. Pym's novels are commonly compared favorably with the work of Jane Austen in their quietly comic focus on the ordinary day-to-day lives of characters, presented with exacting realism and deep sympathy. Her work is also of interest from the perspective of FEMINISM, since her depictions of men are so honest and insightful as to be discomforting to male readers dismayed to recognize the truth in her careful observations of masculine thought and behavior.

BIBLIOGRAPHY

Allen, Orphia Jane. *Barbara Pym: Writing a Life*. Metuchen, N.J.: Scarecrow Press, 1994.

Hazel Holt. *A Lot to Ask: A Life of Barbara Pym*. New York: Dutton, 1990.

Nardin, Jane. *Barbara Pym*. Twayne's English Authors, 406. Boston: Twayne, 1985.

Salwak, Dale, ed. *The Life and Work of Barbara Pym*. New York: Macmillan, 1987.

Wyatt-Brown, Anne M. *Barbara Pym: A Critical Biography*. Columbia: University of Missouri Press, 1992.

Q

QUARANTINE JIM CRACE (1997) The winner of the 1997 WHITBREAD Book of the Year Award, this novel reimages the story of Christ's 40 days of temptation in the wilderness, but in this fictionalized version, Christ is one of several pilgrims, and the other pilgrims remain the central focus of the novel. Instead of Satan, the force of evil in the story is the brutal and feverish merchant Musa, who becomes obsessed with the Galilean's healing powers; Musa's wife, Miri, although pregnant, is eagerly anticipating her liberation upon her husband's apparently imminent death. The other pilgrims include Shim, a half-Jewish Greek; a mute (because tongueless) Badu villager who provides comic relief that ultimately is revealed as wisdom; Aphas, a kind old man dying of a cancer; and Marta, a barren young woman victimized by Musa before the story's end.

Christ is nicknamed "the Gally" in the story; he is portrayed as a teenager who suffers delusional visions and who experiences paroxysms of prayer. The repulsive Musa occupies the central position in the story, partially because of his salesman's calculating charisma, and partially because of his own effusive storytelling talents: He is the born raconteur, but he lacks the bonhomie and warmth that would make him an appealing character. He tells stories because he likes the attention they bring. Musa is an unwilling pilgrim—he and Miri have been abandoned in the desert—but he is the only one to make the association between "the Gally's" actions and the miraculous consequences that follow from them,

and he is the only one to see the resurrected figure—Christ's fasting proves fatal—following the caravan of survivors back to Jerusalem. Musa is a visionary, too: He is able to imagine the worldwide movement of believers who will be drawn to the Galilean, but only because of the opportunities for profit that will follow in the wake of such a focused gathering together of belief.

CRACE'S novel is filled with vivid and original descriptive passages that bring to life the barren Judean desert and the sufferings of the pilgrims seeking redemption through self-torment. Although the author has indicated that he approached his topic intending to debunk the story of Christ's 40 days of temptation in the wilderness, critics have observed that the novel fails to be merely an antireligious treatise. Crace's handling of a complex topic imbued with both sacred and mythic dimensions expands on his original material rather than diminishing it.

BIBLIOGRAPHY

Kermode, Frank. "Into the Wilderness." Review of *Quarantine. New York Times Book Review*, 12 April 1998, 8.

Korn, Eric. "The Galilean." Review of *Quarantine. Times Literary Supplement*, 13 June 1997, 25.

QUEEN OF THE TAMBOURINE, THE JANE GARDAM (1991) Winner of the WHITBREAD Book of the Year Award for 1991, this novel examines the life of a middle-aged suburban housewife, Eliza Peabody. GARDAM'S typical characters are teens moving into adult responsibilities—her novels for young adult readers have won numerous awards—but in *The Queen of the Tambourine* she turns her sympathetic attention to a quieter domain, showing how Eliza copes with the loneliness that plagues her in spite of her marriage. In a series of letters to her neighbor Joan, who has abandoned her husband for travels in the exotic countries of Asia, Eliza relates the details of her life. Without intending to, she also reveals a mind coming unraveled and slipping into instability.

Eliza's correspondence with Joan begins as a series of picky notes and critical comments; when Joan leaves, however, Eliza fears she may have helped push her neighbor away. To assuage her guilt, she invites Joan's abandoned husband to stay in the Peabody home. Their neighborhood is a suburb of the upper-middle-CLASS homes of white-collar professionals. This privileged enclave, however, is no protection from loneliness in an empty and childless marriage or from isolation in a distant suburb. As Eliza continues to write her letters to Joan—who never answers—her anecdotes reveal more and more inconsistencies and contradictions and her stories become wilder. She says that her husband has run off with Joan's husband and that she confides her woes to a young man suffering from AIDS in a hospice. She makes friends, she says, with the children of the new curate. By the middle of the novel, these stories and their variations have established Eliza as an unreliable—and often amusing—narrator, so that the reader must question everything Eliza says. Her stories seem to relate and to reveal, but they may all actually be delusions or futile wishes. Gardam retrieves Eliza's situation as the novel progresses, providing explanations to resolve the AMBIGUITY and INDETERMINACY of the earlier letters.

By all rights, Eliza should be an unsympathetic character as she slips into madness, but Gardam maintains the reader's sympathy for Eliza through comedy and through Eliza's great skill as a storyteller. Her narrative is too absorbing, and the puzzle of the truths it obscures is too compelling; readers are drawn along by the narrative voice and are rewarded with a carefully constructed closure that resolves Eliza's ambiguities.

BIBLIOGRAPHY

Hardy, Barbara. "To the Land of the Dead." Review of *The Queen of the Tambourine*. *Times Literary Supplement*, 12 April 1991, 18.

"Recommended Reading." Review of *The Queen of the Tambourine*. *The New Yorker*, 9 October 1995, 91.

QUESTION OF UPBRINGING, A

ANTHONY POWELL (1951)   Volume one in the 12-volume ROMAN-FLEUVE collectively entitled *A DANCE TO THE MUSIC OF TIME,* this novel introduces the first-person narrator of the entire series, Nicholas Jenkins, as he undergoes the upper-CLASS British tradition of leaving the family circle to be boarded and educated at a PUBLIC SCHOOL as preparation for reading a subject (or what Americans would call declaring and pursuing a "major") at the university level. Powell clearly indicates that Nick's school is a fictional version of Eton, the most distinguished of British public schools and the one traditionally attended by the Prince of Wales; his college is a component of Oxford University.

The series opens (and closes, 12 volumes later) with a scene of workmen warming themselves around a fire, thereby drawing the story line full circle. The novel begins with a meeting between Nicholas and his paternal uncle Giles, a man of no perceivable means of support; Uncle Giles appears in several of the subsequent novels until he dies in *The Kindly Ones,* and he serves as a connection to other recurring characters such as Mrs. Erdleigh, the clairvoyant. While at his school—which his father and uncle had attended before him and in which he later enrolls his own son—and later in his university studies, Nicholas meets the key recurring characters of the series, including the charming and mischievous Charles Stringham, the worldly and handsome Peter Templar, and the ignoble but domineering Kenneth Widmerpool. Nick admires Stringham's easygoing and confident disposition, and he envies Templer's comfortable knowledge of girls and women. The three become friends; Widmerpool is their *bete noir,* an overeager, vain, puritanical, self-absorbed, haughty, vulnerable, and frequently foolish classmate whose overweening ambition more than once leads him to a downfall or a public humiliation.

In addition to the development of social contacts and skills, Nick's school also provides an education to develop the boys' minds and to prepare them for admission to university studies at Oxford or Cambridge; key minor characters include the scholar Le Bas, who supervises the dormitory or "house" in which Nick and many of his friends live, and other teachers of various subjects of study. Stringham plays a trick on Le Bas that gets the pompous housemaster arrested, but school is not all hijinks. There is also the matter of choosing and embracing the "canons of behavior" that will govern future actions. And there is also the matter of love. Nick visits the Templar family and falls secretly in love with Peter's sister Jean; he is on his way to France, where he will reside with the family of a French officer—a friend of Nick's father—in order to perfect his command of the French language and practice the manners suitable to formal society. In France, Nick is surprised to find Widmerpool staying with the same family, and he has a better opportunity for close observation of this competent but distasteful young man.

Nick discovers his interest in writing as a vocation while pursuing his university studies. He frequents the tea parties of the gossipy scholar Sillery, an Oxford don who has taught many young men now in positions of literary and political preeminence (and who loved to talk about them). At these tea parties, Nick meets Mark Members, a poet and a Freudian who serves as POWELL'S target for the occasional satirical jab at this quadrant of the literary world; through Members, he meets J. G. Quiggen, the Marxist. These two characters are interlaced throughout the series in very much the same way that these two influences—Freudianism and Marxism—are entwined in the fabric of the 20th century. The other important minor player introduced appears only by reference: Sir Magnus Donners, a wealthy industrialist who will later employ Widmerpool and who will eventually host a dinner party at which the guests dress up as the Seven Deadly Sins. By the close of the story, Powell has built a strong foundation for the ensuing volumes of his series.

BIBLIOGRAPHY

Frost, Laurie Adams. *Reminiscent Scrutinies: Memory in Anthony Powell's* A Dance to the Music of Time. Troy, N.Y.: Whitson Publishing Co., 1990.

Joyau, Isabelle. *Understanding Powell's* A Dance to the Music of Time. New York: St. Martin's Press, 1994.

Spurling, Hillary. *Invitation to the Dance: A Guide to Anthony Powell's* A Dance to the Music of Time. Boston: Little, Brown, 1977.

QUIET AMERICAN, THE GRAHAM GREENE (1955)

A novel that is almost painfully prescient to American readers coming to it after the Vietnam War, *The Quiet American* is set in Saigon in the early 1950s, when the French are losing control of the farthest outpost of their foray into COLONIALISM. Communism has taken root in the struggle against European colonizers, but other factions also struggle for power and influence in the nation that might yet exist after the French are evicted.

The French, however, are not the focus of the novel and are present as administrative bureaucrats, such as police inspector Vigot, rather than as major players—an indirect comment, perhaps, on the likely outcome of the French war in Indochina. The novel's narrator and protagonist is Thomas Fowler, a middle-aged Englishman serving as a correspondent—he prefers the objectivity of the term *reporter* to describe his connection to the world—for a London newspaper. Fowler is a married man, but his wife is far away in London; they have been separated for several years, but she refuses to divorce her husband. In the meantime, Fowler has a 20-year-old Vietnamese mistress, Phuong—they have lived together for two years. Phuong's sister has an interest in Fowler's intentions and in Phuong's future; she too plays a role in driving the PLOT.

The lives of Fowler and Phuong begin to change with the arrival of the "quiet American" of the title, Alden Pyle, a model of democratic idealism, if not wisdom. Pyle is 32, Harvard-educated, and thoughtful, and he is working for the Economic Aid Mission—and he seems to be an operative of the Central Intelligence Agency. He stands in sharp contrast to Bill Granger, one of Fowler's journalistic competitors and an exemplar of the "ugly American." Fowler likes Pyle; he offers guidance and extends hospitality to the younger man, but when Pyle meets Phuong, the mutual attraction is immediately apparent. It eventually leads to an offer of marriage from Pyle to Phuong. As Fowler learns more of Pyle's hidden life, and as his hold on Phuong weakens, he also acquires both the opportunity and the motive to remove Pyle from the scene. At the same time, he acquires a deep personal obligation to Pyle, who saves Fowler's life while the older man is investigating Pyle's connection to a rogue warlord. The part Fowler plays in eradicating his romantic competitor disgusts him, and yet he plays it.

GREENE structures the novel retrospectively: As the story opens, Pyle's body has been found in the river with an apparent gunshot wound in the chest. Fowler narrates the events and approaches this discovery as a mystery. He himself is a suspect in the murder; Vigot knows that Fowler and Pyle were competing for the love of the same woman. As Fowler continues his story, it becomes apparent that he may be an unreliable narrator, or that he may be rigorously denying and rationalizing his connection to Pyle's death. His need for the youth, beauty, and companionship that Phuong represents is perhaps greater than he wishes to admit. On the other hand, his outrage over the consequences of Pyle's involvement—supplying explosives to an anticommunist warlord—may be genuine. Greene constructs the plot so that Fowler's motives are overdetermined: His betrayal of Pyle might be his last idealistic act, or it might be the spiteful response of a jealous man driven to desperation. Fowler himself does not seem to recognize the complexity of the motives that may have generated his choices with respect to Pyle and Phuong.

The Quiet American is one of Graham Greene's best novels. It features his characteristic exotic locations, political intrigue, ambiguous motives, and romantic entanglements. It has served as the basis of a FILM ADAPTATION twice, both using Greene's original title: In 1958, Joseph Mankiewicz directed Audie Murphy and Michael Redgrave using a script he adapted, and in 2002 Philip Noyce directed Michael Caine as Fowler and Brendan Fraser as Pyle using a screenplay by Christopher Hampton.

BIBLIOGRAPHY

Allot, Miriam. "The Moral Situation in *The Quiet American.*" In *Graham Greene: Some Critical Considerations.* Edited by Robert O. Evans. Lexington: University of Kentucky Press, 1963. 188–206.

West, Richard. "Graham Greene and *The Quiet American,*" *The New York Review of Books* 38, no. 9 (16 May 1991): 49–52.

Whitfield, Stephen J. "Limited Engagement: *The Quiet American* as History," *Journal of American Studies* 30, no. 1 (April 1996): 65–86.

RAINBOW, THE D. H. LAWRENCE (1915)

This novel began as the first half of a project entitled *The Sisters,* which introduced the Brangwen family, established their social, economic, artistic, and educational context, and followed the adventures of the two young women in the family as they searched for love and fulfillment in life. LAWRENCE decided to divide the novel into two parts, which he published as *The Rainbow* and WOMEN IN LOVE (1920). In the first novel, he provides the family and class background of Ursula and Gudrun Brangwen, and he concentrates the latter part of the story on Ursula's coming of age and awakening of personal identity; in the second novel, he follows both sisters through the last stages of establishing themselves as adults.

The Rainbow reaches back to the grandparents of Ursula and Gudrun, then relates the married lives of the sisters' parents, and then explores Ursula's first brush with the emotional and physical effects of love. The Brangwens have been small landholders tilling the soil at Marsh Farm for generations; Tom Brangwen is on the way to being the last of his line, living the solitary life of a bachelor, when Lydia Lensky, a Polish widow with a young daughter, arrives in the parish to serve as housekeeper at the vicarage. Tom offers her daffodils and marriage at his earliest opportunity, and he makes a good home for her and her daughter, Anna. When Anna is 18, Tom's nephew Will Brangwen moves to town to work in the lace factory; he falls in love with Anna, and the two young people marry with assistance from Tom.

Anna, reared in the Brangwen home, becomes a Brangwen in name as well through the marriage. She and Tom have a passionate union, although she is happiest when she is pregnant. The first of their children is Ursula, to whom Will transfers much of the affection that Anna does not have time to appreciate because of her motherly duties. Ursula receives a much better education that would generally be accorded to the daughters of working-CLASS families, and she responds to knowledge joyously. She plans to attend the university after earning enough money to pay her way so as not to be a burden on her family. As she is working at her first job—teaching school—she meets a charming British officer, Anton Skrebensky, who is the son of a friend of Lydia Lensky, Ursula's grandmother. The two fall in love; Ursula is pulled in two directions by her academic ambition and by her passion for Anton, and she is unaccustomed to the power of the emotions she experiences in response to him. He breaks off their relationship because her love for him is more possessive than he is ready to accept.

Six years pass before the two meet again, when they rekindle their love and requite their passion for each other. But where Anton had previously been reluctant to settle into the relationship, this time Ursula is the one to hold back—not physically, for they consummate their love on a holiday, but emotionally. She has nearly completed her studies at the university, and although she neglects them while enjoying Anton's company, she prefers completing her degree to becoming Anton's wife and returning with him to INDIA. This time when Anton leaves, he looks elsewhere for a wife and marries the daughter of his regimental commander. Ursula does not know that he has married someone else when she discovers she is pregnant; she writes to him to accept his proposal, promising to be a good wife, but other events intervene before she can receive his reply. For her, the appearance of a rainbow in the sky at the novel's end is a sign of hope that life would once again be good to her.

Lawrence's novel broke new ground in its frank treatment of women as sexual creatures and in its refusal to present the world as a foregone conclusion. He suspends Ursula and the other characters in the AMBIGUITY of life as it is lived, avoiding the comfortable certainties. Although he focuses on the psychology of his characters, he also sketches the historical context shaping English life in the years covered by his story, 1840–1905: Tom Brangwen is the product of an agricultural world, living a simple life on the land, while Will Brangwen is a product of an industrial world enjoying greater freedom in an urban environment. Neither of them, however, achieves complete fulfillment in their personal lives; that task is left to Ursula, living in the postindustrial world. The change in gender of the narrative's protagonist is significant. The changes that industrialism brought about in the world placed men and women on a more nearly equal footing with respect to the work that they could do, but it did so without instituting a parallel economic and social equality. Ursula has to figure out how to live in the world as the equal of men, not as the dependent, and doing so will require a different set of expectations about human relationships and standards of behavior. Her vision of the rainbow is the metaphor that suggests optimism for the future of men and women together.

BIBLIOGRAPHY
Bloom, Harold, ed. *D. H. Lawrence's* The Rainbow. New York: Chelsea, 1988.
Torgovnick, Marianna. "Narrating Sexuality: *The Rainbow.*" In *The Cambridge Companion to D. H. Lawrence.* Edited by Anne Fernihough. Cambridge: Cambridge University Press, 2001, 33–48.

RAJ QUARTET, THE PAUL SCOTT (1965–1975)

The four volumes of this series include *The JEWEL IN THE CROWN* (1966), *The DAY OF THE SCORPION* (1968), *The TOWERS OF SILENCE* (1971), and *A Division of the SPOILS* (1975). The series is set in INDIA in the last years of British administration—the Raj—and covers the years from 1942 until 1947, when the territory becomes the independent nations of India, dominated by the Hindu religion, and Pakistan, dominated by Islam. The series opens with the rape of an English woman, and that act of violence becomes a key metaphor for the tangled relationship between Britain and India during the waning years of COLONIALISM. The novel does not privilege one group over another, but instead divides the characters and actions between fictional British and Indian people. Its primary focus, however, is the British response to and management of the end of the Raj. SCOTT's last novel, *STAYING ON,* serves as an epilogue to the series, dealing with the British subjects who choose to stay in India after it becomes an independent nation.

British women play key roles in the series: Single women devoted to teaching are in India by choice, but the wives and daughters of British officials are there by their husband's choices, coping with the climate and the growing tensions as best they can. Scott is an insightful creator of female characters, and the women he invents for this series remain complex and believable figures. He also captures effectively the internal divisions within the British men in power, such as police superintendent Merrick, who frames an Indian for the rape that opens the action of the story. The British soul, as Scott depicts it, is hampered by a long history of CLASS snobbery and racism, but it is also benefited by a deep-seated sense of decency. The rocky separation of Britain and India is a record of the uneven struggle between the good and bad impulses on both sides that lead to less than perfect choices and actions, and Scott maps this territory with historical accuracy, psychological realism, and literary sophistication.

BIBLIOGRAPHY

Boyer, Allen. "Love, Sex, and History in *The Raj Quartet*," *Modern Language Quarterly: A Journal of Literary History* 46, no. 1 (March 1985): 64–80.

Hitchens, Christopher. "A Sense of Mission: *The Raj Quartet*," *Grand Street* 4, no. 2 (Winter 1985): 180–99.

Pollard, Arthur. "Twilight of Empire: Paul Scott's *Raj Quartet*." In *Individual and Community in Commonwealth Literature*. Edited by Daniel Massa. Msida: University of Malta Press, 1979.

Swinden, Patrick. *Paul Scott: Images of India.* New York: St. Martin's Press, 1980.

RAZOR'S EDGE, THE W. SOMERSET MAUGHAM (1944)

One of the author's most important works, this novel is also the only one in which he used Americans for nearly all the major characters. The novel's great strength is its character development as MAUGHAM contrasts a man seeking after the true and the good with one seeking after no more in life than pleasure and approbation.

The novel opens with Larry Darrell, a native of Chicago, returning home after serving in WORLD WAR I as an aviator. His exposure to combat and to death has marked him deeply, leaving him with a keen desire to understand the meaning and purpose of life. Although he attempts to pick up the life he was born to, working as a businessman in Chicago, he has lost the values that would have made such a life meaningful, and he soon abandons it to search for spiritual fulfillment in India. His fiancée, Isabel Bradley, eventually marries another businessman, Gray Maturin. She has not fallen out of love with Larry, but she does not understand the force that compels him to seek truth and understanding. For her part, Isabel honestly recognizes that she does not wish to renounce the traditional life for which she has prepared herself: She wants marriage, children, and the material signs of success.

After five years in INDIA, Larry relocates to Europe, eventually winding up in Paris. In the meantime, the 1929 stock market crash that inaugurated the GREAT DEPRESSION wipes out Maturin's business. Isabel's wealthy elderly uncle, Elliot Templeton, allows the newly impoverished couple to stay with him in Paris. Larry is also acquainted with Templeton through his earlier engagement to Isabel. The other major character in the novel, in a distinctly postmodern twist, is Somerset Maugham himself, a well-traveled author who is close friends with Templeton, Isabel, Larry, and the minor characters introduced in Paris.

With these characters in place, the stage is set for Maugham's exploration of life, meaning, love, and human behavior. In Paris, Isabel, Gray, and their children live a pleasant life in Eliot's home, persuading themselves that they are comforting the old man in his last days. Larry becomes acquainted with Sophie, a tragic woman who survived the car crash that killed her husband and children. She has turned to alcohol as an anodyne for her pain and to prostitution as a means of simultaneously feeding her drinking habit and expressing her self-revulsion. Larry wants to help Sophie and offers to marry her, but this arouses Isabel's jealousy—she still feels possessive of Larry, even though she has no intention of abandoning her marriage vows for him. Her actions toward Sophie, and the rationalizations she tries to hide behind, serve as one of the novel's key examinations of moral responsibility. The novel ends more in suspension than in AMBIGUITY: Eliot Templeton dies at the end of a life devoted to his own pleasures, leaving a bequest for Isabel, and Larry decides to return to the United States to work as a laborer and continue his quest for meaning. Maugham expresses his admiration for Larry's search without completely identifying with it.

Published ahead of its time, *The Razor's Edge* found its audience in the youth movements of the 1960s, and it has provided the basis of two FILM ADAPTATIONS. The novel continues to be admired for its sharp character development and for the respect it accords to the examined life in a world increasingly absorbed with materialistic pursuits.

BIBLIOGRAPHY

Burt, Forrest D. *W. Somerset Maugham.* Twayne's English Authors, 399. Boston: Twayne, 1985.

Cordell, Richard A. *Somerset Maugham: A Biographical and Critical Study.* Bloomington: Indiana University Press, 1961.

Singh, Nikky-Guninder Kaur. "Crossing the Razor's Edge: Somerset Maugham and Hindu Philosophy," *Durham University Journal* 87, no. 2 (July 1995): 329–342.

REBECCA DAPHNE DU MAURIER (1938) A popular romance/thriller made into an equally successful film of the same title by Alfred Hitchcock (winner of the Academy Award for best picture in 1940), *Rebecca* illustrates the grip that the dead can exercise over the living and suggests the power with which the past can shape the present.

The nameless first-person narrator of *Rebecca* follows the Cinderella archetype: She is passive, obedient, and beautiful without being aware of her beauty's effect on others. Her isolation and poverty come to an end when an eligible wealthy man, Max de Winter, chooses her to be his wife and brings her to Manderley, his palatial home—a home still under the shadow of his late first wife, the vivacious and gracious socialite Rebecca de Winter. Max has stayed away from the estate since his first wife's death; under the care of Rebecca's devoted lady's maid, Mrs. Danvers, nothing at Manderley has changed.

Max does not concern himself with the house, expecting his new wife to take charge of it and the servants and arrange it all to her liking; his new wife, however, does not know how to fulfill the role of a grand lady, having recently been a servant herself. Her diffidence is so great that soon she feels completely inferior to the dead Rebecca, wondering how Max can love her after being married to such a paragon of women. Mrs. Danvers does what she can to undermine the confidence and the status of her new mistress, who steadily becomes more miserable and desperate to live up to the standard Rebecca seems to have set. Only Max's revelation of the shocking secrets of Rebecca's life and death brings them back together as Mrs. Danvers sets fire to Manderley. Just as Max destroys the edifice of Rebecca's reputation, Mrs. Danvers destroys Manderley, the symbol of Max's social status.

In terms of FREUDIAN CRITICISM, *Rebecca* is an example of the resolution of an Oedipal crisis in the narrator's life. She marries a father figure (Max is much older than the narrator), but finds herself continually thwarted by the domineering shadow of the absent mother figure, Rebecca. Only after Max unequivocally repudiates Rebecca is the narrator released from the prison of her paralyzing self-doubt. The novel also depends on the staple features of the Gothic romance: The endangered heroine, the Byronic hero, the brooding atmosphere in a labyrinthine house by the sea, and a cataclysmic fire. DU MAURIER updates *Jane Eyre* and makes a tale of romance double as a thriller by her quick narrative pace and vivid characterizations.

BIBLIOGRAPHY

Horner, Avril, and Sue Zlosnik. *Daphne du Maurier: Writing, Identity and the Gothic Imagination.* New York: St. Martin's Press, 1998.

Shallcross, Martyn. *The Private World of Daphne Du Maurier.* New York: St Martin's Press, 1992.

REGENERATION TRILOGY, THE PAT BARKER (1991–1995) The three volumes of this series of HISTORICAL novels set during WORLD WAR I are *Regeneration* (1991), *The Eye in the Door* (1993), and *The Ghost Road* (1995), which won the BOOKER PRIZE the year it was published. Although prior to writing this series Pat BARKER had been noted as a writer of fiction about the lives of working-CLASS women, she handles this strikingly different material with skill, historical accuracy, and sensitivity.

Her inspiration for the trilogy originated in the life story of the English poet Siegfried Sassoon, who served as a minor officer in the English war effort until he refused to order men to their deaths any longer. He was confined to a psychiatric hospital in Edinburgh as a consequence of his act of conscience, where he was treated by Dr. William H. R. Rivers, a psychiatrist. Barker fictionalizes the experiences of these real-life characters in the first volume of the trilogy, *Regeneration* (1992), imagining the interaction between the ex-soldier and the psychiatrist charged with healing him and returning him to duty.

Dr. Rivers becomes the protagonist as his work with shell-shocked soldiers continues in the second volume, *The Eye in the Door* (1993), which won the *GUARDIAN* FICTION PRIZE. He treats Billy Prior, a bisexual patient suffering from amnesia, through hypnosis; the treatment allows the soldier to recall events he had pushed out of his mind. The recollection also allows the author to explore the horrors of that most horrific of wars, not the least of which was the persecution of pacifists and homosexuals in England, who were perceived to undermine the war effort. Rivers becomes sensitized by listening to Prior's recollections; he has misgivings about the work he does in healing men so they can once again face death.

In *The Ghost Road,* Dr. Rivers has relocated to London and his patient, Billy Prior, is on his way back to the front. There, Prior has a chance meeting with the doomed poet Wilfred Owen, one of the many gifted Englishmen who became casualties of the war. Dr. Rivers works in a virtual wasteland of devastation, and in quiet moments he remembers a time he spent in Melanesia studying the Polynesian headhunting culture of Eddystone Island—a practice that had been outlawed, ironically, by the same British EMPIRE that was slaughtering its young men by the thousands in France. In Melanesia, Rivers had learned about the local belief that those who are soon to be dead are already marked out in life: They have already branched off onto the ghost road as their journey winds to its end. Prior's return to the front is just such a journey of a nearly dead soul to its inevitable end.

Throughout the *Regeneration Trilogy,* Barker takes a firmly antiwar stand; her use of one of the most pointless wars of the 20th century helps to magnify the futility of war in general. The inhumane waste of lives, of resources, of skills, and of sanity is inescapable as she brings Prior's experiences back into his consciousness, thereby introducing his suffering into the reader's consciousness as well. As he heads back to France, even he seems to understand that he is traveling to his death, while Barker makes her point implicitly: a culture that will willingly engage in such wholesale and wanton destruction of life and sanity can hardly claim to be the least bit superior to the death-worshipping cannibals of remote tribes.

BIBLIOGRAPHY

Klein, Holger Michael. *The First World War in Fiction: A Collection of Critical Essays.* London: Macmillan, 1976.

Lanone, Catherine. "Scattering the Seed of Abraham: The Motif of Sacrifice in Pat Barker's *Regeneration* and *The Ghost Road,*" *Literature and Theology: An International Journal of Theory, Criticism, and Culture* 13, no. 3 (1999): 259–268.

REMAINS OF THE DAY, THE KAZUO ISHIGURO (1989)   Winner of the BOOKER PRIZE in the year it was published, this novel explores the detailed exactitude of a butler's quiet life and uses these materials to fill in the canvas of the historical events going on in the larger world throughout the 30 years before, during, and after WORLD WAR II. The novel bears a family resemblance to Ishiguro's earlier work, *An ARTIST OF THE FLOATING WORLD:* Both feature a first-person narrator who reflects back over the war years, thinking about the small role he played in facilitating the development of conflict and examining the personal consequences of that limited involvement. Although the earlier narrator is a Japanese artist and the later is an English butler, their resemblances exceed their differences, and the two novels can be beneficially read together, each shedding light on the other.

Stevens the butler worked for Lord Darlington, managing a household staff of dozens and orchestrating every domestic detail that would support Lord Darlington's position in the world. As a "gentleman's gentleman," Stevens could be confident that his work was meaningful since it drew its substance from the status of his employer. When Lord Darlington tries to awaken English sympathy for the punitive reparations imposed on Germany after WORLD WAR I (loosely based on the real-life activities of Oswald Mosley), involving his house and his large staff in the project, he enters onto the stage of international politics and ultimately becomes a pawn in a game he does not fully understand. Darlington Hall becomes the focal point of pro-German activity in England during the years of Hitler's rise to power; with the onset of open war, Lord Darlington undergoes a reversal of fortune and finds himself accused of treason toward his homeland. He dies in disgrace, and Darlington Hall is bought by a wealthy American who reduces the staff to a handful.

Stevens remains in service to this new owner, Mr. Farraday, and does the best he can to adapt to the small scale and the casual routine of this new life. Mr. Farraday urges him to take a vacation and lends him a car for the trip; the novel consists of Stevens's thoughts about the chain of events that has brought him to this vacation. As he recollects the grand old days of Darlington Hall, it becomes apparent that Stevens has made large sacrifices in the service of Lord Darlington, allowing his father to die alone during an important international conference and neglecting the signs of affection from Miss Kenton, an impeccable housekeeper he admired at a distance until it was too late. Underlying this simple story of domestic discipline, however, is the larger search that Stevens is conducting in the attempt to discover whether his life was something more than a pale shadow of Lord Darlington's folly. His vacation takes him to a short encounter with the married woman Miss Kenton has become and he realizes how much he has lost compared to the unworthiness of the cause he lost it in.

But this novel is not a tragedy: Stevens is remaking himself, even though the hour is late. He is adapting to a new world, gradually teaching himself skills he never knew he might need, such as sharing a joke with his employer. The flaw in Lord Darlington does not degrade the quality of Stevens's loyalty, and by attaching that same valuable loyalty to Mr. Farraday, he can in some measure regain the dignity his former employer had squandered. He ends his vacation and his review of his life with new optimism and renewed resolve to fit into the new world.

BIBLIOGRAPHY

Gurewich, David. "Upstairs, Downstairs," *The New Criterion* 8, no. 4 (December 1989): 77–80.

Parkes, Adam. *Kazuo Ishiguro's The Remains of the Day: A Reader's Guide.* New York: Continuum, 2001.

RENDELL, RUTH (1930–)

One of the two women (with P. D. JAMES) who are considered to be the inheritors of Agatha CHRISTIE, Ruth Rendell was born in London on February 17, 1930, as Ruth Grasemann. Beginning in 1948, she worked for four years as a journalist for an Essex newspaper, marrying Donald Rendell during this time. Rendell was unsuccessful in getting her work published until 1964, when *From Doon with Death* appeared, introducing the surprisingly literate Inspector Wexford, a Scotland Yard detective, as her recurring investigator. Since then, Rendell has published more than 60 novels, interspersing the Wexford series with novels of suspense such as *A DARK-ADAPTED EYE,* which recount the growth of a murderous impulse in the psyche of an ordinary individual.

Ruth Rendell began using the pseudonym Barbara Vine in 1986 for some of her books. In a note to the reader appended to *A Dark-Adapted Eye,* she explains that she has always had the two names Ruth and Barbara, used by different sides of her family and therefore by different sets of friends. She sees the two names as representations of two sides of her identity, with Ruth being the tougher and Barbara the more feminine aspect of the one person she is. Ruth invented Inspector Wexford, she says, but Barbara knows the domestic arts that sometimes provide him with clues to the identity of a murderer.

Rendell's novels have won several awards from the Crime Writers' Association and the Mystery Writers of America; her work was also recognized in 1980 with an award for genre fiction from the National Arts Council and in 1990 with the Literary Award from the *Sunday Times.* In 1996, Ruth Rendell was named a Dame Commander of the Order of the British Empire. She continues to live and write in England.

BIBLIOGRAPHY

Bakerman, Jane S. "Ruth Rendell." In *Ten Women of Mystery.* Edited by Earl F. Bargainnier. Bowling Green, Ohio: Bowling Green State University Popular Press, 1981.

Rowland, Susan. *From Agatha Christie to Ruth Rendell.* New York: St. Martin's Press, 2000.

Tallett, Dennis. *The Ruth Rendell Companion.* Santa Barbara, Calif.: Companion Books, 1995.

RETURN OF THE KING, THE J. R. R. TOLKIEN (1955)

Volume three in *The Lord of the Rings* trilogy divides its attention between monumental battles in Gondor and Frodo's private struggle in Mordor. In Minas Tirith, the steward Denethor, sworn to preserve the land until the return of the king, sinks toward madness with grief for the death of his eldest son Boromir and nearly kills his surviving son, Faramir. The foolhardy Pippin Took enters the service of Gondor and finally acquires the maturity that he has lacked throughout the story. Gandalf assumes the leadership of Gondor's defenses with Denethor's emotional collapse, holding off the superior forces of Mordor until aid can come from Rohan and from the army of the dead that only Aragorn can summon. Eowyn, the White Lady of Rohan, secretly rides into battle with Merry and strikes the deadliest and most effective blow of the war, in another of TOLKIEN'S revisions to Shakespeare's *Macbeth*. And in the quiet aftermath of battle, Aragorn again shows his true kingship in the houses of healing. Then, in one last risky gambit, the armies of men mount a hopeless assault against the gates of Mordor on the chance that this attack may aid Frodo in the final stage of his quest to destroy Sauron's ring of power.

The second half of the narrative shifts to Sam and Frodo, briefly separated at the end of *The* TWO TOWERS and menaced by orcs. As the ring slowly consumes Frodo, Sam helps him to stagger on toward the Cracks of Doom, finally carrying him up the last slopes. Gollum shadows them, driven to recover his "precious," and when Frodo faces the final challenge of his quest, Gollum unintentionally fulfills the mission. Evil is destroyed, and Gandalf's allies, the eagles, save Frodo and Sam from an impossible situation. The four hobbits are finally reunited in the city of Minas Tirith during the festivities that accompany the crowning of Aragorn as King Elessar and his marriage to Arwen Undomiel. The novel ends with a long denouement as the king undertakes a progress through his lands. The hobbits travel onward to the Shire only to find it in ruins, ground under the heel of Sharkey—the embittered remnants of what was once Saruman, reduced to petty evil and spiteful destructiveness. The experiences of their quest, however, have reshaped the characters of Frodo, Sam, Merry, and Pippin in the molds of courage and resourcefulness, and they soon liberate their homeland. In the final stages of the trilogy's lengthy ending, Bilbo makes his last journey: At the Grey Havens magic passes out of Middle Earth forever, and the ring bearers are taken to the refuge their sufferings have earned them.

Additional appendices follow the close of the novel in many editions, and in these appendices Tolkien clarifies and amplifies several aspects of his tale. *The Lord of the Rings* tells the story of the ending of the Third Age of Middle Earth, but Tolkien had already imagined the events, cultures, languages, and characters of the preceding ages (presented more fully in *The Silmaril-*lion, posthumously published) and some of those elements shed light on the events recounted in *The Lord of the Rings*. Readers will benefit from reading the appendices: Ironically, they are attached to the end of the epic, but they provide details that pave the way for its events.

BIBLIOGRAPHY

Chance, Jane. The Lord of the Rings: *The Mythology of Power.* Twayne's Masterwork Studies, 99. New York: Twayne Publishers, 1992.

Bassham, Gregory, and Eric Bronson, eds. The Lord of the Rings *and Philosophy: One Book to Rule Them All.* Popular Culture and Philosophy 5. Chicago: Open Court, 2003.

McGrath, Sean. "The Passion According to Tolkien." *Tolkien: A Celebration: Collected Writings on a Literary Legacy.* Edited by Joseph Pearce. San Francisco: Ignatius Press, 1999, 172–182.

RETURN OF THE SOLDIER, THE
REBECCA WEST (1918)   Set at a country estate during WORLD WAR I, the PLOT of this novel turns on the device of the amnesia suffered by the injured soldier who comes home there; when the novel was published, however, this plot device had not yet become a hackneyed cliché, and families in England were indeed coping with such cases as a result of shell shock, along with the other horrible effects of "the war to end all wars."

The novel's central character is Chris Baldry, master of Baldry Court. For 10 years before he went to war, he was married to Kitty, who has devoted herself to making Baldry Court a place denoted by the same fragile beauty she herself possesses. Chris's cousin Jenny also lives at Baldry Court, providing companionship to Kitty. Jenny serves as the novel's first-person narrator, frequently as an almost voyeuristic onlooker to her cousin's life, home, and marriage. The action of the story is set in motion when the two women, awaiting a letter from Chris, receive an unexpected visit from an impoverished and poorly dressed woman, Margaret Grey. She tells them that Chris has suffered an attack of amnesia that has obscured his memory of the past 15 years, taking him back to a period when he had been madly in love with her in spite of the differences in CLASS between them. His letter has gone to the woman he remembers and with whom he wishes to be reunited: to Margaret, not to Kitty.

The ladies in residence at Baldry Court are shocked to learn that Chris has forgotten his wife and even his child that had died before the war, but Chris's arrival home confirms Margaret's report. He does not know Kitty and longs passionately to be reunited with Margaret. The story of their love, including an idyllic visit to Monkey Island in the Thames, comes to Jenny from Chris, and she in turn relates it almost as a third-person narrator, admitting that some of the details have been imagined but feel right. Kitty is repelled by Margaret's tatty clothes and the premature aging that poverty has inflicted on her, but Jenny comes to appreciate the woman Chris fell in love with. Through Jenny's observant eyes, the author draws out a contrast between Kitty and Margaret that illustrates a broader classification of two types of women: the cool and refined but sexually repressed and self-absorbed beauty versus the warm and earthy, sexually giving, and unself-conscious nurturer.

Chris arranges to see Margaret again, but she ultimately realizes that she must do everything she can to restore him to his real life, even at the cost of his love for her. The soldier, having returned to his home, must also be returned to himself, and Margaret finds the way to restore Chris to the life he had left behind and then forgotten. The forgetting had been an anodyne to assuage the painful knowledge of the unhappiness of his marriage, restoring him to a nostalgically cherished past; however, with his "cure" he forgoes the dalliances of the lover and takes up his responsibilities with the fortitude of a soldier.

BIBLIOGRAPHY

Orel, Harold. *The Literary Achievement of Rebecca West*. London: Macmillan, 1986.

Ray, Gordon N. *H. G. Wells and Rebecca West*. New Haven, Conn.: Yale University Press, 1974.

Rollyson, Carl E. *The Literary Legacy of Rebecca West*. San Francisco: International Scholars Publications, 1998.

REVENGE FOR LOVE, THE WYNDHAM LEWIS (1937)

A turning point in the author's career as he moved away from the militant advocacy of MODERNISM that dominated and marred his first novels, *The Revenge for Love* makes effective use of the techniques common to the thriller while also allowing LEWIS to exercise his flair for SATIRE to attack complacency, hypocrisy, and blind zealotry. The PLOT eventually centers on a gunrunning scheme to move arms to the besieged Republicans (who are under the control of Communist leaders) during the SPANISH CIVIL WAR, but first it makes a tour of the varieties of human folly to be found among London's Marxist intelligentsia.

The gunrunners are an odd couple formed by Percy Hardcaster, a Communist ideologue, and Victor Stamp, a down-on-his-luck artist. The third major character is Victor's doomed wife Margot, a mouthpiece for FEMINISM and an admirer of Virginia WOOLF; Lewis sets her up as a target for his satire on the insulated BLOOMSBURY world, the members of which advocate social change while they also soak up the benefits of the status quo. Margot, however, grows and changes, becoming a more complex character worthier of better treatment and ultimately forming the moral center of the novel. She devotes herself to Victor and to his talent with little thought for the hardship she endures as a starving artist's wife. Other key characters include Tristam Phipps, a Marxist artist with an established reputation, and his lascivious wife Gillian; Abershaw and O'Hara, wealthy older men who finance dangerous projects and recruit young men to carry them out; and the sex-starved patsy Jack Cruze, a wealthy tax accountant.

Lewis builds his story slowly through the tough voice of a third-person narrator. He begins with Hardcaster in a Spanish prison planning an ill-fated escape; by the time British diplomats rescue him, he has lost a leg to the cause. London's Marxist community welcomes him as a returning hero, and he, a *bona fide* member of the working CLASS, is drawn into a world of artists and intellectuals he scorns as poseurs, hypocrites, and dim-witted romantics. New characters are added in multichapter sections that function primarily to develop opportunities for satire. In the last quarter of the novel, the story begins to pick up speed as Hardcaster, Victor, and Margot are dispatched to Spain, where all of them will be relieved of their idealism regarding the cause they are fighting for. In 1937, this novel was out of step with the political enthusiasms of educated young English artists. Like the American writer John Dos Passos, who made a similar break with the intellectual status quo after his experiences in the Spanish Civil War, Wyndham Lewis had come to a parting of the ways with communism and with people who substituted ideology for carefully reasoned analysis; this novel marks that moment in his own development as an artist.

BIBLIOGRAPHY

Ayers, David. *Wyndham Lewis and Western Man.* New York: St. Martin's Press, 1992.

Meyers, Jeffrey, ed. *Wyndham Lewis: A Revaluation.* London: Athlone Press, 1980.

REVERSE OF THE MEDAL, THE PATRICK O'BRIAN (1986)   See AUBREY-MATURIN NOVELS.

RHYS, JEAN (1890–1979)   The author of *WIDE SARGASSO SEA, LEAVING MR. McKENZIE,* and other novels that examine the lives of marginalized women, Jean Rhys was born on August 24, 1890, on Dominica in the West Indies. Her early life apparently bore a strong resemblance to the life she created for Antoinette Mason in *Wide Sargasso Sea:* She was close to the African-derived culture of the island's black population, and she was also educated in a convent school. In approximately 1907, she moved to England and lived with an aunt; her father soon died, and her mother, a Creole, died shortly after coming to England. At the age of 18, Rhys briefly studied drama and then went on the road as a chorus girl, traveling from one performance to another throughout England. In her personal life, she was bereft of family and homeland, and in her acting career she saw that women were dependents on the men they attracted, their fortunes varying as their attractiveness varied. This theme of male power and female vulnerability recurs in her fiction, which characteristically features as a protagonist a woman on her own in the world at the mercy of the relationships she is able to establish with men. Not uncommonly, that protagonist shares with Rhys a strong attachment to alcohol and a propensity to rely on it as an escape.

Rhys was married to Jean Lenglet (also known as Edouard de Nève) in 1919. Their married life was unsettled; they moved to numerous European cities, losing their first child, a son, just weeks after his birth in 1919. A daughter arrived in 1922. By 1924, they were living again in Paris, but Lenglet was sentenced to six months in prison for questionable dealings in art. Rhys met Ford Madox FORD during this time of desperate financial need and was soon involved in an affair with him. Ford encouraged her writing—Rhys had been keeping notebooks for years by then—and helped get her first collection of short fiction, *The Left Bank* (1927), published. The relationship was complicated by the involvement of Sheila Bowen, an artist with whom Ford had been living for some time. Rhys used the ménage-a-trois as the basis for her novel *Quartet* (1927): H. J. and Lois Heidler are based on Ford and Bowen. Her marriage ended over this affair, and the affair ended as well, leaving Rhys in the vulnerable position that generally entraps her heroines.

Rhys continued to write, publishing three novels in the 1930s: *After Leaving Mr. McKenzie* (1931); *Voyage in the Dark* (1935), based on her acting experiences; and *Good Morning, Midnight* (1939), about an aging woman trying both to shut out emotional pain and also to find emotional fulfillment. These novels all portray ordinary women at the mercy of a world in which men control the means of financial security. They received positive reviews but did not sell. The impending war drove Rhys back to England; during this period she met a literary agent whom she married in 1934. He died just after the war ended in 1945, and two years later Rhys married his cousin, a lawyer. Like her first husband, her third ran afoul of the law and spent time in prison, leaving Rhys impoverished, alone, and dependent on drink.

Rhys did not write for nearly two decades, but in 1949 *Good Morning, Midnight* was adapted as a dramatic piece. By the late 1950s, she was working again on short fiction and *Wide Sargasso Sea.* A heart attack in 1959 delayed the completion of the book, which was finally published in 1966 to great acclaim. Her earlier novels were reissued, and they found readers to be more receptive in the era of feminist activism and women's consciousness-raising. Rhys also published the short fiction collections *Tigers Are Better Looking* (1968) and *Sleep It Off, Lady* (1976), and some autobiographical materials.

Jean Rhys was named a Dame Commander of the British Empire (CBE) in 1978 and died on May 14, 1979.

BIBLIOGRAPHY

Angiers, Carole. *Jean Rhys: A Life and Work.* London: Deutsch, 1990.

Howells, Coral Ann. *Jean Rhys.* New York: St. Martin's Press, 1991.

Maurel, Sylvie. *Jean Rhys.* New York: St. Martin's Press, 1998.

Savory, Elaine. *Jean Rhys.* New York: Cambridge University Press, 1998.

RICHARDSON, DOROTHY (1873–1957)

An important innovator in narrative technique, Dorothy Richardson is one of the less well-recognized voices of MODERNISM. She was born on May 17, 1873, into a Victorian family of upper-CLASS ambitions; her father had inherited a grocery business, which he sold in order to create a leisured life supported by investments. He was only partially successful; Dorothy and her three sisters grew up alternating between luxurious homes and modest lodgings as their father's fortunes waxed and waned. She received a good education, but by the time she was about 17 she was working as a teacher (and briefly as a governess) to help her family financially. Her father was bankrupt by 1893, and the two years following placed increased burdens on Dorothy as she cared for her mother, who suffered from severe depression. In 1895, while under her daughter's care, Mrs. Richardson committed suicide.

Essentially alone in the world by the time she was 22, Richardson moved to London and found employment as a secretary-assistant to several dentists. Her choice was highly unusual—even bold—for a single woman of good family. While her sisters married, Dorothy remained single and made her own way in the world; in a world that restricted women's employment primarily to teaching—a specialized form of child rearing bearing a similarity to the duties of motherhood—she earned her living in the relatively new field (for women) of secretarial work. Dorothy's social circle included other working women and old friends as well, and she soon met H. G. WELLS, the husband of one of her old friends. She and Wells eventually became lovers; in 1906, when she conceived a child by Wells, she broke off the affair, intending to rear it on her own. She lost the baby through a miscarriage and never had another. She eventually married: in 1917, the artist Alan Odle—15 years younger than Richardson—became her husband. They lived a financially marginal existence as each pursued her or his artistic passion.

By this time, Richardson was contributing articles to periodicals and consciously working toward a new form of fiction that would be distinctively feminine. She hit upon stream-of-consciousness as a point of view, limiting her narration to the mental landscape of a female protagonist. She completed her first novel using this technique, *Pointed Roofs,* in 1913, the year before James JOYCE published his first experimental novel, *A PORTRAIT OF THE ARTIST AS A YOUNG MAN.* Her novel, based on the six months she spent as a pupil-teacher in Germany, was published in 1915; although it received critical attention, it did not turn a profit. Richardson continued to write, however, producing 12 more volumes in the work eventually collected as *PILGRIMAGE.* Essentially an autobiographical novel, the story became more difficult to write as Richardson aged; the final volume, *March Moonlight,* was found unfinished among her things when she died on June 17, 1957. It finally was published in 1967. Although Dorothy Richardson never found a large audience for her highly original novels in her lifetime, the expanding work of academic FEMINISM has preserved the appreciation of Richardson's fiction.

BIBLIOGRAPHY

Fromm, Gloria G. *Dorothy Richardson: A Biography.* Urbana: University of Illinois Press, 1977.

Hanscombe, Gillian E. *The Art of Life: Dorothy Richardson and the Development of Feminist Consciousness.* Athens: Ohio University Press, 1982.

Radford, Jean. *Dorothy Richardson.* Bloomington: Indiana University Press, 1991.

Winning, Joanne. *The Pilgrimage of Dorothy Richardson.* Madison: University of Wisconsin Press, 2000.

RIPPLE FROM THE STORM, A DORIS LESSING (1958)

Volume three in the ROMAN-FLEUVE collectively entitled *CHILDREN OF VIOLENCE, A Ripple From the Storm* follows *A PROPER MARRIAGE* (1954) and precedes *LANDLOCKED* (1965). The protagonist, Martha Quest, has moved through two important phases of her life: the period up to her first marriage in *MARTHA QUEST,* and the events of that marriage and its failure in *A Proper Marriage.* She has struggled to build a unified identity out of the conflicting demands and contrary options available to her in the setting of a British colony in Africa (modeled on Southern Rhodesia).

Having left her first husband and her child, Martha returns to Zambesia and to the life of leftist political activism she had discovered before her marriage, and into which she had thought she was marrying when she united her life with that of Douglas Knowell. She throws herself into the fight, attending meetings, distributing leaflets, and performing secretarial work for the Communist Party of Zambesia. The growing group is unified by its commitment to change but divided regarding the best way to achieve it. At the same time that a centripetal force draws individuals together in a collective purpose, a centrifugal force pushes them apart in individual efforts to gain ascendancy over the group. Lessing uses her minor characters to draw portraits of the kinds of people drawn to socialist activism at that time: workers, refugees, intellectuals, feminists, and others.

Martha works herself into a weakened and fevered state. Once again, she has visions: one is of England, the other of Africa. When she awakens from her distracted state, she discovers that one of the local party members, Anton Hess, is nursing her. Anton is a Jewish refugee from Hitler's destruction of Germany, and slowly a relationship develops between Martha and Anton that is a metaphor for the growth of Martha's political consciousness. When Anton is threatened with deportation, Martha marries him to provide him with citizenship and only afterward realizes that they are at best only poorly matched. She repeats the mistake of her first marriage, binding herself to another too quickly and too quirkily—having reasons to do so, but not the right ones. Martha realizes very nearly from the beginning of her marriage that it is doomed; Lessing uses the disintegration of the couple's political group to illustrate the deterioration of the marriage. Anton is a man of words, ideals, and stern adherence to party doctrine, but the marriage has no basis beyond the shared political talk of the husband and wife; when that dries up, the marriage is essentially over.

BIBLIOGRAPHY

Brown, Ruth Christiani. "Peace at Any Price: *A Ripple from the Storm,*" *Doris Lessing Newsletter* 7, no. 2 (Winter 1983): 7–8+.

Stitzel, Judith G. " 'That's Not Funny': Attitudes Towards Humor in Doris Lessing's *A Proper Marriage and A Ripple from the Storm,*" *The Bulletin of the West Virginia Association of College English Teachers* 5, nos. 1–2 (1979): 40–6.

Taylor, Jenny, ed. *Notebooks/Memoirs/Archives: Reading and Rereading Doris Lessing.* Boston: Routledge, 1982.

RITES OF PASSAGE WILLIAM GOLDING **(1980)** An example of NAUTICAL FICTION set in the early 19th century after the close of the Napoleonic wars, this novel is also a BILDUNGSROMAN and the winner of the BOOKER PRIZE in 1981. The author, working at the height of his powers, adapts the formula of the "ship of fools" narrative (the ship as a miniature reflection of the larger world), alluding strongly to both *Billy Budd, Foretopman* by Herman Melville, and "The Rime of the Ancient Mariner" by Samuel Taylor Coleridge. GOLDING draws on the metaphor of the ship itself as a pattern of society, with the upper ranks berthed on the upper decks and the lower ranks below deck, and on the metaphor of the navigation of the globe as a form of personal development on the part of the first-person narrator as that young man's insight grows, enabling him to judge underlying realities from surface appearances. Golding later produced two further volumes, using the setting and characters of *Rites of Passage* to create a trilogy, *Close Quarters* (1987) and *Fire Down Below* (1989); *Rites of Passage,* however, stands alone as a complete novel without its two sequels.

The story unfolds in the form of the journal of the protagonist, Edmund FitzHenry Talbot, a well-born gentleman recording his impressions of a voyage to Australia (or some other location in "the antipodes") for his aristocratic godfather. Talbot is on his way to begin a career as a colonial official in the still-growing British EMPIRE, but he is young, inexperienced, and untested. He initially mistakes the courtly surface manners of Deverel and Cumbershum, officers born to the upper CLASS, for true nobility, and he overlooks the merits of Summers, an officer born to the working class. He does not see the true connection between Zenobia Brocklebank and the man she addresses as father, although he is initially pleased with his successful seduction of that woman—her virtue, it turns out, has been similarly easy for many men and for many years. Talbot is repelled by the appearance and behavior of Reverend Colley, and he finds it dismaying that the reverend should seem to have an opposite, highly positive opinion of Talbot himself. Despite his repugnance for Colley, Talbot is mystified by the behavior of Captain Anderson toward the reverend: Anderson belies his position as the leader of the ship through his rough, cold treatment of those below him, and through his persecuting denigration of Colley in particular.

The story reaches a crisis as the ship moves into the latitudes of the equatorial region: Passions rise with the temperature and climax when Reverend Colley appears on deck in the manner of barbaric savagery, half clothed and insanely incontinent. When Colley collapses back into his cabin in a depressed silence, Summers urges Talbot to speak to the apparently deranged man. Talbot's attempt is unsuccessful, but he notices some writing of Colley's and takes it when he leaves. Like Talbot, Colley has written a journal for an absent reader. Talbot and Colley have experienced essentially the same events since leaving port, but they are different men with different motivations, desires, and compulsions. Talbot goes to Captain Anderson to inquire into Colley's fate, where he learns that the reverend has died. From the Captain's perspective, the case is closed and requires no further action.

As Talbot begins to read Colley's journal, he relives his own recent life from a completely different perspective. Colley's writing sheds light on the aspects of the other people aboard the ship that had eluded Talbot; additionally, it reveals Colley's struggle with his own forbidden desire—he had been powerfully attracted sexually to one of the crew members, the foretopman Billy Rogers. Just as Talbot has experienced illicit sexual contact during the voyage, "seducing" Zenobia, Colley has engaged in a parallel but different situation. Colley's religious motivation to save Rogers's soul facilitates and complicates his personal reasons for seeking out the young seaman. His religion proscribes his personal attraction yet also enjoins him to save the souls of sinners. Talbot arrives at a clear understanding of Colley's death by combining his own experience with the record of Colley's last days. Although Captain Anderson obviously intends to do nothing, and despite Rogers's callous indifference to Colley's tormented soul, Talbot records the details of the parson's life and death—and of the captain's handling of the entire affair—in his own journal, which is already marked for perusal by other eyes. Despite Talbot's limited youthful powers, the simple act of writing about his life may yet deliver justice from an unexpected quarter.

In addition to this main line of the PLOT, Golding explores numerous minor characters in several subplots that function to illustrate character flaws to Talbot's innocent eyes. The novel can be read as an ALLEGORY of one young man's acquisition of Christian virtue as he makes the crossing into adulthood and comes to understand the complexity of life and of human motivation.

BIBLIOGRAPHY

Boyd, S. J. *The Novels of William Golding*. New York: St. Martin's Press, 1988.

Carey, John, ed. *William Golding: The Man and His Books: A Tribute on His 75th Birthday*. New York: Farrar, Straus & Giroux, 1987.

Gregor, Ian. "The Later Golding," *Twentieth Century Literature: A Scholarly and Critical Journal* 28, no. 2 (Summer 1982): 109–29.

ROBBER BRIDE, THE MARGARET ATWOOD (1993)

This novel, the author's eighth work of fiction, won the Commonwealth Writer's Prize in 1994. It is a study of the forces that shape women's behavior in relation to men, in relation to one another both as friends and as enemies, and in relation to their own pasts. The narrative features a triple set of nice-girl protagonists—the military historian Tony, the earth-mother Charis, and the business executive Roz—who share a single antagonist in the form of the femme fatale Zenia. ATWOOD launches her multilayered plot with the device of a luncheon meeting of the three protagonists, all of whom have been cruelly injured by Zenia's predation on their men. Certain that Zenia is now dead, they are disturbed when they think she has resurfaced.

Each woman's story is revealed with particular attention to the childhood influences that have left her damaged and emotionally vulnerable in ways that Zenia has exploited with wicked relish. The friends share more than their victimization by Zenia: They also share victimized childhoods that have marked and weakened them. Atwood plumbs the psychological depths of each woman's character: Tony had been abandoned first by her mother, who ran off with a lover, and then by her father, who committed suicide; in adulthood, she compensates with rigorous adherence to rational intellectualism. Charis (originally Karen) had been emotionally abused by a mentally ill mother and sexually abused by her guardian uncle; in adulthood, she devotes herself to the suppression of her anger by avoiding rational thought. Roz had been reared as an impoverished Catholic while her father was away at war, but with his return she learned that he is Jewish and wealthy, and her life was turned upside down, giving her financial security and social standing that she lacked the grace and confidence to use effectively; in adulthood, she had allowed a philandering husband to abuse their marriage.

Each woman has lost a man to Zenia. In Tony's case, the predatory Zenia had flattered the gullible young woman into writing a paper for Zenia to submit under her own name and later blackmailed Tony over this incident to steal the passive West from her. Although Zenia had also tired of West, who had returned to Tony, their marriage has been damaged by the suffering that West inflicted on Tony in order to fulfill his desire for Zenia. In Charis's case, Zenia had attached herself to Charis like a parasite, claiming that she suffered from cancer and needed a caretaker. Meanwhile, she had seduced Charis's boyfriend, an American draft dodger, and persuaded him to return home and betray his radical friends; he had abandoned the pregnant Charis, leaving with Zenia. In Roz's case, Zenia had become an employee and then easily seduced Roz's philandering husband only to reject him subsequently, leading to his suicide.

The final section of the book reveals each woman's final meeting with Zenia as they try to put an end to her predatory power over their happiness. As physically beautiful, sexually alluring, and emotionally indifferent as Zenia is, it turns out she is not invulnerable. Each woman also discovers why she has a reason to appreciate Zenia's impact on her life. As human beings, these women have grown, strengthened, and deepened their personalities; the men in their lives are static and flat in comparison. Atwood seems to play with a new perspective on the notion of the fortunate fall, suggesting that the suffering women inflict on one another when they compete for the love and loyalty of men ultimately—painfully—makes them better human beings, able to rise above that competition to find positive emotional bonds with themselves, with their families, and with other women.

BIBLIOGRAPHY

Howells, Carol Ann. "The Robber Bride; or, Who Is a True Canadian?" In Margaret Atwood's Textual Assassinations: Recent Poetry and Fiction. Edited by Sharon Rose Wilson. Columbus: Ohio State University Press, 2003, 88–101.

Murray, Jennifer. "Questioning the Triple Goddess: Myth and Meaning in Margaret Atwood's The Robber Bride," Canadian Literature 173 (Summer 2002): 72–90.

Nischik, Reingard M., ed. Margaret Atwood: Works and Impact. Rochester, N.Y.: Camden House, 2000.

ROMAN-FLEUVE A French term, literally meaning "novel river," used to describe a long fictional series of interconnected novels, or a substantial slow-moving examination of a family across several generations. The roman-fleuve is more integrated than are the episodic adventures occurring to the same characters: Ian FLEMING wrote several novels featuring James BOND, but they do not constitute a roman-fleuve. The French writer Marcel Proust published one of the key examples of this genre, À La Recherche du Temps Perdu (1912–22). Important English examples include Anthony POWELL's 12-volume sequence A DANCE TO THE MUSIC OF TIME (1951–75), C. P. SNOW's 11-volume series entitled STRANGERS AND BROTHERS (1940–70), and John GALSWORTHY's The FORSYTE SAGA (1906–22). The roman-fleuve draws its power from the accumulation of detail that accrues over the volumes as characters grow and change. Names, events, and symbols become more highly charged with meaning from the sheer scale of the work, and the leisurely pace allows a minute examination of behavior, motivations, and consequences.

BIBLIOGRAPHY
Felber, Lynette. *Gender and Genre in Novels Without End: The British Roman-Fleuve*. Gainesville: University Press of Florida, 1995.

ROOM AT THE TOP JOHN BRAINE (1957)

An example of fiction from one of the most noted of the ANGRY YOUNG MEN, *Room at the Top* relates the story of Joe Lampton, a working-CLASS man with ambitions to rise above the class to which he was born. He is also the first-person narrator of his own story, although occasionally he casts a clinical third-person eye over his actions. He relates the events of his story retrospectively, looking back on the crucial period of his first civilian employment and his courtship of a daughter of the class above his.

Joe is industrious, having studied accounting during a period of internment as a prisoner of war during WORLD WAR II. Although born to the union-dominated, left-leaning working class, he gets a white-collar position as a municipal bureaucrat in Warley. To polish his speech and deportment, and to associate with a better set of people, he joins a theater group. He meets Alice, a woman of middle years whose career as a professional actress has ended; they soon enter on an affair that becomes increasingly passionate. Joe, however, subordinates every aspect of his life to his career goals—even his love life—and he knows that Alice's love will not advance his career at the same time he enjoys her favors. John BRAINE captures the double standard of attitudes toward the expression of sexuality: for men, extramarital sex is an acceptable option, but women who pursue the same course of action receive the scorn even of the men who are their partners.

Joe's eye turns to Susan Brown; as a 19-year-old, she is ripe for the kind of marriage Joe wants to acquire, and she is the daughter of a prominent businessman to boot. Joe has a rival for her affections in dull-but-respectable Jack Wales, a young man born to the class Joe aspires to join and to the privileges Joe longs to enjoy. Through no effort of his own, Joe benefits from the characteristic struggle between the generations when Susan drops Jack to avoid pleasing her mother, who finds Jack to be an ideal candidate as a son-in-law. Joe plays a risky game in pursuing relationships with both Alice and Susan, for to him Susan is as dull as Jack is to Susan—he needs the excitement and satisfaction of his affair with Alice.

The situation can only end badly for Alice, but she has few options at her stage of life. When an illness hospitalizes her, Joe takes advantage of her absence from his life to consolidate his pursuit of Susan. He eventually meets with Mr. Brown, a self-made man who has left behind his roots in the working class for the solid comforts of the town's Conservative Club. The two men bargain over the disposition of Susan's future; to Alice's misfortune, Joe's affair with her must be sacrificed if Joe is to put his marriage to Susan on the right footing. As an ethical choice, Joe's treatment of Alice is unwarranted; as a pragmatic choice, his rejection of her "seals the deal" with his future father-in-law.

Room at the Top can be unsettling to contemporary readers in its realistic depiction of the chauvinism and sexual prejudice—both toward women and homosexuals, who enter the story in a short coda of Joe's self-loathing after he strikes his bargain with Mr. Brown—in the middle of the 20th century. Still, it is a realistic portrayal of an important transition in British history as increased social mobility after World War II opens new opportunities to the working class.

BIBLIOGRAPHY
Laing, Stuart. "*Room at the Top*: The Morality of Affluence." In *Popular Fiction and Social Change*. Edited by Christopher Pawling. New York: St. Martin's Press, 1984, 157–84.
Marwick, Arthur. "*Room at the Top*: The Novel and the Film." In *The Arts, Literature, and Society*. Edited by Arthur Marwick. London: Routledge, 1990, 249–279.
Salwak, Dale. *John Braine and John Wain: A Reference Guide*. Boston: G. K. Hall, 1980.

ROOM WITH A VIEW, A E. M. FORSTER (1908)

The protagonist of this BILDUNGSROMAN, Lucy Honeychurch, has traveled with her snobbish cousin Charlotte to Florence, Italy, where they meet the Emersons, an American father and son touring the city at the same time they are. The young women are disappointed that the room they are assigned to at their hotel does not feature a view of the River Arno, but they are taken aback when Mr. Emerson offers them the room with a view that he and his son have. Mr. Emerson, in addressing them with such an offer before he had been formally introduced to them, has broken a key protocol of polite English behavior. Only when an English clergyman vouchsafes the social acceptability of the Emersons do the ladies accept this generous offer.

Lucy encounters George Emerson, the son, in some unusual circumstances, and each time George's spontaneity and casual deportment leave her confused; she is attracted to George physically and yet unable to cope with that attraction because of her conventional repressiveness. When she and Charlotte meet Cecil Vyse in Rome, a socially acceptable and perfectly proper Englishman, he impresses them with his impeccable politeness and reserve. Lucy and Cecil become engaged after they have returned to England. But Cecil brings George into Lucy's life again when he introduces his new acquaintances, the Emersons, to his (and her) social circle. Lucy knows from her one kiss with Cecil that she can never settle for a lifetime with him; her challenge is to find the strength to flout the conventional strictures imposed on her by her social status and choose passionate, joyous love over respectable, repressed propriety. Unexpectedly, her cousin Charlotte has a hand in connecting Lucy to those who can persuade her to follow her heart.

Critics often find fault with *A Room with a View*. Its heroine is a flighty girl, and key characters such as George Emerson are too thinly sketched for the major roles they play. Characters sometimes change their behaviors without apparent motivation. But the charm of the novel and its exploration of the suffocating price of conventionality redeem it, and it makes an interesting comparison with FORSTER'S most important novels, *A PASSAGE TO INDIA* and *HOWARDS END*. *A Room with a View* became a successful FILM ADAPTATION in 1985, with the visual dimension of the movie compensating for some of the weaknesses in the printed text.

BIBLIOGRAPHY

Dowling, David. *Bloomsbury Aesthetics and the Novels of Forster and Woolf*. New York: St. Martin's Press, 1985.

Land, Stephen K. *Challenge and Conventionality in the Fiction of E. M. Forster*. New York: AMS Press, 1990.

Rosecrance, Barbara. *Forster's Narrative Vision*. Ithaca, N.Y.: Cornell University Press, 1982.

ROWLING, J. K. (1966–   )

Author of the *HARRY POTTER* phenomenon, Joanne Rowling was born to a middle-CLASS family in the vicinity of Bristol, England, on July 31, 1965. She attended Exeter University, spending a year studying in Paris before she completed her studies. Although she had trained to be a bilingual secretary, she changed career direction when she was 26, relocating to Portugal to teach English as a second language. There, she was married to a Portuguese journalist and gave birth to her first child. By then, she was already working on her first novel, *HARRY POTTER and the Philosopher's Stone* (published in the United States as *Harry Potter and the Sorcerer's Stone*), with the long-term plan of following her protagonist through his entire secondary school career (age 11 to 17) in seven volumes.

Rowling lived in Portugal for three years; when her marriage ended, she moved to Edinburgh, Scotland, with her daughter. They lived a hand-to-mouth existence for a time; Rowling eventually gained a small arts grant to assist her in completing her novel, and she taught school for a while as well. These adverse financial circumstances ended after young readers took Harry Potter to their hearts and created a popular icon of him through the word-of-mouth playground grapevine, leading to the sale of well over 200 million books worldwide and a film franchise with huge box office receipts. Rowling was married for a second time in 2001. She continues to live and write in Edinburgh, enjoying her growing family and a vast international fan following.

BIBLIOGRAPHY

Farmer, Joy. "The Magician's Niece: The Relationship Between J. K. Rowling and C. S. Lewis," *Mythlore: A Journal of J. R. R. Tolkien, C. S. Lewis, Charles Williams, and Mythopoeic Literature* 23 (Spring 2001): 53–64.

J. K. Rowling. Available online. URL: http://www.jkrowling.com. Accessed on July 6, 2004.

Kirk, Connie Ann. *J. K. Rowling: A Biography.* Westport, Conn.: Greenwood, 2003.

ROY, ARUNDHATI (1961–)

Author of *The GOD OF SMALL THINGS,* which won the BOOKER PRIZE in 1997, Arundhati Roy was born in Kerala (in the south of INDIA) in about 1960. Her parents were educated members of the middle CLASS, one a Syrian Christian and one a Hindu. Roy studied architecture in New Delhi after her parents divorced, but eventually she took up acting and screenwriting. She was married to a filmmaker in about 1993. Her first novel was *The God of Small Things,* for which she negotiated an advance large enough to arouse considerable curiosity about the book that inspired such confidence from a publisher. The novel was a critical and popular success and has been translated into numerous languages. Since its publication, Roy has become a vocal political activist and has published collections of essays that argue her position on a variety of issues, including her opposition to globalization and the proliferation of nuclear weapons. Roy continues to live and write in New Delhi.

BIBLIOGRAPHY

Barsamian, David. "Arundhati Roy," *Progressive* 65, no. 4 (April 2001): 33.

Kingsnorth, Paul. "Arundhati Roy," *Peace Review* 13, no. 4 (December 2001): 591.

Marquand, Robert. "India's Arundhati Roy: Novelist Turned Social Activist," *Christian Science Monitor* 91, no. 183 (17 August 1999): 7.

RUBENS, BERNICE (1928–)

Author of *The ELECTED MEMBER,* which won the BOOKER PRIZE in 1970, the second year the prize was awarded, Bernice Rubens was born on July 26, 1923, in Cardiff, Wales, to a family of Russian Jewish immigrants—a connection that frequently appears in her novels. She was educated at the University of Wales; she was named a fellow of the university in 1982 and received an honorary doctorate there in 1991. Rubens taught English in a Birmingham boys' school in 1948 and 1949. She has also worked as a documentary filmmaker, traveling to Asia and Africa in the course of making nonfiction films.

Rubens published her first novel, *Set on Edge,* in 1960; it is a comedy of suffocating mother-love and guilt, a theme that recurs in several of Rubens' early novels. Her second novel, *Madame Sousatzka* (1962), about an aging music teacher and her Jewish pupil, became the basis of a FILM ADAPTATION in 1988, with a screenplay by Ruth Prawer JHABVALA. *The Elected Member* (published in the United States as *Chosen People*) was Rubens's fourth novel; it continues her exploration of suffocating mothers, but turns the topic to a tragic outcome, using the theories of R. D. Laing about the connection of psychological problems and dysfunctional families.

In a 40-year writing career, Rubens has published more than 20 novels that are highly diverse in subject matter and formal construction. She has explored Jewish experience, Russian experience, and immigrant life in England, but she has also written suspenseful murder thrillers such as *Mr. Wakefield's Crusade* (1985); historical novels such as *Kingdom Come* (1990), about a scholar who promotes himself as a new Messiah; and dark comedies such as *Autobiopsy* (1993), about an aspiring writer who steals the brain of his mentor and drains it of ideas. Bernice Rubens continues to live and write in London.

BIBLIOGRAPHY

Harries, Elbogen. "A Million Miles form Odessa," *The New Welsh Review: Wales's Literary Magazine in English* Autumn (1997): 62–4.

Parnell, Michael. "Interview: Bernice Rubens," *The New Welsh Review* Summer (1990): 46–54.

RUSHDIE, SALMAN (1947–)

One of the most controversial writers in the world, Salman Rushdie was born on June 19, 1947, in Bombay, India. Two months later, India gained its independence from the British EMPIRE and immediately split into the nations of INDIA AND PAKISTAN, dividing along religious lines. Members of the wealthy Rushdie family, as Muslims, found themselves suddenly part of a disempowered minority in Hindu-dominated India; in 1964 the family relocated to Pakistan.

Salman Rushdie attended the prestigious PUBLIC SCHOOL Rugby in England beginning in 1961, and then in 1965 he matriculated at King's College, Cambridge, where he studied history, taking a degree in 1968. Although he returned to his family in Pakistan, he spent less than a year there, incurring official disfavor with a production of the play *The Zoo Story* by the American dramatist Edward Albee. Back in London, Rushdie trained for two years as a professional actor and worked as an advertising copywriter. He began writing fiction, but his first novel, *Grimus* (1975), was a failure in both sales and critical reviews. In 1981, however, his second novel, MIDNIGHT'S CHILDREN, was a tremendous success, winning the BOOKER PRIZE and becoming an international best seller. The novel went on to win the JAMES TAIT BLACK MEMORIAL PRIZE in 1982. His third novel, *Shame* (1983), was also short-listed for the Booker Prize. During the 1980s, Rushdie also wrote a nonfiction book, *The Jaguar's Smile: A Nicaraguan Journey* (1987), in which he harshly criticized the Nicaraguan policies of President Ronald Reagan.

Rushdie's great fame, or infamy, began with the publication of *The SATANIC VERSES* in 1988. Muslims found Rushdie's treatment of Islam and of the prophet Mohammed to be inappropriate, even blasphemous. Sale of the book was quickly banned in India, South Africa, and Arab nations such as Saudi Arabia; in Pakistan, a protest against the book's expected publication in the United States degenerated into violence at the American embassy. Muslims all over the world publicly burned copies of the book, including English Muslims, and riots broke out in some places. The leader of Iran, the Ayatollah Khomeini, declared a "fatwa," putting a price on Rushdie's head of a million dollars or more, and on February 14, 1989, only four and a half months after the publication of *The Satanic Verses,* its author went into hiding. Rushdie did not return to public life until 1996.

In 1995, Rushdie published *The MOOR'S LAST SIGH,* and this time politically extreme Hindus took issue with the story, but without the violence and political disruption that had accompanied the previous novel. Rushdie has continued to publish novels, a volume of short fiction, several works of nonfiction, and a collection of letters. The harsh Muslim response to the fiction he created in *The Satanic Verses,* however, has cast a shadow over his personal life.

BIBLIOGRAPHY

Appignanesi, Lisa, and Sara Maitland, eds. *The Rushdie File.* Syracuse, N.Y.: Syracuse University Press, 1990.

Cohn-Sherbok, Dan, ed. *The Salman Rushdie Controversy in Interreligious Perspective.* Lewiston, N.Y.: E. Mellen Press, 1990.

Fletcher, M. D. ed. *Reading Rushdie: Perspectives on the Fiction of Salman Rushdie.* Amsterdam: Rodopi, 1994.

Harrison, James. *Salman Rushdie.* Twayne's English Authors, 488. New York: Twayne, 1992.

Pipes, Daniel. *The Rushdie Affair: The Novel, the Ayatollah, and the West.* New York: Birch Lane Press/Carol Publishing Group, 1990.

S

SACRED HUNGER BARRY UNSWORTH

(1992) An examination of the profit motive—the sacred hunger of the title—and the desecration of humanity it has produced, Barry UNSWORTH's novel shared the BOOKER PRIZE in 1992 with *The ENGLISH PATIENT*. He begins his story in the late 18th century with the entry into the slave trade of William Kemp, who finds the triple profit points attractive: Exchange cheap manufactured goods in Africa for slaves, then sell the slaves at a substantial profit in the New World and buy luxury goods such as tobacco with the proceeds, and sell those in turn at a substantial profit in England in order to acquire more cheap manufactured goods. He commissions the building of a ship, the *Liverpool Merchant,* to carry this enterprise forward, and hires a brutal seaman, Thurso, to captain the ship. He sends along his nephew, Matthew Paris, as ship's doctor; his son Erasmus, who considers Matthew to be his enemy, remains at home performing as an actor in the role of Ferdinand for a sweetened version of *The Tempest* and courting the play's Miranda, Sarah Wolpert.

Matthew Paris is a man of principle and intellect, and when Captain Thurso throws sick slaves overboard to stem the spread of disease while also qualifying for an insurance claim on the lost cargo, Matthew instigates a revolt that becomes a successful mutiny. The captain is killed in the process, making the mutineers doubly criminal. He lands the survivors in the wilds of Florida and establishes an ad hoc colony there

with the goal of pursuing equality for all citizens regardless of race. In the meantime, the failure of his uncle's business drives the old merchant to suicide, and Erasmus's plans to wed Sarah come to nothing. By the time word of the colony makes its circuitous way to Erasmus some 12 years after the mutiny, he is an embittered man with nothing but his wealth and his thirst for vengeance against his cousin to sustain him. He carries his spite and his hunger for profit on his quest for revenge, stopping to negotiate for Florida land with natives as he makes his way toward his goal. The peaceful colony is an easy target after a dozen years of idyllic life.

Unsworth's attention to historical detail is scrupulous and the details he selects are fascinating and instructive. His narrative emphasizes the sick logic of the sacred hunger that drives modern man onward, implying that those who take slaves for money are mired in a slavery of their own making.

BIBLIOGRAPHY

Sarvan, Charles. "Paradigms of the Slave Trade in Two British Novels," *International Fiction Review* 23, nos. 1–2 (1996), 1–6.

Trimm, Ryan S. "The Logical Errors of Matthew Paris: Or, the Violence of Order in *Sacred Hunger.*" In *The Image of Violence in Literature, the Media, and Society.* Edited by Will Wright and Steven Kaplan. Pueblo, Colo.: Society for the Interdisciplinary Study of Social Imagery, University of Southern Colorado, 1995, 426–430.

Velcic, Vlatka. "Postmodern and Postcolonial Portrayals of Colonial History: Contemporary Novels About the Eighteenth Century," *Tennessee Philological Bulletin: Proceedings of the Annual Meeting of the Tennessee Philological Association* 38 (2001): 41–48.

SATANIC VERSES, THE SALMAN RUSHDIE (1988)

The publication of this novel led to perhaps the most extreme attempt at censorship in the history of literature when the leader of Iran, the Ayatollah Khomeini, issued a "fatwa"—essentially a death warrant—against the author and offered rewards to any Muslim who carried out the sentence; Salman RUSHDIE spent several years in hiding as a result. The novel's title refers to the tradition that the Koran (Qu'ran) had included some verses that had to be emended because Satan had disguised himself as the Archangel Gabriel in order to dictate them. A work of fiction that explored this territory was bound to be controversial, since some of the faithful might regard it as impugning the status of the Koran as the verbatim word of God. Additionally, sections of the novel can be read as a roman à clef featuring a character based on Ayatollah Khomeini. The ultimate result for the novel has been to cast it permanently in the shade of the international stir it created.

The novel has a double structure, with PLOT elements in the present-day world and in the remote past (during the seventh-century founding of Islam), with settings in England and in INDIA, with a pair of characters who occur in both settings and in both times, and with a thematic emphasis on the struggle between good and evil. The double structure extends to the chapter numbering: The odd-numbered chapters are set in the present and follow the lives of Gibreel Farishta, an Indian actor, and Saladin Chamcha, an Indian-born English voice actor, while the even-numbered chapters are set in the past and feature the angel Gibreel/Gabriel and Saladin/Shaitan, the two alter egos of the contemporary characters.

The modern story begins quite dramatically: Gibreel and Saladin are traveling to England on the same Air India jet when a terrorist bomb blows it up 29,000 feet above the English Channel. Miraculously, they survive the explosion and the fall (and the fact that they undergo a fall is symbolically significant); by the time they reach land, Gibreel has acquired a halo and Saladin has acquired cloven feet. But Rushdie subverts the stereotypical association of "angel" with good fortune and "devil" with pure evil. Saladin's fortunes decline at first but then ultimately improve, and he occasionally acts in ways that produce good results; inversely, Gibreel's fortunes at first soar but then ultimately decline, and his judgment sometimes fails him, leading to bad events. Interspersed with the chronicle of their lives after the fall is the recurring motif of racial prejudice and class stereotyping as a corrosive and poisonous force in the modern world.

The minor characters of the novel are as well drawn as are Gibreel and Saladin: Gibreel has a lover, Alleluia Cone (from Cohen), a mountain climber who meets death in a fall from the height of a skyscraper rather than a mountain; Saladin has an unfaithful English wife, Pamela Lovelace—a name drawn from the 18th-century history of the novel, Samuel Richardson's *Pamela,* in which the virtue of the eponymous heroine is wronged by Lovelace, her employer. When his life begins to go to pieces, Gibreel winds up shooting a film producer, the well-intentioned but stuttering Whiskey Sisodia; Saladin loses his job on a television series when he is fired by producer Hal Valence. Driven to vengefulness by his misfortunes, Saladin undermines Gibreel's happy life, helping to drive it to an unhappy end, even though he himself finds reconciliation and renewed interest in life upon returning to India.

Alternating with the chapters that tell the contemporary story of Gibreel and Saladin, the even-numbered stories tell of the Satanic verses. These chapters unfold as a dream vision that troubles the sleep of Gibreel. In his dream he sees "Mahound" (a pejorative epithet for the prophet Mohammed) bargain with Abu Simbel, the leader of pagan Arabia: He strikes a pragmatic deal to identify the local goddesses as minor divinities in return for the chief's support, but later, when his power is sufficient to back his ambition, he reneges on the deal and claims that the verses regarding the goddesses were the work of Shaitan. In another thread, a religious leader who resembles the Ayatollah Khomeini returns to his homeland and calls upon

Gibreel (in his angelic form) for the destruction of Ayesha, a symbolic representative of the United States.

In addition to the complex narrative structure, Rushdie's language is complex, playful, and imaginative. In both form and content, he uses his novel to explore the effects in the modern world of alienation, migration, and cultural clashes, casting these monumental stories in the particular terms of the lives of Gibreel and Saladin. He draws inspiration from a wide variety of texts in the CANONs of both English (Christian) and Indian (both Muslim and Hindu) literature and mythology, including Homer's *Odyssey,* the *Mahabharata,* and the wisdom literature of the three of the world's most populous religions. Rushdie's ambition in *The Satanic Verses* is vast, and his achievement is impressive.

BIBLIOGRAPHY

Booker, M. Keith. *Critical Essays on Salman Rushdie.* New York: G. K. Hall, 1999.

Mortimer, Edward. "*Satanic Verses:* The Aftermath," *The New York Times Book Review,* 22 July 1990, 3, 25.

Taneja, G. R., and R. K. Dhawan, eds. *The Novels of Salman Rushdie.* New Delhi: Indian Society for Commonwealth Studies, 1992.

SATIRE   A form of comic literature designed to chastise human folly, satire comes in two varieties, both named after Roman writers. Sharp, or Juvenalian, satire excoriates and may also humiliate its targets; its intention is to cure foolish behavior by inducing shame in those afflicted with it, holding them up to the scorn of the rest of the world. It is named after Juvenal, the author of the biting and bitter series of poems (*The Satires*) that attack corruption, greed, stupidity, coarseness, and a host of other maladies. Gentle, or Horatian, satire lightly taxes human folly, seeking to cure it by raising the consciousness of its targets through an entertaining kind of education. It is named for the Augustan poet Horace, author of the *Ars Poetica,* which immortalized the dictum that art must be both pleasant and useful—it must entertain *and* teach ("*dulce et utile*").

The availability of satire as a form of creative expression—both its creation by writers and its consumption by readers—has varied throughout human history, since it creates an easy target for censorship. Oppres-sive political systems are generally opposed to the free use of satire, ironically adding grist for the satirist's mill through attempts to suppress the art. Satire on the stage in the English Renaissance was suppressed to protect the monarchy from criticism; Soviet bureaucrats also took a dim view of satire. Writers sometimes couch satirical observations in the guise of realism through representations of situations that actually occur but that are laughable when seen from the distance that a narrative provides; such "indirect satire" may not be immediately apparent to all readers, requiring explication of historical or cultural circumstances. In contrast, writers may use "direct satire" by speaking to readers (or viewers, in the case of drama) with unmistakable criticisms of a situation or a practice they wish to change.

BIBLIOGRAPHY

Connery, Brian A., and Kirk Combe, eds. *Theorizing Satire: Essays in Literary Criticism.* New York: St. Martin's Press, 1995.

Feinberg, Leonard. *Introduction to Satire.* Ames: The Iowa State University Press, 1967.

Frye, Northrop. "The Mythos of Winter: Irony and Satire." In *Modern Satire.* Edited by Alvin B. Kernan. New York: Harcourt, Brace & World, 1962.

Highet, Gilbert. *The Anatomy of Satire.* Princeton, N.J.: Princeton University Press, 1962.

Sutherland, James. *English Satire.* Cambridge: Cambridge University Press, 1958.

SAVILLE **DAVID STOREY (1976)**   An autobiographical novel set among characters of the working CLASS, *Saville* won the BOOKER PRIZE in 1976. The protagonist of the story is Colin Saville; the setting is a coal-mining town in Yorkshire, in the north of England, similar to the one in which the author was born and reared. The action of the novel covers the period from the GREAT DEPRESSION of the 1930s to the DIMINISHING AGE of the two decades following WORLD WAR II. David STOREY uses his training as a painter to capture and represent a vivid picture of the lives of coal miners and the physical environment of the Yorkshire landscape in the earlier portions of the novel. The third-person objective point of view maintains an emotional neutrality in the narrative without marginalizing the story of the protagonist's growth and development.

Colin begins life in the center of a loving family, but his essential differences from them in his abilities and interests—he realizes while he is young that he wants to be an artist rather than an artisan—drive a wedge between the boy and the rest of his family. Balancing the use of visual imagery with psychological realism, Storey begins the novel with the tragic death in childhood of the Saville's first child while Mrs. Saville is pregnant with Colin. Storey divides the novel into five sections that correspond to the stages of Colin's life, first concentrating on the family environment, then introducing his connection to other children at play and following him as he enters school and begins to develop the ambitions that will eventually separate him from his family. Ironically, the very schooling that his parents provide for him is also the primary means by which Colin is able to leave the world of his parents and dare to seek his living in the world as an artist.

Saville is a careful and sympathetic review of the clash that results when children diverge from the path their parents assume they will follow. Additionally, it is a revealing examination of the role education plays—especially for the children of the working class—in nurturing the capacity to strive for and imagine how to achieve a better life. Finally, it makes an accounting of the toll that an artist's growth can take on the world that gave rise to him.

BIBLIOGRAPHY

Brown, Dorothy H. "Breaking Away: A Yorkshire Working Class Family in David Storey's *Saville*," *Round Table of South Central College English Association* 27, no. 1 (Spring 1986): 3–5.

Pittock, Malcolm. "David Storey and *Saville*: A Revaluation," *Forum for Modern Language Studies* 32, no. 3 (July 1996): 208–27.

SAYERS, DOROTHY (1893–1957)

One of the leading writers of English MYSTERY AND DETECTIVE FICTION, and the creator of Lord Peter Wimsey, Dorothy Sayers was a contemporary of Agatha CHRISTIE, writing during the formative period of the genre. She was born June 13, 1893, in Oxford, where her father was the headmaster of Christchurch Cathedral Choir School. Four years later, he removed his family to the fen country of East Anglia when he took a position at Bluntisham; in *The NINE TAILORS* (1934), the book many critics think is her best, Dorothy Sayers recreates the fen country with sincere affection and vivid realism. At the age of six, Dorothy became her father's pupil, first studying Latin and then going on to modern languages with considerable facility. She was boarded at the Godolphin School beginning when she was 15. She had difficulty adjusting to the new social environment after a life as an only child, and in her second year she left, suffering illness and emotional distress. In 1912, she won a Gilchrist scholarship to Oxford and was matriculated at Somerville College. She excelled in modern languages, completing her studies with first-class honors in 1915, and was subsequently among the first women graduated from Oxford in 1920.

After college, Dorothy Sayers taught at Hull High School for Girls (1915–17), followed by two years of employment in Oxford at Blackwell's, a distinguished publishing firm. She met Eric Whelpton, a veteran of WORLD WAR I, and took a position teaching in France at the same school where he was employed; he may have been a partial inspiration for Sayers's creation of Lord Peter Wimsey, her recurring detective. During her year in France, she began writing crime fiction to expand her income. Upon returning to England in 1920, she taught for another two years and then went to work in 1922 for an advertising firm, Benson's, where she remained employed for nine years. While working as an advertising copywriter, she lived in BLOOMSBURY and followed the bohemian lifestyle of that district. She had a child outside wedlock during this period. In 1926, she was married to another war veteran, Oswald "Mac" Fleming, a journalist. By 1931, she had become successful enough as a writer to leave her job and earn her living from her publications.

Sayers's first novel appeared in 1923: *Whose Body?* introduced Lord Peter Wimsey to the world and was the first of 11 novels and several short stories in which he solved a perplexing crime. The last Peter Wimsey story appeared in 1940, to the disappointment of readers thirsting for more. Sayers had moved on to other writing projects associated with her deep religious commitment and did not return to the field of mystery and detective fiction. Between 1923 and 1940, she helped move the genre of crime writing closer to the standards of the serious novel of manners through her fully developed characters, her richly detailed social settings, and her examination of the ethical underpinnings of her complex plots.

Sayers cofounded the Detection Club, and with members such as G. K. CHESTERTON, Agatha Christie, and others she cowrote several mysteries. Among her novels featuring Peter Wimsey, some of her most notable titles are *Clouds of Witnesses* (1925), set partially in Parliament, *The Unpleasantness at the Bellona Club* (1928), set in a gentlemen's club, *Strong Poison* (1930), in which Lord Peter meets Harriet Vane, *Murder Must Advertise* (1933), set in an advertising agency, and *Gaudy Nights* (1935), set in Oxford. Her novels are notable for their effective use of intelligent, capable women—she is perhaps underrated as a proponent of FEMINISM—and for their awareness of social issues needing attention. Critics have caviled at Lord Peter's aristocratic pedigree (Sayers created a family tree for him extending back to William the Conqueror), at his elitism, and at his CLASS snobbery, but in context he is affable and considerate of people high and low with whom his investigations bring him in contact.

Between 1940 and her death on December 17, 1957, Dorothy Sayers wrote numerous essays, speeches, radio dramas, devotional poems, translations of French and Italian works, including Dante's *Divine Comedy,* Christian treatises, and several sacred plays, including a 12-episode cycle of radio plays on the life of Christ. Her work as a crime writer has recently reached a new generation of enthusiasts by providing the basis for a series of television FILM ADAPTATIONS, initiated by the British Broadcasting Corporation.

BIBLIOGRAPHY

Coomes, David. *Dorothy L. Sayers: A Careless Rage for Life.* New York: Lion Publishing, 1992.

Dale, Alzina, ed. *Dorothy L. Sayers: The Centenary Celebration.* New York: Walker, 1993.

Reynolds, Barbara. *Dorothy L. Sayers: Her Life and Soul.* New York: St. Martin's Press, 1993.

SCARLET PIMPERNEL, THE BARONESS ORCZY (1905)

An exciting page-turner in the genre of HISTORICAL FICTION, *The Scarlet Pimpernel* takes the period of the French Revolution for its setting and follows the adventures of Sir Percy Blakeney, an apparently indolent English aristocrat who has a double life rescuing worthy French aristocrats from the guillotine. He is a master of disguise, an excellent swordsman, a crafty strategist, and a boldly courageous adventurer. He also has a nemesis, Citizen Chauvelin, who is also cunning with disguises, and an array of helpers such as Sir Andrew Ffolkes. Sir Percy's wife is the beautiful Frenchwoman Marguerite St. Just, who has no idea of her husband's double life and thereby accidentally betrays his secret to his enemy; Marguerite's brother Armand St. Just eventually joins Sir Percy's underground organization. Rounding out the character list is the beautiful Suzanne de Tourney, who falls in love with Sir Andrew.

At the opening of the story, members of the de Tournay family have been rescued and brought to England by the Scarlet Pimpernel—so called because he leaves a drawing of a small red flower behind when he liberates French aristocrats bound for the guillotine. Unfortunately, the Count remains in the custody of the bloody revolutionary government, therefore requiring another foray into danger. Chauvelin has pursued his quarry into England to no avail; there, he attempts to enlist the help of Marguerite, taking her patriotic attachment to the new government for granted. She rejects his solicitation; later, he acquires information against her brother, which he uses to blackmail her for assistance in gathering further information about the Pimpernel and his ring of cohorts. When Marguerite intercepts a note and hands it on to Chauvelin, she has no idea that she is endangering her husband's life.

Entwined with this story of intrigue and action is the love story between Sir Percy and Marguerite. His love for her has cooled because he thinks she betrayed an aristocratic family to the guillotine; for her part, she is too vulnerable to make an explanation to him about what really happened. Their marriage appears to be a complete mismatch between a beautiful social butterfly and a dull English squire devoted to hunting and country life. When Marguerite learns of Sir Percy's hidden identity, her accidental betrayal has already occurred, and she must prove her courage to help save him. The Scarlet Pimpernel, however, is equal to any challenge Chauvelin can present to him, and the couple enjoys a happy reunion after yet another hair's-breadth escape.

The Scarlet Pimpernel is a minor classic well suited to beginning readers of literature. Its plot is complex and yet clearly presented, and its characters are stereotypes who learn to rise above their limitations. It is a melodrama and so lacks the subtlety that middle and high school readers might miss, yet it can serve as a training ground for sharpening the skill of paying attention to details. It is not without irony, especially in those scenes in which Sir Percy is in his indolent Englishman mode, but its irony is not abstruse. And finally, it is ostensibly inoffensive. Skilled readers (and teachers hoping to shape skilled readers), however, will know how to point up the novel's implicit CLASS bias, gender stereotyping, valorization of violent resolution to social discord, and moral AMBIGUITY.

BIBLIOGRAPHY
Nachison, Beth. Introduction to *The Scarlet Pimpernel.* New York: Acclaim Books, 1997.

SCHINDLER'S ARK THOMAS KENEALLY (1982)

Published in the United States under the title *Schindler's List,* and the basis for the 1993 FILM ADAPTATION of that same name, this novel won the BOOKER PRIZE in 1982. It is a "novelization" or "documentary novel" of historical people and events that centers on the Czech-born German industrialist Oskar Schindler; it preserves a riveting and compelling story of the Holocaust that had been little known before the novel was published. KENEALLY undertook the research and writing of the book after hearing the outline of Schindler's story from Leopold Page, one of the Jews whom Schindler saved from almost certain death as the Nazis undertook Hitler's "Final Solution" and attempted to eradicate a cultural and religious group all over Europe.

The novel recounts the story of Oskar Schindler's choices and actions, beginning in his childhood and extending to his old age and death, but it also chronicles the story of the Jews of Krakow, Poland. Schindler had been a opportunistic businessman when WORLD WAR II began: As a charmer, a womanizer, and a member of the Nazi Party, he did not have the obvious makings of a hero. He acquired a Jewish enamelware factory in Krakow planning to reap huge profits as a defense contractor, and under Nazi regulations he was allowed to use the virtual slave labor of Jews penned in the ghetto of the city. Schindler's factory had a certain degree of protection since it was allegedly serving the great war machine of Germany, and Schindler used his status—and bribed Nazi officials when necessary—to retain Jews in this service who would otherwise have been sent to Auschwitz. His chief assistant in this work was his Jewish accountant, Itzhak Stern.

Schindler saved his workers repeatedly: When the villain of the story, the Gestapo officer Amon Goeth, destroyed the ghetto, killing everyone there or imprisoning them in the Plaszow Labor Camp, Schindler had his factory designated as a "sub-camp" so his employees could work *and* live there, allegedly to churn out war goods at an even faster rate. When Germany began retreating toward the end of the war and Schindler was forced to relocate his factory to Czechoslovakia, a paperwork error sent 300 of his female employees to Auschwitz, and Schindler managed to retrieve the 300 women virtually from the jaws of death. He spent millions of German marks in bribes and personally risked his own safety; in the end, some 1,200 Jews were saved. Schindler was recognized at Yad Vashem, the Israeli memorial to the victims of the Holocaust, as one on the "Righteous Gentiles" in 1962; he is buried in Jerusalem.

Thomas Keneally's recounting of Schindler's story has resulted in several controversies. When he won the Booker Prize, Britain's highest award for a work of fiction, some critics questioned whether a "documentary novel" really qualified as a work of fiction. Like works of POSTMODERNISM, *Schindler's Ark* blurs the (presumed) boundary between history and literature. But the larger quarrel arose over Keneally's qualifications to write the novel in the first place: Keneally is neither a Jew nor a survivor of the Holocaust. The distinguished writer Elie Weisel, who is a Jew and a Holocaust survivor, and whose own memoir of his experiences in a death camp, *Night* (1958), is a classic of the literature about the Holocaust, has recommended that the events of the Holocaust should not be represented in works of fiction. The popular response to the book, however, has been to affirm that the story is important enough that it should be told in a form that makes it accessible to a wide audience, as Keneally's novel does. In calling his work a novel, considering that he made up conversation details for which no direct evidence existed, Keneally retains a respectful attitude toward the material while also fleshing out the story with the full range of narrative devices familiar in the world of literature but less common in strictly historical works. He meets the first mandate about the Holocaust: Never forget.

BIBLIOGRAPHY

Brecher, Elinor J. *Schindler's Legacy: True Stories of the List Survivors.* New York: Dutton, 1994.

Gaffney, Carmel. "Keneally's Faction: *Schindler's Ark,*" *Quadrant* 29, no. 7 (July 1985): 75–77.

Hulse, Michael. "Virtue and the Philosophic Innocent: The British Reception of *Schindler's Ark,*" *Critical Quarterly* 25.4 (Winter 1983): 43–52.

SCIENCE FICTION

A quintessential genre of 20th-century literature, science fiction is little more than a hundred years old, although earlier writers have also occasionally hit on the device of imagining that which has not yet become humanly possible. Science fiction is distinguished as a genre by its application of scientific knowledge to fictional purposes, by its interpretive forecasting of the consequences of technological innovations, and by its fondness for the use of the future as a setting for narratives. Although it is frequently linked with FANTASY literature, the two approaches to storytelling are very nearly opposite. The founders of science fiction literature are the French writer of impossible (at the time) adventure stories, Jules Verne, and the British writer of "scientific romances," H. G. WELLS, whose novels *The Time Machine* and *The War of the Worlds* are crucial early texts in the genre.

Broadly, examples of science fiction novels can usually be settled into one of two classifications, "hard" or "soft" science fiction. In hard science fiction, the exact scientific principles involved in making possible the marvels of the story are made clear, and the PLOT may even hinge on the application of physics, astronomy, mathematics, chemistry, or biology to some hypothetical situation. In soft science fiction, in contrast, smoke and mirrors or hand-waving replaces scientific explanations. Sometimes the same writer works both of these veins productively. Thus Arthur C. CLARKE, Britain's greatest science fiction novelist, uses hard science fiction in his much-anthologized story "The Star": Attentive readers will figure out which star it is that disturbs the faith of the space-traveling priest from references to the date when the story occurs and the distance traveled to reach the star. On the other hand, in his novel *The City and the Stars,* Clarke hypothesizes a UTOPIAN future city in which machines never wear out because they are maintained by "eternity circuits." Clarke is also the author of "Clarke's Laws": (1) "When a distinguished but elderly scientist states that something is possible, he is almost certainly right. When he states that something is impossible, he is very probably wrong"; (2) "The only way to discover the limits of the possible is to venture a little way past them into the impossible"; (3) "Any sufficiently advanced technology is indistinguishable from magic."

Examples of science fiction novels vary greatly in the degree of importance placed on traditional narrative strategies such as character development and symbolism, and science fiction writers vary highly in their command of the literary qualities of diction and syntax. British and COMMONWEALTH writers who have gained critical attention for works of science fiction or works that draw on the conventions of science fiction include Clarke (*2001: A SPACE ODYSSEY* and *CHILDHOOD'S END,* among others), J. G. BALLARD (a quartet of apocalyptic novels and numerous short stories), Douglas ADAMS (*The HITCHHIKER'S GUIDE TO THE GALAXY*), Anthony BURGESS (*A CLOCKWORK ORANGE*), C. S. LEWIS (*The SPACE TRILOGY*), Aldous HUXLEY (*BRAVE NEW WORLD*), Doris LESSING (*The FOUR-GATED CITY, Canopus in Argos,* and other novels), Margaret ATWOOD (*The BLIND ASSASSIN*), and many others.

BIBLIOGRAPHY

Bleiler, Everett Franklin. *Science Fiction Writers: Critical Studies of the Major Authors from the Early Nineteenth Century to the Present Day.* New York: Scribner, 1982.

Bould, Mark, Andrew M. Butler, and Istvan Csicsery-Ronay, Jr., eds. "The British Science-Fiction Boom," *Science Fiction Studies* 30, no. 3 (November 2003): 353–400. Special Issue.

Rose, Mark. *Science Fiction: A Collection of Critical Essays.* Englewood Cliffs, N.J.: Prentice Hall, 1976.

Scholes, Robert E., and Eric S. Rabkin. *Science Fiction: History, Science, Vision.* New York: Oxford University Press, 1977.

SCOTT, PAUL (1920–1978)

Born on March 25, 1920, into a family of artists who maintained a precarious hold on middle-CLASS life by working as painters and designers, Paul Scott is the author of *The Raj Quartet,* one of the finest examinations by an English author of the end of British COLONIALISM in INDIA. Financial exigency forced Scott to leave school at 16 and find a job to help support the family. Although he was already writing poetry, his father encouraged him to pursue accounting. Scott found work in the business world and studied for accounting exams at night; he was successful in this work, but he also continued to read and write poetry.

With the outbreak of WORLD WAR II, Scott was drafted into the army in 1940. He met his future wife in Torquay, where she was serving as a nurse; they were married in 1941. Scott made his first trip to India in 1943, when he was stationed there; to his surprise, the British colonials were arrogant toward the native population, and the Indian nationals were resentful of their British administrators. Scott was deeply affected by what he saw and experienced in this twilight period of the British Raj, and once he started writing fiction, India was a nearly constant component of his stories.

During his military service, Scott continued to write poetry. After the war, he began to write plays and won a prize for *Pillars of Salt* (published 1948). In 1950, he began working as a literary agent, a profession he followed successfully for 10 years. He also began writing fiction in his spare hours, finishing five novels before 1960, when he left his employer to write full-time. His first novel, *Johnny Sahib,* was published in 1952 and won the Eyre and Spottiswoode Literary Fellowship prize. His fascination with India and its connection to Britain continued in *Alien Sky* (1953), *A Male Child* (1956), *The Mark of the Warrior* (1958), *The Chinese Love Pavilion* (1960), and *Birds of Paradise* (1962).

Scott published two novels about work and creativity before traveling again to India in 1964 to do research for the novels now recognized as his masterwork, collectively known as *The Raj Quartet.* In *The Jewel in the Crown* (1966), *The Day of the Scorpion* (1968), *The Towers of Silence* (1971), and *A Division of the Spoils* (1975), Scott explores the lives of British and Indian characters living through the most momentous event in modern Indian history as the subcontinent is liberated and then partitioned along religious lines into India and Pakistan. Scott followed this set of novels with a fifth volume as a kind of epilogue or comic afterword, *Staying On* (1977), about the British who preferred to remain in India after it became a separate nation. This volume won the BOOKER PRIZE in the year it was published. Scott received critical recognition, but his books were not popular successes until television brought them to a mass audience.

Scott taught at the University of Tulsa in 1976 and 1977 as a visiting professor. Suffering from cancer, he died on March 1, 1978. After his death, *The Raj Quartet* become a highly successful adaptation for BBC television and also appeared in the United States on public television. His five last books remain the basis of Scott's literary reputation and constitute one of the best fictional treatments by a British author of the last days of the Raj, admired for their sensitive treatment of race, CLASS, gender, and COLONIALISM, and also for their attention to historical details of how British administration functioned—and in some cases how it failed—on the local level at which most Indians experienced it.

BIBLIOGRAPHY

Gorra, Michael. *After Empire: Scott, Naipaul, Rushdie.* Chicago: University of Chicago Press, 1997.

Rao, K. Bhaskara. *Paul Scott.* Twayne's English Authors, 285. Boston: Twayne Publishers, 1980.

Spurling, Hilary. *Paul Scott: A Life of the Author of* The Raj Quartet New York: W. W. Norton, 1990.

Swindon, Patrick. *Paul Scott.* Windsor, Berks: Profile Books, 1982.

THE SCREWTAPE LETTERS C. S. LEWIS

(1942) This comic epistolary novel consists of a series of letters written by Screwtape, a senior demon in Hell, to his young protégé Wormwood, a demon undertaking his first "field work" on Earth. C. S. LEWIS is among the most effective writers of Christian literature in the 20th century, renowned during his lifetime as the "apostle to skeptics," and while he draws on the conventions of religious ALLEGORY in other works such as *The CHRONICLES OF NARNIA* and *The SPACE TRILOGY,* in *The Screwtape Letters* he carries IRONY as far as it can go by making Screwtape the interpreter of Christian doctrine for the purposes of subverting it. Needless to say, Wormwood turns out to be an ineffective tempter, and Screwtape's explanations reveal much about the misguided incompetence—and dreary, dogged, petty persistence—of evil.

In addition to maximizing his use of irony, C. S. Lewis also carries indirect narrative techniques to their extreme: The novel's characters, PLOT, and setting are all presented obliquely or tangentially as Screwtape undertakes the instruction of Wormwood and as he comments on the younger demon's few successes and many failures. Indeed, the novel's human characters never even receive names, allowing Lewis to universalize his depiction of temptation without resorting to allegorical naming. The man Wormwood is attempting to lead astray could be any man—he could be "Everyman," in the manner of the medieval morality play of that title—but Lewis makes the object of Wormwood's temptations to be simultaneously a single, particular, unique man and also the unnamed representative of all mortals. Because of Lewis's indirect narrative strategy, reading *The Screwtape Letters* is an extended exercise in "reading between the lines" in order to capture all that is implied as well as all that is said.

Lewis's indirect method extends to several contemporary topics that he implicitly satirizes by allowing Screwtape to digress from the main object of keeping Wormwood "on task." Screwtape is an expansive and oracular (and self-important) observer of the human condition in general and of the Christian condition in particular. He never misses an opportunity to sniff at human folly, to denigrate divine providence, or to celebrate the perversion of his infernal "father," to whom he makes frequent obsequious references. Along the way, Lewis indirectly comments on fashionably agnostic people, on the practice of human warfare, on education, on family relations, on love, lust, and marriage, and on religious hypocrisy. Screwtape works his way through the familiar trope of the seven deadly sins (pride, envy, wrath, sloth, avarice, gluttony, and lust) in the course of advising Wormwood; at the same time, Lewis works his way through a litany of indirect criticisms of the ways of the modern world. The effect is a wry, acerbic, and amusing examination of Christianity and human psychology that treats weighty matters lightly without trivializing them.

BIBLIOGRAPHY

Manlove, C. N. *C. S. Lewis: His Literary Achievement.* New York: St. Martin's Press, 1987.

Smith, Robert Houston. *Patches of Godlight: The Pattern of Thought of C. S. Lewis.* Athens: University of Georgia Press, 1981.

SEA, THE SEA, THE IRIS MURDOCH

(1978) Positioned at the intersection of Plato's "Allegory of the Cave" and Shakespeare's *The Tempest,* this novel won the BOOKER PRIZE in 1978; MURDOCH had previously won the WHITBREAD Novel Award for *The Sacred and Profane Love Machine* in 1974 and the JAMES TAIT BLACK MEMORIAL PRIZE in 1973 for *The BLACK PRINCE.* This novel displays the author's characteristic use of a male protagonist of middle- to late years who undergoes a trial that alters his perception of the world and his place in it.

The first-person narrator of the novel is Charles Arrowby, a retired theater director and manager. In his 60s, Charles has retired to a house by the sea where he expects to write his memoirs, particularly with respect to his late mentor, Clement Makin, and to renew an affair with Lizzie Scherer. Charles has devoted his professional life to the world of illusions, but this connection has not deepened his ability to perceive the larger illusion in which he lives contentedly—the illusion that he has any real power to work his will upon the world in any significant way. He thinks he knows what he will do and that he has the wherewithal to do it, but life quickly delivers an entirely different banquet than the one that he had ordered. Absorbed in the minutiae of numbering the stripes of the tulip—thinking even that he must get his magnifying glass to help him see even finer details of the phenomena of the world—Charles is taken by surprise when things beyond his control begin happening.

Charles starts out thinking to review the past and capture it—although his memoir quickly degenerates into a diary focused entirely on the insignificant details of the present—but instead the past asserts itself in an unexpected way and captures him when he discovers that his first love, 60-year-old Hartley Fitch, is also living in the very town he has retired to. By then, Charles has "discovered" that he is actually writing a novel, and when he is seized by the return of his old attachment for Hartley he begins to pursue her, even though she is now a woman in a marriage of many years' standing. Charles goes so far as to kidnap Hartley, deluded by his egotistical fantasy of being able to write the script that can dictate the performance of the entire real world. Charles, however, is grasping at shadows and failing to comprehend the larger reality that casts them.

Murdoch deploys several narrative devices to create Charles's experience, including letters and intensely conversational chapters in the style associated with Ivy COMPTON-BURNETT. With respect to Iris Murdoch's fiction, however, understanding the formal elements of narrative devices that communicate PLOT, characters, theme, and symbolism will provide an understanding only of the story's skeleton. Students wishing to gain a full appreciation for Murdoch's novel should familiarize themselves with the works of Plato, especially the philosophical issues explored in the dialogs entitled *The Phaedrus, The Symposium,* and *The Republic.*

BIBLIOGRAPHY

Heusel, Barbara. *Patterned Aimlessness: Iris Murdoch's Novels of the 1970's and 1980's.* Athens: University of Georgia Press, 1995.

Nolan, Brian. *Iris Murdoch: The Retrospective Fiction.* New York: St. Martin's Press, 1999.

Bove, Cheryl Browning. *Understanding Iris Murdoch.* Understanding Contemporary British Literature Series. Columbia: University of South Carolina Press, 1993.

SECOND TRILOGY JOYCE CARY (1952–1955) See *PRISONER OF GRACE* TRILOGY.

SECRET AGENT, THE JOSEPH CONRAD (1907) With John BUCHAN's *The THIRTY-NINE STEPS,* published in 1915, this story is one of the progenitors of the subgenre of SPY NOVELS. Whereas Buchan's tale is a fast-paced adventure filled with episodes and incidents, CONRAD's novel uses psychological realism to examine the motivations and reactions of characters under stress. The reader looks on during interviews, meetings, and discussions, and additionally can examine thoughts and feelings, but the dramatic actions happen elsewhere.

Although Mr. Verloc is the title character of this novel, his wife, Winnie, becomes the listening post through which his activities are studied. Verloc is an agent provocateur for an unnamed foreign government, and during his tenure in England he has made himself comfortable, blending into the background by marrying an English girl and acquiring a modest shop in Soho. He supports his wife's simple-minded brother, Stevie, and tolerates him since she dotes on the young man. A band of anarchists meets regularly at Mr. Verloc's house, but Winnie takes little notice of them. For Mr. Verloc, this group fulfills part of his job requirements: He helps keep them going so that his own masters can benefit from any damage the anarchists inflict on England. But Mr. Verloc's effectiveness has come under review in the opening section of the novel, and he receives orders to blow up some cultural or educational location, preferably the Greenwich Observatory.

The narrator's focus shifts to Winnie as Verloc begins working out how to fulfill his orders. She wants Stevie and her husband to spend some quality time together to develop a stronger bond, and to her surprise her husband agrees to take Stevie on his walks. Only later does it become apparent what Verloc trains Stevie to attempt, and Winnie has to learn from a police inspector what her brother's tragic fate has been. Winnie is driven to a horrible act and finds herself alone in a world that she is ill-equipped to deal with. When she encounters one of the anarchists and accepts his help, entrusting him with her money, she takes yet another step toward her destruction. The narrative focus shifts to the anarchist, Winnie's betrayer, as the story's final listening post, and readers learn the fate of Winnie only indirectly through him.

Conrad depicts the London of the later 19th century as a hellish place of filth, chaos, grossness, and moral decay. He draws on real-world events as the inspiration for his story, creating personalities for his characters that are capable of performing heinous actions and reacting to heart-rending news with further violence. Through this almost nihilistic lens, Conrad condemns the isolated indifference of the modern urban world by showing the depths of despair and desperation to which it drives otherwise ordinary people.

BIBLIOGRAPHY

Fleishman, Avrom. *Conrad's Politics: Community and Anarchy in the Fiction of Joseph Conrad.* Baltimore: The Johns Hopkins University Press, 1967.

Hay, Eloise Knapp. *The Political Novels of Joseph Conrad: A Study.* Chicago: University of Chicago Press, 1963.

Tillyard, E. M. W. "*The Secret Agent* Reconsidered." In *Conrad: A Collection of Critical Essays.* Edited by Marvin Mudrick. Englewood Cliffs, N.J.: Prentice Hall, 1966.

SEXING THE CHERRY JEANETTE WINTERSON (1989)

A novel that combines aspects of folk tale, MAGIC REALISM, mythic ARCHETYPES, and FEMINISM, *Sexing the Cherry* is a highly imaginative story that begins in the Renaissance and ends in the modern world with new versions—descendants—of the original characters. The protagonist is Jordan, a young man in training under John Tradescant, the Royal Gardener, at a time when the technique of grafting to change the characteristics of fruit trees is beginning to be used. Jordan was an orphan found in the bulrushes by the Dog Woman, his adopted mother. She is a giantess of a girth so vast that musket balls are harmless against her—the sexual symbolism of guns that cannot penetrate their target is significant. The narrative moves back and forth between the mother and son, so that the reader sees the son's interest in the wider world and the mother's pain in setting her child free to be an adult. Jordan eventually sets out on a voyage of adventure and discovery, bringing the first pineapple back to England.

On his voyage, Jordan is also seeking Fortunata, one of the Twelve Dancing Princesses. Winterson is especially imaginative in the passage describing the amazing sights Jordan encounters, such as the word cleaner who mops up tired phrases, or the island that has given up gravity; her imagery here brings to mind the short fiction of the American postmodern writer Donald Barthelme. When Jordan finally locates Fortunata and the other princesses, they tell him new versions of familiar fairy tales. In these versions, however, "happily ever after" does not include the inevitable pairing of Prince Charming and his beloved. Instead, women in the new fairy tales eschew romance and marriage: They manage life perfectly fine without it. Winterson implies that the gender stereotyping of traditional fairy tales may be part of the problem, and that women must develop new narratives if they wish to achieve true equity in the world. The Dog Woman is an example of a woman who has created such a new narrative, giving her the courage to face down her opportunistic Puritan neighbors and the power to succeed in her challenge.

The other woman who follows a new narrative is introduced in the contemporary portion of the story. Winterson universalizes her by not giving her a name, but she is a chemist—bright, passionate about her calling, and idealistic. She has not succumbed to the fantasy of the traditional "happily ever after" fairy tale ending. The modern Jordan has to learn how to interact with this kind of strong woman. In order to love her, he must accommodate his life to hers, not the other way around. The novel ends without resolving whether his attempt to do so will be entirely successful.

BIBLIOGRAPHY

Langland, Elizabeth. "Sexing the Text: Narrative Drag as Feminist Poetics and Politics in Jeanette Winterson's *Sexing the Cherry,*" *Narrative* 5, no. 1 (January 1997): 99–107.

Martin, Sara. "The Power of Monstrous Women: Fay Weldon's *The Life and Loves of a She-Devil*" (1983), Angela CARTER's *Nights at the Circus* (1984), and Jeanette Winterson's *Sexing the Cherry* (1989). *Journal of Gender Studies* 8, no. 2 (July 1999): 193–210.

SHIP OF THE LINE, A C. S. FORESTER
(1938) The second volume in the Horatio HORN-BLOWER series, this novel follows *Beat to Quarters,* and the story's action concludes in *Flying Colours.* FORESTER later collected these three novels under the title *Captain Horatio Hornblower.*

After completing his mission off the Pacific coast of Spanish America in *Beat to Quarters,* Captain Hornblower receives orders to report to the Mediterranean under Admiral Leighton. He had previously escorted Lady Barbara Wellesley, sister of the Duke of Wellington, from Panama to England, and they had fallen in love. As a married man, Hornblower had honored his vows and restrained his attachment to Lady Barbara; now, she is married to Admiral Leighton. In command of a 74-gun frigate, the *Sutherland,* in an episodic series of adventures on the way to join the fleet, Hornblower encounters privateers, captures a French ship, and shells French land forces.

Leighton orders Hornblower to take charge of the siege of Rosas, but the Spanish troops he commands fail to perform adequately. In retreat, he learns of the approach of a four-ship French squadron and decides to give battle, a decision that is later supported by orders from the admiral. The ensuing fight forms the climax of the novel. Hornblower at first prevails, taking on the enemy ships one by one, but he is forced to surrender when the last two French ships are able to join forces before he has been relieved by his own fleet. A prisoner at the town he formerly besieged, he becomes a bystander to the action, looking on from shore when Admiral Leighton arrives and finishes the work Hornblower had begun, suffering a mortal wound in the process.

The narrative ends without concluding, following the cliffhanger technique of serialized stories. Only in the following book does Hornblower escape his captors, find allies, and eventually make his way back to a hero's welcome in England, where his wife had died during his absence, and where Lady Barbara has been left widowed.

Forester delivers admirable, well-developed characters, realistic historical settings, and rousing action throughout the Hornblower series. The stories, examples of escapist literature, provide a mass audience with an absorbing and satisfying reading experience.

BIBLIOGRAPHY
Forester, C. S. *The Hornblower Companion.* Boston: Little, Brown, 1964.
Parkinson, C. Northcote. *The Life and Times of Horatio Hornblower.* London: Joseph, 1970.

SIEGE OF KRISHNAPUR J. G. FARRELL
(1973) An example of HISTORICAL FICTION, this novel helped to revive its genre by attracting critical attention and achieving popular success. It won the BOOKER PRIZE in 1973, establishing the reputation of its author.

The novel is set in British INDIA during the Sepoy Mutiny of 1857–58 in the fictional city of Krishnapur, loosely based on the historical city of Lucknow. The story unfolds through a third-person omniscient narrator and has as its protagonist "the Collector," Mr. Hopkins, who is the chief administrator of the colonial system in the district of Krishnapur. This thoroughly British and thoroughly Victorian gentleman is both a tax collector by profession and a collector of arts and antiquities by preference. He lives in the English settlement where colonial officials have built familiar English homes to house their families in somewhat greater splendor than they could have enjoyed in England. This settlement becomes a besieged garrison with the outbreak of the Sepoy Mutiny (also referred to in historical accounts as the Indian Mutiny).

Mr. Hopkins demonstrates his acuity as a leader first in recognizing the obscure signs that some unusual stir is afoot, second by making preparations for the onset of that unknown stir, and third by the example of his courage and fortitude once the colonials are surrounded by hostile troops. The lull before the storm—the period when the obscure signs begin to appear—allows the narrator to explore the routine lives of the characters, establishing their strengths and weaknesses under ordinary circumstances. Then the long, slow stressful waiting that necessarily accompanies a siege, interrupted by brief but intense battle sequences, provides the opportunity to test the characters by subjecting them to an extended crisis.

The tension mounts as supplies and ammunition run low and the defenders are thrown back on their ingenuity and tenacity. In the process, the author is able to examine the Victorian and colonial mind of the English occupants of Krishnapur. The defenders of the tiny garrison are ultimately able to survive the siege only by the luck of being rescued when military reinforcements arrive: Their achievement lies in holding out long enough to be rescued. Although their lives are saved, their ideals, values, and beliefs do not survive the experience unscathed.

The author uses the array of colonials in Krishnapur to explore character in general and Victorian character in particular. The settlement's two doctors, for example, old-fashioned and self-righteous Dr. Dunstaple, with his dangerously outdated ideas on the proper treatment of cholera, and newfangled and coldly rational Dr. McNab, remain at odds both personally and scientifically. The enthusiasm of Mr. Willoughby for phrenology (the belief that personality can be predicted from knowledge of the placement of slight protrusions on the head) illustrates one of the oddities of 19th-century pseudoscience. Young George Fleury, coincidentally visiting new acquaintants in Krishnapur and trapped there when the rebellion breaks out, learns that he can be courageous under fire. Not all the defenders of the garrison prove to be as resilient in coping with their unexpected transformation from luxury to desperation, and not all of them survive the ordeal.

In the history of British COLONIALISM in India, the Sepoy Mutiny was a turning point that led to the abolishing of the East India Company and the assumption of colonial administrative authority by the British government, including for the first time a degree of input from the people of India over whom British rule had been extended. FARRELL implies much of this in his handling of Mr. Hopkins in particular: The Collector survives the siege, but his faith in the colonial enterprise and in the modern notions of progress is shaken. In the closing chapter, the narrator provides a last glimpse of Mr. Hopkins in London after the glory of his achievement has been largely forgotten. He is somewhat dispirited for a man known as the hero of Krishnapur, and he has withdrawn from the world's stage to a quiet existence; only a few decades later, the entire British colonial system in India makes a similar withdrawal.

BIBLIOGRAPHY

Ellis, Juniper. "The Ends of Empire in J. G. Farrell's *The Siege of Krishnapur.*" In *J. G. Farrell: The Critical Grip.* Edited by Ralph J. Crane. Dublin, Ireland: Four Courts, 1999.

McLeod, John. "Exhibiting Empire in J. G. Farrell's *The Siege of Krishnapur,*" *Journal of Commonwealth Literature* 29, no. 2 (Summer 1994): 117–132.

Singh, Frances B. "Progress and History J. G. Farrell's *The Siege of Krishnapur,*" *Chandrabhaga: A Magazine of World Writing* 2 (1979): 23–39.

SILLITOE, ALAN (1928–)

One of the ANGRY YOUNG MEN who dominated British literature in the wake of WORLD WAR II, Alan Sillitoe was born to a working-CLASS family in the slums of Nottingham on March 4, 1928. Too young to fight in the war, he left school and worked in factory jobs between the ages of 14 and 18 (1942–46), when he joined the Royal Air Force. He was stationed in Malaya for two years, serving as a radio operator. During this time, he read extensively—he had been a good student before leaving school to work—and began writing, especially when he was confined to bed to recuperate from tuberculosis. He destroyed these early drafts of poems and fiction but continued to work on his writing.

For 10 years after completing his military service, Sillitoe traveled in the Mediterranean countries of Spain, Italy, and France. He met the noted writer and mythologist Robert GRAVES in Majorca; Graves befriended Sillitoe and advised him to write about the people and settings with which he was most familiar. With this focus, Sillitoe published his first novel, *Saturday Night and Sunday Morning,* in 1958. It was set in Nottingham and featured working-class characters, and it won the Author's Club award for a first novel. In 1959, Sillitoe continued working with the setting and characters of his own background and published *The LONELINESS OF THE LONG DISTANCE RUNNER,* a book that includes a novella by that title and several other stories, winning the HAWTHORNDEN PRIZE. Also that year, he and the American poet Ruth Fainlight were married and in time became the parents of two children.

Sillitoe's work experience and his political exposure made him a supporter of socialism, but when he visited the Soviet Union in the early 1960s, he was disappointed by what he saw there. He published a nonfiction account of his travels, *The Road to Volgograd,* in 1964. He was also publishing poetry and short fiction in the late 1950s and early 1960s. In his novels, he continued to compose stories of social and political protest that drew on his Nottingham roots, but gradually he diversified his subject matter and developed his narrative strategies without abandoning his stance as a critic of the English status quo. In *Key to the Door* (1961), his protagonist is autobiographical: a proletarian with artistic aspirations and leftist political leanings that lead him to revolutionary sympathies. The protagonist's story continues in the 1989 sequel, *The Open Door,* in which the thematic focus has moved away from politics and is solidly grounded in the development of a creative man's talent. Not all his novels in between were successful with critics and readers, but he is among the first English writers to construct a metafictional plot: In *The Storyteller* (1979), he writes a story about a character who uses stories as a means of survival in an unsympathetic world.

Alan Sillitoe has continued to publish in several genres. His output includes more than 20 novels, four screenplays, more than a dozen volumes of poetry (one in collaboration with Ruth Fainlight and the poet Ted Hughes), seven collections of short fiction, three original plays and an adaptation of a Lope de Vega play, seven works of nonfiction, and a few children's books. He continues to live and write in England.

BIBLIOGRAPHY

Atherton, Stanley S. *Alan Sillitoe: A Critical Assessment.* London: W. H. Allen, 1979.

Hanson, Gillian Mary. *Understanding Alan Sillitoe.* Understanding Contemporary British Literature Series. Columbia: University of South Carolina Press, 1999.

Penner, Allen Richard. *Alan Sillitoe.* Twayne's English Authors, 141. New York: Twayne Publishers, 1972.

SILVER CHAIR, THE C. S. LEWIS (1953)

See *The* CHRONICLES OF NARNIA.

SILVER'S CITY MAURICE LEITCH (1981)

The winner of the WHITBREAD Book of the Year Award in 1981, this novel is set in Belfast, NORTHERN IRELAND, at the height of "the troubles." A third-person narrator dispassionately presents the story from inside the operations of a nameless Protestant militant organization that is indistinguishable from a crime syndicate. William Bonney runs a so-called security company, but his primary occupation is terrorism. In the book's opening chapter, Bonney's cold-blooded hit man, a Scot named Galloway, kills a doctor who is alleged to treat Catholic militants ("Finians"). He is assisted by Bonney's worthless brothers-in-law; their presence underscores the family-based nature of the organization, intensifying its similarity to the Mafia. Later, the scene shifts to a brothel, and other discussions suggest that Bonney also runs a protection racket. Much viciousness is in evidence, unadorned by even the pretence of pursuing a just cause or serving a higher ideal.

In the brothel, the novel's actual protagonist makes his first appearance. Silver Steele is an aging and legendary militant who has been in prison for at least a decade. Through no effort or desire on his part, he has been sprung from a prison hospital and placed under the control of Bonney. Steele is certain that he is a marked man—that his sensational death, done in such a way as to cast blame elsewhere, will serve the purposes of his fellow militants more than will his continued incarceration. He is kept drugged and prevented from seeing news programs, but as he is shuffled among secure locations, he sees his name in graffiti everywhere he goes. For some reason, Bonney is delaying the execution, and in the meantime Silver tries to collect himself, searching, with as much nonchalance as he can muster, for a moment of carelessness or inattention when he can make his escape. What he doesn't know is that he was already marked for death before his liberation: Fatal disease is gnawing at him, and he has mere months to live even if he receives medical treatment.

The novel alternates between a focus on Bonney's organization, especially examining the thoughts and actions of Galloway, and a more sympathetic view of Silver's thoughts, feelings, and actions. Memories fill in their background stories that gradually explain the current state of events. The narration avoids exposition of place and time, and it begins *in medias res,* so the reader must piece together the evidence of the location and circumstances of the action. The tone of the story mirrors the grimness of its historical setting, with characters moving through a virtual wasteland of bomb sites and economic decay, their hearts hardened by violence, hatred, and bigotry. In the midst of this desolation, Silver Steele has one last moment of shared human tenderness, demonstrating that hope of a better life has not been entirely extirpated from the land and its people. The novel bears a kinship to American hard-boiled crime fiction, and yet it also stands as a testimony to one of the smaller violent chapters in the history of the 20th century.

BIBLIOGRAPHY

Leith, Linda. "Subverting the Sectarian Heritage: Recent Novels of Northern Ireland," *Canadian Journal of Irish Studies* 18.1 (1992): 88–106.

SLEEP OF REASON, THE C. P. SNOW (1968)

The 10th and penultimate volume in the ROMAN-FLEUVE entitled STRANGERS AND BROTHERS, *The Sleep of Reason* follows CORRIDORS OF POWER (1964) and precedes LAST THINGS (1970). As always, the first-person narrator is Lewis Eliot; in this volume, he is an active participant in the events of the plot rather than a passive observer of someone else's life as he makes his last foray into the legal system in his role as a barrister.

Eliot has retired to his hometown, a location which has not featured prominently in the series since Eliot had gone out into the larger world. After four years of retirement during which he spends his time writing, he agrees to serve on a committee at his old college in response to a request. He is drawn first into a campus scandal which brings the narrative into contact with the changing sexual values of the 1960s; from there, however, Eliot becomes involved in a sensational case concerning two lesbian lovers accused of torturing and murdering a child. One of these women is the niece of George Passant, Eliot's mentor and a key character in the introductory volume of the series. He and Eliot have renewed their acquaintance, and out of loyalty Eliot endures the spectacle of the trial. The theme of death—and especially the irrational deaths of those victimized by others—emerges. Eliot's elderly father dies, and then Eliot himself faces the possibility of death when he is struck down by illness. His own life reaches the point at which it forces him to meditate on death, and the murder case has turned his thoughts to the persistence of evil in the world. His thoughts on the human race darken, reflecting on the horrors of the Holocaust, and the novel closes on a somber and disheartened tone.

BIBLIOGRAPHY

Morris, Robert K. "The English Way of Life." Review of *The Sleep of Reason* and other titles. *The Nation,* 28 April 1969, 546.

Wain, John. "Ruminating About Freedom." Review of *The Sleep of Reason. The New Republic,* 1 February 1969, 30.

SMALL WORLD DAVID LODGE (1984)

Short-listed for the BOOKER PRIZE in 1984, this novel is a sequel to CHANGING PLACES, and technically a CAMPUS NOVEL, although it does not maintain a permanent setting at any particular campus for long. The story picks up the lives of Philip Swallow of Rummidge University and Morris Zapp of Euphoria State University—the former a British academic, the latter an American— some 10 years after their exchange experiences. But for this COMIC NOVEL, Lodge widens his scope to take in the entire world of academic conferences, and he broadens his cast of characters to include, eventually, scholars of English from all over the world. The omniscient third-person narrator begins the story in Rummidge at a miserable conference attended by only 50-some professors of English. Morris Zapp is the featured speaker, as a special favor to his old friend Philip, now the head of the English Department at Rummidge University. Morris returns the favor and invites Philip to attend a conference of postmodernists in Jerusalem later that summer, even though Philip is a literary critic of the most traditional and least postmodern (see POST-MODERNISM) stripe.

From the pool of attendees at the wintry Rummidge event, two new key characters are introduced, professor Persse McGarrigle, an aspiring poet, and Angelica L. Pabst, a beautiful graduate student. Several minor figures from *Changing Places* are in attendance—old enemies and rivals of Philip—and some new minor figures as well, especially Miss Sybil Maiden, a retired professor of Girton College, Oxford, who had once been a student of Jessie L. Weston, author of *From Ritual to Romance*. Fiction intersects reality with this casual reference in chapter one: *From Ritual to Romance* is a real-world work of literary criticism that sets forth and interprets the legend of the Fisher King and the quest for the Grail in terms of fertility symbolism. Later, when a minor (but important) character appears named Arthur Kingfisher, a man whose fertility and intellectual vigor have dried up, the novel begins to resemble an ALLEGORY, in modern terms, of the medieval quest. Literary scholars have taken the place of knights errant, and the circuit of academic conferences has taken the place of the quest. Some scholars search for truth, some for riches, and some for glory, but a select few, including Morris Zapp and Philip Swallow, are soon on a quest for the UNESCO chair in literature, a newly created position luxuriously endowed with both money and prestige. The novel's comic elements, however, continually convert this allegorical structure into a parody.

When the Rummidge conference breaks up, the characters disperse to various points, and the narrative follows along, fragmenting in multiple directions and adding new characters as the circle widens. Soon letters and phone calls have compounded the reach of personal travel, pulling the story to France, Italy, Japan, Turkey, and other locations. Entire chapters of snippets slowly draw together a large, diverse group of scholars headed for Zapp's summer conference in Jerusalem and then for the December conference of the Modern Language Association in New York City (another real-world element in LODGE'S fiction). As for Persse, his quest has placed him in pursuit of the beautiful Miss Pabst; before he finds her again, he has circled the world by hopping from one literary conference to another, helped by the bottomless depths of the American Express card he acquires along the way and occasionally by unexpected encounters with Miss Sybil Maiden. Meanwhile, a series of accidents boosts Philip Swallow's study of William Hazlitt to the center of a controversy, carrying his career to its zenith when he is nominated for the UNESCO chair. Morris Zapp is kidnapped by radical associates of a wealthy Marxist scholar he meets and feels humbled—temporarily—when his ex-wife, Desiree (a key character in *Changing Places*), bargains with the kidnappers to reduce his ransom. In a final glorious tournament of ideas, the candidates for the UNESCO chair present their positions, and Arthur Kingfisher makes a surprising selection for the post.

Lodge's story is a delight for well-prepared readers who are familiar with such canonical standards as "The Eve of St. Agnes" by John Keats, the Arthurian legends, *The Wasteland* by T. S. Eliot, *The Importance of Being Earnest* by Oscar WILDE, and the novels of the ANGRY YOUNG MEN of the 1950s. Familiarity with the many schools of literary criticism that have arisen in the 20th century is useful, although not necessary—Lodge refers to structuralism, Freudianism, reader response criticism, Marxism, archetypal criticism, and traditional literary appreciation, among others, but he also provides explanations by way of the lectures and conversations various characters undertake. Persse, a "conference virgin" in the opening chapter, becomes the reader's surrogate, soaking up the new languages of criticism while searching for the woman he thinks he loves. He is the first and the last character that the narrator examines, and he figures in both of the novel's endings—the traditional ending that restores lost family members, and the modern ending that suspends the story in AMBIGUITY rather than bringing it to closure.

BIBLIOGRAPHY

Friend, Joshua. " 'Every Decoding Is Another Encoding': Morris Zapp's Post-structural Implication on Our Postmodern World," *English Language Notes* 33, no. 3 (March 1996): 61–7.

Martin, Bruce K. *David Lodge.* Twayne's English Authors, 553. New York: Twayne, 1999.

Mews, Siegfried. "The Professor's Novel: David Lodge's *Small World*." *Modern Language Notes* 104, no. 3 (1989): 713–26.

SMITH, DODIE (1896–1990)

Actress, playwright, novelist, and children's writer, Dorothy Gladys Smith was born on May 3, 1896, in Lancashire. Her father died soon after, and her mother returned to the family home in a suburb of Manchester, where a large variety of aunts, uncles, and grandparents adored the newest addition to the brood. One of Dodie's uncles had an interest in amateur dramatics; he put his niece onstage while she was still a toddler, and as a young teen she played boys' roles. Her mother died when Dodie, then 18, was enrolled in the Academy of Dramatic Arts (now RADA, the Royal Academy of Dramatic Arts).

Dodie set out to be a professional actress, but although her outgoing personality and charm got her some roles, her acting lost them. By 1923, she was working as a department manager in a home-decor and furniture store, where she met her future husband, Alec Beesley. By then she had sold a movie screenplay but had failed to sell a play for the stage. In 1929, after visiting a toy fair in Germany for her employer, she wrote a play set at the inn she had stayed at. This play, *Autumn Crocus,* was a great success, and Dodie followed it with four more. These plays were light social comedies with a broad popular appeal.

In 1938, Dodie and Alec came to the United States with Alec's Dalmatian, Pongo; Alec was a pacifist and wished to avoid contributing to the war effort. He and Dodie were married in 1939, and with the entry of the United States into the war, they were unable to return to England. They wound up staying in America until 1953. At first, Dodie worked as a screenwriter in Hollywood. She befriended the playwright John van Druten and through him became acquainted with the expatriated English writer Christopher ISHERWOOD. Alec Beesley made the suggestion that Isherwood's character Sally Bowles, from *GOODBYE TO BERLIN,* would make an excellent subject for a stage play. John van Druten wrote the play *I Am a Camera,* and its success turned around Isherwood's fortunes; later, the play served as the basis for the hit movie and Broadway musical *Cabaret.*

In 1948, still in America, Dodie began writing a COMIC NOVEL that has since been recognized as a minor masterpiece, *I CAPTURE THE CASTLE.* One of the high points of Dodie's career occurred when her novel was identified in the *Times* as one of the year's best: She had longed to be appreciated as a serious writer, not just the author of light stage comedies. In 1956, Dodie produced another small masterpiece in the genre of children's literature, *The Hundred and One Dalmatians.* Exaggerating the experience she and Alec had had when Pongo's replacements, Buzz and Folly, became the parents of 15 puppies, the story features one of the immortal villains of children's literature, that devilish Cruella De Vil.

Dodie Smith's four volumes of autobiography continue the comic voice she had worked in so successfully in three genres. She lived to the age of 94, leaving a fifth volume of memoirs unfinished at her death in November 1990.

BIBLIOGRAPHY

Grove, Valerie. *Dear Dodie: The Life of Dodie Smith.* London: Chatto & Windus, 1996.

Smith, Dodie. *Look Back with Love: A Manchester Childhood.* London: Heinemann, 1974.

———. *Look Back with Mixed Feelings.* London: W. H. Allen, 1978.

———. *Look Back with Astonishment.* London: W. H. Allen, 1979.

———. *Look Back with Gratitude.* London: Muller, Blond & White, 1985.

SMITH, ZADIE (1975–)

The daughter of a Jamaican mother and an English father, Zadie Smith was born—with the name "Sadie"—in England on October 27, 1975. She was educated at Cambridge University, completing an undergraduate degree in 1998. She had begun writing stories in childhood, and at Cambridge her story "The Newspaper Man" appeared in an anthology of student writing; it drew the attention of publishers. Smith acquired a literary agent on the strength of her writing samples and published her first novel, *WHITE TEETH,* in 1999 at the age of 24. The story contrasts two key characters who have been friends for many years, a white London laborer and a Muslim from Bangladesh. The book received both positive and negative reviews, perhaps the most hostile of which was written by Smith herself under a pen name. The novel was a commercial success and won both the GUARDIAN FICTION PRIZE and the JAMES TAIT BLACK MEMORIAL PRIZE for 2000; it also won the WHITBREAD Best First Novel Award and the COMMONWEALTH Writer's First Book Award in 2000, among other awards and prizes. Smith became something of a literary celebrity overnight. Her next novel, *The Autograph Man*, appeared in 2002; it examines the human fascination with celebrities through the character of a Jewish-Chinese autograph dealer. In both of the novels Smith has published so far, she has reappraised the roles of race and ethnicity in contemporary life by normalizing the existence of differences among human beings.

BIBLIOGRAPHY

Cowley, Jason. "The Tiger Woods of Literature?" *The New Statesman*, 25 January 2001, 57.

Jackson, Kevin. "Next Generation Zadie Smith," *The New Yorker* 75, no. 31 (1999): 182.

O'Grady, Kathleen. "*White Teeth*: A Conversation with Author, Zadie Smith," *Atlantis: A Women's Studies Journal/Revue d'Études sur les Femmes* 27, no. 1 (2002): 105–111.

SNOW, C. P. (1905–1980)

A novelist, essayist, and scientist, Charles Percy Snow was born October 15, 1905, in Leicester, England, into a lower-middle-CLASS family. His mother encouraged him to study and improve himself; she made sure he received a quality education in elite grammar schools. In 1925, Snow received a scholarship that allowed him to matriculate at Leicester University College, where he completed an undergraduate degree in chemistry and a master's degree in physics by 1928. He chose a program of scientific studies for practical reasons, even though he had already conceived an ambition to write novels. Upon completing his master's degree, he entered the doctoral program in physics at Cambridge University, where he worked in the Cavendish Laboratory, a leading center of cutting-edge studies in physics. He completed his doctoral studies in 1930, at the age of 25, and was elected a Fellow of Christ's College at Cambridge, holding this post until 1950.

Snow published his first novel, *Death Under Sail*, in 1932; it is an example of MYSTERY AND DETECTIVE FICTION that rejects the impressionistic narrative techniques of MODERNISM espoused by Virginia WOOLF, D. H. LAWRENCE, and James JOYCE. His plain prose style reaches back to the realism of 19th-century writers, and his content reflects his assertion that art must serve a moral purpose. His early works show that he has settled on the philosophy of writing he wishes to defend, but he is searching for his niche: Leaving behind the mystery and detective genre, his second novel, *New Lives for Old* (1933; published anonymously), explores the possibilities and effects of turning back the clock on human aging, verging on the SCIENCE FICTION themes of H. G. WELLS. In *The Search* (1934), about the lives of research scientists, he broaches material that he will explore again in his masterwork, the 11-volume ROMAN-FLEUVE collectively titled *STRANGERS AND BROTHERS*. Snow began developing his ideas for the series in 1935 and published the initial volume with the same title as the series in 1940. Progress on the series halted while Snow worked, during WORLD WAR II, in the Ministry of Labor. The second volume of the series, *The LIGHT AND THE DARK*, appeared in 1947, followed by *TIME OF HOPE* (1949), *The MASTERS* (1951), *The NEW MEN* (1954), *HOMECOMINGS* (1956), *The CONSCIENCE OF THE RICH* (1958), *The AFFAIR* (1960), *CORRIDORS OF POWER* (1964), *The SLEEP OF REASON* (1968), and *LAST THINGS* (1970). The first volume was reissued under the title *George Passant* in 1972. With quiet realism and plots that frequently hinge on ethical questions, these novels capture the political, social, and economic issues of the era they were written in while also developing the life story of the autobiographical first-person narrator, Lewis Eliot.

In 1950, Snow married a writer, Pamela Hansford Johnson; they collaborated on six original plays and an adaptation published between 1951 and 1967. He had become increasingly involved with the administration of science projects rather than the conducting of laboratory experiments, and he worked for several government agencies and in other forms of public service. He was named a Commander of the Order of the British Empire in 1943, and in 1957 he received a knighthood. He was appointed a life peer and assumed the title Baron Snow of the City of Leicester in 1964. Numerous universities awarded him honorary degrees, and he was named rector of the University of St. Andrew's in Scotland.

In 1959, Snow developed one of his most enduring works—a nonfiction piece—and delivered it as the Rede Lecture at Cambridge University: "The Two Cultures and the Scientific Revolution" is an essay that explores the widening gap between the intellectual spheres of the humanities and the sciences. It detonated an academic debate that raged intensely for a decade and that continues to draw attention to the present day. Snow felt that the ignorance, among those in literary circles, of the language and the concepts of science constituted a negligent corrosion of Western culture and an abandonment of social responsibility. F. R. Leavis, the distinguished Cambridge professor of English and the most influential literary critic of the day, shot back a withering reply, and the cause was taken up on both sides of the issue in numerous articles and books.

Throughout the 1960s, Snow's health declined. He continued answering his critics on the issue of the two cultures, and he completed his great roman-fleuve in 1970. He published three additional novels during the 1970s—*The Malcontents* (1972), *In Their Wisdom* (1974), and *A Coat of Varnish* (1979)—before he died on July 1, 1980. Snow also wrote plays and several works of nonfiction, including examinations of science and government, biographies, and works of literary criticism. Critics are divided on the long-term merit of his fiction, with advocates of realism continuing to admire his novels and advocates of experimentation minimizing his contribution to 20th-century literature. In the end, the ongoing debate over the issue of "the two cultures" may prove to be his most lasting stamp on the world of ideas.

BIBLIOGRAPHY

Boytinck, Paul W. *C. P. Snow: A Reference Guide*. Boston: Hall, 1980.

Cornelius, David K., and Edwin St. Vincent. *Cultures in Conflict: Perspectives on the Snow-Leavis Controversy*. Chicago: Scott, Foresman, 1964.

Halperin, John. *C. P. Snow: An Oral Biography Together with a Conversation with Lady Snow (Pamela Hansford Johnson)*. New York: St. Martin's Press, 1983.

Shusterman, David. *C. P. Snow*. Twayne's English Authors, 179. Rev. ed. Boston: Twayne, 1991.

SOCIALISM   See FABIAN SOCIETY.

SOLDIER'S ART, THE ANTHONY POWELL (1966)

Volume eight in the ROMAN-FLEUVE entitled *A DANCE TO THE MUSIC OF TIME*, this novel is positioned in the middle of the third of four movements in the series, and in the middle of WORLD WAR II as well. It follows *The VALLEY OF BONES* (1964) and precedes *The MILITARY PHILOSOPHERS* (1968). The series narrator, Nicholas Jenkins, is serving in the British army as a middle-aged junior officer and has just been posted, at the end of *The Valley of Bones*, under the wing of Kenneth Widmerpool, for whom he has had little fellow feeling ever since they met in their PUBLIC SCHOOL.

The novel opens, as several others have, with a luncheon. In attendance are Nick, Widmerpool, Colonel Hogbourne-Johnson, and General Liddament, who had caught out the unit Nick serves in by means of an unannounced inspection for which they were unprepared in *The Valley of Bones*. The general recommends that Nick meet Finn, a member of the French resistance; the colonel humiliates Widmerpool. But the biggest surprise, for Nick, is the sight of his best friend from school, the well-born Charles Stringham, serving as a waiter in the mess hall. Charles had sunk into an alcoholic funk when his marriage had broken up in the years before the war, and his family had essentially assigned him to a governess and kept him too poor to buy booze. But the discipline of army life and the urgency of the war seem to have helped Stringham to cope with his own problems. He accepts his humble post with equanimity.

On a visit to London, at the height of the blitzkrieg, Nick meets his brother-in-law, Chips Lovell, for a drink. Chips and his wife, Priscilla, who is the sister of Nick's wife, Isobel, have been estranged for some time, and Priscilla has engaged in an affair; nonetheless, Chips wants to be reconciled to her. Nick meets various other friends for dinner, including the composer Hugh Moreland, and Nick's sister-in-law, Priscilla, who is out with her lover, Odo Stevens. But Priscilla leaves by herself when she becomes upset. Later, Nick learns that Chips has been killed in a bomb explosion, and when he goes to visit Lady Molly, where he expects to find Priscilla, her house also has been destroyed by German bombs. Chips and Priscilla ironically die together and yet apart, killed in two different locations in the same raid.

Jenkins returns to his post to find that chaos has intensified: Lt. Bithel's drunkenness gets him into so much trouble that the efforts of Nick and Charles Stringham to cover for him are ineffectual, and Widmerpool has Bithel dismissed. But another form of trouble is brewing for Widmerpool, and he can do nothing but wait for it to strike. Stringham, too, is headed for trouble: He has been transferred to the mobile laundry, which is soon to be posted to the Far East. Nick's efforts to persuade Stringham to transfer out are ineffectual. Nick's fellow officer, Capt. Biggs, commits suicide by hanging himself, and Nick receives yet another transfer, this time to the War Office.

Midway through the third movement of the story, at Britain's darkest hour, as bombs rain on London and invasion by Germany seems nearly inevitable, Nick's life is a reflection in miniature of England's plight. Characters are killed, or they are doomed to be killed, or they are immersed in a continual fog of chaos, disorder, and mismanagement. The future looks grim as Nick receives his orders and heads for the new chapter in his life that they herald.

BIBLIOGRAPHY

Joyau, Isabelle. *Understanding Powell's* A Dance to the Music of Time. New York: St. Martin's Press, 1994.

Selig, Robert L. *Time and Anthony Powell.* Cranbury, N.J.: Associated University Presses, 1991.

Spurling, Hillary. *Invitation to the Dance: A Guide to Anthony Powell's* A Dance to the Music of Time. Boston: Little, Brown, 1977.

SOME DO NOT . . . FORD MADOX FORD
(1924)   See *PARADE'S END*.

SOMETHING TO ANSWER FOR P. H.
NEWBY (1968)   The first novel to win the BOOKER PRIZE upon its establishment in 1969, this novel is set in the SUEZ CANAL during the crisis of 1956. The protagonist, Townrow, is a former army sergeant who had served in the Canal Zone in 1946, where he had made the acquaintance of the aging Lebanese entrepreneur Elie Khoury, and his gray-haired English wife, generally referred to in Townrow's thoughts as "Mrs. K." The novel opens with Mrs. K.'s cry for help from Townrow, via letter, after her husband is murdered. Townrow is something of a scoundrel, employed by a charitable fund from which he has been embezzling money for some time; still in his 30s, divorced and handsome, he decides that helping Mrs. K., whom he believes to be a rich widow, could lead him to a very comfortable life with prospects of inheriting the resources of the childless Mrs. Khoury. He departs for the Canal Zone on the eve of the action by Egyptian President Nasser to nationalize the Suez Canal, but he knows nothing about this momentous event until after several unsettling incidents have slowed the progress of his journey.

The third-person narrator is limited to Townrow's loquacious thoughts, and although the narrative voice sounds reliable, Townrow himself proves to be a very unreliable protagonist. In his first meeting with Elie Khoury, Townrow had been upside-down on the beach, having been thrown from a horse the first time he had ever ridden one. The narrator emphasizes that Townrow's view of the world is askew; the action of the story will serve to correct that situation and restore some degree of admirable qualities to him. As he journeys to Egypt, Townrow exhibits his personal weaknesses: an excessive fondness for alcohol, an unthinking support of the British government and an unquestioning belief in the essential nobility of the British enterprise, a smart mouth, and a lack of respect for authority, especially that of foreign lands. His first act after finally reaching the Canal Zone is to resort to his favorite former drinking haunt, the Cypress Bar, where old Christou gets him thoroughly drunk. Townrow perceives himself to be launching his investigation of Elie's death, doubting Mrs. K.'s claim of murder, but determined to get to the bottom of it and see justice done if murder can be proved. He wakes up the next day out in the desert—naked, injured, and severely hung over—with no recollection of the previous night's discussion with Christou. The reader is thus placed in the position of knowing more about Townrow's activities than the character himself can recall.

Townrow soon finds a powerful love object: not the presumably wealthy Mrs. K., who of necessity decks him out in her late husband's clothes, but Leah Strauss, the daughter of Mrs. K.'s solicitor, Mr. Abravanel. Leah is a Jew who has become an American citizen by marriage; Townrow is soon madly in love with her, hoping she has no scruples against adultery. The nationalities and religious allegiances of the characters constitute an important aspect of the story, for in miniature form it plays out the larger struggle—the Suez Crisis—that follows from the European response to the nationalization of the canal. Townrow is soon entangled in events he only partially understands, but the seriousness of the situation cannot be doubted: People are dying, and the more deeply he probes into Elie Khoury's death, the greater the threat becomes to himself, to Mrs. K., and to Leah. His experiences are consciousness-raising, so that he comes to despise the man he is and to aspire both to be a better man and to make some restitution for the paltry record of his life so far.

Something to Answer For tells the story of an English antihero's redemption; however, that transformation is occurring in a world that no longer has a place for the British EMPIRE. The end of the novel thus cannot fully resolve Townrow's personal crisis. Some of the people he cares for will reach safety, and Townrow will find the better part of himself, but the story's end suspends him in AMBIGUITY.

BIBLIOGRAPHY

Poss, Stanley. "Manners and Myths in the Novels of P. H. Newby," *Critique: Studies in Modern Fiction* 2, no. 1 (1970): 5–19.

Ragheb, Gelila A. M. "Reality and Illusion in the Egyptian Novels of P. H. Newby." In *Images of Egypt in Twentieth Century Literature.* Edited by Hoda Gindi. Cairo: University of Cairo, 1991.

SONGLINES, THE BRUCE CHATWIN (1987)

Though this experimental book is arguably not a work of fiction at all, POSTMODERNISM makes it possible to call it a novel. The protagonist is a character named Bruce who is undertaking a journey that bears a marked similarity to Bruce Chatwin's own travels in the Australian outback.

The title refers to the tradition among Aboriginal Australians of venerating the invisible paths walked by their ancestors—paths that function as a metaphor for the system of values, beliefs, and practices that binds the people together and connects them to their history. Bruce (the narrator) observes the details of the physical world and the disappearing traditions of the people who have inhabited it for thousands of years, bringing to the task the eye of both an anthropologist and an art collector. Additionally, he presents the theory that the natural state of the human race is one of migratory wandering, and that divergence from this natural state—the formation of settlements and the agricultural systems that make them possible—is at the root of the problems of the modern world, perhaps even a sacrilege offensive to God. The Australian outback and the Aborigines' long migratory history in it provide a pretext for Chatwin's advocacy of a different way for human beings to exist in the world.

BIBLIOGRAPHY

Brown, Ruth. "*The Songlines* and the Empire That Never Happened," *Kunapipi* 13, no. 3 (1991): 5–13.

Texier-Vandamme, Christine. "*The Songlines:* Blurring the Edges of Traditional Genres in Search of New Nomadic Aesthetics," *Commonwealth Essays and Studies* 26, no. 1 (Autumn 2003): 75–82.

Wegner, Hart L. "The Travel Writer as Missionary in Reverse: Bruce Chatwin's *Songlines,*" *West Virginia University Philological Papers* 40 (1994): 77–81.

SOUR SWEET TIMOTHY MO (1982)

The author's second publication, *Sour Sweet* won the HAWTHORNDEN PRIZE and was considered for both the BOOKER PRIZE and the WHITBREAD AWARD. Set in London, the novel explores the experiences of a Chinese immigrant family from Hong Kong. The family members settle into contented isolation, failing to connect either with the provincial English people around them, who all seem to look alike, or with London's thriving Asian community. Chen, the husband, clings to traditional Chinese ways, considering himself to be an outsider in England, while his wife, Lily, makes efforts to connect to the wider world and find a middle ground between the old ways and the new. The birth of their son, Man Kee, leads to a further expansion of the family when Lily's sister Mui joins them to help with the baby. Mui soon fits right into English life by studying it on television.

Chen mysteriously disappears after the family opens a Chinese food stand at a truck stop. In an ironic twist, mild-mannered Chen has been mistakenly identified as a drug thief by the Chinese Triad, an organized crime ring with a long tradition in Hong Kong and a strong position in London. An Asian-style "mob hit" has ended Chen's life. Mo seems to suggest that traditional ways in an alien culture can contribute to the eradication of traditional ways. Never fully informed of her husband's fate, Lily must raise her son to function effectively in the English world without forgetting his roots.

Timothy MO uses his most typical subject matter in this early novel, examining the connection between the Chinese and the English, but using that cultural intersection as a point of departure for the universal human experience of being an outsider in a puzzling and unfamiliar world. Chen fails to solve the problem of his isolation, while the women in the novel accommodate themselves to the circumstances that surround them.

BIBLIOGRAPHY
Rothfork, John. "Confucianism in *Timothy Mo's Sour Sweet,*" *Journal of Commonwealth Literature* 24, no. 1 (1989): 49–64.

SOUTH AFRICA See BOER WAR, EMPIRE (END OF), and COLONIALISM. For significant South African novelists, see Justin CARTWRIGHT, J. M. COETZEE, Nadine GORDIMER, Christopher HOPE, and Alan PATON.

SOUTH WIND NORMAN DOUGLAS (1917)
A huge, popular success during WORLD WAR I, this novel provided war-weary readers with an escape to a charming Mediterranean island. The novel opens with the arrival of the Bishop of Bampopo at the island of Nepenthe (loosely based on Capri and other islands to the west of Italy). He is on his way home to England after a lengthy period of service in Africa, and he is making this call in order to fetch his cousin, Mrs. Meadows, home with him. Traveling with him on the

boat are several other people, two of whom feature in the PLOT: Retlow, whose name suggests his dastardly character, and Don Francesco, a local priest who introduces the bishop to the island and its international community of colorful residents, such as Miss Wilberforce, an English lady afflicted with the need to remove her clothing in public.

The thin plot involves an incident that the bishop witnesses when he sees Mrs. Meadows push Retlow—her former first husband—off the cliff near her home. A native boy is later accused of the murder and a trial ensues at which the boy is acquitted after a rather incompetent defense. During all of this the bishop does not speak out, since he is certain that Retlow got what he deserved and that the world has been made a better place for the loss of such a despicable person. This rather questionable ethical stance, however, is insignificant compared with the novel's main attraction, which is its cheerful narration of pleasantly eccentric characters in an idyllic setting. The narrator delivers lectures on the natural features of the island and on the cultural significance of the antiquities to be found there, relics of earlier glorious civilizations.

Although *South Wind* served as a form of escapist literature when it appeared, it has been surprisingly influential on serious writers such as Graham GREENE, Aldous HUXLEY, and Lawrence DURRELL, all of whom borrowed elements from Douglas's approach to fiction or learned lessons in narrative style from him or shared his Mediterranean enthusiasms. Huxley caricatured Douglas, a learned and sociable man, in *CROME YELLOW* in the figure of Scrogan.

BIBLIOGRAPHY
Dasenbrock, Reed Way. "Norman Douglas and the Denizens of Siren Land," *DL* 5, no. 4 (June 1982): 1–9.

SPACE TRILOGY C. S. LEWIS (1938–1945)
The three volumes that make up this series include *Out of the Silent Planet* (1938), *Perelandra* (1943; republished as *Voyage to Venus* in 1953), and *That Hideous Strength* (1945). It is also referred to as the "Ransom trilogy" or the "Cosmic trilogy." Since it involves travel to other planets of the solar system via space ship, it meets the criteria for inclusion in the genre of SCIENCE

FICTION; however, C. S. LEWIS is primarily interested in developing a religious ALLEGORY that stretches Christian ideology to cover Mars and Venus as well as Earth, while reemphasizing the value of religious faith to its readers. The story is related in the third person, although the omniscient narrator occasionally refers to himself in the first person, especially in the second volume, adding a degree of intimacy in the telling of the tale (a strategy Lewis also uses to good effect in the volumes of The CHRONICLES OF NARNIA). The focus of the narrator's attention remains on the protagonist, Professor Ransom, a philologist modeled on Lewis's friend and fellow Christian (and fellow novelist of FANTASY literature), J. R. R. TOLKIEN.

In the opening of Out of the Silent Planet, Ransom is abducted while trying to do a good deed as he pursues a walking vacation in a remote part of England. He knows one of his abductors, the ironically named Devine (later elevated to the title Lord Feverstone in the third volume of the trilogy), because they attended the same PUBLIC SCHOOL, and he has heard of the other, the renowned physicist Dr. Weston. Before Ransom realizes what is happening, this devilish pair has drugged him, dragged him aboard the ship Weston has built, and launched it for points unknown, but not on Planet Earth. During the long journey, Ransom overhears an ominous reference to the Sorns of Malacandra— wherever they are—and concludes that he is to be handed over to them when the ship reaches its destination. He resolves to flee into that unknown world at the first opportunity and trust to his wits to survive.

Ransom's flight from the Sorn welcoming party is successful, and before long he encounters something that is not a Sorn but that is an intelligent user of language. As a linguist, Ransom is ideally suited to handle this situation and quickly becomes the first philologist in the history of the human species to learn an extraterrestrial language. His rescuer is a Hross; Ransom is soon enjoying a prolonged stay in a Hross community and developing a treatise on Hross grammar and syntax. But his abductors have not given up the search, and Ransom still doesn't know where he is, why he's there, or how the Hross can know so much about the Solar System with their simple technology. By the novel's end, he has overcome his fear of the Sorns and

traveled to face the Oyarsa (or regent) of Malacandra, where he learns many staggering truths that form part of Lewis's allegory and that provide the cosmological backdrop against which the subsequent volumes unfold. He comes to accept the existence of the eldila, invisible ethereal beings who watch over the Malacandrans, and of Maleldil, who rules the universe. In particular, he discovers why he has never heard of any of these beings in his life on his home planet, which he learns is properly known as Thulcandra. The three earthlings are allowed to attempt the return home and barely reach it before their ship disintegrates.

In Perelandra, the narrator moves into the periphery of the story, participating in the opening and closing scenes on Earth and recounting Ransom's adventures in between at second hand. Here, Lewis is reimagining the story of Milton's Paradise Lost. Because of the unique problem with the Oyarsa of Earth, human help is needed on Perelandra; Ransom is dispatched by supernatural means to provide that help. On Perelandra, a new world is in the making, with a new Eve; however, she has become separated from the new Adam. Ransom encounters her, knowing only that he is to provide aid, but not knowing what kind or when or how. Eventually, Weston arrives in a new spaceship, and he unwittingly brings with him an evil tempter. Soon Ransom, Weston, and Eve are locked in a struggle for the fate of the new world. Lewis's creation of that world is highly inventive, and the three-way struggle takes the form of a compelling discussion that touches on numerous philosophical and theological points, and even on the nature of human consciousness. Ransom's subsequent conflict with Weston uses many tropes drawn from the ARCHETYPE of the hero's journey into the underworld and back again, but Lewis presents it with some surprising comic touches that effectively humanize the story without trivializing it. Once again, Ransom makes a safe return to Earth, but not before Lewis finishes his reinterpretation of Christian doctrine to take all the planets into account.

In That Hideous Strength, the story remains entirely on Earth and moves more firmly into the category of fantasy. At a small British university, the sale of campus lands is once again on the agenda; this time, however, a venerated and ancient wood that includes "Merlin's

Well" is for sale to N.I.C.E—the National Institute of Coordinated Experiments. The sale is brokered through deceit and by an appeal to the greed of underpaid young faculty members. One of these, the trusting Mark Studdock, is offered a lucrative position in the organization that will soon raise its towering glass headquarters over Merlin's Well. In the meantime, Mark's intelligent wife, Jane, is beset by nightmares featuring people who show up in the morning newspaper. Eventually, she meets Mr. Fisher King—Ransom's identity since his return from Perelandra—and with his advice she discovers what N.I.C.E. is really up to; Mark and Jane are two innocents caught on the opposite sides of a struggle neither of them would have imagined possible. So powerful is N.I.C.E. that Merlin himself must be summoned to assist Ransom, Jane, and their allies. Evil is ultimately defeated, allowing Ransom to plan his return to the paradise of Perelandra.

In his *Space Trilogy,* Lewis ironically uses the conventions of science fiction to undermine the valorization of science in the modern world. Ransom is a figure of faith ready to lay down his life if necessary in order to defend that faith and defeat evil; in contrast, when evil chooses to incarnate itself, it does so in the body of a scientist. From Lewis's Christian perspective, science has only become useful to humankind as a consequence of the Fall in the Garden of Eden. In the new Eden of Perelandra, where the unfallen king and queen live without sin in a world of abundance and in direct communication with Maleldil, science will never become necessary. Lewis creates a vivid, compelling, and memorable set of circumstances and characters to serve as his stalking horse in presenting what is essentially an antimodernist message.

BIBLIOGRAPHY

Downing, David C. *Planets in Peril: A Critical Study of C. S. Lewis's Ransom Trilogy.* Amherst: University of Massachusetts Press, 1992.

Markos, Louis. "Apologist for the Past: The Medieval Vision of C. S. Lewis' *Space Trilogy* and *The Chronicles of Narnia,*" *Mythlore: A Journal of J. R. R. Tolkien, C. S. Lewis, Charles Williams, and Mythopoeic Literature, no.* 23 (Spring 2001): 24–35.

SPANISH CIVIL WAR   An illustration of the political polarities of WORLD WAR II, the Spanish civil war pitted a leftist Republican government, elected to power in 1936, against a right-wing Nationalist movement eventually headed by General Francisco Franco. The war began when a conservative coup against the government failed to dominate the entire country. Both sides appealed for international aid, and the distribution of support that poured in pointed up the political divisions that would soon lead to global warfare: Germany and Italy supported the conservative Nationalists, using Spain as a theater for trying out new methods of ground and air tactics, while the Soviet Union, France, England, and numerous Americans supported the liberal Republicans. Several of these nations signed a nonintervention pact in August 1936; nonetheless, some 60,000 fighters and support personnel flocked to Spain to serve in the International Brigades. Noted writers such as George ORWELL and Ernest Hemingway were among those drawn to Spain during this war.

The war was notable for the viciousness that characterized the conflict: Assassinations and executions became commonplace on both sides, and the Nationalists engaged in a program of deliberate terror. The Republican faction was hampered by infighting that threatened to splinter the alliance of urban workers, rural agricultural laborers, and much of the educated middle class; among the communist elements on the Republican side, supporters were divided by their allegiance to either Joseph Stalin or his chief rival Leon Trotsky. The Nationalists benefited from greater solidarity among businessmen, Catholics, landowners, and the military. The war ravaged the nation and resulted in a death toll variously estimated to range from 500,000 to 1 million casualties. As the Republican forces were pushed back, a half-million refugees flooded into southern France. The war culminated in bloody street fighting in Madrid that ended in a Nationalist victory, placing Franco in a position of power that continued until his death in 1975.

The Spanish civil war is notable for the effect it had on artists and intellectuals. British novels of the period with any degree of political awareness are likely to make reference to the war or to include characters who join the International Brigades. Anthony POWELL sends a character loosely (and ironically) based on George Orwell to the war in his monumental series, *A Dance to the Music of Time,* and leftist characters in the story—primarily artists, musicians, and writers—establish their political credentials through references to the war. Wyndham Lewis develops his satire of communist posturing in *The Revenge for Love* against the backdrop of this civil strife, and in *The Prime of Miss Jean Brodie,* by Muriel Spark, a minor character's meaningless death during this war becomes a crucial plot element.

BIBLIOGRAPHY

Brenan, Gerald. *The Spanish Labyrinth: An Account of the Social and Political Background of the Civil War.* 2nd ed. 1950. Cambridge: Cambridge University Press, 1993.

Esenwein, George and Adrian Shubert. *Spain at War: The Spanish Civil War in Context, 1931–1939.* London: Longman, 1995.

Perez, Jane, and Wendell Aycock, eds. *The Spanish Civil War in Literature.* Lubbock: Texas Tech University Press, 1990.

SPARK, MURIEL (1918–)

A celebrated 20th-century writer of some 21 novels, along with numerous volumes of short fiction, poetry, and literary scholarship, Muriel Spark was born on February 1, 1918, in Edinburgh, Scotland, with the birth name Muriel Sarah Camberg. Her period of study at James Gillespie's School for Girls provided material for her most famous novel, *The Prime of Miss Jean Brodie* (1961). In 1937, when she was 19 years old, she married and became Muriel Spark, the name she has continued to use; the newlyweds relocated to Rhodesia (modern Zimbabwe). The marriage produced one son and ended in divorce after only two years. In 1944, delayed by the outbreak of World War II, Spark moved to London and took up work with a propaganda agency of the British Foreign Office, producing anti-Nazi materials.

After the war, Muriel Spark served as General Secretary of the Poetry Society; additionally, she edited *Poetry Review* in the late 1940s and cofounded the short-lived journal *Forum Stories and Poems.* She became interested in literary biography, beginning with the inventor of the Frankenstein myth, Mary Wollstonecraft Shelley, in 1951, and turning to Emily Brontë (with a cowriter, Derek Stanford) and then to John Masefield in 1953. During this time, she also edited or coedited (with Stanford) texts of the works of William Wordsworth and of the letters of Mary Shelley, the Brontës, and John Henry Newman. In 1952, she published her first collection of poetry just as her inner life was undergoing an important transformation.

In 1954, Muriel Spark converted to Catholicism, and she also received a commission from a publisher to write a novel. She has credited her conversion experience as a key personal transformation that allowed her to move from poetry and short fiction to the novel; her fiction frequently addresses moral and philosophical issues raised by her theological interests. In 1957, *The Comforters* appeared, telling the self-reflexive story of a woman who begins to hear the thoughts of a writer who is constructing a story using this woman as a character. Spark began publishing steadily, producing *Robinson* in 1958, along with a collection of short stories. In 1959, she published *Memento Mori,* in which messages from Death affect the story's course, and in 1960, she published *The Ballad of Peckham Rye,* in which the protagonist begins interfering in the lives of the people he "studies." In 1961, Spark published a second collection of stories that included her radio plays; she also published *The Prime of Miss Jean Brodie,* which became the basis of a successful FILM ADAPTATION and of the film's popular theme song.

Spark also began traveling in 1961. She spent time in Jerusalem conducting research for her longest novel, *The Mandelbaum Gate,* which won the James Tait Black Memorial Prize in 1965. Between beginning her research and publishing the result of it, she also wrote a play, *Doctor of Philosophy,* which was performed in London in 1962 and published the following year. And in 1963, she published *The Girls of Slender Means,* drawing on her experience of living in a women's hotel in the closing days of World War II. In 1964, she moved to New York City for about a year, and continued from there to a 15-year residence in Rome.

In the 1970s and 1980s, Spark produced a new novel every one to three years. Some of the best received of these include *In the Driver's Seat* (1970), about a woman who intends to die by finding a man to murder her; *The Hothouse by the East River* (1973), about the uses of political propaganda; *The Abbess of Crewe: A Modern Morality Tale* (1974), set in an abbey bugged for eavesdropping; LOITERING WITH INTENT (1981), the story of a novelist who takes a job as the secretary of an autobiographical society and finds her fiction being plagiarized; and *A Far Cry from Kensington* (1988), about a woman's transformation from an unappreciated do-gooder to a fuller but less giving existence. This novel also includes satirical portraits of the British publishing world and of Wilhelm Reich's eccentric psychological theories about human sexuality.

In 1962, Muriel Spark became a Fellow of the Royal Society of Literature, and in 1967 she was awarded the Order of the British Empire. Two of her works were short-listed for the BOOKER PRIZE: *The Public Image,* in 1969, the first year the prize was awarded, examined the power of publicity to make and destroy an actress's career, and *Loitering with Intent,* in 1981. In 1982, she settled in Tuscany, where she continues to live and write. Her autobiography, *Curriculum Vita,* appeared in 1992. In 2000, at the age of 82, she published *Aiding and Abetting.* Critical opinion about Spark's literary merit is stronger among British critics than among American critics, and her strongest admirers include writers of POSTMODERNISM, such as Malcolm BRADBURY and David LODGE, who recognize the sophistication of her economical yet many-layered style.

BIBLIOGRAPHY

Bold, Alan Norman. *Muriel Spark.* London: Methuen, 1986.

Hynes, Joseph, ed. *Critical Essays on Muriel Spark.* New York: G. K. Hall, 1992.

Page, Norman. *Muriel Spark.* Modern Novelists Series. New York: St. Martin's Press, 1990.

Richmond, Velma Bourgeois. *Muriel Spark.* New York: Frederick Ungar, 1984.

Walker, Dorothea. *Muriel Spark.* Twayne's English Authors, 460. Boston: Twayne, 1988.

SPY NOVEL

SPY NOVEL   Like SCIENCE FICTION, this popular genre has developed primarily in the 20th century. It was founded with the 1915 publication of *The THIRTY-NINE STEPS* by John BUCHAN, and spy fiction continues to follow the model laid down in that novel, with some variations on the theme. Key British authors who followed after Buchan include Graham GREENE, Eric Ambler, Ian FLEMING, Len Deighton, and John LE CARRÉ. Interestingly, James Bond is reading a novel by Eric Ambler at one point in *FROM RUSSIA WITH LOVE.*

Spy novels often share the characteristic, with MYSTERY AND DETECTIVE FICTION, of some puzzle that must be solved. Some spies, James BOND in particular, may have access to technological wonders that might fit just as easily into a science fiction story. Spy novels may also share characteristics of the thriller, with some disastrous outcome hanging in the balance that will be averted only if the protagonist acts in a timely manner; saving the day usually immerses the protagonist in the conventions of an adventure story; and, not uncommonly, the protagonist may dawdle in the purlieus of the romance novel—generally not of the chaste courtship variety—on the way to saving the day.

Spy novels easily function with only flat characters and stereotypes, and they thrive on complex plotting with unexpected twists; consequently, this genre is generally not categorized as serious literary fiction. Spy novels flourished during the cold war, when the stage of world politics offered a relatively simple two-part division between the forces of democracy and those of communism. They have varied significantly, however, in the degree of realism and grittiness with which the phenomenon of espionage is treated. John le Carré is noted for realism with respect to the bureaucratic dreariness of the day-to-day functioning of espionage; Graham Greene presents possibly the grittiest examples of the genre, keenly aware of the fundamentally corrupt and corrupting nature of the endeavor. These two authors—particularly Graham Greene—are generally recognized as the most literary writers of this genre.

BIBLIOGRAPHY

Atkins, John Alfred. *The British Spy Novel: Styles in Treachery.* London: Calder; New York: Riverrun Press, 1984.

Bloom, Clive. *Spy Thrillers: From Buchan to Le Carré.* New York: St. Martin's Press, 1990.

Smith, Myron J., and Terry White. *Cloak and Dagger Fiction: An Annotated Guide to Spy Thrillers.* Westport, Conn.: Greenwood Press, 1995.

SPY WHO CAME IN FROM THE COLD, THE JOHN LE CARRÉ (1963)

Written in a style that strips the glamour and adventure from espionage to show the morally ambiguous nature of the game, this SPY NOVEL was the basis of a successful FILM ADAPTATION by the same name that starred Richard Burton as LE CARRÉ's doomed spy Alec Leamas.

The story unfolds through a third-person narrator. At the novel's beginning, Alec Leamas works in Berlin for the British Secret Service as a handler of East German double agents. He is nearing the end of his career at 50 and winding down his operations. His last agent, Karl Riemeck, is shot down virtually at Leamas's feet while attempting what should have been a routine crossing of a Berlin Wall checkpoint. This opening scene of the novel provides the location for the closing scene as well, but in between, Leamas undergoes a labyrinthine journey. In England, he reports to Control, the man in charge of the "Circus"—the entire Secret Service—and receives a new assignment: He will help protect Britain's last double agent in East Germany. Control does not, however, reveal this agent's identity to Leamas, so important and precarious is the man's position in the Communist hierarchy. Through this device, le Carré does not reveal the identity to the reader, either, thereby increasing his opportunities to develop suspense and AMBIGUITY in the remaining PLOT.

Leamas, placed on a desk job in London, embarks on a course of action that destroys his reputation and his apparent utility to the Secret Service through drinking and petty embezzlement. He seems locked in a downward spiral that takes him first to an insignificant job in a library, where he enters into an affair with Liz Gold, a minor official in England's Communist Party, and then to a brief stint in prison. He alerts Liz that he will disappear; after completing his time in jail, he travels to Holland, apparently lured by a Soviet agent attempting to turn him. An unexpected newspaper story proclaiming him to be a defector appears, and Leamas is forced to flee to safety in East Germany. There, he is interrogated by Fiedler, the second-in-command to Hans-Dieter Mundt, deputy director of the East German Secret Service. Fiedler is attempting to establish that Mundt is a double agent, but when Leamas arrives in the court where the case is being tried and finds Liz Gold as a witness, he realizes that he has become a pawn in a much larger game than he had thought he was playing. Soon, his life and Liz's as well are at risk in a characteristically cold-blooded episode in the aptly named cold war.

Le Carré carries the spy novel beyond the formulaic episodes of the adventure story by relying on fully rounded characters who are intensely aware of the larger ethical issues at stake in their espionage careers. Leamas the puppeteer in the end finds himself to be a marionette, but by the time he makes this discovery, another life is entangled in his game—a life he has come to care about deeply and sincerely. Free will seems impossible on the chessboard of the cold war, and yet in the end Leamas finds the courage to make a free choice.

BIBLIOGRAPHY

Barley, Tony. *Taking Sides: The Fiction of John le Carré*. Philadelphia: Open University Press, 1986.

Monaghan, David. *The Novels of John le Carré: The Art of Survival*. New York: Basil Blackwell, 1985.

Wolfe, Peter. *Corridors of Deceit: The World of John le Carré*. Bowling Green, Ohio: Bowling Green University Popular Press, 1987.

STAYING ON PAUL SCOTT (1977)

A kind of comic epilogue to the epic four-volume tragedy of *The RAJ QUARTET*—a novel functioning somewhat like a satyr–play at the end of a triple Greek tragedy—*Staying On* won the BOOKER PRIZE in 1977. The novel relates the story of a British couple who choose to remain in INDIA after its emancipation from the British EMPIRE in 1947, opening with a death in 1972 and then looking back over the previous year and over the previous half century in the memories of the survivor. The protagonists are Tusker and Lucy Smalley; Tusker is a colonel retired from the British army, and the two of them are spending their penurious retirement years in residence at Smith's Hotel in Pankot. The action of the plot is set in motion with the arrival of a letter evicting the Smalleys so that the exciting new Shiraz Hotel (a metaphor for the new postcolonial India) can expand into the space now occupied by Smith's (a metaphor of the outmoded British Raj).

The Smalleys had been minor characters in *The Raj Quartet,* occupying a low social position with respect to the other upper-CLASS colonials. In the new India, they realize that they have actually sunk lower on a much larger scale. Social arrangements of all sorts are different in the new world, so that servants and persons of mixed English and Indian blood can legitimately interact with "respectable" society—the sharp lines that had separated the colonizers from the colonized have eroded or been erased. And the treatment of the body is radically transformed: Scott achieves much of his comic effect through the examination of corporeal existence now that the stifling repressions of ultra-proper colonials, who had struggled to maintain superiority through scrupulous propriety, are thrown off. Sex, for example, becomes a fact of routine life, requiring its own adjustments and strategies, instead of a hushed-up and shameful secret.

The lives of Indians also take on a quality which is simultaneously ordinary and exuberant: They have become the norm against which everything is measured in their own land, and so their self-respect no longer must defer to the status of the colonizers. An Indian man pursuing a foolish passion for an exotic dancer (as the Smalley's landlord does) need not be scorned for revealing the low passions peculiar to his race and thereby lowering the esteem in which his brethren are held. Mr. Bhoolabhoy's passion is his own, and its merits or lack thereof affect only his place in the world. Ibrahim's position as a servant expresses his employment status with respect to the Smalleys without reflecting in any way on his merit as a human being. Accustomed to the privilege of belonging to a ruling class (even if occupying its lowest position) that had considered itself not merely in charge of but also superior to those they ruled, the Smalleys must make a huge adjustment to the postcolonial world. Scott's novel is a comic elegy to the passing of the Raj.

BIBLIOGRAPHY

Gooneratne, Yasmin. "Paul Scott's *Staying On:* Finale in a Minor Key," *Journal of Indian Writing in English* 9, no. 2 (July 1981): 1–12.

Tedesco, Janis. "*Staying On:* The Final Connection," *Western Humanities Review* 39, no. 3 (Autumn 1985): 195–211.

STOREY, DAVID (1933–) Trained as a painter and successful in the genres of both drama and fiction, David Story is an admired writer sometimes classed with Alan SILLITOE, one of the ANGRY YOUNG MEN. Storey shares the commitment of that group to the sympathetic representation of the working CLASS, but his interests as an artist have been more diverse.

Storey was born in Wakefield, Yorkshire—a northern mining town—on July 13, 1933; his father was a coal miner. Although born and reared in a loving family, from an early age Storey's interests in art and his academic abilities pulled him in a direction away from the traditions of his family's class and the occupations available in his hometown. He knew at an early age that he was interested in art and that he possessed the talents to pursue that interest. He was educated at Queen Elizabeth Grammar School and then spent two years at the Wakefield School of Art. His parents opposed his interest in art, and his teachers counseled him to train as a commercial artist. Storey broke with his family to attend the Slade School of Fine Art in London, and to support himself and pay for his education, he played professional sports for Leeds Rugby League Club. In 1956, he completed his diploma at Slade; the same year, he was married. He and his wife have four children.

Storey had won awards for his painting, but he turned his attention to writing and published his first novel, *This Sporting Life,* in 1960. An autobiographical novel about a professional rugby player who falls in love with his landlady, it won the Macmillan Award for Fiction and became the basis for a FILM ADAPTATION. His second novel, *Flight into Camden* (1960), presents the story of a young woman's defiance of her working-class family's values; it won the John Llewellyn Rhys Memorial Prize and a Somerset Maugham Award. In 1963, he published an allegorical novel, *Radcliffe,* which represented British class relations as a homosexual love affair. Before continuing his career as a fiction writer, Storey turned his hand to drama, writing several successful plays, including *In Celebration* and *The Changing Room;* in this arena as well, Storey's work has been well received and has won numerous awards.

In 1973, Storey devoted his third novel, *Pasmore,* to the depiction of the effect a failed marriage has on the former spouses, and the following year the novel won the Geoffrey Faber Memorial Prize. His most admired novel, the autobiographical *SAVILLE,* appeared in 1976 and won the BOOKER PRIZE for that year. Storey continued writing plays and novels in the following years; he published *The Thin-Ice Skater* in 2004, a study of two brothers separated in age by some 40 years. David Storey continues to live and write in London.

BIBLIOGRAPHY

Craig, David. "David Storey's Vision of the Working Class." In *The Uses of Fiction: Essays on the Modern Novel in Honour of Arnold Kettle.* Edited by Douglas Jefferson and Martin Graham. Milton Keynes: Open University Press, 1982.

Haffenden, John. *Novelists in Interview.* London: Methuen, 1985.

Hutchings, William. *David Storey: A Casebook.* New York: Garland Publishers, 1992.

STRANGERS AND BROTHERS SERIES— 11 VOLS. C. P. SNOW (1940–1970)

The 11 volumes of this series include *George Passant* (1972; originally *Strangers and Brothers,* 1940), *The LIGHT AND THE DARK* (1947), *TIME OF HOPE* (1949); *The MASTERS* (1951), *The NEW MEN* (1954), *HOMECOMINGS* (1956; published in the United States as *Homecoming*), *The CONSCIENCE OF THE RICH* (1958), *The AFFAIR* (1960), *CORRIDORS OF POWER* (1964), *The SLEEP OF REASON* (1968), and *LAST THINGS* (1970). The action of the entire series covers some 50 years, from WORLD WAR I to the 1960s, viewing this tumultuous period of history from the perspective of one man living though it and contributing to its events.

The entire series has a first-person narrator, Lewis Eliot; born in a Midlands province in a middle-CLASS family, he rises to a position as a barrister of some power, wealth, and influence both in the academic world and in the political world. Considered as a whole, Eliot's story is a ROMAN-FLEUVE, and as such it is frequently compared to Anthony POWELL's *A DANCE TO THE MUSIC OF TIME,* although the two are very different in tone, subject, and style: *Strangers and Brothers,* for example, contains very little of a comic or satirical nature. The first three volumes and *The Conscience of the Rich* are also examples of the BILDUNGSROMAN or novel of a maturing consciousness. SNOW also creates

memorable examples of CAMPUS NOVELS in *The Masters* and *The Affair* (the two most admired books in the series), and he addresses the moral and practical issues related to the development of atomic weapons in *The New Men.* In some of the volumes, Eliot tells his own story, introspectively examining his emotional response to the challenges he faces in life, in some he is a major force in the development of the events in the PLOT, and in some he is an onlooker, virtually a third-person narrator of the events in someone else's life.

Set in 1925, when Eliot is about 20 years old, the first volume of the series is a novel of observed experience, and the subject of observation is George Passant, a solicitor's clerk, a brilliant lecturer, and an effectively inspiring mentor to students at the local technical college. Although first in the series, this novel occurs *in medias res* with respect to Eliot's life; retrospective narratives, especially in *A Time of Hope,* fill in his childhood, family background, and first marriage. In *Strangers and Brothers,* he becomes part of "the group" of bright young people that develops around George Passant's charisma. The key plot complication begins with a legal case against George's business partner in a small advertising enterprise: Jack Cotery is accused of "corrupting" a 15-year-old boy, the son of the local newspaper's owner, Jack's employer. The boy is Roy Calvert, still boarding at a PUBLIC SCHOOL but home on vacation as the story opens. The case faintly echoes, in a middle-class environment, the trial of Oscar WILDE some 30 years prior to the time of the novel.

George Passant prepares a vigorous and effective defense of Jack, and the novel follows the case carefully, detailing public and private conversations, analyzing strategies, and recording key testimonies and speeches. But the victory is a Pyrrhic one: Accusations in the case spill over to George's personal and professional life, and although these cannot be proved, they stain George's reputation. More important for Eliot, they turn out to be true, or partly true: George Passant is a brilliant man, but he is also insecure, and his advocacy of liberal freedoms is undermined by his need to hold himself and his group above the law. Thus, although strictly speaking Jack's shady business practices should have been censured by George, they are allowed to pass uncorrected because of the benefits that have accrued to the group through them. Eliot learns that George knew what was going on and allowed it to continue—a sin of omission rather than one of commission, but wrong in any light. Furthermore, certain sexual irregularities have also been silently tolerated.

George Passant is the first of several flawed, brilliant men to influence Lewis Eliot, and in this first volume in a lengthy treatment of modern life, C. P. Snow establishes significant oppositions that he will repeatedly revisit. Weaknesses that derail competent men remain key topics of investigation, especially when such men cross into the gray region between right and wrong and are cast into the legal sphere that is Eliot's professional world. Strategies and politics recur throughout the series: the public politics of government officials charged with the well-being of the entire population, and the private politics of businesses, committees, friendships, and families. Snow consistently relates these issues to the larger historical context in which his characters—and the author himself—exist, placing Eliot in a specifically liberal political position. The challenge of living a personally fulfilling and morally sound life in a world shared with the unpredictable remainder of the human race—against whom he must also compete—occupies Lewis Eliot's humane and sensitive thoughts through a long and productive adulthood that begins with the discovery of George Passant's hollow idealism.

BIBLIOGRAPHY

Boytinck, Paul. *C. P. Snow: A Reference Guide*. Boston: Hall, 1980.

De la Mothe, John. *C. P. Snow and the Struggle of Modernity*. Austin: University of Texas Press, 1991.

Graves, Nora C. *The Two Culture Theory in C. P. Snow's Novels*. Hattiesburg: University and College Press of Mississippi, 1972.

Rabinovitz, Rubin. "The Reaction Against Modernism: Amis, Snow, Wilson." In *The Columbia History of the British Novel*. Edited by John Richetti et al. New York: Columbia University Press, 1994. 895–917.

Widdowson, Peter J. "C. P. Snow's *Strangers and Brothers* Sequence: Lewis Eliot and the Failure of Realism," *Renaissance & Modern Studies* 19 (1975): 112–128.

STRUCTURALISM   See POSTMODERNISM.

SUBTLE KNIFE, THE PHILIP PULLMAN (1998)

Volume two in the FANTASY trilogy collectively entitled *HIS DARK MATERIALS, The Subtle Knife* introduces a young man, Will Parry, who will join the heroine of the story, Lyra Silvertongue, and help her to complete a monumental journey. This volume follows *The GOLDEN COMPASS* and paves the way for *The AMBER SPYGLASS*.

The PLOT first brings the two young people together. Will is from a small town near Oxford, England, in the world we are familiar with; Lyra is from an Oxford in a parallel universe. Will is searching for his father just as Lyra is searching for hers. His father disappeared during an arctic exploring mission when Will was a baby, and his mother's mental health has been deteriorating since then. Others—sinister, determined men—are also looking for any way to get to his father, and so Will decides to find him first. While fleeing the sinister men, he finds a window into another world, which turns out to be a kind of crossroads between universes. There he meets Lyra, and the two of them soon realize that their journeys are linked in some mysterious way.

During the first part of the novel, Will and Lyra explore the strange new world they have found, Cittagazze, and make occasional trips back to Will's world, where Lyra meets a physicist, Dr. Mary Malone. Dr. Malone is studying Dust, although she has a different name for it, and soon she too is on a dangerous quest. Lyra unexpectedly loses her aleithiometer to a strangely familiar thief, and Will strikes a devil's bargain to get it back: He must obtain a powerful knife in Cittagazze and trade it for the aleithiometer. The struggle to obtain the knife costs more than Will could have guessed, but in a thrilling sequence he becomes the knife-bearer and regains the aleithiometer as well.

The novel features a key subplot in which the balloonist Lee Scoresby joins the northern witches and, upon learning more about Dr. Stanislaw Grumman, sets out to locate this mysterious figure who has been in the background of the story from the very first chapter. Soon word comes of the great struggle that Lyra's father, Lord Asriel, has undertaken against the Authority itself, and the characters of the subplot decide to join him at his mighty fortress. The plot is slowly drawing all the characters together, but powerful counterforces are working to keep them all apart.

Like other middle books of adventure trilogies, the novel ends without closure. Will and Lyra cross paths with Scoresby, Grumman, and the witches, but Lyra's mother, the wicked Mrs. Coulter, arrives on the scene with a force of zeppelins and armed warriors who have been severed from their "daemons"—the animal companions that house their souls. No sooner has Will made the best friend he has ever known and reached the brink of fulfilling his quest than everyone is driven asunder or killed. Even allies turn out to have fatal impulses.

The Subtle Knife is the story of a boy who is called to do the work of a man before he is entirely ready enough—or old enough—to take on the job. Following the ARCHETYPE of the hero's journey, he sets out on his adventure, acquires helpers, and battles adversity. In the concluding volume of the story, he will be required to make the last leg of the hero's journey as he and Lyra enter the afterlife and struggle to return to the worlds of the living.

BIBLIOGRAPHY

Rustin, Margaret, and Michael Rustin. "A New Kind of Friendship—An Essay on Philip Pullman's *The Subtle Knife*," *Journal of Child Psychotherapy* 29, no. 2 (2003): 227–241.

SUEZ CANAL/SUEZ CRISIS   In the east of Egypt, the narrow isthmus that separates the Mediterranean Sea from the Red Sea has been crossed by canal at various times going back as far as 1850 B.C. The ancient canal came to an end in A.D. 775, when it was buried as part of a military defensive strategy. When Napoleon occupied Egypt in 1798, he ordered a survey of a canal route across the isthmus and investigated the evidence of the ancient canal's path. His surveyor erred in calculating a 33-foot difference in height between the northern and southern ends of the route; if true, this difference would have required an expensive system of locks, and so construction was delayed. In fact, both ends of the canal are at sea level.

With a vigorous sea trade to Asia dominated by British sailing routes around the Cape of Good Hope at the southern tip of Africa, the strategic value of a canal, providing a shortcut to valuable markets, was a strong enticement to undertake the project. In 1854, the viceroy of Egypt, Said Pasha, granted a concession to the French diplomat Ferdinand de Lesseps to build the canal; in 1856, the Suez Canal Company was formed (headquartered in Paris) and given the control of the canal for 99 years after the completion of the building project. Construction finally began in 1859 and continued for 10 years, culminating in an opening ceremony in November 1869. British interest in the canal began in 1875, when Benjamin Disraeli, the British prime minister, authorized the purchase of the Egyptian pasha's shares in the Suez Canal Company. British participation made the canal highly profitable, and numerous British civil servants and others soon settled in Port Said at the northern end of the canal and in Suez at the southern end.

Egypt's role in and profit from the canal disappeared until 1949, when the nation crossed by the canal was invited to rejoin the board of directors. Then on July 26, 1956, Egyptian president Gamal Abdel Nasser nationalized the canal 13 years before the concession was scheduled to end, instigating an international conflict, the Suez Crisis. Nasser was retaliating against an American and British reversal of policy to finance the Aswan High Dam on the Nile River; for their part, American and British politicians were punishing Nasser for his ties to the communist Soviet Union and its allies. With the canal in Egyptian hands, Europeans feared that access to oil imports from the Middle East would be cut off; Britain and France joined in a plan to repossess the Canal Zone and accepted Israel as a partner in the enterprise. Israeli troops invaded on October 29, 1956, defeating Egyptian resistance. British and French troops landed at the northern end of the canal in early November, and the United Nations called for a cease-fire. But this military action did not win popular support in Great Britain, and the Soviet Union threatened to intervene on Egypt's behalf. The United Nations evacuated all British and French troops, along with civilians who had been working or living in the

Canal Zone, on December 22, 1956. Israeli troops withdrew three months later.

Once the strongest European presence in the Middle East, the British essentially ended their influence there with the failure to regain control of the Suez Canal. The Suez Crisis marks a milestone in the 20th-century decline of the British EMPIRE. The cost of maintaining an overseas presence, both in terms of money and lives, had exceeded the willingness of British citizens to pay it. In literature, the events of the Suez Crisis were chronicled in P. H. NEWBY's 1967 novel, *SOMETHING TO ANSWER FOR*, the first novel to receive the BOOKER PRIZE.

BIBLIOGRAPHY

Farnie, D. A. *East and West of Suez: The Suez Canal in History, 1854–1956*. Oxford: Clarendon Press, 1969.

Schonfield, Hugh Joseph. *The Suez Canal in Peace and War, 1869–1969*. Rev. ed. Coral Gables, Fla.: University of Miami Press, 1969.

SURGEON'S MATE, THE PATRICK O'BRIAN (1980)   See AUBREY-MATURIN NOVELS.

SWIFT, GRAHAM (1949–   )   Born in London on May 4, 1949, Graham Swift was educated at Dulwich college (the alma mater of P. G. WODEHOUSE) and at Cambridge University, where he completed an undergraduate degree in 1970 and a master's degree in 1975. He taught part-time in London in the early years of his writing career, which began in 1980 with *The Sweet Shop Owner*, a novel about an elderly shopkeeper's belated rebellion against the routine of his life. His second novel, *Shuttlecock* (1981), uses AMBIGUITY in telling the life of an alleged war hero working as a researcher for the police. Swift had his first important success with his third novel, *Waterland* (1983), in which a history teacher uses his own family tree and personal life (much of it set in the Fens of East Anglia, a location that also served Dorothy SAYERS in *The NINE TAILORS*) to teach his students some important but elusive lessons. This novel was short-listed for the BOOKER PRIZE and won the *GUARDIAN* FICTION PRIZE. It was also the basis for a FILM ADAPTATION that provides visual metaphors for fiction's postmodern interaction of past and present.

Swift had established a characteristic perspective in his use of narrative by this time. His interest in history is typically present in his fiction as characters struggle with the present consequences of past events, actions, and choices: To explain one character's present circumstances, an entire nation's history may be necessary, or at the very least the earlier life of that character must be examined for the trace that leads to the present result. In 1988, Swift published *Out of this World*, a novel about a father and daughter attempting to heal a damaged relationship. In *Ever After* (1992), the protagonist must pull his life together after losing several family members and attempting suicide. In 1996, Swift won the Booker Prize for *LAST ORDERS*, a commemoration of the generation that fought in WORLD WAR II. In addition to novels, Graham Swift has published a collection of short fiction, *Learning to Swim and Other Stories* (1982). He continues to live and write in London.

BIBLIOGRAPHY

Higdon, David Leon. "Double Closures in Postmodern British Fiction: The Example of Graham Swift," *Critical Survey* 3 (1991): 88–95.

Lane, Richard J., Rod Mengham, and Philip Tew. *Contemporary British Fiction*. Cambridge, U.K.: Polity Press; Malden, Mass.: Blackwell Publishers, 2003.

Swift, Graham. "An Interview with Graham Swift." Interview by Catherine Bernard. *Contemporary Literature* 38 (Summer 1997): 217–231.

SWORD OF HONOUR TRILOGY EVELYN WAUGH (1952–1961)   This series of ironic novels about the impact of WORLD WAR II on English life consists of three volumes: *MEN AT ARMS* (1952), *OFFICERS AND GENTLEMEN* (1955), and *The END OF THE BATTLE* (1961; originally published in England as *Unconditional Surrender*). The events of the narrative are drawn from the author's real-life experiences as a somewhat older first-time soldier, and most of the characters correspond to the men with whom WAUGH served.

The protagonist is Guy Crouchback, Waugh's alter ego. Divorced from his wife for her flagrant infidelity, Guy is a member of the educated upper CLASS, descended from an ancient Catholic family; he is a gentleman but not an aristocrat. Waugh's elitism and class snobbery are apparent in his creation of Guy, but his insecurity comes out as well as he endows Guy with everything Waugh himself longed for in social status and family heritage. In the first volume, Guy locates a unit willing to take someone his age—the very unglamorous but honorable Royal Corps of Halberdiers. There, he becomes acquainted with several characters who recur throughout the trilogy: Brigadier-General Ben Ritchie-Hook, Frank de Souza, and Trimmer. The other important character in the first volume, Apthorpe, meets a tragically comic end. Guy's promiscuous ex-wife, Virginia Troy, and his courtly father, Gervase, are also introduced.

In the second volume, Guy relocates to the more exciting unit of the Commandos, also under the command of Ritchie-Hook; new characters include Colonel Blackhouse, the charming Ivor Claire, and Ludovic. The men train in Scotland for frontline action on the island of Crete, but they are defeated when unexpected cowardice nullifies the training Guy's fellow officers received. Guy rejoins the unglamorous but well-trained and efficient Halberdiers.

Guy's last military assignment takes him to Yugoslavia, where the British are supporting, much to Guy's surprise, the Communist rebels rather than the monarchy's loyalists. He finally manages to do some good in the war before returning to London at the war's end. An epilogue brings readers up to date with Guy's life in 1951, happily married and successful.

The Sword of Honour Trilogy shows Waugh at the height of his powers as a comic writer who also has important, serious points to make. As a strong right-wing conservative and a Catholic, Waugh uses humor as a stalking horse for his condemnation of the new ways that are crowding out traditions he cherished. War's mixture of the dangerous and the ridiculous and the military's mixture of pointlessness and efficiency provide Waugh with ample opportunities for verbal and situational IRONY and for passages of SATIRE as well. Even though the occasional coward receives a medal or an egregious mistake turns into a propaganda success, Waugh is not writing an antiwar novel. Instead, he is commemorating the effort of the nation to shake itself out of its GREAT DEPRESSION doldrums and discipline itself to the arduous—and morally compromising—task of winning the war.

BIBLIOGRAPHY
Blow, Robert. "Sword of Honour: A Novel with a Hero," Durham University Journal 80, no. 2 (1988): 305–311.
Heinimann, David. "An Ethical Critique of Waugh's Guy Crouchback." Renascence: Essays on Values in Literature 46, no. 3 (Spring 1994): 175–85.
O'Hare, Colman. "The Sacred and Profane Memories of Evelyn Waugh's Men at War," Papers on Language and Literature 20, no. 3 (1984): 301–311.
Phillips, Gene D. Evelyn Waugh's Officers, Gentlemen, and Rogues: The Fact Behind His Fiction. Chicago: Nelson-Hall, 1975.

SYRETT, NETTA (1865–1945)

A prolific novelist, short story writer, and playwright, Netta Syrett's first stories appeared in The Yellow Book, the illustrated literary quarterly, during the vibrant 1890s, and during her long career she published 38 novels, 27 short stories, four plays, and 20 children's books. Her themes and subjects were topical ones: socialism, the "woman question," Irish folklore, the labor movement, educational reform, aestheticism, and psychic phenomena.

Born in London, she trained as a teacher, but she soon turned to writing to make her living. Her earliest stories and novels deal with "the marriage question" and the New Woman; These include The Day's Journey (1906), Rose Cottingham (1915), and Drender's Daughter (1911). In 1938, her novel Portrait of a Rebel (1929) was made into a successful movie, A Woman Rebels, starring Katharine Hepburn. Syrett channeled her love for teaching into writing plays, travel books, and fairy tales for young people; typical are The Jam Queen (1914) and Tinkelly Winkle (1923). Her later novels often deal with psychic phenomena. These include Gemini, her last novel (1940). She died at a nursing home in London on December 15, 1943. Her works are not widely available, but they provide a valuable window on the mental, moral, and social climate of her day.

—Jill Jones

BIBLIOGRAPHY

Ardis, Ann. "Toward a Redefinition of 'Experimental Writing': Netta Syrett's Realism, 1908–12." In *Famous Last Words: Changes in Gender and Narrative Closure.* Edited by Alison Booth. London: University Press of Virginia, 1993, 259–279.

Owens, Jill T. "Netta Syrett: A Chronological, Annotated Bibliography of Her Works, 1890–1940," *Bulletin of Bibliography* 45 (March 1988): 8–14.

TEMPORARY KINGS ANTHONY POWELL
(1973) Volume eleven in the 12-volume ROMAN-FLEUVE known as *A DANCE TO THE MUSIC OF TIME*, *Temporary Kings* follows *BOOKS DO FURNISH A ROOM* (1971) and precedes *HEARING SECRET HARMONIES* (1975). The first-person narrator, Nicholas Jenkins, is growing old, along with his friends, relatives, and acquaintances, simultaneously reaching the heights of success and facing the limits imposed by age.

The story opens at an academic conference in Venice, Italy. Sights and sounds in Venice set off memories which in turn develop associative links to other memories, and the recollected scenes and characters from the earlier volumes constitute much of the first chapter. But the dance of life never stands still: Nick soon meets a young American, Russell Gwinnett, who plans to devote his doctoral dissertation to the late English writer X. Trapnel, a major character in *Books Do Furnish a Room*. Nick had been a good friend of Trapnel, and had been present at a key scene involving Kenneth Widmerpool, a kind of tragicomic villain in the series, his wife, Pamela, and her lover, Trapnel. At an exclusive Venetian palace, Nick and Gwinnett encounter Pamela herself, apparently involved with an American movie producer. Her husband soon arrives and an ugly row between them ensues. Pamela's repeated affairs, before and after her marriage to Widmerpool, have been a recurring mystery since she entered time's dance in *The MILITARY PHILOSOPHERS*.

Pamela agrees to tell Gwinnett about X. Trapnel, and they apparently are soon involved in an affair. Nick hears about their meetings at a distance; unlike the scenes that he witnessed during Trapnel's affair with Pamela, he now listens to others' accounts—an aging man, he is still in the dance, but no longer at its center. Insinuations about Widmerpool continue to crop up regarding his personal life and political dealings. Although nearly 15 years have passed since the end of WORLD WAR II, the survivors are still discovering details about it, and when Sunny Farebrother discusses the death of Charles Stringham during the war, he also hints that Widmerpool will be arrested for treason. The weight of suspicion mounts: Pamela has already suggested that Widmerpool will soon fall, so this new story bolsters her low credibility.

The climactic scene of the novel reintroduces Hugh Moreland, the composer who plays a major role in *CASANOVA'S CHINESE RESTAURANT*, one of the most admired books in the series, and who was among the participants acting out the Seven Deadly Sins as an after-dinner entertainment at Stourwater Castle in *The KINDLY ONES*. He is now terminally ill but still active. He conducts Mozart at a private party and afterward witnesses the last confrontation between Pamela and Kenneth Widmerpool, who has escaped prosecution but not public humiliation. Pamela exposes salacious secrets about their life together and about his political double-dealings as the partygoers are leaving. Her own death occurs in a manner that parallels but reverses one of the incidents she reveals. Again, Nick stands outside these events, learning of them later from eye-witnesses. Gwinnett's connection to Pamela becomes as melodramatically disastrous as her connection to Trapnel had been, but readers glean only hints of the details from letters they exchange.

As in other volumes in the series, music, painting, and literature all play key roles in the characters' lives and the plot events of this penultimate volume. Although the pace slows and the tones become sub-dued as memory gains ascendancy over action, the wit remains sharp. POWELL doesn't allow Nick to sink into sentimentality or to indulge in maudlin excess even though his past years vastly outnumber those of his future. As his friends die off and the center of attention passes to the next generation, Nick continues through the turns of life's dance with grace and good humor.

BIBLIOGRAPHY

Joyau, Isabelle. *Understanding Powell's* A Dance to the Music of Time. New York: St. Martin's Press, 1994.

Selig, Robert L. *Time and Anthony Powell.* Cranbury, N.J.: Associated University Presses, 1991.

Spurling, Hillary. *Invitation to the Dance: A Guide to Anthony Powell's* A Dance to the Music of Time. Boston: Little, Brown, 1977.

TEY, JOSEPHINE (1897–1952)

Born Eliza-beth Mackintosh in Inverness, Scotland, Josephine Tey was a private person who made few details of her life available to the reading public. She attended schools in Inverness and studied physical education at Anstey Physical College; afterward, she taught her specialty in English schools until 1926, when she devoted herself to nursing her invalid father.

Tey's first novel was published under the pseudo-nym "Gordon Daviot": *The Man in the Queue* (1929), also known as *Killer in the Crowd*. She introduced the recurring figure of Detective Alan Grant of Scotland Yard in this novel of mystery and detective fiction, bringing him back in varying degrees of importance in five more novels, including the popular success, *The Franchise Affair*. Her second novel in the Alan Grant series was *A Shilling for Candles* (1936); the year after it was published, Alfred Hitchcock used it for a FILM ADAPTATION, *Young and Innocent*. In *The Daughter of Time* (1951), Grant exonerates Richard III of the crimes that have been ascribed to him; the novel was a popular success, but critics fault its polemical condemnation of historians and its slant in favor of Richard's innocence.

Tey's interests in natural landscapes, fishing, and horses— particularly horse races—come through in her novels, but little else of her does. Her approach to detective novels is refreshingly free of formula, so that her novels appeal to general readers rather than to a genre segment of the popular market. She concentrates on character development and plot structure, and since Alan Grant is something of an outsider at Scot-land Yard, there is little emphasis on police procedures. Grant solves mysteries by applying his considerable intelligence, and he displays courtly and decorous behavior in conducting investigations.

Under her masculine pseudonym, Tey also pub-lished three adventure novels, nine plays, seven radio plays, and a volume of nonfiction. As Josephine Tey, she published two novels outside the Alan Grant series, *Miss Pym Disposes* (1946), set in a physical edu-cation school, and *Brat Farrar* (1949), the story of an impostor who takes the identity of the missing heir to a fabulous fortune and who also solves the mystery of the heir's death. Josephine Tey died on February 13, 1952, in London.

BIBLIOGRAPHY

Charney, Hanna. *The Detective Novel of Manners: Hedonism, Morality, and the Life of Reason.* Rutherford, N.J.: Fairleigh Dickinson University Press, 1981.

Roy, Sandra. *Josephine Tey.* Twayne's English Authors, 277. Boston: Twayne, 1980.

Talburt, Nancy Ellen. *Ten Women of Mystery.* Edited by Earl F. Bargainner. Bowling Green, Ohio: Bowling Green State University Popular Press, 1981.

THAT HIDEOUS STRENGTH C. S. LEWIS (1945)

See THE SPACE TRILOGY.

THEORY OF WAR JOAN BRADY (1993)

This novel won the WHITBREAD Book of the Year Award in 1993, making Joan BRADY the second American to win that prize (after Paul THEROUX). An author's note following the novel's text explains the little-known phenomenon of impoverished white children being sold into slavery in the years following the Civil War, indicating that the author's own grandfather fell victim to this abuse. Slavery, she points out, imposes suffering not only on those ensnared in it but also on succeeding generations of family members who are marked by the emotional trauma inflicted on a recent ancestor. In the case of the author's grandfather, several of his children became suicides, and among his grandchildren alcoholism was common. Her grandfather falls into a relatively small number of whites enslaved in this country; by implication, the millions of blacks enslaved in the United States between 1620 and 1863 must have accumulated enough heartache and misery to ruin the hopes of many generations.

The first-person narrator of *Theory of War* is the granddaughter of a white boy—Jonathan Carrick—sold into slavery at the age of about four. The narrator is confined to a wheelchair, a metaphor for the disabled condition her grandfather's suffering has inflicted on his progeny. The novel opens with the narrator attending Columbia University and seeking to understand the concept of truth from faculty members who have tried to reduce it to a method modeled on mathematics. She is sure that truth is something more complex and elusive than equations and proofs; her drive to understand truth in the abstract is entwined with her efforts to understand her grandfather's twisted emotional logic: She is decoding his secret journals with the help of powerful computer algorithms, and the story revealed is one hard to comprehend from the perspective of the modern world.

Her grandfather's owner, Mr. Stoke, had been an abusive, even sadistic man with an equally abusive son, George. Jonathan had been deprived of education in order to convert as much of his time as possible into labor and thereby into profit. He had been chained to the floor at night to prevent him from running away, and he had been beaten and abused in other ways, especially in terms of humiliation and degradation, on a regular basis. Ultimately, the only thing left inside him was hate unending and unmediated by the slightest touch of mercy or compassion. The first time he has an opportunity to fight back against George Stoke, he

attempts to kill him and leaves him for dead sure of success. Only years later does he learn the truth: George survived and went on to a long and distinguished career as a politician of the lowest ilk—which is to say he covered his district with federally funded projects and himself with glory.

Jonathan is virtually a wild boy after his childhood of enslavement. He goes to work as a brakeman on the first train to pull across the Rockies. Rootless and violent, he wanders on until he finds a reason to stop in Maine, where he unexpectedly finds care and receives the education previously denied to him. This education enables his to write the journal; the violence of the thoughts he records persuades him to encode it. Jonathan eventually experiences other changes; he becomes a preacher and a family man, but his soul has been bent from his earliest days, and without meaning to, he bequeaths his suffering to his children and grandchildren. Without any clear plan, he is looking for the opportunity to take his revenge on George Stoke, and when the chance arises he does not make the same mistake twice. Jonathan's life has been a study in emotional war, and he is well prepared for the oily politician his former tormentor has become.

Joan Brady captures the anger and frustration of Jonathan through the voice of her narrator, branded by her grandfather's anger as indeed the whole family had been. Her story is a condemnation not just of slavery but also of cruelty and inhumanity of all sorts, but most especially to children. The realism deployed in her novel prevents readers from dismissing it as fantasy, a hypothetical scenario, or merely imaginary lives: The dysfunctional life of Jonathan Carrick is a model for what the world can expect when cruelty is allowed to flourish unchecked.

BIBLIOGRAPHY

Cunningham, Valentine. "Handing on Hate." Review of *Theory of War. Times Literary Supplement*, 26 February 1993, 20.

THEROUX, PAUL (1941–)

Born on April 10, 1941, in Bedford, Massachusetts, Paul Theroux is one of two Americans (with Joan BRADY) to win the WHITBREAD Book of the Year Award, qualifying because of his lengthy residency in Great Britain. Theroux's novel PICTURE PALACE won this prize in 1978, the second year that a book of the year was selected from among the individual category winners in that competition. He is particularly noted as a travel writer, having produced best-selling nonfiction in this genre, including *The Old Patagonian Express: By Train Through the Americas* (1979) and *The Kingdom by the Sea: A Journey Around Great Britain* (1983). His novel *The Mosquito Coast* was a best seller in 1981 and the basis for an effective FILM ADAPTATION, and in 1985 he collaborated with Bruce CHATWIN on *Patagonia Revisited*. Theroux has also written two studies about V. S. NAIPAUL: An introduction to his work in 1972 and *Sir Vidia's Shadow: A Friendship Across Five Continents* (2000).

Theroux graduated from the University of Massachusetts in 1963 and entered the Peace Corps after a short period of graduate study at Syracuse University. He taught English in Malawi until he was arrested and deported for spying over an incident in which he carried a message for an opponent of the ruling government. Although he lost his post with the Peace Corps, he remained in Africa until 1968, teaching in Uganda. He married an Englishwoman in 1967 and taught in Singapore between 1968 and 1971, when he decided to write full-time. He had been publishing fiction since 1967 without great financial success; however, with the publication in 1975 of *The Great Railway Bazaar: By Train Through Asia*, he had a surprise success in the usually lackluster field of travel books. He resided for several years in England but returned to his home state of Massachusetts when his marriage ended in divorce.

BIBLIOGRAPHY

Amis, Martin. "Paul Theroux's Enthusiasms," *The Moronic Inferno: and Other Visits to America.* New York: Viking, 1987.

Coale, Samuel. *Paul Theroux.* Twayne's United States Authors, 520. Boston: Twayne Publishers, 1987.

THINGS FALL APART CHINUA ACHEBE (1958)

The title of this novel is an allusion to the poem "The Second Coming" (1920), by William Butler Yeats. The line indicates that the modern world is losing its coherence and disintegrating into a chaos that will give birth to unforeseeable new forms of power; considered in the context of the entire poem, however, this decline into chaos is the permanent condition of life, which is always falling apart and always being renewed. ACHEBE draws on this renowned symbolism, applying it not to 20th-century Europe but to 19th-century Africa, specifically to an Ibo (or Igbo) village in the British colonial territory that will eventually become the nation of Nigeria. Achebe's novel is an example of postcolonial literature and testifies to the lasting effects of the colonial experience on those colonized. For example, the novelist chose to write his masterwork in English, the language of the colonizers, in order to reclaim the right to narrate his people's experience in a manner that diverges from that of earlier colonialist writers such as Joyce CARY and Joseph CONRAD. His goal is to tell, as an African, the story of Africa's collision with European culture, and to do so in the language with the greatest political, economic, and cultural influence in the world.

Achebe uses a third-person narrator to tell his story, setting it in the village of Umuofia just before British traders and missionaries begin to transform it. The protagonist is a leading man in the village, Okonkwo. This character represents the old way of Ibo life while also demonstrating that the seeds of its undoing are already present before the colonizers arrive. In this way, Achebe creates a sympathetic yet dispassionate picture of precolonial life: It was not a world of ideal pristine perfection, but it was a coherent and effective form of human social organization. Okonkwo demonstrates both the strengths and weaknesses of that culture.

Ibo village culture emphasized communal harmony and cooperation but also rewarded individual excellence. Okonkwo is the son of a decent but lazy man who shored up no wealth to leave to his son; consequently, the son is thrown on his own resources to achieve his ambitions. Unlike his father, whom he repudiates, Okonkwo is a "self-made man." Through his drive to succeed and garner material comfort and social influence, he dedicates himself to hard work, self-denial, and delayed gratification. He is a strong and courageous man with a strong and inflexible will. Ironically, in the precontact period, he is more similar to Europeans in his self-reliance and individualism than he is to his own neighbors. But Ibo culture has self-correcting mechanisms that can curb and reform excessive individualism. When Okonkwo violates a sacred ceremony and accidentally kills the son of another man, the routine punishment is applied to him: His property is destroyed and he is exiled to the village of his mother's people for seven years.

During his exile in Mbanta, Okonkwo learns the value of communal culture under the patient instruction of his uncle Uchendu. He comes to appreciate the traditions of Ibo life encapsulated in the many proverbs he quotes. But in accommodating himself to the shared life of the village and the clan, he does not lose the inflexible component of his personality. Where previously he was driven by his will to pursue personal success with single-minded concentration, during his exile he shifts his focus to a similarly single-minded valorization of Ibo traditions and religious beliefs. This process is reinforced by the presence of Christian missionaries in Mbanta, who are dividing the spiritual allegiances of the villagers by making converts of some of them.

When Okonkwo completes his seven years of exile and returns to Umuofia, Christian missionaries and British colonial administrators have arrived there as well. Had his village remained in the same condition as it had been when he left it, Okonkwo would have returned in the perfect frame of mind to harmonize and cooperate with his neighbors. Instead, the old ways are already beginning to fade as young men choose the new religion and serve the interests of the new political and economic system the British have instituted. When his son converts to Christianity, Okonkwo must suffer the breaking of the father-son bond that he himself had earlier inflicted on his own father. After another young man publicly violates a sacred ceremony, Okonkwo becomes the doomed defender of his faith, destroying the Christian church. But Ibo culture is flexible and moderate in its values, and other leaders do not support his call for bloodshed and warfare. The Ibo recognize that they can survive by adapting to the new ways, not by clinging to the past. Lacking this characteristic of moderation, Okonkwo will not be able to survive the influence of European religion and culture on African traditions.

Achebe creates a tragic hero in Okonkwo. Like Oedipus and Hamlet, Okonkwo is flawed in a fundamental way that has come about through no fault of his own and that he cannot change with the emotional and cultural resources available to him. In the face of futility, however, he maintains his nobility of character. His experiences are thus universalized rather than particularized. Although he is a quintessentially Ibo man, his fall is not unique to his Ibo identity. Readers can identify with his ambitions, his goals, and his reactions to the stresses life places upon him: They can pity his end and fear that they themselves may be tested in the same way. Achebe's great achievement is to bring African experience to the world stage so comprehensibly and to bring world readers to the African experience so sympathetically as to build a bridge between the two.

BIBLIOGRAPHY

Innes, C. L. *Chinua Achebe.* Cambridge Studies in African and Caribbean Literature. Cambridge: Cambridge University Press, 1990.

Iyasere, Solomon O., ed. *Understanding "Things Fall Apart": Selected Essays and Criticism.* Troy, N.Y.: Whitston, 1998.

Muoneke, Romanus Okey. *Art, Rebellion, and Redemption: A Reading of the Novels of Chinua Achebe.* New York: Peter Lang, 1994.

Wren, Robert M. *Achebe's World: The Historical and Cultural Context of the Novels.* Washington, D.C.: Three Continents Press, 1980.

THIRKELL, ANGELA (1890–1961) A writer of popular fiction from 1933 until her death, Angela Thirkell produced more than 30 novels of English life set in Anthony Trollope's fictional district of Barsetshire. She was born Angela Mackail on January 30, 1890, and was related both to the British writer Rudyard KIPLING and to the Pre-Raphaelite painter Edward Byrne-Jones; both of these artists played a role in her life during her childhood, contributing incidents to her memoir, *Three Houses,* published in 1931.

Angela Mackail was married in 1911 to James Campbell McInnes, a famous singer of that day, and had three children, of whom two survived to adulthood. The marriage ended in divorce in 1917, and the next year she acquired the name she was to write under when she married an Australian military man stationed in England during WORLD WAR I. The couple relocated to Australia in 1920, traveling by troopship; the experience became the basis of *Trooper to the Southern Cross* (1934), the fifth novel Thirkell published (although she used the pseudonym Leslie Parker) and one of the few not devoted to life in Barsetshire. The story of an Australian doctor traveling home, as Thirkell herself did, by troopship, it has recently been republished to an appreciative critical reception.

The Thirkell marriage produced one son and ended in divorce in 1929; Angela Thirkell returned to London. She had already begun publishing stories in Melbourne, Australia, to eke out the family income, and in 1931 she began her professional career by publishing her childhood recollections. Beginning in 1933, Thirkell published vigorously (three books in 1933 alone) nearly every year for the rest of her life, with some disruption during WORLD WAR II (paper was in short supply in Britain, as Anthony POWELL notes in *BOOKS DO FURNISH A ROOM*). Her novels have been compared with the work of Jane Austen, and they appeal to readers in both England and the United States. The novels of her Barsetshire series form the main bulk of her output, chronicling the lives of well-behaved small-town English families in sympathetic detail. Among the most recognized titles are *Pomfret Towers* (1938), *Marling Hall* (1942), *The Headmistress* (1944), *Peace Breaks Out* (1947), and *Love Among the Ruins* (1948). Angela Thirkell also published short fiction in periodicals and a study of Harriette Wilson in 1936. She died on her 71st birthday, January 30, 1961.

BIBLIOGRAPHY

"The Angela Thirkell Society." Available online. URL: www.angelathirkell.org. Accessed on Feb. 9, 2004.

Strickland, Margot. *Angela Thirkell: Portrait of a Lady Novelist.* London: Duckworth, 1977.

THIRTEEN-GUN SALUTE, THE PATRICK O'BRIAN (1989)   See AUBREY-MATURIN NOVELS.

THIRTY-NINE STEPS, THE JOHN BUCHAN (1915)   The famous film directed by Alfred Hitchcock in 1935 bears only a partial resemblance to the novel that provided its hero and a few of the key story elements. Generally recognized as the origin point for the subgenre of the SPY NOVEL, *The Thirty-Nine Steps* follows the adventures of Richard Hannay, a mining engineer who is drawn into an international intrigue through an act of kindness directed toward a neighbor bearing a fantastic tale of conspiracies, impending assassination, and attacks on English soil. When Hannay finds the neighbor dead in his apartment, he must flee from both the police, who suspect him of the murder, and from the conspirators, who suspect him of knowing about their plans. Hannay performs repeated hairbreadth escapes and is actually captured at one point and must blow up a building to get away. All the while he works on deciphering his neighbor's little codebook, gradually figuring out the specifics of the time and place that the conspirators will strike.

Hannay is up against a mysterious organization known as The Black Stone; the ruthlessness of this group becomes apparent early in the story with the murder of Hannay's neighbor. This imaginary evil force allows BUCHAN greater freedom in setting his PLOT since he is not hampered by the need to remain within the bounds of historical facts. He can make his villains more aggressive than the agents of a real nation would be and provide them with all the resources and skills that exaggerate the tension produced by the pursuit of the hero (but that do not succeed in overcoming him). Since the story follows the format of a chase, the plot can be episodic, broken down into mini-adventures along the way, while simultaneously remaining coherent and focused, since all those smaller adventures build to the climax of the main adventure, adding more clues to the solution of the riddle and putting more pieces of the puzzle in place.

The action of the story moves along at a quick pace; the hero is also the first-person narrator. Since Hannay is reporting straight out of his own thoughts and feelings, Buchan is able to develop him as a believably resourceful character who is also a decent chap. Hannay has acquired a small fortune in South Africa, but the events of the story immediately thrust him into the world with very little else but the clothes on his back and the sum of his intelligence and his experience. He resorts to disguises and subterfuges, and Buchan provides him with an adequate supply of luck and a small number of coincidences to help him on his way. Buchan deliberately stretches credulity with the events of the plot—he referred to this kind of story as a "shocker" rather than a thriller—but he does not cross the line into FANTASY. By keeping the surprises and twists flowing rapidly through the story, Buchan sets a new benchmark for suspense in this novel that also became the blueprint for a new form of escapist literature.

BIBLIOGRAPHY

Cawelti, John G., and Bruce A. Rosenberg. *The Spy Story*. Chicago: University of Chicago Press, 1987.

Daniell, David. *The Interpreter's House: A Critical Assessment of John Buchan*. London: Thomas Nelson, 1975.

Webb, Paul. *A Buchan Companion: A Guide to the Novels and Short Stories*. Dover, N.H.: Alan Sutton, 1994.

THOMAS, D. M. (1935–)

Born on January 27, 1935, in Cornwall, Donald Michael Thomas began his writing career as a poet and a translator of Russian poetry (by Anna Akhmatova, Yevgeny Yevtushenko, and Alexander Pushkin) and earned great acclaim among critics in the United States for *The WHITE HOTEL*, which was short-listed for the BOOKER Prize in 1981.

Thomas was matriculated into New College at Oxford University and earned a bachelor's degree there in 1958 and a master's degree in 1961. He taught grammar school in Devonshire from 1960 to 1964 and was then appointed to a position at Hereford College of Education, where he remained until 1979. He began publishing poetry in 1964; his first translations of Russian poetry appeared in 1976. Thomas's first novel was a book for juvenile readers, *The Devil and the Floral Dance* (1978), followed by two works of FANTASY: *The Flute Player* (1979) and *Birthstone* (1980). Critics noted the poetic language of these novels; the books, however, reached only a small readership. In 1980, *The White Hotel* appeared first in England and seemed doomed to the same fate that had befallen his earlier works until American critics received it a little later. By the spring of 1981, the novel had become a best seller in the United States. It reached the Booker Prize short list that same year but did not have quite the same effect on British critics that it had had on Americans.

Thomas's other novels include the five-volume "Russian Nights" series of *Ararat* (1983), *Swallow* (1984), *Sphinx* (1987), *Summit* (1988), and *Lying Together* (1990); these novels constitute an exercise in POSTMODERNISM, for the story is about storytelling (among other things) and frequently reconfigures itself into new narrative channels. His novel *Pictures at an Exhibition* (1993) revisits the Holocaust and is set partly in Auschwitz and partly in London several years later. In *Eating Pavlova* (1994), he fictionalizes the last days of Sigmund Freud's life, once again mixing history and fiction. *Lady with a Laptop* (1996) follows the adventures of an English novelist who is teaching creative writing on a Greek island. Thomas has also written a biography of Alexander Solzhenitsyn. He continues to live and write in Cornwall.

BIBLIOGRAPHY

Brooks, David. "D. M. Thomas," *Helix* 21–22 (Spring 1985): 33–41.

Wetzsteon, Rachel. "D. M. Thomas." In *British Writers: Supplement IV*. New York: Scribner, 1997, 479–497.

TIETJENS TETRALOGY FORD MADOX FORD (1924–1928)

See *PARADE'S END*.

TIME OF HOPE C. P. SNOW (1949)

The third volume in SNOW's 11-volume sequence collectively known as *STRANGERS AND BROTHERS*, this novel provides a flashback, through recollection, to the early life of the first-person narrator of the series, Lewis Eliot. It thus provides the part of the story that would come earliest in the chronology of Eliot's life, making it a BILDUNGSROMAN that begins in 1914 when Eliot is nine years old and that overlaps with events up to 1933 out of *Strangers and Brothers*, *The LIGHT AND THE DARK*, and the early part of *The CONSCIENCE OF THE RICH*.

The events of *A Time of Hope* explain the conditions that set Eliot on the path he chooses and that form his character for better and for worse. The key formative event in Eliot's young life occurs when his father is bankrupted during WORLD WAR I, plunging the family into poverty and leaving young Lewis marked by a sense of insecurity that becomes a driving force in developing his ambition. His frustrated, demanding, doting mother is the other key influence, in addition to the poverty of his childhood, which determines the shape of Eliot's future. By the time his mother dies, during his teenage years, Eliot has already developed an emotional neurosis that will prevent him from finding happiness in marriage and that will cause him compulsively to prefer a woman incapable of loving him. He pursues Sheila Knight and marries her even though he knows that in her he will not find a lasting and meaningful love relationship.

From this marginalized origin in a provincial town as a member of a financially disadvantaged CLASS, Eliot eventually rises to a position of wealth, power, and prestige, but his success in the professional and political world provides only a partial fulfillment for him because of his impaired ability to seek love and claim it for himself. Although *A Time of Hope* is only one part of a much larger series, it succeeds as a reading experience independent of the rest of the books it belongs with: It provides the most intimate view of Lewis Eliot's personal life and thereby produces a greater emotional bond between the reader and the fictional world of the novel. It is critically regarded as second in literary qualities only to the excellence of the fourth volume in the series, *The* MASTERS.

BIBLIOGRAPHY

Ramanathan, Suguna. *The Novels of C. P. Snow: A Critical Introduction.* London: Macmillan, 1978.

Shusterman, David. *C. P. Snow.* Rev. ed. Twayne's English Authors, 179. Boston: Twayne, 1991.

TITUS ALONE MERVYN PEAKE (1959)   See The GORMENGHAST NOVELS.

TITUS GROAN MERVYN PEAKE (1946)   See The GORMENGHAST NOVELS.

TO LET JOHN GALSWORTHY (1921)   The closing volume of *The* FORSYTE SAGA proper, although not the end of GALSWORTHY'S attention to this fictional family, *To Let* rejoins the story of Soames Forsyte 20 years after the close of *IN CHANCERY.* The two children born at the end of that novel, Fleur and Jon, are young adults, but they have never met because of the split in the family that no one ever talks about. They fall in love when they both happen to be visiting two other Forsyte cousins who married, Val and Holly Dartie, at their horse farm. Afterward, they arrange further meetings secretly and even begin to talk of marriage.

Curiosity leads Fleur to learn of the story of Soames, her father, and Irene. Her mother, Annette Lamotte Forsyte, has taken a lover, and he supplies the story of Soames' failed first marriage and the protracted divorce. But Jon also learns this story from his father, Jolyon Forsyte. Jon is the darling of his parents, especially his mother, and he breaks with Fleur rather than bring Soames back into Irene's life. After his father dies, he immigrates to the United States, where the widowed Irene soon joins him. Fleur had inherited her father's possessive nature and felt toward Jon as Soames had felt toward Irene. Her options, however, are more limited, and she soon accepts the proposal of a young man her father approves of, Michael Mont. With this marriage, the wealthy Forsytes acquire a connection to an aristocratic title, since Michael is the heir to a baronetcy.

The title, *To Let,* equates to the American phrase "for rent," and by the novel's end, Soames has come to feel old and empty, like a vacant house. The older generation of Forsytes has passed away, as have some of the members of his own generation. Soames realizes that a way of life has also passed away: He is a Victorian living in a modern world that belongs to the next generation—the generation of Fleur and Michael Mont.

BIBLIOGRAPHY

Gindin, James. *John Galsworthy's Life and Art.* Ann Arbor: University of Michigan Press, 1987.

Sternlicht, Sanford. *John Galsworthy.* Boston: G. K. Hall, 1987.

TOLKIEN, J. R. R. (1892–1973)   A linguist, a medieval scholar, and the author of some of the most important works of FANTASY ever written, John Ronald Reuel Tolkien was born on January 3, 1892, in Bloemfontein, in what is now South Africa. His father worked as a bank clerk; although earlier generations of the family had owned a successful piano factory, it had dissolved in bankruptcy. In 1895, Tolkien's mother brought him and his younger brother home to England, and less than a year later their father died in South Africa, leaving his family virtually penniless.

Tolkien and his brother were educated at their home in Sarehole Mill by their mother, since she could not afford to send them to school, and since she was herself well trained in languages, art, and natural science. In 1900, she converted to Catholicism. Four years later when she died, her sons were reared by Father Francis Xavier Morgan at their mother's request.

Tolkien won a scholarship and entered Exeter College, Oxford, earning an undergraduate degree in 1915. The outbreak of WORLD WAR I interrupted his life: He had fallen in love with Edith Bratt, another orphan, while he was still a teenager, but they had been forbidden to continue seeing each other until after he turned 21. They were married in 1916 just before Tolkien departed for the front with the Lancashire Fusiliers. In France, he experienced the horrors of trench warfare and was present during the battle of the Somme; these experiences inform his descriptions of battles and ravaged landscapes in *The LORD OF THE RINGS*. Suffering from trench fever, he was returned to England to recuperate. During this period, he began writing down the stories that were posthumously published as *The Silmarillion* (1977), although he had been developing his narratives of Middle Earth for many years before then.

After the war, Tolkien worked for two years on the staff of the *Oxford English Dictionary,* and then he taught at the University of Leeds between 1921 and 1925. He concentrated on scholarly works, winning the Oxford position of Rawlinson and Bosworth Professor of Anglo-Saxon Studies in 1925. He held this post until 1945, when he was appointed Merton Professor of English Language and Literature at Oxford; he retired from Oxford in 1959. While living in Oxford, Tolkien became friends with C. S. LEWIS, whom he was influential in reconverting to Christianity, and he belonged to the INKLINGS, an informal association of thinkers and writers interested in imaginative literature and fantasy.

Tolkien made a habit of telling imaginative stories to his four children, and out of that family tradition and the encouragement of the other Inklings grew his first published novel of Middle Earth, *The HOBBIT* (1937). This children's book was a great success, and his publishers asked for more tales of this sort. He worked on the three volumes of *The Lord of the Rings* for some 15 years, including the years of WORLD WAR II, publishing both *The FELLOWSHIP OF THE RING* and *The TWO TOWERS* in 1954, and *The RETURN OF THE KING* in 1955. When a single-volume paperback edition appeared in the United States in the '60s, the books became a cult phenomenon that spread to every corner of the globe. Tolkien's fictional works form the foundation of the genre of modern fantasy: Numerous writers have drawn inspiration from the vast expanse of his imagined world, with varying degrees of success.

Tolkien kept revising and refining his unpublished stories of Middle Earth, seeking to create a MYTHOLOGY for England that would be a worthy but distinctive counterpart to the great mythologies of Greek and Norse traditions. After Tolkien's death in 1973, his son Christopher undertook the task of editing the vast body of notes and drafts his father created into publishable form. Indeed, more of Tolkien's writing has been published since his death than the amount published in his lifetime.

BIBLIOGRAPHY

Bassham, Gregory, and Eric Bronson, eds. The Lord of the Rings *and Philosophy: One Book to Rule Them All.* Popular Culture and Philosophy 5. Chicago: Open Court, 2003.

Carpenter, Humphrey. *Tolkien: A Biography.* London: Allen & Unwin, 1977.

Purtill, Richard L. *J. R. R. Tolkien: Myth, Morality, and Religion.* San Francisco: Harper & Row, 1984.

Shippey, T. A. *J. R. R. Tolkien: Author of the Century.* Boston: Houghton Mifflin, 2001.

TONGUES OF FLAME TIM PARKS (1985)

A mild SATIRE on the enthusiasms of Christian fundamentalist religion, particularly the practice of speaking in tongues, this COMIC NOVEL features a first-person narrator, Richard Bowen, the son of a traditional Anglican vicar. Their quiet routines are suddenly disrupted when Donald Rolandson arrives to take up the curate's position in the parish. A man of vociferous religious passions, Mr. Rolandson has come under the influence of the American evangelist Joy Kandinsky. At first, he makes his fervor known through a resounding "Aymen!" whenever Rev. Bowen makes a good point in his sermon; however, on the day the action of the story opens, Mr. Rolandson falls to his knees and suddenly begins spouting "words without words," as Richard describes it, or speaking in tongues. In a short time, this enthusiasm spreads even to the Reverend and Mrs. Bowen, and life at the vicarage undergoes a radical change as Richard tries to find the inspiration to speak in tongues himself but repeatedly fails to do so.

Although Richard narrates the story, the source of the conflict that drives the PLOT is his older brother, Adrian. A handsome and intelligent young man, Adrian enjoys his father's favor in spite of his rebelliousness, his burgeoning religious skepticism, and the clubfoot that Adrian hides from the world as best he can. Adrian remains untouched by the fervor sweeping through the Reverend Bowen's congregation. In contrast, Anna Bowen, the sister of Adrian and Richard, follows the lead of her parents and becomes one of the most dramatic expostulators of the new approach to expressing faith. When her fiancé, a missionary in training, breaks off their engagement, Anna sets her heart on Mr. Rolandson. The family dynamic becomes even more unstable when Mrs. Bowen takes in a boarder, Maggie. Mrs. Bowen's good nature will not allow her to see that Maggie delights in the manipulative destruction of any positive relationship she encounters.

When these ingredients have reached a full boil, the church goes on its annual holiday—even Adrian is compelled to join. But with Maggie's conniving, the event turns to disaster in unexpected ways and Richard finds himself in a position to help his brother. The comedy quickly converts to drama and just barely falls short of tragedy, and the Bowen family is never the same again. Tim Parks manages a tricky ending with skill, creating a smooth transition from droll witticisms to sober reflection. His introductory note indicates that his story grew out of personal experiences long past, and that he has fictionalized these beyond recognition. His portrait of the group psychology of the Reverend Bowen's church is sympathetic, avoiding easy ridicule, but his ending implicitly condemns the exercise of unbounded emotional enthusiasm.

BIBLIOGRAPHY

Fenwick, Gillian. *Understanding Tim Parks*. Understanding Contemporary British Literature Series. Columbia: University of South Carolina Press, 2002.

TO THE LIGHTHOUSE VIRGINIA WOOLF (1927)

When Virginia WOOLF wrote *To the Lighthouse,* theories of contemporary art consumed her thoughts. With little action and a stream of consciousness narration, Woolf's novel confounded some critics and delighted others. Combining themes of time, the end of time through death, and transcendence afforded by art, she produced an homage to her own mother in the story of Mrs. Ramsay and her family. The book's sections are labeled "The Window," "Time Passes," and "The Lighthouse." The three sections work together but in nonlinear fashion.

With its action completed in a single summer day, "The Window" introduces the Ramsay family on vacation on the Scottish coast. While Mrs. Ramsay's warmth and creativity attract all around her, her husband's cold logical approach to life often disappoints others, particularly his children. Mrs. Ramsay's compassionate character is revealed in her knitting a stocking for the son of the poverty-stricken lighthouse keeper and in her sympathy for his solitary existence. Much as Woolf's family had growing up, the Ramsays entertain a large group that includes painter Lily Briscoe, poet Augustus Carmichael, scientist William Bankes, and the academic Charles Tansley, a protégé to Mrs. Ramsay who irritates her daughters, Prue, Rose, and Nancy. Conflict develops between Mr. and Mrs. Ramsay when he counters his wife's offer for six-year-old James to cross the bay the following day by predicting that bad weather will prevent the trip. Woolf also emphasizes the traditional conflict between art or intuition (the feminine), and science or logic (the masculine). The first portion is further divided into sections, one of which is related from Lily's point of view, as she paints a portrait of Mrs. Ramsay. As the entire brood later sits at the table, Mrs. Ramsay realizes how tiring her job of keeping the family together can be. The children argue before bed about a pig's skull in their room, over which Mrs. Ramsay drapes her shawl, assuring her sons that the shawl represents a magical garden hiding the pig's head beneath it.

In the book's second part, the vacation home sits empty, symbolizing the desolation experienced by the Ramsays over the deaths of both Mrs. Ramsay and James. James's death appears especially tragic, since he was lost in WORLD WAR I, the result of mankind's technological advances. Mrs. Ramsay's shawl symbolically slips a bit from the skull, and droops further upon the death of Prue in childbirth. However, Lily and Augustus, the two artists in the group, return, their creative natures rejuvenating the atmosphere that scientific advances had served to depress.

In the third section of the novel, "The Lighthouse," readers are offered an out-of-sequence event occurring some years after the day celebrated in "The Window." Lily awakens and, dazed and sleepy, wonders why she is once again at the vacation house. At age 16, James convinces his father to take him to the lighthouse, while Lily completes a painting of a nontraditional Madonna inspired by Mrs. Ramsay. When she realizes that Mr. Ramsay and James must have at last reached the lighthouse, she centers a line in her painting, declaring it finished.

Woolf's interaction with her friend, art critic Roger Fry, who had staged London's first display of postimpressionist art, had always lifted and challenged her spirits. More than anything written by Virginia, *To the Lighthouse* proved Roger's theories about art. He had once produced a simplified, cubist version of a Raphael painting of the Christ child that provoked negative public reaction from those who desired a more conventional presentation. Woolf had always considered his painting a heroic act. When the artist Lily Briscoe reduces a Madonna and child to a purple triangle, Virginia pays tribute to her old friend and inspiration. When another character realizes that the shape of the object does not detract from the reverence in which artists hold their subjects, Woolf clearly communicates that readers should come to that same realization. She had drawn a figure in her later published diary, two blocks joined by what she termed a "corridor," which represented Roger's idea of balance in art. Her novel took the same form, with two traditional narratives joined by a nontraditional midsection.

Basing the novel on her own family, the Stephens, who often escaped to the ocean side when she was a child, Virginia developed a series of images depicting the family in various groupings. The novel's Mr. and Mrs. Ramsey clearly represent Woolf's parents, Julia and Leslie Stephen and, like the Stephen family, they have eight children. The lighthouse the Stephens had admired across the bay symbolizes in the novel as many different things as the people who observe it. To the Ramsay children, it offers adventure, and they celebrate their father's promise to take them there. Mr. Ramsay, who uses the lighthouse as an object of control, will never honor that promise. To Mrs. Ramsay, an expert at looking for and finding love, the lighthouse represents the center of her vision of family. To the lighthouse keeper and his handicapped son, it serves only as a place to live.

Despite their weaknesses, Mr. and Mrs. Ramsey hold the family together with a strong bond of love. American writer Eudora Welty later wrote, "Love indeed pervades the whole novel. If reality is what looms, love is what pervades—so much so that it is quite rarely present in the specific; it is both everywhere and nowhere at a given time." "Quite rarely present" describes what bothered many readers about the novel, which did not follow a logical time-directed sequence and hinted at more than it identified. Welty went on to proclaim the novel a work of great rhythm "that moves as waves of the sea move, and the rise and fall of the heavenly bodies that pass over the sleeping house. Rhythm is visible in the silent strokes of light from the Lighthouse, and sounds in the pounding of the waves. . . . It is administered in the blows of chance and fate." Woolf's writer-husband, Leonard, labeled it "a psychological poem," declaring it original, something totally new. Roger Fry stated it was by far the best of Woolf's writings, while writer E. M. FORSTER told Woolf it was "very beautiful both in (non-radiant) colour and shape, it stirs me much more to questions of whether and why than anything else you have written." While contemporary reviews were mixed, the novel outsold Woolf's three previous novels.

—*Virginia Brackett*

BIBLIOGRAPHY

Curtis, Vanessa. *Virginia Woolf's Women*. Madison: University of Wisconsin Press, 2002.

Hussey, Mark. *Virginia Woolf: A–Z.* Oxford: Oxford University Press, 1995.

Woolf, Virginia. *The Diary of Virginia Woolf.* Vol. 3. New York: Harcourt, Brace and Company, 1982.

TOWERS OF SILENCE, THE PAUL SCOTT (1971)

Volume three in *The RAJ QUARTET,* this novel continues the story begun in *The DAY OF THE SCORPION* of the Layton family at their second home in Pankot, an escape from the sweltering heat of the dry season. The narrative focus shifts, however, to the life of a retired schoolteacher, Miss Barbie Batchelor. She is a former colleague of Miss Crane, one of the chief characters in *The JEWEL IN THE CROWN,* and she rents living quarters at Rose Cottage from Mabel Layton, the mother-in-law of Mildred Layton and grandmother of Sarah Layton and Susan Layton Bingham, all characters introduced in the second volume of the series. Miss Batchelor makes the tragic error of accidentally discovering that Mildred, a woman overly fond of gin, is engaged in an affair with a British officer. Mildred decides to destroy Miss Batchelor's social standing and credibility to protect her own; she also wishes to live in Rose Cottage with her daughters in place of Miss Batchelor.

The death of Mabel Layton provides Mildred with a pretext for evicting Miss Batchelor, who makes a chaotic and disastrous retreat and is ultimately stranded in a nursing home. Within sight of the home are the "towers of silence" of the title: the place where the Parsee (or Parsi) CLASS—an upper-class non-Hindu element in Indian society—leaves the bodies of its dead to be stripped to the bones by vultures. The image is a key metaphor for this volume of the series: The Raj is a dead body left exposed to scavengers, and soon even its fleshless bones will be scattered.

Before her own death occurs, Miss Batchelor accidentally encounters Ronald Merrick at Rose Cottage when she goes there to collect her few remaining things. The Laytons are away; Sarah Layton is having an abortion in Calcutta. Merrick is another link to Miss Crane, since he had investigated her death. Miss Batchelor's connection to Miss Crane carries the narrative back to the past in places, providing readers with a new perspective on the events first recounted in *The Jewel in the Crown.* Additional flashbacks fill out the stories of Teddie Bingham and Susan Layton. From *The Day of the Scorpion,* readers know that Teddie has died. Now his widow's vulnerability leads to her complete mental collapse after the birth of her son by Teddie. By the novel's end, when Miss Batchelor dies, the three remaining women face uncertain futures, as does the British Raj and INDIA itself. These stories conclude in *The DIVISION OF THE SPOILS,* the last volume of the series.

BIBLIOGRAPHY

Childs, Peter. *Paul Scott's* Raj Quartet: *History and Division.* Victoria, B.C.: University of Victoria, 1998.

Rao, K. Bhaskara. *Paul Scott.* Twayne's English Authors, 285. Boston: Twayne, 1980.

TRAINSPOTTING IRVINE WELSH (1993)

The American edition of this novel partially written in Scottish dialect includes a useful glossary, although most words unfamiliar to American readers will eventually be explained by contextual clues or overt glosses. In terms of its reading comprehension challenge, the novel resembles *A CLOCKWORK ORANGE* by Anthony BURGESS; its characters also share more than a passing similarity to that novel's protagonist, Alex, and his gang of droogs as they commit mayhem in the opening sequences. The key difference is that Alex seems to belong to a DYSTOPIAN future, while the characters of *Trainspotting* seem to belong to the kind of present-day sordid news stories that appeal to media outlets specializing in sensationalism. In Welsh's vision, dystopian literature comes to roost in a realistically rendered present-day world: Dystopia is no longer the thing that we fear may come to pass but is instead the world around us in the here and now.

This story of working-CLASS "schemies"—people reared in the ghettoized environment of Edinburgh schemes, or public housing projects—focuses on the joblessness and hopelessness of young adults on public welfare who self-medicate with drugs and alcohol. The nickname "schemies" seems doubly apt, since some of the characters are involved in illicit activities such as welfare fraud, and their lives are plunging downward on trajectories that seem to be aimed, albeit artlessly, at death or prison. The novel features the raw language and degraded behaviors of heroin addicts and soccer hooligans: Readers repulsed by the idea of a scene involving a junkie retrieving heroin suppositories from a backed-up toilet should stop before reaching chapter two. The author seems to make a point of violating every taboo, short of necrophilia, regarding the bodies and bodily functions of men and to a lesser extent of women.

The novel is constructed as a series of interlinking short stories featuring a cast of recurring characters who grew up and attended school together and who are spending their 20s unavoidably unemployed and stoned or drunk or both. The author's narrative strategy changes from one segment to another, frequently taking the form of first-person point of view; as the novel unfolds, however, the first-person narrator is slowly displaced by a third-person observer. The most frequent narrator—and the character with whom the novel opens and closes—is Mark Renton, also known as Rents or Rent Boy. Mark's best friend through the first half of the book is Sick Boy, or Simon Williamson, but slowly the more mundane Danny "Spud" Murphy fills the best-friend slot. At various times, these young men are either addicted to heroin or in withdrawal—intended or enforced—from it, as are their friends Rab "Second Prize" McLaughlin, Frank Begbie, Matty Connell, Tommy Laurence, and Johnny "Mother Superior" Swan. Before the novel's end, some of the main characters have become infected with HIV, some have lost limbs to gangrene, some have died, and some have amplified their drugged isolation through the betrayal of friends.

WELSH'S grim picture is relieved by the cynical humor of his characters, by Mark's clear-sighted honesty about himself, and by darkly comic episodes that are frequently as painful as they are funny. The characters are steeped—marinated—*pickled*—in irony; however, Welsh is almost old-fashioned in his avoidance of AMBIGUITY. He constructs a logical decline for each character: The handsome ladies' man turns to pimping, the angry boy becomes a thief, the weak-willed and the slow-witted die, and the ubiquitous friend betrays his mates. Along the way, Welsh finds moments of mercy and glimmers of humanity in these grotesquely hardened castaways of the modern urban world.

BIBLIOGRAPHY

Freeman, Alan. "Ghosts in Sunny Leith: Irvine Welsh's *Trainspotting*." In *Studies in Scottish Fiction, 1945 to the Present.* Edited by Susanne Hagemann. Frankfurt: Peter Lang, 1996, 251–62.

Milne, Drew. "The Fiction of James Kelman and Irvine Welsh: Accents, Speech and Writing." In *Contemporary British Fiction.* Edited by Richard J. Lane, Rod Mengham, and Philip Tew. Cambridge, U.K.: Polity Press, 2003, 158–173.

Paget, Derek. "Speaking Out: The Transformations of *Trainspotting*." In *Adaptations: From Text to Screen, Screen to Text.* Edited by Deborah Cartmell and Imelda Whelehan. London: Routledge, 1999, 128–140.

TREASON'S HARBOR PATRICK O'BRIAN (1982)   See AUBREY-MATURIN NOVELS.

TREMAIN, ROSE (1943–)   Born Rose Thomson on August 2, 1943, Rose Tremain is the author of numerous award-winning novels, radio plays, teleplays, short stories, and plays. She was educated at the Sorbonne and at East Anglia University, where she earned a bachelor's degree in 1967; upon completing her undergraduate studies, she taught school for two years, followed by nine years of working as an editor or part-time researcher. Beginning in 1979, she taught at the University of Essex for a year and then part-time at East Anglia University, specializing in the teaching of creative writing. She has been a full-time writer since 1980. Tremain has been married and divorced twice and is the mother of one child.

Rose Tremain began her publishing career in 1973 with a work of FEMINISM, *The Fight for Freedom for Women,* followed in 1975 by a biography of Joseph Stalin. In 1976, she published her first novel, *Sadler's Birthday,* an unsentimental study of a former servant's life viewed from the vantage point of old age. Her next novel, *Letter to Sister Benedicta* (1978), recounts a transformation in the life of middle-aged Ruby when disasters strike her husband and children, requiring her to take the leading role in managing the family. *Restoration* (1989) is an example of HISTORICAL FICTION set during the reign of King Charles II; it was short-listed for the BOOKER PRIZE the year it was published. It follows the adventures of Robert Merivel, who establishes a minor role at court until he loses the king's favor and then must restore his life to some degree of order. Tremain turned to the difficult subject of gender identity in *Sacred Country* (1992), winning the JAMES TAIT BLACK MEMORIAL PRIZE for her exploration of Mary Ward's fictional quest to turn herself into Martin Ward in body as well as name. In 1997, *The Way I Found Her,* a BILDUNGSROMAN, was published; it tells of a precocious boy's summer in Paris where he develops a crush on a Russian novelist who disappears. Tremain's next publication, *MUSIC AND SILENCE* (2000), another historical novel, won the WHITBREAD Book of the Year Award for its narrative of an English lute player serving in the 17th-century court of the Danish monarch Christian IV.

Rose Tremain continues to live and write in England, dividing her time between homes in London and Norwich.

BIBLIOGRAPHY

Field, Michele, and Sybil Steinberg. "Rose Tremain." Interview. *Publishers Weekly* 240, no. 14 (5 April 1993): 50.

TREVOR, WILLIAM (1928–)   Born under the name William Trevor Cox on May 24, 1928, in County Cork, IRELAND, William Trevor has published some 15 collections of short fiction and 17 novels, along with several plays, adaptations of his work for other media, and two volumes of nonfiction. He matriculated at Trinity College in Dublin, earning a bachelor's degree in 1950. His creative impulses first found an outlet in sculpture while he earned his living teaching school. In 1952, having won an award for his sculpture, he relocated to England; in that year, he also was married. Increasingly, he turned his attention to fiction, publishing his first novel, *A Standard of Behavior,* in 1958; his second novel, *The Old Boys,* appeared in 1964 and won the HAWTHORNDEN PRIZE.

Trevor relocated to England in search of better employment opportunities: He taught at the PUBLIC SCHOOLS of Rugby and Taunton, and he also worked in advertising for a time. His early fiction focused on England and the English, but by 1978, in *Lovers of Their Time and Other Stories,* he turned his eye on the characters and customs of his homeland. He frequently examines marginalized characters or misfits in—even outcasts from—the social order. They are protagonists rather than heroes, and Trevor depicts then by means of psychological realism. Readers can understand the limitations and the failures of such characters because of the narrative skill Trevor brings to his stories, but he balances characterization with well-crafted PLOTS. He presents his ordinary working people of the middle and lower CLASSES in such a way that he keeps their dignity intact, avoiding SATIRE or caricature while also steering clear of maudlin sentimentality.

The excellence of Trevor's fiction, particularly his short fiction, has brought him numerous awards. He is a member of the Irish Academy of Letters and a recipient of the Royal Society of Literature Award, the Allied Irish Banks' Prize for Literature, and the Irish Community Prize. His novel *FOOLS OF FORTUNE* won the WHITBREAD Book of the Year Award in 1983; he received the same award in 1994 for *FELICIA'S JOURNEY,* a novel that also won the Sunday Express Book of the Year Award. He was named a Commander of the Order of the British Empire in 1979, and he has received numerous honorary doctorate degrees. Trevor settled in Devon when he became a full-time writer, and he continues to live and write there with frequent trips to Ireland, Italy, and Switzerland.

BIBLIOGRAPHY

MacKenna, Dolores. *William Trevor: The Writer and His Work.* Dublin: New Island, 1999.

Morrison, Kristin. *William Trevor.* Twayne's English Authors, 501. New York: Twayne, 1993.

Schirmer, Gregory A. *William Trevor: A Study of His Fiction.* New York: Routledge, 1990.

TRUELOVE, THE PATRICK O'BRIAN (1992)   Published in England under the title *Clarissa Oakes.* See AUBREY-MATURIN NOVELS.

27TH KINGDOM, THE ALICE THOMAS ELLIS (1982)   This novel is set in London, at Dancing Master House, in 1954. Aunt Irene (pronounced "Irina") owns this bohemian establishment and presides over an unusual collection of residents, visitors, and occasional invaders. As the story opens, the house shelters Aunt Irene's handsome but vain nephew Kyril,

her prescient white cat Focus, and little Mr. Sirocco, who came to visit and never left again. It is cleaned by Mrs. Mason, the painfully CLASS-conscious wife of a military man who has become a drunkard after losing his men in the war; it is supplied with both necessities and luxuries by a clan of Cockney dealers in second-hand goods and pilfered merchandise, the O'Connors. True to her bohemian ethos, Aunt Irene is an artist, but the media in which she excels—cooking and home-making—require a large and continually available audience, and so she keeps Dancing Master House at its full occupancy.

Irene's sister Berthe, the reverend mother of a convent in Wales, sends a guest for an indefinite stay—an 18-year-old postulant from the West Indies who lost her family in a tragedy. At first, Aunt Irene sees only Valentine's race, but others soon see Valentine's saintly quality: The cynical Kyril longs to seduce her, the superstitious Mrs. O'Connor is very nearly ready to worship her, Mr. Mason is miraculously resuscitated by her so that he swears off drink, and girls ready to fling their lives away in loose living consider taking the veil after talking to Valentine.

Although Aunt Irene is a likeable, generous, free-spirited woman, her choices are in fact usually either illegal or immoral or unjust: She herself creates the problems she suffers from. Valentine quietly expends her powers in fixing the problems Aunt Irene creates through her indiscriminate bonhomie, and she heals every other ill she encounters as well. She heals every one, that is, except one suicide: Valentine's saintliness encounters the limits of its powers in the face of self-willed death.

Nominated for the BOOKER PRIZE in 1982, this novel is more a character study than a tightly plotted narrative. Initially the story seems to be a satirical treatment of a realistic, albeit unusual, household; gradually, however, Valentine's supernatural abilities add a FANTASY element to the story without sacrificing realism. Although the novel opens with a single first-person sentence and closes in the same way, purporting to be an eyewitness account, the incidents and ironies that grow into a story are told by a third-person omniscient narrator who takes the reader into the minds of the key characters to expose their weaknesses and flaws. The voice of this narrator is the novel's most compelling attraction—wry, witty, truthful, poetic, and ironic—and is characteristic of the author's writing style.

BIBLIOGRAPHY

Allen, Brooke. "Saints and Sinners." Review of *The 27th Kingdom* by Alice Thomas Ellis. *New York Times Book Review*, 24 October 1999, 22.

Sceats, Sarah. *Food, Consumption, and the Body in Contemporary Women's Fiction.* Cambridge: Cambridge University Press, 2000.

2001: A SPACE ODYSSEY ARTHUR C. CLARKE (1968)   One of the most famous films of the 1960s began when director Stanley Kubrick contacted Arthur C. CLARKE in 1964 to discuss ideas for a movie about man's place in the universe. The narrative began with Clarke's short story "The Sentinel," about an alien artifact found on the moon; additional ideas were drawn from another Clarke story, "Expedition to Earth," but much new material was required as well. The screenplay for the film, which credits both Clarke and Kubrick as coauthors, and the novel, for which Clarke is the sole author, both came into existence out of the same creative process, in an intimate interconnection that is unusual either for FILM ADAPTATIONS of novels or for "novelizations" of films. *2001: A Space Odyssey* seems to be a story that took form simultaneously in the two media preferred by the collaborators who created it.

The story opens in the prehistoric past as early hominids hover on the brink of extinction. One day a crystal monolith appears along their path, searching for signs of potential intelligence. The monolith also changes the minds it probes, silently "teaching" the primitive man-apes to use tools, to eat meat, and to slay predators. Warfare is born, and thousands of years of adaptive changes ensue from it. Those changes in turn launch the human race into the solar system, and explorers on the moon make a stunning discovery when they excavate a crystal monolith. Since humans could not have placed it there, it must be an alien artifact, providing the answer to the question of whether other intelligent life exists in the universe—it does. Scientists examining the monolith receive the same treatment that their primitive ancestors did: It probes their minds and subtly changes them.

Without understanding what they will find, the American space agency mounts a mission to Saturn (Jupiter in the film version) without revealing the monolith's existence to the two astronauts, David Bowman and Frank Poole, who will head the mission. Because the purpose of their mission is kept from them but not from HAL 9000, the computer that runs the ship, Dave and Frank are soon threatened; in fact, only Dave survives the mission (although Clarke revives Frank Poole to observe the world of this novel's third sequel, *3001: Final Odyssey*). Dave continues the mission alone; his target is the moon of Saturn known as Iapetus, where he spots a monolith created on a huge scale. He decides to approach it in a space pod, broadcasting a running commentary back to Earth. Suddenly, his perspective seems to shift and he realizes that the monolith is some kind of a gate.

As he is drawn mysteriously along, he passes the flotsam and jetsam of unimaginable technologies. Then, in an unknown binary star system, Dave's ship settles down on the floor of a comfortable hotel room stocked with nourishing food, pure water, and television transmissions from Earth. Dave realizes that somehow he is being incubated within the larger of the two stars in this system, and the time slowly passes until one day it seems to run backward. He has been transformed by his stay in the "hotel" and has become the Star Child—no longer human and no longer limited by the constraints of matter and time. He floats at large in his home solar system, and his first act is to destroy the arsenal of nuclear weapons launched against this mysterious new resident of the sky. He doesn't know what he will do or what he is supposed to do, but he knows he has evolved to become an entity capable of fulfilling human destiny.

BIBLIOGRAPHY

Clarke, Arthur C. *The Odyssey File*. New York: Fawcett, 1984.

Hollow, John. *Against the Night, the Stars: The Science Fiction of Arthur C. Clarke*. San Diego: Harcourt, 1983.

Reid, Robin Anne. *Arthur C. Clarke: A Critical Companion*. Greenwood, Conn.: Greenwood Press, 1997.

TWO TOWERS, THE J. R. R. TOLKIEN (1954)

Volume two in *The LORD OF THE RINGS* trilogy, this novel splits the fellowship into three smaller units headed in disparate directions. As the story opens, the hobbits Frodo Baggins and Samwise Gamgee have slipped away from their friends to continue the quest to Mordor alone. Boromir is mortally wounded by orcs who kidnap Merry and Pippin, the other hobbits. Not knowing that Frodo has departed, Aragorn, Legolas, and Gimli follow the trail of the orcs westward, away from Mordor. The Nine Companions become the Three Hunters, racing to save their friends from certain death.

The pursuit carries them to the northern borders of Rohan, a kingdom of men granted separate sovereignty under Gondor with pledges of mutual aid in warfare. When the Rohirrim attack the orcs, the hobbits escape into nearby Fangorn Forest, encountering Ents, ancient treelike creatures. An unexpected reunion in the depths of the forest restores a previously lost member of the fellowship to his companions. With Merry and Pippin in the care of the Ents, the story shifts to the court of Theoden, King of Rohan.

The corruption of Gandalf's fellow wizard Saruman is a key element of the complex PLOT: Before any military action can proceed against Mordor, Saruman must be defeated. He has entered into a wicked alliance with Sauron, hoping to gain power over Middle Earth for himself, and he has marked Rohan as his first conquest. The battle takes the form of a siege at Helm's Deep; there the outnumbered forces of Theoden fight for survival. This battle would be lost were it not for the efforts of the Ents and the wild trees, the Huorns, bent on avenging their injuries at the hands of the orcs. Tolkien's dissatisfaction with Shakespeare's handling of story details in *Macbeth* inspired his resolution of the siege of Helm's Deep: His version of Birnham Wood really *does* come to Middle Earth's Dunsinane. The threat of Isengard—Saruman's seat of power—is neutralized, but not before one last plot twist sends Gandalf racing toward Minas Tirith with Pippin Took.

Frodo and Sam become entangled with Gollum, who agrees to guide them through Mordor; like Saruman, however, he is serving his own purposes. He knows of the evil that lurks atop the pass into Mordor, and his real plan is to lead the hobbits to their destruction. Along the way, the party is intercepted by warriors from Gondor under the command of Boromir's brother, Faramir, a friend and student of Gandalf.

When he learns of Frodo's mission to destroy the Ring, he tells them he would not stoop to pick it up if he saw it beside the road. Frodo, Sam, and Gollum continue into Mordor over the pass at Cirith Ungol, where the voracious Shelob keeps her lair.

As the middle volume of a unified trilogy, the novel ends without closure. Frodo and Sam escape death in Shelob's lair, but they are separated from each other; Frodo is separated from the ring and under the control of orcs in the closing paragraphs, leaving Sam at the gates of an evil fortress wondering how he can rescue his master. TOLKIEN splits this complex plot into two books of 10 and 11 chapters apiece. With careful attention to time, topographic detail, and the cardinal points, he spreads his characters out to their greatest dispersion, stretching the bond of the fellowship across Rohan, Fangorn, Gondor, Ithilien, and Mordor. Two master strategists, Gandalf and Sauron, are matching wits, enlisting allies, deploying forces, fighting, feinting, and regrouping for the even greater battles that will unfold in *The Return of the King*.

BIBLIOGRAPHY

Isaacs, Neil D., and Rose A. Zimbardo, eds. *Tolkien and the Critics: Essays on J. R. R. Tolkien's* The Lord of the Rings. Notre Dame, Ind.: University of Notre Dame Press, 1968.

Stanton, Michael N. "Humankind." In *Hobbits, Elves, and Wizards: Exploring the Wonders and Worlds of J. R. R. Tolkien's* The Lord of the Rings. Edited by Michael N. Stanton. New York: Palgrave/Macmillan, 2001, 121–130.

U

ULYSSES JAMES JOYCE (1922) One of the monumental literary achievements of the 20th century, second only to JOYCE'S _FINNEGANS WAKE_ in difficulty, _Ulysses_ recounts the events of a single day, June 16, 1904, in the lives of Stephen Dedalus and Leopold Bloom. The story is set in Dublin, Joyce's hometown, and makes effective use of that setting to evoke Irish history and culture while also condensing an epic journey into a single day's events.

Loosely, Leopold Bloom equates to Ulysses, the Roman version of the Greek hero Odysseus, and Stephen Dedalus to Telemachus, the son of Odysseus. The novel extends the story of Stephen's artistic development and maturation begun in _A PORTRAIT OF THE ARTIST AS A YOUNG MAN_. The episodic PLOT parallels the events of _The Odyssey_ metaphorically while also exploring personal and family relations, the role of art in life, the mystery of human sexuality, and numerous other themes. Joyce uses distinctive styles in each of the 18 episodes in the novel, the most noted of which is stream of consciousness narration—a technique in which he was a pioneer, along with Dorothy RICHARDSON and Virginia WOOLF.

The novel begins in the morning with Stephen Dedalus, who had been summoned from Paris to Dublin when his mother was dying. Stephen has rejected religion and had refused to pray for his mother's soul when she had begged him to. Catholicism, however, has left its mark on him, and his refusal to pray—and the effect it had on his dying mother—haunts him. As the novel opens, it is early morning; Stephen is staying with Buck Mulligan, a medical student, who begins his day with the ritual of shaving. Joyce's description of the implements, the towel, the water, and Buck's use of these items endows them with the sacredness associated with religious ritual and its comforting familiarity. Stephen is uncomfortable at home and enjoys the companionship of his peers, but the dissolute lives of college students seem to undermine his ambition and his intellectual ideals. His distaste, however, does not prevent him from accompanying his friends to pubs and even to a brothel later this day.

The narrative dwells a bit longer on Stephen, following him to his job as a teacher, where he is reminded of his own childhood as he works with a dilatory pupil. On this particular day, the school has a half-day off, making the students restless and disruptive. When work is finally over at midday, Stephen walks to the beach, where Leopold will later surreptitiously observe Gertie McDowell while Molly keeps her tryst with Blazes Boylan. All Stephen sees at this hour is the surf rolling the decaying carcass of a dead dog, reminding him of childhood fears that in turn lead to self-doubt as to his abilities.

The narrative shifts to the other main character as Leopold Bloom gets up to prepare breakfast for his soon-to-be-unfaithful wife, Marion Tweedy Bloom, or Molly. Leopold is an advertising salesman and a Jew, while Molly is a singer of limited abilities and larger aspirations. She is planning a concert tour managed by the unscrupulous Blazes Boylan, with whom she is also embarking on an affair. They have a meeting planned for later that day—ostensibly a business meeting between professionals, but betrayal is in the air. Like Stephen's mixed distaste and acquiescence for his student friends, Leopold feels a mixture of frustration and resignation with respect to Molly's singing career and the people with whom it brings her in contact—and the very likely possibility that she will not resist certain erotic solicitations. His love for Molly is tinged with his fear that he will not be able to retain his place in her life, either emotionally or sexually. Over breakfast, Leopold reads a letter from Milly, the Bloom's grown daughter; Milly's young adulthood places her parents in midlife, a ridiculous age when the desires of youth have not entirely worn off and the infirmities of age have not entirely set in. Leopold thinks of his other child as well—a son who died in infancy.

Leopold sets out on his day in Dublin, and his first order of business is to call in at the post office. It turns out that Leopold Bloom has an alter ego named Henry Flower, Esq.; under this name, the man who fears his wife's adultery is flirting with "Martha," the writer of the letter Bloom receives. He continues on, stopping idly at a church and then visiting friends on the way to a funeral. The theme of mortality reminds Bloom of his dead infant son and of his dead father, who had committed suicide. Stephen and Leopold cross paths at a newspaper office where Leopold is conducting some advertising business, and although they do not speak, it becomes apparent that Leopold knows who Stephen is. After a chat about the funeral with Mrs. Breen and a cheese sandwich in a pub, Leopold encounters Stephen again in the National Library. These glimpses of Stephen mark his progress through the day as he rejoins his friends and embarks on an afternoon and evening of carousing and dissipation.

In one of the comic set pieces in the book, Leopold gets swept into a disorderly brawl at a pub upon the mention of Blazes Boylan's good fortune from betting on a boxing match—he had earlier seen this man in a pub shortly before the appointed time for Molly's meeting with her "manager." Upon escaping from his tormentors, Leopold wandered on the beach where Stephen had paused for reflection on the dead dog earlier in the day. In the following scene, which is unobjectionable by contemporary standards, Leopold witnesses lonely Gertie McDowell as she experiences an erotic moment with herself. (This scene was a significant target of complaint in efforts to ban the publication of *Ulysses* in the United States.) While Leopold sits on the beach as a voyeur of another person's private pleasure, he knows that Molly is at that moment meeting Blazes Boylan to share pleasure that should by rights be his, and he is resigned to the fact that he has been cuckolded.

Leopold stops by the hospital to call on Mrs. Purefoy, who is there to deliver a baby. (Mrs. Breen had passed along the news in response to Leopold's news of the funeral—death and birth coinciding in their conversation.) He is concerned to see Stephen, the son of his old friend, still drinking with Buck Mulligan and other young men: Stephen appears to be living the life of a wastrel. Leopold joins the young men as they go to a pub for more drinks, where Stephen argues with Buck Mulligan. Afterward, Stephen and another student go to a brothel, Leopold trailing slowly behind, wishing to intervene and not sure how or whether he should. Each man has a nightmarish vision: Leopold compulsively pictures Molly and Boylan together, while Stephen imagines his mother's ghost pursuing him in the brothel to ask him to pray for her soul. Running from this vision, Stephen gets into a fight with two British soldiers, and Leopold brings him home for safekeeping.

Although Stephen is withdrawn and sullen, Leopold talks about art and ideas, attempting to draw Stephen out of his funk. He invites Stephen to take up residence in the Bloom home—in the space of a day, Leopold has begun to have a fatherly protective feeling toward Stephen, seeing him as a kind of proxy-son. Stephen refuses the offer, however, and leaves as church bells toll. He knows that he cannot remain in IRELAND and also pursue his ambitions and develop his talents. In the final segment of the novel, a highly lyrical coda to the wanderings of the two men, Leopold is asleep and Molly reminisces about her lovers, Leopold's courtship, and their years of married life. Her response to life is a resounding "Yes!"

A plot summary does not begin to capture the many layers and dimensions of the novel; students should plan to read it more than once in order to comprehend and appreciate it. The novel invites reflective pondering and repays the effort of a little research into its sources. Joyce published a chart or "schema" of the structure of the novel, listing the episodes, their parallels to Homer's *Odyssey,* the time when each episode occurs during the day, and the symbols, literary styles, and themes developed in each; however, Joyce's chart can be deceptive in its AMBIGUITIES.

BIBLIOGRAPHY

Benstock, Bernard, ed. *Critical Essays on James Joyce's* Ulysses. Boston: G. K. Hall, 1989.

Blamires, Harry. *The Bloomsday Book: A Guide through Joyce's* Ulysses. London: Methuen & Co Ltd., 1966.

Bloom, Harold. *James Joyce's* Ulysses. New York: Chelsea House, 1987.

Gillespie, Michael Patrick, and Paula F. Gillespie. *Recent Criticism of James Joyce's* Ulysses: *An Analytical Review.* Rochester, N.Y.: Camden House, 2000.

Hart, Clive, and David Hayman, eds. *James Joyce's* Ulysses: *Critical Essays.* Berkeley: University of California Press, 1974.

Kenner, Hugh. Ulysses: *A Study.* Baltimore: The Johns Hopkins University Press, 1987.

McCarthy, Patrick A. Ulysses—*Portals of Discoveries.* Twayne's Masterwork Studies, 41. Boston: Twayne, 1990.

Newman, Robert D., and Weldon Thornton, eds. *Joyce's* Ulysses: *The Larger Perspective.* Newark: University of Delaware Press, 1987.

Thornton, Weldon. *Voices and Values in Joyce's* Ulysses. Gainesville: University Press of Florida, 2000.

UNDER THE VOLCANO MALCOLM LOWRY (1947)

In this novel of an alcoholic's descent into a living hell on the Catholic holiday of the Day of the Dead—which is also the day of his own death—the protagonist is Geoffrey Firmin, a former British consul in Quauhnahuac (kwanAHwuhk), Mexico. The novel opens on November 2, 1939, exactly a year after Firmin's death had occurred. That day in turn had followed by one year the breakup of Firmin's marriage to Yvonne Constable. During that year without his wife, Geoffrey Firmin had slid into despair and self-loathing, resigning his position as consul and spending as much time as possible in a state of inebriation.

The narrative connection to the dead consul occurs through the recollections of his friend, Jacques Laruelle, a French film director. In a conversation with Dr. Vigil, who had met the consul once, they recall the events of the previous year by way of commemorating one man among the countless dead. Firmin had been murdered at the close of a nightmarish day, and as Laruelle continues on his own way, he reviews the events of the 11 hours that preceded the murder. The two men had been boyhood friends, together with Firmin's half brother Hugh Firmin, a left-wing journalist and possibly a gunrunner for the Republicans (loyalists to the ousted elected government and their Communist supporters) in the SPANISH CIVIL WAR. They had also been rivals in adulthood: Jacques Laruelle had had an affair with Yvonne during her marriage to Geoffrey Firmin, as had Hugh. In spite of these many years of familiarity, Laruelle learns something new when he hears Señor Bustamente's suspicion that Firmin had been a spy.

On the day of his death, Geoffrey had been drinking as usual, longing for his ex-wife and yet unable to forgive her unfaithfulness to him. Unexpectedly, she arrives in Quauhnahuac, and soon afterward Hugh Firmin arrives as well, looking for Yvonne and unaware that she had been gone for a year and had divorced Geoffrey. The three travel together to Tomalin, stopping for a visit at Jacques Laruelle's house; Geoffrey is distressed to see his half brother and his ex-wife together, and his distress provides a suitable motivation for further drinking. In a drunken hallucination, he sees two angels, one good and one bad, fighting to possess his conscience through persuasion, but Geoffrey lacks the will to follow the good angel's exhortations.

As the day unwinds, the travelers encounter a dying man whom they decline to help, only to see him robbed even in his moment of direst need. As Geoffrey's sense of his own wounded condition and of the world's futility increases, he begins to drink mescal, a beverage he associates with death. After a violent outburst against Yvonne and Hugh, he runs out in rage and they follow—stopping for a drink at every cantina they encounter. They become lost in a forested tract as they search, and eventually they hear a gunshot, not realizing that it was the sound of Geoffrey's execution in a nearby ravine. By this time they are stumbling drunk themselves, and Yvonne trips and falls, only to be trampled by a horse that had escaped from Geoffrey earlier.

Malcolm Lowry envisioned this novel as the centerpiece of a larger project inspired by Dante's *Divine Comedy* but also influenced by the legends of Faust, the overachiever who sells his soul to Satan in order to fulfill all his desires. Dante visits Hell in his epic poem of Christian exegesis; Faust is hauled off to Hell as part of his infernal contract. Geoffrey Firmin, it seems, chooses to go to Hell like Dante and yet is penned there against his will like Faust. Firmin also suffers from the existential dilemma of the modern world: Everyone has "dirty hands," as Jean Paul Sartre noted, and Firmin's hands may have on them the blood of inhuman deeds done during WORLD WAR I. Yvonne has her infidelities on her hands; Hugh has his gunrunning and the piece of incriminating evidence he leaves in the pocket of Geoffrey's jacket while wearing it. There is no lack of guilt to spread around among the characters, and no shortage of cruelty at large in the world they occupy, but there is a great gaping need for love, self-love, and forgiveness. Lowry's own life was very nearly as disastrous as that of Geoffrey Firmin, and so *Under the Volcano* stands alone, a fragment of the intended larger story set at the nadir of the hero's journey, allowing him to reach Hell but providing him with no road back.

BIBLIOGRAPHY

Asals, Frederick. *The Making of Malcolm Lowry's* Under the Volcano. Athens: University of Georgia Press, 1997.

Markson, David. *Malcolm Lowry's Volcano: Myth, Symbol, Meaning.* New York: Times Books, 1978.

THE UNNAMABLE   SAMUEL BECKETT (1953)   The third volume in BECKETT'S *Trilogy*, this novel follows *MALONE DIES*; it was first published in French and then translated into English by the author in 1958.

The title character is also the first-person narrator and the protagonist of the loose, surreal, and comically absurd story. He speaks to readers of his awareness of his existence, but his description of that existence is not specific—he is aware of pressure points and infers from this awareness that he has a body of some sort. At times, he is reminiscent of the first-person narrator in *Malone Dies,* who seems to expire at the end of that novel; one way to approach this novel is to take the Unnamable as the lingering postmortem consciousness of Malone. Doing so, however, limits other aspects of the story. The narrator at one point, for example, seems to be trapped in the cave that Plato made famous in an ALLEGORY in *The Republic;* the consciousness of any individual is constrained to view the world through the body's eyes in much the same way that the prisoners in the cave are constrained to view the shadows cast directly before them on the wall of their cave prison. In any case, the Unnamable believes that he is being punished, just as prisoners are punished, although he does not know the nature of the offence for which he is punished. He thinks that if he can perform the proper penance (even though he does not know what that penance is), those who have power over him will finally allow him to sink into the nonexistence he longs to achieve.

Stories of other characters are intertwined with the Unnamable's torrent of self-examination; some of these characters have appeared elsewhere in the *Trilogy,* and some have appeared in other writings by Beckett, adding a possibly autobiograhical element to the story. Journey plays an important part in these stories: The character of Mahood, who eventually seems to be some incarnation of the Unnamable, returns from a journey so belatedly that all his family members have died before his arrival. Helplessness is also a key theme: at one point, Mahood is confined to a large jar near a restaurant, rather like a fetus in utero. Since he has lost his limbs and his power of speech, he must depend on the charity of others to feed, clean, and shelter him. The Unnamable is determined not to be deceived by these stories into believing that he has a life. Whereas Malone's narrative lurched to an ending in a more or less linear fashion, the Unnamable is on a recursive path, and his story terminates as it began, focused on the tears of hopeless frustration that he sheds as he realizes he will never be free of the burden of his tormented existence.

BIBLIOGRAPHY

Fletcher, John. *The Novels of Samuel Beckett.* New York: Barnes & Noble, Inc., 1970.

O'Hara, John. *Twentieth Century Interpretations of* Malloy, Malone Dies, The Unnamable: *A Collection of Critical Essays.* Englewood Cliffs, N.J.: Prentice Hall, 1970.

Webb, Eugene. *Samuel Beckett: A Study of His Novels.* Seattle: University of Washington Press, 1970.

UNSWORTH, BARRY (1930–)

Author of SACRED HUNGER, which was a cowinner of the BOOKER PRIZE in 1992, with *The* ENGLISH PATIENT, Barry Forster Unsworth is noted as a historical novelist. He was born to a middle-CLASS family on August 10, 1930, in Durham, England, and educated at the University of Manchester, where he earned an undergraduate degree in 1951. Immediately after college, he served for two years in the British Army's Royal Corps of Signals, at the rank of lieutenant. In 1959, he was married; he and his wife have three children. Unsworth spent several years at a variety of teaching posts, including the University of Athens in Greece, Norwood Technical College, the University of Istanbul in Turkey, Liverpool University, Lund University in Sweden, and the Iowa Writers' Workshop, among others.

Barry Unsworth has published some 15 novels, beginning in 1966 with *The Partnership,* a contemporary story about two men whose business alliance is ruined by a repressed homosexual desire on the part of one of them. His third novel, *The Hide* (1970), about a rape, is also set in the contemporary world, but Unsworth's typical location is in the past. In 1974, he won the Heinemann Award for his novel *Mooncranker's Gift,* about a work of art that challenges the concept of the sacred. He has set two novels in the dying days of the Ottoman Empire during the early 20th century: *Pascali's Island* (1980; published in the United States as *The Idol Hunter*) and *The Rage of the Vulture* (1982). He also uses Italian settings with some frequency: *Stone Virgin* (1985) and *After Hannibal* (1997) are both set in Italy, but each draws on events at differing times. Two of his novels are about writers: In *Losing Nelson* (1999), the protagonist is obsessed by the hero of the Battle of Trafalgar, and in *Sugar and Rum* (1988), a writer working on a book about the English slave trade of the 18th century suffers from writers' block. Writing that novel led Unsworth to write his most famous novel, *Sacred Hunger,* which is the novel that had blocked the protagonist of *Sugar and Rum.* Unsworth has also written a novel set during the medieval era, *Morality Play,* that draws on some of the conventions of MYSTERY AND DETECTIVE convention while also serving as a commentary on art—particularly theatrical art—and its role in the larger world.

Unsworth bought a house in Italy after winning the Booker Prize. He is a fellow of the Royal Society of Literature and has received several writing fellowships and an honorary doctorate from his alma mater. He continues to live and write at his home in Umbria.

BIBLIOGRAPHY

Kemp, Peter. "Barry Unsworth." In *British Writers: Supplement VII.* Edited by Jay Parini. New York: Scribner, 2002, 353–367.

UTOPIAN NOVELS

Speculative fictional works that present a world perfected of social, economic, and political flaws are categorized as utopian novels and contrasted with DYSTOPIAN NOVELS, their opposites. A utopia is an artifact of human ingenuity designed to facilitate human well-being; it is engineering applied to behaviors, institutions, and organizations rather than to materials and landscapes, and it is created for the purpose of maximizing human happiness and social stability. Utopian stories are as old as the Garden of Eden and Plato's *Republic,* but as a literary genre they date to the 1516 publication of Sir Thomas More's *Utopia* (originally in Latin). More coined the word from Greek words meaning "good place" and "no place." Francis Bacon developed his own utopia in *New Atlantis* (1627), as did several other writers in the wake of the discovery of the New World.

The late 19th and early 20th centuries provided fertile ground for utopian fiction as socialism rose in importance and COLONIALISM began to decline. In 1872, Samuel BUTLER published *Erewhon* (an anagram for "nowhere"); in 1888 Edward Bellamy's *Looking Backward* appeared; William Morris's specifically socialistic text *News From Nowhere* was published in 1891; and in 1905, H. G. WELLS published *A New*

Utopia. SCIENCE FICTION novels frequently feature elements of utopianism. Key plot elements include a mechanism for getting an outsider to the utopia and back again (or at least getting back some writing that forms the basis for the story). The outsider describes the features of this amazing world, interacting with the inhabitants of it, and provides the story to his or her own people as a service and a guidebook for improving their own world. Utopian fiction is generally optimistic and oriented toward solving problems and improving the human condition; dystopian fiction is pessimistic and implies that no improvement is possible.

BIBLIOGRAPHY

Carey, John, ed. *The Faber Book of Utopias.* London: Faber & Faber, 1999.

Manuel, Frank Edward and Fritzie Prigohzy. *Utopian Thought in the Western World.* Cambridge, Mass.: Belknap Press, 1979.

Nelson, William. *Twentieth Century Interpretations of Utopia: A Collection of Critical Essays.* Englewood Cliffs, N.J.: Prentice Hall, 1968.

Rabkin, Eric S., Martin Harry Greenberg, and Joseph D. Olander, eds. *No Place Else: Explorations in Utopian and Dystopian Fiction.* Carbondale: Southern Illinois University Press, 1983.

Snodgrass, Mary Ellen. *Encyclopedia of Utopian Literature.* Santa Barbara, Calif.: ABC-CLIO, 1995.

V

VALLEY OF BONES, THE ANTHONY POWELL (1964)

Volume seven in the 12-volume ROMAN-FLEUVE entitled *A DANCE TO THE MUSIC OF TIME, The Valley of Bones* begins the third of four movements in the series as WORLD WAR II comes to dominate the life of the world. The novel follows *The KINDLY ONES* (1962) and precedes *The SOLDIER'S ART* (1966). In it, POWELL introduces new characters who are thrown into the life of Nicholas Jenkins, the first-person narrator of the entire series, by the chaos and upheaval of war, but he also deploys familiar characters as well, maintaining the core focus of the novel on the lives of Nick and the young men he met in school such as Kenneth Widmerpool, Charles Stringham, and Peter Templer, all of whom are entering middle age as the war descends on them.

Having secured a commission in a regiment of the British army at the end of *The Kindly Ones,* Nick meets his unit in Wales. He has already reached the fullness of maturity, having published his first books and married Isobel Tolland; the war has separated the two of them as their first child is due. In Nick's new life, he comes under the charge of the morose and unfortunate Captain Rowland Gwatkin; another lieutenant in the unit, Bithel, is a chronic alcoholic—a theme that has already arisen earlier in the series in relation to Charles Stringham. The unit relocates for training in NORTHERN IRELAND, where Captain Gwatkin runs afoul of General Liddament.

Nick is on his way for training at Aldershot, in England, when he befriends David Pennistone, who will recur in further volumes. During training, he becomes acquainted with Jimmy Brent, who relates the story of an affair with Jean Templer Duport—the woman with whom Nick had first fallen in love and who had ended her affair with Nick in order, she said, to return to her husband. Nick gets a ride with Odo Stevens to visit the Tollands, many of whom are staying at the home of Fredericka Tolland Budd. There, he spends a short visit with Isobel and gets to see his new son. In the novel's closing episode, he returns to his regiment to find it in no better shape: Capt. Gwatkin is in love with an Irish barmaid and embroiled in a dispute with Lt. Bithel. Nick is relieved to be assigned to the DAAG in London, but when he arrives, he discovers that this person is none other than his bête noir, the tirelessly self-promoting Kenneth Widmerpool.

The exigencies of war take a toll on English life in this volume, and especially on English intellectual life. Gone are the evenings at art galleries and concerts, dinner parties and dress balls. Gone, too, is the order of the world that should allot responsibilities and abilities in correspondence to each other. Chaos breeds opportunism, and the Widmerpools of the world benefit.

BIBLIOGRAPHY

Joyau, Isabelle. *Understanding Powell's* A Dance to the Music of Time. New York: St. Martin's Press, 1994.

Selig, Robert L. *Time and Anthony Powell.* Cranbury, N.J.: Associated University Presses, 1991.

Spurling, Hillary. *Invitation to the Dance: A Guide to Anthony Powell's* A Dance to the Music of Time. Boston: Little, Brown, 1977.

VILE BODIES EVELYN WAUGH (1930)

A SATIRE that takes aim at the young adults of the Roaring Twenties referred to as "the bright young things," this novel recycles some minor characters from WAUGH'S previous novel, *DECLINE AND FALL* (1928), and uses a third-person narrator in various ways, including the creation of objectively described scene collections that resemble the cinematic technique of montage.

The protagonist, Adam Fenwick-Symes, tries to secure the finances to marry his fiancée, Nina Blount, repeatedly coming very close to success before bottomless naiveté or improbable events leave him penniless again. Adam finally trades his "interest" in Nina—a comment perhaps on the stock-trading madness of the era—to Captain Eddy Littlejohn (also known as Ginger, a character Adam had made up for his gossip column) for enough money to settle his bill at Shepheard's Hotel. War breaks out on Christmas Eve; Waugh explains in a prefatory note that the novel is set in the near future, so he is not referring to any real war. The novel leaves Adam stranded after a disastrous battle with an unscrupulous military man, a former singing angel from the choir of the American evangelist Mrs. Melrose Ape (a spoof on the notorious scandal-magnet Aimee Semple McPherson), and a case of champagne.

The novel's most compelling point is not its thin PLOT, nor its eccentric characters; instead it is the exposure and expulsion of human folly. As the story rambles from one popular venue to another (nightclubs, horse races, auto races, film showings, and other trendy spots), some of the supporting characters meet their deaths in gruesome or ridiculous ways; these deaths, however, are so distanced by the narration that readers' sympathies are not aroused. One young lady, swinging on a chandelier at Shepheard's, falls to her death; another is humiliated upon leaving No. 10 Downing Street (the British equivalent of the White House) in a grass skirt at an inopportune moment for attention to her attire. A gossip columnist, Baron Balcalm, commits suicide by turning on the gas after filing a completely fictitious story. And a leading light of the Bright Young Things, Agatha Runcible, fades away in a convalescent home after crashing a sports car at a race. Throughout the novel, the Bright Young Things, for all their sprightliness, turn out to be fools in the ordering of their day-to-day lives.

Another target of the novel's satire is religion. Mrs. Ape, on tour in Europe with her angelic choir, drinks hard and lives loose for all the pieties she mouths. Father Rothschild, a Jesuit member of the wealthy Jewish banking family, plots and schemes at posh gatherings of aristocrats. And Nina's father, Colonel Blount, backs a film ostensibly based on the biography of John Wesley, except that the plot bears no resemblance to the life of the founder of the Methodism.

The novel's great attraction is the tone that Waugh creates to make such folly laughable. The dry, straight-faced, droll delivery of ludicrous details redeems the weak plot and silly characters. Readers can see that these conventions are merely the superficial representations of deeper problems, such as shallowness and materialism, that Waugh's humor skewers, roasts, and serves up piping hot.

BIBLIOGRAPHY

Davis, Robert Murray. "Title, Theme, and Structure in *Vile Bodies," Southern Humanities Review* 11 (Winter 1977): 21–27.

Jervis, Steven A. "Evelyn Waugh, *Vile Bodies* and the Younger Generation," *South Atlantic Quarterly* 66 (Summer 1967): 440–448.

VON ARNIM, ELIZABETH (1866–1941)

Born Mary Annette Beauchamp in Australia and reared in England, Elizabeth von Arnim is noted for her novels of women's lives. At the age of 24 she married a German aristocrat and went to live at his estate in Pomerania, where the family remained until 1908, when debt forced them back to England. During this period, von Arnim began writing, and when she needed English tutors for her children, she hired the young E. M. FORSTER, among other future notables. She published her first novel, *Elizabeth and Her German Garden,* in 1898. This thinly disguised comic treatment of her life and her garden remains one of her best-known works.

Von Arnim's husband died in 1910, and she lived in Switzerland until the onset of WORLD WAR I, when she returned to England yet again. She had a short marriage to the elder brother—Earl Russell—of the famed philosopher Bertrand Russell; since the marriage produced no children, the title eventually passed to the younger brother. An autobiographical novel about this doomed marriage, *Vera,* appeared in 1921 and makes an interesting contrast to the comments about the marriage in Bertrand Russell's *Autobiography.* In the following year, von Arnim published *The* ENCHANTED APRIL, a sentimental work that took on a new life toward the end of the 20th century, when it became a FILM ADAPTATION as well as a stage adaptation on Broadway. Von Arnim also published a novel about an affair between an older woman and a younger man, *Love,* in 1925.

Although von Arnim's colorful life straddles the latter part of the Victorian era and the early part of the 20th century, her work has attracted very little critical attention. She was acquainted with many leading figures of her day and published fiction for more than 30 years. Elizabeth von Arnim died in the United States, her last home, in 1941.

BIBLIOGRAPHY

De Charms, Leslie. *Elizabeth of the German Gardens: A Biography.* Garden City, N.Y.: Doubleday, 1958.

Usborne, Karen. *"Elizabeth": The Author of* Elizabeth and Her German Garden. London: Bodley Head, 1987.

VOYAGE OF THE DAWN TREADER, *THE* C. S. LEWIS (1952)

See *The* CHRONICLES OF NARNIA.

W

WAIN, JOHN (1925–1994) Identified over his objections with the movement of ANGRY YOUNG MEN in the 1950s, along with Kingsley AMIS, Iris MURDOCH, and John BRAINE, John Wain was born on March 14, 1925, in Stoke-on-Trent, England. He matriculated at St. John's College, Oxford, where he became acquainted with some of the INKLINGS; C. S. LEWIS was his tutor, and his circle of friends included the future Shakespearean actor and film star Richard Burton. Wain was graduated in 1946 with a B.A. degree and continued his studies, receiving the M.A. in 1949. He married his first wife during graduate school, and immediately afterward he received an appointment as lecturer at the University of Reading. He left the academic profession in 1955 to earn his living from writing, and in 1956 his first marriage ended in divorce.

Wain began to establish his literary reputation with the publication of a book of poems, *Mixed Feelings,* in 1951. His first novel, *Hurry on Down,* appeared in 1953; it depicted the struggles of a university graduate to fit into a social structure that had no place for him and was quickly categorized with the works of the Angry Young Men. He produced a steady stream of novels; collections of poems, short stories, and essays; works of literary criticism; and autobiography. His second marriage began in 1960 and inaugurated a period of happy contentment, reflected in the title and content of his first autobiographical work, *Sprightly Running,* published to great praise in 1962. Wain received an appointment as professor of poetry at Oxford in 1973, and in 1974 his biographical work *Samuel Johnson* won the JAMES TAIT BLACK MEMORIAL PRIZE.

Wain's early writings set high expectations that his middle works did not always satisfy as he experimented with poetic and narrative forms, but his critical reception rose again in the later part of his career. *Lizzie's Floating Shop,* his only work of children's literature, won the WHITBREAD AWARD in that category in 1981, and in 1982 *YOUNG SHOULDERS* won the Whitbread Book of the Year Award. Wain continued to publish novels and poetry to the end of his life; he died on May 24, 1994, in Oxford.

BIBLIOGRAPHY
Gerard, David E. *John Wain.* Westport, Conn.: Meckler, 1987.

Heptonstall, Geoffrey. "Remembering John Wain," *Contemporary Review* 266 (March 1995): 144–147.

Salwak, Dale. *Interviews with Britain's Angry Young Men.* San Bernardino, Calif.: Borgo Press, 1984.

———. *John Wain.* Twayne's English Authors, 316. Boston: Twayne, 1981.

WARNER, REX (1905–1986) Born on March 19, 1905, in Birmingham, England, Rex Warner was the son of a dissenting cleric and a teacher. He was educated at an English PUBLIC SCHOOL, St. George's School in Harpenden, where he excelled in academics—especially the classical languages of Greek and Latin—and sports. He earned a scholarship to Wadham College, Oxford University; there, his tutor was one of the greatest classicists of the 20th century, Sir Maurice Bowra. His classmates and friends included the poets C. Day Lewis and W. H. Auden. Warner became interested in social causes and supported socialism as a better system of government than the British constitutional monarchy. He wrote political tracts advocating a worldwide alliance of socialist countries united behind the leadership of Great Britain.

Warner began his publishing career as a writer of children's literature and of allegorical novels, a poet, a polemicist, and a translator of Greek classics such as *Medea* and *Prometheus Bound.* In 1937, he published his first novel, *The Wild Goose Chase: An Allegory,* followed the next year by *The Professor: A Forecast,* and in 1941 by his most noted work, *The AERODROME: A LOVE STORY.* In this novel, Warner anticipates elements of George ORWELL'S DYSTOPIAN fiction *NINETEEN EIGHTY-FOUR.* In his later career as a novelist, Warner wrote historical fiction set in the classical world and featuring actual persons from the records of the real world.

From 1945 until 1947, Warner directed the British Institute in Athens. He spent several years teaching in the United States at Bowdoin College and later at the University of Connecticut. He wrote several scholarly books about the classical world and continued producing translations of notable ancient Greek playwrights and later of Roman writers as well. His prose was admired for its direct "Attic" style, and his novels continued to express his idealistic hopes for a better human world. Although his politics leaned to the left, as a writer, Warner opposed the subject matter explored so frankly by D. H. LAWRENCE. This stand makes him something of an opponent of literary modernism, but with respect to politics, Warner was opposed to the rising power of the most intractable opponent of modernism in the 20th century, Adolf Hitler. Rex Warner retired from teaching in 1974 and returned to live and write in England, where he died on June 14, 1986.

BIBLIOGRAPHY

Johnstone, Richard. "Novelists of Revolutionary Commitment: Edward Upward and Rex Warner," *The Will to Believe: Novelists of the Nineteen-Thirties.* Oxford: Oxford University Press, 1982.

McLeod, A. L. *A Garland for Rex Warner: Essays in Honour of His Eightieth Birthday.* Mysore, India: Literary Half-Yearly Press, 1985.

Tabachnick, Stephen E. *Fiercer Than Tigers: The Life and Works of Rex Warner.* East Lansing: Michigan State University Press, 2002.

WATERSHIP DOWN RICHARD ADAMS (1972)

The protagonists of this novel are rabbits who come to occupy the meadows of Watership Down in Berkshire, England. The novel had a double success in England and the United States: ADAMS'S English publisher sold it successfully as a children's book, while his American publisher marketed it to adult readers with equal success. The novel serves as an elaborate political and psychological ALLEGORY that examines several forms of government, contrasts differing kinds of character traits, and personifies the abstract ideas of courage, honor, loyalty, and kingship.

When the novel opens, the rabbits of Sandleford Warren have had a happy and secure life, but their leader, the old alpha rabbit, King, is losing interest in his duties just at a time when the world of men is about to impinge on the world of rabbits in a disastrous manner. A new development of houses for people is to be built on the land where Sandleford Warren is nestled, and the first task in the construction project will be the extermination of the native wildlife by pumping poison gas into their burrows. A clairvoyant rabbit, Fiver, sees the danger the future has in store, and several young buck rabbits decide to take their chances in the wilderness outside the warren and form a band to undertake this quest; they include the natural leaders of Hazel and Bigwig—Hazel reluctant to undertake the mantle of power, but an outstanding leader when he must be, and Bigwig more ambitious than his considerable talents warrant but ultimately realistic enough to concede to and serve the better leader.

In their travels, the rabbits encounter other groups before finding their own new home site. They visit a band of unhappy rabbits who have no leader, and at the opposite extreme they meet with rabbits under the thumb of a tyrant, Woundwart. There are struggles for power, threats to safety, and the bereaved homelessness of creatures who have lost their niche and cannot settle until they locate another one just as suitable for them. Adams treats his rabbit protagonists with complete seriousness, giving them all the accoutrements of civilized life, including a remembered history and an imagined future, a MYTHOLOGY and a language, a set of shared and valued customs, and a standard of ethical behavior. These protagonists strive and suffer and change, and they finally succeed in establishing their new home under the wise rule of a great leader.

Richard Adams has identified a key source of factual information for his fiction as R. M. Lockley's book *The Private Life of the Rabbit,* and he has denied that the novel is allegorical in nature. He began the novel as entertainment for his daughters on long car rides and other idle moments of family life and brought it to publication at their insistence. Despite the author's protests to the contrary, *Watership Down* makes an eloquent study of individual and social behavior, yet it can serve as a younger reader's introduction to the complexity of novelistic structure and literary conventions.

BIBLIOGRAPHY

Adams, Richard. "To the Order of Two Little Girls: The Oral and Written Versions of *Watership Down*." In *The Voice of the Narrator in Children's Literature: Insights from Writers and Critics.* Edited by Charlotte Otten and Gary D. Schmidt. New York: Greenwood, 1989.

Baldwin, Mark D. "The Birth of Self and Society: The Language of the Unconscious in Richard Adams's *Watership Down*," *International Fiction Review* 21.1–2 (1994): 39–43.

Miltner, Robert. "*Watership Down*: A Genre Study," *Journal of the Fantastic in the Arts* 6, no. 1 (1993): 63–70.

WAUGH, EVELYN (1903–1966)

A member of a literary family—his father was a writer and a managing director of a major publishing firm and his elder brother was a writer—Evelyn Waugh was born in London on October 28, 1903. He matriculated at Hertford College, Oxford, and was graduated in 1925, taking a degree in history. He taught at two PUBLIC SCHOOLS but was miserable in this profession, which he skewered soon after in his first novel, a SATIRE, *DECLINE AND FALL* (1928).

Waugh was married in 1927, but the marriage ended within two years. In 1930, his second novel, *VILE BODIES,* appeared; it was a satire of the "bright young things"—the hedonistic youth culture of the Roaring Twenties in England. In that year, he also converted to Catholicism, and was granted a dispensation for his first marriage and divorce in 1937, allowing him to remarry. After his first marriage ended, Waugh traveled in Abyssinia (modern Ethiopia and Eritrea), Africa, and South America, remaining abroad for three years. His experiences provided material for three collections of travel writing and for the novel *A HANDFUL OF DUST* (1934), a satire on frivolous aristocrats who come to tragic ends. His historical study *Edmund Campion,* about a Catholic martyr of the Elizabethan era, won the HAWTHORNDEN PRIZE in 1935.

Happily established in a union that would eventually produce six children, Waugh sought active duty in WORLD WAR II even though he was already in his late 30s when the war began. He continued writing and publishing during the war, and in 1945 one of his most important novels was published, *BRIDESHEAD REVISITED.* A popular success in terms of sales, the novel was less well received by critics. Waugh produced some shorter works immediately after the war, including *The LOVED ONE,* a satire that uses overblown American funeral practices as a stalking horse for his attack on modern hedonistic materialism. As with his earlier experiences teaching and traveling, Waugh's military experience became grist for his satirical mill, and he published a trilogy of satires on the war: *Men at Arms* (1952), *Officers and Gentlemen* (1955), and *Unconditional Surrender* (1961; published in the United States as *The End of the Battle*). These three were published under the collective title *SWORD OF HONOUR* in 1965.

A curmudgeonly critic of modern life and liberal values, Evelyn Waugh produced the most important and most successful satirical works in 20th-century English literature. He died of a heart attack on April 10, 1966, at his country home.

BIBLIOGRAPHY

Carens, James F., ed. *Critical Essays on Evelyn Waugh.* Boston: G. K. Hall, 1987.

Crabbe, Katharyn. *Evelyn Waugh.* New York: Continuum, 1988.

Greenblatt, Stephen J. *Three Modern Satirists: Waugh, Orwell, and Huxley.* New Haven, Conn.: Yale University Press, 1965.

Hastings, Selina. *Evelyn Waugh: A Biography.* Boston: Houghton Mifflin, 1994.

Lane, Calvin W. *Evelyn Waugh.* Twayne's English Authors, 30. Boston: Twayne, 1981.

WAVES, THE VIRGINIA WOOLF (1931)

The author's seventh novel, *The Waves* builds on the experimental framework of WOOLF's fourth novel, MRS. DALLOWAY (1925), in which she moved from the more traditional novel format found in her first novel, *The Voyage Out* (1915). Many critics consider *The Waves* to be Woolf's first mature work; in it, she attempts to capture the movement of the sea, a rhythm that had fascinated her since childhood. With *The Waves,* Woolf continued to develop the style and format that would eventually make her the most famous proponent of FEMINISM in the English language.

The idea for the novel had slowly grown in Woolf's imagination. On November 28, 1928, she wrote that she would wait to write until her next idea had "grown heavy in my mind like a ripe pear . . . asking to be cut . . . The Moths still haunts me." She referred to a story idea, "The Moths," that would eventually become her novel, retitled *The Waves.* By January 26, 1930, deep into the writing of the novel, she noted with discouragement that she felt "like a fly on gummed paper" when it came to *The Waves.* However, by February 16, she expressed optimism, feeling "the moth shaking its wings in me." In another month, she felt so exhilarated that she declared, "Children are nothing to this," as she, who had no children, gave birth to a work that by now seemed entirely correct. By April, she celebrated having "turned the corner" where she could "see the last lap straight ahead" on *The Waves.*

The Waves broke new ground in writing, as Woolf had intended. It focused on the lives of three men and three women. A seventh character, based on her dead brother Thoby Stephen, has a relationship with all six, and an important part of their stories is based on that friendship. Written in nine episodes separated by descriptions of time passing from morning to night, the novel was rooted in the vision of a sea creature's fin that Woolf had seen during a bout with depression. The fin could symbolize either hope or death, depending on whether it belonged to a dolphin or a shark. She had also envisioned her novel at different times in the form of a flower center that had lost its petals. Another image that had caught her imagination came from her sister's description of enormous moths flying about during one of her stays in France. With her artist's eye, Woolf hoped to incorporate all these visions in the manner of a postimpressionistic artist. Her final version she called a "series of dramatic soliloquies" written according to a rhythm of waves.

In the first interlude, the predominant imagery is the sun rising over the sea, as a woman casts light in a garden, awakening birds. Woolf incorporates much traditional symbolism, with the sea representing life and rebirth, light representing knowledge, and the birds representing the promise of freedom of spirit. The characters as children gather, speaking of subjects and images that will recur throughout the novel, including water, butterflies, flowers, and death, both of humans and animals; as flowers open, the sea is heard striking the shore, and readers are ushered into the second interlude. Various episodes follow each descriptive interlude, during which the children mature while in school, on vacations, and in chapel. They consider self-identity and their futures, with the women planning for families, the men for work. One female character, Rhoda, remains terrified of society, while another, Jinny, finds it strange that people sleep at night while she is exulting in dancing and parties, the very scenes where Rhoda feels assaulted by both men and women. By the fifth interlude, noon has arrived and sunlight abounds in the descriptions of various countries Woolf enumerates; she also focuses on shadows and the whiteness of house walls, as the ocean thuds like a beast on the shore. In the fifth episode, the character Percival dies while in INDIA, and the other characters lapse into grief. The sixth episode brings love to the character Louis as Ginny continues to party, and Neville, the most interior of the characters, expresses sadness over the weak ability of Christianity to affect the human condition. As the characters reunite in the eighth episode at dinner, they have become friendly strangers, some trying to impress others with their accomplishments. The ninth episode, set at night, represents a "summing up," concluding with imagery of waves breaking against the shore.

A carefully written novel that more closely resembled poetry than prose at times, *The Wave's* theme of alienation as a part of the human condition echoes that of Woolf's other novels. Although she predicted the novel would fail, critics appreciated its format, the beautiful word choice and imagery, and eventually declared it her masterpiece. Like Woolf's other books, it never went out of print. After Woolf's death, her husband, Leonard, placed a lead sculpture of her head close to the tree in their garden they had nicknamed "Virginia." He posted as her epitaph the closing words of *The Waves:* "Against you I will fling myself, unvanquished and unyielding, O Death!"

—*Virginia Brackett*

BIBLIOGRAPHY

Brackett, Virginia. *Restless Genius: The Story of Virginia Woolf.* Greensboro, N.C.: Morgan Reynolds, 2004.

Hussey, Mark. *Virginia Woolf: A–Z.* New York: Facts On File, 1995.

Marsh, Nicholas. *Virginia Woolf: The Novels.* New York: St. Martin's Press, 1998.

Woolf, Virginia. *The Diary of Virginia Woolf.* Edited by Anne Oliver Bell. Vol. 3. New York: Harcourt, Brace, 1982.

WAY OF ALL FLESH, THE SAMUEL BUTLER (1903)

Written during the late 19th century but published after the author's death in the early 20th century, *The Way of All Flesh* marks a departure from the uncritical celebration in literature of Victorian values; in fact, it is a sharp SATIRE on the institutions most revered by the Victorians, such as church and family, British formal education systems, and middle-class enterprise. BUTLER worked on the novel between 1873 and 1885 and was influenced by the theories of Charles Darwin; his insight into the ways new theories and discoveries would affect society makes him a prescient observer of the changes about to transpire in science and politics.

The narrator of the novel is Mr. Overton, the godfather of Ernest Pontifex, the novel's protagonist. Overton (his name is symbolic) has been a friend of the Pontifex family for years, and so he is able to provide an overview of the two generations of Pontifexes before Ernest, as well as Ernest's generation and that of his children. Ernest's grandfather, George, had been a publisher of religious books, and he coerced his second son, Theobald (Ernest's father) to become ordained in the Anglican Church in spite of the young man's resistance to this profession. Theobald is manipulated into courting the girl his father had selected for him, and the two of them rear three children through vigorous application of the rod. Ernest is naïve when he is sent off to the PUBLIC SCHOOL of Roughborough. Only the presence of a kindly spinster aunt makes his life more tolerable; without his knowledge, his aunt leaves a large inheritance for Ernest that will become his on his 28th birthday. Ernest's presence at school, and later at the university where he obediently studies for the ministry into which, like his father, he is ordained, provides satirical targets for Butler's acerbic attacks.

Ernest's misadventures take him to London, where he is betrayed by a friend for the small funds he has, leading to Ernest's arrest and imprisonment, after which his father disowns him. When he has served his prison term, still ignorant of the fortune that has been left to him, he marries a former serving girl to his family and they have two children, but the woman is a drunkard and makes life miserable. Ernest had thought to improve his lot in life through marriage and family, but his innocence leaves him unable to judge the true nature of other people or to see them in an unflattering light. Only through a chance discovery, with the subsequent intervention of Mr. Overton, does Ernest free himself from a fraudulent marriage. Rather than rear his children himself, he turns them over to a family with a better record of success than the Pontifex family has ever established. This PLOT twist essentially asserts that blood is not thicker than water, and that effective parenting is more important than the filial bonds of nature.

The Way of All Flesh appeared posthumously because Samuel Butler patterned the foolish Pontifex family on his own, even lifting particularly egregious passages from letters Butler's parents had written to him to serve as letters to Ernest from his parents. Literarily, it slams the door on Victorian assumptions and leaves open to the first generation of 20th-century novelists the possibility that rejecting the past and experimenting with the present can perhaps lead the world to a better future. In any case, Butler asserts, repeating the past and venerating its conventions can only lead to misery and suffering.

BIBLIOGRAPHY

Cole, G. D. H. *Samuel Butler and* The Way of All Flesh. London: Home & Van Thal, 1948.

Harris, John F. *Samuel Butler, Author of* Erewhon: *The Man and His Work.* Folcroft, Pa.: Folcroft Library Editions, 1973.

WELDON, FAY (1931–)   Born on September 22, 1931, in Alvechurch, Worcestershire, England, with the name Franklin Birkinshaw, Fay Weldon is a successful writer of short fiction, novels, teleplays, radio plays, stage drama, nonfiction, and children's literature. Her mother, an uncle, and her mother's father were all writers, and her father was a doctor. She spent her early years in New Zealand and returned to England at 14 to attend Hampstead Girl's High School; she then went on to St. Andrew's University in Fife, Scotland, where she completed master's degrees in the fields of economics and psychology in 1952. She gave birth to a son in 1955 and struggled as a single mother, finding jobs in journalism and advertising. Her experience of composing catchy, pithy tag lines for advertisements influenced her prose style, which features compact, epigrammatic sentences laden with information and insight. Fay Weldon has been thrice married, once briefly in 1958, again from 1960 until 1994, in a union that produced three sons, and a third time in a marriage that began in 1994.

During the 1950s and early 1960s, Weldon was already writing extensively in her spare time, but in 1966 three of her plays appeared on British television, and in 1967 she adapted one of them into her first novel, *The Fat Woman's Joke* (also known as . . . *And the Wife Ran Away*). Weldon's quintessential fictional subject is women, and the most common target of her SATIRE is injustice and inequity in the social arrangements between the sexes, although she also turns a keen eye on the injustices that arise among women as they cope with the injustices of the larger world in which they are contextualized. Her second novel was *Down Among the Women* (1971), followed, with a growing reputation, by *Female Friends* (1974). In Weldon's novels, women sometimes get revenge for what they have suffered from men; in *Remember Me* (1976), the ghost of a divorced woman haunts the husband who dumped her. In 1978, after an additional novel and numerous plays for various media, her novel *Praxis* was short-listed for the BOOKER PRIZE.

In addition to COMIC NOVELS and satire, Weldon has drawn on the conventions of the thriller in novels such as *The President's Child* (1982). Her most famous novel is THE LIFE AND LOVES OF A SHE-DEVIL (1983), which served as the inspiration for a 1990 FILM ADAPTATION, *She-Devil*. Other notable titles among the 24 novels she has published include *The Shrapnel Academy* (1986), about a group of visitors trapped at a military academy by a spell of bad weather; *The Cloning of Joanna May* (1989); *Life Force* (1992), a work of POSTMODERNISM that experiments with a fictional narrator who creates a narration for a further fictional character; *Affliction* (1993), about the changes in a long childless relationship when the wife finally gets pregnant (published in the United States as *Troubles*); *Worst Fears* (1996), nominated for the WHITBREAD AWARD; and *Big Women* (1997), published in the United States as *Big Girls Don't Cry*.

Weldon's nonfiction includes a hybrid work of fiction and literary criticism about Jane Austen that purports to be letters from the author to a niece (*Letters to Alice on First Reading Jane Austen;* 1984) and a biography of Rebecca West (1985), a writer whose life shares some similarities with Weldon's own. Weldon adapted Jane Austen's *Pride and Prejudice* into the popular BBC television version broadcast in 1980, and she has written more than 50 dramatic works. She has published five collections of short fiction and three works of children's literature, and she has edited a story collection for the British Council. Fay Weldon continues to live and write in London.

BIBLIOGRAPHY

Faulks, Lana. *Fay Weldon.* Twayne's English Authors, 551. New York: Twayne, 1998.

Herbert, Ann-Marie. "Rewriting the Feminine Script: Fay Weldon's Wicked Laughter," *Critical Matrix* 7, no. 1 (1993): 21–40.

Weldon, Fay. "Towards a Humorous View of the Universe." In *Last Laughs: Perspectives on Women and Comedy*. Edited by Regina Barreca. New York: Gordon & Breach, 1988.

WELL OF LONELINESS, THE RADCLYFFE HALL (1928)

A key text in the genre of lesbian literature, *The Well of Loneliness* was banned in England as a work of obscenity when it was first published, and it remained unavailable for the next two decades. The novel is a BILDUNGSROMAN, relating the development of a woman's "inverted" sexual identity as a natural outgrowth of family choices and parental influences. The protagonist, Stephen Gordon, acquired her masculine name when she was born instead of the expected boy. As an only child, she spends more time with her father than many girls might, learning to ride and hunt. In her first experience of love, she develops a crush on a family servant; she is seized with jealousy to see this woman flirting with a man. Her father recognizes what has happened to his daughter, but he cannot speak of it even on his deathbed. When Stephen responds to the attentions of Martin Hallam, it seems that all might be well yet, but Martin's proposal of marriage evokes only rage and revulsion. Stephen senses that something about her is amiss, but she doesn't clearly understand her situation until she falls in love with Angela, a married woman. This affair ends in betrayal, and Stephen is exiled from the family estate by her mother.

Stephen compensates for her empty personal life by constant work, and she succeeds as a novelist. During WORLD WAR I, she volunteers with an ambulance unit serving on the front lines, and although she cannot fight the war, she is wounded and decorated for valor. She meets Mary, another volunteer, and they fall in love and eventually live together as if married. Since they are shunned by "respectable" society, they socialize with others like themselves. Stephen has her work, but Mary is lonely. Unfortunately, the life of nightclubs and bars is no more fulfilling than the cold rejection they have received from mainstream heterosexuals. When they encounter Martin Hallam and he is obviously attracted to Mary, Stephen decides to make a sacrifice worthy of the woman she loves.

Radclyffe HALL's novel broke new ground in its sympathetic portrayal of lesbianism (a term she does not use in her novel) as a possible result of child-rearing practices; however, her picture of adult lesbian life is conflicted. It is a world rife with alcoholism, loneliness, and despair from which Stephen wishes to save her beloved Mary. In depicting Stephen in heroic—even saintly—tones, Hall sets her apart from and above both heterosexual and lesbian life. Stephen's sexual orientation is a cross upon which she martyrs herself and her love for Mary, but this effect is only achieved through a tacit collusion with and acceptance of the societal rejection of homosexuality as an abnormality or a disease. Nonetheless, the depiction of Stephen as a person of honor, courage, and nobility is a daring affirmation of the choices that a woman of strong character may make in spite of societal disapproval.

BIBLIOGRAPHY

Franks, Claudia Stillman. *Beyond* The Well of Loneliness. Aldershot, England: Avebury, 1984.

Newton, Esther. "The 'Mythic Mannish Lesbian': Radclyffe Hall and the New Woman," *Signs* 9 (1984): 557–575.

O'Rourke, Rebecca. *Reflecting on* The Well of Loneliness. London: Routledge, 1989.

WELLS, H. G. (1866–1946)

A prolific writer in numerous genres, Herbert George Wells was born on September 21, 1866, in Bromley, Kent, England. His parents were shopkeepers of modest financial means, and Wells had to work for a living from his early youth. He resolved to rise above the station to which he was born by becoming educated; in 1884, he earned a scholarship to the London Normal School of Science. There, he studied under the noted biologist Thomas Henry Huxley, an early defender of Darwin's theory of evolution and the grandfather of Aldous HUXLEY. Wells began a career as a teacher after earning a bachelor's degree from London University in 1890, but tuberculosis forced him into a convalescence during which he began writing. He published his first professional work—an essay—in 1891; in that year, he was also married to his first wife, a cousin. By 1893, he had completed *A Textbook of Biology,* which remained a teaching standard for several years. His first marriage had deteriorated into a separation by this time, and it ended in divorce in 1895, still an uncommon and socially unacceptable course of action. He was soon married for the second time to Amy Catherine Robbins, one of his former students; they became the parents of two sons.

In 1895, Wells also began producing the novels and short stories that gained him a place in the CANON of modern literature. *The Time Machine: An Invention* appeared in that year and marks the founding of English SCIENCE FICTION. Wells referred to this kind of story as a "scientific romance," distinguishing it from the writings of the French novelist Jules Verne by insisting on the importance of political relevance and psychological development. His other most important novels of this sort include *The Island of Dr. Moreau* (1896), *The Invisible Man: A Grotesque Romance* (1897), *The War of the Worlds* (1898), and *The First Men in the Moon* (1901). Many readers know Wells only as a writer of science fiction, but he also wrote numerous other novels that fall into two broad categories: novels of working-class aspirations to rise in the world, including *The Wheels of Chance: A Holiday Adventure* (1896) and *Love and Mr. Lewisham* (1900), and novels that Wells called "social fables," including *Marriage* (1912) and *Mr. Britling Sees It Through* (1916). His novel *Tono-Bungay* (1908) satirizes the CLASS prejudices and materialistic folly of contemporary British life.

In 1912, Wells sought out the young writer Rebecca WEST after she published a review of his novel *Marriage*. They entered into an affair that lasted some 10 years and produced a son in 1914; West raised the boy as an adopted child in order to spare him the social prejudices that could accompany illegitimacy. During this period Wells wrote one of his greatest popular successes, *The Outline of History: Being a Plain History of Life and Mankind* (1920), which sold phenomenally well and was translated into several languages. About the time his affair with West ended, Wells became interested in politics. He had been writing political treatises among his nonfiction works and he had belonged to the socialist FABIAN SOCIETY for a period early in its existence. In 1922 and again in 1923, he campaigned unsuccessfully, as a Labour Party candidate, for a seat in the House of Commons.

Wells withdrew from active politics but continued to write political works. He ultimately rejected socialism as a viable form of social governance. He also wrote extensively on the sciences, extending his reputation as a visionary. He predicted the development of massively destructive weapons and their use on civilian populations and lived just long enough to see history confirm his prediction. Wells died on August 13, 1946, in London.

BIBLIOGRAPHY

Batchelor, John. *H. G. Wells*. Cambridge: Cambridge University Press, 1985.

Hammond, J. R. *A Preface to H. G. Wells*. New York: Longman, 2001.

Parrinder, Patrick, and Christopher Rolfe, eds. *H. G. Wells. Under Revision: Proceedings of the International H. G. Wells Symposium, London, July 1986*. Selinsgrove, Pa.: Susquehanna University Press, 1990.

WELSH, IRVINE (1958–)

Author of *TRAINSPOTTING, Marabou Stork Nightmares* (1995), *Filth* (1998), and *Porno* (2002), Irvine Welsh was born in Edinburgh in 1958 and educated at Heriot-Watt University, where he completed an M.B.A. degree. He had earlier dropped out of high school and worked at various jobs; his talents include music as well as fiction writing. During the early years of the London punk scene (effectively described in Hanif KUREISHI's novel *The BUDDHA OF SUBURBIA*), Welsh relocated there and immersed himself in that emotionally volatile youth movement.

Welsh's fiction is noted for its raw language and its crude situations, but these features cannot hide the underlying keen intelligence that observes and reports on the seedier side of human existence. His uninhibited use of language is fresh and powerful and deliberately shocking, presented in a voice as distinctive in its own Scottish idiom as that of Holden Caulfield or Huck Finn is in American English. His plots present effective examinations of unsavory and even despicable characters: In *Marabou Stork Nightmares,* the narrator participates in a gang rape, attempts a suicide, and finds so much enlightenment in his coma that he resists efforts to restore him to consciousness, and in *Filth* the narration of a feckless police detective's investigation of a murder is occasionally hijacked by the narrator's introspective tapeworm. Welsh's depiction of drug addiction and other self-destructive recreational pursuits has been compared with the work of American writers such as William Burroughs; additionally, his prose draws heavily on the icons of popular culture. Welsh has also published short fiction and adapted some of his stories for presentation on television. He continues to live and write in Edinburgh.

BIBLIOGRAPHY

Berman, Jennifer. "Irvine Welsh," *Bomb* 56 (Summer 1996): 56–61.

Black, Alan. "Irvine Welsh," *San Francisco Review of Books* 20, no. 3 (July–August 1995): 30–31.

WEST, REBECCA (1892–1983)

Born Cicily Isabel Fairfield on December 21, 1892, in London, Rebecca West chose her pseudonym in 1912 from a play by Henrik Ibsen, *Rosmersholm,* and used it for the rest of her life. Her father, a charming man but never a financially successful provider, abandoned his family in 1901 when she was 10; Rebecca, with her mother and two older sisters, was left in genteel poverty at a crucial period in her young life, and by the time she was an adult she had resolved to improve her lot. She thought first to become an actress, but lacking the gifts to make a success of that profession she turned to journalism, with a modest beginning as a book reviewer in 1911 at the age of 19. She was a strong advocate of FEMINISM and produced a remarkably diverse literary record in a life lived on her own terms.

Rebecca West continued her work as a reviewer until the end of her life, writing more than a thousand reviews; these, however, form only a minor component of her life's work as a woman of letters. One of the first results of this work, however, was a personal rather than a literary event: H. G. WELLS sought an introduction to West after she reviewed his novel *Marriage* (1912), and the two of them entered into an affair that produced a son in 1914 and lasted some 10 years. In 1916, West undertook a work of literary criticism—a highly unusual project for a 24-year-old woman with no academic background—and published an insightful volume on the novels of Henry JAMES. Her first novel, *The RETURN OF THE SOLDIER,* appeared in 1918 and was well reviewed. In 1922, she published *The Judge,* a novel in two sections that combines a young woman's BILDUNGSROMAN with the story of an older woman's decline into suicide; the two women's stories are linked by the man who is engaged to the young woman and who is the son of the older one.

West continued her journalistic writing in the meantime, publishing a collection of essays in 1928 entitled *The Strange Necessity: Essays and Reviews.* By this time, her affair with Wells had ended, as had a subsequent relationship with a wealthy newspaper publisher. In 1929, her novel *Harriet Hume: A London Fantasy* took a new direction for her, adding a psychic element to a romance between a pianist and the politician she loves. West was married in 1930 to a banker, Henry Maxwell Andrews, who proved to be a devoted and supportive spouse. In 1931, she published *Ending in Ernest: A Literary Log,* another collection of her essays; in 1933, she published a biography of St. Augustine. By this time, West had begun to study Yugoslavia, that complex crossroads of cultures and religions, developing her studies into a monumental book that combines travel and history. Still considered to be an important work for understanding a difficult corner of Europe, *Black Lamb and Grey Falcon* appeared in 1941. In recognition of her work, West had already received the Order of St Sava from the Yugoslav government in 1937.

After WORLD WAR II, West covered the Nuremberg trials of Nazi war criminals as a journalist. She became interested in the issues of truth and justice, betrayal and treason. Her essays on the trials and on further issues of justice and criminality appeared in *The Meaning of Treason* (1947) and *A Train of Powder* (1955). West took a strong stand against communism during the 1950s, correctly perceiving that Stalin's totalitarian regime was no ally to art; in an era when many influential writers in Britain and the United States were liberals, leftists, fellow travelers, or outright supporters of communism, West's opposition alienated her from much of the literary world. She was honored by both the French and British governments in 1959, being named a Chevalier of the Legion of Honor in the former and a Dame Commander, Order of the British Empire, in the latter.

Rebecca West returned to fiction in 1956 with *The Fountain Overflows,* the first installment of a four-book series, the second and third volumes of which, *This Real Night* and *Cousin Rosamund,* were published posthumously, with the fourth never being completed. In the first volume, West reaches into her own childhood to draw a portrait of the Aubreys, a mother with three girls and a boy abandoned by their father. In 1957, she published a work of literary criticism, *The Court and the Castle,* a study of the connection between art and government from the Renaissance to the 20th century that she had presented as a lecture series at Yale University. The last novel published during West's lifetime, *The Birds Fall Down,* was published in 1966 and enjoyed a popular success; it is another young woman's bildungsroman, combined in this case with historical intrigues related to the declining empire of Russia in 1905.

In 1968, Rebecca West became a widow upon the death of Henry Andrews. She was named a Companion of Literature in the Royal Society of Literature in that same year, and in 1972 she was elected to honorary membership in the American Academy of Arts and Letters. She continued to work on fiction and journalism to the end of her life. Rebecca West died in London on March 15, 1983, at the age of 90. Her literary achievement continues to provide materials for scholarly study, combining as it does fiction, travel writing, history, literary criticism, ethical studies, journalism, and personal memoir. Although *The Return of the Soldier* is recognized as a minor classic, her novels do not place her in the front ranks of British fiction writers of the 20th century; her complete works, however, stand as a monument to one of the most important women, both as a writer and as a thinker, of that period.

BIBLIOGRAPHY

Deakin, Motley F. *Rebecca West.* Twayne's English Authors, 296. Boston: Twayne, 1980.

Glendinning, Victoria. *Rebecca West: A Life.* New York: Alfred A. Knopf, 1986.

———. *Rebecca West: A Life.* New York: Scribner, 1996.

WHITBREAD AWARD A prestigious British literary award founded in 1971, the Whitbread Book Awards receive funding from Whitbread PLC, a large corporation primarily focused on products and services for leisure activities. Whitbread owns breweries, pubs, pizza parlors, coffee shops, upscale restaurants, and both luxury and budget hotels, and it operates a chain of health clubs. Providing enjoyment to consumers is Whitbread's link to literary prizes: The company uses its funds to recognize outstanding achievement and receives good publicity in the process. The awards are administered by the Booksellers Association of Great Britain and IRELAND; any authors who have lived in either country for at least three years are eligible to enter the competition in the year their book is published. Between 1971 and 1977, separate prizes were awarded in five categories of literary achievement with no overall prize selected.

Since 1977, six prizes have been awarded annually with the addition of a "book of the year" category to the five areas previously established: Five panels of judges in five areas choose a best book in that area, and from those five books a further panel selects the Whitbread Book of the Year. The five categories at present include Best First Novel, Best Children's Book, Best Poetry Book, Best Biography, and Best Novel. The selection panel for each category is composed of an author, a journalist, and a bookseller. The winner in each of these categories receives a 5,000-pound prize and advances to the final competition. The final selection panel consists of the authors who judged the five preliminary categories, three public figures who enjoy reading, and a chair. The author of the single book chosen as Book of the Year receives a 25,000-pound award in addition to the previous award.

The Whitbread Literary Awards were founded only two years after the BOOKER PRIZE began recognizing outstanding contemporary literature. Generally, the Whitbread Book of the Year addresses more unusual subject matter than do the winners of the Booker Prize. Some critics consider the Whitbread Award to be secondary to the Booker Prize, but others see the difference between them as minimal. Both prizes are among the highest cash awards offered in the world for a single work of literature.

BIBLIOGRAPHY

Book Trust Guide to Literary Prizes. London: Book Trust, Published annually.

Todd, Richard. *Consuming Fictions: The Booker Prize and Fiction in Britain Today.* London: Bloomsbury, 1996.

WHITE HOTEL, THE D. M. THOMAS

(1981) The main character of *The White Hotel* a novel that interleaves history and fiction, is Lisa Erdman, a troubled young woman undergoing treatment for hysteria with Sigmund Freud. Thomas draws on actual case histories of some of Freud's patients to invent Lisa's psychoanalysis under the name "Anna G," and he deploys multiple narrative devices to examine her case in different ways. The resulting novel is a striking example of POSTMODERNISM that moves from the personal tragedy of Lisa's psychological problems to the human tragedy of the massacre of Jews at Babi Yar, in Kiev, during WORLD WAR II—one particularly ugly incident in the much larger nightmare of the Holocaust.

The narrative is presented in a prologue and six sections. The prologue looks like the beginning of an epistolary novel, except that the fictional exchange of letters occurs among the historical figures of Freud and his followers Ferenczi and Sachs. Ferenczi makes reference to the growing stresses between Freud and C. G. Jung that would ultimately lead Jung to remove himself from Freud's influence and develop his own theories, including that of the collective unconscious. The letters make what seems to be an innocuous start, presenting professional psychiatrists exchanging friendly gossip and examining the intriguing case of "Anna G."—Lisa Erdman. By the novel's end, however, readers familiar with Jung's theories will realize that *he* might have provided a better analysis of the cause of her psychosomatic pain in her left breast and ovary than Freud (or in any case the author's fictionalization of Freud) did himself.

The novel's first section, "Don Giovanni," takes the form of a poem composed amateurishly in blank verse that relates a sexual FANTASY in graphic detail without losing its poetic quality. The poem represents an uninhibited unleashing of the speaker's libidinal desires; the significance of the title is revealed in subsequent sections of the novel. The poem is crammed with imagery that will recur throughout the novel as the story presented in the poem is retold, examined, analyzed, and repudiated. The first retelling occurs in the novel's second section, "The Gastein Journal," which features a third-person narrator who primarily relates the experiences of the young woman from the poem but who also reveals the contents of several postcards dispatched from "the white hotel." The story presented has a dreamlike quality: Impossible things happen, and there is a discontinuity between the events that occur and the emotions that those events evoke from the participants. Ostensibly, the story relates a rapturous affair conducted at a resort—the white hotel—devastated by disasters. Fire, flood, landslide, and other tragedies beset the guests at the hotel, who also must deal with inexplicable sightings of whales in the lake and other uncanny phenomena. Eventually, readers learn that the third-person narrator of this section is actually Lisa Erdman, who is also the author of the shockingly explicit poem of the first section.

The novel's third section is entitled "Anna G." and is an imitation of an English translation of a case study by Freud, who serves both as the first-person narrator and the analyst of the problems that underlie Lisa's recurring pains and her rejection of her loving husband. The fictional Freud teases out the hidden layers of signification in Lisa's poem and in the story she creates (section two) to interpret it, presenting her with an explanation she is unwilling to accept. The analytic process does not occur without reversals, but by the end Freud and Lisa part on good terms, satisfied that her symptoms have been alleviated.

Section four presents Lisa some years after her analysis. An anonymous third-person narrator follows her to the high point of her career—a performance at the famous Italian opera house La Scala. There, she meets Vera and Victor Berenstein, and she is treated like visiting royalty. She is to replace Vera, who has broken her arm in a fall, for the last few performances of the season; she and Victor feel attracted to each other without entering on a course of action that would destroy Vera's happiness. Vera returns to Kiev, the cultured old city that had been Lisa's original home before she relocated with her family to Odessa and then to Vienna for her career. Vera and Victor are expecting their first child, and the world seems to be a joyous place, if not a perfect one. This narrative gives way to an exchange of letters between Freud and Lisa: He is planning to publish "Anna G," along with her poem and story, so he writes to request her assistance in reviewing the manuscript. The letter and the rereading of her own writing lead Lisa to an unexpected confession, and she reveals everything she had held back from Freud during the analysis. She had a deeper secret hidden below the subterfuge of sexual dysfunction. Events soon take her to Kiev and to the life she thought she would never have as a wife and mother, but the prospects for happiness are limited by the onslaught of war and the atrocities it brought to Kiev and other places.

In the novel's fifth section, the realism of the third-person narration reaches its highest point as the reader experiences the brutality of the killing fields at Babi Yar. On the morning of September 29, 1941, Lisa and her stepson prepare to reach the station in time to get a good seat on the train; instead, they find themselves caught in a crush of more than 30,000 people—all Jews—expecting to be transported to Palestine. The author draws his scene from eyewitness accounts of the horror of this mass extermination of human life. The imagery of Lisa's poem and her story are now fully explicated: Her pain in life has been a premonitory signifier of her death. Although this section is shorter than Freud's analysis or the narration of Lisa's subsequent life, the powerful writing gives it greater weight as vague metaphors are converted into brutal realities. In the novel's tranquil last section, Lisa seems to have reached Palestine, but readers should note that the only people "on the lists" here are those known to be dead from events that occurred in the earlier narrative sections of the story. D. M. THOMAS effectively demonstrates what the founding of Israel must have meant to the people who had survived the death camps and the firing squads: It must have seemed like the promised land or like heaven itself.

The White Hotel is a powerful, deeply affecting novel, but it is also complex and highly sophisticated in narrative structure, poetic imagery, historical awareness, and psychological acuity. Readers must be prepared to examine monstrous things in both the imaginary world of the disordered mind and the real world of human history. The novel does not present an easy reading experience, but it repays careful study and thoughtful engagement with its issues and the formal devices in which they are couched.

BIBLIOGRAPHY

Cross, Richard K. "The Soul Is a Far Country: D. M. Thomas and *The White Hotel*," *Journal of Modern Literature* 18, no. 1 (Winter 1992): 19–47.

Lougy, Robert E. "The Wolf-Man, Freud, and D. M. Thomas: Intertextuality, Interpretation, and Narration in *The White Hotel*," *Modern Language Studies* 21, no. 3 (Summer 1991): 91–106.

Wren, James A. "Thomas's *The White Hotel*," *Explicator* 54, no. 2 (1996): 123–126.

WHITE, PATRICK (1912–1990)

Born on May 28, 1912, to wealthy Australian parents visiting in England, Patrick White became the first Australian to win the NOBEL PRIZE for Literature. He attended Cheltenham PUBLIC SCHOOL in England and then completed an undergraduate degree in languages at Cambridge University. In the middle and late 1930s, he lived in London and traveled on the European continent, especially to Germany, then in the early years of Hitler's rule. White was already aware of his homosexuality while he was still in public school; that combined with his Australian nationality kept him isolated from mainstream society.

In London, he began writing unsuccessful novels and plays, hoping to establish himself as a playwright but failing to place his work with publishers or performers until 1939, when *Happy Valley* appeared. He traveled to New York that year, where he completed *The Living and the Dead,* published in 1941. He returned to England to serve in the armed forces and was commissioned in the Royal Air Force as an intelligence officer. During WORLD WAR II, he served in the Mediterranean theater in northern Africa, Egypt, the Middle East, and Greece, where he met the man who became his lifelong partner. In 1947, they settled permanently in Sydney, Australia.

By that time, White had completed the manuscript for *The Aunt's Story,* one of the novels considered to be among his masterpieces. It was published the following year. In it, White demonstrates his insight into human psychology by making the quiet life of a spinster come alive from within her own thoughts. In 1955, White extended his reputation with *The Tree of Man,* an epic story that covers Australia's history through the experiences of a young pioneer couple struggling to establish a farm in "the Outback." Two years later, in 1957, White published *Voss,* an epic of exploration and love in Australia, and another masterpiece. He then turned to other subject matter in his next three novels, *Riders in the Chariot* (1961), *The Solid Mandala* (1966), and *The Vivisector* (1970), returning to his greatest subject, Australia, in *The EYE OF THE STORM* (1973). That year, White won the Nobel Prize, the first awarded to an author writing in English from a country other than Great Britain or the United States.

Patrick White did not achieve a great financial success through his writing, which appeals to educated, experienced readers of serious literature. His characters display a kind of religious mysticism that draws on the theories of Carl Jung, mixed with concepts of Christian and Jewish theology. He wrote three additional novels after winning the Nobel Prize; of those only one, *A Fringe of Leaves* (1976), is considered to be among his greatest works, and it too maintains its focus on Australia's past. White also wrote short fiction, publishing three volumes of it, a book of verse, a screenplay, three autobiographical volumes, and nine plays. He died in Sydney on September 30, 1990.

BIBLIOGRAPHY

Bliss, Carolyn. *Patrick White's Fiction: The Paradox of Fortunate Failure.* New York: St. Martin's Press, 1986.

Marr, David. *Patrick White: A Life.* New York: Knopf, 1992.

Weigel, John A. *Patrick White.* Twayne's World Authors, 711. Boston: Twayne, 1983.

Williams, Mark. *Patrick White.* New York: St. Martin's Press, 1993.

WHITE TEETH ZADIE SMITH (2000)

This novel presents a contemporary view of London's multicultural, multiethnic, and multiracial aspects. *White Teeth* was the author's first novel; it was widely praised when it was published, becoming a best seller and winning both a WHITBREAD First Novel Award and the *GUARDIAN* First Book Award.

The novel features double protagonists: Archie Jones, a middle-aged working-CLASS Englishman, and Samad Iqbal, his age peer and a Muslim working as a waiter in his cousin's restaurant. The two are an unlikely pair of friends. They had met while serving in the British military at the end of WORLD War II, when Archie saved Samad from committing suicide, and their friendship had continued and grown when Samad immigrated to England with his family in 1973. Their bond is founded on their shared maleness rather than on any characteristic of race, religion, or nationality. They enjoy their pints of ale in the comfortably masculine environment of McConnell's Pool House, and eventually they settle their families only steps away from each other in a mixed-race neighborhood of London.

The novel opens with Archie's aborted suicide attempt on New Year's Day, 1975. After his first marriage, his job, and his suicide attempt fail miserably, Archie meets and nearly immediately marries Clara Bowden, a strapping young Jamaican woman missing her front teeth after a motor-scooter accident: he is 47, and she is 19. Clara's mother belongs to the Jehovah's Witnesses and enjoys anticipating the end of the world. The marriage allows Clara to escape both her mother and her mother's religion. Archie and Clara move to a modest house in north London, where they bring up their daughter Irie ("peace"), and soon Samad and his wife, Alsana, are rearing their twin sons, Magid and Millat, nearby.

Archie's disregard for traditional English ways (other than the pub) contrasts with Samad's desperate need to preserve the traditions of his cultural and religious heritage. Zadie SMITH emphasizes the chance qualities of that heritage: Samad had been a subject of the British EMPIRE when he became acquainted with Archie, but with the end of the war he became a citizen of the newly liberated countries of INDIA AND PAKISTAN, and by the time he relocated to England in 1973, shifting political borders had made him a citizen of Bangladesh. As he rears his sons in the secularized environment of contemporary London, Samad conceives a plan to save one of them from the godless influences of the West, and without telling his wife he sends Magid to be boarded at a Muslim school in his native country. While his son is away, Samad cultivates his idea of the perfect Muslim that young Magid will become; to a certain extent, Samad sacrifices Magid to compensate for his own inadequate abilities to follow the moral strictures of his religion. To his dismay, Magid grows up at his old-country school to become the impeccable model of a British gentleman, while Millat finds Muslim fundamentalism in London (after numerous experiments with many other kinds of extreme behavior).

Smith turns the clock back to explore the ancestors of her main characters, and by this technique she illustrates the ways that the past imposes itself on the present and exerts a shaping force on the perpetual stream of new events. Samad's Hindu ancestor, for example, had fired the first shot in the Sepoy Mutiny of 1857 (a historical event fictionalized in THE SIEGE OF KRISHNAPUR, by J. G. FARRELL). Eventually several generations of the protagonists' families come into the story, covering more than 100 years of history. But the story also has a strongly futuristic thread involving the Chalfens, Marcus and Julia. He is a molecular biologist and she is a horticulturalist; their project for a special genetically altered creature known as "FutureMouse" provides the setting for the novel's climax. On the millennial celebration of New Year's Eve in 1999, the main characters are drawn together in various roles to witness the debut of FutureMouse, while outside the biggest party in 1,000 years counts down the seconds to midnight while the Jehovah's Witnesses once again await the end of the world.

Zadie Smith displays a virtuoso command of the many voices in which contemporary English is spoken, presenting characters of differing socioeconomic classes, wide-ranging linguistic influences, varying degrees and styles of education, and numerous ethnic backgrounds. Her attitude toward these characters is sympathetic and affectionate, even when they display the excessive extent of their human frailties. Modern English life, she shows, is a difficult and complicated struggle between the longing for the familiar and the fear of the exotic. Smith's sympathy for her characters suggests one effective way to cope with the gulfs that subdivide the human species into so many different islands of alien otherness.

BIBLIOGRAPHY

Jackson, Kevin. "Next Generation Zadie Smith." *The New Yorker* 75, no. 31 (1999): 182.

O'Grady, Kathleen. "*White Teeth*: A Conversation with Author Zadie Smith." *Atlantis: A Women's Studies Journal/Revue d'Études sur les Femmes* 27, no. 1 (2002): 105–111.

WHITE, T. H. (1906–1964)

Writing at the same time, in the same genre, and with the same intent of developing a mythic epic for England, T. H. White and J. R. R. TOLKIEN both produced multivolume works of FANTASY tinged by the anxieties that WORLD WAR II brought to the British homeland. Of these two, White came to be seen as a children's author and eventually accepted that classification, while Tolkien became recognized as the modern reinventor of the fantasy genre.

Born Terence Hanbury White on May 29, 1906, in Bombay (now Mumbai), INDIA, the future author of *The ONCE AND FUTURE KING* was the son and grandson of British colonial civil servants. India, however, formed only a small influence on White: His mother removed him to England with her when he was five years old. There, she formally separated from White's father and lived with another man; White's childhood and adulthood were tragically marked by his experience of his mother's emotional instability. As an adult, he never married, suffering from alcoholism, fear of his homosexual desires, and persistent fantasies of sadomasochism.

In 1920, White boarded at Cheltenham College for a period, where he maintained an isolated existence and felt ostracized and tormented by his classmates. He entered Queen's College at Cambridge University, but when he contracted tuberculosis in his second year he left to recuperate in Italy, assisted by donations from his teachers. His illness made him determined to pursue a healthy life, and upon returning to England he devoted himself to hunting, fishing, and other sports—pastimes he frequently shared with his friend the poet Siegfried Sassoon. White completed his studies at Cambridge in 1929 and eventually became a teacher at Stowe Ridings (1932–36), a distinguished PUBLIC SCHOOL.

White had already written a novel while regaining his health in Italy, and in the first half of the 1930s he published two collections of poetry and several novels, some under the pseudonym "James Aston." Frustrated by his suppressed homosexuality, White entered into psychoanalysis in 1935 with the intention of becoming "cured" of a condition considered at the time to be a form of mental aberration. In 1936, his first volume of autobiography, *England Have My Bones,* succeeded well enough to garner for him a publishing contract. After 1937, White supported himself as a full-time writer. He began developing the Arthurian legends into the series of novels that was eventually consolidated under the title *The Once and Future King.* In 1938, he published the first volume, *The Sword in the Stone.* Like John Cooper Powys, author of *Glastonbury Romance,* and J. R. R. Tolkien, White was working on a MYTHOLOGY for England.

Resigning his teaching position, White stayed on at Stowe for some time, renting a cottage on the school grounds. With the outbreak of WORLD WAR II, however, he relocated to IRELAND, a neutral country in the war. As a pacifist, he wanted no part of the conflict, but as a British resident he was at risk of being drafted into the armed forces. In Ireland, he continued working on his Arthurian series, publishing *The Witch in the Wood,* an unflattering portrait of his mother, in 1939, and *The Ill-Made Knight* in 1940. His publisher declined to publish the fourth volume, *A Candle in the Wind,* and White's career stalled until 1946, when his classic work of children's literature, *Mistress Masham's Repose,* appeared. In that year, he also relocated to the Channel Islands, crown possessions off the northern coast of France. He continued to write books for children and completed publishing his Arthurian series in the 1950s, except for the fifth volume, *The Book of Merlyn,* which appeared posthumously in 1977.

White published two histories of notable scandals, *The Age of Scandal: An Excursion Through a Minor Period* (1950) and *The Scandalmongers* (1952), and two additional volumes of autobiography, *The Godstone and the Blackymor* (1959) and *America at Last* (1965). When his work became the basis of the musical stage adaptation *Camelot* in 1960, and the Disney animated FILM ADAPTATION *The Sword in the Stone* (1963), White

achieved financial independence and recognition. He died on January 17, 1964, of an apparent heart attack while on a cruise in the Aegean Islands of Greece.

BIBLIOGRAPHY

Crane, John K. *T. H. White.* Twayne's English Authors, 172. New York: Twayne, 1974.

Garnett, David, ed. *The White-Garnett Letters.* New York: Viking Press, 1968.

Warner, Sylvia Townsend. *T. H. White: A Biography.* London: Cape/Chatto & Windus, 1967.

WIDE SARGASSO SEA JEAN RHYS (1966)

Taking inspiration from the pivotal but demonized character in *Jane Eyre* of the mad wife hidden away in the attic, Jean RHYS imagines a backstory for this misunderstood woman. Where Charlotte Bontë barely sketches an outline of Bertha Mason's existence, Rhys elaborates a life, a family, and a historical context. Drawing on her own knowledge of the Caribbean, where she was born and reared, Rhys enables readers to see the madwoman in the attic sympathetically as a beautiful girl trapped in hostile circumstances.

Rhys gives Bertha the more appealing name Antoinette (Bertha is Antoinette's middle name) and makes her the daughter of a plantation owner and his beautiful but fragile wife. Using the historical detail of a successful slave revolt, Rhys portrays the precarious circumstances of the European colonizers who survive the revolt: They are hated by the former slaves and cut off from their traditional sources of power and wealth. When Antoinette's father dies, his family and servants are on the verge of starvation until Mr. Mason marries Antoinette's mother. The plantation once again hums with life and hope, but in the unstable political, racial, and economic situation, danger continues to threaten the family.

Antoinette's mother soon degenerates into madness—a family affliction. Antoinette goes to board at a convent school; at 17, her stepfather brings her out and marries her to Edward Rochester, a landless younger son. Antoinette inherits her mother's long-abandoned property on another island, and the newlyweds settle into a derelict plantation high in the mountains. Rochester's attachment to Antoinette, never very strongly developed, cools and turns to revulsion for her carnality; he hates the entire tropical world to which he feels exiled. He insists on calling his wife Bertha rather than the more "exotic" Antoinette, which is also her mother's name, a further effort to distance himself from his wife's West Indian past. When his father and older brother die, he suddenly acquires everything—land, wealth, and status—that had previously been denied to him. Giving his wife no options, he takes her to the dreary, gray cold of England and seals her away in the attic of the family estate. There, she waits for her opportunity to re-create the light and warmth she craves. Rhys's closing chapter brilliantly captures the mind of Bertha in the final days of her life, seamlessly integrating the story into the details Brontë originally created.

An outstanding example of INTERTEXTUALITY, *Wide Sargasso Sea* bridges 19th- and 20th-century literary fiction, bringing to it the modern interest in race, CLASS, COLONIALISM and its effects, and FEMINISM. Rhys's novel deepens the experience of reading Brontë's classic, casting an invigorating new light on a key canonical text.

BIBLIOGRAPHY

Lykiard, Alexis. *Jean Rhys Revisited.* Exeter, Devon: Stride Publications, 2000.

Staley, Thomas F. *Jean Rhys: A Critical Study.* Austin: University of Texas Press, 1979.

Wolfe, Peter. *Jean Rhys.* Boston: Twayne Publishers, 1980.

WILDE, OSCAR (1854–1900)

Born Oscar Fingal O'Flaherty Wills Wilde in Dublin, Oscar Wilde died in exile and disgrace as the 20th century began. His parents were titled aristocrats: Sir William Robert Wilde and Lady Jane Francesca Wilde. Wilde began his education in Dublin at the Portora Royal School, excelling in classical Greek. He continued these studies at Trinity College; with his tutor, he toured Italy and visited the city of Ravenna, site of numerous early Christian cathedrals in the Romanesque and early Gothic style, and also the burial place of Dante. In 1874, Wilde entered Oxford with a scholarship to Magdalene College, and in 1878 he won the Newdigate Prize for a poem he wrote about Ravenna.

In the employ of Richard D'Oyly Carte, Wilde visited the United States on a lecture tour designed to publicize the Gilbert and Sullivan light opera *Patience.* On this tour, he met many of the leading American literary figures of the day. At Oxford, he had already begun to indulge in the dandyish dress for which he became famous, and on his American tour he sported a glamorous fur coat and articulated the new theories of AESTHETICISM, or "art for art's sake." When this tour concluded, he traveled to France and met many of the leading literary figures there while writing a play. In 1884, Wilde married Constance Lloyd of Dublin; they had two sons.

In the late 1880s, Wilde edited magazines and contributed features to leading periodicals. He published his most important novel, *The Picture of Dorian Gray,* in 1891 and also published two books of fairy tales. Wilde's most important works are the plays he wrote in the middle 1890s: *Lady Windemere's Fan* (1893), *A Woman of No Importance* (1894), *An Ideal Husband* (1895), and his greatest dramatic work, *The Importance of Being Earnest* (1895). He was also renowned as a conversationalist of great wit, quick in repartee.

Wilde had formed a relationship in the 1890s with a young aristocrat, Lord Alfred Douglas, during his great creative period. In 1895, the young man's father, the marquess of Queensbury, accused Wilde of being a sodomite—of engaging in homosexual relations, which were specifically criminalized by British law. Wilde sued for libel, but the case did not go well. He withdrew his legal proceedings, but he was arrested on criminal charges, and after a sensational pair of trials he was found guilty and sentenced to the harshest penalty allowed for that crime, two years of hard labor. His wife fled from England with the two boys during these humiliating events, further crushing his spirit. Wilde was imprisoned in Reading Gaol, and although he was able to write, producing "De Profundis," the two years aged him. He was released in 1897 and traveled to Europe, living in France, Switzerland, and Italy; the relationship with Lord Alfred Douglas was also resumed. Oscar Wilde died in Paris on November 30, 1900.

Although Wilde did not publish literary works during the 20th century, the catalyst for his tragic downfall—homosexuality—has become an important theme in many creative fields. In film, in novels, in memoirs, and in the scholarly field of literary studies known as queer theory, the exploration of mainstream and peripheral human sexuality has drawn much serious attention. Following from the political advocacy conducted in the second half of the 20th century for improved race relations, and ideologically related to FEMINISM, sexual orientation has become a contested ground for human rights. Too late to help Oscar Wilde, some places and professions have begun to practice tolerance with respect to sexual orientation.

BIBLIOGRAPHY

Belford, Barbara. *Oscar Wilde: A Certain Genius.* New York: Random House, 2000.

WILLIAMS, CHARLES (1886–1945)

Admired by his contemporaries as a literary scholar, a biographical historian, a theological philosopher, a poet, and a novelist, Charles Williams was born in London on September 20, 1886. His father published poetry under a pseudonym, but the family's limited financial resources prevented Williams from completing more than two years of a formal college education. To earn a living, he entered the publishing trade, working for many years as an editor for Oxford University Press, but he continued to study on his own, developing a formidable erudition without earning the degrees that are usually the hallmark of such intellectual dedication.

The earliest published works of Charles Williams were books of poetry produced between 1912 and 1924. He also began writing plays, publishing his first dramatic work, *A Myth of Shakespeare,* in 1928. In the next 10 years, he published prolifically in several genres, producing 18 books of criticism, history, fiction, drama, and theology. He returned to poetry in 1938 and again in 1944, composing two books of poems inspired by the cycle of Arthurian legends. He also produced two critical works on Dante that are still noted for their interpretive insight.

The novels of Charles Williams display his interest in the supernatural, in witchcraft, and in the occult. They depend on suspenseful otherworldly thrills, but use realistic representations of contemporary English life for settings rather than the usual FANTASY settings of the remote past or an imaginary world. As to PLOT, the novels unfold stories of the struggle between good and evil. His titles reflect the theological issues the stories examine: *War in Heaven* (1930), *Many Dimensions* (1931), *The Place of the Lion* (1931), *The Greater Trumps* (1932), *Shadows of Ecstasy* (1933), DESCENT INTO HELL (1937), and *All Hallows' Eve* (1945), published just before his death.

The intrusion of WORLD WAR II forced Williams to relocate to Oxford when his office was moved there for safety; in Oxford, he became acquainted with the INKLINGS, exchanging ideas with such deeply religious authors as C. S. LEWIS, J. R. R. TOLKIEN, and others. During his lifetime, Williams did not find the wide audience that these writers had reached. When he died in Oxford on May 15, 1945, however, he was lauded by these authors and by important poets such as T. S. Eliot and W. H. Auden. He left a large amount of unpublished writing behind, much of it devoted to his studies of Arthurian literature. C. S. Lewis edited a posthumous volume of this aspect of Williams's work, publishing it under the title *Arthurian Torso.* Other posthumous works include a novel, two collections of plays, and a collection of essays.

BIBLIOGRAPHY

Carpenter, Humphrey. *The Inklings.* Boston: Houghton Mifflin, 1978.

Hadfield, Alice Mary. *Charles Williams: An Exploration of His Life and Work.* New York: Oxford University Press, 1982.

Sibley, Agnes Marie. *Charles Williams.* Twayne's English Authors, 322. Boston: Twayne Publishers, 1982.

Spencer, Kathleen. *Charles Williams.* Mercer Island, Wash.: Starmont House, 1986.

WILSON, ANGUS (1913–1991)

Born August 11, 1913, the youngest of six sons, and 13 years behind his next oldest brother, Angus Frank Johnstone Wilson grew up in the late middle life of his parents, relatively isolated from other children and consequently lonely. Although the family had once enjoyed prosperity, Angus Wilson was reared during years of increasing financial distress that his parents ineffectually denied. After completing his university studies at Merton College, Oxford, where he was influenced by Marxist political philosophy, he eventually went to work at the British Museum in the Department of Printed Books, remaining there until the middle 1950s, when he became a full-time writer, critic, and leftist social activist.

Wilson's earliest literary efforts were short stories that he wrote in his 30s as therapy following a nervous breakdown, and they were well received critically. His first novel, *Hemlock and After,* appeared in 1952; it is a chronicle of a middle-aged man's failure in dealing with a life crisis. His characters frequently fail, becoming reconciled to lives of loneliness; however, since Wilson presents loneliness as an inescapable and even necessary fact of human existence, the reconciliation to it is also a kind of sad triumph that restores dignity and some degree of meaning to his protagonists' lives. He tells their stories in novels that experiment with form in imitation of James JOYCE—especially Joyce's novel *ULYSSES.* As a storyteller, Wilson depends on interior monologue, extending it as a literary technique by his mastery of different characters' unique voices. His masterpiece is generally thought to be *NO LAUGHING MATTER* (1967), the story of a dysfunctional family in which the numerous children all grow up to be professionally successful without ever succeeding—without finding happiness—in their personal lives.

After establishing his literary reputation, Wilson taught during the 1960s and 1970s at the University of East Anglia, and he served frequently as a guest lecturer at American universities such as the University of California at Berkeley, Johns Hopkins, and several others. He was named a Commander of the British Empire in 1968 and a Companion of Literature in 1972. He continued his experimental approach to fictional narration, but critics did not receive his final novels with warmth. When he died on June 1, 1991, his recent work was less well known than his earliest stories, even though in his life he had been compared to as great a writer as Charles Dickens. He published insightful critical studies of Dickens, Rudyard KIPLING, and the French novelist Emile Zola; he has himself been studied by the novelist Margaret DRABBLE, whose biography of him in 1995 was intended to restore Wilson's literary status.

BIBLIOGRAPHY

Drabble, Margaret. *Angus Wilson: A Biography.* New York: St. Martin's Press, 1995.

Gardner, Averil. *Angus Wilson.* Twayne's English Authors, 401. Boston: Twayne, 1985.

Halio, Jay L. *Angus Wilson.* Edinburgh: Oliver & Boyd, 1964.

WINE-DARK SEA, THE PATRICK O'BRIAN (1993)   See AUBREY-MATURIN NOVELS.

WINGS OF THE DOVE, THE HENRY JAMES (1902)

A novel that examines the cost of emotional duplicity and of doing a right thing for the wrong reason, *The Wings of the Dove* presents a contrast between a wealthy but doomed American girl, Milly Theale, and an English girl, Kate Croy, who is the poor relation of a wealthy family. Each of these young women has an older female associate, and these women provide a further contrastive layer to the story while also furthering the development of the PLOT: Milly's American friend and companion, the widow and writer Mrs. Stringham, is also an old school friend of Mrs. Lowder, the wealthy aunt who is grooming her niece Kate for an advantageous marriage to the dissipated Lord Mark. These two friends eventually bring Kate and Milly together, and the young women then form their own fast friendship.

Before the young women become acquainted, however, the plot is thickened by a further level of complication that develops into an unusual love triangle. Kate is reluctant to fulfill her aunt's ambition to marry her into wealth and social status because she is in love with a poor journalist, Merton Densher. He is respectable enough to be received in the Lowder home, but Mrs. Lowder will abandon Kate to poverty if the young couple gets married against her wishes. When Morton's newspaper sends him to New York to write a series of feature stories, Mrs. Lowder is relieved. In New York, Merton meets Milly Theale, who has just inherited a large fortune. Events draw all the major characters together in London, where Mrs. Stringham introduces Milly to polite society through social events at the home of her friend, Mrs. Lowder. Lord Mark, Mrs. Lowder's intended spouse for Kate, becomes attracted to the beautiful Milly; she in turn becomes an accomplice in aiding her friends Kate and Merton to continue meeting in secret.

The final tragic element of the plot is put in place when Milly learns that she is terminally ill. Sir Luke Strett, a prominent London physician, tells the unfortunate young woman that she should enjoy life as much as she can in the little time she has left and advises her to spend the winter months in Venice. Milly shares the information of her condition only with Kate, Mrs. Stringham, and Mrs. Lowder, asking them to keep it secret, since she does not want to be an object of pity. She goes to Venice accompanied by her friends and intending to enjoy an ordinary life to the end. But when Kate realizes that her wealthy friend is developing a romantic attachment to Merton, she sees this connection as a way to escape her aunt's control: If Merton were to marry Milly, he would inherit a fortune upon her death in the near future. As a widower with a fortune, he would then be an acceptable suitor for Kate in Mrs. Lowder's eyes. Kate becomes a scheming matchmaker in the money-driven mold of her aunt. The lie at the heart of the arrangement seems insignificant to her, since Milly would enjoy a loving relationship in her dying months, while Kate and Merton would enjoy her fortune and resume their love after Milly's death.

For his part, Merton is a reluctant participant in Kate's plan. Kate and her aunt return to England, but first Kate secures Merton's promise to pursue a marriage to Milly. He is repelled by the idea of lying about love for the sake of money. Soon Lord Mark reenters the story as well, having come to Venice and decided to propose marriage to Milly himself; she rejects him, but he also has learned that Kate and Merton are engaged, and he reveals this information to Milly just as she has begun to hope for a proposal from Merton. Milly is crushed and dies in Venice knowing of her friend's plot, but she is also a merciful and generous woman. She leaves a large bequest for Merton so he can marry Kate. Merton had earlier felt that carrying out Kate's plan would change them both from the persons with whom each had fallen in love; in the end, even knowing of the plan has the same effect, and Milly's generosity in death is the final blow to the relationship.

The fact that Kate had perceived her scheme to be an acceptable plan reveals the degree to which she had already been coopted by the desire for wealth and status. She is not willing to sacrifice her aunt's wealth to her love for Merton, and she is not willing to sacrifice love by submitting to a wealthy marriage with Lord Mark. Kate wants both wealth and Merton, and she sees Milly's imminent death as a way to achieve her double objective. In a deeply ironic twist, Kate and Merton are divided by Milly's posthumous effort to give Kate freely that which she had previously tried to take by deceit.

BIBLIOGRAPHY

Cargill, Oscar. *The Novels of Henry James.* New York: Macmillan, 1961.

Fowler, Virginia. "The Later Fiction." In *A Companion to Henry James Studies.* Edited by Daniel Mark Fogel. Westport, Conn.: Greenwood Press, 1993.

Wagenknecht, Edward. *The Novels of Henry James.* New York: Frederick Ungar, 1983.

WINTERSON, JEANETTE (1959–)

Born on August 27, 1959, Jeanette Winterson was an adopted child reared in a conservative religious environment. In her youth, she embraced the faith of her family and prepared herself for a possible calling as a missionary or some other form of religious service, preaching sermons at a precocious age. When, as a young woman, she realized her lesbian sexual orientation, both her family and her church rejected her. Following a job interview during which she regaled a personnel officer with stories of her life, she began crafting those stories into her first novel, *Oranges Are Not the Only Fruit* (1985). The title refers to a famous scene in the movie *Spartacus* between Marcus Lucinius Crassus, played by Laurence Olivier, and Antoninus, played by Tony Curtis; the scene depicts an understated and highly metaphorical homosexual seduction. Winterson's autobiographical book won the WHITBREAD First Novel Award and brought its frank treatment of homoerotic desire and its forthright criticism of religious hypocrisy to a wide readership.

Winterson's other novels include *Boating for Beginners* (1985), a comic retelling of Noah's adventures;

The Passion (1987), partly an example of HISTORICAL FIC-
TION set during the age of Napoleon and partly a work
of MAGIC REALISM; *SEXING THE CHERRY* (1989), another
mixing of history and FANTASY; *WRITTEN ON THE BODY*
(1992), an experimental work narrated by a seductive
person whose gender is never identified; *Art and Lies*
(1994), a fictional examination of art narrated by the
artists Handel, Picasso, and Sappho; and *Gut Symme-
tries* (1997), about an adulterous marriage. Winterson
has also published poetry and essays and a novel
inspired by her laptop computer, *The Powerbook*
(2000). She has also developed a sophisticated Web
site—having won a controversial legal battle for the
right to her own name after it (and the names of many
other authors) had been claimed by an Internet entrepreneur—and incorporated technology into her art.
Jeanette Winterson continues to live and write in England.

BIBLIOGRAPHY

Bengston, Helene, Børch, Marianne, and Cindie Maagaarde,
    eds. *Sponsored by Demons: The Art of Jeanette Winterson.*
    Agedrup, Denmark: Scholars, 1999.

Hinds, Hillary. "Oranges Are Not the Only Fruit: Reaching
    Audiences Other Lesbian Texts Cannot Reach," *New Les-
    bian Criticism: Literary and Cultural Readings.* New York:
    Columbia University Press, 1992.

Wood, Michael. *Children of Silence: On Contemporary Fiction.*
    New York: Columbia University Press, 1998.

WODEHOUSE, P. G. (1881–1975) One of
the most prolific of 20th-century humorists, Pelham
Grenville Wodehouse (pronounced wood-house) was
born in Guildford, England, on October 15, 1881, at
the height of the British EMPIRE, into the family of a civil
servant employed in Hong Kong. He was educated in
English boarding schools and housed during vacations
with various relatives in England. In 1900, he graduated from Dulwich College. Although he had been writing stories as a child and had already published a
prize-winning story, his father found him a position as
a bank clerk in Hong Kong; after two years, however,
during which he continued to write and publish his
stories, he found employment in 1902 as a columnist
for the English newspaper the *Globe.* He also published

his first novel, *The Pothunters,* that year, and soon after,
he began writing lyrics for musical plays.

In 1909, Wodehouse first visited the United States,
and he found an English wife there in 1914. He relocated permanently to the United States in 1947 and
became an American citizen in 1955. During his first
American visit, Wodehouse became the theater critic
for *Vanity Fair* and was soon collaborating on Broadway musicals with Jerome Kern and Guy Bolton. Ultimately, he contributed to some 52 productions,
including works by Cole Porter and George and Ira
Gershwin. He also gained an enthusiastic American
readership for his novels—a connection that was to
prove valuable at a crucial junction in his life.

In the period leading up to WORLD WAR II, Wodehouse lived in France. Accepting an honorary doctorate at Oxford took him back to England briefly in
1939, but he returned to the Continent only to be
caught up in the hostilities. He was captured in the
lightning onslaught of the German army and detained
in a prisoner-of-war camp until strident protests from
his American readers persuaded authorities to treat
him more gently. He was moved to a Berlin hotel under
a kind of house arrest. There, he agreed to broadcast
radio addresses to the United States; however, because
his talks were carried over German radio frequencies,
his countrymen in England perceived Wodehouse to
be a traitor. The condemnation of him was widespread
and deeply outraged: Londoners suffering under the
blitzkrieg could not tolerate the idea of a British novelist ensconced in a Berlin hotel broadcasting humorous
anecdotes over German radio. Writers who came to
Wodehouse's defense included George ORWELL, but at
the war's end a warrant for his arrest was issued: If he
returned to England, he would be tried for treason.
Wodehouse left the Continent for the United States
and ultimately became an American citizen. Queen
Elizabeth II officially pardoned Wodehouse prior to
conferring knighthood on him shortly before he died.

Over a career of some 70 years, Wodehouse produced one or more novels, several short stories, and
some kind of dramatic production, musical or not,
every year. Although much of his earliest work has
been lost, a large body of fiction remains yet unpublished. His most famous work is probably the JEEVES

and Wooster series of COMIC NOVELS that chronicle the misadventures of Bertie Wooster and his "gentleman's gentleman," or valet, Jeeves. In story after story, the well-meaning Bertie gets himself into a fix and the ever-competent Jeeves discreetly extricates him, frequently drawing on his vast reservoir of arcane knowledge and unsuspected skills. Wodehouse creates an even more eccentric upper-class menagerie in the Blandings series, set at Blandings Castle and featuring the owner's prize hog, the ravishing Empress of Blandings. Two other important series are the Psmith novels (pronounced "Smith") and the school novels, which share a connection to life in the British PUBLIC SCHOOL system.

BIBLIOGRAPHY

Green, Benny. *P. G. Wodehouse: A Literary Biography.* New York: Rutledge Press, 1981.

Hall, Robert A., Jr. *The Comic Style of P. G. Wodehouse.* Hamden, Conn.: Archon Books, 1974.

Phelps, Barry. *P. G. Wodehouse: Man and Myth.* London: Constable, 1992.

Sproat, Iain. *Wodehouse at War.* New Haven, Conn.: Ticknor & Fields, 1981.

WOMEN IN LOVE D. H. LAWRENCE (1920)

Continuing and expanding the family narrative begun in *The RAINBOW* (1915), this novel explores the early adulthood of Ursula and Gudrun Brangwen and their romantic attachments to Rupert Birkin and Gerald Crich, respectively. Critics widely regard *Women in Love* to be the greatest novel LAWRENCE produced; his prose breaks new ground in finding metaphors to express erotic experiences, and his narrative style continues the "great tradition" of psychological realism identified by F. R. Leavis as the height of English literary achievement.

This novel is thickly textured with contrastive oppositions: nature and industry, love and sex, romanticism and MODERNISM, male and female essences, heterosexual and homosexual desire, upper-CLASS and working-class values, and others. The story draws the two sisters into the circle of the wealthy, domineering Hermione Roddice (a caricature of the society maven, Lady Ottoline Morrell) and the mine-owning Crich family. Birkin is Gerald's best friend and has been a suitor to Hermione for some time, although that relationship is emotionally volatile. Gerald is shaking up the old ways of the mining community by introducing modern machinery and insisting on higher standards of performance for his employees. His father operated the mine by functioning as a kind of feudal lord in a fiefdom, but Gerald is more of a Social Darwinist, retaining only the most fit, and therefore most profitable, workers. Birkin, who partially represents Lawrence himself, is inspired by nature, not machinery, and is pessimistic about the human race; he advocates spontaneity, unconventionality, and freely expressed honesty. Although Birkin and Gerald are opposites in many ways, the two have an intense friendship, and they are keenly interested in resolving the mysteries of love. But where Gerald resorts to casual affairs and substitutes sex for love, Birkin is searching for fulfillment through intense emotional bonds both to women and men.

During a weekend stay with Hermione, the four protagonists get to know one another better, and the stresses in the relationship between Birkin and Hermione finally break them apart. Like Gerald, Hermione is modern, cosmopolitan, and sophisticated, but Birkin increasingly finds her cold, artificial, and calculating. Ursula is free of upper-class snobbery and lacks the drive to dominate those around her, so Birkin is soon pursuing her, seeking an experience deeper than love. Ursula is more conventional than Birkin, especially in her jealousy of Hermione, but she is also quick to repent and forgive. The connection between Gerald and Gudrun is more tentative at first, and more destructive in the long run. She is attracted to his powerful will yet reluctant to be under its sway, even to her own benefit.

The relationships between these two couples become intensified after a summer party when Gerald's newlywed sister Laura drowns with her husband. The death of the young lovers drives Birkin and Ursula toward a mutual understanding. When Gerald's father dies in the wake of this tragedy, the bereaved son seeks solace in Gudrun's bed, sneaking into the Brangwen home uninvited. But where Birkin and Ursula accommodate themselves to marriage despite Birkin's longing for unconventionality, Gudrun and Gerald are both too strong-willed to circumscribe their lives on a permanent basis. In an ironic reversal, Birkin, the character most passionately devoted to unconventional spontaneity, settles comfortably into domesticity, while his conventional best friend refuses to pledge himself to anyone. But on a vacation in the Alps, when Gudrun takes an interest in another artist she meets there, Gerald walks off into the frozen mountains and dies of exposure. The characters associated with spontaneity, unconventionality, the values of romanticism, and the love of nature thrive in a traditional marriage, while those associated with modernity, indulgence in libidinal urges, and willfulness perish or decay.

Lawrence's frank treatment of sexual desire and his skillful use of dialogue and description to insinuate erotic ideas and experiences caused this novel's publication to be delayed (and later led to the suppression of LADY CHATTERLEY'S LOVER). But his understanding of the new ideas of Sigmund Freud and his success in exploring previously taboo aspects of human experience also influenced other writers to do the same, widening the range of topics addressed by the 20th-century English novel.

BIBLIOGRAPHY

Bloom, Harold, ed. *D. H. Lawrence.* New York: Chelsea House, 1986.

Kondo, Kyoko Kay. "Metaphor in *Women in Love.*" In *D. H. Lawrence: New Worlds.* Edited by Keith Cushman and Earl G. Ingersoll. Madison, N.J.: Fairleigh Dickinson University Press, 2003, 168–82.

Levy, Eric P. "The Paradoxes of Love in *Women in Love,*" *Centennial Review* 43, no. 3 (Fall 1999): 575–84.

WOOLF, VIRGINIA (1882–1941)

One of the most important feminist voices in the 20th century, Virginia Woolf was the daughter of Sir Leslie Stephen, the editor of the *Dictionary of National Biography* (a kind of British *Who's Who* of important but deceased individuals). Born Adeline Virginia Stephen, Virginia Woolf matured in a dynamic household in which her father emphasized the importance of an intellectual life. Considered England's most important Victorian man of letters after Matthew Arnold, Stephen had first married Harriet Marian Thackeray, younger daughter to novelist William Makepeace Thackeray. The couple had one daughter, whose mental deficiency later required her institutionalization. Left a young widower at Minnie's death, Stephen married the young widow and mother of three Julia Prinsep Duckworth. In addition to their four children from previous marriages, the couple had four children together, Vanessa, Virginia, Thoby, and Adrian. Virginia always felt closer to Vanessa and Thoby than to Adrian, whose attention from his mother as the baby made Virginia jealous. She also felt close to her half sister, Stella Duckworth, who served as surrogate mother for the growing family during Julia Stephen's absences to care for her own mother and also to perform social services. Her social activism earned her much admiration, including Coventry Patmore's use of her as the model for his series of poems titled *The Angel in the House.*

The dynamic household welcomed frequent visitors, authors, historians, philosophers, editors, and critics of the era, as they visited with Stephen. Luminaries such as the American poet James Russell Lowell; Stephen's former father-in-law, W. M. Thackeray; the famous British writers George Meredith and Thomas Hardy; and the American writer Henry JAMES all encouraged Virginia's writing as a child. She and Vanessa were, for the most part, schooled at home, where Virginia wrote and Vanessa painted. Julia Stephen's death in 1895 ended what Virginia described as an idyllic life, although her later comments indicated that her half brothers might have sexually abused her. Virginia suffered the first of several nervous breakdowns following her mother's death. Stephen would never recover from her loss, becoming more demanding of Stella and, after she married and moved out, Vanessa and Virginia.

Virginia's fragile security was shattered again in 1897, when Stella died just three months after marriage. Rumors that she had been pregnant at the time added to Virginia's growing distrust of men, sex, and childbearing. In the absence of the brothers, who all attended school, Virginia and Vanessa grew closer than ever, both rebelling against their father's demands and the societal constraints of creative women. Woolf began a study of Greek at King's College in Kensington, later studying privately with Clara Pater. In 1899, the sisters visited Thoby at Trinity College in Cambridge, where they would first meet Clive Bell, Lytton Strachey, Saxon

Sydney-Turner, and Leonard Woolf, all members of what would become the famed BLOOMSBURY GROUP.

Woolf began an intimate relationship with Violet Dickinson, a friend of Stella's, that would last for years and may have involved her first lesbian experiences. Leslie Stephen became ill with cancer in 1900, requiring a surgery that left him weak and irritable. After a slow decline, he died in 1904, once again leaving Virginia bereft. The young women escaped their grief through one of many trips they would make to Europe, eventually celebrating the newfound freedom their father's absence offered them. Although Virginia seemed to recover, later biographers surmised that Stephen's death added to the threat to Virginia's mental health, compounded perhaps by sexual confusion and her early molestations. She suffered another depression in 1904, which, like later breakdowns, involved horrendous headaches, blackouts, suicide attempts, and hallucinations. As she convalesced with a relative, Vanessa, Thoby, and Adrian moved from their parents' home in Hyde Park Gate to 46 Gordon Square in Bloomsbury, considered an unfashionable neighborhood, a move that alarmed several relatives and acquaintances. In December 1904, Virginia published her first article, an unsigned review in the *Guardian*.

In 1905, Virginia's life changed drastically when she accepted a teaching position at Morley College and Thoby began holding "Thursday Evenings" with friends. The intellectual discussions at those gatherings thrilled Virginia and included many individuals later in the Bloomsbury group. In March she sailed with Adrian to Portugal and enjoyed a country that would offer the setting for her first novel, *The Voyage Out*. She wrote and taught for two years while Vanessa began developing a life as a painter, rejecting Clive Bell's marriage proposal. Family members became concerned that Virginia might never marry, although she also had received proposals, which she rejected.

Vanessa and others became ill during a family outing to Greece and, while she recovered at home, Thoby Stephen died, shattering Virginia's world. She had loved Thoby as much as she disliked Adrian, but managed to escape her usual depression, perhaps by living out a denial of his death through fictional reports to Violet Dickinson, also ill, of Thoby's recovery. Three

days after Thoby's death, Vanessa agreed to marry Clive, and Virginia's life again changed. Left with only Adrian in their house, she feared they could never get along, but her work on *Melymbrosia,* later published as *The Voyage Out* in 1915, occupied her, as did her relationships with Strachey, the artist Roger Fry, Sydney-Turner, and writers E. M. FORSTER and Desmond MacCarthy.

Virginia began contributing regularly to various periodicals and moved with Adrian to 29 Fitzroy Square. While her relatives protested her irregular lifestyle, Virginia's growing self-confidence helped her ignore them. Vanessa suffered a miscarriage and began a long-running affair with Roger Fry, while Clive became a regularly practicing bisexual, although he would have two sons with Vanessa. Duncan Grant fathered Vanessa's daughter, Angelica, but Clive posed as her father for stability's sake, and she did not find out the truth until her teen years. During one of Virginia's visits to the Bell home, she dined with Leonard Woolf, home on leave from his seven years of highly successful civil service in Ceylon (Sri Lanka). The two eventually married, beginning the relationship that many believed saved Virginia from an early death. Virginia felt secure in the company of the Jewish Leonard, and the two developed pet names for each other.

Leonard found marriage to Virginia demanding as he nursed her through several illnesses while finding time for his own growing writing career. The two began a publishing business together, the Hogarth Press, named for Hogarth House in London, where they lived after 1915. The press would publish seminal works by important writers including T. S. Eliot and Katherine Mansfield. Virginia continued to publish, turning out experimental novels that sometimes confounded her readers. In the middle of a world torn by war, Leonard attempted to enlist, but was rejected, due to a tremor. He began writing against the war in a learned manner that attracted much positive attention. *Two Stories,* published in 1917, included the story "The Mark on the Wall" by Virginia and "Three Jews" by Leonard. Leonard accepted an appointment as secretary of the Labour Party Advisory Committee on International Questions, publishing works that proved important in postwar England. His writings would later become part of the founding of the League of

Nations, and both Leonard and Virginia remained antifascist and antiwar voices for the next several decades.

In 1919, Virginia published *Night and Day,* just before the Woolfs bought Monk's House in Rodmell, Sussex, where they spent most summers for decades. Gerald Duckworth, Virginia's half brother, published her first two novels, but the Hogarth Press published all her additional work.

In 1921, the Hogarth Press issued Virginia's *Monday or Tuesday,* as she finished another novel, *Jacob's Room,* issued in 1922. That year, Virginia met her future lover and lifelong friend, Vita Sackville-West, married to Harold Nicolson. Two years later, the Woolfs moved again, to 52 Tavistock Square, and Virginia lectured at Cambridge, delivering her essay "Mr. Bennett and Mrs. Brown," later published by Hogarth. *The Common Reader* and Mrs. DALLOWAY would follow in 1925 and TO THE LIGHTHOUSE in 1927. Virginia kept voluminous diaries containing plans for her novels, as well as a wealth of commentary on famous literary and political figures that Leonard would publish after her death. Among those comments is her description of a huge moth that inspired her next novel.

Although she had become a formidable force in fiction, introducing experimental methods that proved crucial in the development of the novel, Virginia occasionally doubted her own talents. Those doubts were assuaged in 1928, when *To the Lighthouse* won the Femina-vie Heureuse prize. Her fictional ORLANDO, A BIOGRAPHY (1928) featured a male protagonist who, over several centuries, metamorphosed into a female, a book she said celebrated Vita's life. Later that year, she delivered lectures at Cambridge that would afterward be printed as the tremendously important *A Room of One's Own* (1929). The work would prove an invaluable call-to-arms for feminists: Woolf suggested women needed rooms of their own and incomes of 500 pounds. She also famously wrote of having to kill the angel in the house, a seeming reference to her mother, before feeling free to write, and of an imaginary sister to playwright William Shakespeare, musing on her likely fate in a society that suppressed the creative bent of women. Although the lectures created some controversy, suggesting only

upper-CLASS women can write, the book remains a stalwart of women's literature studies.

In 1930, Woolf developed yet another close friendship with a woman named Ethyl Smyth, who would lend her support to Woolf's career, although Woolf sometimes found Smyth's attentions stifling. During that decade, she and Leonard seemed to enjoy a happy relationship, although most biographers agree they did not have sexual relations. In 1931, the book that grew from Woolf's vision of a moth titled *The WAVES* (1931) was published. Although again devastated by loss with the death in 1932 of Lytton Strachey and subsequent suicide of his lover, Dora Carrington, Woolf managed to publish "A Letter to a Young Poet" and *The Common Reader, Second Series.* She published the ironic *Flush: A Biography,* a supposed life of the pet dog of Elizabeth Barrett Browning in 1933, and became quite depressed as she worked on *The Years,* at last published in 1937, her depression intensified by the death of Roger Fry in 1934. When Fry's sister asked Woolf to publish his biography, she at first hesitated, not knowing how much of the truth of Fry's bisexuality and his affair with Vanessa to include. She began work on it, however, as well as on her next novel, *Three Guineas.* She would face a shattering death again when her beloved nephew, Vanessa's son Julian Bell, died fighting as part of the SPANISH CIVIL WAR.

Three Guineas was published in 1938, and the following year, the Woolfs met with Sigmund Freud, who sought sanctuary in London from the Nazis. As the war became a reality in England, the Woolfs agreed to commit suicide together should the Nazis invade. They moved again in 1940, relocating to 37 Mecklenburgh Square, and Virginia published *Roger Fry: A Biography* and delivered the lecture "The Leaning Tower" to the Worker's Educational Association. She continued work on her final novel, *Between the Acts,* but began to suffer delusions after many years of relatively good health. In 1941, fearful that she would descend permanently into madness, she wrote two notes to Leonard and on March 28 filled her coat with rocks, drowning herself in the River Ouse. After the recovery of her body three weeks later, Leonard had Virginia cremated and buried her ashes beneath one of the two oaks in his garden they had named for themselves.

Leonard would see to the publication of Virginia's final novel later that year and began the enormous task of organizing her many works. He released various edited editions of her essays as well as selections from her diaries. By the 1950s, public sentiment had turned against Virginia, mainly due to rumors regarding her sexual orientation. Because Leonard could find no English library that wanted her papers, most of them went to the New York Public Library.

Virginia Woolf later inspired an industry in repeated publications of her works, numerous biographies, a multitude of literary criticism, and various media versions of her own writings. Her name has become synonymous with the critical theories of FEMINISM, and many college courses devote themselves to the study of her ideas and their development.

—*Virginia Brackett*

BIBLIOGRAPHY

Bell, Quentin. *Virginia Woolf; A Biography.* Vol. 1, *Virginia Stephen 1882–1912.* Vol. 2, *Mrs. Woolf 1912–1941.* London: Hogarth Press, 1973.

Caramagno, Thomas. *The Flight of the Mind: Virginia Woolf's Art and Manic-Depressive Illness.* Berkeley: University of California Press, 1992.

Gordon, Lyndall. *Virginia Woolf: A Writer's Life.* Oxford: Oxford University Press, 1984.

Marder, Herbert. *The Measure of Life: Virginia Woolf's Last Years.* Ithaca, N.Y.: Cornell University Press, 2000.

Spater, George, and Ian Parsons. *A Marriage of True Minds: An Intimate Portrait of Leonard and Virginia Woolf.* New York: Harcourt Brace Jovanovich, 1977.

WORLD OF WONDERS ROBERTSON DAVIES (1975) See *THE DEPTFORD TRILOGY.*

WORLD WAR I (1914–NOVEMBER 11, 1918)

When the Austrian archduke Francis Ferdinand, presumed heir to the throne of the Austro-Hungarian Empire, was assassinated in the Bosnian capital of Sarajevo on June 28, 1914, Great Britain had no direct obligation to join the military preparations and declarations of war that immediately followed. Austria-Hungary, Germany, France, Russia (then ruled by a deteriorating monarchy), and several Balkan states made declarations of war beginning on July 28. The German strategy against France called for a wide flanking assault through Belgium (the "Schlieffen plan"); when German soldiers entered that country on August 4, Britain was obliged by treaty to enter the war in defense of its Belgian ally. Over the next several weeks, further declarations of war followed until nations as far away as Japan became embroiled in a war of unprecedented scope and complexity. On September 5, 1914, the Treaty of London established Great Britain, France, and Russia as the "Allies" opposed to the Central Powers constituted by Germany, Austria-Hungary, and eventually the Ottoman Empire (modern Turkey and its conquered territories). The United States remained officially neutral until April 6, 1917, when German submarine attacks on American shipping inflamed public and political support for entering the war on the side of the Allies.

The technological innovation of the machine gun soon brought the opposing sides to a stalemate: Rapid-fire guns effectively neutralized direct frontal assaults, leading to defensive trench warfare that stretched from the Alps to the Atlantic. After only a few months of fighting, during which German forces overran Belgium and parts of northern France, both sides took up entrenched defensive positions: Neither side could break through the lines of the other side, and for three years (1915–17) the conflict ground virtually to a halt. Skirmishes might win or lose a few yards of the blasted terrain between the entrenched opponents known as "no man's land," but the deciding factors in the ultimate resolution of the war had more to do with economic welfare, efficiency of communications and distribution systems, and the spread of disease. The great clash of opposing national superiorities settled into a demeaning war of attrition: Whoever first ran out of men, money, and materials would be the losing side.

While armies remained immobilized, war planners tried to come up with strategies for breaking the deadlock. Chemical warfare with mustard gas was used as a method of clearing trenches. British planners, including Winston Churchill, began developing ways to resume a mobile offense by means of a fortified vehicle eventually known as the tank. Although tanks were in use by 1916, this machine did not become a decisive weapon until WORLD WAR II. Cutting supplies to entrenched enemy soldiers was crucial; the British navy lead the world in the battleships and destroyers available for naval blockades, and the Germans countered with submarine warfare—a strategy applied against the British, their allies, and any other nations doing business with them, thereby bringing the United States into the war and tipping the balance of power against the Germans.

As the stalemate in Europe stretched on, colonial outposts became targets as means of undermining national economies, and the recent German presence in Africa was very nearly eradicated. Strategists looked for new fronts in order to divide opposing forces. The Allies attempted to develop a front in the Dardanelles on the Gallipoli peninsula, but the results were disastrous and the Anzac forces (Australian and New Zealand soldiers) deployed there were decimated before the British abandoned the effort. Warfare also moved into the skies for the first time: As early as 1914, each side had deployed reconnaissance planes to collect intelligence and then began using planes to drop bombs on strategic targets. German planes bombed London for the first time on the night of May 31, 1915, and German zeppelins assaulted coastal towns in southeastern England from 1915 to 1916. In turn, British planes bombed German dirigible facilities, submarine bases, and industrial sites in southwestern Germany. The effectiveness of German bombing runs led the British to create the world's first military unit specialized for warfare in the skies: the Royal Air Force was founded beginning in 1917.

By 1916, the American president Woodrow Wilson began trying to make peace in Europe. Through diplomatic overtures and public speeches, Wilson advocated a policy of "peace without victory," and although the British and the Austrians were interested in responding to Wilson's overtures, the German decision to pursue unrestricted submarine warfare brought the United States into the war. A key factor was the infamous "Zimmermann telegram," in which the German secretary of state offered Mexico the chance to reclaim Texas, New Mexico, and Arizona in exchange for its allegiance if the United States entered the war against

Germany. American soldiers soon joined British and French forces in Europe; more important, American credit revived the exhausted economies of the Allies with several billion dollars in support. On November 11, 1918, World War I ended when German representatives signed the armistice agreement. The war ended without a decisive battle: dispirited Germans had lost confidence in their ability to prevail over the Allies, and so Germany accepted very harsh terms of surrender. The terms were designed to cripple German military and economic power so that Germany could never again invade its European neighbors; instead, they established conditions that led Europe and the rest of the world into another war only 20 years later.

World War I had a devastating effect on Europe and on Britain. Four empires fell in 1918 as revolutions disrupted Russia, Austria-Hungary, the Ottoman Empire, and the German Empire, and the British Empire was terminally weakened, although it persisted until after World War II. More than 65 million combatants fought in the war: Some 42 million soldiers fought for the Allies, including 12 million Russians, more than 8 million soldiers apiece from Great Britain and France, more than 5.5 million Italians, and nearly 4.5 million Americans. On the other side, nearly 23 million soldiers fought for the Central Powers, about half from Germany and the rest from Austria-Hungary, Turkey, and Bulgaria. Estimates place the total military casualties at some 8.5 million killed by weapons or disease, and civilian casualties may have reached 13 million. Great Britain suffered the largest single-day loss of life in history on July 1, 1916, during the Battle of the Somme when 57,470 British soldiers were killed; the total wartime casualties for the British, however, were smaller (somewhat less than 1 million) than those suffered by Russian, French, German, or Austro-Hungarian forces.

World War I left a deep stamp on 20th-century British literature. Numerous poets created literary impressions of the war, such as Thomas Hardy's "Channel Firing," and many young poets were killed in action. The Welsh poet and novelist David JONES memorialized his wartime experiences (he was wounded at the Somme) in his poem-novel IN PAREN-THESIS, and Ford Madox FORD created a fictional tetralogy, PARADE'S END, about the war. Other novelists, such as J. R. R. TOLKIEN, C. S. LEWIS, Robert GRAVES, and Wyndham LEWIS, fought in the war but turned their creative efforts in other directions; Robert Graves wrote an acclaimed nonfiction work, *Goodbye to All That,* about the war before turning his attention to history and MYTHOLOGY. Numerous older writers contributed to the war effort in various supporting capacities: E. M. FORSTER worked for the Red Cross in Alexandria, Egypt, and W. Somerset MAUGHAM served as a spy, later basing his Ashenden stories on his experiences. John BUCHAN served as a correspondent for the London *Times* newspaper, Agatha CHRISTIE worked as a nurse, Arthur Conan DOYLE organized civilian defenses and wrote about his tours of the front lines, and H. G. WELLS produced propaganda against Germany.

Those not directly connected to the fighting or the war effort were nonetheless affected by it and frequently expressed their experiences in fictional form. In the aftermath of the war, as a bereaved nation entered the Roaring Twenties under the shadow of grief, novelists captured the search for solace in books such as Virginia WOOLF's *MRS. DALLOWAY,* Rebecca WEST's *RETURN OF THE SOLDIER,* and Aldous HUXLEY's *ANTIC HAY.* James BARRIE captured the experience of those waiting at home during the war in some of his plays. The desire to escape from the gloom and death of the war helped propel an escapist novel by Norman DOUGLAS, *SOUTH WIND,* to best-seller status. And for many British citizens, the most lasting effect of the war was to remove a loved one from their lives. Ian FLEMING lost his father at the battle of the Somme; Rudyard KIPLING lost his only son in the war, commemorating him in the poem "My Boy Jack" in 1916.

Many artists and intellectuals opposed the war and were willing to suffer the consequences of such opposition. The philosopher Bertrand Russell sat in jail during much of the war in protest against it. The novelist David GARNETT was a conscientious objector and worked with Quaker objectors to rebuild devastated French villages. Henry JAMES, already near the end of his life, became a British citizen to protest the American reluctance to enter the war expeditiously. D. H. LAWRENCE failed to qualify for military service because of poor health, and then during the war he and his German wife were ostracized in the small Cornish town where they lived; Lawrence's bitterness caused him to become expatriated from his homeland after the war ended.

World War I has provided a wealth of material for later writers as well. Radclyffe HALL used the war to provide her female protagonist with masculinizing wartime experience as an ambulance driver in *THE WELL OF LONELINESS.* One of the greatest novels in Anthony POWELL's 12-volume ROMAN-FLEUVE is *The KINDLY ONES,* and in it he recounts a child's view of World War I as the adult narrator, preoccupied with the onset of World War II, recollects the earlier war. In Pat BARKER's award-winning *REGENERATION TRILOGY,* the author fictionalizes the historical experiences of the soldier-turned-protester Siegfried Sassoon to focus on the psychological damage wrought by the war. In *THE GREENGAGE SUMMER,* Rumer GODDEN imagines a British mother taking her children on a vacation to the site of the Battle of the Marne in order to teach them to appreciate the life they have that was made possible by so many sacrifices.

BIBLIOGRAPHY

Ferro, Marc. *The Great War, 1914–1918.* London: Routledge & Kegan Paul, 1973.

Fussell, Paul. *The Great War and Modern Memory.* New York: Oxford University Press, 1975.

Lee, Dwight E., ed. *The Outbreak of the First World War: Causes and Responsibilities.* 4th ed. Lexington, Mass.: Heath, 1975.

Strachan, Hew. *World War I: A History.* Oxford: Oxford University Press, 1998.

Winter, J. M. *The Experience of World War I.* New York: Oxford University Press, 1989.

WORLD WAR II (1939–1945)

In the aftermath of WORLD WAR I, national economies around the world first boomed during the 1920s and then collapsed during the 1930s as the GREAT DEPRESSION began in the United States and spread to the rest of the globe. In Europe, the effects of the reparations exacted from Germany through the 1919 Treaty of Versailles were made even more punitive as the world economic situation worsened. Rampant inflation made German currency virtually worthless, and widespread unemployment freed cadres of young men from the demands of jobs and careers. A radical new political movement rose to power, eventually led by Adolf Hitler, who was determined to rebuild Germany, restore it to power, and regain territories seized during the early days of World War I and then ceded at the surrender. In the long term, Hitler's ambition was to dominate the entire world.

German-speaking settlements had developed throughout eastern Europe for some time; driven by theories of "Aryan" superiority, especially to Slavs and Jews, and representing himself as a bulwark against communist expansion, Hitler initially presented his goal to be the uniting of all Germans within the boundaries of a single nation. Under the banner of *Lebensraum* (living-space, or elbow-room), he made aggressive claims against territories in Poland, on Germany's eastern border, in particular. Hitler purchased the quiescence of the Soviet Union by promising, in a secret nonaggression pact signed in late August of 1939, that the eastern two-thirds of Poland would become the property of the Russians when Germany took possession of the western third. In the meantime, Poland signed defense treaties with Great Britain and France. On September 1, German troops marched into Poland; on September 3, Britain and France declared war on Germany.

As a consequence of World War I, German military commanders had altered their strategies to take advantage of the new technologies developed by 1918, particularly the tank and the airplane. The Germans, in losing World War I, took action to adapt themselves into a better fighting force, creating armored tank divisions (the panzers) and powerful units of fighter planes and bombers (the Luftwaffe), while the Allies continued the outmoded systems of organization and weapons with which they had prevailed in World War I thanks to American intervention. German tanks quickly overran Austria, Poland, Norway, Belgium, Holland, France, and Czechoslovakia; meanwhile, Italy mounted a weak assault on southeastern France in support of its membership in the "Axis Powers." German and Italian units were also attacking targets in northern Africa in order to regain colonial territories lost at the end of World War I. By May 26, 1940, when the British evacuated their troops from Europe at the port of Dunkirk, German forces controlled Europe from the Atlantic to the Soviet border and from the Alps to the North Sea. On June 14, 1940, German troops entered Paris, and France was quickly reduced to a puppet state under Marshal Petain (the Vichy government).

In England, the war became a defensive operation on land as the Battle of Britain brought waves of German bombers over British cities, especially London. Thousands of children in London and southern England were evacuated to more remote rural areas. King George VI and his wife, Elizabeth, declared that they would share the suffering of their fellow citizens, refusing to leave London and frequently visiting bombed sites to encourage their beleaguered subjects. British fighter pilots were initially unsuccessful in encounters with German aircraft, suffering devastating losses of men and planes. At sea, the British navy continued the war more effectively, blockading or mining German ports, escorting supply convoys partway across the Atlantic, and engaging German battleships, although German submarines (U-boats) took a heavy toll on merchant shipping.

England seemed to be next on Hitler's target list, and political observers expected the island nation to fall quickly. The situation seemed hopeless. Before Hitler could mount an invasion of England, however, he turned his attention to the east. The Soviet Union had moved against Finland in the north and had expanded its forces to Bessarabia and other oil-rich territories in the south. Germany was dependent on Romanian oilfields for the fuel to power its tanks and aircraft, and in order to protect his existing supplies and to secure new ones, Hitler opened a second front in June of 1941 by violating his nonaggression pact with the Soviet Union. The British were further relieved by American supplies of food and weapons when the Lend-Lease act was passed in early in 1941; later that year, when Japan's attack against Pearl Harbor brought the United States into the war on the side of the Allies, Britain's security was more firmly established.

When the Germans opened the eastern front, Hitler's commanders expected the Red Army to fall in a matter of months, and Hitler himself believed that the communist regime would quickly collapse.

Instead, an early winter set in, and the Russians brought up unexpectedly large reserves of troops. German troops advanced briefly to the suburbs of Moscow, but could not hold that position. The war on the eastern front came to a head in the lengthy battle for Stalingrad, causing enormous casualties and inflicting intense suffering on troops unprepared for a prolonged winter siege.

Despite being divided between eastern and western fronts, Hitler joined Japan in declaring war on the United States on December 11, 1941, after the attack on Pearl Harbor, Hawaii. British fortifications at Hong Kong and Burma fell in 1941, and then in early 1942, with the fall of Singapore to Japanese troops, the large British population of colonial merchants and administrators was interned in Japanese prisoner-of-war camps. With attention focused on the new Pacific theater of war and on the eastern front, Britain developed itself into a staging ground for an eventual assault on the European continent. American pilots and planes joined British aviators in increasing numbers and flew from British bases against continental targets, hammering German military positions, distribution systems, ports, industrial complexes, and cities. The British began to see the tide of war turning in late 1942 with a victory directed by Field Marshal Montgomery against German tank divisions commanded by Field Marshal Rommel in northern Africa. British troops fought to victory in Sicily and Italy in 1943 and joined American troops and other allies in sailing the largest armada in history across the English Channel for the historic D-day invasion.

As the European war ground to its end, Winston Churchill maintained Britain's diplomatic position in strategic talks with Franklin D. Roosevelt and Joseph Stalin. British air power steadily expanded, and on the night of February 13–14, 1945, 800 Royal Air Force bombers began a series of bombing runs over Dresden, Germany, continued in the following days by American planes, in the most destructive attack in history. Hitler called unsuccessfully for German civilians to die rather than submit to Allied troops as they drove toward Berlin; similarly, his countrymen ignored his attempt to institute a German version of the scorched-earth policy the Russians had used against him on the east-

ern front. Many Germans preferred conquest by the American and British wing of the Allies and so did nothing to stop the eastward sweep of Allied troops. Hitler committed suicide on April 30, 1945.

When the Germans surrendered on May 7, 1945, and the Japanese on August 14 of that year, Great Britain had suffered more than 450,000 war-related deaths; Germany, 3.5 million; Russia, 11 million; the United States, nearly 300,000; and Japan, nearly 2 million. Figures are disputed because of impaired record-keeping, but the worldwide casualties from the war may have amounted to more than 35 million lives— and possibly as many as 25 million more—and the total cost of the war may have exceeded $1 trillion. In the number of British lives lost, World War II was about half as costly as World War I, although property destruction due to aerial bombardment was much greater. In the years following 1945, the British dismantled their EMPIRE, finally establishing the COMMONWEALTH in its place. While Americans instituted the Marshall Plan in continental Europe, in Great Britain the period from the end of the war to 1965 came to be called the "DIMINISHING AGE" as the British coped with their expensive victory.

The British literary legacy of World War II includes a number of excellent novels about the war, including Evelyn WAUGH's SWORD OF HONOUR trilogy and the three volumes of the third movement of Anthony POWELL's A DANCE TO THE MUSIC OF TIME (The VALLEY OF BONES, The SOLDIER'S ART, and The MILITARY PHILOSOPHERS); C. P. SNOW uses the war as a background in The NEW MEN, about the race to build an atomic weapon, and in The LIGHT AND THE DARK, about a self-destructive man who volunteers as an aviator during the most disastrous phase of the air war. Autobiographical novels include EMPIRE OF THE SUN, by J. G. BALLARD, recounting his interment in a Japanese prisoner-of-war camp after the fall of Singapore. Fictionalized accounts of historical events include SCHINDLER'S ARK, by Thomas KENEALLY, and The WHITE HOTEL, by D. M. THOMAS, both of which examine aspects of the Holocaust.

Novels of retrospection, in which characters affected by the war reminisce about their experiences, include Penelope LIVELY's MOON TIGER, set in the North African campaign, The REMAINS OF THE DAY, by Kazuo ISHIGURO, and *LAST ORDERS,* by Graham SWIFT. The war serves as a tumultuous background for love stories in Michael ONDAATJE's *The ENGLISH PATIENT* and Lawrence DURRELL's *CLEA,* the closing volume of *The ALEXANDRIA QUARTET;* it creates a metaphorically important backstory for the title character in *The MAGUS,* by John FOWLES. The civilian risks of the war form key elements in Henry GREEN's *LOVING* and in Muriel SPARK's *THE GIRLS OF SLENDER MEANS.* P. G. WODEHOUSE did not write war stories or serve in the British armed forces, but his life was drastically changed by the war when he was captured as a civilian in the German onslaught across France. Radio broadcasts he made from Germany were deemed treasonous in England, and after the war he relocated to the United States, eventually becoming an American citizen.

BIBLIOGRAPHY

Churchill, Sir Winston. *The Second World War.* 6 volumes. Boston: Houghton Mifflin, 1948–1953.

Budiansky, Stephen. *Battle of Wits: The Complete Story of Codebreaking in World War II.* New York: Free Press, 2000.

Hough, Richard Alexander and Denis Richards. *The Battle of Britain: The Greatest Air Battle of World War II.* New York: W. W. Norton, 1989.

Keegan, John. *The Second World War.* New York: Viking, 1990.

Taylor, A. J. P. *The Origins of the Second World War.* New York: Atheneum, 1961.

WRITTEN ON THE BODY JEANETTE WINTERSON (1992)

The first-person narrator of this novel is passionate about love and has had lovers of both sexes; however, the discussion of these events and people never quite gets around to a statement of the narrator's own gender. The narrator offers self-descriptive metaphors suggesting sometimes a male, and sometimes a female, identity. Nothing in the story mitigates against either a male or a female narrator; the concealment of this detail in the midst of an outpouring of heartfelt devotion to love becomes a kind of teasing game with the reader, who is in the same condition: could be male—could be female. The lack of a specific gender tends to universalize the narrator's commentary on love.

The narrator's immediate objective is a meditation on the resolution of a current love affair with a married woman, Louise, who is suffering from a cancer that will probably be terminal. Her husband, Elgin, is a physician who specializes in cancer treatment. The narrator and Louise live together for a time, each leaving a partner to be with the other, but when Elgin reveals Louise's medical condition to the narrator, nothing short of sacrifice is enough in the effort to save Louise. Love and life seem to become mutual exclusives: If Louise stays with the narrator, her condition will worsen until it deprives her of life, but they will enjoy love in the meantime; or, if Louise can be returned to Elgin and her treatment program, she may extend her life and yet lose her love. The narrator chooses for her, and afterward Louise finds the strength to make choices of her own.

Intertwined into the story of Louise and the narrator are the many stories of the narrator's other lovers, as well as references to the narrator's family. The narrative shifts abruptly in the middle of the story to become a kind of anatomy textbook comprising of associations of body parts and the diseases to which they are susceptible, each brought home to Louise's case, but in intensely poetic and, as appropriate, erotic language. The story resumes to present the narrator's suffering and determination to find and unite with true love. In a conclusion awash with yearning and romance and the promise of fulfillment, Louise appears again.

The novel presents a provocative and refreshing examination of love as both an emotional and as a sexual phenomenon. In parts, it is an adoring paean to female sexuality, but the frank enjoyment of physical pleasure never loses sight of the emotional bonding that completes the physical act. WINTERSON brings love alive and cleanses it of the shopworn formulas of romance fiction, re-creating romance in the process.

BIBLIOGRAPHY

Anna, Gabriele. Review of *Written on the Body,* *The New York Review of Books* 40, no. 5 (March 4, 1993): 22.

Doan, Laura and Robyn Wiegman, eds. *The Lesbian Postmodern.* New York: Columbia University Press, 1994.

Petro, Pamela. Review of *Written on the Body,* *The Atlantic* 271, no. 2 (February 1993): 112.

Y

YELLOW ADMIRAL, THE PATRICK
O'BRIAN (1996)   See AUBREY-MATURIN NOVELS.

YOUNG SHOULDERS JOHN WAIN (1982)

This novel, the author's 10th work of long fiction, won
the WHITBREAD Book of the Year Award in 1982; it
appeared in the United States under the title *The Free
Zone Starts Here.* Related in the stream-of-consciousness manner by a first-person narrator who is also the
17-year-old protagonist, *Young Shoulders* tells the story
of a small family bereaved of its youngest member, a
12-year-old daughter, Clare Waterford, in an airplane
crash. The daughter, enrolled at a boarding school, has
died with a planeload of her classmates and two teachers as they were taking an educational tour of Portugal
and Spain, and now the airline is bringing two planes
full of bereaved parents and siblings to a memorial
service in Lisbon. Paul Waterford recounts the events
of the 24-hour journey, slipping in and out of imaginary conversations with Clare, who has become a kind
of transcendent, all-knowing presence for him.

As Paul copes with his grief and evades it by escaping into his fantasies of founding the World Free Zone,
he reveals the condition that the family has sunk to:
His parents seem to be on the edge of divorce, with his
mother on one side drinking to ease the emptiness of
her life, and his father on the other musing vaguely
about his aesthetic interests. He is an architect,
although only modestly successful, and she once

hoped for a career on the stage; now their youth is fad-
ing, their love is faltering, and one of their children is
dead. Paul avoids them as much as possible and soon
falls in with Gerald, a rather smarmy journalist who
says his wife is too bedridden to attend the funeral of
their only son, Charlie, a boy two years younger than
Paul. Gerald is actually divorced and had placed Charlie in the boarding school so he could visit him without seeing the ex-wife. Paul eventually realizes that
Gerald is trying to live out an event that Charlie's death
has stolen: taking his son to a brothel for his induction
into manhood. Paul has an EPIPHANY, but it is hardly the
sort Gerald could understand.

The magnitude of the tragedy is vast, and Paul sees
adults pushed to the edge of endurance and beyond.
As some of the parents begin to collapse from the strain
of their uncomprehending grief, Paul gains a new perspective on his own life. The narrative voice moves
from the jaded nonchalance of adolescence in the
novel's beginning through an intoxicated and chaotic
dark night of the soul in Lisbon's red-light district and
finally achieves the maturity of a young adult at the
end, mirroring Paul's process of growth through the
events of a single day.

BIBLIOGRAPHY

Heptonstall, Geoffrey. "Remembering John Wain," *Contemporary Review* 266, no. 1550 (March 1995): 144–147.

Z

ZIMBABWE/FORMER SOUTHERN RHO-DESIA See EMPIRE and COLONIALISM. For a British novelist with a significant connection to this part of Africa, see Doris LESSING.

ZULEIKA DOBSON: OR, AN OXFORD LOVE STORY MAX BEERBOHM (1911)

By the end of this COMIC NOVEL, the author reveals that Zuleika Dobson is indeed a femme fatale: Oxford undergraduates commit suicide in droves for love of the beautiful Zuleika. This paragon of beauty comes to Oxford to reconcile with her grandfather, the Warden of Judas; he had refused to support her when she became an orphan, forcing her to earn her own living first as a governess and then as a performer of tired magic tricks rejuvenated by her irresistible beauty. Zuleika becomes the toast of Europe and America, and at the height of her fame her grandfather extends the olive branch of an invitation to comfort him with a visit in his declining years.

A third-person omniscient narrator delivers this slight PLOT and the archly sardonic descriptions of the characters. The narrative voice is in fact the greatest pleasure of the novel, since the narrator wraps his droll descriptions together with wry evaluations, ornamenting the resulting package with snippets of conversation. What happens and to whom it happens are not as important as the manner by which events and characters are bodied forth in words. BEERBOHM'S vocabulary is both vast in extent and precise in application, and these word-level skills are amplified by an equal talent in imitating the syntactic patterns of classical rhetorical manuals of style. From anaphora to zeugma, Beerbohm's sentences are crafted with masterly skill.

In Zuleika's day, the artistry of the well-turned phrase was admired and emulated, but since then critics have rezoned BELLES LETTRES through lower and lower appraisals of its properties. What seemed charming in the "oughties" and teens of the early 20th century now seems mannered, exaggerated, or even forced. The polished is now—to some—the belabored. Readers should engage *Zuleika Dobson* ready to admire the exquisite faceting of its prose rather than to be absorbed in the detail of its PLOT or the verisimilitude of its characters. And to experience the book most fully, the extra effort to find an illustrated edition in order to enjoy Beerbohm's 80 line drawings will be amply rewarded.

BIBLIOGRAPHY

Danson, Lawrence. *Max Beerbohm and the Act of Writing.* New York: Oxford University Press, 1989.

Hall, N. John. "Introduction." In *The Illustrated Zuleika Dobson: Or, An Oxford Love Story.* Max Beerbohm. New Haven, Conn.: Yale Nota Bene/Yale University Press, 2002.

Nicholson, Harold. "*Zuleika Dobson*: A Revaluation." In *The Surprise of Excellence: Modern Essays on Max Beerbohm.* Edited by J. G. Riewald. Hamden, Conn.: Archon, 1974, 30–37.

APPENDIX I

PRIZE-WINNING BRITISH AND COMMONWEALTH LITERATURE

I. The Booker Prize: awarded in October for the "best full-length novel" (as defined by the judges) published in the year preceding the deadline

1969: P. H. Newby, *Something to Answer For*
1970: Bernice Rubens, *The Elected Member*
1971: V. S. Naipaul, *In a Free State*
1972: John Berger, *G.*
1973: J. G. Farrell, *Siege of Krishnapur*
1974: Stanley Middleton, *Holiday*
1975: Nadine Gordimer, *The Conversationalist* and Ruth Prawer Jhabvala, *Heat and Dust*
1976: David Storey, *Saville*
1977: Paul Scott, *Staying On*
1978: Iris Murdoch, *The Sea, The Sea*
1979: Penelope Fitzgerald, *Offshore*
1980: William Golding, *Rites of Passage*
1981: Salman Rushdie, *Midnight's Children*
1982: Thomas Keneally, *Schindler's Ark*
1983: J. M. Coetzee, *Life and Times of Michael K.*
1984: Anita Brookner, *Hotel du Lac*
1985: Keri Hulme, *Bone People*
1986: Kingsley Amis, *The Old Devils*
1987: Penelope Lively, *Moon Tiger*
1988: Peter Carey, *Oscar and Lucinda*
1989: Kazuo Ishiguro, *The Remains of the Day*
1990: A. S. Byatt, *Possession*

1991: Ben Okri, *The Famished Road*
1992: Michael Ondaatje, *The English Patient* and Barry Unsworth, *Sacred Hunger*
1993: Roddy Doyle, *Paddy Clarke Ha Ha Ha*
1994: James Kelman, *How Late It Was, How Late*
1995: Pat Barker, *The Ghost Road*
1996: Graham Swift, *Last Orders*
1997: Arundhati Roy, *The God of Small Things*
1998: Ian McEwan, *Amsterdam*
1999: J. M. Coetzee, *Disgrace*
2000: Margaret Atwood, *The Blind Assassin*
2001: Peter Carey, *True History of the Kelly Gang*
2002: Yann Martel, *Life of Pi*
2003: DBC Pierre, *Vernon God Little*
2004: Alan Hollingsworth, *The Line of Beauty*

II. The Whitbread Award—Best Book of the Year: Beginning in 1985, five panels of judges select winners that are "well-written, enjoyable books that they would strongly recommend anyone to read" in the five categories of First Novel, Novel, Biography, Poetry, and Children's Book (quoting from the official Web site). A further panel selects the Whitbread Book of the Year from these five category winners.

1971: Best Novel: Gerda Charles, *The Destiny Waltz*
1972: Best Novel: Susan Hill, *The Bird of Night*
1973: Best Novel: Shiva Naipaul, *The Chip Chip Gatherers*
1974: Best Novel: Irish Murdoch, *The Sacred and Profane Love Machine*

1975: Best Novel: William McIlvanney, *Docherty*

1976: Best Novel: William Trevor, *The Children of Dynmouth*

1977: Best Novel: Beryl Bainbridge, *Injury Time*

1978: Best Novel: Paul Theroux, *Picture Palace*

1979: Best Novel: Jennifer Johnston, *The Old Jest*

1980: Best Novel and Book of the Year: David Lodge, *How Far Can You Go*

1981: Best Novel: Maurice Leitch, *Silver's City*

1982: Best Novel: John Wain, *Young Shoulders*

1983: Best Novel: William Trevor, *Fools of Fortune*

1984: Best Novel: Christopher Hope, *Kruger's Alp*

1985: Book of the Year: Douglas Dunn, *Elegies* (poetry)

1985: Best Novel: Peter Ackroyd, *Hawksmoor*

1986: Best Novel and Book of the Year: Kazuo Ishiguro, *An Artist of the Floating World*

1987: Book of the Year: Christopher Nolan, *Under the Eye of the Clock* (biography)

1987: Best Novel: Ian McEwan, *The Child in Time*

1988: Book of the Year: Paul Sayer, *The Comforts of Madness* (first novel)

1988: Best Novel: Salman Rushdie, *The Satanic Verses*

1989: Book of the Year: Richard Holmes, *Coleridge: Early Visions* (biography)

1989: Best Novel: Lindsay Clarke, *The Chymical Wedding*

1990: Best Novel and Book of the Year: Nicholas Mosley, *Hopeful Monsters*

1991: Book of the Year: John Richardson, *A Life of Picasso* (biography)

1991: Best Novel: Jane Gardam, *The Queen of the Tambourine*

1992: Book of the Year: Jeff Torrington, *Swing Hammer Swing!* (first novel)

1992: Best Novel: Alasdair Gray, *Poor Things*

1993: Best Novel and Book of the Year: Joan Brady, *Theory of War*

1994: Best Novel and Book of the Year: William Trevor, *Felicia's Journey*

1995: Book of the Year: Kate Atkinson, *Behind the Scenes at the Museum* (first novel)

1995: Best Novel: Salman Rushdie, *The Moor's Last Sigh*

1996: Book of the Year: Seamus Heaney, *The Spirit Level* (poetry)

1996: Best Novel: Beryl Bainbridge, *Every Man for Himself*

1997: Book of the Year: Ted Hughes, *Tales from Ovid* (poetry)

1997: Best Novel: Jim Crace, *Quarantine*

1998: Book of the Year: Ted Hughes, *Birthday Letters* (poetry)

1998: Best Novel: Justin Cartwright, *Leading the Cheers*

1999: Book of the Year: Seamus Heaney, *Beowulf* (poetry)

1999: Best Novel: Rose Tremain, *Music and Silence*

2000: Best Novel and Book of the Year: Matthew Kneale, *English Passengers*

2001: Best Children's Novel and Book of the Year: Philip Pullman, *The Amber Spyglass*

2002: Book of the Year: Clare Tomalin, *Samuel Pepys: The Unequaled Self* (biography)

2002: Best Novel: Michael Frayn, *Spies*

2003: Best Novel and Book of the Year: Mark Haddon, *The Curious Incident of the Dog in the Night-Time*

III. *Guardian* Fiction Prize: Awarded between 1965 and 1998 by the *Guardian* newspaper under the direction of its literary editor. In 1999, the prize became the *Guardian* First Book Award and was no longer limited to fiction.

1965: Clive Barry, *Crumb Borne*

1966: Archie Hind, *The Dear Green Place*

1967: Eva Figes, *Winter Journey*

1968: P. J. Kavanagh, *A Song and a Dance*

1969: Maurice Leitch, *Poor Lazarus*

1970: Margaret Blount, *Where Did You Last See your Father?*

1971: Thomas Kilroy, *The Big Chapel*

1972: John Berger, *G.*

1973: Peter Redgrove, *In the Country of the Skin*

1974: Beryl Bainbridge, *The Bottle Factory Outing*

1975: Sylvia Clayton, *Friends and Romans*

1976: Robert Nye, *Falstaff*

1977: Michael Moorcock, *The Condition of Muzak*

1978: Neil Jordan, *Night in Tunisia*

1979: Dambudzo Merechera, *The House of Hunger*

1980: J. L. Carr, *A Month in the Country*

1981: John Banville, *Kepler*

1982: Glyn Hughes, *Where I Used to Play on the Green*
1983: Graham Swift, *Waterland*
1984: J. G. Ballard, *Empire of the Sun*
1985: Peter Ackroyd, *Hawksmoor*
1986: Jim Crace, *Continent*
1987: Peter Benson, *The Levels*
1988: Lucy Ellman, *Sweet Desserts*
1989: Carol Lake, *Rosehill: Portrait from a Midlands City*
1990: Pauline Melville, *Shape-Shifter*
1991: Alan Judd, *The Devil's Own Work*
1992: Alasdair Gray, *Poor Things*
1993: Pat Barker, *The Eye in the Door*
1994: Candia McWilliam, *Debatable Land*
1995: James Buchan, *Heart's Journey in Winter*
1996: Seamus Deane, *Reading in the Dark*
1997: Anne Michaels, *Fugitive Pieces*
1998: Jackie Kay, *Trumpet*
1999: Philip Gourevitch, *We Wish to Inform You That Tomorrow We Will be Killed with Our Families*
2000: Zadie Smith, *White Teeth*
2001: Chris Ware, *Jimmy Corrigan, or the Smartest Kid on Earth*
2002: Jonathan Safran Foer, *Everything Is Illuminated*
2003: Robert MacFarlane, *Mountains of the Mind*

IV. Hawthornden Prize (no award given in 1945–57, 1959, 1966, 1971–73, or 1984–87): awarded to the best work of imaginative literature published in the preceding year selected from fiction, poetry, biography, drama, and other imaginative forms at the discretion of a panel of judges

1919: Edward Shanks, *The Queen of China*
1920: John Freeman, *Poems New and Old*
1921: Romer Wilson, *The Death of Society*
1922: Edmund Blunden, *The Shepherd*
1923: David Garnett, *Lady into Fox*
1924: Ralph Hale Mottram, *The Spanish Farm*
1925: Sean O'Casey, *Juno and the Paycock*
1926: V. Sackville-West, *The Land*
1927: Henry Williamson, *Tarka the Otter*
1928: Sigfried Sassoon, *Memoirs of a Fox-Hunting Man*
1929: Lord David Cecil, *The Stricken Deer*
1930: Geoffrey Dennis, *The End of the World*
1931: Kate O'Brien, *Without My Cloak*

1932: Charles Morgan, *The Fountain*
1933: V. Sackville-West, *Collected Poems*
1934: James Hilton, *Lost Horizon*
1935: Robert Graves, *I, Claudius*
1936: Evelyn Waugh, *Edmund Campion*
1937: Ruth Pitter, *A Trophy of Arms*
1938: David Jones, *In Parenthesis*
1939: Christopher Hassall, *Penthesperon*
1940: James Pope-Hennessy, *London Fabric*
1941: Graham Greene, *The Power and the Glory*
1942: John Llewellyn Rhys, *England Is My Village*
1943: Sidney Keyes, *The Cruel Solstice and the Iron Laurel*
1944: Martyn Skinner, *Letters to Malaya*
1958: Dom Moraes, *A Beginning*
1960: Alan Sillitoe, *The Loneliness of the Long Distance Runner*
1961: Ted Hughes, *Lupercal*
1962: Robert Shaw, *The Sun Doctor*
1963: Alistair Horne, *The Price of Glory: Verdun 1916*
1964: V. S. Naipaul, *Mr. Stone and the Knight's Companion*
1965: William Trevor, *The Old Boys*
1967: Michael Frayn, *The Russian Interpreter*
1968: Michael Levey, *Early Renaissance*
1969: Geoffrey Hill, *King Log*
1970: Piers Paul Read, *Monk Dawson*
1974: Oliver Sacks, *Awakenings*
1975: David Lodge, *Changing Places*
1976: Robert Nye, *Falstaff*
1977: Bruce Chatwin, *In Patagonia*
1978: David Cook, *Walter*
1979: P. S. Rushforth, *Kindergarten*
1980: Christopher Reid, *Arcadia*
1981: Douglas Dunn, *St. Kilda's Parliament*
1982: Timothy Mo, *Sour Sweet*
1983: Jonathan Keates, *Allegro Postillions*
1988: Colin Thubron, *Behind the Wall*
1989: Alan Bennett, *Talking Heads*
1990: Kit Wright, *Short Afternoons*
1991: Claire Tomalin, *The Invisible Woman*
1992: Ferdinand Mount, *Of Love and Asthma*
1993: Andrew Barrow, *The Top Dancer*
1994: Tim Pears, *In the Place of Fallen Leaves*
1995: James Michie, *The Collected Poems*
1996: Hilary Mantel, *An Experiment in Love*
1997: John Lanchester, *The Debt to Pleasure*

1998: Charles Nicholl, *Somebody Else*
1999: Antony Beevor, *Stalingrad*
2000: Michael Longley, *The Weather in Japan*
2001: Helen Simpson, *Hey Yeah Right Get a Life*
2002: Eamon Duffy, *The Voices of Morebath: Reformation and Rebellion in an English Village*
2003: William Fiennes, *The Snow Geese*

V. James Tait Black Memorial Award: Given annually in memory of the publisher James Tait Black to a work of fiction and a work of biography published in Britain by writers of any nationality. Prize winners are selected by the professor of English Literature at the University of Edinburgh.

1919: Hugh Walpole, *The Secret City*
1920: D. H. Lawrence, *The Lost Girl*
1921: Walter de la Mare, *Memoirs of a Midget*
1922: David Garnett, *Lady into Fox*
1923: Arnold Bennett, *Riceyman Steps*
1924: E. M. Forster, *A Passage to India*
1925: Liam O'Flaherty, *The Informer*
1926: Radclyffe Hall, *Adam's Breed*
1927: Francis Brett Young, *The Portrait of Clare*
1928: Siegfried Sassoon, *Memoirs of a Foxhunting Man*
1929: J. B. Priestley, *The Good Companions*
1930: E. H. Young, *Miss Mole*
1931: Kate O'Brien, *Without My Cloak*
1932: Helen Simpson, *Boomerang*
1933: A. G. Macdonnell, *England, Their England*
1934: Robert Graves, *I, Claudius* and *Claudius the God*
1935: L. H. Myers, *The Root and the Flower*
1936: Winifred Holtby, *South Riding*
1937: Neil M. Gunn, *Highland River*
1938: C. S. Forester, *A Ship of the Line* and *Flying Colours*
1939: Aldous Huxley, *After Many a Summer Dies the Swan*
1940: Charles Morgan, *The Voyage*
1941: Joyce Cary, *A House of Children*
1942: Arthur Waley, Translation of *Monkey* by Wu Ch'êng-ên
1943: Mary Lavin, *Tales from Bective Bridge*
1944: Forrest Reid, *Young Tom*
1945: L. A. G. Strong, *Travellers*

1946: Oliver Onions, *Poor Man's Tapestry*
1947: L. P. Hartley, *Eustace and Hilda*
1948: Graham Greene, *The Heart of the Matter*
1949: Emma Smith, *The Far Cry*
1950: Robert Henriquez, *Through the Valley*
1951: W. C. Chapman-Mortimer, *Father Goose*
1952: Evelyn Waugh, *Men at Arms*
1953: Margaret Kennedy, *Troy Chimneys*
1954: C. P. Snow, *The New Men* and *The Masters*
1955: Ivy Compton-Burnett, *Mother and Son*
1956: Rose Macauley, *The Towers of Trebizond*
1957: Anthony Powell, *At Lady Molly's*
1958: Angus Wilson, *The Middle Age of Mrs. Eliot*
1959: Morris West, *The Devil's Advocate*
1960: Rex Warner, *Imperial Caesar*
1961: Jennifer Dawson, *The Ha-Ha*
1962: Ronald Hardy, *Act of Destruction*
1963: Gerda Charles, *A Slanting Light*
1964: Frank Tuohy, *The Ice Saints*
1965: Muriel Spark, *The Mandelbaum Gate*
1966: Christine Brooke-Rose, *Langrishe,* and Aidan Higgins, *Go Down*
1967: Margaret Drabble, *Jerusalem The Golden*
1968: Maggie Ross, *The Gasteropod*
1969: Elizabeth Bowen, *Eva Trout*
1970: Lily Powell, *The Bird of Paradise*
1971: Nadine Gordimer, *A Guest of Honour*
1972: John Berger, *G.*
1973: Iris Murdoch, *The Black Prince*
1974: Lawrence Durrell, *Monsieur, or the Prince of Darkness*
1975: Brian Moore, *The Great Victorian Collection*
1976: John Banville, *Doctor Copernicus*
1977: John le Carré, *The Honourable Schoolboy*
1978: Maurice Gee, *Plumb*
1979: William Golding, *Darkness Visible*
1980: J. M. Coetzee, *Waiting for the Barbarians*
1981: Salman Rushdie, *Midnight's Children,* and Paul Theroux, *The Mosquito Coast*
1982: Bruce Chatwin, *On the Black Hill*
1983: Jonathan Keates, *Allegro Postillions*
1984: J. G. Ballard, *Empire of the Sun,* and Angela Carter, *Nights at the Circus*
1985: Robert Edric, *Winter Garden*
1986: Jenny Joseph, *Persephone*

1987: George Mackay Brown, *The Golden Bird: Two Orkney Stories*

1988: Piers Paul Read, *A Season in the West*

1989: James Kelman, *A Disaffection*

1990: William Boyd, *Brazzaville Beach*

1991: Iain Sinclair, *Downriver*

1992: Rose Tremain, *Sacred Country*

1993: Caryl Phillips, *Crossing the River*

1994: Alan Hollinghurst, *The Folding Star*

1995: Christopher Priest, *The Prestige*

1996: Graham Swift, *Last Orders,* and Alice Thompson, *Justine*

1997: Andrew Miller, *Ingenious Pain*

1998: Beryl Bainbridge, *Master Georgie*

1999: Timothy Mo, *Renegade,* or *Halo2*

2000: Zadie Smith, *White Teeth*

2001: Sid Smith, *Something Like a House*

2002: Jonathan Franzen, *The Corrections*

2003: Andrew O'Hagan, *Personality*

VI. The Nobel Prize: British and Commonwealth Novelists writing in English

1907: Rudyard Kipling

1932: John Galsworthy

1969: Samuel Beckett

1973: Patrick White

1983: William Golding

1991: Nadine Gordimer

2001: V. S. Naipaul

2003: J. M. Coetzee

APPENDIX II

GLOSSARY OF COMMON LITERARY TERMS

The following entries define and discuss the common literary terms used often in this book. Terms in SMALL CAPS refer to entries in the main text.

ALLUSION At the simplest level, writers use allusion when they refer to something outside their texts that they assume their readers will recognize and understand. Writers and readers of literature inevitably share several important features: At a minimum, they must share a language, and not uncommonly they also share a nationality and a cultural identity. Since writers can expect their readers to share the pool of knowledge from which they themselves draw, they can use allusion to extend a new work by embedding in it references to older works, historical events, cultural artifacts, social customs, and other aspects of human existence. The greater the shared knowledge between writers and readers, the more effective will the use of allusion be to extend the meaning of the work that contains the allusion. Universal common education has facilitated the use of allusion, since most literate people will have read many of the same texts in their school days; Shakespeare's near ubiquity in the American high school curriculum means that references to his most commonly taught plays will, for most readers, add an extra layer of signification to works that feature such references. Similarly, the Bible and the classical pantheon of mythological figures provide numerous examples.

Short quotations and indirect references are the most typical kinds of allusion; for example, Julian BARNES alludes to a 19th-century French writer and to a short story by that writer in the title of his novel *FLAUBERT'S PARROT*. But several 20th-century authors have adopted a more extreme form of this literary device by borrowing historical events and real people and applying them to fictional uses, or by employing entire characters created by earlier writers. Beryl BAINBRIDGE makes an allusion to a historical event—the sinking of the *Titanic*—in choosing it as the setting of her novel *EVERY MAN FOR HIMSELF*. In *WIDE SARGASSO SEA*, Jean RHYS adopts the character of Antoinette Bertha Mason, originally created by Charlotte Brontë for *Jane Eyre* (1847), as the protagonist of a story that views the world from Bertha's point of view. The popular phenomenon of "fan fiction" is a kind of amateur version of this strategy: Fans who admire the characters in a popular movie, TV show, comic strip, or novel, and who also have an urge to write stories, now commonly publish their own versions of their favorite characters' adventures on the Internet or in fanzines. Risqué and pornographic versions of such stories are referred to as "slash" fiction.

Allusion also occurs in art forms other than literature. Film directors may use a camera angle, lighting scheme, prop, or other aspect of an earlier director's work in order to allude to it, and painters may allude to earlier works through compositional strategies, color combinations, brush techniques, or actual images. A collage is a total allusion, since everything in it is a clipping that comes from somewhere else, simultaneously pointing back to its origin while also constituting some new original work of art; the links that knit together the World Wide Web constitute a network of allusions. The critical position that every new work of art is an allusion to things that came before is generally distinguished by the term INTERTEXTUALITY.

When the pool of knowledge shared between readers and writers is small, problems can arise. Erudite writers may exploit this fact to select erudite audiences by deliberately choosing learned and obscure references. When literary texts cross cultural boundaries in space or time, as India's *Mahabarata* and England's *Beowulf* have done, allusion can begin to fail. In such cases, annotations by translators and scholars can help readers recover a full appreciation for an exotic text. Like *ALLEGORY*, however, allusion can work at a minimal level even when readers don't recognize it: Failing to recognize the sentence "The readiness is all" as a quotation from Shakespeare's *Hamlet* will not prevent a reader from understanding the resolution that it expresses. But without the reader's recognition of the allusion, the text loses some of its richness.

BIBLIOGRAPHY

Hebel, Udo J. *Intertextuality, Allusion, and Quotation: An International Bibliography of Critical Studies.* New York: Greenwood Press, 1989.

Pasco, Allen H. *Allusion: A Literary Graft.* Toronto: University of Toronto Press, 1994.

Pucci, Joseph Michael. *The Full-Knowing Reader: Allusion and the Power of the Reader in the Western Literary Tradition.* New Haven, Conn.: Yale University Press, 1998.

CHARACTER/CHARACTERS   The creatures— generally human, though not exclusively—to whom the events of the PLOT happen are the characters of a fictional *narrative* (see below). Examples of nonhuman characters include animals in a beast fable such as *WATERSHIP DOWN,* but since they generally talk, behave, and react just as humans would, and since their choices by design illustrate human foibles, they hardly constitute a separate category. Imaginary creatures, usually in FANTASY literature, may include trolls, gods and goddesses, elves, a hobbit or two, dragons, witches and wizards, giants, dwarves, borrowers, leprechauns, or any other form authors are capable of imagining, but these creatures, too, display human characteristics, often in stereotyped or idealized extremes. But by far, the majority of the characters in 20th-century British literature are examples of realism: They look, think, and act like ordinary people, and their experiences are similar to the experiences anyone might have in quotidian life.

When writers develop their characters in detail, so that readers feel these fictional creations to be personal acquaintances, they are said to be *round* characters; those with little development of individuality are *flat* characters and may even be stereotypes or one-dimensional figures. Flat characters are useful for advancing the plot economically by creating or contributing to situations that fully developed round characters must cope with. Characters of either the round or flat sort may also be constructed on the pattern of ARCHETYPES such as the hero, the ingénue, the wicked stepmother, or the unreliable trickster. Character development can dominate a novel to the point that plot events are insignificant or inconsequential: 20th-century novels of interiority may focus intensely on how characters think and feel rather than on what they do.

BIBLIOGRAPHY

Forster, E. M. *Aspects of the Novel.* New York: Harcourt, Brace & Company, 1927.

IMAGERY   A literary device crucially important to poetry, imagery serves novelists well also, functioning either descriptively or metaphorically. Writers most often employ imagery in descriptive passages that appeal to the five senses: sight, hearing, smell, touch, and taste. Of these five, sight is the most important. The writer's goal in using descriptive imagery is to represent some object of the senses accurately and clearly, rendering it in literal terms that capture colors, sounds, odors, textures, and flavors, bringing them to life in the reader's imagination. Imagery in descriptive passages helps a fictional person or scene to be more vivid in the reader's mind; effective imagery can linger in the memory long after the specifics of PLOT and character have faded away.

Metaphorical imagery functions to make abstract ideas more comprehensible by associating them with concrete objects of the senses that suggestively correlate with the aspects of the abstract idea the writer wishes to emphasize. Symbolism is a common form of metaphorical imagery. Writers draw on the figures of speech in the canon of traditional rhetoric when they are creating metaphorical images, including such figures as metonymy, synecdoche, personification, and simile. These figures all work by describing an unfamiliar thing (the abstract idea) in terms of a familiar thing (the concrete object of the senses) with well-known characteristics; by analogy, the unfamiliar thing must have characteristics similar to those of the familiar thing.

Imagery served as a key concept to New Criticism in the middle of the 20th century. An interpretation of a literary work that relies on the imagery of the work usually reaches for a "deeper" or less obvious meaning than the surface events of the plot may first suggest. Writers' claims about the intended meaning of the work generally carry little weight for a critic using imagery to interpret the work. Theoretically, imagery may develop in a work as it is written and then may affect a reader as it is read without conscious awareness in either case of the full range of meanings implied by the images. Most recently, imagery has become a field of investigation in the cognitive sciences exploring the way the mind functions.

BIBLIOGRAPHY

Collins, Christopher. *The Poetics of the Mind's Eye: Literature and the Psychology of the Imagination.* Philadelphia: University of Pennsylvania Press, 1991.

Dennett, Daniel C. "Two Approaches to Mental Images." In *Imagery.* Edited by Ned Joel Block. A Bradford Book. Cambridge, Mass.: MIT Press, 1981.

Lindauer, Martin S. "Imagery and the Arts." In *Imagery: Current Theory, Research, and Application.* Edited by Anees A. Sheikh. New York: John Wiley & Sons, 1983.

Scarry, Elaine. *Dreaming by the Book.* New York: Farrar, Straus, Giroux, 1991.

NARRATOR/NARRATIVE   Every story is a narrative about someone in some place doing something for some reason—a formula that gives rise to the basic elements of fiction: character, setting, PLOT, and theme. Narratives about real people are either news reports (or gossip, if the characters are known to the recipient of the narrative) if they are set in the present, or histories if they are set in the past. Narratives about fictional people may be myths if they include the actions of supernatural divinities, or folktales if they extend to characters others than human beings but less powerful than deities (trolls, witches, unicorns, or wicked stepmothers, for example). Narratives set in the future are usually examples of SCIENCE FICTION or DYSTOPIAN NOVELS; narratives set in the past may be examples of FANTASY FICTION if they include supernatural elements, or HISTORICAL FICTION if not. Narratives set in the present or in the world contemporary to the author at the time of composition have been dominated by the conventions of realism for the past 200 years, presenting ordinary people—in settings that duplicate the features of the world that readers live in—dealing with challenges that readers might expect to face themselves at some point in their lives.

In order for a narrative to report its events to an audience, a metaphorical speaker (metaphorical because most stories are now received silently in the mental act of reading and interpreting) must transmit the details to an implied listener. The narrator is not necessarily identical with the author of a narrative: In the case of first-person *point of view* (see below), the narrator is a *character* (see above) created by the author and involved in some way, either as a major player or an observer, in the events occurring in the narrative, and in the case of third-person point of view, the narrator who views and reports the events is also the expression of a fictional voice created by or assumed by the author in order to tell the events of the story most effectively. The implied listener is similarly not necessarily identical with the readership of a narrative: Some narratives are specifically addressed to someone other than the reader, such as a fictional recipient of fictional letters. When narratives are addressed to fictional listeners such as psychiatrists, priests, friends, or enemies of the narrator, the reader stands in the position of an eavesdropper who listens in on a story meant for other ears.

Real readers, as opposed to implied listeners, can most effectively receive and enjoy a narrative through suspension of disbelief, allowing the characters and events of the story to dictate the terms of the narrative's world and reserving judgment until the reading is complete.

BIBLIOGRAPHY

Halperin, John. *The Theory of the Novel: New Essays.* New York: Oxford University Press, 1974.

Hardy, Barbara Nathan. *Tellers and Listeners: The Narrative Imagination.* London: Athlone Press, 1975.

Miller, J. Hillis. "Narrative." In *Critical Terms for Literary Study.* Edited by Frank Lentricchia and Thomas McLaughlin. Chicago: University of Chicago Press, 1990.

Scholes, Robert E., and Robert Kellogg. *The Nature of Narrative.* New York: Oxford University Press, 1966.

POINT OF VIEW   This technical term refers to a novel's mode of *narration* (see above). Readers should take care not to conflate point of view with terms such as "perspective" or "attitude" that refer specifically to the state of mind of a *character* (see above) with respect to the other characters and the events of the PLOT. Writers select a point of view from which to narrate a story in order to control the flow of information to the reader and to shape the quality of the reader's perception of that information.

Point of view occurs in two broad types, known as first-person and third-person point of view. First-person point of view features a narrator identified as "I" or "we" who is a witness to the events of the plot either at firsthand (an eyewitness) or at secondhand (a reporter of others' eyewitness accounts) and who may also be directly involved in the action, possibly even as the *protagonist* (see below). Readers are in intimate contact with the first-person narrator, having access to his or her thoughts and attitudes, at least so far as the character is a reliable narrator. This narrator relates to the world of the story in the same way that real people relate to the real world: Just as we cannot see into the minds of other people but must judge the contents of minds—the true thoughts and feelings of other people—by the external evidence of speech and actions, so too the first-person narrator must interpret the mental acts of the other characters from the physical phenomena of words and deeds.

Third-person point of view is a less intimate connection to the story, but it is a more complex narrative strategy. The third-person narrator is not involved in the story as a character, yet has as much influence on the reader's perception of the story as do any of the participants in the plot. The third-person narrator is an onlooker to the action who may also seem to be the creator of the story, but critics distinguish carefully between the author and the narrator of a fiction; after all, the narrator is, like the characters enmeshed in the plot, a creation of the author. The third-person narrator refers to the characters as "he," "she," or "they"; this narrative mode is generally devoid of self-referential pronouns. Authors control the flow of information to the readers by shaping the third-person narrator's access to the characters' minds; the narrator's access is either omniscient, providing godlike unlimited access to all the thoughts of all the characters, or it is limited to the mind of only one character (usually the protagonist), or it is objective, depending on the observation of words and actions to report on the characters and leaving the interpretation of their mental states to the reader.

A special form of third-person narration developed in the early 20th century in the fiction of Dorothy RICHARDSON, Virginia WOOLF, and James JOYCE and has been widely imitated since then: stream-of-consciousness narration. In this storytelling mode, the thoughts of the character under observation by the narrator tumble forth in the chaotic and associative form that occurs in real-world thinking. The wide-ranging swarm of a character's thoughts contextualizes the events of the plot and embeds them in the development of that character's thoughts and feelings. Stream-of-consciousness narration provides writers with a way to *show* a story rather than merely *tell* it. It can fragment a narrative text in the way that a cubist painting fragments the planes of vision in translating it into a painting; it can also provide a vast array of tiny details that adds up to more than the sum of its parts, just as a pointillist painting creates a coherent large image from a welter of tiny dots. The hallmark of stream-of-consciousness narration is the rambling, seemingly disorderly, associative quality of the thoughts that pour through a character's mind. In a few cases, this narrative form has been used for a first-person narrator; it is an effective technique for *suggesting* madness or emotional instability rather than explaining it through exposition.

Recognizing a third-person narrator is as easy as noticing the presence of third-person pronouns to refer to the characters; deciding which kind of third-person narrator is telling a story requires careful attention to the passages that refer to mental acts, if there are any. Mental acts include thinking, wishing, planning, reasoning, feeling emotions, reflecting, understanding, recognizing, inferring, deducing, and a host of other brain activities that can occur without the necessity of audible words or physical acts. Omniscient third-person narrators report these mental acts for any of the characters, so the reader must note the distribution of the reports of mental acts. When all the reports refer to a single character, readers are in the hands of a limited third-person narrator. When the narrative is devoid of any direct observation of mental acts and features only descriptions of the characters' words and actions that would be available if the reader were actually living the story instead of reading it, then the author has deployed a third-person objective narrator.

BIBLIOGRAPHY

Friedman, Melvin J. *Stream of Consciousness: A Study in Literary Method.* New Haven, Conn.: Yale University Press, 1955.

Jacobs, Carol, and Henry Sussman, eds. *Acts of Narrative.* Stanford, Calif.: Stanford University Press, 2003.

Leaska, Mitchell A. "The Concept of Point of View." In *Essentials of the Theory of Fiction.* Edited by Michael J. Hoffman and Patrick D. Murphy. 2nd ed. Durham, N.C.: Duke University Press, 1996, 158–71.

PROTAGONIST   In any work of fiction, the central *character* (see above) who experiences the *conflict* (see above) of the PLOT is the protagonist; the opponent to this character is the antagonist. The terms *hero* or *heroine* are too narrow to cover the range of characters about whom novelists construct a *narrative* (see above), since the central character in 20th-century fiction may think, feel, and behave in distinctly unheroic ways. For example, the quintessential protagonist in a novel by Jean RHYS is a desperate but fragile woman who drinks too much and trades sexual favors for economic security; she is hardly a heroine, and yet her plight compels the reader's attention and may even elicit a degree of sympathy. Novels of psychological realism may focus intensely on flawed or even villainous characters; these, too, have thoughts and feelings and undergo transformation, for better or worse, in response to life's pressures. Additionally, the central character may be a passive observer to larger events who performs none of the actions associated with heroism, but who is transformed internally by the very act of witnessing and reflecting on these events. Kazuo ISHIGURO's protagonists in *An ARTIST OF THE FLOATING WORLD* and *The REMAINS OF THE DAY* are such onlookers, but they occupy center stage in the structure of each of these novels.

BIBLIOGRAPHY

Palmer, Alan. "The Construction of Fictional Minds," *Narrative* 10, no. 1 (January 2002): 28–46.

Paris, Bernard J. *Imagined Human Beings: A Psychological Approach to Character and Conflict in Literature.* New York: New York University Press, 1997.

VOICE   The distinctive use of language by any particular *narrator* (see above) in a work of literature, voice stamps the work with a kind of linguistic personal signature. The voice of Alex, the first-person narrator in *A CLOCKWORK ORANGE,* is distinctive in being unlike any other narrator while also recognizably young. The voice of Nicholas Jenkins, the first-person narrator of the 12 volumes in *A DANCE TO THE MUSIC OF TIME,* is consistent in capturing his upper-CLASS origins and PUBLIC SCHOOL education, and additionally it changes subtly over the course of the series as Nick ages and undergoes new experiences. Authors control voice by choosing a consistent vocabulary and attitude on the part of the narrator they create to tell the story (although in the case of a deranged narrator, inconsistency of voice would be equally appropriate).

BIBLIOGRAPHY

Aczel, Richard. "Understanding as Overhearing: Towards a Dialogics of Voice," *New Literary History: A Journal of Theory and Interpretation* 32, no. 3 (Summer 2001): 597–617.

Hobbs, Catherine L. "Finding Voice in English Studies," *JAC: A Journal of Composition Theory* 21, no. 1 (Winter 2001): 193–200.

APPENDIX III

SELECTED BIBLIOGRAPHY

Abel, Elizabeth, Marianne Hirsch, and Elizabeth Langland. *The Voyage In: Fictions of Female Development.* Hanover, N.H.: University Press of New England, 1983.

Allen, Graham. *Intertextuality.* The New Critical Idiom Series. London: Routledge, 2000.

Ashcroft, Bill, Gareth Griffiths, and Helen Tiffin. *The Empire Writes Back: Theory and Practice in Post-Colonial Literature.* London: Routledge, 1989.

Bartlett, C. J. *A History of Postwar Britain, 1945–1974.* London: Longman, 1977.

Batchelor, John. *The Edwardian Novelists.* New York: St. Martin's Press, 1982.

Bell-Villada, Gene H. *Art for Art's Sake and Literary Life: How Politics and Markets Helped Shape the Ideology and Culture of Aestheticism, 1790–1990.* Lincoln: University of Nebraska Press, 1996.

Bertens, Hans, Douwe Fokkema, and Mario J. Valdes, eds. *International Postmodernism: Theory and Literary Practice.* Comparative History of Literatures in European Languages Series 11. Amsterdam: Benjamins, 1997.

Bertens, Hans, and Joseph P. Natoli, eds. *Postmodernism: The Key Figures.* Malden, Mass.: Blackwell Publishers, 2002.

Bevan, David, ed. *University Fiction.* Rodopi Perspectives on Modern Literature 5. Amsterdam; Atlanta: Rodopi, 1990.

Boehmer, Elleke. *Colonial and Postcolonial Literature.* Oxford: Oxford University Press, 1995.

Booker, Keith M. *Colonial Texts: India in the Modern British Novel.* Ann Arbor: University of Michigan Press, 1997.

———. *Dystopian Literature: A Theory and Research Guide.* Westport, Conn.: Greenwood Press, 1994.

Bradbury, Malcolm, and James McFarlane, eds. *Modernism 1890–1930.* London: Penguin, 1976.

Brombert, Victor H. *In Praise of Antiheroes: Figures and Themes in Modern European Literature, 1830–1980.* Chicago: University of Chicago Press, 1999.

Buckley, Jerome Hamilton. *Season of Youth: The Bildungsroman from Dickens to Golding.* Cambridge, Mass.: Harvard University Press, 1974.

Burgess, Anthony. *99 Novels: The Best in English Since 1939.* New York: Summit Books, 1984.

———. *The Novel Now.* London: Faber & Faber, 1967.

Calinescu, Matei, and Douwe Fokkeman, eds. *Exploring Postmodernism.* Amsterdam: J. Benjamins, 1987.

Campbell, Joseph. *The Hero with a Thousand Faces.* Princeton, N.J.: Princeton University Press, 1949.

Carpenter, Humphrey. *The Brideshead Generation.* London; Faber and Faber, 1989.

Cheyette, Bryan. *Constructions of "the Jew" in English Literature and Society: Racial Representations, 1875–1945.* Cambridge: Cambridge University Press, 1993.

Collins, Christopher. *The Poetics of the Mind's Eye: Literature and the Psychology of the Imagination.* Philadelphia: University of Pennsylvania Press, 1991.

Connery, Brian A., and Kirk Combe, eds. *Theorizing Satire: Essays in Literary Criticism.* New York: St. Martin's Press, 1995.

Culler, Jonathan D. *On Deconstruction: Theory and Criticism after Structuralism.* Ithaca, N.Y.: Cornell University Press, 1982.

Davies, Norman. *The Isles: A History*. Oxford: Oxford University Press, 1999.

Donoghue, Denis. *We Irish: Essays on Irish Literature and Society*. New York: Knopf—dist. by Random House, 1986.

Edel, Leon. *Bloomsbury: A House of Lions*. Philadelphia: Lippincott, 1979.

Felber, Lynette. *Gender and Genre in Novels Without End: The British Roman-Fleuve*. Gainesville: University Press of Florida, 1995.

Fernandez-Armesto, Felipe, ed. *England 1945–2000*. London: The Folio Society, 2001.

Ferres, John H., and Martin Tucker, eds. *Modern Commonwealth Literature*. New York: Ungar, 1977.

Forster, E. M. *Aspects of the Novel*. New York: Harcourt, Brace & Company, 1927.

Fraiman, Susan. *Unbecoming Women: British Woman Writers and the Novel of Development*. New York: Columbia University Press, 1993.

Frazer, James George. *The Golden Bough: A Study in Magic and Religion*. Oxford World's Classics. Oxford: Oxford University Press, 1998.

Freiburg, Rudolph, and Jan Schnitker. *"Do You Consider Yourself a Postmodern Author?" Interviews with Contemporary English Writers*. Piscataway, N.J.: Transaction Publishers, 1999.

Friedman, Melvin J. *Stream of Consciousness: A Study in Literary Method*. New Haven, Conn.: Yale University Press, 1955.

Frye, Northrop. *Anatomy of Criticism: Four Essays*. Princeton, N.J.: Princeton University Press, 1957.

Giddens, Anthony, and David Held, eds. *Classes, Power, and Conflict: Classical and Contemporary Debates*. Berkeley: University of California Press, 1982.

Gilbert, Sandra M., and Susan Gubar. *The Madwoman in the Attic: The Woman Writer and the Nineteenth-Century Literary Imagination*. New Haven, Conn.: Yale University Press, 1979.

———. *No Man's Land: The Place of the Woman Writer in the Twentieth Century*. 3 vols. New Haven, Conn.: Yale University Press, 1988–94.

Gorra, Michael. *The English Novel at Mid-Century: From the Leaning Tower*. New York: Macmillan, 1990.

Graff, Gerald. *Literature Against Itself: Literary Ideas in Modern Society*. Chicago: University of Chicago Press, 1979.

Gray, Nancy. *Language Unbound: On Experimental Writing by Women*. Urbana: University of Illinois Press, 1992.

Guillory, John. *Cultural Capital: The Problem of Literary Canon Formation*. Chicago: University of Chicago Press, 1993.

Guy, Josephine M. *The British Avant-Garde: The Theory and Politics of Tradition*. New York: Harvester Wheatsheaf, 1991.

Haffenden, John. *Novelists in Interview*. London: Methuen, 1985.

Halperin, John. *The Theory of the Novel: New Essays*. New York: Oxford University Press, 1974.

Hardin, James N. *Reflection and Action: Essays on the Bildungsroman*. Columbia: University of South Carolina Press, 1991.

Harmon, William. *A Handbook to Literature*. 9th ed. Upper Saddle River, N.J.: Prentice Hall, 2003.

Harper, Graeme, ed. *Comedy, Fantasy, and Colonialism*. London: Continuum, 2002.

Havighurst, Alfred F. *Britain in Transition: The Twentieth Century*. Chicago: University of Chicago Press, 1985.

Hoffman, Michael J., and Patrick D. Murphy, eds. *Essentials of the Theory of Fiction*. 2nd ed. Durham, N.C.: Duke University Press, 1996.

Holland, Jack. *Hope Against History: The Course of Conflict in Northern Ireland*. New York: Henry Holt, 1999.

Hosmer, Robert E., Jr., ed. *Contemporary British Women Writers: Narrative Strategies*. New York: St. Martin's Press, 1993.

Hunter, Jefferson. *Edwardian Fiction*. Cambridge, Mass.: Harvard University Press, 1982.

Jacobs, Carol, and Henry Sussman, eds. *Acts of Narrative*. Stanford, Calif.: Stanford University Press, 2003.

James, Lawrence. *The Rise and Fall of the British Empire*. New York: St. Martin's Press, 1996.

Joannu, Maroula. *Women Writers of the Thirties: Gender, Politics, and History*. Edinburgh: Edinburgh University Press, 1999.

Johnson, Barbara. *A World of Difference*. Baltimore: Johns Hopkins University Press, 1987.

Karl, Frederick R. *A Reader's Guide to the Contemporary English Novel*. New York: Farrar, Straus & Giroux—The Noonday Press, 1962.

Kiberd, Declan. *Inventing Ireland*. Cambridge, Mass.: Harvard University Press, 1996.

King, Bruce Alvin. *The New English Literatures: Cultural Nationalisms in a Changing World*. New York: St. Martin's Press, 1980.

Klaus, H. Gustav. *The Socialist Novel in Britain: Towards the Recovery of a Tradition.* New York: St. Martin's Press, 1982.

Knaplund, Paul. *Britain: Commonwealth and Empire, 1901–1955.* New York: Harper, 1957.

Knapp, Bettina Liebowitz. *A Jungian Approach to Literature.* Carbondale, Ill.: Southern Illinois University Press, 1984.

Lane, Richard J., Rod Mengham, and Philip Tew. *Contemporary British Fiction.* Cambridge, U.K.: Polity Press; Malden, Mass.: Blackwell Publishers, 2003.

Leavis, F. R. *The Great Tradition: George Eliot, Henry James, Joseph Conrad.* London: Chatto & Windus, 1948.

Levenson, Michael H. *A Genealogy of Modernism: A Study of English Literary Doctrine, 1908–1922.* Cambridge: Cambridge University Press, 1984.

Lodge, David. *The Art of Fiction: Illustrated From Classic and Modern Texts.* New York: Viking, 1993.

Maassen, Irmgard, and Anna Maria Stuby. *(Sub)versions of Realism: Recent Women's Fiction in Britain.* Heidelberg: Universitätsverlag C. Winter, 1997.

McFarlane, Brian. *Novel to Film: An Introduction to the Art of Adaptation.* Oxford: Clarendon Press; New York: Oxford University Press, 1996.

McGowan, John. *Postmodernism and Its Critics.* Ithaca, N.Y.: Cornell University Press, 1991.

Miller, Laura, with Adam Begley. *The salon.com Reader's Guide to Contemporary Authors.* New York: Penguin, 2000.

Muecke, D. C. *Irony.* The Critical Idiom 13. London: Methuen, 1970.

Naik, M. K. *A History of Indian English Literature.* New Delhi: Sahitya Akademi, 1982.

Norris, Christopher. *Deconstruction: Theory and Practice.* London: Methuen, 1982.

Nowell-Smith, Simon, ed. *Edwardian England, 1901–1914.* London: Oxford University Press, 1964.

Paris, Bernard J. *Imagined Human Beings: A Psychological Approach to Character and Conflict in Literature.* Literature and Psychoanalysis 9. New York: New York University Press, 1997.

Peppis, Paul. *Literature, Politics, and the English Avant-Garde: Nation and Empire, 1901–1918.* Cambridge: Cambridge University Press, 2000.

Perez, Jane, and Wendell Aycock, eds. *The Spanish Civil War in Literature.* Lubbock: Texas Tech University Press, 1990.

Phelan, James. *Reading People, Reading Plots: Character, Progression, and the Interpretation of Narrative.* Chicago: University of Chicago Press, 1989.

Pucci, Joseph Michael. *The Full-Knowing Reader: Allusion and the Power of the Reader in the Western Literary Tradition.* New Haven, Conn.: Yale University Press, 1998.

Quilligan, Maureen. *The Language of Allegory: Defining the Genre.* Ithaca, N.Y.: Cornell University Press, 1979.

Rabkin, Eric S., Martin Harry Greenberg, and Joseph D. Olander, eds. *No Place Else: Explorations in Utopian and Dystopian Fiction.* Carbondale: Southern Illinois University Press, 1983.

Ransom, John Crowe. *The New Criticism.* Norfolk, Conn.: New Directions, 1941.

Richardson, Brian. *Narrative Dynamics: Essays on Time, Plot, Closure, and Frames.* Columbus: Ohio State University Press, 2002.

Richetti, John, ed. *The Columbia History of the British Novel.* New York: Columbia University Press, 1994.

Roberts, J. M. *Twentieth Century: The History of the World, 1901–2000.* New York: Viking, 1999.

Rose, Margaret A. *Parody: Ancient, Modern, and Post-Modern.* Cambridge: Cambridge University Press, 1993.

Rothermund, Dietmar. *The Global Impact of the Great Depression, 1929–1939.* London: Routledge, 1996.

Salwak, Dale. *Interviews with Britain's Angry Young Men.* San Bernardino, Calif.: Borgo Press, 1984.

Schlueter, Paul, and June Schlueter, eds. *An Encyclopedia of British Women Writers.* Rev. and expanded ed. New Brunswick, N.J.: Rutgers University Press, 1998.

Schmidt, Richard, and Thomas E. Moody. *Alienation and Social Criticism.* Atlantic Highlands, N.J.: Humanities Press, 1994.

Scholes, Robert. *Fabulation and Metafiction.* Urbana: University of Illinois Press, 1979.

Scholes, Robert, and Robert Kellogg. *The Nature of Narrative.* London: Oxford University Press, 1966.

Scholes, Robert. *Semiotics and Interpretation.* New Haven, Conn.: Yale University Press, 1982.

———. *Structuralism in Literature: An Introduction.* New Haven, Conn.: Yale University Press, 1974.

Skura, Meredith Anne. *The Literary Use of the Psychoanalytic Process.* New Haven, Conn.: Yale University Press, 1981.

Stevenson, Randall. *The British Novel Since the Thirties: An Introduction.* Athens: The University of Georgia Press, 1986.

Stringer, Jennie, ed. *The Oxford Companion to Twentieth-Century Literature in English.* Oxford: Oxford University Press, 1996.

Strongman, Luke. *The Booker Prize and the Legacy of Empire.* Cross-Cultures: Readings in the Post-Colonial Literatures in English 54. Amsterdam: Rodopi, 2002.

Sutherland, James. *English Satire.* Cambridge: Cambridge University Press, 1958.

Swinnerton, Frank. *The Georgian Literary Scene, 1910–1935: A Panorama.* New York: Farrar, Straus, 1950.

Taylor, A. J. P. *England 1914–1945.* London: The Folio Society, 2000.

Thormählen, Marianne, ed. *Rethinking Modernism.* Basingstoke, U.K.: Palgrave Macmillan, 2003.

Thornton, A. P. *Imperialism in the Twentieth Century.* Minneapolis: University of Minnesota Press, 1977.

Tigges, Wim. *Moments of Moment: Aspects of the Literary Epiphany.* Studies in Literature 25. Amsterdam: Rodopi, 1999.

Todd, Richard. *Consuming Fictions: The Booker Prize and Fiction in Britain Today.* London: Bloomsbury, 1996.

Turner, Barry A. *Industrialism.* Harlow, U.K.: Longman, 1975.

Vanneman, Reeve, and Lynn Weber Cannon. *The American Perception of Class.* Philadelphia: Temple University Press, 1987.

Vorda, Allan. *Face to Face: Interviews with Contemporary Novelists.* Houston: Rice University Press, 1993.

Walker, William. *Dialectics and Passive Resistance: The Comic Antihero in Modern Fiction.* New York: P. Lang, 1985.

Walsh, Timothy. *The Dark Matter of Words: Absence, Unknowing, and Emptiness in Literature.* Carbondale: Southern Illinois University Press, 1998.

Walsh, William. *Commonwealth Literature.* London: Oxford University Press, 1973.

Waugh, Patricia. *Metafiction: The Theory and Practice of Self-Conscious Fiction.* New Accents Series. New York: Methuen, 1984.

Wellek, René. *A History of Modern Criticism: 1750–1950.* New Haven, Conn.: Yale University Press, 1955.

Wood, James. *The Irresponsible Self: On Laughter and the Novel.* New York: Farrar, Straus & Giroux, 2004.

Wood, Michael. *Children of Silence: On Contemporary Fiction.* New York: Columbia University Press, 1998.

Zamora, Lois Parkinson, and Wendy B. Faris, eds. *Magical Realism: Theory, History, Community.* Durham, N.C.: Duke University Press, 1995.

INDEX